Collins Spanish Dictionary

Published by Collins
An imprint of HarperCollins
Publishers
Westerhill Road
Bishopbriggs
Glasgow G64 2QT
www.harpercollins.co.uk

This Edition 2014

10 9 8 7 6 5 4 3 2 1

ISBN 978-0-00-794282-4
ISBN 978-0-00-794286-2
ISBN 978-0-00-758334-8
ISBN 978-0-00-794237-4

Collins® is a registered trademark of
HarperCollins Publishers Limited

www.collins.co.uk
www.collinsdictionary.com

Printed in Great Britain by Clays Ltd, St Ives plc

A catalogue record for this book is available from the British Library.

If you would like to comment on any aspect of this book, please contact us at the above address or online.
E-mail: dictionaries@harpercollins.co.uk

Acknowledgements
We would like to thank those authors and publishers who kindly gave permission for copyright material to be used in the Collins Corpus.
We would also like to thank Times Newspapers Ltd for providing valuable data.

ÍNDICE

CONTENTS

INTRODUCCIÓN

Estamos muy satisfechos de que hayas decidido comprar este diccionario y esperamos que lo disfrutes y que te sirva de gran ayuda ya sea en el colegio, en el trabajo, en tus vacaciones o en casa.

INTRODUCTION

We are delighted that you have decided to buy this Spanish dictionary and hope you will enjoy and benefit from using it at school, at home, on holiday or at work.

ABREVIATURAS / ABBREVIATIONS

ABREVIATURAS		ABBREVIATIONS
abreviatura	*ab(b)r*	abbreviation
adjetivo, locución adjetiva	*adj*	adjective, adjectival phrase
administración	*Admin*	administration
adverbio, locución adverbial	*adv*	adverb, adverbial phrase
agricultura	*Agr*	agriculture
anatomía	*Anat*	anatomy
Argentina	*Arg*	Argentina
arquitectura	*Arq, Arch*	architecture
el automóvil	*Aut(o)*	the motor car and motoring
aviación, viajes aéreos	*Aviac, Aviat*	flying, air travel
biología	*Bio(l)*	biology
botánica, flores	*Bot*	botany
inglés británico	BRIT	British English
Centroamérica	CAM	Central America
química	*Chem*	chemistry
comercio, finanzas, banca	*Com(m)*	commerce, finance, banking
informática	*Comput*	computing
conjunción	*conj*	conjunction
construcción	*Constr*	building
compuesto	*cpd*	compound element
Cono Sur	CS	Southern Cone
cocina	*Culin*	cookery
economía	*Econ*	economics
eletricidad, electrónica	*Elec*	electricity, electronics
enseñanza, sistema escolar y universitario	*Escol*	schooling, schools and universities
España	ESP	Spain
especialmente	*esp*	especially
exclamación, interjección	*excl*	exclamation, interjection
femenino	*f*	feminine
lengua familiar (! vulgar)	*fam(!)*	colloquial usage (! particularly offensive)
ferrocarril	*Ferro*	railways
uso figurado	*fig*	figurative use
fotografía	*Foto*	photography
(verbo inglés) del cual la partícula es inseparable	*fus*	(phrasal verb) where the particle is inseparable
generalmente	*gen*	generally
geografía, geología	*Geo*	geography, geology
geometría	*Geom*	geometry
historia	*Hist*	history
uso familiar (! vulgar)	*inf(!)*	colloquial usage (! particularly offensive)
infinitivo	*infin*	infinitive
informática	*Inform*	computing
invariable	*inv*	invariable
irregular	*irreg*	irregular
lo jurídico	*Jur*	law
América Latina	LAM	Latin America
gramática, lingüística	*Ling*	grammar, linguistics

ABREVIATURAS		ABBREVIATIONS
masculino	*m*	masculine
matemáticas	*Mat(h)*	mathematics
masculino/femenino	*m/f*	masculine/feminine
medicina	*Med*	medicine
México	MÉX, MEX	Mexico
lo militar, ejército	*Mil*	military matters
música	*Mús, Mus*	music
substantivo, nombre	*n*	noun
navegación, náutica	*Náut, Naut*	sailing, navigation
sustantivo numérico	*num*	numeral noun
complemento	*obj*	(grammatical) object
	o.s.	oneself
peyorativo	*pey, pej*	derogatory, pejorative
fotografía	*Phot*	photography
fisiología	*Physiol*	physiology
plural	*pl*	plural
política	*Pol*	politics
participio de pasado	*pp*	past participle
preposición	*prep*	preposition
pronombre	*pron*	pronoun
psicología, psiquiatría	*Psico, Psych*	psychology, psychiatry
tiempo pasado	*pt*	past tense
química	*Quím*	chemistry
ferrocarril	*Rail*	railways
religión	*Rel*	religion
Río de la Plata	RPL	River Plate
	sb	somebody
Cono Sur	SC	Southern Cone
enseñanza, sistema escolar y universitario	*Scol*	schooling, schools and universities
singular	*sg*	singular
España	SP	Spain
	sth	something
sujeto	*su(b)j*	(grammatical) subject
subjuntivo	*subjun*	subjunctive
tauromaquia	*Taur*	bullfighting
también	*tb*	also
técnica, tecnología	*Tec(h)*	technical term, technology
telecomunicaciones	*Telec, Tel*	telecommunications
imprenta, tipografía	*Tip, Typ*	typography, printing
televisión	*TV*	television
universidad	*Univ*	university
inglés norteamericano	US	American English
verbo	*vb*	verb
verbo intransitivo	*vi*	intransitive verb
verbo pronominal	*vr*	reflexive verb
verbo transitivo	*vt*	transitive verb
zoología	*Zool*	zoology
marca registrada	®	registered trademark
indica un equivalente cultural	≈	introduces a cultural equivalent

SPANISH PRONUNCIATION

VOWELS

a	[a]	pata	not as long as *a* in f*a*r. When followed by a consonant in the same syllable (i.e. in a closed syllable), as in *a*mante, the *a* is short, as in b*a*t
e	[e]	me	like *e* in th*e*y. In a closed syllable, as in g*e*nte, the *e* is short as in p*e*t
i	[i]	pino	as in m*ea*n or mach*i*ne
o	[o]	lo	as in l*o*cal. In a closed syllable, as in c*o*ntrol, the *o* is short as in c*o*t
u	[u]	lunes	as in r*u*le. It is silent after q, and in g*u*e, g*u*i, unless marked g*ü*e, g*ü*i e.g. antigüedad, when it is pronounced like *w* in *w*olf

SEMIVOWELS

i, y	[j]	bien hielo yunta	pronounced like *y* in yes
u	[w]	huevo fuento antig*ü*edad	unstressed *u* between consonant and vowel is pronounced like *w* in *w*ell. See notes on *u* above.

DIPHTHONGS

ai, ay	[ai]	baile	as *i* in r*i*de
au	[au]	auto	as *ou* in sh*ou*t
ei, ey	[ei]	buey	as *ey* in gr*ey*
eu	[eu]	deuda	both elements pronounced independently [e] + [u]
oi, oy	[oi]	hoy	as *oy* in t*oy*

CONSONANTS

b	[b, β]	boda *b*om*b*a la*b*or	see notes on *v* below
c	[k]	caja	*c* before *a*, *o*, *u* is pronounced as in *c*at
ce, ci	[θe, θi]	cero *c*ielo	*c* before *e* or *i* is pronounced as in *th*in
ch	[tʃ]	chiste	*ch* is pronounced as *ch* in *ch*air
d	[d, ð]	danés ciudad	at the beginning of a phrase or after *l* or *n*, *d* is pronounced as in English. In any other position it is pronounced like *th* in *th*e

g	[g,ɣ]	**ga**fas pa**g**a	*g* before *a*, *o* or *u* is pronounced as in *g*ap, if at the beginning of a phrase or after *n*. In other positions the sound is softened
ge, gi	[xe, xi]	**ge**nte **gi**rar	*g* before *e* or *i* is pronounced similar to *ch* in Scottish lo*ch*
h		**h**aber	*h* is always silent in Spanish
j	[x]	**j**ugar	*j* is pronounced similar to *ch* in Scottish lo*ch*
ll	[ʎ]	ta**ll**e	*ll* is pronounced like the *y* in *y*et or the *lli* in mi*lli*on
ñ	[ʃ]	ni**ñ**o	*ñ* is pronounced like the *ni* in o*ni*on
q	[k]	**q**ue	*q* is pronounced as *k* in *k*ing
r, rr	[r, rr]	qui**t**ar ga**rr**a	*r* is always pronounced in Spanish, unlike the silent *r* in dance*r*. *rr* is trilled, like a Scottish *r*
s	[s]	quizá**s** i**s**la	*s* is usually pronounced as in pa*ss*, but before *b*, *d*, *g*, *l*, *m* or *n* it is pronounced as in ro*s*e
v	[b,β]	**v**ía	*v* is pronounced something like *b*. At the beginning of a phrase or after *m* or *n* it is pronounced as *b* in *b*oy. In any other position the sound is softened
z	[θ]	tena**z**	*z* is pronounced as *th* in *th*in

f, k, l, m, n, p, t and x are pronounced as in English.

STRESS

The rules of stress in Spanish are as follows:

(a) when a word ends in a vowel or in *n* or *s*, the second last syllable is stressed:
pa*ta*ta, pa*ta*tas; *co*me, *co*men

(b) when a word ends in a consonant other than *n* or *s*, the stress falls on the last syllable:
pa*red*, ha*blar*

(c) when the rules set out in (a) and (b) are not applied, an acute accent appears over the stressed vowel:
co*mún*, geogra*fía*, in*glés*

In the phonetic transcription, the symbol [ˈ] precedes the syllable on which the stress falls.

LA PRONUNCIACIÓN INGLESA

VOCALES

	Ejemplo inglés	*Explicación*
[ɑː]	father	Entre *a* de padre y *o* de noche
[ʌ]	but, come	*a* muy breve
[æ]	man, cat	Con los labios en la posición de *e* en pena y luego se pronuncia el sonido *a* parecido a la *a* de carro
[ə]	father, ago	Vocal neutra parecida a una *e* u *o* casi muda
[əː]	bird, heard	Entre *e* abierta y *o* cerrada, sonido alargado
[ɛ]	get, bed	Como en perro
[ɪ]	it, big	Más breve que en *si*
[iː]	tea, see	Como en fino
[ɔ]	hot, wash	Como en torre
[ɔː]	saw, all	Como en por
[u]	put, book	Sonido breve, más cerrado que burro
[uː]	too, you	Sonido largo, como en uno

DIPTONGOS

	Ejemplo inglés	*Explicación*
[aɪ]	fly, high	Como en fraile
[au]	how, house	Como en pausa
[ɛə]	there, bear	Casi como en *vea*, pero el sonido *a* se mezcla con el indistinto [ə]
[eɪ]	day, obey	*e* cerrada seguida por una *i* débil
[ɪə]	here, hear	Como en man*ía*, mezclándose el sonido *a* con el indistinto [ə]
[əu]	go, note	[ə] seguido por una breve *u*
[ɔɪ]	boy, oil	Como en v*oy*
[uə]	poor, sure	*u* bastante larga más el sonido indistinto [ə]

CONSONANTES

	Ejemplo inglés	*Explicación*
[b]	**big, lobby**	Como en tum*b*an
[d]	**mended**	Como en con*d*e, an*d*ar
[g]	**go, get, big**	Como en *g*rande, *g*ol
[dʒ]	**gin, judge**	Como en la *ll* andaluza y en Generalitat (*catalán*)
[ŋ]	**sing**	Como en ví*n*culo
[h]	**house, he**	Como la jota hispanoamericana
[j]	**young, yes**	Como en *y*a
[k]	**come, mock**	Como en *c*aña, Es*c*ocia
[r]	**red, tread**	Se pronuncia con la punta de la lengua hacia atrás y sin hacerla vibrar
[s]	**sand, yes**	Como en ca*s*a, *s*esión
[z]	**rose, zebra**	Como en de*s*de, mi*s*mo
[ʃ]	**she, machine**	Como en *ch*ambre (*francés*), roxo (*portugués*)
[tʃ]	**chin, rich**	Como en *ch*ocolate
[v]	**valley**	Como *f*, pero se retiran los dientes superiores vibrándolos contra el labio inferior
[w]	**water, which**	Como la *u* de h*u*evo, p*u*ede
[ʒ]	**vision**	Como en *j*ournal (*francés*)
[θ]	**think, myth**	Como en re*c*eta, *z*apato
[ð]	**this, the**	Como en habla*d*o, verda*d*

f, l, m, n, p, t y x iguales que en español.

El signo [*] indica que la r final escrita apenas se pronuncia en inglés británico cuando la palabra siguiente empieza con vocal.
El signo [ˈ] indica la sílaba acentuada.

SPANISH VERB TABLES

1 Gerund **2** Imperative **3** Present **4** Preterite **5** Future **6** Present subjunctive **7** Imperfect subjunctive **8** Past participle **9** Imperfect

Etc indicates that the irregular root is used for all persons of the tense, e.g. **oír**: 6 oiga, oigas, oigamos, oigáis, oigan

agradecer 3 agradezco **6** agradezca *etc*
aprobar 2 aprueba **3** apruebo, apruebas, aprueba, aprueban **6** apruebe, apruebes, apruebe, aprueben
atravesar 2 atraviesa **3** atravieso, atraviesas, atraviesa, atraviesan **6** atraviese, atravieses, atraviese, atraviesen
caber 3 quepo **4** cupe, cupiste, cupo, cupimos, cupisteis, cupieron **5** cabré *etc* **6** quepa *etc* **7** cupiera *etc*
caer 1 cayendo **3** caigo **4** cayó, cayeron **6** caiga *etc* **7** cayera *etc*
cerrar 2 cierra **3** cierro, cierras, cierra, cierran **6** cierre, cierres, cierre, cierren
COMER 1 comiendo **2** come, comed **3** como, comes, come, comemos, coméis, comen **4** comí, comiste, comió, comimos, comisteis, comieron **5** comeré, comerás, comerá, comeremos, comeréis, comerán **6** coma, comas, coma, comamos, comáis, coman **7** comiera, comieras, comiera, comiéramos, comierais, comieran **8** comido **9** comía, comías, comía, comíamos, comíais, comían
conocer 3 conozco **6** conozca *etc*
contar 2 cuenta **3** cuento, cuentas, cuenta, cuentan **6** cuente, cuentes, cuente, cuenten
dar 3 doy **4** di, diste, dio, dimos, disteis, dieron **7** diera *etc*
decir 2 di **3** digo **4** dije, dijiste, dijo, dijimos, dijisteis, dijeron **5** diré *etc* **6** diga *etc* **7** dijera *etc* **8** dicho
despertar 2 despierta **3** despierto, despiertas, despierta, despiertan **6** despierte, despiertes, despierte, despierten
divertir 1 divirtiendo **2** divierte **3** divierto, diviertes, divierte, divierten **4** divirtió, divirtieron **6** divierta, diviertas, divierta, divirtamos, divirtáis, diviertan **7** divirtiera *etc*
dormir 1 durmiendo **2** duerme **3** duermo, duermes, duerme, duermen **4** durmió, durmieron **6** duerma, duermas, duerma, durmamos, durmáis, duerman **7** durmiera *etc*
empezar 2 empieza **3** empiezo, empiezas, empieza, empiezan **4** empecé **6** empiece, empieces, empiece, empecemos, empecéis, empiecen
entender 2 entiende **3** entiendo, entiendes, entiende, entienden **6** entienda, entiendas, entienda, entiendan
ESTAR 2 está **3** estoy, estás, está, están **4** estuve, estuviste,

estuvo, estuvimos, estuvisteis, estuvieron **6** esté, estés, esté, estén **7** estuviera *etc*

HABER 3 he, has, ha, hemos, han **4** hube, hubiste, hubo, hubimos, hubisteis, hubieron **5** habré *etc* **6** haya *etc* **7** hubiera *etc*

HABLAR 1 hablando **2** habla, hablad **3** hablo, hablas, habla, hablamos, habláis, hablan **4** hablé, hablaste, habló, hablamos, hablasteis, hablaron **5** hablaré, hablarás, hablará, hablaremos, hablaréis, hablarán **6** hable, hables, hable, hablemos, habléis, hablen **7** hablara, hablaras, hablara, habláramos, hablarais, hablaran **8** hablado **9** hablaba, hablabas, hablaba, hablábamos, hablabais, hablaban

hacer 2 haz **3** hago **4** hice, hiciste, hizo, hicimos, hicisteis, hicieron **5** haré *etc* **6** haga *etc* **7** hiciera *etc* **8** hecho

instruir 1 instruyendo **2** instruye **3** instruyo, instruyes, instruye, instruyen **4** instruyó, instruyeron **6** instruya *etc* **7** instruyera *etc*

ir 1 yendo **2** ve **3** voy, vas, va, vamos, vais, van **4** fui, fuiste, fue, fuimos, fuisteis, fueron **6** vaya, vayas, vaya, vayamos, vayáis, vayan **7** fuera *etc* **9** iba, ibas, iba, íbamos, ibais, iban

jugar 2 juega **3** juego, juegas, juega, juegan **4** jugué **6** juegue *etc*

leer 1 leyendo **4** leyó, leyeron **7** leyera *etc*

morir 1 muriendo **2** muere **3** muero, mueres, muere, mueren **4** murió, murieron **6** muera, mueras, muera, muramos, muráis, mueran **7** muriera *etc* **8** muerto

mover 2 mueve **3** muevo, mueves,mueve,mueven **6** mueva, muevas, mueva, muevan

negar 2 niega **3** niego, niegas, niega, niegan **4** negué **6** niegue, niegues, niegue, neguemos, neguéis, nieguen

ofrecer 3 ofrezco **6** ofrezca *etc*

oír 1 oyendo **2** oye **3** oigo, oyes, oye, oyen **4** oyó, oyeron **6** oiga *etc* **7** oyera *etc*

oler 2 huele **3** huelo, hueles, huele, huelen **6** huela, huelas, huela, huelan

parecer 3 parezco **6** parezca *etc*

pedir 1 pidiendo **2** pide **3** pido, pides, pide, piden **4** pidió, pidieron **6** pida *etc* **7** pidiera *etc*

pensar 2 piensa **3** pienso, piensas, piensa, piensan **6** piense, pienses, piense, piensen

perder 2 pierde **3** pierdo, pierdes, pierde, pierden **6** pierda, pierdas, pierda, pierdan

poder 1 pudiendo **2** puede **3** puedo, puedes, puede, pueden **4** pude, pudiste, pudo, pudimos, pudisteis, pudieron **5** podré *etc* **6** pueda, puedas, pueda, puedan **7** pudiera *etc*

poner 2 pon **3** pongo **4** puse, pusiste, puso, pusimos, pusisteis, pusieron **5** pondré *etc* **6** ponga *etc* **7** pusiera *etc* **8** puesto

preferir 1 prefiriendo **2** prefiere **3** prefiero, prefieres, prefiere, prefieren **4** prefirió, prefirieron **6** prefiera, prefieras, prefiera, prefiramos, prefiráis, prefieran **7** prefiriera *etc*

querer 2 quiere **3** quiero, quieres, quiere, quieren **4** quise, quisiste, quiso, quisimos, quisisteis, quisieron **5** querré *etc* **6** quiera, quieras, quiera, quieran **7** quisiera *etc*
reír 2 ríe **3** río, ríes, ríe, ríen **4** reí, rieron **6** ría, rías, ría, riamos, riáis, rían **7** riera *etc*
repetir 1 repitiendo **2** repite **3** repito, repites, repite, repiten **4** repitió, repitieron **6** repita *etc* **7** repitiera *etc*
rogar 2 ruega **3** ruego, ruegas, ruega, ruegan **4** rogué **6** ruegue, ruegues, ruegue, roguemos, roguéis, rueguen
saber 3 sé **4** supe, supiste, supo, supimos, supisteis, supieron **5** sabré *etc* **6** sepa *etc* **7** supiera *etc*
salir 2 sal **3** salgo **5** saldré *etc* **6** salga *etc*
seguir 1 siguiendo **2** sigue **3** sigo, sigues, sigue, siguen **4** siguió, siguieron **6** siga *etc* **7** siguiera *etc*
sentar 2 sienta **3** siento, sientas, sienta, sientan **6** siente, sientes, siente, sienten
sentir 1 sintiendo **2** siente **3** siento, sientes, siente, sienten **4** sintió, sintieron **6** sienta, sientas, sienta, sintamos, sintáis, sientan **7** sintiera *etc*
SER 2 sé **3** soy, eres, es, somos, sois, son **4** fui, fuiste, fue, fuimos, fuisteis, fueron **6** sea *etc* **7** fuera *etc* **9** era, eras, era, éramos, erais, eran
servir 1 sirviendo **2** sirve **3** sirvo, sirves, sirve, sirven **4** sirvió, sirvieron **6** sirva *etc* **7** sirviera *etc*
soñar 2 sueña **3** sueño, sueñas, sueña, sueñan **6** sueñe, sueñes, sueñe, sueñen
tener 2 ten **3** tengo, tienes, tiene, tienen **4** tuve, tuviste, tuvo, tuvimos, tuvisteis, tuvieron **5** tendré *etc* **6** tenga *etc* **7** tuviera *etc*
traer 1 trayendo **3** traigo **4** traje, trajiste, trajo, trajimos, trajisteis, trajeron **6** traiga *etc* **7** trajera *etc*
valer 2 vale **3** valgo **5** valdré *etc* **6** valga *etc*
venir 2 ven **3** vengo, vienes, viene, vienen **4** vine, viniste, vino, vinimos, vinisteis, vinieron **5** vendré *etc* **6** venga *etc* **7** viniera *etc*
ver 3 veo **6** vea *etc* **8** visto **9** veía *etc*
vestir 1 vistiendo **2** viste **3** visto, vistes, viste, visten **4** vistió, vistieron **6** vista *etc* **7** vistiera *etc*
VIVIR 1 viviendo **2** vive, vivid **3** vivo, vives, vive, vivimos, vivís, viven **4** viví, viviste, vivió, vivimos, vivisteis, vivieron **5** viviré, vivirás, vivirá, viviremos, viviréis, vivirán **6** viva, vivas, viva, vivamos, viváis, vivan **7** viviera, vivieras, viviera, viviéramos, vivierais, vivieran **8** vivido **9** vivía, vivías, vivía, vivíamos, vivías, vivían
volver 2 vuelve **3** vuelvo, vuelves, vuelve, vuelven **6** vuelva, vuelvas, vuelva, vuelvan **8** vuelto

VERBOS IRREGULARES EN INGLÉS

PRESENTE	PASADO	PARTICIPIO	PRESENTE	PASADO	PARTICIPIO
arise	arose	arisen	**fall**	fell	fallen
awake	awoke	awoken	**feed**	fed	fed
be (am, is,	was, were	been	**feel**	felt	felt
are; being)			**fight**	fought	fought
bear	bore	born(e)	**find**	found	found
beat	beat	beaten	**flee**	fled	fled
become	became	become	**fling**	flung	flung
begin	began	begun	**fly**	flew	flown
bend	bent	bent	**forbid**	forbad(e)	forbidden
bet	bet,	bet,	**forecast**	forecast	forecast
	betted	betted	**forget**	forgot	forgotten
bid (*at auction,*	bid	bid	**forgive**	forgave	forgiven
cards)			**forsake**	forsook	forsaken
bid (*say*)	bade	bidden	**freeze**	froze	frozen
bind	bound	bound	**get**	got	got,
bite	bit	bitten			(*us*) gotten
bleed	bled	bled	**give**	gave	given
blow	blew	blown	**go** (goes)	went	gone
break	broke	broken	**grind**	ground	ground
breed	bred	bred	**grow**	grew	grown
bring	brought	brought	**hang**	hung	hung
build	built	built	**hang** (*suspend*)	hanged	hanged
burn	burnt,	burnt,	(execute)		
	burned	burned	**have**	had	had
burst	burst	burst	**hear**	heard	heard
buy	bought	bought	**hide**	hid	hidden
can	could	(been able)	**hit**	hit	hit
cast	cast	cast	**hold**	held	held
catch	caught	caught	**hurt**	hurt	hurt
choose	chose	chosen	**keep**	kept	kept
cling	clung	clung	**kneel**	knelt,	knelt,
come	came	come		kneeled	kneeled
cost (*be*	cost	cost	**know**	knew	known
valued at)			**lay**	laid	laid
cost (*work*	costed	costed	**lead**	led	led
out price of)			**lean**	leant,	leant,
creep	crept	crept		leaned	leaned
cut	cut	cut	**leap**	leapt,	leapt,
deal	dealt	dealt		leaped	leaped
dig	dug	dug	**learn**	learnt,	learnt,
do (does)	did	done		learned	learned
draw	drew	drawn	**leave**	left	left
dream	dreamed,	dreamed,	**lend**	lent	lent
	dreamt	dreamt	**let**	let	let
drink	drank	drunk	**lie** (lying)	lay	lain
drive	drove	driven	**light**	lit,	lit,
dwell	dwelt	dwelt		lighted	lighted
eat	ate	eaten	**lose**	lost	lost

PRESENTE	PASADO	PARTICIPIO
make	made	made
may	might	–
mean	meant	meant
meet	met	met
mistake	mistook	mistaken
mow	mowed	mown, mowed
must	(had to)	(had to)
pay	paid	paid
put	put	put
quit	quit, quitted	quit, quitted
read	read	read
rid	rid	rid
ride	rode	ridden
ring	rang	rung
rise	rose	risen
run	ran	run
saw	sawed	sawed, sawn
say	said	said
see	saw	seen
seek	sought	sought
sell	sold	sold
send	sent	sent
set	set	set
sew	sewed	sewn
shake	shook	shaken
shear	sheared	shorn, sheared
shed	shed	shed
shine	shone	shone
shoot	shot	shot
show	showed	shown
shrink	shrank	shrunk
shut	shut	shut
sing	sang	sung
sink	sank	sunk
sit	sat	sat
slay	slew	slain
sleep	slept	slept
slide	slid	slid
sling	slung	slung
slit	slit	slit
smell	smelt, smelled	smelt, smelled
sow	sowed	sown, sowed
speak	spoke	spoken

PRESENTE	PASADO	PARTICIPIO
speed	sped, speeded	sped, speeded
spell	spelt, spelled	spelt, spelled
spend	spent	spent
spill	spilt, spilled	spilt, spilled
spin	spun	spun
spit	spat	spat
spoil	spoiled, spoilt	spoiled, spoilt
spread	spread	spread
spring	sprang	sprung
stand	stood	stood
steal	stole	stolen
stick	stuck	stuck
sting	stung	stung
stink	stank	stunk
stride	strode	stridden
strike	struck	struck
strive	strove	striven
swear	swore	sworn
sweep	swept	swept
swell	swelled	swollen, swelled
swim	swam	swum
swing	swung	swung
take	took	taken
teach	taught	taught
tear	tore	torn
tell	told	told
think	thought	thought
throw	threw	thrown
thrust	thrust	thrust
tread	trod	trodden
wake	woke, waked	woken, waked
wear	wore	worn
weave (*on loom*)	wove	woven
weave (*wind*)	weaved	weaved
wed	wedded, wed	wedded, wed
weep	wept	wept
win	won	won
wind	wound	wound
wring	wrung	wrung
write	wrote	written

a

PALABRA CLAVE

a [a] (*a + el = al*) *prep* **1** (*dirección*) to; **fueron a Madrid/Grecia** they went to Madrid/ Greece; **me voy a casa** I'm going home
2 (*distancia*): **está a 15 km de aquí** it's 15 kms from here
3 (*posición*): **estar a la mesa** to be at table; **al lado de** next to, beside; *V tb* **puerta**
4 (*tiempo*): **a las 10/a medianoche** at 10/ midnight; **a la mañana siguiente** the following morning; **a los pocos días** after a few days; **estamos a 9 de julio** it's the ninth of July; **a los 24 años** at the age of 24; **al año/a la semana** a year/week later
5 (*manera*): **a la francesa** the French way; **a caballo** on horseback; **a oscuras** in the dark
6 (*medio, instrumento*): **a lápiz** in pencil; **a mano** by hand; **cocina a gas** gas stove
7 (*razón*): **a 30 céntimos el kilo** at 30 cents a kilo; **a más de 50 km/h** at more than 50 kms per hour
8 (*dativo*): **se lo di a él** I gave it to him; **vi al policía** I saw the policeman; **se lo compré a él** I bought it from him
9 (*tras ciertos verbos*): **voy a verle** I'm going to see him; **empezó a trabajar** he started working *o* to work
10 (*+ infin*): **al verlo, lo reconocí inmediatamente** when I saw him I recognized him at once; **el camino a recorrer** the distance we *etc* have to travel; **¡a callar!** keep quiet!; **¡a comer!** let's eat!

abad, esa [a'βað, 'ðesa] *nm/f* abbot/ abbess; **abadía** *nf* abbey
abajo [a'βaxo] *adv* (*situación*) (down) below, underneath; (*en edificio*) downstairs; (*dirección*) down, downwards; **el piso de ~** the downstairs flat; **la parte de ~** the lower part; **¡~ el gobierno!** down with the government!; **cuesta/río ~** downhill/ downstream; **de arriba ~** from top to bottom; **el ~ firmante** the undersigned; **más ~** lower *o* further down
abalanzarse [aβalan'θarse] *vr*: **~ sobre** *o* **contra** to throw o.s. at
abanderado, -a [aβande'raðo] *nm/f* (*portaestandarte*) standard bearer; (*de un movimiento*) champion, leader; (*MÉX: linier*) linesman, assistant referee
abandonado, -a [aβando'naðo, a] *adj* derelict; (*desatendido*) abandoned; (*desierto*) deserted; (*descuidado*) neglected
abandonar [aβando'nar] *vt* to leave; (*persona*) to abandon, desert; (*cosa*) to abandon, leave behind; (*descuidar*) to neglect; (*renunciar a*) to give up; (*Inform*) to quit; **abandonarse** *vr*: **~se a** to abandon o.s. to; **abandono** *nm* (*acto*) desertion, abandonment; (*estado*) abandon, neglect; (*renuncia*) withdrawal, retirement; **ganar por abandono** to win by default
abanico [aβa'niko] *nm* fan; (*Náut*) derrick
abarcar [aβar'kar] *vt* to include, embrace; (*LAM: acaparar*) to monopolize
abarrotado, -a [aβarro'taðo, a] *adj* packed
abarrotar [aβarro'tar] *vt* (*local, estadio, teatro*) to fill, pack
abarrotero, -a [aβarro'tero, a] (*MÉX*) *nm/f* grocer; **abarrotes** (*MÉX*) *nmpl* groceries; **tienda de abarrotes** (*MÉX, CAM*) grocery store
abastecer [aβaste'θer] *vt*: **~ (de)** to supply (with); **abastecimiento** *nm* supply
abasto [a'βasto] *nm* supply; **no dar ~ a** to be unable to cope with
abatible [aβa'tiβle] *adj*: **asiento ~** tip-up seat; (*Auto*) reclining seat
abatido, -a [aβa'tiðo, a] *adj* dejected, downcast
abatir [aβa'tir] *vt* (*muro*) to demolish; (*pájaro*) to shoot *o* bring down; (*fig*) to depress
abdicar [aβði'kar] *vi* to abdicate
abdomen [aβ'ðomen] *nm* abdomen; **abdominales** *nmpl* (*tb*: **ejercicios abdominales**) sit-ups
abecedario [aβeθe'ðarjo] *nm* alphabet
abedul [aβe'ðul] *nm* birch
abeja [a'βexa] *nf* bee
abejorro [aβe'xorro] *nm* bumblebee
abertura [aβer'tura] *nf* = **apertura**
abeto [a'βeto] *nm* fir
abierto, -a [a'βjerto, a] *pp de* **abrir** ▷ *adj* open
abismal [aβis'mal] *adj* (*fig*) vast, enormous

abismo [a'βismo] *nm* abyss
ablandar [aβlan'dar] *vt* to soften; **ablandarse** *vr* to get softer
abocado, -a [aβo'kaðo, a] *adj* (*vino*) smooth, pleasant
abochornar [aβotʃor'nar] *vt* to embarrass
abofetear [aβofete'ar] *vt* to slap (in the face)
abogado, -a [aβo'ɣaðo, a] *nm/f* lawyer; (*notario*) solicitor; (*en tribunal*) barrister (BRIT), attorney (US); **abogado defensor** defence lawyer *o* (US) attorney
abogar [aβo'ɣar] *vi*: **~ por** to plead for; (*fig*) to advocate
abolir [aβo'lir] *vt* to abolish; (*cancelar*) to cancel
abolladura [aβoʎa'ðura] *nf* dent
abollar [aβo'ʎar] *vt* to dent
abombarse [aβom'barse] (LAM) *vr* to go bad
abominable [aβomi'naβle] *adj* abominable
abonado, -a [aβo'naðo, a] *adj* (*deuda*) paid(-up) ▷*nm/f* subscriber
abonar [aβo'nar] *vt* (*deuda*) to settle; (*terreno*) to fertilize; (*idea*) to endorse; **abonarse** *vr* to subscribe; **abono** *nm* payment; fertilizer; subscription
abordar [aβor'ðar] *vt* (*barco*) to board; (*asunto*) to broach
aborigen [aβo'rixen] *nmf* aborigine
aborrecer [aβorre'θer] *vt* to hate, loathe
abortar [aβor'tar] *vi* (*malparir*) to have a miscarriage; (*deliberadamente*) to have an abortion; **aborto** *nm* miscarriage; abortion
abovedado, -a [aβoβe'ðaðo, a] *adj* vaulted, domed
abrasar [aβra'sar] *vt* to burn (up); (*Agr*) to dry up, parch
abrazar [aβra'θar] *vt* to embrace, hug
abrazo [a'βraθo] *nm* embrace, hug; **un ~** (*en carta*) with best wishes
abrebotellas [aβreβo'teʎas] *nm inv* bottle opener
abrecartas [aβre'kartas] *nm inv* letter opener
abrelatas [aβre'latas] *nm inv* tin (BRIT) *o* can opener
abreviatura [aβreβja'tura] *nf* abbreviation
abridor [aβri'ðor] *nm* bottle opener; (*de latas*) tin (BRIT) *o* can opener
abrigador, a [aβriga'ðor, a] (MÉX) *adj* warm
abrigar [aβri'ɣar] *vt* (*proteger*) to shelter; (*ropa*) to keep warm; (*fig*) to cherish
abrigo [a'βriɣo] *nm* (*prenda*) coat, overcoat; (*lugar protegido*) shelter
abril [a'βril] *nm* April
abrillantador [aβriʎanta'ðor] *nm* polish
abrillantar [aβriʎan'tar] *vt* to polish
abrir [a'βrir] *vt* to open (up) ▷*vi* to open; **abrirse** *vr* to open (up); (*extenderse*) to open out; (*cielo*) to clear; **~se paso** to find *o* force a way through
abrochar [aβro'tʃar] *vt* (*con botones*) to button (up); (*zapato, con broche*) to do up
abrupto, -a [a'βrupto, a] *adj* abrupt; (*empinado*) steep
absoluto, -a [aβso'luto, a] *adj* absolute; **en ~** *adv* not at all
absolver [aβsol'βer] *vt* to absolve; (*Jur*) to pardon; (: *acusado*) to acquit
absorbente [aβsor'βente] *adj* absorbent; (*interesante*) absorbing
absorber [aβsor'βer] *vt* to absorb; (*embeber*) to soak up
absorción [aβsor'θjon] *nf* absorption; (*Com*) takeover
abstemio, -a [aβs'temjo, a] *adj* teetotal
abstención [aβsten'θjon] *nf* abstention
abstenerse [aβste'nerse] *vr*: **~ (de)** to abstain *o* refrain (from)
abstinencia [aβsti'nenθja] *nf* abstinence; (*ayuno*) fasting
abstracto, -a [aβ'strakto, a] *adj* abstract
abstraer [aβstra'er] *vt* to abstract; **abstraerse** *vr* to be *o* become absorbed
abstraído, -a [aβstra'iðo, a] *adj* absent-minded
absuelto [aβ'swelto] *pp de* **absolver**
absurdo, -a [aβ'surðo, a] *adj* absurd
abuchear [aβutʃe'ar] *vt* to boo
abuelo, -a [a'βwelo, a] *nm/f* grandfather(-mother); **abuelos** *nmpl* grandparents
abultado, -a [aβul'taðo, a] *adj* bulky
abultar [aβul'tar] *vi* to be bulky
abundancia [aβun'danθja] *nf*: **una ~ de** plenty of; **abundante** *adj* abundant, plentiful
abundar [aβun'dar] *vi* to abound, be plentiful
aburrido, -a [aβu'rriðo, a] *adj* (*hastiado*) bored; (*que aburre*) boring; **aburrimiento** *nm* boredom, tedium
aburrir [aβu'rrir] *vt* to bore; **aburrirse** *vr* to be bored, get bored
abusado, -a [aβu'saðo, a] (MÉX: *fam*) *adj* (*astuto*) sharp, cunning ▷*excl*: **¡~!** (*inv*) look out!, careful!
abusar [aβu'sar] *vi* to go too far; **~ de** to abuse
abusivo, -a [aβu'siβo, a] *adj* (*precio*)

exorbitant

abuso [a'βuso] *nm* abuse

acá [a'ka] *adv* (*lugar*) here

acabado, -a [aka'βaðo, a] *adj* finished, complete; (*perfecto*) perfect; (*agotado*) worn out; (*fig*) masterly ▷ *nm* finish

acabar [aka'βar] *vt* (*llevar a su fin*) to finish, complete; (*consumir*) to use up; (*rematar*) to finish off ▷ *vi* to finish, end; **acabarse** *vr* to finish, stop; (*terminarse*) to be over; (*agotarse*) to run out; **~ con** to put an end to; **~ de llegar** to have just arrived; **~ por hacer** to end (up) by doing; **¡se acabó!** it's all over!; (*¡basta!*) that's enough!

acabóse [aka'βose] *nm*: **esto es el ~** this is the last straw

academia [aka'ðemja] *nf* academy; **academia de idiomas** language school; **académico, -a** *adj* academic

acalorado, -a [akalo'raðo, a] *adj* (*discusión*) heated

acampar [akam'par] *vi* to camp

acantilado [akanti'laðo] *nm* cliff

acaparar [akapa'rar] *vt* to monopolize; (*acumular*) to hoard

acariciar [akari'θjar] *vt* to caress; (*esperanza*) to cherish

acarrear [akarre'ar] *vt* to transport; (*fig*) to cause, result in

acaso [a'kaso] *adv* perhaps, maybe; **(por) si ~** (just) in case

acatar [aka'tar] *vt* to respect; (*ley*) obey

acatarrarse [akata'rrarse] *vr* to catch a cold

acceder [akθe'ðer] *vi*: **~ a** (*petición etc*) to agree to; (*tener acceso a*) to have access to; (*Inform*) to access

accesible [akθe'siβle] *adj* accessible

acceso [ak'θeso] *nm* access, entry; (*camino*) access, approach; (*Med*) attack, fit

accesorio, -a [akθe'sorjo, a] *adj, nm* accessory

accidentado, -a [akθiðen'taðo, a] *adj* uneven; (*montañoso*) hilly; (*azaroso*) eventful ▷ *nm/f* accident victim

accidental [akθiðen'tal] *adj* accidental

accidente [akθi'ðente] *nm* accident; **accidentes** *nmpl* (*de terreno*) unevenness *sg*; **accidente laboral** *o* **de trabajo/de tráfico** industrial/road *o* traffic accident

acción [ak'θjon] *nf* action; (*acto*) action, act; (*Com*) share; (*Jur*) action, lawsuit; **accionar** *vt* to work, operate; (*Inform*) to drive

accionista [akθjo'nista] *nmf* shareholder, stockholder

acebo [a'θeβo] *nm* holly; (*árbol*) holly tree

acechar [aθe'tʃar] *vt* to spy on; (*aguardar*) to lie in wait for; **acecho** *nm*: **estar al acecho (de)** to lie in wait (for)

aceite [a'θeite] *nm* oil; **aceite de girasol/oliva** olive/sunflower oil; **aceitera** *nf* oilcan; **aceitoso, -a** *adj* oily

aceituna [aθei'tuna] *nf* olive; **aceituna rellena** stuffed olive

acelerador [aθelera'ðor] *nm* accelerator

acelerar [aθele'rar] *vt* to accelerate

acelga [a'θelɣa] *nf* chard, beet

acento [a'θento] *nm* accent; (*acentuación*) stress

acentuar [aθen'twar] *vt* to accent; to stress; (*fig*) to accentuate

acepción [aθep'θjon] *nf* meaning

aceptable [aθep'taβle] *adj* acceptable

aceptación [aθepta'θjon] *nf* acceptance; (*aprobación*) approval

aceptar [aθep'tar] *vt* to accept; (*aprobar*) to approve; **~ hacer algo** to agree to do sth

acequia [a'θekja] *nf* irrigation ditch

acera [a'θera] *nf* pavement (BRIT), sidewalk (US)

acerca [a'θerka]: **~ de** *prep* about, concerning

acercar [aθer'kar] *vt* to bring *o* move nearer; **acercarse** *vr* to approach, come near

acero [a'θero] *nm* steel

acérrimo, -a [a'θerrimo, a] *adj* (*partidario*) staunch; (*enemigo*) bitter

acertado, -a [aθer'taðo, a] *adj* correct; (*apropiado*) apt; (*sensato*) sensible

acertar [aθer'tar] *vt* (*blanco*) to hit; (*solución*) to get right; (*adivinar*) to guess ▷ *vi* to get it right, be right; **~ a** to manage to; **~ con** to happen *o* hit on

acertijo [aθer'tixo] *nm* riddle, puzzle

achacar [atʃa'kar] *vt* to attribute

achacoso, -a [atʃa'koso, a] *adj* sickly

achicar [atʃi'kar] *vt* to reduce; (*Náut*) to bale out

achicharrar [atʃitʃa'rrar] *vt* to scorch, burn

achichincle [atʃi'tʃinkle] (MÉX: *fam*) *nmf* minion

achicoria [atʃi'korja] *nf* chicory

achuras [a'tʃuras] (RPL) *nfpl* offal *sg*

acicate [aθi'kate] *nm* spur

acidez [aθi'ðeθ] *nf* acidity

ácido, -a ['aθiðo, a] *adj* sour, acid ▷ *nm* acid

acierto *etc* [a'θjerto] *vb V* **acertar** ▷ *nm* success; (*buen paso*) wise move; (*solución*) solution; (*habilidad*) skill, ability

acitronar [aθitro'nar] (MÉX: *fam*) *vt* to brown

aclamar [akla'mar] *vt* to acclaim;

(*aplaudir*) to applaud
aclaración [aklara'θjon] *nf* clarification, explanation
aclarar [akla'rar] *vt* to clarify, explain; (*ropa*) to rinse ▷ *vi* to clear up; **aclararse** *vr* (*explicarse*) to understand; **~se la garganta** to clear one's throat
aclimatación [aklimata'θjon] *nf* acclimatization
aclimatar [aklima'tar] *vt* to acclimatize; **aclimatarse** *vr* to become acclimatized
acné [ak'ne] *nm* acne
acobardar [akoβar'ðar] *vt* to intimidate
acogedor, a [akoxe'ðor, a] *adj* welcoming; (*hospitalario*) hospitable
acoger [ako'xer] *vt* to welcome; (*abrigar*) to shelter
acogida [ako'xiða] *nf* reception; refuge
acomedido, -a [akome'ðiðo, a] (MÉX) *adj* helpful, obliging
acometer [akome'ter] *vt* to attack; (*emprender*) to undertake; **acometida** *nf* attack, assault
acomodado, -a [akomo'ðaðo, a] *adj* (*persona*) well-to-do
acomodador, a [akomoða'ðor, a] *nm/f* usher(ette)
acomodar [akomo'ðar] *vt* to adjust; (*alojar*) to accommodate; **acomodarse** *vr* to conform; (*instalarse*) to install o.s.; (*adaptarse*): **~se (a)** to adapt (to)
acompañar [akompa'ɲar] *vt* to accompany; (*documentos*) to enclose
acondicionar [akondiθjo'nar] *vt* to arrange, prepare; (*pelo*) to condition
aconsejar [akonse'xar] *vt* to advise, counsel; **~ a algn hacer** *o* **que haga algo** to advise sb to do sth
acontecer [akonte'θer] *vi* to happen, occur; **acontecimiento** *nm* event
acopio [a'kopjo] *nm* store, stock
acoplar [ako'plar] *vt* to fit; (*Elec*) to connect; (*vagones*) to couple
acorazado, -a [akora'θaðo, a] *adj* armour-plated, armoured ▷ *nm* battleship
acordar [akor'ðar] *vt* (*resolver*) to agree, resolve; (*recordar*) to remind; **acordarse** *vr* to agree; **~ hacer algo** to agree to do sth; **~se (de algo)** to remember (sth); **acorde** *adj* (*Mús*) harmonious; **acorde con** (*medidas etc*) in keeping with ▷ *nm* chord
acordeón [akorðe'on] *nm* accordion
acordonado, -a [akorðo'naðo, a] *adj* (*calle*) cordoned-off
acorralar [akorra'lar] *vt* to round up, corral
acortar [akor'tar] *vt* to shorten; (*duración*) to cut short; (*cantidad*) to reduce; **acortarse** *vr* to become shorter
acosar [ako'sar] *vt* to pursue relentlessly; (*fig*) to hound, pester; **acoso** *nm* harassment; **acoso sexual** sexual harassment
acostar [akos'tar] *vt* (*en cama*) to put to bed; (*en suelo*) to lay down; **acostarse** *vr* to go to bed; to lie down; **~se con algn** to sleep with sb
acostumbrado, -a [akostum'braðo, a] *adj* usual; **~ a** used to
acostumbrar [akostum'brar] *vt*: **~ a algn a algo** to get sb used to sth ▷ *vi*: **~ (a) hacer** to be in the habit of doing; **acostumbrarse** *vr*: **~se a** to get used to
acotación [akota'θjon] *nf* marginal note; (*Geo*) elevation mark; (*de límite*) boundary mark; (*Teatro*) stage direction
acotamiento [akota'mjento] (MÉX) *nm* hard shoulder (BRIT), berm (US)
acre ['akre] *adj* (*olor*) acrid; (*fig*) biting ▷ *nm* acre
acreditar [akreði'tar] *vt* (*garantizar*) to vouch for, guarantee; (*autorizar*) to authorize; (*dar prueba de*) to prove; (*Com: abonar*) to credit; (*embajador*) to accredit
acreedor, a [akree'ðor, a] *nm/f* creditor
acribillar [akriβi'ʎar] *vt*: **~ a balazos** to riddle with bullets
acróbata [a'kroβata] *nmf* acrobat
acta ['akta] *nf* certificate; (*de comisión*) minutes *pl*, record; **acta de matrimonio/nacimiento** (MÉX) marriage/birth certificate; **acta notarial** affidavit
actitud [akti'tuð] *nf* attitude; (*postura*) posture
activar [akti'βar] *vt* to activate; (*acelerar*) to speed up
actividad [aktiβi'ðað] *nf* activity
activo, -a [ak'tiβo, a] *adj* active; (*vivo*) lively ▷ *nm* (*Com*) assets *pl*
acto ['akto] *nm* act, action; (*ceremonia*) ceremony; (*Teatro*) act; **en el ~** immediately
actor [ak'tor] *nm* actor; (*Jur*) plaintiff ▷ *adj*: **parte ~a** prosecution
actriz [ak'triθ] *nf* actress
actuación [aktwa'θjon] *nf* action; (*comportamiento*) conduct, behaviour; (*Jur*) proceedings *pl*; (*desempeño*) performance
actual [ak'twal] *adj* present(-day), current

> No confundir **actual** con la palabra inglesa *actual*.

actualidad *nf* present; **actualidades** *nfpl* (*noticias*) news *sg*; **en la actualidad** at present; (*hoy día*) nowadays; **actualizar** [aktwali'θar] *vt* to update, modernize; **actualmente** [aktwal'mente] *adv* at present; (*hoy día*) nowadays

No confundir **actualmente** con la palabra inglesa *actually*.

actuar [ak'twar] *vi* (*obrar*) to work, operate; (*actor*) to act, perform ▷*vt* to work, operate; **~ de** to act as

acuarela [akwa'rela] *nf* watercolour

acuario [a'kwarjo] *nm* aquarium; (*Astrología*): **A~** Aquarius

acuático, -a [a'kwatiko, a] *adj* aquatic

acudir [aku'ðir] *vi* (*asistir*) to attend; (*ir*) to go; **~ a** (*fig*) to turn to; **~ a una cita** to keep an appointment; **~ en ayuda de** to go to the aid of

acuerdo *etc* [a'kwerðo] *vb V* **acordar** ▷*nm* agreement; **¡de ~!** agreed!; **de ~ con** (*persona*) in agreement with; (*acción, documento*) in accordance with; **estar de ~** to be agreed, agree

acumular [akumu'lar] *vt* to accumulate, collect

acuñar [aku'ɲar] *vt* (*moneda*) to mint; (*frase*) to coin

acupuntura [akupun'tura] *nf* acupuncture

acurrucarse [akurru'karse] *vr* to crouch; (*ovillarse*) to curl up

acusación [akusa'θjon] *nf* accusation

acusar [aku'sar] *vt* to accuse; (*revelar*) to reveal; (*denunciar*) to denounce

acuse [a'kuse] *nm*: **~ de recibo** acknowledgement of receipt

acústica [a'kustika] *nf* acoustics *pl*

acústico, -a [a'kustiko, a] *adj* acoustic

adaptación [aðapta'θjon] *nf* adaptation

adaptador [aðapta'ðor] *nm* (*Elec*) adapter, adaptor; **adaptador universal** universal adapter *o* adaptor

adaptar [aðap'tar] *vt* to adapt; (*acomodar*) to fit

adecuado, -a [aðe'kwaðo, a] *adj* (*apto*) suitable; (*oportuno*) appropriate

a. de J.C. *abr* (= *antes de Jesucristo*) B.C.

adelantado, -a [aðelan'taðo, a] *adj* advanced; (*reloj*) fast; **pagar por ~** to pay in advance

adelantamiento [aðelanta'mjento] *nm* (*Auto*) overtaking

adelantar [aðelan'tar] *vt* to move forward; (*avanzar*) to advance; (*acelerar*) to speed up; (*Auto*) to overtake ▷*vi* to go forward, advance; **adelantarse** *vr* to go forward, advance

adelante [aðe'lante] *adv* forward(s), ahead ▷*excl* come in!; **de hoy en ~** from now on; **más ~** later on; (*más allá*) further on

adelanto [aðe'lanto] *nm* advance; (*mejora*) improvement; (*progreso*) progress

adelgazar [aðelɣa'θar] *vt* to thin (down) ▷*vi* to get thin; (*con régimen*) to slim down, lose weight

ademán [aðe'man] *nm* gesture; **ademanes** *nmpl* manners

además [aðe'mas] *adv* besides; (*por otra parte*) moreover; (*también*) also; **~ de** besides, in addition to

adentrarse [aðen'trarse] *vr*: **~ en** to go into, get inside; (*penetrar*) to penetrate (into)

adentro [a'ðentro] *adv* inside, in; **mar ~** out at sea; **tierra ~** inland

adepto, -a [a'ðepto, a] *nm/f* supporter

aderezar [aðere'θar] *vt* (*ensalada*) to dress; (*comida*) to season; **aderezo** *nm* dressing; seasoning

adeudar [aðeu'ðar] *vt* to owe

adherirse [aðe'rirse] *vr*: **~ a** to adhere to; (*partido*) to join

adhesión [aðe'sjon] *nf* adhesion; (*fig*) adherence

adicción [aðik'θjon] *nf* addiction

adición [aði'θjon] *nf* addition

adicto, -a [a'ðikto, a] *adj*: **~ a** addicted to; (*dedicado*) devoted to ▷*nm/f* supporter, follower; (*toxicómano*) addict

adiestrar [aðjes'trar] *vt* to train, teach; (*conducir*) to guide, lead

adinerado, -a [aðine'raðo, a] *adj* wealthy

adiós [a'ðjos] *excl* (*para despedirse*) goodbye!, cheerio!; (*al pasar*) hello!

aditivo [aði'tiβo] *nm* additive

adivinanza [aðiβi'nanθa] *nf* riddle

adivinar [aðiβi'nar] *vt* to prophesy; (*conjeturar*) to guess; **adivino, -a** *nm/f* fortune-teller

adj *abr* (= *adjunto*) encl

adjetivo [aðxe'tiβo] *nm* adjective

adjudicar [aðxuði'kar] *vt* to award; **adjudicarse** *vr*: **~se algo** to appropriate sth

adjuntar [aðxun'tar] *vt* to attach, enclose; **adjunto, -a** *adj* attached, enclosed ▷*nm/f* assistant

administración [aðministra'θjon] *nf* administration; (*dirección*) management; **administrador, a** *nm/f* administrator, manager(ess)

administrar [aðminis'trar] *vt* to administer; **administrativo, -a** *adj* administrative

admirable [aðmi'raβle] *adj* admirable

admiración [aðmira'θjon] *nf* admiration; (*asombro*) wonder; (*Ling*) exclamation mark

admirar [aðmi'rar] *vt* to admire; (*extrañar*) to surprise

admisible [aðmi'siβle] *adj* admissible

admisión [aðmi'sjon] *nf* admission; (*reconocimiento*) acceptance
admitir [aðmi'tir] *vt* to admit; (*aceptar*) to accept
adobar [aðo'βar] *vt* (*Culin*) to season
adobe [a'ðoβe] *nm* adobe, sun-dried brick
adolecer [aðole'θer] *vi*: **~ de** to suffer from
adolescente [aðoles'θente] *nmf* adolescent, teenager
adonde [a'ðonðe] *conj* (to) where
adónde [a'ðonde] *adv* = **dónde**
adopción [aðop'θjon] *nf* adoption
adoptar [aðop'tar] *vt* to adopt
adoptivo, -a [aðop'tiβo, a] *adj* (*padres*) adoptive; (*hijo*) adopted
adoquín [aðo'kin] *nm* paving stone
adorar [aðo'rar] *vt* to adore
adornar [aðor'nar] *vt* to adorn
adorno [a'ðorno] *nm* ornament; (*decoración*) decoration
adosado, -a [aðo'saðo, a] *adj*: **casa adosada** semi-detached house
adosar [aðo'sar] (*MÉX*) *vt* (*adjuntar*) to attach, enclose (*with a letter*)
adquiero *etc vb V* **adquirir**
adquirir [aðki'rir] *vt* to acquire, obtain
adquisición [aðkisi'θjon] *nf* acquisition
adrede [a'ðreðe] *adv* on purpose
ADSL *nm abr* broadband
aduana [a'ðwana] *nf* customs *pl*
aduanero, -a [aðwa'nero, a] *adj* customs *cpd* ▷ *nm/f* customs officer
adueñarse [aðwe'ɲarse] *vr*: **~ de** to take possession of
adular [aðu'lar] *vt* to flatter
adulterar [aðulte'rar] *vt* to adulterate
adulterio [aðul'terjo] *nm* adultery
adúltero, -a [a'ðultero, a] *adj* adulterous ▷ *nm/f* adulterer/adulteress
adulto, -a [a'ðulto, a] *adj, nm/f* adult
adverbio [að'βerβjo] *nm* adverb
adversario, -a [aðβer'sarjo, a] *nm/f* adversary
adversidad [aðβersi'ðað] *nf* adversity; (*contratiempo*) setback
adverso, -a [að'βerso, a] *adj* adverse
advertencia [aðβer'tenθja] *nf* warning; (*prefacio*) preface, foreword
advertir [aðβer'tir] *vt* to notice; (*avisar*): **~ a algn de** to warn sb about *o* of
Adviento [að'βjento] *nm* Advent
advierto *etc vb V* **advertir**
aéreo, -a [a'ereo, a] *adj* aerial
aerobic [ae'roβik] *nm* aerobics *sg*; **aerobics** (*MÉX*) *nmpl* aerobics *sg*
aeromozo, -a [aero'moθo, a] (*LAM*) *nm/f* air steward(ess)
aeronáutica [aero'nautika] *nf* aeronautics *sg*
aeronave [aero'naβe] *nm* spaceship
aeroplano [aero'plano] *nm* aeroplane
aeropuerto [aero'pwerto] *nm* airport
aerosol [aero'sol] *nm* aerosol
afamado, -a [afa'maðo, a] *adj* famous
afán [a'fan] *nm* hard work; (*deseo*) desire
afanador, a [afana'ðor, a] (*MÉX*) *nm/f* (*de limpieza*) cleaner
afanar [afa'nar] *vt* to harass; (*fam*) to pinch
afear [afe'ar] *vt* to disfigure
afección [afek'θjon] *nf* (*Med*) disease
afectado, -a [afek'taðo, a] *adj* affected
afectar [afek'tar] *vt* to affect
afectísimo, -a [afek'tisimo, a] *adj* affectionate; **suyo ~** yours truly
afectivo, -a [afek'tiβo, a] *adj* (*problema etc*) emotional
afecto [a'fekto] *nm* affection; **tenerle ~ a algn** to be fond of sb
afectuoso, -a [afek'twoso, a] *adj* affectionate
afeitar [afei'tar] *vt* to shave; **afeitarse** *vr* to shave
afeminado, -a [afemi'naðo, a] *adj* effeminate
Afganistán [afɣanis'tan] *nm* Afghanistan
afianzar [afjan'θar] *vt* to strengthen; to secure; **afianzarse** *vr* to become established
afiche [a'fitʃe] (*RPL*) *nm* poster
afición [afi'θjon] *nf* fondness, liking; **la ~** the fans *pl*; **pinto por ~** I paint as a hobby;
aficionado, -a *adj* keen, enthusiastic; (*no profesional*) amateur ▷ *nm/f* enthusiast, fan; amateur; **ser aficionado a algo** to be very keen on *o* fond of sth
aficionar [afiθjo'nar] *vt*: **~ a algn a algo** to make sb like sth; **aficionarse** *vr*: **~se a algo** to grow fond of sth
afilado, -a [afi'laðo, a] *adj* sharp
afilar [afi'lar] *vt* to sharpen
afiliarse [afi'ljarse] *vr* to affiliate
afín [a'fin] *adj* (*parecido*) similar; (*conexo*) related
afinar [afi'nar] *vt* (*Tec*) to refine; (*Mús*) to tune ▷ *vi* (*tocar*) to play in tune; (*cantar*) to sing in tune
afincarse [afin'karse] *vr* to settle
afinidad [afini'ðað] *nf* affinity; (*parentesco*) relationship; **por ~** by marriage
afirmación [afirma'θjon] *nf* affirmation
afirmar [afir'mar] *vt* to affirm, state; **afirmativo, -a** *adj* affirmative
afligir [afli'xir] *vt* to afflict; (*apenar*) to distress

aflojar [aflo'xar] *vt* to slacken; (*desatar*) to loosen, undo; (*relajar*) to relax ▷ *vi* to drop; (*bajar*) to go down; **aflojarse** *vr* to relax

afluente [aflu'ente] *adj* flowing ▷ *nm* tributary

afmo, -a *abr* (= *afectísimo(a) suyo(a)*) Yours

afónico, -a ['afoniko, a] *adj*: **estar ~** to have a sore throat; to have lost one's voice

aforo [a'foro] *nm* (*de teatro etc*) capacity

afortunado, -a [afortu'naðo, a] *adj* fortunate, lucky

África ['afrika] *nf* Africa; **África del Sur** South Africa; **africano, -a** *adj, nm/f* African

afrontar [afron'tar] *vt* to confront; (*poner cara a cara*) to bring face to face

afrutado, -a [afru'taðo, a] *adj* fruity

after ['after] (*pl* **~s**) *nm* after-hours club; **afterhours** [after'aurs] *nm inv* = **after**

afuera [a'fwera] *adv* out, outside; **afueras** *nfpl* outskirts

agachar [aɤa'tʃar] *vt* to bend, bow; **agacharse** *vr* to stoop, bend

agalla [a'ɤaʎa] *nf* (*Zool*) gill; **tener ~s** (*fam*) to have guts

agarradera [aɤarra'ðera] (*MÉX*) *nf* handle

agarrado, -a [aɤa'rraðo, a] *adj* mean, stingy

agarrar [aɤa'rrar] *vt* to grasp, grab; (*LAM*: *tomar*) to take, catch; (*recoger*) to pick up ▷ *vi* (*planta*) to take root; **agarrarse** *vr* to hold on (tightly)

agencia [a'xenθja] *nf* agency; **agencia de viajes** travel agency; **agencia inmobiliaria** estate (*BRIT*) *o* real estate (*US*) agent's (office)

agenciarse [axen'θjarse] *vr* to obtain, procure

agenda [a'xenda] *nf* diary; **~ electronica** PDA

> No confundir **agenda** con la palabra inglesa *agenda*.

agente [a'xente] *nmf* agent; (*tb*: **~ de policía**) policeman/policewoman; **agente de seguros** insurance agent; **agente de tránsito** (*MÉX*) traffic cop; **agente inmobiliario** estate agent (*BRIT*), realtor (*US*)

ágil ['axil] *adj* agile, nimble; **agilidad** *nf* agility, nimbleness

agilizar [axili'θar] *vt* (*trámites*) to speed up

agiotista [axjo'tista] (*MÉX*) *nmf* (*usurero*) usurer

agitación [axita'θjon] *nf* (*de mano etc*) shaking, waving; (*de líquido etc*) stirring; (*fig*) agitation

agitado, -a [axi'aðo, a] *adj* hectic; (*viaje*) bumpy

agitar [axi'tar] *vt* to wave, shake; (*líquido*) to stir; (*fig*) to stir up, excite; **agitarse** *vr* to get excited; (*inquietarse*) to get worried *o* upset

aglomeración [aɤlomera'θjon] *nf* agglomeration; **aglomeración de gente/tráfico** mass of people/traffic jam

agnóstico, -a [aɤ'nostiko, a] *adj, nm/f* agnostic

agobiar [aɤo'βjar] *vt* to weigh down; (*oprimir*) to oppress; (*cargar*) to burden

agolparse [aɤol'parse] *vr* to crowd together

agonía [aɤo'nia] *nf* death throes *pl*; (*fig*) agony, anguish

agonizante [aɤoni'θante] *adj* dying

agonizar [aɤoni'θar] *vi* to be dying

agosto [a'ɤosto] *nm* August

agotado, -a [aɤo'taðo, a] *adj* (*persona*) exhausted; (*libros*) out of print; (*acabado*) finished; (*Com*) sold out; **agotador, a** [aɤota'ðor, a] *adj* exhausting

agotamiento [aɤota'mjento] *nm* exhaustion

agotar [aɤo'tar] *vt* to exhaust; (*consumir*) to drain; (*recursos*) to use up, deplete; **agotarse** *vr* to be exhausted; (*acabarse*) to run out; (*libro*) to go out of print

agraciado, -a [aɤra'θjaðo, a] *adj* (*atractivo*) attractive; (*en sorteo etc*) lucky

agradable [aɤra'ðaβle] *adj* pleasant, nice

agradar [aɤra'ðar] *vt*: **él me agrada** I like him

agradecer [aɤraðe'θer] *vt* to thank; (*favor etc*) to be grateful for; **agradecido, -a** *adj* grateful; **¡muy agradecido!** thanks a lot!; **agradecimiento** *nm* thanks *pl*; gratitude

agradezco *etc vb V* **agradecer**

agrado [a'ɤraðo] *nm*: **ser de tu** *etc* **~** to be to your *etc* liking

agrandar [aɤran'dar] *vt* to enlarge; (*fig*) to exaggerate; **agrandarse** *vr* to get bigger

agrario, -a [a'ɤrarjo, a] *adj* agrarian, land *cpd*; (*política*) agricultural, farming

agravante [aɤra'βante] *adj* aggravating ▷ *nm*: **con el ~ de que ...** with the further difficulty that ...

agravar [aɤra'βar] *vt* (*pesar sobre*) to make heavier; (*irritar*) to aggravate; **agravarse** *vr* to worsen, get worse

agraviar [aɤra'βjar] *vt* to offend; (*ser injusto con*) to wrong

agredir [aɤre'ðir] *vt* to attack

agregado, -a [aɤre'ɤaðo, a] *nm/f*: **A~** ≈ teacher (*who is not head of department*) ▷ *nm* aggregate; (*persona*) attaché

agregar [aɤre'ɤar] *vt* to gather; (*añadir*) to add; (*persona*) to appoint

agresión [aɤre'sjon] *nf* aggression

agresivo, -a [aɤre'siβo, a] *adj* aggressive

agriar [a'ɣrjar] *vt* to (turn) sour
agrícola [a'ɣrikola] *adj* farming *cpd*, agricultural
agricultor, a [aɣrikul'tor, a] *nm/f* farmer
agricultura [aɣrikul'tura] *nf* agriculture, farming
agridulce [aɣri'ðulθe] *adj* bittersweet; (*Culin*) sweet and sour
agrietarse [aɣrje'tarse] *vr* to crack; (*piel*) to chap
agrio, -a ['aɣrjo, a] *adj* bitter
agrupación [aɣrupa'θjon] *nf* group; (*acto*) grouping
agrupar [aɣru'par] *vt* to group
agua ['aɣwa] *nf* water; (*Náut*) wake; (*Arq*) slope of a roof; **aguas** *nfpl* (*de piedra*) water *sg*, sparkle *sg*; (*Med*) water *sg*, urine *sg*; (*Náut*) waters; **agua bendita/destilada/potable** holy/distilled/drinking water; **agua caliente** hot water; **agua corriente** running water; **agua de colonia** eau de cologne; **agua mineral (con/sin gas)** (sparkling/still) mineral water; **agua oxigenada** hydrogen peroxide; **aguas abajo/arriba** downstream/upstream; **aguas jurisdiccionales** territorial waters
aguacate [aɣwa'kate] *nm* avocado (pear)
aguacero [aɣwa'θero] *nm* (heavy) shower, downpour
aguado, -a [a'ɣwaðo, a] *adj* watery, watered down
aguafiestas [aɣwa'fjestas] *nmf inv* spoilsport, killjoy
aguamiel [aɣwa'mjel] (MÉX) *nf* fermented maguey *o* agave juice
aguanieve [aɣwa'njeβe] *nf* sleet
aguantar [aɣwan'tar] *vt* to bear, put up with; (*sostener*) to hold up ▷ *vi* to last; **aguantarse** *vr* to restrain o.s.; **aguante** *nm* (*paciencia*) patience; (*resistencia*) endurance
aguar [a'ɣwar] *vt* to water down
aguardar [aɣwar'ðar] *vt* to wait for
aguardiente [aɣwar'ðjente] *nm* brandy, liquor
aguarrás [aɣwa'rras] *nm* turpentine
aguaviva [aɣwa'βiβa] (RPL) *nf* jellyfish
agudeza [aɣu'ðeθa] *nf* sharpness; (*ingenio*) wit
agudo, -a [a'ɣuðo, a] *adj* sharp; (*voz*) high-pitched, piercing; (*dolor, enfermedad*) acute
agüero [a'ɣwero] *nm*: **buen/mal ~** good/bad omen
aguijón [aɣi'xon] *nm* sting; (*fig*) spur
águila ['aɣila] *nf* eagle; (*fig*) genius
aguileño, -a [aɣi'leɲo, a] *adj* (*nariz*) aquiline; (*rostro*) sharp-featured
aguinaldo [aɣi'naldo] *nm* Christmas box
aguja [a'ɣuxa] *nf* needle; (*de reloj*) hand; (*Arq*) spire; (*Tec*) firing-pin; **agujas** *nfpl* (*Zool*) ribs; (*Ferro*) points
agujerear [aɣuxere'ar] *vt* to make holes in
agujero [aɣu'xero] *nm* hole
agujetas [aɣu'xetas] *nfpl* stitch *sg*; (*rigidez*) stiffness *sg*
ahí [a'i] *adv* there; **de ~ que** so that, with the result that; **~ llega** here he comes; **por ~** that way; (*allá*) over there; **200 o por ~** 200 or so
ahijado, -a [ai'xaðo, a] *nm/f* godson/daughter
ahogar [ao'ɣar] *vt* to drown; (*asfixiar*) to suffocate, smother; (*fuego*) to put out; **ahogarse** *vr* (*en el agua*) to drown; (*por asfixia*) to suffocate
ahogo [a'oɣo] *nm* breathlessness; (*fig*) financial difficulty
ahondar [aon'dar] *vt* to deepen, make deeper; (*fig*) to study thoroughly ▷ *vi*: **~ en** to study thoroughly
ahora [a'ora] *adv* now; (*hace poco*) a moment ago, just now; (*dentro de poco*) in a moment; **~ voy** I'm coming; **~ mismo** right now; **~ bien** now then; **por ~** for the present
ahorcar [aor'kar] *vt* to hang
ahorita [ao'rita] (*fam*) *adv* (LAM: *en este momento*) right now; (MÉX: *hace poco*) just now; (: *dentro de poco*) in a minute
ahorrar [ao'rrar] *vt* (*dinero*) to save; (*esfuerzos*) to save, avoid; **ahorro** *nm* (*acto*) saving; **ahorros** *nmpl* (*dinero*) savings
ahuecar [awe'kar] *vt* to hollow (out); (*voz*) to deepen; **ahuecarse** *vr* to give o.s. airs
ahumar [au'mar] *vt* to smoke, cure; (*llenar de humo*) to fill with smoke ▷ *vi* to smoke; **ahumarse** *vr* to fill with smoke
ahuyentar [aujen'tar] *vt* to drive off, frighten off; (*fig*) to dispel
aire ['aire] *nm* air; (*viento*) wind; (*corriente*) draught; (*Mús*) tune; **al ~ libre** in the open air; **aire acondicionado** air conditioning; **airear** *vt* to air; **airearse** *vr* (*persona*) to go out for a breath of fresh air; **airoso, -a** *adj* windy; draughty; (*fig*) graceful
aislado, -a [ais'laðo, a] *adj* isolated; (*incomunicado*) cut-off; (*Elec*) insulated
aislar [ais'lar] *vt* to isolate; (*Elec*) to insulate
ajardinado, -a [axarði'naðo, a] *adj* landscaped
ajedrez [axe'ðreθ] *nm* chess
ajeno, -a [a'xeno, a] *adj* (*que pertenece a otro*) somebody else's; **~ a** foreign to
ajetreado, -a [axetre'aðo, a] *adj* busy

ajetreo [axe'treo] *nm* bustle

ají [a'xi] (cs) *nm* chil(l)i, red pepper; (*salsa*) chil(l)i sauce

ajillo [a'xiʎo] *nm*: **gambas al ~** garlic prawns

ajo ['axo] *nm* garlic

ajuar [a'xwar] *nm* household furnishings *pl*; (*de novia*) trousseau; (*de niño*) layette

ajustado, -a [axus'taðo, a] *adj* (*tornillo*) tight; (*cálculo*) right; (*ropa*) tight(-fitting); (*resultado*) close

ajustar [axus'tar] *vt* (*adaptar*) to adjust; (*encajar*) to fit; (*Tec*) to engage; (*Imprenta*) to make up; (*apretar*) to tighten; (*concertar*) to agree (on); (*reconciliar*) to reconcile; (*cuentas, deudas*) to settle ▷ *vi* to fit; **ajustarse** *vr*: **~se a** (*precio etc*) to be in keeping with, fit in with; **~ las cuentas a algn** to get even with sb

ajuste [a'xuste] *nm* adjustment; (*Costura*) fitting; (*acuerdo*) compromise; (*de cuenta*) settlement

al [al] = **a + el**; *V* **a**

ala ['ala] *nf* wing; (*de sombrero*) brim; winger; **ala delta** *nf* hang-glider

alabanza [ala'βanθa] *nf* praise

alabar [ala'βar] *vt* to praise

alacena [ala'θena] *nf* kitchen cupboard (BRIT) *o* closet (US)

alacrán [ala'kran] *nm* scorpion

alambrada [alam'braða] *nf* wire fence; (*red*) wire netting

alambre [a'lambre] *nm* wire; **alambre de púas** barbed wire

alameda [ala'meða] *nf* (*plantío*) poplar grove; (*lugar de paseo*) avenue, boulevard

álamo ['alamo] *nm* poplar

alarde [a'larðe] *nm* show, display; **hacer ~ de** to boast of

alargador [alarɣa'ðor] *nm* (*Elec*) extension lead

alargar [alar'ɣar] *vt* to lengthen, extend; (*paso*) to hasten; (*brazo*) to stretch out; (*cuerda*) to pay out; (*conversación*) to spin out; **alargarse** *vr* to get longer

alarma [a'larma] *nf* alarm; **alarma de incendios** fire alarm; **alarmar** *vt* to alarm; **alarmarse** to get alarmed; **alarmante** [alar'mante] *adj* alarming

alba ['alβa] *nf* dawn

albahaca [al'βaka] *nf* basil

Albania [al'βanja] *nf* Albania

albañil [alβa'ɲil] *nm* bricklayer; (*cantero*) mason

albarán [alβa'ran] *nm* (*Com*) delivery note, invoice

albaricoque [alβari'koke] *nm* apricot

albedrío [alβe'ðrio] *nm*: **libre ~** free will

alberca [al'βerka] *nf* reservoir; (MÉX: *piscina*) swimming pool

albergar [alβer'ɣar] *vt* to shelter

albergue *etc* [al'βerɣe] *vb V* **albergar** ▷ *nm* shelter, refuge; **albergue juvenil** youth hostel

albóndiga [al'βondiɣa] *nf* meatball

albornoz [alβor'noθ] *nm* (*de los árabes*) burnous; (*para el baño*) bathrobe

alborotar [alβoro'tar] *vi* to make a row ▷ *vt* to agitate, stir up; **alborotarse** *vr* to get excited; (*mar*) to get rough; **alboroto** *nm* row, uproar

álbum ['alβum] (*pl* **~s, ~es**) *nm* album; **álbum de recortes** scrapbook

albur [al'βur] (MÉX) *nm* (*juego de palabras*) pun; (*doble sentido*) double entendre

alcachofa [alka'tʃofa] *nf* artichoke

alcalde, -esa [al'kalde, esa] *nm/f* mayor(ess)

alcaldía [alkal'dia] *nf* mayoralty; (*lugar*) mayor's office

alcance *etc* [al'kanθe] *vb V* **alcanzar** ▷ *nm* reach; (*Com*) adverse balance; **al ~ de algn** available to sb

alcancía [alkan'θia] (LAM) *nf* (*para ahorrar*) money box; (*para colectas*) collection box

alcantarilla [alkanta'riʎa] *nf* (*de aguas cloacales*) sewer; (*en la calle*) gutter

alcanzar [alkan'θar] *vt* (*algo: con la mano, el pie*) to reach; (*alguien: en el camino etc*) to catch up (with); (*autobús*) to catch; (*bala*) to hit, strike ▷ *vi* (*ser suficiente*) to be enough; **~ a hacer** to manage to do

alcaparra [alka'parra] *nf* caper

alcayata [alka'jata] *nf* hook

alcázar [al'kaθar] *nm* fortress; (*Náut*) quarter-deck

alcoba [al'koβa] *nf* bedroom

alcohol [al'kol] *nm* alcohol; **alcohol metílico** methylated spirits *pl* (BRIT), wood alcohol (US); **alcohólico, -a** *adj, nm/f* alcoholic; **alcoholímetro** [alko'limetro] *nm* Breathalyser® (BRIT), drunkometer (US); **alcoholismo** [alko'lismo] *nm* alcoholism

alcornoque [alkor'noke] *nm* cork tree; (*fam*) idiot

aldea [al'dea] *nf* village; **aldeano, -a** *adj* village *cpd* ▷ *nm/f* villager

aleación [alea'θjon] *nf* alloy

aleatorio, -a [alea'torjo, a] *adj* random

aleccionar [alekθjo'nar] *vt* to instruct; (*adiestrar*) to train

alegar [ale'ɣar] *vt* to claim; (*Jur*) to plead ▷ *vi* (LAM: *discutir*) to argue

alegoría [aleɣo'ria] *nf* allegory

alegrar [ale'ɣrar] *vt* (*causar alegría*) to cheer (up); (*fuego*) to poke; (*fiesta*) to liven

up; **alegrarse** *vr* (*fam*) to get merry *o* tight; **~se de** to be glad about
alegre [a'leɣre] *adj* happy, cheerful; (*fam*) merry, tight; (*chiste*) risqué, blue; **alegría** *nf* happiness; merriment
alejar [ale'xar] *vt* to remove; (*fig*) to estrange; **alejarse** *vr* to move away
alemán, -ana [ale'man, ana] *adj, nm/f* German ▷ *nm* (*Ling*) German
Alemania [ale'manja] *nf* Germany
alentador, a [alenta'ðor, a] *adj* encouraging
alentar [alen'tar] *vt* to encourage
alergia [a'lerxja] *nf* allergy
alero [a'lero] *nm* (*de tejado*) eaves *pl*; (*guardabarros*) mudguard
alerta [a'lerta] *adj, nm* alert
aleta [a'leta] *nf* (*de pez*) fin; (*ala*) wing; (*de foca, Deporte*) flipper; (*Auto*) mudguard
aletear [alete'ar] *vi* to flutter
alevín [ale'βin] *nm* fry, young fish
alevosía [aleβo'sia] *nf* treachery
alfabeto [alfa'βeto] *nm* alphabet
alfalfa [al'falfa] *nf* alfalfa, lucerne
alfarería [alfare'ria] *nf* pottery; (*tienda*) pottery shop; **alfarero, -a** *nm/f* potter
alféizar [al'feiθar] *nm* window-sill
alférez [al'fereθ] *nm* (*Mil*) second lieutenant; (*Náut*) ensign
alfil [al'fil] *nm* (*Ajedrez*) bishop
alfiler [alfi'ler] *nm* pin; (*broche*) clip
alfombra [al'fombra] *nf* carpet; (*más pequeña*) rug; **alfombrilla** *nf* rug, mat; (*Inform*) mouse mat *o* pad
alforja [al'forxa] *nf* saddlebag
algas ['alɣas] *nfpl* seaweed
álgebra ['alxeβra] *nf* algebra
algo ['alɣo] *pron* something; anything ▷ *adv* somewhat, rather; **¿~ más?** anything else?; (*en tienda*) is that all?; **por ~ será** there must be some reason for it
algodón [alɣo'ðon] *nm* cotton; (*planta*) cotton plant; **algodón de azúcar** candy floss (BRIT), cotton candy (US); **algodón hidrófilo** cotton wool (BRIT), absorbent cotton (US)
alguien ['alɣjen] *pron* someone, somebody; (*en frases interrogativas*) anyone, anybody
alguno, -a [al'ɣuno, a] *adj* (*delante de nm*): **algún** some; (*después de n*): **no tiene talento ~** he has no talent, he doesn't have any talent ▷ *pron* (*alguien*) someone, somebody; **algún que otro libro** some book or other; **algún día iré** I'll go one *o* some day; **sin interés ~** without the slightest interest; **~ que otro** an occasional one; **~s piensan** some (people) think
alhaja [a'laxa] *nf* jewel; (*tesoro*) precious object, treasure
alhelí [ale'li] *nm* wallflower, stock
aliado, -a [a'ljaðo, a] *adj* allied
alianza [a'ljanθa] *nf* alliance; (*anillo*) wedding ring
aliar [a'ljar] *vt* to ally; **aliarse** *vr* to form an alliance
alias ['aljas] *adv* alias
alicatado [alika'taðo] (ESP) *nm* tiling
alicates [ali'kates] *nmpl* pliers
aliciente [ali'θjente] *nm* incentive; (*atracción*) attraction
alienación [aljena'θjon] *nf* alienation
aliento [a'ljento] *nm* breath; (*respiración*) breathing; **sin ~** breathless
aligerar [alixe'rar] *vt* to lighten; (*reducir*) to shorten; (*aliviar*) to alleviate; (*mitigar*) to ease; (*paso*) to quicken
alijo [a'lixo] *nm* consignment
alimaña [ali'maɲa] *nf* pest
alimentación [alimenta'θjon] *nf* (*comida*) food; (*acción*) feeding; (*tienda*) grocer's (shop)
alimentar [alimen'tar] *vt* to feed; (*nutrir*) to nourish; **alimentarse** *vr* to feed
alimenticio, -a [alimen'tiθjo, a] *adj* food *cpd*; (*nutritivo*) nourishing, nutritious
alimento [ali'mento] *nm* food; (*nutrición*) nourishment
alineación [alinea'θjon] *nf* alignment; (*Deporte*) line-up
alinear [aline'ar] *vt* to align; (*Deporte*) to select, pick
aliñar [ali'ɲar] *vt* (*Culin*) to season; **aliño** *nm* (*Culin*) dressing
alioli [ali'oli] *nm* garlic mayonnaise
alisar [ali'sar] *vt* to smooth
alistarse [alis'tarse] *vr* to enlist; (*inscribirse*) to enrol
aliviar [ali'βjar] *vt* (*carga*) to lighten; (*persona*) to relieve; (*dolor*) to relieve, alleviate
alivio [a'liβjo] *nm* alleviation, relief
aljibe [al'xiβe] *nm* cistern
allá [a'ʎa] *adv* (*lugar*) there; (*por ahí*) over there; (*tiempo*) then; **~ abajo** down there; **más ~** further on; **más ~ de** beyond; **¡~ tú!** that's your problem!; **¡~ voy!** I'm coming!
allanamiento [aʎana'mjento] *nm* (LAM: *de policía*) raid; **allanamiento de morada** burglary
allanar [aʎa'nar] *vt* to flatten, level (out); (*igualar*) to smooth (out); (*fig*) to subdue; (*Jur*) to burgle, break into
allegado, -a [aʎe'ɣaðo, a] *adj* near, close ▷ *nm/f* relation
allí [a'ʎi] *adv* there; **~ mismo** right there;

por ~ over there; (*por ese camino*) that way
alma ['alma] *nf* soul; (*persona*) person
almacén [alma'θen] *nm* (*depósito*) warehouse, store; (*Mil*) magazine; (cs: *de comestibles*) grocer's (shop); **grandes almacenes** department store *sg*; **almacenaje** *nm* storage
almacenar [almaθe'nar] *vt* to store, put in storage; (*proveerse*) to stock up with
almanaque [alma'nake] *nm* almanac
almeja [al'mexa] *nf* clam
almendra [al'mendra] *nf* almond; **almendro** *nm* almond tree
almíbar [al'miβar] *nm* syrup
almidón [almi'ðon] *nm* starch
almirante [almi'rante] *nm* admiral
almohada [almo'aða] *nf* pillow; (*funda*) pillowcase; **almohadilla** *nf* cushion; (*para alfileres*) pincushion; (*Tec*) pad
almohadón [almoa'ðon] *nm* large pillow; bolster
almorranas [almo'rranas] *nfpl* piles, haemorrhoids
almorzar [almor'θar] *vt*: **~ una tortilla** to have an omelette for lunch ▷ *vi* to (have) lunch
almuerzo *etc* [al'mwerθo] *vb V* **almorzar** ▷ *nm* lunch
alocado, -a [alo'kaðo, a] *adj* crazy
alojamiento [aloxa'mjento] *nm* lodging(s) *pl*; (*viviendas*) housing
alojar [alo'xar] *vt* to lodge; **alojarse** *vr* to lodge, stay
alondra [a'londra] *nf* lark, skylark
alpargata [alpar'ɣata] *nf* rope-soled sandal, espadrille
Alpes ['alpes] *nmpl*: **los ~** the Alps
alpinismo [alpi'nismo] *nm* mountaineering, climbing; **alpinista** *nmf* mountaineer, climber
alpiste [al'piste] *nm* birdseed
alquilar [alki'lar] *vt* (*propietario*: *inmuebles*) to let, rent (out); (: *coche*) to hire out; (: *TV*) to rent (out); (*alquilador*: *inmuebles*, *TV*) to rent; (: *coche*) to hire; **"se alquila casa"** "house to let (BRIT) *o* for rent (US)"
alquiler [alki'ler] *nm* renting; letting; hiring; (*arriendo*) rent; hire charge; **de ~** for hire; **alquiler de automóviles** *o* **coches** car hire
alquimia [al'kimja] *nf* alchemy
alquitrán [alki'tran] *nm* tar
alrededor [alreðe'ðor] *adv* around, about; **~ de** around, about; **mirar a su ~** to look (round) about one; **alrededores** *nmpl* surroundings
alta ['alta] *nf* (certificate of) discharge
altar [al'tar] *nm* altar
altavoz [alta'βoθ] *nm* loudspeaker; (*amplificador*) amplifier
alteración [altera'θjon] *nf* alteration; (*alboroto*) disturbance
alterar [alte'rar] *vt* to alter; to disturb; **alterarse** *vr* (*persona*) to get upset
altercado [alter'kaðo] *nm* argument
alternar [alter'nar] *vt* to alternate ▷ *vi* to alternate; (*turnar*) to take turns; **alternarse** *vr* to alternate; to take turns; **~ con** to mix with; **alternativa** *nf* alternative; (*elección*) choice; **alternativo, -a** *adj* alternative; (*alterno*) alternating; **alterno, -a** *adj* alternate; (*Elec*) alternating
Alteza [al'teθa] *nf* (*tratamiento*) Highness
altibajos [alti'βaxos] *nmpl* ups and downs
altiplano [alti'plano] *nm* = **altiplanicie**
altisonante [altiso'nante] *adj* high-flown, high-sounding
altitud [alti'tuð] *nf* height; (*Aviac*, *Geo*) altitude
altivo, -a [al'tiβo, a] *adj* haughty, arrogant
alto, -a ['alto, a] *adj* high; (*persona*) tall; (*sonido*) high, sharp; (*noble*) high, lofty ▷ *nm* halt; (*Mús*) alto; (*Geo*) hill ▷ *adv* (*de sitio*) high; (*de sonido*) loud, loudly ▷ *excl* halt!; **la pared tiene 2 metros de ~** the wall is 2 metres high; **en alta mar** on the high seas; **en voz alta** in a loud voice; **las altas horas de la noche** the small *o* wee hours; **en lo ~ de** at the top of; **pasar por ~** to overlook; **altoparlante** [altopar'lante] (LAM) *nm* loudspeaker
altura [al'tura] *nf* height; (*Náut*) depth; (*Geo*) latitude; **la pared tiene 1.80 de ~** the wall is 1 metre 80cm high; **a estas ~s** at this stage; **a estas ~s del año** at this time of the year
alubia [a'luβja] *nf* bean
alucinación [aluθina'θjon] *nf* hallucination
alucinar [aluθi'nar] *vi* to hallucinate ▷ *vt* to deceive; (*fascinar*) to fascinate
alud [a'luð] *nm* avalanche; (*fig*) flood
aludir [alu'ðir] *vi*: **~ a** to allude to; **darse por aludido** to take the hint
alumbrado [alum'braðo] *nm* lighting
alumbrar [alum'brar] *vt* to light (up) ▷ *vi* (*Med*) to give birth
aluminio [alu'minjo] *nm* aluminium (BRIT), aluminum (US)
alumno, -a [a'lumno, a] *nm/f* pupil, student
alusión [alu'sjon] *nf* allusion
alusivo, -a [alu'siβo, a] *adj* allusive
aluvión [alu'βjon] *nm* alluvium; (*fig*) flood
alverja [al'βerxa] (LAM) *nf* pea

alza ['alθa] *nf* rise; (*Mil*) sight
alzamiento [alθa'mjento] *nm* (*rebelión*) rising
alzar [al'θar] *vt* to lift (up); (*precio, muro*) to raise; (*cuello de abrigo*) to turn up; (*Agr*) to gather in; (*Imprenta*) to gather; **alzarse** *vr* to get up, rise; (*rebelarse*) to revolt; (*Com*) to go fraudulently bankrupt; (*Jur*) to appeal
ama ['ama] *nf* lady of the house; (*dueña*) owner; (*institutriz*) governess; (*madre adoptiva*) foster mother; **ama de casa** housewife; **ama de llaves** housekeeper
amabilidad [amaβili'ðað] *nf* kindness; (*simpatía*) niceness; **amable** *adj* kind; nice; **es usted muy amable** that's very kind of you
amaestrado, -a [amaes'traðo, a] *adj* (*animal: en circo etc*) performing
amaestrar [amaes'trar] *vt* to train
amago [a'maɣo] *nm* threat; (*gesto*) threatening gesture; (*Med*) symptom
amainar [amai'nar] *vi* (*viento*) to die down
amamantar [amaman'tar] *vt* to suckle, nurse
amanecer [amane'θer] *vi* to dawn ▷*nm* dawn; **~ afiebrado** to wake up with a fever
amanerado, -a [amane'raðo, a] *adj* affected
amante [a'mante] *adj*: **~ de** fond of ▷*nmf* lover
amapola [ama'pola] *nf* poppy
amar [a'mar] *vt* to love
amargado, -a [amar'ɣaðo, a] *adj* bitter
amargar [amar'ɣar] *vt* to make bitter; (*fig*) to embitter; **amargarse** *vr* to become embittered
amargo, -a [a'marɣo, a] *adj* bitter
amarillento, -a [amari'ʎento, a] *adj* yellowish; (*tez*) sallow; **amarillo, -a** *adj, nm* yellow
amarrado, -a [ama'rraðo, a] (*MÉX: fam*) *adj* mean, stingy
amarrar [ama'rrar] *vt* to moor; (*sujetar*) to tie up
amarras [a'marras] *nfpl*: **soltar ~** to set sail
amasar [ama'sar] *vt* (*masa*) to knead; (*mezclar*) to mix, prepare; (*confeccionar*) to concoct
amateur [ama'ter] *nmf* amateur
amazona [ama'θona] *nf* horsewoman; **Amazonas** *nm*: **el Amazonas** the Amazon
ámbar ['ambar] *nm* amber
ambición [ambi'θjon] *nf* ambition; **ambicionar** *vt* to aspire to; **ambicioso, -a** *adj* ambitious
ambidextro, -a [ambi'ðekstro, a] *adj* ambidextrous
ambientación [ambjenta'θjon] *nf* (*Cine, Teatro etc*) setting; (*Radio*) sound effects
ambiente [am'bjente] *nm* atmosphere; (*medio*) environment
ambigüedad [ambiɣwe'ðað] *nf* ambiguity; **ambiguo, -a** *adj* ambiguous
ámbito ['ambito] *nm* (*campo*) field; (*fig*) scope
ambos, -as ['ambos, as] *adj pl, pron pl* both
ambulancia [ambu'lanθja] *nf* ambulance
ambulante [ambu'lante] *adj* travelling *cpd*, itinerant
ambulatorio [ambula'torio] *nm* state health-service clinic
amén [a'men] *excl* amen; **~ de** besides
amenaza [ame'naθa] *nf* threat; **amenazar** [amena'θar] *vt* to threaten ▷*vi*: **amenazar con hacer** to threaten to do
ameno, -a [a'meno, a] *adj* pleasant
América [a'merika] *nf* America; **América Central/Latina** Central/Latin America; **América del Norte/del Sur** North/South America; **americana** *nf* coat, jacket; *V tb* **americano**; **americano, -a** *adj, nm/f* American
ametralladora [ametraʎa'ðora] *nf* machine gun
amigable [ami'ɣaβle] *adj* friendly
amígdala [a'miɣðala] *nf* tonsil; **amigdalitis** *nf* tonsillitis
amigo, -a [a'miɣo, a] *adj* friendly ▷*nm/f* friend; (*amante*) lover; **ser ~ de algo** to be fond of sth; **ser muy ~s** to be close friends
aminorar [amino'rar] *vt* to diminish; (*reducir*) to reduce; **~ la marcha** to slow down
amistad [amis'tað] *nf* friendship; **amistades** *nfpl* (*amigos*) friends; **amistoso, -a** *adj* friendly
amnesia [am'nesja] *nf* amnesia
amnistía [amnis'tia] *nf* amnesty
amo ['amo] *nm* owner; (*jefe*) boss
amolar [amo'lar] (*MÉX: fam*) *vt* to ruin, damage
amoldar [amol'dar] *vt* to mould; (*adaptar*) to adapt
amonestación [amonesta'θjon] *nf* warning; **amonestaciones** *nfpl* (*Rel*) marriage banns
amonestar [amones'tar] *vt* to warn; (*Rel*) to publish the banns of
amontonar [amonto'nar] *vt* to collect, pile up; **amontonarse** *vr* to crowd together; (*acumularse*) to pile up
amor [a'mor] *nm* love; (*amante*) lover;

hacer el ~ to make love; **amor propio** self-respect
amoratado, -a [amora'taðo, a] *adj* purple
amordazar [amorða'θar] *vt* to muzzle; (*fig*) to gag
amorfo, -a [a'morfo, a] *adj* amorphous, shapeless
amoroso, -a [amo'roso, a] *adj* affectionate, loving
amortiguador [amortigwa'ðor] *nm* shock absorber; (*parachoques*) bumper; **amortiguadores** *nmpl* (*Auto*) suspension *sg*
amortiguar [amorti'ɣwar] *vt* to deaden; (*ruido*) to muffle; (*color*) to soften
amotinar [amoti'nar] *vt* to stir up, incite (to riot); **amotinarse** *vr* to mutiny
amparar [ampa'rar] *vt* to protect; **ampararse** *vr* to seek protection; (*de la lluvia etc*) to shelter; **amparo** *nm* help, protection; **al amparo de** under the protection of
amperio [am'perjo] *nm* ampère, amp
ampliación [amplja'θjon] *nf* enlargement; (*extensión*) extension
ampliar [am'pljar] *vt* to enlarge; to extend
amplificador [amplifika'ðor] *nm* amplifier
amplificar [amplifi'kar] *vt* to amplify
amplio, -a ['ampljo, a] *adj* spacious; (*de falda etc*) full; (*extenso*) extensive; (*ancho*) wide; **amplitud** *nf* spaciousness; extent; (*fig*) amplitude
ampolla [am'poʎa] *nf* blister; (*Med*) ampoule
amputar [ampu'tar] *vt* to cut off, amputate
amueblar [amwe'βlar] *vt* to furnish
anales [a'nales] *nmpl* annals
analfabetismo [analfaβe'tismo] *nm* illiteracy; **analfabeto, -a** *adj, nm/f* illiterate
analgésico [anal'xesiko] *nm* painkiller, analgesic
análisis [a'nalisis] *nm inv* analysis
analista [ana'lista] *nmf* (*gen*) analyst
analizar [anali'θar] *vt* to analyse
analógico, -a [ana'loxiko, a] *adj* (*Inform*) analog; (*reloj*) analogue (BRIT), analog (US)
análogo, -a [a'naloɣo, a] *adj* analogous, similar
ananá [ana'na] (RPL) *nm* pineapple
anarquía [anar'kia] *nf* anarchy; **anarquista** *nmf* anarchist
anatomía [anato'mia] *nf* anatomy
anca ['anka] *nf* rump, haunch; **ancas** *nfpl* (*fam*) behind *sg*
ancho, -a ['antʃo, a] *adj* wide; (*falda*) full; (*fig*) liberal ▷ *nm* width; (*Ferro*) gauge; **ponerse ~** to get conceited; **estar a sus anchas** to be at one's ease
anchoa [an'tʃoa] *nf* anchovy
anchura [an'tʃura] *nf* width; (*extensión*) wideness
anciano, -a [an'θjano, a] *adj* old, aged ▷ *nm/f* old man/woman; elder
ancla ['ankla] *nf* anchor
Andalucía [andalu'θia] *nf* Andalusia; **andaluz, -a** *adj, nm/f* Andalusian
andamio [an'damjo] *nm* scaffold(ing)
andar [an'dar] *vt* to go, cover, travel ▷ *vi* to go, walk, travel; (*funcionar*) to go, work; (*estar*) to be ▷ *nm* walk, gait, pace; **andarse** *vr* to go away; **~ a pie/a caballo/en bicicleta** to go on foot/on horseback/by bicycle; **~ haciendo algo** to be doing sth; **¡anda!** (*sorpresa*) go on!; **anda por** *o* **en los 40** he's about 40
andén [an'den] *nm* (*Ferro*) platform; (*Náut*) quayside; (CAM: *de la calle*) pavement (BRIT), sidewalk (US)
Andes ['andes] *nmpl*: **los ~** the Andes
andinismo [andi'nismo] (LAM) *nm* mountaineering, climbing
Andorra [an'dorra] *nf* Andorra
andrajoso, -a [andra'xoso, a] *adj* ragged
anduve *etc vb V* **andar**
anécdota [a'nekðota] *nf* anecdote, story
anegar [ane'ɣar] *vt* to flood; (*ahogar*) to drown
anemia [a'nemja] *nf* anaemia
anestesia [anes'tesja] *nf* (*sustancia*) anaesthetic; (*proceso*) anaesthesia; **anestesia general/local** general/local anaesthetic
anexar [anek'sar] *vt* to annex; (*documento*) to attach; **anexión** *nf* annexation; **anexo, -a** *adj* attached ▷ *nm* annexe
anfibio, -a [an'fiβjo, a] *adj* amphibious ▷ *nm* amphibian
anfiteatro [anfite'atro] *nm* amphitheatre; (*Teatro*) dress circle
anfitrión, -ona [anfi'trjon, ona] *nm/f* host(ess)
ánfora ['anfora] *nf* (*cántaro*) amphora; (MÉX *Pol*) ballot box
ángel ['anxel] *nm* angel; **ángel de la guarda** guardian angel
angina [an'xina] *nf* (*Med*) inflammation of the throat; **tener ~s** to have tonsillitis; **angina de pecho** angina
anglicano, -a [angli'kano, a] *adj, nm/f* Anglican
anglosajón, -ona [anglosa'xon, ona] *adj*

Anglo-Saxon
anguila [an'gila] *nf* eel
angula [an'gula] *nf* elver, baby eel
ángulo ['angulo] *nm* angle; (*esquina*) corner; (*curva*) bend
angustia [an'gustja] *nf* anguish
anhelar [ane'lar] *vt* to be eager for; (*desear*) to long for, desire ▷ *vi* to pant, gasp; **anhelo** *nm* eagerness; desire
anidar [ani'ðar] *vi* to nest
anillo [a'niʎo] *nm* ring; **anillo de boda/compromiso** wedding/engagement ring
animación [anima'θjon] *nf* liveliness; (*vitalidad*) life; (*actividad*) activity; bustle
animado, -a [ani'maðo, a] *adj* lively; (*vivaz*) animated; **animador, a** *nm/f* (*TV*) host(ess), compère; (*Deporte*) cheerleader
animal [ani'mal] *adj* animal; (*fig*) stupid ▷ *nm* animal; (*fig*) fool; (*bestia*) brute
animar [ani'mar] *vt* (*Bio*) to animate, give life to; (*fig*) to liven up, brighten up, cheer up; (*estimular*) to stimulate; **animarse** *vr* to cheer up; to feel encouraged; (*decidirse*) to make up one's mind
ánimo ['animo] *nm* (*alma*) soul; (*mente*) mind; (*valentía*) courage ▷ *excl* cheer up!
animoso, -a [ani'moso, a] *adj* brave; (*vivo*) lively
aniquilar [aniki'lar] *vt* to annihilate, destroy
anís [a'nis] *nm* aniseed; (*licor*) anisette
aniversario [aniβer'sarjo] *nm* anniversary
anoche [a'notʃe] *adv* last night; **antes de ~** the night before last
anochecer [anotʃe'θer] *vi* to get dark ▷ *nm* nightfall, dark; **al ~** at nightfall
anodino, -a [ano'ðino, a] *adj* dull, anodyne
anomalía [anoma'lia] *nf* anomaly
anonadado, -a [anona'ðaðo, a] *adj*: **estar ~** to be overwhelmed *o* amazed
anonimato [anoni'mato] *nm* anonymity
anónimo, -a [a'nonimo, a] *adj* anonymous; (*Com*) limited ▷ *nm* (*carta anónima*) anonymous letter; (*: maliciosa*) poison-pen letter
anormal [anor'mal] *adj* abnormal
anotación [anota'θjon] *nf* note; annotation
anotar [ano'tar] *vt* to note down; (*comentar*) to annotate
ansia ['ansja] *nf* anxiety; (*añoranza*) yearning; **ansiar** *vt* to long for
ansiedad [ansje'ðað] *nf* anxiety
ansioso, -a [an'sjoso, a] *adj* anxious; (*anhelante*) eager; **~ de** *o* **por algo** greedy for sth
antaño [an'taɲo] *adv* long ago, formerly
Antártico [an'tartiko] *nm*: **el ~** the Antarctic
ante ['ante] *prep* before, in the presence of; (*problema etc*) faced with ▷ *nm* (*piel*) suede; **~ todo** above all
anteanoche [antea'notʃe] *adv* the night before last
anteayer [antea'jer] *adv* the day before yesterday
antebrazo [ante'βraθo] *nm* forearm
antecedente [anteθe'ðente] *adj* previous ▷ *nm* antecedent; **antecedentes** *nmpl* (*historial*) record *sg*; **antecedentes penales** criminal record
anteceder [anteθe'ðer] *vt* to precede, go before
antecesor, a [anteθe'sor, a] *nm/f* predecessor
antelación [antela'θjon] *nf*: **con ~** in advance
antemano [ante'mano]: **de ~** *adv* beforehand, in advance
antena [an'tena] *nf* antenna; (*de televisión etc*) aerial; **antena parabólica** satellite dish
antenoche [ante'notʃe] (LAM) *adv* the night before last
anteojo [ante'oxo] *nm* eyeglass; **anteojos** *nmpl* (LAM: *gafas*) glasses, spectacles
antepasados [antepa'saðos] *nmpl* ancestors
anteponer [antepo'ner] *vt* to place in front; (*fig*) to prefer
anterior [ante'rjor] *adj* preceding, previous; **anterioridad** *nf*: **con anterioridad a** prior to, before
antes ['antes] *adv* (*con prioridad*) before ▷ *prep*: **~ de** before ▷ *conj*: **~ de ir/de que te vayas** before going/before you go; **~ bien** (but) rather; **dos días ~** two days before *o* previously; **no quiso venir ~** she didn't want to come any earlier; **tomo el avión ~ que el barco** I take the plane rather than the boat; **~ de** *o* **que nada** (*en el tiempo*) first of all; (*indicando preferencia*) above all; **~ que yo** before me; **lo ~ posible** as soon as possible; **cuanto ~ mejor** the sooner the better
antibalas [anti'βalas] *adj inv*: **chaleco ~** bullet-proof jacket
antibiótico [anti'βjotiko] *nm* antibiotic
anticaspa [anti'kaspa] *adj inv* anti-dandruff *cpd*
anticipación [antiθipa'θjon] *nf* anticipation; **con 10 minutos de ~** 10 minutes early
anticipado, -a [antiθi'paðo, a] *adj* (*pago*) advance; **por ~** in advance
anticipar [antiθi'par] *vt* to anticipate;

(*adelantar*) to bring forward; (*Com*) to advance; **anticiparse** *vr*: **~se a su época** to be ahead of one's time
anticipo [anti'θipo] *nm* (*Com*) advance
anticonceptivo, -a [antikonθep'tiβo, a] *adj, nm* contraceptive
anticongelante [antikonxe'lante] *nm* antifreeze
anticuado, -a [anti'kwaðo, a] *adj* out-of-date, old-fashioned; (*desusado*) obsolete
anticuario [anti'kwarjo] *nm* antique dealer
anticuerpo [anti'kwerpo] *nm* (*Med*) antibody
antidepresivo [antiðepre'siβo] *nm* antidepressant
antidóping [anti'dopin] *adj inv*: **control ~** drugs test
antídoto [an'tiðoto] *nm* antidote
antiestético, -a [anties'tetiko, a] *adj* unsightly
antifaz [anti'faθ] *nm* mask; (*velo*) veil
antiglobalización [antigloβaliθa'θjon] *nf* anti-globalization; **antiglobalizador, a** *adj* anti-globalization *cpd*
antiguamente [antiɣwa'mente] *adv* formerly; (*hace mucho tiempo*) long ago
antigüedad [antiɣwe'ðað] *nf* antiquity; (*artículo*) antique; (*rango*) seniority
antiguo, -a [an'tiɣwo, a] *adj* old, ancient; (*que fue*) former
Antillas [an'tiʎas] *nfpl*: **las ~** the West Indies
antílope [an'tilope] *nm* antelope
antinatural [antinatu'ral] *adj* unnatural
antipatía [antipa'tia] *nf* antipathy, dislike; **antipático, -a** *adj* disagreeable, unpleasant
antirrobo [anti'rroβo] *adj inv* (*alarma etc*) anti-theft
antisemita [antise'mita] *adj* anti-Semitic ▷ *nmf* anti-Semite
antiséptico, -a [anti'septiko, a] *adj* antiseptic ▷ *nm* antiseptic
antivirus [anti'birus] *nm inv* (*Comput*) antivirus program
antojarse [anto'xarse] *vr* (*desear*): **se me antoja comprarlo** I have a mind to buy it; (*pensar*): **se me antoja que ...** I have a feeling that ...
antojitos [anto'xitos] (*MÉX*) *nmpl* snacks, nibbles
antojo [an'toxo] *nm* caprice, whim; (*rosa*) birthmark; (*lunar*) mole
antología [antolo'xia] *nf* anthology
antorcha [an'tortʃa] *nf* torch
antro ['antro] *nm* cavern
antropología [antropolo'xia] *nf* anthropology
anual [a'nwal] *adj* annual
anuario [a'nwarjo] *nm* yearbook
anulación [anula'θjon] *nf* annulment; (*cancelación*) cancellation
anular [anu'lar] *vt* (*contrato*) to annul, cancel; (*ley*) to revoke, repeal; (*suscripción*) to cancel ▷ *nm* ring finger
anunciar [anun'θjar] *vt* to announce; (*proclamar*) to proclaim; (*Com*) to advertise
anuncio [a'nunθjo] *nm* announcement; (*señal*) sign; (*Com*) advertisement; (*cartel*) poster
anzuelo [an'θwelo] *nm* hook; (*para pescar*) fish hook
añadidura [aɲaði'ðura] *nf* addition, extra; **por ~** besides, in addition
añadir [aɲa'ðir] *vt* to add
añejo, -a [a'ɲexo, a] *adj* old; (*vino*) mellow
añicos [a'ɲikos] *nmpl*: **hacer ~** to smash, shatter
año ['aɲo] *nm* year; **¡Feliz A~ Nuevo!** Happy New Year!; **tener 15 ~s** to be 15 (years old); **los ~s 90** the nineties; **el ~ que viene** next year; **año bisiesto/escolar/fiscal/sabático** leap/school/tax/sabbatical year
añoranza [aɲo'ranθa] *nf* nostalgia; (*anhelo*) longing
apa ['apa] (*MÉX*) *excl* goodness me!, good gracious!
apabullar [apaβu'ʎar] *vt* to crush, squash
apacible [apa'θiβle] *adj* gentle, mild
apaciguar [apaθi'ɣwar] *vt* to pacify, calm (down)
apadrinar [apaðri'nar] *vt* to sponsor, support; (*Rel*) to be godfather to
apagado, -a [apa'ɣaðo, a] *adj* (*volcán*) extinct; (*color*) dull; (*voz*) quiet; (*sonido*) muted, muffled; (*persona*: *apático*) listless; **estar ~** (*fuego, luz*) to be out; (*Radio, TV etc*) to be off
apagar [apa'ɣar] *vt* to put out; (*Elec, Radio, TV*) to turn off; (*sonido*) to silence, muffle; (*sed*) to quench
apagón [apa'ɣon] *nm* blackout; power cut
apalabrar [apala'βrar] *vt* to agree to; (*contratar*) to engage
apalear [apale'ar] *vt* to beat, thrash
apantallar [apanta'ʎar] (*MÉX*) *vt* to impress
apañar [apa'ɲar] *vt* to pick up; (*asir*) to take hold of, grasp; (*reparar*) to mend, patch up; **apañarse** *vr* to manage, get along
apapachar [apapa'tʃar] (*MÉX*: *fam*) *vt* to cuddle, hug
aparador [apara'ðor] *nm* sideboard; (*MÉX*: *escaparate*) shop window
aparato [apa'rato] *nm* apparatus;

(*máquina*) machine; (*doméstico*) appliance; (*boato*) ostentation; **aparato digestivo** (*Anat*) digestive system; **aparatoso, -a** *adj* showy, ostentatious

aparcamiento [aparka'mjento] *nm* car park (BRIT), parking lot (US)

aparcar [apar'kar] *vt, vi* to park

aparear [apare'ar] *vt* (*objetos*) to pair, match; (*animales*) to mate; **aparearse** *vr* to make a pair; to mate

aparecer [apare'θer] *vi* to appear; **aparecerse** *vr* to appear

aparejador, a [aparexa'ðor, a] *nm/f* (*Arq*) master builder

aparejo [apa'rexo] *nm* harness; rigging; (*de poleas*) block and tackle

aparentar [aparen'tar] *vt* (*edad*) to look; (*fingir*): **~ tristeza** to pretend to be sad

aparente [apa'rente] *adj* apparent; (*adecuado*) suitable

aparezco *etc vb V* **aparecer**

aparición [apari'θjon] *nf* appearance; (*de libro*) publication; (*espectro*) apparition

apariencia [apa'rjenθja] *nf* (outward) appearance; **en ~** outwardly, seemingly

apartado, -a [apar'taðo, a] *adj* separate; (*lejano*) remote ▷ *nm* (*tipográfico*) paragraph; **apartado de correos** (ESP) post office box; **apartado postal** (LAM) post office box

apartamento [aparta'mento] *nm* apartment, flat (BRIT)

apartar [apar'tar] *vt* to separate; (*quitar*) to remove; **apartarse** *vr* to separate, part; (*irse*) to move away; to keep away

aparte [a'parte] *adv* (*separadamente*) separately; (*además*) besides ▷ *nm* aside; (*tipográfico*) new paragraph

aparthotel [aparto'tel] *nm* serviced apartments

apasionado, -a [apasjo'naðo, a] *adj* passionate

apasionar [apasjo'nar] *vt* to excite; **le apasiona el fútbol** she's crazy about football; **apasionarse** *vr* to get excited

apatía [apa'tia] *nf* apathy

apático, -a [a'patiko, a] *adj* apathetic

Apdo *abr* (= *Apartado (de Correos)*) PO Box

apeadero [apea'ðero] *nm* halt, stop, stopping place

apearse [ape'arse] *vr* (*jinete*) to dismount; (*bajarse*) to get down *o* out; (*Auto, Ferro*) to get off *o* out

apechugar [apetʃu'ɣar] *vr*: **~ con algo** to face up to sth

apegarse [ape'ɣarse] *vr*: **~ a** to become attached to; **apego** *nm* attachment, devotion

apelar [ape'lar] *vi* to appeal; **~ a** (*fig*) to resort to

apellidar [apeʎi'ðar] *vt* to call, name; **apellidarse** *vr*: **se apellida Pérez** her (sur) name's Pérez

apellido [ape'ʎiðo] *nm* surname

apenar [ape'nar] *vt* to grieve, trouble; (LAM: *avergonzar*) to embarrass; **apenarse** *vr* to grieve; (LAM: *avergonzarse*) to be embarrassed

apenas [a'penas] *adv* scarcely, hardly ▷ *conj* as soon as, no sooner

apéndice [a'pendiθe] *nm* appendix; **apendicitis** *nf* appendicitis

aperitivo [aperi'tiβo] *nm* (*bebida*) aperitif; (*comida*) appetizer

apertura [aper'tura] *nf* opening; (*Pol*) liberalization

apestar [apes'tar] *vt* to infect ▷ *vi*: **~ (a)** to stink (of)

apetecer [apete'θer] *vt*: **¿te apetece un café?** do you fancy a (cup of) coffee?; **apetecible** *adj* desirable; (*comida*) appetizing

apetito [ape'tito] *nm* appetite; **apetitoso, -a** *adj* appetizing; (*fig*) tempting

apiadarse [apja'ðarse] *vr*: **~ de** to take pity on

ápice ['apiθe] *nm* whit, iota

apilar [api'lar] *vt* to pile *o* heap up

apiñarse [api'ɲarse] *vr* to crowd *o* press together

apio ['apjo] *nm* celery

apisonadora [apisona'ðora] *nf* steamroller

aplacar [apla'kar] *vt* to placate

aplastante [aplas'tante] *adj* overwhelming; (*lógica*) compelling

aplastar [aplas'tar] *vt* to squash (flat); (*fig*) to crush

aplaudir [aplau'ðir] *vt* to applaud

aplauso [a'plauso] *nm* applause; (*fig*) approval, acclaim

aplazamiento [aplaθa'mjento] *nm* postponement

aplazar [apla'θar] *vt* to postpone, defer

aplicación [aplika'θjon] *nf* application; (*esfuerzo*) effort

aplicado, -a [apli'kaðo, a] *adj* diligent, hard-working

aplicar [apli'kar] *vt* (*ejecutar*) to apply; **aplicarse** *vr* to apply o.s.

aplique *etc* [a'plike] *vb V* **aplicar** ▷ *nm* wall light

aplomo [a'plomo] *nm* aplomb, self-assurance

apodar [apo'ðar] *vt* to nickname

apoderado [apoðe'raðo] *nm* agent,

representative

apoderarse [apoðe'rarse] *vr*: **~ de** to take possession of

apodo [a'poðo] *nm* nickname

apogeo [apo'xeo] *nm* peak, summit

apoquinar [apoki'nar] (*fam*) *vt* to fork out, cough up

aporrear [aporre'ar] *vt* to beat (up)

aportar [apor'tar] *vt* to contribute ▷ *vi* to reach port; **aportarse** *vr* (LAM: *llegar*) to arrive, come

aposta [a'posta] *adv* deliberately, on purpose

apostar [apos'tar] *vt* to bet, stake; (*tropas etc*) to station, post ▷ *vi* to bet

apóstol [a'postol] *nm* apostle

apóstrofo [a'postrofo] *nm* apostrophe

apoyar [apo'jar] *vt* to lean, rest; (*fig*) to support, back; **apoyarse** *vr*: **~se en** to lean on; **apoyo** *nm* (*gen*) support; backing, help

apreciable [apre'θjaβle] *adj* considerable; (*fig*) esteemed

apreciar [apre'θjar] *vt* to evaluate, assess; (*Com*) to appreciate, value; (*persona*) to respect; (*tamaño*) to gauge, assess; (*detalles*) to notice

aprecio [a'preθjo] *nm* valuation, estimate; (*fig*) appreciation

aprehender [apreen'der] *vt* to apprehend, detain

apremio [a'premjo] *nm* urgency

aprender [apren'der] *vt, vi* to learn; **~ algo de memoria** to learn sth (off) by heart

aprendiz, a [apren'diθ, a] *nm/f* apprentice; (*principiante*) learner; **aprendizaje** *nm* apprenticeship

aprensión [apren'sjon] *nm* apprehension, fear; **aprensivo, -a** *adj* apprehensive

apresar [apre'sar] *vt* to seize; (*capturar*) to capture

apresurado, -a [apresu'raðo, a] *adj* hurried, hasty

apresurar [apresu'rar] *vt* to hurry, accelerate; **apresurarse** *vr* to hurry, make haste

apretado, -a [apre'taðo, a] *adj* tight; (*escritura*) cramped

apretar [apre'tar] *vt* to squeeze; (*Tec*) to tighten; (*presionar*) to press together, pack ▷ *vi* to be too tight

apretón [apre'ton] *nm* squeeze; **apretón de manos** handshake

aprieto [a'prjeto] *nm* squeeze; (*dificultad*) difficulty; **estar en un ~** to be in a fix

aprisa [a'prisa] *adv* quickly, hurriedly

aprisionar [aprisjo'nar] *vt* to imprison

aprobación [aproβa'θjon] *nf* approval

aprobar [apro'βar] *vt* to approve (of); (*examen, materia*) to pass ▷ *vi* to pass

apropiado, -a [apro'pjaðo, a] *adj* suitable

apropiarse [apro'pjarse] *vr*: **~ de** to appropriate

aprovechado, -a [aproβe'tʃaðo, a] *adj* industrious, hard-working; (*económico*) thrifty; (*pey*) unscrupulous

aprovechar [aproβe'tʃar] *vt* to use; (*explotar*) to exploit; (*experiencia*) to profit from; (*oferta, oportunidad*) to take advantage of ▷ *vi* to progress, improve; **aprovecharse** *vr*: **~se de** to make use of; to take advantage of; **¡que aproveche!** enjoy your meal!

aproximación [aproksima'θjon] *nf* approximation; (*de lotería*) consolation prize

aproximar [aproksi'mar] *vt* to bring nearer; **aproximarse** *vr* to come near, approach

apruebo *etc vb V* **aprobar**

aptitud [apti'tuð] *nf* aptitude

apto, -a ['apto, a] *adj* suitable

apuesta [a'pwesta] *nf* bet, wager

apuesto, -a [a'pwesto, a] *adj* neat, elegant

apuntar [apun'tar] *vt* (*con arma*) to aim at; (*con dedo*) to point at *o* to; (*anotar*) to note (down); (*Teatro*) to prompt; **apuntarse** *vr* (*Deporte*: *tanto, victoria*) to score; (*Escol*) to enrol

No confundir **apuntar** con la palabra inglesa *appoint*.

apunte [a'punte] *nm* note

apuñalar [apuɲa'lar] *vt* to stab

apurado, -a [apu'raðo, a] *adj* needy; (*difícil*) difficult; (*peligroso*) dangerous; (LAM: *con prisa*) hurried, rushed

apurar [apu'rar] *vt* (*agotar*) to drain; (*recursos*) to use up; (*molestar*) to annoy; **apurarse** *vr* (*preocuparse*) to worry; (LAM: *darse prisa*) to hurry

apuro [a'puro] *nm* (*aprieto*) fix, jam; (*escasez*) want, hardship; (*vergüenza*) embarrassment; (LAM: *prisa*) haste, urgency

aquejado, -a [ake'xaðo, a] *adj*: **~ de** (*Med*) afflicted by

aquel, aquella [a'kel, a'keʎa] *adj* that; **~los(as)** those

aquél, aquélla [a'kel, a'keʎa] *pron* that (one); **~los(as)** those (ones)

aquello [a'keʎo] *pron* that, that business

aquí [a'ki] *adv* (*lugar*) here; (*tiempo*) now; **~ arriba** up here; **~ mismo** right here; **~ yace** here lies; **de ~ a siete días** a week from now

ara ['ara] *nf*: **en ~s de** for the sake of

árabe ['araβe] *adj, nmf* Arab ▷ *nm* (*Ling*) Arabic

Arabia [a'raβja] *nf* Arabia; **Arabia Saudí** *o* **Saudita** Saudi Arabia
arado [a'raðo] *nm* plough
Aragón [ara'ɣon] *nm* Aragon; **aragonés, -esa** *adj, nm/f* Aragonese
arancel [aran'θel] *nm* tariff, duty
arandela [aran'dela] *nf* (*Tec*) washer
araña [a'raɲa] *nf* (*Zool*) spider; (*lámpara*) chandelier
arañar [ara'ɲar] *vt* to scratch
arañazo [ara'ɲaθo] *nm* scratch
arbitrar [arβi'trar] *vt* to arbitrate in; (*Deporte*) to referee ▷ *vi* to arbitrate
arbitrario, -a [arβi'trarjo, a] *adj* arbitrary
árbitro ['arβitro] *nm* arbitrator; (*Deporte*) referee; (*Tenis*) umpire
árbol ['arβol] *nm* (*Bot*) tree; (*Náut*) mast; (*Tec*) axle, shaft; **árbol de Navidad** Christmas tree
arboleda [arβo'leða] *nf* grove, plantation
arbusto [ar'βusto] *nm* bush, shrub
arca ['arka] *nf* chest, box
arcada [ar'kaða] *nf* arcade; (*de puente*) arch, span; **arcadas** *nfpl* (*náuseas*) retching *sg*
arcaico, -a [ar'kaiko, a] *adj* archaic
arce ['arθe] *nm* maple tree
arcén [ar'θen] *nm* (*de autopista*) hard shoulder; (*de carretera*) verge
archipiélago [artʃi'pjelaɣo] *nm* archipelago
archivador [artʃiβa'ðor] *nm* filing cabinet
archivar [artʃi'βar] *vt* to file (away); **archivo** *nm* file, archive(s) *pl*; **archivo adjunto** (*Inform*) attachment; **archivo de seguridad** (*Inform*) backup file
arcilla [ar'θiʎa] *nf* clay
arco ['arko] *nm* arch; (*Mat*) arc; (*Mil, Mús*) bow; **arco iris** rainbow
arder [ar'ðer] *vi* to burn; **estar que arde** (*persona*) to fume
ardid [ar'ðið] *nm* ploy, trick
ardiente [ar'ðjente] *adj* burning, ardent
ardilla [ar'ðiʎa] *nf* squirrel
ardor [ar'ðor] *nm* (*calor*) heat; (*fig*) ardour; **ardor de estómago** heartburn
arduo, -a ['arðwo, a] *adj* arduous
área ['area] *nf* area; (*Deporte*) penalty area
arena [a'rena] *nf* sand; (*de una lucha*) arena; **arenas movedizas** quicksand *sg*; **arenal** [are'nal] *nm* (*terreno arenoso*) sandy spot
arenisca [are'niska] *nf* sandstone; (*cascajo*) grit
arenoso, -a [are'noso, a] *adj* sandy
arenque [a'renke] *nm* herring
arete [a'rete] (*MÉX*) *nm* earring
Argel [ar'xel] *n* Algiers; **Argelia** *nf* Algeria; **argelino, -a** *adj, nm/f* Algerian
Argentina [arxen'tina] *nf* (*tb*: **la ~**) Argentina
argentino, -a [arxen'tino, a] *adj* Argentinian; (*de plata*) silvery ▷ *nm/f* Argentinian
argolla [ar'ɣoʎa] *nf* (large) ring
argot [ar'ɣo] (*pl* **~s**) *nm* slang
argucia [ar'ɣuθja] *nf* subtlety, sophistry
argumentar [arɣumen'tar] *vt, vi* to argue
argumento [arɣu'mento] *nm* argument; (*razonamiento*) reasoning; (*de novela etc*) plot; (*Cine, TV*) storyline
aria ['arja] *nf* aria
aridez [ari'ðeθ] *nf* aridity, dryness
árido, -a ['ariðo, a] *adj* arid, dry
Aries ['arjes] *nm* Aries
arisco, -a [a'risko, a] *adj* surly; (*insociable*) unsociable
aristócrata [aris'tokrata] *nmf* aristocrat
arma ['arma] *nf* arm; **armas** *nfpl* arms; **arma blanca** blade, knife; **arma de doble filo** double-edged sword; **arma de fuego** firearm; **armas de destrucción masiva** weapons of mass destruction
armada [ar'maða] *nf* armada; (*flota*) fleet
armadillo [arma'ðiʎo] *nm* armadillo
armado, -a [ar'maðo, a] *adj* armed; (*Tec*) reinforced
armadura [arma'ðura] *nf* (*Mil*) armour; (*Tec*) framework; (*Zool*) skeleton; (*Física*) armature
armamento [arma'mento] *nm* armament; (*Náut*) fitting-out
armar [ar'mar] *vt* (*soldado*) to arm; (*máquina*) to assemble; (*navío*) to fit out; **~la, ~ un lío** to start a row, kick up a fuss
armario [ar'marjo] *nm* wardrobe; (*de cocina, baño*) cupboard; **armario empotrado** built-in cupboard
armatoste [arma'toste] *nm* (*mueble*) monstrosity; (*máquina*) contraption
armazón [arma'θon] *nf o m* body, chassis; (*de mueble etc*) frame; (*Arq*) skeleton
armiño [ar'miɲo] *nm* stoat; (*piel*) ermine
armisticio [armis'tiθjo] *nm* armistice
armonía [armo'nia] *nf* harmony
armónica [ar'monika] *nf* harmonica
armonizar [armoni'θar] *vt* to harmonize; (*diferencias*) to reconcile
aro ['aro] *nm* ring; (*tejo*) quoit; (*cs*: *pendiente*) earring
aroma [a'roma] *nm* aroma, scent; **aromaterapia** *n* aromatherapy; **aromático, -a** [aro'matiko, a] *adj* aromatic
arpa ['arpa] *nf* harp

arpía [ar'pia] *nf* shrew
arpón [ar'pon] *nm* harpoon
arqueología [arkeolo'xia] *nf* archaeology; **arqueólogo, -a** *nm/f* archaeologist
arquetipo [arke'tipo] *nm* archetype
arquitecto [arki'tekto] *nm* architect; **arquitectura** *nf* architecture
arrabal [arra'βal] *nm* poor suburb, slum; **arrabales** *nmpl* (*afueras*) outskirts
arraigar [arrai'ɣar] *vt* to establish ▷*vi* to take root
arrancar [arran'kar] *vt* (*sacar*) to extract, pull out; (*arrebatar*) to snatch (away); (*Inform*) to boot; (*fig*) to extract ▷*vi* (*Auto, máquina*) to start; (*ponerse en marcha*) to get going; **~ de** to stem from
arranque *etc* [a'rranke] *vb V* **arrancar** ▷*nm* sudden start; (*Auto*) start; (*fig*) fit, outburst
arrasar [arra'sar] *vt* (*aplanar*) to level, flatten; (*destruir*) to demolish
arrastrar [arras'trar] *vt* to drag (along); (*fig*) to drag down, degrade; (*agua, viento*) to carry away ▷*vi* to drag, trail on the ground; **arrastrarse** *vr* to crawl; (*fig*) to grovel; **llevar algo arrastrado** to drag sth along
arrear [arre'ar] *vt* to drive on, urge on ▷*vi* to hurry along
arrebatar [arreβa'tar] *vt* to snatch (away), seize; (*fig*) to captivate
arrebato [arre'βato] *nm* fit of rage, fury; (*éxtasis*) rapture
arrecife [arre'θife] *nm* reef
arreglado, -a [arre'ɣlaðo, a] *adj* (*ordenado*) neat, orderly; (*moderado*) moderate, reasonable
arreglar [arre'ɣlar] *vt* (*poner orden*) to tidy up; (*algo roto*) to fix, repair; (*problema*) to solve; **arreglarse** *vr* to reach an understanding; **arreglárselas** (*fam*) to get by, manage
arreglo [a'rreɣlo] *nm* settlement; (*orden*) order; (*acuerdo*) agreement; (*Mús*) arrangement, setting
arremangar [arreman'gar] *vt* to roll up, turn up; **arremangarse** *vr* to roll up one's sleeves
arremeter [arreme'ter] *vi*: **~ contra** to attack, rush at
arrendamiento [arrenda'mjento] *nm* letting; (*alquilar*) hiring; (*contrato*) lease; (*alquiler*) rent; **arrendar** *vt* to let, lease; to rent; **arrendatario, -a** *nm/f* tenant
arreos [a'rreos] *nmpl* (*de caballo*) harness *sg*, trappings
arrepentimiento [arrepenti'mjento] *nm* regret, repentance
arrepentirse [arrepen'tirse] *vr* to repent; **~ de** to regret
arresto [a'rresto] *nm* arrest; (*Mil*) detention; (*audacia*) boldness, daring; **arresto domiciliario** house arrest
arriar [a'rrjar] *vt* (*velas*) to haul down; (*bandera*) to lower, strike; (*cable*) to pay out

PALABRA CLAVE

arriba [a'rriβa] *adv* **1** (*posición*) above; **desde arriba** from above; **arriba de todo** at the very top, right on top; **Juan está arriba** Juan is upstairs; **lo arriba mencionado** the aforementioned
2 (*dirección*): **calle arriba** up the street
3 **de arriba abajo** from top to bottom; **mirar a algn de arriba abajo** to look sb up and down
4 **para arriba: de 5000 euros para arriba** from 5000 euros up(wards)
▷*adj*: **de arriba: el piso de arriba** the upstairs (BRIT) flat *o* apartment; **la parte de arriba** the top *o* upper part
▷*prep*: **arriba de** (LAM: *por encima de*) above; **arriba de 200 dólares** more than 200 dollars
▷*excl*: **¡arriba!** up!; **¡manos arriba!** hands up!; **¡arriba España!** long live Spain!

arribar [arri'βar] *vi* to put into port; (*llegar*) to arrive
arriendo *etc* [a'rrjendo] *vb V* **arrendar** ▷*nm* = **arrendamiento**
arriesgado, -a [arrjes'ɣaðo, a] *adj* (*peligroso*) risky; (*audaz*) bold, daring
arriesgar [arrjes'ɣar] *vt* to risk; (*poner en peligro*) to endanger; **arriesgarse** *vr* to take a risk
arrimar [arri'mar] *vt* (*acercar*) to bring close; (*poner de lado*) to set aside; **arrimarse** *vr* to come close *o* closer; **~se a** to lean on
arrinconar [arrinko'nar] *vt* (*colocar*) to put in a corner; (*enemigo*) to corner; (*fig*) to put on one side; (*abandonar*) to push aside
arroba [a'rroβa] *nf* (*Internet*) at (sign)
arrodillarse [arroði'ʎarse] *vr* to kneel (down)
arrogante [arro'ɣante] *adj* arrogant
arrojar [arro'xar] *vt* to throw, hurl; (*humo*) to emit, give out; (*Com*) to yield, produce; **arrojarse** *vr* to throw *o* hurl o.s.
arrojo [a'rroxo] *nm* daring
arrollador, a [arroʎa'ðor, a] *adj* overwhelming
arrollar [arro'ʎar] *vt* (*Auto etc*) to run over, knock down; (*Deporte*) to crush
arropar [arro'par] *vt* to cover, wrap up;

arroparse *vr* to wrap o.s. up
arroyo [a'rrojo] *nm* stream; (*de la calle*) gutter
arroz [a'rroθ] *nm* rice; **arroz con leche** rice pudding
arruga [a'rruɣa] *nf* (*de cara*) wrinkle; (*de vestido*) crease; **arrugar** [arru'ɣar] *vt* to wrinkle; to crease; **arrugarse** *vr* to get creased
arruinar [arrwi'nar] *vt* to ruin, wreck; **arruinarse** *vr* to be ruined, go bankrupt
arsenal [arse'nal] *nm* naval dockyard; (*Mil*) arsenal
arte ['arte] (*gen m en sg y siempre f en pl*) *nm* art; (*maña*) skill, guile; **artes** *nfpl* (*bellas artes*) arts
artefacto [arte'fakto] *nm* appliance
arteria [ar'terja] *nf* artery
artesanía [artesa'nia] *nf* craftsmanship; (*artículos*) handicrafts *pl*; **artesano, -a** *nm/f* artisan, craftsman(-woman)
ártico, -a ['artiko, a] *adj* Arctic ▷*nm*: **el Á~** the Arctic
articulación [artikula'θjon] *nf* articulation; (*Med, Tec*) joint
artículo [ar'tikulo] *nm* article; (*cosa*) thing, article; **artículos** *nmpl* (*Com*) goods; **artículos de escritorio** stationery
artífice [ar'tifiθe] *nmf* (*fig*) architect
artificial [artifi'θjal] *adj* artificial
artillería [artiʎe'ria] *nf* artillery
artilugio [arti'luxjo] *nm* gadget
artimaña [arti'maɲa] *nf* trap, snare; (*astucia*) cunning
artista [ar'tista] *nmf* (*pintor*) artist, painter; (*Teatro*) artist, artiste; **artista de cine** film actor/actress; **artístico, -a** *adj* artistic
artritis [ar'tritis] *nf* arthritis
arveja [ar'βexa] (LAM) *nf* pea
arzobispo [arθo'βispo] *nm* archbishop
as [as] *nm* ace
asa ['asa] *nf* handle; (*fig*) lever
asado [a'saðo] *nm* roast (meat); (LAM: *barbacoa*) barbecue

ASADO

Traditional Latin American barbecues, especially in the River Plate area, are celebrated in the open air around a large grill which is used to grill mainly beef and various kinds of spicy pork sausage. They are usually very common during the summer and can go on for several days. The head cook is nearly always a man.

asador [asa'ðor] *nm* spit
asadura [asa'ðura] *nf* entrails *pl*, offal
asalariado, -a [asala'rjaðo, a] *adj* paid, salaried ▷*nm/f* wage earner
asaltar [asal'tar] *vt* to attack, assault; (*fig*) to assail; **asalto** *nm* attack, assault; (*Deporte*) round
asamblea [asam'blea] *nf* assembly; (*reunión*) meeting
asar [a'sar] *vt* to roast
ascendencia [asθen'denθja] *nf* ancestry; (LAM: *influencia*) ascendancy; **de ~ francesa** of French origin
ascender [asθen'der] *vi* (*subir*) to ascend, rise; (*ser promovido*) to gain promotion ▷*vt* to promote; **~ a** to amount to; **ascendiente** *nm* influence ▷*nmf* ancestor
ascensión [asθen'sjon] *nf* ascent; (*Rel*): **la A~** the Ascension
ascenso [as'θenso] *nm* ascent; (*promoción*) promotion
ascensor [asθen'sor] *nm* lift (BRIT), elevator (US)
asco ['asko] *nm*: **¡qué ~!** how revolting *o* disgusting; **el ajo me da ~** I hate *o* loathe garlic; **estar hecho un ~** to be filthy
ascua ['askwa] *nf* ember
aseado, -a [ase'aðo, a] *adj* clean; (*arreglado*) tidy; (*pulcro*) smart
asear [ase'ar] *vt* to clean, wash; to tidy (up)
asediar [ase'ðjar] *vt* (*Mil*) to besiege, lay siege to; (*fig*) to chase, pester; **asedio** *nm* siege; (*Com*) run
asegurado, -a [aseɣu'raðo, a] *adj* insured
asegurador, a [aseɣura'ðor, a] *nm/f* insurer
asegurar [aseɣu'rar] *vt* (*consolidar*) to secure, fasten; (*dar garantía de*) to guarantee; (*preservar*) to safeguard; (*afirmar, dar por cierto*) to assure, affirm; (*tranquilizar*) to reassure; (*tomar un seguro*) to insure; **asegurarse** *vr* to assure o.s., make sure
asemejarse [aseme'xarse] *vr* to be alike; **~ a** to be like, resemble
asentado, -a [asen'taðo, a] *adj* established, settled
asentar [asen'tar] *vt* (*sentar*) to seat, sit down; (*poner*) to place, establish; (*alisar*) to level, smooth down *o* out; (*anotar*) to note down ▷*vi* to be suitable, suit
asentir [asen'tir] *vi* to assent, agree; **~ con la cabeza** to nod (one's head)
aseo [a'seo] *nm* cleanliness; **aseos** *nmpl* (*servicios*) toilet *sg* (BRIT), cloakroom *sg* (BRIT), restroom *sg* (US)
aséptico, -a [a'septiko, a] *adj* germ-free,

free from infection
asequible [ase'kiβle] *adj* (*precio*) reasonable; (*meta*) attainable; (*persona*) approachable
asesinar [asesi'nar] *vt* to murder; (*Pol*) to assassinate; **asesinato** *nm* murder; assassination
asesino, -a [ase'sino, a] *nm/f* murderer, killer; (*Pol*) assassin
asesor, a [ase'sor, a] *nm/f* adviser, consultant; **asesorar** [aseso'rar] *vt* (*Jur*) to advise, give legal advice to; (*Com*) to act as consultant to; **asesorarse** *vr*: **asesorarse con** *o* **de** to take advice from, consult; **asesoría** *nf* (*cargo*) consultancy; (*oficina*) consultant's office
asestar [ases'tar] *vt* (*golpe*) to deal, strike
asfalto [as'falto] *nm* asphalt
asfixia [as'fiksja] *nf* asphyxia, suffocation; **asfixiar** [asfik'sjar] *vt* to asphyxiate, suffocate; **asfixiarse** *vr* to be asphyxiated, suffocate
así [a'si] *adv* (*de esta manera*) in this way, like this, thus; (*aunque*) although; (*tan pronto como*) as soon as; **~ que** so; **~ como** as well as; **~ y todo** even so; **¿no es ~?** isn't it?, didn't you? *etc*; **~ de grande** this big
Asia ['asja] *nf* Asia; **asiático, -a** *adj, nm/f* Asian, Asiatic
asiduo, -a [a'siðwo, a] *adj* assiduous; (*frecuente*) frequent ▷*nm/f* regular (customer)
asiento [a'sjento] *nm* (*mueble*) seat, chair; (*de coche, en tribunal etc*) seat; (*localidad*) seat, place; (*fundamento*) site; **asiento delantero/trasero** front/back seat
asignación [asiɣna'θjon] *nf* (*atribución*) assignment; (*reparto*) allocation; (*sueldo*) salary; **asignación (semanal)** pocket money
asignar [asiɣ'nar] *vt* to assign, allocate
asignatura [asiɣna'tura] *nf* subject; course
asilo [a'silo] *nm* (*refugio*) asylum, refuge; (*establecimiento*) home, institution; **asilo político** political asylum
asimilar [asimi'lar] *vt* to assimilate
asimismo [asi'mismo] *adv* in the same way, likewise
asistencia [asis'tenθja] *nf* audience; (*Med*) attendance; (*ayuda*) assistance; **asistencia en carretera** roadside assistance; **asistente** *nmf* assistant; **los asistentes** those present; **asistente social** social worker
asistido, -a [asis'tiðo, a] *adj*: **~ por ordenador** computer-assisted
asistir [asis'tir] *vt* to assist, help ▷*vi*: **~ a** to attend, be present at
asma ['asma] *nf* asthma
asno ['asno] *nm* donkey; (*fig*) ass
asociación [asoθja'θjon] *nf* association; (*Com*) partnership; **asociado, -a** *adj* associate ▷*nm/f* associate; (*Com*) partner
asociar [aso'θjar] *vt* to associate
asomar [aso'mar] *vt* to show, stick out ▷*vi* to appear; **asomarse** *vr* to appear, show up; **~ la cabeza por la ventana** to put one's head out of the window
asombrar [asom'brar] *vt* to amaze, astonish; **asombrarse** *vr* (*sorprenderse*) to be amazed; (*asustarse*) to get a fright; **asombro** *nm* amazement, astonishment; (*susto*) fright; **asombroso, -a** *adj* astonishing, amazing
asomo [a'somo] *nm* hint, sign
aspa ['aspa] *nf* (*cruz*) cross; (*de molino*) sail; **en ~** X-shaped
aspaviento [aspa'βjento] *nm* exaggerated display of feeling; (*fam*) fuss
aspecto [as'pekto] *nm* (*apariencia*) look, appearance; (*fig*) aspect
áspero, -a ['aspero, a] *adj* rough; bitter; sour; harsh
aspersión [asper'sjon] *nf* sprinkling
aspiración [aspira'θjon] *nf* breath, inhalation; (*Mús*) short pause; **aspiraciones** *nfpl* (*ambiciones*) aspirations
aspirador [aspira'ðor] *nm* = **aspiradora**
aspiradora [aspira'ðora] *nf* vacuum cleaner, Hoover®
aspirante [aspi'rante] *nmf* (*candidato*) candidate; (*Deporte*) contender
aspirar [aspi'rar] *vt* to breathe in ▷*vi*: **~ a** to aspire to
aspirina [aspi'rina] *nf* aspirin
asqueroso, -a [aske'roso, a] *adj* disgusting, sickening
asta ['asta] *nf* lance; (*arpón*) spear; (*mango*) shaft, handle; (*Zool*) horn; **a media ~** at half mast
asterisco [aste'risko] *nm* asterisk
astilla [as'tiʎa] *nf* splinter; (*pedacito*) chip; **astillas** *nfpl* (*leña*) firewood *sg*
astillero [asti'ʎero] *nm* shipyard
astro ['astro] *nm* star
astrología [astrolo'xia] *nf* astrology; **astrólogo, -a** *nm/f* astrologer
astronauta [astro'nauta] *nmf* astronaut
astronomía [astrono'mia] *nf* astronomy
astucia [as'tuθja] *nf* astuteness; (*ardid*) clever trick
asturiano, -a [astu'rjano, a] *adj, nm/f* Asturian
astuto, -a [as'tuto, a] *adj* astute; (*taimado*) cunning

asumir [asu'mir] *vt* to assume
asunción [asun'θjon] *nf* assumption; (*Rel*): **A~** Assumption
asunto [a'sunto] *nm* (*tema*) matter, subject; (*negocio*) business
asustar [asus'tar] *vt* to frighten; **asustarse** *vr* to be (*o* become) frightened
atacar [ata'kar] *vt* to attack
atadura [ata'ðura] *nf* bond, tie
atajar [ata'xar] *vt* (*enfermedad, mal*) to stop ▷ *vi* (*persona*) to take a short cut
atajo [a'taxo] *nm* short cut
atañer [ata'ɲer] *vi*: **~ a** to concern
ataque *etc* [a'take] *vb V* **atacar** ▷ *nm* attack; **ataque cardíaco** heart attack
atar [a'tar] *vt* to tie, tie up
atarantado, -a [ataran'taðo, a] (*MÉX*) *adj* (*aturdido*) dazed
atardecer [atarðe'θer] *vi* to get dark ▷ *nm* evening; (*crepúsculo*) dusk
atareado, -a [atare'aðo, a] *adj* busy
atascar [atas'kar] *vt* to clog up; (*obstruir*) to jam; (*fig*) to hinder; **atascarse** *vr* to stall; (*cañería*) to get blocked up; **atasco** *nm* obstruction; (*Auto*) traffic jam
ataúd [ata'uð] *nm* coffin
ataviar [ata'βjar] *vt* to deck, array
atemorizar [atemori'θar] *vt* to frighten, scare
Atenas [a'tenas] *n* Athens
atención [aten'θjon] *nf* attention; (*bondad*) kindness ▷ *excl* (be) careful!, look out!
atender [aten'der] *vt* to attend to, look after; (*Tel*) to answer ▷ *vi* to pay attention
atenerse [ate'nerse] *vr*: **~ a** to abide by, adhere to
atentado [aten'taðo] *nm* crime, illegal act; (*asalto*) assault; (*tb*: **~ terrorista**) terrorist attack; **~ contra la vida de algn** attempt on sb's life; **atentado suicida** suicide bombing
atentamente [atenta'mente] *adv*: **Le saluda ~** Yours faithfully
atentar [aten'tar] *vi*: **~ a** *o* **contra** to commit an outrage against
atento, -a [a'tento, a] *adj* attentive, observant; (*cortés*) polite, thoughtful; **estar ~ a** (*explicación*) to pay attention to
atenuar [ate'nwar] *vt* (*disminuir*) to lessen, minimize
ateo, -a [a'teo, a] *adj* atheistic ▷ *nm/f* atheist
aterrador, a [aterra'ðor, a] *adj* frightening
aterrizaje [aterri'θaxe] *nm* landing; **aterrizaje forzoso** emergency *o* forced landing
aterrizar [aterri'θar] *vi* to land
aterrorizar [aterrori'θar] *vt* to terrify
atesorar [ateso'rar] *vt* to hoard
atestar [ates'tar] *vt* to pack, stuff; (*Jur*) to attest, testify to
atestiguar [atesti'ɣwar] *vt* to testify to, bear witness to
atiborrar [atiβo'rrar] *vt* to fill, stuff; **atiborrarse** *vr* to stuff o.s.
ático ['atiko] *nm* (*desván*) attic; (*apartamento*) penthouse
atinado, -a [ati'naðo, a] *adj* (*sensato*) wise; (*correcto*) right, correct
atinar [ati'nar] *vi* (*al disparar*): **~ al blanco** to hit the target; (*fig*) to be right
atizar [ati'θar] *vt* to poke; (*horno etc*) to stoke; (*fig*) to stir up, rouse
atlántico, -a [at'lantiko, a] *adj* Atlantic ▷ *nm*: **el (océano) A~** the Atlantic (Ocean)
atlas ['atlas] *nm inv* atlas
atleta [at'leta] *nm* athlete; **atlético, -a** *adj* athletic; **atletismo** *nm* athletics *sg*
atmósfera [at'mosfera] *nf* atmosphere
atolladero [atoʎa'ðero] *nm* (*fig*) jam, fix
atómico, -a [a'tomiko, a] *adj* atomic
átomo ['atomo] *nm* atom
atónito, -a [a'tonito, a] *adj* astonished, amazed
atontado, -a [aton'taðo, a] *adj* stunned; (*bobo*) silly, daft
atormentar [atormen'tar] *vt* to torture; (*molestar*) to torment; (*acosar*) to plague, harass
atornillar [atorni'ʎar] *vt* to screw on *o* down
atosigar [atosi'ɣar] *vt* to harass, pester
atracador, a [atraka'ðor, a] *nm/f* robber
atracar [atra'kar] *vt* (*Náut*) to moor; (*robar*) to hold up, rob ▷ *vi* to moor; **atracarse** *vr*: **~se (de)** to stuff o.s. (with)
atracción [atrak'θjon] *nf* attraction
atraco [a'trako] *nm* holdup, robbery
atracón [atra'kon] *nm*: **darse** *o* **pegarse un ~ (de)** (*fam*) to stuff o.s. (with)
atractivo, -a [atrak'tiβo, a] *adj* attractive ▷ *nm* appeal
atraer [atra'er] *vt* to attract
atragantarse [atraɣan'tarse] *vr*: **~ (con)** to choke (on); **se me ha atragantado el chico** I can't stand the boy
atrancar [atran'kar] *vt* (*puerta*) to bar, bolt
atrapar [atra'par] *vt* to trap; (*resfriado etc*) to catch
atrás [a'tras] *adv* (*movimiento*) back(-wards); (*lugar*) behind; (*tiempo*) previously; **ir hacia ~** to go back(wards), to go to the rear; **estar ~** to be behind *o* at the back
atrasado, -a [atra'saðo, a] *adj* slow;

(*pago*) overdue, late; (*país*) backward
atrasar [atra'sar] *vi* to be slow; **atrasarse** *vr* to remain behind; (*tren*) to be *o* run late; **atraso** *nm* slowness; lateness, delay; (*de país*) backwardness; **atrasos** *nmpl* (*Com*) arrears
atravesar [atraβe'sar] *vt* (*cruzar*) to cross (over); (*traspasar*) to pierce; to go through; (*poner al través*) to lay *o* put across; **atravesarse** *vr* to come in between; (*intervenir*) to interfere
atravieso *etc vb V* **atravesar**
atreverse [atre'βerse] *vr* to dare; (*insolentarse*) to be insolent; **atrevido, -a** *adj* daring; insolent; **atrevimiento** *nm* daring; insolence
atribución [atriβu'θjon] *nf* attribution; **atribuciones** *nfpl* (*Pol*) powers; (*Admin*) responsibilities
atribuir [atriβu'ir] *vt* to attribute; (*funciones*) to confer
atributo [atri'βuto] *nm* attribute
atril [a'tril] *nm* (*para libro*) lectern; (*Mús*) music stand
atropellar [atrope'ʎar] *vt* (*derribar*) to knock over *o* down; (*empujar*) to push (aside); (*Auto*) to run over, run down; (*agraviar*) to insult; **atropello** *nm* (*Auto*) accident; (*empujón*) push; (*agravio*) wrong; (*atrocidad*) outrage
atroz [a'troθ] *adj* atrocious, awful
ATS *nmf abr* (= *Ayudante Técnico Sanitario*) nurse
atuendo [a'twendo] *nm* attire
atún [a'tun] *nm* tuna
aturdir [atur'ðir] *vt* to stun; (*de ruido*) to deafen; (*fig*) to dumbfound, bewilder
audacia [au'ðaθja] *nf* boldness, audacity; **audaz** *adj* bold, audacious
audición [auði'θjon] *nf* hearing; (*Teatro*) audition
audiencia [au'ðjenθja] *nf* audience; (*Jur: tribunal*) court
audífono [au'ðifono] *nm* (*para sordos*) hearing aid
auditor [auði'tor] *nm* (*Jur*) judge advocate; (*Com*) auditor
auditorio [auði'torjo] *nm* audience; (*sala*) auditorium
auge ['auxe] *nm* boom; (*clímax*) climax
augurar [auɣu'rar] *vt* to predict; (*presagiar*) to portend
augurio [au'ɣurjo] *nm* omen
aula ['aula] *nf* classroom; (*en universidad etc*) lecture room
aullar [au'ʎar] *vi* to howl, yell
aullido [au'ʎiðo] *nm* howl, yell
aumentar [aumen'tar] *vt* to increase; (*precios*) to put up; (*producción*) to step up; (*con microscopio, anteojos*) to magnify ▷ *vi* to increase, be on the increase; **aumentarse** *vr* to increase, be on the increase; **aumento** *nm* increase; rise
aun [a'un] *adv* even; **~ así** even so; **~ más** even *o* yet more
aún [a'un] *adv*: **~ está aquí** he's still here; **~ no lo sabemos** we don't know yet; **¿no ha venido ~?** hasn't she come yet?
aunque [a'unke] *conj* though, although, even though
aúpa [a'upa] *excl* come on!
auricular [auriku'lar] *nm* (*Tel*) receiver; **auriculares** *nmpl* (*cascos*) headphones
aurora [au'rora] *nf* dawn
ausencia [au'senθja] *nf* absence
ausentarse [ausen'tarse] *vr* to go away; (*por poco tiempo*) to go out
ausente [au'sente] *adj* absent
austero, -a [aus'tero, a] *adj* austere
austral [aus'tral] *adj* southern ▷ *nm monetary unit of Argentina*
Australia [aus'tralja] *nf* Australia; **australiano, -a** *adj, nm/f* Australian
Austria ['austrja] *nf* Austria; **austríaco, -a** *adj, nm/f* Austrian
auténtico, -a [au'tentiko, a] *adj* authentic
auto ['auto] *nm* (*Jur*) edict, decree; (*: orden*) writ; (*Auto*) car; **autos** *nmpl* (*Jur*) proceedings; (*: acta*) court record *sg*
autoadhesivo [autoaðe'siβo] *adj* self-adhesive; (*sobre*) self-sealing
autobiografía [autoβjoɣra'fia] *nf* autobiography
autobomba [auto'bomba] (RPL) *nm* fire engine
autobronceador [autoβronθea'ðor] *adj* self-tanning
autobús [auto'βus] *nm* bus; **autobús de línea** long-distance coach
autocar [auto'kar] *nm* coach (BRIT), (passenger) bus (US)
autóctono, -a [au'toktono, a] *adj* native, indigenous
autodefensa [autoðe'fensa] *nf* self-defence
autodidacta [autoði'ðakta] *adj* self-taught
autoescuela [autoes'kwela] (ESP) *nf* driving school
autógrafo [au'toɣrafo] *nm* autograph
autómata [au'tomata] *nm* automaton
automático, -a [auto'matiko, a] *adj* automatic ▷ *nm* press stud
automóvil [auto'moβil] *nm* (motor) car (BRIT), automobile (US); **automovilismo** *nm*

(*actividad*) motoring; (*Deporte*) motor racing; **automovilista** *nmf* motorist, driver
autonomía [autono'mia] *nf* autonomy; **autónomo, -a** (ESP), **autonómico, -a** (ESP) *adj* (*Pol*) autonomous
autopista [auto'pista] *nf* motorway (BRIT), freeway (US); **autopista de cuota** (ESP) *o* **peaje** (MÉX) toll (BRIT) *o* turnpike (US) road
autopsia [au'topsja] *nf* autopsy, postmortem
autor, a [au'tor, a] *nm/f* author
autoridad [autori'ðað] *nf* authority; **autoritario, -a** *adj* authoritarian
autorización [autoriθa'θjon] *nf* authorization; **autorizado, -a** *adj* authorized; (*aprobado*) approved
autorizar [autori'θar] *vt* to authorize; (*aprobar*) to approve
autoservicio [autoser'βiθjo] *nm* (*tienda*) self-service shop (BRIT) *o* store (US); (*restaurante*) self-service restaurant
autostop [auto'stop] *nm* hitch-hiking; **hacer ~** to hitch-hike; **autostopista** *nmf* hitch-hiker
autovía [auto'βia] *nf* ≈ A-road (BRIT), dual carriageway (BRIT), ≈ state highway (US)
auxiliar [auksi'ljar] *vt* to help ▷ *nmf* assistant; **auxilio** *nm* assistance, help; **primeros auxilios** first aid *sg*
Av *abr* (= *Avenida*) Av(e)
aval [a'βal] *nm* guarantee; (*persona*) guarantor
avalancha [aβa'lantʃa] *nf* avalanche
avance [a'βanθe] *nm* advance; (*pago*) advance payment; (*Cine*) trailer
avanzar [aβan'θar] *vt, vi* to advance
avaricia [aβa'riθja] *nf* avarice, greed; **avaricioso, -a** *adj* avaricious, greedy
avaro, -a [a'βaro, a] *adj* miserly, mean ▷ *nm/f* miser
Avda *abr* (= *Avenida*) Av(e)
AVE ['aβe] *nm abr* (= *Alta Velocidad Española*) ≈ bullet train
ave ['aβe] *nf* bird; **ave de rapiña** bird of prey
avecinarse [aβeθi'narse] *vr* (*tormenta: fig*) to be on the way
avellana [aβe'ʎana] *nf* hazelnut; **avellano** *nm* hazel tree
avemaría [aβema'ria] *nm* Hail Mary, Ave Maria
avena [a'βena] *nf* oats *pl*
avenida [aβe'niða] *nf* (*calle*) avenue
aventajar [aβenta'xar] *vt* (*sobrepasar*) to surpass, outstrip
aventón [aβen'ton] (MÉX: *fam*) *nm* ride; **dar ~ a algn** to give sb a ride
aventura [aβen'tura] *nf* adventure; **aventurero, -a** *adj* adventurous
avergonzar [aβerɣon'θar] *vt* to shame; (*desconcertar*) to embarrass; **avergonzarse** *vr* to be ashamed; to be embarrassed
avería [aβe'ria] *nf* (*Tec*) breakdown, fault
averiado, -a [aβe'rjaðo, a] *adj* broken down; **"~"** "out of order"
averiguar [aβeri'ɣwar] *vt* to investigate; (*descubrir*) to find out, ascertain
avestruz [aβes'truθ] *nm* ostrich
aviación [aβja'θjon] *nf* aviation; (*fuerzas aéreas*) air force
aviador, a [aβja'ðor, a] *nm/f* aviator, airman(-woman)
ávido, -a ['aβiðo, a] *adj* avid, eager
avinagrado, -a [aβina'ɣraðo, a] *adj* sour, acid
avión [a'βjon] *nm* aeroplane; (*ave*) martin; **avión de reacción** jet (plane)
avioneta [aβjo'neta] *nf* light aircraft
avisar [aβi'sar] *vt* (*advertir*) to warn, notify; (*informar*) to tell; (*aconsejar*) to advise, counsel; **aviso** *nm* warning; (*noticia*) notice
avispa [a'βispa] *nf* wasp
avispado, -a [aβis'paðo, a] *adj* sharp, clever
avivar [aβi'βar] *vt* to strengthen, intensify
axila [ak'sila] *nf* armpit
ay [ai] *excl* (*dolor*) ow!, ouch!; (*aflicción*) oh!, oh dear!; **¡~ de mi!** poor me!
ayer [a'jer] *adv, nm* yesterday; **antes de ~** the day before yesterday; **~ mismo** only yesterday
ayote [a'jote] (CAM) *nm* pumpkin
ayuda [a'juða] *nf* help, assistance ▷ *nm* page; **ayudante** *nmf* assistant, helper; (*Escol*) assistant; (*Mil*) adjutant
ayudar [aju'ðar] *vt* to help, assist
ayunar [aju'nar] *vi* to fast; **ayunas** *nfpl*: **estar en ayunas** to be fasting; **ayuno** *nm* fast; fasting
ayuntamiento [ajunta'mjento] *nm* (*consejo*) town (*o* city) council; (*edificio*) town (*o* city) hall
azafata [aθa'fata] *nf* air stewardess
azafrán [aθa'fran] *nm* saffron
azahar [aθa'ar] *nm* orange/lemon blossom
azar [a'θar] *nm* (*casualidad*) chance, fate; (*desgracia*) misfortune, accident; **por ~** by chance; **al ~** at random
Azores [a'θores] *nfpl*: **las ~** the Azores
azotar [aθo'tar] *vt* to whip, beat; (*pegar*) to spank; **azote** *nm* (*látigo*) whip; (*latigazo*) lash, stroke; (*en las nalgas*) spank; (*calamidad*) calamity
azotea [aθo'tea] *nf* (flat) roof

azteca [aθ'teka] *adj, nmf* Aztec
azúcar [a'θukar] *nm* sugar; **azucarado, -a** *adj* sugary, sweet
azucarero, -a [aθuka'rero, a] *adj* sugar *cpd* ▷ *nm* sugar bowl
azucena [aθu'θena] *nf* white lily
azufre [a'θufre] *nm* sulphur
azul [a'θul] *adj, nm* blue; **azul celeste/marino** sky/navy blue
azulejo [aθu'lexo] *nm* tile
azuzar [aθu'θar] *vt* to incite, egg on

B.A. *abr* (= *Buenos Aires*) B.A.
baba ['baβa] *nf* spittle, saliva; **babear** *vi* to drool, slaver
babero [ba'βero] *nm* bib
babor [ba'βor] *nm* port (side)
babosada [baβo'saða] (*MÉX, CAM*: *fam*) *nf* drivel; **baboso, -a** [ba'βoso, a] (*LAM*: *fam*) *adj* silly
baca ['baka] *nf* (*Auto*) luggage *o* roof rack
bacalao [baka'lao] *nm* cod(fish)
bache ['batʃe] *nm* pothole, rut; (*fig*) bad patch
bachillerato [batʃiʎe'rato] *nm* *higher secondary school course*
bacinica [baθi'nika] (*LAM*) *nf* potty
bacteria [bak'terja] *nf* bacterium, germ
Bahama [ba'ama]: **las (Islas) ~** *nfpl* the Bahamas
bahía [ba'ia] *nf* bay
bailar [bai'lar] *vt, vi* to dance; **bailarín, -ina** *nm/f* (ballet) dancer; **baile** *nm* dance; (*formal*) ball
baja ['baxa] *nf* drop, fall; (*Mil*) casualty; **dar de ~** (*soldado*) to discharge; (*empleado*) to dismiss
bajada [ba'xaða] *nf* descent; (*camino*) slope; (*de aguas*) ebb
bajar [ba'xar] *vi* to go down, come down; (*temperatura, precios*) to drop, fall ▷ *vt* (*cabeza*) to bow; (*escalera*) to go down, come down; (*precio, voz*) to lower; (*llevar abajo*) to take down; **bajarse** *vr* (*de coche*) to get out; (*de autobús, tren*) to get off; **~ de** (*coche*) to get out of; (*autobús, tren*) to get off; **~se algo de Internet** to download sth from the Internet
bajío [ba'xio] (*LAM*) *nm* lowlands *pl*
bajo, -a ['baxo] *adj* (*mueble, número, precio*) low; (*piso*) ground; (*de estatura*) small, short; (*color*) pale; (*sonido*) faint, soft, low; (*voz: en tono*) deep; (*metal*) base; (*humilde*) low, humble ▷ *adv* (*hablar*) softly, quietly; (*volar*)

low ▷ *prep* under, below, underneath ▷ *nm* (*Mús*) bass; **~ la lluvia** in the rain
bajón [ba'xon] *nm* fall, drop
bakalao [baka'lao] (*ESP*: *fam*) *nm* rave (music)
bala ['bala] *nf* bullet
balacear [balaθe'ar] (*MÉX, CAM*) *vt* to shoot
balance [ba'lanθe] *nm* (*Com*) balance; (: *libro*) balance sheet; (: *cuenta general*) stocktaking
balancear [balanθe'ar] *vt* to balance ▷ *vi* to swing (to and fro); (*vacilar*) to hesitate; **balancearse** *vr* to swing (to and fro), to hesitate
balanza [ba'lanθa] *nf* scales *pl*, balance; **balanza comercial** balance of trade; **balanza de pagos** balance of payments
balaustrada [balaus'traða] *nf* balustrade; (*pasamanos*) banisters *pl*
balazo [ba'laθo] *nm* (*golpe*) shot; (*herida*) bullet wound
balbucear [balβuθe'ar] *vi, vt* to stammer, stutter
balcón [bal'kon] *nm* balcony
balde ['balde] *nm* bucket, pail; **de ~** (for) free, for nothing; **en ~** in vain
baldosa [bal'dosa] *nf* (*azulejo*) floor tile; (*grande*) flagstone; **baldosín** *nm* (small) tile
Baleares [bale'ares] *nfpl*: **las (Islas) ~** the Balearic Islands
balero [ba'lero] (*LAM*) *nm* (*juguete*) cup-and-ball toy
baliza [ba'liθa] *nf* (*Aviac*) beacon; (*Náut*) buoy
ballena [ba'ʎena] *nf* whale
ballet [ba'le] (*pl* **~s**) *nm* ballet
balneario [balne'arjo] *nm* spa; (*CS*: *en la costa*) seaside resort
balón [ba'lon] *nm* ball
baloncesto [balon'θesto] *nm* basketball
balonmano [balon'mano] *nm* handball
balsa ['balsa] *nf* raft; (*Bot*) balsa wood
bálsamo ['balsamo] *nm* balsam, balm
baluarte [ba'lwarte] *nm* bastion, bulwark
bambú [bam'bu] *nm* bamboo
banana [ba'nana] (*LAM*) *nf* banana; **banano** *nm* (*LAM*: *árbol*) banana tree; (*CAM*: *fruta*) banana
banca ['banka] *nf* (*Com*) banking
bancario, -a [ban'karjo, a] *adj* banking *cpd*, bank *cpd*
bancarrota [banka'rrota] *nf* bankruptcy; **hacer ~** to go bankrupt
banco ['banko] *nm* bench; (*Escol*) desk; (*Com*) bank; (*Geo*) stratum; **banco de arena** sandbank; **banco de crédito** credit bank; **banco de datos** databank
banda ['banda] *nf* band; (*pandilla*) gang; (*Náut*) side, edge; **banda ancha** broadband; **banda sonora** soundtrack
bandada [ban'daða] *nf* (*de pájaros*) flock; (*de peces*) shoal
bandazo [ban'daθo] *nm*: **dar ~s** to sway from side to side
bandeja [ban'dexa] *nf* tray
bandera [ban'dera] *nf* flag
banderilla [bande'riʎa] *nf* banderilla
bandido [ban'diðo] *nm* bandit
bando ['bando] *nm* (*edicto*) edict, proclamation; (*facción*) faction; **bandos** *nmpl* (*Rel*) banns
bandolera [bando'lera] *nf*: **llevar en ~** to wear across one's chest
banquero [ban'kero] *nm* banker
banqueta [ban'keta] *nf* stool; (*MÉX*: *en calle*) pavement (*BRIT*), sidewalk (*US*)
banquete [ban'kete] *nm* banquet; (*para convidados*) formal dinner; **banquete de boda(s)** wedding reception
banquillo [ban'kiʎo] *nm* (*Jur*) dock, prisoner's bench; (*banco*) bench; (*para los pies*) footstool
banquina [ban'kina] (*RPL*) *nf* hard shoulder (*BRIT*), berm (*US*)
bañadera [baɲa'ðera] (*RPL*) *nf* bathtub
bañador [baɲa'ðor] (*ESP*) *nm* swimming costume (*BRIT*), bathing suit (*US*)
bañar [ba'ɲar] *vt* to bath, bathe; (*objeto*) to dip; (*de barniz*) to coat; **bañarse** *vr* (*en el mar*) to bathe, swim; (*en la bañera*) to have a bath
bañera [ba'ɲera] (*ESP*) *nf* bath(tub)
bañero, -a [ba'ɲero, a] (*CS*) *nm/f* lifeguard
bañista [ba'ɲista] *nmf* bather
baño ['baɲo] *nm* (*en bañera*) bath; (*en río*) dip, swim; (*cuarto*) bathroom; (*bañera*) bath(tub); (*capa*) coating; **darse** *o* **tomar un ~** (*en bañera*) to have *o* take a bath; (*en mar, piscina*) to have a swim; **baño María** bain-marie
bar [bar] *nm* bar
barahúnda [bara'unda] *nf* uproar, hubbub
baraja [ba'raxa] *nf* pack (of cards); **barajar** *vt* (*naipes*) to shuffle; (*fig*) to jumble up
baranda [ba'randa] *nf* = **barandilla**
barandilla [baran'diʎa] *nf* rail, railing
barata [ba'rata] (*MÉX*) *nf* (bargain) sale
baratillo [bara'tiʎo] *nm* (*tienda*) junkshop; (*subasta*) bargain sale; (*conjunto de cosas*) secondhand goods *pl*
barato, -a [ba'rato, a] *adj* cheap ▷ *adv* cheap, cheaply
barba ['barβa] *nf* (*mentón*) chin; (*pelo*) beard

barbacoa [barβa'koa] *nf* (*parrilla*) barbecue; (*carne*) barbecued meat
barbaridad [barβari'ðað] *nf* barbarity; (*acto*) barbarism; (*atrocidad*) outrage; **una ~** (*fam*) loads; **¡qué ~!** (*fam*) how awful!
barbarie [bar'βarje] *nf* barbarism, savagery; (*crueldad*) barbarity
bárbaro, -a ['barβaro, a] *adj* barbarous, cruel; (*grosero*) rough, uncouth ▷*nm/f* barbarian ▷*adv*: **lo pasamos ~** (*fam*) we had a great time; **¡qué ~!** (*fam*) how marvellous!; **un éxito ~** (*fam*) a terrific success; **es un tipo ~** (*fam*) he's a great bloke
barbero [bar'βero] *nm* barber, hairdresser
barbilla [bar'βiʎa] *nf* chin, tip of the chin
barbudo, -a [bar'βuðo, a] *adj* bearded
barca ['barka] *nf* (small) boat; **barcaza** *nf* barge
Barcelona [barθe'lona] *n* Barcelona
barco ['barko] *nm* boat; (*grande*) ship; **barco de carga/pesca** cargo/fishing boat; **barco de vela** sailing ship
barda ['barða] (*MÉX*) *nf* (*de madera*) fence
baremo [ba'remo] *nm* (*Mat*: *fig*) scale
barítono [ba'ritono] *nm* baritone
barman ['barman] *nm* barman
barniz [bar'niθ] *nm* varnish; (*en loza*) glaze; (*fig*) veneer; **barnizar** *vt* to varnish; (*loza*) to glaze
barómetro [ba'rometro] *nm* barometer
barquillo [bar'kiʎo] *nm* cone, cornet
barra ['barra] *nf* bar, rod; (*de un bar, café*) bar; (*de pan*) French stick; (*palanca*) lever; **barra de labios** lipstick; **barra libre** free bar
barraca [ba'rraka] *nf* hut, cabin
barranco [ba'rranko] *nm* ravine; (*fig*) difficulty
barrena [ba'rrena] *nf* drill
barrer [ba'rrer] *vt* to sweep; (*quitar*) to sweep away
barrera [ba'rrera] *nf* barrier
barriada [ba'rrjaða] *nf* quarter, district
barricada [barri'kaða] *nf* barricade
barrida [ba'rriða] *nf* sweep, sweeping
barriga [ba'rriɣa] *nf* belly; (*panza*) paunch; **barrigón, -ona** *adj* potbellied; **barrigudo, -a** *adj* potbellied
barril [ba'rril] *nm* barrel, cask
barrio ['barrjo] *nm* (*vecindad*) area, neighborhood (*US*); (*en afueras*) suburb; **barrio chino** (*ESP*) red-light district
barro ['barro] *nm* (*lodo*) mud; (*objetos*) earthenware; (*Med*) pimple
barroco, -a [ba'rroko, a] *adj*, *nm* baroque
barrote [ba'rrote] *nm* (*de ventana*) bar
bartola [bar'tola] *nf*: **tirarse** *o* **tumbarse a la ~** to take it easy, be lazy
bártulos ['bartulos] *nmpl* things, belongings
barullo [ba'ruʎo] *nm* row, uproar
basar [ba'sar] *vt* to base; **basarse** *vr*: **~se en** to be based on
báscula ['baskula] *nf* (platform) scales
base ['base] *nf* base; **a ~ de** on the basis of; (*mediante*) by means of; **base de datos** (*Inform*) database
básico, -a ['basiko, a] *adj* basic
basílica [ba'silika] *nf* basilica
básquetbol ['basketbol] (*LAM*) *nm* basketball

PALABRA CLAVE

bastante [bas'tante] *adj* **1** (*suficiente*) enough; **bastante dinero** enough *o* sufficient money; **bastantes libros** enough books
2 (*valor intensivo*): **bastante gente** quite a lot of people; **tener bastante calor** to be rather hot
▷*adv*: **bastante bueno/malo** quite good/rather bad; **bastante rico** pretty rich; **(lo) bastante inteligente (como) para hacer algo** clever enough *o* sufficiently clever to do sth

bastar [bas'tar] *vi* to be enough *o* sufficient; **bastarse** *vr* to be self-sufficient; **~ para** to be enough to; **¡basta!** (that's) enough!
bastardo, -a [bas'tarðo, a] *adj*, *nm/f* bastard
bastidor [basti'ðor] *nm* frame; (*de coche*) chassis; (*Teatro*) wing; **entre ~es** (*fig*) behind the scenes
basto, -a ['basto, a] *adj* coarse, rough; **bastos** *nmpl* (*Naipes*) ≈ clubs
bastón [bas'ton] *nm* stick, staff; (*para pasear*) walking stick
bastoncillo [baston'θiʎo] *nm* cotton bud
basura [ba'sura] *nf* rubbish (*BRIT*), garbage (*US*) ▷*adj*: **comida/televisión ~** junk food/TV
basurero [basu'rero] *nm* (*hombre*) dustman (*BRIT*), garbage man (*US*); (*lugar*) dump; (*cubo*) (rubbish) bin (*BRIT*), trash can (*US*)
bata ['bata] *nf* (*gen*) dressing gown; (*cubretodo*) smock, overall; (*Med, Tec etc*) lab(oratory) coat
batalla [ba'taʎa] *nf* battle; **de ~** (*fig*) for everyday use; **batalla campal** pitched battle
batallón [bata'ʎon] *nm* battalion
batata [ba'tata] *nf* sweet potato
batería [bate'ria] *nf* battery; (*Mús*) drums;

batería de cocina kitchen utensils
batido, -a [ba'tiðo, a] *adj* (*camino*) beaten, well-trodden ▷ *nm* (*Culin*: *de leche*) milk shake
batidora [bati'ðora] *nf* beater, mixer; **batidora eléctrica** food mixer, blender
batir [ba'tir] *vt* to beat, strike; (*vencer*) to beat, defeat; (*revolver*) to beat, mix; **batirse** *vr* to fight; **~ palmas** to applaud
batuta [ba'tuta] *nf* baton; **llevar la ~** (*fig*) to be the boss, be in charge
baúl [ba'ul] *nm* trunk; (*Auto*) boot (BRIT), trunk (US)
bautismo [bau'tismo] *nm* baptism, christening
bautizar [bauti'θar] *vt* to baptize, christen; (*fam*: *diluir*) to water down; **bautizo** *nm* baptism, christening
bayeta [ba'jeta] *nf* floorcloth
baza ['baθa] *nf* trick; **meter ~** to butt in
bazar [ba'θar] *nm* bazaar
bazofia [ba'θofja] *nf* trash
be [be] *nf name of the letter* B; **be chica/grande** (MÉX) V/B; **be larga** (LAM) B
beato, -a [be'ato, a] *adj* blessed; (*piadoso*) pious
bebé [be'βe] (*pl* **~s**) *nm* baby
bebedero [beβe'ðero, a] (MÉX, CS) *nm* drinking fountain
bebedor, a [beβe'ðor, a] *adj* hard-drinking
beber [be'βer] *vt*, *vi* to drink
bebida [be'βiða] *nf* drink; **bebido, -a** *adj* drunk
beca ['beka] *nf* grant, scholarship; **becario, -a** [be'karjo, a] *nm/f* scholarship holder, grant holder
bedel [be'ðel] *nm* (*Escol*) janitor; (*Univ*) porter
béisbol ['beisβol] *nm* baseball
Belén [be'len] *nm* Bethlehem; **belén** *nm* (*de Navidad*) nativity scene, crib
belga ['belɣa] *adj*, *nmf* Belgian
Bélgica ['belxika] *nf* Belgium
bélico, -a ['beliko, a] *adj* (*actitud*) warlike
belleza [be'ʎeθa] *nf* beauty
bello, -a ['beʎo, a] *adj* beautiful, lovely; **Bellas Artes** Fine Art
bellota [be'ʎota] *nf* acorn
bemol [be'mol] *nm* (*Mús*) flat; **esto tiene ~es** (*fam*) this is a tough one
bencina [ben'θina] *nf* (*Quím*) benzine
bendecir [bende'θir] *vt* to bless
bendición [bendi'θjon] *nf* blessing
bendito, -a [ben'dito, a] *pp de* **bendecir** ▷ *adj* holy; (*afortunado*) lucky; (*feliz*) happy; (*sencillo*) simple ▷ *nm/f* simple soul
beneficencia [benefi'θenθja] *nf* charity
beneficiario, -a [benefi'θjarjo, a] *nm/f* beneficiary
beneficio [bene'fiθjo] *nm* (*bien*) benefit, advantage; (*ganancia*) profit, gain; **a ~ de algn** in aid of sb; **beneficioso, -a** *adj* beneficial
benéfico, -a [be'nefiko, a] *adj* charitable
beneplácito [bene'plaθito] *nm* approval, consent
benévolo, -a [be'neβolo, a] *adj* benevolent, kind
benigno, -a [be'niɣno, a] *adj* kind; (*suave*) mild; (*Med*: *tumor*) benign, non-malignant
berberecho [berβe'retʃo] *nm* (*Zool*, *Culin*) cockle
berenjena [beren'xena] *nf* aubergine (BRIT), eggplant (US)
Berlín [ber'lin] *n* Berlin
berlinesa [berli'nesa] (RPL) *nf* doughnut, donut (US)
bermudas [ber'muðas] *nfpl* Bermuda shorts
berrido [be'rriðo] *nm* bellow(ing)
berrinche [be'rrintʃe] (*fam*) *nm* temper, tantrum
berro ['berro] *nm* watercress
berza ['berθa] *nf* cabbage
besamel [besa'mel] *nf* (*Culin*) white sauce, bechamel sauce
besar [be'sar] *vt* to kiss; (*fig*: *tocar*) to graze; **besarse** *vr* to kiss (one another); **beso** *nm* kiss
bestia ['bestja] *nf* beast, animal; (*fig*) idiot; **bestia de carga** beast of burden; **bestial** [bes'tjal] *adj* bestial; (*fam*) terrific; **bestialidad** *nf* bestiality; (*fam*) stupidity
besugo [be'suɣo] *nm* sea bream; (*fam*) idiot
besuquear [besuke'ar] *vt* to cover with kisses; **besuquearse** *vr* to kiss and cuddle
betabel [beta'bel] (MÉX) *nm* beetroot (BRIT), beet (US)
betún [be'tun] *nm* shoe polish; (*Quím*) bitumen
biberón [biβe'ron] *nm* feeding bottle
Biblia ['biβlja] *nf* Bible
bibliografía [biβljoɣra'fia] *nf* bibliography
biblioteca [biβljo'teka] *nf* library; (*mueble*) bookshelves; **biblioteca de consulta** reference library; **bibliotecario, -a** *nm/f* librarian
bicarbonato [bikarβo'nato] *nm* bicarbonate
bicho ['bitʃo] *nm* (*animal*) small animal; (*sabandija*) bug, insect; (*Taur*) bull
bici ['biθi] (*fam*) *nf* bike
bicicleta [biθi'kleta] *nf* bicycle, cycle; **ir**

en ~ to cycle
bidé [bi'ðe] (*pl* **~s**) *nm* bidet
bidón [bi'ðon] *nm* (*de aceite*) drum; (*de gasolina*) can

PALABRA CLAVE

bien [bjen] *nm* **1** (*bienestar*) good; **te lo digo por tu bien** I'm telling you for your own good; **el bien y el mal** good and evil
2 (*posesión*): **bienes** goods; **bienes de consumo** consumer goods; **bienes inmuebles** *o* **raíces/bienes muebles** real estate *sg*/personal property *sg* ▷ *adv*
1 (*de manera satisfactoria, correcta etc*) well; **trabaja/come bien** she works/eats well; **contestó bien** he answered correctly; **me siento bien** I feel fine; **no me siento bien** I don't feel very well; **se está bien aquí** it's nice here
2 (*frases*): **hiciste bien en llamarme** you were right to call me
3 (*valor intensivo*) very; **un cuarto bien caliente** a nice warm room; **bien se ve que ...** it's quite clear that ...
4 estar bien: estoy muy bien aquí I feel very happy here; **está bien que vengan** it's all right for them to come; **¡está bien! lo haré** oh all right, I'll do it
5 (*de buena gana*): **yo bien que iría pero ...** I'd gladly go but ... ▷ *excl*: **¡bien!** (*aprobación*) O.K.!; **¡muy bien!** well done! ▷ *adj inv* (*matiz despectivo*): **gente bien** posh people ▷ *conj*
1 bien ... bien: bien en coche bien en tren either by car or by train
2 (LAM): **no bien: no bien llegue te llamaré** as soon as I arrive I'll call you
3 si bien even though; *V tb* **más**

bienal [bje'nal] *adj* biennial
bienestar [bjenes'tar] *nm* well-being, welfare
bienvenida [bjembe'niða] *nf* welcome; **dar la ~ a algn** to welcome sb
bienvenido [bjembe'niðo] *excl* welcome!
bife ['bife] (CS) *nm* steak
bifurcación [bifurka'θjon] *nf* fork
bígamo, -a ['biɣamo, a] *adj* bigamous ▷ *nm/f* bigamist
bigote [bi'ɣote] *nm* moustache; **bigotudo, -a** *adj* with a big moustache
bikini [bi'kini] *nm* bikini; (*Culin*) toasted ham and cheese sandwich
bilingüe [bi'lingwe] *adj* bilingual
billar [bi'ʎar] *nm* billiards *sg*; **billares** *nmpl* (*lugar*) billiard hall; (*sala de juegos*) amusement arcade; **billar americano** pool
billete [bi'ʎete] *nm* ticket; (*de banco*) (bank)note (BRIT), bill (US); (*carta*) note; **~ de 20 libras** £20 note; **billete de ida y vuelta** return (BRIT) *o* round-trip (US) ticket; **billete sencillo** *o* **de ida** single (BRIT) *o* one-way (US) ticket; **billete electrónico** e-ticket
billetera [biʎe'tera] *nf* wallet
billón [bi'ʎon] *nm* billion
bimensual [bimen'swal] *adj* twice monthly
bingo ['bingo] *nm* bingo
biodegradable [bioðeɣra'ðaβle] *adj* biodegradable
biografía [bjoɣra'fia] *nf* biography
biología [bjolo'xia] *nf* biology; **biológico, -a** *adj* biological; (*cultivo, producto*) organic; **biólogo, -a** *nm/f* biologist
biombo ['bjombo] *nm* (folding) screen
bioterrorismo [bjoterro'rismo] *nm* bioterrorism
biquini [bi'kini] *nm o* (RPL) *f* bikini
birlar [bir'lar] (*fam*) *vt* to pinch
Birmania [bir'manja] *nf* Burma
birome [bi'rome] (RPL) *nf* ballpoint (pen)
birria ['birrja] *nf*: **ser una ~** (*película, libro*) to be rubbish
bis [bis] *excl* encore!
bisabuelo, -a [bisa'βwelo, a] *nm/f* great-grandfather(-mother)
bisagra [bi'saɣra] *nf* hinge
bisiesto [bi'sjesto] *adj*: **año ~** leap year
bisnieto, -a [bis'njeto, a] *nm/f* great-grandson/daughter
bisonte [bi'sonte] *nm* bison
bisté [bis'te] *nm* = **bistec**
bistec [bis'tek] *nm* steak
bisturí [bistu'ri] *nm* scalpel
bisutería [bisute'ria] *nf* imitation *o* costume jewellery
bit [bit] *nm* (*Inform*) bit
bizco, -a ['biθko, a] *adj* cross-eyed
bizcocho [biθ'kotʃo] *nm* (*Culin*) sponge cake
blanca ['blanka] *nf* (*Mús*) minim; **estar sin ~** (ESP: *fam*) to be broke; *V tb* **blanco**
blanco, -a ['blanko, a] *adj* white ▷ *nm/f* white man/woman, white ▷ *nm* (*color*) white; (*en texto*) blank; (*Mil, fig*) target; **en ~** blank; **noche en ~** sleepless night
blandir [blan'dir] *vt* to brandish
blando, -a ['blando, a] *adj* soft; (*tierno*) tender, gentle; (*carácter*) mild; (*fam*) cowardly
blanqueador [blankea'ðor] (MÉX) *nm* bleach
blanquear [blanke'ar] *vt* to whiten; (*fachada*) to whitewash; (*paño*) to bleach ▷ *vi* to turn white
blanquillo [blan'kiʎo] (MÉX, CAM) *nm* egg

blasfemar [blasfe'mar] *vi* to blaspheme, curse
bledo ['bleðo] *nm*: **me importa un ~** I couldn't care less
blindado, -a [blin'daðo, a] *adj* (*Mil*) armour-plated; (*antibala*) bullet-proof; **coche** (ESP) *o* **carro** (LAM) **~** armoured car
bloc [blok] (*pl* **~s**) *nm* writing pad
blof [blof] (MÉX) *nm* bluff; **blofear** (MÉX) *vi* to bluff
blog [bloɣ] (*pl* **~s**) *nm* blog
bloque ['bloke] *nm* block; (*Pol*) bloc
bloquear [bloke'ar] *vt* to blockade; **bloqueo** *nm* blockade; (*Com*) freezing, blocking; **bloqueo mental** mental block
blusa ['blusa] *nf* blouse
bobada [bo'βaða] *nf* foolish action; foolish statement; **decir ~s** to talk nonsense
bobina [bo'βina] *nf* (*Tec*) bobbin; (*Foto*) spool; (*Elec*) coil
bobo, -a ['boβo, a] *adj* (*tonto*) daft, silly; (*cándido*) naôve ▷ *nm/f* fool, idiot ▷ *nm* (*Teatro*) clown, funny man
boca ['boka] *nf* mouth; (*de crustáceo*) pincer; (*de cañón*) muzzle; (*entrada*) mouth, entrance; **bocas** *nfpl* (*de río*) mouth *sg*; **~ abajo/arriba** face down/up; **se me hace la ~ agua** my mouth is watering; **boca de incendios** hydrant; **boca del estómago** pit of the stomach; **boca de metro** underground (BRIT) *o* subway (US) entrance
bocacalle [boka'kaʎe] *nf* (entrance to a) street; **la primera ~** the first turning *o* street
bocadillo [boka'ðiʎo] *nm* sandwich
bocado [bo'kaðo] *nm* mouthful, bite; (*de caballo*) bridle
bocajarro [boka'xarro]: **a ~** *adv* (*disparar*) point-blank
bocanada [boka'naða] *nf* (*de vino*) mouthful, swallow; (*de aire*) gust, puff
bocata [bo'kata] (*fam*) *nm* sandwich
bocazas [bo'kaθas] (*fam*) *nm inv* bigmouth
boceto [bo'θeto] *nm* sketch, outline
bochorno [bo'tʃorno] *nm* (*vergüenza*) embarrassment; (*calor*): **hace ~** it's very muggy
bocina [bo'θina] *nf* (*Mús*) trumpet; (*Auto*) horn; (*para hablar*) megaphone
boda ['boða] *nf* (*tb*: **~s**) wedding, marriage; (*fiesta*) wedding reception; **bodas de oro/plata** golden/silver wedding *sg*
bodega [bo'ðeɣa] *nf* (*de vino*) (wine) cellar; (*depósito*) storeroom; (*de barco*) hold
bodegón [boðe'ɣon] *nm* (*Arte*) still life
bofetada [bofe'taða] *nf* slap (in the face)
boga ['boɣa] *nf*: **en ~** (*fig*) in vogue
Bogotá [boɣo'ta] *n* Bogotá
bohemio, -a [bo'emjo, a] *adj, nm/f* Bohemian
bohío [bo'io] (CAM) *nm* shack, hut
boicot [boi'kot] (*pl* **~s**) *nm* boycott; **boicotear** *vt* to boycott
bóiler ['boiler] (MÉX) *nm* boiler
boina ['boina] *nf* beret
bola ['bola] *nf* ball; (*canica*) marble; (*Naipes*) (grand) slam; (*betún*) shoe polish; (*mentira*) tale, story; **bolas** *nfpl* (LAM: *caza*) bolas *sg*; **bola de billar** billiard ball; **bola de nieve** snowball
boleadoras [bolea'ðoras] *nfpl* bolas *sg*
bolear [bole'ar] (MÉX) *vt* (*zapatos*) to polish, shine
bolera [bo'lera] *nf* skittle *o* bowling alley
bolero, -a (MÉX) [bo'lero] *nm/f* (*limpiabotas*) shoeshine boy/girl
boleta [bo'leta] (LAM) *nf* (*de rifa*) ticket; (CS: *recibo*) receipt; **boleta de calificaciones** (MÉX) report card
boletería [bolete'ria] (LAM) *nf* ticket office
boletín [bole'tin] *nm* bulletin; (*periódico*) journal, review; **boletín de noticias** news bulletin
boleto [bo'leto] *nm* (LAM) ticket; **boleto de ida y vuelta** (LAM) round trip ticket; **boleto electrónico** (LAM) e-ticket; **boleto redondo** (MÉX) round trip ticket
boli ['boli] (*fam*) *nm* Biro®
bolígrafo [bo'liɣrafo] *nm* ball-point pen, Biro®
bolilla [bo'liʎa] (RPL) *nf* topic
bolillo [bo'liʎo] (MÉX) *nm* (bread) roll
bolita [bo'lita] (CS) *nf* marble
bolívar [bo'liβar] *nm* *monetary unit of Venezuela*
Bolivia [bo'liβja] *nf* Bolivia; **boliviano, -a** *adj, nm/f* Bolivian
bollería [boʎe'ria] *nf* cakes *pl* and pastries *pl*
bollo ['boʎo] *nm* (*pan*) roll; (*bulto*) bump, lump; (*abolladura*) dent
bolo ['bolo] *nm* skittle; (*píldora*) (large) pill; **(juego de) bolos** *nmpl* skittles *sg*
bolsa ['bolsa] *nf* (*para llevar algo*) bag; (MÉX, CAM: *bolsillo*) pocket; (MÉX: *de mujer*) handbag; (*Anat*) cavity, sac; (*Com*) stock exchange; (*Minería*) pocket; **de ~** pocket *cpd*; **bolsa de agua caliente** hot water bottle; **bolsa de aire** air pocket; **bolsa de dormir** (MÉX, RPL) sleeping bag; **bolsa de la compra** shopping bag; **bolsa de papel/plástico** paper/plastic bag
bolsear [bolse'ar] (MÉX, CAM) *vt*: **~ a algn** to pick sb's pocket
bolsillo [bol'siʎo] *nm* pocket; (*cartera*) purse; **de ~** pocket(-size)
bolso ['bolso] *nm* (*bolsa*) bag; (*de mujer*)

handbag
bomba ['bomba] *nf* (*Mil*) bomb; (*Tec*) pump ▷ *adj* (*fam*): **noticia ~** bombshell ▷ *adv* (*fam*): **pasarlo ~** to have a great time; **bomba atómica/de efecto retardado/de humo** atomic/time/smoke bomb
bombacha [bom'batʃa] (RPL) *nf* panties *pl*
bombardear [bombarðe'ar] *vt* to bombard; (*Mil*) to bomb; **bombardeo** *nm* bombardment; bombing
bombazo [bom'baθo] (MÉX) *nm* (*explosión*) explosion; (*fam*: *notición*) bombshell; (: *éxito*) smash hit
bombear [bombe'ar] *vt* (*agua*) to pump (out *o* up)
bombero [bom'bero] *nm* fireman
bombilla [bom'biʎa] (ESP) *nf* (light) bulb
bombita [bom'bita] (RPL) *nf* (light) bulb
bombo ['bombo] *nm* (*Mús*) bass drum; (*Tec*) drum
bombón [bom'bon] *nm* chocolate; (MÉX: *de caramelo*) marshmallow
bombona [bom'bona] (ESP) *nf* (*de butano, oxígeno*) cylinder
bonachón, -ona [bona'tʃon, ona] *adj* good-natured, easy-going
bonanza [bo'nanθa] *nf* (*Náut*) fair weather; (*fig*) bonanza; (*Minería*) rich pocket *o* vein
bondad [bon'dað] *nf* goodness, kindness; **tenga la ~ de** (please) be good enough to
bonito, -a [bo'nito, a] *adj* pretty; (*agradable*) nice ▷ *nm* (*atún*) tuna (fish)
bono ['bono] *nm* voucher; (*Finanzas*) bond
bonobús [bono'βus] (ESP) *nm* bus pass
bonoloto [bono'loto] *nf* *state-run weekly lottery*
boquerón [boke'ron] *nm* (*pez*) (kind of) anchovy; (*agujero*) large hole
boquete [bo'kete] *nm* gap, hole
boquiabierto, -a [bokia'βjerto, a] *adj*: **quedarse ~** to be amazed *o* flabbergasted
boquilla [bo'kiʎa] *nf* (*para riego*) nozzle; (*para cigarro*) cigarette holder; (*Mús*) mouthpiece
borbotón [borβo'ton] *nm*: **salir a borbotones** to gush out
borda ['borða] *nf* (*Náut*) (ship's) rail; **tirar algo/caerse por la ~** to throw sth/fall overboard
bordado [bor'ðaðo] *nm* embroidery
bordar [bor'ðar] *vt* to embroider
borde ['borðe] *nm* edge, border; (*de camino etc*) side; (*en la costura*) hem; **al ~ de** (*fig*) on the verge *o* brink of; **ser ~** (ESP: *fam*) to be rude; **bordear** *vt* to border
bordillo [bor'ðiʎo] *nm* kerb (BRIT), curb (US)
bordo ['borðo] *nm* (*Náut*) side; **a ~** on board
borlote [bor'lote] (MÉX) *nm* row, uproar
borrachera [borra'tʃera] *nf* (*ebriedad*) drunkenness; (*orgía*) spree, binge
borracho, -a [bo'rratʃo, a] *adj* drunk ▷ *nm/f* (*habitual*) drunkard, drunk; (*temporal*) drunk, drunk man/woman
borrador [borra'ðor] *nm* (*escritura*) first draft, rough sketch; (*goma*) rubber (BRIT), eraser
borrar [bo'rrar] *vt* to erase, rub out
borrasca [bo'rraska] *nf* storm
borrego, -a [bo'rreɣo, a] *nm/f* (*Zool*: *joven*) (yearling) lamb; (*adulto*) sheep ▷ *nm* (MÉX: *fam*) false rumour
borrico, -a [bo'rriko, a] *nm/f* donkey/she-donkey; (*fig*) stupid man/woman
borrón [bo'rron] *nm* (*mancha*) stain
borroso, -a [bo'rroso, a] *adj* vague, unclear; (*escritura*) illegible
bosque ['boske] *nm* wood; (*grande*) forest
bostezar [boste'θar] *vi* to yawn; **bostezo** *nm* yawn
bota ['bota] *nf* (*calzado*) boot; (*para vino*) leather wine bottle; **botas de agua** *o* **goma** Wellingtons
botana [bo'tana] (MÉX) *nf* snack, appetizer
botánica [bo'tanika] *nf* (*ciencia*) botany; *V tb* **botánico**
botánico, -a [bo'taniko, a] *adj* botanical ▷ *nm/f* botanist
botar [bo'tar] *vt* to throw, hurl; (*Náut*) to launch; (LAM: *echar*) to throw out ▷ *vi* (ESP: *saltar*) to bounce
bote ['bote] *nm* (*salto*) bounce; (*golpe*) thrust; (ESP: *envase*) tin, can; (*embarcación*) boat; (MÉX, CAM: *pey*: *cárcel*) jail; **de ~ en ~** packed, jammed full; **bote de la basura** (MÉX) dustbin (BRIT), trashcan (US); **bote salvavidas** lifeboat
botella [bo'teʎa] *nf* bottle; **botellín** *nm* small bottle; **botellón** *nm* (ESP: *fam*) outdoor drinking session
botijo [bo'tixo] *nm* (earthenware) jug
botín [bo'tin] *nm* (*calzado*) half boot; (*polaina*) spat; (*Mil*) booty
botiquín [boti'kin] *nm* (*armario*) medicine cabinet; (*portátil*) first-aid kit
botón [bo'ton] *nm* button; (*Bot*) bud
botones [bo'tones] *nm inv* bellboy (BRIT), bellhop (US)
bóveda ['boβeða] *nf* (*Arq*) vault
boxeador [boksea'ðor] *nm* boxer
boxeo [bok'seo] *nm* boxing
boya ['boja] *nf* (*Náut*) buoy; (*de caña*) float
boyante [bo'jante] *adj* prosperous
bozal [bo'θal] *nm* (*para caballos*) halter; (*de*

perro) muzzle
bragas ['braɣas] *nfpl* (*de mujer*) panties, knickers (BRIT)
bragueta [bra'ɣeta] *nf* fly, flies *pl*
braille [breil] *nm* braille
brasa ['brasa] *nf* live *o* hot coal
brasero [bra'sero] *nm* brazier
brasier [bra'sjer] (MÉX) *nm* bra
Brasil [bra'sil] *nm* (*tb*: **el ~**) Brazil; **brasileño, -a** *adj, nm/f* Brazilian
brassier [bra'sjer] (MÉX) *nm* V **brasier**
bravo, -a ['braβo, a] *adj* (*valiente*) brave; (*feroz*) ferocious; (*salvaje*) wild; (*mar etc*) rough, stormy ▷ *excl* bravo!; **bravura** *nf* bravery; ferocity
braza ['braθa] *nf* fathom; **nadar a ~** to swim breast-stroke
brazalete [braθa'lete] *nm* (*pulsera*) bracelet; (*banda*) armband
brazo ['braθo] *nm* arm; (*Zool*) foreleg; (*Bot*) limb, branch; **luchar a ~ partido** to fight hand-to-hand; **ir cogidos del ~** to walk arm in arm
brebaje [bre'βaxe] *nm* potion
brecha ['bretʃa] *nf* (*hoyo, vacío*) gap, opening; (*Mil, fig*) breach
brega ['breɣa] *nf* (*lucha*) struggle; (*trabajo*) hard work
breva ['breβa] *nf* early fig
breve ['breβe] *adj* short, brief ▷ *nf* (*Mús*) breve; **en ~** (*pronto*) shortly, before long; **brevedad** *nf* brevity, shortness
bribón, -ona [bri'βon, ona] *adj* idle, lazy ▷ *nm/f* (*pícaro*) rascal, rogue
bricolaje [briko'laxe] *nm* do-it-yourself, DIY
brida ['briða] *nf* bridle, rein; (*Tec*) clamp
bridge [britʃ] *nm* bridge
brigada [bri'ɣaða] *nf* (*unidad*) brigade; (*de trabajadores*) squad, gang ▷ *nm* ≈ staff-sergeant, sergeant-major
brillante [bri'ʎante] *adj* brilliant ▷ *nm* diamond
brillar [bri'ʎar] *vi* to shine; (*joyas*) to sparkle
brillo ['briʎo] *nm* shine; (*brillantez*) brilliance; (*fig*) splendour; **sacar ~ a** to polish
brincar [brin'kar] *vi* to skip about, hop about, jump about
brinco ['brinko] *nm* jump, leap
brindar [brin'dar] *vi*: **~ a** *o* **por** to drink (a toast) to ▷ *vt* to offer, present
brindis ['brindis] *nm inv* toast
brío ['brio] *nm* spirit, dash
brisa ['brisa] *nf* breeze
británico, -a [bri'taniko, a] *adj* British ▷ *nm/f* Briton, British person
brizna ['briθna] *nf* (*de hierba, paja*) blade; (*de tabaco*) leaf
broca ['broka] *nf* (*Tec*) drill, bit
brocha ['brotʃa] *nf* (large) paintbrush; **brocha de afeitar** shaving brush
broche ['brotʃe] *nm* brooch
broma ['broma] *nf* joke; **de** *o* **en ~** in fun, as a joke; **broma pesada** practical joke; **bromear** *vi* to joke
bromista [bro'mista] *adj* fond of joking ▷ *nmf* joker, wag
bronca ['bronka] *nf* row; **echar una ~ a algn** to tick sb off
bronce ['bronθe] *nm* bronze; **bronceado, -a** *adj* bronze; (*por el sol*) tanned ▷ *nm* (sun) tan; (*Tec*) bronzing
bronceador [bronθea'ðor] *nm* suntan lotion
broncearse [bronθe'arse] *vr* to get a suntan
bronquio ['bronkjo] *nm* (*Anat*) bronchial tube
bronquitis [bron'kitis] *nf inv* bronchitis
brotar [bro'tar] *vi* (*Bot*) to sprout; (*aguas*) to gush (forth); (*Med*) to break out
brote ['brote] *nm* (*Bot*) shoot; (*Med, fig*) outbreak
bruces ['bruθes]: **de bruces** *adv*: **caer** *o* **dar de ~** to fall headlong, fall flat
bruja ['bruxa] *nf* witch; **brujería** *nf* witchcraft
brujo ['bruxo] *nm* wizard, magician
brújula ['bruxula] *nf* compass
bruma ['bruma] *nf* mist
brusco, -a ['brusko, a] *adj* (*súbito*) sudden; (*áspero*) brusque
Bruselas [bru'selas] *n* Brussels
brutal [bru'tal] *adj* brutal; **brutalidad** [brutali'ðað] *nf* brutality
bruto, -a ['bruto, a] *adj* (*idiota*) stupid; (*bestial*) brutish; (*peso*) gross; **en ~** raw, unworked
Bs.As. *abr* (= *Buenos Aires*) B.A.
bucal [bu'kal] *adj* oral; **por vía ~** orally
bucear [buθe'ar] *vi* to dive ▷ *vt* to explore; **buceo** *nm* diving
bucle ['bukle] *nm* curl
budismo [bu'ðismo] *nm* Buddhism
buen [bwen] *adj m* V **bueno**
buenamente [bwena'mente] *adv* (*fácilmente*) easily; (*voluntariamente*) willingly
buenaventura [bwenaβen'tura] *nf* (*suerte*) good luck; (*adivinación*) fortune
buenmozo [bwen'moθo] (MÉX) *adj* handsome

PALABRA CLAVE

bueno, -a ['bweno, a] (*antes de nmsg:* **buen**) *adj* **1** (*excelente etc*) good; **es un libro bueno, es un buen libro** it's a good book; **hace bueno, hace buen tiempo** the weather is fine, it is fine; **el bueno de Paco** good old Paco; **fue muy bueno conmigo** he was very nice *o* kind to me
2 (*apropiado*): **ser bueno para** to be good for; **creo que vamos por buen camino** I think we're on the right track
3 (*irónico*): **le di un buen rapapolvo** I gave him a good *o* real ticking off; **¡buen conductor estás hecho!** some *o* a fine driver you are!; **¡estaría bueno que ...!** a fine thing it would be if ...!
4 (*atractivo, sabroso*): **está bueno este bizcocho** this sponge is delicious; **Carmen está muy buena** Carmen is gorgeous
5 (*saludos*): **¡buen día!, ¡buenos días!** (good) morning!; **¡buenas (tardes)!** (good) afternoon!; (*más tarde*) (good) evening!; **¡buenas noches!** good night!
6 (*otras locuciones*): **estar de buenas** to be in a good mood; **por las buenas o por las malas** by hook or by crook; **de buenas a primeras** all of a sudden ▷*excl*: **¡bueno!** all right!; **bueno, ¿y qué?** well, so what?

Buenos Aires [bweno'saires] *nm* Buenos Aires
buey [bwei] *nm* ox
búfalo ['bufalo] *nm* buffalo
bufanda [bu'fanda] *nf* scarf
bufete [bu'fete] *nm* (*despacho de abogado*) lawyer's office
bufón [bu'fon] *nm* clown
buhardilla [buar'ðiʎa] *nf* attic
búho ['buo] *nm* owl; (*fig*) hermit, recluse
buitre ['bwitre] *nm* vulture
bujía [bu'xia] *nf* (*vela*) candle; (*Elec*) candle (power); (*Auto*) spark plug
bula ['bula] *nf* (papal) bull
bulbo ['bulβo] *nm* bulb
bulevar [bule'βar] *nm* boulevard
Bulgaria [bul'ɣarja] *nf* Bulgaria; **búlgaro, -a** *adj, nm/f* Bulgarian
bulla ['buʎa] *nf* (*ruido*) uproar; (*de gente*) crowd
bullicio [bu'ʎiθjo] *nm* (*ruido*) uproar; (*movimiento*) bustle
bulto ['bulto] *nm* (*paquete*) package; (*fardo*) bundle; (*tamaño*) size, bulkiness; (*Med*) swelling, lump; (*silueta*) vague shape
buñuelo [bu'ɲwelo] *nm* ≈ doughnut (BRIT), ≈ donut (US); (*fruta de sartén*) fritter
buque ['buke] *nm* ship, vessel; **buque de guerra** warship
burbuja [bur'βuxa] *nf* bubble
burdel [bur'ðel] *nm* brothel
burgués, -esa [bur'ɣes, esa] *adj* middle-class, bourgeois; **burguesía** *nf* middle class, bourgeoisie
burla ['burla] *nf* (*mofa*) gibe; (*broma*) joke; (*engaño*) trick; **burlar** [bur'lar] *vt* (*engañar*) to deceive ▷*vi* to joke; **burlarse** *vr* to joke; **burlarse de** to make fun of
burlón, -ona [bur'lon, ona] *adj* mocking
buró [bu'ro] (MÉX) *nm* bedside table
burocracia [buro'kraθja] *nf* civil service
burrada [bu'rraða] *nf*: **decir** *o* **soltar ~s** to talk nonsense; **hacer ~s** to act stupid; **una ~** (ESP: *mucho*) a (hell of a) lot
burro, -a ['burro, a] *nm/f* donkey/she-donkey; (*fig*) ass, idiot
bursátil [bur'satil] *adj* stock-exchange *cpd*
bus [bus] *nm* bus
busca ['buska] *nf* search, hunt ▷*nm* (*Tel*) bleeper; **en ~ de** in search of
buscador [buska'ðor] *nm* (*Internet*) search engine
buscar [bus'kar] *vt* to look for, search for, seek ▷*vi* to look, search, seek; **se busca secretaria** secretary wanted
busque *etc vb V* **buscar**
búsqueda ['buskeða] *nf* = **busca**
busto ['busto] *nm* (*Anat, Arte*) bust
butaca [bu'taka] *nf* armchair; (*de cine, teatro*) stall, seat
butano [bu'tano] *nm* butane (gas)
buzo ['buθo] *nm* diver
buzón [bu'θon] *nm* (*en puerta*) letter box; (*en calle*) pillar box

C. *abr* (=*centígrado*) C; (*compañía*) Co.

C/ *abr* (=*calle*) St

cabal [ka'βal] *adj* (*exacto*) exact; (*correcto*) right, proper; (*acabado*) finished, complete; **cabales** *nmpl*: **no está en sus cabales** she isn't in her right mind

cábalas ['kaβalas] *nfpl*: **hacer ~** to guess

cabalgar [kaβal'ɣar] *vt, vi* to ride

cabalgata [kaβal'ɣata] *nf* procession

caballa [ka'βaʎa] *nf* mackerel

caballería [kaβaʎe'ria] *nf* mount; (*Mil*) cavalry

caballero [kaβa'ʎero] *nm* gentleman; (*de la orden de caballería*) knight; (*trato directo*) sir

caballete [kaβa'ʎete] *nm* (*Arte*) easel; (*Tec*) trestle

caballito [kaβa'ʎito] *nm* (*caballo pequeño*) small horse, pony; **caballitos** *nmpl* (*en verbena*) roundabout, merry-go-round

caballo [ka'βaʎo] *nm* horse; (*Ajedrez*) knight; (*Naipes*) queen; **ir en ~** to ride; **caballo de carreras** racehorse; **caballo de fuerza** *o* **vapor** horsepower

cabaña [ka'βaɲa] *nf* (*casita*) hut, cabin

cabecear [kaβeθe'ar] *vt, vi* to nod

cabecera [kaβe'θera] *nf* head; (*Imprenta*) headline

cabecilla [kaβe'θiʎa] *nm* ringleader

cabellera [kaβe'ʎera] *nf* (head of) hair; (*de cometa*) tail

cabello [ka'βeʎo] *nm* (*tb*: **~s**) hair; **cabello de ángel** *confectionery and pastry filling made of pumpkin and syrup*

caber [ka'βer] *vi* (*entrar*) to fit, go; **caben 3 más** there's room for 3 more

cabestrillo [kaβes'triʎo] *nm* sling

cabeza [ka'βeθa] *nf* head; (*Pol*) chief, leader; **cabeza de ajo** bulb of garlic; **cabeza de familia** head of the household; **cabeza rapada** skinhead; **cabezada** *nf* (*golpe*) butt; **dar cabezadas** to nod off; **cabezón, -ona** *adj* (*vino*) heady; (*fam*: *persona*) pig-headed

cabida [ka'βiða] *nf* space

cabina [ka'βina] *nf* cabin; (*de avión*) cockpit; (*de camión*) cab; **cabina telefónica** telephone (BRIT) box *o* booth

cabizbajo, -a [kaβiθ'βaxo, a] *adj* crestfallen, dejected

cable ['kaβle] *nm* cable

cabo ['kaβo] *nm* (*de objeto*) end, extremity; (*Mil*) corporal; (*Náut*) rope, cable; (*Geo*) cape; **al ~ de 3 días** after 3 days; **llevar a ~** to carry out

cabra ['kaβra] *nf* goat

cabré *etc vb V* **caber**

cabrear [kaβre'ar] (*fam*) *vt* to bug; **cabrearse** *vr* (*enfadarse*) to fly off the handle

cabrito [ka'βrito] *nm* kid

cabrón [ka'βron] *nm* cuckold; (*fam!*) bastard (*!*)

caca ['kaka] (*fam*) *nf* pooh

cacahuete [kaka'wete] (ESP) *nm* peanut

cacao [ka'kao] *nm* cocoa; (*Bot*) cacao

cacarear [kakare'ar] *vi* (*persona*) to boast; (*gallina*) to crow

cacería [kaθe'ria] *nf* hunt

cacarizo, -a [kaka'riθo, a] (MÉX) *adj* pockmarked

cacerola [kaθe'rola] *nf* pan, saucepan

cachalote [katʃa'lote] *nm* (*Zool*) sperm whale

cacharro [ka'tʃarro] *nm* earthenware pot; **cacharros** *nmpl* pots and pans

cachear [katʃe'ar] *vt* to search, frisk

cachemir [katʃe'mir] *nm* cashmere

cachetada [katʃe'taða] (LAM: *fam*) *nf* (*bofetada*) slap

cachete [ka'tʃete] *nm* (*Anat*) cheek; (ESP: *bofetada*) slap (in the face)

cachivache [katʃi'βatʃe] *nm* (*trasto*) piece of junk; **cachivaches** *nmpl* junk *sg*

cacho ['katʃo] *nm* (small) bit; (LAM: *cuerno*) horn

cachondeo [katʃon'deo] (ESP: *fam*) *nm* farce, joke

cachondo, -a [ka'tʃondo, a] *adj* (*Zool*) on heat; (*fam*: *sexualmente*) randy; (: *gracioso*) funny

cachorro, -a [ka'tʃorro, a] *nm/f* (*perro*) pup, puppy; (*león*) cub

cachucha [ka'tʃuka] (MÉX: *fam*) *nf* cap

cacique [ka'θike] *nm* chief, local ruler; (*Pol*) local party boss

cactus ['kaktus] *nm inv* cactus

cada ['kaða] *adj inv* each; (*antes de número*) every; **~ día** each day, every day; **~ dos días** every other day; **~ uno/a** each one, every one; **~ vez más/menos** more and more/ less and less; **~ vez que ...** whenever, every time (that) ...; **uno de ~ diez** one out of every ten

cadáver [ka'ðaβer] *nm* (dead) body, corpse

cadena [ka'ðena] *nf* chain; (*TV*) channel; **trabajo en ~** assembly line work; **cadena montañosa** mountain range; **cadena perpetua** (*Jur*) life imprisonment

cadera [ka'ðera] *nf* hip

cadete [ka'ðete] *nm* cadet

caducar [kaðu'kar] *vi* to expire; **caduco, -a** *adj* expired; (*persona*) very old

caer [ka'er] *vi* to fall (down); **caerse** *vr* to fall (down); **me cae bien/mal** I get on well with him/I can't stand him; **~ en la cuenta** to realize; **dejar ~** to drop; **su cumpleaños cae en viernes** her birthday falls on a Friday

café [ka'fe] (*pl* **~s**) *nm* (*bebida, planta*) coffee; (*lugar*) café ▷ *adj* (MÉX: *color*) brown, tan; **café con leche** white coffee; **café negro** (LAM) black coffee; **café solo** (ESP) black coffee

cafetera [kafe'tera] *nf* coffee pot

cafetería [kafete'ria] *nf* (*gen*) café

cafetero, -a [kafe'tero, a] *adj* coffee *cpd*; **ser muy ~** to be a coffee addict

cafishio [ka'fiʃjo] (CS) *nm* pimp

cagar [ka'ɣar] (*fam!*) *vt* to bungle, mess up ▷ *vi* to have a shit (*!*)

caída [ka'iða] *nf* fall; (*declive*) slope; (*disminución*) fall, drop

caído, -a [ka'iðo, a] *adj* drooping

caiga *etc vb V* **caer**

caimán [kai'man] *nm* alligator

caja ['kaxa] *nf* box; (*para reloj*) case; (*de ascensor*) shaft; (*Com*) cashbox; (*donde se hacen los pagos*) cashdesk; (*: en supermercado*) checkout, till; **caja de ahorros** savings bank; **caja de cambios** gearbox; **caja de fusibles** fuse box; **caja fuerte** *o* **de caudales** safe, strongbox

cajero, -a [ka'xero, a] *nm/f* cashier; **cajero automático** cash dispenser

cajetilla [kaxe'tiʎa] *nf* (*de cigarrillos*) packet

cajón [ka'xon] *nm* big box; (*de mueble*) drawer

cajuela (MÉX) *nf* (*Auto*) boot (BRIT), trunk (US)

cal [kal] *nf* lime

cala ['kala] *nf* (*Geo*) cove, inlet; (*de barco*) hold

calabacín [kalaβa'θin] *nm* (*Bot*) baby marrow; (*: más pequeño*) courgette (BRIT), zucchini (US)

calabacita [kalaβa'θita] (MÉX) *nf* courgette (BRIT), zucchini (US)

calabaza [kala'βaθa] *nf* (*Bot*) pumpkin

calabozo [kala'βoθo] *nm* (*cárcel*) prison; (*celda*) cell

calada [ka'laða] (ESP) *nf* (*de cigarrillo*) puff

calado, -a [ka'laðo, a] *adj* (*prenda*) lace *cpd* ▷ *nm* (*Náut*) draught

calamar [kala'mar] *nm* squid *no pl*

calambre [ka'lambre] *nm* (*Elec*) shock

calar [ka'lar] *vt* to soak, drench; (*penetrar*) to pierce, penetrate; (*comprender*) to see through; (*vela*) to lower; **calarse** *vr* (*Auto*) to stall; **~se las gafas** to stick one's glasses on

calavera [kala'βera] *nf* skull

calcar [kal'kar] *vt* (*reproducir*) to trace; (*imitar*) to copy

calcetín [kalθe'tin] *nm* sock

calcio ['kalθjo] *nm* calcium

calcomanía [kalkoma'nia] *nf* transfer

calculador, a [kalkula'ðor, a] *adj* (*persona*) calculating; **calculadora** [kalkula'ðora] *nf* calculator

calcular [kalku'lar] *vt* (*Mat*) to calculate, compute; **~ que ...** to reckon that ...

caldera [kal'dera] *nf* boiler

calderilla [kalde'riʎa] *nf* (*moneda*) small change

caldo ['kaldo] *nm* stock; (*consomé*) consommé

calefacción [kalefak'θjon] *nf* heating; **calefacción central** central heating

calefón [kale'fon] (RPL) *nm* boiler

calendario [kalen'darjo] *nm* calendar

calentador [kalenta'ðor] *nm* heater

calentamiento [kalenta'mjento] *nm* (*Deporte*) warm-up; **calentamiento global** global warming

calentar [kalen'tar] *vt* to heat (up); **calentarse** *vr* to heat up, warm up; (*fig: discusión etc*) to get heated

calentón [kalen'ton] (RPL: *fam*) *adj* (*sexualmente*) horny, randy (BRIT)

calentura [kalen'tura] *nf* (*Med*) fever, (high) temperature

calesita [kale'sita] (RPL) *nf* merry-go-round, carousel

calibre [ka'liβre] *nm* (*de cañón*) calibre, bore; (*diámetro*) diameter; (*fig*) calibre

calidad [kali'ðað] *nf* quality; **de ~** quality *cpd*; **en ~ de** in the capacity of, as

cálido, -a ['kaliðo, a] *adj* hot; (*fig*) warm

caliente *etc* [ka'ljente] *vb V* **calentar** ▷ *adj* hot; (*fig*) fiery; (*disputa*) heated; (*fam: cachondo*) randy

calificación [kalifika'θjon] *nf* qualification; (*de alumno*) grade, mark

calificado, -a [kalifi'kaðo, a] (LAM) *adj* (*competente*) qualified; (*obrero*) skilled

calificar [kalifi'kar] *vt* to qualify; (*alumno*) to grade, mark; **~ de** to describe as

C

calima [ka'lima] *nf* (*cerca del mar*) mist
cáliz ['kaliθ] *nm* chalice
caliza [ka'liθa] *nf* limestone
callado, -a [ka'ʎaðo, a] *adj* quiet
callar [ka'ʎar] *vt* (*asunto delicado*) to keep quiet about, say nothing about; (*persona, opinión*) to silence ▷*vi* to keep quiet, be silent; **callarse** *vr* to keep quiet, be silent; **¡cállate!** be quiet!, shut up!
calle ['kaʎe] *nf* street; (*Deporte*) lane; **~ arriba/abajo** up/down the street; **calle de sentido único** one-way street; **calle mayor** (ESP) high (BRIT) *o* main (US) street; **calle peatonal** pedestrianized *o* pedestrian street; **calle principal** (LAM) high (BRIT) *o* main (US) street; **callejear** *vi* to wander (about) the streets; **callejero, -a** *adj* street *cpd* ▷*nm* street map; **callejón** *nm* alley, passage; **callejón sin salida** cul-de-sac; **callejuela** *nf* side-street, alley
callista [ka'ʎista] *nmf* chiropodist
callo ['kaʎo] *nm* callus; (*en el pie*) corn; **callos** *nmpl* (*Culin*) tripe *sg*
calma ['kalma] *nf* calm
calmante [kal'mante] *nm* sedative, tranquillizer
calmar [kal'mar] *vt* to calm, calm down ▷*vi* (*tempestad*) to abate; (*mente etc*) to become calm
calor [ka'lor] *nm* heat; (*agradable*) warmth; **hace ~** it's hot; **tener ~** to be hot
caloría [kalo'ria] *nf* calorie
calumnia [ka'lumnja] *nf* calumny, slander
caluroso, -a [kalu'roso, a] *adj* hot; (*sin exceso*) warm; (*fig*) enthusiastic
calva ['kalβa] *nf* bald patch; (*en bosque*) clearing
calvario [kal'βarjo] *nm* stations *pl* of the cross
calvicie [kal'βiθje] *nf* baldness
calvo, -a ['kalβo, a] *adj* bald; (*terreno*) bare, barren; (*tejido*) threadbare
calza ['kalθa] *nf* wedge, chock
calzada [kal'θaða] *nf* roadway, highway
calzado, -a [kal'θaðo, a] *adj* shod ▷*nm* footwear
calzador [kalθa'ðor] *nm* shoehorn
calzar [kal'θar] *vt* (*zapatos etc*) to wear; (*mueble*) to put a wedge under; **calzarse** *vr*: **~se los zapatos** to put on one's shoes; **¿qué (número) calza?** what size do you take?
calzón [kal'θon] *nm* (ESP: *pantalón corto*) shorts; (LAM: *ropa interior: de hombre*) underpants, pants (BRIT), shorts (US); (: *de mujer*) panties, knickers (BRIT)
calzoncillos [kalθon'θiʎos] *nmpl* underpants
cama ['kama] *nf* bed; **hacer la ~** to make the bed; **cama individual/de matrimonio** single/double bed
camaleón [kamale'on] *nm* chameleon
cámara ['kamara] *nf* chamber; (*habitación*) room; (*sala*) hall; (*Cine*) cine camera; (*fotográfica*) camera; **cámara de aire** (ESP) inner tube; **cámara de comercio** chamber of commerce; **cámara de gas** gas chamber; **cámara digital** digital camera; **cámara frigorífica** cold-storage room
camarada [kama'raða] *nmf* comrade, companion
camarera [kama'rera] *nf* (*en restaurante*) waitress; (*en casa, hotel*) maid
camarero [kama'rero] *nm* waiter
camarógrafo, -a [kama'rografo, a] (LAM) *nm/f* cameraman/camerawoman
camarón [kama'ron] *nm* shrimp
camarote [kama'rote] *nm* cabin
cambiable [kam'bjaβle] *adj* (*variable*) changeable, variable; (*intercambiable*) interchangeable
cambiante [kam'bjante] *adj* variable
cambiar [kam'bjar] *vt* to change; (*dinero*) to exchange ▷*vi* to change; **cambiarse** *vr* (*mudarse*) to move; (*de ropa*) to change; **~ de idea** *u* **opinión** to change one's mind; **~se de ropa** to change (one's clothes)
cambio ['kambjo] *nm* change; (*trueque*) exchange; (*Com*) rate of exchange; (*oficina*) bureau de change; (*dinero menudo*) small change; **a ~ de** in return *o* exchange for; **en ~** on the other hand; (*en lugar de*) instead; **cambio climático** climate change; **cambio de divisas** foreign exchange; **cambio de marchas** *o* **velocidades** gear lever
camelar [kame'lar] *vt* to sweet-talk
camello [ka'meʎo] *nm* camel; (*fam: traficante*) pusher
camerino [kame'rino] *nm* dressing room
camilla [ka'miʎa] *nf* (*Med*) stretcher
caminar [kami'nar] *vi* (*marchar*) to walk, go ▷*vt* (*recorrer*) to cover, travel
caminata [kami'nata] *nf* long walk; (*por el campo*) hike
camino [ka'mino] *nm* way, road; (*sendero*) track; **a medio ~** halfway (there); **en el ~** on the way, en route; **~ de** on the way to; **Camino de Santiago** Way of St James; **camino particular** private road

CAMINO DE SANTIAGO

The **Camino de Santiago** is a medieval pilgrim route stretching from the Pyrenees to Santiago de Compostela

- in north-west Spain, where tradition
- has it the body of the Apostle James is
- buried. Nowadays it is a popular tourist
- route as well as a religious one.

camión [ka'mjon] *nm* lorry (BRIT), truck (US); (MÉX: *autobús*) bus; **camión cisterna** tanker; **camión de la basura** dustcart, refuse lorry; **camión de mudanzas** removal (BRIT) *o* moving (US) van; **camionero, -a** *nm/f* lorry *o* truck driver
camioneta [kamjo'neta] *nf* van, light truck
camisa [ka'misa] *nf* shirt; (*Bot*) skin; **camisa de fuerza** straitjacket
camiseta [kami'seta] *nf* (*prenda*) tee-shirt; (*ropa interior*) vest; (*de deportista*) top
camisón [kami'son] *nm* nightdress, nightgown
camorra [ka'morra] *nf*: **buscar ~** to look for trouble
camote [ka'mote] *nm* (MÉX, CS: *batata*) sweet potato, yam; (MÉX: *bulbo*) tuber, bulb; (CS: *fam*: *enamoramiento*) crush
campamento [kampa'mento] *nm* camp
campana [kam'pana] *nf* bell; **campanada** *nf* peal; **campanario** *nm* belfry
campanilla [kampa'niʎa] *nf* small bell
campaña [kam'paɲa] *nf* (*Mil, Pol*) campaign; **campaña electoral** election campaign
campechano, -a [kampe'tʃano, a] *adj* (*franco*) open
campeón, -ona [kampe'on, ona] *nm/f* champion; **campeonato** *nm* championship
cámper ['kamper] (LAM) *nm o f* caravan (BRIT), trailer (US)
campera [kam'pera] (RPL) *nf* anorak
campesino, -a [kampe'sino, a] *adj* country *cpd*, rural; (*gente*) peasant *cpd* ▷ *nm/f* countryman/woman; (*agricultor*) farmer
campestre [kam'pestre] *adj* country *cpd*, rural
camping ['kampin] (*pl* **~s**) *nm* camping; (*lugar*) campsite; **ir** *o* **estar de ~** to go camping
campo ['kampo] *nm* (*fuera de la ciudad*) country, countryside; (*Agr, Elec*) field; (*de fútbol*) pitch; (*de golf*) course; (*Mil*) camp; **campo de batalla** battlefield; **campo de concentración** concentration camp; **campo de deportes** sports ground, playing field; **campo visual** field of vision, visual field
camuflaje [kamu'flaxe] *nm* camouflage
cana ['kana] *nf* white *o* grey hair; **tener ~s** to be going grey
Canadá [kana'ða] *nm* Canada; **canadiense** *adj, nmf* Canadian ▷ *nf* fur-lined jacket
canal [ka'nal] *nm* canal; (*Geo*) channel, strait; (*de televisión*) channel; (*de tejado*) gutter; **canal de Panamá** Panama Canal
canaleta [kana'leta] (LAM) *nf* (*de tejado*) gutter
canalizar [kanali'θar] *vt* to channel
canalla [ka'naʎa] *nf* rabble, mob ▷ *nm* swine
canapé [kana'pe] (*pl* **~s**) *nm* sofa, settee; (*Culin*) canapé
Canarias [ka'narjas] *nfpl* (*tb*: **las Islas ~**) the Canary Islands, the Canaries
canario, -a [ka'narjo, a] *adj, nm/f* (native) of the Canary Isles ▷ *nm* (*Zool*) canary
canasta [ka'nasta] *nf* (round) basket
canasto [ka'nasto] *nm* large basket
cancela [kan'θela] *nf* gate
cancelación [kanθela'θjon] *nf* cancellation
cancelar [kanθe'lar] *vt* to cancel; (*una deuda*) to write off
cáncer ['kanθer] *nm* (*Med*) cancer; **C~** (*Astrología*) Cancer
cancha ['kantʃa] *nf* (*de baloncesto*) court; (LAM: *campo*) pitch; **cancha de tenis** (LAM) tennis court
canciller [kanθi'ʎer] *nm* chancellor
canción [kan'θjon] *nf* song; **canción de cuna** lullaby
candado [kan'daðo] *nm* padlock
candente [kan'dente] *adj* red-hot; (*fig*: *tema*) burning
candidato, -a [kandi'ðato, a] *nm/f* candidate
cándido, -a ['kandiðo, a] *adj* simple; naive

> No confundir **cándido** con la palabra inglesa *candid*.

candil [kan'dil] *nm* oil lamp; **candilejas** *nfpl* (*Teatro*) footlights
canela [ka'nela] *nf* cinnamon
canelones [kane'lones] *nmpl* cannelloni
cangrejo [kan'grexo] *nm* crab
canguro [kan'guro] *nm* kangaroo; **hacer de ~** to babysit
caníbal [ka'niβal] *adj, nmf* cannibal
canica [ka'nika] *nf* marble
canijo, -a [ka'nixo, a] *adj* frail, sickly
canilla [ka'niʎa] (RPL) *nf* tap (BRIT), faucet (US)
canjear [kanxe'ar] *vt* to exchange
canoa [ka'noa] *nf* canoe
canon ['kanon] *nm* canon; (*pensión*) rent;

(*Com*) tax
canonizar [kanoni'θar] *vt* to canonize
canoso, -a [ka'noso, a] *adj* grey-haired
cansado, -a [kan'saðo, a] *adj* tired, weary; (*tedioso*) tedious, boring
cansancio [kan'sanθjo] *nm* tiredness, fatigue
cansar [kan'sar] *vt* (*fatigar*) to tire, tire out; (*aburrir*) to bore; (*fastidiar*) to bother; **cansarse** *vr* to tire, get tired; (*aburrirse*) to get bored
cantábrico, -a [kan'taβriko, a] *adj* Cantabrian
cantante [kan'tante] *adj* singing ▷*nmf* singer
cantar [kan'tar] *vt* to sing ▷*vi* to sing; (*insecto*) to chirp ▷*nm* (*acción*) singing; (*canción*) song; (*poema*) poem
cántaro ['kantaro] *nm* pitcher, jug; **llover a ~s** to rain cats and dogs
cante ['kante] *nm* (*Mús*) *Andalusian folk song*; **cante jondo** flamenco singing
cantera [kan'tera] *nf* quarry
cantero [kan'tero] (RPL) *nm* (*arriate*) border
cantidad [kanti'ðað] *nf* quantity, amount; **~ de** lots of
cantimplora [kantim'plora] *nf* (*frasco*) water bottle, canteen
cantina [kan'tina] *nf* canteen; (*de estación*) buffet; (LAM: *bar*) bar
cantinero, -a [kanti'nero, a] (MÉX) *nm/f* barman/barmaid, bartender (US)
canto ['kanto] *nm* singing; (*canción*) song; (*borde*) edge, rim; (*de cuchillo*) back; **canto rodado** boulder
cantor, a [kan'tor, a] *nm/f* singer
canturrear [kanturre'ar] *vi* to sing softly
canuto [ka'nuto] *nm* (*tubo*) small tube; (*fam: droga*) joint
caña ['kaɲa] *nf* (*Bot: tallo*) stem, stalk; (*carrizo*) reed; (*vaso*) tumbler; (*de cerveza*) glass of beer; (*Anat*) shinbone; **caña de azúcar** sugar cane; **caña de pescar** fishing rod
cañada [ka'ɲaða] *nf* (*entre dos montañas*) gully, ravine; (*camino*) cattle track
cáñamo ['kaɲamo] *nm* hemp
cañería [kaɲe'ria] *nf* (*tubo*) pipe
caño ['kaɲo] *nm* (*tubo*) tube, pipe; (*de albañal*) sewer; (*Mús*) pipe; (*de fuente*) jet
cañón [ka'ɲon] *nm* (*Mil*) cannon; (*de fusil*) barrel; (*Geo*) canyon, gorge
caoba [ka'oβa] *nf* mahogany
caos ['kaos] *nm* chaos
capa ['kapa] *nf* cloak, cape; (*Geo*) layer, stratum; **capa de ozono** ozone layer
capacidad [kapaθi'ðað] *nf* (*medida*) capacity; (*aptitud*) capacity, ability
caparazón [kapara'θon] *nm* shell
capataz [kapa'taθ] *nm* foreman
capaz [ka'paθ] *adj* able, capable; (*amplio*) capacious, roomy
capellán [kape'ʎan] *nm* chaplain; (*sacerdote*) priest
capicúa [kapi'kua] *adj inv* (*número, fecha*) reversible
capilla [ka'piʎa] *nf* chapel
capital [kapi'tal] *adj* capital ▷*nm* (*Com*) capital ▷*nf* (*ciudad*) capital; **capital social** share *o* authorized capital
capitalismo [kapita'lismo] *nm* capitalism; **capitalista** *adj, nmf* capitalist
capitán [kapi'tan] *nm* captain
capítulo [ka'pitulo] *nm* chapter
capó [ka'po] *nm* (*Auto*) bonnet
capón [ka'pon] *nm* (*gallo*) capon
capota [ka'pota] *nf* (*de mujer*) bonnet; (*Auto*) hood (BRIT), top (US)
capote [ka'pote] *nm* (*abrigo: de militar*) greatcoat; (*de torero*) cloak
capricho [ka'pritʃo] *nm* whim, caprice; **caprichoso, -a** *adj* capricious
Capricornio [kapri'kornjo] *nm* Capricorn
cápsula ['kapsula] *nf* capsule
captar [kap'tar] *vt* (*comprender*) to understand; (*Radio*) to pick up; (*atención, apoyo*) to attract
captura [kap'tura] *nf* capture; (*Jur*) arrest; **capturar** *vt* to capture; to arrest
capucha [ka'putʃa] *nf* hood, cowl
capuchón [kapu'tʃon] (ESP) *nm* (*de bolígrafo*) cap
capullo [ka'puʎo] *nm* (*Bot*) bud; (*Zool*) cocoon; (*fam*) idiot
caqui ['kaki] *nm* khaki
cara ['kara] *nf* (*Anat: de moneda*) face; (*de disco*) side; (*descaro*) boldness; **~ a** facing; **de ~** opposite, facing; **dar la ~** to face the consequences; **¿~ o cruz?** heads or tails?; **¡qué ~ (más dura)!** what a nerve!
Caracas [ka'rakas] *n* Caracas
caracol [kara'kol] *nm* (*Zool*) snail; (*concha*) (sea) shell
carácter [ka'rakter] (*pl* **caracteres**) *nm* character; **tener buen/mal ~** to be good natured/bad tempered
característica [karakte'ristika] *nf* characteristic
característico, -a [karakte'ristiko, a] *adj* characteristic
caracterizar [karakteri'θar] *vt* to characterize, typify
caradura [kara'ðura] *nmf*: **es un ~** he's got a nerve
carajillo [kara'xiʎo] *nm* *coffee with a dash*

C

of brandy
carajo [ka'raxo] (*fam!*) *nm*: **¡~!** shit! (*!*)
caramba [ka'ramba] *excl* good gracious!
caramelo [kara'melo] *nm* (*dulce*) sweet; (*azúcar fundida*) caramel
caravana [kara'βana] *nf* caravan; (*fig*) group; (*Auto*) tailback
carbón [kar'βon] *nm* coal; **papel ~** carbon paper
carbono [kar'βono] *nm* carbon
carburador [karβura'ðor] *nm* carburettor
carburante [karβu'rante] *nm* (*para motor*) fuel
carcajada [karka'xaða] *nf* (loud) laugh, guffaw
cárcel ['karθel] *nf* prison, jail; (*Tec*) clamp
carcoma [kar'koma] *nf* woodworm
cardar [kar'ðar] *vt* (*pelo*) to backcomb
cardenal [karðe'nal] *nm* (*Rel*) cardinal; (*Med*) bruise
cardíaco, -a [kar'ðiako, a] *adj* cardiac, heart *cpd*
cardinal [karði'nal] *adj* cardinal
cardo ['karðo] *nm* thistle
carecer [kare'θer] *vi*: **~ de** to lack, be in need of
carencia [ka'renθja] *nf* lack; (*escasez*) shortage; (*Med*) deficiency
careta [ka'reta] *nf* mask
carga ['karɣa] *nf* (*peso, Elec*) load; (*de barco*) cargo, freight; (*Mil*) charge; (*responsabilidad*) duty, obligation
cargado, -a [kar'ɣaðo, a] *adj* loaded; (*Elec*) live; (*café, té*) strong; (*cielo*) overcast
cargamento [karɣa'mento] *nm* (*acción*) loading; (*mercancías*) load, cargo
cargar [kar'ɣar] *vt* (*barco, arma*) to load; (*Elec*) to charge; (*Com: algo en cuenta*) to charge; (*Inform*) to load ▷ *vi* (*Mil*) to charge; (*Auto*) to load (up); **~ con** to pick up, carry away; (*peso: fig*) to shoulder, bear; **cargarse** *vr* (*fam: estropear*) to break; (*: matar*) to bump off
cargo ['karɣo] *nm* (*puesto*) post, office; (*responsabilidad*) duty, obligation; (*Jur*) charge; **hacerse ~ de** to take charge of *o* responsibility for
carguero [kar'ɣero] *nm* freighter, cargo boat; (*avión*) freight plane
Caribe [ka'riβe] *nm*: **el ~** the Caribbean; **del ~** Caribbean; **caribeño, -a** [kari'βeɲo, a] *adj* Caribbean
caricatura [karika'tura] *nf* caricature
caricia [ka'riθja] *nf* caress
caridad [kari'ðað] *nf* charity
caries ['karjes] *nf inv* tooth decay
cariño [ka'riɲo] *nm* affection, love; (*caricia*) caress; (*en carta*) love ...; **tener ~ a** to be fond of; **cariñoso, -a** *adj* affectionate
carisma [ka'risma] *nm* charisma
caritativo, -a [karita'tiβo, a] *adj* charitable
cariz [ka'riθ] *nm*: **tener** *o* **tomar buen/mal ~** to look good/bad
carmín [kar'min] *nm* lipstick
carnal [kar'nal] *adj* carnal; **primo ~** first cousin
carnaval [karna'βal] *nm* carnival

CARNAVAL

Carnaval is the traditional period of fun, feasting and partying which takes place in the three days before the start of Lent ("Cuaresma"). Although in decline during the Franco years the carnival has grown in popularity recently in Spain. Cádiz and Tenerife are particularly well-known for their flamboyant celebrations with fancy-dress parties, parades and firework displays being the order of the day.

carne ['karne] *nf* flesh; (*Culin*) meat; **se me pone la ~ de gallina sólo verlo** I get the creeps just seeing it; **carne de cerdo/cordero/ternera/vaca** pork/lamb/veal/beef; **carne de gallina** (*fig*) gooseflesh; **carne molida** (LAM) mince (BRIT), ground meat (US); **carne picada** (ESP, RPL) mince (BRIT), ground meat (US)
carné [kar'ne] (ESP) (*pl* **~s**) *nm*: **~ de conducir** driving licence (BRIT), driver's license (US); **~ de identidad** identity card; **~ de socio** membership card
carnero [kar'nero] *nm* sheep, ram; (*carne*) mutton
carnet [kar'ne] (ESP) (*pl* **~s**) *nm* = **carné**
carnicería [karniθe'ria] *nf* butcher's (shop); (*fig: matanza*) carnage, slaughter
carnicero, -a [karni'θero, a] *adj* carnivorous ▷ *nm/f* butcher; (*carnívoro*) carnivore
carnívoro, -a [kar'niβoro, a] *adj* carnivorous
caro, -a ['karo, a] *adj* dear; (*Com*) dear, expensive ▷ *adv* dear, dearly
carpa ['karpa] *nf* (*pez*) carp; (*de circo*) big top; (LAM: *tienda de campaña*) tent
carpeta [kar'peta] *nf* folder, file; **carpeta de anillas** ring binder
carpintería [karpinte'ria] *nf* carpentry, joinery; **carpintero** *nm* carpenter
carraspear [karraspe'ar] *vi* to clear one's throat
carraspera [karras'pera] *nf* hoarseness

carrera [ka'rrera] *nf* (*acción*) run(ning); (*espacio recorrido*) run; (*competición*) race; (*trayecto*) course; (*profesión*) career; (*licenciatura*) degree; **a la ~** at (full) speed; **carrera de obstáculos** (*Deporte*) steeplechase
carrete [ka'rrete] *nm* reel, spool; (*Tec*) coil
carretera [karre'tera] *nf* (main) road, highway; **carretera de circunvalación** ring road; **carretera nacional** ≈ A road (BRIT), ≈ state highway (US)
carretilla [karre'tiʎa] *nf* trolley; (*Agr*) (wheel)barrow
carril [ka'rril] *nm* furrow; (*de autopista*) lane; (*Ferro*) rail; **carril-bici** cycle lane
carrito [ka'rrito] *nm* trolley
carro ['karro] *nm* cart, wagon; (*Mil*) tank; (LAM: *coche*) car; **carro patrulla** (LAM) patrol *o* panda (BRIT) car
carrocería [karroθe'ria] *nf* bodywork, coachwork
carroña [ka'rroɲa] *nf* carrion *no pl*
carroza [ka'rroθa] *nf* (*carruaje*) coach
carrusel [karru'sel] *nm* merry-go-round, roundabout
carta ['karta] *nf* letter; (*Culin*) menu; (*naipe*) card; (*mapa*) map; (*Jur*) document; **carta certificada/urgente** registered/special-delivery letter
cartabón [karta'βon] *nm* set square
cartel [kar'tel] *nm* (*anuncio*) poster, placard; (*Escol*) wall chart; (*Com*) cartel; **cartelera** *nf* hoarding, billboard; (*en periódico etc*) entertainments guide; **"en cartelera"** "showing"
cartera [kar'tera] *nf* (*de bolsillo*) wallet; (*de colegial, cobrador*) satchel; (*de señora*) handbag; (*para documentos*) briefcase; (*Com*) portfolio; **ocupa la ~ de Agricultura** she is Minister of Agriculture
carterista [karte'rista] *nmf* pickpocket
cartero [kar'tero] *nm* postman
cartilla [kar'tiʎa] *nf* primer, first reading book; **cartilla de ahorros** savings book
cartón [kar'ton] *nm* cardboard; **cartón piedra** papier-mâché
cartucho [kar'tutʃo] *nm* (*Mil*) cartridge
cartulina [kartu'lina] *nf* card
casa ['kasa] *nf* house; (*hogar*) home; (*Com*) firm, company; **en ~** at home; **casa consistorial** town hall; **casa de campo** country house; **casa de huéspedes** boarding house; **casa de socorro** first aid post; **casa rodante** (CS) caravan (BRIT), trailer (US)
casado, -a [ka'saðo, a] *adj* married ▷ *nm/f* married man/woman
casar [ka'sar] *vt* to marry; (*Jur*) to quash, annul; **casarse** *vr* to marry, get married
cascabel [kaska'βel] *nm* (small) bell
cascada [kas'kaða] *nf* waterfall
cascanueces [kaska'nweθes] *nm inv* nutcrackers *pl*
cascar [kas'kar] *vt* to crack, split, break (open); **cascarse** *vr* to crack, split, break (open)
cáscara ['kaskara] *nf* (*de huevo, fruta seca*) shell; (*de fruta*) skin; (*de limón*) peel
casco ['kasko] *nm* (*de bombero, soldado*) helmet; (*Náut*: *de barco*) hull; (*Zool*: *de caballo*) hoof; (*botella*) empty bottle; (*de ciudad*): **el ~ antiguo** the old part; **el ~ urbano** the town centre; **los ~s azules** the UN peace-keeping force, the blue berets
cascote [kas'kote] *nm* rubble
caserío [kase'rio] (ESP) *nm* farmhouse; (*casa*) country mansion
casero, -a [ka'sero, a] *adj* (*pan etc*) home-made ▷ *nm/f* (*propietario*) landlord/lady; **ser muy ~** to be home-loving; **"comida casera"** "home cooking"
caseta [ka'seta] *nf* hut; (*para bañista*) cubicle; (*de feria*) stall
casete [ka'sete] *nm o f* cassette
casi ['kasi] *adv* almost, nearly; **~ nada** hardly anything; **~ nunca** hardly ever, almost never; **~ te caes** you almost fell
casilla [ka'siʎa] *nf* (*casita*) hut, cabin; (*Ajedrez*) square; (*para cartas*) pigeonhole; **casilla de correo** (CS) P.O. Box; **casillero** *nm* (*para cartas*) pigeonholes *pl*
casino [ka'sino] *nm* club; (*de juego*) casino
caso ['kaso] *nm* case; **en ~ de** in case of; **en ~ de que ...** in case ...; **el ~ es que ...** the fact is that ...; **en ese/todo ~** in that/any case; **hacer ~ a** to pay attention to; **venir al ~** to be relevant
caspa ['kaspa] *nf* dandruff
cassette [ka'sete] *nm o f* = **casete**
castaña [kas'taɲa] *nf* chestnut
castaño, -a [kas'taɲo, a] *adj* chestnut(-coloured), brown ▷ *nm* chestnut tree
castañuelas [kasta'ɲwelas] *nfpl* castanets
castellano, -a [kaste'ʎano, a] *adj, nm/f* Castilian ▷ *nm* (*Ling*) Castilian, Spanish
castigar [kasti'ɣar] *vt* to punish; (*Deporte*) to penalize; **castigo** *nm* punishment; (*Deporte*) penalty
Castilla [kas'tiʎa] *nf* Castille
castillo [kas'tiʎo] *nm* castle
castizo, -a [kas'tiθo, a] *adj* (*Ling*) pure
casto, -a ['kasto, a] *adj* chaste, pure
castor [kas'tor] *nm* beaver
castrar [kas'trar] *vt* to castrate

casual [ka'swal] *adj* chance, accidental

No confundir **casual** con la palabra inglesa *casual*.

casualidad *nf* chance, accident; (*combinación de circunstancias*) coincidence; **da la casualidad de que ...** it (just) so happens that ...; **¡qué casualidad!** what a coincidence!

cataclismo [kata'klismo] *nm* cataclysm

catador, a [kata'ðor, a] *nm/f* wine taster

catalán, -ana [kata'lan, ana] *adj, nm/f* Catalan ▷ *nm* (*Ling*) Catalan

catalizador [kataliθa'ðor] *nm* catalyst; (*Auto*) catalytic convertor

catalogar [katalo'ɣar] *vt* to catalogue; **~ a algn (de)** (*fig*) to categorize sb (as)

catálogo [ka'taloɣo] *nm* catalogue

Cataluña [kata'luɲa] *nf* Catalonia

catar [ka'tar] *vt* to taste, sample

catarata [kata'rata] *nf* (*Geo*) waterfall; (*Med*) cataract

catarro [ka'tarro] *nm* catarrh; (*constipado*) cold

catástrofe [ka'tastrofe] *nf* catastrophe

catear [kate'ar] (*fam*) *vt* (*examen, alumno*) to fail

cátedra ['kateðra] *nf* (*Univ*) chair, professorship

catedral [kate'ðral] *nf* cathedral

catedrático, -a [kate'ðratiko, a] *nm/f* professor

categoría [kateɣo'ria] *nf* category; (*rango*) rank, standing; (*calidad*) quality; **de ~** (*hotel*) top-class

cateto, -a ['kateto, a] (ESP: *pey*) *nm/f* peasant

catolicismo [katoli'θismo] *nm* Catholicism

católico, -a [ka'toliko, a] *adj, nm/f* Catholic

catorce [ka'torθe] *num* fourteen

cauce ['kauθe] *nm* (*de río*) riverbed; (*fig*) channel

caucho ['kautʃo] (ESP) *nm* rubber

caudal [kau'ðal] *nm* (*de río*) volume, flow; (*fortuna*) wealth; (*abundancia*) abundance

caudillo [kau'ðiʎo] *nm* leader, chief

causa ['kausa] *nf* cause; (*razón*) reason; (*Jur*) lawsuit, case; **a ~ de** because of; **causar** [kau'sar] *vt* to cause

cautela [kau'tela] *nf* caution, cautiousness; **cauteloso, -a** *adj* cautious, wary

cautivar [kauti'βar] *vt* to capture; (*atraer*) to captivate

cautiverio [kauti'βerjo] *nm* captivity

cautividad [kautiβi'ðað] *nf* = **cautiverio**

cautivo, -a [kau'tiβo, a] *adj, nm/f* captive

cauto, -a ['kauto, a] *adj* cautious, careful

cava ['kaβa] *nm* *champagne-type wine*

cavar [ka'βar] *vt* to dig

caverna [ka'βerna] *nf* cave, cavern

cavidad [kaβi'ðað] *nf* cavity

cavilar [kaβi'lar] *vt* to ponder

cayendo *etc vb V* **caer**

caza ['kaθa] *nf* (*acción: gen*) hunting; (*: con fusil*) shooting; (*una caza*) hunt, chase; (*de animales*) game ▷ *nm* (*Aviac*) fighter; **ir de ~** to go hunting; **caza mayor** game hunting; **cazador, a** [kaθa'ðor, a] *nm/f* hunter; **cazadora** *nf* jacket; **cazar** [ka'θar] *vt* to hunt; (*perseguir*) to chase; (*prender*) to catch

cazo ['kaθo] *nm* saucepan

cazuela [ka'θwela] *nf* (*vasija*) pan; (*guisado*) casserole

CD *nm abr* (= *compact disc*) CD

CD-ROM [θeðe'rom] *nm abr* CD-ROM

CE *nf abr* (= *Comunidad Europea*) EC

cebada [θe'βaða] *nf* barley

cebar [θe'βar] *vt* (*animal*) to fatten (up); (*anzuelo*) to bait; (*Mil, Tec*) to prime

cebo ['θeβo] *nm* (*para animales*) feed, food; (*para peces, fig*) bait; (*de arma*) charge

cebolla [θe'βoʎa] *nf* onion; **cebolleta** *nf* spring onion

cebra ['θeβra] *nf* zebra

cecear [θeθe'ar] *vi* to lisp

ceder [θe'ðer] *vt* to hand over, give up, part with ▷ *vi* (*renunciar*) to give in, yield; (*disminuir*) to diminish, decline; (*romperse*) to give way

cedro ['θeðro] *nm* cedar

cédula ['θeðula] *nf* certificate, document; **cédula de identidad** (LAM) identity card; **cédula electoral** (LAM) ballot

cegar [θe'ɣar] *vt* to blind; (*tubería etc*) to block up, stop up ▷ *vi* to go blind; **cegarse** *vr*: **~se (de)** to be blinded (by)

ceguera [θe'ɣera] *nf* blindness

ceja ['θexa] *nf* eyebrow

cejar [θe'xar] *vi* (*fig*) to back down

celador, a [θela'ðor, a] *nm/f* (*de edificio*) watchman; (*de museo etc*) attendant

celda ['θelda] *nf* cell

celebración [θeleβra'θjon] *nf* celebration

celebrar [θele'βrar] *vt* to celebrate; (*alabar*) to praise ▷ *vi* to be glad; **celebrarse** *vr* to occur, take place

célebre ['θelebre] *adj* famous

celebridad [θeleβri'ðað] *nf* fame; (*persona*) celebrity

celeste [θe'leste] *adj* (*azul*) sky-blue

celestial [θeles'tjal] *adj* celestial, heavenly

celo[1] ['θelo] *nm* zeal; (*Rel*) fervour; (*Zool*): **en ~** on heat; **celos** *nmpl* jealousy *sg*; **dar ~s a algn** to make sb jealous; **tener ~s** to be

jealous
celo²® ['θelo] *nm* Sellotape®
celofán [θelo'fan] *nm* cellophane
celoso, -a [θe'loso, a] *adj* jealous; (*trabajador*) zealous
celta ['θelta] *adj* Celtic ▷*nmf* Celt
célula ['θelula] *nf* cell
celulitis [θelu'litis] *nf* cellulite
cementerio [θemen'terjo] *nm* cemetery, graveyard
cemento [θe'mento] *nm* cement; (*hormigón*) concrete; (LAM: *cola*) glue
cena ['θena] *nf* evening meal, dinner;
cenar [θe'nar] *vt* to have for dinner ▷*vi* to have dinner
cenicero [θeni'θero] *nm* ashtray
ceniza [θe'niθa] *nf* ash, ashes *pl*
censo ['θenso] *nm* census; **censo electoral** electoral roll
censura [θen'sura] *nf* (*Pol*) censorship;
censurar [θensu'rar] *vt* (*idea*) to censure; (*cortar: película*) to censor
centella [θen'teʎa] *nf* spark
centenar [θente'nar] *nm* hundred
centenario, -a [θente'narjo, a] *adj* centenary; hundred-year-old ▷*nm* centenary
centeno [θen'teno] *nm* (*Bot*) rye
centésimo, -a [θen'tesimo, a] *adj* hundredth
centígrado [θen'tiɣraðo] *adj* centigrade
centímetro [θen'timetro] *nm* centimetre (BRIT), centimeter (US)
céntimo ['θentimo] *nm* cent
centinela [θenti'nela] *nm* sentry, guard
centollo [θen'toʎo] *nm* spider crab
central [θen'tral] *adj* central ▷*nf* head office; (*Tec*) plant; (*Tel*) exchange; **central eléctrica** power station; **central nuclear** nuclear power station; **central telefónica** telephone exchange
centralita [θentra'lita] *nf* switchboard
centralizar [θentrali'θar] *vt* to centralize
centrar [θen'trar] *vt* to centre
céntrico, -a ['θentriko, a] *adj* central
centrifugar [θentrifu'ɣar] *vt* to spin-dry
centro ['θentro] *nm* centre; **centro comercial** shopping centre; **centro de atención al cliente** call centre; **centro de salud** health centre; **centro escolar** school; **centro juvenil** youth club; **centro turístico** (*lugar muy visitado*) tourist centre; **centro urbano** urban area, city
centroamericano, -a [θentroameri'kano, a] *adj, nm/f* Central American
ceñido, -a [θe'ɲiðo, a] *adj* (*chaqueta, pantalón*) tight(-fitting)
ceñir [θe'ɲir] *vt* (*rodear*) to encircle, surround; (*ajustar*) to fit (tightly)
ceño ['θeɲo] *nm* frown, scowl; **fruncir el ~** to frown, knit one's brow
cepillar [θepi'ʎar] *vt* to brush; (*madera*) to plane (down)
cepillo [θe'piʎo] *nm* brush; (*para madera*) plane; **cepillo de dientes** toothbrush
cera ['θera] *nf* wax
cerámica [θe'ramika] *nf* pottery; (*arte*) ceramics
cerca ['θerka] *nf* fence ▷*adv* near, nearby, close; **~ de** near, close to
cercanías [θerka'nias] *nfpl* (*afueras*) outskirts, suburbs
cercano, -a [θer'kano, a] *adj* close, near
cercar [θer'kar] *vt* to fence in; (*rodear*) to surround
cerco ['θerko] *nm* (*Agr*) enclosure; (LAM: *valla*) fence; (*Mil*) siege
cerdo, -a ['θerðo, a] *nm/f* pig/sow
cereal [θere'al] *nm* cereal; **cereales** *nmpl* cereals, grain *sg*
cerebro [θe'reβro] *nm* brain; (*fig*) brains *pl*
ceremonia [θere'monja] *nf* ceremony;
ceremonioso, -a *adj* ceremonious
cereza [θe'reθa] *nf* cherry
cerilla [θe'riʎa] *nf* (*fósforo*) match
cerillo [θe'riʎo] (MÉX) *nm* match
cero ['θero] *nm* nothing, zero
cerquillo [θer'kiʎo] (CAM, RPL) *nm* fringe (BRIT), bangs *pl* (US)
cerrado, -a [θe'rraðo, a] *adj* closed, shut; (*con llave*) locked; (*tiempo*) cloudy, overcast; (*curva*) sharp; (*acento*) thick, broad
cerradura [θerra'ðura] *nf* (*acción*) closing; (*mecanismo*) lock
cerrajero [θerra'xero] *nm* locksmith
cerrar [θe'rrar] *vt* to close, shut; (*paso, carretera*) to close; (*grifo*) to turn off; (*cuenta, negocio*) to close ▷*vi* to close, shut; (*noche*) to come down; **cerrarse** *vr* to close, shut; **~ con llave** to lock; **~ un trato** to strike a bargain
cerro ['θerro] *nm* hill
cerrojo [θe'rroxo] *nm* (*herramienta*) bolt; (*de puerta*) latch
certamen [θer'tamen] *nm* competition, contest
certero, -a [θer'tero, a] *adj* (*gen*) accurate
certeza [θer'teθa] *nf* certainty
certidumbre [θerti'ðumβre] *nf* = **certeza**
certificado, -a [θertifi'kaðo, a] *adj* (*carta, paquete*) registered; (*aprobado*) certified ▷*nm* certificate; **certificado médico** medical certificate
certificar [θertifi'kar] *vt* (*asegurar, atestar*) to certify

cervatillo [θerβa'tiʎo] *nm* fawn
cervecería [θerβeθe'ria] *nf* (*fábrica*) brewery; (*bar*) public house, pub
cerveza [θer'βeθa] *nf* beer
cesar [θe'sar] *vi* to cease, stop ▷ *vt* (*funcionario*) to remove from office
cesárea [θe'sarea] *nf* (*Med*) Caesarean operation *o* section
cese ['θese] *nm* (*de trabajo*) dismissal; (*de pago*) suspension
césped ['θespeð] *nm* grass, lawn
cesta ['θesta] *nf* basket
cesto ['θesto] *nm* (large) basket, hamper
cfr *abr* (= *confróntese*) cf.
chabacano, -a [tʃaβa'kano, a] *adj* vulgar, coarse
chabola [tʃa'βola] (ESP) *nf* shack; **barrio de chabolas** shanty town
chacal [tʃa'kal] *nm* jackal
chacha ['tʃatʃa] (*fam*) *nf* maid
cháchara ['tʃatʃara] *nf* chatter; **estar de ~** to chatter away
chacra ['tʃakra] (CS) *nf* smallholding
chafa ['tʃafa] (MÉX: *fam*) *adj* useless, dud
chafar [tʃa'far] *vt* (*aplastar*) to crush; (*plan etc*) to ruin
chal [tʃal] *nm* shawl
chalado, -a [tʃa'lado, a] (*fam*) *adj* crazy
chalé [tʃa'le] (*pl* **~s**) *nm* villa, ≈ detached house
chaleco [tʃa'leko] *nm* waistcoat, vest (US); **chaleco de seguridad** (*Aut*) reflective safety vest; **chaleco salvavidas** life jacket
chalet [tʃa'le] (*pl* **~s**) *nm* = **chalé**
chamaco, -a (MÉX) [tʃa'mako, a] *nm/f* (*niño*) kid
chambear [tʃambe'ar] (MÉX: *fam*) *vi* to earn one's living
champán [tʃam'pan] *nm* champagne
champiñón [tʃampi'ɲon] *nm* mushroom
champú [tʃam'pu] (*pl* **~es, ~s**) *nm* shampoo
chamuscar [tʃamus'kar] *vt* to scorch, sear, singe
chance ['tʃanθe] (LAM) *nm* chance
chancho, -a ['tʃantʃo, a] (LAM) *nm/f* pig
chanchullo [tʃan'tʃuʎo] (*fam*) *nm* fiddle
chandal [tʃan'dal] *nm* tracksuit
chantaje [tʃan'taxe] *nm* blackmail
chapa ['tʃapa] *nf* (*de metal*) plate, sheet; (*de madera*) board, panel; (RPL *Auto*) number (BRIT) *o* license (US) plate; **chapado, -a** *adj*: **chapado en oro** gold-plated
chaparrón [tʃapa'rron] *nm* downpour, cloudburst
chaperón [tʃape'ron] (MÉX) *nm*: **hacer de ~** to play gooseberry; **chaperona** (LAM) *nf*: **hacer de chaperona** to play gooseberry
chapopote [tʃapo'pote] (MÉX) *nm* tar
chapulín [tʃapu'lin] (MÉX, CAM) *nm* grasshopper
chapurrear [tʃapurre'ar] *vt* (*idioma*) to speak badly
chapuza [tʃa'puθa] *nf* botched job
chapuzón [tʃapu'θon] *nm*: **darse un ~** to go for a dip
chaqueta [tʃa'keta] *nf* jacket
chaquetón [tʃake'ton] *nm* long jacket
charca ['tʃarka] *nf* pond, pool
charco ['tʃarko] *nm* pool, puddle
charcutería [tʃarkute'ria] *nf* (*tienda*) *shop selling chiefly pork meat products*; (*productos*) cooked pork meats *pl*
charla ['tʃarla] *nf* talk, chat; (*conferencia*) lecture; **charlar** [tʃar'lar] *vi* to talk, chat; **charlatán, -ana** [tʃarla'tan, ana] *nm/f* (*hablador*) chatterbox; (*estafador*) trickster
charol [tʃa'rol] *nm* varnish; (*cuero*) patent leather
charola [tʃa'rola] (MÉX) *nf* tray
charro ['tʃarro, a] (MÉX) *nm* typical Mexican
chasco ['tʃasko] *nm* (*desengaño*) disappointment
chasis ['tʃasis] *nm inv* chassis
chasquido [tʃas'kiðo] *nm* crack; click
chat [tʃat] *nm* (*Internet*) chat room
chatarra [tʃa'tarra] *nf* scrap (metal)
chatear [tʃate'ar] *vi* (*Internet*) to chat
chato, -a ['tʃato, a] *adj* flat; (*nariz*) snub
chaucha ['tʃautʃa] (RPL) *nf* runner (BRIT) *o* pole (US) bean
chaval, a [tʃa'βal, a] (ESP) *nm/f* kid, lad/lass
chavo, -a ['tʃaβo] (MÉX: *fam*) *nm/f* guy/girl
checar [tʃe'kar] (MÉX) *vt*: **~ tarjeta** (*al entrar*) to clock in *o* on; (: *al salir*) to clock off *o* out
checo, -a ['tʃeko, a] *adj, nm/f* Czech ▷ *nm* (*Ling*) Czech
checoslovaco, -a [tʃekoslo'βako, a] *adj, nm/f* Czech, Czechoslovak
Checoslovaquia [tʃekoslo'βakja] *nf* (*Hist*) Czechoslovakia
cheque ['tʃeke] *nm* cheque (BRIT), check (US); **cobrar un ~** to cash a cheque; **cheque al portador** cheque payable to bearer; **cheque de viaje** traveller's cheque (BRIT), traveler's check (US); **cheque en blanco** blank cheque
chequeo [tʃe'keo] *nm* (*Med*) check-up; (*Auto*) service
chequera [tʃe'kera] (LAM) *nf* chequebook (BRIT), checkbook (US)
chévere ['tʃeβere] (LAM: *fam*) *adj* great
chícharo ['tʃitʃaro] (MÉX, CAM) *nm* pea

chichón [tʃi'tʃon] *nm* bump, lump
chicle ['tʃikle] *nm* chewing gum
chico, -a ['tʃiko, a] *adj* small, little ▷*nm/f* (*niño*) child; (*muchacho*) boy/girl
chiflado, -a [tʃi'flaðo, a] *adj* crazy
chiflar [tʃi'flar] *vt* to hiss, boo
chilango, -a [tʃi'lango, a] (MÉX) *adj* of o from Mexico City
Chile ['tʃile] *nm* Chile; **chileno, -a** *adj, nm/f* Chilean
chile ['tʃile] *nm* chilli pepper
chillar [tʃi'ʎar] *vi* (*persona*) to yell, scream; (*animal salvaje*) to howl; (*cerdo*) to squeal
chillido [tʃi'ʎiðo] *nm* (*de persona*) yell, scream; (*de animal*) howl
chimenea [tʃime'nea] *nf* chimney; (*hogar*) fireplace
China ['tʃina] *nf* (*tb*: **la ~**) China
chinche ['tʃintʃe] *nf* (*insecto*) (bed)bug; (*Tec*) drawing pin (BRIT), thumbtack (US) ▷*nmf* nuisance, pest
chincheta [tʃin'tʃeta] *nf* drawing pin (BRIT), thumbtack (US)
chingada [tʃin'gaða] (MÉX: *fam!*) *nf*: **hijo de la ~** bastard
chino, -a ['tʃino, a] *adj, nm/f* Chinese ▷*nm* (*Ling*) Chinese
chipirón [tʃipi'ron] *nm* (*Zool, Culin*) squid
Chipre ['tʃipre] *nf* Cyprus; **chipriota** *adj, nmf* Cypriot
chiquillo, -a [tʃi'kiʎo, a] *nm/f* (*fam*) kid
chirimoya [tʃiri'moja] *nf* custard apple
chiringuito [tʃirin'ɣito] *nm* small open-air bar
chiripa [tʃi'ripa] *nf* fluke
chirriar [tʃi'rrjar] *vi* to creak, squeak
chirrido [tʃi'rriðo] *nm* creak(ing), squeak(ing)
chisme ['tʃisme] *nm* (*habladurías*) piece of gossip; (*fam*: *objeto*) thingummyjig
chismoso, -a [tʃis'moso, a] *adj* gossiping ▷*nm/f* gossip
chispa ['tʃispa] *nf* spark; (*fig*) sparkle; (*ingenio*) wit; (*fam*) drunkenness
chispear [tʃispe'ar] *vi* (*lloviznar*) to drizzle
chiste ['tʃiste] *nm* joke, funny story
chistoso, -a [tʃis'toso, a] *adj* funny, amusing
chivo, -a ['tʃiβo, a] *nm/f* (billy-/nanny-) goat; **chivo expiatorio** scapegoat
chocante [tʃo'kante] *adj* startling; (*extraño*) odd; (*ofensivo*) shocking
chocar [tʃo'kar] *vi* (*coches etc*) to collide, crash ▷*vt* to shock; (*sorprender*) to startle; **~ con** to collide with; (*fig*) to run into, run up against; **¡chócala!** (*fam*) put it there!
chochear [tʃotʃe'ar] *vi* to be senile
chocho, -a ['tʃotʃo, a] *adj* doddering, senile; (*fig*) soft, doting
choclo ['tʃoklo] (CS) *nm* (*grano*) sweet corn; (*mazorca*) corn on the cob
chocolate [tʃoko'late] *adj, nm* chocolate; **chocolatina** *nf* chocolate
chofer [tʃo'fer] *nm* = **chófer**
chófer ['tʃofer] *nm* driver
chollo ['tʃoʎo] (ESP: *fam*) *nm* bargain, snip
choque *etc* ['tʃoke] *vb V* **chocar** ▷*nm* (*impacto*) impact; (*golpe*) jolt; (*Auto*) crash; (*fig*) conflict; **choque frontal** head-on collision
chorizo [tʃo'riθo] *nm* *hard pork sausage*, (type of) salami
chorrada [tʃo'rraða] (ESP: *fam*) *nf*: **¡es una ~!** that's crap! (*!*); **decir ~s** to talk crap (*!*)
chorrear [tʃorre'ar] *vi* to gush (out), spout (out); (*gotear*) to drip, trickle
chorro ['tʃorro] *nm* jet; (*fig*) stream
choza ['tʃoθa] *nf* hut, shack
chubasco [tʃu'βasko] *nm* squall
chubasquero [tʃuβas'kero] *nm* lightweight raincoat
chuchería [tʃutʃe'ria] *nf* trinket
chuleta [tʃu'leta] *nf* chop, cutlet
chulo ['tʃulo] *nm* (*de prostituta*) pimp
chupaleta [tʃupa'leta] (MÉX) *nf* lollipop
chupar [tʃu'par] *vt* to suck; (*absorber*) to absorb; **chuparse** *vr* to grow thin
chupete [tʃu'pete] (ESP, CS) *nm* dummy (BRIT), pacifier (US)
chupetín [tʃupe'tin] (RPL) *nf* lollipop
chupito [tʃu'pito] (*fam*) *nm* shot
chupón [tʃu'pon] *nm* (*piruleta*) lollipop; (LAM: *chupete*) dummy (BRIT), pacifier (US)
churro ['tʃurro] *nm* (type of) fritter
chusma ['tʃusma] *nf* rabble, mob
chutar [tʃu'tar] *vi* to shoot (at goal)
Cía *abr* (= *compañía*) Co.
cianuro [θja'nuro] *nm* cyanide
cibercafé [θiβerka'fe] *nm* cybercafé
cibernauta [θiβer'nauta] *nmf* web surfer, Internet user
ciberterrorista [θiβerterro'rista] *nmf* cyberterrorist
cicatriz [θika'triθ] *nf* scar; **cicatrizarse** *vr* to heal (up), form a scar
ciclismo [θi'klismo] *nm* cycling
ciclista [θi'klista] *adj* cycle *cpd* ▷*nmf* cyclist
ciclo ['θiklo] *nm* cycle; **cicloturismo** *nm* touring by bicycle
ciclón [θi'klon] *nm* cyclone
ciego, -a ['θjeɣo, a] *adj* blind ▷*nm/f* blind man/woman
cielo ['θjelo] *nm* sky; (*Rel*) heaven; **¡~s!** good heavens!
ciempiés [θjem'pjes] *nm inv* centipede

cien [θjen] *num V* **ciento**
ciencia ['θjenθja] *nf* science; **ciencias** *nfpl* (*Escol*) science *sg*; **ciencia-ficción** *nf* science fiction
científico, -a [θjen'tifiko, a] *adj* scientific ▷ *nm/f* scientist
ciento ['θjento] *num* hundred; **pagar al 10 por ~** to pay at 10 per cent; *V tb* **cien**
cierre *etc* ['θjerre] *vb V* **cerrar** ▷ *nm* closing, shutting; (*con llave*) locking; (LAM: *cremallera*) zip (fastener)
cierro *etc vb V* **cerrar**
cierto, -a ['θjerto, a] *adj* sure, certain; (*un tal*) a certain; (*correcto*) right, correct; **por ~** by the way; **~ hombre** a certain man; **ciertas personas** certain *o* some people; **sí, es ~** yes, that's correct
ciervo ['θjerβo] *nm* deer; (*macho*) stag
cifra ['θifra] *nf* number; (*secreta*) code; **cifrar** [θi'frar] *vt* to code, write in code
cigala [θi'ɣala] *nf* Norway lobster
cigarra [θi'ɣarra] *nf* cicada
cigarrillo [θiɣa'rriʎo] *nm* cigarette
cigarro [θi'ɣarro] *nm* cigarette; (*puro*) cigar
cigüeña [θi'ɣweɲa] *nf* stork
cilíndrico, -a [θi'lindriko, a] *adj* cylindrical
cilindro [θi'lindro] *nm* cylinder
cima ['θima] *nf* (*de montaña*) top, peak; (*de árbol*) top; (*fig*) height
cimentar [θimen'tar] *vt* to lay the foundations of; (*fig: fundar*) to found
cimiento [θi'mjento] *nm* foundation
cincel [θin'θel] *nm* chisel
cinco ['θinko] *num* five
cincuenta [θin'kwenta] *num* fifty
cine ['θine] *nm* cinema; **cinematográfico, -a** [θinemato'ɣrafiko, a] *adj* cine-, film *cpd*
cínico, -a ['θiniko, a] *adj* cynical ▷ *nm/f* cynic
cinismo [θi'nismo] *nm* cynicism
cinta ['θinta] *nf* band, strip; (*de tela*) ribbon; (*película*) reel; (*de máquina de escribir*) ribbon; **cinta adhesiva/aislante** sticky/insulating tape; **cinta de vídeo** videotape; **cinta magnetofónica** tape; **cinta métrica** tape measure
cintura [θin'tura] *nf* waist
cinturón [θintu'ron] *nm* belt; **cinturón de seguridad** safety belt
ciprés [θi'pres] *nm* cypress (tree)
circo ['θirko] *nm* circus
circuito [θir'kwito] *nm* circuit
circulación [θirkula'θjon] *nf* circulation; (*Auto*) traffic
circular [θirku'lar] *adj, nf* circular ▷ *vi, vt* to circulate ▷ *vi* (*Auto*) to drive; **"circule por la derecha"** "keep (to the) right"
círculo ['θirkulo] *nm* circle; **círculo vicioso** vicious circle
circunferencia [θirkunfe'renθja] *nf* circumference
circunstancia [θirkuns'tanθja] *nf* circumstance
cirio ['θirjo] *nm* (wax) candle
ciruela [θi'rwela] *nf* plum; **ciruela pasa** prune
cirugía [θiru'xia] *nf* surgery; **cirugía estética** *o* **plástica** plastic surgery
cirujano [θiru'xano] *nm* surgeon
cisne ['θisne] *nm* swan
cisterna [θis'terna] *nf* cistern, tank
cita ['θita] *nf* appointment, meeting; (*de novios*) date; (*referencia*) quotation
citación [θita'θjon] *nf* (*Jur*) summons *sg*
citar [θi'tar] *vt* (*gen*) to make an appointment with; (*Jur*) to summons; (*un autor, texto*) to quote; **citarse** *vr*: **se ~on en el cine** they arranged to meet at the cinema
cítricos ['θitrikos] *nmpl* citrus fruit(s)
ciudad [θju'ðað] *nf* town; (*más grande*) city; **ciudadano, -a** *nm/f* citizen
cívico, -a ['θiβiko, a] *adj* civic
civil [θi'βil] *adj* civil ▷ *nm* (*guardia*) policeman; **civilización** [θiβiliθa'θjon] *nf* civilization; **civilizar** [θiβili'θar] *vt* to civilize
cizaña [θi'θaɲa] *nf* (*fig*) discord
cl. *abr* (= *centilitro*) cl.
clamor [kla'mor] *nm* clamour, protest
clandestino, -a [klandes'tino, a] *adj* clandestine; (*Pol*) underground
clara ['klara] *nf* (*de huevo*) egg white
claraboya [klara'βoja] *nf* skylight
clarear [klare'ar] *vi* (*el día*) to dawn; (*el cielo*) to clear up, brighten up; **clarearse** *vr* to be transparent
claridad [klari'ðað] *nf* (*de día*) brightness; (*de estilo*) clarity
clarificar [klarifi'kar] *vt* to clarify
clarinete [klari'nete] *nm* clarinet
claro, -a ['klaro, a] *adj* clear; (*luminoso*) bright; (*color*) light; (*evidente*) clear, evident; (*poco espeso*) thin ▷ *nm* (*en bosque*) clearing ▷ *adv* clearly ▷ *excl*: **¡~ que sí!** of course!; **¡~ que no!** of course not!
clase ['klase] *nf* class; **dar ~(s)** to teach; **clase alta/media/obrera** upper/middle/working class; **clases particulares** private lessons *o* tuition *sg*
clásico, -a ['klasiko, a] *adj* classical
clasificación [klasifika'θjon] *nf* classification; (*Deporte*) league (table)
clasificar [klasifi'kar] *vt* to classify
claustro ['klaustro] *nm* cloister

C

cláusula ['klausula] *nf* clause
clausura [klau'sura] *nf* closing, closure
clavar [kla'βar] *vt* (*clavo*) to hammer in; (*cuchillo*) to stick, thrust
clave ['klaβe] *nf* key; (*Mús*) clef; **clave de acceso** password; **clave lada** (MÉX) dialling (BRIT) *o* area (US) code
clavel [kla'βel] *nm* carnation
clavícula [kla'βikula] *nf* collar bone
clavija [kla'βixa] *nf* peg, dowel, pin; (*Elec*) plug
clavo ['klaβo] *nm* (*de metal*) nail; (*Bot*) clove
claxon ['klakson] (*pl* **~s**) *nm* horn
clérigo ['kleriɣo] *nm* priest
clero ['klero] *nm* clergy
clicar [kli'kar] *vi* (*Internet*) to click; **~ en el icono** to click on an icon; **~ dos veces** to double-click
cliché [kli'tʃe] *nm* cliché; (*Foto*) negative
cliente, -a ['kljente, a] *nm/f* client, customer; **clientela** [kljen'tela] *nf* clientele, customers *pl*
clima ['klima] *nm* climate; **climatizado, -a** [klimati'θaðo, a] *adj* air-conditioned
clímax ['klimaks] *nm inv* climax
clínica ['klinika] *nf* clinic; (*particular*) private hospital
clip [klip] (*pl* **~s**) *nm* paper clip
clítoris ['klitoris] *nm inv* (*Anat*) clitoris
cloaca [klo'aka] *nf* sewer
clonar [klo'nar] *vt* to clone
cloro ['kloro] *nm* chlorine
clóset ['kloset] (MÉX) *nm* cupboard
club [klub] (*pl* **~s** *o* **~es**) *nm* club; **club nocturno** night club
cm *abr* (= *centímetro, centímetros*) cm
coágulo [ko'aɣulo] *nm* clot
coalición [koali'θjon] *nf* coalition
coartada [koar'taða] *nf* alibi
coartar [koar'tar] *vt* to limit, restrict
coba ['koβa] *nf*: **dar ~ a algn** (*adular*) to suck up to sb
cobarde [ko'βarðe] *adj* cowardly ▷ *nm* coward; **cobardía** *nf* cowardice
cobaya [ko'βaja] *nf* guinea pig
cobertizo [koβer'tiθo] *nm* shelter
cobertura [koβer'tura] *nf* cover; **aquí no hay ~** (*Tel*) I can't get a signal
cobija [ko'βixa] (LAM) *nf* blanket; **cobijar** [koβi'xar] *vt* (*cubrir*) to cover; (*proteger*) to shelter; **cobijo** *nm* shelter
cobra ['koβra] *nf* cobra
cobrador, a [koβra'ðor, a] *nm/f* (*de autobús*) conductor/conductress; (*de impuestos, gas*) collector
cobrar [ko'βrar] *vt* (*cheque*) to cash; (*sueldo*) to collect, draw; (*objeto*) to recover; (*precio*) to charge; (*deuda*) to collect ▷ *vi* to be paid; **cóbrese al entregar** cash on delivery; **¿me cobra, por favor?** how much do I owe you?, can I have the bill, please?
cobre ['koβre] *nm* copper; **cobres** *nmpl* (*Mús*) brass instruments
cobro ['koβro] *nm* (*de cheque*) cashing; **presentar al ~** to cash
cocaína [koka'ina] *nf* cocaine
cocción [kok'θjon] *nf* (*Culin*) cooking; (*en agua*) boiling
cocer [ko'θer] *vt, vi* to cook; (*en agua*) to boil; (*en horno*) to bake
coche ['kotʃe] *nm* (*Auto*) car (BRIT), automobile (US); (*de tren, de caballos*) coach, carriage; (*para niños*) pram (BRIT), baby carriage (US); **ir en ~** to drive; **coche celular** police van; **coche de bomberos** fire engine; **coche de carreras** racing car; **coche fúnebre** hearse; **coche-cama** (*pl* **coches-cama**) *nm* (*Ferro*) sleeping car, sleeper
cochera [ko'tʃera] *nf* garage; (*de autobuses, trenes*) depot
coche restaurante (*pl* **coches restaurante**) *nm* (*Ferro*) dining car, diner
cochinillo [kotʃi'niʎo] *nm* (*Culin*) suckling pig, sucking pig
cochino, -a [ko'tʃino, a] *adj* filthy, dirty ▷ *nm/f* pig
cocido [ko'θiðo] *nm* stew
cocina [ko'θina] *nf* kitchen; (*aparato*) cooker, stove; (*acto*) cookery; **cocina eléctrica/de gas** electric/gas cooker; **cocina francesa** French cuisine; **cocinar** *vt, vi* to cook
cocinero, -a [koθi'nero, a] *nm/f* cook
coco ['koko] *nm* coconut
cocodrilo [koko'ðrilo] *nm* crocodile
cocotero [koko'tero] *nm* coconut palm
cóctel ['koktel] *nm* cocktail; **cóctel molotov** petrol bomb, Molotov cocktail
codazo [ko'ðaθo] *nm*: **dar un ~ a algn** to nudge sb
codicia [ko'ðiθja] *nf* greed; **codiciar** *vt* to covet
código ['koðiɣo] *nm* code; **código civil** common law; **código de barras** bar code; **código de circulación** highway code; **código de la zona** (LAM) dialling (BRIT) *o* area (US) code; **código postal** postcode
codillo [ko'ðiʎo] *nm* (*Zool*) knee; (*Tec*) elbow (joint)
codo ['koðo] *nm* (*Anat, de tubo*) elbow; (*Zool*) knee
codorniz [koðor'niθ] *nf* quail
coexistir [koe(k)sis'tir] *vi* to coexist
cofradía [kofra'ðia] *nf* brotherhood, fraternity
cofre ['kofre] *nm* (*de joyas*) case; (*de dinero*)

chest
coger [ko'xer] (ESP) *vt* to take (hold of); (*objeto caído*) to pick up; (*frutas*) to pick, harvest; (*resfriado, ladrón, pelota*) to catch ▷ *vi*: **~ por el buen camino** to take the right road; **cogerse** *vr* (*el dedo*) to catch; **~se a algo** to get hold of sth
cogollo [ko'ɣoʎo] *nm* (*de lechuga*) heart
cogote [ko'ɣote] *nm* back *o* nape of the neck
cohabitar [koaβi'tar] *vi* to live together, cohabit
coherente [koe'rente] *adj* coherent
cohesión [koe'sjon] *nm* cohesion
cohete [ko'ete] *nm* rocket
cohibido, -a [koi'βiðo, a] *adj* (*Psico*) inhibited; (*tímido*) shy
coincidencia [koinθi'ðenθja] *nf* coincidence
coincidir [koinθi'ðir] *vi* (*en idea*) to coincide, agree; (*en lugar*) to coincide
coito ['koito] *nm* intercourse, coitus
coja *etc vb V* **coger**
cojear [koxe'ar] *vi* (*persona*) to limp, hobble; (*mueble*) to wobble, rock
cojera [ko'xera] *nf* limp
cojín [ko'xin] *nm* cushion
cojo, -a *etc* ['koxo, a] *vb V* **coger** ▷ *adj* (*que no puede andar*) lame, crippled; (*mueble*) wobbly ▷ *nm/f* lame person, cripple
cojón [ko'xon] (*fam!*) *nm*: **¡cojones!** shit! (*!*); **cojonudo, -a** (*fam*) *adj* great, fantastic
col [kol] *nf* cabbage; **coles de Bruselas** Brussels sprouts
cola ['kola] *nf* tail; (*de gente*) queue; (*lugar*) end, last place; (*para pegar*) glue, gum; **hacer ~** to queue (up)
colaborador, a [kolaβora'ðor, a] *nm/f* collaborator
colaborar [kolaβo'rar] *vi* to collaborate
colada [ko'laða] (ESP) *nf*: **hacer la ~** to do the washing
colador [kola'ðor] *nm* (*para líquidos*) strainer; (*para verduras etc*) colander
colapso [ko'lapso] *nm* collapse
colar [ko'lar] *vt* (*líquido*) to strain off; (*metal*) to cast ▷ *vi* to ooze, seep (through); **colarse** *vr* to jump the queue; **~se en** to get into without paying; (*fiesta*) to gatecrash
colcha ['koltʃa] *nf* bedspread
colchón [kol'tʃon] *nm* mattress; **colchón inflable** air bed *o* mattress
colchoneta [koltʃo'neta] *nf* (*en gimnasio*) mat; (*de playa*) air bed
colección [kolek'θjon] *nf* collection; **coleccionar** *vt* to collect; **coleccionista** *nmf* collector
colecta [ko'lekta] *nf* collection
colectivo, -a [kolek'tiβo, a] *adj* collective, joint ▷ *nm* (ARG: *autobús*) (small) bus
colega [ko'leɣa] *nmf* colleague; (ESP: *amigo*) mate
colegial, a [kole'xjal, a] *nm/f* schoolboy(-girl)
colegio [ko'lexjo] *nm* college; (*escuela*) school; (*de abogados etc*) association; **colegio electoral** polling station; **colegio mayor** (ESP) hall of residence

COLEGIO

A **colegio** is normally a private primary or secondary school. In the state system it means a primary school although these are also called **escuelas**. State secondary schools are called **institutos**.

cólera ['kolera] *nf* (*ira*) anger; (*Med*) cholera
colesterol [koleste'rol] *nm* cholesterol
coleta [ko'leta] *nf* pigtail
colgante [kol'ɣante] *adj* hanging ▷ *nm* (*joya*) pendant
colgar [kol'ɣar] *vt* to hang (up); (*ropa*) to hang out ▷ *vi* to hang; (*Tel*) to hang up
cólico ['koliko] *nm* colic
coliflor [koli'flor] *nf* cauliflower
colilla [ko'liʎa] *nf* cigarette end, butt
colina [ko'lina] *nf* hill
colisión [koli'sjon] *nf* collision; **colisión frontal** head-on crash
collar [ko'ʎar] *nm* necklace; (*de perro*) collar
colmar [kol'mar] *vt* to fill to the brim; (*fig*) to fulfil, realize
colmena [kol'mena] *nf* beehive
colmillo [kol'miʎo] *nm* (*diente*) eye tooth; (*de elefante*) tusk; (*de perro*) fang
colmo ['kolmo] *nm*: **¡es el ~!** it's the limit!
colocación [koloka'θjon] *nf* (*acto*) placing; (*empleo*) job, position
colocar [kolo'kar] *vt* to place, put, position; (*dinero*) to invest; (*poner en empleo*) to find a job for; **colocarse** *vr* to get a job
Colombia [ko'lombja] *nf* Colombia; **colombiano, -a** *adj, nm/f* Colombian
colonia [ko'lonja] *nf* colony; (*agua de colonia*) cologne; (MÉX: *de casas*) residential area; **colonia proletaria** (MÉX) shantytown
colonización [koloniθa'θjon] *nf* colonization; **colonizador, a** [koloniθa'ðor, a] *adj* colonizing ▷ *nm/f* colonist, settler
colonizar [koloni'θar] *vt* to colonize
coloquio [ko'lokjo] *nm* conversation; (*congreso*) conference

color [ko'lor] *nm* colour
colorado, -a [kolo'raðo, a] *adj* (*rojo*) red; (*MÉX: chiste*) smutty, rude
colorante [kolo'rante] *nm* colouring
colorear [kolore'ar] *vt* to colour
colorete [kolo'rete] *nm* blusher
colorido [kolo'riðo] *nm* colouring
columna [ko'lumna] *nf* column; (*pilar*) pillar; (*apoyo*) support; (*tb*: **~ vertebral**) spine, spinal column; (*fig*) backbone
columpiar [kolum'pjar] *vt* to swing; **columpiarse** *vr* to swing; **columpio** *nm* swing
coma ['koma] *nf* comma ▷ *nm* (*Med*) coma
comadre [ko'maðre] *nf* (*madrina*) godmother; (*chismosa*) gossip; **comadrona** *nf* midwife
comal [ko'mal] (*MÉX, CAM*) *nm* griddle
comandante [koman'dante] *nm* commandant
comarca [ko'marka] *nf* region
comba ['komba] (*ESP*) *nf* (*cuerda*) skipping rope; **saltar a la ~** to skip
combate [kom'bate] *nm* fight
combatir [komba'tir] *vt* to fight, combat
combinación [kombina'θjon] *nf* combination; (*Quím*) compound; (*prenda*) slip
combinar [kombi'nar] *vt* to combine
combustible [kombus'tiβle] *nm* fuel
comedia [ko'meðja] *nf* comedy; (*Teatro*) play, drama; **comediante** [kome'ðjante] *nmf* (comic) actor/actress
comedido, -a [kome'ðiðo, a] *adj* moderate
comedor, a [kome'ðor, a] *nm* (*habitación*) dining room; (*cantina*) canteen
comensal [komen'sal] *nmf* fellow guest (*o* diner)
comentar [komen'tar] *vt* to comment on; **comentario** [komen'tarjo] *nm* comment, remark; (*literario*) commentary; **comentarios** *nmpl* (*chismes*) gossip *sg*; **comentarista** [komenta'rista] *nmf* commentator
comenzar [komen'θar] *vt, vi* to begin, start; **~ a hacer algo** to begin *o* start doing sth
comer [ko'mer] *vt* to eat; (*Damas, Ajedrez*) to take, capture ▷ *vi* to eat; (*ESP, MÉX: almorzar*) to have lunch; **comerse** *vr* to eat up
comercial [komer'θjal] *adj* commercial; (*relativo al negocio*) business *cpd*; **comercializar** *vt* (*producto*) to market; (*pey*) to commercialize
comerciante [komer'θjante] *nmf* trader, merchant
comerciar [komer'θjar] *vi* to trade, do business
comercio [ko'merθjo] *nm* commerce, trade; (*tienda*) shop, store; (*negocio*) business; (*fig*) dealings *pl*; **comercio electrónico** e-commerce; **comercio exterior/interior** foreign/domestic trade
comestible [komes'tiβle] *adj* eatable, edible; **comestibles** *nmpl* food *sg*, foodstuffs
cometa [ko'meta] *nm* comet ▷ *nf* kite
cometer [kome'ter] *vt* to commit
cometido [kome'tiðo] *nm* task, assignment
cómic ['komik] *nm* comic
comicios [ko'miθjos] *nmpl* elections
cómico, -a ['komiko, a] *adj* comic(al) ▷ *nm/f* comedian
comida [ko'miða] *nf* (*alimento*) food; (*almuerzo, cena*) meal; (*de mediodía*) lunch; **comida basura** junk food; **comida chatarra** (*MÉX*) junk food
comidilla [komi'ðiʎa] *nf*: **ser la ~ del barrio** *o* **pueblo** to be the talk of the town
comienzo *etc* [ko'mjenθo] *vb V* **comenzar** ▷ *nm* beginning, start
comillas [ko'miʎas] *nfpl* quotation marks
comilona [komi'lona] (*fam*) *nf* blow-out
comino [ko'mino] *nm*: **(no) me importa un ~** I don't give a damn
comisaría [komisa'ria] *nf* (*de policía*) police station; (*Mil*) commissariat
comisario [komi'sarjo] *nm* (*Mil etc*) commissary; (*Pol*) commissar
comisión [komi'sjon] *nf* commission; **Comisiones Obreras** (*ESP*) Communist trade union
comité [komi'te] (*pl* **~s**) *nm* committee
comitiva [komi'tiβa] *nf* retinue
como ['komo] *adv* as; (*tal* **~**) like; (*aproximadamente*) about, approximately ▷ *conj* (*ya que, puesto que*) as, since; **¡~ no!** of course!; **~ no lo haga hoy** unless he does it today; **~ si** as if; **es tan alto ~ ancho** it is as high as it is wide
cómo ['komo] *adv* how?, why? ▷ *excl* what?, I beg your pardon? ▷ *nm*: **el ~ y el porqué** the whys and wherefores
cómoda ['komoða] *nf* chest of drawers
comodidad [komoði'ðað] *nf* comfort
comodín [komo'ðin] *nm* joker
cómodo, -a ['komoðo, a] *adj* comfortable; (*práctico, de fácil uso*) convenient
compact [kom'pakt] (*pl* **~s**) *nm* (*tb*: **~ disc**) compact disk player
compacto, -a [kom'pakto, a] *adj*

compact
compadecer [kompaðe'θer] *vt* to pity, be sorry for; **compadecerse** *vr*: **~se de** to pity, be *o* feel sorry for
compadre [kom'paðre] *nm* (*padrino*) godfather; (*amigo*) friend, pal
compañero, -a [kompa'ɲero, a] *nm/f* companion; (*novio*) boy/girlfriend; **compañero de clase** classmate
compañía [kompa'ɲia] *nf* company; **hacer ~ a algn** to keep sb company
comparación [kompara'θjon] *nf* comparison; **en ~ con** in comparison with
comparar [kompa'rar] *vt* to compare
comparecer [kompare'θer] *vi* to appear (in court)
comparsa [kom'parsa] *nmf* (*Teatro*) extra
compartimiento [komparti'mjento] *nm* (*Ferro*) compartment
compartir [kompar'tir] *vt* to share; (*dinero, comida etc*) to divide (up), share (out)
compás [kom'pas] *nm* (*Mús*) beat, rhythm; (*Mat*) compasses *pl*; (*Náut etc*) compass
compasión [kompa'sjon] *nf* compassion, pity
compasivo, -a [kompa'siβo, a] *adj* compassionate
compatible [kompa'tiβle] *adj* compatible
compatriota [kompa'trjota] *nmf* compatriot, fellow countryman/woman
compenetrarse [kompene'trarse] *vr* to be in tune
compensación [kompensa'θjon] *nf* compensation
compensar [kompen'sar] *vt* to compensate
competencia [kompe'tenθja] *nf* (*incumbencia*) domain, field; (*Jur, habilidad*) competence; (*rivalidad*) competition
competente [kompe'tente] *adj* competent
competición [kompeti'θjon] *nf* competition
competir [kompe'tir] *vi* to compete
compinche [kom'pintʃe] (LAM) *nmf* mate, buddy (US)
complacer [kompla'θer] *vt* to please; **complacerse** *vr* to be pleased
complaciente [kompla'θjente] *adj* kind, obliging, helpful
complejo, -a [kom'plexo, a] *adj, nm* complex
complementario, -a [komplemen'tarjo, a] *adj* complementary
completar [komple'tar] *vt* to complete
completo, -a [kom'pleto, a] *adj* complete; (*perfecto*) perfect; (*lleno*) full ▷ *nm* full complement
complicado, -a [kompli'kaðo, a] *adj* complicated; **estar ~ en** to be mixed up in
cómplice ['kompliθe] *nmf* accomplice
complot [kom'plo(t)] (*pl* **~s**) *nm* plot
componer [kompo'ner] *vt* (*Mús, Literatura, Imprenta*) to compose; (*algo roto*) to mend, repair; (*arreglar*) to arrange; **componerse** *vr*: **~se de** to consist of
comportamiento [komporta'mjento] *nm* behaviour, conduct
comportarse [kompor'tarse] *vr* to behave
composición [komposi'θjon] *nf* composition
compositor, a [komposi'tor, a] *nm/f* composer
compostura [kompos'tura] *nf* (*actitud*) composure
compra ['kompra] *nf* purchase; **hacer la ~** to do the shopping; **ir de ~s** to go shopping; **comprador, a** *nm/f* buyer, purchaser; **comprar** [kom'prar] *vt* to buy, purchase
comprender [kompren'der] *vt* to understand; (*incluir*) to comprise, include
comprensión [kompren'sjon] *nf* understanding; **comprensivo, -a** *adj* (*actitud*) understanding
compresa [kom'presa] *nf* (*para mujer*) sanitary towel (BRIT) *o* napkin (US)
comprimido, -a [kompri'miðo, a] *adj* compressed ▷ *nm* (*Med*) pill, tablet
comprimir [kompri'mir] *vt* to compress; (*Internet*) to zip
comprobante [kompro'βante] *nm* proof; (*Com*) voucher; **comprobante de compra** proof of purchase
comprobar [kompro'βar] *vt* to check; (*probar*) to prove; (*Tec*) to check, test
comprometer [komprome'ter] *vt* to compromise; (*poner en peligro*) to endanger; **comprometerse** *vr* (*involucrarse*) to get involved
compromiso [kompro'miso] *nm* (*obligación*) obligation; (*cometido*) commitment; (*convenio*) agreement; (*apuro*) awkward situation
compuesto, -a [kom'pwesto, a] *adj*: **~ de** composed of, made up of ▷ *nm* compound
computadora [komputa'ðora] (LAM) *nf* computer; **computadora central** mainframe (computer); **computadora personal** personal computer
cómputo ['komputo] *nm* calculation
comulgar [komul'ɣar] *vi* to receive communion
común [ko'mun] *adj* common ▷ *nm*: **el ~** the community

C

comunicación [komunika'θjon] *nf* communication; (*informe*) report
comunicado [komuni'kado] *nm* announcement; **comunicado de prensa** press release
comunicar [komuni'kar] *vt, vi* to communicate; **comunicarse** *vr* to communicate; **está comunicando** (*Tel*) the line's engaged (BRIT) *o* busy (US); **comunicativo, -a** *adj* communicative
comunidad [komuni'ðað] *nf* community; **comunidad autónoma** (ESP) autonomous region; **Comunidad (Económica) Europea** European (Economic) Community; **comunidad de vecinos** residents' association
comunión [komu'njon] *nf* communion
comunismo [komu'nismo] *nm* communism; **comunista** *adj, nmf* communist

PALABRA CLAVE

con [kon] *prep* **1** (*medio, compañía*) with; **comer con cuchara** to eat with a spoon; **pasear con algn** to go for a walk with sb
2 (*a pesar de*): **con todo, merece nuestros respetos** all the same, he deserves our respect
3 (*para con*): **es muy bueno para con los niños** he's very good with (the) children
4 (*+ infin*): **con llegar a las seis estará bien** if you come by six it will be fine ▷ *conj*: **con que: será suficiente con que le escribas** it will be sufficient if you write to her

concebir [konθe'βir] *vt, vi* to conceive
conceder [konθe'ðer] *vt* to concede
concejal, a [konθe'xal, a] *nm/f* town councillor
concentración [konθentra'θjon] *nf* concentration
concentrar [konθen'trar] *vt* to concentrate; **concentrarse** *vr* to concentrate
concepto [kon'θepto] *nm* concept
concernir [konθer'nir] *vi* to concern; **en lo que concierne a ...** as far as ... is concerned; **en lo que a mí concierne** as far as I'm concerned
concertar [konθer'tar] *vt* (*Mús*) to harmonize; (*acordar: precio*) to agree; (*: tratado*) to conclude; (*trato*) to arrange, fix up; (*combinar: esfuerzos*) to coordinate ▷ *vi* to harmonize, be in tune
concesión [konθe'sjon] *nf* concession
concesionario [konθesjo'narjo] *nm* (licensed) dealer, agent
concha ['kontʃa] *nf* shell
conciencia [kon'θjenθja] *nf* conscience; **tomar ~ de** to become aware of; **tener la ~ tranquila** to have a clear conscience
concienciar [konθjen'θjar] *vt* to make aware; **concienciarse** *vr* to become aware
concienzudo, -a [konθjen'θuðo, a] *adj* conscientious
concierto *etc* [kon'θjerto] *vb V* **concertar** ▷ *nm* concert; (*obra*) concerto
conciliar [konθi'ljar] *vt* to reconcile; **~ el sueño** to get to sleep
concilio [kon'θiljo] *nm* council
conciso, -a [kon'θiso, a] *adj* concise
concluir [konklu'ir] *vt, vi* to conclude; **concluirse** *vr* to conclude
conclusión [konklu'sjon] *nf* conclusion
concordar [konkor'ðar] *vt* to reconcile ▷ *vi* to agree, tally
concordia [kon'korðja] *nf* harmony
concretar [konkre'tar] *vt* to make concrete, make more specific; **concretarse** *vr* to become more definite
concreto, -a [kon'kreto, a] *adj, nm* (LAM: *hormigón*) concrete; **en ~** (*en resumen*) to sum up; (*específicamente*) specifically; **no hay nada en ~** there's nothing definite
concurrido, -a [konku'rriðo, a] *adj* (*calle*) busy; (*local, reunión*) crowded
concursante [konkur'sante] *nmf* competitor
concurso [kon'kurso] *nm* (*de público*) crowd; (*Escol, Deporte, competencia*) competition; (*ayuda*) help, cooperation
condal [kon'dal] *adj*: **la Ciudad C~** Barcelona
conde ['konde] *nm* count
condecoración [kondekora'θjon] *nf* (*Mil*) medal
condena [kon'dena] *nf* sentence; **condenación** [kondena'θjon] *nf* condemnation; (*Rel*) damnation; **condenar** [konde'nar] *vt* to condemn; (*Jur*) to convict; **condenarse** *vr* (*Rel*) to be damned
condesa [kon'desa] *nf* countess
condición [kondi'θjon] *nf* condition; **a ~ de que ...** on condition that ...; **condicional** *adj* conditional
condimento [kondi'mento] *nm* seasoning
condominio [kondo'minjo] (LAM) *nm* condominium
condón [kon'don] *nm* condom
conducir [kondu'θir] *vt* to take, convey; (*Auto*) to drive ▷ *vi* to drive; (*fig*) to lead; **conducirse** *vr* to behave
conducta [kon'dukta] *nf* conduct,

behaviour
conducto [kon'dukto] *nm* pipe, tube; (*fig*) channel
conductor, a [konduk'tor, a] *adj* leading, guiding ▷ *nm* (*Física*) conductor; (*de vehículo*) driver
conduje *etc vb V* **conducir**
conduzco *etc vb V* **conducir**
conectado, -a [konek'taðo, a] *adj* (*Inform*) on-line
conectar [konek'tar] *vt* to connect (up); (*enchufar*) plug in
conejillo [kone'xiʎo] *nm*: **~ de Indias** guinea pig
conejo [ko'nexo] *nm* rabbit
conexión [konek'sjon] *nf* connection
confección [confe(k)'θjon] *nf* preparation; (*industria*) clothing industry
confeccionar [konfekθjo'nar] *vt* to make (up)
conferencia [konfe'renθja] *nf* conference; (*lección*) lecture; (ESP *Tel*) call; **conferencia de prensa** press conference
conferir [konfe'rir] *vt* to award
confesar [konfe'sar] *vt* to confess, admit
confesión [konfe'sjon] *nf* confession
confesionario [konfesjo'narjo] *nm* confessional
confeti [kon'feti] *nm* confetti
confiado, -a [kon'fjaðo, a] *adj* (*crédulo*) trusting; (*seguro*) confident
confianza [kon'fjanθa] *nf* trust; (*seguridad*) confidence; (*familiaridad*) intimacy, familiarity
confiar [kon'fjar] *vt* to entrust ▷ *vi* to trust; **~ en algn** to trust sb; **~ en que ...** to hope that ...
confidencial [konfiðen'θjal] *adj* confidential
confidente [konfi'ðente] *nmf* confidant/e; (*policial*) informer
configurar [konfiɣu'rar] *vt* to shape, form
confín [kon'fin] *nm* limit; **confines** *nmpl* confines, limits
confirmar [konfir'mar] *vt* to confirm
confiscar [konfis'kar] *vt* to confiscate
confite [kon'fite] *nm* sweet (BRIT), candy (US); **confitería** [konfite'ria] *nf* (*tienda*) confectioner's (shop)
confitura [konfi'tura] *nf* jam
conflictivo, -a [konflik'tiβo, a] *adj* (*asunto, propuesta*) controversial; (*país, situación*) troubled
conflicto [kon'flikto] *nm* conflict; (*fig*) clash
confluir [kon'flwir] *vi* (*ríos*) to meet; (*gente*) to gather
conformar [konfor'mar] *vt* to shape, fashion ▷ *vi* to agree; **conformarse** *vr* to conform; (*resignarse*) to resign o.s.; **~se con algo** to be happy with sth
conforme [kon'forme] *adj* (*correspondiente*): **~ con** in line with; (*de acuerdo*): **estar ~s (con algo)** to be in agreement (with sth) ▷ *adv* as ▷ *excl* agreed! ▷ *prep*: **~ a** in accordance with; **quedarse ~ (con algo)** to be satisfied (with sth)
confortable [konfor'taβle] *adj* comfortable
confortar [konfor'tar] *vt* to comfort
confrontar [konfron'tar] *vt* to confront; (*dos personas*) to bring face to face; (*cotejar*) to compare
confundir [konfun'dir] *vt* (*equivocar*) to mistake, confuse; (*turbar*) to confuse; **confundirse** *vr* (*turbarse*) to get confused; (*equivocarse*) to make a mistake; (*mezclarse*) to mix
confusión [konfu'sjon] *nf* confusion
confuso, -a [kon'fuso, a] *adj* confused
congelado, -a [konxe'laðo, a] *adj* frozen; **congelados** *nmpl* frozen food(s); **congelador** *nm* (*aparato*) freezer, deep freeze
congelar [konxe'lar] *vt* to freeze; **congelarse** *vr* (*sangre, grasa*) to congeal
congeniar [konxe'njar] *vi* to get on (BRIT) *o* along (US) well
congestión [konxes'tjon] *nf* congestion
congestionar [konxestjo'nar] *vt* to congest
congraciarse [kongra'θjarse] *vr* to ingratiate o.s.
congratular [kongratu'lar] *vt* to congratulate
congregar [kongre'ɣar] *vt* to gather together; **congregarse** *vr* to gather together
congresista [kongre'sista] *nmf* delegate, congressman/woman
congreso [kon'greso] *nm* congress
conjetura [konxe'tura] *nf* guess; **conjeturar** *vt* to guess
conjugar [konxu'ɣar] *vt* to combine, fit together; (*Ling*) to conjugate
conjunción [konxun'θjon] *nf* conjunction
conjunto, -a [kon'xunto, a] *adj* joint, united ▷ *nm* whole; (*Mús*) band; **en ~** as a whole
conmemoración [konmemora'θjon] *nf* commemoration
conmemorar [konmemo'rar] *vt* to commemorate

C

conmigo [kon'miɣo] *pron* with me
conmoción [konmo'θjon] *nf* shock; (*fig*) upheaval; **conmoción cerebral** (*Med*) concussion
conmovedor, a [konmoβe'ðor, a] *adj* touching, moving; (*emocionante*) exciting
conmover [konmo'βer] *vt* to shake, disturb; (*fig*) to move
conmutador [konmuta'ðor] *nm* switch; (LAM: *centralita*) switchboard; (: *central*) telephone exchange
cono ['kono] *nm* cone; **Cono Sur** Southern Cone
conocedor, a [konoθe'ðor, a] *adj* expert, knowledgeable ▷ *nm/f* expert
conocer [kono'θer] *vt* to know; (*por primera vez*) to meet, get to know; (*entender*) to know about; (*reconocer*) to recognize; **conocerse** *vr* (*una persona*) to know o.s.; (*dos personas*) to (get to) know each other; **~ a algn de vista** to know sb by sight
conocido, -a [kono'θiðo, a] *adj* (well-) known ▷ *nm/f* acquaintance
conocimiento [konoθi'mjento] *nm* knowledge; (*Med*) consciousness; **conocimientos** *nmpl* (*saber*) knowledge *sg*
conozco *etc vb V* **conocer**
conque ['konke] *conj* and so, so then
conquista [kon'kista] *nf* conquest; **conquistador, a** *adj* conquering ▷ *nm* conqueror; **conquistar** [konkis'tar] *vt* to conquer
consagrar [konsa'ɣrar] *vt* (*Rel*) to consecrate; (*fig*) to devote
consciente [kons'θjente] *adj* conscious
consecución [konseku'θjon] *nf* acquisition; (*de fin*) attainment
consecuencia [konse'kwenθja] *nf* consequence, outcome; (*coherencia*) consistency
consecuente [konse'kwente] *adj* consistent
consecutivo, -a [konseku'tiβo, a] *adj* consecutive
conseguir [konse'ɣir] *vt* to get, obtain; (*objetivo*) to attain
consejero, -a [konse'xero, a] *nm/f* adviser, consultant; (*Pol*) councillor
consejo [kon'sexo] *nm* advice; (*Pol*) council; **consejo de administración** (*Com*) board of directors; **consejo de guerra** court martial; **consejo de ministros** cabinet meeting
consenso [kon'senso] *nm* consensus
consentimiento [konsenti'mjento] *nm* consent
consentir [konsen'tir] *vt* (*permitir, tolerar*) to consent to; (*mimar*) to pamper, spoil; (*aguantar*) to put up with ▷ *vi* to agree, consent; **~ que algn haga algo** to allow sb to do sth
conserje [kon'serxe] *nm* caretaker; (*portero*) porter
conservación [konserβa'θjon] *nf* conservation; (*de alimentos, vida*) preservation
conservador, a [konserβa'ðor, a] *adj* (*Pol*) conservative ▷ *nm/f* conservative
conservante [konser'βante] *nm* preservative
conservar [konser'βar] *vt* to conserve, keep; (*alimentos, vida*) to preserve; **conservarse** *vr* to survive
conservas [kon'serβas] *nfpl* canned food(s) *pl*
conservatorio [konserβa'torjo] *nm* (*Mús*) conservatoire, conservatory
considerable [konsiðe'raβle] *adj* considerable
consideración [konsiðera'θjon] *nf* consideration; (*estimación*) respect
considerado, -a [konsiðe'raðo, a] *adj* (*atento*) considerate; (*respetado*) respected
considerar [konsiðe'rar] *vt* to consider
consigna [kon'siɣna] *nf* (*orden*) order, instruction; (*para equipajes*) left-luggage office
consigo *etc* [kon'siɣo] *vb V* **conseguir** ▷ *pron* (*m*) with him; (*f*) with her; (*Vd*) with you; (*reflexivo*) with o.s.
consiguiendo *etc vb V* **conseguir**
consiguiente [konsi'ɣjente] *adj* consequent; **por ~** and so, therefore, consequently
consistente [konsis'tente] *adj* consistent; (*sólido*) solid, firm; (*válido*) sound
consistir [konsis'tir] *vi*: **~ en** (*componerse de*) to consist of
consola [kon'sola] *nf* (*mueble*) console table; (*de videojuegos*) console
consolación [konsola'θjon] *nf* consolation
consolar [konso'lar] *vt* to console
consolidar [konsoli'ðar] *vt* to consolidate
consomé [konso'me] (*pl* **~s**) *nm* consommé, clear soup
consonante [konso'nante] *adj* consonant, harmonious ▷ *nf* consonant
consorcio [kon'sorθjo] *nm* consortium
conspiración [konspira'θjon] *nf* conspiracy
conspirar [konspi'rar] *vi* to conspire
constancia [kon'stanθja] *nf* constancy; **dejar ~ de** to put on record
constante [kons'tante] *adj, nf* constant
constar [kons'tar] *vi* (*evidenciarse*) to be

clear *o* evident; **~ de** to consist of
constipado, -a [konsti'paðo, a] *adj*: **estar ~** to have a cold ▷ *nm* cold
No confundir **constipado** con la palabra inglesa *constipated*.
constitución [konstitu'θjon] *nf* constitution
constituir [konstitu'ir] *vt* (*formar, componer*) to constitute, make up; (*fundar, erigir, ordenar*) to constitute, establish
construcción [konstruk'θjon] *nf* construction, building
constructor, a [konstruk'tor, a] *nm/f* builder
construir [konstru'ir] *vt* to build, construct
construyendo *etc vb V* **construir**
consuelo [kon'swelo] *nm* consolation, solace
cónsul ['konsul] *nm* consul; **consulado** *nm* consulate
consulta [kon'sulta] *nf* consultation; (*Med*): **horas de ~** surgery hours; **consultar** [konsul'tar] *vt* to consult; **consultar algo con algn** to discuss sth with sb; **consultorio** [konsul'torjo] *nm* (*Med*) surgery
consumición [konsumi'θjon] *nf* consumption; (*bebida*) drink; (*comida*) food; **consumición mínima** cover charge
consumidor, a [konsumi'ðor, a] *nm/f* consumer
consumir [konsu'mir] *vt* to consume; **consumirse** *vr* to be consumed; (*persona*) to waste away
consumismo [konsu'mismo] *nm* consumerism
consumo [kon'sumo] *nm* consumption
contabilidad [kontaβili'ðað] *nf* accounting, book-keeping; (*profesión*) accountancy; **contable** *nmf* accountant
contacto [kon'takto] *nm* contact; (*Auto*) ignition; **estar/ponerse en ~ con algn** to be/to get in touch with sb
contado, -a [kon'taðo, a] *adj*: **~s** (*escasos*) numbered, scarce, few ▷ *nm*: **pagar al ~** to pay (in) cash
contador [konta'ðor] *nm* (ESP: *aparato*) meter ▷ *nmf* (LAM *Com*) accountant
contagiar [konta'xjar] *vt* (*enfermedad*) to pass on, transmit; (*persona*) to infect; **contagiarse** *vr* to become infected
contagio [kon'taxjo] *nm* infection; **contagioso, -a** *adj* infectious; (*fig*) catching
contaminación [kontamina'θjon] *nf* contamination; (*polución*) pollution
contaminar [kontami'nar] *vt* to contaminate; (*aire, agua*) to pollute
contante [kon'tante] *adj*: **dinero ~ (y sonante)** cash
contar [kon'tar] *vt* (*páginas, dinero*) to count; (*anécdota, chiste etc*) to tell ▷ *vi* to count; **~ con** to rely on, count on
contemplar [kontem'plar] *vt* to contemplate; (*mirar*) to look at
contemporáneo, -a [kontempo'raneo, a] *adj, nm/f* contemporary
contenedor [kontene'ðor] *nm* container
contener [konte'ner] *vt* to contain, hold; (*retener*) to hold back, contain; **contenerse** *vr* to control *o* restrain o.s.
contenido, -a [konte'niðo, a] *adj* (*moderado*) restrained; (*risa etc*) suppressed ▷ *nm* contents *pl*, content
contentar [konten'tar] *vt* (*satisfacer*) to satisfy; (*complacer*) to please; **contentarse** *vr* to be satisfied
contento, -a [kon'tento, a] *adj* (*alegre*) pleased; (*feliz*) happy
contestación [kontesta'θjon] *nf* answer, reply
contestador [kontesta'ðor] *nm* (*tb*: **~ automático**) answering machine
contestar [kontes'tar] *vt* to answer, reply; (*Jur*) to corroborate, confirm
No confundir **contestar** con la palabra inglesa *contest*.
contexto [kon'te(k)sto] *nm* context
contigo [kon'tiɣo] *pron* with you
contiguo, -a [kon'tiɣwo, a] *adj* adjacent, adjoining
continente [konti'nente] *adj, nm* continent
continuación [kontinwa'θjon] *nf* continuation; **a ~** then, next
continuar [konti'nwar] *vt* to continue, go on with ▷ *vi* to continue, go on; **~ hablando** to continue talking *o* to talk
continuidad [kontinwi'ðað] *nf* continuity
continuo, -a [kon'tinwo, a] *adj* (*sin interrupción*) continuous; (*acción perseverante*) continual
contorno [kon'torno] *nm* outline; (*Geo*) contour; **contornos** *nmpl* neighbourhood *sg*, surrounding area *sg*
contra ['kontra] *prep, adv* against ▷ *nm inv* con ▷ *nf*: **la C~** (*de Nicaragua*) the Contras *pl*
contraataque [kontraa'take] *nm* counter-attack
contrabajo [kontra'βaxo] *nm* double bass
contrabandista [kontraβan'dista] *nmf* smuggler
contrabando [kontra'βando] *nm* (*acción*)

smuggling; (*mercancías*) contraband
contracción [kontrak'θjon] *nf* contraction
contracorriente [kontrako'rrjente] *nf* cross-current
contradecir [kontraðe'θir] *vt* to contradict
contradicción [kontraðik'θjon] *nf* contradiction
contradictorio, -a [kontraðik'torjo, a] *adj* contradictory
contraer [kontra'er] *vt* to contract; (*limitar*) to restrict; **contraerse** *vr* to contract; (*limitarse*) to limit o.s.
contraluz [kontra'luθ] *nm* view against the light
contrapartida [kontrapar'tiða] *nf*: **como ~ (de)** in return (for)
contrapelo [kontra'pelo]: **a ~** *adv* the wrong way
contrapeso [kontra'peso] *nm* counterweight
contraportada [kontrapor'taða] *nf* (*de revista*) back cover
contraproducente [kontraproðu'θente] *adj* counterproductive
contrario, -a [kon'trarjo, a] *adj* contrary; (*persona*) opposed; (*sentido, lado*) opposite ▷ *nm/f* enemy, adversary; (*Deporte*) opponent; **al** *o* **por el ~** on the contrary; **de lo ~** otherwise
contrarreloj [kontrarre'lo] *nf* (*tb*: **prueba ~**) time trial
contrarrestar [kontrarres'tar] *vt* to counteract
contrasentido [kontrasen'tiðo] *nm* (*contradicción*) contradiction
contraseña [kontra'seɲa] *nf* (*Inform*) password
contrastar [kontras'tar] *vt, vi* to contrast
contraste [kon'traste] *nm* contrast
contratar [kontra'tar] *vt firmar un acuerdo para*, to contract for; (*empleados, obreros*) to hire, engage
contratiempo [kontra'tjempo] *nm* setback
contratista [kontra'tista] *nmf* contractor
contrato [kon'trato] *nm* contract
contraventana [kontraβen'tana] *nf* shutter
contribución [kontriβu'θjon] *nf* (*municipal etc*) tax; (*ayuda*) contribution
contribuir [kontriβu'ir] *vt, vi* to contribute; (*Com*) to pay (in taxes)
contribuyente [kontriβu'jente] *nmf* (*Com*) taxpayer; (*que ayuda*) contributor
contrincante [kontrin'kante] *nmf* opponent
control [kon'trol] *nm* control; (*inspección*) inspection, check; **control de pasaportes** passport inspection; **controlador, a** *nm/f* controller; **controlador aéreo** air-traffic controller; **controlar** [kontro'lar] *vt* to control; (*inspeccionar*) to inspect, check
contundente [kontun'dente] *adj* (*instrumento*) blunt; (*argumento, derrota*) overwhelming
contusión [kontu'sjon] *nf* bruise
convalecencia [kombale'θenθja] *nf* convalescence
convalecer [kombale'θer] *vi* to convalesce, get better
convalidar [kombali'ðar] *vt* (*título*) to recognize
convencer [komben'θer] *vt* to convince; **~ a algn (de** *o* **para hacer algo)** to persuade sb (to do sth)
convención [komben'θjon] *nf* convention
conveniente [kombe'njente] *adj* suitable; (*útil*) useful
convenio [kom'benjo] *nm* agreement, treaty
convenir [kombe'nir] *vi* (*estar de acuerdo*) to agree; (*venir bien*) to suit, be suitable

> No confundir **convenir** con la palabra inglesa *convene*.

convento [kom'bento] *nm* convent
convenza *etc vb V* **convencer**
convergir [komber'xir] *vi* = **converger**
conversación [kombersa'θjon] *nf* conversation
conversar [komber'sar] *vi* to talk, converse
conversión [komber'sjon] *nf* conversion
convertir [komber'tir] *vt* to convert
convidar [kombi'ðar] *vt* to invite; **~ a algn a una cerveza** to buy sb a beer
convincente [kombin'θente] *adj* convincing
convite [kom'bite] *nm* invitation; (*banquete*) banquet
convivencia [kombi'βenθja] *nf* coexistence, living together
convivir [kombi'βir] *vi* to live together
convocar [kombo'kar] *vt* to summon, call (together)
convocatoria [komboka'torja] *nf* (*de oposiciones, elecciones*) notice; (*de huelga*) call
cónyuge ['konjuxe] *nmf* spouse
coñac [ko'ɲa(k)] (*pl* **~s**) *nm* cognac, brandy
coño ['koɲo] (*fam!*) *excl* (*enfado*) shit! (!); (*sorpresa*) bloody hell! (!)
cool [kul] *adj* (*fam*) cool
cooperación [koopera'θjon] *nf* cooperation

cooperar [koope'rar] *vi* to cooperate
cooperativa [koopera'tiβa] *nf* cooperative
coordinadora [koorðina'ðora] *nf* (*comité*) coordinating committee
coordinar [koorði'nar] *vt* to coordinate
copa ['kopa] *nf* cup; (*vaso*) glass; (*bebida*): **tomar una ~** (to have a) drink; (*de árbol*) top; (*de sombrero*) crown; **copas** *nfpl* (*Naipes*) ≈ hearts
copia ['kopja] *nf* copy; **copia de respaldo o seguridad** (*Inform*) back-up copy; **copiar** *vt* to copy
copla ['kopla] *nf* verse; (*canción*) (popular) song
copo ['kopo] *nm*: **~ de nieve** snowflake; **~s de maíz** cornflakes
coqueta [ko'keta] *adj* flirtatious, coquettish; **coquetear** *vi* to flirt
coraje [ko'raxe] *nm* courage; (*ánimo*) spirit; (*ira*) anger
coral [ko'ral] *adj* choral ▷ *nf* (*Mús*) choir ▷ *nm* (*Zool*) coral
coraza [ko'raθa] *nf* (*armadura*) armour; (*blindaje*) armour-plating
corazón [kora'θon] *nm* heart
corazonada [koraθo'naða] *nf* impulse; (*presentimiento*) hunch
corbata [kor'βata] *nf* tie
corchete [kor'tʃete] *nm* catch, clasp
corcho ['kortʃo] *nm* cork; (*Pesca*) float
cordel [kor'ðel] *nm* cord, line
cordero [kor'ðero] *nm* lamb
cordial [kor'ðjal] *adj* cordial
cordillera [korði'ʎera] *nf* range (of mountains)
Córdoba ['korðoβa] *n* Cordova
cordón [kor'ðon] *nm* (*cuerda*) cord, string; (*de zapatos*) lace; (*Mil etc*) cordon; **cordón umbilical** umbilical cord
cordura [kor'ðura] *nf*: **con ~** (*obrar, hablar*) sensibly
corneta [kor'neta] *nf* bugle
cornisa [kor'nisa] *nf* (*Arq*) cornice
coro ['koro] *nm* chorus; (*conjunto de cantores*) choir
corona [ko'rona] *nf* crown; (*de flores*) garland
coronel [koro'nel] *nm* colonel
coronilla [koro'niʎa] *nf* (*Anat*) crown (of the head)
corporal [korpo'ral] *adj* corporal, bodily
corpulento, -a [korpu'lento, a] *adj* (*persona*) heavily-built
corral [ko'rral] *nm* farmyard
correa [ko'rrea] *nf* strap; (*cinturón*) belt; (*de perro*) lead, leash; **correa del ventilador** (*Auto*) fan belt
corrección [korrek'θjon] *nf* correction; (*reprensión*) rebuke; **correccional** *nm* reformatory
correcto, -a [ko'rrekto, a] *adj* correct; (*persona*) well-mannered
corredizo, -a [korre'ðiθo, a] *adj* (*puerta etc*) sliding
corredor, a [korre'ðor, a] *nm* (*pasillo*) corridor; (*balcón corrido*) gallery; (*Com*) agent, broker ▷ *nm/f* (*Deporte*) runner
corregir [korre'xir] *vt* (*error*) to correct; **corregirse** *vr* to reform
correo [ko'rreo] *nm* post, mail; (*persona*) courier; **Correos** *nmpl* (ESP) Post Office *sg*; **correo aéreo** airmail; **correo basura** (*Inform*) spam; **correo electrónico** e-mail, electronic mail; **correo web** webmail
correr [ko'rrer] *vt* to run; (*cortinas*) to draw; (*cerrojo*) to shoot ▷ *vi* to run; (*líquido*) to run, flow; **correrse** *vr* to slide, move; (*colores*) to run
correspondencia [korrespon'denθja] *nf* correspondence; (*Ferro*) connection
corresponder [korrespon'der] *vi* to correspond; (*convenir*) to be suitable; (*pertenecer*) to belong; (*concernir*) to concern; **corresponderse** *vr* (*por escrito*) to correspond; (*amarse*) to love one another
correspondiente [korrespon'djente] *adj* corresponding
corresponsal [korrespon'sal] *nmf* correspondent
corrida [ko'rriða] *nf* (*de toros*) bullfight
corrido, -a [ko'rriðo, a] *adj* (*avergonzado*) abashed; **un kilo ~** a good kilo
corriente [ko'rrjente] *adj* (*agua*) running; (*dinero etc*) current; (*común*) ordinary, normal ▷ *nf* current ▷ *nm* current month; **estar al ~ de** to be informed about; **corriente eléctrica** electric current
corrija *etc vb V* **corregir**
corro ['korro] *nm* ring, circle (of people)
corromper [korrom'per] *vt* (*madera*) to rot; (*fig*) to corrupt
corrosivo, -a [korro'siβo, a] *adj* corrosive
corrupción [korrup'θjon] *nf* rot, decay; (*fig*) corruption
corsé [kor'se] *nm* corset
cortacésped [korta'θespeð] *nm* lawn mower
cortado, -a [kor'taðo, a] *adj* (*gen*) cut; (*leche*) sour; (*tímido*) shy; (*avergonzado*) embarrassed ▷ *nm* coffee (with a little milk)
cortafuegos [korta'fweɣos] *nm inv* (*en el bosque*) firebreak, fire lane (*US*); (*Internet*) firewall
cortar [kor'tar] *vt* to cut; (*suministro*) to

cut off; (*un pasaje*) to cut out ▷ *vi* to cut; **cortarse** *vr* (*avergonzarse*) to become embarrassed; (*leche*) to turn, curdle; **~se el pelo** to have one's hair cut

cortauñas [korta'uɲas] *nm inv* nail clippers *pl*

corte ['korte] *nm* cut, cutting; (*de tela*) piece, length ▷ *nf*: **las C~s** the Spanish Parliament; **corte de luz** power cut; **corte y confección** dressmaking

cortejo [kor'texo] *nm* entourage; **cortejo fúnebre** funeral procession

cortés [kor'tes] *adj* courteous, polite

cortesía [korte'sia] *nf* courtesy

corteza [kor'teθa] *nf* (*de árbol*) bark; (*de pan*) crust

cortijo [kor'tixo] (ESP) *nm* farm, farmhouse

cortina [kor'tina] *nf* curtain

corto, -a ['korto, a] *adj* (*breve*) short; (*tímido*) bashful; **~ de luces** not very bright; **~ de vista** short-sighted; **estar ~ de fondos** to be short of funds; **cortocircuito** *nm* short circuit; **cortometraje** *nm* (*Cine*) short

cosa ['kosa] *nf* thing; **~ de** about; **eso es ~ mía** that's my business

coscorrón [kosko'rron] *nm* bump on the head

cosecha [ko'setʃa] *nf* (*Agr*) harvest; (*de vino*) vintage; **cosechar** [kose'tʃar] *vt* to harvest, gather (in)

coser [ko'ser] *vt* to sew

cosmético, -a [kos'metiko, a] *adj, nm* cosmetic

cosquillas [kos'kiʎas] *nfpl*: **hacer ~** to tickle; **tener ~** to be ticklish

costa ['kosta] *nf* (*Geo*) coast; **a toda ~** at all costs; **Costa Brava** Costa Brava; **Costa Cantábrica** Cantabrian Coast; **Costa del Sol** Costa del Sol

costado [kos'taðo] *nm* side

costanera [kosta'nera] (CS) *nf* promenade, sea front

costar [kos'tar] *vt* (*valer*) to cost; **me cuesta hablarle** I find it hard to talk to him

Costa Rica [kosta'rika] *nf* Costa Rica; **costarricense** *adj, nmf* Costa Rican; **costarriqueño, -a** *adj, nm/f* Costa Rican

coste ['koste] *nm* = **costo**

costear [koste'ar] *vt* to pay for

costero, -a [kos'tero, a] *adj* (*pueblecito, camino*) coastal

costilla [kos'tiʎa] *nf* rib; (*Culin*) cutlet

costo ['kosto] *nm* cost, price; **costo de (la) vida** cost of living; **costoso, -a** *adj* costly, expensive

costra ['kostra] *nf* (*corteza*) crust; (*Med*) scab

costumbre [kos'tumbre] *nf* custom, habit

costura [kos'tura] *nf* sewing, needlework; (*zurcido*) seam

costurera [kostu'rera] *nf* dressmaker

costurero [kostu'rero] *nm* sewing box *o* case

cotidiano, -a [koti'ðjano, a] *adj* daily, day to day

cotilla [ko'tiʎa] (ESP: *fam*) *nmf* gossip; **cotillear** (ESP) *vi* to gossip; **cotilleo** (ESP) *nm* gossip(ing)

cotizar [koti'θar] *vt* (*Com*) to quote, price; **cotizarse** *vr*: **~se a** to sell at, fetch; (*Bolsa*) to stand at, be quoted at

coto ['koto] *nm* (*terreno cercado*) enclosure; (*de caza*) reserve

cotorra [ko'torra] *nf* parrot

coyote [ko'jote] *nm* coyote, prairie wolf

coz [koθ] *nf* kick

crack [krak] *nm* (*droga*) crack

cráneo ['kraneo] *nm* skull, cranium

cráter ['krater] *nm* crater

crayón [kra'jon] (MÉX, RPL) *nm* crayon, chalk

creación [krea'θjon] *nf* creation

creador, a [krea'ðor, a] *adj* creative ▷ *nm/f* creator

crear [kre'ar] *vt* to create, make

crecer [kre'θer] *vi* to grow; (*precio*) to rise

creces ['kreθes]: **con ~** *adv* amply, fully

crecido, -a [kre'θiðo, a] *adj* (*persona, planta*) full-grown; (*cantidad*) large

crecimiento [kreθi'mjento] *nm* growth; (*aumento*) increase

credencial [kreðen'θjal] *nf* (LAM: *tarjeta*) card; **credenciales** *nfpl* credentials; **credencial de socio** (LAM) membership card

crédito ['kreðito] *nm* credit

credo ['kreðo] *nm* creed

creencia [kre'enθja] *nf* belief

creer [kre'er] *vt, vi* to think, believe; **creerse** *vr* to believe o.s. (to be); **~ en** to believe in; **creo que sí/no** I think/don't think so; **¡ya lo creo!** I should think so!

creído, -a [kre'iðo, a] *adj* (*engreído*) conceited

crema ['krema] *nf* cream; **crema batida** (LAM) whipped cream; **crema pastelera** (confectioner's) custard

cremallera [krema'ʎera] *nf* zip (fastener)

crepe ['krepe] (ESP) *nf* pancake

cresta ['kresta] *nf* (*Geo, Zool*) crest

creyendo *etc vb V* **creer**

creyente [kre'jente] *nmf* believer

creyó *etc vb V* **creer**

crezco *etc vb V* **crecer**

cría *etc* ['kria] *vb V* **criar** ▷ *nf* (*de animales*)

rearing, breeding; (*animal*) young; *V tb* **crío**
criadero [kria'ðero] *nm* (*Zool*) breeding place
criado, -a [kri'aðo, a] *nm* servant ▷ *nf* servant, maid
criador [kria'ðor] *nm* breeder
crianza [kri'anθa] *nf* rearing, breeding; (*fig*) breeding
criar [kri'ar] *vt* (*educar*) to bring up; (*producir*) to grow, produce; (*animales*) to breed
criatura [kria'tura] *nf* creature; (*niño*) baby, (small) child
cribar [kri'βar] *vt* to sieve
crimen ['krimen] *nm* crime
criminal [krimi'nal] *adj, nmf* criminal
crines ['krines] *nfpl* mane
crío, -a ['krio, a] (*fam*) *nm/f* (*niño*) kid
crisis ['krisis] *nf inv* crisis; **crisis nerviosa** nervous breakdown
crismas ['krismas] (ESP) *nm inv* Christmas card
cristal [kris'tal] *nm* crystal; (*de ventana*) glass, pane; (*lente*) lens; **cristalino, -a** *adj* crystalline; (*fig*) clear ▷ *nm* lens (of the eye)
cristianismo [kristja'nismo] *nm* Christianity
cristiano, -a [kris'tjano, a] *adj, nm/f* Christian
Cristo ['kristo] *nm* Christ; (*crucifijo*) crucifix
criterio [kri'terjo] *nm* criterion; (*juicio*) judgement
crítica ['kritika] *nf* criticism; *V tb* **crítico**
criticar [kriti'kar] *vt* to criticize
crítico, -a ['kritiko, a] *adj* critical ▷ *nm/f* critic
Croacia [kro'aθja] *nf* Croatia
cromo ['kromo] *nm* chrome
crónica ['kronika] *nf* chronicle, account
crónico, -a ['kroniko, a] *adj* chronic
cronómetro [kro'nometro] *nm* stopwatch
croqueta [kro'keta] *nf* croquette
cruce *etc* ['kruθe] *vb V* **cruzar** ▷ *nm* (*para peatones*) crossing; (*de carreteras*) crossroads
crucero [kru'θero] *nm* (*viaje*) cruise
crucificar [kruθifi'kar] *vt* to crucify
crucifijo [kruθi'fixo] *nm* crucifix
crucigrama [kruθi'ɣrama] *nm* crossword (puzzle)
cruda ['kruða] (MÉX, CAM: *fam*) *nf* hangover
crudo, -a ['kruðo, a] *adj* raw; (*no maduro*) unripe; (*petróleo*) crude; (*rudo, cruel*) cruel ▷ *nm* crude (oil)
cruel [krwel] *adj* cruel; **crueldad** *nf* cruelty
crujiente [kru'xjente] *adj* (*galleta etc*) crunchy
crujir [kru'xir] *vi* (*madera etc*) to creak; (*dedos*) to crack; (*dientes*) to grind; (*nieve, arena*) to crunch
cruz [kruθ] *nf* cross; (*de moneda*) tails *sg*; **cruz gamada** swastika
cruzada [kru'θaða] *nf* crusade
cruzado, -a [kru'θaðo, a] *adj* crossed ▷ *nm* crusader
cruzar [kru'θar] *vt* to cross; **cruzarse** *vr* (*líneas etc*) to cross; (*personas*) to pass each other
Cruz Roja *nf* Red Cross
cuaderno [kwa'ðerno] *nm* notebook; (*de escuela*) exercise book; (*Náut*) logbook
cuadra ['kwaðra] *nf* (*caballeriza*) stable; (LAM: *entre calles*) block
cuadrado, -a [kwa'ðraðo, a] *adj* square ▷ *nm* (*Mat*) square
cuadrar [kwa'ðrar] *vt* to square ▷ *vi*: **~ con** to square with, tally with; **cuadrarse** *vr* (*soldado*) to stand to attention
cuadrilátero [kwaðri'latero] *nm* (*Deporte*) boxing ring; (*Geom*) quadrilateral
cuadrilla [kwa'ðriʎa] *nf* party, group
cuadro ['kwaðro] *nm* square; (*Arte*) painting; (*Teatro*) scene; (*diagrama*) chart; (*Deporte, Med*) team; **tela a ~s** checked (BRIT) *o* chequered (US) material
cuajar [kwa'xar] *vt* (*leche*) to curdle; (*sangre*) to congeal; (*Culin*) to set; **cuajarse** *vr* to curdle; to congeal; to set; (*llenarse*) to fill up
cuajo ['kwaxo] *nm*: **de ~** (*arrancar*) by the roots; (*cortar*) completely
cual [kwal] *adv* like, as ▷ *pron*: **el** *etc* **~** which; (*persona sujeto*) who; (*: objeto*) whom ▷ *adj* such as; **cada ~** each one; **déjalo tal ~** leave it just as it is
cuál [kwal] *pron interr* which (one)
cualesquier, a [kwales'kjer(a)] *pl de* **cualquier(a)**
cualidad [kwali'ðað] *nf* quality
cualquier [kwal'kjer] *adj V* **cualquiera**
cualquiera [kwal'kjera] (*pl* **cualesquiera**) *adj* (*delante de nm y f* **cualquier**) any ▷ *pron* anybody; **un coche ~ servirá** any car will do; **no es un hombre ~** he isn't just anybody; **cualquier día/libro** any day/ book; **eso ~ lo sabe hacer** anybody can do that; **es un ~** he's a nobody
cuando ['kwando] *adv* when; (*aún si*) if, even if ▷ *conj* (*puesto que*) since ▷ *prep*: **yo, ~ niño ...** when I was a child ...; **~ no sea así** even if it is not so; **~ más** at (the) most; **~ menos** at least; **~ no** if not, otherwise; **de ~ en ~** from time to time
cuándo ['kwando] *adv* when; **¿desde ~?**

since when?
cuantía [kwan'tia] *nf* extent

PALABRA CLAVE

cuanto, -a ['kwanto, a] *adj* **1** (*todo*): **tiene todo cuanto desea** he's got everything he wants; **le daremos cuantos ejemplares necesite** we'll give him as many copies as *o* all the copies he needs; **cuantos hombres la ven** all the men who see her
2 **unos cuantos: había unos cuantos periodistas** there were a few journalists
3 (+ *más*): **cuanto más vino bebes peor te sentirás** the more wine you drink the worse you'll feel
▷ *pron*: **tiene cuanto desea** he has everything he wants; **tome cuanto/cuantos quiera** take as much/many as you want
▷ *adv*: **en cuanto: en cuanto profesor** as a teacher; **en cuanto a mí** as for me; *V tb* **antes**
▷ *conj* **1** **cuanto más gana menos gasta** the more he earns the less he spends; **cuanto más joven más confiado** the younger you are the more trusting you are
2 **en cuanto: en cuanto llegue/llegué** as soon as I arrive/arrived

cuánto, -a ['kwanto, a] *adj* (*exclamación*) what a lot of; (*interr: sg*) how much?; (*: pl*) how many? ▷ *pron*, *adv* how; (*: interr: sg*) how much?; (*: pl*) how many?; **¡cuánta gente!** what a lot of people!; **¿~ cuesta?** how much does it cost?; **¿a ~s estamos?** what's the date?
cuarenta [kwa'renta] *num* forty
cuarentena [kwaren'tena] *nf* quarantine
cuaresma [kwa'resma] *nf* Lent
cuarta ['kwarta] *nf* (*Mat*) quarter, fourth; (*palmo*) span
cuartel [kwar'tel] *nm* (*Mil*) barracks *pl*; **cuartel de bomberos** (RPL) fire station; **cuartel general** headquarters *pl*
cuarteto [kwar'teto] *nm* quartet
cuarto, -a ['kwarto, a] *adj* fourth ▷ *nm* (*Mat*) quarter, fourth; (*habitación*) room; **cuarto de baño** bathroom; **cuarto de estar** living room; **cuarto de hora** quarter (of an) hour; **cuarto de kilo** quarter kilo; **cuartos de final** quarter finals
cuatro ['kwatro] *num* four
Cuba ['kuβa] *nf* Cuba
cuba ['kuβa] *nf* cask, barrel
cubano, -a [ku'βano, a] *adj*, *nm/f* Cuban
cubata [ku'βata] *nm* (*fam*) large drink (*of rum and coke etc*)
cubeta [ku'βeta] (ESP, MÉX) *nf* (*balde*) bucket, tub
cúbico, -a ['kuβiko, a] *adj* cubic
cubierta [ku'βjerta] *nf* cover, covering; (*neumático*) tyre; (*Náut*) deck
cubierto, -a [ku'βjerto, a] *pp de* **cubrir** ▷ *adj* covered ▷ *nm* cover; (*lugar en la mesa*) place; **cubiertos** *nmpl* cutlery *sg*; **a ~** under cover
cubilete [kuβi'lete] *nm* (*en juegos*) cup
cubito [ku'βito] *nm* (*tb*: **~ de hielo**) ice-cube
cubo ['kuβo] *nm* (*Mat*) cube; (ESP: *balde*) bucket, tub; (*Tec*) drum; **cubo de (la) basura** dustbin (BRIT), trash can (US)
cubrir [ku'βrir] *vt* to cover; **cubrirse** *vr* (*cielo*) to become overcast
cucaracha [kuka'ratʃa] *nf* cockroach
cuchara [ku'tʃara] *nf* spoon; (*Tec*) scoop; **cucharada** *nf* spoonful; **cucharadita** *nf* teaspoonful
cucharilla [kutʃa'riʎa] *nf* teaspoon
cucharón [kutʃa'ron] *nm* ladle
cuchilla [ku'tʃiʎa] *nf* (large) knife; (*de arma blanca*) blade; **cuchilla de afeitar** razor blade
cuchillo [ku'tʃiʎo] *nm* knife
cuchitril [kutʃi'tril] *nm* hovel
cuclillas [ku'kliʎas] *nfpl*: **en ~** squatting
cuco, -a ['kuko, a] *adj* pretty; (*astuto*) sharp ▷ *nm* cuckoo
cucurucho [kuku'rutʃo] *nm* cornet
cueca ['kweka] *nf* *Chilean national dance*
cuello ['kweʎo] *nm* (*Anat*) neck; (*de vestido, camisa*) collar
cuenca ['kwenka] *nf* (*Anat*) eye socket; (*Geo*) bowl, deep valley
cuenco ['kwenko] *nm* bowl
cuenta *etc* ['kwenta] *vb V* **contar** ▷ *nf* (*cálculo*) count, counting; (*en café, restaurante*) bill (BRIT), check (US); (*Com*) account; (*de collar*) bead; **a fin de ~s** in the end; **caer en la ~** to catch on; **darse ~ de** to realize; **tener en ~** to bear in mind; **echar ~s** to take stock; **cuenta atrás** countdown; **cuenta corriente/de ahorros** current/savings account; **cuenta de correo (electrónica)** (*Inform*) email account; **cuentakilómetros** *nm inv* ≈ milometer; (*de velocidad*) speedometer
cuento *etc* ['kwento] *vb V* **contar** ▷ *nm* story; **cuento chino** tall story; **cuento de hadas** a fairy tale
cuerda ['kwerða] *nf* rope; (*fina*) string; (*de reloj*) spring; **dar ~ a un reloj** to wind up a clock; **cuerda floja** tightrope; **cuerdas vocales** vocal cords
cuerdo, -a ['kwerðo, a] *adj* sane;

(*prudente*) wise, sensible
cuerno ['kwerno] *nm* horn
cuero ['kwero] *nm* leather; **en ~s** stark naked; **cuero cabelludo** scalp
cuerpo ['kwerpo] *nm* body
cuervo ['kwerβo] *nm* crow
cuesta *etc* ['kwesta] *vb V* **costar** ▷ *nf* slope; (*en camino etc*) hill; **~ arriba/abajo** uphill/downhill; **a ~s** on one's back
cueste *etc vb V* **costar**
cuestión [kwes'tjon] *nf* matter, question
cuete ['kwete] *adj* (MÉX: *fam*) drunk ▷ *nm* (LAM: *cohete*) rocket; (MÉX, RPL: *fam: embriaguez*) drunkenness; (MÉX: Culin) steak
cueva ['kweβa] *nf* cave
cuidado [kwi'ðaðo] *nm* care, carefulness; (*preocupación*) care, worry ▷ *excl* careful!, look out!; **eso me tiene sin ~** I'm not worried about that
cuidadoso, -a [kwiða'ðoso, a] *adj* careful; (*preocupado*) anxious
cuidar [kwi'ðar] *vt* (*Med*) to care for; (*ocuparse de*) to take care of, look after ▷ *vi*: **~ de** to take care of, look after; **cuidarse** *vr* to look after o.s.; **~se de hacer algo** to take care to do sth
culata [ku'lata] *nf* (*de fusil*) butt
culebra [ku'leβra] *nf* snake
culebrón [kule'βron] (*fam*) *nm* (*TV*) soap(-opera)
culo ['kulo] *nm* bottom, backside; (*de vaso, botella*) bottom
culpa ['kulpa] *nf* fault; (*Jur*) guilt; **por ~ de** because of; **echar la ~ a algn** to blame sb for sth; **tener la ~ (de)** to be to blame (for); **culpable** *adj* guilty ▷ *nmf* culprit; **culpar** [kul'par] *vt* to blame; (*acusar*) to accuse
cultivar [kulti'βar] *vt* to cultivate
cultivo [kul'tiβo] *nm* (*acto*) cultivation; (*plantas*) crop
culto, -a ['kulto, a] *adj* (*que tiene cultura*) cultured, educated ▷ *nm* (*homenaje*) worship; (*religión*) cult
cultura [kul'tura] *nf* culture
culturismo [kultu'rismo] *nm* body-building
cumbia ['kumbja] *nf popular Colombian dance*
cumbre ['kumbre] *nf* summit, top
cumpleaños [kumple'aɲos] *nm inv* birthday
cumplido, -a [kum'pliðo, a] *adj* (*abundante*) plentiful; (*cortés*) courteous ▷ *nm* compliment; **visita de ~** courtesy call
cumplidor, a [kumpli'ðor, a] *adj* reliable
cumplimiento [kumpli'mjento] *nm* (*de un deber*) fulfilment; (*acabamiento*) completion
cumplir [kum'plir] *vt* (*orden*) to carry out, obey; (*promesa*) to carry out, fulfil; (*condena*) to serve ▷ *vi*: **~ con** (*deber*) to carry out, fulfil; **cumplirse** *vr* (*plazo*) to expire; **hoy cumple dieciocho años** he is eighteen today
cuna ['kuna] *nf* cradle, cot
cundir [kun'dir] *vi* (*noticia, rumor, pánico*) to spread; (*rendir*) to go a long way
cuneta [ku'neta] *nf* ditch
cuña ['kuɲa] *nf* wedge
cuñado, -a [ku'ɲaðo, a] *nm/f* brother-/sister-in-law
cuota ['kwota] *nf* (*parte proporcional*) share; (*cotización*) fee, dues *pl*
cupe *etc vb V* **caber**
cupiera *etc vb V* **caber**
cupo ['kupo] *vb V* **caber** ▷ *nm* quota
cupón [ku'pon] *nm* coupon
cúpula ['kupula] *nf* dome
cura ['kura] *nf* (*curación*) cure; (*método curativo*) treatment ▷ *nm* priest
curación [kura'θjon] *nf* cure
curandero, -a [kuran'dero, a] *nm/f* quack
curar [ku'rar] *vt* (*Med: herida*) to treat, dress; (*: enfermo*) to cure; (*Culin*) to cure, salt; (*cuero*) to tan; **curarse** *vr* to get well, recover
curiosear [kurjose'ar] *vt* to glance at, look over ▷ *vi* to look round, wander round; (*explorar*) to poke about
curiosidad [kurjosi'ðað] *nf* curiosity
curioso, -a [ku'rjoso, a] *adj* curious ▷ *nm/f* bystander, onlooker
curita [ku'rita] (LAM) *nf* (sticking) plaster (BRIT), Bandaid® (US)
currante [ku'rrante] (ESP: *fam*) *nmf* worker
currar [ku'rrar] (ESP: *fam*) *vi* to work
currículo [ku'rrikulo] = **curriculum**
curriculum [ku'rrikulum] *nm* curriculum vitae
cursi ['kursi] (*fam*) *adj* affected
cursillo [kur'siʎo] *nm* short course
cursiva [kur'siβa] *nf* italics *pl*
curso ['kurso] *nm* course; **en ~** (*año*) current; (*proceso*) going on, under way
cursor [kur'sor] *nm* (*Inform*) cursor
curul [ku'rul] (MÉX) *nm* (*escaño*) seat
curva ['kurβa] *nf* curve, bend
custodia [kus'toðja] *nf* safekeeping; custody
cutis ['kutis] *nm inv* skin, complexion
cutre ['kutre] (ESP: *fam*) *adj* (*lugar*) grotty
cuyo, -a ['kujo, a] *pron* (*de quien*) whose; (*de que*) whose, of which; **en ~ caso** in which case
C.V. *abr* (= *caballos de vapor*) H.P.

d

D. *abr* (= Don) Esq
dado, -a ['daðo, a] *pp de* **dar** ▷ *nm* die; **dados** *nmpl* dice; **~ que** given that
daltónico, -a [dal'toniko, a] *adj* colour-blind
dama ['dama] *nf* (*gen*) lady; (*Ajedrez*) queen; **damas** *nfpl* (*juego*) draughts *sg*; **dama de honor** bridesmaid
damasco [da'masko] (RPL) *nm* apricot
danés, -esa [da'nes, esa] *adj* Danish ▷ *nm/f* Dane
dañar [da'ɲar] *vt* (*objeto*) to damage; (*persona*) to hurt; **dañarse** *vr* (*objeto*) to get damaged
dañino, -a [da'ɲino, a] *adj* harmful
daño ['daɲo] *nm* (*objeto*) damage; (*persona*) harm, injury; **~s y perjuicios** (*Jur*) damages; **hacer ~ a** to damage; (*persona*) to hurt, injure; **hacerse ~** to hurt o.s.

PALABRA CLAVE

dar [dar] *vt* **1** (*gen*) to give; (*obra de teatro*) to put on; (*film*) to show; (*fiesta*) to hold; **dar algo a algn** to give sb sth *o* sth to sb; **dar de beber a algn** to give sb a drink
2 (*producir: intereses*) to yield; (*fruta*) to produce
3 (*locuciones + n*): **da gusto escucharle** it's a pleasure to listen to him; *V tb* **paseo**
4 (*+ n: = perífrasis de verbo*): **me da asco** it sickens me
5 (*considerar*): **dar algo por descontado/ entendido** to take sth for granted/as read; **dar algo por concluido** to consider sth finished
6 (*hora*): **el reloj dio las 6** the clock struck 6 (o'clock)
7: **me da lo mismo** it's all the same to me; *V tb* **igual, más**
▷ *vi* **1** **dar con: dimos con él dos horas más tarde** we came across him two hours later; **al final di con la solución** I eventually came up with the answer
2: **dar en** (*blanco, suelo*) to hit; **el sol me da en la cara** the sun is shining (right) on my face
3: **dar de sí** (*zapatos etc*) to stretch, give
darse *vr* **1**: **darse por vencido** to give up
2 (*ocurrir*): **se han dado muchos casos** there have been a lot of cases
3: **darse a: se ha dado a la bebida** he's taken to drinking
4: **se me dan bien/mal las ciencias** I'm good/bad at science
5: **dárselas de: se las da de experto** he fancies himself *o* poses as an expert

dardo ['darðo] *nm* dart
dátil ['datil] *nm* date
dato ['dato] *nm* fact, piece of information; **datos personales** personal details
dcha. *abr* (= *derecha*) r.h.
d. de C. *abr* (= *después de Cristo*) A.D.

PALABRA CLAVE

de [de] (*de + el = del*) *prep* **1** (*posesión*) of; **la casa de Isabel/mis padres** Isabel's/my parents' house; **es de ellos** it's theirs
2 (*origen, distancia, con números*) from; **soy de Gijón** I'm from Gijón; **de 8 a 20** from 8 to 20; **salir del cine** to go out of *o* leave the cinema; **de 2 en 2** 2 by 2, 2 at a time
3 (*valor descriptivo*): **una copa de vino** a glass of wine; **la mesa de la cocina** the kitchen table; **un billete de 10 euros** a 10 euro note; **un niño de tres años** a three-year-old (child); **una máquina de coser** a sewing machine; **ir vestido de gris** to be dressed in grey; **la niña del vestido azul** the girl in the blue dress; **trabaja de profesora** she works as a teacher; **de lado** sideways; **de atrás/ delante** rear/front
4 (*hora, tiempo*): **a las 8 de la mañana** at 8 o'clock in the morning; **de día/noche** by day/night; **de hoy en ocho días** a week from now; **de niño era gordo** as a child he was fat
5 (*comparaciones*): **más/menos de cien personas** more/less than a hundred people; **el más caro de la tienda** the most expensive in the shop; **menos/más de lo pensado** less/more than expected
6 (*causa*): **del calor** from the heat
7 (*tema*) about; **clases de inglés** English classes; **¿sabes algo de él?** do you know anything about him?; **un libro de física** a physics book

8 (*adj + de + infin*): **fácil de entender** easy to understand
9 (*oraciones pasivas*): **fue respetado de todos** he was loved by all
10 (*condicional + infin*) if; **de ser posible** if possible; **de no terminarlo hoy** if I *etc* don't finish it today

dé [de] *vb V* **dar**
debajo [de'βaxo] *adv* underneath; **~ de** below, under; **por ~ de** beneath
debate [de'βate] *nm* debate; **debatir** *vt* to debate
deber [de'βer] *nm* duty ▷*vt* to owe ▷*vi*: **debe (de)** it must, it should; **deberes** *nmpl* (*Escol*) homework; **deberse** *vr*: **~se a** to be owing *o* due to; **debo hacerlo** I must do it; **debe de ir** he should go
debido, -a [de'βiðo, a] *adj* proper, just; **~ a** due to, because of
débil ['deβil] *adj* (*persona, carácter*) weak; (*luz*) dim; **debilidad** *nf* weakness; dimness
debilitar [deβili'tar] *vt* to weaken; **debilitarse** *vr* to grow weak
débito ['deβito] *nm* debit; **débito bancario** (LAM) direct debit (BRIT) *o* billing (US)
debutar [deβu'tar] *vi* to make one's debut
década ['dekaða] *nf* decade
decadencia [deka'ðenθja] *nf* (*estado*) decadence; (*proceso*) decline, decay
decaído, -a [deka'iðo, a] *adj*: **estar ~** (*abatido*) to be down
decano, -a [de'kano, a] *nm/f* (*de universidad etc*) dean
decena [de'θena] *nf*: **una ~** ten (or so)
decente [de'θente] *adj* decent
decepción [deθep'θjon] *nf* disappointment

No confundir **decepción** con la palabra inglesa *deception*.

decepcionar [deθepθjo'nar] *vt* to disappoint
decidir [deθi'ðir] *vt, vi* to decide; **decidirse** *vr*: **~se a** to make up one's mind to
décimo, -a ['deθimo, a] *adj* tenth ▷*nm* tenth
decir [de'θir] *vt* to say; (*contar*) to tell; (*hablar*) to speak ▷*nm* saying; **decirse** *vr*: **se dice que** it is said that; **es ~** that is (to say); **~ para sí** to say to o.s.; **querer ~** to mean; **¡dígame!** (*Tel*) hello!; (*en tienda*) can I help you?
decisión [deθi'sjon] *nf* (*resolución*) decision; (*firmeza*) decisiveness
decisivo, -a [deθi'siβo, a] *adj* decisive
declaración [deklara'θjon] *nf* (*manifestación*) statement; (*de amor*) declaration; **declaración fiscal** *o* **de la renta** income-tax return
declarar [dekla'rar] *vt* to declare ▷*vi* to declare; (*Jur*) to testify; **declararse** *vr* to propose
decoración [dekora'θjon] *nf* decoration
decorado [deko'raðo] *nm* (*Cine, Teatro*) scenery, set
decorar [deko'rar] *vt* to decorate; **decorativo, -a** *adj* ornamental, decorative
decreto [de'kreto] *nm* decree
dedal [de'ðal] *nm* thimble
dedicación [deðika'θjon] *nf* dedication
dedicar [deði'kar] *vt* (*libro*) to dedicate; (*tiempo, dinero*) to devote; (*palabras: decir, consagrar*) to dedicate, devote; **dedicatoria** *nf* (*de libro*) dedication
dedo ['deðo] *nm* finger; **hacer ~** (*fam*) to hitch (a lift); **dedo anular** ring finger; **dedo corazón** middle finger; **dedo (del pie)** toe; **dedo gordo** (*de la mano*) thumb; (*del pie*) big toe; **dedo índice** index finger; **dedo meñique** little finger; **dedo pulgar** thumb
deducción [deðuk'θjon] *nf* deduction
deducir [deðu'θir] *vt* (*concluir*) to deduce, infer; (*Com*) to deduct
defecto [de'fekto] *nm* defect, flaw; **defectuoso, -a** *adj* defective, faulty
defender [defen'der] *vt* to defend; **defenderse** *vr* (*desenvolverse*) to get by
defensa [de'fensa] *nf* defence ▷*nm* (*Deporte*) defender, back; **defensivo, -a** *adj* defensive; **a la defensiva** on the defensive
defensor, a [defen'sor, a] *adj* defending ▷*nm/f* (*abogado defensor*) defending counsel; (*protector*) protector
deficiencia [defi'θjenθja] *nf* deficiency
deficiente [defi'θjente] *adj* (*defectuoso*) defective; **~ en** lacking *o* deficient in; **ser un ~ mental** to be mentally handicapped
déficit ['defiθit] (*pl* **~s**) *nm* deficit
definición [defini'θjon] *nf* definition
definir [defi'nir] *vt* (*determinar*) to determine, establish; (*decidir*) to define; (*aclarar*) to clarify; **definitivo, -a** *adj* definitive; **en definitiva** definitively; (*en resumen*) in short
deformación [deforma'θjon] *nf* (*alteración*) deformation; (*Radio etc*) distortion
deformar [defor'mar] *vt* (*gen*) to deform; **deformarse** *vr* to become deformed; **deforme** *adj* (*informe*) deformed; (*feo*) ugly; (*malhecho*) misshapen
defraudar [defrau'ðar] *vt* (*decepcionar*) to disappoint; (*estafar*) to defraud
defunción [defun'θjon] *nf* death, demise
degenerar [dexene'rar] *vi* to degenerate
degradar [deɣra'ðar] *vt* to debase,

degrade; **degradarse** *vr* to demean o.s.
degustación [deɣusta'θjon] *nf* sampling, tasting
dejar [de'xar] *vt* to leave; (*permitir*) to allow, let; (*abandonar*) to abandon, forsake; (*beneficios*) to produce, yield ▷ *vi*: **~ de** (*parar*) to stop; (*no hacer*) to fail to; **~ a un lado** to leave *o* set aside; **~ entrar/salir** to let in/out; **~ pasar** to let through
del [del] (= **de** + **el**) *V* **de**
delantal [delan'tal] *nm* apron
delante [de'lante] *adv* in front; (*enfrente*) opposite; (*adelante*) ahead; **~ de** in front of, before
delantera [delan'tera] *nf* (*de vestido, casa etc*) front part; (*Deporte*) forward line; **llevar la ~ (a algn)** to be ahead (of sb)
delantero, -a [delan'tero, a] *adj* front ▷ *nm* (*Deporte*) forward, striker
delatar [dela'tar] *vt* to inform on *o* against, betray; **delator, a** *nm/f* informer
delegación [deleɣa'θjon] *nf* (*acción, delegados*) delegation; (*Com: oficina*) office, branch; **delegación de policía** (*MÉX*) police station
delegado, -a [dele'ɣaðo, a] *nm/f* delegate; (*Com*) agent
delegar [dele'ɣar] *vt* to delegate
deletrear [deletre'ar] *vt* to spell (out)
delfín [del'fin] *nm* dolphin
delgado, -a [del'ɣaðo, a] *adj* thin; (*persona*) slim, thin; (*tela etc*) light, delicate
deliberar [deliβe'rar] *vt* to debate, discuss
delicadeza [delika'ðeθa] *nf* (*gen*) delicacy; (*refinamiento, sutileza*) refinement
delicado, -a [deli'kaðo, a] *adj* (*gen*) delicate; (*sensible*) sensitive; (*quisquilloso*) touchy
delicia [de'liθja] *nf* delight
delicioso, -a [deli'θjoso, a] *adj* (*gracioso*) delightful; (*exquisito*) delicious
delimitar [delimi'tar] *vt* (*función, responsabilidades*) to define
delincuencia [delin'kwenθja] *nf* delinquency; **delincuente** *nmf* delinquent; (*criminal*) criminal
delineante [deline'ante] *nmf* draughtsman/woman
delirante [deli'rante] *adj* delirious
delirar [deli'rar] *vi* to be delirious, rave
delirio [de'lirjo] *nm* (*Med*) delirium; (*palabras insensatas*) ravings *pl*
delito [de'lito] *nm* (*gen*) crime; (*infracción*) offence
delta ['delta] *nm* delta
demacrado, -a [dema'krado, a] *adj*: **estar ~** to look pale and drawn, be wasted away
demanda [de'manda] *nf* (*pedido, Com*) demand; (*petición*) request; (*Jur*) action, lawsuit; **demandar** [deman'dar] *vt* (*gen*) to demand; (*Jur*) to sue, file a lawsuit against
demás [de'mas] *adj*: **los ~ niños** the other *o* remaining children ▷ *pron*: **los/las ~** the others, the rest (of them); **lo ~** the rest (of it)
demasía [dema'sia] *nf* (*exceso*) excess, surplus; **comer en ~** to eat to excess
demasiado, -a [dema'sjaðo, a] *adj*: **~ vino** too much wine ▷ *adv* (*antes de adj, adv*) too; **~s libros** too many books; **¡esto es ~!** that's the limit!; **hace ~ calor** it's too hot; **~ despacio** too slowly; **~s** too many
demencia [de'menθja] *nf* (*locura*) madness
democracia [demo'kraθja] *nf* democracy
demócrata [de'mokrata] *nmf* democrat; **democrático, -a** *adj* democratic
demoler [demo'ler] *vt* to demolish; **demolición** *nf* demolition
demonio [de'monjo] *nm* devil, demon; **¡~s!** hell!, damn!; **¿cómo ~s?** how the hell?
demora [de'mora] *nf* delay
demos ['demos] *vb V* **dar**
demostración [demostra'θjon] *nf* (*Mat*) proof; (*de afecto*) show, display
demostrar [demos'trar] *vt* (*probar*) to prove; (*mostrar*) to show; (*manifestar*) to demonstrate
den [den] *vb V* **dar**
denegar [dene'ɣar] *vt* (*rechazar*) to refuse; (*Jur*) to reject
denominación [denomina'θjon] *nf* (*acto*) naming; **Denominación de Origen** *see below*

DENOMINACIÓN DE ORIGEN

The **Denominación de Origen**, abbreviated to **D.O.**, is a prestigious classification awarded to food products such as wines, cheeses, sausages and hams which meet the stringent quality and production standards of the designated region. **D.O.** labels serve as a guarantee of quality.

densidad [densi'ðað] *nf* density; (*fig*) thickness
denso, -a ['denso, a] *adj* dense; (*espeso, pastoso*) thick; (*fig*) heavy
dentadura [denta'ðura] *nf* (set of) teeth *pl*; **dentadura postiza** false teeth *pl*
dentera [den'tera] *nf* (*grima*): **dar ~ a algn** to set sb's teeth on edge
dentífrico, -a [den'tifriko, a] *adj* dental ▷ *nm* toothpaste

dentista [den'tista] *nmf* dentist
dentro ['dentro] *adv* inside ▷*prep*: **~ de** in, inside, within; **por ~** (on the) inside; **mirar por ~** to look inside; **~ de tres meses** within three months
denuncia [de'nunθja] *nf* (*delación*) denunciation; (*acusación*) accusation; (*de accidente*) report; **denunciar** *vt* to report; (*delatar*) to inform on *o* against
departamento [departa'mento] *nm* *sección administrativa*, department, section; (LAM: *apartamento*) flat (BRIT), apartment
depender [depen'der] *vi*: **~ de** to depend on; **depende** it (all) depends
dependienta [depen'djenta] *nf* saleswoman, shop assistant
dependiente [depen'djente] *adj* dependent ▷*nm* salesman, shop assistant
depilar [depi'lar] *vt* (*con cera*) to wax; (*cejas*) to pluck
deportar [depor'tar] *vt* to deport
deporte [de'porte] *nm* sport; **hacer ~** to play sports; **deportista** *adj* sports *cpd* ▷*nmf* sportsman/woman; **deportivo, -a** *adj* (*club, periódico*) sports *cpd* ▷*nm* sports car
depositar [deposi'tar] *vt* (*dinero*) to deposit; (*mercancías*) to put away, store; **depositarse** *vr* to settle
depósito [de'posito] *nm* (*gen*) deposit; (*almacén*) warehouse, store; (*de agua, gasolina etc*) tank; **depósito de cadáveres** mortuary
depredador, a [depreða'ðor, a] *adj* predatory ▷*nm* predator
depresión [depre'sjon] *nf* depression; **depresión nerviosa** nervous breakdown
deprimido, -a [depri'miðo, a] *adj* depressed
deprimir [depri'mir] *vt* to depress; **deprimirse** *vr* (*persona*) to become depressed
deprisa [de'prisa] *adv* quickly, hurriedly
depurar [depu'rar] *vt* to purify; (*purgar*) to purge
derecha [de'retʃa] *nf* right(-hand) side; (*Pol*) right; **a la ~** (*estar*) on the right; (*torcer etc*) (to the) right
derecho, -a [de'retʃo, a] *adj* right, right-hand ▷*nm* (*privilegio*) right; (*lado*) right(-hand) side; (*leyes*) law ▷*adv* straight, directly; **derechos** *nmpl* (*de aduana*) duty *sg*; (*de autor*) royalties; **tener ~ a** to have a right to; **derechos de autor** royalties
deriva [de'riβa] *nf*: **ir** *o* **estar a la ~** to drift, be adrift
derivado [deri'βaðo] *nm* (*Com*) by-product
derivar [deri'βar] *vt* to derive; (*desviar*) to direct ▷*vi* to derive, be derived; (*Náut*) to drift; **derivarse** *vr* to derive, be derived; to drift
derramamiento [derrama'mjento] *nm* (*dispersión*) spilling; **derramamiento de sangre** bloodshed
derramar [derra'mar] *vt* to spill; (*verter*) to pour out; (*esparcir*) to scatter; **derramarse** *vr* to pour out
derrame [de'rrame] *nm* (*de líquido*) spilling; (*de sangre*) shedding; (*de tubo etc*) overflow; (*pérdida*) leakage; **derrame cerebral** brain haemorrhage
derredor [derre'ðor] *adv*: **al** *o* **en ~ de** around, about
derretir [derre'tir] *vt* (*gen*) to melt; (*nieve*) to thaw; **derretirse** *vr* to melt
derribar [derri'βar] *vt* to knock down; (*construcción*) to demolish; (*persona, gobierno, político*) to bring down
derrocar [derro'kar] *vt* (*gobierno*) to bring down, overthrow
derrochar [derro'tʃar] *vt* to squander; **derroche** *nm* (*despilfarro*) waste, squandering
derrota [de'rrota] *nf* (*Náut*) course; (*Mil, Deporte etc*) defeat, rout; **derrotar** *vt* (*gen*) to defeat; **derrotero** *nm* (*rumbo*) course
derrumbar [derrum'bar] *vt* (*edificio*) to knock down; **derrumbarse** *vr* to collapse
des *etc vb V* **dar**
desabrochar [desaβro'tʃar] *vt* (*botónes, broches*) to undo, unfasten; **desabrocharse** *vr* (*ropa etc*) to come undone
desacato [desa'kato] *nm* (*falta de respeto*) disrespect; (*Jur*) contempt
desacertado, -a [desaθer'taðo, a] *adj* (*equivocado*) mistaken; (*inoportuno*) unwise
desacierto [desa'θjerto] *nm* mistake, error
desaconsejar [desakonse'xar] *vt* to advise against
desacreditar [desakreði'tar] *vt* (*desprestigiar*) to discredit, bring into disrepute; (*denigrar*) to run down
desacuerdo [desa'kwerðo] *nm* disagreement, discord
desafiar [desa'fjar] *vt* (*retar*) to challenge; (*enfrentarse a*) to defy
desafilado, -a [desafi'laðo, a] *adj* blunt
desafinado, -a [desafi'naðo, a] *adj*: **estar ~** to be out of tune
desafinar [desafi'nar] *vi* (*al cantar*) to be *o* go out of tune
desafío *etc* [desa'fio] *vb V* **desafiar** ▷*nm* (*reto*) challenge; (*combate*) duel; (*resistencia*) defiance
desafortunado, -a [desafortu'naðo, a]

adj (*desgraciado*) unfortunate, unlucky
desagradable [desaɣra'ðaβle] *adj* (*fastidioso, enojoso*) unpleasant; (*irritante*) disagreeable
desagradar [desaɣra'ðar] *vi* (*disgustar*) to displease; (*molestar*) to bother
desagradecido, -a [desaɣraðe'θiðo, a] *adj* ungrateful
desagrado [desa'ɣraðo] *nm* (*disgusto*) displeasure; (*contrariedad*) dissatisfaction
desagüe [des'aɣwe] *nm* (*de un líquido*) drainage; (*cañería*) drainpipe; (*salida*) outlet, drain
desahogar [desao'ɣar] *vt* (*aliviar*) to ease, relieve; (*ira*) to vent; **desahogarse** *vr* (*relajarse*) to relax; (*desfogarse*) to let off steam
desahogo [desa'oɣo] *nm* (*alivio*) relief; (*comodidad*) comfort, ease
desahuciar [desau'θjar] *vt* (*enfermo*) to give up hope for; (*inquilino*) to evict
desairar [desai'rar] *vt* (*menospreciar*) to slight, snub
desalentador, a [desalenta'ðor, a] *adj* discouraging
desaliño [desa'liɲo] *nm* slovenliness
desalmado, -a [desal'maðo, a] *adj* (*cruel*) cruel, heartless
desalojar [desalo'xar] *vt* (*expulsar, echar*) to eject; (*abandonar*) to move out of ▷ *vi* to move out
desamor [desa'mor] *nm* (*frialdad*) indifference; (*odio*) dislike
desamparado, -a [desampa'raðo, a] *adj* (*persona*) helpless; (*lugar: expuesto*) exposed; (*desierto*) deserted
desangrar [desan'grar] *vt* to bleed; (*fig: persona*) to bleed dry; **desangrarse** *vr* to lose a lot of blood
desanimado, -a [desani'maðo, a] *adj* (*persona*) downhearted; (*espectáculo, fiesta*) dull
desanimar [desani'mar] *vt* (*desalentar*) to discourage; (*deprimir*) to depress; **desanimarse** *vr* to lose heart
desapacible [desapa'θiβle] *adj* (*gen*) unpleasant
desaparecer [desapare'θer] *vi* (*gen*) to disappear; (*el sol, el luz*) to vanish; **desaparecido, -a** *adj* missing; **desaparición** *nf* disappearance
desapercibido, -a [desaperθi'βiðo, a] *adj* (*desprevenido*) unprepared; **pasar ~** to go unnoticed
desaprensivo, -a [desapren'siβo, a] *adj* unscrupulous
desaprobar [desapro'βar] *vt* (*reprobar*) to disapprove of; (*condenar*) to condemn; (*no consentir*) to reject
desaprovechado, -a [desaproβe'tʃaðo, a] *adj* (*oportunidad, tiempo*) wasted; (*estudiante*) slack
desaprovechar [desaproβe'tʃar] *vt* to waste
desarmador [desarma'ðor] (*MÉX*) *nm* screwdriver
desarmar [desar'mar] *vt* (*Mil, fig*) to disarm; (*Tec*) to take apart, dismantle; **desarme** *nm* disarmament
desarraigar [desarrai'ɣar] *vt* to uproot; **desarraigo** *nm* uprooting
desarreglar [desarre'ɣlar] *vt* (*desordenar*) to disarrange; (*trastocar*) to upset, disturb
desarrollar [desarro'ʎar] *vt* (*gen*) to develop; **desarrollarse** *vr* to develop; (*ocurrir*) to take place; (*Foto*) to develop; **desarrollo** *nm* development
desarticular [desartiku'lar] *vt* (*hueso*) to dislocate; (*objeto*) to take apart; (*fig*) to break up
desasosegar [desasose'ɣar] *vt* (*inquietar*) to disturb, make uneasy
desasosiego *etc* [desaso'sjeɣo] *vb V* **desasosegar** ▷ *nm* (*intranquilidad*) uneasiness, restlessness; (*ansiedad*) anxiety
desastre [de'sastre] *nm* disaster; **desastroso, -a** *adj* disastrous
desatar [desa'tar] *vt* (*nudo*) to untie; (*paquete*) to undo; (*separar*) to detach; **desatarse** *vr* (*zapatos*) to come untied; (*tormenta*) to break
desatascar [desatas'kar] *vt* (*cañería*) to unblock, clear
desatender [desaten'der] *vt no prestar atención a*, to disregard; (*abandonar*) to neglect
desatino [desa'tino] *nm* (*idiotez*) foolishness, folly; (*error*) blunder
desatornillar [desatorni'ʎar] *vt* to unscrew
desatrancar [desatran'kar] *vt* (*puerta*) to unbolt; (*cañería*) to clear, unblock
desautorizado, -a [desautori'θaðo, a] *adj* unauthorized
desautorizar [desautori'θar] *vt* (*oficial*) to deprive of authority; (*informe*) to deny
desayunar [desaju'nar] *vi* to have breakfast ▷ *vt* to have for breakfast; **desayuno** *nm* breakfast
desazón [desa'θon] *nf* anxiety
desbarajuste [desβara'xuste] *nm* confusion, disorder
desbaratar [desβara'tar] *vt* (*deshacer, destruir*) to ruin
desbloquear [desβloke'ar] *vt* (*negociaciónes, tráfico*) to get going again;

(*Com: cuenta*) to unfreeze
desbordar [desβor'ðar] *vt* (*sobrepasar*) to go beyond; (*exceder*) to exceed; **desbordarse** *vr* (*río*) to overflow; (*entusiasmo*) to erupt
descabellado, -a [deskaβe'ʎaðo, a] *adj* (*disparatado*) wild, crazy
descafeinado, -a [deskafei'naðo, a] *adj* decaffeinated ▷ *nm* decaffeinated coffee
descalabro [deska'laβro] *nm* blow; (*desgracia*) misfortune
descalificar [deskalifi'kar] *vt* to disqualify; (*desacreditar*) to discredit
descalzar [deskal'θar] *vt* (*zapato*) to take off; **descalzo, -a** *adj* barefoot(ed)
descambiar [deskam'bjar] *vt* to exchange
descaminado, -a [deskami'naðo, a] *adj* (*equivocado*) on the wrong road; (*fig*) misguided
descampado [deskam'paðo] *nm* open space
descansado, -a [deskan'saðo, a] *adj* (*gen*) rested; (*que tranquiliza*) restful
descansar [deskan'sar] *vt* (*gen*) to rest ▷ *vi* to rest, have a rest; (*echarse*) to lie down
descansillo [deskan'siʎo] *nm* (*de escalera*) landing
descanso [des'kanso] *nm* (*reposo*) rest; (*alivio*) relief; (*pausa*) break; (*Deporte*) interval, half time
descapotable [deskapo'taβle] *nm* (*tb*: **coche ~**) convertible
descarado, -a [deska'raðo, a] *adj* shameless; (*insolente*) cheeky
descarga [des'karɣa] *nf* (*Arq, Elec, Mil*) discharge; (*Náut*) unloading; **descargar** [deskar'ɣar] *vt* to unload; (*golpe*) to let fly; **descargarse** *vr* to unburden o.s.; **descargarse algo de Internet** to download sth from the Internet
descaro [des'karo] *nm* nerve
descarriar [deska'rrjar] *vt* (*descaminar*) to misdirect; (*fig*) to lead astray; **descarriarse** *vr* (*perderse*) to lose one's way; (*separarse*) to stray; (*pervertirse*) to err, go astray
descarrilamiento [deskarrila'mjento] *nm* (*de tren*) derailment
descarrilar [deskarri'lar] *vi* to be derailed
descartar [deskar'tar] *vt* (*rechazar*) to reject; (*eliminar*) to rule out; **descartarse** *vr* (*Naipes*) to discard; **~se de** to shirk
descendencia [desθen'denθja] *nf* (*origen*) origin, descent; (*hijos*) offspring
descender [desθen'der] *vt* (*bajar: escalera*) to go down ▷ *vi* to descend; (*temperatura, nivel*) to fall, drop; **~ de** to be descended from
descendiente [desθen'djente] *nmf* descendant
descenso [des'θenso] *nm* descent; (*de temperatura*) drop
descifrar [desθi'frar] *vt* to decipher; (*mensaje*) to decode
descolgar [deskol'ɣar] *vt* (*bajar*) to take down; (*teléfono*) to pick up; **descolgarse** *vr* to let o.s. down
descolorido, -a [deskolo'riðo, a] *adj* faded; (*pálido*) pale
descompasado, -a [deskompa'saðo, a] *adj* (*sin proporción*) out of all proportion; (*excesivo*) excessive
descomponer [deskompo'ner] *vt* (*desordenar*) to disarrange, disturb; (*Tec*) to put out of order; (*dividir*) to break down (into parts); (*fig*) to provoke; **descomponerse** *vr* (*corromperse*) to rot, decompose; (*LAM Tec*) to break down
descomposición [deskomposi'θjon] *nf* (*de un objeto*) breakdown; (*de fruta etc*) decomposition; **descomposición de vientre** (*ESP*) stomach upset, diarrhoea
descompostura [deskompos'tura] *nf* (*MÉX: avería*) breakdown, fault; (*LAM: diarrea*) diarrhoea
descomprimir [deskompri'mir] (*Internet*) to unzip
descompuesto, -a [deskom'pwesto, a] *adj* (*corrompido*) decomposed; (*roto*) broken
desconcertado, -a [deskonθer'taðo, a] *adj* disconcerted, bewildered
desconcertar [deskonθer'tar] *vt* (*confundir*) to baffle; (*incomodar*) to upset, put out; **desconcertarse** *vr* (*turbarse*) to be upset
desconchado, -a [deskon'tʃaðo, a] *adj* (*pintura*) peeling
desconcierto *etc* [deskon'θjerto] *vb V* **desconcertar** ▷ *nm* (*gen*) disorder; (*desorientación*) uncertainty; (*inquietud*) uneasiness
desconectar [deskonek'tar] *vt* to disconnect
desconfianza [deskon'fjanθa] *nf* distrust
desconfiar [deskon'fjar] *vi* to be distrustful; **~ de** to distrust, suspect
descongelar [deskonxe'lar] *vt* to defrost; (*Com, Pol*) to unfreeze
descongestionar [deskonxestjo'nar] *vt* (*cabeza, tráfico*) to clear
desconocer [deskono'θer] *vt* (*ignorar*) not to know, be ignorant of
desconocido, -a [deskono'θiðo, a] *adj* unknown ▷ *nm/f* stranger
desconocimiento [deskonoθi'mjento]

nm falta de conocimientos, ignorance
desconsiderado, -a [deskonsiðe'raðo, a] *adj* inconsiderate; (*insensible*) thoughtless
desconsuelo *etc* [deskon'swelo] *vb V* **desconsolar** ▷ *nm* (*tristeza*) distress; (*desesperación*) despair
descontado, -a [deskon'taðo, a] *adj*: **dar por ~ (que)** to take (it) for granted (that)
descontar [deskon'tar] *vt* (*deducir*) to take away, deduct; (*rebajar*) to discount
descontento, -a [deskon'tento, a] *adj* dissatisfied ▷ *nm* dissatisfaction, discontent
descorchar [deskor'tʃar] *vt* to uncork
descorrer [desko'rrer] *vt* (*cortinas, cerrojo*) to draw back
descortés [deskor'tes] *adj* (*mal educado*) discourteous; (*grosero*) rude
descoser [desko'ser] *vt* to unstitch; **descoserse** *vr* to come apart (at the seams)
descosido, -a [desko'siðo, a] *adj* (*Costura*) unstitched
descreído, -a [deskre'iðo, a] *adj* (*incrédulo*) incredulous; (*falto de fe*) unbelieving
descremado, -a [deskre'maðo, a] *adj* skimmed
describir [deskri'βir] *vt* to describe; **descripción** [deskrip'θjon] *nf* description
descrito [des'krito] *pp de* **describir**
descuartizar [deskwarti'θar] *vt* (*animal*) to cut up
descubierto, -a [desku'βjerto, a] *pp de* **descubrir** ▷ *adj* uncovered, bare; (*persona*) bareheaded ▷ *nm* (*bancario*) overdraft; **al ~** in the open
descubrimiento [deskuβri'mjento] *nm* (*hallazgo*) discovery; (*revelación*) revelation
descubrir [desku'βrir] *vt* to discover, find; (*inaugurar*) to unveil; (*vislumbrar*) to detect; (*revelar*) to reveal, show; (*destapar*) to uncover; **descubrirse** *vr* to reveal o.s.; (*quitarse sombrero*) to take off one's hat; (*confesar*) to confess
descuento *etc* [des'kwento] *vb V* **descontar** ▷ *nm* discount
descuidado, -a [deskwi'ðaðo, a] *adj* (*sin cuidado*) careless; (*desordenado*) untidy; (*olvidadizo*) forgetful; (*dejado*) neglected; (*desprevenido*) unprepared
descuidar [deskwi'ðar] *vt* (*dejar*) to neglect; (*olvidar*) to overlook; **descuidarse** *vr* (*distraerse*) to be careless; (*abandonarse*) to let o.s. go; (*desprevenirse*) to drop one's guard; **¡descuida!** don't worry!; **descuido** *nm* (*dejadez*) carelessness; (*olvido*) negligence

PALABRA CLAVE

desde ['desðe] *prep* **1** (*lugar*) from; **desde Burgos hasta mi casa hay 30 km** it's 30 km from Burgos to my house
2 (*posición*): **hablaba desde el balcón** she was speaking from the balcony
3 (*tiempo*: + *adv, n*): **desde ahora** from now on; **desde la boda** since the wedding; **desde niño** since I *etc* was a child; **desde 3 años atrás** since 3 years ago
4 (*tiempo*: + *vb, fecha*) since; for; **nos conocemos desde 1992/desde hace 20 años** we've known each other since 1992/ for 20 years; **no le veo desde 1997/desde hace 5 años** I haven't seen him since 1997/ for 5 years
5 (*gama*): **desde los más lujosos hasta los más económicos** from the most luxurious to the most reasonably priced
6: **desde luego (que no)** of course (not)
▷ *conj*: **desde que: desde que recuerdo** for as long as I can remember; **desde que llegó no ha salido** he hasn't been out since he arrived

desdén [des'ðen] *nm* scorn
desdeñar [desðe'ɲar] *vt* (*despreciar*) to scorn
desdicha [des'ðitʃa] *nf* (*desgracia*) misfortune; (*infelicidad*) unhappiness; **desdichado, -a** *adj* (*sin suerte*) unlucky; (*infeliz*) unhappy
desear [dese'ar] *vt* to want, desire, wish for
desechar [dese'tʃar] *vt* (*basura*) to throw out *o* away; (*ideas*) to reject, discard; **desechos** *nmpl* rubbish *sg*, waste *sg*
desembalar [desemba'lar] *vt* to unpack
desembarazar [desembara'θar] *vt* (*desocupar*) to clear; (*desenredar*) to free; **desembarazarse** *vr*: **~se de** to free o.s. of, get rid of
desembarcar [desembar'kar] *vt* (*mercancías etc*) to unload ▷ *vi* to disembark
desembocadura [desemboka'ðura] *nf* (*de río*) mouth; (*de calle*) opening
desembocar [desembo'kar] *vi* (*río*) to flow into; (*fig*) to result in
desembolso [desem'bolso] *nm* payment
desembrollar [desembro'ʎar] *vt* (*madeja*) to unravel; (*asunto, malentendido*) to sort out
desemejanza [deseme'xanθa] *nf* dissimilarity
desempaquetar [desempake'tar] *vt* (*regalo*) to unwrap; (*mercancía*) to unpack

desempate [desem'pate] *nm* (*Fútbol*) replay, play-off; (*Tenis*) tie-break(er)
desempeñar [desempe'ɲar] *vt* (*cargo*) to hold; (*papel*) to perform; (*lo empeñado*) to redeem; **~ un papel** (*fig*) to play (a role)
desempleado, -a [desemple'aðo, a] *nm/f* unemployed person; **desempleo** *nm* unemployment
desencadenar [desenkaðe'nar] *vt* to unchain; (*ira*) to unleash; **desencadenarse** *vr* to break loose; (*tormenta*) to burst; (*guerra*) to break out
desencajar [desenka'xar] *vt* (*hueso*) to dislocate; (*mecanismo, pieza*) to disconnect, disengage
desencanto [desen'kanto] *nm* disillusionment
desenchufar [desentʃu'far] *vt* to unplug
desenfadado, -a [desenfa'ðaðo, a] *adj* (*desenvuelto*) uninhibited; (*descarado*) forward; **desenfado** *nm* (*libertad*) freedom; (*comportamiento*) free and easy manner; (*descaro*) forwardness
desenfocado, -a [desenfo'kaðo, a] *adj* (*Foto*) out of focus
desenfreno [desen'freno] *nm* wildness; (*de las pasiones*) lack of self-control
desenganchar [desengan'tʃar] *vt* (*gen*) to unhook; (*Ferro*) to uncouple
desengañar [desenga'ɲar] *vt* to disillusion; **desengañarse** *vr* to become disillusioned; **desengaño** *nm* disillusionment; (*decepción*) disappointment
desenlace [desen'laθe] *nm* outcome
desenmascarar [desenmaska'rar] *vt* to unmask
desenredar [desenre'ðar] *vt* (*pelo*) to untangle; (*problema*) to sort out
desenroscar [desenros'kar] *vt* to unscrew
desentenderse [desenten'derse] *vr*: **~ de** to pretend not to know about; (*apartarse*) to have nothing to do with
desenterrar [desente'rrar] *vt* to exhume; (*tesoro, fig*) to unearth, dig up
desentonar [desento'nar] *vi* (*Mús*) to sing (*o* play) out of tune; (*color*) to clash
desentrañar [desentra'ɲar] *vt* (*misterio*) to unravel
desenvoltura [desenβol'tura] *nf* ease
desenvolver [desenβol'βer] *vt* (*paquete*) to unwrap; (*fig*) to develop; **desenvolverse** *vr* (*desarrollarse*) to unfold, develop; (*arreglárselas*) to cope
deseo [de'seo] *nm* desire, wish; **deseoso, -a** *adj*: **estar deseoso de** to be anxious to
desequilibrado, -a [desekili'βraðo, a] *adj* unbalanced
desertar [deser'tar] *vi* to desert
desértico, -a [de'sertiko, a] *adj* desert *cpd*
desesperación [desespera'θjon] *nf* (*impaciencia*) desperation, despair; (*irritación*) fury
desesperar [desespe'rar] *vt* to drive to despair; (*exasperar*) to drive to distraction ▷ *vi*: **~ de** to despair of; **desesperarse** *vr* to despair, lose hope
desestabilizar [desestaβili'θar] *vt* to destabilize
desestimar [desesti'mar] *vt* (*menospreciar*) to have a low opinion of; (*rechazar*) to reject
desfachatez [desfatʃa'teθ] *nf* (*insolencia*) impudence; (*descaro*) rudeness
desfalco [des'falko] *nm* embezzlement
desfallecer [desfaʎe'θer] *vi* (*perder las fuerzas*) to become weak; (*desvanecerse*) to faint
desfasado, -a [desfa'saðo, a] *adj* (*anticuado*) old-fashioned; **desfase** *nm* (*diferencia*) gap
desfavorable [desfaβo'raβle] *adj* unfavourable
desfigurar [desfiɤu'rar] *vt* (*cara*) to disfigure; (*cuerpo*) to deform
desfiladero [desfila'ðero] *nm* gorge
desfilar [desfi'lar] *vi* to parade; **desfile** *nm* procession; **desfile de modelos** fashion show
desgana [des'ɤana] *nf* (*falta de apetito*) loss of appetite; (*apatía*) unwillingness; **desganado, -a** *adj*: **estar desganado** (*sin apetito*) to have no appetite; (*sin entusiasmo*) to have lost interest
desgarrar [desɤa'rrar] *vt* to tear (up); (*fig*) to shatter; **desgarro** *nm* (*en tela*) tear; (*aflicción*) grief
desgastar [desɤas'tar] *vt* (*deteriorar*) to wear away *o* down; (*estropear*) to spoil; **desgastarse** *vr* to get worn out; **desgaste** *nm* wear (and tear)
desglosar [desɤlo'sar] *vt* (*factura*) to break down
desgracia [des'ɤraθja] *nf* misfortune; (*accidente*) accident; (*vergüenza*) disgrace; (*contratiempo*) setback; **por ~** unfortunately; **desgraciado, -a** [desɤra'θjaðo, a] *adj* (*sin suerte*) unlucky, unfortunate; (*miserable*) wretched; (*infeliz*) miserable
desgravar [desɤra'βar] *vt* (*impuestos*) to reduce the tax *o* duty on
desguace [des'ɤwaθe] (ESP) *nm* junkyard
deshabitado, -a [desaβi'taðo, a] *adj* uninhabited

deshacer [desa'θer] *vt* (*casa*) to break up; (*Tec*) to take apart; (*enemigo*) to defeat; (*diluir*) to melt; (*contrato*) to break; (*intriga*) to solve; **deshacerse** *vr* (*disolverse*) to melt; (*despedazarse*) to come apart *o* undone; **~se de** to get rid of; **~se en lágrimas** to burst into tears
deshecho, -a [des'etʃo, a] *adj* undone; (*roto*) smashed; (*persona*): **estar ~** to be shattered
desheredar [desere'ðar] *vt* to disinherit
deshidratar [desiðra'tar] *vt* to dehydrate
deshielo [des'jelo] *nm* thaw
deshonesto, -a [deso'nesto, a] *adj* indecent
deshonra [des'onra] *nf* (*deshonor*) dishonour; (*vergüenza*) shame
deshora [des'ora]: **a ~** *adv* at the wrong time
deshuesadero [deswesa'ðero] (*MÉX*) *nm* junkyard
deshuesar [deswe'sar] *vt* (*carne*) to bone; (*fruta*) to stone
desierto, -a [de'sjerto, a] *adj* (*casa, calle, negocio*) deserted ▷ *nm* desert
designar [desiɣ'nar] *vt* (*nombrar*) to designate; (*indicar*) to fix
desigual [desi'ɣwal] *adj* (*terreno*) uneven; (*lucha etc*) unequal
desilusión [desilu'sjon] *nf* disillusionment; (*decepción*) disappointment; **desilusionar** *vt* to disillusion; to disappoint; **desilusionarse** *vr* to become disillusioned
desinfectar [desinfek'tar] *vt* to disinfect
desinflar [desin'flar] *vt* to deflate
desintegración [desinteɣra'θjon] *nf* disintegration
desinterés [desinte'res] *nm* (*desgana*) lack of interest; (*altruismo*) unselfishness
desintoxicarse [desintoksi'karse] *vr* (*drogadicto*) to undergo detoxification
desistir [desis'tir] *vi* (*renunciar*) to stop, desist
desleal [desle'al] *adj* (*infiel*) disloyal; (*Com: competencia*) unfair; **deslealtad** *nf* disloyalty
desligar [desli'ɣar] *vt* (*desatar*) to untie, undo; (*separar*) to separate; **desligarse** *vr* (*de un compromiso*) to extricate o.s.
desliz [des'liθ] *nm* (*fig*) lapse; **deslizar** *vt* to slip, slide
deslumbrar [deslum'brar] *vt* to dazzle
desmadrarse [desma'ðrarse] (*fam*) *vr* (*descontrolarse*) to run wild; (*divertirse*) to let one's hair down; **desmadre** (*fam*) *nm* (*desorganización*) chaos; (*jaleo*) commotion
desmán [des'man] *nm* (*exceso*) outrage; (*abuso de poder*) abuse
desmantelar [desmante'lar] *vt* (*deshacer*) to dismantle; (*casa*) to strip
desmaquillador [desmakiʎa'ðor] *nm* make-up remover
desmayar [desma'jar] *vi* to lose heart; **desmayarse** *vr* (*Med*) to faint; **desmayo** *nm* (*Med: acto*) faint; (*: estado*) unconsciousness
desmemoriado, -a [desmemo'rjado, a] *adj* forgetful
desmentir [desmen'tir] *vt* (*contradecir*) to contradict; (*refutar*) to deny
desmenuzar [desmenu'θar] *vt* (*deshacer*) to crumble; (*carne*) to chop; (*examinar*) to examine closely
desmesurado, -a [desmesu'raðo, a] *adj* disproportionate
desmontable [desmon'taβle] *adj* (*que se quita: pieza*) detachable; (*plegable*) collapsible, folding
desmontar [desmon'tar] *vt* (*deshacer*) to dismantle; (*tierra*) to level ▷ *vi* to dismount
desmoralizar [desmorali'θar] *vt* to demoralize
desmoronar [desmoro'nar] *vt* to wear away, erode; **desmoronarse** *vr* (*edificio, dique*) to collapse; (*economía*) to decline
desnatado, -a [desna'taðo, a] *adj* skimmed
desnivel [desni'βel] *nm* (*de terreno*) unevenness
desnudar [desnu'ðar] *vt* (*desvestir*) to undress; (*despojar*) to strip; **desnudarse** *vr* (*desvestirse*) to get undressed; **desnudo, -a** *adj* naked ▷ *nm/f* nude; **desnudo de** devoid *o* bereft of
desnutrición [desnutri'θjon] *nf* malnutrition; **desnutrido, -a** *adj* undernourished
desobedecer [desoβeðe'θer] *vt, vi* to disobey; **desobediencia** *nf* disobedience
desocupado, -a [desoku'paðo, a] *adj* at leisure; (*desempleado*) unemployed; (*deshabitado*) empty, vacant
desodorante [desoðo'rante] *nm* deodorant
desolación [desola'θjon] *nf* (*de lugar*) desolation; (*fig*) grief
desolar [deso'lar] *vt* to ruin, lay waste
desorbitado, -a [desorβi'taðo, a] *adj* (*excesivo: ambición*) boundless; (*deseos*) excessive; (*: precio*) exorbitant
desorden [des'orðen] *nm* confusion; (*político*) disorder, unrest
desorganización [desorɣaniθa'θjon] *nf* (*de persona*) disorganization; (*en empresa, oficina*) disorder, chaos

desorientar [desorjen'tar] *vt* (*extraviar*) to mislead; (*confundir, desconcertar*) to confuse; **desorientarse** *vr* (*perderse*) to lose one's way

despabilado, -a [despaβi'laðo, a] *adj* (*despierto*) wide-awake; (*fig*) alert, sharp

despachar [despa'tʃar] *vt* (*negocio*) to do, complete; (*enviar*) to send, dispatch; (*vender*) to sell, deal in; (*billete*) to issue; (*mandar ir*) to send away

despacho [des'patʃo] *nm* (*oficina*) office; (*de paquetes*) dispatch; (*venta*) sale; (*comunicación*) message

despacio [des'paθjo] *adv* slowly

desparpajo [despar'paxo] *nm* self-confidence; (*pey*) nerve

desparramar [desparra'mar] *vt* (*esparcir*) to scatter; (*líquido*) to spill

despecho [des'petʃo] *nm* spite

despectivo, -a [despek'tiβo, a] *adj* (*despreciativo*) derogatory; (*Ling*) pejorative

despedida [despe'ðiða] *nf* (*adiós*) farewell; (*de obrero*) sacking

despedir [despe'ðir] *vt* (*visita*) to see off, show out; (*empleado*) to dismiss; (*inquilino*) to evict; (*objeto*) to hurl; (*olor etc*) to give out *o* off; **despedirse** *vr*: **~se de** to say goodbye to

despegar [despe'ɣar] *vt* to unstick ▷ *vi* (*avión*) to take off; **despegarse** *vr* to come loose, come unstuck; **despego** *nm* detachment

despegue *etc* [des'peɣe] *vb V* **despegar** ▷ *nm* takeoff

despeinado, -a [despei'naðo, a] *adj* dishevelled, unkempt

despejado, -a [despe'xaðo, a] *adj* (*lugar*) clear, free; (*cielo*) clear; (*persona*) wide-awake, bright

despejar [despe'xar] *vt* (*gen*) to clear; (*misterio*) to clear up ▷ *vi* (*el tiempo*) to clear; **despejarse** *vr* (*tiempo, cielo*) to clear (up); (*misterio*) to become clearer; (*cabeza*) to clear

despensa [des'pensa] *nf* larder

despeñarse [despe'ɲarse] *vr* to hurl o.s. down; (*coche*) to tumble over

desperdicio [desper'ðiθjo] *nm* (*despilfarro*) squandering; **desperdicios** *nmpl* (*basura*) rubbish *sg* (BRIT), garbage *sg* (US); (*residuos*) waste *sg*

desperezarse [despere'θarse] *vr* to stretch

desperfecto [desper'fekto] *nm* (*deterioro*) slight damage; (*defecto*) flaw, imperfection

despertador [desperta'ðor] *nm* alarm clock

despertar [desper'tar] *nm* awakening ▷ *vt* (*persona*) to wake up; (*recuerdos*) to revive; (*sentimiento*) to arouse ▷ *vi* to awaken, wake up; **despertarse** *vr* to awaken, wake up

despido *etc* [des'piðo] *vb V* **despedir** ▷ *nm* dismissal, sacking

despierto, -a *etc* [des'pjerto, a] *vb V* **despertar** ▷ *adj* awake; (*fig*) sharp, alert

despilfarro [despil'farro] *nm* (*derroche*) squandering; (*lujo desmedido*) extravagance

despistar [despis'tar] *vt* to throw off the track *o* scent; (*confundir*) to mislead, confuse; **despistarse** *vr* to take the wrong road; (*confundirse*) to become confused

despiste [des'piste] *nm* absent-mindedness; **un ~** a mistake *o* slip

desplazamiento [desplaθa'mjento] *nm* displacement

desplazar [despla'θar] *vt* to move; (*Náut*) to displace; (*Inform*) to scroll; (*fig*) to oust; **desplazarse** *vr* (*persona*) to travel

desplegar [desple'ɣar] *vt* (*tela, papel*) to unfold, open out; (*bandera*) to unfurl; **despliegue** *etc* [des'pleɣe] *vb V* **desplegar** ▷ *nm* display

desplomarse [desplo'marse] *vr* (*edificio, gobierno, persona*) to collapse

desplumar [desplu'mar] *vt* (*ave*) to pluck; (*fam: estafar*) to fleece

despoblado, -a [despo'βlaðo, a] *adj* (*sin habitantes*) uninhabited

despojar [despo'xar] *vt* (*alguien: de sus bienes*) to divest of, deprive of; (*casa*) to strip, leave bare; (*alguien: de su cargo*) to strip of

despojo [des'poxo] *nm* (*acto*) plundering; (*objetos*) plunder, loot; **despojos** *nmpl* (*de ave, res*) offal *sg*

desposado, -a [despo'saðo, a] *adj, nm/f* newly-wed

despreciar [despre'θjar] *vt* (*desdeñar*) to despise, scorn; (*afrentar*) to slight; **desprecio** *nm* scorn, contempt; slight

desprender [despren'der] *vt* (*broche*) to unfasten; (*olor*) to give off; **desprenderse** *vr* (*botón: caerse*) to fall off; (*broche*) to come unfastened; (*olor, perfume*) to be given off; **~se de algo que ...** to draw from sth that ...

desprendimiento [desprendi'mjento] *nm* (*gen*) loosening; (*generosidad*) disinterestedness; (*de tierra, rocas*) landslide; **desprendimiento de retina** detachment of the retina

despreocupado, -a [despreoku'paðo, a] *adj* (*sin preocupación*) unworried, nonchalant; (*negligente*) careless

despreocuparse [despreoku'parse] *vr* not to worry; **~ de** to have no interest in

desprestigiar [desprestі'xjar] *vt* (*criticar*) to run down; (*desacreditar*) to discredit

desprevenido, -a [despreβe'niðo, a] *adj* (*no preparado*) unprepared, unready
desproporcionado, -a [desproporθjo'naðo, a] *adj* disproportionate, out of proportion
desprovisto, -a [despro'βisto, a] *adj*: **~ de** devoid of
después [des'pwes] *adv* afterwards, later; (*próximo paso*) next; **~ de comer** after lunch; **un año ~** a year later; **~ se debatió el tema** next the matter was discussed; **~ de corregido el texto** after the text had been corrected; **~ de todo** after all
desquiciado, -a [deski'θjaðo, a] *adj* deranged
destacar [desta'kar] *vt* to emphasize, point up; (*Mil*) to detach, detail ▷ *vi* (*resaltarse*) to stand out; (*persona*) to be outstanding *o* exceptional; **destacarse** *vr* to stand out; to be outstanding *o* exceptional
destajo [des'taxo] *nm*: **trabajar a ~** to do piecework
destapar [desta'par] *vt* (*botella*) to open; (*cacerola*) to take the lid off; (*descubrir*) to uncover; **destaparse** *vr* (*revelarse*) to reveal one's true character
destartalado, -a [destarta'laðo, a] *adj* (*desordenado*) untidy; (*ruinoso*) tumbledown
destello [des'teʎo] *nm* (*de estrella*) twinkle; (*de faro*) signal light
destemplado, -a [destem'plaðo, a] *adj* (*Mús*) out of tune; (*voz*) harsh; (*Med*) out of sorts; (*tiempo*) unpleasant, nasty
desteñir [deste'ɲir] *vt* to fade ▷ *vi* to fade; **desteñirse** *vr* to fade; **esta tela no destiñe** this fabric will not run
desternillarse [desterni'ʎarse] *vr*: **~ de risa** to split one's sides laughing
desterrar [deste'rrar] *vt* (*exiliar*) to exile; (*fig*) to banish, dismiss
destiempo [des'tjempo]: **a ~** *adv* out of turn
destierro *etc* [des'tjerro] *vb V* **desterrar** ▷ *nm* exile
destilar [desti'lar] *vt* to distil; **destilería** *nf* distillery
destinar [desti'nar] *vt* (*funcionario*) to appoint, assign; (*fondos*): **~ (a)** to set aside (for)
destinatario, -a [destina'tarjo, a] *nm/f* addressee
destino [des'tino] *nm* (*suerte*) destiny; (*de avión, viajero*) destination; **con ~ a Londres** (*barco*) (bound) for London; (*avión, carta*) to London
destituir [destitu'ir] *vt* to dismiss
destornillador [destorniʎa'ðor] *nm* screwdriver
destornillar [destorni'ʎar] *vt* (*tornillo*) to unscrew; **destornillarse** *vr* to unscrew
destreza [des'treθa] *nf* (*habilidad*) skill; (*maña*) dexterity
destrozar [destro'θar] *vt* (*romper*) to smash, break (up); (*estropear*) to ruin; (*nervios*) to shatter
destrozo [des'troθo] *nm* (*acción*) destruction; (*desastre*) smashing; **destrozos** *nmpl* (*pedazos*) pieces; (*daños*) havoc *sg*
destrucción [destruk'θjon] *nf* destruction
destruir [destru'ir] *vt* to destroy
desuso [des'uso] *nm* disuse; **caer en ~** to become obsolete
desvalijar [desvali'xar] *vt* (*persona*) to rob; (*casa, tienda*) to burgle; (*coche*) to break into
desván [des'βan] *nm* attic
desvanecer [desβane'θer] *vt* (*disipar*) to dispel; (*borrar*) to blur; **desvanecerse** *vr* (*humo etc*) to vanish, disappear; (*color*) to fade; (*recuerdo, sonido*) to fade away; (*Med*) to pass out; (*duda*) to be dispelled
desvariar [desβa'rjar] *vi* (*enfermo*) to be delirious
desvelar [desβe'lar] *vt* to keep awake; **desvelarse** *vr* (*no poder dormir*) to stay awake; (*preocuparse*) to be vigilant *o* watchful
desventaja [desβen'taxa] *nf* disadvantage
desvergonzado, -a [desβerɣon'θaðo, a] *adj* shameless
desvestir [desβes'tir] *vt* to undress; **desvestirse** *vr* to undress
desviación [desβja'θjon] *nf* deviation; (*Auto*) diversion, detour
desviar [des'βjar] *vt* to turn aside; (*río*) to alter the course of; (*navío*) to divert, re-route; (*conversación*) to sidetrack; **desviarse** *vr* (*apartarse del camino*) to turn aside; (*: barco*) to go off course
desvío *etc* [des'βio] *vb V* **desviar** ▷ *nm* (*desviación*) detour, diversion; (*fig*) indifference
desvivirse [desβi'βirse] *vr*: **~ por** (*anhelar*) to long for, crave for; (*hacer lo posible por*) to do one's utmost for
detallar [deta'ʎar] *vt* to detail
detalle [de'taʎe] *nm* detail; (*gesto*) gesture, token; **al ~** in detail; (*Com*) retail
detallista [deta'ʎista] *nmf* (*Com*) retailer
detective [detek'tiβe] *nmf* detective; **detective privado** private detective
detener [dete'ner] *vt* (*gen*) to stop; (*Jur*) to arrest; (*objeto*) to keep; **detenerse** *vr* to stop; (*demorarse*): **~se en** to delay over,

linger over
detenidamente [deteniða'mente] *adv* (*minuciosamente*) carefully; (*extensamente*) at great length
detenido, -a [dete'niðo, a] *adj* (*arrestado*) under arrest ▷ *nm/f* person under arrest, prisoner
detenimiento [deteni'mjento] *nm*: **con ~** thoroughly; (*observar, considerar*) carefully
detergente [deter'xente] *nm* detergent
deteriorar [deterjo'rar] *vt* to spoil, damage; **deteriorarse** *vr* to deteriorate; **deterioro** *nm* deterioration
determinación [determina'θjon] *nf* (*empeño*) determination; (*decisión*) decision; **determinado, -a** *adj* specific
determinar [determi'nar] *vt* (*plazo*) to fix; (*precio*) to settle; **determinarse** *vr* to decide
detestar [detes'tar] *vt* to detest
detractor, a [detrak'tor, a] *nm/f* slanderer, libeller
detrás [de'tras] *adv* (*tb*: **por ~**) behind; (*atrás*) at the back; **~ de** behind
detrimento [detri'mento] *nm*: **en ~ de** to the detriment of
deuda ['deuða] *nf* debt; **deuda exterior/pública** foreign/national debt
devaluación [deβalwa'θjon] *nf* devaluation
devastar [deβas'tar] *vt* (*destruir*) to devastate
deveras [de'βeras] (*MÉX*) *nf inv*: **un amigo de (a) ~** a true *o* real friend
devoción [deβo'θjon] *nf* devotion
devolución [deβolu'θjon] *nf* (*reenvío*) return, sending back; (*reembolso*) repayment; (*Jur*) devolution
devolver [deβol'βer] *vt* to return; (*lo extraviado, lo prestado*) to give back; (*carta al correo*) to send back; (*Com*) to repay, refund ▷ *vi* (*vomitar*) to be sick
devorar [deβo'rar] *vt* to devour
devoto, -a [de'βoto, a] *adj* devout ▷ *nm/f* admirer
devuelto *pp de* **devolver**
devuelva *etc vb V* **devolver**
di *etc vb V* **dar; decir**
día ['dia] *nm* day; **¿qué ~ es?** what's the date?; **estar/poner al ~** to be/keep up to date; **el ~ de hoy/de mañana** today/tomorrow; **al ~ siguiente** (on) the following day; **vivir al ~** to live from hand to mouth; **de ~** by day, in daylight; **en pleno ~** in full daylight; **Día de la Independencia** Independence Day; **Día de los Muertos** (*MÉX*) All Souls' Day; **Día de Reyes** Epiphany; **día feriado** (*LAM*) holiday; **día festivo** (*ESP*) holiday; **día lectivo** teaching day; **día libre** day off
diabetes [dja'βetes] *nf* diabetes
diablo ['djaβlo] *nm* devil; **diablura** *nf* prank
diadema [dja'ðema] *nf* tiara
diafragma [dja'fraɣma] *nm* diaphragm
diagnóstico [diaɣ'nostiko] *nm* = **diagnosis**
diagonal [djaɣo'nal] *adj* diagonal
diagrama [dja'ɣrama] *nm* diagram
dial [djal] *nm* dial
dialecto [dja'lekto] *nm* dialect
dialogar [djalo'ɣar] *vi*: **~ con** (*Pol*) to hold talks with
diálogo ['djaloɣo] *nm* dialogue
diamante [dja'mante] *nm* diamond
diana ['djana] *nf* (*Mil*) reveille; (*de blanco*) centre, bull's-eye
diapositiva [djaposi'tiβa] *nf* (*Foto*) slide, transparency
diario, -a ['djarjo, a] *adj* daily ▷ *nm* newspaper; **a ~** daily; **de ~** everyday
diarrea [dja'rrea] *nf* diarrhoea
dibujar [diβu'xar] *vt* to draw, sketch; **dibujo** *nm* drawing; **dibujos animados** cartoons
diccionario [dikθjo'narjo] *nm* dictionary
dice *etc vb V* **decir**
dicho, -a ['ditʃo, a] *pp de* **decir** ▷ *adj*: **en ~s países** in the aforementioned countries ▷ *nm* saying
dichoso, -a [di'tʃoso, a] *adj* happy
diciembre [di'θjembre] *nm* December
dictado [dik'taðo] *nm* dictation
dictador [dikta'ðor] *nm* dictator; **dictadura** *nf* dictatorship
dictar [dik'tar] *vt* (*carta*) to dictate; (*Jur: sentencia*) to pronounce; (*decreto*) to issue; (*LAM: clase*) to give
didáctico, -a [di'ðaktiko, a] *adj* educational
diecinueve [djeθi'nweβe] *num* nineteen
dieciocho [djeθi'otʃo] *num* eighteen
dieciséis [djeθi'seis] *num* sixteen
diecisiete [djeθi'sjete] *num* seventeen
diente ['djente] *nm* (*Anat, Tec*) tooth; (*Zool*) fang; (*: de elefante*) tusk; (*de ajo*) clove
diera *etc vb V* **dar**
diesel ['disel] *adj*: **motor ~** diesel engine
diestro, -a ['djestro, a] *adj* (*derecho*) right; (*hábil*) skilful
dieta ['djeta] *nf* diet; **estar a ~** to be on a diet
diez [djeθ] *num* ten
diferencia [dife'renθja] *nf* difference; **a ~ de** unlike; **diferenciar** *vt* to differentiate between ▷ *vi* to differ; **diferenciarse**

d

vr to differ, be different; (*distinguirse*) to distinguish o.s.
diferente [dife'rente] *adj* different
diferido [dife'riðo] *nm*: **en ~** (*TV etc*) recorded
difícil [di'fiθil] *adj* difficult
dificultad [difikul'tað] *nf* difficulty; (*problema*) trouble
dificultar [difikul'tar] *vt* (*complicar*) to complicate, make difficult; (*estorbar*) to obstruct
difundir [difun'dir] *vt* (*calor, luz*) to diffuse; (*Radio, TV*) to broadcast; **~ una noticia** to spread a piece of news; **difundirse** *vr* to spread (out)
difunto, -a [di'funto, a] *adj* dead, deceased ▷ *nm/f* deceased (person)
difusión [difu'sjon] *nf* (*Radio, TV*) broadcasting
diga *etc vb V* **decir**
digerir [dixe'rir] *vt* to digest; (*fig*) to absorb; **digestión** *nf* digestion; **digestivo, -a** *adj* digestive
digital [dixi'tal] *adj* digital
dignarse [diɣ'narse] *vr* to deign to
dignidad [diɣni'ðað] *nf* dignity
digno, -a ['diɣno, a] *adj* worthy
digo *etc vb V* **decir**
dije *etc vb V* **decir**
dilatar [dila'tar] *vt* (*cuerpo*) to dilate; (*prolongar*) to prolong
dilema [di'lema] *nm* dilemma
diluir [dilu'ir] *vt* to dilute
diluvio [di'luβjo] *nm* deluge, flood
dimensión [dimen'sjon] *nf* dimension
diminuto, -a [dimi'nuto, a] *adj* tiny, diminutive
dimitir [dimi'tir] *vi* to resign
dimos *vb V* **dar**
Dinamarca [dina'marka] *nf* Denmark
dinámico, -a [di'namiko, a] *adj* dynamic
dinamita [dina'mita] *nf* dynamite
dínamo ['dinamo] *nf* dynamo
dineral [dine'ral] *nm* large sum of money, fortune
dinero [di'nero] *nm* money; **dinero en efectivo** *o* **metálico** cash; **dinero suelto** (loose) change
dio *vb V* **dar**
dios [djos] *nm* god; **¡D~ mío!** (oh,) my God!; **¡por D~!** for heaven's sake!; **diosa** ['djosa] *nf* goddess
diploma [di'ploma] *nm* diploma
diplomacia [diplo'maθja] *nf* diplomacy; (*fig*) tact
diplomado, -a [diplo'maðo, a] *adj* qualified
diplomático, -a [diplo'matiko, a] *adj* diplomatic ▷ *nm/f* diplomat
diputación [diputa'θjon] *nf* (*tb*: **~ provincial**) ≈ county council
diputado, -a [dipu'taðo, a] *nm/f* delegate; (*Pol*) ≈ member of parliament (BRIT) ≈ representative (US)
dique ['dike] *nm* dyke
diré *etc vb V* **decir**
dirección [direk'θjon] *nf* direction; (*señas*) address; (*Auto*) steering; (*gerencia*) management; (*Pol*) leadership; **dirección única/prohibida** one-way street/no entry
direccional [direkθjo'nal] (MÉX) *nf* (*Auto*) indicator
directa [di'rekta] *nf* (*Auto*) top gear
directiva [direk'tiβa] *nf* (*tb*: **junta ~**) board of directors
directo, -a [di'rekto, a] *adj* direct; (*Radio, TV*) live; **transmitir en ~** to broadcast live
director, a [direk'tor, a] *adj* leading ▷ *nm/f* director; (*Escol*) head(teacher) (BRIT), principal (US); (*gerente*) manager/ess; (*Prensa*) editor; **director de cine** film director; **director general** managing director
directorio [direk'torjo] (MÉX) *nm* (*telefónico*) phone book
dirigente [diri'xente] *nmf* (*Pol*) leader
dirigir [diri'xir] *vt* to direct; (*carta*) to address; (*obra de teatro, film*) to direct; (*Mús*) to conduct; (*negocio*) to manage; **dirigirse** *vr*: **~se a** to go towards, make one's way towards; (*hablar con*) to speak to
dirija *etc vb V* **dirigir**
disciplina [disθi'plina] *nf* discipline
discípulo, -a [dis'θipulo, a] *nm/f* disciple
Discman® ['diskman] *nm* Discman®
disco ['disko] *nm* disc; (*Deporte*) discus; (*Tel*) dial; (*Auto*: *semáforo*) light; (*Mús*) record; **disco compacto/de larga duración** compact disc/long-playing record; **disco de freno** brake disc; **disco flexible/duro** *o* **rígido** (*Inform*) floppy/hard disk
disconforme [diskon'forme] *adj* differing; **estar ~ (con)** to be in disagreement (with)
discordia [dis'korðja] *nf* discord
discoteca [disko'teka] *nf* disco(theque)
discreción [diskre'θjon] *nf* discretion; (*reserva*) prudence; **comer a ~** to eat as much as one wishes
discreto, -a [dis'kreto, a] *adj* discreet
discriminación [diskrimina'θjon] *nf* discrimination
disculpa [dis'kulpa] *nf* excuse; (*pedir perdón*) apology; **pedir ~s a/por** to apologize to/for; **disculpar** *vt* to excuse, pardon; **disculparse** *vr* to excuse o.s.; to

apologize
discurso [dis'kurso] *nm* speech
discusión [disku'sjon] *nf* (*diálogo*) discussion; (*riña*) argument
discutir [disku'tir] *vt* (*debatir*) to discuss; (*pelear*) to argue about; (*contradecir*) to argue against ▷*vi* (*debatir*) to discuss; (*pelearse*) to argue
disecar [dise'kar] *vt* (*conservar: animal*) to stuff; (*: planta*) to dry
diseñar [dise'ɲar] *vt, vi* to design
diseño [di'seɲo] *nm* design
disfraz [dis'fraθ] *nm* (*máscara*) disguise; (*excusa*) pretext; **disfrazar** *vt* to disguise; **disfrazarse** *vr*: **disfrazarse de** to disguise o.s. as
disfrutar [disfru'tar] *vt* to enjoy ▷*vi* to enjoy o.s.; **~ de** to enjoy, possess
disgustar [disɣus'tar] *vt* (*no gustar*) to displease; (*contrariar, enojar*) to annoy, upset; **disgustarse** *vr* (*enfadarse*) to get upset; (*dos personas*) to fall out

No confundir **disgustar** con la palabra inglesa *disgust*.

disgusto [dis'ɣusto] *nm* (*contrariedad*) annoyance; (*tristeza*) grief; (*riña*) quarrel
disimular [disimu'lar] *vt* (*ocultar*) to hide, conceal ▷*vi* to dissemble
dislocarse [dislo'karse] *vr* (*articulación*) to sprain, dislocate
disminución [disminu'θjon] *nf* decrease, reduction
disminuido, -a [disminu'iðo, a] *nm/f*: **~ mental/físico** mentally/physically handicapped person
disminuir [disminu'ir] *vt* to decrease, diminish
disolver [disol'βer] *vt* (*gen*) to dissolve; **disolverse** *vr* to dissolve; (*Com*) to go into liquidation
dispar [dis'par] *adj* different
disparar [dispa'rar] *vt, vi* to shoot, fire
disparate [dispa'rate] *nm* (*tontería*) foolish remark; (*error*) blunder; **decir ~s** to talk nonsense
disparo [dis'paro] *nm* shot
dispersar [disper'sar] *vt* to disperse; **dispersarse** *vr* to scatter
disponer [dispo'ner] *vt* (*arreglar*) to arrange; (*ordenar*) to put in order; (*preparar*) to prepare, get ready ▷*vi*: **~ de** to have, own; **disponerse** *vr*: **~se a** *o* **para hacer** to prepare to do
disponible [dispo'niβle] *adj* available
disposición [disposi'θjon] *nf* arrangement, disposition; (*voluntad*) willingness; (*Inform*) layout; **a su ~** at your service
dispositivo [disposi'tiβo] *nm* device, mechanism
dispuesto, -a [dis'pwesto, a] *pp de* **disponer** ▷*adj* (*arreglado*) arranged; (*preparado*) disposed
disputar [dispu'tar] *vt* (*carrera*) to compete in
disquete [dis'kete] *nm* floppy disk, diskette
distancia [dis'tanθja] *nf* distance; **distanciar** [distan'θjar] *vt* to space out; **distanciarse** *vr* to become estranged; **distante** [dis'tante] *adj* distant
diste *vb V* **dar**
disteis *vb V* **dar**
distinción [distin'θjon] *nf* distinction; (*elegancia*) elegance; (*honor*) honour
distinguido, -a [distin'giðo, a] *adj* distinguished
distinguir [distin'gir] *vt* to distinguish; (*escoger*) to single out; **distinguirse** *vr* to be distinguished
distintivo [distin'tiβo] *nm* badge; (*fig*) characteristic
distinto, -a [dis'tinto, a] *adj* different; (*claro*) clear
distracción [distrak'θjon] *nf* distraction; (*pasatiempo*) hobby, pastime; (*olvido*) absent-mindedness, distraction
distraer [distra'er] *vt* (*atención*) to distract; (*divertir*) to amuse; (*fondos*) to embezzle; **distraerse** *vr* (*entretenerse*) to amuse o.s.; (*perder la concentración*) to allow one's attention to wander
distraído, -a [distra'iðo, a] *adj* (*gen*) absent-minded; (*entretenido*) amusing
distribuidor, a [distriβui'ðor, a] *nm/f* distributor; **distribuidora** *nf* (*Com*) dealer, agent; (*Cine*) distributor
distribuir [distriβu'ir] *vt* to distribute
distrito [dis'trito] *nm* (*sector, territorio*) region; (*barrio*) district; **Distrito Federal** (*MÉX*) Federal District; **distrito postal** postal district
disturbio [dis'turβjo] *nm* disturbance; (*desorden*) riot
disuadir [diswa'ðir] *vt* to dissuade
disuelto [di'swelto] *pp de* **disolver**
DIU *nm abr* (= *dispositivo intrauterino*) IUD
diurno, -a ['djurno, a] *adj* day *cpd*
divagar [diβa'ɣar] *vi* (*desviarse*) to digress
diván [di'βan] *nm* divan
diversidad [diβersi'ðað] *nf* diversity, variety
diversión [diβer'sjon] *nf* (*gen*) entertainment; (*actividad*) hobby, pastime
diverso, -a [di'βerso, a] *adj* diverse; **~s libros** several books; **diversos** *nmpl*

d

sundries

divertido, -a [diβer'tiðo, a] *adj* (*chiste*) amusing; (*fiesta etc*) enjoyable

divertir [diβer'tir] *vt* (*entretener, recrear*) to amuse; **divertirse** *vr* (*pasarlo bien*) to have a good time; (*distraerse*) to amuse o.s.

dividendos [diβi'ðendos] *nmpl* (*Com*) dividends

dividir [diβi'ðir] *vt* (*gen*) to divide; (*distribuir*) to distribute, share out

divierta *etc vb V* **divertir**

divino, -a [di'βino, a] *adj* divine

divirtiendo *etc vb V* **divertir**

divisa [di'βisa] *nf* (*emblema*) emblem, badge; **divisas** *nfpl* foreign exchange *sg*

divisar [diβi'sar] *vt* to make out, distinguish

división [diβi'sjon] *nf* (*gen*) division; (*de partido*) split; (*de país*) partition

divorciar [diβor'θjar] *vt* to divorce; **divorciarse** *vr* to get divorced; **divorcio** *nm* divorce

divulgar [diβul'ɣar] *vt* (*ideas*) to spread; (*secreto*) to divulge

DNI (ESP) *nm abr* (*= Documento Nacional de Identidad*) *national identity card*

DNI

The **Documento Nacional de Identidad** is a Spanish ID card which must be carried at all times and produced on request for the police. It contains the holder's photo, fingerprints and personal details. It is also known as the **DNI** or "carnet de identidad".

Dña. *abr* (*= doña*) Mrs

do [do] *nm* (*Mús*) do, C

dobladillo [doβla'ðiʎo] *nm* (*de vestido*) hem; (*de pantalón: vuelta*) turn-up (BRIT), cuff (US)

doblar [do'βlar] *vt* to double; (*papel*) to fold; (*caño*) to bend; (*la esquina*) to turn, go round; (*film*) to dub ▷ *vi* to turn; (*campana*) to toll; **doblarse** *vr* (*plegarse*) to fold (up), crease; (*encorvarse*) to bend; **~ a la derecha/izquierda** to turn right/left

doble ['doβle] *adj* double; (*de dos aspectos*) dual; (*fig*) two-faced ▷ *nm* double ▷ *nmf* (*Teatro*) double, stand-in; **dobles** *nmpl* (*Deporte*) doubles *sg*; **con ~ sentido** with a double meaning

doce ['doθe] *num* twelve; **docena** *nf* dozen

docente [do'θente] *adj*: **centro/personal ~** teaching establishment/staff

dócil ['doθil] *adj* (*pasivo*) docile; (*obediente*) obedient

doctor, a [dok'tor, a] *nm/f* doctor

doctorado [dokto'raðo] *nm* doctorate

doctrina [dok'trina] *nf* doctrine, teaching

documentación [dokumenta'θjon] *nf* documentation, papers *pl*

documental [dokumen'tal] *adj, nm* documentary

documento [doku'mento] *nm* (*certificado*) document; **documento adjunto** (*Inform*) attachment; **documento nacional de identidad** identity card

dólar ['dolar] *nm* dollar

doler [do'ler] *vt, vi* to hurt; (*fig*) to grieve; **dolerse** *vr* (*de su situación*) to grieve, feel sorry; (*de las desgracias ajenas*) to sympathize; **me duele el brazo** my arm hurts

dolor [do'lor] *nm* pain; (*fig*) grief, sorrow; **dolor de cabeza/estómago/muelas** headache/stomachache/toothache

domar [do'mar] *vt* to tame

domesticar [domesti'kar] *vt* = **domar**

doméstico, -a [do'mestiko, a] *adj* (*vida, servicio*) home; (*tareas*) household; (*animal*) tame, pet

domicilio [domi'θiljo] *nm* home; **servicio a ~** home delivery service; **sin ~ fijo** of no fixed abode; **domicilio particular** private residence

dominante [domi'nante] *adj* dominant; (*persona*) domineering

dominar [domi'nar] *vt* (*gen*) to dominate; (*idiomas*) to be fluent in ▷ *vi* to dominate, prevail

domingo [do'mingo] *nm* Sunday; **Domingo de Ramos/Resurrección** Palm/Easter Sunday

dominio [do'minjo] *nm* (*tierras*) domain; (*autoridad*) power, authority; (*de las pasiones*) grip, hold; (*de idiomas*) command

don [don] *nm* (*talento*) gift; **~ Juan Gómez** Mr Juan Gómez, Juan Gómez Esq (BRIT)

DON/DOÑA

The term **don/doña** often abbreviated to **D./Dña** is placed before the first name as a mark of respect to an older or more senior person – eg Don Diego, Doña Inés. Although becoming rarer in Spain it is still used with names and surnames on official documents and formal correspondence – eg "Sr. D. Pedro Rodríguez Hernández", "Sra. Dña. Inés Rodríguez Hernández".

dona ['dona] (*MÉX*) *nf* doughnut, donut (*US*)
donar [do'nar] *vt* to donate
donativo [dona'tiβo] *nm* donation
donde ['donde] *adv* where ▷*prep*: **el coche está allí ~ el farol** the car is over there by the lamppost *o* where the lamppost is; **en ~** where, in which
dónde ['donde] *adv* where?; **¿a ~ vas?** where are you going (to)?; **¿de ~ vienes?** where have you been?; **¿por ~?** where?, whereabouts?
dondequiera [donde'kjera] *adv* anywhere; **por ~** everywhere, all over the place ▷*conj*: **~ que** wherever
donut® [do'nut] (*ESP*) *nm* doughnut, donut (*US*)
doña ['doɲa] *nf*: **~ Alicia** Alicia; **~ Victoria Benito** Mrs Victoria Benito
dorado, -a [do'raðo, a] *adj* (*color*) golden; (*Tec*) gilt
dormir [dor'mir] *vt*: **~ la siesta** to have an afternoon nap ▷*vi* to sleep; **dormirse** *vr* to fall asleep
dormitorio [dormi'torjo] *nm* bedroom
dorsal [dor'sal] *nm* (*Deporte*) number
dorso ['dorso] *nm* (*de mano*) back; (*de hoja*) other side
dos [dos] *num* two
dosis ['dosis] *nf inv* dose, dosage
dotado, -a [do'taðo, a] *adj* gifted; **~ de** endowed with
dotar [do'tar] *vt* to endow; **dote** *nf* dowry; **dotes** *nfpl* (*talentos*) gifts
doy [doj] *vb V* **dar**
drama ['drama] *nm* drama; **dramaturgo** [drama'turɣo] *nm* dramatist, playwright
drástico, -a ['drastiko, a] *adj* drastic
drenaje [dre'naxe] *nm* drainage
droga ['droɣa] *nf* drug; **drogadicto, -a** [droɣa'ðikto, a] *nm/f* drug addict
droguería [droɣe'ria] *nf* hardware shop (*BRIT*) *o* store (*US*)
ducha ['dutʃa] *nf* (*baño*) shower; (*Med*) douche; **ducharse** *vr* to take a shower
duda ['duða] *nf* doubt; **no cabe ~** there is no doubt about it; **dudar** *vt, vi* to doubt; **dudoso, -a** [du'ðoso, a] *adj* (*incierto*) hesitant; (*sospechoso*) doubtful
duela *etc vb V* **doler**
duelo ['dwelo] *vb V* **doler** ▷*nm* (*combate*) duel; (*luto*) mourning
duende ['dwende] *nm* imp, goblin
dueño, -a ['dweɲo, a] *nm/f* (*propietario*) owner; (*de pensión, taberna*) landlord/lady; (*empresario*) employer
duermo *etc vb V* **dormir**
dulce ['dulθe] *adj* sweet ▷*adv* gently, softly ▷*nm* sweet
dulcería [dulθe'ria] (*LAM*) *nf* confectioner's (shop)
dulzura [dul'θura] *nf* sweetness; (*ternura*) gentleness
dúo ['duo] *nm* duet
duplicar [dupli'kar] *vt* (*hacer el doble de*) to duplicate
duque ['duke] *nm* duke; **duquesa** *nf* duchess
duración [dura'θjon] *nf* (*de película, disco etc*) length; (*de pila etc*) life; (*curso: de acontecimientos etc*) duration
duradero, -a [dura'ðero, a] *adj* (*tela etc*) hard-wearing; (*fe, paz*) lasting
durante [du'rante] *prep* during
durar [du'rar] *vi* to last; (*recuerdo*) to remain
durazno [du'raθno] (*LAM*) *nm* (*fruta*) peach; (*árbol*) peach tree
durex ['dureks] (*MÉX, ARG*) *nm* (*tira adhesiva*) Sellotape® (*BRIT*), Scotch tape® (*US*)
dureza [du'reθa] *nf* (*calidad*) hardness
duro, -a ['duro, a] *adj* hard; (*carácter*) tough ▷*adv* hard ▷*nm* (*moneda*) five-peseta coin *o* piece
DVD *nm abr* (= *disco de vídeo digital*) DVD

d

E *abr* (= *este*) E
e [e] *conj* and
ébano ['eβano] *nm* ebony
ebrio, -a ['eβrjo, a] *adj* drunk
ebullición [eβuʎi'θjon] *nf* boiling
echar [e'tʃar] *vt* to throw; (*agua, vino*) to pour (out); (*empleado: despedir*) to fire, sack; (*hojas*) to sprout; (*cartas*) to post; (*humo*) to emit, give out ▷ *vi*: **~ a correr** to run off; **echarse** *vr* to lie down; **~ llave a** to lock (up); **~ abajo** (*gobierno*) to overthrow; (*edificio*) to demolish; **~ mano a** to lay hands on; **~ una mano a algn** (*ayudar*) to give sb a hand; **~ de menos** to miss; **~se atrás** (*fig*) to back out
eclesiástico, -a [ekle'sjastiko, a] *adj* ecclesiastical
eco ['eko] *nm* echo; **tener ~** to catch on
ecología [ekolo'ɣia] *nf* ecology; **ecológico, -a** *adj* (*producto, método*) environmentally-friendly; (*agricultura*) organic; **ecologista** *adj* ecological, environmental ▷ *nmf* environmentalist
economía [ekono'mia] *nf* (*sistema*) economy; (*carrera*) economics
económico, -a [eko'nomiko, a] *adj* (*barato*) cheap, economical; (*ahorrativo*) thrifty; (*Com: año etc*) financial; (*: situación*) economic
economista [ekono'mista] *nmf* economist
Ecuador [ekwa'ðor] *nm* Ecuador; **ecuador** *nm* (*Geo*) equator
ecuatoriano, -a [ekwato'rjano, a] *adj, nm/f* Ecuadorian
ecuestre [e'kwestre] *adj* equestrian
edad [e'ðað] *nf* age; **¿qué ~ tienes?** how old are you?; **tiene ocho años de ~** he's eight (years old); **de ~ mediana/avanzada** middle-aged/advanced in years; **la E~ Media** the Middle Ages
edición [eði'θjon] *nf* (*acto*) publication; (*ejemplar*) edition
edificar [edifi'kar] *vt, vi* to build
edificio [eði'fiθjo] *nm* building; (*fig*) edifice, structure
Edimburgo [eðim'burɣo] *nm* Edinburgh
editar [eði'tar] *vt* (*publicar*) to publish; (*preparar textos*) to edit
editor, a [eði'tor, a] *nm/f* (*que publica*) publisher; (*redactor*) editor ▷ *adj* publishing *cpd*; **editorial** *adj* editorial ▷ *nm* leading article, editorial; **casa editorial** publisher
edredón [eðre'ðon] *nm* duvet
educación [eðuka'θjon] *nf* education; (*crianza*) upbringing; (*modales*) (good) manners *pl*
educado, -a [eðu'kaðo, a] *adj*: **bien/mal ~** well/badly behaved
educar [eðu'kar] *vt* to educate; (*criar*) to bring up; (*voz*) to train
EE. UU. *nmpl abr* (= *Estados Unidos*) US(A)
efectivamente [efectiβa'mente] *adv* (*como respuesta*) exactly, precisely; (*verdaderamente*) really; (*de hecho*) in fact
efectivo, -a [efek'tiβo, a] *adj* effective; (*real*) actual, real ▷ *nm*: **pagar en ~** to pay (in) cash; **hacer ~ un cheque** to cash a cheque
efecto [e'fekto] *nm* effect, result; **efectos** *nmpl* (*efectos personales*) effects; (*bienes*) goods; (*Com*) assets; **en ~** in fact; (*respuesta*) exactly, indeed; **efecto invernadero** greenhouse effect; **efectos especiales/secundarios/sonoros** special/side/sound effects
efectuar [efek'twar] *vt* to carry out; (*viaje*) to make
eficacia [efi'kaθja] *nf* (*de persona*) efficiency; (*de medicamento etc*) effectiveness
eficaz [efi'kaθ] *adj* (*persona*) efficient; (*acción*) effective
eficiente [efi'θjente] *adj* efficient
egipcio, -a [e'xipθjo, a] *adj, nm/f* Egyptian
Egipto [e'xipto] *nm* Egypt
egoísmo [eɣo'ismo] *nm* egoism
egoísta [eɣo'ista] *adj* egoistical, selfish ▷ *nmf* egoist
Eire ['eire] *nm* Eire
ej. *abr* (= *ejemplo*) eg
eje ['exe] *nm* (*Geo, Mat*) axis; (*de rueda*) axle; (*de máquina*) shaft, spindle
ejecución [exeku'θjon] *nf* execution; (*cumplimiento*) fulfilment; (*Mús*) performance; (*Jur: embargo de deudor*) attachment
ejecutar [exeku'tar] *vt* to execute, carry out; (*matar*) to execute; (*cumplir*) to fulfil;

(*Mús*) to perform; (*Jur: embargar*) to attach, distrain (on)

ejecutivo, -a [exeku'tiβo, a] *adj* executive; **el (poder) ~** the executive (power)

ejemplar [exem'plar] *adj* exemplary ▷ *nm* example; (*Zool*) specimen; (*de libro*) copy; (*de periódico*) number, issue

ejemplo [e'xemplo] *nm* example; **por ~** for example

ejercer [exer'θer] *vt* to exercise; (*influencia*) to exert; (*un oficio*) to practise ▷ *vi* (*practicar*): **~ (de)** to practise (as)

ejercicio [exer'θiθjo] *nm* exercise; (*período*) tenure; **hacer ~** to take exercise; **ejercicio comercial** financial year

ejército [e'xerθito] *nm* army; **entrar en el ~** to join the army, join up; **ejército del aire/de tierra** Air Force/Army

ejote [e'xote] (*MÉX*) *nm* green bean

PALABRA CLAVE

el [el] (*f* **la**, *pl* **los, las,** *neutro* **lo**) *art def* **1** the; **el libro/la mesa/los estudiantes** the book/table/students

2 (*con n abstracto: no se traduce*): **el amor/la juventud** love/youth

3 (*posesión: se traduce a menudo por adj posesivo*): **romperse el brazo** to break one's arm; **levantó la mano** he put his hand up; **se puso el sombrero** she put her hat on

4 (*valor descriptivo*): **tener la boca grande/los ojos azules** to have a big mouth/blue eyes

5 (*con días*) on; **me iré el viernes** I'll leave on Friday; **los domingos suelo ir a nadar** on Sundays I generally go swimming

6 (*lo +adj*): **lo difícil/caro** what is difficult/expensive; (*cuán*): **no se da cuenta de lo pesado que es** he doesn't realise how boring he is

▷ *pron demos* **1**: **mi libro y el de usted** my book and yours; **las de Pepe son mejores** Pepe's are better; **no la(s) blanca(s) sino la(s) gris(es)** not the white one(s) but the grey one(s)

2: **lo de: lo de ayer** what happened yesterday; **lo de las facturas** that business about the invoices

▷ *pron relativo* **1** (*indef*): **el que: el (los) que quiera(n) que se vaya(n)** anyone who wants to can leave; **llévese el que más le guste** take the one you like best

2 (*def*): **el que: el que compré ayer** the one I bought yesterday; **los que se van** those who leave

3: **lo que: lo que pienso yo/más me gusta** what I think/like most

▷ *conj*: **el que: el que lo diga** the fact that he says so; **el que sea tan vago me molesta** his being so lazy bothers me

▷ *excl*: **¡el susto que me diste!** what a fright you gave me!

▷ *pron personal* **1** (*persona: m*) him; (*: f*) her; (*: pl*) them; **lo/las veo** I can see him/them

2 (*animal, cosa: sg*) it; (*: pl*) them; **lo (*o* la) veo** I can see it; **los (*o* las) veo** I can see them

3 (*como sustituto de frase*): **lo: no lo sabía** I didn't know; **ya lo entiendo** I understand now

él [el] *pron* (*persona*) he; (*cosa*) it; (*después de prep: persona*) him; (*: cosa*) it; **de ~** his

elaborar [elaβo'rar] *vt* (*producto*) to make, manufacture; (*preparar*) to prepare; (*madera, metal etc*) to work; (*proyecto etc*) to work on *o* out

elástico, -a [e'lastiko, a] *adj* elastic; (*flexible*) flexible ▷ *nm* elastic; (*un elástico*) elastic band

elección [elek'θjon] *nf* election; (*selección*) choice, selection; **elecciones generales** general election *sg*

electorado [elekto'raðo] *nm* electorate, voters *pl*

electricidad [elektriθi'ðað] *nf* electricity

electricista [elektri'θista] *nmf* electrician

eléctrico, -a [e'lektriko, a] *adj* electric

electro... [elektro] *prefijo* electro...; **electrocardiograma** *nm* electrocardiogram; **electrocutar** *vt* to electrocute; **electrodo** *nm* electrode; **electrodomésticos** *nmpl* (electrical) household appliances

electrónica [elek'tronika] *nf* electronics *sg*

electrónico, -a [elek'troniko, a] *adj* electronic

elefante [ele'fante] *nm* elephant

elegancia [ele'ɣanθja] *nf* elegance, grace; (*estilo*) stylishness

elegante [ele'ɣante] *adj* elegant, graceful; (*estiloso*) stylish, fashionable

elegir [ele'xir] *vt* (*escoger*) to choose, select; (*optar*) to opt for; (*presidente*) to elect

elemental [elemen'tal] *adj* (*claro, obvio*) elementary; (*fundamental*) elemental, fundamental

elemento [ele'mento] *nm* element; (*fig*) ingredient; **elementos** *nmpl* elements, rudiments

elevación [eleβa'θjon] *nf* elevation; (*acto*) raising, lifting; (*de precios*) rise; (*Geo etc*) height, altitude

elevar [ele'βar] *vt* to raise, lift (up); (*precio*)

to put up; **elevarse** *vr* (*edificio*) to rise; (*precios*) to go up
eligiendo *etc vb V* **elegir**
elija *etc vb V* **elegir**
eliminar [elimi'nar] *vt* to eliminate, remove
eliminatoria [elimina'torja] *nf* heat, preliminary (round)
élite ['elite] *nf* elite
ella ['eʎa] *pron* (*persona*) she; (*cosa*) it; (*después de prep: persona*) her; (*: cosa*) it; **de ~** hers
ellas ['eʎas] *pron* (*personas y cosas*) they; (*después de prep*) them; **de ~** theirs
ello ['eʎo] *pron* it
ellos ['eʎos] *pron* they; (*después de prep*) them; **de ~** theirs
elogiar [elo'xjar] *vt* to praise; **elogio** *nm* praise
elote [e'lote] (MÉX) *nm* corn on the cob
eludir [elu'ðir] *vt* to avoid
email [i'mel] *nm* email; (*dirección*) email address; **mandar un ~ a algn** to email sb, send sb an email
embajada [emba'xaða] *nf* embassy
embajador, a [embaxa'ðor, a] *nm/f* ambassador/ambassadress
embalar [emba'lar] *vt* to parcel, wrap (up); **embalarse** *vr* to go fast
embalse [em'balse] *nm* (*presa*) dam; (*lago*) reservoir
embarazada [embara'θaða] *adj* pregnant ▷ *nf* pregnant woman

No confundir **embarazada** con la palabra inglesa *embarrassed*.

embarazo [emba'raθo] *nm* (*de mujer*) pregnancy; (*impedimento*) obstacle, obstruction; (*timidez*) embarrassment; **embarazoso, -a** *adj* awkward, embarrassing
embarcación [embarka'θjon] *nf* (*barco*) boat, craft; (*acto*) embarkation, boarding
embarcadero [embarka'ðero] *nm* pier, landing stage
embarcar [embar'kar] *vt* (*cargamento*) to ship, stow; (*persona*) to embark, put on board; **embarcarse** *vr* to embark, go on board
embargar [embar'ɣar] *vt* (*Jur*) to seize, impound
embargo [em'barɣo] *nm* (*Jur*) seizure; (*Com, Pol*) embargo
embargue *etc vb V* **embargar**
embarque *etc* [em'barke] *vb V* **embarcar** ▷ *nm* shipment, loading
embellecer [embeʎe'θer] *vt* to embellish, beautify
embestida [embes'tiða] *nf* attack, onslaught; (*carga*) charge
embestir [embes'tir] *vt* to attack, assault; to charge, attack ▷ *vi* to attack
emblema [em'blema] *nm* emblem
embobado, -a [embo'βaðo, a] *adj* (*atontado*) stunned, bewildered
embolia [em'bolja] *nf* (*Med*) clot
émbolo ['embolo] *nm* (*Auto*) piston
emborrachar [emborra'tʃar] *vt* to make drunk, intoxicate; **emborracharse** *vr* to get drunk
emboscada [embos'kaða] *nf* ambush
embotar [embo'tar] *vt* to blunt, dull
embotellamiento [emboteʎa'mjento] *nm* (*Auto*) traffic jam
embotellar [embote'ʎar] *vt* to bottle
embrague [em'braɣe] *nm* (*tb*: **pedal de ~**) clutch
embrión [em'brjon] *nm* embryo
embrollo [em'broʎo] *nm* (*enredo*) muddle, confusion; (*aprieto*) fix, jam
embrujado, -a [embru'xado, a] *adj* bewitched; **casa embrujada** haunted house
embrutecer [embrute'θer] *vt* (*atontar*) to stupefy
embudo [em'buðo] *nm* funnel
embuste [em'buste] *nm* (*mentira*) lie; **embustero, -a** *adj* lying, deceitful ▷ *nm/f* (*mentiroso*) liar
embutido [embu'tiðo] *nm* (*Culin*) sausage; (*Tec*) inlay
emergencia [emer'xenθja] *nf* emergency; (*surgimiento*) emergence
emerger [emer'ɣer] *vi* to emerge, appear
emigración [emiɣra'θjon] *nf* emigration; (*de pájaros*) migration
emigrar [emi'ɣrar] *vi* (*personas*) to emigrate; (*pájaros*) to migrate
eminente [emi'nente] *adj* eminent, distinguished; (*elevado*) high
emisión [emi'sjon] *nf* (*acto*) emission; (*Com etc*) issue; (*Radio, TV: acto*) broadcasting; (*: programa*) broadcast, programme (BRIT), program (US)
emisora [emi'sora] *nf* radio *o* broadcasting station
emitir [emi'tir] *vt* (*olor etc*) to emit, give off; (*moneda etc*) to issue; (*opinión*) to express; (*Radio*) to broadcast
emoción [emo'θjon] *nf* emotion; (*excitación*) excitement; (*sentimiento*) feeling
emocionante [emoθjo'nante] *adj* (*excitante*) exciting, thrilling
emocionar [emoθjo'nar] *vt* (*excitar*) to excite, thrill; (*conmover*) to move, touch; (*impresionar*) to impress
emoticón [emoti'kon], **emoticono**

[emoti'kono] *nm* smiley
emotivo, -a [emo'tiβo, a] *adj* emotional
empacho [em'patʃo] *nm* (*Med*) indigestion; (*fig*) embarrassment
empalagoso, -a [empala'ɣoso, a] *adj* cloying; (*fig*) tiresome
empalmar [empal'mar] *vt* to join, connect ▷ *vi* (*dos caminos*) to meet, join; **empalme** *nm* joint, connection; junction; (*de trenes*) connection
empanada [empa'naða] *nf* pie, pasty
empañarse [empa'ɲarse] *vr* (*cristales etc*) to steam up
empapar [empa'par] *vt* (*mojar*) to soak, saturate; (*absorber*) to soak up, absorb; **empaparse** *vr*: **~se de** to soak up
empapelar [empape'lar] *vt* (*paredes*) to paper
empaquetar [empake'tar] *vt* to pack, parcel up
empastar [empas'tar] *vt* (*embadurnar*) to paste; (*diente*) to fill
empaste [em'paste] *nm* (*de diente*) filling
empatar [empa'tar] *vi* to draw, tie; **~on a dos** they drew two-all; **empate** *nm* draw, tie
empecé *etc vb V* **empezar**
empedernido, -a [empeðer'niðo, a] *adj* hard, heartless; (*fumador*) inveterate
empeine [em'peine] *nm* (*de pie, zapato*) instep
empeñado, -a [empe'ɲaðo, a] *adj* (*persona*) determined; (*objeto*) pawned
empeñar [empe'ɲar] *vt* (*objeto*) to pawn, pledge; (*persona*) to compel; **empeñarse** *vr* (*endeudarse*) to get into debt; **~se en** to be set on, be determined to
empeño [em'peɲo] *nm* (*determinación, insistencia*) determination, insistence; **casa de ~s** pawnshop
empeorar [empeo'rar] *vt* to make worse, worsen ▷ *vi* to get worse, deteriorate
empezar [empe'θar] *vt, vi* to begin, start
empiece *etc vb V* **empezar**
empiezo *etc vb V* **empezar**
emplasto [em'plasto] *nm* (*Med*) plaster
emplazar [empla'θar] *vt* (*ubicar*) to site, place, locate; (*Jur*) to summons; (*convocar*) to summon
empleado, -a [emple'aðo, a] *nm/f* (*gen*) employee; (*de banco etc*) clerk
emplear [emple'ar] *vt* (*usar*) to use, employ; (*dar trabajo a*) to employ; **emplearse** *vr* (*conseguir trabajo*) to be employed; (*ocuparse*) to occupy o.s.
empleo [em'pleo] *nm* (*puesto*) job; (*puestos: colectivamente*) employment; (*uso*) use, employment
empollar [empo'ʎar] (ESP: *fam*) *vt, vi* to swot (up); **empollón, -ona** (ESP: *fam*) *nm/f* swot
emporio [em'porjo] (LAM) *nm* (*gran almacén*) department store
empotrado, -a [empo'traðo, a] *adj* (*armario etc*) built-in
emprender [empren'der] *vt* (*empezar*) to begin, embark on; (*acometer*) to tackle, take on
empresa [em'presa] *nf* (*de espíritu etc*) enterprise; (*Com*) company, firm; **empresariales** *nfpl* business studies; **empresario, -a** *nm/f* (*Com*) businessman(-woman)
empujar [empu'xar] *vt* to push, shove
empujón [empu'xon] *nm* push, shove
empuñar [empu'ɲar] *vt* (*asir*) to grasp, take (firm) hold of

PALABRA CLAVE

en [en] *prep* **1** (*posición*) in; (: *sobre*) on; **está en el cajón** it's in the drawer; **en Argentina/La Paz** in Argentina/La Paz; **en la oficina/el colegio** at the office/school; **está en el suelo/quinto piso** it's on the floor/the fifth floor
2 (*dirección*) into; **entró en el aula** she went into the classroom; **meter algo en el bolso** to put sth into one's bag
3 (*tiempo*) in; on; **en 1605/3 semanas/invierno** in 1605/3 weeks/winter; **en (el mes de) enero** in (the month of) January; **en aquella ocasión/época** on that occasion/at that time
4 (*precio*) for; **lo vendió en 20 dólares** he sold it for 20 dollars
5 (*diferencia*) by; **reducir/aumentar en una tercera parte/un 20 por ciento** to reduce/increase by a third/20 per cent
6 (*manera*): **en avión/autobús** by plane/bus; **escrito en inglés** written in English
7 (*después de vb que indica gastar etc*) on; **han cobrado demasiado en dietas** they've charged too much to expenses; **se le va la mitad del sueldo en comida** he spends half his salary on food
8 (*tema, ocupación*): **experto en la materia** expert on the subject; **trabaja en la construcción** he works in the building industry
9 (*adj + en + infin*): **lento en reaccionar** slow to react

enaguas [e'naɣwas] *nfpl* petticoat *sg*, underskirt *sg*
enajenación [enaxena'θjon] *nf* (*Psico*: *tb*:

~ mental) mental derangement
enamorado, -a [enamo'raðo, a] *adj* in love ▷ *nm/f* lover; **estar ~ (de)** to be in love (with)
enamorar [enamo'rar] *vt* to win the love of; **enamorarse** *vr*: **~se de algn** to fall in love with sb
enano, -a [e'nano, a] *adj* tiny ▷ *nm/f* dwarf
encabezamiento [enkaβeθa'mjento] *nm* (*de carta*) heading; (*de periódico*) headline
encabezar [enkaβe'θar] *vt* (*movimiento, revolución*) to lead, head; (*lista*) to head, be at the top of; (*carta*) to put a heading to
encadenar [enkaðe'nar] *vt* to chain (together); (*poner grilletes a*) to shackle
encajar [enka'xar] *vt* (*ajustar*): **~ (en)** to fit (into); (*fam*: *golpe*) to take ▷ *vi* to fit (well); (*fig*: *corresponder a*) to match
encaje [en'kaxe] *nm* (*labor*) lace
encallar [enka'ʎar] *vi* (*Náut*) to run aground
encaminar [enkami'nar] *vt* to direct, send
encantado, -a [enkan'taðo, a] *adj* (*hechizado*) bewitched; (*muy contento*) delighted; **¡~!** how do you do, pleased to meet you
encantador, a [enkanta'ðor, a] *adj* charming, lovely ▷ *nm/f* magician, enchanter/enchantress
encantar [enkan'tar] *vt* (*agradar*) to charm, delight; (*hechizar*) to bewitch, cast a spell on; **me encanta eso** I love that; **encanto** *nm* (*hechizo*) spell, charm; (*fig*) charm, delight
encarcelar [enkarθe'lar] *vt* to imprison, jail
encarecer [enkare'θer] *vt* to put up the price of; **encarecerse** *vr* to get dearer
encargado, -a [enkar'ɣaðo, a] *adj* in charge ▷ *nm/f* agent, representative; (*responsable*) person in charge
encargar [enkar'ɣar] *vt* to entrust; (*recomendar*) to urge, recommend; **encargarse** *vr*: **~se de** to look after, take charge of; **~ algo a algn** to put sb in charge of sth; **~ a algn que haga algo** to ask sb to do sth
encargo [en'karɣo] *nm* (*tarea*) assignment, job; (*responsabilidad*) responsibility; (*Com*) order
encariñarse [enkari'ɲarse] *vr*: **~ con** to grow fond of, get attached to
encarnación [enkarna'θjon] *nf* incarnation, embodiment
encarrilar [enkarri'lar] *vt* (*tren*) to put back on the rails; (*fig*) to correct, put on the right track
encasillar [enkasi'ʎar] *vt* (*fig*) to pigeonhole; (*actor*) to typecast
encendedor [enθende'ðor] *nm* lighter
encender [enθen'der] *vt* (*con fuego*) to light; (*luz, radio*) to put on, switch on; (*avivar*: *pasión*) to inflame; **encenderse** *vr* to catch fire; (*excitarse*) to get excited; (*de cólera*) to flare up; (*el rostro*) to blush
encendido [enθen'diðo] *nm* (*Auto*) ignition
encerado [enθe'raðo] *nm* (*Escol*) blackboard
encerrar [enθe'rrar] *vt* (*confinar*) to shut in, shut up; (*comprender, incluir*) to include, contain
encharcado, -a [entʃar'kaðo, a] *adj* (*terreno*) flooded
encharcarse [entʃar'karse] *vr* to get flooded
enchufado, -a [entʃu'faðo, a] (*fam*) *nm/f* well-connected person
enchufar [entʃu'far] *vt* (*Elec*) to plug in; (*Tec*) to connect, fit together; **enchufe** *nm* (*Elec*: *clavija*) plug; (: *toma*) socket; (*de dos tubos*) joint, connection; (*fam*: *influencia*) contact, connection; (: *puesto*) cushy job
encía [en'θia] *nf* gum
encienda *etc vb V* **encender**
encierro *etc* [en'θjerro] *vb V* **encerrar** ▷ *nm* shutting in, shutting up; (*calabozo*) prison
encima [en'θima] *adv* (*sobre*) above, over; (*además*) besides; **~ de** (*en*) on, on top of; (*sobre*) above, over; (*además de*) besides, on top of; **por ~ de** over; **¿llevas dinero ~?** have you (got) any money on you?; **se me vino ~** it took me by surprise
encina [en'θina] *nf* holm oak
encinta [en'θinta] *adj* pregnant
enclenque [en'klenke] *adj* weak, sickly
encoger [enko'xer] *vt* to shrink, contract; **encogerse** *vr* to shrink, contract; (*fig*) to cringe; **~se de hombros** to shrug one's shoulders
encomendar [enkomen'dar] *vt* to entrust, commend; **encomendarse** *vr*: **~se a** to put one's trust in
encomienda *etc* [enko'mjenda] *vb V* **encomendar** ▷ *nf* (*encargo*) charge, commission; (*elogio*) tribute; **encomienda postal** (LAM) package
encontrar [enkon'trar] *vt* (*hallar*) to find; (*inesperadamente*) to meet, run into; **encontrarse** *vr* to meet (each other); (*situarse*) to be (situated); **~se con** to meet; **~se bien (de salud)** to feel well
encrucijada [enkruθi'xaða] *nf*

crossroads *sg*
encuadernación [enkwaðerna'θjon] *nf* binding
encuadrar [enkwa'ðrar] *vt* (*retrato*) to frame; (*ajustar*) to fit, insert; (*contener*) to contain
encubrir [enku'βrir] *vt* (*ocultar*) to hide, conceal; (*criminal*) to harbour, shelter
encuentro *etc* [en'kwentro] *vb V* **encontrar** ▷ *nm* (*de personas*) meeting; (*Auto etc*) collision, crash; (*Deporte*) match, game; (*Mil*) encounter
encuerado, -a (MÉX) [enkwe'raðo, a] *adj* nude, naked
encuesta [en'kwesta] *nf* inquiry, investigation; (*sondeo*) (public) opinion poll
encumbrar [enkum'brar] *vt* (*persona*) to exalt
endeble [en'deβle] *adj* (*persona*) weak; (*argumento, excusa, persona*) weak
endemoniado, -a [endemo'njaðo, a] *adj* possessed (of the devil); (*travieso*) devilish
enderezar [endere'θar] *vt* (*poner derecho*) to straighten (out); (*: verticalmente*) to set upright; (*situación*) to straighten *o* sort out; (*dirigir*) to direct; **enderezarse** *vr* (*persona sentada*) to straighten up
endeudarse [endeu'ðarse] *vr* to get into debt
endiablado, -a [endja'βlaðo, a] *adj* devilish, diabolical; (*travieso*) mischievous
endilgar [endil'ɣar] (*fam*) *vt*: **~le algo a algn** to lumber sb with sth
endiñar [endi'ɲar] (ESP: *fam*) *vt* (*boféton*) to land, belt
endosar [endo'sar] *vt* (*cheque etc*) to endorse
endulzar [endul'θar] *vt* to sweeten; (*suavizar*) to soften
endurecer [endure'θer] *vt* to harden; **endurecerse** *vr* to harden, grow hard
enema [e'nema] *nm* (*Med*) enema
enemigo, -a [ene'miɣo, a] *adj* enemy, hostile ▷ *nm/f* enemy
enemistad [enemis'tað] *nf* enmity
enemistar [enemis'tar] *vt* to make enemies of, cause a rift between; **enemistarse** *vr* to become enemies; (*amigos*) to fall out
energía [ener'xia] *nf* (*vigor*) energy, drive; (*empuje*) push; (*Tec, Elec*) energy, power; **energía eólica** wind power; **energía solar** solar energy *o* power
enérgico, -a [e'nerxiko, a] *adj* (*gen*) energetic; (*voz, modales*) forceful
energúmeno, -a [ener'ɣumeno, a] (*fam*) *nm/f* (*fig*) madman(-woman)
enero [e'nero] *nm* January
enfadado, -a [enfa'ðaðo, a] *adj* angry, annoyed
enfadar [enfa'ðar] *vt* to anger, annoy; **enfadarse** *vr* to get angry *o* annoyed
enfado [en'faðo] *nm* (*enojo*) anger, annoyance; (*disgusto*) trouble, bother
énfasis ['enfasis] *nm* emphasis, stress
enfático, -a [en'fatiko, a] *adj* emphatic
enfermar [enfer'mar] *vt* to make ill ▷ *vi* to fall ill, be taken ill
enfermedad [enferme'ðað] *nf* illness; **enfermedad venérea** venereal disease
enfermera [enfer'mera] *nf* nurse
enfermería [enferme'ria] *nf* infirmary; (*de colegio etc*) sick bay
enfermero [enfer'mero] *nm* (male) nurse
enfermizo, -a [enfer'miθo, a] *adj* (*persona*) sickly, unhealthy; (*fig*) unhealthy
enfermo, -a [en'fermo, a] *adj* ill, sick ▷ *nm/f* invalid, sick person; (*en hospital*) patient; **caer** *o* **ponerse ~** to fall ill
enfocar [enfo'kar] *vt* (*foto etc*) to focus; (*problema etc*) to approach
enfoque *etc* [en'foke] *vb V* **enfocar** ▷ *nm* focus
enfrentar [enfren'tar] *vt* (*peligro*) to face (up to), confront; (*oponer*) to bring face to face; **enfrentarse** *vr* (*dos personas*) to face *o* confront each other; (*Deporte: dos equipos*) to meet; **~se a** *o* **con** to face up to, confront
enfrente [en'frente] *adv* opposite; **la casa de ~** the house opposite, the house across the street; **~ de** opposite, facing
enfriamiento [enfria'mjento] *nm* chilling, refrigeration; (*Med*) cold, chill
enfriar [enfri'ar] *vt* (*alimentos*) to cool, chill; (*algo caliente*) to cool down; **enfriarse** *vr* to cool down; (*Med*) to catch a chill; (*amistad*) to cool
enfurecer [enfure'θer] *vt* to enrage, madden; **enfurecerse** *vr* to become furious, fly into a rage; (*mar*) to get rough
enganchar [engan'tʃar] *vt* to hook; (*dos vagones*) to hitch up; (*Tec*) to couple, connect; (*Mil*) to recruit; **engancharse** *vr* (*Mil*) to enlist, join up
enganche [en'gantʃe] *nm* hook; (ESP *Tec*) coupling, connection; (*acto*) hooking (up); (*Mil*) recruitment, enlistment; (MÉX: *depósito*) deposit
engañar [enga'ɲar] *vt* to deceive; (*estafar*) to cheat, swindle; **engañarse** *vr* (*equivocarse*) to be wrong; (*disimular la verdad*) to deceive o.s.
engaño [en'gaɲo] *nm* deceit; (*estafa*) trick, swindle; (*error*) mistake, misunderstanding; (*ilusión*) delusion; **engañoso, -a** *adj* (*tramposo*) crooked; (*mentiroso*) dishonest,

e

deceitful; (*aspecto*) deceptive; (*consejo*) misleading
engatusar [engatu'sar] (*fam*) *vt* to coax
engendro [en'xendro] *nm* (*Bio*) foetus; (*fig*) monstrosity
englobar [englo'βar] *vt* to include, comprise
engordar [engor'ðar] *vt* to fatten ▷*vi* to get fat, put on weight
engorroso, -a [engo'rroso, a] *adj* bothersome, trying
engranaje [engra'naxe] *nm* (*Auto*) gear
engrasar [engra'sar] *vt* (*Tec: poner grasa*) to grease; (*: lubricar*) to lubricate, oil; (*manchar*) to make greasy
engreído, -a [engre'iðo, a] *adj* vain, conceited
enhebrar [ene'βrar] *vt* to thread
enhorabuena [enora'βwena] *excl*: **¡~!** congratulations! ▷*nf*: **dar la ~ a** to congratulate
enigma [e'niɤma] *nm* enigma; (*problema*) puzzle; (*misterio*) mystery
enjambre [en'xambre] *nm* swarm
enjaular [enxau'lar] *vt* to (put in a) cage; (*fam*) to jail, lock up
enjuagar [enxwa'ɤar] *vt* (*ropa*) to rinse (out)
enjuague *etc* [en'xwaɤe] *vb* *V* **enjuagar** ▷*nm* (*Med*) mouthwash; (*de ropa*) rinse, rinsing
enlace [en'laθe] *nm* link, connection; (*relación*) relationship; (*tb*: **~ matrimonial**) marriage; (*de carretera, trenes*) connection; **enlace sindical** shop steward
enlatado, -a [enla'taðo, a] *adj* (*alimentos, productos*) tinned, canned
enlazar [enla'θar] *vt* (*unir con lazos*) to bind together; (*atar*) to tie; (*conectar*) to link, connect; (LAM: *caballo*) to lasso
enloquecer [enloke'θer] *vt* to drive mad ▷*vi* to go mad
enmarañar [enmara'ɲar] *vt* (*enredar*) to tangle (up), entangle; (*complicar*) to complicate; (*confundir*) to confuse
enmarcar [enmar'kar] *vt* (*cuadro*) to frame
enmascarar [enmaska'rar] *vt* to mask; **enmascararse** *vr* to put on a mask
enmendar [enmen'dar] *vt* to emend, correct; (*constitución etc*) to amend; (*comportamiento*) to reform; **enmendarse** *vr* to reform, mend one's ways; **enmienda** *nf* correction; amendment; reform
enmudecer [enmuðe'θer] *vi* (*perder el habla*) to fall silent; (*guardar silencio*) to remain silent
ennoblecer [ennoβle'θer] *vt* to ennoble
enojado, -a [eno'xaðo, a] (LAM) *adj* angry
enojar [eno'xar] *vt* (*encolerizar*) to anger; (*disgustar*) to annoy, upset; **enojarse** *vr* to get angry; to get annoyed
enojo [e'noxo] *nm* (*cólera*) anger; (*irritación*) annoyance
enorme [e'norme] *adj* enormous, huge; (*fig*) monstrous
enredadera [enreða'ðera] *nf* (*Bot*) creeper, climbing plant
enredar [enre'ðar] *vt* (*cables, hilos etc*) to tangle (up), entangle; (*situación*) to complicate, confuse; (*meter cizaña*) to sow discord among *o* between; (*implicar*) to embroil, implicate; **enredarse** *vr* to get entangled, get tangled (up); (*situación*) to get complicated; (*persona*) to get embroiled; (LAM: *fam*) to meddle
enredo [en'reðo] *nm* (*maraña*) tangle; (*confusión*) mix-up, confusion; (*intriga*) intrigue
enriquecer [enrike'θer] *vt* to make rich, enrich; **enriquecerse** *vr* to get rich
enrojecer [enroxe'θer] *vt* to redden ▷*vi* (*persona*) to blush; **enrojecerse** *vr* to blush
enrollar [enro'ʎar] *vt* to roll (up), wind (up)
ensalada [ensa'laða] *nf* salad; **ensaladilla (rusa)** *nf* Russian salad
ensanchar [ensan'tʃar] *vt* (*hacer más ancho*) to widen; (*agrandar*) to enlarge, expand; (*Costura*) to let out; **ensancharse** *vr* to get wider, expand
ensayar [ensa'jar] *vt* to test, try (out); (*Teatro*) to rehearse
ensayo [en'sajo] *nm* test, trial; (*Quím*) experiment; (*Teatro*) rehearsal; (*Deporte*) try; (*Escol, Literatura*) essay
enseguida [ense'ɤiða] *adv* at once, right away
ensenada [ense'naða] *nf* inlet, cove
enseñanza [ense'ɲanθa] *nf* (*educación*) education; (*acción*) teaching; (*doctrina*) teaching, doctrine; **enseñanza (de) primaria/secundaria** elementary/ secondary education
enseñar [ense'ɲar] *vt* (*educar*) to teach; (*mostrar, señalar*) to show
enseres [en'seres] *nmpl* belongings
ensuciar [ensu'θjar] *vt* (*manchar*) to dirty, soil; (*fig*) to defile; **ensuciarse** *vr* to get dirty; (*bebé*) to dirty one's nappy
entablar [enta'βlar] *vt* (*recubrir*) to board (up); (*Ajedrez, Damas*) to set up; (*conversación*) to strike up; (*Jur*) to file ▷*vi* to draw
ente ['ente] *nm* (*organización*) body, organization; (*fam: persona*) odd character
entender [enten'der] *vt* (*comprender*) to

understand; (*darse cuenta*) to realize ▷ *vi* to understand; (*creer*) to think, believe; **entenderse** *vr* (*comprenderse*) to be understood; (*ponerse de acuerdo*) to agree, reach an agreement; **~ de** to know all about; **~ algo de** to know a little about; **~ en** to deal with, have to do with; **~ mal** to misunderstand; **~se con algn** (*llevarse bien*) to get on *o* along with sb; **~se mal** (*dos personas*) to get on badly

entendido, -a [enten'diðo, a] *adj* (*comprendido*) understood; (*hábil*) skilled; (*inteligente*) knowledgeable ▷ *nm/f* (*experto*) expert ▷ *excl* agreed!; **entendimiento** *nm* (*comprensión*) understanding; (*inteligencia*) mind, intellect; (*juicio*) judgement

enterado, -a [ente'raðo, a] *adj* well-informed; **estar ~ de** to know about, be aware of

enteramente [entera'mente] *adv* entirely, completely

enterar [ente'rar] *vt* (*informar*) to inform, tell; **enterarse** *vr* to find out, get to know

enterito [ente'rito] (RPL) *nm* boiler suit (BRIT), overalls (US)

entero, -a [en'tero, a] *adj* (*total*) whole, entire; (*fig: honesto*) honest; (*: firme*) firm, resolute ▷ *nm* (*Com: punto*) point

enterrar [ente'rrar] *vt* to bury

entidad [enti'ðað] *nf* (*empresa*) firm, company; (*organismo*) body; (*sociedad*) society; (*Filosofía*) entity

entiendo *etc vb V* **entender**

entierro [en'tjerro] *nm* (*acción*) burial; (*funeral*) funeral

entonación [entona'θjon] *nf* (*Ling*) intonation

entonar [ento'nar] *vt* (*canción*) to intone; (*colores*) to tone; (*Med*) to tone up ▷ *vi* to be in tune

entonces [en'tonθes] *adv* then, at that time; **desde ~** since then; **en aquel ~** at that time; **(pues) ~** and so

entornar [entor'nar] *vt* (*puerta, ventana*) to half-close, leave ajar; (*los ojos*) to screw up

entorpecer [entorpe'θer] *vt* (*entendimiento*) to dull; (*impedir*) to obstruct, hinder; (*: tránsito*) to slow down, delay

entrada [en'traða] *nf* (*acción*) entry, access; (*sitio*) entrance, way in; (*Inform*) input; (*Com*) receipts *pl*, takings *pl*; (*Culin*) starter; (*Deporte*) innings *sg*; (*Teatro*) house, audience; (*billete*) ticket; **~s y salidas** (*Com*) income and expenditure; **de ~** from the outset; **entrada de aire** (*Tec*) air intake *o* inlet

entrado, -a [en'traðo, a] *adj*: **~ en años** elderly; **una vez ~ el verano** in the summer(time), when summer comes

entramparse [entram'parse] *vr* to get into debt

entrante [en'trante] *adj* next, coming; **mes/año ~** next month/year; **entrantes** *nmpl* starters

entraña [en'traɲa] *nf* (*fig: centro*) heart, core; (*raíz*) root; **entrañas** *nfpl* (*Anat*) entrails; (*fig*) heart *sg*; **entrañable** *adj* close, intimate; **entrañar** *vt* to entail

entrar [en'trar] *vt* (*introducir*) to bring in; (*Inform*) to input ▷ *vi* (*meterse*) to go in, come in, enter; (*comenzar*): **~ diciendo** to begin by saying; **hacer ~** to show in; **me entró sed/sueño** I started to feel thirsty/sleepy; **no me entra** I can't get the hang of it

entre ['entre] *prep* (*dos*) between; (*más de dos*) among(st)

entreabrir [entrea'βrir] *vt* to half-open, open halfway

entrecejo [entre'θexo] *nm*: **fruncir el ~** to frown

entredicho [entre'ðitʃo] *nm* (*Jur*) injunction; **poner en ~** to cast doubt on; **estar en ~** to be in doubt

entrega [en'treɣa] *nf* (*de mercancías*) delivery; (*de novela etc*) instalment; **entregar** [entre'ɣar] *vt* (*dar*) to hand (over), deliver; **entregarse** *vr* (*rendirse*) to surrender, give in, submit; (*dedicarse*) to devote o.s.

entremeses [entre'meses] *nmpl* hors d'œuvres

entremeter [entreme'ter] *vt* to insert, put in; **entremeterse** *vr* to meddle, interfere; **entremetido, -a** *adj* meddling, interfering

entremezclar [entremeθ'klar] *vt* to intermingle; **entremezclarse** *vr* to intermingle

entrenador, a [entrena'ðor, a] *nm/f* trainer, coach

entrenarse [entre'narse] *vr* to train

entrepierna [entre'pjerna] *nf* crotch

entresuelo [entre'swelo] *nm* mezzanine

entretanto [entre'tanto] *adv* meanwhile, meantime

entretecho [entre'tetʃo] (CS) *nm* attic

entretejer [entrete'xer] *vt* to interweave

entretener [entrete'ner] *vt* (*divertir*) to entertain, amuse; (*detener*) to hold up, delay; **entretenerse** *vr* (*divertirse*) to amuse o.s.; (*retrasarse*) to delay, linger; **entretenido, -a** *adj* entertaining, amusing; **entretenimiento** *nm* entertainment, amusement

entrever [entre'βer] *vt* to glimpse, catch a glimpse of

entrevista [entre'βista] *nf* interview;

e

entrevistar *vt* to interview; **entrevistarse** *vr* to have an interview
entristecer [entriste'θer] *vt* to sadden, grieve; **entristecerse** *vr* to grow sad
entrometerse [entrome'terse] *vr*: **~ (en)** to interfere (in *o* with)
entumecer [entume'θer] *vt* to numb, benumb; **entumecerse** *vr* (*por el frío*) to go *o* become numb
enturbiar [entur'βjar] *vt* (*el agua*) to make cloudy; (*fig*) to confuse; **enturbiarse** *vr* (*oscurecerse*) to become cloudy; (*fig*) to get confused, become obscure
entusiasmar [entusjas'mar] *vt* to excite, fill with enthusiasm; (*gustar mucho*) to delight; **entusiasmarse** *vr*: **~se con** *o* **por** to get enthusiastic *o* excited about
entusiasmo [entu'sjasmo] *nm* enthusiasm; (*excitación*) excitement
entusiasta [entu'sjasta] *adj* enthusiastic ▷ *nmf* enthusiast
enumerar [enume'rar] *vt* to enumerate
envainar [embai'nar] *vt* to sheathe
envalentonar [embalento'nar] *vt* to give courage to; **envalentonarse** *vr* (*pey*: *jactarse*) to boast, brag
envasar [emba'sar] *vt* (*empaquetar*) to pack, wrap; (*enfrascar*) to bottle; (*enlatar*) to can; (*embolsar*) to pocket
envase [em'base] *nm* (*en paquete*) packing, wrapping; (*en botella*) bottling; (*en lata*) canning; (*recipiente*) container; (*paquete*) package; (*botella*) bottle; (*lata*) tin (BRIT), can
envejecer [embexe'θer] *vt* to make old, age ▷ *vi* (*volverse viejo*) to grow old; (*parecer viejo*) to age
envenenar [embene'nar] *vt* to poison; (*fig*) to embitter
envergadura [emberɣa'ðura] *nf* (*fig*) scope, compass
enviar [em'bjar] *vt* to send; **~ un mensaje a algn** (*por movil*) to text sb, to send sb a text message
enviciarse [embi'θjarse] *vr*: **~ (con)** to get addicted (to)
envidia [em'biðja] *nf* envy; **tener ~ a** to envy, be jealous of; **envidiar** *vt* to envy
envío [em'bio] *nm* (*acción*) sending; (*de mercancías*) consignment; (*de dinero*) remittance
enviudar [embju'ðar] *vi* to be widowed
envoltura [embol'tura] *nf* (*cobertura*) cover; (*embalaje*) wrapper, wrapping; **envoltorio** *nm* package
envolver [embol'βer] *vt* to wrap (up); (*cubrir*) to cover; (*enemigo*) to surround; (*implicar*) to involve, implicate
envuelto [em'bwelto] *pp de* **envolver**
enyesar [enje'sar] *vt* (*pared*) to plaster; (*Med*) to put in plaster
enzarzarse [enθar'θarse] *vr*: **~ en** (*pelea*) to get mixed up in; (*disputa*) to get involved in
épica ['epika] *nf* epic
epidemia [epi'ðemja] *nf* epidemic
epilepsia [epi'lepsja] *nf* epilepsy
episodio [epi'soðjo] *nm* episode
época ['epoka] *nf* period, time; (*Hist*) age, epoch; **hacer ~** to be epoch-making
equilibrar [ekili'βrar] *vt* to balance; **equilibrio** *nm* balance, equilibrium; **mantener/perder el equilibrio** to keep/ lose one's balance; **equilibrista** *nmf* (*funámbulo*) tightrope walker; (*acróbata*) acrobat
equipaje [eki'paxe] *nm* luggage; (*avíos*): **hacer el ~** to pack; **equipaje de mano** hand luggage
equipar [eki'par] *vt* (*proveer*) to equip
equipararse [ekipa'rarse] *vr*: **~ con** to be on a level with
equipo [e'kipo] *nm* (*conjunto de cosas*) equipment; (*Deporte*) team; (*de obreros*) shift
equis ['ekis] *nf inv* (the letter) X
equitación [ekita'θjon] *nf* horse riding
equivalente [ekiβa'lente] *adj, nm* equivalent
equivaler [ekiβa'ler] *vi* to be equivalent *o* equal
equivocación [ekiβoka'θjon] *nf* mistake, error
equivocado, -a [ekiβo'kaðo, a] *adj* wrong, mistaken
equivocarse [ekiβo'karse] *vr* to be wrong, make a mistake; **~ de camino** to take the wrong road
era ['era] *vb V* **ser** ▷ *nf* era, age
erais *vb V* **ser**
éramos *vb V* **ser**
eran *vb V* **ser**
eras *vb V* **ser**
erección [erek'θjon] *nf* erection
eres *vb V* **ser**
erigir [eri'xir] *vt* to erect, build; **erigirse** *vr*: **~se en** to set o.s. up as
erizo [e'riθo] *nm* (*Zool*) hedgehog; **erizo de mar** sea-urchin
ermita [er'mita] *nf* hermitage; **ermitaño, -a** [ermi'taɲo, a] *nm/f* hermit
erosión [ero'sjon] *nf* erosion
erosionar [erosjo'nar] *vt* to erode
erótico, -a [e'rotiko, a] *adj* erotic; **erotismo** *nm* eroticism
errante [e'rrante] *adj* wandering, errant
erróneo, -a [e'rroneo, a] *adj* (*equivocado*) wrong, mistaken
error [e'rror] *nm* error, mistake; (*Inform*)

bug; **error de imprenta** misprint
eructar [eruk'tar] *vt* to belch, burp
erudito, -a [eru'ðito, a] *adj* erudite, learned
erupción [erup'θjon] *nf* eruption; (*Med*) rash
es *vb V* **ser**
esa ['esa] (*pl* **~s**) *adj demos V* **ese**
ésa ['esa] (*pl* **~s**) *pron V* **ése**
esbelto, -a [es'βelto, a] *adj* slim, slender
esbozo [es'βoθo] *nm* sketch, outline
escabeche [eska'βetʃe] *nm* brine; (*de aceitunas etc*) pickle; **en ~** pickled
escabullirse [eskaβu'ʎirse] *vr* to slip away, to clear out
escafandra [eska'fandra] *nf* (*buzo*) diving suit; (*escafandra espacial*) space suit
escala [es'kala] *nf* (*proporción, Mús*) scale; (*de mano*) ladder; (*Aviac*) stopover; **hacer ~ en** to stop *o* call in at
escalafón [eskala'fon] *nm* (*escala de salarios*) salary scale, wage scale
escalar [eska'lar] *vt* to climb, scale
escalera [eska'lera] *nf* stairs *pl*, staircase; (*escala*) ladder; (*Naipes*) run; **escalera de caracol** spiral staircase; **escalera de incendios** fire escape; **escalera mecánica** escalator
escalfar [eskal'far] *vt* (*huevos*) to poach
escalinata [eskali'nata] *nf* staircase
escalofriante [eskalo'frjante] *adj* chilling
escalofrío [eskalo'frio] *nm* (*Med*) chill; **escalofríos** *nmpl* (*fig*) shivers
escalón [eska'lon] *nm* step, stair; (*de escalera*) rung
escalope [eska'lope] *nm* (*Culin*) escalope
escama [es'kama] *nf* (*de pez, serpiente*) scale; (*de jabón*) flake; (*fig*) resentment
escampar [eskam'par] *vb impers* to stop raining
escandalizar [eskandali'θar] *vt* to scandalize, shock; **escandalizarse** *vr* to be shocked; (*ofenderse*) to be offended
escándalo [es'kandalo] *nm* scandal; (*alboroto, tumulto*) row, uproar; **escandaloso, -a** *adj* scandalous, shocking
escandinavo, -a [eskandi'naβo, a] *adj, nm/f* Scandinavian
escanear [eskane'ar] *vt* to scan
escaño [es'kaɲo] *nm* bench; (*Pol*) seat
escapar [eska'par] *vi* (*gen*) to escape, run away; (*Deporte*) to break away; **escaparse** *vr* to escape, get away; (*agua, gas*) to leak (out)
escaparate [eskapa'rate] *nm* shop window
escape [es'kape] *nm* (*de agua, gas*) leak; (*de motor*) exhaust
escarabajo [eskara'βaxo] *nm* beetle
escaramuza [eskara'muθa] *nf* skirmish
escarbar [eskar'βar] *vt* (*tierra*) to scratch
escarceos [eskar'θeos] *nmpl*: **en mis ~ con la política ...** in my dealings with politics ...; **escarceos amorosos** love affairs
escarcha [es'kartʃa] *nf* frost; **escarchado, -a** [eskar'tʃaðo, a] *adj* (*Culin: fruta*) crystallized
escarlatina [eskarla'tina] *nf* scarlet fever
escarmentar [eskarmen'tar] *vt* to punish severely ▷ *vi* to learn one's lesson
escarmiento *etc* [eskar'mjento] *vb V* **escarmentar** ▷ *nm* (*ejemplo*) lesson; (*castigo*) punishment
escarola [eska'rola] *nf* endive
escarpado, -a [eskar'paðo, a] *adj* (*pendiente*) sheer, steep; (*rocas*) craggy
escasear [eskase'ar] *vi* to be scarce
escasez [eska'seθ] *nf* (*falta*) shortage, scarcity; (*pobreza*) poverty
escaso, -a [es'kaso, a] *adj* (*poco*) scarce; (*raro*) rare; (*ralo*) thin, sparse; (*limitado*) limited
escatimar [eskati'mar] *vt* to skimp (on), be sparing with
escayola [eska'jola] *nf* plaster
escena [es'θena] *nf* scene; **escenario** [esθe'narjo] *nm* (*Teatro*) stage; (*Cine*) set; (*fig*) scene

> No confundir **escenario** con la palabra inglesa *scenery*.

escenografía *nf* set design
escéptico, -a [es'θeptiko, a] *adj* sceptical ▷ *nm/f* sceptic
esclarecer [esklare'θer] *vt* (*misterio, problema*) to shed light on
esclavitud [esklaβi'tuð] *nf* slavery
esclavizar [esklaβi'θar] *vt* to enslave
esclavo, -a [es'klaβo, a] *nm/f* slave
escoba [es'koβa] *nf* broom; **escobilla** *nf* brush
escocer [esko'θer] *vi* to burn, sting; **escocerse** *vr* to chafe, get chafed
escocés, -esa [esko'θes, esa] *adj* Scottish ▷ *nm/f* Scotsman(-woman), Scot
Escocia [es'koθja] *nf* Scotland
escoger [esko'xer] *vt* to choose, pick, select; **escogido, -a** *adj* chosen, selected
escolar [esko'lar] *adj* school *cpd* ▷ *nmf* schoolboy(-girl), pupil
escollo [es'koʎo] *nm* (*obstáculo*) pitfall
escolta [es'kolta] *nf* escort; **escoltar** *vt* to escort
escombros [es'kombros] *nmpl* (*basura*) rubbish *sg*; (*restos*) debris *sg*
esconder [eskon'der] *vt* to hide, conceal; **esconderse** *vr* to hide; **escondidas** (LAM)

nfpl: **a escondidas** secretly; **escondite** *nm* hiding place; (ESP: *juego*) hide-and-seek; **escondrijo** *nm* hiding place, hideout
escopeta [esko'peta] *nf* shotgun
escoria [es'korja] *nf* (*de alto horno*) slag; (*fig*) scum, dregs *pl*
Escorpio [es'korpjo] *nm* Scorpio
escorpión [eskor'pjon] *nm* scorpion
escotado, -a [esko'taðo, a] *adj* low-cut
escote [es'kote] *nm* (*de vestido*) low neck; **pagar a ~** to share the expenses
escotilla [esko'tiʎa] *nf* (*Náut*) hatch(way)
escozor [esko'θor] *nm* (*dolor*) sting(ing)
escribible [eskri'βiβle] *adj* writable
escribir [eskri'βir] *vt, vi* to write; **~ a máquina** to type; **¿cómo se escribe?** how do you spell it?
escrito, -a [es'krito, a] *pp de* **escribir** ▷ *nm* (*documento*) document; (*manuscrito*) text, manuscript; **por ~** in writing
escritor, a [eskri'tor, a] *nm/f* writer
escritorio [eskri'torjo] *nm* desk
escritura [eskri'tura] *nf* (*acción*) writing; (*caligrafía*) (hand)writing; (*Jur*: *documento*) deed
escrúpulo [es'krupulo] *nm* scruple; (*minuciosidad*) scrupulousness; **escrupuloso, -a** *adj* scrupulous
escrutinio [eskru'tinjo] *nm* (*examen atento*) scrutiny; (*Pol*: *recuento de votos*) count(ing)
escuadra [es'kwaðra] *nf* (*Mil etc*) squad; (*Náut*) squadron; (*flota*: *de coches etc*) fleet; **escuadrilla** *nf* (*de aviones*) squadron; (LAM: *de obreros*) gang
escuadrón [eskwa'ðron] *nm* squadron
escuálido, -a [es'kwaliðo, a] *adj* skinny, scraggy; (*sucio*) squalid
escuchar [esku'tʃar] *vt* to listen to ▷ *vi* to listen
escudo [es'kuðo] *nm* shield
escuela [es'kwela] *nf* school; **escuela de artes y oficios** (ESP) ≈ technical college; **escuela de choferes** (LAM) driving school; **escuela de manejo** (MÉX) driving school
escueto, -a [es'kweto, a] *adj* plain; (*estilo*) simple
escuincle, -a [es'kwinkle, a] (MÉX: *fam*) *nm/f* kid
esculpir [eskul'pir] *vt* to sculpt; (*grabar*) to engrave; (*tallar*) to carve; **escultor, a** *nm/f* sculptor(-tress); **escultura** *nf* sculpture
escupidera [eskupi'ðera] *nf* spittoon
escupir [esku'pir] *vt, vi* to spit (out)
escurreplatos [eskurre'platos] (ESP) *nm inv* draining board (BRIT), drainboard (US)
escurridero [eskurri'ðero] (LAM) *nm* draining board (BRIT), drainboard (US)
escurridizo, -a [eskurri'ðiθo, a] *adj* slippery
escurridor [eskurri'ðor] *nm* colander
escurrir [esku'rrir] *vt* (*ropa*) to wring out; (*verduras, platos*) to drain ▷ *vi* (*líquidos*) to drip; **escurrirse** *vr* (*secarse*) to drain; (*resbalarse*) to slip, slide; (*escaparse*) to slip away
ese ['ese] (*f* **esa**, *pl* **esos, esas**) *adj demos* (*sg*) that; (*pl*) those
ése ['ese] (*f* **ésa**, *pl* **ésos, ésas**) *pron* (*sg*) that (one); (*pl*) those (ones); **~ ... éste ...** the former ... the latter ...; **no me vengas con ésas** don't give me any more of that nonsense
esencia [e'senθja] *nf* essence; **esencial** *adj* essential
esfera [es'fera] *nf* sphere; (*de reloj*) face; **esférico, -a** *adj* spherical
esforzarse [esfor'θarse] *vr* to exert o.s., make an effort
esfuerzo *etc* [es'fwerθo] *vb* V **esforzarse** ▷ *nm* effort
esfumarse [esfu'marse] *vr* (*apoyo, esperanzas*) to fade away
esgrima [es'ɣrima] *nf* fencing
esguince [es'ɣinθe] *nm* (*Med*) sprain
eslabón [esla'βon] *nm* link
eslip [ez'lip] *nm* pants *pl* (BRIT), briefs *pl*
eslovaco, -a [eslo'βako, a] *adj, nm/f* Slovak, Slovakian ▷ *nm* (*Ling*) Slovak, Slovakian
Eslovaquia [eslo'βakja] *nf* Slovakia
esmalte [es'malte] *nm* enamel; **esmalte de uñas** nail varnish *o* polish
esmeralda [esme'ralda] *nf* emerald
esmerarse [esme'rarse] *vr* (*aplicarse*) to take great pains, exercise great care; (*afanarse*) to work hard
esmero [es'mero] *nm* (great) care
esnob [es'nob] (*pl* **~s**) *adj* (*persona*) snobbish ▷ *nmf* snob
eso ['eso] *pron* that, that thing *o* matter; **~ de su coche** that business about his car; **~ de ir al cine** all that about going to the cinema; **a ~ de las cinco** at about five o'clock; **en ~** thereupon, at that point; **~ es** that's it; **¡~ sí que es vida!** now that is really living!; **por ~ te lo dije** that's why I told you; **y ~ que llovía** in spite of the fact it was raining
esos *adj demos* V **ese**
ésos *pron* V **ése**
espabilar *etc* [espaβi'lar] = **despabilar etc**
espacial [espa'θjal] *adj* (*del espacio*) space *cpd*
espaciar [espa'θjar] *vt* to space (out)
espacio [es'paθjo] *nm* space; (*Mús*)

interval; (*Radio, TV*) programme (BRIT), program (US); **el ~** space; **espacio aéreo/exterior** air/outer space; **espacioso, -a** *adj* spacious, roomy
espada [es'paða] *nf* sword; **espadas** *nfpl* (*Naipes*) spades
espaguetis [espa'ɣetis] *nmpl* spaghetti *sg*
espalda [es'palda] *nf* (*gen*) back; **espaldas** *nfpl* (*hombros*) shoulders; **a ~s de algn** behind sb's back; **estar de ~s** to have one's back turned; **tenderse de ~s** to lie (down) on one's back; **volver la ~ a algn** to cold-shoulder sb
espantajo [espan'taxo] *nm* = **espantapájaros**
espantapájaros [espanta'paxaros] *nm inv* scarecrow
espantar [espan'tar] *vt* (*asustar*) to frighten, scare; (*ahuyentar*) to frighten off; (*asombrar*) to horrify, appal; **espantarse** *vr* to get frightened *o* scared; to be appalled
espanto [es'panto] *nm* (*susto*) fright; (*terror*) terror; (*asombro*) astonishment; **espantoso, -a** *adj* frightening; terrifying; astonishing
España [es'paɲa] *nf* Spain; **español, a** *adj* Spanish ▷ *nm/f* Spaniard ▷ *nm* (*Ling*) Spanish
esparadrapo [espara'ðrapo] *nm* (sticking) plaster (BRIT), adhesive tape (US)
esparcir [espar'θir] *vt* to spread; (*diseminar*) to scatter; **esparcirse** *vr* to spread (out), to scatter; (*divertirse*) to enjoy o.s.
espárrago [es'parraɣo] *nm* asparagus
esparto [es'parto] *nm* esparto (grass)
espasmo [es'pasmo] *nm* spasm
espátula [es'patula] *nf* spatula
especia [es'peθja] *nf* spice
especial [espe'θjal] *adj* special; **especialidad** *nf* speciality (BRIT), specialty (US)
especie [es'peθje] *nf* (*Bio*) species; (*clase*) kind, sort; **en ~** in kind
especificar [espeθifi'kar] *vt* to specify; **específico, -a** *adj* specific
espécimen [es'peθimen] (*pl* **especímenes**) *nm* specimen
espectáculo [espek'takulo] *nm* (*gen*) spectacle; (*Teatro etc*) show
espectador, a [espekta'ðor, a] *nm/f* spectator
especular [espeku'lar] *vt, vi* to speculate
espejismo [espe'xismo] *nm* mirage
espejo [es'pexo] *nm* mirror; **(espejo) retrovisor** rear-view mirror
espeluznante [espeluθ'nante] *adj* horrifying, hair-raising
espera [es'pera] *nf* (*pausa, intervalo*) wait; (*Jur: plazo*) respite; **en ~ de** waiting for; (*con expectativa*) expecting
esperanza [espe'ranθa] *nf* (*confianza*) hope; (*expectativa*) expectation; **hay pocas ~s de que venga** there is little prospect of his coming; **esperanza de vida** life expectancy
esperar [espe'rar] *vt* (*aguardar*) to wait for; (*tener expectativa de*) to expect; (*desear*) to hope for ▷ *vi* to wait; to expect; to hope; **hacer ~ a algn** to keep sb waiting; **~ un bebé** to be expecting (a baby)
esperma [es'perma] *nf* sperm
espeso, -a [es'peso, a] *adj* thick; **espesor** *nm* thickness
espía [es'pia] *nmf* spy; **espiar** *vt* (*observar*) to spy on
espiga [es'piɣa] *nf* (*Bot: de trigo etc*) ear
espigón [espi'ɣon] *nm* (*Bot*) ear; (*Náut*) breakwater
espina [es'pina] *nf* thorn; (*de pez*) bone; **espina dorsal** (*Anat*) spine
espinaca [espi'naka] *nf* spinach
espinazo [espi'naθo] *nm* spine, backbone
espinilla [espi'niʎa] *nf* (*Anat: tibia*) shin(bone); (*grano*) blackhead
espinoso, -a [espi'noso, a] *adj* (*planta*) thorny, prickly; (*asunto*) difficult
espionaje [espjo'naxe] *nm* spying, espionage
espiral [espi'ral] *adj, nf* spiral
espirar [espi'rar] *vt* to breathe out, exhale
espiritista [espiri'tista] *adj, nmf* spiritualist
espíritu [es'piritu] *nm* spirit; **Espíritu Santo** Holy Ghost *o* Spirit; **espiritual** *adj* spiritual
espléndido, -a [es'plendiðo, a] *adj* (*magnífico*) magnificent, splendid; (*generoso*) generous
esplendor [esplen'dor] *nm* splendour
espolvorear [espolβore'ar] *vt* to dust, sprinkle
esponja [es'ponxa] *nf* sponge; (*fig*) sponger; **esponjoso, -a** *adj* spongy
espontaneidad [espontanei'ðað] *nf* spontaneity; **espontáneo, -a** *adj* spontaneous
esposa [es'posa] *nf* wife; **esposas** *nfpl* handcuffs; **esposar** *vt* to handcuff
esposo [es'poso] *nm* husband
espray [es'prai] *nm* spray
espuela [es'pwela] *nf* spur
espuma [es'puma] *nf* foam; (*de cerveza*) froth, head; (*de jabón*) lather; **espuma de afeitar** shaving foam; **espumadera** *nf* (*utensilio*) skimmer; **espumoso, -a** *adj*

frothy, foamy; (*vino*) sparkling
esqueleto [eske'leto] *nm* skeleton
esquema [es'kema] *nm* (*diagrama*) diagram; (*dibujo*) plan; (*Filosofía*) schema
esquí [es'ki] (*pl* **~s**) *nm* (*objeto*) ski; (*Deporte*) skiing; **esquí acuático** water-skiing; **esquiar** *vi* to ski
esquilar [eski'lar] *vt* to shear
esquimal [eski'mal] *adj, nmf* Eskimo
esquina [es'kina] *nf* corner; **esquinazo** [eski'naθo] *nm*: **dar esquinazo a algn** to give sb the slip
esquirol [eski'rol] (ESP) *nm* strikebreaker, scab
esquivar [eski'βar] *vt* to avoid
esta ['esta] *adj demos V* **este**[2]
está *vb V* **estar**
ésta *pron V* **éste**
estabilidad [estaβili'ðað] *nf* stability; **estable** *adj* stable
establecer [estaβle'θer] *vt* to establish; **establecerse** *vr* to establish o.s.; (*echar raíces*) to settle (down); **establecimiento** *nm* establishment
establo [es'taβlo] *nm* (*Agr*) stable
estaca [es'taka] *nf* stake, post; (*de tienda de campaña*) peg
estacada [esta'kaða] *nf* (*cerca*) fence, fencing; (*palenque*) stockade
estación [esta'θjon] *nf* station; (*del año*) season; **estación balnearia** seaside resort; **estación de autobuses** bus station; **estación de servicio** service station
estacionamiento [estaθjona'mjento] *nm* (*Auto*) parking; (*Mil*) stationing
estacionar [estaθjo'nar] *vt* (*Auto*) to park; (*Mil*) to station
estadía [esta'ðia] (LAM) *nf* stay
estadio [es'taðjo] *nm* (*fase*) stage, phase; (*Deporte*) stadium
estadista [esta'ðista] *nm* (*Pol*) statesman; (*Mat*) statistician
estadística [esta'ðistika] *nf* figure, statistic; (*ciencia*) statistics *sg*
estado [es'taðo] *nm* (*Pol*: *condición*) state; **estar en ~** to be pregnant; **estado civil** marital status; **estado de ánimo** state of mind; **estado de cuenta** bank statement; **estado de sitio** state of siege; **estado mayor** staff; **Estados Unidos** United States (of America)
estadounidense [estaðouni'ðense] *adj* United States *cpd*, American ▷*nmf* American
estafa [es'tafa] *nf* swindle, trick; **estafar** *vt* to swindle, defraud
estáis *vb V* **estar**
estallar [esta'ʎar] *vi* to burst; (*bomba*) to explode; go off; (*epidemia, guerra, rebelión*) to break out; **~ en llanto** to burst into tears;
estallido *nm* explosion; (*fig*) outbreak
estampa [es'tampa] *nf* print, engraving;
estampado, -a [estam'paðo, a] *adj* printed ▷*nm* (*impresión*: *acción*) printing; (: *efecto*) print; (*marca*) stamping
estampar [estam'par] *vt* (*imprimir*) to print; (*marcar*) to stamp; (*metal*) to engrave; (*poner sello en*) to stamp; (*fig*) to stamp, imprint
estampida [estam'piða] *nf* stampede
estampido [estam'piðo] *nm* bang, report
estampilla [estam'piʎa] (LAM) *nf* (postage) stamp
están *vb V* **estar**
estancado, -a [estan'kaðo, a] *adj* stagnant
estancar [estan'kar] *vt* (*aguas*) to hold up, hold back; (*Com*) to monopolize; (*fig*) to block, hold up; **estancarse** *vr* to stagnate
estancia [es'tanθja] *nf* (ESP, MÉX: *permanencia*) stay; (*sala*) room; (RPL: *de ganado*) farm, ranch; **estanciero** (RPL) *nm* farmer, rancher
estanco, -a [es'tanko, a] *adj* watertight ▷*nm* tobacconist's (shop), cigar store (US)

ESTANCO

Cigarettes, tobacco, postage stamps and official forms are all sold under state monopoly in shops called **estancos**. Although tobacco products can also be bought in bars and quioscos they are generally more expensive.

estándar [es'tandar] *adj, nm* standard
estandarte [estan'darte] *nm* banner, standard
estanque [es'tanke] *nm* (*lago*) pool, pond; (*Agr*) reservoir
estanquero, -a [estan'kero, a] *nm/f* tobacconist
estante [es'tante] *nm* (*armario*) rack, stand; (*biblioteca*) bookcase; (*anaquel*) shelf; **estantería** *nf* shelving, shelves *pl*

PALABRA CLAVE

estar [es'tar] *vi* **1** (*posición*) to be; **está en la plaza** it's in the square; **¿está Juan?** is Juan in?; **estamos a 30 km de Junín** we're 30 kms from Junín
2 (*+ adj*: *estado*) to be; **estar enfermo** to be ill; **está muy elegante** he's looking very smart; **¿cómo estás?** how are you keeping?
3 (*+ gerundio*) to be; **estoy leyendo** I'm

reading
4 (*uso pasivo*): **está condenado a muerte** he's been condemned to death; **está envasado en ...** it's packed in ...
5 (*con fechas*): **¿a cuántos estamos?** what's the date today?; **estamos a 5 de mayo** it's the 5th of May
6 (*locuciones*): **¿estamos?** (*¿de acuerdo?*) okay?; (*¿listo?*) ready?
7: **estar de: estar de vacaciones/viaje** to be on holiday/away *o* on a trip; **está de camarero** he's working as a waiter
8: **estar para: está para salir** he's about to leave; **no estoy para bromas** I'm not in the mood for jokes
9: **estar por** (*propuesta etc*) to be in favour of; (*persona etc*) to support, side with; **está por limpiar** it still has to be cleaned
10: **estar sin: estar sin dinero** to have no money; **está sin terminar** it isn't finished yet
estarse *vr*: **se estuvo en la cama toda la tarde** he stayed in bed all afternoon

estas ['estas] *adj demos V* **este²**
éstas *pron V* **éste**
estatal [esta'tal] *adj* state *cpd*
estático, -a [es'tatiko, a] *adj* static
estatua [es'tatwa] *nf* statue
estatura [esta'tura] *nf* stature, height
este¹ ['este] *nm* east
este² ['este] (*f* **esta**, *pl* **estos, estas**) *adj demos* (*sg*) this; (*pl*) these
esté *etc vb V* **estar**
éste ['este] (*f* **ésta**, *pl* **éstos, éstas**) *pron* (*sg*) this (one); (*pl*) these (ones); **ése ... ~ ...** the former ... the latter ...
estén *etc vb V* **estar**
estepa [es'tepa] *nf* (*Geo*) steppe
estera [es'tera] *nf* mat(ting)
estéreo [es'tereo] *adj inv, nm* stereo; **estereotipo** *nm* stereotype
estéril [es'teril] *adj* sterile, barren; (*fig*) vain, futile; **esterilizar** *vt* to sterilize
esterlina [ester'lina] *adj*: **libra ~** pound sterling
estés *etc vb V* **estar**
estética [es'tetika] *nf* aesthetics *sg*
estético, -a [es'tetiko, a] *adj* aesthetic
estiércol [es'tjerkol] *nm* dung, manure
estigma [es'tiɣma] *nm* stigma
estilo [es'tilo] *nm* style; (*Tec*) stylus; (*Natación*) stroke; **algo por el ~** something along those lines
estima [es'tima] *nf* esteem, respect; **estimación** [estima'θjon] *nf* (*evaluación*) estimation; (*aprecio, afecto*) esteem, regard; **estimado, a** *adj* esteemed; **E~ señor** Dear Sir
estimar [esti'mar] *vt* (*evaluar*) to estimate; (*valorar*) to value; (*apreciar*) to esteem, respect; (*pensar, considerar*) to think, reckon
estimulante [estimu'lante] *adj* stimulating ▷ *nm* stimulant
estimular [estimu'lar] *vt* to stimulate; (*excitar*) to excite
estímulo [es'timulo] *nm* stimulus; (*ánimo*) encouragement
estirar [esti'rar] *vt* to stretch; (*dinero, suma etc*) to stretch out; **estirarse** *vr* to stretch
estirón [esti'ron] *nm* pull, tug; (*crecimiento*) spurt, sudden growth; **dar** *o* **pegar un ~** (*fam: niño*) to shoot up (*inf*)
estirpe [es'tirpe] *nf* stock, lineage
estival [esti'βal] *adj* summer *cpd*
esto ['esto] *pron* this, this thing *o* matter; **~ de la boda** this business about the wedding
Estocolmo [esto'kolmo] *nm* Stockholm
estofado [esto'faðo] *nm* stew
estómago [es'tomaɣo] *nm* stomach; **tener ~** to be thick-skinned
estorbar [estor'βar] *vt* to hinder, obstruct; (*molestar*) to bother, disturb ▷ *vi* to be in the way; **estorbo** *nm* (*molestia*) bother, nuisance; (*obstáculo*) hindrance, obstacle
estornudar [estornu'ðar] *vi* to sneeze
estos ['estos] *adj demos V* **este²**
éstos *pron V* **éste**
estoy *vb V* **estar**
estrado [es'traðo] *nm* platform
estrafalario, -a [estrafa'larjo, a] *adj* odd, eccentric
estrago [es'traɣo] *nm* ruin, destruction; **hacer ~s en** to wreak havoc among
estragón [estra'ɣon] *nm* tarragon
estrambótico, -a [estram'botiko, a] *adj* (*persona*) eccentric; (*peinado, ropa*) outlandish
estrangular [estrangu'lar] *vt* (*persona*) to strangle; (*Med*) to strangulate
estratagema [estrata'xema] *nf* (*Mil*) stratagem; (*astucia*) cunning
estrategia [estra'texja] *nf* strategy; **estratégico, -a** *adj* strategic
estrato [es'trato] *nm* stratum, layer
estrechar [estre'tʃar] *vt* (*reducir*) to narrow; (*Costura*) to take in; (*abrazar*) to hug, embrace; **estrecharse** *vr* (*reducirse*) to narrow, grow narrow; (*abrazarse*) to embrace; **~ la mano** to shake hands
estrechez [estre'tʃeθ] *nf* narrowness; (*de ropa*) tightness; **estrecheces** *nfpl* (*dificultades económicas*) financial difficulties
estrecho, -a [es'tretʃo, a] *adj* narrow; (*apretado*) tight; (*íntimo*) close, intimate; (*miserable*) mean ▷ *nm* strait; **~ de miras**

e

narrow-minded
estrella [es'treʎa] *nf* star; **estrella de mar** (*Zool*) starfish; **estrella fugaz** shooting star
estrellar [estre'ʎar] *vt* (*hacer añicos*) to smash (to pieces); (*huevos*) to fry; **estrellarse** *vr* to smash; (*chocarse*) to crash; (*fracasar*) to fail
estremecer [estreme'θer] *vt* to shake; **estremecerse** *vr* to shake, tremble
estrenar [estre'nar] *vt* (*vestido*) to wear for the first time; (*casa*) to move into; (*película, obra de teatro*) to première; **estrenarse** *vr* (*persona*) to make one's début; **estreno** *nm* (*Cine etc*) première
estreñido, -a [estre'ɲiðo, a] *adj* constipated
estreñimiento [estreɲi'mjento] *nm* constipation
estrepitoso, -a [estrepi'toso, a] *adj* noisy; (*fiesta*) rowdy
estría [es'tria] *nf* groove
estribar [estri'βar] *vi*: **~ en** to lie on
estribillo [estri'βiʎo] *nm* (*Literatura*) refrain; (*Mús*) chorus
estribo [es'triβo] *nm* (*de jinete*) stirrup; (*de coche, tren*) step; (*de puente*) support; (*Geo*) spur; **perder los ~s** to fly off the handle
estribor [estri'βor] *nm* (*Náut*) starboard
estricto, -a [es'trikto, a] *adj* (*riguroso*) strict; (*severo*) severe
estridente [estri'ðente] *adj* (*color*) loud; (*voz*) raucous
estropajo [estro'paxo] *nm* scourer
estropear [estrope'ar] *vt* to spoil; (*dañar*) to damage; **estropearse** *vr* (*objeto*) to get damaged; (*persona, piel*) to be ruined
estructura [estruk'tura] *nf* structure
estrujar [estru'xar] *vt* (*apretar*) to squeeze; (*aplastar*) to crush; (*fig*) to drain, bleed
estuario [es'twarjo] *nm* estuary
estuche [es'tutʃe] *nm* box, case
estudiante [estu'ðjante] *nmf* student; **estudiantil** *adj* student *cpd*
estudiar [estu'ðjar] *vt* to study
estudio [es'tuðjo] *nm* study; (*Cine, Arte, Radio*) studio; **estudios** *nmpl* studies; (*erudición*) learning *sg*; **estudioso, -a** *adj* studious
estufa [es'tufa] *nf* heater, fire
estupefaciente [estupefa'θjente] *nm* drug, narcotic
estupefacto, -a [estupe'fakto, a] *adj* speechless, thunderstruck
estupendo, -a [estu'pendo, a] *adj* wonderful, terrific; (*fam*) great; **¡~!** that's great!, fantastic!
estupidez [estupi'ðeθ] *nf* (*torpeza*) stupidity; (*acto*) stupid thing (to do)
estúpido, -a [es'tupiðo, a] *adj* stupid, silly
estuve *etc vb V* **estar**
ETA ['eta] (ESP) *nf abr* (= *Euskadi ta Askatasuna*) ETA
etapa [e'tapa] *nf* (*de viaje*) stage; (*Deporte*) leg; (*parada*) stopping place; (*fase*) stage, phase
etarra [e'tarra] *nmf* member of ETA
etc. *abr* (= *etcétera*) etc
etcétera [et'θetera] *adv* etcetera
eternidad [eterni'ðað] *nf* eternity; **eterno, -a** *adj* eternal, everlasting
ética ['etika] *nf* ethics *pl*
ético, -a ['etiko, a] *adj* ethical
etiqueta [eti'keta] *nf* (*modales*) etiquette; (*rótulo*) label, tag
Eucaristía [eukaris'tia] *nf* Eucharist
euforia [eu'forja] *nf* euphoria
euro ['euro] *nm* (*moneda*) euro
eurodiputado, -a [eurodipu'taðo, a] *nm/f* Euro MP, MEP
Europa [eu'ropa] *nf* Europe; **europeo, -a** *adj, nm/f* European
Euskadi [eus'kaði] *nm* the Basque Country *o* Provinces *pl*
euskera [eus'kera] *nm* (*Ling*) Basque
evacuación [eβakwa'θjon] *nf* evacuation
evacuar [eβa'kwar] *vt* to evacuate
evadir [eβa'ðir] *vt* to evade, avoid; **evadirse** *vr* to escape
evaluar [eβa'lwar] *vt* to evaluate
evangelio [eβan'xeljo] *nm* gospel
evaporar [eβapo'rar] *vt* to evaporate; **evaporarse** *vr* to vanish
evasión [eβa'sjon] *nf* escape, flight; (*fig*) evasion; **evasión de capitales** flight of capital
evasiva [eβa'siβa] *nf* (*pretexto*) excuse
evento [e'βento] *nm* event
eventual [eβen'twal] *adj* possible, conditional (upon circumstances); (*trabajador*) casual, temporary

No confundir **eventual** con la palabra inglesa *eventual*.

evidencia [eβi'ðenθja] *nf* evidence, proof
evidente [eβi'ðente] *adj* obvious, clear, evident
evitar [eβi'tar] *vt* (*evadir*) to avoid; (*impedir*) to prevent; **~ hacer algo** to avoid doing sth
evocar [eβo'kar] *vt* to evoke, call forth
evolución [eβolu'θjon] *nf* (*desarrollo*) evolution, development; (*cambio*) change; (*Mil*) manoeuvre; **evolucionar** *vi* to evolve; to manoeuvre
ex [eks] *adj* ex-; **el ~ ministro** the former minister, the ex-minister
exactitud [eksakti'tuð] *nf* exactness;

(*precisión*) accuracy; (*puntualidad*) punctuality; **exacto, -a** *adj* exact; accurate; punctual; **¡exacto!** exactly!
exageración [eksaxera'θjon] *nf* exaggeration
exagerar [eksaxe'rar] *vt, vi* to exaggerate
exaltar [eksal'tar] *vt* to exalt, glorify; **exaltarse** *vr* (*excitarse*) to get excited *o* worked up
examen [ek'samen] *nm* examination; **examen de conducir** driving test; **examen de ingreso** entrance examination
examinar [eksami'nar] *vt* to examine; **examinarse** *vr* to be examined, take an examination
excavadora [ekskaβa'ðora] *nf* excavator
excavar [ekska'βar] *vt* to excavate
excedencia [eksθe'ðenθja] *nf*: **estar en ~** to be on leave; **pedir** *o* **solicitar la ~** to ask for leave
excedente [eksθe'ðente] *adj, nm* excess, surplus
exceder [eksθe'ðer] *vt* to exceed, surpass; **excederse** *vr* (*extralimitarse*) to go too far
excelencia [eksθe'lenθja] *nf* excellence; **su E~** his Excellency; **excelente** *adj* excellent
excéntrico, -a [eks'θentriko, a] *adj, nm/f* eccentric
excepción [eksθep'θjon] *nf* exception; **a ~ de** with the exception of, except for; **excepcional** *adj* exceptional
excepto [eks'θepto] *adv* excepting, except (for)
exceptuar [eksθep'twar] *vt* to except, exclude
excesivo, -a [eksθe'siβo, a] *adj* excessive
exceso [eks'θeso] *nm* (*gen*) excess; (*Com*) surplus; **exceso de equipaje/peso** excess luggage/weight; **exceso de velocidad** speeding
excitado, -a [eksθi'taðo, a] *adj* excited; (*emociónes*) aroused
excitar [eksθi'tar] *vt* to excite; (*incitar*) to urge; **excitarse** *vr* to get excited
exclamación [eksklama'θjon] *nf* exclamation
exclamar [ekscla'mar] *vi* to exclaim
excluir [eksklu'ir] *vt* to exclude; (*dejar fuera*) to shut out; (*descartar*) to reject
exclusiva [eksklu'siβa] *nf* (*Prensa*) exclusive, scoop; (*Com*) sole right
exclusivo, -a [eksklu'siβo, a] *adj* exclusive; **derecho ~** sole *o* exclusive right
Excmo. *abr* = **excelentísmo**
excomulgar [ekskomul'ɣar] *vt* (*Rel*) to excommunicate
excomunión [ekskomu'njon] *nf* excommunication
excursión [ekskur'sjon] *nf* excursion, outing; **excursionista** *nmf* (*turista*) sightseer
excusa [eks'kusa] *nf* excuse; (*disculpa*) apology; **excusar** [eksku'sar] *vt* to excuse
exhaustivo, -a [eksaus'tiβo, a] *adj* (*análisis*) thorough; (*estudio*) exhaustive
exhausto, -a [ek'sausto, a] *adj* exhausted
exhibición [eksiβi'θjon] *nf* exhibition, display, show
exhibir [eksi'βir] *vt* to exhibit, display, show
exigencia [eksi'xenθja] *nf* demand, requirement; **exigente** *adj* demanding
exigir [eksi'xir] *vt* (*gen*) to demand, require; **~ el pago** to demand payment
exiliado, -a [eksi'ljaðo, a] *adj* exiled ▷ *nm/f* exile
exilio [ek'siljo] *nm* exile
eximir [eksi'mir] *vt* to exempt
existencia [eksis'tenθja] *nf* existence; **existencias** *nfpl* stock(s) *pl*
existir [eksis'tir] *vi* to exist, be
éxito ['eksito] *nm* (*triunfo*) success; (*Mús etc*) hit; **tener ~** to be successful

No confundir **éxito** con la palabra inglesa *exit*.

exorbitante [eksorβi'tante] *adj* (*precio*) exorbitant; (*cantidad*) excessive
exótico, -a [ek'sotiko, a] *adj* exotic
expandir [ekspan'dir] *vt* to expand
expansión [ekspan'sjon] *nf* expansion
expansivo, -a [ekspan'siβo, a] *adj*: **onda expansiva** shock wave
expatriarse [ekspa'trjarse] *vr* to emigrate; (*Pol*) to go into exile
expectativa [ekspekta'tiβa] *nf* (*espera*) expectation; (*perspectiva*) prospect
expedición [ekspeði'θjon] *nf* (*excursión*) expedition
expediente [ekspe'ðjente] *nm* expedient; (*Jur: procedimento*) action, proceedings *pl*; (*: papeles*) dossier, file, record
expedir [ekspe'ðir] *vt* (*despachar*) to send, forward; (*pasaporte*) to issue
expensas [eks'pensas] *nfpl*: **a ~ de** at the expense of
experiencia [ekspe'rjenθja] *nf* experience
experimentado, -a [eksperimen'taðo, a] *adj* experienced
experimentar [eksperimen'tar] *vt* (*en laboratorio*) to experiment with; (*probar*) to test, try out; (*notar, observar*) to experience; (*deterioro, pérdida*) to suffer; **experimento** *nm* experiment

experto, -a [eks'perto, a] *adj* expert, skilled ▷ *nm/f* expert
expirar [ekspi'rar] *vi* to expire
explanada [eskpla'naða] *nf* (*llano*) plain
explayarse [ekspla'jarse] *vr* (*en discurso*) to speak at length; **~ con algn** to confide in sb
explicación [eksplika'θjon] *nf* explanation
explicar [ekspli'kar] *vt* to explain; **explicarse** *vr* to explain (o.s.)
explícito, -a [eks'pliθito, a] *adj* explicit
explique *etc vb V* **explicar**
explorador, a [eksplora'ðor, a] *nm/f* (*pionero*) explorer; (*Mil*) scout ▷ *nm* (*Med*) probe; (*Tec*) (radar) scanner
explorar [eksplo'rar] *vt* to explore; (*Med*) to probe; (*radar*) to scan
explosión [eksplo'sjon] *nf* explosion; **explosivo, -a** *adj* explosive
explotación [eksplota'θjon] *nf* exploitation; (*de planta etc*) running
explotar [eksplo'tar] *vt* to exploit to run, operate ▷ *vi* to explode
exponer [ekspo'ner] *vt* to expose; (*cuadro*) to display; (*vida*) to risk; (*idea*) to explain; **exponerse** *vr*: **~se a (hacer) algo** to run the risk of (doing) sth
exportación [eksporta'θjon] *nf* (*acción*) export; (*mercancías*) exports *pl*
exportar [ekspor'tar] *vt* to export
exposición [eksposi'θjon] *nf* (*gen*) exposure; (*de arte*) show, exhibition; (*explicación*) explanation; (*declaración*) account, statement
expresamente [ekspresa'mente] *adv* (*decir*) clearly; (*a propósito*) expressly
expresar [ekspre'sar] *vt* to express; **expresión** *nf* expression
expresivo, -a [ekspre'siβo, a] *adj* (*persona, gesto, palabras*) expressive; (*cariñoso*) affectionate
expreso, -a [eks'preso, a] *pp de* **expresar** ▷ *adj* (*explícito*) express; (*claro*) specific, clear; (*tren*) fast ▷ *adv*: **enviar ~** to send by express (delivery)
express [eks'pres] (LAM) *adv*: **enviar algo ~** to send sth special delivery
exprimidor [eksprimi'ðor] *nm* squeezer
exprimir [ekspri'mir] *vt* (*fruta*) to squeeze; (*zumo*) to squeeze out
expuesto, -a [eks'pwesto, a] *pp de* **exponer** ▷ *adj* exposed; (*cuadro etc*) on show, on display
expulsar [ekspul'sar] *vt* (*echar*) to eject, throw out; (*alumno*) to expel; (*despedir*) to sack, fire; (*Deporte*) to send off; **expulsión** *nf* expulsion; sending-off
exquisito, -a [ekski'sito, a] *adj* exquisite; (*comida*) delicious
éxtasis ['ekstasis] *nm* ecstasy
extender [eksten'der] *vt* to extend; (*los brazos*) to stretch out, hold out; (*mapa, tela*) to spread (out), open (out); (*mantequilla*) to spread; (*certificado*) to issue; (*cheque, recibo*) to make out; (*documento*) to draw up; **extenderse** *vr* (*gen*) to extend; (*persona*: *en el suelo*) to stretch out; (*epidemia*) to spread; **extendido, -a** *adj* (*abierto*) spread out, open; (*brazos*) outstretched; (*costumbre*) widespread
extensión [eksten'sjon] *nf* (*de terreno, mar*) expanse, stretch; (*de tiempo*) length, duration; (*Tel*) extension; **en toda la ~ de la palabra** in every sense of the word
extenso, -a [eks'tenso, a] *adj* extensive
exterior [ekste'rjor] *adj* (*de fuera*) external; (*afuera*) outside, exterior; (*apariencia*) outward; (*deuda, relaciónes*) foreign ▷ *nm* (*gen*) exterior, outside; (*aspecto*) outward appearance; (*Deporte*) wing(er); (*países extranjeros*) abroad; **en el ~** abroad; **al ~** outwardly, on the surface
exterminar [ekstermi'nar] *vt* to exterminate
externo, -a [eks'terno, a] *adj* (*exterior*) external, outside; (*superficial*) outward ▷ *nm/f* day pupil
extinguir [ekstin'gir] *vt* (*fuego*) to extinguish, put out; (*raza, población*) to wipe out; **extinguirse** *vr* (*fuego*) to go out; (*Bio*) to die out, become extinct
extintor [ekstin'tor] *nm* (fire) extinguisher
extirpar [ekstir'par] *vt* (*Med*) to remove (surgically)
extra ['ekstra] *adj inv* (*tiempo*) extra; (*chocolate, vino*) good-quality ▷ *nmf* extra ▷ *nm* extra; (*bono*) bonus
extracción [ekstrak'θjon] *nf* extraction; (*en lotería*) draw
extracto [eks'trakto] *nm* extract
extradición [ekstraði'θjon] *nf* extradition
extraer [ekstra'er] *vt* to extract, take out
extraescolar [ekstraesko'lar] *adj*: **actividad ~** extracurricular activity
extranjero, -a [ekstran'xero, a] *adj* foreign ▷ *nm/f* foreigner ▷ *nm* foreign countries *pl*; **en el ~** abroad

No confundir **extranjero** con la palabra inglesa *stranger*.

extrañar [ekstra'ɲar] *vt* (*sorprender*) to find strange *o* odd; (*echar de menos*) to miss; **extrañarse** *vr* (*sorprenderse*) to be amazed, be surprised; **me extraña** I'm surprised

extraño, -a [eks'traɲo, a] *adj* (*extranjero*) foreign; (*raro, sorprendente*) strange, odd
extraordinario, -a [ekstraorði'narjo, a] *adj* extraordinary; (*edición, número*) special ▷ *nm* (*de periódico*) special edition; **horas extraordinarias** overtime *sg*
extrarradio [ekstra'rraðjo] *nm* suburbs
extravagante [ekstraβa'ɣante] *adj* (*excéntrico*) eccentric; (*estrafalario*) outlandish
extraviado, -a [ekstra'βjaðo, a] *adj* lost, missing
extraviar [ekstra'βjar] *vt* (*persona: desorientar*) to mislead, misdirect; (*perder*) to lose, misplace; **extraviarse** *vr* to lose one's way, get lost
extremar [ekstre'mar] *vt* to carry to extremes
extremaunción [ekstremaun'θjon] *nf* extreme unction
extremidad [ekstremi'ðað] *nf* (*punta*) extremity; **extremidades** *nfpl* (*Anat*) extremities
extremo, -a [eks'tremo, a] *adj* extreme; (*último*) last ▷ *nm* end; (*límite, grado sumo*) extreme; **en último ~** as a last resort
extrovertido, -a [ekstroβer'tiðo, a] *adj, nm/f* extrovert
exuberante [eksuβe'rante] *adj* exuberant; (*fig*) luxuriant, lush
eyacular [ejaku'lar] *vt, vi* to ejaculate

f

fa [fa] *nm* (*Mús*) fa, F
fabada [fa'βaða] *nf* bean and sausage stew
fábrica ['faβrika] *nf* factory; **marca de ~** trademark; **precio de ~** factory price

> No confundir **fábrica** con la palabra inglesa *fabric*.

fabricación [faβrika'θjon] *nf* (*manufactura*) manufacture; (*producción*) production; **de ~ casera** home-made; **fabricación en serie** mass production
fabricante [faβri'kante] *nmf* manufacturer
fabricar [faβri'kar] *vt* (*manufacturar*) to manufacture, make; (*construir*) to build; (*cuento*) to fabricate, devise
fábula ['faβula] *nf* (*cuento*) fable; (*chisme*) rumour; (*mentira*) fib
fabuloso, -a [faβu'loso, a] *adj* (*oportunidad, tiempo*) fabulous, great
facción [fak'θjon] *nf* (*Pol*) faction; **facciones** *nfpl* (*de rostro*) features
faceta [fa'θeta] *nf* facet
facha ['fatʃa] (*fam*) *nf* (*aspecto*) look; (*cara*) face
fachada [fa'tʃaða] *nf* (*Arq*) façade, front
fácil ['faθil] *adj* (*simple*) easy; (*probable*) likely
facilidad [faθili'ðað] *nf* (*capacidad*) ease; (*sencillez*) simplicity; (*de palabra*) fluency; **facilidades** *nfpl* facilities; **facilidades de pago** credit facilities
facilitar [faθili'tar] *vt* (*hacer fácil*) to make easy; (*proporcionar*) to provide
factor [fak'tor] *nm* factor
factura [fak'tura] *nf* (*cuenta*) bill; **facturación** *nf* (*de equipaje*) check-in; **facturar** *vt* (*Com*) to invoice, charge for; (*equipaje*) to check in
facultad [fakul'tað] *nf* (*aptitud, Escol etc*) faculty; (*poder*) power

faena [fa'ena] *nf* (*trabajo*) work; (*quehacer*) task, job
faisán [fai'san] *nm* pheasant
faja ['faxa] *nf* (*para la cintura*) sash; (*de mujer*) corset; (*de tierra*) strip
fajo ['faxo] *nm* (*de papeles*) bundle; (*de billetes*) wad
falda ['falda] *nf* (*prenda de vestir*) skirt; **falda pantalón** culottes *pl*, split skirt
falla ['faʎa] *nf* (*defecto*) fault, flaw; **falla humana** (LAM) human error
fallar [fa'ʎar] *vt* (*Jur*) to pronounce sentence on ▷ *vi* (*memoria*) to fail; (*motor*) to miss
Fallas ['faʎas] *nfpl* *Valencian celebration of the feast of St Joseph*

FALLAS

In the week of 19 March (the feast of San José), Valencia honours its patron saint with a spectacular fiesta called **Las Fallas**. The **Fallas** are huge papier-mâché, cardboard and wooden sculptures which are built by competing teams throughout the year. They depict politicians and well-known public figures and are thrown onto bonfires and set alight once a jury has judged them – only the best sculpture escapes the flames.

fallecer [faʎe'θer] *vi* to pass away, die; **fallecimiento** *nm* decease, demise
fallido, -a [fa'ʎiðo, a] *adj* (*gen*) frustrated, unsuccessful
fallo ['faʎo] *nm* (*Jur*) verdict, ruling; (*fracaso*) failure; **fallo cardíaco** heart failure; **fallo humano** (ESP) human error
falsificar [falsifi'kar] *vt* (*firma etc*) to forge; (*moneda*) to counterfeit
falso, -a ['falso, a] *adj* false; (*documento, moneda etc*) fake; **en ~** falsely
falta ['falta] *nf* (*defecto*) fault, flaw; (*privación*) lack, want; (*ausencia*) absence; (*carencia*) shortage; (*equivocación*) mistake; (*Deporte*) foul; **echar en ~** to miss; **hacer ~ hacer algo** to be necessary to do sth; **me hace ~ una pluma** I need a pen; **falta de educación** bad manners *pl*; **falta de ortografía** spelling mistake
faltar [fal'tar] *vi* (*escasear*) to be lacking, be wanting; (*ausentarse*) to be absent, be missing; **faltan 2 horas para llegar** there are 2 hours to go till arrival; **~ al respeto a algn** to be disrespectful to sb; **¡no faltaba más!** (*no hay de qué*) don't mention it
fama ['fama] *nf* (*renombre*) fame; (*reputación*) reputation
familia [fa'milja] *nf* family; **familia numerosa** large family; **familia política** in-laws *pl*
familiar [fami'ljar] *adj* (*relativo a la familia*) family *cpd*; (*conocido, informal*) familiar ▷ *nm* relative, relation
famoso, -a [fa'moso, a] *adj* (*renombrado*) famous
fan [fan] (*pl* **~s**) *nmf* fan
fanático, -a [fa'natiko, a] *adj* fanatical ▷ *nm/f* fanatic; (*Cine, Deporte*) fan
fanfarrón, -ona [fanfa'rron, ona] *adj* boastful
fango ['fango] *nm* mud
fantasía [fanta'sia] *nf* fantasy, imagination; **joyas de ~** imitation jewellery *sg*
fantasma [fan'tasma] *nm* (*espectro*) ghost, apparition; (*fanfarrón*) show-off
fantástico, -a [fan'tastiko, a] *adj* fantastic
farmacéutico, -a [farma'θeutiko, a] *adj* pharmaceutical ▷ *nm/f* chemist (BRIT), pharmacist
farmacia [far'maθja] *nf* chemist's (shop) (BRIT), pharmacy; **farmacia de guardia** all-night chemist
fármaco ['farmako] *nm* drug
faro ['faro] *nm* (*Náut: torre*) lighthouse; (*Auto*) headlamp; **faros antiniebla** fog lamps; **faros delanteros/traseros** headlights/rear lights
farol [fa'rol] *nm* lantern, lamp
farola [fa'rola] *nf* street lamp (BRIT) *o* light (US)
farra ['farra] (LAM: *fam*) *nf* party; **ir de ~** to go on a binge
farsa ['farsa] *nf* (*gen*) farce
farsante [far'sante] *nmf* fraud, fake
fascículo [fas'θikulo] *nm* (*de revista*) part, instalment
fascinar [fasθi'nar] *vt* (*gen*) to fascinate
fascismo [fas'θismo] *nm* fascism; **fascista** *adj, nmf* fascist
fase ['fase] *nf* phase
fashion ['faʃon] *adj* (*fam*) trendy
fastidiar [fasti'ðjar] *vt* (*molestar*) to annoy, bother; (*estropear*) to spoil; **fastidiarse** *vr*: **¡que se fastidie!** (*fam*) he'll just have to put up with it!
fastidio [fas'tiðjo] *nm* (*molestia*) annoyance; **fastidioso, -a** *adj* (*molesto*) annoying
fatal [fa'tal] *adj* (*gen*) fatal; (*desgraciado*) ill-fated; (*fam: malo, pésimo*) awful; **fatalidad** *nf* (*destino*) fate; (*mala suerte*) misfortune
fatiga [fa'tiɣa] *nf* (*cansancio*) fatigue,

weariness
fatigar [fati'ɣar] *vt* to tire, weary
fatigoso, -a [fati'ɣoso, a] *adj* (*cansador*) tiring
fauna ['fauna] *nf* fauna
favor [fa'βor] *nm* favour; **estar a ~ de** to be in favour of; **haga el ~ de ...** would you be so good as to ..., kindly ...; **por ~** please; **favorable** *adj* favourable
favorecer [faβore'θer] *vt* to favour; (*vestido etc*) to become, flatter; **este peinado le favorece** this hairstyle suits him
favorito, -a [faβo'rito, a] *adj, nm/f* favourite
fax [faks] *nm inv* fax; **mandar por ~** to fax
fe [fe] *nf* (*Rel*) faith; (*documento*) certificate; **actuar con buena/mala ~** to act in good/bad faith
febrero [fe'βrero] *nm* February
fecha ['fetʃa] *nf* date; **con ~ adelantada** postdated; **en ~ próxima** soon; **hasta la ~** to date, so far; **poner ~** to date; **fecha de caducidad** (*de producto alimenticio*) sell-by date; (*de contrato etc*) expiry date; **fecha de nacimiento** date of birth; **fecha límite** *o* **tope** deadline
fecundo, -a [fe'kundo, a] *adj* (*fértil*) fertile; (*fig*) prolific; (*productivo*) productive
federación [feðera'θjon] *nf* federation
felicidad [feliθi'ðað] *nf* happiness; **¡~es!** (*deseos*) best wishes, congratulations!; (*en cumpleaños*) happy birthday!
felicitación [feliθita'θjon] *nf* (*tarjeta*) greeting(s) card
felicitar [feliθi'tar] *vt* to congratulate
feliz [fe'liθ] *adj* happy
felpudo [fel'puðo] *nm* doormat
femenino, -a [feme'nino, a] *adj, nm* feminine
feminista [femi'nista] *adj, nmf* feminist
fenómeno [fe'nomeno] *nm* phenomenon; (*fig*) freak, accident ▷ *adj* great ▷ *excl* great!, marvellous!; **fenomenal** *adj* = **fenómeno**
feo, -a ['feo, a] *adj* (*gen*) ugly; (*desagradable*) bad, nasty
féretro ['feretro] *nm* (*ataúd*) coffin; (*sarcófago*) bier
feria ['ferja] *nf* (*gen*) fair; (*descanso*) holiday, rest day; (*MÉX*: *cambio*) small *o* loose change; (*CS*: *mercado*) village market
feriado [fe'rjaðo] (*LAM*) *nm* holiday
fermentar [fermen'tar] *vi* to ferment
feroz [fe'roθ] *adj* (*cruel*) cruel; (*salvaje*) fierce
férreo, -a ['ferreo, a] *adj* iron
ferretería [ferrete'ria] *nf* (*tienda*) ironmonger's (shop) (*BRIT*), hardware store (*US*)
ferrocarril [ferroka'rril] *nm* railway
ferroviario, -a [ferro'βjarjo, a] *adj* rail *cpd*
ferry ['ferri] (*pl* **~s** *o* **ferries**) *nm* ferry
fértil ['fertil] *adj* (*productivo*) fertile; (*rico*) rich; **fertilidad** *nf* (*gen*) fertility; (*productividad*) fruitfulness
fervor [fer'βor] *nm* fervour
festejar [feste'xar] *vt* (*celebrar*) to celebrate
festejo [fes'texo] *nm* celebration; **festejos** *nmpl* (*fiestas*) festivals
festín [fes'tin] *nm* feast, banquet
festival [festi'βal] *nm* festival
festividad [festiβi'ðað] *nf* festivity
festivo, -a [fes'tiβo, a] *adj* (*de fiesta*) festive; (*Cine, Literatura*) humorous; **día ~** holiday
feto ['feto] *nm* foetus
fiable ['fjaβle] *adj* (*persona*) trustworthy; (*máquina*) reliable
fiambre ['fjambre] *nm* cold meat
fiambrera [fjam'brera] *nf* (*para almuerzo*) lunch box
fianza ['fianθa] *nf* surety; (*Jur*): **libertad bajo ~** release on bail
fiar [fi'ar] *vt* (*salir garante de*) to guarantee; (*vender a crédito*) to sell on credit ▷ *vi* to trust; **fiarse** *vr* to trust (in), rely on; **~ a** (*secreto*) to confide (to); **~se de algn** to rely on sb
fibra ['fiβra] *nf* fibre; **fibra óptica** optical fibre
ficción [fik'θjon] *nf* fiction
ficha ['fitʃa] *nf* (*Tel*) token; (*en juegos*) counter, marker; (*tarjeta*) (index) card; **fichaje** *nm* (*Deporte*) signing; **fichar** *vt* (*archivar*) to file, index; (*Deporte*) to sign; **estar fichado** to have a record; **fichero** *nm* box file; (*Inform*) file
ficticio, -a [fik'tiθjo, a] *adj* (*imaginario*) fictitious; (*falso*) fabricated
fidelidad [fiðeli'ðað] *nf* (*lealtad*) fidelity, loyalty; **alta ~** high fidelity, hi-fi
fideos [fi'ðeos] *nmpl* noodles
fiebre ['fjeβre] *nf* (*Med*) fever; (*fig*) fever, excitement; **tener ~** to have a temperature; **fiebre aftosa** foot-and-mouth disease
fiel [fjel] *adj* (*leal*) faithful, loyal; (*fiable*) reliable; (*exacto*) accurate, faithful ▷ *nm*: **los ~es** the faithful
fieltro ['fjeltro] *nm* felt
fiera ['fjera] *nf* (*animal feroz*) wild animal *o* beast; (*fig*) dragon; *V tb* **fiero**
fiero, -a ['fjero, a] *adj* (*cruel*) cruel; (*feroz*) fierce; (*duro*) harsh
fierro ['fjerro] (*LAM*) *nm* (*hierro*) iron

fiesta ['fjesta] *nf* party; (*de pueblo*) festival; (*vacaciones*: *tb*: **~s**) holiday *sg*; **fiesta mayor** annual festival; **fiesta patria** (*LAM*) independence day

FIESTAS

Fiestas can be official public holidays or holidays set by each autonomous region, many of which coincide with religious festivals. There are also many **fiestas** all over Spain for a local patron saint or the Virgin Mary. These often last several days and can include religious processions, carnival parades, bullfights and dancing.

figura [fi'ɣura] *nf* (*gen*) figure; (*forma, imagen*) shape, form; (*Naipes*) face card

figurar [fiɣu'rar] *vt* (*representar*) to represent; (*fingir*) to figure ▷ *vi* to figure; **figurarse** *vr* (*imaginarse*) to imagine; (*suponer*) to suppose

fijador [fixa'ðor] *nm* (*Foto etc*) fixative; (*de pelo*) gel

fijar [fi'xar] *vt* (*gen*) to fix; (*estampilla*) to affix, stick (on); **fijarse** *vr*: **~se en** to notice

fijo, -a ['fixo, a] *adj* (*gen*) fixed; (*firme*) firm; (*permanente*) permanent ▷ *adv*: **mirar ~** to stare

fila ['fila] *nf* row; (*Mil*) rank; **ponerse en ~** to line up, get into line; **fila india** single file

filatelia [fila'telja] *nf* philately, stamp collecting

filete [fi'lete] *nm* (*de carne*) fillet steak; (*de pescado*) fillet

filiación [filja'θjon] *nf* (*Pol*) affiliation

filial [fi'ljal] *adj* filial ▷ *nf* subsidiary

Filipinas [fili'pinas] *nfpl*: **las (Islas) ~** the Philippines; **filipino, -a** *adj, nm/f* Philippine

filmar [fil'mar] *vt* to film, shoot

filo ['filo] *nm* (*gen*) edge; **sacar ~ a** to sharpen; **al ~ del mediodía** at about midday; **de doble ~** double-edged

filología [filolo'ɣia] *nf* philology; **filología inglesa** (*Univ*) English Studies

filón [fi'lon] *nm* (*Minería*) vein, lode; (*fig*) goldmine

filosofía [filoso'fia] *nf* philosophy; **filósofo, -a** *nm/f* philosopher

filtrar [fil'trar] *vt, vi* to filter, strain; **filtrarse** *vr* to filter; **filtro** *nm* (*Tec, utensilio*) filter

fin [fin] *nm* end; (*objetivo*) aim, purpose; **al ~ y al cabo** when all's said and done; **a ~ de** in order to; **por ~** finally; **en ~** in short; **fin de semana** weekend

final [fi'nal] *adj* final ▷ *nm* end, conclusion ▷ *nf* final; **al ~** in the end; **a ~es de** at the end of; **finalidad** *nf* (*propósito*) purpose, intention; **finalista** *nmf* finalist; **finalizar** *vt* to end, finish; (*Inform*) to log out *o* off ▷ *vi* to end, come to an end

financiar [finan'θjar] *vt* to finance; **financiero, -a** *adj* financial ▷ *nm/f* financier

finca ['finka] *nf* (*casa de campo*) country house; (*ESP*: *bien inmueble*) property, land; (*LAM*: *granja*) farm

finde ['finde] *nm abr* (*fam*: *fin de semana*) weekend

fingir [fin'xir] *vt* (*simular*) to simulate, feign ▷ *vi* (*aparentar*) to pretend

finlandés, -esa [finlan'des, esa] *adj* Finnish ▷ *nm/f* Finn ▷ *nm* (*Ling*) Finnish

Finlandia [fin'landja] *nf* Finland

fino, -a ['fino, a] *adj* fine; (*delgado*) slender; (*de buenas maneras*) polite, refined; (*jerez*) fino, dry

firma ['firma] *nf* signature; (*Com*) firm, company

firmamento [firma'mento] *nm* firmament

firmar [fir'mar] *vt* to sign

firme ['firme] *adj* firm; (*estable*) stable; (*sólido*) solid; (*constante*) steady; (*decidido*) resolute ▷ *nm* road (surface); **firmeza** *nf* firmness; (*constancia*) steadiness; (*solidez*) solidity

fiscal [fis'kal] *adj* fiscal ▷ *nmf* public prosecutor; **año ~** tax *o* fiscal year

fisgonear [fisɣone'ar] *vt* to poke one's nose into ▷ *vi* to pry, spy

física ['fisika] *nf* physics *sg*; *V tb* **físico**

físico, -a ['fisiko, a] *adj* physical ▷ *nm* physique ▷ *nm/f* physicist

fisura [fi'sura] *nf* crack; (*Med*) fracture

flác(c)ido, -a ['fla(k)θiðo, a] *adj* flabby

flaco, -a ['flako, a] *adj* (*muy delgado*) skinny, thin; (*débil*) weak, feeble

flagrante [fla'ɣrante] *adj* flagrant

flama ['flama] (*MÉX*) *nf* flame; **flamable** (*MÉX*) *adj* flammable

flamante [fla'mante] (*fam*) *adj* brilliant; (*nuevo*) brand-new

flamenco, -a [fla'menko, a] *adj* (*de Flandes*) Flemish; (*baile, música*) flamenco ▷ *nm* (*baile, música*) flamenco; (*Zool*) flamingo

flamingo [fla'mingo] (*MÉX*) *nm* flamingo

flan [flan] *nm* creme caramel

No confundir **flan** con la palabra inglesa *flan*.

flash [flaʃ] (*pl* **~** *o* **~es**) *nm* (*Foto*) flash

flauta ['flauta] *nf* (*Mús*) flute

flecha ['fletʃa] *nf* arrow
flechazo [fle'tʃaθo] *nm* love at first sight
fleco ['fleko] *nm* fringe
flema ['flema] *nm* phlegm
flequillo [fle'kiʎo] *nm* (*pelo*) fringe
flexible [flek'siβle] *adj* flexible
flexión [flek'sjon] *nf* press-up
flexo ['flekso] *nm* adjustable table-lamp
flirtear [flirte'ar] *vi* to flirt
flojera [flo'xera] (*LAM*: *fam*) *nf*: **me da ~** I can't be bothered
flojo, -a ['floxo, a] *adj* (*gen*) loose; (*sin fuerzas*) limp; (*débil*) weak
flor [flor] *nf* flower; **a ~ de** on the surface of; **flora** *nf* flora; **florecer** *vi* (*Bot*) to flower, bloom; (*fig*) to flourish; **florería** (*LAM*) *nf* florist's (shop); **florero** *nm* vase; **floristería** *nf* florist's (shop)
flota ['flota] *nf* fleet
flotador [flota'ðor] *nm* (*gen*) float; (*para nadar*) rubber ring
flotar [flo'tar] *vi* (*gen*) to float; **flote** *nm*: **a flote** afloat; **salir a flote** (*fig*) to get back on one's feet
fluidez [flui'ðeθ] *nf* fluidity; (*fig*) fluency
fluido, -a ['fluiðo, a] *adj, nm* fluid
fluir [flu'ir] *vi* to flow
flujo ['fluxo] *nm* flow; **flujo y reflujo** ebb and flow
flúor ['fluor] *nm* fluoride
fluorescente [flwores'θente] *adj* fluorescent ▷*nm* fluorescent light
fluvial [fluβi'al] *adj* (*navegación, cuenca*) fluvial, river *cpd*
fobia ['fobja] *nf* phobia; **fobia a las alturas** fear of heights
foca ['foka] *nf* seal
foco ['foko] *nm* focus; (*Elec*) floodlight; (*MÉX*: *bombilla*) (light) bulb
fofo, -a ['fofo, a] *adj* soft, spongy; (*carnes*) flabby
fogata [fo'ɣata] *nf* bonfire
fogón [fo'ɣon] *nm* (*de cocina*) ring, burner
folio ['foljo] *nm* folio, page
follaje [fo'ʎaxe] *nm* foliage
folleto [fo'ʎeto] *nm* (*Pol*) pamphlet
follón [fo'ʎon] (*ESP*: *fam*) *nm* (*lío*) mess; (*conmoción*) fuss; **armar un ~** to kick up a row
fomentar [fomen'tar] *vt* (*Med*) to foment
fonda ['fonda] *nf* inn
fondo ['fondo] *nm* (*de mar*) bottom; (*de coche, sala*) back; (*Arte etc*) background; (*reserva*) fund; **fondos** *nmpl* (*Com*) funds, resources; **una investigación a ~** a thorough investigation; **en el ~** at bottom, deep down
fonobuzón [fonoβu'θon] *nm* voice mail
fontanería [fontane'ria] *nf* plumbing; **fontanero, -a** *nm/f* plumber
footing ['futın] *nm* jogging; **hacer ~** to jog, go jogging
forastero, -a [foras'tero, a] *nm/f* stranger
forcejear [forθexe'ar] *vi* (*luchar*) to struggle
forense [fo'rense] *nmf* pathologist
forma ['forma] *nf* (*figura*) form, shape; (*Med*) fitness; (*método*) way, means; **las ~s** the conventions; **estar en ~** to be fit; **de ~ que ...** so that ...; **de todas ~s** in any case
formación [forma'θjon] *nf* (*gen*) formation; (*educación*) education; **formación profesional** vocational training
formal [for'mal] *adj* (*gen*) formal; (*fig*: *serio*) serious; (: *de fiar*) reliable; **formalidad** *nf* formality; seriousness; **formalizar** *vt* (*Jur*) to formalize; (*situación*) to put in order, regularize; **formalizarse** *vr* (*situación*) to be put in order, be regularized
formar [for'mar] *vt* (*componer*) to form, shape; (*constituir*) to make up, constitute; (*Escol*) to train, educate; **formarse** *vr* (*Escol*) to be trained, educated; (*cobrar forma*) to form, take form; (*desarrollarse*) to develop
formatear [formate'ar] *vt* to format
formato [for'mato] *nm* format
formidable [formi'ðaβle] *adj* (*temible*) formidable; (*estupendo*) tremendous
fórmula ['formula] *nf* formula
formulario [formu'larjo] *nm* form
fornido, -a [for'niðo, a] *adj* well-built
foro ['foro] *nm* (*Pol, Inform etc*) forum
forrar [fo'rrar] *vt* (*abrigo*) to line; (*libro*) to cover; **forro** *nm* (*de cuaderno*) cover; (*Costura*) lining; (*de sillón*) upholstery; **forro polar** fleece
fortalecer [fortale'θer] *vt* to strengthen
fortaleza [forta'leθa] *nf* (*Mil*) fortress, stronghold; (*fuerza*) strength; (*determinación*) resolution
fortuito, -a [for'twito, a] *adj* accidental
fortuna [for'tuna] *nf* (*suerte*) fortune, (good) luck; (*riqueza*) fortune, wealth
forzar [for'θar] *vt* (*puerta*) to force (open); (*compeler*) to compel
forzoso, -a [for'θoso, a] *adj* necessary
fosa ['fosa] *nf* (*sepultura*) grave; (*en tierra*) pit; **fosas nasales** nostrils
fósforo ['fosforo] *nm* (*Quím*) phosphorus; (*cerilla*) match
fósil ['fosil] *nm* fossil
foso ['foso] *nm* ditch; (*Teatro*) pit; (*Auto*) inspection pit
foto ['foto] *nf* photo, snap(shot); **sacar una ~** to take a photo *o* picture; **foto (de)**

carné passport(-size) photo
fotocopia [foto'kopja] *nf* photocopy; **fotocopiadora** *nf* photocopier; **fotocopiar** *vt* to photocopy
fotografía [fotoɤra'fia] *nf* (*Arte*) photography; (*una fotografía*) photograph; **fotografiar** *vt* to photograph
fotógrafo, -a [fo'toɤrafo, a] *nm/f* photographer
fotomatón [fotoma'ton] *nm* photo booth
FP (ESP) *nf abr* (= *Formación Profesional*) *vocational courses for 14- to 18-year-olds*
fracasar [fraka'sar] *vi* (*gen*) to fail
fracaso [fra'kaso] *nm* failure
fracción [frak'θjon] *nf* fraction
fractura [frak'tura] *nf* fracture, break
fragancia [fra'ɤanθja] *nf* (*olor*) fragrance, perfume
frágil ['fraxil] *adj* (*débil*) fragile; (*Com*) breakable
fragmento [fraɤ'mento] *nm* (*pedazo*) fragment
fraile ['fraile] *nm* (*Rel*) friar; (: *monje*) monk
frambuesa [fram'bwesa] *nf* raspberry
francés, -esa [fran'θes, esa] *adj* French ▷ *nm/f* Frenchman(-woman) ▷ *nm* (*Ling*) French
Francia ['franθja] *nf* France
franco, -a ['franko, a] *adj* (*cándido*) frank, open; (*Com*: *exento*) free ▷ *nm* (*moneda*) franc
francotirador, a [frankotira'ðor, a] *nm/f* sniper
franela [fra'nela] *nf* flannel
franja ['franxa] *nf* fringe
franquear [franke'ar] *vt* (*camino*) to clear; (*carta, paquete postal*) to frank, stamp; (*obstáculo*) to overcome
franqueo [fran'keo] *nm* postage
franqueza [fran'keθa] *nf* (*candor*) frankness
frasco ['frasko] *nm* bottle, flask
frase ['frase] *nf* sentence; **frase hecha** set phrase; (*pey*) stock phrase
fraterno, -a [fra'terno, a] *adj* brotherly, fraternal
fraude ['frauðe] *nm* (*cualidad*) dishonesty; (*acto*) fraud
frazada [fra'saða] (LAM) *nf* blanket
frecuencia [fre'kwenθja] *nf* frequency; **con ~** frequently, often
frecuentar [frekwen'tar] *vt* to frequent
frecuente [fre'kwente] *adj* (*gen*) frequent
fregadero [freɤa'ðero] *nm* (kitchen) sink
fregar [fre'ɤar] *vt* (*frotar*) to scrub; (*platos*) to wash (up); (LAM: *fam*: *fastidiar*) to annoy; (: *malograr*) to screw up
fregona [fre'ɤona] *nf* mop
freír [fre'ir] *vt* to fry
frenar [fre'nar] *vt* to brake; (*fig*) to check
frenazo [fre'naθo] *nm*: **dar un ~** to brake sharply
frenesí [frene'si] *nm* frenzy
freno ['freno] *nm* (*Tec, Auto*) brake; (*de cabalgadura*) bit; (*fig*) check; **freno de mano** handbrake
frente ['frente] *nm* (*Arq, Pol*) front; (*de objeto*) front part ▷ *nf* forehead, brow; **~ a** in front of; (*en situación opuesta de*) opposite; **al ~ de** (*fig*) at the head of; **chocar de ~** to crash head-on; **hacer ~ a** to face up to
fresa ['fresa] (ESP) *nf* strawberry
fresco, -a ['fresko, a] *adj* (*nuevo*) fresh; (*frío*) cool; (*descarado*) cheeky ▷ *nm* (*aire*) fresh air; (*Arte*) fresco; (LAM: *jugo*) fruit drink ▷ *nm/f* (*fam*): **ser un ~** to have a nerve; **tomar el ~** to get some fresh air; **frescura** *nf* freshness; (*descaro*) cheek, nerve
frialdad [frial'dað] *nf* (*gen*) coldness; (*indiferencia*) indifference
frigidez [frixi'ðeθ] *nf* frigidity
frigorífico [frixo'rifiko] *nm* refrigerator
frijol [fri'xol] *nm* kidney bean
frío, -a *etc* ['frio, a] *vb V* **freír** ▷ *adj* cold; (*indiferente*) indifferent ▷ *nm* cold; indifference; **hace ~** it's cold; **tener ~** to be cold
frito, -a ['frito, a] *adj* fried; **me trae ~ ese hombre** I'm sick and tired of that man; **fritos** *nmpl* fried food
frívolo, -a ['friβolo, a] *adj* frivolous
frontal [fron'tal] *adj* frontal; **choque ~** head-on collision
frontera [fron'tera] *nf* frontier; **fronterizo, -a** *adj* frontier *cpd*; (*contiguo*) bordering
frontón [fron'ton] *nm* (*Deporte*: *cancha*) pelota court; (: *juego*) pelota
frotar [fro'tar] *vt* to rub; **frotarse** *vr*: **~se las manos** to rub one's hands
fructífero, -a [fruk'tifero, a] *adj* fruitful
fruncir [frun'θir] *vt* to pucker; (*Costura*) to pleat; **~ el ceño** to knit one's brow
frustrar [frus'trar] *vt* to frustrate
fruta ['fruta] *nf* fruit; **frutería** *nf* fruit shop; **frutero, -a** *adj* fruit *cpd* ▷ *nm/f* fruiterer ▷ *nm* fruit bowl
frutilla [fru'tiʎa] (CS) *nf* strawberry
fruto ['fruto] *nm* fruit; (*fig*: *resultado*) result; (: *beneficio*) benefit; **frutos secos** nuts and dried fruit *pl*
fucsia ['fuksja] *nf* fuchsia
fue [fwe] *vb V* **ser; ir**
fuego ['fweɤo] *nm* (*gen*) fire; **a ~ lento** on a low heat; **¿tienes ~?** have you (got) a light?; **fuego amigo** friendly fire; **fuegos artificiales** fireworks

fuente ['fwente] *nf* fountain; (*manantial: fig*) spring; (*origen*) source; (*plato*) large dish
fuera *etc* ['fwera] *vb V* **ser; ir** ▷ *adv* out(side); (*en otra parte*) away; (*excepto, salvo*) except, save ▷ *prep*: **~ de** outside; (*fig*) besides; **~ de sí** beside o.s.; **por ~** (on the) outside
fuera-borda [fwera'βorða] *nm* speedboat
fuerte ['fwerte] *adj* strong; (*golpe*) hard; (*ruido*) loud; (*comida*) rich; (*lluvia*) heavy; (*dolor*) intense ▷ *adv* strongly; hard; loud(ly)
fuerza *etc* ['fwerθa] *vb V* **forzar** ▷ *nf* (*fortaleza*) strength; (*Tec, Elec*) power; (*coacción*) force; (*Mil, Pol*) force; **a ~ de** by dint of; **cobrar ~s** to recover one's strength; **tener ~s para** to have the strength to; **a la ~** forcibly, by force; **por ~** of necessity; **fuerza de voluntad** willpower; **fuerzas aéreas** air force *sg*; **fuerzas armadas** armed forces
fuga ['fuɣa] *nf* (*huida*) flight, escape; (*de gas etc*) leak
fugarse [fu'ɣarse] *vr* to flee, escape
fugaz [fu'ɣaθ] *adj* fleeting
fugitivo, a [fuxi'tiβo, a] *adj, nm/f* fugitive
fui [fwi] *vb V* **ser; ir**
fulano, -a [fu'lano, a] *nm/f* so-and-so, what's-his-name/what's-her-name
fulminante [fulmi'nante] *adj* (*fig: mirada*) fierce; (*Med: enfermedad, ataque*) sudden; (*fam: éxito, golpe*) sudden
fumador, a [fuma'ðor, a] *nm/f* smoker
fumar [fu'mar] *vt, vi* to smoke; **~ en pipa** to smoke a pipe
función [fun'θjon] *nf* function; (*en trabajo*) duties *pl*; (*espectáculo*) show; **entrar en funciones** to take up one's duties
funcionar [funθjo'nar] *vi* (*gen*) to function; (*máquina*) to work; **"no funciona"** "out of order"
funcionario, -a [funθjo'narjo, a] *nm/f* civil servant
funda ['funda] *nf* (*gen*) cover; (*de almohada*) pillowcase
fundación [funda'θjon] *nf* foundation
fundamental [fundamen'tal] *adj* fundamental, basic
fundamento [funda'mento] *nm* (*base*) foundation
fundar [fun'dar] *vt* to found; **fundarse** *vr*: **~se en** to be founded on
fundición [fundi'θjon] *nf* fusing; (*fábrica*) foundry
fundir [fun'dir] *vt* (*gen*) to fuse; (*metal*) to smelt, melt down; (*nieve etc*) to melt; (*Com*) to merge; (*estatua*) to cast; **fundirse** *vr* (*colores etc*) to merge, blend; (*unirse*) to fuse together; (*Elec: fusible, lámpara etc*) to fuse, blow; (*nieve etc*) to melt
fúnebre ['funeβre] *adj* funeral *cpd*, funereal
funeral [fune'ral] *nm* funeral; **funeraria** *nf* undertaker's
funicular [funiku'lar] *nm* (*tren*) funicular; (*teleférico*) cable car
furgón [fur'ɣon] *nm* wagon; **furgoneta** *nf* (*Auto, Com*) (transit) van (BRIT), pick-up (truck) (US)
furia ['furja] *nf* (*ira*) fury; (*violencia*) violence; **furioso, -a** *adj* (*iracundo*) furious; (*violento*) violent
furtivo, -a [fur'tiβo, a] *adj* furtive ▷ *nm* poacher
fusible [fu'siβle] *nm* fuse
fusil [fu'sil] *nm* rifle; **fusilar** *vt* to shoot
fusión [fu'sjon] *nf* (*gen*) melting; (*unión*) fusion; (*Com*) merger
fútbol ['futβol] *nm* football (BRIT), soccer (US); **fútbol americano** American football (BRIT), football (US); **fútbol sala** indoor football (BRIT) *o* soccer (US); **futbolín** *nm* table football; **futbolista** *nmf* footballer
futuro, -a [fu'turo, a] *adj, nm* future

f

g

gabardina [gaβar'ðina] *nf* raincoat, gabardine
gabinete [gaβi'nete] *nm* (*Pol*) cabinet; (*estudio*) study; (*de abogados etc*) office
gachas ['gatʃas] *nfpl* porridge *sg*
gafas ['gafas] *nfpl* glasses; **gafas de sol** sunglasses
gafe ['gafe] (ESP) *nmf* jinx
gaita ['gaita] *nf* bagpipes *pl*
gajes ['gaxes] *nmpl*: **~ del oficio** occupational hazards
gajo ['gaxo] *nm* (*de naranja*) segment
gala ['gala] *nf* (*traje de etiqueta*) full dress; **galas** *nfpl* (*ropa*) finery *sg*; **estar de ~** to be in one's best clothes; **hacer ~ de** to display
galápago [ga'lapaɣo] *nm* (*Zool*) turtle
galardón [galar'ðon] *nm* award, prize
galaxia [ga'laksja] *nf* galaxy
galera [ga'lera] *nf* (*nave*) galley; (*carro*) wagon; (*Imprenta*) galley
galería [gale'ria] *nf* (*gen*) gallery; (*balcón*) veranda(h); (*pasillo*) corridor; **galería comercial** shopping mall
Gales ['gales] *nm* (*tb*: **País de ~**) Wales; **galés, -esa** *adj* Welsh ▷*nm/f* Welshman(-woman) ▷*nm* (*Ling*) Welsh
galgo, -a ['galɣo, a] *nm/f* greyhound
gallego, -a [ga'ʎeɣo, a] *adj, nm/f* Galician
galleta [ga'ʎeta] *nf* biscuit (BRIT), cookie (US)
gallina [ga'ʎina] *nf* hen ▷*nmf* (*fam: cobarde*) chicken; **gallinero** *nm* henhouse; (*Teatro*) top gallery
gallo ['gaʎo] *nm* cock, rooster
galopar [galo'par] *vi* to gallop
gama ['gama] *nf* (*fig*) range
gamba ['gamba] *nf* prawn (BRIT), shrimp (US)
gamberro, -a [gam'berro, a] (ESP) *nm/f* hooligan, lout
gamuza [ga'muθa] *nf* chamois
gana ['gana] *nf* (*deseo*) desire, wish; (*apetito*) appetite; (*voluntad*) will; (*añoranza*) longing; **de buena ~** willingly; **de mala ~** reluctantly; **me da ~s de** I feel like, I want to; **no me da la ~** I don't feel like it; **tener ~s de** to feel like
ganadería [ganaðe'ria] *nf* (*ganado*) livestock; (*ganado vacuno*) cattle *pl*; (*cría, comercio*) cattle raising
ganadero, -a [gana'ðero, a] (ESP) *nm/f* (*hacendado*) rancher
ganado [ga'naðo] *nm* livestock; **ganado porcino** pigs *pl*
ganador, a [gana'ðor, a] *adj* winning ▷*nm/f* winner
ganancia [ga'nanθja] *nf* (*lo ganado*) gain; (*aumento*) increase; (*beneficio*) profit; **ganancias** *nfpl* (*ingresos*) earnings; (*beneficios*) profit *sg*, winnings
ganar [ga'nar] *vt* (*obtener*) to get, obtain; (*sacar ventaja*) to gain; (*salario etc*) to earn; (*Deporte, premio*) to win; (*derrotar a*) to beat; (*alcanzar*) to reach ▷*vi* (*Deporte*) to win; **ganarse** *vr*: **~se la vida** to earn one's living
ganchillo [gan'tʃiʎo] *nm* crochet
gancho ['gantʃo] *nm* (*gen*) hook; (*colgador*) hanger
gandul, a [gan'dul, a] *adj, nm/f* good-for-nothing, layabout
ganga ['ganga] *nf* bargain
gangrena [gan'grena] *nf* gangrene
ganso, -a ['ganso, a] *nm/f* (*Zool*) goose; (*fam*) idiot
ganzúa [gan'θua] *nf* skeleton key
garabato [gara'βato] *nm* (*escritura*) scrawl, scribble
garaje [ga'raxe] *nm* garage
garantía [garan'tia] *nf* guarantee
garantizar [garanti'θar] *vt* to guarantee
garbanzo [gar'βanθo] *nm* chickpea (BRIT), garbanzo (US)
garfio ['garfjo] *nm* grappling iron
garganta [gar'ɣanta] *nf* (*Anat*) throat; (*de botella*) neck; **gargantilla** *nf* necklace
gárgaras ['garɣaras] *nfpl*: **hacer ~** to gargle
gargarear [garɣare'ar] (LAM) *vi* to gargle
garita [ga'rita] *nf* cabin, hut; (*Mil*) sentry box
garra ['garra] *nf* (*de gato, Tec*) claw; (*de ave*) talon; (*fam: mano*) hand, paw
garrafa [ga'rrafa] *nf* carafe, decanter
garrapata [garra'pata] *nf* tick
gas [gas] *nm* gas; **gases lacrimógenos** tear gas *sg*
gasa ['gasa] *nf* gauze
gaseosa [gase'osa] *nf* lemonade
gaseoso, -a [gase'oso, a] *adj* gassy, fizzy

gasoil [ga'soil] *nm* diesel (oil)
gasóleo [ga'soleo] *nm* = **gasoil**
gasolina [gaso'lina] *nf* petrol (BRIT), gas(oline) (US); **gasolinera** *nf* petrol (BRIT) *o* gas (US) station
gastado, -a [gas'taðo, a] *adj* (*dinero*) spent; (*ropa*) worn out; (*usado: frase etc*) trite
gastar [gas'tar] *vt* (*dinero, tiempo*) to spend; (*fuerzas*) to use up; (*desperdiciar*) to waste; (*llevar*) to wear; **gastarse** *vr* to wear out; (*estropearse*) to waste; **~ en** to spend on; **~ bromas** to crack jokes; **¿qué número gastas?** what size (shoe) do you take?
gasto ['gasto] *nm* (*desembolso*) expenditure, spending; (*consumo, uso*) use; **gastos** *nmpl* (*desembolsos*) expenses; (*cargos*) charges, costs
gastronomía [gastrono'mia] *nf* gastronomy
gatear [gate'ar] *vi* (*andar a gatas*) to go on all fours
gatillo [ga'tiʎo] *nm* (*de arma de fuego*) trigger; (*de dentista*) forceps
gato, -a ['gato, a] *nm/f* cat ▷ *nm* (*Tec*) jack; **andar a gatas** to go on all fours
gaucho ['gautʃo] *nm* gaucho

GAUCHO

Gauchos are the herdsmen or riders of the Southern Cone plains. Although popularly associated with Argentine folklore, **gauchos** belong equally to the cattle-raising areas of Southern Brazil and Uruguay. **Gauchos'** traditions and clothing reflect their mixed ancestry and cultural roots. Their baggy trousers are Arabic in origin, while the horse and guitar are inherited from the Spanish conquistadors; the poncho, maté and **boleadoras** (strips of leather weighted at either end with stones) form part of the Indian tradition.

gaviota [ga'βjota] *nf* seagull
gay [ge] *adj inv, nm* gay, homosexual
gazpacho [gaθ'patʃo] *nm* gazpacho
gel [xel] *nm*: **~ de baño/ducha** bath/shower gel
gelatina [xela'tina] *nf* jelly; (*polvos etc*) gelatine
gema ['xema] *nf* gem
gemelo, -a [xe'melo, a] *adj, nm/f* twin; **gemelos** *nmpl* (*de camisa*) cufflinks; (*prismáticos*) field glasses, binoculars
gemido [xe'miðo] *nm* (*quejido*) moan, groan; (*aullido*) howl
Géminis ['xeminis] *nm* Gemini
gemir [xe'mir] *vi* (*quejarse*) to moan, groan; (*aullar*) to howl
generación [xenera'θjon] *nf* generation
general [xene'ral] *adj* general ▷ *nm* general; **por lo** *o* **en ~** in general; **Generalitat** *nf Catalan parliament*; **generalizar** *vt* to generalize; **generalizarse** *vr* to become generalized, spread
generar [xene'rar] *vt* to generate
género ['xenero] *nm* (*clase*) kind, sort; (*tipo*) type; (*Bio*) genus; (*Ling*) gender; (*Com*) material; **género humano** human race
generosidad [xenerosi'ðað] *nf* generosity; **generoso, -a** *adj* generous
genial [xe'njal] *adj* inspired; (*idea*) brilliant; (*estupendo*) wonderful
genio ['xenjo] *nm* (*carácter*) nature, disposition; (*humor*) temper; (*facultad creadora*) genius; **de mal ~** bad-tempered
genital [xeni'tal] *adj* genital; **genitales** *nmpl* genitals
genoma [xe'noma] *nm* genome
gente ['xente] *nf* (*personas*) people *pl*; (*parientes*) relatives *pl*
gentil [xen'til] *adj* (*elegante*) graceful; (*encantador*) charming

No confundir **gentil** con la palabra inglesa *gentle*.

genuino, -a [xe'nwino, a] *adj* genuine
geografía [xeoɤra'fia] *nf* geography
geología [xeolo'xia] *nf* geology
geometría [xeome'tria] *nf* geometry
gerente [xe'rente] *nmf* (*supervisor*) manager; (*jefe*) director
geriatría [xeria'tria] *nf* (*Med*) geriatrics *sg*
germen ['xermen] *nm* germ
gesticular [xestiku'lar] *vi* to gesticulate; (*hacer muecas*) to grimace; **gesticulación** *nf* gesticulation; (*mueca*) grimace
gestión [xes'tjon] *nf* management; (*diligencia, acción*) negotiation
gesto ['xesto] *nm* (*mueca*) grimace; (*ademán*) gesture
Gibraltar [xiβral'tar] *nm* Gibraltar; **gibraltareño, -a** *adj, nm/f* Gibraltarian
gigante [xi'ɤante] *adj, nmf* giant; **gigantesco, -a** *adj* gigantic
gilipollas [xili'poʎas] (*fam*) *adj inv* daft ▷ *nmf inv* wally
gimnasia [xim'nasja] *nf* gymnastics *pl*; **gimnasio** *nm* gymnasium; **gimnasta** *nmf* gymnast
ginebra [xi'neβra] *nf* gin
ginecólogo, -a [xine'koloɤo, a] *nm/f* gynaecologist
gira ['xira] *nf* tour, trip
girar [xi'rar] *vt* (*dar la vuelta*) to turn

(around); (: *rápidamente*) to spin; (*Com*: *giro postal*) to draw; (: *letra de cambio*) to issue ▷ *vi* to turn (round); (*rápido*) to spin
girasol [xira'sol] *nm* sunflower
giratorio, -a [xira'torjo, a] *adj* revolving
giro ['xiro] *nm* (*movimiento*) turn, revolution; (*Ling*) expression; (*Com*) draft; **giro bancario/postal** bank draft/money order
gis [xis] (MÉX) *nm* chalk
gitano, -a [xi'tano, a] *adj, nm/f* gypsy
glacial [gla'θjal] *adj* icy, freezing
glaciar [gla'θjar] *nm* glacier
glándula ['glandula] *nf* gland
global [glo'βal] *adj* global; **globalización** *nf* globalization
globo ['gloβo] *nm* (*esfera*) globe, sphere; (*aerostato, juguete*) balloon
glóbulo ['gloβulo] *nm* globule; (*Anat*) corpuscle
gloria ['glorja] *nf* glory
glorieta [glo'rjeta] *nf* (*de jardín*) bower, arbour; (*plazoleta*) roundabout (BRIT), traffic circle (US)
glorioso, -a [glo'rjoso, a] *adj* glorious
glotón, -ona [glo'ton, ona] *adj* gluttonous, greedy ▷ *nm/f* glutton
glucosa [glu'kosa] *nf* glucose
gobernador, a [goβerna'ðor, a] *adj* governing ▷ *nm/f* governor; **gobernante** *adj* governing
gobernar [goβer'nar] *vt* (*dirigir*) to guide, direct; (*Pol*) to rule, govern ▷ *vi* to govern; (*Náut*) to steer
gobierno *etc* [go'βjerno] *vb V* **gobernar** ▷ *nm* (*Pol*) government; (*dirección*) guidance, direction; (*Náut*) steering
goce *etc* ['goθe] *vb V* **gozar** ▷ *nm* enjoyment
gol [gol] *nm* goal
golf [golf] *nm* golf
golfa ['golfa] (*fam!*) *nf* (*mujer*) slut, whore
golfo, -a ['golfo, a] *nm* (*Geo*) gulf ▷ *nm/f* (*fam*: *niño*) urchin; (*gamberro*) lout
golondrina [golon'drina] *nf* swallow
golosina [golo'sina] *nf* (*dulce*) sweet; **goloso, -a** *adj* sweet-toothed
golpe ['golpe] *nm* blow; (*de puño*) punch; (*de mano*) smack; (*de remo*) stroke; (*fig*: *choque*) clash; **no dar ~** to be bone idle; **de un ~** with one blow; **de ~** suddenly; **golpe (de estado)** coup (d'état); **golpear** *vt, vi* to strike, knock; (*asestar*) to beat; (*de puño*) to punch; (*golpetear*) to tap
goma ['goma] *nf* (*caucho*) rubber; (*elástico*) elastic; (*una goma*) elastic band; **goma de borrar** eraser, rubber (BRIT); **goma espuma** foam rubber
gomina [go'mina] *nf* hair gel
gomita [go'mita] (RPL) *nf* rubber band
gordo, -a ['gorðo, a] *adj* (*gen*) fat; (*fam*) enormous; **el (premio) ~** (*en lotería*) first prize
gorila [go'rila] *nm* gorilla
gorra ['gorra] *nf* cap; (*de bebé*) bonnet; (*militar*) bearskin; **entrar de ~** (*fam*) to gatecrash; **ir de ~** to sponge
gorrión [go'rrjon] *nm* sparrow
gorro ['gorro] *nm* (*gen*) cap; (*de bebé, mujer*) bonnet
gorrón, -ona [go'rron, ona] *nm/f* scrounger; **gorronear** (*fam*) *vi* to scrounge
gota ['gota] *nf* (*gen*) drop; (*de sudor*) bead; (*Med*) gout; **gotear** *vi* to drip; (*lloviznar*) to drizzle; **gotera** *nf* leak
gozar [go'θar] *vi* to enjoy o.s.; **~ de** (*disfrutar*) to enjoy; (*poseer*) to possess
gr. *abr* (= *gramo, gramos*) g
grabación [graβa'θjon] *nf* recording
grabado [gra'βaðo] *nm* print, engraving
grabadora [graβa'ðora] *nf* tape-recorder; **grabadora de CD/DVD** CD/DVD writer
grabar [gra'βar] *vt* to engrave; (*discos, cintas*) to record
gracia ['graθja] *nf* (*encanto*) grace, gracefulness; (*humor*) humour, wit; **¡(muchas) ~s!** thanks (very much)!; **~s a** thanks to; **dar las ~s a algn por algo** to thank sb for sth; **tener ~** (*chiste etc*) to be funny; **no me hace ~** I am not keen; **gracioso, -a** *adj* (*divertido*) funny, amusing; (*cómico*) comical ▷ *nm/f* (*Teatro*) comic character
grada ['graða] *nf* (*de escalera*) step; (*de anfiteatro*) tier, row; **gradas** *nfpl* (*Deporte*: *de estadio*) terraces
grado ['graðo] *nm* degree; (*de aceite, vino*) grade; (*grada*) step; (*Mil*) rank; **de buen ~** willingly; **grado centígrado/Fahrenheit** degree centigrade/Fahrenheit
graduación [graðwa'θjon] *nf* (*del alcohol*) proof, strength; (*Escol*) graduation; (*Mil*) rank
gradual [gra'ðwal] *adj* gradual
graduar [gra'ðwar] *vt* (*gen*) to graduate; (*Mil*) to commission; **graduarse** *vr* to graduate; **~se la vista** to have one's eyes tested
gráfica ['grafika] *nf* graph
gráfico, -a ['grafiko, a] *adj* graphic ▷ *nm* diagram; **gráficos** *nmpl* (*Inform*) graphics
grajo ['graxo] *nm* rook
gramática [gra'matika] *nf* grammar
gramo ['gramo] *nm* gramme (BRIT), gram (US)
gran [gran] *adj V* **grande**

grana ['grana] *nf* (*color, tela*) scarlet
granada [gra'naða] *nf* pomegranate; (*Mil*) grenade
granate [gra'nate] *adj* deep red
Gran Bretaña [-bre'taɲa] *nf* Great Britain
grande ['grande] (*antes de nmsg* **gran**) *adj* (*de tamaño*) big, large; (*alto*) tall; (*distinguido*) great; (*impresionante*) grand ▷ *nm* grandee
granel [gra'nel]: **a ~** *adv* (*Com*) in bulk
granero [gra'nero] *nm* granary, barn
granito [gra'nito] *nm* (*Agr*) small grain; (*roca*) granite
granizado [grani'θaðo] *nm* iced drink
granizar [grani'θar] *vi* to hail; **granizo** *nm* hail
granja ['granxa] *nf* (*gen*) farm; **granjero, -a** *nm/f* farmer
grano ['grano] *nm* grain; (*semilla*) seed; (*de café*) bean; (*Med*) pimple, spot
granuja [gra'nuxa] *nmf* rogue; (*golfillo*) urchin
grapa ['grapa] *nf* staple; (*Tec*) clamp; **grapadora** *nf* stapler
grasa ['grasa] *nf* (*gen*) grease; (*de cocinar*) fat, lard; (*sebo*) suet; (*mugre*) filth; **grasiento, -a** *adj* greasy; (*de aceite*) oily; **graso, -a** *adj* (*leche, queso, carne*) fatty; (*pelo, piel*) greasy
gratinar [grati'nar] *vt* to cook au gratin
gratis ['gratis] *adv* free
grato, -a ['grato, a] *adj* (*agradable*) pleasant, agreeable
gratuito, -a [gra'twito, a] *adj* (*gratis*) free; (*sin razón*) gratuitous
grave ['graβe] *adj* heavy; (*serio*) grave, serious; **gravedad** *nf* gravity
Grecia ['greθja] *nf* Greece
gremio ['gremjo] *nm* trade, industry
griego, -a ['grjeɤo, a] *adj, nm/f* Greek
grieta ['grjeta] *nf* crack
grifo ['grifo] (ESP) *nm* tap (BRIT), faucet (US)
grillo ['griʎo] *nm* (*Zool*) cricket
gripa ['gripa] (MÉX) *nf* flu, influenza
gripe ['gripe] *nf* flu, influenza; **gripe aviar** bird flu
gris [gris] *adj* (*color*) grey
gritar [gri'tar] *vt, vi* to shout, yell; **grito** *nm* shout, yell; (*de horror*) scream
grosella [gro'seʎa] *nf* (red)currant
grosero, -a [gro'sero, a] *adj* (*poco cortés*) rude, bad-mannered; (*ordinario*) vulgar, crude
grosor [gro'sor] *nm* thickness
grúa ['grua] *nf* (*Tec*) crane; (*de petróleo*) derrick
grueso, -a ['grweso, a] *adj* thick; (*persona*) stout ▷ *nm* bulk; **el ~ de** the bulk of
grulla ['gruʎa] *nf* crane
grumo ['grumo] *nm* clot, lump
gruñido [gru'ɲiðo] *nm* grunt; (*de persona*) grumble
gruñir [gru'ɲir] *vi* (*animal*) to growl; (*persona*) to grumble
grupo ['grupo] *nm* group; (*Tec*) unit, set; **grupo de presión** pressure group; **grupo sanguíneo** blood group
gruta ['gruta] *nf* grotto
guacho, -a ['gwatʃo, a] (CS) *nm/f* homeless child
guajolote [gwaxo'lote] (MÉX) *nm* turkey
guante ['gwante] *nm* glove; **guantes de goma** rubber gloves; **guantera** *nf* glove compartment
guapo, -a ['gwapo, a] *adj* good-looking, attractive; (*elegante*) smart
guarda ['gwarða] *nmf* (*persona*) guard, keeper ▷ *nf* (*acto*) guarding; (*custodia*) custody; **guarda jurado** (armed) security guard; **guardabarros** *nm inv* mudguard (BRIT), fender (US); **guardabosques** *nm inv* gamekeeper; **guardacostas** *nm inv* coastguard vessel ▷ *nmf* guardian, protector; **guardaespaldas** *nmf inv* bodyguard; **guardameta** *nmf* goalkeeper; **guardar** *vt* (*gen*) to keep; (*vigilar*) to guard, watch over; (*dinero: ahorrar*) to save; **guardarse** *vr* (*preservarse*) to protect o.s.; (*evitar*) to avoid; **guardar cama** to stay in bed; **guardarropa** *nm* (*armario*) wardrobe; (*en establecimiento público*) cloakroom
guardería [gwarðe'ria] *nf* nursery
guardia ['gwarðja] *nf* (*Mil*) guard; (*cuidado*) care, custody ▷ *nmf* guard; (*policía*) policeman(-woman); **estar de ~** to be on guard; **montar ~** to mount guard; **Guardia Civil** Civil Guard
guardián, -ana [gwar'ðjan, ana] *nm/f* (*gen*) guardian, keeper
guarida [gwa'riða] *nf* (*de animal*) den, lair; (*refugio*) refuge
guarnición [gwarni'θjon] *nf* (*de vestimenta*) trimming; (*de piedra*) mount; (*Culin*) garnish; (*arneses*) harness; (*Mil*) garrison
guarro, -a ['gwarro, a] *nm/f* pig
guasa ['gwasa] *nf* joke; **guasón, -ona** *adj* (*bromista*) joking ▷ *nm/f* wit; joker
Guatemala [gwate'mala] *nf* Guatemala
guay [gwai] (*fam*) *adj* super, great
güero, -a ['gwero, a] (MÉX) *adj* blond(e)
guerra ['gerra] *nf* war; **dar ~** to annoy; **guerra civil** civil war; **guerra fría** cold war; **guerrero, -a** *adj* fighting; (*carácter*) warlike ▷ *nm/f* warrior
guerrilla [ge'rriʎa] *nf* guerrilla warfare; (*tropas*) guerrilla band *o* group
guía *etc* ['gia] *vb V* **guiar** ▷ *nmf* (*persona*)

g

guide; (*nf*: *libro*) guidebook; **guía telefónica** telephone directory; **guía turística** tourist guide
guiar [gi'ar] *vt* to guide, direct; (*Auto*) to steer; **guiarse** *vr*: **~se por** to be guided by
guinda ['ginda] *nf* morello cherry
guindilla [gin'diʎa] *nf* chilli pepper
guiñar [gi'ɲar] *vt* to wink
guión [gi'on] *nm* (*Ling*) hyphen, dash; (*Cine*) script; **guionista** *nmf* scriptwriter
guiri ['giri] (*ESP*: *fam, pey*) *nmf* foreigner
guirnalda [gir'nalda] *nf* garland
guisado [gi'saðo] *nm* stew
guisante [gi'sante] *nm* pea
guisar [gi'sar] *vt, vi* to cook; **guiso** *nm* cooked dish
guitarra [gi'tarra] *nf* guitar
gula ['gula] *nf* gluttony, greed
gusano [gu'sano] *nm* worm; (*lombriz*) earthworm
gustar [gus'tar] *vt* to taste, sample ▷ *vi* to please, be pleasing; **~ de algo** to like *o* enjoy sth; **me gustan las uvas** I like grapes; **le gusta nadar** she likes *o* enjoys swimming
gusto ['gusto] *nm* (*sentido, sabor*) taste; (*placer*) pleasure; **tiene ~ a menta** it tastes of mint; **tener buen ~** to have good taste; **coger el** *o* **tomar ~ a algo** to take a liking to sth; **sentirse a ~** to feel at ease; **mucho ~ (en conocerle)** pleased to meet you; **el ~ es mío** the pleasure is mine; **con ~** willingly, gladly

ha *vb V* **haber**
haba ['aβa] *nf* bean
Habana [a'βana] *nf*: **la ~** Havana
habano [a'βano] *nm* Havana cigar
habéis *vb V* **haber**

PALABRA CLAVE

haber [a'βer] *vb aux* **1** (*tiempos compuestos*) to have; **había comido** I had eaten; **antes/después de haberlo visto** before seeing/after seeing *o* having seen it
2: **¡haberlo dicho antes!** you should have said so before!
3: **haber de: he de hacerlo** I have to do it; **ha de llegar mañana** it should arrive tomorrow
▷ *vb impers* **1** (*existencia*: *sg*) there is; (: *pl*) there are; **hay un hermano/dos hermanos** there is one brother/there are two brothers; **¿cuánto hay de aquí a Sucre?** how far is it from here to Sucre?
2 (*obligación*): **hay que hacer algo** something must be done; **hay que apuntarlo para acordarse** you have to write it down to remember
3: **¡hay que ver!** well I never!
4: **¡no hay de** *o* **por** (*LAM*) **qué!** don't mention it!, not at all!
5: **¿qué hay?** (*¿qué pasa?*) what's up?, what's the matter?; (*¿qué tal?*) how's it going?
▷ *vt*: **he aquí unas sugerencias** here are some suggestions; **no hay cintas blancas pero sí las hay rojas** there aren't any white ribbons but there are some red ones
▷ *nm* (*en cuenta*) credit side; **haberes** *nmpl* assets; **¿cuánto tengo en el haber?** how much do I have in my account?; **tiene varias novelas en su haber** he has several novels to his credit
haberse *vr*: **habérselas con algn** to have

hoy [oi] *adv* (*este día*) today; (*la actualidad*) now(adays) ▷*nm* present time; **~ (en) día** now(adays)
hoyo ['ojo] *nm* hole, pit
hoz [oθ] *nf* sickle
hube *etc vb V* **haber**
hucha ['utʃa] *nf* money box
hueco, -a ['weko, a] *adj* (*vacío*) hollow, empty; (*resonante*) booming ▷*nm* hollow, cavity
huelga *etc* ['welɣa] *vb V* **holgar** ▷*nf* strike; **declararse en ~** to go on strike, come out on strike; **huelga de hambre** hunger strike; **huelga general** general strike
huelguista [wel'ɣista] *nmf* striker
huella ['weʎa] *nf* (*pisada*) tread; (*marca del paso*) footprint, footstep; (*: de animal, máquina*) track; **huella dactilar** fingerprint
huelo *etc vb V* **oler**
huérfano, -a ['werfano, a] *adj* orphan(ed) ▷*nm/f* orphan
huerta ['werta] *nf* market garden; (*en Murcia y Valencia*) irrigated region
huerto ['werto] *nm* kitchen garden; (*de árboles frutales*) orchard
hueso ['weso] *nm* (*Anat*) bone; (*de fruta*) stone
huésped ['wespeð] *nmf* guest
hueva ['weβa] *nf* roe
huevera [we'βera] *nf* eggcup
huevo ['weβo] *nm* egg; **huevo a la copa** (CS) soft-boiled egg; **huevo duro/escalfado** hard-boiled/poached egg; **huevo estrellado** (LAM) fried egg; **huevo frito** (ESP) fried egg; **huevo pasado por agua** soft-boiled egg; **huevos revueltos** scrambled eggs; **huevo tibio** (MÉX) soft-boiled egg
huida [u'iða] *nf* escape, flight
huir [u'ir] *vi* (*escapar*) to flee, escape; (*evitar*) to avoid
hule ['ule] *nm* oilskin; (*MÉX: goma*) rubber
hulera [u'lera] (*MÉX*) *nf* catapult
humanidad [umani'ðað] *nf* (*género humano*) man(kind); (*cualidad*) humanity
humanitario, -a [umani'tarjo, a] *adj* humanitarian
humano, -a [u'mano, a] *adj* (*gen*) human; (*humanitario*) humane ▷*nm* human; **ser ~** human being
humareda [uma'reða] *nf* cloud of smoke
humedad [ume'ðað] *nf* (*de clima*) humidity; (*de pared etc*) dampness; **a prueba de ~** damp-proof; **humedecer** *vt* to moisten, wet; **humedecerse** *vr* to get wet
húmedo, -a ['umeðo, a] *adj* (*mojado*) damp, wet; (*tiempo etc*) humid
humilde [u'milde] *adj* humble, modest
humillación [umiʎa'θjon] *nf* humiliation; **humillante** *adj* humiliating
humillar [umi'ʎar] *vt* to humiliate
humo ['umo] *nm* (*de fuego*) smoke; (*gas nocivo*) fumes *pl*; (*vapor*) steam, vapour; **humos** *nmpl* (*fig*) conceit *sg*
humor [u'mor] *nm* (*disposición*) mood, temper; (*lo que divierte*) humour; **de buen/mal ~** in a good/bad mood; **humorista** *nmf* comic; **humorístico, -a** *adj* funny, humorous
hundimiento [undi'mjento] *nm* (*gen*) sinking; (*colapso*) collapse
hundir [un'dir] *vt* to sink; (*edificio, plan*) to ruin, destroy; **hundirse** *vr* to sink, collapse
húngaro, -a ['ungaro, a] *adj, nm/f* Hungarian
Hungría [un'gria] *nf* Hungary
huracán [ura'kan] *nm* hurricane
huraño, -a [u'raɲo, a] *adj* (*antisocial*) unsociable
hurgar [ur'ɣar] *vt* to poke, jab; (*remover*) to stir (up); **hurgarse** *vr*: **~se (las narices)** to pick one's nose
hurón, -ona [u'ron, ona] *nm* (*Zool*) ferret
hurtadillas [urta'ðiʎas]: **a ~** *adv* stealthily, on the sly
hurtar [ur'tar] *vt* to steal; **hurto** *nm* theft, stealing
husmear [usme'ar] *vt* (*oler*) to sniff out, scent; (*fam*) to pry into
huyo *etc vb V* **huir**

h

iba *etc vb V* **ir**
ibérico, -a [i'βeriko, a] *adj* Iberian
iberoamericano, -a [iβeroameri'kano, a] *adj, nm/f* Latin American
Ibiza [i'βiθa] *nf* Ibiza
iceberg [iθe'βer] *nm* iceberg
icono [i'kono] *nm* ikon, icon
ida ['iða] *nf* going, departure; **~ y vuelta** round trip, return
idea [i'ðea] *nf* idea; **no tengo la menor ~** I haven't a clue
ideal [iðe'al] *adj, nm* ideal; **idealista** *nmf* idealist; **idealizar** *vt* to idealize
ídem ['iðem] *pron* ditto
idéntico, -a [i'ðentiko, a] *adj* identical
identidad [iðenti'ðað] *nf* identity
identificación [iðentifika'θjon] *nf* identification
identificar [iðentifi'kar] *vt* to identify; **identificarse** *vr*: **~se con** to identify with
ideología [iðeolo'xia] *nf* ideology
idilio [i'ðiljo] *nm* love-affair
idioma [i'ðjoma] *nm* (*gen*) language

> No confundir **idioma** con la palabra inglesa *idiom*.

idiota [i'ðjota] *adj* idiotic ▷ *nmf* idiot
ídolo ['iðolo] *nm* (*tb fig*) idol
idóneo, -a [i'ðoneo, a] *adj* suitable
iglesia [i'ɣlesja] *nf* church
ignorante [iɣno'rante] *adj* ignorant, uninformed ▷ *nmf* ignoramus
ignorar [iɣno'rar] *vt* not to know, be ignorant of; (*no hacer caso a*) to ignore
igual [i'ɣwal] *adj* (*gen*) equal; (*similar*) like, similar; (*mismo*) (the) same; (*constante*) constant; (*temperatura*) even ▷ *nmf* equal; **~ que** like, the same as; **me da** *o* **es ~** I don't care; **son ~es** they're the same; **al ~ que** (*prep, conj*) like, just like
igualar [iɣwa'lar] *vt* (*gen*) to equalize, make equal; (*allanar, nivelar*) to level (off), even (out); **igualarse** *vr* (*platos de balanza*) to balance out
igualdad [iɣwal'dað] *nf* equality; (*similaridad*) sameness; (*uniformidad*) uniformity
igualmente [iɣwal'mente] *adv* equally; (*también*) also, likewise ▷ *excl* the same to you!
ilegal [ile'ɣal] *adj* illegal
ilegítimo, -a [ile'xitimo, a] *adj* illegitimate
ileso, -a [i'leso, a] *adj* unhurt
ilimitado, -a [ilimi'taðo, a] *adj* unlimited
iluminación [ilumina'θjon] *nf* illumination; (*alumbrado*) lighting
iluminar [ilumi'nar] *vt* to illuminate, light (up); (*fig*) to enlighten
ilusión [ilu'sjon] *nf* illusion; (*quimera*) delusion; (*esperanza*) hope; **hacerse ilusiones** to build up one's hopes; **ilusionado, -a** *adj* excited; **ilusionar** *vi*: **le ilusiona ir de vacaciones** he's looking forward to going on holiday; **ilusionarse** *vr*: **ilusionarse (con)** to get excited (about)
iluso, -a [i'luso, a] *adj* easily deceived ▷ *nm/f* dreamer
ilustración [ilustra'θjon] *nf* illustration; (*saber*) learning, erudition; **la I~** the Enlightenment; **ilustrado, -a** *adj* illustrated; learned
ilustrar [ilus'trar] *vt* to illustrate; (*instruir*) to instruct; (*explicar*) to explain, make clear
ilustre [i'lustre] *adj* famous, illustrious
imagen [i'maxen] *nf* (*gen*) image; (*dibujo*) picture
imaginación [imaxina'θjon] *nf* imagination
imaginar [imaxi'nar] *vt* (*gen*) to imagine; (*idear*) to think up; (*suponer*) to suppose; **imaginarse** *vr* to imagine; **imaginario, -a** *adj* imaginary; **imaginativo, -a** *adj* imaginative
imán [i'man] *nm* magnet
imbécil [im'beθil] *nmf* imbecile, idiot
imitación [imita'θjon] *nf* imitation; **de ~** imitation *cpd*
imitar [imi'tar] *vt* to imitate; (*parodiar, remedar*) to mimic, ape
impaciente [impa'θjente] *adj* impatient; (*nervioso*) anxious
impacto [im'pakto] *nm* impact
impar [im'par] *adj* odd
imparcial [impar'θjal] *adj* impartial, fair
impecable [impe'kaβle] *adj* impeccable
impedimento [impeði'mento] *nm* impediment, obstacle
impedir [impe'ðir] *vt* (*obstruir*) to impede, obstruct; (*estorbar*) to prevent; **~ a algn**

hacer *o* **que algn haga algo** to prevent sb (from) doing sth, stop sb doing sth
imperativo, -a [impera'tiβo, a] *adj* (*urgente, Ling*) imperative
imperdible [imper'ðiβle] *nm* safety pin
imperdonable [imperðo'naβle] *adj* unforgivable, inexcusable
imperfecto, -a [imper'fekto, a] *adj* imperfect
imperio [im'perjo] *nm* empire; (*autoridad*) rule, authority; (*fig*) pride, haughtiness
impermeable [imperme'aβle] *adj* waterproof ▷ *nm* raincoat, mac (BRIT)
impersonal [imperso'nal] *adj* impersonal
impertinente [imperti'nente] *adj* impertinent
ímpetu ['impetu] *nm* (*impulso*) impetus, impulse; (*impetuosidad*) impetuosity; (*violencia*) violence
implantar [implan'tar] *vt* to introduce
implemento [imple'mento] (LAM) *nm* tool, implement
implicar [impli'kar] *vt* to involve; (*entrañar*) to imply
implícito, -a [im'pliθito, a] *adj* (*tácito*) implicit; (*sobreentendido*) implied
imponente [impo'nente] *adj* (*impresionante*) impressive, imposing; (*solemne*) grand
imponer [impo'ner] *vt* (*gen*) to impose; (*exigir*) to exact; **imponerse** *vr* to assert o.s.; (*prevalecer*) to prevail; **imponible** *adj* (*Com*) taxable
impopular [impopu'lar] *adj* unpopular
importación [importa'θjon] *nf* (*acto*) importing; (*mercancías*) imports *pl*
importancia [impor'tanθja] *nf* importance; (*valor*) value, significance; (*extensión*) size, magnitude; **no tiene ~** it's nothing; **importante** *adj* important; valuable, significant
importar [impor'tar] *vt* (*del extranjero*) to import; (*costar*) to amount to ▷ *vi* to be important, matter; **me importa un rábano** I couldn't care less; **no importa** it doesn't matter; **¿le importa que fume?** do you mind if I smoke?
importe [im'porte] *nm* (*total*) amount; (*valor*) value
imposible [impo'siβle] *adj* (*gen*) impossible; (*insoportable*) unbearable, intolerable
imposición [imposi'θjon] *nf* imposition; (*Com: impuesto*) tax; (*: inversión*) deposit
impostor, a [impos'tor, a] *nm/f* impostor
impotencia [impo'tenθja] *nf* impotence; **impotente** *adj* impotent
impreciso, -a [impre'θiso, a] *adj* imprecise, vague
impregnar [impreɣ'nar] *vt* to impregnate; **impregnarse** *vr* to become impregnated
imprenta [im'prenta] *nf* (*acto*) printing; (*aparato*) press; (*casa*) printer's; (*letra*) print
imprescindible [impresθin'diβle] *adj* essential, vital
impresión [impre'sjon] *nf* (*gen*) impression; (*Imprenta*) printing; (*edición*) edition; (*Foto*) print; (*marca*) imprint; **impresión digital** fingerprint
impresionante [impresjo'nante] *adj* impressive; (*tremendo*) tremendous; (*maravilloso*) great, marvellous
impresionar [impresjo'nar] *vt* (*conmover*) to move; (*afectar*) to impress, strike; (*película fotográfica*) to expose; **impresionarse** *vr* to be impressed; (*conmoverse*) to be moved
impreso, -a [im'preso, a] *pp de* **imprimir** ▷ *adj* printed; **impresos** *nmpl* printed matter; **impresora** *nf* printer
imprevisto, -a [impre'βisto, a] *adj* (*gen*) unforeseen; (*inesperado*) unexpected
imprimir [impri'mir] *vt* to imprint, impress, stamp; (*textos*) to print; (*Inform*) to output, print out
improbable [impro'βaβle] *adj* improbable; (*inverosímil*) unlikely
impropio, -a [im'propjo, a] *adj* improper
improvisado, -a [improβi'saðo, a] *adj* improvised
improvisar [improβi'sar] *vt* to improvise
improviso, -a [impro'βiso, a] *adj*: **de ~** unexpectedly, suddenly
imprudencia [impru'ðenθja] *nf* imprudence; (*indiscreción*) indiscretion; (*descuido*) carelessness; **imprudente** *adj* unwise, imprudent; (*indiscreto*) indiscreet
impuesto, -a [im'pwesto, a] *adj* imposed ▷ *nm* tax; **impuesto al valor agregado** *o* **añadido** (LAM) value added tax (BRIT) ≈ sales tax (US); **impuesto sobre el valor añadido** (ESP) value added tax (BRIT) ≈ sales tax (US)
impulsar [impul'sar] *vt* to drive; (*promover*) to promote, stimulate
impulsivo, -a [impul'siβo, a] *adj* impulsive; **impulso** *nm* impulse; (*fuerza, empuje*) thrust, drive; (*fig: sentimiento*) urge, impulse
impureza [impu'reθa] *nf* impurity; **impuro, -a** *adj* impure
inaccesible [inakθe'siβle] *adj* inaccessible
inaceptable [inaθep'taβle] *adj* unacceptable
inactivo, -a [inak'tiβo, a] *adj* inactive
inadecuado, -a [inaðe'kwaðo, a] *adj*

i

(*insuficiente*) inadequate; (*inapto*) unsuitable
inadvertido, -a [inaðβer'tiðo, a] *adj* (*no visto*) unnoticed
inaguantable [inaɤwan'taβle] *adj* unbearable
inanimado, -a [inani'maðo, a] *adj* inanimate
inaudito, -a [inau'ðito, a] *adj* unheard-of
inauguración [inauɤura'θjon] *nf* inauguration; opening
inaugurar [inauɤu'rar] *vt* to inaugurate; (*exposición*) to open
inca ['inka] *nmf* Inca
incalculable [inkalku'laβle] *adj* incalculable
incandescente [inkandes'θente] *adj* incandescent
incansable [inkan'saβle] *adj* tireless, untiring
incapacidad [inkapaθi'ðað] *nf* incapacity; (*incompetencia*) incompetence; **incapacidad física/mental** physical/ mental disability
incapacitar [inkapaθi'tar] *vt* (*inhabilitar*) to incapacitate, render unfit; (*descalificar*) to disqualify
incapaz [inka'paθ] *adj* incapable
incautarse [inkau'tarse] *vr*: **~ de** to seize, confiscate
incauto, -a [in'kauto, a] *adj* (*imprudente*) incautious, unwary
incendiar [inθen'djar] *vt* to set fire to; (*fig*) to inflame; **incendiarse** *vr* to catch fire; **incendiario, -a** *adj* incendiary
incendio [in'θendjo] *nm* fire
incentivo [inθen'tiβo] *nm* incentive
incertidumbre [inθerti'ðumbre] *nf* (*inseguridad*) uncertainty; (*duda*) doubt
incesante [inθe'sante] *adj* incessant
incesto [in'θesto] *nm* incest
incidencia [inθi'ðenθja] *nf* (*Mat*) incidence
incidente [inθi'ðente] *nm* incident
incidir [inθi'ðir] *vi* (*influir*) to influence; (*afectar*) to affect
incienso [in'θjenso] *nm* incense
incierto, -a [in'θjerto, a] *adj* uncertain
incineración [inθinera'θjon] *nf* incineration; (*de cadáveres*) cremation
incinerar [inθine'rar] *vt* to burn; (*cadáveres*) to cremate
incisión [inθi'sjon] *nf* incision
incisivo, -a [inθi'siβo, a] *adj* sharp, cutting; (*fig*) incisive
incitar [inθi'tar] *vt* to incite, rouse
inclemencia [inkle'menθja] *nf* (*severidad*) harshness, severity; (*del tiempo*) inclemency
inclinación [inklina'θjon] *nf* (*gen*) inclination; (*de tierras*) slope, incline; (*de cabeza*) nod, bow; (*fig*) leaning, bent
inclinar [inkli'nar] *vt* to incline; (*cabeza*) to nod, bow ▷ *vi* to lean, slope; **inclinarse** *vr* to bow; (*encorvarse*) to stoop; **~se a** (*parecerse a*) to take after, resemble; **~se ante** to bow down to; **me inclino a pensar que ...** I'm inclined to think that ...
incluir [inklu'ir] *vt* to include; (*incorporar*) to incorporate; (*meter*) to enclose
inclusive [inklu'siβe] *adv* inclusive ▷ *prep* including
incluso [in'kluso] *adv* even
incógnita [in'koɤnita] *nf* (*Mat*) unknown quantity
incógnito [in'koɤnito] *nm*: **de ~** incognito
incoherente [inkoe'rente] *adj* incoherent
incoloro, -a [inko'loro, a] *adj* colourless
incomodar [inkomo'ðar] *vt* to inconvenience; (*molestar*) to bother, trouble; (*fastidiar*) to annoy
incomodidad [inkomoði'ðað] *nf* inconvenience; (*fastidio, enojo*) annoyance; (*de vivienda*) discomfort
incómodo, -a [in'komoðo, a] *adj* (*inconfortable*) uncomfortable; (*molesto*) annoying; (*inconveniente*) inconvenient
incomparable [inkompa'raβle] *adj* incomparable
incompatible [inkompa'tiβle] *adj* incompatible
incompetente [inkompe'tente] *adj* incompetent
incompleto, -a [inkom'pleto, a] *adj* incomplete, unfinished
incomprensible [inkompren'siβle] *adj* incomprehensible
incomunicado, -a [inkomuni'kaðo, a] *adj* (*aislado*) cut off, isolated; (*confinado*) in solitary confinement
incondicional [inkondiθjo'nal] *adj* unconditional; (*apoyo*) wholehearted; (*partidario*) staunch
inconfundible [inkonfun'diβle] *adj* unmistakable
incongruente [inkon'grwente] *adj* incongruous
inconsciente [inkons'θjente] *adj* unconscious; thoughtless
inconsecuente [inkonse'kwente] *adj* inconsistent
inconstante [inkons'tante] *adj* inconstant
incontable [inkon'taβle] *adj* countless, innumerable
inconveniencia [inkombe'njenθja] *nf* unsuitability, inappropriateness;

(*descortesía*) impoliteness; **inconveniente** *adj* unsuitable; impolite ▷ *nm* obstacle; (*desventaja*) disadvantage; **el inconveniente es que ...** the trouble is that ...
incordiar [inkor'ðjar] (*fam*) *vt* to bug, annoy
incorporar [inkorpo'rar] *vt* to incorporate; **incorporarse** *vr* to sit up; **~se a** to join
incorrecto, -a [inko'rrekto, a] *adj* (*gen*) incorrect, wrong; (*comportamiento*) bad-mannered
incorregible [inkorre'xiβle] *adj* incorrigible
incrédulo, -a [in'kreðulo, a] *adj* incredulous, unbelieving; sceptical
increíble [inkre'iβle] *adj* incredible
incremento [inkre'mento] *nm* increment; (*aumento*) rise, increase
increpar [inkre'par] *vt* to reprimand
incruento, -a [in'krwento, a] *adj* bloodless
incrustar [inkrus'tar] *vt* to incrust; (*piedras: en joya*) to inlay
incubar [inku'βar] *vt* to incubate
inculcar [inkul'kar] *vt* to inculcate
inculto, -a [in'kulto, a] *adj* (*persona*) uneducated; (*grosero*) uncouth ▷ *nm/f* ignoramus
incumplimiento [inkumpli'mjento] *nm* non-fulfilment; **incumplimiento de contrato** breach of contract
incurrir [inku'rrir] *vi*: **~ en** to incur; (*crimen*) to commit
indagar [inda'ɣar] *vt* to investigate; to search; (*averiguar*) to ascertain
indecente [inde'θente] *adj* indecent, improper; (*lascivo*) obscene
indeciso, -a [inde'θiso, a] *adj* (*por decidir*) undecided; (*vacilante*) hesitant
indefenso, -a [inde'fenso, a] *adj* defenceless
indefinido, -a [indefi'niðo, a] *adj* indefinite; (*vago*) vague, undefined
indemne [in'demne] *adj* (*objeto*) undamaged; (*persona*) unharmed, unhurt
indemnizar [indemni'θar] *vt* to indemnify; (*compensar*) to compensate
independencia [indepen'denθja] *nf* independence
independiente [indepen'djente] *adj* (*libre*) independent; (*autónomo*) self-sufficient
indeterminado, -a [indetermi'naðo, a] *adj* indefinite; (*desconocido*) indeterminate
India ['indja] *nf*: **la ~** India
indicación [indika'θjon] *nf* indication; (*señal*) sign; (*sugerencia*) suggestion, hint
indicado, -a [indi'kaðo, a] *adj* (*momento, método*) right; (*tratamiento*) appropriate; (*solución*) likely
indicador [indika'ðor] *nm* indicator; (*Tec*) gauge, meter
indicar [indi'kar] *vt* (*mostrar*) to indicate, show; (*termómetro etc*) to read, register; (*señalar*) to point to
índice ['indiθe] *nm* index; (*catálogo*) catalogue; (*Anat*) index finger, forefinger; **índice de materias** table of contents
indicio [in'diθjo] *nm* indication, sign; (*en pesquisa etc*) clue
indiferencia [indife'renθja] *nf* indifference; (*apatía*) apathy; **indiferente** *adj* indifferent
indígena [in'dixena] *adj* indigenous, native ▷ *nmf* native
indigestión [indixes'tjon] *nf* indigestion
indigesto, -a [indi'xesto, a] *adj* (*alimento*) indigestible; (*fig*) turgid
indignación [indiɣna'θjon] *nf* indignation
indignar [indiɣ'nar] *vt* to anger, make indignant; **indignarse** *vr*: **~se por** to get indignant about
indigno, -a [in'diɣno, a] *adj* (*despreciable*) low, contemptible; (*inmerecido*) unworthy
indio, -a ['indjo, a] *adj, nm/f* Indian
indirecta [indi'rekta] *nf* insinuation, innuendo; (*sugerencia*) hint
indirecto, -a [indi'rekto, a] *adj* indirect
indiscreción [indiskre'θjon] *nf* (*imprudencia*) indiscretion; (*irreflexión*) tactlessness; (*acto*) gaffe, faux pas
indiscreto, -a [indis'kreto, a] *adj* indiscreet
indiscutible [indisku'tiβle] *adj* indisputable, unquestionable
indispensable [indispen'saβle] *adj* indispensable, essential
indispuesto, -a [indis'pwesto, a] *adj* (*enfermo*) unwell, indisposed
indistinto, -a [indis'tinto, a] *adj* indistinct; (*vago*) vague
individual [indiβi'ðwal] *adj* individual; (*habitación*) single ▷ *nm* (*Deporte*) singles *sg*
individuo, -a [indi'βiðwo, a] *adj, nm* individual
índole ['indole] *nf* (*naturaleza*) nature; (*clase*) sort, kind
inducir [indu'θir] *vt* to induce; (*inferir*) to infer; (*persuadir*) to persuade
indudable [indu'ðaβle] *adj* undoubted; (*incuestionable*) unquestionable
indultar [indul'tar] *vt* (*perdonar*) to pardon, reprieve; (*librar de pago*) to exempt;

indulto *nm* pardon; exemption
industria [in'dustrja] *nf* industry; (*habilidad*) skill; **industrial** *adj* industrial ▷ *nm* industrialist
inédito, -a [in'eðito, a] *adj* (*texto*) unpublished; (*nuevo*) new
ineficaz [inefi'kaθ] *adj* (*inútil*) ineffective; (*ineficiente*) inefficient
ineludible [inelu'ðiβle] *adj* inescapable, unavoidable
ineptitud [inepti'tuð] *nf* ineptitude, incompetence; **inepto, -a** *adj* inept, incompetent
inequívoco, -a [ine'kiβoko, a] *adj* unequivocal; (*inconfundible*) unmistakable
inercia [in'erθja] *nf* inertia; (*pasividad*) passivity
inerte [in'erte] *adj* inert; (*inmóvil*) motionless
inesperado, -a [inespe'raðo, a] *adj* unexpected, unforeseen
inestable [ines'taβle] *adj* unstable
inevitable [ineβi'taβle] *adj* inevitable
inexacto, -a [inek'sakto, a] *adj* inaccurate; (*falso*) untrue
inexperto, -a [inek'sperto, a] *adj* (*novato*) inexperienced
infalible [infa'liβle] *adj* infallible; (*plan*) foolproof
infame [in'fame] *adj* infamous; (*horrible*) dreadful; **infamia** *nf* infamy; (*deshonra*) disgrace
infancia [in'fanθja] *nf* infancy, childhood
infantería [infante'ria] *nf* infantry
infantil [infan'til] *adj* (*pueril, aniñado*) infantile; (*cándido*) childlike; (*literatura, ropa etc*) children's
infarto [in'farto] *nm* (*tb*: **~ de miocardio**) heart attack
infatigable [infati'ɣaβle] *adj* tireless, untiring
infección [infek'θjon] *nf* infection; **infeccioso, -a** *adj* infectious
infectar [infek'tar] *vt* to infect; **infectarse** *vr* to become infected
infeliz [infe'liθ] *adj* unhappy, wretched ▷ *nmf* wretch
inferior [infe'rjor] *adj* inferior; (*situación*) lower ▷ *nmf* inferior, subordinate
inferir [infe'rir] *vt* (*deducir*) to infer, deduce; (*causar*) to cause
infidelidad [infiðeli'ðað] *nf* (*gen*) infidelity, unfaithfulness
infiel [in'fjel] *adj* unfaithful, disloyal; (*erróneo*) inaccurate ▷ *nmf* infidel, unbeliever
infierno [in'fjerno] *nm* hell
infiltrarse [infil'trarse] *vr*: **~ en** to infiltrate in(to); (*persona*) to work one's way in(to)
ínfimo, -a ['infimo, a] *adj* (*más bajo*) lowest; (*despreciable*) vile, mean
infinidad [infini'ðað] *nf* infinity; (*abundancia*) great quantity
infinito, -a [infi'nito, a] *adj*, *nm* infinite
inflación [infla'θjon] *nf* (*hinchazón*) swelling; (*monetaria*) inflation; (*fig*) conceit
inflamable [infl'maβle] *adj* flammable
inflamar [infla'mar] *vt* (*Med*: *fig*) to inflame; **inflamarse** *vr* to catch fire; to become inflamed
inflar [in'flar] *vt* (*hinchar*) to inflate, blow up; (*fig*) to exaggerate; **inflarse** *vr* to swell (up); (*fig*) to get conceited
inflexible [inflek'siβle] *adj* inflexible; (*fig*) unbending
influencia [influ'enθja] *nf* influence
influir [influ'ir] *vt* to influence
influjo [in'fluxo] *nm* influence
influya *etc vb V* **influir**
influyente [influ'jente] *adj* influential
información [informa'θjon] *nf* information; (*noticias*) news *sg*; (*Jur*) inquiry; **I~** (*oficina*) Information Office; (*mostrador*) Information Desk; (*Tel*) Directory Enquiries
informal [infor'mal] *adj* (*gen*) informal
informar [infor'mar] *vt* (*gen*) to inform; (*revelar*) to reveal, make known ▷ *vi* (*Jur*) to plead; (*denunciar*) to inform; (*dar cuenta de*) to report on; **informarse** *vr* to find out; **~se de** to inquire into
informática [infor'matika] *nf* computer science, information technology
informe [in'forme] *adj* shapeless ▷ *nm* report
infracción [infrak'θjon] *nf* infraction, infringement
infravalorar [infrabalo'rar] *vt* to undervalue, underestimate
infringir [infrin'xir] *vt* to infringe, contravene
infundado, -a [infun'daðo, a] *adj* groundless, unfounded
infundir [infun'dir] *vt* to infuse, instil
infusión [infu'sjon] *nf* infusion; **infusión de manzanilla** camomile tea
ingeniería [inxenje'ria] *nf* engineering; **ingeniería genética** genetic engineering; **ingeniero, -a** *nm/f* engineer; **ingeniero civil** *o* **de caminos** civil engineer
ingenio [in'xenjo] *nm* (*talento*) talent; (*agudeza*) wit; (*habilidad*) ingenuity, inventiveness; **ingenio azucarero** (LAM) sugar refinery; **ingenioso, -a** [inxe'njoso, a] *adj* ingenious, clever; (*divertido*) witty; **ingenuo, -a** *adj* ingenuous

ingerir [inxe'rir] *vt* to ingest; (*tragar*) to swallow; (*consumir*) to consume
Inglaterra [ingla'terra] *nf* England
ingle ['ingle] *nf* groin
inglés, -esa [in'gles, esa] *adj* English ▷ *nm/f* Englishman(-woman) ▷ *nm* (*Ling*) English
ingrato, -a [in'grato, a] *adj* (*gen*) ungrateful
ingrediente [ingre'ðjente] *nm* ingredient
ingresar [ingre'sar] *vt* (*dinero*) to deposit ▷ *vi* to come in; **~ en el hospital** to go into hospital
ingreso [in'greso] *nm* (*entrada*) entry; (*en hospital etc*) admission; **ingresos** *nmpl* (*dinero*) income *sg*; (*Com*) takings *pl*
inhabitable [inaβi'taβle] *adj* uninhabitable
inhalar [ina'lar] *vt* to inhale
inhibir [ini'βir] *vt* to inhibit
inhóspito, -a [i'nospito, a] *adj* (*región, paisaje*) inhospitable
inhumano, -a [inu'mano, a] *adj* inhuman
inicial [ini'θjal] *adj, nf* initial
iniciar [ini'θjar] *vt* (*persona*) to initiate; (*empezar*) to begin, commence; (*conversación*) to start up
iniciativa [iniθja'tiβa] *nf* initiative; **iniciativa privada** private enterprise
ininterrumpido, -a [ininterrum'piðo, a] *adj* uninterrupted
injertar [inxer'tar] *vt* to graft; **injerto** *nm* graft
injuria [in'xurja] *nf* (*agravio, ofensa*) offence; (*insulto*) insult

No confundir **injuria** con la palabra inglesa *injury*.

injusticia [inxus'tiθja] *nf* injustice
injusto, -a [in'xusto, a] *adj* unjust, unfair
inmadurez [inmaðu'reθ] *nf* immaturity
inmediaciones [inmeðja'θjones] *nfpl* neighbourhood *sg*, environs
inmediato, -a [inme'ðjato, a] *adj* immediate; (*contiguo*) adjoining; (*rápido*) prompt; (*próximo*) neighbouring, next; **de ~** immediately
inmejorable [inmexo'raβle] *adj* unsurpassable; (*precio*) unbeatable
inmenso, -a [in'menso, a] *adj* immense, huge
inmigración [inmiɣra'θjon] *nf* immigration
inmobiliaria [inmoβi'ljarja] *nf* estate agency
inmolar [inmo'lar] *vt* to immolate, sacrifice
inmoral [inmo'ral] *adj* immoral
inmortal [inmor'tal] *adj* immortal; **inmortalizar** *vt* to immortalize
inmóvil [in'moβil] *adj* immobile
inmueble [in'mweβle] *adj*: **bienes ~s** real estate, landed property ▷ *nm* property
inmundo, -a [in'mundo, a] *adj* filthy
inmune [in'mune] *adj*: **~ (a)** (*Med*) immune (to)
inmunidad [inmuni'ðað] *nf* immunity
inmutarse [inmu'tarse] *vr* to turn pale; **no se inmutó** he didn't turn a hair
innato, -a [in'nato, a] *adj* innate
innecesario, -a [inneθe'sarjo, a] *adj* unnecessary
innovación [innoβa'θjon] *nf* innovation
innovar [inno'βar] *vt* to introduce
inocencia [ino'θenθja] *nf* innocence
inocentada [inoθen'taða] *nf* practical joke
inocente [ino'θente] *adj* (*ingenuo*) naive, innocent; (*inculpable*) innocent; (*sin malicia*) harmless ▷ *nmf* simpleton; **el día de los (Santos) I~s** ≈ April Fools' Day

DÍA DE LOS (SANTOS) INOCENTES

The 28th December, el **día de los (Santos) Inocentes**, is when the Church commemorates the story of Herod's slaughter of the innocent children of Judaea. On this day Spaniards play **inocentadas** (practical jokes) on each other, much like our April Fool's Day pranks.

inodoro [ino'ðoro] *nm* toilet, lavatory (BRIT)
inofensivo, -a [inofen'siβo, a] *adj* inoffensive, harmless
inolvidable [inolβi'ðaβle] *adj* unforgettable
inoportuno, -a [inopor'tuno, a] *adj* untimely; (*molesto*) inconvenient
inoxidable [inoksi'ðaβle] *adj*: **acero ~** stainless steel
inquietar [inkje'tar] *vt* to worry, trouble; **inquietarse** *vr* to worry, get upset; **inquieto, -a** *adj* anxious, worried; **inquietud** *nf* anxiety, worry
inquilino, -a [inki'lino, a] *nm/f* tenant
insaciable [insa'θjaβle] *adj* insatiable
inscribir [inskri'βir] *vt* to inscribe; **~ a algn en** (*lista*) to put sb on; (*censo*) to register sb on
inscripción [inskrip'θjon] *nf* inscription; (*Escol etc*) enrolment; (*en censo*) registration
insecticida [insekti'θiða] *nm* insecticide

insecto [in'sekto] *nm* insect
inseguridad [inseɤuri'ðað] *nf* insecurity; **inseguridad ciudadana** lack of safety in the streets
inseguro, -a [inse'ɤuro, a] *adj* insecure; (*inconstante*) unsteady; (*incierto*) uncertain
insensato, -a [insen'sato, a] *adj* foolish, stupid
insensible [insen'siβle] *adj* (*gen*) insensitive; (*movimiento*) imperceptible; (*sin sentido*) numb
insertar [inser'tar] *vt* to insert
inservible [inser'βiβle] *adj* useless
insignia [in'siɤnja] *nf* (*señal distintiva*) badge; (*estandarte*) flag
insignificante [insiɤnifi'kante] *adj* insignificant
insinuar [insi'nwar] *vt* to insinuate, imply
insípido, -a [in'sipiðo, a] *adj* insipid
insistir [insis'tir] *vi* to insist; **~ en algo** to insist on sth; (*enfatizar*) to stress sth
insolación [insola'θjon] *nf* (*Med*) sunstroke
insolente [inso'lente] *adj* insolent
insólito, -a [in'solito, a] *adj* unusual
insoluble [inso'luβle] *adj* insoluble
insomnio [in'somnjo] *nm* insomnia
insonorizado, -a [insonori'θaðo, a] *adj* (*cuarto etc*) soundproof
insoportable [insopor'taβle] *adj* unbearable
inspección [inspek'θjon] *nf* inspection, check; **inspeccionar** *vt* (*examinar*) to inspect, examine; (*controlar*) to check
inspector, a [inspek'tor, a] *nm/f* inspector
inspiración [inspira'θjon] *nf* inspiration
inspirar [inspi'rar] *vt* to inspire; (*Med*) to inhale; **inspirarse** *vr*: **~se en** to be inspired by
instalación [instala'θjon] *nf* (*equipo*) fittings *pl*, equipment; **instalación eléctrica** wiring
instalar [insta'lar] *vt* (*establecer*) to instal; (*erguir*) to set up, erect; **instalarse** *vr* to establish o.s.; (*en una vivienda*) to move into
instancia [ins'tanθja] *nf* (*Jur*) petition; (*ruego*) request; **en última ~** as a last resort
instantáneo, -a [instan'taneo, a] *adj* instantaneous; **café ~** instant coffee
instante [ins'tante] *nm* instant, moment; **al ~** right now
instar [ins'tar] *vt* to press, urge
instaurar [instau'rar] *vt* (*costumbre*) to establish; (*normas, sistema*) to bring in, introduce; (*gobierno*) to instal
instigar [insti'ɤar] *vt* to instigate
instinto [ins'tinto] *nm* instinct; **por ~** instinctively
institución [institu'θjon] *nf* institution, establishment
instituir [institu'ir] *vt* to establish; (*fundar*) to found; **instituto** *nm* (*gen*) institute; (ESP *Escol*) ≈ comprehensive (BRIT) *o* high (US) school
institutriz [institu'triθ] *nf* governess
instrucción [instruk'θjon] *nf* instruction
instruir [instru'ir] *vt* (*gen*) to instruct; (*enseñar*) to teach, educate
instrumento [instru'mento] *nm* (*gen*) instrument; (*herramienta*) tool, implement
insubordinarse [insuβorði'narse] *vr* to rebel
insuficiente [insufi'θjente] *adj* (*gen*) insufficient; (*Escol*: *calificación*) unsatisfactory
insular [insu'lar] *adj* insular
insultar [insul'tar] *vt* to insult; **insulto** *nm* insult
insuperable [insupe'raβle] *adj* (*excelente*) unsurpassable; (*problema etc*) insurmountable
insurrección [insurrek'θjon] *nf* insurrection, rebellion
intachable [inta'tʃaβle] *adj* irreproachable
intacto, -a [in'takto, a] *adj* intact
integral [inte'ɤral] *adj* integral; (*completo*) complete; **pan ~** wholemeal (BRIT) *o* wholewheat (US) bread
integrar [inte'ɤrar] *vt* to make up, compose; (*Mat*: *fig*) to integrate
integridad [inteɤri'ðað] *nf* wholeness; (*carácter*) integrity; **íntegro, -a** *adj* whole, entire; (*honrado*) honest
intelectual [intelek'twal] *adj*, *nmf* intellectual
inteligencia [inteli'xenθja] *nf* intelligence; (*ingenio*) ability; **inteligente** *adj* intelligent
intemperie [intem'perje] *nf*: **a la ~** out in the open, exposed to the elements
intención [inten'θjon] *nf* (*gen*) intention, purpose; **con segundas intenciones** maliciously; **con ~** deliberately
intencionado, -a [intenθjo'naðo, a] *adj* deliberate; **mal ~** ill-disposed, hostile
intensidad [intensi'ðað] *nf* (*gen*) intensity; (*Elec, Tec*) strength; **llover con ~** to rain hard
intenso, -a [in'tenso, a] *adj* intense; (*sentimiento*) profound, deep
intentar [inten'tar] *vt* (*tratar*) to try, attempt; **intento** *nm* attempt
interactivo, -a [interak'tiβo, a] *adj*

(*Inform*) interactive
intercalar [interka'lar] *vt* to insert
intercambio [inter'kambjo] *nm* exchange, swap
interceder [interθe'ðer] *vi* to intercede
interceptar [interθep'tar] *vt* to intercept
interés [inte'res] *nm* (*gen*) interest; (*parte*) share, part; (*pey*) self-interest; **intereses creados** vested interests
interesado, -a [intere'saðo, a] *adj* interested; (*prejuiciado*) prejudiced; (*pey*) mercenary, self-seeking
interesante [intere'sante] *adj* interesting
interesar [intere'sar] *vt, vi* to interest, be of interest to; **interesarse** *vr*: **~se en** *o* **por** to take an interest in
interferir [interfe'rir] *vt* to interfere with; (*Tel*) to jam ▷ *vi* to interfere
interfón [inter'fon] (*MÉX*) *nm* entry phone
interino, -a [inte'rino, a] *adj* temporary ▷ *nm/f* temporary holder of a post; (*Med*) locum; (*Escol*) supply teacher
interior [inte'rjor] *adj* inner, inside; (*Com*) domestic, internal ▷ *nm* interior, inside; (*fig*) soul, mind; **Ministerio del I~** ≈ Home Office (*BRIT*), ≈ Department of the Interior (*US*); **interiorista** (*ESP*) *nmf* interior designer
interjección [interxek'θjon] *nf* interjection
interlocutor, a [interloku'tor, a] *nm/f* speaker
intermedio, -a [inter'meðjo, a] *adj* intermediate ▷ *nm* interval
interminable [intermi'naβle] *adj* endless
intermitente [intermi'tente] *adj* intermittent ▷ *nm* (*Auto*) indicator
internacional [internaθjo'nal] *adj* international
internado [inter'naðo] *nm* boarding school
internar [inter'nar] *vt* to intern; (*en un manicomio*) to commit; **internarse** *vr* (*penetrar*) to penetrate
internauta [inter'nauta] *nmf* web surfer, Internet user
Internet, internet [inter'net] *nm o f* Internet
interno, -a [in'terno, a] *adj* internal, interior; (*Pol etc*) domestic ▷ *nm/f* (*alumno*) boarder
interponer [interpo'ner] *vt* to interpose, put in; **interponerse** *vr* to intervene
interpretación [interpreta'θjon] *nf* interpretation
interpretar [interpre'tar] *vt* to interpret; (*Teatro, Mús*) to perform, play; **intérprete** *nmf* (*Ling*) interpreter, translator; (*Mús, Teatro*) performer, artist(e)
interrogación [interroɣa'θjon] *nf* interrogation; (*Ling*: *tb*: **signo de ~**) question mark
interrogar [interro'ɣar] *vt* to interrogate, question
interrumpir [interrum'pir] *vt* to interrupt
interrupción [interrup'θjon] *nf* interruption
interruptor [interrup'tor] *nm* (*Elec*) switch
intersección [intersek'θjon] *nf* intersection
interurbano, -a [interur'βano, a] *adj*: **llamada interurbana** long-distance call
intervalo [inter'βalo] *nm* interval; (*descanso*) break
intervenir [interβe'nir] *vt* (*controlar*) to control, supervise; (*Med*) to operate on ▷ *vi* (*participar*) to take part, participate; (*mediar*) to intervene
interventor, a [interβen'tor, a] *nm/f* inspector; (*Com*) auditor
intestino [intes'tino] *nm* (*Med*) intestine
intimar [inti'mar] *vi* to become friendly
intimidad [intimi'ðað] *nf* intimacy; (*familiaridad*) familiarity; (*vida privada*) private life; (*Jur*) privacy
íntimo, -a ['intimo, a] *adj* intimate
intolerable [intole'raβle] *adj* intolerable, unbearable
intoxicación [intoksika'θjon] *nf* poisoning; **intoxicación alimenticia** food poisoning
intranet [intra'net] *nf* intranet
intranquilo, -a [intran'kilo, a] *adj* worried
intransitable [intransi'taβle] *adj* impassable
intrépido, -a [in'trepiðo, a] *adj* intrepid
intriga [in'triɣa] *nf* intrigue; (*plan*) plot; **intrigar** *vt, vi* to intrigue
intrínseco, -a [in'trinseko, a] *adj* intrinsic
introducción [introðuk'θjon] *nf* introduction
introducir [introðu'θir] *vt* (*gen*) to introduce; (*moneda etc*) to insert; (*Inform*) to input, enter
intromisión [intromi'sjon] *nf* interference, meddling
introvertido, -a [introβer'tiðo, a] *adj, nm/f* introvert

i

intruso, -a [in'truso, a] *adj* intrusive ▷ *nm/f* intruder
intuición [intwi'θjon] *nf* intuition
inundación [inunda'θjon] *nf* flood(ing); **inundar** *vt* to flood; (*fig*) to swamp, inundate
inusitado, -a [inusi'taðo, a] *adj* unusual, rare
inútil [in'util] *adj* useless; (*esfuerzo*) vain, fruitless
inutilizar [inutili'θar] *vt* to make *o* render useless
invadir [imba'ðir] *vt* to invade
inválido, -a [im'baliðo, a] *adj* invalid ▷ *nm/f* invalid
invasión [imba'sjon] *nf* invasion
invasor, a [imba'sor, a] *adj* invading ▷ *nm/f* invader
invención [imben'θjon] *nf* invention
inventar [imben'tar] *vt* to invent
inventario [imben'tarjo] *nm* inventory
invento [im'bento] *nm* invention
inventor, a [imben'tor, a] *nm/f* inventor
invernadero [imberna'ðero] *nm* greenhouse
inverosímil [imbero'simil] *adj* implausible
inversión [imber'sjon] *nf* (*Com*) investment
inverso, -a [im'berso, a] *adj* inverse, opposite; **en el orden ~** in reverse order; **a la inversa** inversely, the other way round
inversor, a [imber'sor, a] *nm/f* (*Com*) investor
invertir [imber'tir] *vt* (*Com*) to invest; (*volcar*) to turn upside down; (*tiempo etc*) to spend
investigación [imbestiɣa'θjon] *nf* investigation; (*Escol*) research; **investigación y desarrollo** research and development
investigar [imbesti'ɣar] *vt* to investigate; (*Escol*) to do research into
invierno [im'bjerno] *nm* winter
invisible [imbi'siβle] *adj* invisible
invitado, -a [imbi'taðo, a] *nm/f* guest
invitar [imbi'tar] *vt* to invite; (*incitar*) to entice; (*pagar*) to buy, pay for
invocar [imbo'kar] *vt* to invoke, call on
involucrar [imbolu'krar] *vt*: **~ en** to involve in; **involucrarse** *vr* (*persona*): **~se en** to get mixed up in
involuntario, -a [imbolun'tarjo, a] *adj* (*movimiento, gesto*) involuntary; (*error*) unintentional
inyección [injek'θjon] *nf* injection
inyectar [injek'tar] *vt* to inject
iPod® ['ipoð] (*pl* **~s**) *nm* iPod®

PALABRA CLAVE

ir [ir] *vi* **1** to go; (*a pie*) to walk; (*viajar*) to travel; **ir caminando** to walk; **fui en tren** I went *o* travelled by train; **¡(ahora) voy!** (I'm just) coming!
2: **ir (a) por: ir (a) por el médico** to fetch the doctor
3 (*progresar: persona, cosa*) to go; **el trabajo va muy bien** work is going very well; **¿cómo te va?** how are things going?; **me va muy bien** I'm getting on very well; **le fue fatal** it went awfully badly for him
4 (*funcionar*): **el coche no va muy bien** the car isn't running very well
5: **te va estupendamente ese color** that colour suits you fantastically well
6 (*locuciones*): **¿vino? – ¡que va!** did he come? – of course not!; **vamos, no llores** come on, don't cry; **¡vaya coche!** what a car!, that's some car!
7: **no vaya a ser: tienes que correr, no vaya a ser que pierdas el tren** you'll have to run so as not to miss the train
8 (+ *pp*): **iba vestido muy bien** he was very well dressed
9: **ni me** *etc* **va ni me** *etc* **viene** I *etc* don't care
▷ *vb aux* **1 ir a: voy/iba a hacerlo hoy** I am/was going to do it today
2 (+ *gerundio*): **iba anocheciendo** it was getting dark; **todo se me iba aclarando** everything was gradually becoming clearer to me
3 (+ *pp*: = *pasivo*): **van vendidos 300 ejemplares** 300 copies have been sold so far
irse *vr* **1**: **¿por dónde se va al zoológico?** which is the way to the zoo?
2 (*marcharse*) to leave; **ya se habrán ido** they must already have left *o* gone

ira ['ira] *nf* anger, rage
Irak [i'rak] *nm* = **Iraq**
Irán [i'ran] *nm* Iran; **iraní** *adj, nmf* Iranian
Iraq [i'rak] *nm* Iraq; **iraquí** *adj, nmf* Iraqi
iris ['iris] *nm inv* (*tb*: **arco ~**) rainbow; (*Anat*) iris
Irlanda [ir'landa] *nf* Ireland; **irlandés, -esa** *adj* Irish ▷ *nm/f* Irishman(-woman); **los irlandeses** the Irish
ironía [iro'nia] *nf* irony; **irónico, -a** *adj* ironic(al)
IRPF *nm abr* (= *Impuesto sobre la Renta de las Personas Físicas*) (personal) income tax
irreal [irre'al] *adj* unreal
irregular [irreɣu'lar] *adj* (*gen*) irregular; (*situación*) abnormal
irremediable [irreme'ðjaβle] *adj*

irremediable; (*vicio*) incurable
irreparable [irrepa'raβle] *adj* (*daños*) irreparable; (*pérdida*) irrecoverable
irrespetuoso, -a [irrespe'twoso, a] *adj* disrespectful
irresponsable [irrespon'saβle] *adj* irresponsible
irreversible [irreβer'sible] *adj* irreversible
irrigar [irri'ɣar] *vt* to irrigate
irrisorio, -a [irri'sorjo, a] *adj* derisory, ridiculous
irritar [irri'tar] *vt* to irritate, annoy
irrupción [irrup'θjon] *nf* irruption; (*invasión*) invasion
isla ['isla] *nf* island
Islam [is'lam] *nm* Islam; **las enseñanzas del ~** the teachings of Islam; **islámico, -a** *adj* Islamic
islandés, -esa [islan'des, esa] *adj* Icelandic ▷ *nm/f* Icelander
Islandia [is'landja] *nf* Iceland
isleño, -a [is'leɲo, a] *adj* island *cpd* ▷ *nm/f* islander
Israel [isra'el] *nm* Israel; **israelí** *adj, nmf* Israeli
istmo ['istmo] *nm* isthmus
Italia [i'talja] *nf* Italy; **italiano, -a** *adj, nm/f* Italian
itinerario [itine'rarjo] *nm* itinerary, route
ITV (ESP) *nf abr* (= *inspección técnica de vehículos*) roadworthiness test, ≈ MOT (BRIT)
IVA ['iβa] *nm abr* (= *impuesto sobre el valor añadido*) VAT
izar [i'θar] *vt* to hoist
izdo, -a *abr* (= *izquierdo, a*) l
izquierda [iθ'kjerda] *nf* left; (*Pol*) left (wing); **a la ~** (*estar*) on the left; (*torcer etc*) (to the) left
izquierdo, -a [iθ'kjerðo, a] *adj* left

jabalí [xaβa'li] *nm* wild boar
jabalina [xaβa'lina] *nf* javelin
jabón [xa'βon] *nm* soap
jaca ['xaka] *nf* pony
jacal [xa'kal] (MÉX) *nm* shack
jacinto [xa'θinto] *nm* hyacinth
jactarse [xak'tarse] *vr* to boast, brag
jadear [xaðe'ar] *vi* to pant, gasp for breath
jaguar [xa'ɣwar] *nm* jaguar
jaiba ['xaiβa] (LAM) *nf* crab
jalar [xa'lar] (LAM) *vt* to pull
jalea [xa'lea] *nf* jelly
jaleo [xa'leo] *nm* racket, uproar; **armar un ~** to kick up a racket
jalón [xa'lon] (LAM) *nm* tug
jamás [xa'mas] *adv* never
jamón [xa'mon] *nm* ham; **jamón dulce** *o* **de York** cooked ham; **jamón serrano** cured ham
Japón [xa'pon] *nm* Japan; **japonés, -esa** *adj, nm/f* Japanese ▷ *nm* (*Ling*) Japanese
jaque ['xake] *nm* (*Ajedrez*) check; **jaque mate** checkmate
jaqueca [xa'keka] *nf* (very bad) headache, migraine
jarabe [xa'raβe] *nm* syrup
jardín [xar'ðin] *nm* garden; **jardín infantil** *o* **de infancia** nursery (school); **jardinería** *nf* gardening; **jardinero, -a** *nm/f* gardener
jarra ['xarra] *nf* jar; (*jarro*) jug
jarro ['xarro] *nm* jug
jarrón [xa'rron] *nm* vase
jaula ['xaula] *nf* cage
jauría [xau'ria] *nf* pack of hounds
jazmín [xaθ'min] *nm* jasmine
J.C. *abr* (= *Jesucristo*) J.C.
jeans [jins, dʒins] (LAM) *nmpl* jeans, denims; **unos ~** a pair of jeans
jefatura [xefa'tura] *nf* (*tb*: **~ de policía**) police headquarters *sg*
jefe, -a ['xefe, a] *nm/f* (*gen*) chief, head;

(*patrón*) boss; **jefe de cocina** chef; **jefe de estación** stationmaster; **jefe de Estado** head of state; **jefe de estudios** (*Escol*) director of studies; **jefe de gobierno** head of government
jengibre [xen'xiβre] *nm* ginger
jeque ['xeke] *nm* sheik
jerárquico, -a [xe'rarkiko, a] *adj* hierarchic(al)
jerez [xe'reθ] *nm* sherry
jerga ['xerɤa] *nf* jargon
jeringa [xe'ringa] *nf* syringe; (LAM: *molestia*) annoyance, bother; **jeringuilla** *nf* syringe
jeroglífico [xero'ɤlifiko] *nm* hieroglyphic
jersey [xer'sei] (*pl* **~s**) *nm* jersey, pullover, jumper
Jerusalén [xerusa'len] *n* Jerusalem
Jesucristo [xesu'kristo] *nm* Jesus Christ
jesuita [xe'swita] *adj, nm* Jesuit
Jesús [xe'sus] *nm* Jesus; **¡~!** good heavens!; (*al estornudar*) bless you!
jinete [xi'nete] *nmf* horseman(-woman), rider
jipijapa [xipi'xapa] (LAM) *nm* straw hat
jirafa [xi'rafa] *nf* giraffe
jirón [xi'ron] *nm* rag, shred
jitomate [xito'mate] (MÉX) *nm* tomato
joder [xo'ðer] (*fam!*) *vt, vi* to fuck (*!*)
jogging ['joɤin] (RPL) *nm* tracksuit (BRIT), sweat suit (US)
jornada [xor'naða] *nf* (*viaje de un día*) day's journey; (*camino o viaje entero*) journey; (*día de trabajo*) working day
jornal [xor'nal] *nm* (day's) wage; **jornalero** *nm* (day) labourer
joroba [xo'roβa] *nf* hump, hunched back; **jorobado, -a** *adj* hunchbacked ▷ *nm/f* hunchback
jota ['xota] *nf* (the letter) J; (*danza*) *Aragonese dance*; **no saber ni ~** to have no idea
joven ['xoβen] (*pl* **jóvenes**) *adj* young ▷ *nm* young man, youth ▷ *nf* young woman, girl
joya ['xoja] *nf* jewel, gem; (*fig: persona*) gem; **joyas de fantasía** costume *o* imitation jewellery; **joyería** *nf* (*joyas*) jewellery; (*tienda*) jeweller's (shop); **joyero** *nm* (*persona*) jeweller; (*caja*) jewel case
juanete [xwa'nete] *nm* (*del pie*) bunion
jubilación [xuβila'θjon] *nf* (*retiro*) retirement
jubilado, -a [xuβi'laðo, a] *adj* retired ▷ *nm/f* pensioner (BRIT), senior citizen
jubilar [xuβi'lar] *vt* to pension off, retire; (*fam*) to discard; **jubilarse** *vr* to retire
júbilo ['xuβilo] *nm* joy, rejoicing; **jubiloso, -a** *adj* jubilant
judía [xu'ðia] (ESP) *nf* (*Culin*) bean; **judía blanca/verde** haricot/French bean; *V tb* **judío**
judicial [xuði'θjal] *adj* judicial
judío, -a [xu'ðio, a] *adj* Jewish ▷ *nm/f* Jew(ess)
judo ['juðo] *nm* judo
juego *etc* ['xweɤo] *vb V* **jugar** ▷ *nm* (*gen*) play; (*pasatiempo, partido*) game; (*en casino*) gambling; (*conjunto*) set; **fuera de ~** (*Deporte: persona*) offside; (*: pelota*) out of play; **juego de palabras** pun, play on words; **Juegos Olímpicos** Olympic Games
juerga ['xwerɤa] (ESP: *fam*) *nf* binge; (*fiesta*) party; **ir de ~** to go out on a binge
jueves ['xweβes] *nm inv* Thursday
juez [xweθ] *nmf* judge; **juez de instrucción** examining magistrate; **juez de línea** linesman; **juez de salida** starter
jugada [xu'ɤaða] *nf* play; **buena ~** good move *o* shot *o* stroke *etc*
jugador, a [xuɤa'ðor, a] *nm/f* player; (*en casino*) gambler
jugar [xu'ɤar] *vt, vi* to play; (*en casino*) to gamble; (*apostar*) to bet; **~ al fútbol** to play football
juglar [xu'ɤlar] *nm* minstrel
jugo ['xuɤo] *nm* (*Bot*) juice; (*fig*) essence, substance; **jugo de naranja** (LAM) orange juice; **jugoso, -a** *adj* juicy; (*fig*) substantial, important
juguete [xu'ɤete] *nm* toy; **juguetear** *vi* to play; **juguetería** *nf* toyshop
juguetón, -ona [xuɤe'ton, ona] *adj* playful
juicio ['xwiθjo] *nm* judgement; (*razón*) sanity, reason; (*opinión*) opinion
julio ['xuljo] *nm* July
jumper ['dʒumper] (LAM) *nm* pinafore dress (BRIT), jumper (US)
junco ['xunko] *nm* rush, reed
jungla ['xungla] *nf* jungle
junio ['xunjo] *nm* June
junta ['xunta] *nf* (*asamblea*) meeting, assembly; (*comité, consejo*) council, committee; (*Com, Finanzas*) board; (*Tec*) joint; **junta directiva** board of directors
juntar [xun'tar] *vt* to join, unite; (*maquinaria*) to assemble, put together; (*dinero*) to collect; **juntarse** *vr* to join, meet; (*reunirse: personas*) to meet, assemble; (*arrimarse*) to approach, draw closer; **~se con algn** to join sb
junto, -a ['xunto, a] *adj* joined; (*unido*) united; (*anexo*) near, close; (*contiguo, próximo*) next, adjacent ▷ *adv*: **todo ~** all at once; **~s** together; **~ a** near (to), next to; **~**

con (together) with
jurado [xu'raðo] *nm* (*Jur*: *individuo*) juror; (: *grupo*) jury; (*de concurso*: *grupo*) panel (of judges); (: *individuo*) member of a panel
juramento [xura'mento] *nm* oath; (*maldición*) oath, curse; **prestar ~** to take the oath; **tomar ~ a** to swear in, administer the oath to
jurar [xu'rar] *vt, vi* to swear; **~ en falso** to commit perjury; **tenérsela jurada a algn** to have it in for sb
jurídico, -a [xu'riðiko, a] *adj* legal
jurisdicción [xurisðik'θjon] *nf* (*poder, autoridad*) jurisdiction; (*territorio*) district
justamente [xusta'mente] *adv* justly, fairly; (*precisamente*) just, exactly
justicia [xus'tiθja] *nf* justice; (*equidad*) fairness, justice
justificación [xustifika'θjon] *nf* justification; **justificar** *vt* to justify
justo, -a ['xusto, a] *adj* (*equitativo*) just, fair, right; (*preciso*) exact, correct; (*ajustado*) tight ▷ *adv* (*precisamente*) exactly, precisely; (*LAM*: *apenas a tiempo*) just in time
juvenil [xuβe'nil] *adj* youthful
juventud [xuβen'tuð] *nf* (*adolescencia*) youth; (*jóvenes*) young people *pl*
juzgado [xuθ'ɣaðo] *nm* tribunal; (*Jur*) court
juzgar [xuθ'ɣar] *vt* to judge; **a ~ por ...** to judge by ..., judging by ...

kárate ['karate] *nm* karate
kg *abr* (= *kilogramo*) kg
kilo ['kilo] *nm* kilo; **kilogramo** *nm* kilogramme; **kilometraje** *nm* distance in kilometres ≈ mileage; **kilómetro** *nm* kilometre; **kilovatio** *nm* kilowatt
kiosco ['kjosko] *nm* = **quiosco**
kleenex® [kli'neks] *nm* paper handkerchief, tissue
Kosovo [ko'soβo] *nm* Kosovo
km *abr* (= *kilómetro*) km
kv *abr* (= *kilovatio*) kw

L

l *abr* (= *litro*) l

la [la] *art def* the ▷ *pron* her; (*Ud.*) you; (*cosa*) it ▷ *nm* (*Mús*) la; **~ del sombrero rojo** the girl in the red hat; *V tb* **el**

laberinto [laβe'rinto] *nm* labyrinth

labio ['laβjo] *nm* lip

labor [la'βor] *nf* labour; (*Agr*) farm work; (*tarea*) job, task; (*Costura*) needlework; **labores domésticas** *o* **del hogar** household chores; **laborable** *adj* (*Agr*) workable; **día laborable** working day; **laboral** *adj* (*accidente*) at work; (*jornada*) working

laboratorio [laβora'torjo] *nm* laboratory

laborista [laβo'rista] *adj*: **Partido L~** Labour Party

labrador, a [laβra'ðor, a] *adj* farming *cpd* ▷ *nm/f* farmer

labranza [la'βranθa] *nf* (*Agr*) cultivation

labrar [la'βrar] *vt* (*gen*) to work; (*madera etc*) to carve; (*fig*) to cause, bring about

laca ['laka] *nf* lacquer

lacio, -a ['laθjo, a] *adj* (*pelo*) straight

lacón [la'kon] *nm* shoulder of pork

lactancia [lak'tanθja] *nf* lactation

lácteo, -a ['lakteo, a] *adj*: **productos ~s** dairy products

ladear [laðe'ar] *vt* to tip, tilt ▷ *vi* to tilt; **ladearse** *vr* to lean

ladera [la'ðera] *nf* slope

lado ['laðo] *nm* (*gen*) side; (*fig*) protection; (*Mil*) flank; **al ~ de** beside; **poner de ~** to put on its side; **poner a un ~** to put aside; **por todos ~s** on all sides, all round (BRIT)

ladrar [la'ðrar] *vi* to bark; **ladrido** *nm* bark, barking

ladrillo [la'ðriʎo] *nm* (*gen*) brick; (*azulejo*) tile

ladrón, -ona [la'ðron, ona] *nm/f* thief

lagartija [laɣar'tixa] *nf* (*Zool*) (small) lizard

lagarto [la'ɣarto] *nm* (*Zool*) lizard

lago ['laɣo] *nm* lake

lágrima ['laɣrima] *nf* tear

laguna [la'ɣuna] *nf* (*lago*) lagoon; (*hueco*) gap

lamentable [lamen'taβle] *adj* lamentable, regrettable; (*miserable*) pitiful

lamentar [lamen'tar] *vt* (*sentir*) to regret; (*deplorar*) to lament; **lamentarse** *vr* to lament; **lo lamento mucho** I'm very sorry

lamer [la'mer] *vt* to lick

lámina ['lamina] *nf* (*plancha delgada*) sheet; (*para estampar, estampa*) plate

lámpara ['lampara] *nf* lamp; **lámpara de alcohol/gas** spirit/gas lamp; **lámpara de pie** standard lamp

lana ['lana] *nf* wool

lancha ['lantʃa] *nf* launch; **lancha motora** motorboat, speedboat

langosta [lan'gosta] *nf* (*crustáceo*) lobster; (: *de río*) crayfish; **langostino** *nm* Dublin Bay prawn

lanza ['lanθa] *nf* (*arma*) lance, spear

lanzamiento [lanθa'mjento] *nm* (*gen*) throwing; (*Náut, Com*) launch, launching; **lanzamiento de peso** putting the shot

lanzar [lan'θar] *vt* (*gen*) to throw; (*Deporte*: *pelota*) to bowl; (*Náut, Com*) to launch; (*Jur*) to evict; **lanzarse** *vr* to throw o.s.

lapa ['lapa] *nf* limpet

lapicero [lapi'θero] (CAM) *nm* (*bolígrafo*) ballpoint pen, Biro®

lápida ['lapiða] *nf* stone; **lápida mortuoria** headstone

lápiz ['lapiθ] *nm* pencil; **lápiz de color** coloured pencil; **lápiz de labios** lipstick; **lápiz de ojos** eyebrow pencil

largar [lar'ɣar] *vt* (*soltar*) to release; (*aflojar*) to loosen; (*lanzar*) to launch; (*fam*) to let fly; (*velas*) to unfurl; (LAM: *lanzar*) to throw; **largarse** *vr* (*fam*) to beat it; **~se a** (CS: *empezar*) to start to

largo, -a ['larɣo, a] *adj* (*longitud*) long; (*tiempo*) lengthy; (*fig*) generous ▷ *nm* length; (*Mús*) largo; **dos años ~s** two long years; **tiene 9 metros de ~** it is 9 metres long; **a la larga** in the long run; **a lo ~ de** along; (*tiempo*) all through, throughout

> No confundir **largo** con la palabra inglesa *large*.

largometraje *nm* feature film

laringe [la'rinxe] *nf* larynx; **laringitis** *nf* laryngitis

las [las] *art def* the ▷ *pron* them; **~ que cantan** the ones *o* women *o* girls who sing; *V tb* **el**

lasaña [la'saɲa] *nf* lasagne, lasagna

láser ['laser] *nm* laser

lástima ['lastima] *nf* (*pena*) pity; **dar ~** to be pitiful; **es una ~ que ...** it's a pity that ...; **¡qué ~!** what a pity!; **está hecha una ~** she looks pitiful
lastimar [lasti'mar] *vt* (*herir*) to wound; (*ofender*) to offend; **lastimarse** *vr* to hurt o.s.
lata ['lata] *nf* (*metal*) tin; (*caja*) tin (BRIT), can; (*fam*) nuisance; **en ~** tinned (BRIT), canned; **dar la ~** to be a nuisance
latente [la'tente] *adj* latent
lateral [late'ral] *adj* side *cpd*, lateral ▷ *nm* (*Teatro*) wings
latido [la'tiðo] *nm* (*de corazón*) beat
latifundio [lati'fundjo] *nm* large estate
latigazo [lati'ɣaθo] *nm* (*golpe*) lash; (*sonido*) crack
látigo ['latiɣo] *nm* whip
latín [la'tin] *nm* Latin
latino, -a [la'tino, a] *adj* Latin; **latinoamericano, -a** *adj, nm/f* Latin-American
latir [la'tir] *vi* (*corazón, pulso*) to beat
latitud [lati'tuð] *nf* (*Geo*) latitude
latón [la'ton] *nm* brass
laurel [lau'rel] *nm* (*Bot*) laurel; (*Culin*) bay
lava ['laβa] *nf* lava
lavabo [la'βaβo] *nm* (*pila*) washbasin; (*tb*: **~s**) toilet
lavado [la'βaðo] *nm* washing; (*de ropa*) laundry; (*Arte*) wash; **lavado de cerebro** brainwashing; **lavado en seco** dry-cleaning
lavadora [laβa'ðora] *nf* washing machine
lavanda [la'βanda] *nf* lavender
lavandería [laβande'ria] *nf* laundry; (*automática*) launderette
lavaplatos [laβa'platos] *nm inv* dishwasher
lavar [la'βar] *vt* to wash; (*borrar*) to wipe away; **lavarse** *vr* to wash o.s.; **~se las manos** to wash one's hands; **~se los dientes** to brush one's teeth; **~ y marcar** (*pelo*) to shampoo and set; **~ en seco** to dry-clean; **~ los platos** to wash the dishes
lavarropas [laβa'rropas] (RPL) *nm inv* washing machine
lavavajillas [laβaβa'xiʎas] *nm inv* dishwasher
laxante [lak'sante] *nm* laxative
lazarillo [laθa'riʎo] *nm* (*tb*: **perro ~**) guide dog
lazo ['laθo] *nm* knot; (*lazada*) bow; (*para animales*) lasso; (*trampa*) snare; (*vínculo*) tie
le [le] *pron* (*directo*) him (*o* her); (: *usted*) you; (*indirecto*) to him (*o* her *o* it); (: *usted*) to you
leal [le'al] *adj* loyal; **lealtad** *nf* loyalty
lección [lek'θjon] *nf* lesson
leche ['letʃe] *nf* milk; **tiene mala ~** (*fam!*) he's a swine (*!*); **leche condensada** condensed milk; **leche desnatada** skimmed milk
lecho ['letʃo] *nm* (*cama*: *de río*) bed; (*Geo*) layer
lechón [le'tʃon] *nm* sucking (BRIT) *o* suckling (US) pig
lechoso, -a [le'tʃoso, a] *adj* milky
lechuga [le'tʃuɣa] *nf* lettuce
lechuza [le'tʃuθa] *nf* owl
lector, a [lek'tor, a] *nm/f* reader ▷ *nm*: **~ de discos compactos** CD player
lectura [lek'tura] *nf* reading
leer [le'er] *vt* to read
legado [le'ɣaðo] *nm* (*don*) bequest; (*herencia*) legacy; (*enviado*) legate
legajo [le'ɣaxo] *nm* file
legal [le'ɣal] *adj* (*gen*) legal; (*persona*) trustworthy; **legalizar** [leɣali'θar] *vt* to legalize; (*documento*) to authenticate
legaña [le'ɣaɲa] *nf* sleep (*in eyes*)
legión [le'xjon] *nf* legion; **legionario, -a** *adj* legionary ▷ *nm* legionnaire
legislación [lexisla'θjon] *nf* legislation
legislar [lexis'lar] *vi* to legislate
legislatura [lexisla'tura] *nf* (*Pol*) period of office
legítimo, -a [le'xitimo, a] *adj* (*genuino*) authentic; (*legal*) legitimate
legua ['leɣwa] *nf* league
legumbres [le'ɣumbres] *nfpl* pulses
leído, -a [le'iðo, a] *adj* well-read
lejanía [lexa'nia] *nf* distance; **lejano, -a** *adj* far-off; (*en el tiempo*) distant; (*fig*) remote
lejía [le'xia] *nf* bleach
lejos ['lexos] *adv* far, far away; **a lo ~** in the distance; **de** *o* **desde ~** from afar; **~ de** far from
lema ['lema] *nm* motto; (*Pol*) slogan
lencería [lenθe'ria] *nf* linen, drapery
lengua ['lengwa] *nf* tongue; (*Ling*) language; **morderse la ~** to hold one's tongue
lenguado [len'gwaðo] *nm* sole
lenguaje [len'gwaxe] *nm* language; **lenguaje de programación** program(m) ing language
lengüeta [len'gweta] *nf* (*Anat*) epiglottis; (*zapatos*) tongue; (*Mús*) reed
lente ['lente] *nf* lens; (*lupa*) magnifying glass; **lentes** *nfpl* lenses ▷ *nmpl* (LAM: *gafas*) glasses; **lentes bifocales/de sol** (LAM) bifocals/sunglasses; **lentes de contacto** contact lenses
lenteja [len'texa] *nf* lentil; **lentejuela** *nf* sequin
lentilla [len'tiʎa] *nf* contact lens
lentitud [lenti'tuð] *nf* slowness; **con ~**

slowly

lento, -a ['lento, a] *adj* slow

leña ['leɲa] *nf* firewood; **leñador, a** *nm/f* woodcutter

leño ['leɲo] *nm* (*trozo de árbol*) log; (*madero*) timber; (*fig*) blockhead

Leo ['leo] *nm* Leo

león [le'on] *nm* lion; **león marino** sea lion

leopardo [leo'parðo] *nm* leopard

leotardos [leo'tarðos] *nmpl* tights

lepra ['lepra] *nf* leprosy; **leproso, -a** *nm/f* leper

les [les] *pron* (*directo*) them; (: *ustedes*) you; (*indirecto*) to them; (: *ustedes*) to you

lesbiana [les'βjana] *adj, nf* lesbian

lesión [le'sjon] *nf* wound, lesion; (*Deporte*) injury; **lesionado, -a** *adj* injured ▷ *nm/f* injured person

letal [le'tal] *adj* lethal

letanía [leta'nia] *nf* litany

letra ['letra] *nf* letter; (*escritura*) handwriting; (*Mús*) lyrics *pl*; **letra de cambio** bill of exchange; **letra de imprenta** print; **letrado, -a** *adj* learned ▷ *nm/f* lawyer; **letrero** *nm* (*cartel*) sign; (*etiqueta*) label

letrina [le'trina] *nf* latrine

leucemia [leu'θemja] *nf* leukaemia

levadura [leβa'ðura] *nf* (*para el pan*) yeast; (*de cerveza*) brewer's yeast

levantar [leβan'tar] *vt* (*gen*) to raise; (*del suelo*) to pick up; (*hacia arriba*) to lift (up); (*plan*) to make, draw up; (*mesa*) to clear; (*campamento*) to strike; (*fig*) to cheer up, hearten; **levantarse** *vr* to get up; (*enderezarse*) to straighten up; (*rebelarse*) to rebel; **~ el ánimo** to cheer up

levante [le'βante] *nm* east coast; **el L~** *region of Spain extending from Castellón to Murcia*

levar [le'βar] *vt* to weigh

leve ['leβe] *adj* light; (*fig*) trivial

levita [le'βita] *nf* frock coat

léxico ['leksiko] *nm* (*vocabulario*) vocabulary

ley [lei] *nf* (*gen*) law; (*metal*) standard

leyenda [le'jenda] *nf* legend

leyó *etc vb V* **leer**

liar [li'ar] *vt* to tie (up); (*unir*) to bind; (*envolver*) to wrap (up); (*enredar*) to confuse; (*cigarrillo*) to roll; **liarse** *vr* (*fam*) to get involved; **~se a palos** to get involved in a fight

Líbano ['liβano] *nm*: **el ~** the Lebanon

libélula [li'βelula] *nf* dragonfly

liberación [liβera'θjon] *nf* liberation; (*de la cárcel*) release

liberal [liβe'ral] *adj, nmf* liberal

liberar [liβe'rar] *vt* to liberate

libertad [liβer'tað] *nf* liberty, freedom; **libertad bajo fianza** bail; **libertad bajo palabra** parole; **libertad condicional** probation; **libertad de culto/de prensa/ de comercio** freedom of worship/of the press/of trade

libertar [liβer'tar] *vt* (*preso*) to set free; (*de una obligación*) to release; (*eximir*) to exempt

libertino, -a [liβer'tino, a] *adj* permissive ▷ *nm/f* permissive person

libra ['liβra] *nf* pound; **L~** (*Astrología*) Libra; **libra esterlina** pound sterling

libramiento [liβra'mjento] (*MÉX*) *nm* ring road (*BRIT*), beltway (*US*)

librar [li'βrar] *vt* (*de peligro*) to save; (*batalla*) to wage, fight; (*de impuestos*) to exempt; (*cheque*) to make out; (*Jur*) to exempt; **librarse** *vr*: **~se de** to escape from, free o.s. from

libre ['liβre] *adj* free; (*lugar*) unoccupied; (*asiento*) vacant; (*de deudas*) free of debts; **~ de impuestos** free of tax; **tiro ~** free kick; **los 100 metros ~s** the 100 metres free-style (race); **al aire ~** in the open air

librería [liβre'ria] *nf* (*tienda*) bookshop

> No confundir **librería** con la palabra inglesa *library*.

librero, -a *nm/f* bookseller

libreta [li'βreta] *nf* notebook

libro ['liβro] *nm* book; **libro de bolsillo** paperback; **libro de texto** textbook; **libro electrónico** e-book

Lic. *abr* = **licenciado, a**

licencia [li'θenθja] *nf* (*gen*) licence; (*permiso*) permission; **licencia de caza** game licence; **licencia por enfermedad** (*MÉX, RPL*) sick leave; **licenciado, -a** *adj* licensed ▷ *nm/f* graduate; **licenciar** *vt* (*empleado*) to dismiss; (*permitir*) to permit, allow; (*soldado*) to discharge; (*estudiante*) to confer a degree upon; **licenciarse** *vr*: **licenciarse en Derecho** to graduate in law

lícito, -a ['liθito, a] *adj* (*legal*) lawful; (*justo*) fair, just; (*permisible*) permissible

licor [li'kor] *nm* spirits *pl* (*BRIT*), liquor (*US*); (*de frutas etc*) liqueur

licuadora [likwa'ðora] *nf* blender

líder ['liðer] *nmf* leader; **liderato** *nm* leadership; **liderazgo** *nm* leadership

lidia ['liðja] *nf* bullfighting; (*una lidia*) bullfight; **toros de ~** fighting bulls; **lidiar** *vt, vi* to fight

liebre ['ljeβre] *nf* hare

lienzo ['ljenθo] *nm* linen; (*Arte*) canvas; (*Arq*) wall

liga ['liɣa] *nf* (*de medias*) garter, suspender; (*LAM*: *goma*) rubber band; (*confederación*)

league
ligadura [liɣa'ðura] *nf* bond, tie; (*Med, Mús*) ligature
ligamento [liɣa'mento] *nm* ligament
ligar [li'ɣar] *vt* (*atar*) to tie; (*unir*) to join; (*Med*) to bind up; (*Mús*) to slur ▷ *vi* to mix, blend; (*fam*): **(él) liga mucho** he pulls a lot of women; **ligarse** *vr* to commit o.s.
ligero, -a [li'xero, a] *adj* (*de peso*) light; (*tela*) thin; (*rápido*) swift, quick; (*ágil*) agile, nimble; (*de importancia*) slight; (*de carácter*) flippant, superficial ▷ *adv*: **a la ligera** superficially
liguero [li'ɣero] *nm* suspender (BRIT) *o* garter (US) belt
lija ['lixa] *nf* (*Zool*) dogfish; (*tb*: **papel de ~**) sandpaper
lila ['lila] *nf* lilac
lima ['lima] *nf* file; (*Bot*) lime; **lima de uñas** nailfile; **limar** *vt* to file
limitación [limita'θjon] *nf* limitation, limit
limitar [limi'tar] *vt* to limit; (*reducir*) to reduce, cut down ▷ *vi*: **~ con** to border on; **limitarse** *vr*: **~se a** to limit o.s. to
límite ['limite] *nm* (*gen*) limit; (*fin*) end; (*frontera*) border; **límite de velocidad** speed limit
limítrofe [li'mitrofe] *adj* neighbouring
limón [li'mon] *nm* lemon ▷ *adj*: **amarillo ~** lemon-yellow; **limonada** *nf* lemonade
limosna [li'mosna] *nf* alms *pl*; **vivir de ~** to live on charity
limpiador [limpja'ðor] (MÉX) *nm* = **limpiaparabrisas**
limpiaparabrisas [limpjapara'βrisas] *nm inv* windscreen (BRIT) *o* windshield (US) wiper
limpiar [lim'pjar] *vt* to clean; (*con trapo*) to wipe; (*quitar*) to wipe away; (*zapatos*) to shine, polish; (*fig*) to clean up
limpieza [lim'pjeθa] *nf* (*estado*) cleanliness; (*acto*) cleaning; (*: de las calles*) cleansing; (*: de zapatos*) polishing; (*habilidad*) skill; (*fig: Policía*) clean-up; (*pureza*) purity; (*Mil*): **operación de ~** mopping-up operation; **limpieza en seco** dry cleaning
limpio, -a ['limpjo, a] *adj* clean; (*moralmente*) pure; (*Com*) clear, net; (*fam*) honest ▷ *adv*: **jugar ~** to play fair; **pasar a** (ESP) *o* **en** (LAM) **~** to make a clean copy of
lince ['linθe] *nm* lynx
linchar [lin'tʃar] *vt* to lynch
lindar [lin'dar] *vi* to adjoin; **~ con** to border on
lindo, -a ['lindo, a] *adj* pretty, lovely ▷ *adv*: **nos divertimos de lo ~** we had a marvellous time; **canta muy ~** (LAM) he sings beautifully
línea ['linea] *nf* (*gen*) line; **en ~** (*Inform*) on line; **línea aérea** airline; **línea de meta** goal line; (*en carrera*) finishing line; **línea discontinua** (*Auto*) broken line; **línea recta** straight line
lingote [lin'gote] *nm* ingot
lingüista [lin'gwista] *nmf* linguist; **lingüística** *nf* linguistics *sg*
lino ['lino] *nm* linen; (*Bot*) flax
linterna [lin'terna] *nf* torch (BRIT), flashlight (US)
lío ['lio] *nm* bundle; (*fam*) fuss; (*desorden*) muddle, mess; **armar un ~** to make a fuss
liquen ['liken] *nm* lichen
liquidación [likiða'θjon] *nf* liquidation; **venta de ~** clearance sale
liquidar [liki'ðar] *vt* (*mercancías*) to liquidate; (*deudas*) to pay off; (*empresa*) to wind up
líquido, -a ['likiðo, a] *adj* liquid; (*ganancia*) net ▷ *nm* liquid; **líquido imponible** net taxable income
lira ['lira] *nf* (*Mús*) lyre; (*moneda*) lira
lírico, -a ['liriko, a] *adj* lyrical
lirio ['lirjo] *nm* (*Bot*) iris
lirón [li'ron] *nm* (*Zool*) dormouse; (*fig*) sleepyhead
Lisboa [lis'βoa] *n* Lisbon
lisiar [li'sjar] *vt* to maim
liso, -a ['liso, a] *adj* (*terreno*) flat; (*cabello*) straight; (*superficie*) even; (*tela*) plain
lista ['lista] *nf* list; (*de alumnos*) school register; (*de libros*) catalogue; (*de platos*) menu; (*de precios*) price list; **pasar ~** to call the roll; **tela de ~s** striped material; **lista de espera** waiting list; **lista de precios** price list; **listín** *nm* (*tb*: **listín telefónico** *o* **de teléfonos**) telephone directory
listo, -a ['listo, a] *adj* (*perspicaz*) smart, clever; (*preparado*) ready
listón [lis'ton] *nm* (*de madera, metal*) strip
litera [li'tera] *nf* (*en barco, tren*) berth; (*en dormitorio*) bunk, bunk bed
literal [lite'ral] *adj* literal
literario, -a [lite'rarjo, a] *adj* literary
literato, -a [lite'rato, a] *adj* literary ▷ *nm/f* writer
literatura [litera'tura] *nf* literature
litigio [li'tixjo] *nm* (*Jur*) lawsuit; (*fig*): **en ~ con** in dispute with
litografía [litoɣra'fia] *nf* lithography; (*una litografía*) lithograph
litoral [lito'ral] *adj* coastal ▷ *nm* coast, seaboard
litro ['litro] *nm* litre
lívido, -a ['liβiðo, a] *adj* livid
llaga ['ʎaɣa] *nf* wound

l

llama ['ʎama] *nf* flame; (*Zool*) llama
llamada [ʎa'maða] *nf* call; **llamada a cobro revertido** reverse-charge (BRIT) *o* collect (US) call; **llamada al orden** call to order; **llamada de atención** warning; **llamada local** (LAM) local call; **llamada metropolitana** (ESP) local call; **llamada por cobrar** (MÉX) reverse-charge (BRIT) *o* collect (US) call
llamamiento [ʎama'mjento] *nm* call
llamar [ʎa'mar] *vt* to call; (*atención*) to attract ▷ *vi* (*por teléfono*) to telephone; (*a la puerta*) to knock (*o* ring); (*por señas*) to beckon; (*Mil*) to call up; **llamarse** *vr* to be called, be named; **¿cómo se llama (usted)?** what's your name?
llamativo, -a [ʎama'tiβo, a] *adj* showy; (*color*) loud
llano, -a ['ʎano, a] *adj* (*superficie*) flat; (*persona*) straightforward; (*estilo*) clear ▷ *nm* plain, flat ground
llanta ['ʎanta] *nf* (ESP) (wheel) rim; **llanta (de goma)** (LAM: *neumático*) tyre; (: *cámara*) inner (tube); **llanta de repuesto** (LAM) spare tyre
llanto ['ʎanto] *nm* weeping
llanura [ʎa'nura] *nf* plain
llave ['ʎaβe] *nf* key; (*del agua*) tap; (*Mecánica*) spanner; (*de la luz*) switch; (*Mús*) key; **echar la ~ a** to lock up; **llave de contacto** (ESP *Auto*) ignition key; **llave de encendido** (LAM *Auto*) ignition key; **llave de paso** stopcock; **llave inglesa** monkey wrench; **llave maestra** master key; **llavero** *nm* keyring
llegada [ʎe'ɣaða] *nf* arrival
llegar [ʎe'ɣar] *vi* to arrive; (*alcanzar*) to reach; (*bastar*) to be enough; **llegarse** *vr*: **~se a** to approach; **~ a** to manage to, succeed in; **~ a saber** to find out; **~ a ser** to become; **~ a las manos de** to come into the hands of
llenar [ʎe'nar] *vt* to fill; (*espacio*) to cover; (*formulario*) to fill in *o* up; (*fig*) to heap
lleno, -a ['ʎeno, a] *adj* full, filled; (*repleto*) full up ▷ *nm* (*Teatro*) full house; **dar de ~ contra un muro** to hit a wall head-on
llevadero, -a [ʎeβa'ðero, a] *adj* bearable, tolerable
llevar [ʎe'βar] *vt* to take; (*ropa*) to wear; (*cargar*) to carry; (*quitar*) to take away; (*en coche*) to drive; (*transportar*) to transport; (*traer: dinero*) to carry; (*conducir*) to lead; (*Mat*) to carry ▷ *vi* (*suj: camino etc*): **~ a** to lead to; **llevarse** *vr* to carry off, take away; **llevamos dos días aquí** we have been here for two days; **él me lleva 2 años** he's 2 years older than me; **~ los libros** (*Com*) to keep the books; **~se bien** to get on well (together)
llorar [ʎo'rar] *vt, vi* to cry, weep; **~ de risa** to cry with laughter
llorón, -ona [ʎo'ron, ona] *adj* tearful ▷ *nm/f* cry-baby
lloroso, -a [ʎo'roso, a] *adj* (*gen*) weeping, tearful; (*triste*) sad, sorrowful
llover [ʎo'βer] *vi* to rain
llovizna [ʎo'βiθna] *nf* drizzle; **lloviznar** *vi* to drizzle
llueve *etc vb V* **llover**
lluvia ['ʎuβja] *nf* rain; **lluvia radioactiva** (radioactive) fallout; **lluvioso, -a** *adj* rainy
lo [lo] *art def*: **~ bel~** the beautiful, what is beautiful, that which is beautiful ▷ *pron* (*persona*) him; (*cosa*) it; **~ que sea** whatever; *V tb* **el**
loable [lo'aβle] *adj* praiseworthy
lobo ['loβo] *nm* wolf; **lobo de mar** (*fig*) sea dog
lóbulo ['loβulo] *nm* lobe
local [lo'kal] *adj* local ▷ *nm* place, site; (*oficinas*) premises *pl*; **localidad** *nf* (*barrio*) locality; (*lugar*) location; (*Teatro*) seat, ticket; **localizar** *vt* (*ubicar*) to locate, find; (*restringir*) to localize; (*situar*) to place
loción [lo'θjon] *nf* lotion
loco, -a ['loko, a] *adj* mad ▷ *nm/f* lunatic, mad person; **estar ~ con** *o* **por algo/por algn** to be mad about sth/sb
locomotora [lokomo'tora] *nf* engine, locomotive
locuaz [lo'kwaθ] *adj* loquacious
locución [loku'θjon] *nf* expression
locura [lo'kura] *nf* madness; (*acto*) crazy act
locutor, a [loku'tor, a] *nm/f* (*Radio*) announcer; (*comentarista*) commentator; (*TV*) newsreader
locutorio [loku'torjo] *nm* (*en telefónica*) telephone booth
lodo ['loðo] *nm* mud
lógica ['loxika] *nf* logic
lógico, -a ['loxiko, a] *adj* logical
login ['loxin] *nm* login
logística [lo'xistika] *nf* logistics *sg*
logotipo [loðo'tipo] *nm* logo
logrado, -a [lo'ðraðo, a] *adj* (*interpretación, reproducción*) polished, excellent
lograr [lo'ɣrar] *vt* to achieve; (*obtener*) to get, obtain; **~ hacer** to manage to do; **~ que algn venga** to manage to get sb to come
logro ['loɣro] *nm* achievement, success
lóker ['loker] (LAM) *nm* locker
loma ['loma] *nf* hillock (BRIT), small hill
lombriz [lom'briθ] *nf* worm
lomo ['lomo] *nm* (*de animal*) back; (*Culin: de*

cerdo) pork loin; (: *de vaca*) rib steak; (*de libro*) spine
lona ['lona] *nf* canvas
loncha ['lontʃa] *nf* = **lonja**
lonchería [lontʃe'ria] (LAM) *nf* snack bar, diner (US)
Londres ['londres] *n* London
longaniza [longa'niθa] *nf* pork sausage
longitud [lonxi'tuð] *nf* length; (*Geo*) longitude; **tener 3 metros de ~** to be 3 metres long; **longitud de onda** wavelength
lonja ['lonxa] *nf* slice; (*de tocino*) rasher; **lonja de pescado** fish market
loro ['loro] *nm* parrot
los [los] *art def* the ▷ *pron* them; (*ustedes*) you; **mis libros y ~ tuyos** my books and yours; *V tb* **el**
losa ['losa] *nf* stone
lote ['lote] *nm* portion; (*Com*) lot
lotería [lote'ria] *nf* lottery; (*juego*) lotto

LOTERÍA

Millions of pounds are spent on lotteries each year in Spain, two of which are state-run: the **Lotería Primitiva** and the **Lotería Nacional**, with money raised going directly to the government. One of the most famous lotteries is run by the wealthy and influential society for the blind, "la ONCE".

loza ['loθa] *nf* crockery
lubina [lu'βina] *nf* sea bass
lubricante [luβri'kante] *nm* lubricant
lubricar [luβri'kar] *vt* to lubricate
lucha ['lutʃa] *nf* fight, struggle; **lucha de clases** class struggle; **lucha libre** wrestling; **luchar** *vi* to fight
lúcido, -a ['luθido, a] *adj* (*persona*) lucid; (*mente*) logical; (*idea*) crystal-clear
luciérnaga [lu'θjernaɣa] *nf* glow-worm
lucir [lu'θir] *vt* to illuminate, light (up); (*ostentar*) to show off ▷ *vi* (*brillar*) to shine; **lucirse** *vr* (*irónico*) to make a fool of o.s.
lucro ['lukro] *nm* profit, gain
lúdico, -a ['ludiko, a] *adj* (*aspecto, actividad*) play *cpd*
luego ['lweɣo] *adv* (*después*) next; (*más tarde*) later, afterwards
lugar [lu'ɣar] *nm* place; (*sitio*) spot; **en primer ~** in the first place, firstly; **en ~ de** instead of; **hacer ~** to make room; **fuera de ~** out of place; **sin ~ a dudas** without doubt, undoubtedly; **dar ~ a** to give rise to; **tener ~** to take place; **yo en su ~** if I were him; **lugar común** commonplace
lúgubre ['luɣuβre] *adj* mournful
lujo ['luxo] *nm* luxury; (*fig*) profusion, abundance; **de ~** luxury *cpd*, de luxe; **lujoso, -a** *adj* luxurious
lujuria [lu'xurja] *nf* lust
lumbre ['lumbre] *nf* fire; (*para cigarrillo*) light
luminoso, -a [lumi'noso, a] *adj* luminous, shining
luna ['luna] *nf* moon; (*de un espejo*) glass; (*de gafas*) lens; (*fig*) crescent; **estar en la ~** to have one's head in the clouds; **luna de miel** honeymoon; **luna llena/nueva** full/new moon
lunar [lu'nar] *adj* lunar ▷ *nm* (*Anat*) mole; **tela de ~es** spotted material
lunes ['lunes] *nm inv* Monday
lupa ['lupa] *nf* magnifying glass
lustre ['lustre] *nm* polish; (*fig*) lustre; **dar ~ a** to polish
luto ['luto] *nm* mourning; **llevar el** *o* **vestirse de ~** to be in mourning
Luxemburgo [luksem'burɣo] *nm* Luxembourg
luz [luθ] (*pl* **luces**) *nf* light; **dar a ~ un niño** to give birth to a child; **sacar a la ~** to bring to light; **dar** *o* **encender** (ESP) *o* **prender** (LAM)**/apagar la ~** to switch the light on/off; **tener pocas luces** to be dim *o* stupid; **traje de luces** bullfighter's costume; **luces de tráfico** traffic lights; **luz de freno** brake light; **luz roja/verde** red/green light

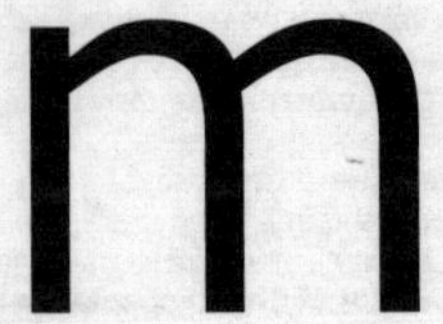

m *abr* (= *metro*) m; (= *minuto*) m
macana [ma'kana] (MÉX) *nf* truncheon (BRIT), billy club (US)
macarrones [maka'rrones] *nmpl* macaroni *sg*
macedonia [maθe'ðonja] *nf* (*tb*: **~ de frutas**) fruit salad
maceta [ma'θeta] *nf* (*de flores*) pot of flowers; (*para plantas*) flowerpot
machacar [matʃa'kar] *vt* to crush, pound ▷ *vi* (*insistir*) to go on, keep on
machete [ma'tʃete] *nm* machete, (large) knife
machetear [matʃete'ar] (MÉX) *vt* to swot (BRIT), grind away (US)
machismo [ma'tʃismo] *nm* male chauvinism; **machista** *adj, nm* sexist
macho ['matʃo] *adj* male; (*fig*) virile ▷ *nm* male; (*fig*) he-man
macizo, -a [ma'θiθo, a] *adj* (*grande*) massive; (*fuerte, sólido*) solid ▷ *nm* mass, chunk
madeja [ma'ðexa] *nf* (*de lana*) skein, hank; (*de pelo*) mass, mop
madera [ma'ðera] *nf* wood; (*fig*) nature, character; **una ~** a piece of wood
madrastra [ma'ðrastra] *nf* stepmother
madre ['maðre] *adj* mother *cpd* ▷ *nf* mother; (*de vino etc*) dregs *pl*; **madre política/soltera** mother-in-law/unmarried mother
Madrid [ma'ðrið] *n* Madrid
madriguera [maðri'ɣera] *nf* burrow
madrileño, -a [maðri'leɲo, a] *adj* of o from Madrid ▷ *nm/f* native of Madrid
madrina [ma'ðrina] *nf* godmother; (*Arq*) prop, shore; (*Tec*) brace; (*de boda*) bridesmaid
madrugada [maðru'ɣaða] *nf* early morning; (*alba*) dawn, daybreak
madrugador, a [maðruɣa'ðor, a] *adj* early-rising
madrugar [maðru'ɣar] *vi* to get up early; (*fig*) to get ahead
madurar [maðu'rar] *vt, vi* (*fruta*) to ripen; (*fig*) to mature; **madurez** *nf* ripeness; maturity; **maduro, -a** *adj* ripe; mature
maestra *nf* *V* **maestro**
maestría [maes'tria] *nf* mastery; (*habilidad*) skill, expertise
maestro, -a [ma'estro, a] *adj* masterly; (*principal*) main ▷ *nm/f* master/mistress; (*profesor*) teacher ▷ *nm* (*autoridad*) authority; (*Mús*) maestro; (*experto*) master; **maestro albañil** master mason
magdalena [maɣða'lena] *nf* fairy cake
magia ['maxja] *nf* magic; **mágico, -a** *adj* magic(al) ▷ *nm/f* magician
magisterio [maxis'terjo] *nm* (*enseñanza*) teaching; (*profesión*) teaching profession; (*maestros*) teachers *pl*
magistrado [maxis'traðo] *nm* magistrate
magistral [maxis'tral] *adj* magisterial; (*fig*) masterly
magnate [maɣ'nate] *nm* magnate, tycoon
magnético, -a [maɣ'netiko, a] *adj* magnetic
magnetofón [maɣneto'fon] *nm* tape recorder
magnetófono [maɣne'tofono] *nm* = **magnetofón**
magnífico, -a [maɣ'nifiko, a] *adj* splendid, magnificent
magnitud [maɣni'tuð] *nf* magnitude
mago, -a ['maɣo, a] *nm/f* magician; **los Reyes M~s** the Three Wise Men
magro, -a ['maɣro, a] *adj* (*carne*) lean
mahonesa [mao'nesa] *nf* mayonnaise
maître ['metre] *nm* head waiter
maíz [ma'iθ] *nm* maize (BRIT), corn (US); sweet corn
majestad [maxes'tað] *nf* majesty
majo, -a ['maxo, a] *adj* nice; (*guapo*) attractive, good-looking; (*elegante*) smart
mal [mal] *adv* badly; (*equivocadamente*) wrongly ▷ *adj* = **malo** ▷ *nm* evil; (*desgracia*) misfortune; (*daño*) harm, damage; (*Med*) illness; **~ que bien** rightly or wrongly; **ir de ~ en peor** to get worse and worse
malabarista [malaβa'rista] *nmf* juggler
malaria [ma'larja] *nf* malaria
malcriado, -a [mal'krjaðo, a] *adj* spoiled
maldad [mal'dað] *nf* evil, wickedness
maldecir [malde'θir] *vt* to curse
maldición [maldi'θjon] *nf* curse
maldito, -a [mal'dito, a] *adj* (*condenado*) damned; (*perverso*) wicked; **¡~ sea!** damn it!
malecón [male'kon] (LAM) *nm* sea front,

promenade
maleducado, -a [maleðu'kaðo, a] *adj* bad-mannered, rude
malentendido [malenten'diðo] *nm* misunderstanding
malestar [males'tar] *nm* (*gen*) discomfort; (*fig: inquietud*) uneasiness; (*Pol*) unrest
maleta [ma'leta] *nf* case, suitcase; (*Auto*) boot (BRIT), trunk (US); **hacer las ~s** to pack; **maletero** *nm* (*Auto*) boot (BRIT), trunk (US); **maletín** *nm* small case, bag
maleza [ma'leθa] *nf* (*malas hierbas*) weeds *pl*; (*arbustos*) thicket
malgastar [malɣas'tar] *vt* (*tiempo, dinero*) to waste; (*salud*) to ruin
malhechor, a [male'tʃor, a] *nm/f* delinquent
malhumorado, -a [malumo'raðo, a] *adj* bad-tempered
malicia [ma'liθja] *nf* (*maldad*) wickedness; (*astucia*) slyness, guile; (*mala intención*) malice, spite; (*carácter travieso*) mischievousness
maligno, -a [ma'liɣno, a] *adj* evil; (*malévolo*) malicious; (*Med*) malignant
malla ['maʎa] *nf* mesh; (*de baño*) swimsuit; (*de ballet, gimnasia*) leotard; **mallas** *nfpl* tights; **malla de alambre** wire mesh
Mallorca [ma'ʎorka] *nf* Majorca
malo, -a ['malo, a] *adj* bad, false ▷ *nm/f* villain; **estar ~** to be ill
malograr [malo'ɣrar] *vt* to spoil; (*plan*) to upset; (*ocasión*) to waste
malparado, -a [malpa'raðo, a] *adj*: **salir ~** to come off badly
malpensado, -a [malpen'saðo, a] *adj* nasty
malteada [malte'aða] (LAM) *nf* milkshake
maltratar [maltra'tar] *vt* to ill-treat, mistreat
malvado, -a [mal'βaðo, a] *adj* evil, villainous
Malvinas [mal'βinas] *nfpl* (*tb*: **Islas ~**) Falklands, Falkland Islands
mama ['mama] *nf* (*de animal*) teat; (*de mujer*) breast
mamá [ma'ma] (*pl* **~s**) (*fam*) *nf* mum, mummy
mamar [ma'mar] *vt, vi* to suck
mamarracho [mama'rratʃo] *nm* sight, mess
mameluco [mameluko] (RPL) *nm* dungarees *pl* (BRIT), overalls *pl* (US)
mamífero [ma'mifero] *nm* mammal
mampara [mam'para] *nf* (*entre habitaciones*) partition; (*biombo*) screen
mampostería [mamposte'ria] *nf* masonry
manada [ma'naða] *nf* (*Zool*) herd; (*: de leones*) pride; (*: de lobos*) pack
manantial [manan'tjal] *nm* spring
mancha ['mantʃa] *nf* stain, mark; (*Zool*) patch; **manchar** *vt* (*gen*) to stain, mark; (*ensuciar*) to soil, dirty
manchego, -a [man'tʃeɣo, a] *adj* of o from La Mancha
manco, -a ['manko, a] *adj* (*de un brazo*) one-armed; (*de una mano*) one-handed; (*fig*) defective, faulty
mancuernas [man'kwernas] (MÉX) *nfpl* cufflinks
mandado [man'daðo] (LAM) *nm* errand
mandamiento [manda'mjento] *nm* (*orden*) order, command; (*Rel*) commandment
mandar [man'dar] *vt* (*ordenar*) to order; (*dirigir*) to lead, command; (*enviar*) to send; (*pedir*) to order, ask for ▷ *vi* to be in charge; (*pey*) to be bossy; **¿mande?** (MÉX: *¿cómo dice?*) pardon?, excuse me?; **~ hacer un traje** to have a suit made
mandarina [manda'rina] (ESP) *nf* tangerine, mandarin (orange)
mandato [man'dato] *nm* (*orden*) order; (*Pol: período*) term of office; (*: territorio*) mandate
mandíbula [man'diβula] *nf* jaw
mandil [man'dil] *nm* apron
mando ['mando] *nm* (*Mil*) command; (*de país*) rule; (*el primer lugar*) lead; (*Pol*) term of office; (*Tec*) control; **~ a la izquierda** left-hand drive; **mando a distancia** remote control
mandón, -ona [man'don, ona] *adj* bossy, domineering
manejar [mane'xar] *vt* to manage; (*máquina*) to work, operate; (*caballo etc*) to handle; (*casa*) to run, manage; (LAM: *coche*) to drive; **manejarse** *vr* (*comportarse*) to act, behave; (*arreglárselas*) to manage; **manejo** *nm* (*de bicicleta*) handling; (*de negocio*) management, running; (LAM *Auto*) driving; (*facilidad de trato*) ease, confidence; **manejos** *nmpl* (*intrigas*) intrigues
manera [ma'nera] *nf* way, manner, fashion; **maneras** *nfpl* (*modales*) manners; **su ~ de ser** the way he is; (*aire*) his manner; **de ninguna ~** no way, by no means; **de otra ~** otherwise; **de todas ~s** at any rate; **no hay ~ de persuadirle** there's no way of convincing him
manga ['manga] *nf* (*de camisa*) sleeve; (*de riego*) hose
mango ['mango] *nm* handle; (*Bot*) mango
manguera [man'gera] *nf* hose
maní [ma'ni] (LAM) *nm* peanut

m

manía [ma'nia] *nf* (*Med*) mania; (*fig: moda*) rage, craze; (*disgusto*) dislike; (*malicia*) spite; **coger ~ a algn** to take a dislike to sb; **tener ~ a algn** to dislike sb; **maníaco, -a** *adj* maniac(al) ▷*nm/f* maniac

maniático, -a [ma'njatiko, a] *adj* maniac(al) ▷*nm/f* maniac

manicomio [mani'komjo] *nm* mental hospital (BRIT), insane asylum (US)

manifestación [manifesta'θjon] *nf* (*declaración*) statement, declaration; (*de emoción*) show, display; (*Pol: desfile*) demonstration; (*: concentración*) mass meeting

manifestar [manifes'tar] *vt* to show, manifest; (*declarar*) to state, declare; **manifiesto, -a** *adj* clear, manifest ▷*nm* manifesto

manillar [mani'ʎar] *nm* handlebars *pl*

maniobra [ma'njoβra] *nf* manoeuvre; **maniobras** *nfpl* (*Mil*) manoeuvres; **maniobrar** *vt* to manoeuvre

manipulación [manipula'θjon] *nf* manipulation

manipular [manipu'lar] *vt* to manipulate; (*manejar*) to handle

maniquí [mani'ki] *nm* dummy ▷*nmf* model

manivela [mani'βela] *nf* crank

manjar [man'xar] *nm* (tasty) dish

mano ['mano] *nf* hand; (*Zool*) foot, paw; (*de pintura*) coat; (*serie*) lot, series; **a ~** by hand; **a ~ derecha/izquierda** on the right(-hand side)/left(-hand side); **de primera ~** (at) first hand; **de segunda ~** (at) second hand; **robo a ~ armada** armed robbery; **estrechar la ~ a algn** to shake sb's hand; **mano de obra** labour, manpower; **manos libres** *adj inv* (*teléfono, dispositivo*) hands-free ▷*nm inv* hands-free kit

manojo [ma'noxo] *nm* handful, bunch; (*de llaves*) bunch

manopla [ma'nopla] *nf* mitten

manosear [manose'ar] *vt* (*tocar*) to handle, touch; (*desordenar*) to mess up, rumple; (*insistir en*) to overwork; (LAM: *acariciar*) to caress, fondle

manotazo [mano'taθo] *nm* slap, smack

mansalva [man'salβa]: **a ~** *adv* indiscriminately

mansión [man'sjon] *nf* mansion

manso, -a ['manso, a] *adj* gentle, mild; (*animal*) tame

manta ['manta] (ESP) *nf* blanket

manteca [man'teka] *nf* fat; (CS: *mantequilla*) butter; **manteca de cerdo** lard

mantecado [mante'kaðo] (ESP) *nm* *Christmas sweet made from flour, almonds and lard*

mantel [man'tel] *nm* tablecloth

mantendré *etc vb V* **mantener**

mantener [mante'ner] *vt* to support, maintain; (*alimentar*) to sustain; (*conservar*) to keep; (*Tec*) to maintain, service; **mantenerse** *vr* (*seguir de pie*) to be still standing; (*no ceder*) to hold one's ground; (*subsistir*) to sustain o.s., keep going; **mantenimiento** *nm* maintenance; sustenance; (*sustento*) support

mantequilla [mante'kiʎa] *nf* butter

mantilla [man'tiʎa] *nf* mantilla; **mantillas** *nfpl* (*de bebé*) baby clothes

manto ['manto] *nm* (*capa*) cloak; (*de ceremonia*) robe, gown

mantuve *etc vb V* **mantener**

manual [ma'nwal] *adj* manual ▷*nm* manual, handbook

manuscrito, -a [manus'krito, a] *adj* handwritten ▷*nm* manuscript

manutención [manuten'θjon] *nf* maintenance; (*sustento*) support

manzana [man'θana] *nf* apple; (*Arq*) block (of houses)

manzanilla [manθa'niʎa] *nf* (*planta*) camomile; (*infusión*) camomile tea

manzano [man'θano] *nm* apple tree

maña ['maɲa] *nf* (*gen*) skill, dexterity; (*pey*) guile; (*destreza*) trick, knack

mañana [ma'ɲana] *adv* tomorrow ▷*nm* future ▷*nf* morning; **de** *o* **por la ~** in the morning; **¡hasta ~!** see you tomorrow!; **~ por la ~** tomorrow morning

mapa ['mapa] *nm* map

maple ['maple] (LAM) *nm* maple

maqueta [ma'keta] *nf* (scale) model

maquiladora [makila'ðora] (MÉX) *nf* (*Com*) bonded assembly plant

maquillaje [maki'ʎaxe] *nm* make-up; (*acto*) making up

maquillar [maki'ʎar] *vt* to make up; **maquillarse** *vr* to put on (some) make-up

máquina ['makina] *nf* machine; (*de tren*) locomotive, engine; (*Foto*) camera; (*fig*) machinery; **escrito a ~** typewritten; **máquina de coser** sewing machine; **máquina de escribir** typewriter; **máquina fotográfica** camera

maquinaria [maki'narja] *nf* (*máquinas*) machinery; (*mecanismo*) mechanism, works *pl*

maquinilla [maki'niʎa] (ESP) *nf* (*tb:* **~ de afeitar**) razor

maquinista [maki'nista] *nmf* (*de tren*) engine driver; (*Tec*) operator; (*Náut*) engineer

mar [mar] *nm o f* sea; **~ adentro** out at sea; **en alta ~** on the high seas; **la ~ de** (*fam*) lots of; **el Mar Negro/Báltico** the Black/ Baltic Sea

maraña [ma'raɲa] *nf* (*maleza*) thicket; (*confusión*) tangle

maravilla [mara'βiʎa] *nf* marvel, wonder; (*Bot*) marigold; **maravillar** *vt* to astonish, amaze; **maravillarse** *vr* to be astonished, be amazed; **maravilloso, -a** *adj* wonderful, marvellous

marca ['marka] *nf* (*gen*) mark; (*sello*) stamp; (*Com*) make, brand; **de ~** excellent, outstanding; **marca de fábrica** trademark; **marca registrada** registered trademark

marcado, -a [mar'kaðo, a] *adj* marked, strong

marcador [marka'ðor] *nm* (*Deporte*) scoreboard; (*: persona*) scorer

marcapasos [marka'pasos] *nm inv* pacemaker

marcar [mar'kar] *vt* (*gen*) to mark; (*número de teléfono*) to dial; (*gol*) to score; (*números*) to record, keep a tally of; (*pelo*) to set ▷ *vi* (*Deporte*) to score; (*Tel*) to dial

marcha ['martʃa] *nf* march; (*Tec*) running, working; (*Auto*) gear; (*velocidad*) speed; (*fig*) progress; (*dirección*) course; **poner en ~** to put into gear; (*fig*) to set in motion, get going; **dar ~ atrás** to reverse, put into reverse; **estar en ~** to be under way, be in motion

marchar [mar'tʃar] *vi* (*ir*) to go; (*funcionar*) to work, go; **marcharse** *vr* to go (away), leave

marchitar [martʃi'tar] *vt* to wither, dry up; **marchitarse** *vr* (*Bot*) to wither; (*fig*) to fade away; **marchito, -a** *adj* withered, faded; (*fig*) in decline

marciano, -a [mar'θjano, a] *adj, nm/f* Martian

marco ['marko] *nm* frame; (*moneda*) mark; (*fig*) framework

marea [ma'rea] *nf* tide; **marea negra** oil slick

marear [mare'ar] *vt* (*fig*) to annoy, upset; (*Med*): **~ a algn** to make sb feel sick; **marearse** *vr* (*tener náuseas*) to feel sick; (*desvanecerse*) to feel faint; (*aturdirse*) to feel dizzy; (*fam: emborracharse*) to get tipsy

maremoto [mare'moto] *nm* tidal wave

mareo [ma'reo] *nm* (*náusea*) sick feeling; (*en viaje*) travel sickness; (*aturdimiento*) dizziness; (*fam: lata*) nuisance

marfil [mar'fil] *nm* ivory

margarina [marɣa'rina] *nf* margarine

margarita [marɣa'rita] *nf* (*Bot*) daisy; (*Tip*) daisywheel

margen ['marxen] *nm* (*borde*) edge, border; (*fig*) margin, space ▷ *nf* (*de río etc*) bank; **dar ~ para** to give an opportunity for; **mantenerse al ~** to keep out (of things)

marginar [marxi'nar] *vt* (*socialmente*) to marginalize, ostracize

mariachi [ma'rjatʃi] *nm* (*persona*) mariachi musician; (*grupo*) mariachi band

MARIACHI

Mariachi music is the musical style most characteristic of Mexico. From the state of Jalisco in the 19th century, this music spread rapidly throughout the country, until each region had its own particular style of the Mariachi "sound". A Mariachi band can be made up of several singers, up to eight violins, two trumpets, guitars, a "vihuela" (an old form of guitar), and a harp. The dance associated with this music is called the "zapateado".

marica [ma'rika] (*fam*) *nm* sissy

maricón [mari'kon] (*fam*) *nm* queer

marido [ma'riðo] *nm* husband

marihuana [mari'wana] *nf* marijuana, cannabis

marina [ma'rina] *nf* navy; **marina mercante** merchant navy

marinero, -a [mari'nero, a] *adj* sea *cpd* ▷ *nm* sailor, seaman

marino, -a [ma'rino, a] *adj* sea *cpd*, marine ▷ *nm* sailor

marioneta [marjo'neta] *nf* puppet

mariposa [mari'posa] *nf* butterfly

mariquita [mari'kita] *nf* ladybird (BRIT), ladybug (US)

marisco [ma'risko] (ESP) *nm* shellfish *inv*, seafood; **mariscos** (LAM) *nmpl* = **marisco**

marítimo, -a [ma'ritimo, a] *adj* sea *cpd*, maritime

mármol ['marmol] *nm* marble

marqués, -esa [mar'kes, esa] *nm/f* marquis/marchioness

marrón [ma'rron] *adj* brown

marroquí [marro'ki] *adj, nmf* Moroccan ▷ *nm* Morocco (leather)

Marruecos [ma'rrwekos] *nm* Morocco

martes ['martes] *nm inv* Tuesday; **~ y trece** ≈ Friday 13th

MARTES Y TRECE

According to Spanish superstition Tuesday is an unlucky day, even more so if it falls on the 13th of the month.

martillo [mar'tiʎo] *nm* hammer
mártir ['martir] *nmf* martyr; **martirio** *nm* martyrdom; (*fig*) torture, torment
marxismo [mark'sismo] *nm* Marxism
marzo ['marθo] *nm* March

PALABRA CLAVE

más [mas] *adj, adv* **1**: **más (que** *o* **de)** (*compar*) more (than), ...+ er (than); **más grande/inteligente** bigger/more intelligent; **trabaja más (que yo)** he works more (than me); *V tb* **cada**
2 (*superl*): **el más** the most, ...+ est; **el más grande/inteligente (de)** the biggest/most intelligent (in)
3 (*negativo*): **no tengo más dinero** I haven't got any more money; **no viene más por aquí** he doesn't come round here any more
4 (*adicional*): **no le veo más solución que ...** I see no other solution than to ...; **¿quién más?** anybody else?
5 (*+ adj*: *valor intensivo*): **¡qué perro más sucio!** what a filthy dog!; **¡es más tonto!** he's so stupid!
6 (*locuciones*): **más o menos** more or less; **los más** most people; **es más** furthermore; **más bien** rather; **¡qué más da!** what does it matter!; *V tb* **no**
7: **por más: por más que te esfuerces** no matter how hard you try; **por más que quisiera ...** much as I should like to ...
8: **de más: veo que aquí estoy de más** I can see I'm not needed here; **tenemos uno de más** we've got one extra ▷ *prep*: **2 más 2 son 4** 2 and *o* plus 2 are 4
▷ *nm inv*: **este trabajo tiene sus más y sus menos** this job's got its good points and its bad points

mas [mas] *conj* but
masa ['masa] *nf* (*mezcla*) dough; (*volumen*) volume, mass; (*Física*) mass; **en ~** en masse; **las ~s** (*Pol*) the masses
masacre [ma'sakre] *nf* massacre
masaje [ma'saxe] *nm* massage
máscara ['maskara] *nf* mask; **máscara antigás/de oxígeno** gas/oxygen mask; **mascarilla** *nf* (*de belleza, Med*) mask
masculino, -a [masku'lino, a] *adj* masculine; (*Bio*) male
masía [ma'sia] *nf* farmhouse
masivo, -a [ma'siβo, a] *adj* mass *cpd*
masoquista [maso'kista] *nmf* masochist
máster ['master] (ESP) *nm* master
masticar [masti'kar] *vt* to chew
mástil ['mastil] *nm* (*de navío*) mast; (*de guitarra*) neck
mastín [mas'tin] *nm* mastiff
masturbarse [mastur'βarse] *vr* to masturbate
mata ['mata] *nf* (*arbusto*) bush, shrub; (*de hierba*) tuft
matadero [mata'ðero] *nm* slaughterhouse, abattoir
matamoscas [mata'moskas] *nm inv* (*pala*) fly swat
matanza [ma'tanθa] *nf* slaughter
matar [ma'tar] *vt, vi* to kill; **matarse** *vr* (*suicidarse*) to kill o.s., commit suicide; (*morir*) to be *o* get killed; **~ el hambre** to stave off hunger
matasellos [mata'seʎos] *nm inv* postmark
mate ['mate] *adj* matt ▷ *nm* (*en ajedrez*) (check)mate; (LAM: *hierba*) maté; (: *vasija*) gourd
matemáticas [mate'matikas] *nfpl* mathematics; **matemático, -a** *adj* mathematical ▷ *nm/f* mathematician
materia [ma'terja] *nf* (*gen*) matter; (*Tec*) material; (*Escol*) subject; **en ~ de** on the subject of; **materia prima** raw material; **material** *adj* material ▷ *nm* material; (*Tec*) equipment; **materialista** *adj* materialist(ic); **materialmente** *adv* materially; (*fig*) absolutely
maternal [mater'nal] *adj* motherly, maternal
maternidad [materni'ðað] *nf* motherhood, maternity; **materno, -a** *adj* maternal; (*lengua*) mother *cpd*
matinal [mati'nal] *adj* morning *cpd*
matiz [ma'tiθ] *nm* shade; **matizar** *vt* (*variar*) to vary; (*Arte*) to blend; **matizar de** to tinge with
matón [ma'ton] *nm* bully
matorral [mato'rral] *nm* thicket
matrícula [ma'trikula] *nf* (*registro*) register; (*Auto*) registration number; (: *placa*) number plate; **matrícula de honor** (*Univ*) *top marks in a subject at university with the right to free registration the following year*; **matricular** *vt* to register, enrol
matrimonio [matri'monjo] *nm* (*pareja*) (married) couple; (*unión*) marriage
matriz [ma'triθ] *nf* (*Anat*) womb; (*Tec*) mould
matrona [ma'trona] *nf* (*persona de edad*) matron; (*comadrona*) midwife
matufia [ma'tufja] (RPL: *fam*) *nf* put-up job
maullar [mau'ʎar] *vi* to mew, miaow
maxilar [maksi'lar] *nm* jaw(bone)
máxima ['maksima] *nf* maxim
máximo, -a ['maksimo, a] *adj*

maximum; (*más alto*) highest; (*más grande*) greatest ▷*nm* maximum; **como ~** at most
mayo ['majo] *nm* May
mayonesa [majo'nesa] *nf* mayonnaise
mayor [ma'jor] *adj* main, chief; (*adulto*) adult; (*de edad avanzada*) elderly; (*Mús*) major; (*compar*: *de tamaño*) bigger; (: *de edad*) older; (*superl*: *de tamaño*) biggest; (: *de edad*) oldest ▷*nm* (*adulto*) adult; **mayores** *nmpl* (*antepasados*) ancestors; **al por ~** wholesale; **mayor de edad** adult
mayoral [majo'ral] *nm* foreman
mayordomo [major'ðomo] *nm* butler
mayoría [majo'ria] *nf* majority, greater part
mayorista [majo'rista] *nmf* wholesaler
mayoritario, -a [majori'tarjo, a] *adj* majority *cpd*
mayúscula [ma'juskula] *nf* capital letter
mazapán [maθa'pan] *nm* marzipan
mazo ['maθo] *nm* (*martillo*) mallet; (*de flores*) bunch; (*Deporte*) bat
me [me] *pron* (*directo*) me; (*indirecto*) (to) me; (*reflexivo*) (to) myself; **¡dá~lo!** give it to me!
mear [me'ar] (*fam*) *vi* to pee, piss (*!*)
mecánica [me'kanika] *nf* (*Escol*) mechanics *sg*; (*mecanismo*) mechanism; *V tb* **mecánico**
mecánico, -a [me'kaniko, a] *adj* mechanical ▷*nm/f* mechanic
mecanismo [meka'nismo] *nm* mechanism; (*marcha*) gear
mecanografía [mekanoɣra'fia] *nf* typewriting; **mecanógrafo, -a** *nm/f* typist
mecate [me'kate] (*MÉX, CAM*) *nm* rope
mecedora [meθe'ðora] *nf* rocking chair
mecer [me'θer] *vt* (*cuna*) to rock; **mecerse** *vr* to rock; (*rama*) to sway
mecha ['metʃa] *nf* (*de vela*) wick; (*de bomba*) fuse
mechero [me'tʃero] *nm* (cigarette) lighter
mechón [me'tʃon] *nm* (*gen*) tuft; (*de pelo*) lock
medalla [me'ðaʎa] *nf* medal
media ['meðja] *nf* stocking; (*LAM*: *calcetín*) sock; (*promedio*) average
mediado, -a [me'ðjaðo, a] *adj* half-full; (*trabajo*) half-completed; **a ~s de** in the middle of, halfway through
mediano, -a [me'ðjano, a] *adj* (*regular*) medium, average; (*mediocre*) mediocre
medianoche [meðja'notʃe] *nf* midnight
mediante [me'ðjante] *adv* by (means of), through
mediar [me'ðjar] *vi* (*interceder*) to mediate, intervene
medicamento [meðika'mento] *nm* medicine, drug
medicina [meði'θina] *nf* medicine
médico, -a ['meðiko, a] *adj* medical ▷*nm/f* doctor
medida [me'ðiða] *nf* measure; (*medición*) measurement; (*prudencia*) moderation, prudence; **en cierta/gran ~** up to a point/ to a great extent; **un traje a la ~** a made-to-measure suit; **~ de cuello** collar size; **a ~ de** in proportion to; (*de acuerdo con*) in keeping with; **a ~ que** (*conforme*) as; **medidor** (*LAM*) *nm* meter
medio, -a ['meðjo, a] *adj* half (a); (*punto*) mid, middle; (*promedio*) average ▷*adv* half ▷*nm* (*centro*) middle, centre; (*promedio*) average; (*método*) means, way; (*ambiente*) environment; **medios** *nmpl* means, resources; **~ litro** half a litre; **las tres y media** half past three; **a ~ terminar** half finished; **pagar a medias** to share the cost; **medio ambiente** environment; **medio de transporte** means of transport; **Medio Oriente** Middle East; **medios de comunicación** media; **medioambiental** *adj* (*política, efectos*) environmental
mediocre [me'ðjokre] *adj* mediocre
mediodía [meðjo'ðia] *nm* midday, noon
medir [me'ðir] *vt, vi* (*gen*) to measure
meditar [meði'tar] *vt* to ponder, think over, meditate on; (*planear*) to think out
mediterráneo, -a [meðite'rraneo, a] *adj* Mediterranean ▷*nm*: **el M~** the Mediterranean
médula ['meðula] *nf* (*Anat*) marrow; **médula espinal** spinal cord
medusa [me'ðusa] (*ESP*) *nf* jellyfish
megáfono [me'ɣafono] *nm* megaphone
megapíxel [meɣa'piksel] (*pl* **megapixels** *or* **~es**) *nm* megapixel
mejilla [me'xiʎa] *nf* cheek
mejillón [mexi'ʎon] *nm* mussel
mejor [me'xor] *adj, adv* (*compar*) better; (*superl*) best; **a lo ~** probably; (*quizá*) maybe; **~ dicho** rather; **tanto ~** so much the better
mejora [me'xora] *nf* improvement; **mejorar** *vt* to improve, make better ▷*vi* to improve, get better; **mejorarse** *vr* to improve, get better
melancólico, -a [melan'koliko, a] *adj* (*triste*) sad, melancholy; (*soñador*) dreamy
melena [me'lena] *nf* (*de persona*) long hair; (*Zool*) mane
mellizo, -a [me'ʎiθo, a] *adj, nm/f* twin
melocotón [meloko'ton] (*ESP*) *nm* peach
melodía [melo'ðia] *nf* melody, tune
melodrama [melo'ðrama] *nm* melodrama; **melodramático, -a** *adj* melodramatic

melón [me'lon] *nm* melon
membrete [mem'brete] *nm* letterhead
membrillo [mem'briʎo] *nm* quince; **(carne de) ~** quince jelly
memoria [me'morja] *nf* (*gen*) memory; **memorias** *nfpl* (*de autor*) memoirs; **memorizar** *vt* to memorize
menaje [me'naxe] *nm* (*tb*: **artículos de ~**) household items
mencionar [menθjo'nar] *vt* to mention
mendigo, -a [men'diɣo, a] *nm/f* beggar
menear [mene'ar] *vt* to move; **menearse** *vr* to shake; (*balancearse*) to sway; (*moverse*) to move; (*fig*) to get a move on
menestra [me'nestra] *nf* (*tb*: **~ de verduras**) vegetable stew
menopausia [meno'pausja] *nf* menopause
menor [me'nor] *adj* (*más pequeño*: *compar*) smaller; (: *superl*) smallest; (*más joven*: *compar*) younger; (: *superl*) youngest; (*Mús*) minor ▷ *nmf* (*joven*) young person, juvenile; **no tengo la ~ idea** I haven't the faintest idea; **al por ~** retail; **menor de edad** person under age
Menorca [me'norka] *nf* Minorca

PALABRA CLAVE

menos [menos] *adj* **1**: **menos (que** *o* **de)** (*compar*: *cantidad*) less (than); (: *número*) fewer (than); **con menos entusiasmo** with less enthusiasm; **menos gente** fewer people; *V tb* **cada**
2 (*superl*): **es el que menos culpa tiene** he is the least to blame
▷ *adv* **1** (*compar*): **menos (que** *o* **de)** less (than); **me gusta menos que el otro** I like it less than the other one
2 (*superl*): **es el menos listo (de su clase)** he's the least bright in his class; **de todas ellas es la que menos me agrada** out of all of them she's the one I like least
3 (*locuciones*): **no quiero verle y menos visitarle** I don't want to see him, let alone visit him; **tenemos siete de menos** we're seven short; **(por) lo menos** at (the very) least; **¡menos mal!** thank goodness!
▷ *prep* except; (*cifras*) minus; **todos menos él** everyone except (for) him; **5 menos 2** 5 minus 2
▷ *conj*: **a menos que: a menos que venga mañana** unless he comes tomorrow

menospreciar [menospre'θjar] *vt* to underrate, undervalue; (*despreciar*) to scorn, despise
mensaje [men'saxe] *nm* message; **enviar un ~ a algn** (*por móvil*) to text sb, send sb a text message; **mensaje de texto** text message; **mensajero, -a** *nm/f* messenger
menso, -a ['menso, a] (*MÉX*: *fam*) *adj* stupid
menstruación [menstrua'θjon] *nf* menstruation
mensual [men'swal] *adj* monthly; **100 euros ~es** 100 euros a month; **mensualidad** *nf* (*salario*) monthly salary; (*Com*) monthly payment, monthly instalment
menta ['menta] *nf* mint
mental [men'tal] *adj* mental; **mentalidad** *nf* mentality; **mentalizar** *vt* (*sensibilizar*) to make aware; (*convencer*) to convince; (*padres*) to prepare (mentally); **mentalizarse** *vr* (*concienciarse*) to become aware; **mentalizarse (de)** to get used to the idea (of); **mentalizarse de que ...** (*convencerse*) to get it into one's head that ...
mente ['mente] *nf* mind
mentir [men'tir] *vi* to lie
mentira [men'tira] *nf* (*una mentira*) lie; (*acto*) lying; (*invención*) fiction; **parece mentira que ...** it seems incredible that ..., I can't believe that ...; **mentiroso, -a** [menti'roso, a] *adj* lying ▷ *nm/f* liar
menú [me'nu] (*pl* **~s**) *nm* menu; **menú del día** set menu; **menú turistico** tourist menu
menudencias [menu'ðenθjas] (*LAM*) *nfpl* giblets
menudo, -a [me'nuðo, a] *adj* (*pequeño*) small, tiny; (*sin importancia*) petty, insignificant; **¡~ negocio!** (*fam*) some deal!; **a ~** often, frequently
meñique [me'ɲike] *nm* little finger
mercadillo [merka'ðiʎo] (*ESP*) *nm* flea market
mercado [mer'kaðo] *nm* market; **mercado de pulgas** (*LAM*) flea market
mercancía [merkan'θia] *nf* commodity; **mercancías** *nfpl* goods, merchandise *sg*
mercenario, -a [merθe'narjo, a] *adj, nm* mercenary
mercería [merθe'ria] *nf* haberdashery (*BRIT*), notions *pl* (*US*); (*tienda*) haberdasher's (*BRIT*), notions store (*US*)
mercurio [mer'kurjo] *nm* mercury
merecer [mere'θer] *vt* to deserve, merit ▷ *vi* to be deserving, be worthy; **merece la pena** it's worthwhile; **merecido, -a** *adj* (well) deserved; **llevar su merecido** to get one's deserts
merendar [meren'dar] *vt* to have for tea ▷ *vi* to have tea; (*en el campo*) to have a picnic; **merendero** *nm* open-air cafe
merengue [me'renge] *nm* meringue
meridiano [meri'ðjano] *nm* (*Geo*)

meridian
merienda [me'rjenda] *nf* (light) tea, afternoon snack; (*de campo*) picnic
mérito ['merito] *nm* merit; (*valor*) worth, value
merluza [mer'luθa] *nf* hake
mermelada [merme'laða] *nf* jam
mero, -a ['mero, a] *adj* mere; (MÉX, CAM: *fam*) very
merodear [meroðe'ar] *vi*: **~ por** to prowl about
mes [mes] *nm* month
mesa ['mesa] *nf* table; (*de trabajo*) desk; (*Geo*) plateau; **poner/quitar la ~** to lay/clear the table; **mesa electoral** *officials in charge of a polling station*; **mesa redonda** (*reunión*) round table; **mesero, -a** (LAM) *nm/f* waiter/ waitress
meseta [me'seta] *nf* (*Geo*) plateau, tableland
mesilla [me'siʎa] *nf* (*tb*: **~ de noche**) bedside table
mesón [me'son] *nm* inn
mestizo, -a [mes'tiθo, a] *adj* half-caste, of mixed race ▷*nm/f* half-caste
meta ['meta] *nf* goal; (*de carrera*) finish
metabolismo [metaβo'lismo] *nm* metabolism
metáfora [me'tafora] *nf* metaphor
metal [me'tal] *nm* (*materia*) metal; (*Mús*) brass; **metálico, -a** *adj* metallic; (*de metal*) metal ▷*nm* (*dinero contante*) cash
meteorología [meteorolo'xia] *nf* meteorology
meter [me'ter] *vt* (*colocar*) to put, place; (*introducir*) to put in, insert; (*involucrar*) to involve; (*causar*) to make, cause; **meterse** *vr*: **~se en** to go into, enter; (*fig*) to interfere in, meddle in; **~se a** to start; **~se a escritor** to become a writer; **~se con uno** to provoke sb, pick a quarrel with sb
meticuloso, -a [metiku'loso, a] *adj* meticulous, thorough
metódico, -a [me'toðiko, a] *adj* methodical
método ['metoðo] *nm* method
metralleta [metra'ʎeta] *nf* sub-machine-gun
métrico, -a ['metriko, a] *adj* metric
metro ['metro] *nm* metre; (*tren*) underground (BRIT), subway (US)
metrosexual [metrosek'swal] *adj, nm* metrosexual
mexicano, -a [mexi'kano, a] *adj, nm/f* Mexican
México ['mexiko] *nm* Mexico; **Ciudad de ~** Mexico City
mezcla ['meθkla] *nf* mixture; **mezcladora** (MÉX) *nf* (*tb*: **mezcladora de cemento**) cement mixer; **mezclar** *vt* to mix (up); **mezclarse** *vr* to mix, mingle; **mezclarse en** to get mixed up in, get involved in
mezquino, -a [meθ'kino, a] *adj* mean
mezquita [meθ'kita] *nf* mosque
mg. *abr* (= *miligramo*) mg
mi [mi] *adj pos* my ▷*nm* (*Mús*) E
mí [mi] *pron* me; myself
mía *pron V* **mío**
michelín [mitʃe'lin] (*fam*) *nm* (*de grasa*) spare tyre
microbio [mi'kroβjo] *nm* microbe
micrófono [mi'krofono] *nm* microphone
microondas [mikro'ondas] *nm inv* (*tb*: **horno ~**) microwave (oven)
microscopio [mikro'skopjo] *nm* microscope
miedo ['mjeðo] *nm* fear; (*nerviosismo*) apprehension, nervousness; **tener ~** to be afraid; **de ~** wonderful, marvellous; **hace un frío de ~** (*fam*) it's terribly cold; **miedoso, -a** *adj* fearful, timid
miel [mjel] *nf* honey
miembro ['mjembro] *nm* limb; (*socio*) member; **miembro viril** penis
mientras ['mjentras] *conj* while; (*duración*) as long as ▷*adv* meanwhile; **~ tanto** meanwhile
miércoles ['mjerkoles] *nm inv* Wednesday
mierda ['mjerða] (*fam!*) *nf* shit (!)
miga ['miɣa] *nf* crumb; (*fig*: *meollo*) essence; **hacer buenas ~s** (*fam*) to get on well
mil [mil] *num* thousand; **dos ~ libras** two thousand pounds
milagro [mi'laɣro] *nm* miracle; **milagroso, -a** *adj* miraculous
milésima [mi'lesima] *nf* (*de segundo*) thousandth
mili ['mili] (ESP: *fam*) *nf*: **hacer la ~** to do one's military service
milímetro [mi'limetro] *nm* millimetre
militante [mili'tante] *adj* militant
militar [mili'tar] *adj* military ▷*nmf* soldier ▷*vi* (*Mil*) to serve; (*en un partido*) to be a member
milla ['miʎa] *nf* mile
millar [mi'ʎar] *nm* thousand
millón [mi'ʎon] *num* million; **millonario, -a** *nm/f* millionaire
milusos [mi'lusos] (MÉX) *nm inv* odd-job man
mimar [mi'mar] *vt* to spoil, pamper
mimbre ['mimbre] *nm* wicker
mímica ['mimika] *nf* (*para comunicarse*) sign language; (*imitación*) mimicry
mimo ['mimo] *nm* (*caricia*) caress; (*de niño*)

m

spoiling; (*Teatro*) mime; (*: actor*) mime artist
mina ['mina] *nf* mine
mineral [mine'ral] *adj* mineral ▷ *nm* (*Geo*) mineral; (*mena*) ore
minero, -a [mi'nero, a] *adj* mining *cpd* ▷ *nm/f* miner
miniatura [minja'tura] *adj inv*, *nf* miniature
minidisco [mini'disko] *nm* MiniDisc®
minifalda [mini'falda] *nf* miniskirt
mínimo, -a ['minimo, a] *adj*, *nm* minimum
minino, -a [mi'nino, a] (*fam*) *nm/f* puss, pussy
ministerio [minis'terjo] *nm* Ministry; **Ministerio de Hacienda/de Asuntos Exteriores** Treasury (BRIT), Treasury Department (US)/Foreign Office (BRIT), State Department (US)
ministro, -a [mi'nistro, a] *nm/f* minister
minoría [mino'ria] *nf* minority
minúscula [mi'nuskula] *nf* small letter
minúsculo, -a [mi'nuskulo, a] *adj* tiny, minute
minusválido, -a [minus'βaliðo, a] *adj* (physically) handicapped ▷ *nm/f* (physically) handicapped person
minuta [mi'nuta] *nf* (*de comida*) menu
minutero [minu'tero] *nm* minute hand
minuto [mi'nuto] *nm* minute
mío, -a ['mio, a] *pron*: **el ~/la mía** mine; **un amigo ~** a friend of mine; **lo ~** what is mine
miope [mi'ope] *adj* short-sighted
mira ['mira] *nf* (*de arma*) sight(s) (*pl*); (*fig*) aim, intention
mirada [mi'raða] *nf* look, glance; (*expresión*) look, expression; **clavar la ~ en** to stare at; **echar una ~ a** to glance at
mirado, -a [mi'raðo, a] *adj* (*sensato*) sensible; (*considerado*) considerate; **bien/mal ~** (*estimado*) well/not well thought of; **bien ~ ...** all things considered ...
mirador [mira'ðor] *nm* viewpoint, vantage point
mirar [mi'rar] *vt* to look at; (*observar*) to watch; (*considerar*) to consider, think over; (*vigilar, cuidar*) to watch, look after ▷ *vi* to look; (*Arq*) to face; **mirarse** *vr* (*dos personas*) to look at each other; **~ bien/mal** to think highly of/have a poor opinion of; **~se al espejo** to look at o.s. in the mirror
mirilla [mi'riʎa] *nf* spyhole, peephole
mirlo ['mirlo] *nm* blackbird
misa ['misa] *nf* mass
miserable [mise'raβle] *adj* (*avaro*) mean, stingy; (*nimio*) miserable, paltry; (*lugar*) squalid; (*fam*) vile, despicable ▷ *nmf* (*malvado*) rogue
miseria [mi'serja] *nf* (*pobreza*) poverty; (*tacañería*) meanness, stinginess; (*condiciones*) squalor; **una ~** a pittance
misericordia [miseri'korðja] *nf* (*compasión*) compassion, pity; (*piedad*) mercy
misil [mi'sil] *nm* missile
misión [mi'sjon] *nf* mission; **misionero, -a** *nm/f* missionary
mismo, -a ['mismo, a] *adj* (*semejante*) same; (*después de pron*) -self; (*para enfásis*) very ▷ *adv*: **aquí/hoy ~** right here/this very day; **ahora ~** right now ▷ *conj*: **lo ~ que** just like *o* as; **el ~ traje** the same suit; **en ese ~ momento** at that very moment; **vino el ~ ministro** the minister himself came; **yo ~ lo vi** I saw it myself; **lo ~** the same (thing); **da lo ~** it's all the same; **quedamos en las mismas** we're no further forward; **por lo ~** for the same reason
misterio [mis'terjo] *nm* mystery; **misterioso, -a** *adj* mysterious
mitad [mi'tað] *nf* (*medio*) half; (*centro*) middle; **a ~ de precio** (at) half-price; **en** *o* **a ~ del camino** halfway along the road; **cortar por la ~** to cut through the middle
mitin ['mitin] (*pl* **mítines**) *nm* meeting
mito ['mito] *nm* myth
mixto, -a ['miksto, a] *adj* mixed
ml. *abr* (= *mililitro*) ml
mm. *abr* (= *milímetro*) mm
mobiliario [moβi'ljarjo] *nm* furniture
mochila [mo'tʃila] *nf* rucksack (BRIT), back-pack
moco ['moko] *nm* mucus; **mocos** *nmpl* (*fam*) snot; **limpiarse los ~s de la nariz** (*fam*) to wipe one's nose
moda ['moða] *nf* fashion; (*estilo*) style; **a la** *o* **de ~** in fashion, fashionable; **pasado de ~** out of fashion
modales [mo'ðales] *nmpl* manners
modelar [moðe'lar] *vt* to model
modelo [mo'ðelo] *adj inv*, *nmf* model
módem ['moðem] *nm* (*Inform*) modem
moderado, -a [moðe'raðo, a] *adj* moderate
moderar [moðe'rar] *vt* to moderate; (*violencia*) to restrain, control; (*velocidad*) to reduce; **moderarse** *vr* to restrain o.s., control o.s.
modernizar [moðerni'θar] *vt* to modernize
moderno, -a [mo'ðerno, a] *adj* modern; (*actual*) present-day
modestia [mo'ðestja] *nf* modesty; **modesto, -a** *adj* modest
modificar [moðifi'kar] *vt* to modify
modisto, -a [mo'ðisto, a] *nm/f* (*diseñador*) couturier, designer; (*que confecciona*)

dressmaker
modo ['moðo] *nm* way, manner; (*Mús*) mode; **modos** *nmpl* manners; **de ningún ~** in no way; **de todos ~s** at any rate; **modo de empleo** directions *pl* (for use)
mofarse [mo'farse] *vr*: **~ de** to mock, scoff at
mofle ['mofle] (MÉX, CAM) *nm* silencer (BRIT), muffler (US)
mogollón [moɣo'ʎon] (ESP: *fam*) *adv* a hell of a lot
moho ['moo] *nm* mould, mildew; (*en metal*) rust
mojar [mo'xar] *vt* to wet; (*humedecer*) to damp(en), moisten; (*calar*) to soak; **mojarse** *vr* to get wet
molcajete [molka'xete] (MÉX) *nm* mortar
molde ['molde] *nm* mould; (*Costura*) pattern; (*fig*) model; **moldeado** *nm* soft perm; **moldear** *vt* to mould
mole ['mole] *nf* mass, bulk; (*edificio*) pile
moler [mo'ler] *vt* to grind, crush
molestar [moles'tar] *vt* to bother; (*fastidiar*) to annoy; (*incomodar*) to inconvenience, put out ▷ *vi* to be a nuisance; **molestarse** *vr* to bother; (*incomodarse*) to go to trouble; (*ofenderse*) to take offence; **¿(no) te molesta si ...?** do you mind if ...?

No confundir **molestar** con la palabra inglesa *molest*.

molestia [mo'lestja] *nf* bother, trouble; (*incomodidad*) inconvenience; (*Med*) discomfort; **es una ~** it's a nuisance; **molesto, -a** *adj* (*que fastidia*) annoying; (*incómodo*) inconvenient; (*inquieto*) uncomfortable, ill at ease; (*enfadado*) annoyed
molido, -a [mo'liðo, a] *adj*: **estar ~** (*fig*) to be exhausted *o* dead beat
molinillo [moli'niʎo] *nm* hand mill; **molinillo de café** coffee grinder
molino [mo'lino] *nm* (*edificio*) mill; (*máquina*) grinder
momentáneo, -a [momen'taneo, a] *adj* momentary
momento [mo'mento] *nm* moment; **de ~** at *o* for the moment
momia ['momja] *nf* mummy
monarca [mo'narka] *nmf* monarch, ruler; **monarquía** *nf* monarchy
monasterio [monas'terjo] *nm* monastery
mondar [mon'dar] *vt* to peel; **mondarse** *vr* (ESP): **~se de risa** (*fam*) to split one's sides laughing
mondongo [mon'dongo] (LAM) *nm* tripe
moneda [mo'neða] *nf* (*tipo de dinero*) currency, money; (*pieza*) coin; **una ~ de 2 euros** a 2 euro piece; **monedero** *nm* purse
monitor, a [moni'tor, a] *nm/f* instructor, coach ▷ *nm* (*TV*) set; (*Inform*) monitor
monja ['monxa] *nf* nun
monje ['monxe] *nm* monk
mono, -a ['mono, a] *adj* (*bonito*) lovely, pretty; (*gracioso*) nice, charming ▷ *nm/f* monkey, ape ▷ *nm* dungarees *pl*; (*overoles*) overalls *pl*
monopatín [monopa'tin] *nm* skateboard
monopolio [mono'poljo] *nm* monopoly; **monopolizar** *vt* to monopolize
monótono, -a [mo'notono, a] *adj* monotonous
monstruo ['monstrwo] *nm* monster ▷ *adj inv* fantastic; **monstruoso, -a** *adj* monstrous
montaje [mon'taxe] *nm* assembly; (*Teatro*) décor; (*Cine*) montage
montaña [mon'taɲa] *nf* (*monte*) mountain; (*sierra*) mountains *pl*, mountainous area; **montaña rusa** roller coaster; **montañero, -a** *nm/f* mountaineer; **montañismo** *nm* mountaineering
montar [mon'tar] *vt* (*subir a*) to mount, get on; (*Tec*) to assemble, put together; (*negocio*) to set up; (*arma*) to cock; (*colocar*) to lift on to; (*Culin*) to beat ▷ *vi* to mount, get on; (*sobresalir*) to overlap; **~ en bicicleta** to ride a bicycle; **~ en cólera** to get angry; **~ a caballo** to ride, go horseriding
monte ['monte] *nm* (*montaña*) mountain; (*bosque*) woodland; (*área sin cultivar*) wild area, wild country; **monte de piedad** pawnshop
montón [mon'ton] *nm* heap, pile; (*fig*): **un ~ de** heaps *o* lots of
monumento [monu'mento] *nm* monument
moño ['moɲo] *nm* bun
moqueta [mo'keta] *nf* fitted carpet
mora ['mora] *nf* blackberry; *V tb* **moro**
morado, -a [mo'raðo, a] *adj* purple, violet ▷ *nm* bruise
moral [mo'ral] *adj* moral ▷ *nf* (*ética*) ethics *pl*; (*moralidad*) morals *pl*, morality; (*ánimo*) morale
moraleja [mora'lexa] *nf* moral
morboso, -a [mor'βoso, a] *adj* morbid
morcilla [mor'θiʎa] *nf* blood sausage ≈ black pudding (BRIT)
mordaza [mor'ðaθa] *nf* (*para la boca*) gag; (*Tec*) clamp
morder [mor'ðer] *vt* to bite; (*fig: consumir*) to eat away, eat into; **mordisco** *nm* bite
moreno, -a [mo'reno, a] *adj* (*color*) (dark) brown; (*de tez*) dark; (*de pelo moreno*) dark-

m

haired; (*negro*) black
morfina [mor'fina] *nf* morphine
moribundo, -a [mori'βundo, a] *adj* dying
morir [mo'rir] *vi* to die; (*fuego*) to die down; (*luz*) to go out; **morirse** *vr* to die; (*fig*) to be dying; **murió en un accidente** he was killed in an accident; **~se por algo** to be dying for sth
moro, -a ['moro, a] *adj* Moorish ▷ *nm/f* Moor
moroso, -a [mo'roso, a] *nm/f* bad debtor, defaulter
morraña [mo'raɲa] (MÉX) *nf* (*cambio*) small *o* loose change
morro ['morro] *nm* (*Zool*) snout, nose; (*Auto, Aviac*) nose
morsa ['morsa] *nf* walrus
mortadela [morta'ðela] *nf* mortadella
mortal [mor'tal] *adj* mortal; (*golpe*) deadly; **mortalidad** *nf* mortality
mortero [mor'tero] *nm* mortar
mosca ['moska] *nf* fly
Moscú [mos'ku] *n* Moscow
mosquearse [moske'arse] (*fam*) *vr* (*enojarse*) to get cross; (*ofenderse*) to take offence
mosquitero [moski'tero] *nm* mosquito net
mosquito [mos'kito] *nm* mosquito
mostaza [mos'taθa] *nf* mustard
mosto ['mosto] *nm* (unfermented) grape juice
mostrador [mostra'ðor] *nm* (*de tienda*) counter; (*de café*) bar
mostrar [mos'trar] *vt* to show; (*exhibir*) to display, exhibit; (*explicar*) to explain; **mostrarse** *vr*: **~se amable** to be kind; to prove to be kind; **no se muestra muy inteligente** he doesn't seem (to be) very intelligent
mota ['mota] *nf* speck, tiny piece; (*en diseño*) dot
mote ['mote] *nm* nickname
motín [mo'tin] *nm* (*del pueblo*) revolt, rising; (*del ejército*) mutiny
motivar [moti'βar] *vt* (*causar*) to cause, motivate; (*explicar*) to explain, justify; **motivo** *nm* motive, reason
moto ['moto] (*fam*) *nf* = **motocicleta**
motocicleta [motoθi'kleta] *nf* motorbike (BRIT), motorcycle
motoneta [moto'neta] (CS) *nf* scooter
motor [mo'tor] *nm* motor, engine; **motor a chorro** *o* **de reacción/de explosión** jet engine/internal combustion engine
motora [mo'tora] *nf* motorboat
movedizo, -a *adj* V **arena**
mover [mo'βer] *vt* to move; (*cabeza*) to shake; (*accionar*) to drive; (*fig*) to cause, provoke; **moverse** *vr* to move; (*fig*) to get a move on
móvil ['moβil] *adj* mobile; (*pieza de máquina*) moving; (*mueble*) movable ▷ *nm* (*motivo*) motive; (*teléfono*) mobile
movimiento [moβi'mjento] *nm* movement; (*Tec*) motion; (*actividad*) activity
mozo, -a ['moθo, a] *adj* (*joven*) young ▷ *nm/f* youth, young man/girl; (CS: *mesero*) waiter/waitress
MP3 *nm* MP3; **reproductor (de) ~** MP3 player
mucama [mu'kama] (RPL) *nf* maid
muchacho, -a [mu'tʃatʃo, a] *nm/f* (*niño*) boy/girl; (*criado*) servant; (*criada*) maid
muchedumbre [mutʃe'ðumbre] *nf* crowd

PALABRA CLAVE

mucho, -a ['mutʃo, a] *adj* **1** (*cantidad*) a lot of, much; (*número*) lots of, a lot of, many; **mucho dinero** a lot of money; **hace mucho calor** it's very hot; **muchas amigas** lots *o* a lot of friends
2 (*sg*: *grande*): **ésta es mucha casa para él** this house is much too big for him
▷ *pron*: **tengo mucho que hacer** I've got a lot to do; **muchos dicen que ...** a lot of people say that ...; *V tb* **tener**
▷ *adv* **1 me gusta mucho** I like it a lot; **lo siento mucho** I'm very sorry; **come mucho** he eats a lot; **¿te vas a quedar mucho?** are you going to be staying long?
2 (*respuesta*) very; **¿estás cansado? – ¡mucho!** are you tired? – very!
3 (*locuciones*): **como mucho** at (the) most; **con mucho: el mejor con mucho** by far the best; **ni mucho menos: no es rico ni mucho menos** he's far from being rich
4: **por mucho que: por mucho que le creas** no matter how *o* however much you believe her

muda ['muða] *nf* change of clothes
mudanza [mu'ðanθa] *nf* (*de casa*) move
mudar [mu'ðar] *vt* to change; (*Zool*) to shed ▷ *vi* to change; **mudarse** *vr* (*ropa*) to change; **~se de casa** to move house
mudo, -a ['muðo, a] *adj* dumb; (*callado, Cine*) silent
mueble ['mweβle] *nm* piece of furniture; **muebles** *nmpl* furniture *sg*
mueca ['mweka] *nf* face, grimace; **hacer ~s a** to make faces at
muela ['mwela] *nf* back tooth; **muela del**

juicio wisdom tooth
muelle ['mweʎe] *nm* spring; (*Náut*) wharf; (*malecón*) pier
muero *etc vb V* **morir**
muerte ['mwerte] *nf* death; (*homicidio*) murder; **dar ~ a** to kill
muerto, -a ['mwerto, a] *pp de* **morir** ▷*adj* dead ▷*nm/f* dead man/woman; (*difunto*) deceased; (*cadáver*) corpse; **estar ~ de cansancio** to be dead tired; **Día de los Muertos** (*MÉX*) All Souls' Day

DÍA DE LOS MUERTOS

All Souls' Day (or "Day of the Dead") in Mexico coincides with All Saints' Day, which is celebrated in the Catholic countries of Latin America on November 1st and 2nd. All Souls' Day is actually a celebration which begins in the evening of October 31st and continues until November 2nd. It is a combination of the Catholic tradition of honouring the Christian saints and martyrs, and the ancient Mexican or Aztec traditions, in which death was not something sinister. For this reason all the dead are honoured by bringing offerings of food, flowers and candles to the cemetery.

muestra ['mwestra] *nf* (*señal*) indication, sign; (*demostración*) demonstration; (*prueba*) proof; (*estadística*) sample; (*modelo*) model, pattern; (*testimonio*) token
muestro *etc vb V* **mostrar**
muevo *etc vb V* **mover**
mugir [mu'xir] *vi* (*vaca*) to moo
mugre ['muɣre] *nf* dirt, filth
mujer [mu'xer] *nf* woman; (*esposa*) wife; **mujeriego** *nm* womanizer
mula ['mula] *nf* mule
muleta [mu'leta] *nf* (*para andar*) crutch; (*Taur*) *stick with red cape attached*
multa ['multa] *nf* fine; **poner una ~ a** to fine; **multar** *vt* to fine
multicines [multi'θines] *nmpl* multiscreen cinema *sg*
multinacional [multinaθjo'nal] *nf* multinational
múltiple ['multiple] *adj* multiple; (*pl*) many, numerous
multiplicar [multipli'kar] *vt* (*Mat*) to multiply; (*fig*) to increase; **multiplicarse** *vr* (*Bio*) to multiply; (*fig*) to be everywhere at once
multitud [multi'tuð] *nf* (*muchedumbre*) crowd; **~ de** lots of
mundial [mun'djal] *adj* world-wide, universal; (*guerra, récord*) world *cpd*
mundo ['mundo] *nm* world; **todo el ~** everybody; **tener ~** to be experienced, know one's way around
munición [muni'θjon] *nf* ammunition
municipal [muniθi'pal] *adj* municipal, local
municipio [muni'θipjo] *nm* (*ayuntamiento*) town council, corporation; (*territorio administrativo*) town, municipality
muñeca [mu'ɲeka] *nf* (*Anat*) wrist; (*juguete*) doll
muñeco [mu'ɲeko] *nm* (*figura*) figure; (*marioneta*) puppet; (*fig*) puppet, pawn
mural [mu'ral] *adj* mural, wall *cpd* ▷*nm* mural
muralla [mu'raʎa] *nf* (city) wall(s) (*pl*)
murciélago [mur'θjelaɣo] *nm* bat
murmullo [mur'muʎo] *nm* murmur(ing); (*cuchicheo*) whispering
murmurar [murmu'rar] *vi* to murmur, whisper; (*cotillear*) to gossip
muro ['muro] *nm* wall
muscular [musku'lar] *adj* muscular
músculo ['muskulo] *nm* muscle
museo [mu'seo] *nm* museum; **museo de arte** art gallery
musgo ['musɣo] *nm* moss
música ['musika] *nf* music; *V tb* **músico**
músico, -a ['musiko, a] *adj* musical ▷*nm/f* musician
muslo ['muslo] *nm* thigh
musulmán, -ana [musul'man, ana] *nm/f* Moslem
mutación [muta'θjon] *nf* (*Bio*) mutation; (*cambio*) (sudden) change
mutilar [muti'lar] *vt* to mutilate; (*a una persona*) to maim
mutuo, -a ['mutwo, a] *adj* mutual
muy [mwi] *adv* very; (*demasiado*) too; **M~ Señor mío** Dear Sir; **~ de noche** very late at night; **eso es ~ de él** that's just like him

N *abr* (= *norte*) N
nabo ['naβo] *nm* turnip
nacer [na'θer] *vi* to be born; (*de huevo*) to hatch; (*vegetal*) to sprout; (*río*) to rise; **nací en Barcelona** I was born in Barcelona; **nacido, -a** *adj* born; **recién nacido** newborn; **nacimiento** *nm* birth; (*de Navidad*) Nativity; (*de río*) source
nación [na'θjon] *nf* nation; **nacional** *adj* national; **nacionalismo** *nm* nationalism
nada ['naða] *pron* nothing ▷ *adv* not at all, in no way; **no decir ~** to say nothing, not to say anything; **~ más** nothing else; **de ~** don't mention it
nadador, a [naða'ðor, a] *nm/f* swimmer
nadar [na'ðar] *vi* to swim
nadie ['naðje] *pron* nobody, no-one; **~ habló** nobody spoke; **no había ~** there was nobody there, there wasn't anybody there
nado ['naðo] **a nado**: *adv*: **pasar a ~** to swim across
nafta ['nafta] (RPL) *nf* petrol (BRIT), gas (US)
naipe ['naipe] *nm* (playing) card; **naipes** *nmpl* cards
nalgas ['nalɣas] *nfpl* buttocks
nalguear [nalɣe'ar] (MÉX, CAM) *vt* to spank
nana ['nana] (ESP) *nf* lullaby
naranja [na'ranxa] *adj inv, nf* orange; **media ~** (*fam*) better half; **naranjada** *nf* orangeade; **naranjo** *nm* orange tree
narciso [nar'θiso] *nm* narcissus
narcótico, -a [nar'kotiko, a] *adj, nm* narcotic; **narcotizar** *vt* to drug; **narcotráfico** *nm* drug trafficking *o* running
nariz [na'riθ] *nf* nose; **nariz chata/ respingona** snub/turned-up nose
narración [narra'θjon] *nf* narration
narrar [na'rrar] *vt* to narrate, recount; **narrativa** *nf* narrative
nata ['nata] *nf* cream; **nata montada** whipped cream
natación [nata'θjon] *nf* swimming
natal [na'tal] *adj*: **ciudad ~** home town; **natalidad** *nf* birth rate
natillas [na'tiʎas] *nfpl* custard *sg*
nativo, -a [na'tiβo, a] *adj, nm/f* native
natural [natu'ral] *adj* natural; (*fruta etc*) fresh ▷ *nmf* native ▷ *nm* (*disposición*) nature
naturaleza [natura'leθa] *nf* nature; (*género*) nature, kind; **naturaleza muerta** still life
naturalmente [natural'mente] *adv* (*de modo natural*) in a natural way; **¡~!** of course!
naufragar [naufra'ɣar] *vi* to sink; **naufragio** *nm* shipwreck
nauseabundo, -a [nausea'βundo, a] *adj* nauseating, sickening
náuseas ['nauseas] *nfpl* nausea *sg*; **me da ~** it makes me feel sick
náutico, -a ['nautiko, a] *adj* nautical
navaja [na'βaxa] *nf* knife; (*de barbero, peluquero*) razor
naval [na'βal] *adj* naval
Navarra [na'βarra] *n* Navarre
nave ['naβe] *nf* (*barco*) ship, vessel; (*Arq*) nave; **nave espacial** spaceship; **nave industrial** factory premises *pl*
navegador [naβeɣa'ðor] *nm* (*Inform*) browser
navegante [naβe'ɣante] *nmf* navigator
navegar [naβe'ɣar] *vi* (*barco*) to sail; (*avión*) to fly; **~ por Internet** to surf the Net
Navidad [naβi'ðað] *nf* Christmas; **Navidades** *nfpl* Christmas time; **¡Feliz ~!** Merry Christmas!; **navideño, -a** *adj* Christmas *cpd*
nazca *etc vb V* **nacer**
nazi ['naθi] *adj, nmf* Nazi
NE *abr* (= *nor(d)este*) NE
neblina [ne'βlina] *nf* mist
necesario, -a [neθe'sarjo, a] *adj* necessary
neceser [neθe'ser] *nm* toilet bag; (*bolsa grande*) holdall
necesidad [neθesi'ðað] *nf* need; (*lo inevitable*) necessity; (*miseria*) poverty; **en caso de ~** in case of need *o* emergency; **hacer sus ~es** to relieve o.s.
necesitado, -a [neθesi'taðo, a] *adj* needy, poor; **~ de** in need of
necesitar [neθesi'tar] *vt* to need, require
necio, -a ['neθjo, a] *adj* foolish
nectarina [nekta'rina] *nf* nectarine
nefasto, -a [ne'fasto, a] *adj* ill-fated, unlucky
negación [neɣa'θjon] *nf* negation;

(*rechazo*) refusal, denial
negar [ne'ɣar] *vt* (*renegar, rechazar*) to refuse; (*prohibir*) to refuse, deny; (*desmentir*) to deny; **negarse** *vr*: **~se a** to refuse to
negativa [neɣa'tiβa] *nf* negative; (*rechazo*) refusal, denial
negativo, -a [neɣa'tiβo, a] *adj, nm* negative
negociante [neɣo'θjante] *nmf* businessman/woman
negociar [neɣo'θjar] *vt, vi* to negotiate; **~ en** to deal *o* trade in
negocio [ne'ɣoθjo] *nm* (*Com*) business; (*asunto*) affair, business; (*operación comercial*) deal, transaction; (*lugar*) place of business; **los ~s** business *sg*; **hacer ~** to do business
negra ['neɣra] *nf* (*Mús*) crotchet; *V tb* **negro**
negro, -a ['neɣro, a] *adj* black; (*suerte*) awful ▷ *nm* black ▷ *nm/f* black man/woman
nene, -a ['nene, a] *nm/f* baby, small child
neón [ne'on] *nm*: **luces/lámpara de ~** neon lights/lamp
neoyorquino, -a [neojor'kino, a] *adj* (of) New York
nervio ['nerβjo] *nm* nerve; **nerviosismo** *nm* nervousness, nerves *pl*; **nervioso, -a** *adj* nervous
neto, -a ['neto, a] *adj* net
neumático, -a [neu'matiko, a] *adj* pneumatic ▷ *nm* (ESP) tyre (BRIT), tire (US); **neumático de recambio** spare tyre
neurólogo, -a [neu'roloɣo, a] *nm/f* neurologist
neurona [neu'rona] *nf* nerve cell
neutral [neu'tral] *adj* neutral; **neutralizar** *vt* to neutralize; (*contrarrestar*) to counteract
neutro, -a ['neutro, a] *adj* (*Bio, Ling*) neuter
neutrón [neu'tron] *nm* neutron
nevada [ne'βaða] *nf* snowstorm; (*caída de nieve*) snowfall
nevar [ne'βar] *vi* to snow
nevera [ne'βera] (ESP) *nf* refrigerator (BRIT), icebox (US)
nevería [neβe'ria] (MÉX) *nf* ice-cream parlour
nexo ['nekso] *nm* link, connection
ni [ni] *conj* nor, neither; (*tb*: **~ siquiera**) not ... even; **~ aunque que** not even if; **~ blanco ~ negro** neither white nor black
Nicaragua [nika'raɣwa] *nf* Nicaragua; **nicaragüense** *adj, nmf* Nicaraguan
nicho ['nitʃo] *nm* niche
nicotina [niko'tina] *nf* nicotine
nido ['niðo] *nm* nest
niebla ['njeβla] *nf* fog; (*neblina*) mist
niego *etc vb V* **negar**
nieto, -a ['njeto, a] *nm/f* grandson/daughter; **nietos** *nmpl* grandchildren
nieve *etc* ['njeβe] *vb V* **nevar** ▷ *nf* snow; (MÉX: *helado*) ice cream
NIF *nm abr* (= *Número de Identificación Fiscal*) *personal identification number used for financial and tax purposes*
ninfa ['ninfa] *nf* nymph
ningún *adj V* **ninguno**
ninguno, -a [nin'guno, a] (*adj* **ningún**) no *pron* (*nadie*) nobody; (*ni uno*) none, not one; (*ni uno ni otro*) neither; **de ninguna manera** by no means, not at all
niña ['niɲa] *nf* (*Anat*) pupil; *V tb* **niño**
niñera [ni'ɲera] *nf* nursemaid, nanny
niñez [ni'ɲeθ] *nf* childhood; (*infancia*) infancy
niño, -a ['niɲo, a] *adj* (*joven*) young; (*inmaduro*) immature ▷ *nm/f* child, boy/girl
nipón, -ona [ni'pon, ona] *adj, nm/f* Japanese
níquel ['nikel] *nm* nickel
níspero ['nispero] *nm* medlar
nítido, -a ['nitiðo, a] *adj* clear; sharp
nitrato [ni'trato] *nm* nitrate
nitrógeno [ni'troxeno] *nm* nitrogen
nivel [ni'βel] *nm* (*Geo*) level; (*norma*) level, standard; (*altura*) height; **nivel de aceite** oil level; **nivel de aire** spirit level; **nivel de vida** standard of living; **nivelar** *vt* to level out; (*fig*) to even up; (*Com*) to balance
no [no] *adv* no; not; (*con verbo*) not ▷ *excl* no!; **~ tengo nada** I don't have anything, I have nothing; **~ es el mío** it's not mine; **ahora ~** not now; **¿~ lo sabes?** don't you know?; **~ mucho** not much; **~ bien termine, lo entregaré** as soon as I finish, I'll hand it over; **~ más: ayer ~ más** just yesterday; **¡pase ~ más!** come in!; **¡a que ~ lo sabes!** I bet you don't know!; **¡cómo ~!** of course!; **la ~ intervención** non-intervention
noble ['noβle] *adj, nmf* noble; **nobleza** *nf* nobility
noche ['notʃe] *nf* night, night-time; (*la tarde*) evening; **de ~, por la ~** at night; **es de ~** it's dark; **Noche de San Juan** *see below*

NOCHE DE SAN JUAN

The **Noche de San Juan** on the 24th June is a **fiesta** coinciding with the summer solstice and which has taken the place of other ancient pagan festivals. Traditionally fire plays a major part in these festivities with celebrations and dancing taking place around bonfires in towns and villages across the country.

n

nochebuena [notʃe'βwena] *nf* Christmas Eve

NOCHEBUENA

Traditional Christmas celebrations in Spanish-speaking countries mainly take place on the night of **Nochebuena**, Christmas Eve. Families gather together for a large meal and the more religiously inclined attend Midnight Mass. While presents are traditionally given by **los Reyes Magos** on the 6th January, more and more people are exchanging gifts on Christmas Eve.

nochevieja [notʃe'βjexa] *nf* New Year's Eve
nocivo, -a [no'θiβo, a] *adj* harmful
noctámbulo, -a [nok'tambulo, a] *nm/f* sleepwalker
nocturno, -a [nok'turno, a] *adj* (*de la noche*) nocturnal, night *cpd*; (*de la tarde*) evening *cpd* ▷*nm* nocturne
nogal [no'ɣal] *nm* walnut tree
nómada ['nomaða] *adj* nomadic ▷*nmf* nomad
nombrar [nom'brar] *vt* (*designar*) to name; (*mencionar*) to mention; (*dar puesto a*) to appoint
nombre ['nombre] *nm* name; (*sustantivo*) noun; **~ y apellidos** name in full; **poner ~ a** to call, name; **nombre común/propio** common/proper noun; **nombre de pila/de soltera** Christian/maiden name
nómina ['nomina] *nf* (*lista*) payroll; (*hoja*) payslip
nominal [nomi'nal] *adj* nominal
nominar [nomi'nar] *vt* to nominate
nominativo, -a [nomina'tiβo, a] *adj* (*Com*): **cheque ~ a X** cheque made out to X
nordeste [nor'ðeste] *adj* north-east, north-eastern, north-easterly ▷*nm* north-east
nórdico, -a ['norðiko, a] *adj* Nordic
noreste [no'reste] *adj, nm* = **nordeste**
noria ['norja] *nf* (*Agr*) waterwheel; (*de carnaval*) big (BRIT) *o* Ferris (US) wheel
norma ['norma] *nf* rule (of thumb)
normal [nor'mal] *adj* (*corriente*) normal; (*habitual*) usual, natural; **normalizarse** *vr* to return to normal; **normalmente** *adv* normally
normativa [norma'tiβa] *nf* (set of) rules *pl*, regulations *pl*
noroeste [noro'este] *adj* north-west, north-western, north-westerly ▷*nm* north-west
norte ['norte] *adj* north, northern, northerly ▷*nm* north; (*fig*) guide
norteamericano, -a [norteameri'kano, a] *adj, nm/f* (North) American
Noruega [no'rweɣa] *nf* Norway
noruego, -a [no'rweɣo, a] *adj, nm/f* Norwegian
nos [nos] *pron* (*directo*) us; (*indirecto*) us; to us; for us; from us; (*reflexivo*) (to) ourselves; (*recíproco*) (to) each other; **~ levantamos a las 7** we get up at 7
nosotros, -as [no'sotros, as] *pron* (*sujeto*) we; (*después de prep*) us
nostalgia [nos'talxja] *nf* nostalgia
nota ['nota] *nf* note; (*Escol*) mark
notable [no'taβle] *adj* notable; (*Escol*) outstanding
notar [no'tar] *vt* to notice, note; **notarse** *vr* to be obvious; **se nota que ...** one observes that ...
notario [no'tarjo] *nm* notary
noticia [no'tiθja] *nf* (*información*) piece of news; **las ~s** the news *sg*; **tener ~s de algn** to hear from sb

No confundir **noticia** con la palabra inglesa *notice*.

noticiero [noti'θjero] (LAM) *nm* news bulletin
notificar [notifi'kar] *vt* to notify, inform
notorio, -a [no'torjo, a] *adj* (*público*) well-known; (*evidente*) obvious
novato, -a [no'βato, a] *adj* inexperienced ▷*nm/f* beginner, novice
novecientos, -as [noβe'θjentos, as] *num* nine hundred
novedad [noβe'ðað] *nf* (*calidad de nuevo*) newness; (*noticia*) piece of news; (*cambio*) change, (new) development
novel [no'βel] *adj* new; (*inexperto*) inexperienced ▷*nmf* beginner
novela [no'βela] *nf* novel
noveno, -a [no'βeno, a] *adj* ninth
noventa [no'βenta] *num* ninety
novia *nf V* **novio**
novicio, -a [no'βiθjo, a] *nm/f* novice
noviembre [no'βjembre] *nm* November
novillada [noβi'ʎaða] *nf* (*Taur*) *bullfight with young bulls*; **novillero** *nm* novice bullfighter; **novillo** *nm* young bull, bullock; **hacer novillos** (*fam*) to play truant
novio, -a ['noβjo, a] *nm/f* boyfriend/girlfriend; (*prometido*) fiancé/fiancée; (*recién casado*) bridegroom/bride; **los ~s** the newly-weds
nube ['nuβe] *nf* cloud
nublado, -a [nu'βlaðo, a] *adj* cloudy; **nublarse** *vr* to grow dark
nubosidad [nuβosi'ðað] *nf* cloudiness;

había mucha ~ it was very cloudy
nuca ['nuka] *nf* nape of the neck
nuclear [nukle'ar] *adj* nuclear
núcleo ['nukleo] *nm* (*centro*) core; (*Física*) nucleus; **núcleo urbano** city centre
nudillo [nu'ðiʎo] *nm* knuckle
nudista [nu'ðista] *adj* nudist
nudo ['nuðo] *nm* knot; (*de carreteras*) junction
nuera ['nwera] *nf* daughter-in-law
nuestro, -a ['nwestro, a] *adj pos* our ▷ *pron* ours; **~ padre** our father; **un amigo ~** a friend of ours; **es el ~** it's ours
Nueva York [-jɔrk] *n* New York
Nueva Zelanda [-θe'landa] *nf* New Zealand
nueve ['nweβe] *num* nine
nuevo, -a ['nweβo, a] *adj* (*gen*) new; **de ~** again
nuez [nweθ] *nf* walnut; (*Anat*) Adam's apple; **nuez moscada** nutmeg
nulo, -a ['nulo, a] *adj* (*inepto, torpe*) useless; (*inválido*) (null and) void; (*Deporte*) drawn, tied
núm. *abr* (= *número*) no.
numerar [nume'rar] *vt* to number
número ['numero] *nm* (*gen*) number; (*tamaño: de zapato*) size; (*ejemplar: de diario*) number, issue; **sin ~** numberless, unnumbered; **número atrasado** back number; **número de matrícula/teléfono** registration/telephone number; **número impar/par** odd/even number; **número romano** Roman numeral
numeroso, -a [nume'roso, a] *adj* numerous
nunca ['nunka] *adv* (*jamás*) never; **~ lo pensé** I never thought it; **no viene ~** he never comes; **~ más** never again; **más que ~** more than ever
nupcias ['nupθjas] *nfpl* wedding *sg*, nuptials
nutria ['nutrja] *nf* otter
nutrición [nutri'θjon] *nf* nutrition
nutrir [nu'trir] *vt* (*alimentar*) to nourish; (*dar de comer*) to feed; (*fig*) to strengthen; **nutritivo, -a** *adj* nourishing, nutritious
nylon [ni'lon] *nm* nylon

ñango, -a ['ɲango, a] (MÉX) *adj* puny
ñapa ['ɲapa] (LAM) *nf* extra
ñata ['ɲata] (LAM: *fam*) *nf* nose; *V tb* **ñato**
ñato, -a ['ɲato, a] (LAM) *adj* snub-nosed
ñoñería [ɲoɲe'ria] *nf* insipidness
ñoño, -a ['ɲoɲo, a] *adj* (*fam: tonto*) silly, stupid; (*soso*) insipid; (*persona*) spineless; (ESP: *película, novela*) sentimental

O *abr* (=*oeste*) W
o [o] *conj* or
oasis [o'asis] *nm inv* oasis
obcecarse [oβθe'karse] *vr* to get *o* become stubborn
obedecer [oβeðe'θer] *vt* to obey; **obediente** *adj* obedient
obertura [oβer'tura] *nf* overture
obeso, -a [o'βeso, a] *adj* obese
obispo [o'βispo] *nm* bishop
obituario [oβɪ'twarjo] (LAM) *nm* obituary
objetar [oβxe'tar] *vt, vi* to object
objetivo, -a [oβxe'tiβo, a] *adj, nm* objective
objeto [oβ'xeto] *nm* (*cosa*) object; (*fin*) aim
objetor, a [oβxe'tor, a] *nm/f* objector
obligación [oβliɣa'θjon] *nf* obligation; (*Com*) bond
obligar [oβli'ɣar] *vt* to force; **obligarse** *vr* to bind o.s.; **obligatorio, -a** *adj* compulsory, obligatory
oboe [o'βoe] *nm* oboe
obra ['oβra] *nf* work; (*Arq*) construction, building; (*Teatro*) play; **por ~ de** thanks to (the efforts of); **obra maestra** masterpiece; **obras públicas** public works; **obrar** *vt* to work; (*tener efecto*) to have an effect on ▷ *vi* to act, behave; (*tener efecto*) to have an effect; **la carta obra en su poder** the letter is in his/her possession
obrero, -a [o'βrero, a] *adj* (*clase*) working; (*movimiento*) labour *cpd* ▷ *nm/f* (*gen*) worker; (*sin oficio*) labourer
obsceno, -a [oβs'θeno, a] *adj* obscene
obscu... =**oscu...**
obsequiar [oβse'kjar] *vt* (*ofrecer*) to present with; (*agasajar*) to make a fuss of, lavish attention on; **obsequio** *nm* (*regalo*) gift; (*cortesía*) courtesy, attention
observación [oβserβa'θjon] *nf* observation; (*reflexión*) remark
observador, a [oβserβa'ðor, a] *nm/f* observer
observar [oβser'βar] *vt* to observe; (*anotar*) to notice; **observarse** *vr* to keep to, observe
obsesión [oβse'sjon] *nf* obsession; **obsesivo, -a** *adj* obsessive
obstáculo [oβs'takulo] *nm* obstacle; (*impedimento*) hindrance, drawback
obstante [oβs'tante]: **no ~** *adv* nevertheless
obstinado, -a [oβsti'naðo, a] *adj* obstinate, stubborn
obstinarse [oβsti'narse] *vr* to be obstinate; **~ en** to persist in
obstruir [oβstru'ir] *vt* to obstruct
obtener [oβte'ner] *vt* (*gen*) to obtain; (*premio*) to win
obturador [oβtura'ðor] *nm* (*Foto*) shutter
obvio, -a ['oββjo, a] *adj* obvious
oca ['oka] *nf* (*animal*) goose; (*juego*) ≈ snakes and ladders
ocasión [oka'sjon] *nf* (*oportunidad*) opportunity, chance; (*momento*) occasion, time; (*causa*) cause; **de ~** secondhand; **ocasionar** *vt* to cause
ocaso [o'kaso] *nm* (*fig*) decline
occidente [okθi'ðente] *nm* west
OCDE *nf abr* (=*Organización de Cooperación y Desarrollo Económico*) OECD
océano [o'θeano] *nm* ocean; **Océano Índico** Indian Ocean
ochenta [o'tʃenta] *num* eighty
ocho ['otʃo] *num* eight; **dentro de ~ días** within a week
ocio ['oθjo] *nm* (*tiempo*) leisure; (*pey*) idleness
octavilla [okta'viʎa] *nf* leaflet, pamphlet
octavo, -a [ok'taβo, a] *adj* eighth
octubre [ok'tuβre] *nm* October
oculista [oku'lista] *nmf* oculist
ocultar [okul'tar] *vt* (*esconder*) to hide; (*callar*) to conceal; **oculto, -a** *adj* hidden; (*fig*) secret
ocupación [okupa'θjon] *nf* occupation
ocupado, -a [oku'paðo, a] *adj* (*persona*) busy; (*plaza*) occupied, taken; (*teléfono*) engaged; **ocupar** *vt* (*gen*) to occupy; **ocuparse** *vr*: **ocuparse de** *o* **en** (*gen*) to concern o.s. with; (*cuidar*) to look after
ocurrencia [oku'rrenθja] *nf* (*idea*) bright idea
ocurrir [oku'rrir] *vi* to happen; **ocurrirse** *vr*: **se me ocurrió que ...** it occurred to me that ...
odiar [o'ðjar] *vt* to hate; **odio** *nm* hate, hatred; **odioso, -a** *adj* (*gen*) hateful; (*malo*) nasty

odontólogo, -a [oðon'toloɣo, a] *nm/f* dentist, dental surgeon
oeste [o'este] *nm* west; **una película del ~** a western
ofender [ofen'der] *vt* (*agraviar*) to offend; (*insultar*) to insult; **ofenderse** *vr* to take offence; **ofensa** *nf* offence; **ofensiva** *nf* offensive; **ofensivo, -a** *adj* offensive
oferta [o'ferta] *nf* offer; (*propuesta*) proposal; **la ~ y la demanda** supply and demand; **artículos en ~** goods on offer
oficial [ofi'θjal] *adj* official ▷ *nm* (*Mil*) officer
oficina [ofi'θina] *nf* office; **oficina de correos** post office; **oficina de información** information bureau; **oficina de turismo** tourist office; **oficinista** *nmf* clerk
oficio [o'fiθjo] *nm* (*profesión*) profession; (*puesto*) post; (*Rel*) service; **ser del ~** to be an old hand; **tener mucho ~** to have a lot of experience; **oficio de difuntos** funeral service
ofimática [ofi'matika] *nf* office automation
ofrecer [ofre'θer] *vt* (*dar*) to offer; (*proponer*) to propose; **ofrecerse** *vr* (*persona*) to offer o.s., volunteer; (*situación*) to present itself; **¿qué se le ofrece?, ¿se le ofrece algo?** what can I do for you?, can I get you anything?
ofrecimiento [ofreθi'mjento] *nm* offer
oftalmólogo, -a [oftal'moloɣo, a] *nm/f* ophthalmologist
oída [o'iða] *nf*: **de ~s** by hearsay
oído [o'iðo] *nm* (*Anat*) ear; (*sentido*) hearing
oigo *etc vb V* **oír**
oír [o'ir] *vt* (*gen*) to hear; (*atender a*) to listen to; **¡oiga!** listen!; **~ misa** to attend mass
OIT *nf abr* (= *Organización Internacional del Trabajo*) ILO
ojal [o'xal] *nm* buttonhole
ojalá [oxa'la] *excl* if only (it were so)!, some hope! ▷ *conj* if only ...!, would that ...!; **~ (que) venga hoy** I hope he comes today
ojeada [oxe'aða] *nf* glance
ojera [o'xera] *nf*: **tener ~s** to have bags under one's eyes
ojo ['oxo] *nm* eye; (*de puente*) span; (*de cerradura*) keyhole ▷ *excl* careful!; **tener ~ para** to have an eye for; **ojo de buey** porthole
okey ['okei] (LAM) *excl* O.K.
okupa [o'kupa] (ESP: *fam*) *nmf* squatter
ola ['ola] *nf* wave
olé [o'le] *excl* bravo!, olé!
oleada [ole'aða] *nf* big wave, swell; (*fig*) wave
oleaje [ole'axe] *nm* swell
óleo ['oleo] *nm* oil; **oleoducto** *nm* (oil) pipeline
oler [o'ler] *vt* (*gen*) to smell; (*inquirir*) to pry into; (*fig: sospechar*) to sniff out ▷ *vi* to smell; **~ a** to smell of
olfatear [olfate'ar] *vt* to smell; (*inquirir*) to pry into; **olfato** *nm* sense of smell
olimpiada [olim'piaða] *nf*: **las O~s** the Olympics; **olímpico, -a** [o'limpiko, a] *adj* Olympic
oliva [o'liβa] *nf* (*aceituna*) olive; **aceite de ~** olive oil; **olivo** *nm* olive tree
olla ['oʎa] *nf* pan; (*comida*) stew; **olla exprés** *o* **a presión** (ESP) pressure cooker; **olla podrida** *type of Spanish stew*
olmo ['olmo] *nm* elm (tree)
olor [o'lor] *nm* smell; **oloroso, -a** *adj* scented
olvidar [olβi'ðar] *vt* to forget; (*omitir*) to omit; **olvidarse** *vr* (*fig*) to forget o.s.; **se me olvidó** I forgot
olvido [ol'βiðo] *nm* oblivion; (*despiste*) forgetfulness
ombligo [om'bliɣo] *nm* navel
omelette [ome'lete] (LAM) *nf* omelet(te)
omisión [omi'sjon] *nf* (*abstención*) omission; (*descuido*) neglect
omiso, -a [o'miso, a] *adj*: **hacer caso ~ de** to ignore, pass over
omitir [omi'tir] *vt* to omit
omnipotente [omnipo'tente] *adj* omnipotent
omóplato [o'moplato] *nm* shoulder blade
OMS *nf abr* (= *Organización Mundial de la Salud*) WHO
once ['onθe] *num* eleven; **onces** (CS) *nfpl* tea break *sg*
onda ['onda] *nf* wave; **onda corta/larga/media** short/long/medium wave; **ondear** *vt, vi* to wave; (*tener ondas*) to be wavy; (*agua*) to ripple
ondulación [ondula'θjon] *nf* undulation; **ondulado, -a** *adj* wavy
ONG *nf abr* (= *organización no gubernamental*) NGO
ONU ['onu] *nf abr* (= *Organización de las Naciones Unidas*) UNO
opaco, -a [o'pako, a] *adj* opaque
opción [op'θjon] *nf* (*gen*) option; (*derecho*) right, option
OPEP ['opep] *nf abr* (= *Organización de Países Exportadores de Petróleo*) OPEC
ópera ['opera] *nf* opera; **ópera bufa** *o* **cómica** comic opera
operación [opera'θjon] *nf* (*gen*) operation; (*Com*) transaction, deal
operador, a [opera'ðor, a] *nm/f* operator; (*Cine: de proyección*) projectionist; (*: de rodaje*)

cameraman
operar [ope'rar] *vt* (*producir*) to produce, bring about; (*Med*) to operate on ▷*vi* (*Com*) to operate, deal; **operarse** *vr* to occur; (*Med*) to have an operation
opereta [ope'reta] *nf* operetta
opinar [opi'nar] *vt* to think ▷*vi* to give one's opinion; **opinión** *nf* (*creencia*) belief; (*criterio*) opinion
opio ['opjo] *nm* opium
oponer [opo'ner] *vt* (*resistencia*) to put up, offer; **oponerse** *vr* (*objetar*) to object; (*estar frente a frente*) to be opposed; (*dos personas*) to oppose each other; **~ A a B** to set A against B; **me opongo a pensar que ...** I refuse to believe *o* think that ...
oportunidad [oportuni'ðað] *nf* (*ocasión*) opportunity; (*posibilidad*) chance
oportuno, -a [opor'tuno, a] *adj* (*en su tiempo*) opportune, timely; (*respuesta*) suitable; **en el momento ~** at the right moment
oposición [oposi'θjon] *nf* opposition; **oposiciones** *nfpl* (*Escol*) public examinations
opositor, a [oposi'tor, a] *nm/f* (*adversario*) opponent; (*candidato*): **~ (a)** candidate (for)
opresión [opre'sjon] *nf* oppression; **opresor, a** *nm/f* oppressor
oprimir [opri'mir] *vt* to squeeze; (*fig*) to oppress
optar [op'tar] *vi* (*elegir*) to choose; **~ por** to opt for; **optativo, -a** *adj* optional
óptico, -a ['optiko, a] *adj* optic(al) ▷*nm/f* optician; **óptica** *nf* optician's (shop); **desde esta óptica** from this point of view
optimismo [opti'mismo] *nm* optimism; **optimista** *nmf* optimist
opuesto, -a [o'pwesto, a] *adj* (*contrario*) opposite; (*antagónico*) opposing
oración [ora'θjon] *nf* (*Rel*) prayer; (*Ling*) sentence
orador, a [ora'ðor, a] *nm/f* (*conferenciante*) speaker, orator
oral [o'ral] *adj* oral
orangután [orangu'tan] *nm* orangutan
orar [o'rar] *vi* to pray
oratoria [ora'torja] *nf* oratory
órbita ['orβita] *nf* orbit
orden ['orðen] *nm* (*gen*) order ▷*nf* (*gen*) order; (*Inform*) command; **en ~ de prioridad** in order of priority; **orden del día** agenda
ordenado, -a [orðe'naðo, a] *adj* (*metódico*) methodical; (*arreglado*) orderly
ordenador [orðena'ðor] *nm* computer; **ordenador central** mainframe computer
ordenar [orðe'nar] *vt* (*mandar*) to order; (*poner orden*) to put in order, arrange; **ordenarse** *vr* (*Rel*) to be ordained
ordeñar [orðe'ɲar] *vt* to milk
ordinario, -a [orði'narjo, a] *adj* (*común*) ordinary, usual; (*vulgar*) vulgar, common
orégano [o'reɣano] *nm* oregano
oreja [o'rexa] *nf* ear; (*Mecánica*) lug, flange
orfanato [orfa'nato] *nm* orphanage
orfebrería [orfeβre'ria] *nf* gold/silver work
orgánico, -a [or'ɣaniko, a] *adj* organic
organismo [orɣa'nismo] *nm* (*Bio*) organism; (*Pol*) organization
organización [orɣaniθa'θjon] *nf* organization; **organizar** *vt* to organize
órgano ['orɣano] *nm* organ
orgasmo [or'ɣasmo] *nm* orgasm
orgía [or'xia] *nf* orgy
orgullo [or'ɣuʎo] *nm* pride; **orgulloso, -a** *adj* (*gen*) proud; (*altanero*) haughty
orientación [orjenta'θjon] *nf* (*posición*) position; (*dirección*) direction
oriental [orjen'tal] *adj* eastern; (*del Extremo Oriente*) oriental
orientar [orjen'tar] *vt* (*situar*) to orientate; (*señalar*) to point; (*dirigir*) to direct; (*guiar*) to guide; **orientarse** *vr* to get one's bearings
oriente [o'rjente] *nm* east; **el O~ Medio** the Middle East; **el Próximo/Extremo O~** the Near/Far East
origen [o'rixen] *nm* origin
original [orixi'nal] *adj* (*nuevo*) original; (*extraño*) odd, strange; **originalidad** *nf* originality
originar [orixi'nar] *vt* to start, cause; **originarse** *vr* to originate; **originario, -a** *adj* original; **originario de** native of
orilla [o'riʎa] *nf* (*borde*) border; (*de río*) bank; (*de bosque, tela*) edge; (*de mar*) shore
orina [o'rina] *nf* urine; **orinal** *nm* (chamber) pot; **orinar** *vi* to urinate; **orinarse** *vr* to wet o.s.
oro ['oro] *nm* gold; **oros** *nmpl* (*Naipes*) hearts
orquesta [or'kesta] *nf* orchestra; **orquesta sinfónica** symphony orchestra
orquídea [or'kiðea] *nf* orchid
ortiga [or'tiɣa] *nf* nettle
ortodoxo, -a [orto'ðokso, a] *adj* orthodox
ortografía [ortoɣra'fia] *nf* spelling
ortopedia [orto'peðja] *nf* orthopaedics *sg*; **ortopédico, -a** *adj* orthopaedic
oruga [o'ruɣa] *nf* caterpillar
orzuelo [or'θwelo] *nm* stye
os [os] *pron* (*gen*) you; (*a vosotros*) to you
osa ['osa] *nf* (she-)bear; **Osa Mayor/Menor** Great/Little Bear

osadía [osa'ðia] *nf* daring
osar [o'sar] *vi* to dare
oscilación [osθila'θjon] *nf* (*movimiento*) oscillation; (*fluctuación*) fluctuation
oscilar [osθi'lar] *vi* to oscillate; to fluctuate
oscurecer [oskure'θer] *vt* to darken ▷*vi* to grow dark; **oscurecerse** *vr* to grow *o* get dark
oscuridad [oskuri'ðað] *nf* obscurity; (*tinieblas*) darkness
oscuro, -a [os'kuro, a] *adj* dark; (*fig*) obscure; **a oscuras** in the dark
óseo, -a ['oseo, a] *adj* bone *cpd*
oso ['oso] *nm* bear; **oso de peluche** teddy bear; **oso hormiguero** anteater
ostentar [osten'tar] *vt* (*gen*) to show; (*pey*) to flaunt, show off; (*poseer*) to have, possess
ostión [os'tjon] (*MÉX*) *nm* = **ostra**
ostra ['ostra] *nf* oyster
OTAN ['otan] *nf abr* (= *Organización del Tratado del Atlántico Norte*) NATO
otitis [o'titis] *nf* earache
otoñal [oto'ɲal] *adj* autumnal
otoño [o'toɲo] *nm* autumn
otorgar [otor'ɣar] *vt* (*conceder*) to concede; (*dar*) to grant
otorrino, -a [oto'rrino, a], **otorrinolaringólogo, -a** [otorrinolarin'goloɣo, a] *nm/f* ear, nose and throat specialist

PALABRA CLAVE

otro, -a ['otro, a] *adj* **1** (*distinto*: *sg*) another; (: *pl*) other; **con otros amigos** with other *o* different friends
2 (*adicional*): **tráigame otro café (más), por favor** can I have another coffee please; **otros diez días más** another ten days
▷*pron* **1** **el otro** the other one; **(los) otros** (the) others; **de otro** somebody else's; **que lo haga otro** let somebody else do it
2 (*recíproco*): **se odian (la) una a (la) otra** they hate one another *o* each other
3: **otro tanto: comer otro tanto** to eat the same *o* as much again; **recibió una decena de telegramas y otras tantas llamadas** he got about ten telegrams and as many calls

ovación [oβa'θjon] *nf* ovation
oval [o'βal] *adj* oval; **ovalado, -a** *adj* oval; **óvalo** *nm* oval
ovario [o'βario] *nm* ovary
oveja [o'βexa] *nf* sheep
overol [oβe'rol] (*LAM*) *nm* overalls *pl*
ovillo [o'βiʎo] *nm* (*de lana*) ball of wool
OVNI ['oβni] *nm abr* (= *objeto volante no identificado*) UFO
ovulación [oβula'θjon] *nf* ovulation; **óvulo** *nm* ovum
oxidación [oksiða'θjon] *nf* rusting
oxidar [oksi'ðar] *vt* to rust; **oxidarse** *vr* to go rusty
óxido ['oksiðo] *nm* oxide
oxigenado, -a [oksixe'naðo, a] *adj* (*Quím*) oxygenated; (*pelo*) bleached
oxígeno [ok'sixeno] *nm* oxygen
oyente [o'jente] *nmf* listener
oyes *etc vb V* **oír**
ozono [o'θono] *nm* ozone

p

pabellón [paβe'ʎon] *nm* bell tent; (*Arq*) pavilion; (*de hospital etc*) block, section; (*bandera*) flag

pacer [pa'θer] *vi* to graze

paciencia [pa'θjenθja] *nf* patience

paciente [pa'θjente] *adj, nmf* patient

pacificación [paθifika'θjon] *nf* pacification

pacífico, -a [pa'θifiko, a] *adj* (*persona*) peaceable; (*existencia*) peaceful; **el (Océano) P~** the Pacific (Ocean)

pacifista [paθi'fista] *nmf* pacifist

pacotilla [pako'tiʎa] *nf*: **de ~** (*actor, escritor*) third-rate

pactar [pak'tar] *vt* to agree to *o* on ▷*vi* to come to an agreement

pacto ['pakto] *nm* (*tratado*) pact; (*acuerdo*) agreement

padecer [paðe'θer] *vt* (*sufrir*) to suffer; (*soportar*) to endure, put up with; **padecimiento** *nm* suffering

padrastro [pa'ðrastro] *nm* stepfather

padre ['paðre] *nm* father ▷*adj* (*fam*): **un éxito ~** a tremendous success; **padres** *nmpl* parents; **padre político** father-in-law

padrino [pa'ðrino] *nm* (*Rel*) godfather; (*tb*: **~ de boda**) best man; (*fig*) sponsor, patron; **padrinos** *nmpl* godparents

padrón [pa'ðron] *nm* (*censo*) census, roll

padrote [pa'ðrote] (*MÉX*: *fam*) *nm* pimp

paella [pa'eʎa] *nf* paella, *dish of rice with meat, shellfish etc*

paga ['paɣa] *nf* (*pago*) payment; (*sueldo*) pay, wages *pl*

pagano, -a [pa'ɣano, a] *adj, nm/f* pagan, heathen

pagar [pa'ɣar] *vt* to pay; (*las compras, crimen*) to pay for; (*fig*: *favor*) to repay ▷*vi* to pay; **~ al contado/a plazos** to pay (in) cash/ in instalments

pagaré [paɣa're] *nm* I.O.U.

página ['paxina] *nf* page; **página de inicio** (*Inform*) home page; **página web** (*Inform*) web page

pago ['paɣo] *nm* (*dinero*) payment; **en ~ de** in return for; **pago anticipado/a cuenta/ contra reembolso/en especie** advance payment/payment on account/cash on delivery/payment in kind

pág(s). *abr* (= *página(s)*) p(p).

pague *etc vb V* **pagar**

país [pa'is] *nm* (*gen*) country; (*región*) land; **los P~es Bajos** the Low Countries; **el P~ Vasco** the Basque Country

paisaje [pai'saxe] *nm* landscape, scenery

paisano, -a [pai'sano, a] *adj* of the same country ▷*nm/f* (*compatriota*) fellow countryman/woman; **vestir de ~** (*soldado*) to be in civvies; (*guardia*) to be in plain clothes

paja ['paxa] *nf* straw; (*fig*) rubbish (*BRIT*), trash (*US*)

pajarita [paxa'rita] *nf* (*corbata*) bow tie

pájaro ['paxaro] *nm* bird; **pájaro carpintero** woodpecker

pajita [pa'xita] *nf* (drinking) straw

pala ['pala] *nf* spade, shovel; (*raqueta etc*) bat; (: *de tenis*) racquet; (*Culin*) slice; **pala mecánica** power shovel

palabra [pa'laβra] *nf* word; (*facultad*) (power of) speech; (*derecho de hablar*) right to speak; **tomar la ~** (*en mitin*) to take the floor

palabrota [pala'brota] *nf* swearword

palacio [pa'laθjo] *nm* palace; (*mansión*) mansion, large house; **palacio de justicia** courthouse; **palacio municipal** town *o* city hall

paladar [pala'ðar] *nm* palate; **paladear** *vt* to taste

palanca [pa'lanka] *nf* lever; (*fig*) pull, influence

palangana [palan'gana] *nf* washbasin

palco ['palko] *nm* box

Palestina [pales'tina] *nf* Palestine; **palestino, -a** *nm/f* Palestinian

paleta [pa'leta] *nf* (*de pintor*) palette; (*de albañil*) trowel; (*de ping-pong*) bat; (*MÉX, CAM*: *helado*) ice lolly (*BRIT*), Popsicle® (*US*)

palidecer [paliðe'θer] *vi* to turn pale; **palidez** *nf* paleness; **pálido, -a** *adj* pale

palillo [pa'liʎo] *nm* (*mondadientes*) toothpick; (*para comer*) chopstick

palito [pa'lito] (*RPL*) *nm* (*helado*) ice lolly (*BRIT*), Popsicle® (*US*)

paliza [pa'liθa] *nf* beating, thrashing

palma ['palma] *nf* (*Anat*) palm; (*árbol*) palm tree; **batir** *o* **dar ~s** to clap, applaud; **palmada** *nf* slap; **palmadas** *nfpl* clapping

sg, applause *sg*
palmar [pal'mar] (*fam*) *vi* (*tb*: **~la**) to die, kick the bucket
palmear [palme'ar] *vi* to clap
palmera [pal'mera] *nf* (*Bot*) palm tree
palmo ['palmo] *nm* (*medida*) span; (*fig*) small amount; **~ a ~** inch by inch
palo ['palo] *nm* stick; (*poste*) post; (*de tienda de campaña*) pole; (*mango*) handle, shaft; (*golpe*) blow, hit; (*de golf*) club; (*de béisbol*) bat; (*Náut*) mast; (*Naipes*) suit
paloma [pa'loma] *nf* dove, pigeon
palomitas [palo'mitas] *nfpl* popcorn *sg*
palpar [pal'par] *vt* to touch, feel
palpitar [palpi'tar] *vi* to palpitate; (*latir*) to beat
palta ['palta] (CS) *nf* avocado
paludismo [palu'ðismo] *nm* malaria
pamela [pa'mela] *nf* picture hat, sun hat
pampa ['pampa] *nf* pampas, prairie
pan [pan] *nm* bread; (*una barra*) loaf; **pan integral** wholemeal (BRIT) *o* wholewheat (US) bread; **pan rallado** breadcrumbs *pl*; **pan tostado** (MÉX: *tostada*) toast
pana ['pana] *nf* corduroy
panadería [panaðe'ria] *nf* baker's (shop); **panadero, -a** *nm/f* baker
Panamá [pana'ma] *nm* Panama; **panameño, -a** *adj* Panamanian
pancarta [pan'karta] *nf* placard, banner
panceta [pan'θeta] (ESP, RPL) *nf* bacon
pancho ['pantʃo] (RPL) *nm* hot dog
pancito [pan'θito] *nm* (bread) roll
panda ['panda] *nm* (*Zool*) panda
pandereta [pande'reta] *nf* tambourine
pandilla [pan'diʎa] *nf* set, group; (*de criminales*) gang; (*pey*: *camarilla*) clique
panecillo [pane'θiʎo] (ESP) *nm* (bread) roll
panel [pa'nel] *nm* panel; **panel solar** solar panel
panfleto [pan'fleto] *nm* pamphlet
pánico ['paniko] *nm* panic
panorama [pano'rama] *nm* panorama; (*vista*) view
panqueque [pan'keke] (LAM) *nm* pancake
pantalla [pan'taʎa] *nf* (*de cine*) screen; (*de lámpara*) lampshade
pantalón [panta'lon] *nm* trousers; **pantalones** *nmpl* trousers; **pantalones cortes** shorts
pantano [pan'tano] *nm* (*ciénaga*) marsh, swamp; (*depósito*: *de agua*) reservoir; (*fig*) jam, difficulty
panteón [pante'on] *nm* (*monumento*) pantheon
pantera [pan'tera] *nf* panther
pantimedias [panti'meðjas] (MÉX) *nfpl* = **pantis**
pantis ['pantis] *nmpl* tights (BRIT), pantyhose (US)
pantomima [panto'mima] *nf* pantomime
pantorrilla [panto'rriʎa] *nf* calf (of the leg)
pants [pants] (MÉX) *nmpl* tracksuit (BRIT), sweat suit (US)
pantufla [pan'tufla] *nf* slipper
panty(s) ['panti(s)] *nm(pl)* tights (BRIT), pantyhose (US)
panza ['panθa] *nf* belly, paunch
pañal [pa'ɲal] *nm* nappy (BRIT), diaper (US); **pañales** *nmpl* (*fig*) early stages, infancy *sg*
paño ['paɲo] *nm* (*tela*) cloth; (*pedazo de tela*) (piece of) cloth; (*trapo*) duster, rag; **paños menores** underclothes
pañuelo [pa'ɲwelo] *nm* handkerchief, hanky; (*fam*: *para la cabeza*) (head)scarf
papa ['papa] *nm*: **el P~** the Pope ▷ *nf* (LAM: *patata*) potato; **papas fritas** (LAM) French fries, chips (BRIT); (*de bolsa*) crisps (BRIT), potato chips (US)
papá [pa'pa] (*fam*) *nm* dad(dy), pa (US)
papada [pa'paða] *nf* double chin
papagayo [papa'ɣajo] *nm* parrot
papalote [papa'lote] (MÉX, CAM) *nm* kite
papanatas [papa'natas] (*fam*) *nm inv* simpleton
papaya [pa'paja] *nf* papaya
papear [pape'ar] (*fam*) *vt, vi* to scoff
papel [pa'pel] *nm* paper; (*hoja de papel*) sheet of paper; (*Teatro*: *fig*) role; **papel de aluminio** aluminium (BRIT) *o* aluminum (US) foil; **papel de arroz/envolver/fumar** rice/wrapping/cigarette paper; **papel de estaño** *o* **plata** tinfoil; **papel de lija** sandpaper; **papel higiénico** toilet paper; **papel moneda** paper money; **papel secante** blotting paper
papeleo [pape'leo] *nm* red tape
papelera [pape'lera] *nf* wastepaper basket; (*en la calle*) litter bin; **papelera (de reciclaje)** (*Inform*) wastebasket
papelería [papele'ria] *nf* stationer's (shop)
papeleta [pape'leta] (ESP) *nf* (*Pol*) ballot paper
paperas [pa'peras] *nfpl* mumps *sg*
papilla [pa'piʎa] *nf* (*de bebé*) baby food
paquete [pa'kete] *nm* (*de cigarrillos etc*) packet; (*Correos etc*) parcel
par [par] *adj* (*igual*) like, equal; (*Mat*) even ▷ *nm* equal; (*de guantes*) pair; (*de veces*) couple; (*Pol*) peer; (*Golf, Com*) par; **abrir de ~ en ~** to open wide

para ['para] *prep* for; **no es ~ comer** it's not for eating; **decir ~ sí** to say to o.s.; **¿~ qué lo quieres?** what do you want it for?; **se casaron ~ separarse otra vez** they married only to separate again; **lo tendré ~ mañana** I'll have it (for) tomorrow; **ir ~ casa** to go home, head for home; **~ profesor es muy estúpido** he's very stupid for a teacher; **¿quién es usted ~ gritar así?** who are you to shout like that?; **tengo bastante ~ vivir** I have enough to live on; *V tb* **con**

parabién [para'βjen] *nm* congratulations *pl*

parábola [pa'raβola] *nf* parable; (*Mat*) parabola; **parabólica** *nf* (*tb*: **antena parábolica**) satellite dish

parabrisas [para'βrisas] *nm inv* windscreen (BRIT), windshield (US)

paracaídas [paraka'iðas] *nm inv* parachute; **paracaidista** *nmf* parachutist; (*Mil*) paratrooper

parachoques [para'tʃokes] *nm inv* (*Auto*) bumper; (*Mecánica etc*) shock absorber

parada [pa'raða] *nf* stop; (*acto*) stopping; (*de industria*) shutdown, stoppage; (*lugar*) stopping place; **parada de autobús** bus stop; **parada de taxis** taxi stand *o* rank (BRIT)

paradero [para'ðero] *nm* stopping-place; (*situación*) whereabouts

parado, -a [pa'raðo, a] *adj* (*persona*) motionless, standing still; (*fábrica*) closed, at a standstill; (*coche*) stopped; (LAM: *de pie*) standing (up); (ESP: *sin empleo*) unemployed, idle

paradoja [para'ðoxa] *nf* paradox

parador [para'ðor] *nm* parador, state-run hotel

paragolpes [para'golpes] (RPL) *nm inv* (*Auto*) bumper, fender (US)

paraguas [pa'raɣwas] *nm inv* umbrella

Paraguay [para'ɣwai] *nm* Paraguay; **paraguayo, -a** *adj, nm/f* Paraguayan

paraíso [para'iso] *nm* paradise, heaven

paraje [pa'raxe] *nm* place, spot

paralelo, -a [para'lelo, a] *adj* parallel

parálisis [pa'ralisis] *nf inv* paralysis; **paralítico, -a** *adj, nm/f* paralytic

paralizar [parali'θar] *vt* to paralyse; **paralizarse** *vr* to become paralysed; (*fig*) to come to a standstill

páramo ['paramo] *nm* bleak plateau

paranoico, -a [para'noiko, a] *nm/f* paranoiac

parapente [para'pente] *nm* (*deporte*) paragliding; (*aparato*) paraglider

parapléjico, -a [para'plexiko, a] *adj, nm/f* paraplegic

parar [pa'rar] *vt* to stop; (*golpe*) to ward off ▷ *vi* to stop; **pararse** *vr* to stop; (LAM: *ponerse de pie*) to stand up; **ha parado de llover** it has stopped raining; **van a ir a ~ a comisaría** they're going to end up in the police station; **~se en** to pay attention to

pararrayos [para'rrajos] *nm inv* lightning conductor

parásito, -a [pa'rasito, a] *nm/f* parasite

parcela [par'θela] *nf* plot, piece of ground

parche ['partʃe] *nm* (*gen*) patch

parchís [par'tʃis] *nm* ludo

parcial [par'θjal] *adj* (*pago*) part-; (*eclipse*) partial; (*Jur*) prejudiced, biased; (*Pol*) partisan

parecer [pare'θer] *nm* (*opinión*) opinion, view; (*aspecto*) looks *pl* ▷ *vi* (*tener apariencia*) to seem, look; (*asemejarse*) to look *o* seem like; (*aparecer, llegar*) to appear; **parecerse** *vr* to look alike, resemble each other; **al ~** apparently; **según parece** evidently, apparently; **~se a** to look like, resemble; **me parece que** I think (that), it seems to me that

parecido, -a [pare'θiðo, a] *adj* similar ▷ *nm* similarity, likeness, resemblance; **bien ~** good-looking, nice-looking

pared [pa'reð] *nf* wall

pareja [pa'rexa] *nf* (*par*) pair; (*dos personas*) couple; (*otro*: *de un par*) other one (of a pair); (*persona*) partner

parentesco [paren'tesko] *nm* relationship

paréntesis [pa'rentesis] *nm inv* parenthesis; (*en escrito*) bracket

parezco *etc vb V* **parecer**

pariente [pa'rjente] *nmf* relative, relation

> No confundir **pariente** con la palabra inglesa *parent*.

parir [pa'rir] *vt* to give birth to ▷ *vi* (*mujer*) to give birth, have a baby

París [pa'ris] *n* Paris

parka ['parka] (LAM) *nf* anorak

parking ['parkin] *nm* car park (BRIT), parking lot (US)

parlamentar [parlamen'tar] *vi* to parley

parlamentario, -a [parlamen'tarjo, a] *adj* parliamentary ▷ *nm/f* member of parliament

parlamento [parla'mento] *nm* parliament

parlanchín, -ina [parlan'tʃin, ina] *adj* indiscreet ▷ *nm/f* chatterbox

parlar [par'lar] *vi* to chatter (away)

paro ['paro] *nm* (*huelga*) stoppage (of work), strike; (ESP: *desempleo*) unemployment; (: *subsidio*) unemployment benefit; **estar en ~** (ESP) to be unemployed;

paro cardíaco cardiac arrest
parodia [pa'roðja] *nf* parody; **parodiar** *vt* to parody
parpadear [parpaðe'ar] *vi* (*ojos*) to blink; (*luz*) to flicker
párpado ['parpaðo] *nm* eyelid
parque ['parke] *nm* (*lugar verde*) park; (*MÉX: munición*) ammunition; **parque de atracciones** fairground; **parque de bomberos** (*ESP*) fire station; **parque infantil/temático/zoológico** playground/ theme park/zoo
parqué [par'ke] *nm* parquet (flooring)
parquímetro [par'kimetro] *nm* parking meter
parra ['parra] *nf* (grape)vine
párrafo ['parrafo] *nm* paragraph; **echar un ~** (*fam*) to have a chat
parranda [pa'rranda] (*fam*) *nf* spree, binge
parrilla [pa'rriʎa] *nf* (*Culin*) grill; (*de coche*) grille; **(carne a la) ~** barbecue; **parrillada** *nf* barbecue
párroco ['parroko] *nm* parish priest
parroquia [pa'rrokja] *nf* parish; (*iglesia*) parish church; (*Com*) clientele, customers *pl*; **parroquiano, -a** *nm/f* parishioner; (*Com*) client, customer
parte ['parte] *nm* message; (*informe*) report ▷ *nf* part; (*lado, cara*) side; (*de reparto*) share; (*Jur*) party; **en alguna ~ de Europa** somewhere in Europe; **en** *o* **por todas ~s** everywhere; **en gran ~** to a large extent; **la mayor ~ de los españoles** most Spaniards; **de un tiempo a esta ~** for some time past; **de ~ de algn** on sb's behalf; **¿de ~ de quién?** (*Tel*) who is speaking?; **por ~ de** on the part of; **yo por mí ~** I for my part; **por otra ~** on the other hand; **dar ~** to inform; **tomar ~** to take part; **parte meteorológico** weather forecast *o* report
participación [partiθipa'θjon] *nf* (*acto*) participation, taking part; (*parte, Com*) share; (*de lotería*) shared prize; (*aviso*) notice, notification
participante [partiθi'pante] *nmf* participant
participar [partiθi'par] *vt* to notify, inform ▷ *vi* to take part, participate
partícipe [par'tiθipe] *nmf* participant
particular [partiku'lar] *adj* (*especial*) particular, special; (*individual, personal*) private, personal ▷ *nm* (*punto, asunto*) particular, point; (*individuo*) individual; **tiene coche ~** he has a car of his own
partida [par'tiða] *nf* (*salida*) departure; (*Com*) entry, item; (*juego*) game; (*grupo de personas*) band, group; **mala ~** dirty trick; **partida de nacimiento/matrimonio/ defunción** (*ESP*) birth/marriage/death certificate
partidario, -a [parti'ðarjo, a] *adj* partisan ▷ *nm/f* supporter, follower
partido [par'tiðo] *nm* (*Pol*) party; (*Deporte*) game, match; **sacar ~ de** to profit *o* benefit from; **tomar ~** to take sides
partir [par'tir] *vt* (*dividir*) to split, divide; (*compartir, distribuir*) to share (out), distribute; (*romper*) to break open, split open; (*rebanada*) to cut (off) ▷ *vi* (*ponerse en camino*) to set off *o* out; (*comenzar*) to start (off *o* out); **partirse** *vr* to crack *o* split *o* break (in two *etc*); **a ~ de** (starting) from
partitura [parti'tura] *nf* (*Mús*) score
parto ['parto] *nm* birth; (*fig*) product, creation; **estar de ~** to be in labour
parvulario [parβu'larjo] (*ESP*) *nm* nursery school, kindergarten
pasa ['pasa] *nf* raisin; **pasa de Corinto** currant
pasacintas [pasa'θintas] (*LAM*) *nm* cassette player
pasada [pa'saða] *nf* passing, passage; **de ~** in passing, incidentally; **una mala ~** a dirty trick
pasadizo [pasa'ðiθo] *nm* (*pasillo*) passage, corridor; (*callejuela*) alley
pasado, -a [pa'saðo, a] *adj* past; (*malo: comida, fruta*) bad; (*muy cocido*) overdone; (*anticuado*) out of date ▷ *nm* past; **~ mañana** the day after tomorrow; **el mes ~** last month
pasador [pasa'ðor] *nm* (*cerrojo*) bolt; (*de pelo*) hair slide; (*horquilla*) grip
pasaje [pa'saxe] *nm* passage; (*pago de viaje*) fare; (*los pasajeros*) passengers *pl*; (*pasillo*) passageway
pasajero, -a [pasa'xero, a] *adj* passing; (*situación, estado*) temporary; (*amor, enfermedad*) brief ▷ *nm/f* passenger
pasamontañas [pasamon'taɲas] *nm inv* balaclava helmet
pasaporte [pasa'porte] *nm* passport
pasar [pa'sar] *vt* to pass; (*tiempo*) to spend; (*desgracias*) to suffer, endure; (*noticia*) to give, pass on; (*río*) to cross; (*barrera*) to pass through; (*falta*) to overlook, tolerate; (*contrincante*) to surpass, do better than; (*coche*) to overtake; (*Cine*) to show; (*enfermedad*) to give, infect with ▷ *vi* (*gen*) to pass; (*terminarse*) to be over; (*ocurrir*) to happen; **pasarse** *vr* (*flores*) to fade; (*comida*) to go bad *o* off; (*fig*) to overdo it, go too far; **~ de** to go beyond, exceed; **~ por** (*LAM*) to fetch; **~lo bien/mal** to have a good/bad time; **¡pase!** come in!; **hacer ~** to show in;

P

lo que pasa es que ... the thing is ...; **~se al enemigo** to go over to the enemy; **se me pasó** I forgot; **no se le pasa nada** he misses nothing; **pase lo que pase** come what may; **¿qué pasa?** what's going on?, what's up?; **¿qué te pasa?** what's wrong?

pasarela [pasa'rela] *nf* footbridge; (*en barco*) gangway

pasatiempo [pasa'tjempo] *nm* pastime, hobby

Pascua ['paskwa] *nf* (*en Semana Santa*) Easter; **Pascuas** *nfpl* Christmas (time); **¡felices ~s!** Merry Christmas!

pase ['pase] *nm* pass; (*Cine*) performance, showing

pasear [pase'ar] *vt* to take for a walk; (*exhibir*) to parade, show off ▷*vi* to walk, go for a walk; **pasearse** *vr* to walk, go for a walk; **~ en coche** to go for a drive; **paseo** *nm* (*avenida*) avenue; (*distancia corta*) walk, stroll; **dar un** *o* **ir de paseo** to go for a walk; **paseo marítimo** (ESP) promenade

pasillo [pa'siʎo] *nm* passage, corridor

pasión [pa'sjon] *nf* passion

pasivo, -a [pa'siβo, a] *adj* passive; (*inactivo*) inactive ▷*nm* (*Com*) liabilities *pl*, debts *pl*

pasmoso, -a [pas'moso, a] *adj* amazing, astonishing

paso, -a ['paso, a] *adj* dried ▷*nm* step; (*modo de andar*) walk; (*huella*) footprint; (*rapidez*) speed, pace, rate; (*camino accesible*) way through, passage; (*cruce*) crossing; (*pasaje*) passing, passage; (*Geo*) pass; (*estrecho*) strait; **a ese ~** (*fig*) at that rate; **salir al ~ de** *o* **a** to waylay; **estar de ~** to be passing through; **prohibido el ~** no entry; **ceda el ~** give way; **paso a nivel** (*Ferro*) level-crossing; **paso (de) cebra** (ESP) zebra crossing; **paso de peatones** pedestrian crossing; **paso elevado** flyover

pasota [pa'sota] (ESP: *fam*) *adj, nmf* ≈ dropout; **ser un ~** to be a bit of a dropout; (*ser indiferente*) not to care about anything

pasta ['pasta] *nf* paste; (*Culin: masa*) dough; (: *de bizcochos etc*) pastry; (*fam*) dough; **pastas** *nfpl* (*bizcochos*) pastries, small cakes; (*fideos, espaguetis etc*) pasta; **pasta dentífrica** *o* **de dientes** toothpaste

pastar [pas'tar] *vt, vi* to graze

pastel [pas'tel] *nm* (*dulce*) cake; (*Arte*) pastel; **pastel de carne** meat pie; **pastelería** *nf* cake shop

pastilla [pas'tiʎa] *nf* (*de jabón, chocolate*) bar; (*píldora*) tablet, pill

pasto ['pasto] *nm* (*hierba*) grass; (*lugar*) pasture, field; **pastor, a** [pas'tor, a] *nm/f* shepherd/ess ▷*nm* (*Rel*) clergyman, pastor; **pastor alemán** Alsatian

pata ['pata] *nf* (*pierna*) leg; (*pie*) foot; (*de muebles*) leg; **~s arriba** upside down; **metedura de ~** (*fam*) gaffe; **meter la ~** (*fam*) to put one's foot in it; **tener buena/mala ~** to be lucky/unlucky; **pata de cabra** (*Tec*) crowbar; **patada** *nf* kick; (*en el suelo*) stamp

patata [pa'tata] *nf* potato; **patatas fritas** chips, French fries; (*de bolsa*) crisps

paté [pa'te] *nm* pâté

patente [pa'tente] *adj* obvious, evident; (*Com*) patent ▷*nf* patent

paternal [pater'nal] *adj* fatherly, paternal; **paterno, -a** *adj* paternal

patético, -a [pa'tetiko, a] *adj* pathetic, moving

patilla [pa'tiʎa] *nf* (*de gafas*) side(piece); **patillas** *nfpl* sideburns

patín [pa'tin] *nm* skate; (*de trineo*) runner; **patín de ruedas** roller skate; **patinaje** *nm* skating; **patinar** *vi* to skate; (*resbalarse*) to skid, slip; (*fam*) to slip up, blunder

patineta [pati'neta] *nf* (MÉX: *patinete*) scooter; (CS: *monopatín*) skateboard

patinete [pati'nete] *nm* scooter

patio ['patjo] *nm* (*de casa*) patio, courtyard; **patio de recreo** playground

pato ['pato] *nm* duck; **pagar el ~** (*fam*) to take the blame, carry the can

patoso, -a [pa'toso, a] (*fam*) *adj* clumsy

patotero [pato'tero] (CS) *nm* hooligan, lout

patraña [pa'traɲa] *nf* story, fib

patria ['patrja] *nf* native land, mother country

patrimonio [patri'monjo] *nm* inheritance; (*fig*) heritage

patriota [pa'trjota] *nmf* patriot

patrocinar [patroθi'nar] *vt* to sponsor

patrón, -ona [pa'tron, ona] *nm/f* (*jefe*) boss, chief, master(mistress); (*propietario*) landlord/lady; (*Rel*) patron saint ▷*nm* (*Tec, Costura*) pattern

patronato [patro'nato] *nm* sponsorship; (*acto*) patronage; (*fundación benéfica*) trust, foundation

patrulla [pa'truʎa] *nf* patrol

pausa ['pausa] *nf* pause, break

pauta ['pauta] *nf* line, guide line

pava ['paβa] (RPL) *nf* kettle

pavimento [paβi'mento] *nm* (*de losa*) pavement, paving

pavo ['paβo] *nm* turkey; **pavo real** peacock

payaso, -a [pa'jaso, a] *nm/f* clown

payo, -a ['pajo, a] *nm/f* non-gipsy

paz [paθ] *nf* peace; (*tranquilidad*) peacefulness, tranquillity; **hacer las paces** to make peace; (*fig*) to make up; **¡déjame en**

~! leave me alone!
PC *nm* PC, personal computer
P.D. *abr* (= *posdata*) P.S., p.s.
peaje [pe'axe] *nm* toll
peatón [pea'ton] *nm* pedestrian; **peatonal** *adj* pedestrian
peca ['peka] *nf* freckle
pecado [pe'kaðo] *nm* sin; **pecador, a** *adj* sinful ▷ *nm/f* sinner
pecaminoso, -a [pekami'noso, a] *adj* sinful
pecar [pe'kar] *vi* (*Rel*) to sin; **peca de generoso** he is generous to a fault
pecera [pe'θera] *nf* fish tank; (*redonda*) goldfish bowl
pecho ['petʃo] *nm* (*Anat*) chest; (*de mujer*) breast; **dar el ~ a** to breast-feed; **tomar algo a ~** to take sth to heart
pechuga [pe'tʃuɣa] *nf* breast
peculiar [peku'ljar] *adj* special, peculiar; (*característico*) typical, characteristic
pedal [pe'ðal] *nm* pedal; **pedalear** *vi* to pedal
pedante [pe'ðante] *adj* pedantic ▷ *nmf* pedant
pedazo [pe'ðaθo] *nm* piece, bit; **hacerse ~s** to smash, shatter
pediatra [pe'ðjatra] *nmf* paediatrician
pedido [pe'ðiðo] *nm* (*Com*) order; (*petición*) request
pedir [pe'ðir] *vt* to ask for, request; (*comida, Com: mandar*) to order; (*necesitar*) to need, demand, require ▷ *vi* to ask; **me pidió que cerrara la puerta** he asked me to shut the door; **¿cuánto piden por el coche?** how much are they asking for the car?
pedo ['peðo] (*fam!*) *nm* fart
pega ['peɣa] *nf* snag; **poner ~s (a)** to complain (about)
pegadizo, -a [peɣa'ðiθo, a] *adj* (*Mús*) catchy
pegajoso, -a [peɣa'xoso, a] *adj* sticky, adhesive
pegamento [peɣa'mento] *nm* gum, glue
pegar [pe'ɣar] *vt* (*papel, sellos*) to stick (on); (*cartel*) to stick up; (*coser*) to sew (on); (*unir: partes*) to join, fix together; (*Comput*) to paste; (*Med*) to give, infect with; (*dar: golpe*) to give, deal ▷ *vi* (*adherirse*) to stick, adhere; (*ir juntos: colores*) to match, go together; (*golpear*) to hit; (*quemar: el sol*) to strike hot, burn; **pegarse** *vr* (*gen*) to stick; (*dos personas*) to hit each other, fight; (*fam*): **~ un grito** to let out a yell; **~ un salto** to jump (with fright); **~ en** to touch; **~se un tiro** to shoot o.s.
pegatina [peɣa'tina] *nf* sticker
pegote [pe'ɣote] (*fam*) *nm* eyesore, sight
peinado [pei'naðo] *nm* hairstyle
peinar [pei'nar] *vt* to comb; (*hacer estilo*) to style; **peinarse** *vr* to comb one's hair
peine ['peine] *nm* comb; **peineta** *nf* ornamental comb
p.ej. *abr* (= *por ejemplo*) e.g.
Pekín [pe'kin] *n* Pekin(g)
pelado, -a [pe'laðo, a] *adj* (*fruta, patata etc*) peeled; (*cabeza*) shorn; (*campo, fig*) bare; (*fam: sin dinero*) broke
pelar [pe'lar] *vt* (*fruta, patatas etc*) to peel; (*cortar el pelo a*) to cut the hair of; (*quitar la piel: animal*) to skin; **pelarse** *vr* (*la piel*) to peel off; **voy a ~me** I'm going to get my hair cut
peldaño [pel'daɲo] *nm* step
pelea [pe'lea] *nf* (*lucha*) fight; (*discusión*) quarrel, row; **peleado, -a** [pele'aðo, a] *adj*: **estar peleado (con algn)** to have fallen out (with sb); **pelear** [pele'ar] *vi* to fight; **pelearse** *vr* to fight; (*reñirse*) to fall out, quarrel
pelela [pe'lela] (cs) *nf* potty
peletería [pelete'ria] *nf* furrier's, fur shop
pelícano [pe'likano] *nm* pelican
película [pe'likula] *nf* film; (*cobertura ligera*) thin covering; (*Foto: rollo*) roll *o* reel of film; **película de dibujos (animados)/del oeste** cartoon/western
peligro [pe'liɣro] *nm* danger; (*riesgo*) risk; **correr ~ de** to run the risk of; **peligroso, -a** *adj* dangerous; risky
pelirrojo, -a [peli'rroxo, a] *adj* red-haired, red-headed ▷ *nm/f* redhead
pellejo [pe'ʎexo] *nm* (*de animal*) skin, hide
pellizcar [peʎiθ'kar] *vt* to pinch, nip
pelma ['pelma] (*ESP: fam*) *nmf* pain (in the neck)
pelmazo [pel'maθo] (*fam*) *nm* = **pelma**
pelo ['pelo] *nm* (*cabellos*) hair; (*de barba, bigote*) whisker; (*de animal: pellejo*) hair, fur, coat; **venir al ~** to be exactly what one needs; **un hombre de ~ en pecho** a brave man; **por los ~s** by the skin of one's teeth; **no tener ~s en la lengua** to be outspoken, not to mince one's words; **con ~s y señales** in minute detail; **tomar el ~ a algn** to pull sb's leg
pelota [pe'lota] *nf* ball; **en ~** stark naked; **hacer la ~ (a algn)** (*ESP: fam*) to creep (to sb); **pelota vasca** pelota
pelotón [pelo'ton] *nm* (*Mil*) squad, detachment
peluca [pe'luka] *nf* wig
peluche [pe'lutʃe] *nm*: **oso/muñeco de ~** teddy bear/soft toy
peludo, -a [pe'luðo, a] *adj* hairy, shaggy
peluquería [peluke'ria] *nf* hairdresser's;

P

peluquero, -a *nm/f* hairdresser
pelusa [pe'lusa] *nf* (*Bot*) down; (*en tela*) fluff
pena ['pena] *nf* (*congoja*) grief, sadness; (*remordimiento*) regret; (*dificultad*) trouble; (*dolor*) pain; (*Jur*) sentence; **merecer** *o* **valer la ~** to be worthwhile; **a duras ~s** with great difficulty; **¡qué ~!** what a shame!; **pena capital** capital punishment; **pena de muerte** death penalty
penal [pe'nal] *adj* penal ▷*nm* (*cárcel*) prison
penalidad [penali'ðað] *nf* (*problema, dificultad*) trouble, hardship; (*Jur*) penalty, punishment; **penalidades** *nfpl* trouble *sg*, hardship *sg*
penalti [pe'nalti] *nm* =**penalty**
penalty [pe'nalti] (*pl* **~s** *o* **penalties**) *nm* penalty (kick)
pendiente [pen'djente] *adj* pending, unsettled ▷*nm* earring ▷*nf* hill, slope
pene ['pene] *nm* penis
penetrante [pene'trante] *adj* (*herida*) deep; (*persona, arma*) sharp; (*sonido*) penetrating, piercing; (*mirada*) searching; (*viento, ironía*) biting
penetrar [pene'trar] *vt* to penetrate, pierce; (*entender*) to grasp ▷*vi* to penetrate, go in; (*entrar*) to enter, go in; (*líquido*) to soak in; (*fig*) to pierce
penicilina [peniθi'lina] *nf* penicillin
península [pe'ninsula] *nf* peninsula; **peninsular** *adj* peninsular
penique [pe'nike] *nm* penny
penitencia [peni'tenθja] *nf* penance
penoso, -a [pe'noso, a] *adj* (*lamentable*) distressing; (*difícil*) arduous, difficult
pensador, a [pensa'ðor, a] *nm/f* thinker
pensamiento [pensa'mjento] *nm* thought; (*mente*) mind; (*idea*) idea
pensar [pen'sar] *vt* to think; (*considerar*) to think over, think out; (*proponerse*) to intend, plan; (*imaginarse*) to think up, invent ▷*vi* to think; **~ en** to aim at, aspire to; **pensativo, -a** *adj* thoughtful, pensive
pensión [pen'sjon] *nf* (*casa*) boarding *o* guest house; (*dinero*) pension; (*cama y comida*) board and lodging; **media ~** half-board; **pensión completa** full board; **pensionista** *nmf* (*jubilado*) (old-age) pensioner; (*huésped*) lodger
penúltimo, -a [pe'nultimo, a] *adj* penultimate, last but one
penumbra [pe'numbra] *nf* half-light
peña ['peɲa] *nf* (*roca*) rock; (*cuesta*) cliff, crag; (*grupo*) group, circle; (*LAM*: *club*) folk club
peñasco [pe'ɲasco] *nm* large rock, boulder
peñón [pe'ɲon] *nm* wall of rock; **el P~** the Rock (of Gibraltar)
peón [pe'on] *nm* labourer; (*LAM Agr*) farm labourer, farmhand; (*Ajedrez*) pawn
peonza [pe'onθa] *nf* spinning top
peor [pe'or] *adj* (*comparativo*) worse; (*superlativo*) worst ▷*adv* worse; worst; **de mal en ~** from bad to worse
pepinillo [pepi'niʎo] *nm* gherkin
pepino [pe'pino] *nm* cucumber; **(no) me importa un ~** I don't care one bit
pepita [pe'pita] *nf* (*Bot*) pip; (*Minería*) nugget
pepito [pe'pito] (*ESP*) *nm* (*tb*: **~ de ternera**) steak sandwich
pequeño, -a [pe'keɲo, a] *adj* small, little
pera ['pera] *nf* pear; **peral** *nm* pear tree
percance [per'kanθe] *nm* setback, misfortune
percatarse [perka'tarse] *vr*: **~ de** to notice, take note of
percebe [per'θeβe] *nm* barnacle
percepción [perθep'θjon] *nf* (*vista*) perception; (*idea*) notion, idea
percha ['pertʃa] *nf* (coat)hanger; (*ganchos*) coat hooks *pl*; (*de ave*) perch
percibir [perθi'βir] *vt* to perceive, notice; (*Com*) to earn, get
percusión [perku'sjon] *nf* percussion
perdedor, a [perðe'ðor, a] *adj* losing ▷*nm/f* loser
perder [per'ðer] *vt* to lose; (*tiempo, palabras*) to waste; (*oportunidad*) to lose, miss; (*tren*) to miss ▷*vi* to lose; **perderse** *vr* (*extraviarse*) to get lost; (*desaparecer*) to disappear, be lost to view; (*arruinarse*) to be ruined; **echar a ~** (*comida*) to spoil, ruin; (*oportunidad*) to waste
pérdida ['perðiða] *nf* loss; (*de tiempo*) waste; **pérdidas** *nfpl* (*Com*) losses
perdido, -a [per'ðiðo, a] *adj* lost
perdiz [per'ðiθ] *nf* partridge
perdón [per'ðon] *nm* (*disculpa*) pardon, forgiveness; (*clemencia*) mercy; **¡~!** sorry!, I beg your pardon!; **perdonar** *vt* to pardon, forgive; (*la vida*) to spare; (*excusar*) to exempt, excuse; **¡perdone (usted)!** sorry!, I beg your pardon!
perecedero, -a [pereθe'ðero, a] *adj* perishable
perecer [pere'θer] *vi* to perish, die
peregrinación [pereɣrina'θjon] *nf* (*Rel*) pilgrimage
peregrino, -a [pere'ɣrino, a] *adj* (*idea*) strange, absurd ▷*nm/f* pilgrim
perejil [pere'xil] *nm* parsley
perenne [pe'renne] *adj* everlasting, perennial

pereza [pe'reθa] *nf* laziness, idleness; **perezoso, -a** *adj* lazy, idle
perfección [perfek'θjon] *nf* perfection; **perfeccionar** *vt* to perfect; (*mejorar*) to improve; (*acabar*) to complete, finish
perfecto, -a [per'fekto, a] *adj* perfect; (*total*) complete
perfil [per'fil] *nm* profile; (*contorno*) silhouette, outline; (*Arq*) (cross) section; **perfiles** *nmpl* features
perforación [perfora'θjon] *nf* perforation; (*con taladro*) drilling; **perforadora** *nf* punch
perforar [perfo'rar] *vt* to perforate; (*agujero*) to drill, bore; (*papel*) to punch a hole in ▷*vi* to drill, bore
perfume [per'fume] *nm* perfume, scent
periferia [peri'ferja] *nf* periphery; (*de ciudad*) outskirts *pl*
periférico [peri'feriko] (LAM) *nm* ring road (BRIT), beltway (US)
perilla [pe'riʎa] *nf* (*barba*) goatee; (LAM: *de puerta*) doorknob, door handle
perímetro [pe'rimetro] *nm* perimeter
periódico, -a [pe'rjoðiko, a] *adj* periodic(al) ▷*nm* newspaper
periodismo [perjo'ðismo] *nm* journalism; **periodista** *nmf* journalist
periodo [pe'rjoðo] *nm* period
período [pe'rioðo] *nm* = **periodo**
periquito [peri'kito] *nm* budgerigar, budgie
perito, -a [pe'rito, a] *adj* (*experto*) expert; (*diestro*) skilled, skilful ▷*nm/f* expert; skilled worker; (*técnico*) technician
perjudicar [perxuði'kar] *vt* (*gen*) to damage, harm; **perjudicial** *adj* damaging, harmful; (*en detrimento*) detrimental; **perjuicio** *nm* damage, harm
perjurar [perxu'rar] *vi* to commit perjury
perla ['perla] *nf* pearl; **me viene de ~s** it suits me fine
permanecer [permane'θer] *vi* (*quedarse*) to stay, remain; (*seguir*) to continue to be
permanente [perma'nente] *adj* permanent, constant ▷*nf* perm
permiso [per'miso] *nm* permission; (*licencia*) permit, licence; **con ~** excuse me; **estar de ~** (*Mil*) to be on leave; **permiso de conducir** driving licence (BRIT), driver's license (US); **permiso por enfermedad** (LAM) sick leave
permitir [permi'tir] *vt* to permit, allow
pernera [per'nera] *nf* trouser leg
pero ['pero] *conj* but; (*aún*) yet ▷*nm* (*defecto*) flaw, defect; (*reparo*) objection
perpendicular [perpendiku'lar] *adj* perpendicular
perpetuo, -a [per'petwo, a] *adj* perpetual
perplejo, -a [per'plexo, a] *adj* perplexed, bewildered
perra ['perra] *nf* (*Zool*) bitch; **estar sin una ~** (ESP: *fam*) to be flat broke
perrera [pe'rrera] *nf* kennel
perrito [pe'rrito] *nm* (*tb*: **~ caliente**) hot dog
perro ['perro] *nm* dog
persa ['persa] *adj, nmf* Persian
persecución [perseku'θjon] *nf* pursuit, chase; (*Rel, Pol*) persecution
perseguir [perse'ɣir] *vt* to pursue, hunt; (*cortejar*) to chase after; (*molestar*) to pester, annoy; (*Rel, Pol*) to persecute
persiana [per'sjana] *nf* (Venetian) blind
persistente [persis'tente] *adj* persistent
persistir [persis'tir] *vi* to persist
persona [per'sona] *nf* person; **persona mayor** elderly person
personaje [perso'naxe] *nm* important person, celebrity; (*Teatro etc*) character
personal [perso'nal] *adj* (*particular*) personal; (*para una persona*) single, for one person ▷*nm* personnel, staff; **personalidad** *nf* personality
personarse [perso'narse] *vr* to appear in person
personificar [personifi'kar] *vt* to personify
perspectiva [perspek'tiβa] *nf* perspective; (*vista, panorama*) view, panorama; (*posibilidad futura*) outlook, prospect
persuadir [perswa'ðir] *vt* (*gen*) to persuade; (*convencer*) to convince; **persuadirse** *vr* to become convinced; **persuasión** *nf* persuasion
pertenecer [pertene'θer] *vi* to belong; (*fig*) to concern; **perteneciente** *adj*: **perteneciente a** belonging to; **pertenencia** *nf* ownership; **pertenencias** *nfpl* (*bienes*) possessions, property *sg*
pertenezca *etc vb V* **pertenecer**
pértiga ['pertiɣa] *nf*: **salto de ~** pole vault
pertinente [perti'nente] *adj* relevant, pertinent; (*apropiado*) appropriate; **~ a** concerning, relevant to
perturbación [perturβa'θjon] *nf* (*Pol*) disturbance; (*Med*) upset, disturbance
Perú [pe'ru] *nm* Peru; **peruano, -a** *adj, nm/f* Peruvian
perversión [perβer'sjon] *nf* perversion; **perverso, -a** *adj* perverse; (*depravado*) depraved
pervertido, -a [perβer'tiðo, a] *adj* perverted ▷*nm/f* pervert
pervertir [perβer'tir] *vt* to pervert,

P

corrupt
pesa ['pesa] *nf* weight; (*Deporte*) shot
pesadez [pesa'ðeθ] *nf* (*peso*) heaviness; (*lentitud*) slowness; (*aburrimiento*) tediousness
pesadilla [pesa'ðiʎa] *nf* nightmare, bad dream
pesado, -a [pe'saðo, a] *adj* heavy; (*lento*) slow; (*difícil, duro*) tough, hard; (*aburrido*) boring, tedious; (*tiempo*) sultry
pésame ['pesame] *nm* expression of condolence, message of sympathy; **dar el ~** to express one's condolences
pesar [pe'sar] *vt* to weigh ▷ *vi* to weigh; (*ser pesado*) to weigh a lot, be heavy; (*fig: opinión*) to carry weight; **no pesa mucho** it's not very heavy ▷ *nm* (*arrepentimiento*) regret; (*pena*) grief, sorrow; **a ~ de** *o* **pese a (que)** in spite of, despite
pesca ['peska] *nf* (*acto*) fishing; (*lo pescado*) catch; **ir de ~** to go fishing
pescadería [peskaðe'ria] *nf* fish shop, fishmonger's (BRIT)
pescadilla [peska'ðiʎa] *nf* whiting
pescado [pes'kaðo] *nm* fish
pescador, a [peska'ðor, a] *nm/f* fisherman/woman
pescar [pes'kar] *vt* (*tomar*) to catch; (*intentar tomar*) to fish for; (*conseguir: trabajo*) to manage to get ▷ *vi* to fish, go fishing
pesebre [pe'seβre] *nm* manger
peseta [pe'seta] *nf* (*Hist*) peseta
pesimista [pesi'mista] *adj* pessimistic ▷ *nmf* pessimist
pésimo, -a ['pesimo, a] *adj* awful, dreadful
peso ['peso] *nm* weight; (*balanza*) scales *pl*; (*moneda*) peso; **vender al ~** to sell by weight; **peso bruto/neto** gross/net weight; **peso pesado/pluma** heavyweight/featherweight
pesquero, -a [pes'kero, a] *adj* fishing *cpd*
pestaña [pes'taɲa] *nf* (*Anat*) eyelash; (*borde*) rim
peste ['peste] *nf* plague; (*mal olor*) stink, stench
pesticida [pesti'θiða] *nm* pesticide
pestillo [pes'tiʎo] *nm* (*cerrojo*) bolt; (*picaporte*) door handle
petaca [pe'taka] *nf* (*de cigarros*) cigarette case; (*de pipa*) tobacco pouch; (MÉX: *maleta*) suitcase
pétalo ['petalo] *nm* petal
petardo [pe'tardo] *nm* firework, firecracker
petición [peti'θjon] *nf* (*pedido*) request, plea; (*memorial*) petition; (*Jur*) plea
peto ['peto] (ESP) *nm* dungarees *pl*, overalls *pl* (US)
petróleo [pe'troleo] *nm* oil, petroleum; **petrolero, -a** *adj* petroleum *cpd* ▷ *nm* (oil) tanker
peyorativo, -a [pejora'tiβo, a] *adj* pejorative
pez [peθ] *nm* fish; **pez espada** swordfish
pezón [pe'θon] *nm* teat, nipple
pezuña [pe'θuɲa] *nf* hoof
pianista [pja'nista] *nmf* pianist
piano ['pjano] *nm* piano
piar [pjar] *vi* to cheep
pibe, -a ['piβe, a] (RPL) *nm/f* boy/girl
picadero [pika'ðero] *nm* riding school
picadillo [pika'ðiʎo] *nm* mince, minced meat
picado, -a [pi'kaðo, a] *adj* pricked, punctured; (*Culin*) minced, chopped; (*mar*) choppy; (*diente*) bad; (*tabaco*) cut; (*enfadado*) cross
picador [pika'ðor] *nm* (*Taur*) picador; (*minero*) faceworker
picadura [pika'ðura] *nf* (*pinchazo*) puncture; (*de abeja*) sting; (*de mosquito*) bite; (*tabaco picado*) cut tobacco
picante [pi'kante] *adj* hot; (*comentario*) racy, spicy
picaporte [pika'porte] *nm* (*manija*) doorhandle; (*pestillo*) latch
picar [pi'kar] *vt* (*agujerear, perforar*) to prick, puncture; (*abeja*) to sting; (*mosquito, serpiente*) to bite; (*Culin*) to mince, chop; (*incitar*) to incite, goad; (*dañar, irritar*) to annoy, bother; (*quemar: lengua*) to burn, sting ▷ *vi* (*pez*) to bite, take the bait; (*sol*) to burn, scorch; (*abeja, Med*) to sting; (*mosquito*) to bite; **picarse** *vr* (*agriarse*) to turn sour, go off; (*ofenderse*) to take offence
picardía [pikar'ðia] *nf* villainy; (*astucia*) slyness, craftiness; (*una picardía*) dirty trick; (*palabra*) rude/bad word *o* expression
pícaro, -a ['pikaro, a] *adj* (*malicioso*) villainous; (*travieso*) mischievous ▷ *nm* (*astuto*) crafty sort; (*sinvergüenza*) rascal, scoundrel
pichi ['pitʃi] (ESP) *nm* pinafore dress (BRIT), jumper (US)
pichón [pi'tʃon] *nm* young pigeon
pico ['piko] *nm* (*de ave*) beak; (*punta*) sharp point; (*Tec*) pick, pickaxe; (*Geo*) peak, summit; **y ~** and a bit; **las seis y ~** six and a bit
picor [pi'kor] *nm* itch
picoso, -a [pi'koso, a] (MÉX) *adj* (*comida*) hot
picudo, -a [pi'kuðo, a] *adj* pointed, with a point
pidió *etc vb V* **pedir**

pido *etc vb V* **pedir**
pie [pje] (*pl* **~s**) *nm* foot; (*fig: motivo*) motive, basis; (*: fundamento*) foothold; **ir a ~** to go on foot, walk; **estar de ~** to be standing (up); **ponerse de ~** to stand up; **de ~s a cabeza** from top to bottom; **al ~ de la letra** (*citar*) literally, verbatim; (*copiar*) exactly, word for word; **en ~ de guerra** on a war footing; **dar ~ a** to give cause for; **hacer ~** (*en el agua*) to touch (the) bottom
piedad [pje'ðað] *nf* (*lástima*) pity, compassion; (*clemencia*) mercy; (*devoción*) piety, devotion
piedra ['pjeðra] *nf* stone; (*roca*) rock; (*de mechero*) flint; (*Meteorología*) hailstone; **piedra preciosa** precious stone
piel [pjel] *nf* (*Anat*) skin; (*Zool*) skin, hide, fur; (*cuero*) leather; (*Bot*) skin, peel
pienso *etc vb V* **pensar**
pierdo *etc vb V* **perder**
pierna ['pjerna] *nf* leg
pieza ['pjeθa] *nf* piece; (*habitación*) room; **pieza de recambio** *o* **repuesto** spare (part)
pigmeo, -a [piɣ'meo, a] *adj, nm/f* pigmy
pijama [pi'xama] *nm* pyjamas *pl* (BRIT), pajamas *pl* (US)
pila ['pila] *nf* (*Elec*) battery; (*montón*) heap, pile; (*lavabo*) sink
píldora ['pildora] *nf* pill; **la ~ (anticonceptiva)** the (contraceptive) pill
pileta [pi'leta] (RPL) *nf* (*fregadero*) (kitchen) sink; (*piscina*) swimming pool
pillar [pi'ʎar] *vt* (*saquear*) to pillage, plunder; (*fam: coger*) to catch; (*: agarrar*) to grasp, seize; (*: entender*) to grasp, catch on to; **pillarse** *vr*: **~se un dedo con la puerta** to catch one's finger in the door
pillo, -a ['piʎo, a] *adj* villainous; (*astuto*) sly, crafty ▷ *nm/f* rascal, rogue, scoundrel
piloto [pi'loto] *nm* pilot; (*de aparato*) (pilot) light; (*Auto: luz*) tail *o* rear light; (*: conductor*) driver; **piloto automático** automatic pilot
pimentón [pimen'ton] *nm* paprika
pimienta [pi'mjenta] *nf* pepper
pimiento [pi'mjento] *nm* pepper, pimiento
pin [pin] (*pl* **~s**) *nm* badge
pinacoteca [pinako'teka] *nf* art gallery
pinar [pi'nar] *nm* pine forest (BRIT), pine grove (US)
pincel [pin'θel] *nm* paintbrush
pinchadiscos [pintʃa'ðiskos] (ESP) *nmf inv* disc-jockey, DJ
pinchar [pin'tʃar] *vt* (*perforar*) to prick, pierce; (*neumático*) to puncture; (*fig*) to prod; (*Inform*) to click
pinchazo [pin'tʃaθo] *nm* (*perforación*) prick; (*de neumático*) puncture; (*fig*) prod
pincho ['pintʃo] *nm* savoury (snack); **pincho de tortilla** small slice of omelette; **pincho moruno** shish kebab
ping-pong ['pin'pon] *nm* table tennis
pingüino [pin'gwino] *nm* penguin
pino ['pino] *nm* pine (tree)
pinta ['pinta] *nf* spot; (*de líquidos*) spot, drop; (*aspecto*) appearance, look(s) (*pl*); **pintado, -a** *adj* spotted; (*de colores*) colourful; **pintadas** *nfpl* graffiti *sg*
pintalabios [pinta'laβjos] (ESP) *nm inv* lipstick
pintar [pin'tar] *vt* to paint ▷ *vi* to paint; (*fam*) to count, be important; **pintarse** *vr* to put on make-up
pintor, a [pin'tor, a] *nm/f* painter
pintoresco, -a [pinto'resko, a] *adj* picturesque
pintura [pin'tura] *nf* painting; **pintura al óleo** oil painting
pinza ['pinθa] *nf* (*Zool*) claw; (*para colgar ropa*) clothes peg; (*Tec*) pincers *pl*; **pinzas** *nfpl* (*para depilar etc*) tweezers *pl*
piña ['piɲa] *nf* (*de pino*) pine cone; (*fruta*) pineapple; (*fig*) group
piñata [pi'ɲata] *nf* *container hung up at parties to be beaten with sticks until sweets or presents fall out*

PIÑATA

Piñata is a very popular party game in Mexico. The **piñata** itself is a hollow figure made of papier maché, or, traditionally, from adobe, in the shape of an object, a star, a person or an animal. It is filled with either sweets and toys, or fruit and yam beans. The game consists of hanging the **piñata** from the ceiling, and beating it with a stick, blindfolded, until it breaks and the presents fall out.

piñón [pi'ɲon] *nm* (*fruto*) pine nut; (*Tec*) pinion
pío, -a ['pio, a] *adj* (*devoto*) pious, devout; (*misericordioso*) merciful
piojo ['pjoxo] *nm* louse
pipa ['pipa] *nf* pipe; **pipas** *nfpl* (*Bot*) (edible) sunflower seeds
pipí [pi'pi] (*fam*) *nm*: **hacer ~** to have a wee(-wee) (BRIT), have to go (wee-wee) (US)
pique ['pike] *nm* (*resentimiento*) pique, resentment; (*rivalidad*) rivalry, competition; **irse a ~** to sink; (*esperanza, familia*) to be ruined
piqueta [pi'keta] *nf* pick(axe)
piquete [pi'kete] *nm* (*Mil*) squad, party;

(*de obreros*) picket; (MÉX: *de insecto*) bite; **piquetear** (LAM) *vt* to picket
pirado, -a [pi'raðo, a] (*fam*) *adj* round the bend ▷ *nm/f* nutter
piragua [pi'raɣwa] *nf* canoe; **piragüismo** *nm* canoeing
pirámide [pi'ramiðe] *nf* pyramid
pirata [pi'rata] *adj, nmf* pirate; **pirata informático** hacker
Pirineo(s) [piri'neo(s)] *nm(pl)* Pyrenees *pl*
pirómano, -a [pi'romano, a] *nm/f* (*Med, Jur*) arsonist
piropo [pi'ropo] *nm* compliment, (piece of) flattery
pirueta [pi'rweta] *nf* pirouette
piruleta [piru'leta] (ESP) *nf* lollipop
pis [pis] (*fam*) *nm* pee, piss; **hacer ~** to have a pee; (*para niños*) to wee-wee
pisada [pi'saða] *nf* (*paso*) footstep; (*huella*) footprint
pisar [pi'sar] *vt* (*caminar sobre*) to walk on, tread on; (*apretar con el pie*) to press; (*fig*) to trample on, walk all over ▷ *vi* to tread, step, walk
piscina [pis'θina] *nf* swimming pool
Piscis ['pisθis] *nm* Pisces
piso ['piso] *nm* (*suelo, planta*) floor; (ESP: *apartamento*) flat (BRIT), apartment; **primer ~** (ESP) first floor; (LAM: *planta baja*) ground floor
pisotear [pisote'ar] *vt* to trample (on *o* underfoot)
pista ['pista] *nf* track, trail; (*indicio*) clue; **pista de aterrizaje** runway; **pista de baile** dance floor; **pista de hielo** ice rink; **pista de tenis** (ESP) tennis court
pistola [pis'tola] *nf* pistol; (*Tec*) spray-gun
pistón [pis'ton] *nm* (*Tec*) piston; (*Mús*) key
pitar [pi'tar] *vt* (*silbato*) to blow; (*rechiflar*) to whistle at, boo ▷ *vi* to whistle; (*Auto*) to sound *o* toot one's horn; (LAM: *fumar*) to smoke
pitillo [pi'tiʎo] *nm* cigarette
pito ['pito] *nm* whistle; (*de coche*) horn
pitón [pi'ton] *nm* (*Zool*) python
pitonisa [pito'nisa] *nf* fortune-teller
pitorreo [pito'rreo] *nm* joke; **estar de ~** to be joking
píxel ['piksel] (*pl* **pixels** *or* **~es**) *nm* pixel
piyama [pi'jama] (LAM) *nm* pyjamas *pl* (BRIT), pajamas *pl* (US)
pizarra [pi'θarra] *nf* (*piedra*) slate; (ESP: *encerado*) blackboard; **pizarra blanca** whiteboard; **pizarra interactiva** interactive whiteboard
pizarrón [piθa'rron] (LAM) *nm* blackboard
pizca ['piθka] *nf* pinch, spot; (*fig*) spot, speck; **ni ~** not a bit
placa ['plaka] *nf* plate; (*distintivo*) badge, insignia; **placa de matrícula** (LAM) number plate
placard [pla'kar] (RPL) *nm* cupboard
placer [pla'θer] *nm* pleasure ▷ *vt* to please
plaga ['plaɣa] *nf* pest; (*Med*) plague; (*abundancia*) abundance
plagio ['plaxjo] *nm* plagiarism
plan [plan] *nm* (*esquema, proyecto*) plan; (*idea, intento*) idea, intention; **tener ~** (*fam*) to have a date; **tener un ~** (*fam*) to have an affair; **en ~ económico** (*fam*) on the cheap; **vamos en ~ de turismo** we're going as tourists; **si te pones en ese ~ ...** if that's your attitude ...
plana ['plana] *nf* sheet (of paper), page; (*Tec*) trowel; **en primera ~** on the front page
plancha ['plantʃa] *nf* (*para planchar*) iron; (*rótulo*) plate, sheet; (*Náut*) gangway; **a la ~** (*Culin*) grilled; **planchar** *vt* to iron ▷ *vi* to do the ironing
planear [plane'ar] *vt* to plan ▷ *vi* to glide
planeta [pla'neta] *nm* planet
plano, -a ['plano, a] *adj* flat, level, even ▷ *nm* (*Mat, Tec*) plane; (*Foto*) shot; (*Arq*) plan; (*Geo*) map; (*de ciudad*) map, street plan; **primer ~** close-up
planta ['planta] *nf* (*Bot, Tec*) plant; (*Anat*) sole of the foot, foot; (*piso*) floor; (LAM: *personal*) staff; **planta baja** ground floor
plantar [plan'tar] *vt* (*Bot*) to plant; (*levantar*) to erect, set up; **plantarse** *vr* to stand firm; **~ a algn en la calle** to throw sb out; **dejar plantado a algn** (*fam*) to stand sb up
plantear [plante'ar] *vt* (*problema*) to pose; (*dificultad*) to raise
plantilla [plan'tiʎa] *nf* (*de zapato*) insole; (ESP: *personal*) personnel; **ser de ~** (ESP) to be on the staff
plantón [plan'ton] *nm* (*Mil*) guard, sentry; (*fam*) long wait; **dar (un) ~ a algn** to stand sb up
plasta ['plasta] (ESP: *fam*) *adj inv* boring ▷ *nmf* bore
plástico, -a ['plastiko, a] *adj* plastic ▷ *nm* plastic
Plastilina® [plasti'lina] *nf* Plasticine®
plata ['plata] *nf* (*metal*) silver; (*cosas hechas de plata*) silverware; (CS: *dinero*) cash, dough
plataforma [plata'forma] *nf* platform; **plataforma de lanzamiento/perforación** launch(ing) pad/drilling rig
plátano ['platano] *nm* (*fruta*) banana; (*árbol*) plane tree; banana tree
platea [pla'tea] *nf* (*Teatro*) pit
plática ['platika] *nf* talk, chat; **platicar** *vi*

to talk, chat

platillo [pla'tiʎo] *nm* saucer; **platillos** *nmpl* (*Mús*) cymbals; **platillo volante** flying saucer

platino [pla'tino] *nm* platinum; **platinos** *nmpl* (*Auto*) contact points

plato ['plato] *nm* plate, dish; (*parte de comida*) course; (*comida*) dish; **primer ~** first course; **plato combinado** set main course (*served on one plate*); **plato fuerte** main course

playa ['plaja] *nf* beach; (*costa*) seaside; **playa de estacionamiento** (CS) car park (BRIT), parking lot (US)

playera [pla'jera] *nf* (MÉX: *camiseta*) T-shirt; **playeras** *nfpl* (*zapatos*) canvas shoes

plaza ['plaθa] *nf* square; (*mercado*) market(place); (*sitio*) room, space; (*de vehículo*) seat, place; (*colocación*) post, job; **plaza de toros** bullring

plazo ['plaθo] *nm* (*lapso de tiempo*) time, period; (*fecha de vencimiento*) expiry date; (*pago parcial*) instalment; **a corto/largo ~** short-/long-term; **comprar algo a ~s** to buy sth on hire purchase (BRIT) *o* on time (US)

plazoleta [plaθo'leta] *nf* small square

plebeyo, -a [ple'βejo, a] *adj* plebeian; (*pey*) coarse, common

plegable [ple'ɣaβle] *adj* collapsible; (*silla*) folding

pleito ['pleito] *nm* (*Jur*) lawsuit, case; (*fig*) dispute, feud

plenitud [pleni'tuð] *nf* plenitude, fullness; (*abundancia*) abundance

pleno, -a ['pleno, a] *adj* full; (*completo*) complete ▷*nm* plenum; **en ~ día** in broad daylight; **en ~ verano** at the height of summer; **en plena cara** full in the face

pliego *etc* ['pljeɣo] *vb V* **plegar** ▷*nm* (*hoja*) sheet (of paper); (*carta*) sealed letter/document; **pliego de condiciones** details *pl*, specifications *pl*

pliegue *etc* ['pljeɣe] *vb V* **plegar** ▷*nm* fold, crease; (*de vestido*) pleat

plomería [plome'ria] (LAM) *nf* plumbing; **plomero** (LAM) *nm* plumber

plomo ['plomo] *nm* (*metal*) lead; (*Elec*) fuse; **sin ~** unleaded

pluma ['pluma] *nf* feather; (*para escribir*): **~ (estilográfica)** ink pen; **~ fuente** (LAM) fountain pen

plumero [plu'mero] *nm* (*para el polvo*) feather duster

plumón [plu'mon] *nm* (*de ave*) down

plural [plu'ral] *adj* plural

pluriempleo [pluriem'pleo] *nm* having more than one job

plus [plus] *nm* bonus

población [poβla'θjon] *nf* population; (*pueblo, ciudad*) town, city

poblado, -a [po'βlaðo, a] *adj* inhabited ▷*nm* (*aldea*) village; (*pueblo*) (small) town; **densamente ~** densely populated

poblador, a [poβla'ðor, a] *nm/f* settler, colonist

pobre ['poβre] *adj* poor ▷*nmf* poor person; **pobreza** *nf* poverty

pocilga [po'θilɣa] *nf* pigsty

PALABRA CLAVE

poco, -a ['poko, a] *adj* **1** (*sg*) little, not much; **poco tiempo** little *o* not much time; **de poco interés** of little interest, not very interesting; **poca cosa** not much

2 (*pl*) few, not many; **unos pocos** a few, some; **pocos niños comen lo que les conviene** few children eat what they should

▷*adv* **1** little, not much; **cuesta poco** it doesn't cost much

2 (*+ adj: negativo, antónimo*): **poco amable/inteligente** not very nice/intelligent

3: **por poco me caigo** I almost fell

4: **a poco: a poco de haberse casado** shortly after getting married

5: **poco a poco** little by little

▷*nm* a little, a bit; **un poco triste/de dinero** a little sad/money

podar [po'ðar] *vt* to prune

PALABRA CLAVE

poder [po'ðer] *vi* **1** (*tener capacidad*) can, be able to; **no puedo hacerlo** I can't do it, I'm unable to do it

2 (*tener permiso*) can, may, be allowed to; **¿se puede?** may I (*o* we)?; **puedes irte ahora** you may go now; **no se puede fumar en este hospital** smoking is not allowed in this hospital

3 (*tener posibilidad*) may, might, could; **puede llegar mañana** he may *o* might arrive tomorrow; **pudiste haberte hecho daño** you might *o* could have hurt yourself; **¡podías habérmelo dicho antes!** you might have told me before!

4: **puede ser** perhaps; **puede ser que lo sepa Tomás** Tomás may *o* might know

5: **¡no puedo más!** I've had enough!; **es tonto a más no poder** he's as stupid as they come

6: **poder con: no puedo con este crío** this kid's too much for me

P

▷ *nm* power; **detentar** *o* **ocupar** *o* **estar en el poder** to be in power; **poder adquisitivo/ejecutivo/legislativo** purchasing/executive/legislative power; **poder judicial** judiciary

poderoso, -a [poðeroso, a] *adj* (*político, país*) powerful
podio ['poðjo] *nm* (*Deporte*) podium
podium ['poðjum] = **podio**
podrido, -a [po'ðriðo, a] *adj* rotten, bad; (*fig*) rotten, corrupt
podrir [po'ðrir] = **pudrir**
poema [po'ema] *nm* poem
poesía [poe'sia] *nf* poetry
poeta [po'eta] *nmf* poet; **poético, -a** *adj* poetic(al)
poetisa [poe'tisa] *nf* (woman) poet
póker ['poker] *nm* poker
polaco, -a [po'lako, a] *adj* Polish ▷ *nm/f* Pole
polar [po'lar] *adj* polar
polea [po'lea] *nf* pulley
polémica [po'lemika] *nf* polemics *sg*; (*una polémica*) controversy, polemic
polen ['polen] *nm* pollen
policía [poli'θia] *nmf* policeman/woman ▷ *nf* police; **policíaco, -a** *adj* police *cpd*; **novela policíaca** detective story; **policial** *adj* police *cpd*
polideportivo [poliðepor'tiβo] *nm* sports centre *o* complex
polígono [po'liɣono] *nm* (*Mat*) polygon; **polígono industrial** (ESP) industrial estate
polilla [po'liʎa] *nf* moth
polio ['poljo] *nf* polio
política [po'litika] *nf* politics *sg*; (*económica, agraria etc*) policy; *V tb* **político**
político, -a [po'litiko, a] *adj* political; (*discreto*) tactful; (*de familia*) ...-in-law ▷ *nm/f* politician; **padre ~** father-in-law
póliza ['poliθa] *nf* certificate, voucher; (*impuesto*) tax stamp; **póliza de seguro(s)** insurance policy
polizón [poli'θon] *nm* stowaway
pollera [po'ʎera] (CS) *nf* skirt
pollo ['poʎo] *nm* chicken
polo ['polo] *nm* (*Geo, Elec*) pole; (*helado*) ice lolly (BRIT), Popsicle® (US); (*Deporte*) polo; (*suéter*) polo-neck; **polo Norte/Sur** North/ South Pole
Polonia [po'lonja] *nf* Poland
poltrona [pol'trona] *nf* easy chair
polución [polu'θjon] *nf* pollution
polvera [pol'βera] *nf* powder compact
polvo ['polβo] *nm* dust; (*Quím, Culin, Med*) powder; **polvos** *nmpl* (*maquillaje*) powder *sg*; **en ~** powdered; **quitar el ~** to dust; **estar hecho ~** (*fam*) to be worn out *o* exhausted; **polvos de talco** talcum powder *sg*
pólvora ['polβora] *nf* gunpowder
polvoriento, -a [polβo'rjento, a] *adj* (*superficie*) dusty; (*sustancia*) powdery
pomada [po'maða] *nf* cream, ointment
pomelo [po'melo] *nm* grapefruit
pómez ['pomeθ] *nf*: **piedra ~** pumice stone
pomo ['pomo] *nm* doorknob
pompa ['pompa] *nf* (*burbuja*) bubble; (*bomba*) pump; (*esplendor*) pomp, splendour
pómulo ['pomulo] *nm* cheekbone
pon [pon] *vb V* **poner**
ponchadura [pontʃa'dura] (MÉX) *nf* puncture (BRIT), flat (US); **ponchar** (MÉX) *vt* (*llanta*) to puncture
ponche ['pontʃe] *nm* punch
poncho ['pontʃo] *nm* poncho
pondré *etc vb V* **poner**

PALABRA CLAVE

poner [po'ner] *vt* **1** (*colocar*) to put; (*telegrama*) to send; (*obra de teatro*) to put on; (*película*) to show; **ponlo más fuerte** turn it up; **¿qué ponen en el Excelsior?** what's on at the Excelsior?
2 (*tienda*) to open; (*instalar*: *gas etc*) to put in; (*radio, TV*) to switch *o* turn on
3 (*suponer*): **pongamos que ...** let's suppose that ...
4 (*contribuir*): **el gobierno ha puesto otro millón** the government has contributed another million
5 (*Tel*): **póngame con el Sr. López** can you put me through to Mr. López?
6: **poner de: le han puesto de director general** they've appointed him general manager
7 (*+ adj*) to make; **me estás poniendo nerviosa** you're making me nervous
8 (*dar nombre*): **al hijo le pusieron Diego** they called their son Diego
▷ *vi* (*gallina*) to lay
ponerse *vr* **1** (*colocarse*): **se puso a mi lado** he came and stood beside me; **tú ponte en esa silla** you go and sit on that chair
2 (*vestido, cosméticos*) to put on; **¿por qué no te pones el vestido nuevo?** why don't you put on *o* wear your new dress?
3 (*+ adj*) to turn; to get, become; **se puso muy serio** he got very serious; **después de lavarla la tela se puso azul** after washing it the material turned blue
4: **ponerse a: se puso a llorar** he started to cry; **tienes que ponerte a estudiar** you must get down to studying

pongo *etc vb V* **poner**
poniente [po'njente] *nm* (*occidente*) west; (*viento*) west wind
pontífice [pon'tifiθe] *nm* pope, pontiff
popa ['popa] *nf* stern
popote [po'pote] (*MÉX*) *nm* straw
popular [popu'lar] *adj* popular; (*cultura*) of the people, folk *cpd*; **popularidad** *nf* popularity

PALABRA CLAVE

por [por] *prep* **1** (*objetivo*) for; **luchar por la patria** to fight for one's country
2 (*+ infin*): **por no llegar tarde** so as not to arrive late; **por citar unos ejemplos** to give a few examples
3 (*causa*) out of, because of; **por escasez de fondos** through *o* for lack of funds
4 (*tiempo*): **por la mañana/noche** in the morning/at night; **se queda por una semana** she's staying (for) a week
5 (*lugar*): **pasar por Madrid** to pass through Madrid; **ir a Guayaquil por Quito** to go to Guayaquil via Quito; **caminar por la calle** to walk along the street; *V tb* **todo**
6 (*cambio, precio*): **te doy uno nuevo por el que tienes** I'll give you a new one (in return) for the one you've got
7 (*valor distributivo*): **6 euros por hora/cabeza** 6 euros an *o* per hour/a *o* per head
8 (*modo, medio*) by; **por correo/avión** by post/air; **entrar por la entrada principal** to go in through the main entrance
9: **10 por 10 son 100** 10 times 10 is 100
10 (*en lugar de*): **vino él por su jefe** he came instead of his boss
11: **por mí que revienten** as far as I'm concerned they can drop dead
12: **¿por qué?** why?; **¿por qué no?** why not?

porcelana [porθe'lana] *nf* porcelain; (*china*) china
porcentaje [porθen'taxe] *nm* percentage
porción [por'θjon] *nf* (*parte*) portion, share; (*cantidad*) quantity, amount
porfiar [por'fjar] *vi* to persist, insist; (*disputar*) to argue stubbornly
pormenor [porme'nor] *nm* detail, particular
pornografía [pornoɣra'fia] *nf* pornography
poro ['poro] *nm* pore
pororó [poro'ro] (*RPL*) *nm* popcorn
poroso, -a [po'roso, a] *adj* porous
poroto [po'roto] (*CS*) *nm* bean
porque ['porke] *conj* (*a causa de*) because; (*ya que*) since; (*con el fin de*) so that, in order that
porqué [por'ke] *nm* reason, cause
porquería [porke'ria] *nf* (*suciedad*) filth, dirt; (*acción*) dirty trick; (*objeto*) small thing, trifle; (*fig*) rubbish
porra ['porra] (*ESP*) *nf* (*arma*) stick, club
porrazo [po'rraθo] *nm* blow, bump
porro ['porro] (*fam*) *nm* (*droga*) joint (*fam*)
porrón [po'rron] *nm* *glass wine jar with a long spout*
portaaviones [porta'(a)βjones] *nm inv* aircraft carrier
portada [por'taða] *nf* (*de revista*) cover
portador, a [porta'ðor, a] *nm/f* carrier, bearer; (*Com*) bearer, payee
portaequipajes [portaeki'paxes] *nm inv* (*Auto: maletero*) boot; (: *baca*) luggage rack
portafolio [porta'foljo] (*LAM*) *nm* briefcase
portal [por'tal] *nm* (*entrada*) vestibule, hall; (*portada*) porch, doorway; (*puerta de entrada*) main door; (*Internet*) portal; **portales** *nmpl* (*LAM*) arcade *sg*
portamaletas [portama'letas] *nm inv* (*Auto: maletero*) boot; (: *baca*) roof rack
portarse [por'tarse] *vr* to behave, conduct o.s.
portátil [por'tatil] *adj* portable
portavoz [porta'βoθ] *nmf* spokesman/woman
portazo [por'taθo] *nm*: **dar un ~** to slam the door
porte ['porte] *nm* (*Com*) transport; (*precio*) transport charges *pl*
portentoso, -a [porten'toso, a] *adj* marvellous, extraordinary
porteño, -a [por'teɲo, a] *adj* of *o* from Buenos Aires
portería [porte'ria] *nf* (*oficina*) porter's office; (*Deporte*) goal
portero, -a [por'tero, a] *nm/f* porter; (*conserje*) caretaker; (*ujier*) doorman; (*Deporte*) goalkeeper; **portero automático** (*ESP*) entry phone
pórtico ['portiko] *nm* (*patio*) portico, porch; (*fig*) gateway; (*arcada*) arcade
portorriqueño, -a [portorri'keɲo, a] *adj* Puerto Rican
Portugal [portu'ɣal] *nm* Portugal; **portugués, -esa** *adj, nm/f* Portuguese ▷ *nm* (*Ling*) Portuguese
porvenir [porβe'nir] *nm* future
pos [pos] *prep*: **en ~ de** after, in pursuit of
posaderas [posa'ðeras] *nfpl* backside *sg*, buttocks
posar [po'sar] *vt* (*en el suelo*) to lay down, put down; (*la mano*) to place, put gently ▷ *vi* (*modelo*) to sit, pose; **posarse** *vr* to settle;

P

(*pájaro*) to perch; (*avión*) to land, come down
posavasos [posa'basos] *nm inv* coaster; (*para cerveza*) beermat
posdata [pos'ðata] *nf* postscript
pose ['pose] *nf* pose
poseedor, a [posee'ðor, a] *nm/f* owner, possessor; (*de récord, puesto*) holder
poseer [pose'er] *vt* to possess, own; (*ventaja*) to enjoy; (*récord, puesto*) to hold
posesivo, -a [pose'siβo, a] *adj* possessive
posibilidad [posiβili'ðað] *nf* possibility; (*oportunidad*) chance; **posibilitar** *vt* to make possible; (*hacer realizable*) to make feasible
posible [po'siβle] *adj* possible; (*realizable*) feasible; **de ser ~** if possible; **en lo ~** as far as possible
posición [posi'θjon] *nf* position; (*rango social*) status
positivo, -a [posi'tiβo, a] *adj* positive
poso ['poso] *nm* sediment; (*heces*) dregs *pl*
posponer [pospo'ner] *vt* (*relegar*) to put behind/below; (*aplazar*) to postpone
posta ['posta] *nf*: **a ~** deliberately, on purpose
postal [pos'tal] *adj* postal ▷ *nf* postcard
poste ['poste] *nm* (*de telégrafos etc*) post, pole; (*columna*) pillar
póster ['poster] (*pl* **~es, ~s**) *nm* poster
posterior [poste'rjor] *adj* back, rear; (*siguiente*) following, subsequent; (*más tarde*) later
postgrado [post'graðo] *nm* = **posgrado**
postizo, -a [pos'tiθo, a] *adj* false, artificial ▷ *nm* hairpiece
postre ['postre] *nm* sweet, dessert
póstumo, -a ['postumo, a] *adj* posthumous
postura [pos'tura] *nf* (*del cuerpo*) posture, position; (*fig*) attitude, position
potable [po'taβle] *adj* drinkable; **agua ~** drinking water
potaje [po'taxe] *nm* thick vegetable soup
potencia [po'tenθja] *nf* power; **potencial** [poten'θjal] *adj, nm* potential
potente [po'tente] *adj* powerful
potro, -a ['potro, a] *nm/f* (*Zool*) colt/filly ▷ *nm* (*de gimnasia*) vaulting horse
pozo ['poθo] *nm* well; (*de río*) deep pool; (*de mina*) shaft
PP (ESP) *nm abr* = **Partido Popular**
práctica ['praktika] *nf* practice; (*método*) method; (*arte, capacidad*) skill; **en la ~** in practice
practicable [prakti'kaβle] *adj* practicable; (*camino*) passable
practicante [prakti'kante] *nmf* (*Med: ayudante de doctor*) medical assistant; (*: enfermero*) nurse; (*quien practica algo*) practitioner ▷ *adj* practising
practicar [prakti'kar] *vt* to practise; (*Deporte*) to play; (*realizar*) to carry out, perform
práctico, -a ['praktiko, a] *adj* practical; (*instruído: persona*) skilled, expert
practique *etc vb V* **practicar**
pradera [pra'ðera] *nf* meadow; (*US etc*) prairie
prado ['praðo] *nm* (*campo*) meadow, field; (*pastizal*) pasture
Praga ['praɣa] *n* Prague
pragmático, -a [praɣ'matiko, a] *adj* pragmatic
precario, -a [pre'karjo, a] *adj* precarious
precaución [prekau'θjon] *nf* (*medida preventiva*) preventive measure, precaution; (*prudencia*) caution, wariness
precedente [preθe'ðente] *adj* preceding; (*anterior*) former ▷ *nm* precedent
preceder [preθe'ðer] *vt, vi* to precede, go before, come before
precepto [pre'θepto] *nm* precept
precinto [pre'θinto] *nm* (*tb*: **~ de garantía**) seal
precio ['preθjo] *nm* price; (*costo*) cost; (*valor*) value, worth; (*de viaje*) fare; **precio al contado/de coste/de oportunidad** cash/cost/bargain price; **precio al por menor** retail price; **precio de ocasión** bargain price; **precio de venta al público** retail price; **precio tope** top price
preciosidad [preθjosi'ðað] *nf* (*valor*) (high) value, (great) worth; (*encanto*) charm; (*cosa bonita*) beautiful thing; **es una ~** it's lovely, it's really beautiful
precioso, -a [pre'θjoso, a] *adj* precious; (*de mucho valor*) valuable; (*fam*) lovely, beautiful
precipicio [preθi'piθjo] *nm* cliff, precipice; (*fig*) abyss
precipitación [preθipita'θjon] *nf* haste; (*lluvia*) rainfall
precipitado, -a [preθipi'taðo, a] *adj* (*conducta*) hasty, rash; (*salida*) hasty, sudden
precipitar [preθipi'tar] *vt* (*arrojar*) to hurl down, throw; (*apresurar*) to hasten; (*acelerar*) to speed up, accelerate; **precipitarse** *vr* to throw o.s.; (*apresurarse*) to rush; (*actuar sin pensar*) to act rashly
precisamente [preθisa'mente] *adv* precisely; (*exactamente*) precisely, exactly
precisar [preθi'sar] *vt* (*necesitar*) to need, require; (*fijar*) to determine exactly, fix; (*especificar*) to specify
precisión [preθi'sjon] *nf* (*exactitud*) precision

preciso, -a [pre'θiso, a] *adj* (*exacto*) precise; (*necesario*) necessary, essential
preconcebido, -a [prekonθe'βiðo, a] *adj* preconceived
precoz [pre'koθ] *adj* (*persona*) precocious; (*calvicie etc*) premature
predecir [preðe'θir] *vt* to predict, forecast
predestinado, -a [preðesti'naðo, a] *adj* predestined
predicar [preði'kar] *vt, vi* to preach
predicción [preðik'θjon] *nf* prediction
predilecto, -a [preði'lekto, a] *adj* favourite
predisposición [preðisposi'θjon] *nf* inclination; prejudice, bias
predominar [preðomi'nar] *vt* to dominate ▷*vi* to predominate; (*prevalecer*) to prevail; **predominio** *nm* predominance; prevalence
preescolar [pre(e)sko'lar] *adj* preschool
prefabricado, -a [prefaβri'kaðo, a] *adj* prefabricated
prefacio [pre'faθjo] *nm* preface
preferencia [prefe'renθja] *nf* preference; **de ~** preferably, for preference
preferible [prefe'riβle] *adj* preferable
preferir [prefe'rir] *vt* to prefer
prefiero *etc vb V* **preferir**
prefijo [pre'fixo] *nm* (*Tel*) (dialling) code
pregunta [pre'ɣunta] *nf* question; **hacer una ~** to ask a question; **preguntas frecuentes** FAQs, frequently asked questions
preguntar [preɣun'tar] *vt* to ask; (*cuestionar*) to question ▷*vi* to ask; **preguntarse** *vr* to wonder; **preguntar por algn** to ask for sb; **preguntón, -ona** [preɣun'ton, ona] *adj* inquisitive
prehistórico, -a [preis'toriko, a] *adj* prehistoric
prejuicio [pre'xwiθjo] *nm* (*acto*) prejudgement; (*idea preconcebida*) preconception; (*parcialidad*) prejudice, bias
preludio [pre'luðjo] *nm* prelude
prematuro, -a [prema'turo, a] *adj* premature
premeditar [premeði'tar] *vt* to premeditate
premiar [pre'mjar] *vt* to reward; (*en un concurso*) to give a prize to
premio ['premjo] *nm* reward; prize; (*Com*) premium
prenatal [prena'tal] *adj* antenatal, prenatal
prenda ['prenda] *nf* (*ropa*) garment, article of clothing; (*garantía*) pledge; **prendas** *nfpl* (*talentos*) talents, gifts
prender [pren'der] *vt* (*captar*) to catch, capture; (*detener*) to arrest; (*Costura*) to pin, attach; (*sujetar*) to fasten ▷*vi* to catch; (*arraigar*) to take root; **prenderse** *vr* (*encenderse*) to catch fire
prendido, -a [pren'diðo, a] (LAM) *adj* (*luz etc*) on
prensa ['prensa] *nf* press; **la ~** the press
preñado, -a [pre'ɲaðo, a] *adj* pregnant; **~ de** pregnant with, full of
preocupación [preokupa'θjon] *nf* worry, concern; (*ansiedad*) anxiety
preocupado, -a [preoku'paðo, a] *adj* worried, concerned; (*ansioso*) anxious
preocupar [preoku'par] *vt* to worry; **preocuparse** *vr* to worry; **~se de algo** (*hacerse cargo*) to take care of sth
preparación [prepara'θjon] *nf* (*acto*) preparation; (*estado*) readiness; (*entrenamiento*) training
preparado, -a [prepa'raðo, a] *adj* (*dispuesto*) prepared; (*Culin*) ready (to serve) ▷*nm* preparation
preparar [prepa'rar] *vt* (*disponer*) to prepare, get ready; (*Tec: tratar*) to prepare, process; (*entrenar*) to teach, train; **prepararse** *vr*: **~se a** *o* **para** to prepare to *o* for, get ready to *o* for; **preparativo, -a** *adj* preparatory, preliminary; **preparativos** *nmpl* preparations; **preparatoria** (MÉX) *nf* sixth-form college (BRIT), senior high school (US)
presa ['presa] *nf* (*cosa apresada*) catch; (*víctima*) victim; (*de animal*) prey; (*de agua*) dam
presagiar [presa'xjar] *vt* to presage, forebode; **presagio** *nm* omen
prescindir [presθin'dir] *vi*: **~ de** (*privarse de*) to do *o* go without; (*descartar*) to dispense with
prescribir [preskri'βir] *vt* to prescribe
presencia [pre'senθja] *nf* presence; **presenciar** *vt* to be present at; (*asistir a*) to attend; (*ver*) to see, witness
presentación [presenta'θjon] *nf* presentation; (*introducción*) introduction
presentador, a [presenta'ðor, a] *nm/f* presenter, compère
presentar [presen'tar] *vt* to present; (*ofrecer*) to offer; (*mostrar*) to show, display; (*a una persona*) to introduce; **presentarse** *vr* (*llegar inesperadamente*) to appear, turn up; (*ofrecerse: como candidato*) to run, stand; (*aparecer*) to show, appear; (*solicitar empleo*) to apply
presente [pre'sente] *adj* present ▷*nm* present; **hacer ~** to state, declare; **tener ~** to remember, bear in mind
presentimiento [presenti'mjento] *nm*

P

premonition, presentiment
presentir [presen'tir] *vt* to have a premonition of
preservación [preserβa'θjon] *nf* protection, preservation
preservar [preser'βar] *vt* to protect, preserve; **preservativo** *nm* sheath, condom
presidencia [presi'ðenθja] *nf* presidency; (*de comité*) chairmanship
presidente [presi'ðente] *nmf* president; (*de comité*) chairman/woman
presidir [presi'ðir] *vt* (*dirigir*) to preside at, preside over; (: *comité*) to take the chair at; (*dominar*) to dominate, rule ▷ *vi* to preside; to take the chair
presión [pre'sjon] *nf* pressure; **presión atmosférica** atmospheric *o* air pressure; **presionar** *vt* to press; (*fig*) to press, put pressure on ▷ *vi*: **presionar para** to press for
preso, -a ['preso, a] *nm/f* prisoner; **tomar** *o* **llevar ~ a algn** to arrest sb, take sb prisoner
prestación [presta'θjon] *nf* service; (*subsidio*) benefit; **prestaciones** *nfpl* (*Tec, Auto*) performance features
prestado, -a [pres'taðo, a] *adj* on loan; **pedir ~** to borrow
prestamista [presta'mista] *nmf* moneylender
préstamo ['prestamo] *nm* loan; **préstamo hipotecario** mortgage
prestar [pres'tar] *vt* to lend, loan; (*atención*) to pay; (*ayuda*) to give
prestigio [pres'tixjo] *nm* prestige; **prestigioso, -a** *adj* (*honorable*) prestigious; (*famoso, renombrado*) renowned, famous
presumido, -a [presu'miðo, a] *adj* (*persona*) vain
presumir [presu'mir] *vt* to presume ▷ *vi* (*tener aires*) to be conceited; **presunto, -a** *adj* (*supuesto*) supposed, presumed; (*así llamado*) so-called; **presuntuoso, -a** *adj* conceited, presumptuous
presupuesto [presu'pwesto] *pp de* **presuponer** ▷ *nm* (*Finanzas*) budget; (*estimación*: *de costo*) estimate
pretencioso, -a [preten'θjoso, a] *adj* pretentious
pretender [preten'der] *vt* (*intentar*) to try to, seek to; (*reivindicar*) to claim; (*buscar*) to seek, try for; (*cortejar*) to woo, court; **~ que** to expect that

No confundir **pretender** con la palabra inglesa *pretend*.

pretendiente *nmf* (*amante*) suitor; (*al trono*) pretender; **pretensión** *nf* (*aspiración*) aspiration; (*reivindicación*) claim; (*orgullo*) pretension
pretexto [pre'teksto] *nm* pretext; (*excusa*) excuse
prevención [preβen'θjon] *nf* prevention; (*precaución*) precaution
prevenido, -a [preβe'niðo, a] *adj* prepared, ready; (*cauteloso*) cautious
prevenir [preβe'nir] *vt* (*impedir*) to prevent; (*predisponer*) to prejudice, bias; (*avisar*) to warn; (*preparar*) to prepare, get ready; **prevenirse** *vr* to get ready, prepare; **~se contra** to take precautions against; **preventivo, -a** *adj* preventive, precautionary
prever [pre'βer] *vt* to foresee
previo, -a ['preβjo, a] *adj* (*anterior*) previous; (*preliminar*) preliminary ▷ *prep*: **~ acuerdo de los otros** subject to the agreement of the others
previsión [preβi'sjon] *nf* (*perspicacia*) foresight; (*predicción*) forecast; **previsto, -a** *adj* anticipated, forecast
prima ['prima] *nf* (*Com*) bonus; (*de seguro*) premium; *V tb* **primo**
primario, -a [pri'marjo, a] *adj* primary
primavera [prima'βera] *nf* spring(-time)
primera [pri'mera] *nf* (*Auto*) first gear; (*Ferro*: *tb*: **~ clase**) first class; **de ~** (*fam*) first-class, first-rate
primero, -a [pri'mero, a] (*adj* **primer**) first; (*principal*) prime *adv* first; (*más bien*) sooner, rather; **primera plana** front page
primitivo, -a [primi'tiβo, a] *adj* primitive; (*original*) original
primo, -a ['primo, a] *adj* prime ▷ *nm/f* cousin; (*fam*) fool, idiot; **materias primas** raw materials; **primo hermano** first cousin
primogénito, -a [primo'xenito, a] *adj* first-born
primoroso, -a [primo'roso, a] *adj* exquisite, delicate
princesa [prin'θesa] *nf* princess
principal [prinθi'pal] *adj* principal, main ▷ *nm* (*jefe*) chief, principal
príncipe ['prinθipe] *nm* prince
principiante [prinθi'pjante] *nmf* beginner
principio [prin'θipjo] *nm* (*comienzo*) beginning, start; (*origen*) origin; (*primera etapa*) rudiment, basic idea; (*moral*) principle; **desde el ~** from the first; **en un ~** at first; **a ~s de** at the beginning of
pringue ['pringe] *nm* (*grasa*) grease, fat, dripping
prioridad [priori'ðað] *nf* priority
prisa ['prisa] *nf* (*apresuramiento*) hurry, haste; (*rapidez*) speed; (*urgencia*) (sense of) urgency; **a** *o* **de ~** quickly; **correr ~** to be

urgent; **darse ~** to hurry up; **tener ~** to be in a hurry
prisión [pri'sjon] *nf* (*cárcel*) prison; (*período de cárcel*) imprisonment; **prisionero, -a** *nm/f* prisoner
prismáticos [pris'matikos] *nmpl* binoculars
privado, -a [pri'βaðo, a] *adj* private
privar [pri'βar] *vt* to deprive; **privativo, -a** *adj* exclusive
privilegiar [priβile'xjar] *vt* to grant a privilege to; (*favorecer*) to favour
privilegio [priβi'lexjo] *nm* privilege; (*concesión*) concession
pro [pro] *nm o f* profit, advantage ▷ *prep*: **asociación ~ ciegos** association for the blind ▷ *prefijo*: **~ americano** pro-American; **en ~ de** on behalf of, for; **los ~s y los contras** the pros and cons
proa ['proa] *nf* bow, prow; **de ~** bow *cpd*, fore
probabilidad [proβaβili'ðað] *nf* probability, likelihood; (*oportunidad, posibilidad*) chance, prospect; **probable** *adj* probable, likely
probador [proβa'ðor] *nm* (*en tienda*) fitting room
probar [pro'βar] *vt* (*demostrar*) to prove; (*someter a prueba*) to test, try out; (*ropa*) to try on; (*comida*) to taste ▷ *vi* to try; **~se un traje** to try on a suit
probeta [pro'βeta] *nf* test tube
problema [pro'βlema] *nm* problem
procedente [proθe'ðente] *adj* (*razonable*) reasonable; (*conforme a derecho*) proper, fitting; **~ de** coming from, originating in
proceder [proθe'ðer] *vi* (*avanzar*) to proceed; (*actuar*) to act; (*ser correcto*) to be right (and proper), be fitting ▷ *nm* (*comportamiento*) behaviour, conduct; **~ de** to come from, originate in; **procedimiento** *nm* procedure; (*proceso*) process; (*método*) means *pl*, method
procesador [proθesa'ðor] *nm* processor; **procesador de textos** word processor
procesar [proθe'sar] *vt* to try, put on trial
procesión [proθe'sjon] *nf* procession
proceso [pro'θeso] *nm* process; (*Jur*) trial
proclamar [prokla'mar] *vt* to proclaim
procrear [prokre'ar] *vt, vi* to procreate
procurador, a [prokura'ðor, a] *nm/f* attorney
procurar [proku'rar] *vt* (*intentar*) to try, endeavour; (*conseguir*) to get, obtain; (*asegurar*) to secure; (*producir*) to produce
prodigio [pro'ðixjo] *nm* prodigy; (*milagro*) wonder, marvel; **prodigioso, -a** *adj* prodigious, marvellous
pródigo, -a ['proðiɣo, a] *adj*: **hijo ~** prodigal son
producción [proðuk'θjon] *nf* (*gen*) production; (*producto*) output; **producción en serie** mass production
producir [proðu'θir] *vt* to produce; (*causar*) to cause, bring about; **producirse** *vr* (*cambio*) to come about; (*accidente*) to take place; (*problema etc*) to arise; (*hacerse*) to be produced, be made; (*estallar*) to break out
productividad [proðuktiβi'ðað] *nf* productivity; **productivo, -a** *adj* productive; (*provechoso*) profitable
producto [pro'ðukto] *nm* product
productor, a [proðuk'tor, a] *adj* productive, producing ▷ *nm/f* producer
proeza [pro'eθa] *nf* exploit, feat
profano, -a [pro'fano, a] *adj* profane ▷ *nm/f* layman/woman
profecía [profe'θia] *nf* prophecy
profesión [profe'sjon] *nf* profession; (*en formulario*) occupation; **profesional** *adj* professional
profesor, a [profe'sor, a] *nm/f* teacher; **profesorado** *nm* teaching profession
profeta [pro'feta] *nmf* prophet
prófugo, -a ['profuɣo, a] *nm/f* fugitive; (*Mil: desertor*) deserter
profundidad [profundi'ðað] *nf* depth; **profundizar** *vi*: **profundizar en** to go deeply into; **profundo, -a** *adj* deep; (*misterio, pensador*) profound
progenitor [proxeni'tor] *nm* ancestor; **progenitores** *nmpl* (*padres*) parents
programa [pro'ɣrama] *nm* programme (BRIT), program (US); **programa de estudios** curriculum, syllabus; **programación** *nf* programming; **programador, a** *nm/f* programmer; **programar** *vt* to program
progresar [proɣre'sar] *vi* to progress, make progress; **progresista** *adj, nmf* progressive; **progresivo, -a** *adj* progressive; (*gradual*) gradual; (*continuo*) continuous; **progreso** *nm* progress
prohibición [proiβi'θjon] *nf* prohibition, ban
prohibir [proi'βir] *vt* to prohibit, ban, forbid; **prohibido** *o* **se prohibe fumar** no smoking; **"prohibido el paso"** "no entry"
prójimo, -a ['proximo, a] *nm/f* fellow man; (*vecino*) neighbour
prólogo ['proloɣo] *nm* prologue
prolongar [prolon'ɣar] *vt* to extend; (*reunión etc*) to prolong; (*calle, tubo*) to extend
promedio [pro'meðjo] *nm* average; (*de distancia*) middle, mid-point
promesa [pro'mesa] *nf* promise
prometer [prome'ter] *vt* to promise ▷ *vi*

to show promise; **prometerse** *vr* (*novios*) to get engaged; **prometido, -a** *adj* promised; engaged ▷ *nm/f* fiancé/fiancée
prominente [promi'nente] *adj* prominent
promoción [promo'θjon] *nf* promotion
promotor [promo'tor] *nm* promoter; (*instigador*) instigator
promover [promo'βer] *vt* to promote; (*causar*) to cause; (*instigar*) to instigate, stir up
promulgar [promul'ɣar] *vt* to promulgate; (*anunciar*) to proclaim
pronombre [pro'nombre] *nm* pronoun
pronosticar [pronosti'kar] *vt* to predict, foretell, forecast; **pronóstico** *nm* prediction, forecast; **pronóstico del tiempo** weather forecast
pronto, -a ['pronto, a] *adj* (*rápido*) prompt, quick; (*preparado*) ready ▷ *adv* quickly, promptly; (*en seguida*) at once, right away; (*dentro de poco*) soon; (*temprano*) early ▷ *nm*: **tiene unos ~s muy malos** he gets ratty all of a sudden (*inf*); **de ~** suddenly; **por lo ~** meanwhile, for the present
pronunciación [pronunθja'θjon] *nf* pronunciation
pronunciar [pronun'θjar] *vt* to pronounce; (*discurso*) to make, deliver; **pronunciarse** *vr* to revolt, rebel; (*declararse*) to declare o.s.
propagación [propaɣa'θjon] *nf* propagation
propaganda [propa'ɣanda] *nf* (*Pol*) propaganda; (*Com*) advertising
propenso, -a [pro'penso, a] *adj* inclined to; **ser ~ a** to be inclined to, have a tendency to
propicio, -a [pro'piθjo, a] *adj* favourable, propitious
propiedad [propje'ðað] *nf* property; (*posesión*) possession, ownership; **propiedad particular** private property
propietario, -a [propje'tarjo, a] *nm/f* owner, proprietor
propina [pro'pina] *nf* tip
propio, -a ['propjo, a] *adj* own, of one's own; (*característico*) characteristic, typical; (*debido*) proper; (*mismo*) selfsame, very; **el ~ ministro** the minister himself; **¿tienes casa propia?** have you a house of your own?
proponer [propo'ner] *vt* to propose, put forward; (*problema*) to pose; **proponerse** *vr* to propose, intend
proporción [propor'θjon] *nf* proportion; (*Mat*) ratio; **proporciones** *nfpl* (*dimensiones*) dimensions; (*fig*) size *sg*; **proporcionado, -a** *adj* proportionate; (*regular*) medium, middling; (*justo*) just right; **proporcionar** *vt* (*dar*) to give, supply, provide
proposición [proposi'θjon] *nf* proposition; (*propuesta*) proposal
propósito [pro'posito] *nm* purpose; (*intento*) aim, intention ▷ *adv*: **a ~** by the way, incidentally; (*a posta*) on purpose, deliberately; **a ~ de** about, with regard to
propuesta [pro'pwesta] *vb V* **proponer** ▷ *nf* proposal
propulsar [propul'sar] *vt* to drive, propel; (*fig*) to promote, encourage; **propulsión** *nf* propulsion; **propulsión a chorro** *o* **por reacción** jet propulsion
prórroga ['prorroɣa] *nf* extension; (*Jur*) stay; (*Com*) deferment; (*Deporte*) extra time; **prorrogar** *vt* (*período*) to extend; (*decisión*) to defer, postpone
prosa ['prosa] *nf* prose
proseguir [prose'ɣir] *vt* to continue, carry on ▷ *vi* to continue, go on
prospecto [pros'pekto] *nm* prospectus
prosperar [prospe'rar] *vi* to prosper, thrive, flourish; **prosperidad** *nf* prosperity; (*éxito*) success; **próspero, -a** *adj* prosperous, flourishing; (*que tiene éxito*) successful
prostíbulo [pros'tiβulo] *nm* brothel (BRIT), house of prostitution (US)
prostitución [prostitu'θjon] *nf* prostitution
prostituir [prosti'twir] *vt* to prostitute; **prostituirse** *vr* to prostitute o.s., become a prostitute
prostituta [prosti'tuta] *nf* prostitute
protagonista [protaɣo'nista] *nmf* protagonist
protección [protek'θjon] *nf* protection
protector, a [protek'tor, a] *adj* protective, protecting ▷ *nm/f* protector
proteger [prote'xer] *vt* to protect; **protegido, -a** *nm/f* protégé/protégée
proteína [prote'ina] *nf* protein
protesta [pro'testa] *nf* protest; (*declaración*) protestation
protestante [protes'tante] *adj* Protestant
protestar [protes'tar] *vt* to protest, declare ▷ *vi* to protest
protocolo [proto'kolo] *nm* protocol
prototipo [proto'tipo] *nm* prototype
provecho [pro'βetʃo] *nm* advantage, benefit; (*Finanzas*) profit; **¡buen ~!** bon appétit!; **en ~ de** to the benefit of; **sacar ~ de** to benefit from, profit by
provenir [proβe'nir] *vi*: **~ de** to come *o* stem from
proverbio [pro'βerβjo] *nm* proverb

providencia [proβi'ðenθja] *nf* providence
provincia [pro'βinθja] *nf* province
provisión [proβi'sjon] *nf* provision; (*abastecimiento*) provision, supply; (*medida*) measure, step
provisional [proβisjo'nal] *adj* provisional
provocar [proβo'kar] *vt* to provoke; (*alentar*) to tempt, invite; (*causar*) to bring about, lead to; (*promover*) to promote; (*estimular*) to rouse, stimulate; **¿te provoca un café?** (CAM) would you like a coffee?; **provocativo, -a** *adj* provocative
proxeneta [prokse'neta] *nm* pimp
próximamente [proksima'mente] *adv* shortly, soon
proximidad [proksimi'ðað] *nf* closeness, proximity; **próximo, -a** *adj* near, close; (*vecino*) neighbouring; (*siguiente*) next
proyectar [projek'tar] *vt* (*objeto*) to hurl, throw; (*luz*) to cast, shed; (*Cine*) to screen, show; (*planear*) to plan
proyectil [projek'til] *nm* projectile, missile
proyecto [pro'jekto] *nm* plan; (*estimación de costo*) detailed estimate
proyector [projek'tor] *nm* (*Cine*) projector
prudencia [pru'ðenθja] *nf* (*sabiduría*) wisdom; (*cuidado*) care; **prudente** *adj* sensible, wise; (*conductor*) careful
prueba *etc* ['prweβa] *vb V* **probar** ▷ *nf* proof; (*ensayo*) test, trial; (*degustación*) tasting, sampling; (*de ropa*) fitting; **a ~** on trial; **a ~ de** proof against; **a ~ de agua/fuego** waterproof/fireproof; **someter a ~** to put to the test
psico... [siko] *prefijo* psycho...; **psicología** *nf* psychology; **psicológico, -a** *adj* psychological; **psicólogo, -a** *nm/f* psychologist; **psicópata** *nmf* psychopath; **psicosis** *nf inv* psychosis
psiquiatra [si'kjatra] *nmf* psychiatrist; **psiquiátrico, -a** *adj* psychiatric
PSOE [pe'soe] (ESP) *nm abr* = **Partido Socialista Obrero Español**
púa ['pua] *nf* (*Bot, Zool*) prickle, spine; (*para guitarra*) plectrum (BRIT), pick (US); **alambre de ~** barbed wire
pubertad [puβer'tað] *nf* puberty
publicación [puβlika'θjon] *nf* publication
publicar [puβli'kar] *vt* (*editar*) to publish; (*hacer público*) to publicize; (*divulgar*) to make public, divulge
publicidad [puβliθi'ðað] *nf* publicity; (*Com: propaganda*) advertising; **publicitario, -a** *adj* publicity *cpd*; advertising *cpd*
público, -a ['puβliko, a] *adj* public ▷ *nm* public; (*Teatro etc*) audience
puchero [pu'tʃero] *nm* (*Culin: guiso*) stew; (*: olla*) cooking pot; **hacer ~s** to pout
pucho ['putʃo] (CS: *fam*) *nm* cigarette, fag (BRIT)
pude *etc vb V* **poder**
pudiente [pu'ðjente] *adj* (*rico*) wealthy, well-to-do
pudiera *etc vb V* **poder**
pudor [pu'ðor] *nm* modesty
pudrir [pu'ðrir] *vt* to rot; **pudrirse** *vr* to rot, decay
pueblo ['pweβlo] *nm* people; (*nación*) nation; (*aldea*) village
puedo *etc vb V* **poder**
puente ['pwente] *nm* bridge; **hacer ~** (*fam*) *to take extra days off work between 2 public holidays*; to take a long weekend; **puente aéreo** shuttle service; **puente colgante** suspension bridge; **puente levadizo** drawbridge

HACER PUENTE

When a public holiday in Spain falls on a Tuesday or Thursday it is common practice for employers to make the Monday or Friday a holiday as well and to give everyone a four-day weekend. This is known as **hacer puente**. When a named public holiday such as the **Día de la Constitución** falls on a Tuesday or Thursday, people refer to the whole holiday period as e.g. the **puente de la Constitución**.

puerco, -a ['pwerko, a] *nm/f* pig/sow ▷ *adj* (*sucio*) dirty, filthy; (*obsceno*) disgusting; **puerco espín** porcupine
pueril [pwe'ril] *adj* childish
puerro ['pwerro] *nm* leek
puerta ['pwerta] *nf* door; (*de jardín*) gate; (*portal*) doorway; (*fig*) gateway; (*portería*) goal; **a la ~** at the door; **a ~ cerrada** behind closed doors; **puerta giratoria** revolving door
puerto ['pwerto] *nm* port; (*paso*) pass; (*fig*) haven, refuge
Puerto Rico [pwerto'riko] *nm* Puerto Rico; **puertorriqueño, -a** *adj, nm/f* Puerto Rican
pues [pwes] *adv* (*entonces*) then; (*bueno*) well, well then; (*así que*) so ▷ *conj* (*ya que*) since; **¡~ sí!** yes!, certainly!
puesta ['pwesta] *nf* (*apuesta*) bet, stake; **puesta al día** updating; **puesta a punto** fine tuning; **puesta de sol** sunset; **puesta en marcha** starting
puesto, -a ['pwesto, a] *pp de* **poner**

▷ *adj*: **tener algo ~** to have sth on, be wearing sth ▷ *nm* (*lugar, posición*) place; (*trabajo*) post, job; (*Com*) stall ▷ *conj*: **~ que** since, as

púgil ['puxil] *nm* boxer

pulga ['pulɣa] *nf* flea

pulgada [pul'ɣaða] *nf* inch

pulgar [pul'ɣar] *nm* thumb

pulir [pu'lir] *vt* to polish; (*alisar*) to smooth; (*fig*) to polish up, touch up

pulmón [pul'mon] *nm* lung; **pulmonía** *nf* pneumonia

pulpa ['pulpa] *nf* pulp; (*de fruta*) flesh, soft part

pulpería [pulpe'ria] (LAM) *nf* (*tienda*) small grocery store

púlpito ['pulpito] *nm* pulpit

pulpo ['pulpo] *nm* octopus

pulque ['pulke] *nm* pulque

PULQUE

Pulque is a thick, white, alcoholic drink which is very popular in Mexico. In ancient times it was considered sacred by the Aztecs. It is produced by fermenting the juice of the **maguey**, a Mexican cactus similar to the agave. It can be drunk by itself or mixed with fruit or vegetable juice.

pulsación [pulsa'θjon] *nf* beat; **pulsaciones** pulse rate

pulsar [pul'sar] *vt* (*tecla*) to touch, tap; (*Mús*) to play; (*botón*) to press, push ▷ *vi* to pulsate; (*latir*) to beat, throb

pulsera [pul'sera] *nf* bracelet

pulso ['pulso] *nm* (*Anat*) pulse; (*fuerza*) strength; (*firmeza*) steadiness, steady hand

pulverizador [pulβeriθa'ðor] *nm* spray, spray gun

pulverizar [pulβeri'θar] *vt* to pulverize; (*líquido*) to spray

puna ['puna] (CAM) *nf* mountain sickness

punta ['punta] *nf* point, tip; (*extremo*) end; (*fig*) touch, trace; **horas ~** peak *o* rush hours; **sacar ~ a** to sharpen

puntada [pun'taða] *nf* (*Costura*) stitch

puntal [pun'tal] *nm* prop, support

puntapié [punta'pje] *nm* kick

puntería [punte'ria] *nf* (*de arma*) aim, aiming; (*destreza*) marksmanship

puntero, -a [pun'tero, a] *adj* leading ▷ *nm* (*palo*) pointer

puntiagudo, -a [puntja'ɣuðo, a] *adj* sharp, pointed

puntilla [pun'tiʎa] *nf* (*encaje*) lace edging *o* trim; **(andar) de ~s** (to walk) on tiptoe

punto ['punto] *nm* (*gen*) point; (*señal diminuta*) spot, dot; (*Costura, Med*) stitch; (*lugar*) spot, place; (*momento*) point, moment; **a ~** ready; **estar a ~ de** to be on the point of *o* about to; **en ~** on the dot; **hasta cierto ~** to some extent; **hacer ~** (ESP: *tejer*) to knit; **dos ~s** (*Ling*) colon; **punto de interrogación** question mark; **punto de vista** point of view, viewpoint; **punto final** full stop (BRIT), period (US); **punto muerto** dead center; (*Auto*) neutral (gear); **punto y aparte** (*en dictado*) full stop, new paragraph; **punto y coma** semicolon

puntocom [punto'kom] *adj inv, nf inv* dotcom

puntuación [puntwa'θjon] *nf* punctuation; (*puntos: en examen*) mark(s) (*pl*); (*Deporte*) score

puntual [pun'twal] *adj* (*a tiempo*) punctual; (*exacto*) exact, accurate; **puntualidad** *nf* punctuality; exactness, accuracy

puntuar [pun'twar] *vi* (*Deporte*) to score, count

punzante [pun'θante] *adj* (*dolor*) shooting, sharp; (*herramienta*) sharp

puñado [pu'ɲaðo] *nm* handful

puñal [pu'ɲal] *nm* dagger; **puñalada** *nf* stab

puñetazo [puɲe'taθo] *nm* punch

puño ['puɲo] *nm* (*Anat*) fist; (*cantidad*) fistful, handful; (*Costura*) cuff; (*de herramienta*) handle

pupila [pu'pila] *nf* pupil

pupitre [pu'pitre] *nm* desk

puré [pu're] *nm* purée; (*sopa*) (thick) soup; **puré de papas** (LAM) mashed potatoes; **puré de patatas** (ESP) mashed potatoes

purga ['purɣa] *nf* purge; **purgante** *adj, nm* purgative

purgatorio [purɣa'torjo] *nm* purgatory

purificar [purifi'kar] *vt* to purify; (*refinar*) to refine

puritano, -a [puri'tano, a] *adj* (*actitud*) puritanical; (*iglesia, tradición*) puritan ▷ *nm/f* puritan

puro, -a ['puro, a] *adj* pure; (*verdad*) simple, plain ▷ *nm* cigar

púrpura ['purpura] *nf* purple

pus [pus] *nm* pus

puse *etc vb V* **poder**

pusiera *etc vb V* **poder**

puta ['puta] (*fam!*) *nf* whore, prostitute

putrefacción [putrefak'θjon] *nf* rotting, putrefaction

PVP *nm abr* (= *precio de venta al público*) RRP

pyme, PYME ['pime] *nf abr* (= *Pequeña y Mediana Empresa*) SME

q

PALABRA CLAVE

que [ke] *conj* **1** (*con oración subordinada: muchas veces no se traduce*) that; **dijo que vendría** he said (that) he would come; **espero que lo encuentres** I hope (that) you find it; *V tb* **el**
2 (*en oración independiente*): **¡que entre!** send him in; **¡que aproveche!** enjoy your meal!; **¡que se mejore tu padre!** I hope your father gets better
3 (*enfático*): **¿me quieres? – ¡que sí!** do you love me? – of course!
4 (*consecutivo: muchas veces no se traduce*) that; **es tan grande que no lo puedo levantar** it's so big (that) I can't lift it
5 (*comparaciones*) than; **yo que tú/él** if I were you/him; *V tb* **más, menos, mismo**
6 (*valor disyuntivo*): **que le guste o no** whether he likes it or not; **que venga o que no venga** whether he comes or not
7 (*porque*): **no puedo, que tengo que quedarme en casa** I can't, I've got to stay in
▷ *pron* **1** (*cosa*) that, which; (*+ prep*) which; **el sombrero que te compraste** the hat (that *o* which) you bought; **la cama en que dormí** the bed (that *o* which) I slept in
2 (*persona: suj*) that, who; (*: objeto*) that, whom; **el amigo que me acompañó al museo** the friend that *o* who went to the museum with me; **la chica que invité** the girl (that *o* whom) I invited

qué [ke] *adj* what?, which? ▷ *pron* what?; **¡~ divertido!** how funny!; **¿~ edad tienes?** how old are you?; **¿de ~ me hablas?** what are you saying to me?; **¿~ tal?** how are you?, how are things?; **¿~ hay (de nuevo)?** what's new?
quebrado, -a [ke'βraðo, a] *adj* (*roto*) broken ▷ *nm/f* bankrupt ▷ *nm* (*Mat*) fraction
quebrantar [keβran'tar] *vt* (*infringir*) to violate, transgress
quebrar [ke'βrar] *vt* to break, smash ▷ *vi* to go bankrupt
quedar [ke'ðar] *vi* to stay, remain; (*encontrarse: sitio*) to be; (*haber aún*) to remain, be left; **quedarse** *vr* to remain, stay (behind); **~se (con) algo** to keep sth; **~ en** (*acordar*) to agree on/to; **~ en nada** to come to nothing; **~ por hacer** to be still to be done; **~ ciego/mudo** to be left blind/dumb; **no te queda bien ese vestido** that dress doesn't suit you; **eso queda muy lejos** that's a long way (away); **quedamos a las seis** we agreed to meet at six
quedo, -a ['keðo, a] *adj* still ▷ *adv* softly, gently
quehacer [kea'θer] *nm* task, job; **quehaceres (domésticos)** *nmpl* household chores
queja ['kexa] *nf* complaint; **quejarse** *vr* (*enfermo*) to moan, groan; (*protestar*) to complain; **quejarse de que** to complain that; **quejido** *nm* moan
quemado, -a [ke'maðo, a] *adj* burnt
quemadura [kema'ðura] *nf* burn, scald
quemar [ke'mar] *vt* to burn; (*fig: malgastar*) to burn up, squander ▷ *vi* to be burning hot; **quemarse** *vr* (*consumirse*) to burn (up); (*del sol*) to get sunburnt
quemarropa [kema'rropa]: **a ~** *adv* point-blank
quepo *etc vb V* **caber**
querella [ke'reʎa] *nf* (*Jur*) charge; (*disputa*) dispute

PALABRA CLAVE

querer [ke'rer] *vt* **1** (*desear*) to want; **quiero más dinero** I want more money; **quisiera** *o* **querría un té** I'd like a tea; **sin querer** unintentionally; **quiero ayudar/que vayas** I want to help/you to go
2 (*preguntas: para pedir algo*): **¿quiere abrir la ventana?** could you open the window?; **¿quieres echarme una mano?** can you give me a hand?
3 (*amar*) to love; (*tener cariño a*) to be fond of; **te quiero** I love you; **quiere mucho a sus hijos** he's very fond of his children
4 **le pedí que me dejara ir pero no quiso** I asked him to let me go but he refused

querido, -a [ke'riðo, a] *adj* dear ▷ *nm/f* darling; (*amante*) lover
queso ['keso] *nm* cheese; **queso crema** (LAM) cream cheese; **queso de untar** (ESP)

cream cheese; **queso manchego** *sheep's milk cheese made in La Mancha*
quicio ['kiθjo] *nm* hinge; **sacar a algn de ~** to get on sb's nerves
quiebra ['kjeβra] *nf* break, split; (*Com*) bankruptcy; (*Econ*) slump
quiebro ['kjeβro] *nm* (*del cuerpo*) swerve
quien [kjen] *pron* who; **hay ~ piensa que** there are those who think that; **no hay ~ lo haga** no-one will do it
quién [kjen] *pron* who, whom; **¿~ es?** who's there?
quienquiera [kjen'kjera] (*pl* **quienesquiera**) *pron* whoever
quiero *etc vb V* **querer**
quieto, -a ['kjeto, a] *adj* still; (*carácter*) placid

No confundir **quieto** con la palabra inglesa *quiet*.

quietud *nf* stillness
químico, -a ['kimiko, a] *adj* chemical ▷ *nm/f* chemist ▷ *nf* chemistry
quincalla [kin'kaʎa] *nf* hardware, ironmongery (BRIT)
quince ['kinθe] *num* fifteen; **~ días** a fortnight; **quinceañero, -a** *nm/f* teenager; **quincena** *nf* fortnight; (*pago*) fortnightly pay; **quincenal** *adj* fortnightly
quiniela [ki'njela] *nf* football pools *pl*; **quinielas** *nfpl* (*impreso*) pools coupon *sg*
quinientos, -as [ki'njentos, as] *adj, num* five hundred
quinto, -a ['kinto, a] *adj* fifth ▷ *nf* country house; (*Mil*) call-up, draft
quiosco ['kjosko] *nm* (*de música*) bandstand; (*de periódicos*) news stand
quirófano [ki'rofano] *nm* operating theatre
quirúrgico, -a [ki'rurxiko, a] *adj* surgical
quise *etc vb V* **querer**
quisiera *etc vb V* **querer**
quisquilloso, -a [kiski'ʎoso, a] *adj* (*susceptible*) touchy; (*meticuloso*) pernickety
quiste ['kiste] *nm* cyst
quitaesmalte [kitaes'malte] *nm* nail-polish remover
quitamanchas [kita'mantʃas] *nm inv* stain remover
quitanieves [kita'njeβes] *nm inv* snowplough (BRIT), snowplow (US)
quitar [ki'tar] *vt* to remove, take away; (*ropa*) to take off; (*dolor*) to relieve; **¡quita de ahí!** get away!; **quitarse** *vr* to withdraw; (*ropa*) to take off; **se quitó el sombrero** he took off his hat
Quito ['kito] *n* Quito
quizá(s) [ki'θa(s)] *adv* perhaps, maybe

rábano ['raβano] *nm* radish; **me importa un ~** I don't give a damn
rabia ['raβja] *nf* (*Med*) rabies *sg*; (*ira*) fury, rage; **rabiar** *vi* to have rabies; to rage, be furious; **rabiar por algo** to long for sth
rabieta [ra'βjeta] *nf* tantrum, fit of temper
rabino [ra'βino] *nm* rabbi
rabioso, -a [ra'βjoso, a] *adj* rabid; (*fig*) furious
rabo ['raβo] *nm* tail
racha ['ratʃa] *nf* gust of wind; **buena/mala ~** spell of good/bad luck
racial [ra'θjal] *adj* racial, race *cpd*
racimo [ra'θimo] *nm* bunch
ración [ra'θjon] *nf* portion; **raciones** *nfpl* rations
racional [raθjo'nal] *adj* (*razonable*) reasonable; (*lógico*) rational
racionar [raθjo'nar] *vt* to ration (out)
racismo [ra'θismo] *nm* racism; **racista** *adj, nm* racist
radar [ra'ðar] *nm* radar
radiador [raðja'ðor] *nm* radiator
radiante [ra'ðjante] *adj* radiant
radical [raði'kal] *adj, nmf* radical
radicar [raði'kar] *vi*: **~ en** (*dificultad, problema*) to lie in; (*solución*) to consist in
radio ['raðjo] *nf* radio; (*aparato*) radio (set) ▷ *nm* (*Mat*) radius; (*Quím*) radium; **radioactividad** *nf* radioactivity; **radioactivo, -a** *adj* radioactive; **radiografía** *nf* X-ray; **radioterapia** *nf* radiotherapy; **radioyente** *nmf* listener
ráfaga ['rafaɣa] *nf* gust; (*de luz*) flash; (*de tiros*) burst
raíz [ra'iθ] *nf* root; **a ~ de** as a result of; **raíz cuadrada** square root
raja ['raxa] *nf* (*de melón etc*) slice; (*grieta*) crack; **rajar** *vt* to split; (*fam*) to slash; **rajarse** *vr* to split, crack; **rajarse de** to back out of

rajatabla [raxa'taβla]: **a ~** *adv* (*estrictamente*) strictly, to the letter
rallador [raʎa'ðor] *nm* grater
rallar [ra'ʎar] *vt* to grate
rama ['rama] *nf* branch; **ramaje** *nm* branches *pl*, foliage; **ramal** *nm* (*de cuerda*) strand; (*Ferro*) branch line (BRIT); (*Auto*) branch (road) (BRIT)
rambla ['rambla] *nf* (*avenida*) avenue
ramo ['ramo] *nm* branch; (*sección*) department, section
rampa ['rampa] *nf* ramp; **rampa de acceso** entrance ramp
rana ['rana] *nf* frog; **salto de ~** leapfrog
ranchero [ran'tʃero] (MÉX) *nm* (*hacendado*) rancher; smallholder
rancho ['rantʃo] *nm* (*grande*) ranch; (*pequeño*) small farm
rancio, -a ['ranθjo, a] *adj* (*comestibles*) rancid; (*vino*) aged, mellow; (*fig*) ancient
rango ['rango] *nm* rank, standing
ranura [ra'nura] *nf* groove; (*de teléfono etc*) slot
rapar [ra'par] *vt* to shave; (*los cabellos*) to crop
rapaz [ra'paθ] (*nf* **~a**) *nmf* young boy/girl ▷ *adj* (*Zool*) predatory
rape ['rape] *nm* (*pez*) monkfish; **al ~** cropped
rapé [ra'pe] *nm* snuff
rapidez [rapi'ðeθ] *nf* speed, rapidity; **rápido, -a** *adj* fast, quick ▷ *adv* quickly ▷ *nm* (*Ferro*) express; **rápidos** *nmpl* rapids
rapiña [ra'piɲa] *nm* robbery; **ave de ~** bird of prey
raptar [rap'tar] *vt* to kidnap; **rapto** *nm* kidnapping; (*impulso*) sudden impulse; (*éxtasis*) ecstasy, rapture
raqueta [ra'keta] *nf* racquet
raquítico, -a [ra'kitiko, a] *adj* stunted; (*fig*) poor, inadequate
rareza [ra'reθa] *nf* rarity; (*fig*) eccentricity
raro, -a ['raro, a] *adj* (*poco común*) rare; (*extraño*) odd, strange; (*excepcional*) remarkable
ras [ras] *nm*: **a ~ de** level with; **a ~ de tierra** at ground level
rasar [ra'sar] *vt* (*igualar*) to level
rascacielos [raska'θjelos] *nm inv* skyscraper
rascar [ras'kar] *vt* (*con las uñas etc*) to scratch; (*raspar*) to scrape; **rascarse** *vr* to scratch (o.s.)
rasgar [ras'ɣar] *vt* to tear, rip (up)
rasgo ['rasɣo] *nm* (*con pluma*) stroke; **rasgos** *nmpl* (*facciones*) features, characteristics; **a grandes ~s** in outline, broadly
rasguño [ras'ɣuɲo] *nm* scratch
raso, -a ['raso, a] *adj* (*liso*) flat, level; (*a baja altura*) very low ▷ *nm* satin; **cielo ~** clear sky
raspadura [raspa'ðura] *nf* (*acto*) scrape, scraping; (*marca*) scratch; **raspaduras** *nfpl* (*de papel etc*) scrapings
raspar [ras'par] *vt* to scrape; (*arañar*) to scratch; (*limar*) to file
rastra ['rastra] *nf* (*Agr*) rake; **a ~s** by dragging; (*fig*) unwillingly
rastrear [rastre'ar] *vt* (*seguir*) to track
rastrero, -a [ras'trero, a] *adj* (*Bot, Zool*) creeping; (*fig*) despicable, mean
rastrillo [ras'triʎo] *nm* rake
rastro ['rastro] *nm* (*Agr*) rake; (*pista*) track, trail; (*vestigio*) trace; **el R~** (ESP) the Madrid fleamarket
rasurado [rasu'raðo] (MÉX) *nm* shaving; **rasuradora** [rasura'ðora] (MÉX) *nf* electric shaver; **rasurar** [rasu'rar] (MÉX) *vt* to shave; **rasurarse** *vr* to shave
rata ['rata] *nf* rat
ratear [rate'ar] *vt* (*robar*) to steal
ratero, -a [ra'tero, a] *adj* light-fingered ▷ *nm/f* (*carterista*) pickpocket; (*ladrón*) petty thief
rato ['rato] *nm* while, short time; **a ~s** from time to time; **hay para ~** there's still a long way to go; **al poco ~** soon afterwards; **pasar el ~** to kill time; **pasar un buen/mal ~** to have a good/rough time; **en mis ~s libres** in my spare time
ratón [ra'ton] *nm* mouse; **ratonera** *nf* mousetrap
raudal [rau'ðal] *nm* torrent; **a ~es** in abundance
raya ['raja] *nf* line; (*marca*) scratch; (*en tela*) stripe; (*de pelo*) parting; (*límite*) boundary; (*pez*) ray; (*puntuación*) dash; **a ~s** striped; **pasarse de la ~** to go too far; **tener a ~** to keep in check; **rayar** *vt* to line; to scratch; (*subrayar*) to underline ▷ *vi*: **rayar en** *o* **con** to border on
rayo ['rajo] *nm* (*del sol*) ray, beam; (*de luz*) shaft; (*en una tormenta*) (flash of) lightning; **rayos X** X-rays
raza ['raθa] *nf* race; **raza humana** human race
razón [ra'θon] *nf* reason; (*justicia*) right, justice; (*razonamiento*) reasoning; (*motivo*) reason, motive; (*Mat*) ratio; **a ~ de 10 cada día** at the rate of 10 a day; **en ~ de** with regard to; **dar ~ a algn** to agree that sb is right; **tener ~** to be right; **razón de ser** raison d'être; **razón directa/inversa** direct/inverse proportion; **razonable** *adj* reasonable; (*justo, moderado*) fair; **razonamiento** *nm* (*juicio*) judg(e)ment;

r

(*argumento*) reasoning; **razonar** *vt, vi* to reason, argue
re [re] *nm* (*Mús*) D
reacción [reak'θjon] *nf* reaction; **avión a ~** jet plane; **reacción en cadena** chain reaction; **reaccionar** *vi* to react
reacio, -a [re'aθjo, a] *adj* stubborn
reactivar [reakti'βar] *vt* to revitalize
reactor [reak'tor] *nm* reactor
real [re'al] *adj* real; (*del rey, fig*) royal
realidad [reali'ðað] *nf* reality, fact; (*verdad*) truth
realista [rea'lista] *nmf* realist
realización [realiθa'θjon] *nf* fulfilment
realizador, a [realiθa'ðor, a] *nm/f* film-maker
realizar [reali'θar] *vt* (*objetivo*) to achieve; (*plan*) to carry out; (*viaje*) to make, undertake; **realizarse** *vr* to come about, come true
realmente [real'mente] *adv* really, actually
realzar [real'θar] *vt* to enhance; (*acentuar*) to highlight
reanimar [reani'mar] *vt* to revive; (*alentar*) to encourage; **reanimarse** *vr* to revive
reanudar [reanu'ðar] *vt* (*renovar*) to renew; (*historia, viaje*) to resume
reaparición [reapari'θjon] *nf* reappearance
rearme [re'arme] *nm* rearmament
rebaja [re'βaxa] *nf* (*Com*) reduction; (*: descuento*) discount; **rebajas** *nfpl* (*Com*) sale; **rebajar** *vt* (*bajar*) to lower; (*reducir*) to reduce; (*disminuir*) to lessen; (*humillar*) to humble
rebanada [reβa'naða] *nf* slice
rebañar [reβa'ɲar] *vt* (*comida*) to scrape up; (*plato*) to scrape clean
rebaño [re'βaɲo] *nm* herd; (*de ovejas*) flock
rebatir [reβa'tir] *vt* to refute
rebeca [re'βeka] *nf* cardigan
rebelarse [reβe'larse] *vr* to rebel, revolt
rebelde [re'βelde] *adj* rebellious; (*niño*) unruly ▷*nmf* rebel; **rebeldía** *nf* rebelliousness; (*desobediencia*) disobedience
rebelión [reβe'ljon] *nf* rebellion
reblandecer [reβlande'θer] *vt* to soften
rebobinar [reβoβi'nar] *vt* (*cinta, película de video*) to rewind
rebosante [reβo'sante] *adj* overflowing
rebosar [reβo'sar] *vi* (*líquido, recipiente*) to overflow; (*abundar*) to abound, be plentiful
rebotar [reβo'tar] *vt* to bounce; (*rechazar*) to repel ▷*vi* (*pelota*) to bounce; (*bala*) to ricochet; **rebote** *nm* rebound; **de rebote** on the rebound
rebozado, -a [reβo'θaðo, a] *adj* fried in batter *o* breadcrumbs
rebozar [reβo'θar] *vt* to wrap up; (*Culin*) to fry in batter *o* breadcrumbs
rebuscado, -a [reβus'kaðo, a] *adj* (*amanerado*) affected; (*palabra*) recherché; (*idea*) far-fetched
rebuscar [reβus'kar] *vi*: **~ (en/por)** to search carefully (in/for)
recado [re'kaðo] *nm* (*mensaje*) message; (*encargo*) errand; **tomar un ~** (*Tel*) to take a message
recaer [reka'er] *vi* to relapse; **~ en** to fall to *o* on; (*criminal etc*) to fall back into, relapse into; **recaída** *nf* relapse
recalcar [rekal'kar] *vt* (*fig*) to stress, emphasize
recalentar [rekalen'tar] *vt* (*volver a calentar*) to reheat; (*calentar demasiado*) to overheat
recámara [re'kamara] (MÉX) *nf* bedroom
recambio [re'kambjo] *nm* spare; (*de pluma*) refill
recapacitar [rekapaθi'tar] *vi* to reflect
recargado, -a [rekar'ɣaðo, a] *adj* overloaded
recargar [rekar'ɣar] *vt* to overload; (*batería*) to recharge; **~ el saldo de** (*Tel*) to top up; **recargo** *nm* surcharge; (*aumento*) increase
recatado, -a [reka'taðo, a] *adj* (*modesto*) modest, demure; (*prudente*) cautious
recaudación [rekauða'θjon] *nf* (*acción*) collection; (*cantidad*) takings *pl*; (*en deporte*) gate; **recaudador, a** *nm/f* tax collector
recelar [reθe'lar] *vt*: **~ que ...** (*sospechar*) to suspect that ...; (*temer*) to fear that ... ▷*vi*: **~ de** to distrust; **recelo** *nm* distrust, suspicion
recepción [reθep'θjon] *nf* reception; **recepcionista** *nmf* receptionist
receptor, a [reθep'tor, a] *nm/f* recipient ▷*nm* (*Tel*) receiver
recesión [reθe'sjon] *nf* (*Com*) recession
receta [re'θeta] *nf* (*Culin*) recipe; (*Med*) prescription

> No confundir **receta** con la palabra inglesa *receipt*.

rechazar [retʃa'θar] *vt* to reject; (*oferta*) to turn down; (*ataque*) to repel
rechazo [re'tʃaθo] *nm* rejection
rechinar [retʃi'nar] *vi* to creak; (*dientes*) to grind
rechistar [retʃis'tar] *vi*: **sin ~** without a murmur
rechoncho, -a [re'tʃontʃo, a] (*fam*) *adj* thickset (BRIT), heavy-set (US)
rechupete [retʃu'pete]: **de ~** *adj* (*comida*)

delicious, scrumptious
recibidor [reθiβi'ðor] *nm* entrance hall
recibimiento [reθiβi'mjento] *nm* reception, welcome
recibir [reθi'βir] *vt* to receive; (*dar la bienvenida*) to welcome ▷ *vi* to entertain; **recibo** *nm* receipt
reciclable [reθı'klaβle] *adj* recyclable
reciclar [reθi'klar] *vt* to recycle
recién [re'θjen] *adv* recently, newly; **los ~ casados** the newly-weds; **el ~ llegado** the newcomer; **el ~ nacido** the newborn child
reciente [re'θjente] *adj* recent; (*fresco*) fresh
recinto [re'θinto] *nm* enclosure; (*área*) area, place
recio, -a ['reθjo, a] *adj* strong, tough; (*voz*) loud ▷ *adv* hard, loud(ly)
recipiente [reθi'pjente] *nm* receptacle
recíproco, -a [re'θiproco, a] *adj* reciprocal
recital [reθi'tal] *nm* (*Mús*) recital; (*Literatura*) reading
recitar [reθi'tar] *vt* to recite
reclamación [reklama'θjon] *nf* claim, demand; (*queja*) complaint
reclamar [rekla'mar] *vt* to claim, demand ▷ *vi*: **~ contra** to complain about; **reclamo** *nm* (*anuncio*) advertisement; (*tentación*) attraction
reclinar [rekli'nar] *vt* to recline, lean; **reclinarse** *vr* to lean back
reclusión [reklu'sjon] *nf* (*prisión*) prison; (*refugio*) seclusion
recluta [re'kluta] *nmf* recruit ▷ *nf* recruitment; **reclutar** *vt* (*datos*) to collect; (*dinero*) to collect up; **reclutamiento** *nm* recruitment
recobrar [reko'βrar] *vt* (*salud*) to recover; (*rescatar*) to get back; **recobrarse** *vr* to recover
recodo [re'koðo] *nm* (*de río, camino*) bend
recogedor [rekoxe'ðor] *nm* dustpan
recoger [reko'xer] *vt* to collect; (*Agr*) to harvest; (*levantar*) to pick up; (*juntar*) to gather; (*pasar a buscar*) to come for, get; (*dar asilo*) to give shelter to; (*faldas*) to gather up; (*pelo*) to put up; **recogerse** *vr* (*retirarse*) to retire; **recogido, -a** *adj* (*lugar*) quiet, secluded; (*pequeño*) small ▷ *nf* (*Correos*) collection; (*Agr*) harvest
recolección [rekolek'θjon] *nf* (*Agr*) harvesting; (*colecta*) collection
recomendación [rekomenda'θjon] *nf* (*sugerencia*) suggestion, recommendation; (*referencia*) reference
recomendar [rekomen'dar] *vt* to suggest, recommend; (*confiar*) to entrust
recompensa [rekom'pensa] *nf* reward, recompense; **recompensar** *vt* to reward, recompense
reconciliación [rekonθilja'θjon] *nf* reconciliation
reconciliar [rekonθi'ljar] *vt* to reconcile; **reconciliarse** *vr* to become reconciled
recóndito, -a [re'kondito, a] *adj* (*lugar*) hidden, secret
reconocer [rekono'θer] *vt* to recognize; (*registrar*) to search; (*Med*) to examine; **reconocido, -a** *adj* recognized; (*agradecido*) grateful; **reconocimiento** *nm* recognition; search; examination; gratitude; (*confesión*) admission
reconquista [rekon'kista] *nf* reconquest; **la R~** the Reconquest (of Spain)
reconstituyente [rekonstitu'jente] *nm* tonic
reconstruir [rekonstru'ir] *vt* to reconstruct
reconversión [rekonβer'sjon] *nf* (*reestructuración*) restructuring; **reconversión industrial** industrial rationalization
recopilación [rekopila'θjon] *nf* (*resumen*) summary; (*compilación*) compilation; **recopilar** *vt* to compile
récord ['rekorð] (*pl* **~s**) *adj inv, nm* record
recordar [rekor'ðar] *vt* (*acordarse de*) to remember; (*acordar a otro*) to remind ▷ *vi* to remember

No confundir **recordar** con la palabra inglesa *record*.

recorrer [reko'rrer] *vt* (*país*) to cross, travel through; (*distancia*) to cover; (*registrar*) to search; (*repasar*) to look over; **recorrido** *nm* run, journey; **tren de largo recorrido** main-line train
recortar [rekor'tar] *vt* to cut out; **recorte** *nm* (*acción, de prensa*) cutting; (*de telas, chapas*) trimming; **recorte presupuestario** budget cut
recostar [rekos'tar] *vt* to lean; **recostarse** *vr* to lie down
recoveco [reko'βeko] *nm* (*de camino, río etc*) bend; (*en casa*) cubby hole
recreación [rekrea'θjon] *nf* recreation
recrear [rekre'ar] *vt* (*entretener*) to entertain; (*volver a crear*) to recreate; **recreativo, -a** *adj* recreational; **recreo** *nm* recreation; (*Escol*) break, playtime
recriminar [rekrimi'nar] *vt* to reproach ▷ *vi* to recriminate; **recriminarse** *vr* to reproach each other
recrudecer [rekruðe'θer] *vt, vi* to worsen; **recrudecerse** *vr* to worsen
recta ['rekta] *nf* straight line

rectángulo, -a [rek'tangulo, a] *adj* rectangular ▷ *nm* rectangle
rectificar [rektifi'kar] *vt* to rectify; (*volverse recto*) to straighten ▷ *vi* to correct o.s.
rectitud [rekti'tuð] *nf* straightness
recto, -a ['rekto, a] *adj* straight; (*persona*) honest, upright; **siga todo ~** go straight on ▷ *nm* rectum
rector, a [rek'tor, a] *adj* governing
recuadro [re'kwaðro] *nm* box; (*Tip*) inset
recubrir [reku'βrir] *vt*: **~ (con)** (*pintura, crema*) to cover (with)
recuento [re'kwento] *nm* inventory; **hacer el ~ de** to count *o* reckon up
recuerdo [re'kwerðo] *nm* souvenir; **recuerdos** *nmpl* (*memorias*) memories; **¡~s a tu madre!** give my regards to your mother!
recular [reku'lar] *vi* to back down
recuperación [rekupera'θjon] *nf* recovery
recuperar [rekupe'rar] *vt* to recover; (*tiempo*) to make up; **recuperarse** *vr* to recuperate
recurrir [reku'rrir] *vi* (*Jur*) to appeal; **~ a** to resort to; (*persona*) to turn to; **recurso** *nm* resort; (*medios*) means *pl*, resources *pl*; (*Jur*) appeal
red [reð] *nf* net, mesh; (*Ferro etc*) network; (*trampa*) trap; **la R~** (*Internet*) the Net
redacción [reðak'θjon] *nf* (*acción*) editing; (*personal*) editorial staff; (*Escol*) essay, composition
redactar [reðak'tar] *vt* to draw up, draft; (*periódico*) to edit
redactor, a [reðak'tor, a] *nm/f* editor
redada [re'ðaða] *nf* (*de policía*) raid, round-up
rededor [reðe'ðor] *nm*: **al** *o* **en ~** around, round about
redoblar [reðo'βlar] *vt* to redouble ▷ *vi* (*tambor*) to roll
redonda [re'ðonda] *nf*: **a la ~** around, round about
redondear [reðonde'ar] *vt* to round, round off
redondel [reðon'del] *nm* (*círculo*) circle; (*Taur*) bullring, arena
redondo, -a [re'ðondo, a] *adj* (*circular*) round; (*completo*) complete
reducción [reðuk'θjon] *nf* reduction
reducido, -a [reðu'θiðo, a] *adj* reduced; (*limitado*) limited; (*pequeño*) small
reducir [reðu'θir] *vt* to reduce; to limit; **reducirse** *vr* to diminish
redundancia [reðun'danθja] *nf* redundancy
reembolsar [re(e)mbol'sar] *vt* (*persona*) to reimburse; (*dinero*) to repay, pay back; (*depósito*) to refund; **reembolso** *nm* reimbursement; refund
reemplazar [re(e)mpla'θar] *vt* to replace; **reemplazo** *nm* replacement; **de reemplazo** (*Mil*) reserve
reencuentro [re(e)n'kwentro] *nm* reunion
reescribible [reeskri'βiβle] *adj* rewritable
refacción [refak'θjon] (MÉX) *nf* spare (part)
referencia [refe'renθja] *nf* reference; **con ~ a** with reference to
referéndum [refe'rendum] (*pl* **~s**) *nm* referendum
referente [refe'rente] *adj*: **~ a** concerning, relating to
réferi ['referi] (LAM) *nmf* referee
referir [refe'rir] *vt* (*contar*) to tell, recount; (*relacionar*) to refer, relate; **referirse** *vr*: **~se a** to refer to
refilón [refi'lon]: **de ~** *adv* obliquely
refinado, -a [refi'naðo, a] *adj* refined
refinar [refi'nar] *vt* to refine; **refinería** *nf* refinery
reflejar [refle'xar] *vt* to reflect; **reflejo, -a** *adj* reflected; (*movimiento*) reflex ▷ *nm* reflection; (*Anat*) reflex
reflexión [reflek'sjon] *nf* reflection; **reflexionar** *vt* to reflect on ▷ *vi* to reflect; (*detenerse*) to pause (to think)
reflexivo, -a [reflek'siβo, a] *adj* thoughtful; (*Ling*) reflexive
reforma [re'forma] *nf* reform; (*Arq etc*) repair; **reforma agraria** agrarian reform
reformar [refor'mar] *vt* to reform; (*modificar*) to change, alter; (*Arq*) to repair; **reformarse** *vr* to mend one's ways
reformatorio [reforma'torjo] *nm* reformatory
reforzar [refor'θar] *vt* to strengthen; (*Arq*) to reinforce; (*fig*) to encourage
refractario, -a [refrak'tarjo, a] *adj* (*Tec*) heat-resistant
refrán [re'fran] *nm* proverb, saying
refregar [refre'ɣar] *vt* to scrub
refrescante [refres'kante] *adj* refreshing, cooling
refrescar [refres'kar] *vt* to refresh ▷ *vi* to cool down; **refrescarse** *vr* to get cooler; (*tomar aire fresco*) to go out for a breath of fresh air; (*beber*) to have a drink
refresco [re'fresko] *nm* soft drink, cool drink; **"~s"** "refreshments"
refriega [re'frjeɣa] *nf* scuffle, brawl
refrigeración [refrixera'θjon] *nf* refrigeration; (*de sala*) air-conditioning

refrigerador [refrixera'ðor] *nm* refrigerator (BRIT), icebox (US)
refrigerar [refrixe'rar] *vt* to refrigerate; (*sala*) to air-condition
refuerzo [re'fwerθo] *nm* reinforcement; (*Tec*) support
refugiado, -a [refu'xjaðo, a] *nm/f* refugee
refugiarse [refu'xjarse] *vr* to take refuge, shelter
refugio [re'fuxjo] *nm* refuge; (*protección*) shelter
refunfuñar [refunfu'ɲar] *vi* to grunt, growl; (*quejarse*) to grumble
regadera [reɤa'ðera] *nf* watering can
regadío [rega'ðio] *nm* irrigated land
regalado, -a [reɤa'laðo, a] *adj* comfortable, luxurious; (*gratis*) free, for nothing
regalar [reɤa'lar] *vt* (*dar*) to give (as a present); (*entregar*) to give away; (*mimar*) to pamper, make a fuss of
regaliz [reɤa'liθ] *nm* liquorice
regalo [re'ɤalo] *nm* (*obsequio*) gift, present; (*gusto*) pleasure
regañadientes [reɤaɲa'ðjentes]: **a ~** *adv* reluctantly
regañar [reɤa'ɲar] *vt* to scold ▷ *vi* to grumble; **regañón, -ona** *adj* nagging
regar [re'ɤar] *vt* to water, irrigate; (*fig*) to scatter, sprinkle
regatear [reɤate'ar] *vt* (*Com*) to bargain over; (*escatimar*) to be mean with ▷ *vi* to bargain, haggle; (*Deporte*) to dribble; **regateo** *nm* bargaining; dribbling; (*del cuerpo*) swerve, dodge
regazo [re'ɤaθo] *nm* lap
regenerar [rexene'rar] *vt* to regenerate
régimen ['reximen] (*pl* **regímenes**) *nm* regime; (*Med*) diet
regimiento [rexi'mjento] *nm* regiment
regio, -a ['rexjo, a] *adj* royal, regal; (*fig: suntuoso*) splendid; (*cs: fam*) great, terrific
región [re'xjon] *nf* region
regir [re'xir] *vt* to govern, rule; (*dirigir*) to manage, run ▷ *vi* to apply, be in force
registrar [rexis'trar] *vt* (*buscar*) to search; (*: en cajón*) to look through; (*inspeccionar*) to inspect; (*anotar*) to register, record; (*Inform*) to log; **registrarse** *vr* to register; (*ocurrir*) to happen
registro [re'xistro] *nm* (*acto*) registration; (*Mús, libro*) register; (*inspección*) inspection, search; **registro civil** registry office
regla ['reɤla] *nf* (*ley*) rule, regulation; (*de medir*) ruler, rule; (*Med: período*) period; **en ~** in order
reglamentación [reɤlamenta'θjon] *nf* (*acto*) regulation; (*lista*) rules *pl*
reglamentar [reɤlamen'tar] *vt* to regulate; **reglamentario, -a** *adj* statutory; **reglamento** *nm* rules *pl*, regulations *pl*
regocijarse [reɤoθi'xarse] *vr* (*alegrarse*) to rejoice; **regocijo** *nm* joy, happiness
regrabadora [regraβa'ðora] *nf* rewriter; **regrabadora de DVD** DVD rewriter
regresar [reɤre'sar] *vi* to come back, go back, return; **regreso** *nm* return
reguero [re'ɤero] *nm* (*de sangre etc*) trickle; (*de humo*) trail
regulador [reɤula'ðor] *nm* regulator; (*de radio etc*) knob, control
regular [reɤu'lar] *adj* regular; (*normal*) normal, usual; (*común*) ordinary; (*organizado*) regular, orderly; (*mediano*) average; (*fam*) not bad, so-so ▷ *adv* so-so, alright ▷ *vt* (*controlar*) to control, regulate; (*Tec*) to adjust; **por lo ~** as a rule; **regularidad** *nf* regularity; **regularizar** *vt* to regularize
rehabilitación [reaβilita'θjon] *nf* rehabilitation; (*Arq*) restoration
rehabilitar [reaβili'tar] *vt* to rehabilitate; (*Arq*) to restore; (*reintegrar*) to reinstate
rehacer [rea'θer] *vt* (*reparar*) to mend, repair; (*volver a hacer*) to redo, repeat; **rehacerse** *vr* (*Med*) to recover
rehén [re'en] *nm* hostage
rehuir [reu'ir] *vt* to avoid, shun
rehusar [reu'sar] *vt, vi* to refuse
reina ['reina] *nf* queen; **reinado** *nm* reign
reinar [rei'nar] *vi* to reign
reincidir [reinθi'ðir] *vi* to relapse
reincorporarse [reinkorpo'rarse] *vr*: **~ a** to rejoin
reino ['reino] *nm* kingdom; **reino animal/vegetal** animal/plant kingdom; **el Reino Unido** the United Kingdom
reintegrar [reinte'ɤrar] *vt* (*reconstituir*) to reconstruct; (*persona*) to reinstate; (*dinero*) to refund, pay back; **reintegrarse** *vr*: **~se a** to return to
reír [re'ir] *vi* to laugh; **reírse** *vr* to laugh; **~se de** to laugh at
reiterar [reite'rar] *vt* to reiterate
reivindicación [reiβindika'θjon] *nf* (*demanda*) claim, demand; (*justificación*) vindication
reivindicar [reiβindi'kar] *vt* to claim
reja ['rexa] *nf* (*de ventana*) grille, bars *pl*; (*en la calle*) grating
rejilla [re'xiʎa] *nf* grating, grille; (*muebles*) wickerwork; (*de ventilación*) vent; (*de coche etc*) luggage rack
rejoneador [rexonea'ðor] *nm* mounted bullfighter

r

rejuvenecer [rexuβene'θer] *vt, vi* to rejuvenate
relación [rela'θjon] *nf* relation, relationship; (*Mat*) ratio; (*narración*) report; **con ~ a, en ~ con** in relation to; **relaciones públicas** public relations; **relacionar** *vt* to relate, connect; **relacionarse** *vr* to be connected, be linked
relajación [relaxa'θjon] *nf* relaxation
relajar [rela'xar] *vt* to relax; **relajarse** *vr* to relax
relamerse [rela'merse] *vr* to lick one's lips
relámpago [re'lampaɣo] *nm* flash of lightning; **visita ~** lightning visit
relatar [rela'tar] *vt* to tell, relate
relativo, -a [rela'tiβo, a] *adj* relative; **en lo ~ a** concerning
relato [re'lato] *nm* (*narración*) story, tale
relegar [rele'ɣar] *vt* to relegate
relevante [rele'βante] *adj* eminent, outstanding
relevar [rele'βar] *vt* (*sustituir*) to relieve; **relevarse** *vr* to relay; **~ a algn de un cargo** to relieve sb of his post
relevo [re'leβo] *nm* relief; **carrera de ~s** relay race
relieve [re'ljeβe] *nm* (*Arte, Tec*) relief; (*fig*) prominence, importance; **bajo ~** bas-relief
religión [reli'xjon] *nf* religion; **religioso, -a** *adj* religious ▷ *nm/f* monk/nun
relinchar [relin'tʃar] *vi* to neigh
reliquia [re'likja] *nf* relic; **reliquia de familia** heirloom
rellano [re'ʎano] *nm* (*Arq*) landing
rellenar [reʎe'nar] *vt* (*llenar*) to fill up; (*Culin*) to stuff; (*Costura*) to pad; **relleno, -a** *adj* full up; stuffed ▷ *nm* stuffing; (*de tapicería*) padding
reloj [re'lo(x)] *nm* clock; **poner el ~ (en hora)** to set one's watch (*o* the clock); **reloj (de pulsera)** wristwatch; **reloj despertador** alarm (clock); **reloj digital** digital watch; **relojero, -a** *nm/f* clockmaker; watchmaker
reluciente [relu'θjente] *adj* brilliant, shining
relucir [relu'θir] *vi* to shine; (*fig*) to excel
remachar [rema'tʃar] *vt* to rivet; (*fig*) to hammer home, drive home; **remache** *nm* rivet
remangar [reman'gar] *vt* to roll up
remanso [re'manso] *nm* pool
remar [re'mar] *vi* to row
rematado, -a [rema'taðo, a] *adj* complete, utter
rematar [rema'tar] *vt* to finish off; (*Com*) to sell off cheap ▷ *vi* to end, finish off; (*Deporte*) to shoot
remate [re'mate] *nm* end, finish; (*punta*) tip; (*Deporte*) shot; (*Arq*) top; **de** *o* **para ~** to crown it all (BRIT), to top it off
remedar [reme'ðar] *vt* to imitate
remediar [reme'ðjar] *vt* to remedy; (*subsanar*) to make good, repair; (*evitar*) to avoid
remedio [re'meðjo] *nm* remedy; (*alivio*) relief, help; (*Jur*) recourse, remedy; **poner ~ a** to correct, stop; **no tener más ~** to have no alternative; **¡qué ~!** there's no choice!; **sin ~** hopeless
remendar [remen'dar] *vt* to repair; (*con parche*) to patch
remiendo [re'mjendo] *nm* mend; (*con parche*) patch; (*cosido*) darn
remilgado, -a [remil'ɣaðo, a] *adj* prim; (*afectado*) affected
remiso, -a [re'miso, a] *adj* slack, slow
remite [re'mite] *nm* (*en sobre*) name and address of sender
remitir [remi'tir] *vt* to remit, send ▷ *vi* to slacken; (*en carta*): **remite: X** sender: X; **remitente** *nmf* sender
remo ['remo] *nm* (*de barco*) oar; (*Deporte*) rowing
remojar [remo'xar] *vt* to steep, soak; (*galleta etc*) to dip, dunk
remojo [re'moxo] *nm*: **dejar la ropa en ~** to leave clothes to soak
remolacha [remo'latʃa] *nf* beet, beetroot
remolcador [remolka'ðor] *nm* (*Náut*) tug; (*Auto*) breakdown lorry
remolcar [remol'kar] *vt* to tow
remolino [remo'lino] *nm* eddy; (*de agua*) whirlpool; (*de viento*) whirlwind; (*de gente*) crowd
remolque [re'molke] *nm* tow, towing; (*cuerda*) towrope; **llevar a ~** to tow
remontar [remon'tar] *vt* to mend; **remontarse** *vr* to soar; **~se a** (*Com*) to amount to; **~ el vuelo** to soar
remorder [remor'ðer] *vt* to distress, disturb; **~le la conciencia a algn** to have a guilty conscience; **remordimiento** *nm* remorse
remoto, -a [re'moto, a] *adj* remote
remover [remo'βer] *vt* to stir; (*tierra*) to turn over; (*objetos*) to move round
remuneración [remunera'θjon] *nf* remuneration
remunerar [remune'rar] *vt* to remunerate; (*premiar*) to reward
renacer [rena'θer] *vi* to be reborn; (*fig*) to revive; **renacimiento** *nm* rebirth; **el Renacimiento** the Renaissance
renacuajo [rena'kwaxo] *nm* (*Zool*) tadpole

renal [re'nal] *adj* renal, kidney *cpd*
rencilla [ren'θiʎa] *nf* quarrel
rencor [ren'kor] *nm* rancour, bitterness; **rencoroso, -a** *adj* spiteful
rendición [rendi'θjon] *nf* surrender
rendido, -a [ren'diðo, a] *adj* (*sumiso*) submissive; (*cansado*) worn-out, exhausted
rendija [ren'dixa] *nf* (*hendedura*) crack, cleft
rendimiento [rendi'mjento] *nm* (*producción*) output; (*Tec, Com*) efficiency
rendir [ren'dir] *vt* (*vencer*) to defeat; (*producir*) to produce; (*dar beneficio*) to yield; (*agotar*) to exhaust ▷ *vi* to pay; **rendirse** *vr* (*someterse*) to surrender; (*cansarse*) to wear o.s. out; **~ homenaje** *o* **culto a** to pay homage to
renegar [rene'ɣar] *vi* (*renunciar*) to renounce; (*blasfemar*) to blaspheme; (*quejarse*) to complain
RENFE ['renfe] *nf abr* (= *Red Nacional de los Ferrocarriles Españoles*)
renglón [ren'glon] *nm* (*línea*) line; (*Com*) item, article; **a ~ seguido** immediately after
renombre [re'nombre] *nm* renown
renovación [renoβa'θjon] *nf* (*de contrato*) renewal; (*Arq*) renovation
renovar [reno'βar] *vt* to renew; (*Arq*) to renovate
renta ['renta] *nf* (*ingresos*) income; (*beneficio*) profit; (*alquiler*) rent; **renta vitalicia** annuity; **rentable** *adj* profitable
renuncia [re'nunθja] *nf* resignation; **renunciar** [renun'θjar] *vt* to renounce; (*tabaco, alcohol etc*): **renunciar a** to give up; (*oferta, oportunidad*) to turn down; (*puesto*) to resign ▷ *vi* to resign
reñido, -a [re'ɲiðo, a] *adj* (*batalla*) bitter, hard-fought; **estar ~ con algn** to be on bad terms with sb
reñir [re'ɲir] *vt* (*regañar*) to scold ▷ *vi* (*estar peleado*) to quarrel, fall out; (*combatir*) to fight
reo ['reo] *nmf* culprit, offender; (*acusado*) accused, defendant
reojo [re'oxo]: **de ~** *adv* out of the corner of one's eye
reparación [repara'θjon] *nf* (*acto*) mending, repairing; (*Tec*) repair; (*fig*) amends *pl*, reparation
reparar [repa'rar] *vt* to repair; (*fig*) to make amends for; (*observar*) to observe ▷ *vi*: **~ en** (*darse cuenta de*) to notice; (*prestar atención a*) to pay attention to
reparo [re'paro] *nm* (*advertencia*) observation; (*duda*) doubt; (*dificultad*) difficulty; **poner ~s (a)** to raise objections (to)

repartidor, a [reparti'ðor, a] *nm/f* distributor
repartir [repar'tir] *vt* to distribute, share out; (*Correos*) to deliver; **reparto** *nm* distribution; delivery; (*Teatro, Cine*) cast; (CAM: *urbanización*) housing estate (BRIT), real estate development (US)
repasar [repa'sar] *vt* (*Escol*) to revise; (*Mecánica*) to check, overhaul; (*Costura*) to mend; **repaso** *nm* revision; overhaul, checkup; mending
repecho [re'petʃo] *nm* steep incline
repelente [repe'lente] *adj* repellent, repulsive
repeler [repe'ler] *vt* to repel
repente [re'pente] *nm*: **de ~** suddenly
repentino, -a [repen'tino, a] *adj* sudden
repercusión [reperku'sjon] *nf* repercussion
repercutir [reperku'tir] *vi* (*objeto*) to rebound; (*sonido*) to echo; **~ en** (*fig*) to have repercussions on
repertorio [reper'torjo] *nm* list; (*Teatro*) repertoire
repetición [repeti'θjon] *nf* repetition
repetir [repe'tir] *vt* to repeat; (*plato*) to have a second helping of ▷ *vi* to repeat; (*sabor*) to come back; **repetirse** *vr* (*volver sobre un tema*) to repeat o.s.
repetitivo, -a [repeti'tiβo, a] *adj* repetitive, repetitious
repique [re'pike] *nm* pealing, ringing; **repiqueteo** *nm* pealing; (*de tambor*) drumming
repisa [re'pisa] *nf* ledge, shelf; (*de ventana*) windowsill; **la ~ de la chimenea** the mantelpiece
repito *etc vb V* **repetir**
replantearse [replante'arse] *vr*: **~ un problema** to reconsider a problem
repleto, -a [re'pleto, a] *adj* replete, full up
réplica ['replika] *nf* answer; (*Arte*) replica
replicar [repli'kar] *vi* to answer; (*objetar*) to argue, answer back
repliegue [re'pljeɣe] *nm* (*Mil*) withdrawal
repoblación [repoβla'θjon] *nf* repopulation; (*de río*) restocking; **repoblación forestal** reafforestation
repoblar [repo'βlar] *vt* to repopulate; (*con árboles*) to reafforest
repollito [repo'ʎito] (CS) *nm*: **~s de Bruselas** (Brussels) sprouts
repollo [re'poʎo] *nm* cabbage
reponer [repo'ner] *vt* to replace, put back; (*Teatro*) to revive; **reponerse** *vr* to recover; **~ que ...** to reply that ...
reportaje [repor'taxe] *nm* report, article
reportero, -a [repor'tero, a] *nm/f*

reporter
reposacabezas [reposaka'βeθas] *nm inv* headrest
reposar [repo'sar] *vi* to rest, repose
reposera [repo'sera] (RPL) *nf* deck chair
reposición [reposi'θjon] *nf* replacement; (*Cine*) remake
reposo [re'poso] *nm* rest
repostar [repos'tar] *vt* to replenish; (*Auto*) to fill up (with petrol (BRIT) *o* gasoline (US))
repostería [reposte'ria] *nf* confectioner's (shop)
represa [re'presa] *nf* dam; (*lago artificial*) lake, pool
represalia [repre'salja] *nf* reprisal
representación [representa'θjon] *nf* representation; (*Teatro*) performance; **representante** *nmf* representative; performer
representar [represen'tar] *vt* to represent; (*Teatro*) to perform; (*edad*) to look; **representarse** *vr* to imagine; **representativo, -a** *adj* representative
represión [repre'sjon] *nf* repression
reprimenda [repri'menda] *nf* reprimand, rebuke
reprimir [repri'mir] *vt* to repress
reprobar [repro'βar] *vt* to censure, reprove
reprochar [repro'tʃar] *vt* to reproach; **reproche** *nm* reproach
reproducción [reproðuk'θjon] *nf* reproduction
reproducir [reproðu'θir] *vt* to reproduce; **reproducirse** *vr* to breed; (*situación*) to recur
reproductor, a [reproðuk'tor, a] *adj* reproductive ▷ *nm* player; **reproductor de CD** CD player
reptil [rep'til] *nm* reptile
república [re'puβlika] *nf* republic; **República Dominicana** Dominican Republic; **republicano, -a** *adj, nm* republican
repudiar [repu'ðjar] *vt* to repudiate; (*fe*) to renounce
repuesto [re'pwesto] *nm* (*pieza de recambio*) spare (part); (*abastecimiento*) supply; **rueda de ~** spare wheel
repugnancia [repuɣ'nanθja] *nf* repugnance; **repugnante** *adj* repugnant, repulsive
repugnar [repuɣ'nar] *vt* to disgust
repulsa [re'pulsa] *nf* rebuff
repulsión [repul'sjon] *nf* repulsion, aversion; **repulsivo, -a** *adj* repulsive
reputación [reputa'θjon] *nf* reputation
requerir [reke'rir] *vt* (*pedir*) to ask, request; (*exigir*) to require; (*llamar*) to send for, summon
requesón [reke'son] *nm* cottage cheese
requete... [re'kete] *prefijo* extremely
réquiem ['rekjem] (*pl* **~s**) *nm* requiem
requisito [reki'sito] *nm* requirement, requisite
res [res] *nf* beast, animal
resaca [re'saka] *nf* (*de mar*) undertow, undercurrent; (*fam*) hangover
resaltar [resal'tar] *vi* to project, stick out; (*fig*) to stand out
resarcir [resar'θir] *vt* to compensate; **resarcirse** *vr* to make up for
resbaladero [resβala'ðero] (MÉX) *nm* slide
resbaladizo, -a [resβala'ðiθo, a] *adj* slippery
resbalar [resβa'lar] *vi* to slip, slide; (*fig*) to slip (up); **resbalarse** *vr* to slip, slide; to slip (up); **resbalón** *nm* (*acción*) slip
rescatar [reska'tar] *vt* (*salvar*) to save, rescue; (*objeto*) to get back, recover; (*cautivos*) to ransom
rescate [res'kate] *nm* rescue; (*de objeto*) recovery; **pagar un ~** to pay a ransom
rescindir [resθin'dir] *vt* to rescind
rescisión [resθi'sjon] *nf* cancellation
resecar [rese'kar] *vt* to dry thoroughly; (*Med*) to cut out, remove; **resecarse** *vr* to dry up
reseco, -a [re'seko, a] *adj* very dry; (*fig*) skinny
resentido, -a [resen'tiðo, a] *adj* resentful
resentimiento [resenti'mjento] *nm* resentment, bitterness
resentirse [resen'tirse] *vr* (*debilitarse: persona*) to suffer; **~ de** (*consecuencias*) to feel the effects of; **~ de (*o* por) algo** to resent sth, be bitter about sth
reseña [re'seɲa] *nf* (*cuenta*) account; (*informe*) report; (*Literatura*) review
reseñar [rese'ɲar] *vt* to describe; (*Literatura*) to review
reserva [re'serβa] *nf* reserve; (*reservación*) reservation
reservado, -a [reser'βaðo, a] *adj* reserved; (*retraído*) cold, distant ▷ *nm* private room
reservar [reser'βar] *vt* (*guardar*) to keep; (*habitación, entrada*) to reserve; **reservarse** *vr* to save o.s.; (*callar*) to keep to o.s.
resfriado [resfri'aðo] *nm* cold; **resfriarse** *vr* to cool; (*Med*) to catch a cold
resguardar [resɣwar'ðar] *vt* to protect, shield; **resguardarse** *vr*: **~se de** to guard against; **resguardo** *nm* defence; (*vale*) voucher; (*recibo*) receipt, slip

residencia [resi'ðenθja] *nf* residence; **residencia de ancianos** residential home, old people's home; **residencia universitaria** hall of residence; **residencial** *nf* (*urbanización*) housing estate
residente [resi'ðente] *adj, nmf* resident
residir [resi'ðir] *vi* to reside, live; **~ en** to reside in, lie in
residuo [re'siðwo] *nm* residue
resignación [resiɣna'θjon] *nf* resignation; **resignarse** *vr*: **resignarse a** *o* **con** to resign o.s. to, be resigned to
resina [re'sina] *nf* resin
resistencia [resis'tenθja] *nf* (*dureza*) endurance, strength; (*oposición, Elec*) resistance; **resistente** *adj* strong, hardy; resistant
resistir [resis'tir] *vt* (*soportar*) to bear; (*oponerse a*) to resist, oppose; (*aguantar*) to put up with ▷ *vi* to resist; (*aguantar*) to last, endure; **resistirse** *vr*: **~se a** to refuse to, resist
resoluto, -a [reso'luto, a] *adj* resolute
resolver [resol'βer] *vt* to resolve; (*solucionar*) to solve, resolve; (*decidir*) to decide, settle; **resolverse** *vr* to make up one's mind
resonar [reso'nar] *vi* to ring, echo
resoplar [reso'plar] *vi* to snort; **resoplido** *nm* heavy breathing
resorte [re'sorte] *nm* spring; (*fig*) lever
resortera [resor'tera] (*MÉX*) *nf* catapult
respaldar [respal'dar] *vt* to back (up), support; **respaldarse** *vr* to lean back; **~se con** *o* **en** (*fig*) to take one's stand on; **respaldo** *nm* (*de sillón*) back; (*fig*) support, backing
respectivo, -a [respek'tiβo, a] *adj* respective; **en lo ~ a** with regard to
respecto [res'pekto] *nm*: **al ~** on this matter; **con ~ a, ~ de** with regard to, in relation to
respetable [respe'taβle] *adj* respectable
respetar [respe'tar] *vt* to respect; **respeto** *nm* respect; (*acatamiento*) deference; **respetos** *nmpl* respects; **respetuoso, -a** *adj* respectful
respingo [res'pingo] *nm* start, jump
respiración [respira'θjon] *nf* breathing; (*Med*) respiration; (*ventilación*) ventilation; **respiración asistida** artificial respiration (*by machine*)
respirar [respi'rar] *vi* to breathe; **respiratorio, -a** *adj* respiratory; **respiro** *nm* breathing; (*fig: descanso*) respite
resplandecer [resplande'θer] *vi* to shine; **resplandeciente** *adj* resplendent, shining; **resplandor** *nm* brilliance, brightness; (*de luz, fuego*) blaze
responder [respon'der] *vt* to answer ▷ *vi* to answer; (*fig*) to respond; (*pey*) to answer back; **~ de** *o* **por** to answer for; **respondón, -ona** *adj* cheeky
responsabilidad [responsaβili'ðað] *nf* responsibility
responsabilizarse [responsaβili'θarse] *vr* to make o.s. responsible, take charge
responsable [respon'saβle] *adj* responsible
respuesta [res'pwesta] *nf* answer, reply
resquebrajar [reskeβra'xar] *vt* to crack, split; **resquebrajarse** *vr* to crack, split
resquicio [res'kiθjo] *nm* chink; (*hendedura*) crack
resta ['resta] *nf* (*Mat*) remainder
restablecer [restaβle'θer] *vt* to re-establish, restore; **restablecerse** *vr* to recover
restante [res'tante] *adj* remaining; **lo ~** the remainder
restar [res'tar] *vt* (*Mat*) to subtract; (*fig*) to take away ▷ *vi* to remain, be left
restauración [restaura'θjon] *nf* restoration
restaurante [restau'rante] *nm* restaurant
restaurar [restau'rar] *vt* to restore
restituir [restitu'ir] *vt* (*devolver*) to return, give back; (*rehabilitar*) to restore
resto ['resto] *nm* (*residuo*) rest, remainder; (*apuesta*) stake; **restos** *nmpl* remains
restorán [resto'ran] *nm* (*Lam*) restaurant
restregar [restre'ɣar] *vt* to scrub, rub
restricción [restrik'θjon] *nf* restriction
restringir [restrin'xir] *vt* to restrict, limit
resucitar [resuθi'tar] *vt, vi* to resuscitate, revive
resuelto, -a [re'swelto, a] *pp de* **resolver** ▷ *adj* resolute, determined
resultado [resul'taðo] *nm* result; (*conclusión*) outcome; **resultante** *adj* resulting, resultant
resultar [resul'tar] *vi* (*ser*) to be; (*llegar a ser*) to turn out to be; (*salir bien*) to turn out well; (*Com*) to amount to; **~ de** to stem from; **me resulta difícil hacerlo** it's difficult for me to do it
resumen [re'sumen] (*pl* **resúmenes**) *nm* summary, résumé; **en ~** in short
resumir [resu'mir] *vt* to sum up; (*cortar*) to abridge, cut down; (*condensar*) to summarize

No confundir **resumir** con la palabra inglesa *resume*.

resurgir [resur'xir] *vi* (*reaparecer*) to reappear

r

resurrección [resurre(k)'θjon] *nf* resurrection
retablo [re'taβlo] *nm* altarpiece
retaguardia [reta'ɣwarðja] *nf* rearguard
retahíla [reta'ila] *nf* series, string
retal [re'tal] *nm* remnant
retar [re'tar] *vt* to challenge; (*desafiar*) to defy, dare
retazo [re'taθo] *nm* snippet (BRIT), fragment
retención [reten'θjon] *nf* (*tráfico*) hold-up; **retención fiscal** deduction for tax purposes
retener [rete'ner] *vt* (*intereses*) to withhold
reticente [reti'θente] *adj* (*tono*) insinuating; (*postura*) reluctant; **ser ~ a hacer algo** to be reluctant *o* unwilling to do sth
retina [re'tina] *nf* retina
retintín [retin'tin] *nm* jangle, jingle
retirada [reti'raða] *nf* (*Mil, refugio*) retreat; (*de dinero*) withdrawal; (*de embajador*) recall; **retirado, -a** *adj* (*lugar*) remote; (*vida*) quiet; (*jubilado*) retired
retirar [reti'rar] *vt* to withdraw; (*quitar*) to remove; (*jubilar*) to retire, pension off; **retirarse** *vr* to retreat, withdraw; to retire; (*acostarse*) to retire, go to bed; **retiro** *nm* retreat; retirement; (*pago*) pension
reto ['reto] *nm* dare, challenge
retocar [reto'kar] *vt* (*fotografía*) to touch up, retouch
retoño [re'toɲo] *nm* sprout, shoot; (*fig*) offspring, child
retoque [re'toke] *nm* retouching
retorcer [retor'θer] *vt* to twist; (*manos, lavado*) to wring; **retorcerse** *vr* to become twisted; (*mover el cuerpo*) to writhe
retorcido, -a [retor'θiðo, a] *adj* (*persona*) devious
retorcijón [retorθi'jon] (LAM) *nm* (*tb*: **~ de tripas**) stomach cramp
retórica [re'torika] *nf* rhetoric; (*pey*) affectedness
retorno [re'torno] *nm* return
retortijón [retorti'xon] (ESP) *nm* (*tb*: **~ de tripas**) stomach cramp
retozar [reto'θar] *vi* (*juguetear*) to frolic, romp; (*saltar*) to gambol
retracción [retrak'θjon] *nf* retraction
retraerse [retra'erse] *vr* to retreat, withdraw; **retraído, -a** *adj* shy, retiring; **retraimiento** *nm* retirement; (*timidez*) shyness
retransmisión [retransmi'sjon] *nf* repeat (broadcast)
retransmitir [retransmi'tir] *vt* (*mensaje*) to relay; (*TV etc*) to repeat, retransmit; (*: en vivo*) to broadcast live
retrasado, -a [retra'saðo, a] *adj* late; (*Med*) mentally retarded; (*país etc*) backward, underdeveloped
retrasar [retra'sar] *vt* (*demorar*) to postpone, put off; (*retardar*) to slow down ▷ *vi* (*atrasarse*) to be late; (*reloj*) to be slow; (*producción*) to fall (off); (*quedarse atrás*) to lag behind; **retrasarse** *vr* to be late; to be slow; to fall (off); to lag behind
retraso [re'traso] *nm* (*demora*) delay; (*lentitud*) slowness; (*tardanza*) lateness; (*atraso*) backwardness; **retrasos** *nmpl* (*Finanzas*) arrears; **llegar con ~** to arrive late; **retraso mental** mental deficiency
retratar [retra'tar] *vt* (*Arte*) to paint the portrait of; (*fotografiar*) to photograph; (*fig*) to depict, describe; **retrato** *nm* portrait; (*fig*) likeness; **retrato-robot** (ESP) *nm* Identikit®
retrete [re'trete] *nm* toilet
retribuir [retri'βwir] *vt* (*recompensar*) to reward; (*pagar*) to pay
retro... ['retro] *prefijo* retro...
retroceder [retroθe'ðer] *vi* (*echarse atrás*) to move back(wards); (*fig*) to back down
retroceso [retro'θeso] *nm* backward movement; (*Med*) relapse; (*fig*) backing down
retrospectivo, -a [retrospek'tiβo, a] *adj* retrospective
retrovisor [retroβi'sor] *nm* (*tb*: **espejo ~**) rear-view mirror
retumbar [retum'bar] *vi* to echo, resound
reúma [re'uma], **reuma** ['reuma] *nm* rheumatism
reunión [reu'njon] *nf* (*asamblea*) meeting; (*fiesta*) party
reunir [reu'nir] *vt* (*juntar*) to reunite, join (together); (*recoger*) to gather (together); (*personas*) to get together; (*cualidades*) to combine; **reunirse** *vr* (*personas: en asamblea*) to meet, gather
revalidar [reβali'ðar] *vt* (*ratificar*) to confirm, ratify
revalorizar [reβalori'θar] *vt* to revalue, reassess
revancha [re'βantʃa] *nf* revenge
revelación [reβela'θjon] *nf* revelation
revelado [reβe'laðo] *nm* developing
revelar [reβe'lar] *vt* to reveal; (*Foto*) to develop
reventa [re'βenta] *nf* (*de entradas: para concierto*) touting
reventar [reβen'tar] *vt* to burst, explode
reventón [reβen'ton] *nm* (*Auto*) blow-out (BRIT), flat (US)
reverencia [reβe'renθja] *nf* reverence; **reverenciar** *vt* to revere

reverendo, -a [reβe'rendo, a] *adj* reverend
reverente [reβe'rente] *adj* reverent
reversa [re'βersa] (*MÉX, CAM*) *nf* reverse (gear)
reversible [reβer'siβle] *adj* (*prenda*) reversible
reverso [re'βerso] *nm* back, other side; (*de moneda*) reverse
revertir [reβer'tir] *vi* to revert
revés [re'βes] *nm* back, wrong side; (*fig*) reverse, setback; (*Deporte*) backhand; **al ~** the wrong way round; (*de arriba abajo*) upside down; (*ropa*) inside out; **volver algo del ~** to turn sth round; (*ropa*) to turn sth inside out
revisar [reβi'sar] *vt* (*examinar*) to check; (*texto etc*) to revise; **revisión** *nf* revision; **revisión salarial** wage review
revisor, a [reβi'sor, a] *nm/f* inspector; (*Ferro*) ticket collector
revista [re'βista] *nf* magazine, review; (*Teatro*) revue; (*inspección*) inspection; **pasar ~ a** to review, inspect; **revista del corazón** *magazine featuring celebrity gossip and real-life romance stories*
revivir [reβi'βir] *vi* to revive
revolcarse [reβol'karse] *vr* to roll about
revoltijo [reβol'tixo] *nm* mess, jumble
revoltoso, -a [reβol'toso, a] *adj* (*travieso*) naughty, unruly
revolución [reβolu'θjon] *nf* revolution; **revolucionario, -a** *adj, nm/f* revolutionary
revolver [reβol'βer] *vt* (*desordenar*) to disturb, mess up; (*mover*) to move about ▷*vi*: **~ en** to go through, rummage (about) in; **revolverse** *vr* (*volver contra*) to turn on *o* against
revólver [re'βolβer] *nm* revolver
revuelo [re'βwelo] *nm* fluttering; (*fig*) commotion
revuelta [re'βwelta] *nf* (*motín*) revolt; (*agitación*) commotion
revuelto, -a [re'βwelto, a] *pp de* **revolver** ▷*adj* (*mezclado*) mixed-up, in disorder
rey [rei] *nm* king; **Día de R~es** Twelfth Night; **los R~es Magos** the Three Wise Men, the Magi

REYES MAGOS

On the night before the 6th January (the Epiphany), children go to bed expecting **los Reyes Magos** (the Three Wise Men) to bring them presents. Twelfth Night processions, known as **cabalgatas**, take place that evening when 3 people dressed as **los Reyes Magos** arrive in the town by land or sea to the delight of the children.

reyerta [re'jerta] *nf* quarrel, brawl
rezagado, -a [reθa'ɣaðo, a] *nm/f* straggler
rezar [re'θar] *vi* to pray; **~ con** (*fam*) to concern, have to do with; **rezo** *nm* prayer
rezumar [reθu'mar] *vt* to ooze
ría ['ria] *nf* estuary
riada [ri'aða] *nf* flood
ribera [ri'βera] *nf* (*de río*) bank; (*: área*) riverside
ribete [ri'βete] *nm* (*de vestido*) border; (*fig*) addition
ricino [ri'θino] *nm*: **aceite de ~** castor oil
rico, -a ['riko, a] *adj* rich; (*adinerado*) wealthy, rich; (*lujoso*) luxurious; (*comida*) delicious; (*niño*) lovely, cute ▷*nm/f* rich person
ridiculez [riðiku'leθ] *nf* absurdity
ridiculizar [riðikuli'θar] *vt* to ridicule
ridículo, -a [ri'ðikulo, a] *adj* ridiculous; **hacer el ~** to make a fool of o.s.; **poner a algn en ~** to make a fool of sb
riego ['rjeɣo] *nm* (*aspersión*) watering; (*irrigación*) irrigation; **riego sanguíneo** blood flow *o* circulation
riel [rjel] *nm* rail
rienda ['rjenda] *nf* rein; **dar ~ suelta a** to give free rein to
riesgo ['rjesɣo] *nm* risk; **correr el ~ de** to run the risk of
rifa ['rifa] *nf* (*lotería*) raffle; **rifar** *vt* to raffle
rifle ['rifle] *nm* rifle
rigidez [rixi'ðeθ] *nf* rigidity, stiffness; (*fig*) strictness; **rígido, -a** *adj* rigid, stiff; strict, inflexible
rigor [ri'ɣor] *nm* strictness, rigour; (*inclemencia*) harshness; **de ~** de rigueur, essential; **riguroso, -a** *adj* rigorous; harsh; (*severo*) severe
rimar [ri'mar] *vi* to rhyme
rimbombante [rimbom'bante] *adj* pompous
rímel ['rimel] *nm* mascara
rímmel ['rimel] *nm* = **rímel**
rin [rin] (*MÉX*) *nm* (wheel) rim
rincón [rin'kon] *nm* corner (*inside*)
rinoceronte [rinoθe'ronte] *nm* rhinoceros
riña ['riɲa] *nf* (*disputa*) argument; (*pelea*) brawl
riñón [ri'ɲon] *nm* kidney
río *etc* ['rio] *vb V* **reír** ▷*nm* river; (*fig*) torrent, stream; **río abajo/arriba** downstream/upstream; **Río de la Plata** River Plate

r

rioja [ri'oxa] *nm* (*vino*) rioja (wine)
rioplatense [riopla'tense] *adj* of o from the River Plate region
riqueza [ri'keθa] *nf* wealth, riches *pl*; (*cualidad*) richness
risa ['risa] *nf* laughter; (*una risa*) laugh; **¡qué ~!** what a laugh!
risco ['risko] *nm* crag, cliff
ristra ['ristra] *nf* string
risueño, -a [ri'sweɲo, a] *adj* (*sonriente*) smiling; (*contento*) cheerful
ritmo ['ritmo] *nm* rhythm; **a ~ lento** slowly; **trabajar a ~ lento** to go slow; **ritmo cardíaco** heart rate
rito ['rito] *nm* rite
ritual [ri'twal] *adj, nm* ritual
rival [ri'βal] *adj, nmf* rival; **rivalidad** *nf* rivalry; **rivalizar** *vi*: **rivalizar con** to rival, vie with
rizado, -a [ri'θaðo, a] *adj* curly ▷ *nm* curls *pl*
rizar [ri'θar] *vt* to curl; **rizarse** *vr* (*pelo*) to curl; (*agua*) to ripple; **rizo** *nm* curl; ripple
RNE *nf abr* = **Radio Nacional de España**
robar [ro'βar] *vt* to rob; (*objeto*) to steal; (*casa etc*) to break into; (*Naipes*) to draw
roble ['roβle] *nm* oak; **robledal** *nm* oakwood
robo ['roβo] *nm* robbery, theft
robot [ro'βot] *nm* robot; **robot (de cocina)** (ESP) food processor
robustecer [roβuste'θer] *vt* to strengthen
robusto, -a [ro'βusto, a] *adj* robust, strong
roca ['roka] *nf* rock
roce ['roθe] *nm* (*caricia*) brush; (*Tec*) friction; (*en la piel*) graze; **tener ~ con** to be in close contact with
rociar [ro'θjar] *vt* to spray
rocín [ro'θin] *nm* nag, hack
rocío [ro'θio] *nm* dew
rocola [ro'kola] (LAM) *nf* jukebox
rocoso, -a [ro'koso, a] *adj* rocky
rodaballo [roða'baʎo] *nm* turbot
rodaja [ro'ðaxa] *nf* slice
rodaje [ro'ðaxe] *nm* (*Cine*) shooting, filming; (*Auto*): **en ~** running in
rodar [ro'ðar] *vt* (*vehículo*) to wheel (along); (*escalera*) to roll down; (*viajar por*) to travel (over) ▷ *vi* to roll; (*coche*) to go, run; (*Cine*) to shoot, film
rodear [roðe'ar] *vt* to surround ▷ *vi* to go round; **rodearse** *vr*: **~se de amigos** to surround o.s. with friends
rodeo [ro'ðeo] *nm* (*ruta indirecta*) detour; (*evasión*) evasion; (*Deporte*) rodeo; **hablar sin ~s** to come to the point, speak plainly
rodilla [ro'ðiʎa] *nf* knee; **de ~s** kneeling; **ponerse de ~s** to kneel (down)
rodillo [ro'ðiʎo] *nm* roller; (*Culin*) rolling-pin
roedor, a [roe'ðor, a] *adj* gnawing ▷ *nm* rodent
roer [ro'er] *vt* (*masticar*) to gnaw; (*corroer, fig*) to corrode
rogar [ro'ɣar] *vt, vi* (*pedir*) to ask for; (*suplicar*) to beg, plead; **se ruega no fumar** please do not smoke
rojizo, -a [ro'xiθo, a] *adj* reddish
rojo, -a ['roxo, a] *adj, nm* red; **al ~ vivo** red-hot
rol [rol] *nm* list, roll; (*papel*) role
rollito [ro'ʎito] *nm* (*tb*: **~ de primavera**) spring roll
rollizo, -a [ro'ʎiθo, a] *adj* (*objeto*) cylindrical; (*persona*) plump
rollo ['roʎo] *nm* roll; (*de cuerda*) coil; (*madera*) log; (ESP: *fam*) bore; **¡qué ~!** (ESP: *fam*) what a carry-on!
Roma ['roma] *n* Rome
romance [ro'manθe] *nm* (*amoroso*) romance; (*Literatura*) ballad
romano, -a [ro'mano, a] *adj, nm/f* Roman; **a la romana** in batter
romanticismo [romanti'θismo] *nm* romanticism
romántico, -a [ro'mantiko, a] *adj* romantic
rombo ['rombo] *nm* (*Geom*) rhombus
romería [rome'ria] *nf* (*Rel*) pilgrimage; (*excursión*) trip, outing

ROMERÍA

Originally a pilgrimage to a shrine or church to express devotion to the Virgin Mary or a local Saint, the **romería** has also become a rural festival which accompanies the pilgrimage. People come from all over to attend, bringing their own food and drink, and spend the day in celebration.

romero, -a [ro'mero, a] *nm/f* pilgrim ▷ *nm* rosemary
romo, -a ['romo, a] *adj* blunt; (*fig*) dull
rompecabezas [rompeka'βeθas] *nm inv* riddle, puzzle; (*juego*) jigsaw (puzzle)
rompehuelgas [rompe'welɣas] (LAM) *nm inv* strikebreaker, scab
rompeolas [rompe'olas] *nm inv* breakwater
romper [rom'per] *vt* to break; (*hacer pedazos*) to smash; (*papel, tela etc*) to tear, rip ▷ *vi* (*olas*) to break; (*sol, diente*) to break through; **romperse** *vr* to break; **~ un**

contrato to break a contract; **~ a** (*empezar a*) to start (suddenly) to; **~ a llorar** to burst into tears; **~ con algn** to fall out with sb
ron [ron] *nm* rum
roncar [ron'kar] *vi* to snore
ronco, -a ['ronko, a] *adj* (*afónico*) hoarse; (*áspero*) raucous
ronda ['ronda] *nf* (*gen*) round; (*patrulla*) patrol; **rondar** *vt* to patrol ▷*vi* to patrol; (*fig*) to prowl round
ronquido [ron'kiðo] *nm* snore, snoring
ronronear [ronrone'ar] *vi* to purr
roña ['roɲa] *nf* (*Veterinaria*) mange; (*mugre*) dirt, grime; (*óxido*) rust
roñoso, -a [ro'ɲoso, a] *adj* (*mugriento*) filthy; (*tacaño*) mean
ropa ['ropa] *nf* clothes *pl*, clothing; **ropa blanca** linen; **ropa de cama** bed linen; **ropa de color** coloureds *pl*; **ropa interior** underwear; **ropa sucia** dirty washing; **ropaje** *nm* gown, robes *pl*
ropero [ro'pero] *nm* linen cupboard; (*guardarropa*) wardrobe
rosa ['rosa] *adj* pink ▷*nf* rose
rosado, -a [ro'saðo, a] *adj* pink ▷*nm* rosé
rosal [ro'sal] *nm* rosebush
rosario [ro'sarjo] *nm* (*Rel*) rosary; **rezar el ~** to say the rosary
rosca ['roska] *nf* (*de tornillo*) thread; (*de humo*) coil, spiral; (*pan, postre*) ring-shaped roll/pastry
rosetón [rose'ton] *nm* rosette; (*Arq*) rose window
rosquilla [ros'kiʎa] *nf* doughnut-shaped fritter
rostro ['rostro] *nm* (*cara*) face
rotativo, -a [rota'tiβo, a] *adj* rotary
roto, -a ['roto, a] *pp de* **romper** ▷*adj* broken
rotonda [ro'tonda] *nf* roundabout
rótula ['rotula] *nf* kneecap; (*Tec*) ball-and-socket joint
rotulador [rotula'ðor] *nm* felt-tip pen
rótulo ['rotulo] *nm* heading, title; label; (*letrero*) sign
rotundamente [rotunda'mente] *adv* (*negar*) flatly; (*responder, afirmar*) emphatically; **rotundo, -a** *adj* round; (*enfático*) emphatic
rotura [ro'tura] *nf* (*acto*) breaking; (*Med*) fracture
rozadura [roθa'ðura] *nf* abrasion, graze
rozar [ro'θar] *vt* (*frotar*) to rub; (*arañar*) to scratch; (*tocar ligeramente*) to shave, touch lightly; **rozarse** *vr* to rub (together); **~se con** (*fam*) to rub shoulders with
rte. *abr* (= *remite, remitente*) sender
RTVE *nf abr* = **Radiotelevisión Española**

rubí [ru'βi] *nm* ruby; (*de reloj*) jewel
rubio, -a ['ruβjo, a] *adj* fair-haired, blond(e) ▷*nm/f* blond/blonde; **tabaco ~** Virginia tobacco
rubor [ru'βor] *nm* (*sonrojo*) blush; (*timidez*) bashfulness; **ruborizarse** *vr* to blush
rúbrica ['ruβrika] *nf* (*de la firma*) flourish; **rubricar** *vt* (*firmar*) to sign with a flourish; (*concluir*) to sign and seal
rudimentario, -a [ruðimen'tarjo, a] *adj* rudimentary
rudo, -a ['ruðo, a] *adj* (*sin pulir*) unpolished; (*grosero*) coarse; (*violento*) violent; (*sencillo*) simple
rueda ['rweða] *nf* wheel; (*círculo*) ring, circle; (*rodaja*) slice, round; **rueda de auxilio** (RPL) spare tyre; **rueda delantera/trasera/de repuesto** front/back/spare wheel; **rueda de prensa** press conference; **rueda gigante** (LAM) big (BRIT) *o* Ferris (US) wheel
ruedo ['rweðo] *nm* (*círculo*) circle; (*Taur*) arena, bullring
ruego *etc* ['rweɣo] *vb V* **rogar** ▷*nm* request
rugby ['ruɣβi] *nm* rugby
rugido [ru'xiðo] *nm* roar
rugir [ru'xir] *vi* to roar
rugoso, -a [ru'ɣoso, a] *adj* (*arrugado*) wrinkled; (*áspero*) rough; (*desigual*) ridged
ruido ['rwiðo] *nm* noise; (*sonido*) sound; (*alboroto*) racket, row; (*escándalo*) commotion, rumpus; **ruidoso, -a** *adj* noisy, loud; (*fig*) sensational
ruin [rwin] *adj* contemptible, mean
ruina ['rwina] *nf* ruin; (*colapso*) collapse; (*de persona*) ruin, downfall
ruinoso, -a [rwi'noso, a] *adj* ruinous; (*destartalado*) dilapidated, tumbledown; (*Com*) disastrous
ruiseñor [rwise'ɲor] *nm* nightingale
rulero [ru'lero] (RPL) *nm* roller
ruleta [ru'leta] *nf* roulette
rulo ['rulo] *nm* (*para el pelo*) curler
Rumanía [ruma'nia] *nf* Rumania
rumba ['rumba] *nf* rumba
rumbo ['rumbo] *nm* (*ruta*) route, direction; (*ángulo de dirección*) course, bearing; (*fig*) course of events; **ir con ~ a** to be heading for
rumiante [ru'mjante] *nm* ruminant
rumiar [ru'mjar] *vt* to chew; (*fig*) to chew over ▷*vi* to chew the cud
rumor [ru'mor] *nm* (*ruido sordo*) low sound; (*murmuración*) murmur, buzz; **rumorearse** *vr*: **se rumorea que ...** it is rumoured that ...
rupestre [ru'pestre] *adj* rock *cpd*
ruptura [rup'tura] *nf* rupture
rural [ru'ral] *adj* rural

Rusia ['rusja] *nf* Russia; **ruso, -a** *adj, nm/f* Russian
rústico, -a ['rustiko, a] *adj* rustic; (*ordinario*) coarse, uncouth ▷ *nm/f* yokel
ruta ['ruta] *nf* route
rutina [ru'tina] *nf* routine

S

S *abr* (= *santo, a*) St; (= *sur*) S
s. *abr* (= *siglo*) C.; (= *siguiente*) foll
S.A. *abr* (= *Sociedad Anónima*) Ltd. (BRIT), Inc. (US)
sábado ['saβaðo] *nm* Saturday
sábana ['saβana] *nf* sheet
sabañón [saβa'ɲon] *nm* chilblain
saber [sa'βer] *vt* to know; (*llegar a conocer*) to find out, learn; (*tener capacidad de*) to know how to ▷ *vi*: **~ a** to taste of, taste like ▷ *nm* knowledge, learning; **a ~** namely; **¿sabes conducir/nadar?** can you drive/swim?; **¿sabes francés?** do you speak French?; **~ de memoria** to know by heart; **hacer ~ algo a algn** to inform sb of sth, let sb know sth
sabiduría [saβiðu'ria] *nf* (*conocimientos*) wisdom; (*instrucción*) learning
sabiendas [sa'βjendas]: **a ~** *adv* knowingly
sabio, -a ['saβjo, a] *adj* (*docto*) learned; (*prudente*) wise, sensible
sabor [sa'βor] *nm* taste, flavour; **saborear** *vt* to taste, savour; (*fig*) to relish
sabotaje [saβo'taxe] *nm* sabotage
sabré *etc vb V* **saber**
sabroso, -a [sa'βroso, a] *adj* tasty; (*fig: fam*) racy, salty
sacacorchos [saka'kortʃos] *nm inv* corkscrew
sacapuntas [saka'puntas] *nm inv* pencil sharpener
sacar [sa'kar] *vt* to take out; (*fig: extraer*) to get (out); (*quitar*) to remove, get out; (*hacer salir*) to bring out; (*conclusión*) to draw; (*novela etc*) to publish, bring out; (*ropa*) to take off; (*obra*) to make; (*premio*) to receive; (*entradas*) to get; (*Tenis*) to serve; **~ adelante** (*niño*) to bring up; (*negocio*) to carry on, go on with; **~ a algn a bailar** to get sb up to dance; **~ una foto** to take a photo; **~ la lengua** to stick out one's tongue; **~ buenas/malas**

notas to get good/bad marks
sacarina [saka'rina] *nf* saccharin(e)
sacerdote [saθer'ðote] *nm* priest
saciar [sa'θjar] *vt* (*hambre, sed*) to satisfy; **saciarse** *vr* (*de comida*) to get full up
saco ['sako] *nm* bag; (*grande*) sack; (*su contenido*) bagful; (LAM: *chaqueta*) jacket; **saco de dormir** sleeping bag
sacramento [sakra'mento] *nm* sacrament
sacrificar [sakrifi'kar] *vt* to sacrifice; **sacrificio** *nm* sacrifice
sacristía [sakris'tia] *nf* sacristy
sacudida [saku'ðiða] *nf* (*agitación*) shake, shaking; (*sacudimiento*) jolt, bump; **sacudida eléctrica** electric shock
sacudir [saku'ðir] *vt* to shake; (*golpear*) to hit
Sagitario [saxi'tarjo] *nm* Sagittarius
sagrado, -a [sa'ɣraðo, a] *adj* sacred, holy
Sáhara ['saara] *nm*: **el ~** the Sahara (desert)
sal [sal] *vb V* **salir** ▷ *nf* salt; **sales de baño** bath salts
sala ['sala] *nf* room; (*tb*: **~ de estar**) living room; (*Teatro*) house, auditorium; (*de hospital*) ward; **sala de espera** waiting room; **sala de estar** living room; **sala de fiestas** dance hall
salado, -a [sa'laðo, a] *adj* salty; (*fig*) witty, amusing; **agua salada** salt water
salar [sa'lar] *vt* to salt, add salt to
salario [sa'larjo] *nm* wage, pay
salchicha [sal'tʃitʃa] *nf* (pork) sausage; **salchichón** *nm* (salami-type) sausage
saldo ['saldo] *nm* (*pago*) settlement; (*de una cuenta*) balance; (*lo restante*) remnant(s) (*pl*), remainder; (*de móvil*) credit; **saldos** *nmpl* (*en tienda*) sale
saldré *etc vb V* **salir**
salero [sa'lero] *nm* salt cellar
salgo *etc vb V* **salir**
salida [sa'liða] *nf* (*puerta etc*) exit, way out; (*acto*) leaving, going out; (*de tren, Aviac*) departure; (*Tec*) output, production; (*fig*) way out; (*Com*) opening; (*Geo, válvula*) outlet; (*de gas*) leak; **calle sin ~** cul-de-sac; **salida de baño** (RPL) bathrobe; **salida de emergencia/incendios** emergency exit/ fire escape

PALABRA CLAVE

salir [sa'lir] *vi* **1** (*partir*: *tb*: **salir de**) to leave; **Juan ha salido** Juan is out; **salió de la cocina** he came out of the kitchen
2 (*aparecer*) to appear; (*disco, libro*) to come out; **anoche salió en la tele** she appeared *o* was on TV last night; **salió en todos los periódicos** it was in all the papers
3 (*resultar*): **la muchacha nos salió muy trabajadora** the girl turned out to be a very hard worker; **la comida te ha salido exquisita** the food was delicious; **sale muy caro** it's very expensive
4: **salirle a uno algo: la entrevista que hice me salió bien/mal** the interview I did went *o* turned out well/badly
5: **salir adelante: no sé como haré para salir adelante** I don't know how I'll get by
salirse *vr* (*líquido*) to spill; (*animal*) to escape

saliva [sa'liβa] *nf* saliva
salmo ['salmo] *nm* psalm
salmón [sal'mon] *nm* salmon
salmonete [salmo'nete] *nm* red mullet
salón [sa'lon] *nm* (*de casa*) living room, lounge; (*muebles*) lounge suite; **salón de baile** dance hall; **salón de belleza** beauty parlour
salpicadera [salpika'ðera] (MÉX) *nf* mudguard (BRIT), fender (US)
salpicadero [salpika'ðero] *nm* (*Auto*) dashboard
salpicar [salpi'kar] *vt* (*rociar*) to sprinkle, spatter; (*esparcir*) to scatter
salpicón [salpi'kon] *nm* (*tb*: **~ de marisco**) seafood salad
salsa ['salsa] *nf* sauce; (*con carne asada*) gravy; (*fig*) spice
saltamontes [salta'montes] *nm inv* grasshopper
saltar [sal'tar] *vt* to jump (over), leap (over); (*dejar de lado*) to skip, miss out ▷ *vi* to jump, leap; (*pelota*) to bounce; (*al aire*) to fly up; (*quebrarse*) to break; (*al agua*) to dive; (*fig*) to explode, blow up
salto ['salto] *nm* jump, leap; (*al agua*) dive; **salto de agua** waterfall; **salto de altura/ longitud** high/long jump
salud [sa'luð] *nf* health; **¡(a su) ~!** cheers!, good health!; **saludable** *adj* (*de buena salud*) healthy; (*provechoso*) good, beneficial
saludar [salu'ðar] *vt* to greet; (*Mil*) to salute; **saludo** *nm* greeting; **"saludos"** (*en carta*) "best wishes", "regards"
salvación [salβa'θjon] *nf* salvation; (*rescate*) rescue
salvado [sal'βaðo] *nm* bran
salvaje [sal'βaxe] *adj* wild; (*tribu*) savage
salvamanteles [salβaman'teles] *nm inv* table mat
salvamento [salβa'mento] *nm* rescue
salvapantallas [salβapan'taʎas] *nm inv* screen saver
salvar [sal'βar] *vt* (*rescatar*) to save, rescue; (*resolver*) to overcome, resolve; (*cubrir*

distancias) to cover, travel; (*hacer excepción*) to except, exclude; (*barco*) to salvage
salvavidas [salβa'βiðas] *adj inv*: **bote/chaleco ~** lifeboat/life jacket
salvo, -a ['salβo, a] *adj* safe ▷ *adv* except (for), save; **a ~** out of danger; **~ que** unless
san [san] *adj* saint; **S~ Juan** St John
sanar [sa'nar] *vt* (*herida*) to heal; (*persona*) to cure ▷ *vi* (*persona*) to get well, recover; (*herida*) to heal
sanatorio [sana'torjo] *nm* sanatorium
sanción [san'θjon] *nf* sanction
sancochado, -a [sanko'tʃado, a] (MÉX) *adj* (*Culin*) underdone, rare
sandalia [san'dalja] *nf* sandal
sandía [san'dia] *nf* watermelon
sandwich ['sandwitʃ] (*pl* **~s, ~es**) *nm* sandwich
sanfermines [sanfer'mines] *nmpl* *festivities in celebration of San Fermín (Pamplona)*

SANFERMINES

The **Sanfermines** is a week-long festival in Pamplona made famous by Ernest Hemingway. From the 7th July, the feast of "San Fermín", crowds of mainly young people take to the streets drinking, singing and dancing. Early in the morning bulls are released along the narrow streets leading to the bullring, and young men risk serious injury to show their bravery by running out in front of them, a custom which is also typical of many Spanish villages.

sangrar [san'grar] *vt, vi* to bleed; **sangre** *nf* blood
sangría [san'gria] *nf* sangria, *sweetened drink of red wine with fruit*
sangriento, -a [san'grjento, a] *adj* bloody
sanguíneo, -a [san'gineo, a] *adj* blood *cpd*
sanidad [sani'ðað] *nf* (*tb*: **~ pública**) public health
San Isidro [sani'sidro] *nm* *patron saint of Madrid*

SAN ISIDRO

San Isidro is the patron saint of Madrid, and gives his name to the week-long festivities which take place around the 15th May. Originally an 18th-century trade fair, the **San Isidro** celebrations now include music, dance, a famous **romería**, theatre and bullfighting.

sanitario, -a [sani'tarjo, a] *adj* health *cpd*; **sanitarios** *nmpl* toilets (BRIT), washroom (US)
sano, -a ['sano, a] *adj* healthy; (*sin daños*) sound; (*comida*) wholesome; (*entero*) whole, intact; **~ y salvo** safe and sound

No confundir **sano** con la palabra inglesa *sane*.

Santiago [san'tjaɣo] *nm*: **~ (de Chile)** Santiago
santiamén [santja'men] *nm*: **en un ~** in no time at all
santidad [santi'ðað] *nf* holiness, sanctity
santiguarse [santi'ɣwarse] *vr* to make the sign of the cross
santo, -a ['santo, a] *adj* holy; (*fig*) wonderful, miraculous ▷ *nm/f* saint ▷ *nm* saint's day; **~ y seña** password
santuario [san'twarjo] *nm* sanctuary, shrine
sapo ['sapo] *nm* toad
saque ['sake] *nm* (*Tenis*) service, serve; (*Fútbol*) throw-in; **saque de esquina** corner (kick)
saquear [sake'ar] *vt* (*Mil*) to sack; (*robar*) to loot, plunder; (*fig*) to ransack
sarampión [saram'pjon] *nm* measles *sg*
sarcástico, -a [sar'kastiko, a] *adj* sarcastic
sardina [sar'ðina] *nf* sardine
sargento [sar'xento] *nm* sergeant
sarmiento [sar'mjento] *nm* (*Bot*) vine shoot
sarna ['sarna] *nf* itch; (*Med*) scabies
sarpullido [sarpu'ʎiðo] *nm* (*Med*) rash
sarro ['sarro] *nm* (*en dientes*) tartar, plaque
sartén [sar'ten] *nf* frying pan
sastre ['sastre] *nm* tailor; **sastrería** *nf* (*arte*) tailoring; (*tienda*) tailor's (shop)
Satanás [sata'nas] *nm* Satan
satélite [sa'telite] *nm* satellite
sátira ['satira] *nf* satire
satisfacción [satisfak'θjon] *nf* satisfaction
satisfacer [satisfa'θer] *vt* to satisfy; (*gastos*) to meet; (*pérdida*) to make good; **satisfacerse** *vr* to satisfy o.s., be satisfied; (*vengarse*) to take revenge; **satisfecho, -a** *adj* satisfied; (*contento*) content(ed), happy; (*tb*: **satisfecho de sí mismo**) self-satisfied, smug
saturar [satu'rar] *vt* to saturate; **saturarse** *vr* (*mercado, aeropuerto*) to reach saturation point
sauce ['sauθe] *nm* willow; **sauce llorón**

weeping willow
sauna ['sauna] *nf* sauna
savia ['saβja] *nf* sap
saxofón [sakso'fon] *nm* saxophone
sazonar [saθo'nar] *vt* to ripen; (*Culin*) to flavour, season
scooter [e'skuter] (ESP) *nf* scooter
Scotch® [skotʃ] (LAM) *nm* Sellotape® (BRIT), Scotch tape® (US)
SE *abr* (= *sudeste*) SE

PALABRA CLAVE

se [se] *pron* **1** (*reflexivo: sg: m*) himself; (: *f*) herself; (: *pl*) themselves; (: *cosa*) itself; (: *de Vd*) yourself; (: *de Vds*) yourselves; **se está preparando** she's preparing herself
2 (*con complemento indirecto*) to him; to her; to them; to it; to you; **a usted se lo dije ayer** I told you yesterday; **se compró un sombrero** he bought himself a hat; **se rompió la pierna** he broke his leg
3 (*uso recíproco*) each other, one another; **se miraron (el uno al otro)** they looked at each other *o* one another
4 (*en oraciones pasivas*): **se han vendido muchos libros** a lot of books have been sold
5 (*impers*): **se dice que ...** people say that ..., it is said that ...; **allí se come muy bien** the food there is very good, you can eat very well there

sé *etc* [se] *vb V* **saber; ser**
sea *etc vb V* **ser**
sebo ['seβo] *nm* fat, grease
secador [seka'ðor] *nm*: **~ de pelo** hair-dryer
secadora [seka'ðora] *nf* tumble dryer
secar [se'kar] *vt* to dry; **secarse** *vr* to dry (off); (*río, planta*) to dry up
sección [sek'θjon] *nf* section
seco, -a ['seko, a] *adj* dry; (*carácter*) cold; (*respuesta*) sharp, curt; **parar en ~** to stop dead; **decir algo a secas** to say sth curtly
secretaría [sekreta'ria] *nf* secretariat
secretario, -a [sekre'tarjo, a] *nm/f* secretary
secreto, -a [se'kreto, a] *adj* secret; (*persona*) secretive ▷*nm* secret; (*calidad*) secrecy
secta ['sekta] *nf* sect
sector [sek'tor] *nm* sector
secuela [se'kwela] *nf* consequence
secuencia [se'kwenθja] *nf* sequence
secuestrar [sekwes'trar] *vt* to kidnap; (*bienes*) to seize, confiscate; **secuestro** *nm* kidnapping; seizure, confiscation
secundario, -a [sekun'darjo, a] *adj* secondary
sed [seð] *nf* thirst; **tener ~** to be thirsty
seda ['seða] *nf* silk
sedal [se'ðal] *nm* fishing line
sedán [se'ðan] (LAM) *nm* saloon (BRIT), sedan (US)
sedante [se'ðante] *nm* sedative
sede ['seðe] *nf* (*de gobierno*) seat; (*de compañía*) headquarters *pl*; **Santa S~** Holy See
sedentario, -a [seðen'tario, a] *adj* sedentary
sediento, -a [se'ðjento, a] *adj* thirsty
sedimento [seði'mento] *nm* sediment
seducción [seðuk'θjon] *nf* seduction
seducir [seðu'θir] *vt* to seduce; (*cautivar*) to charm, fascinate; (*atraer*) to attract; **seductor, a** *adj* seductive; charming, fascinating; attractive ▷*nm/f* seducer
segar [se'ɣar] *vt* (*mies*) to reap, cut; (*hierba*) to mow, cut
seglar [se'ɣlar] *adj* secular, lay
seguida [se'ɣiða] *nf*: **en ~** at once, right away
seguido, -a [se'ɣiðo, a] *adj* (*continuo*) continuous, unbroken; (*recto*) straight ▷*adv* (*directo*) straight (on); (*después*) after; (LAM: *a menudo*) often; **~s** consecutive, successive; **5 días ~s** 5 days running, 5 days in a row
seguir [se'ɣir] *vt* to follow; (*venir después*) to follow on, come after; (*proseguir*) to continue; (*perseguir*) to chase, pursue ▷*vi* (*gen*) to follow; (*continuar*) to continue, carry *o* go on; **seguirse** *vr* to follow; **sigo sin comprender** I still don't understand; **sigue lloviendo** it's still raining
según [se'ɣun] *prep* according to ▷*adv*: **¿irás? – ~** are you going? – it all depends ▷*conj* as; **~ caminamos** while we walk
segundo, -a [se'ɣundo, a] *adj* second ▷*nm* second ▷*nf* second meaning; **de segunda mano** second-hand; **segunda (clase)** second class; **segunda (marcha)** (*Auto*) second (gear)
seguramente [seɣura'mente] *adv* surely; (*con certeza*) for sure, with certainty
seguridad [seɣuri'ðað] *nf* safety; (*del estado, de casa etc*) security; (*certidumbre*) certainty; (*confianza*) confidence; (*estabilidad*) stability; **seguridad social** social security
seguro, -a [se'ɣuro, a] *adj* (*cierto*) sure, certain; (*fiel*) trustworthy; (*libre de peligro*) safe; (*bien defendido, firme*) secure ▷*adv* for sure, certainly ▷*nm* (*Com*) insurance; **seguro contra terceros/a todo riesgo** third party/comprehensive insurance;

seguros sociales social security *sg*
seis [seis] *num* six
seísmo [se'ismo] *nm* tremor, earthquake
selección [selek'θjon] *nf* selection; **seleccionar** *vt* to pick, choose, select
selectividad [selektiβi'ðað] (ESP) *nf* university entrance examination
selecto, -a [se'lekto, a] *adj* select, choice; (*escogido*) selected
sellar [se'ʎar] *vt* (*documento oficial*) to seal; (*pasaporte, visado*) to stamp
sello ['seʎo] *nm* stamp; (*precinto*) seal
selva ['selβa] *nf* (*bosque*) forest, woods *pl*; (*jungla*) jungle
semáforo [se'maforo] *nm* (*Auto*) traffic lights *pl*; (*Ferro*) signal
semana [se'mana] *nf* week; **entre ~** during the week; **Semana Santa** Holy Week; **semanal** *adj* weekly; **semanario** *nm* weekly magazine

SEMANA SANTA

In Spain celebrations for **Semana Santa** (Holy Week) are often spectacular. "Viernes Santo", "Sábado Santo" and "Domingo de Resurrección" (Good Friday, Holy Saturday, Easter Sunday) are all national public holidays, with additional days being given as local holidays. There are fabulous **procesiones** all over the country, with members of "cofradías" (brotherhoods) dressing in hooded robes and parading their "pasos" (religious floats and sculptures) through the streets. Seville has the most famous Holy Week processions.

sembrar [sem'brar] *vt* to sow; (*objetos*) to sprinkle, scatter about; (*noticias etc*) to spread
semejante [seme'xante] *adj* (*parecido*) similar ▷*nm* fellow man, fellow creature; **~s** alike, similar; **nunca hizo cosa ~** he never did any such thing; **semejanza** *nf* similarity, resemblance
semejar [seme'xar] *vi* to seem like, resemble; **semejarse** *vr* to look alike, be similar
semen ['semen] *nm* semen
semestral [semes'tral] *adj* half-yearly, bi-annual
semicírculo [semi'θirkulo] *nm* semicircle
semidesnatado, -a [semiðesna'taðo, a] *adj* semi-skimmed
semifinal [semifi'nal] *nf* semifinal
semilla [se'miʎa] *nf* seed
seminario [semi'narjo] *nm* (*Rel*) seminary; (*Escol*) seminar
sémola ['semola] *nf* semolina
senado [se'naðo] *nm* senate; **senador, a** *nm/f* senator
sencillez [senθi'ʎeθ] *nf* simplicity; (*de persona*) naturalness; **sencillo, -a** *adj* simple; natural, unaffected
senda ['senda] *nf* path, track
senderismo [sende'rismo] *nm* hiking
sendero [sen'dero] *nm* path, track
sendos, -as ['sendos, as] *adj pl*: **les dio ~ golpes** he hit both of them
senil [se'nil] *adj* senile
seno ['seno] *nm* (*Anat*) bosom, bust; (*fig*) bosom; **~s** breasts
sensación [sensa'θjon] *nf* sensation; (*sentido*) sense; (*sentimiento*) feeling; **sensacional** *adj* sensational
sensato, -a [sen'sato, a] *adj* sensible
sensible [sen'sible] *adj* sensitive; (*apreciable*) perceptible, appreciable; (*pérdida*) considerable

> No confundir **sensible** con la palabra inglesa *sensible*.

sensiblero, -a *adj* sentimental
sensitivo, -a [sensi'tiβo, a] *adj* sense *cpd*
sensorial [senso'rjal] *adj* sensory
sensual [sen'swal] *adj* sensual
sentada [sen'taða] *nf* sitting; (*protesta*) sit-in
sentado, -a [sen'taðo, a] *adj*: **estar ~** to sit, be sitting (down); **dar por ~** to take for granted, assume
sentar [sen'tar] *vt* to sit, seat; (*fig*) to establish ▷*vi* (*vestido*) to suit; (*alimento*): **~ bien/mal a** to agree/disagree with; **sentarse** *vr* (*persona*) to sit, sit down; (*los depósitos*) to settle
sentencia [sen'tenθja] *nf* (*máxima*) maxim, saying; (*Jur*) sentence; **sentenciar** *vt* to sentence
sentido, -a [sen'tiðo, a] *adj* (*pérdida*) regrettable; (*carácter*) sensitive ▷*nm* sense; (*sentimiento*) feeling; (*significado*) sense, meaning; (*dirección*) direction; **mi más ~ pésame** my deepest sympathy; **tener ~** to make sense; **sentido común** common sense; **sentido del humor** sense of humour; **sentido único** one-way (street)
sentimental [sentimen'tal] *adj* sentimental; **vida ~** love life
sentimiento [senti'mjento] *nm* feeling
sentir [sen'tir] *vt* to feel; (*percibir*) to perceive, sense; (*lamentar*) to regret, be sorry for ▷*vi* (*tener la sensación*) to feel; (*lamentarse*) to feel sorry ▷*nm* opinion, judgement; **~se bien/mal** to feel well/ill; **lo**

siento I'm sorry
seña ['seɲa] *nf* sign; (*Mil*) password; **señas** *nfpl* (*dirección*) address *sg*; **señas personales** personal description *sg*
señal [se'ɲal] *nf* sign; (*síntoma*) symptom; (*Ferro, Tel*) signal; (*marca*) mark; (*Com*) deposit; **en ~ de** as a token *o* sign of; **señalar** *vt* to mark; (*indicar*) to point out, indicate
señor [se'ɲor] *nm* (*hombre*) man; (*caballero*) gentleman; (*dueño*) owner, master; (*trato: antes de nombre propio*) Mr; (*: hablando directamente*) sir; **muy ~ mío** Dear Sir; **el ~ alcalde/presidente** the mayor/president
señora [se'ɲora] *nf* (*dama*) lady; (*trato: antes de nombre propio*) Mrs; (*: hablando directamente*) madam; (*esposa*) wife; **Nuestra S~** Our Lady
señorita [seɲo'rita] *nf* (*con nombre y/o apellido*) Miss; (*mujer joven*) young lady
señorito [seɲo'rito] *nm* young gentleman; (*pey*) rich kid
sepa *etc vb V* **saber**
separación [separa'θjon] *nf* separation; (*división*) division; (*hueco*) gap
separar [sepa'rar] *vt* to separate; (*dividir*) to divide; **separarse** *vr* (*parte*) to come away; (*partes*) to come apart; (*persona*) to leave, go away; (*matrimonio*) to separate; **separatismo** *nm* separatism
sepia ['sepja] *nf* cuttlefish
septentrional [septentrjo'nal] *adj* northern
septiembre [sep'tjembre] *nm* September
séptimo, -a ['septimo, a] *adj, nm* seventh
sepulcral [sepul'kral] *adj* (*fig: silencio, atmósfera*) deadly; **sepulcro** *nm* tomb, grave
sepultar [sepul'tar] *vt* to bury; **sepultura** *nf* (*acto*) burial; (*tumba*) grave, tomb
sequía [se'kia] *nf* drought
séquito ['sekito] *nm* (*de rey etc*) retinue; (*seguidores*) followers *pl*

PALABRA CLAVE

ser [ser] *vi* **1** (*descripción*) to be; **es médica/muy alta** she's a doctor/very tall; **la familia es de Cuzco** his (*o* her *etc*) family is from Cuzco; **soy Ana** (*Tel*) Ana speaking *o* here
2 (*propiedad*): **es de Joaquín** it's Joaquín's, it belongs to Joaquín
3 (*horas, fechas, números*): **es la una** it's one o'clock; **son las seis y media** it's half-past six; **es el 1 de junio** it's the first of June; **somos/son seis** there are six of us/them
4 (*en oraciones pasivas*): **ha sido descubierto ya** it's already been discovered
5: **es de esperar que ...** it is to be hoped *o* I *etc* hope that ...
6 (*locuciones con sub*): **o sea** that is to say; **sea él sea su hermana** either him or his sister
7: **a no ser por él ...** but for him ...
8: **a no ser que: a no ser que tenga uno ya** unless he's got one already ▷ *nm* being; **ser humano** human being

sereno, -a [se'reno, a] *adj* (*persona*) calm, unruffled; (*el tiempo*) fine, settled; (*ambiente*) calm, peaceful ▷ *nm* night watchman
serial [ser'jal] *nm* serial
serie ['serje] *nf* series; (*cadena*) sequence, succession; **fuera de ~** out of order; (*fig*) special, out of the ordinary; **fabricación en ~** mass production
seriedad [serje'ðað] *nf* seriousness; (*formalidad*) reliability; **serio, -a** *adj* serious; reliable, dependable; grave, serious; **en serio** *adv* seriously
serigrafía [seriɣra'fia] *nf* silk-screen printing
sermón [ser'mon] *nm* (*Rel*) sermon
seropositivo, -a [seroposi'tiβo] *adj* HIV positive
serpentear [serpente'ar] *vi* to wriggle; (*camino, río*) to wind, snake
serpentina [serpen'tina] *nf* streamer
serpiente [ser'pjente] *nf* snake; **serpiente de cascabel** rattlesnake
serranía [serra'nia] *nf* mountainous area
serrar [se'rrar] *vt* = **aserrar**
serrín [se'rrin] *nm* sawdust
serrucho [se'rrutʃo] *nm* saw
service ['serβis] (RPL) *nm* (*Auto*) service
servicio [ser'βiθjo] *nm* service; (LAM *Auto*) service; **servicios** *nmpl* (ESP) toilet(s); **servicio incluido** service charge included; **servicio militar** military service
servidumbre [serβi'ðumbre] *nf* (*sujeción*) servitude; (*criados*) servants *pl*, staff
servil [ser'βil] *adj* servile
servilleta [serβi'ʎeta] *nf* serviette, napkin
servir [ser'βir] *vt* to serve ▷ *vi* to serve; (*tener utilidad*) to be of use, be useful; **servirse** *vr* to serve *o* help o.s.; **~se de algo** to make use of sth, use sth; **sírvase pasar** please come in
sesenta [se'senta] *num* sixty
sesión [se'sjon] *nf* (*Pol*) session, sitting; (*Cine*) showing
seso ['seso] *nm* brain; **sesudo, -a** *adj* sensible, wise
seta ['seta] *nf* mushroom; **seta venenosa** toadstool
setecientos, -as [sete'θjentos, as] *adj, num* seven hundred
setenta [se'tenta] *num* seventy
seto ['seto] *nm* hedge

severo, -a [se'βero, a] *adj* severe
Sevilla [se'βiʎa] *n* Seville; **sevillano, -a** *adj* of *o* from Seville ▷*nm/f* native *o* inhabitant of Seville
sexo ['sekso] *nm* sex
sexto, -a ['seksto, a] *adj, nm* sixth
sexual [sek'swal] *adj* sexual; **vida ~** sex life
si [si] *conj* if ▷*nm* (*Mús*) B; **me pregunto ~ ...** I wonder if *o* whether ...
sí [si] *adv* yes ▷*nm* consent ▷*pron* (*uso impersonal*) oneself; (*sg*: *m*) himself; (: *f*) herself; (: *de cosa*) itself; (*de usted*) yourself; (*pl*) themselves; (*de ustedes*) yourselves; (*recíproco*) each other; **él no quiere pero yo ~** he doesn't want to but I do; **ella ~ vendrá** she will certainly come, she is sure to come; **claro que ~** of course; **creo que ~** I think so
siamés, -esa [sja'mes, esa] *adj, nm/f* Siamese
SIDA ['siða] *nm abr* (= *Síndrome de Inmunodeficiencia Adquirida*) AIDS
siderúrgico, -a [siðe'rurxico, a] *adj* iron and steel *cpd*
sidra ['siðra] *nf* cider
siembra ['sjembra] *nf* sowing
siempre ['sjempre] *adv* always; (*todo el tiempo*) all the time; **~ que** (*cada vez*) whenever; (*dado que*) provided that; **como ~** as usual; **para ~** for ever
sien [sjen] *nf* temple
siento *etc* ['sjento] *vb V* **sentar; sentir**
sierra ['sjerra] *nf* (*Tec*) saw; (*cadena de montañas*) mountain range
siervo, -a ['sjerβo, a] *nm/f* slave
siesta ['sjesta] *nf* siesta, nap; **echar la ~** to have an afternoon nap *o* a siesta
siete ['sjete] *num* seven
sifón [si'fon] *nm* syphon
sigla ['siɣla] *nf* abbreviation; acronym
siglo ['siɣlo] *nm* century; (*fig*) age
significado [siɣnifi'kaðo] *nm* (*de palabra etc*) meaning
significar [siɣnifi'kar] *vt* to mean, signify; (*notificar*) to make known, express
signo ['siɣno] *nm* sign; **signo de admiración** *o* **exclamación** exclamation mark; **signo de interrogación** question mark
sigo *etc vb V* **seguir**
siguiente [si'ɣjente] *adj* next, following
siguió *etc vb V* **seguir**
sílaba ['silaβa] *nf* syllable
silbar [sil'βar] *vt, vi* to whistle; **silbato** *nm* whistle; **silbido** *nm* whistle, whistling
silenciador [silenθja'ðor] *nm* silencer
silenciar [silen'θjar] *vt* (*persona*) to silence; (*escándalo*) to hush up; **silencio** *nm* silence, quiet; **silencioso, -a** *adj* silent, quiet
silla ['siʎa] *nf* (*asiento*) chair; (*tb*: **~ de montar**) saddle; **silla de ruedas** wheelchair
sillón [si'ʎon] *nm* armchair, easy chair
silueta [si'lweta] *nf* silhouette; (*de edificio*) outline; (*figura*) figure
silvestre [sil'βestre] *adj* wild
simbólico, -a [sim'boliko, a] *adj* symbolic(al)
simbolizar [simboli'θar] *vt* to symbolize
símbolo ['simbolo] *nm* symbol
similar [simi'lar] *adj* similar
simio ['simjo] *nm* ape
simpatía [simpa'tia] *nf* liking; (*afecto*) affection; (*amabilidad*) kindness; **simpático, -a** *adj* nice, pleasant; kind

> No confundir **simpático** con la palabra inglesa *sympathetic*.

simpatizante [simpati'θante] *nmf* sympathizer
simpatizar [simpati'θar] *vi*: **~ con** to get on well with
simple ['simple] *adj* simple; (*elemental*) simple, easy; (*mero*) mere; (*puro*) pure, sheer ▷*nmf* simpleton; **simpleza** *nf* simpleness; (*necedad*) silly thing; **simplificar** *vt* to simplify
simposio [sim'posjo] *nm* symposium
simular [simu'lar] *vt* to simulate
simultáneo, -a [simul'taneo, a] *adj* simultaneous
sin [sin] *prep* without; **la ropa está ~ lavar** the clothes are unwashed; **~ que** without; **~ embargo** however, still
sinagoga [sina'ɣoɣa] *nf* synagogue
sinceridad [sinθeri'ðað] *nf* sincerity; **sincero, -a** *adj* sincere
sincronizar [sinkroni'θar] *vt* to synchronize
sindical [sindi'kal] *adj* union *cpd*, trade-union *cpd*; **sindicalista** *adj, nmf* trade unionist
sindicato [sindi'kato] *nm* (*de trabajadores*) trade(s) union; (*de negociantes*) syndicate
síndrome ['sinðrome] *nm* (*Med*) syndrome; **síndrome de abstinencia** (*Med*) withdrawal symptoms; **síndrome de la clase turista** (*Med*) economy-class syndrome
sinfín [sin'fin] *nm*: **un ~ de** a great many, no end of
sinfonía [sinfo'nia] *nf* symphony
singular [singu'lar] *adj* singular; (*fig*) outstanding, exceptional; (*raro*) peculiar, odd
siniestro, -a [si'njestro, a] *adj* sinister ▷*nm* (*accidente*) accident
sinnúmero [sin'numero] *nm* = **sinfín**

sino ['sino] *nm* fate, destiny ▷ *conj* (*pero*) but; (*salvo*) except, save
sinónimo, -a [si'nonimo, a] *adj* synonymous ▷ *nm* synonym
síntesis ['sintesis] *nf* synthesis; **sintético, -a** *adj* synthetic
sintió *vb V* **sentir**
síntoma ['sintoma] *nm* symptom
sintonía [sinto'nia] *nf* (*Radio, Mús: de programa*) tuning; **sintonizar** *vt* (*Radio: emisora*) to tune (in)
sinvergüenza [simber'ɣwenθa] *nmf* rogue, scoundrel; **¡es un ~!** he's got a nerve!
siquiera [si'kjera] *conj* even if, even though ▷ *adv* at least; **ni ~** not even
Siria ['sirja] *nf* Syria
sirviente, -a [sir'βjente, a] *nm/f* servant
sirvo *etc vb V* **servir**
sistema [sis'tema] *nm* system; (*método*) method; **sistema educativo** education system; **sistemático, -a** *adj* systematic

SISTEMA EDUCATIVO

The reform of the Spanish **sistema educativo** (education system) begun in the early 90s has replaced the courses **EGB**, **BUP** and **COU** with the following: "Primaria" a compulsory 6 years; "Secundaria" a compulsory 4 years and "Bachillerato" an optional 2-year secondary school course, essential for those wishing to go on to higher education.

sitiar [si'tjar] *vt* to besiege, lay siege to
sitio ['sitjo] *nm* (*lugar*) place; (*espacio*) room, space; (*Mil*) siege; **sitio de taxis** (*MÉX: parada*) taxi stand *o* rank (*BRIT*); **sitio web** (*Inform*) website
situación [sitwa'θjon] *nf* situation, position; (*estatus*) position, standing
situado, -a [situ'aðo] *adj* situated, placed
situar [si'twar] *vt* to place, put; (*edificio*) to locate, situate
slip [slip] *nm* pants *pl*, briefs *pl*
smoking ['smokin, es'mokin] (*pl* **~s**) *nm* dinner jacket (*BRIT*), tuxedo (*US*)
No confundir **smoking** con la palabra inglesa *smoking*.
SMS *nm* (*mensaje*) text message, SMS message
snob [es'nob] = **esnob**
SO *abr* (= *suroeste*) SW
sobaco [so'βako] *nm* armpit
sobar [so'βar] *vt* (*ropa*) to rumple; (*comida*) to play around with
soberanía [soβera'nia] *nf* sovereignty; **soberano, -a** *adj* sovereign; (*fig*) supreme ▷ *nm/f* sovereign
soberbia [so'βerβja] *nf* pride; haughtiness, arrogance; magnificence
soberbio, -a [so'βerβjo, a] *adj* (*orgulloso*) proud; (*altivo*) arrogant; (*estupendo*) magnificent, superb
sobornar [soβor'nar] *vt* to bribe; **soborno** *nm* bribe
sobra ['soβra] *nf* excess, surplus; **sobras** *nfpl* left-overs, scraps; **de ~** surplus, extra; **tengo de ~** I've more than enough; **sobrado, -a** *adj* (*más que suficiente*) more than enough; (*superfluo*) excessive; **sobrante** *adj* remaining, extra ▷ *nm* surplus, remainder
sobrar [so'βrar] *vt* to exceed, surpass ▷ *vi* (*tener de más*) to be more than enough; (*quedar*) to remain, be left (over)
sobrasada [soβra'saða] *nf* *pork sausage spread*
sobre ['soβre] *prep* (*gen*) on; (*encima*) on (top of); (*por encima de, arriba de*) over, above; (*más que*) more than; (*además*) in addition to, besides; (*alrededor de*) about ▷ *nm* envelope; **~ todo** above all
sobrecama [soβre'kama] *nf* bedspread
sobrecargar [soβrekar'ɣar] *vt* (*camión*) to overload; (*Com*) to surcharge
sobredosis [soβre'ðosis] *nf inv* overdose
sobreentender [soβre(e)nten'der] *vt* to deduce, infer; **sobreentenderse** *vr*: **se sobreentiende que ...** it is implied that ...
sobrehumano, -a [soβreu'mano, a] *adj* superhuman
sobrellevar [soβreʎe'βar] *vt* to bear, endure
sobremesa [soβre'mesa] *nf*: **durante la ~** after dinner
sobrenatural [soβrenatu'ral] *adj* supernatural
sobrenombre [soβre'nombre] *nm* nickname
sobrepasar [soβrepa'sar] *vt* to exceed, surpass
sobreponerse [soβrepo'nerse] *vr*: **~ a** to overcome
sobresaliente [soβresa'ljente] *adj* outstanding, excellent
sobresalir [soβresa'lir] *vi* to project, jut out; (*fig*) to stand out, excel
sobresaltar [soβresal'tar] *vt* (*asustar*) to scare, frighten; (*sobrecoger*) to startle; **sobresalto** *nm* (*movimiento*) start; (*susto*) scare; (*turbación*) sudden shock
sobretodo [soβre'toðo] *nm* overcoat
sobrevenir [soβreβe'nir] *vi* (*ocurrir*) to happen (unexpectedly); (*resultar*) to follow,

S

ensue

sobrevivir [soβreβi'βir] *vi* to survive

sobrevolar [soβreβo'lar] *vt* to fly over

sobriedad [soβrje'ðað] *nf* sobriety, soberness; (*moderación*) moderation, restraint

sobrino, -a [so'βrino, a] *nm/f* nephew/niece

sobrio, -a ['soβrjo, a] *adj* sober; (*moderado*) moderate, restrained

socarrón, -ona [soka'rron, ona] *adj* (*sarcástico*) sarcastic, ironic(al)

socavón [soka'βon] *nm* (*hoyo*) hole

sociable [so'θjaβle] *adj* (*persona*) sociable, friendly; (*animal*) social

social [so'θjal] *adj* social; (*Com*) company *cpd*

socialdemócrata [soθjalde'mokrata] *nmf* social democrat

socialista [soθja'lista] *adj, nm* socialist

socializar [soθjali'θar] *vt* to socialize

sociedad [soθje'ðað] *nf* society; (*Com*) company; **sociedad anónima** limited company; **sociedad de consumo** consumer society

socio, -a ['soθjo, a] *nm/f* (*miembro*) member; (*Com*) partner

sociología [soθjolo'xia] *nf* sociology; **sociólogo, -a** *nm/f* sociologist

socorrer [soko'rrer] *vt* to help; **socorrista** *nmf* first aider; (*en piscina, playa*) lifeguard; **socorro** *nm* (*ayuda*) help, aid; (*Mil*) relief; **¡socorro!** help!

soda ['soða] *nf* (*sosa*) soda; (*bebida*) soda (water)

sofá [so'fa] (*pl* **~s**) *nm* sofa, settee; **sofá-cama** *nm* studio couch; sofa bed

sofocar [sofo'kar] *vt* to suffocate; (*apagar*) to smother, put out; **sofocarse** *vr* to suffocate; (*fig*) to blush, feel embarrassed; **sofoco** *nm* suffocation; embarrassment

sofreír [sofre'ir] *vt* (*Culin*) to fry lightly

soga ['soɣa] *nf* rope

sois *etc vb V* **ser**

soja ['soxa] *nf* soya

sol [sol] *nm* sun; (*luz*) sunshine, sunlight; (*Mús*) G; **hace ~** it's sunny

solamente [sola'mente] *adv* only, just

solapa [so'lapa] *nf* (*de chaqueta*) lapel; (*de libro*) jacket

solapado, -a [sola'paðo, a] *adj* (*intenciónes*) underhand; (*gestos, movimiento*) sly

solar [so'lar] *adj* solar, sun *cpd*

soldado [sol'daðo] *nm* soldier; **soldado raso** private

soldador [solda'ðor] *nm* soldering iron; (*persona*) welder

soldar [sol'dar] *vt* to solder, weld

soleado, -a [sole'aðo, a] *adj* sunny

soledad [sole'ðað] *nf* solitude; (*estado infeliz*) loneliness

solemne [so'lemne] *adj* solemn

soler [so'ler] *vi* to be in the habit of, be accustomed to; **suele salir a las ocho** she usually goes out at eight o'clock

solfeo [sol'feo] *nm* solfa

solicitar [soliθi'tar] *vt* (*permiso*) to ask for, seek; (*puesto*) to apply for; (*votos*) to canvass for; (*atención*) to attract

solícito, -a [so'liθito, a] *adj* (*diligente*) diligent; (*cuidadoso*) careful; **solicitud** *nf* (*calidad*) great care; (*petición*) request; (*a un puesto*) application

solidaridad [soliðari'ðað] *nf* solidarity; **solidario, -a** *adj* (*participación*) joint, common; (*compromiso*) mutually binding

sólido, -a ['soliðo, a] *adj* solid

soliloquio [soli'lokjo] *nm* soliloquy

solista [so'lista] *nmf* soloist

solitario, -a [soli'tarjo, a] *adj* (*persona*) lonely, solitary; (*lugar*) lonely, desolate ▷ *nm/f* (*recluso*) recluse; (*en la sociedad*) loner ▷ *nm* solitaire

sollozar [soʎo'θar] *vi* to sob; **sollozo** *nm* sob

solo, -a ['solo, a] *adj* (*único*) single, sole; (*sin compañía*) alone; (*solitario*) lonely; **hay una sola dificultad** there is just one difficulty; **a solas** alone, by oneself

sólo ['solo] *adv* only, just

solomillo [solo'miʎo] *nm* sirloin

soltar [sol'tar] *vt* (*dejar ir*) to let go of; (*desprender*) to unfasten, loosen; (*librar*) to release, set free; (*risa etc*) to let out

soltero, -a [sol'tero, a] *adj* single, unmarried ▷ *nm/f* bachelor/single woman; **solterón, -ona** *nm/f* old bachelor/spinster

soltura [sol'tura] *nf* looseness, slackness; (*de los miembros*) agility, ease of movement; (*en el hablar*) fluency, ease

soluble [so'luβle] *adj* (*Quím*) soluble; (*problema*) solvable; **~ en agua** soluble in water

solución [solu'θjon] *nf* solution; **solucionar** *vt* (*problema*) to solve; (*asunto*) to settle, resolve

solventar [solβen'tar] *vt* (*pagar*) to settle, pay; (*resolver*) to resolve; **solvente** *adj* (*Econ: empresa, persona*) solvent

sombra ['sombra] *nf* shadow; (*como protección*) shade; **sombras** *nfpl* (*oscuridad*) darkness *sg*, shadows; **tener buena/mala ~** to be lucky/unlucky

sombrero [som'brero] *nm* hat

sombrilla [som'briʎa] *nf* parasol,

sunshade

sombrío, -a [som'brio, a] *adj* (*oscuro*) dark; (*triste*) sombre, sad; (*persona*) gloomy

someter [some'ter] *vt* (*país*) to conquer; (*persona*) to subject to one's will; (*informe*) to present, submit; **someterse** *vr* to give in, yield, submit; **~ a** to subject to

somier [so'mjer] (*pl* **~s**) *n* spring mattress

somnífero [som'nifero] *nm* sleeping pill

somos *vb V* **ser**

son [son] *vb V* **ser** ▷ *nm* sound

sonaja [so'naxa] (*MÉX*) *nf* = **sonajero**

sonajero [sona'xero] *nm* (baby's) rattle

sonambulismo [sonambu'lismo] *nm* sleepwalking; **sonámbulo, -a** *nm/f* sleepwalker

sonar [so'nar] *vt* to ring ▷ *vi* to sound; (*hacer ruido*) to make a noise; (*pronunciarse*) to be sounded, be pronounced; (*ser conocido*) to sound familiar; (*campana*) to ring; (*reloj*) to strike, chime; **sonarse** *vr*: **~se (las narices)** to blow one's nose; **me suena ese nombre** that name rings a bell

sonda ['sonda] *nf* (*Náut*) sounding; (*Tec*) bore, drill; (*Med*) probe

sondear [sonde'ar] *vt* to sound; to bore (into), drill; to probe, sound; (*fig*) to sound out; **sondeo** *nm* sounding; boring, drilling; (*fig*) poll, enquiry

sonido [so'niðo] *nm* sound

sonoro, -a [so'noro, a] *adj* sonorous; (*resonante*) loud, resonant

sonreír [sonre'ir] *vi* to smile; **sonreírse** *vr* to smile; **sonriente** *adj* smiling; **sonrisa** *nf* smile

sonrojarse [sonro'xarse] *vr* to blush, go red; **sonrojo** *nm* blush

soñador, a [soɲa'ðor, a] *nm/f* dreamer

soñar [so'ɲar] *vt, vi* to dream; **~ con** to dream about *o* of

soñoliento, -a [soɲo'ljento, a] *adj* sleepy, drowsy

sopa ['sopa] *nf* soup

soplar [so'plar] *vt* (*polvo*) to blow away, blow off; (*inflar*) to blow up; (*vela*) to blow out ▷ *vi* to blow; **soplo** *nm* blow, puff; (*de viento*) puff, gust

soplón, -ona [so'plon, ona] (*fam*) *nm/f* (*niño*) telltale; (*de policía*) grass (*fam*)

soporífero [sopo'rifero] *nm* sleeping pill

soportable [sopor'taβle] *adj* bearable

soportar [sopor'tar] *vt* to bear, carry; (*fig*) to bear, put up with

No confundir **soportar** con la palabra inglesa *support*.

soporte *nm* support; (*fig*) pillar, support

soprano [so'prano] *nf* soprano

sorber [sor'βer] *vt* (*chupar*) to sip; (*absorber*) to soak up, absorb

sorbete [sor'βete] *nm* iced fruit drink

sorbo ['sorβo] *nm* (*trago: grande*) gulp, swallow; (*: pequeño*) sip

sordera [sor'ðera] *nf* deafness

sórdido, -a ['sorðiðo, a] *adj* dirty, squalid

sordo, -a ['sorðo, a] *adj* (*persona*) deaf ▷ *nm/f* deaf person; **sordomudo, -a** *adj* deaf and dumb

sorna ['sorna] *nf* sarcastic tone

soroche [so'rotʃe] (*CAM*) *nm* mountain sickness

sorprendente [sorpren'dente] *adj* surprising

sorprender [sorpren'der] *vt* to surprise; **sorpresa** *nf* surprise

sortear [sorte'ar] *vt* to draw lots for; (*rifar*) to raffle; (*dificultad*) to avoid; **sorteo** *nm* (*en lotería*) draw; (*rifa*) raffle

sortija [sor'tixa] *nf* ring; (*rizo*) ringlet, curl

sosegado, -a [sose'ɣaðo, a] *adj* quiet, calm

sosiego [so'sjeɣo] *nm* quiet(ness), calm(ness)

soso, -a ['soso, a] *adj* (*Culin*) tasteless; (*aburrido*) dull, uninteresting

sospecha [sos'petʃa] *nf* suspicion; **sospechar** *vt* to suspect; **sospechoso, -a** *adj* suspicious; (*testimonio, opinión*) suspect ▷ *nm/f* suspect

sostén [sos'ten] *nm* (*apoyo*) support; (*sujetador*) bra; (*alimentación*) sustenance, food

sostener [soste'ner] *vt* to support; (*mantener*) to keep up, maintain; (*alimentar*) to sustain, keep going; **sostenerse** *vr* to support o.s.; (*seguir*) to continue, remain; **sostenido, -a** *adj* continuous, sustained; (*prolongado*) prolonged

sotana [so'tana] *nf* (*Rel*) cassock

sótano ['sotano] *nm* basement

soy [soi] *vb V* **ser**

soya ['soja] (*LAM*) *nf* soya (*BRIT*), soy (*US*)

Sr. *abr* (= *Señor*) Mr

Sra. *abr* (= *Señora*) Mrs

Sres. *abr* (= *Señores*) Messrs

Srta. *abr* (= *Señorita*) Miss

Sta. *abr* (= *Santa*) St

Sto. *abr* (= *Santo*) St

su [su] *pron* (*de él*) his; (*de ella*) her; (*de una cosa*) its; (*de ellos, ellas*) their; (*de usted, ustedes*) your

suave ['swaβe] *adj* gentle; (*superficie*) smooth; (*trabajo*) easy; (*música, voz*) soft, sweet; **suavidad** *nf* gentleness; smoothness; softness, sweetness; **suavizante** *nm* (*de ropa*) softener; (*del pelo*) conditioner; **suavizar** *vt* to soften; (*quitar*

S

la aspereza) to smooth (out)
subasta [su'βasta] *nf* auction; **subastar** *vt* to auction (off)
subcampeón, -ona [suβkampe'on, ona] *nm/f* runner-up
subconsciente [suβkon'sθjente] *adj, nm* subconscious
subdesarrollado, -a [suβðesarro'ʎaðo, a] *adj* underdeveloped
subdesarrollo [suβðesa'rroʎo] *nm* underdevelopment
subdirector, a [suβðirek'tor, a] *nm/f* assistant director
súbdito, -a ['suβðito, a] *nm/f* subject
subestimar [suβesti'mar] *vt* to underestimate, underrate
subida [su'βiða] *nf* (*de montaña etc*) ascent, climb; (*de precio*) rise, increase; (*pendiente*) slope, hill
subir [su'βir] *vt* (*objeto*) to raise, lift up; (*cuesta, calle*) to go up; (*colina, montaña*) to climb; (*precio*) to raise, put up ▷*vi* to go up, come up; (*a un coche*) to get in; (*a un autobús, tren o avión*) to get on, board; (*precio*) to rise, go up; (*río, marea*) to rise; **subirse** *vr* to get up, climb
súbito, -a ['suβito, a] *adj* (*repentino*) sudden; (*imprevisto*) unexpected
subjetivo, -a [suβxe'tiβo, a] *adj* subjective
sublevar [suβle'βar] *vt* to rouse to revolt; **sublevarse** *vr* to revolt, rise
sublime [su'βlime] *adj* sublime
submarinismo [suβmari'nismo] *nm* scuba diving
submarino, -a [suβma'rino, a] *adj* underwater ▷*nm* submarine
subnormal [suβnor'mal] *adj* subnormal ▷*nmf* subnormal person
subordinado, -a [suβorði'naðo, a] *adj, nm/f* subordinate
subrayar [suβra'jar] *vt* to underline
subsanar [suβsa'nar] *vt* to rectify
subsidio [suβ'siðjo] *nm* (*ayuda*) aid, financial help; (*subvención*) subsidy, grant; (*de enfermedad, paro etc*) benefit, allowance
subsistencia [suβsis'tenθja] *nf* subsistence
subsistir [suβsis'tir] *vi* to subsist; (*sobrevivir*) to survive, endure
subte ['suβte] (RPL) *nm* underground (BRIT), subway (US)
subterráneo, -a [suβte'rraneo, a] *adj* underground, subterranean ▷*nm* underpass, underground passage
subtítulo [suβ'titulo] *nm* (*Cine*) subtitle
suburbio [su'βurβjo] *nm* (*barrio*) slum quarter
subvención [suββen'θjon] *nf* (*Econ*) subsidy, grant; **subvencionar** *vt* to subsidize
sucedáneo, -a [suθe'ðaneo, a] *adj* substitute ▷*nm* substitute (food)
suceder [suθe'ðer] *vt, vi* to happen; (*seguir*) to succeed, follow; **lo que sucede es que ...** the fact is that ...; **sucesión** *nf* succession; (*serie*) sequence, series
sucesivamente [suθesiβa'mente] *adv*: **y así ~** and so on
sucesivo, -a [suθe'siβo, a] *adj* successive, following; **en lo ~** in future, from now on
suceso [su'θeso] *nm* (*hecho*) event, happening; (*incidente*) incident

> No confundir **suceso** con la palabra inglesa *success*.

suciedad [suθje'ðað] *nf* (*estado*) dirtiness; (*mugre*) dirt, filth
sucio, -a ['suθjo, a] *adj* dirty
suculento, -a [suku'lento, a] *adj* succulent
sucumbir [sukum'bir] *vi* to succumb
sucursal [sukur'sal] *nf* branch (office)
sudadera [suða'ðera] *nf* sweatshirt
Sudáfrica [suð'afrika] *nf* South Africa
Sudamérica [suða'merika] *nf* South America; **sudamericano, -a** *adj, nm/f* South American
sudar [su'ðar] *vt, vi* to sweat
sudeste [su'ðeste] *nm* south-east
sudoeste [suðo'este] *nm* south-west
sudor [su'ðor] *nm* sweat; **sudoroso, -a** *adj* sweaty, sweating
Suecia ['sweθja] *nf* Sweden; **sueco, -a** *adj* Swedish ▷*nm/f* Swede
suegro, -a ['sweɣro, a] *nm/f* father-/mother-in-law
suela ['swela] *nf* sole
sueldo ['sweldo] *nm* pay, wage(s) (*pl*)
suele *etc vb V* **soler**
suelo ['swelo] *nm* (*tierra*) ground; (*de casa*) floor
suelto, -a ['swelto, a] *adj* loose; (*libre*) free; (*separado*) detached; (*ágil*) quick, agile ▷*nm* (loose) change, small change
sueñito [swe'ɲito] (LAM) *nm* nap
sueño *etc* ['sweɲo] *vb V* **soñar** ▷*nm* sleep; (*somnolencia*) sleepiness, drowsiness; (*lo soñado, fig*) dream; **tener ~** to be sleepy
suero ['swero] *nm* (*Med*) serum; (*de leche*) whey
suerte ['swerte] *nf* (*fortuna*) luck; (*azar*) chance; (*destino*) fate, destiny; (*especie*) sort, kind; **tener ~** to be lucky
suéter ['sweter] *nm* sweater
suficiente [sufi'θjente] *adj* enough, sufficient ▷*nm* (*Escol*) pass

sufragio [su'fraxjo] *nm* (*voto*) vote; (*derecho de voto*) suffrage
sufrido, -a [su'friðo, a] *adj* (*persona*) tough; (*paciente*) long-suffering, patient
sufrimiento [sufri'mjento] *nm* (*dolor*) suffering
sufrir [su'frir] *vt* (*padecer*) to suffer; (*soportar*) to bear, put up with; (*apoyar*) to hold up, support ▷*vi* to suffer
sugerencia [suxe'renθja] *nf* suggestion
sugerir [suxe'rir] *vt* to suggest; (*sutilmente*) to hint
sugestión [suxes'tjon] *nf* suggestion; (*sutil*) hint; **sugestionar** *vt* to influence
sugestivo, -a [suxes'tiβo, a] *adj* stimulating; (*fascinante*) fascinating
suicida [sui'θiða] *adj* suicidal ▷*nmf* suicidal person; (*muerto*) suicide, person who has committed suicide; **suicidarse** *vr* to commit suicide, kill o.s.; **suicidio** *nm* suicide
Suiza ['swiθa] *nf* Switzerland; **suizo, -a** *adj, nm/f* Swiss
sujeción [suxe'θjon] *nf* subjection
sujetador [suxeta'ðor] *nm* (*sostén*) bra
sujetar [suxe'tar] *vt* (*fijar*) to fasten; (*detener*) to hold down; **sujetarse** *vr* to subject o.s.; **sujeto, -a** *adj* fastened, secure ▷*nm* subject; (*individuo*) individual; **sujeto a** subject to
suma ['suma] *nf* (*cantidad*) total, sum; (*de dinero*) sum; (*acto*) adding (up), addition; **en ~** in short
sumamente [suma'mente] *adv* extremely, exceedingly
sumar [su'mar] *vt* to add (up) ▷*vi* to add up
sumergir [sumer'xir] *vt* to submerge; (*hundir*) to sink
suministrar [sumini'strar] *vt* to supply, provide; **suministro** *nm* supply; (*acto*) supplying, providing
sumir [su'mir] *vt* to sink, submerge; (*fig*) to plunge
sumiso, -a [su'miso, a] *adj* submissive, docile
sumo, -a ['sumo, a] *adj* great, extreme; (*autoridad*) highest, supreme
suntuoso, -a [sun'twoso, a] *adj* sumptuous, magnificent
supe *etc vb V* **saber**
super... [super] *prefijo* super..., over...
superbueno, -a [super'bweno, a] *adj* great, fantastic
súper ['super] *nf* (*gasolina*) four-star (petrol)
superar [supe'rar] *vt* (*sobreponerse a*) to overcome; (*rebasar*) to surpass, do better than; (*pasar*) to go beyond; **superarse** *vr* to excel o.s.
superficial [superfi'θjal] *adj* superficial; (*medida*) surface *cpd*, of the surface
superficie [super'fiθje] *nf* surface; (*área*) area
superfluo, -a [su'perflwo, a] *adj* superfluous
superior [supe'rjor] *adj* (*piso, clase*) upper; (*temperatura, número, nivel*) higher; (*mejor: calidad, producto*) superior, better ▷*nmf* superior; **superioridad** *nf* superiority
supermercado [supermer'kaðo] *nm* supermarket
superponer [superpo'ner] *vt* to superimpose
superstición [supersti'θjon] *nf* superstition; **supersticioso, -a** *adj* superstitious
supervisar [superβi'sar] *vt* to supervise
supervivencia [superβi'βenθja] *nf* survival
superviviente [superβi'βjente] *adj* surviving
supiera *etc vb V* **saber**
suplantar [suplan'tar] *vt* to supplant
suplemento [suple'mento] *nm* supplement
suplente [su'plente] *adj, nm* substitute
supletorio, -a [suple'torjo, a] *adj* supplementary ▷*nm* supplement; **teléfono ~** extension
súplica ['suplika] *nf* request; (*Jur*) petition
suplicar [supli'kar] *vt* (*cosa*) to beg (for), plead for; (*persona*) to beg, plead with
suplicio [su'pliθjo] *nm* torture
suplir [su'plir] *vt* (*compensar*) to make good, make up for; (*reemplazar*) to replace, substitute ▷*vi*: **~ a** to take the place of, substitute for
supo *etc vb V* **saber**
suponer [supo'ner] *vt* to suppose; **suposición** *nf* supposition
suprimir [supri'mir] *vt* to suppress; (*derecho, costumbre*) to abolish; (*palabra etc*) to delete; (*restricción*) to cancel, lift
supuesto, -a [su'pwesto, a] *pp de* **suponer** ▷*adj* (*hipotético*) supposed ▷*nm* assumption, hypothesis; **~ que** since; **por ~** of course
sur [sur] *nm* south
surcar [sur'kar] *vt* to plough; **surco** *nm* (*en metal, disco*) groove; (*Agr*) furrow
surgir [sur'xir] *vi* to arise, emerge; (*dificultad*) to come up, crop up
suroeste [suro'este] *nm* south-west
surtido, -a [sur'tiðo, a] *adj* mixed,

S

assorted ▷ *nm* (*selección*) selection, assortment; (*abastecimiento*) supply, stock; **surtidor** *nm* (*tb*: **surtidor de gasolina**) petrol pump (BRIT), gas pump (US)
surtir [sur'tir] *vt* to supply, provide ▷ *vi* to spout, spurt
susceptible [susθep'tiβle] *adj* susceptible; (*sensible*) sensitive; **~ de** capable of
suscitar [susθi'tar] *vt* to cause, provoke; (*interés, sospechas*) to arouse
suscribir [suskri'βir] *vt* (*firmar*) to sign; (*respaldar*) to subscribe to, endorse; **suscribirse** *vr* to subscribe; **suscripción** *nf* subscription
susodicho, -a [suso'ðitʃo, a] *adj* above-mentioned
suspender [suspen'der] *vt* (*objeto*) to hang (up), suspend; (*trabajo*) to stop, suspend; (*Escol*) to fail; (*interrumpir*) to adjourn; (*atrasar*) to postpone
suspense [sus'pense] (ESP) *nm* suspense; **película/novela de ~** thriller
suspensión [suspen'sjon] *nf* suspension; (*fig*) stoppage, suspension
suspenso, -a [sus'penso, a] *adj* hanging, suspended; (ESP *Escol*) failed ▷ *nm* (ESP *Escol*) fail; **película** *o* **novela de ~** (LAM) thriller; **quedar** *o* **estar en ~** to be pending
suspicaz [suspi'kaθ] *adj* suspicious, distrustful
suspirar [suspi'rar] *vi* to sigh; **suspiro** *nm* sigh
sustancia [sus'tanθja] *nf* substance
sustento [sus'tento] *nm* support; (*alimento*) sustenance, food
sustituir [sustitu'ir] *vt* to substitute, replace; **sustituto, -a** *nm/f* substitute, replacement
susto ['susto] *nm* fright, scare
sustraer [sustra'er] *vt* to remove, take away; (*Mat*) to subtract
susurrar [susu'rrar] *vi* to whisper; **susurro** *nm* whisper
sutil [su'til] *adj* (*aroma, diferencia*) subtle; (*tenue*) thin; (*inteligencia, persona*) sharp
suyo, -a ['sujo, a] (*con artículo o después del verbo* **ser**) *adj* (*de él*) his; (*de ella*) hers; (*de ellos, ellas*) theirs; (*de Ud, Uds*) yours; **un amigo ~** a friend of his (*o* hers *o* theirs *o* yours)

Tabacalera [taβaka'lera] *nf Spanish state tobacco monopoly*
tabaco [ta'βako] *nm* tobacco; (ESP: *fam*) cigarettes *pl*
tabaquería [tabake'ria] (LAM) *nf* tobacconist's (shop) (BRIT), smoke shop (US); **tabaquero, -a** (LAM) *nm/f* tobacconist
taberna [ta'βerna] *nf* bar, pub (BRIT)
tabique [ta'βike] *nm* partition (wall)
tabla ['taβla] *nf* (*de madera*) plank; (*estante*) shelf; (*de vestido*) pleat; (*Arte*) panel; **tablas** *nfpl*: **estar** *o* **quedar en ~s** to draw; **tablado** *nm* (*plataforma*) platform; (*Teatro*) stage
tablao [ta'βlao] *nm* (*tb*: **~ flamenco**) flamenco show
tablero [ta'βlero] *nm* (*de madera*) plank, board; (*de ajedrez, damas*) board; **tablero de mandos** (LAM *Auto*) dashboard
tableta [ta'βleta] *nf* (*Med*) tablet; (*de chocolate*) bar
tablón [ta'βlon] *nm* (*de suelo*) plank; (*de techo*) beam; **tablón de anuncios** notice (BRIT) *o* bulletin (US) board
tabú [ta'βu] *nm* taboo
taburete [taβu'rete] *nm* stool
tacaño, -a [ta'kaɲo, a] *adj* mean
tacha ['tatʃa] *nf* flaw; (*Tec*) stud; **tachar** *vt* (*borrar*) to cross out; **tachar de** to accuse of
tacho ['tatʃo] (CS) *nm* (*balde*) bucket; **tacho de la basura** rubbish bin (BRIT), trash can (US)
taco ['tako] *nm* (*Billar*) cue; (*de billetes*) book; (CS: *de zapato*) heel; (*tarugo*) peg; (*palabrota*) swear word
tacón [ta'kon] *nm* heel; **de ~ alto** high-heeled
táctica ['taktika] *nf* tactics *pl*
táctico, -a ['taktiko, a] *adj* tactical
tacto ['takto] *nm* touch; (*fig*) tact
tajada [ta'xaða] *nf* slice
tajante [ta'xante] *adj* sharp

tajo ['taxo] *nm* (*corte*) cut; (*Geo*) cleft

tal [tal] *adj* such ▷ *pron* (*persona*) someone, such a one; (*cosa*) something, such a thing ▷ *adv*: **~ como** (*igual*) just as ▷ *conj*: **con ~ de que** provided that; **~ cual** (*como es*) just as it is; **~ vez** perhaps; **~ como** such as; **~ para cual** (*dos iguales*) two of a kind; **¿qué ~?** how are things?; **¿qué ~ te gusta?** how do you like it?

taladrar [tala'ðrar] *vt* to drill; **taladro** *nm* drill

talante [ta'lante] *nm* (*humor*) mood; (*voluntad*) will, willingness

talar [ta'lar] *vt* to fell, cut down; (*devastar*) to devastate

talco ['talko] *nm* (*polvos*) talcum powder

talento [ta'lento] *nm* talent; (*capacidad*) ability

TALGO ['talɣo] (ESP) *nm abr* (= *tren articulado ligero Goicoechea-Oriol*) ≈ HST (BRIT)

talismán [talis'man] *nm* talisman

talla ['taʎa] *nf* (*estatura, fig, Med*) height, stature; (*palo*) measuring rod; (*Arte*) carving; (*medida*) size

tallar [ta'ʎar] *vt* (*madera*) to carve; (*metal etc*) to engrave; (*medir*) to measure

tallarines [taʎa'rines] *nmpl* noodles

talle ['taʎe] *nm* (*Anat*) waist; (*fig*) appearance

taller [ta'ʎer] *nm* (*Tec*) workshop; (*de artista*) studio

tallo ['taʎo] *nm* (*de planta*) stem; (*de hierba*) blade; (*brote*) shoot

talón [ta'lon] *nm* (*Anat*) heel; (*Com*) counterfoil; (*cheque*) cheque (BRIT), check (US)

talonario [talo'narjo] *nm* (*de cheques*) chequebook (BRIT), checkbook (US); (*de recibos*) receipt book

tamaño, -a [ta'maɲo, a] *adj* (*tan grande*) such a big; (*tan pequeño*) such a small ▷ *nm* size; **de ~ natural** full-size

tamarindo [tama'rindo] *nm* tamarind

tambalearse [tambale'arse] *vr* (*persona*) to stagger; (*vehículo*) to sway

también [tam'bjen] *adv* (*igualmente*) also, too, as well; (*además*) besides

tambor [tam'bor] *nm* drum; (*Anat*) eardrum; **tambor del freno** brake drum

tamizar [tami'θar] *vt* to sieve

tampoco [tam'poko] *adv* nor, neither; **yo ~ lo compré** I didn't buy it either

tampón [tam'pon] *nm* tampon

tan [tan] *adv* so; **~ es así que ...** so much so that ...

tanda ['tanda] *nf* (*gen*) series; (*turno*) shift

tangente [tan'xente] *nf* tangent

tangerina [tanxe'rina] (LAM) *nf* tangerine

tangible [tan'xiβle] *adj* tangible

tanque ['tanke] *nm* (*cisterna, Mil*) tank; (*Auto*) tanker

tantear [tante'ar] *vt* (*calcular*) to reckon (up); (*medir*) to take the measure of; (*probar*) to test, try out; (*tomar la medida: persona*) to take the measurements of; (*situación*) to weigh up; (*persona: opinión*) to sound out ▷ *vi* (*Deporte*) to score; **tanteo** *nm* (*cálculo*) (rough) calculation; (*prueba*) test, trial; (*Deporte*) scoring

tanto, -a ['tanto, a] *adj* (*cantidad*) so much, as much ▷ *adv* (*cantidad*) so much, as much; (*tiempo*) so long, as long ▷ *conj*: **en ~ que** while ▷ *nm* (*suma*) certain amount; (*proporción*) so much; (*punto*) point; (*gol*) goal; **un ~ perezoso** somewhat lazy ▷ *pron*: **cado uno paga ~** each one pays so much; **~s** so many, as many; **20 y ~s** 20-odd; **hasta ~ (que)** until such time as; **~ tú como yo** both you and I; **~ como eso** as much as that; **~ más ... cuanto que** all the more ... because; **~ mejor/peor** so much the better/the worse; **~ si viene como si va** whether he comes or whether he goes; **~ es así que** so much so that; **por (lo) ~** therefore; **entre ~** meanwhile; **estar al ~** to be up to date; **me he vuelto ronco de** *o* **con ~ hablar** I have become hoarse with so much talking; **a ~s de agosto** on such and such a day in August

tapa ['tapa] *nf* (*de caja, olla*) lid; (*de botella*) top; (*de libro*) cover; (*comida*) snack

tapadera [tapa'ðera] *nf* lid, cover

tapar [ta'par] *vt* (*cubrir*) to cover; (*envolver*) to wrap *o* cover up; (*la vista*) to obstruct; (*persona, falta*) to conceal; (*MÉX, CAM: diente*) to fill; **taparse** *vr* to wrap o.s. up

taparrabo [tapa'rraβo] *nm* loincloth

tapete [ta'pete] *nm* table cover

tapia ['tapja] *nf* (garden) wall

tapicería [tapiθe'ria] *nf* tapestry; (*para muebles*) upholstery; (*tienda*) upholsterer's (shop)

tapiz [ta'piθ] *nm* (*alfombra*) carpet; (*tela tejida*) tapestry; **tapizar** *vt* (*muebles*) to upholster

tapón [ta'pon] *nm* (*de botella*) top; (*de lavabo*) plug; **tapón de rosca** screw-top

taquigrafía [takiɣra'fia] *nf* shorthand; **taquígrafo, -a** *nm/f* shorthand writer, stenographer

taquilla [ta'kiʎa] *nf* (*donde se compra*) booking office; (*suma recogida*) takings *pl*

tarántula [ta'rantula] *nf* tarantula

tararear [tarare'ar] *vi* to hum

tardar [tar'ðar] *vi* (*tomar tiempo*) to take a

t

long time; (*llegar tarde*) to be late; (*demorar*) to delay; **¿tarda mucho el tren?** does the train take (very) long?; **a más ~** at the latest; **no tardes en venir** come soon

tarde ['tarðe] *adv* late ▷ *nf* (*de día*) afternoon; (*al anochecer*) evening; **de ~ en ~** from time to time; **¡buenas ~s!** good afternoon!; **a** *o* **por la ~** in the afternoon; in the evening

tardío, -a [tar'ðio, a] *adj* (*retrasado*) late; (*lento*) slow (to arrive)

tarea [ta'rea] *nf* task; (*faena*) chore; (*Escol*) homework

tarifa [ta'rifa] *nf* (*lista de precios*) price list; (*precio*) tariff

tarima [ta'rima] *nf* (*plataforma*) platform

tarjeta [tar'xeta] *nf* card; **tarjeta de crédito/de Navidad/postal/telefónica** credit card/Christmas card/postcard/phonecard; **tarjeta de embarque** boarding pass; **tarjeta de memoria** memory card; **tarjeta prepago** top-up card; **tarjeta SIM** SIM card

tarro ['tarro] *nm* jar, pot

tarta ['tarta] *nf* (*pastel*) cake; (*de base dura*) tart

tartamudear [tartamuðe'ar] *vi* to stammer; **tartamudo, -a** *adj* stammering ▷ *nm/f* stammerer

tártaro, -a ['tartaro, a] *adj*: **salsa tártara** tartar(e) sauce

tasa ['tasa] *nf* (*precio*) (fixed) price, rate; (*valoración*) valuation; (*medida, norma*) measure, standard; **tasa de cambio/interés** exchange/interest rate; **tasas de aeropuerto** airport tax; **tasas universitarias** university fees

tasar [ta'sar] *vt* (*arreglar el precio*) to fix a price for; (*valorar*) to value, assess

tasca ['taska] (*fam*) *nf* pub

tatarabuelo, -a [tatara'βwelo, a] *nm/f* great-great-grandfather/mother

tatuaje [ta'twaxe] *nm* (*dibujo*) tattoo; (*acto*) tattooing

tatuar [ta'twar] *vt* to tattoo

taurino, -a [tau'rino, a] *adj* bullfighting *cpd*

Tauro ['tauro] *nm* Taurus

tauromaquia [tauro'makja] *nf* tauromachy, (art of) bullfighting

taxi ['taksi] *nm* taxi; **taxista** [tak'sista] *nmf* taxi driver

taza ['taθa] *nf* cup; (*de retrete*) bowl; **~ para café** coffee cup; **taza de café** cup of coffee; **tazón** *nm* (*taza grande*) mug, large cup; (*de fuente*) basin

te [te] *pron* (*complemento de objeto*) you; (*complemento indirecto*) (to) you; (*reflexivo*) (to) yourself; **¿~ duele mucho el brazo?** does your arm hurt a lot?; **~ equivocas** you're wrong; **¡cálma~!** calm down!

té [te] *nm* tea

teatral [tea'tral] *adj* theatre *cpd*; (*fig*) theatrical

teatro [te'atro] *nm* theatre; (*Literatura*) plays *pl*, drama

tebeo [te'βeo] *nm* comic

techo ['tetʃo] *nm* (*externo*) roof; (*interno*) ceiling; **techo corredizo** sunroof

tecla ['tekla] *nf* key; **teclado** *nm* keyboard; **teclear** *vi* (*Mús*) to strum; (*con los dedos*) to tap ▷ *vt* (*Inform*) to key in

técnica ['teknika] *nf* technique; (*tecnología*) technology; *V tb* **técnico**

técnico, -a ['tekniko, a] *adj* technical ▷ *nm/f* technician; (*experto*) expert

tecnología [teknolo'xia] *nf* technology; **tecnológico, -a** *adj* technological

tecolote [teko'lote] (MÉX) *nm* owl

tedioso, -a [te'ðjoso, a] *adj* boring, tedious

teja ['texa] *nf* tile; (*Bot*) lime (tree); **tejado** *nm* (tiled) roof

tejemaneje [texema'nexe] *nm* (*lío*) fuss; (*intriga*) intrigue

tejer [te'xer] *vt* to weave; (*hacer punto*) to knit; (*fig*) to fabricate; **tejido** *nm* (*tela*) material, fabric; (*telaraña*) web; (*Anat*) tissue

tel [tel] *abr* (= *teléfono*) tel

tela ['tela] *nf* (*tejido*) material; (*telaraña*) web; (*en líquido*) skin; **telar** *nm* (*máquina*) loom

telaraña [tela'raɲa] *nf* cobweb

tele ['tele] (*fam*) *nf* telly (BRIT), tube (US)

tele... ['tele] *prefijo* tele...; **telebasura** *nf* trash TV; **telecomunicación** *nf* telecommunication; **telediario** *nm* television news; **teledirigido, -a** *adj* remote-controlled

teleférico [tele'feriko] *nm* (*de esquí*) ski-lift

telefonear [telefone'ar] *vi* to telephone

telefónico, -a [tele'foniko, a] *adj* telephone *cpd*

telefonillo [telefo'niʎo] *nm* (*de puerta*) intercom

telefonista [telefo'nista] *nmf* telephonist

teléfono [te'lefono] *nm* (tele)phone; **estar hablando al ~** to be on the phone; **llamar a algn por ~** to ring sb (up) *o* phone sb (up); **teléfono celular** (LAM) mobile phone; **teléfono con cámara** camera phone; **teléfono inalámbrico** cordless phone; **teléfono móvil** (ESP) mobile phone

telégrafo [te'leɣrafo] *nm* telegraph

telegrama [tele'ɣrama] *nm* telegram

tele: telenovela *nf* soap (opera); **teleobjetivo** *nm* telephoto lens; **telepatía** *nf* telepathy; **telepático, -a** *adj* telepathic; **telerrealidad** *nf* reality TV; **telescopio** *nm* telescope; **telesilla** *nm* chairlift; **telespectador, a** *nm/f* viewer; **telesquí** *nm* ski-lift; **teletarjeta** *nf* phonecard; **teletipo** *nm* teletype; **teletrabajador, a** *nm/f* teleworker; **teletrabajo** *nm* teleworking; **televentas** *nfpl* telesales
televidente [teleβi'ðente] *nmf* viewer
televisar [teleβi'sar] *vt* to televise
televisión [teleβi'sjon] *nf* television; **televisión digital** digital television
televisor [teleβi'sor] *nm* television set
télex ['teleks] *nm inv* telex
telón [te'lon] *nm* curtain; **telón de acero** (*Pol*) iron curtain; **telón de fondo** backcloth, background
tema ['tema] *nm* (*asunto*) subject, topic; (*Mús*) theme; **temático, -a** *adj* thematic
temblar [tem'blar] *vi* to shake, tremble; (*por frío*) to shiver; **temblor** *nm* trembling; (*de tierra*) earthquake; **tembloroso, -a** *adj* trembling
temer [te'mer] *vt* to fear ▷ *vi* to be afraid; **temo que llegue tarde** I am afraid he may be late
temible [te'miβle] *adj* fearsome
temor [te'mor] *nm* (*miedo*) fear; (*duda*) suspicion
témpano ['tempano] *nm* (*tb*: **~ de hielo**) ice-floe
temperamento [tempera'mento] *nm* temperament
temperatura [tempera'tura] *nf* temperature
tempestad [tempes'tað] *nf* storm
templado, -a [tem'plaðo, a] *adj* (*moderado*) moderate; (*frugal*) frugal; (*agua*) lukewarm; (*clima*) mild; (*Mús*) well-tuned; **templanza** *nf* moderation; mildness
templar [tem'plar] *vt* (*moderar*) to moderate; (*furia*) to restrain; (*calor*) to reduce; (*afinar*) to tune (up); (*acero*) to temper; (*tuerca*) to tighten up; **temple** *nm* (*ajuste*) tempering; (*afinación*) tuning; (*pintura*) tempera
templo ['templo] *nm* (*iglesia*) church; (*pagano etc*) temple
temporada [tempo'raða] *nf* time, period; (*estación*) season
temporal [tempo'ral] *adj* (*no permanente*) temporary ▷ *nm* storm
temprano, -a [tem'prano, a] *adj* early; (*demasiado pronto*) too soon, too early
ten *vb V* **tener**
tenaces [te'naθes] *adj pl V* **tenaz**
tenaz [te'naθ] *adj* (*material*) tough; (*persona*) tenacious; (*creencia, resistencia*) stubborn
tenaza(s) [te'naθa(s)] *nf(pl)* (*Med*) forceps; (*Tec*) pliers; (*Zool*) pincers
tendedero [tende'ðero] *nm* (*para ropa*) drying place; (*cuerda*) clothes line
tendencia [ten'denθja] *nf* tendency; **tener ~ a** to tend to, have a tendency to
tender [ten'der] *vt* (*extender*) to spread out; (*colgar*) to hang out; (*vía férrea, cable*) to lay; (*estirar*) to stretch ▷ *vi*: **~ a** to tend to, have a tendency towards; **tenderse** *vr* to lie down; **~ la cama/mesa** (LAM) to make the bed/lay (BRIT) *o* set (US) the table
tenderete [tende'rete] *nm* (*puesto*) stall; (*exposición*) display of goods
tendero, -a [ten'dero, a] *nm/f* shopkeeper
tendón [ten'don] *nm* tendon
tendré *etc vb V* **tener**
tenebroso, -a [tene'βroso, a] *adj* (*oscuro*) dark; (*fig*) gloomy
tenedor [tene'ðor] *nm* (*Culin*) fork
tenencia [te'nenθja] *nf* (*de casa*) tenancy; (*de oficio*) tenure; (*de propiedad*) possession

PALABRA CLAVE

tener [te'ner] *vt* **1** (*poseer, gen*) to have; (*en la mano*) to hold; **¿tienes un boli?** have you got a pen?; **va a tener un niño** she's going to have a baby; **¡ten (*o* tenga)!, ¡aquí tienes (*o* tiene)!** here you are!
2 (*edad, medidas*) to be; **tiene 7 años** she's 7 (years old); **tiene 15 cm de largo** it's 15 cm long; *V* **calor; hambre etc**
3 (*considerar*): **lo tengo por brillante** I consider him to be brilliant; **tener en mucho a algn** to think very highly of sb
4 (+ *pp*: = *pretérito*): **tengo terminada ya la mitad del trabajo** I've done half the work already
5: **tener que hacer algo** to have to do sth; **tengo que acabar este trabajo hoy** I have to finish this job today
6: **¿qué tienes, estás enfermo?** what's the matter with you, are you ill?
tenerse *vr* **1** **tenerse en pie** to stand up
2 **tenerse por** to think o.s.

tengo *etc vb V* **tener**
tenia ['tenja] *nf* tapeworm
teniente [te'njente] *nm* (*rango*) lieutenant; (*ayudante*) deputy
tenis ['tenis] *nm* tennis; **tenis de mesa** table tennis; **tenista** *nmf* tennis player
tenor [te'nor] *nm* (*sentido*) meaning; (*Mús*)

tenor; **a ~ de** on the lines of
tensar [ten'sar] *vt* to tighten; (*arco*) to draw
tensión [ten'sjon] *nf* tension; (*Tec*) stress; **tener la ~ alta** to have high blood pressure; **tensión arterial** blood pressure
tenso, -a ['tenso, a] *adj* tense
tentación [tenta'θjon] *nf* temptation
tentáculo [ten'takulo] *nm* tentacle
tentador, a [tenta'ðor, a] *adj* tempting
tentar [ten'tar] *vt* (*seducir*) to tempt; (*atraer*) to attract
tentempié [tentem'pje] *nm* snack
tenue ['tenwe] *adj* (*delgado*) thin, slender; (*neblina*) light; (*lazo, vínculo*) slight
teñir [te'ɲir] *vt* to dye; (*fig*) to tinge; **teñirse** *vr* to dye; **~se el pelo** to dye one's hair
teología [teolo'xia] *nf* theology
teoría [teo'ria] *nf* theory; **en ~** in theory; **teórico, -a** *adj* theoretic(al) ▷ *nm/f* theoretician, theorist; **teorizar** *vi* to theorize
terapéutico, -a [tera'peutiko, a] *adj* therapeutic
terapia [te'rapja] *nf* therapy
tercer *adj V* **tercero**
tercermundista [terθermun'dista] *adj* Third World *cpd*
tercero, -a [ter'θero, a] (*delante de nmsg:* **tercer**) *adj* third ▷ *nm* (*Jur*) third party
terceto [ter'θeto] *nm* trio
terciar [ter'θjar] *vi* (*participar*) to take part; (*hacer de árbitro*) to mediate; **terciario, -a** *adj* tertiary
tercio ['terθjo] *nm* third
terciopelo [terθjo'pelo] *nm* velvet
terco, -a ['terko, a] *adj* obstinate
tergal® [ter'ɣal] *nm type of polyester*
tergiversar [terxiβer'sar] *vt* to distort
termal [ter'mal] *adj* thermal
termas ['termas] *nfpl* hot springs
térmico, -a ['termiko, a] *adj* thermal
terminal [termi'nal] *adj, nm, nf* terminal
terminante [termi'nante] *adj* (*final*) final, definitive; (*tajante*) categorical; **terminantemente** *adv*: **terminantemente prohibido** strictly forbidden
terminar [termi'nar] *vt* (*completar*) to complete, finish; (*concluir*) to end ▷ *vi* (*llegar a su fin*) to end; (*parar*) to stop; (*acabar*) to finish; **terminarse** *vr* to come to an end; **~ por hacer algo** to end up (by) doing sth
término ['termino] *nm* end, conclusion; (*parada*) terminus; (*límite*) boundary; **en último ~** (*a fin de cuentas*) in the last analysis; (*como último recurso*) as a last resort; **término medio** average; (*fig*) middle way
termómetro [ter'mometro] *nm* thermometer
termo(s)® ['termo(s)] *nm* Thermos®
termostato [termo'stato] *nm* thermostat
ternero, -a [ter'nero, a] *nm/f* (*animal*) calf ▷ *nf* (*carne*) veal
ternura [ter'nura] *nf* (*trato*) tenderness; (*palabra*) endearment; (*cariño*) fondness
terrado [te'rraðo] *nm* terrace
terraplén [terra'plen] *nm* embankment
terrateniente [terrate'njente] *nmf* landowner
terraza [te'rraθa] *nf* (*balcón*) balcony; (*tejado*) (flat) roof; (*Agr*) terrace
terremoto [terre'moto] *nm* earthquake
terrenal [terre'nal] *adj* earthly
terreno [te'rreno] *nm* (*tierra*) land; (*parcela*) plot; (*suelo*) soil; (*fig*) field; **un ~** a piece of land
terrestre [te'rrestre] *adj* terrestrial; (*ruta*) land *cpd*
terrible [te'rriβle] *adj* terrible, awful
territorio [terri'torjo] *nm* territory
terrón [te'rron] *nm* (*de azúcar*) lump; (*de tierra*) clod, lump
terror [te'rror] *nm* terror; **terrorífico, -a** *adj* terrifying; **terrorista** *adj, nmf* terrorist; **terrorista suicida** suicide bomber
terso, -a ['terso, a] *adj* (*liso*) smooth; (*pulido*) polished
tertulia [ter'tulja] *nf* (*reunión informal*) social gathering; (*grupo*) group, circle
tesis ['tesis] *nf inv* thesis
tesón [te'son] *nm* (*firmeza*) firmness; (*tenacidad*) tenacity
tesorero, -a [teso'rero, a] *nm/f* treasurer
tesoro [te'soro] *nm* treasure; (*Com, Pol*) treasury
testamento [testa'mento] *nm* will
testarudo, -a [testa'ruðo, a] *adj* stubborn
testículo [tes'tikulo] *nm* testicle
testificar [testifi'kar] *vt* to testify; (*fig*) to attest ▷ *vi* to give evidence
testigo [tes'tiɣo] *nmf* witness; **testigo de cargo/descargo** witness for the prosecution/defence; **testigo ocular** eye witness
testimonio [testi'monjo] *nm* testimony
teta ['teta] *nf* (*de biberón*) teat; (*Anat: fam*) breast
tétanos ['tetanos] *nm* tetanus
tetera [te'tera] *nf* teapot
tétrico, -a ['tetriko, a] *adj* gloomy, dismal
textil [teks'til] *adj* textile
texto ['teksto] *nm* text; **textual** *adj* textual

textura [teks'tura] *nf* (*de tejido*) texture
tez [teθ] *nf* (*cutis*) complexion
ti [ti] *pron* you; (*reflexivo*) yourself
tía ['tia] *nf* (*pariente*) aunt; (*fam*) chick, bird
tibio, -a ['tiβjo, a] *adj* lukewarm
tiburón [tiβu'ron] *nm* shark
tic [tik] *nm* (*ruido*) click; (*de reloj*) tick; (*Med*): **~ nervioso** nervous tic
tictac [tik'tak] *nm* (*de reloj*) tick tock
tiempo ['tjempo] *nm* time; (*época, período*) age, period; (*Meteorología*) weather; (*Ling*) tense; (*Deporte*) half; **a ~** in time; **a un** *o* **al mismo ~** at the same time; **al poco ~** very soon (after); **se quedó poco ~** he didn't stay very long; **hace poco ~** not long ago; **mucho ~** a long time; **de ~ en ~** from time to time; **hace buen/mal ~** the weather is fine/bad; **estar a ~** to be in time; **hace ~** some time ago; **hacer ~** to while away the time; **motor de 2 ~s** two-stroke engine; **primer ~** first half
tienda ['tjenda] *nf* shop, store; **tienda de abarrotes** (MÉX, CAM) grocer's (BRIT), grocery store (US); **tienda de alimentación** *o* **comestibles** grocer's (BRIT), grocery store (US); **tienda de campaña** tent
tienes *etc vb V* **tener**
tienta *etc* ['tjenta] *vb V* **tentar** ▷ *nf*: **andar a ~s** to grope one's way along
tiento *etc* ['tjento] *vb V* **tentar** ▷ *nm* (*tacto*) touch; (*precaución*) wariness
tierno, -a ['tjerno, a] *adj* (*blando*) tender; (*fresco*) fresh; (*amable*) sweet
tierra ['tjerra] *nf* earth; (*suelo*) soil; (*mundo*) earth, world; (*país*) country, land; **~ adentro** inland
tieso, -a ['tjeso, a] *adj* (*rígido*) rigid; (*duro*) stiff; (*fam: orgulloso*) conceited
tiesto ['tjesto] *nm* flowerpot
tifón [ti'fon] *nm* typhoon
tifus ['tifus] *nm* typhus
tigre ['tiɣre] *nm* tiger
tijera [ti'xera] *nf* scissors *pl*; (*Zool*) claw; **tijeras** *nfpl* scissors; (*para plantas*) shears
tila ['tila] *nf* lime blossom tea
tildar [til'dar] *vt*: **~ de** to brand as
tilde ['tilde] *nf* (*Tip*) tilde
tilín [ti'lin] *nm* tinkle
timar [ti'mar] *vt* (*estafar*) to swindle
timbal [tim'bal] *nm* small drum
timbre ['timbre] *nm* (*sello*) stamp; (*campanilla*) bell; (*tono*) timbre; (*Com*) stamp duty
timidez [timi'ðeθ] *nf* shyness; **tímido, -a** *adj* shy
timo ['timo] *nm* swindle
timón [ti'mon] *nm* helm, rudder; **timonel** *nm* helmsman
tímpano ['timpano] *nm* (*Anat*) eardrum; (*Mús*) small drum
tina ['tina] *nf* tub; (*baño*) bath(tub); **tinaja** *nf* large jar
tinieblas [ti'njeβlas] *nfpl* darkness *sg*; (*sombras*) shadows
tino ['tino] *nm* (*habilidad*) skill; (*juicio*) insight
tinta ['tinta] *nf* ink; (*Tec*) dye; (*Arte*) colour
tinte ['tinte] *nm* dye
tintero [tin'tero] *nm* inkwell
tinto ['tinto] *nm* red wine
tintorería [tintore'ria] *nf* dry cleaner's
tío ['tio] *nm* (*pariente*) uncle; (*fam: individuo*) bloke (BRIT), guy
tiovivo [tio'βiβo] *nm* merry-go-round
típico, -a ['tipiko, a] *adj* typical
tipo ['tipo] *nm* (*clase*) type, kind; (*hombre*) fellow; (*Anat: de hombre*) build; (*: de mujer*) figure; (*Imprenta*) type; **tipo bancario/de descuento/de interés/de cambio** bank/discount/interest/exchange rate
tipografía [tipoɣra'fia] *nf* printing *cpd*
tíquet ['tiket] (*pl* **~s**) *nm* ticket; (*en tienda*) cash slip
tiquismiquis [tikis'mikis] *nm inv* fussy person ▷ *nmpl* (*querellas*) squabbling *sg*; (*escrúpulos*) silly scruples
tira ['tira] *nf* strip; (*fig*) abundance; **tira y afloja** give and take
tirabuzón [tiraβu'θon] *nm* (*rizo*) curl
tirachinas [tira'tʃinas] *nm inv* catapult
tirada [ti'raða] *nf* (*acto*) cast, throw; (*serie*) series; (*Tip*) printing, edition; **de una ~** at one go
tirado, -a [ti'raðo, a] *adj* (*barato*) dirt-cheap; (*fam: fácil*) very easy
tirador [tira'ðor] *nm* (*mango*) handle
tirano, -a [ti'rano, a] *adj* tyrannical ▷ *nm/f* tyrant
tirante [ti'rante] *adj* (*cuerda etc*) tight, taut; (*relaciónes*) strained ▷ *nm* (*Arq*) brace; (*Tec*) stay; **tirantes** *nmpl* (*de pantalón*) braces (BRIT), suspenders (US); **tirantez** *nf* tightness; (*fig*) tension
tirar [ti'rar] *vt* to throw; (*dejar caer*) to drop; (*volcar*) to upset; (*derribar*) to knock down *o* over; (*desechar*) to throw out *o* away; (*dinero*) to squander; (*imprimir*) to print ▷ *vi* (*disparar*) to shoot; (*de la puerta etc*) to pull; (*fam: andar*) to go; (*tender a, buscar realizar*) to tend to; (*Deporte*) to shoot; **tirarse** *vr* to throw o.s.; **~ abajo** to bring down, destroy; **tira más a su padre** he takes more after his father; **ir tirando** to manage
tirita [ti'rita] *nf* (sticking) plaster (BRIT), Bandaid® (US)
tiritar [tiri'tar] *vi* to shiver

tiro ['tiro] *nm* (*lanzamiento*) throw; (*disparo*) shot; (*Deporte*) shot; (*Golf, Tenis*) drive; (*alcance*) range; **caballo de ~** cart-horse; **tiro al blanco** target practice
tirón [ti'ron] *nm* (*sacudida*) pull, tug; **de un ~** in one go, all at once
tiroteo [tiro'teo] *nm* exchange of shots, shooting
tisis ['tisis] *nf inv* consumption, tuberculosis
títere ['titere] *nm* puppet
titubear [tituβe'ar] *vi* to stagger; to stammer; (*fig*) to hesitate; **titubeo** *nm* staggering; stammering; hesitation
titulado, -a [titu'laðo, a] *adj* (*libro*) entitled; (*persona*) titled
titular [titu'lar] *adj* titular ▷*nmf* holder ▷*nm* headline ▷*vt* to title; **titularse** *vr* to be entitled; **título** *nm* title; (*de diario*) headline; (*certificado*) professional qualification; (*universitario*) (university) degree; **a título de** in the capacity of
tiza ['tiθa] *nf* chalk
toalla [to'aʎa] *nf* towel
tobillo [to'βiʎo] *nm* ankle
tobogán [toβo'ɣan] *nm* (*montaña rusa*) roller-coaster; (*de niños*) chute, slide
tocadiscos [toka'ðiskos] *nm inv* record player
tocado, -a [to'kaðo, a] *adj* (*fam*) touched ▷*nm* headdress
tocador [toka'ðor] *nm* (*mueble*) dressing table; (*cuarto*) boudoir; (*fam*) ladies' toilet (BRIT) *o* room (US)
tocar [to'kar] *vt* to touch; (*Mús*) to play; (*referirse a*) to allude to; (*timbre*) to ring ▷*vi* (*a la puerta*) to knock (on *o* at the door); (*ser de turno*) to fall to, be the turn of; (*ser hora*) to be due; **tocarse** *vr* (*cubrirse la cabeza*) to cover one's head; (*tener contacto*) to touch (each other); **por lo que a mí me toca** as far as I am concerned; **te toca a ti** it's your turn
tocayo, -a [to'kajo, a] *nm/f* namesake
tocino [to'θino] *nm* bacon
todavía [toða'βia] *adv* (*aun*) even; (*aún*) still, yet; **~ más** yet more; **~ no** not yet

PALABRA CLAVE

todo, -a ['toðo, a] *adj* **1** (*con artículo sg*) all; **toda la carne** all the meat; **toda la noche** all night, the whole night; **todo el libro** the whole book; **toda una botella** a whole bottle; **todo lo contrario** quite the opposite; **está toda sucia** she's all dirty; **por todo el país** throughout the whole country
2 (*con artículo pl*) all; every; **todos los libros** all the books; **todas las noches** every night; **todos los que quieran salir** all those who want to leave
▷*pron* **1** everything, all; **todos** everyone, everybody; **lo sabemos todo** we know everything; **todos querían más tiempo** everybody *o* everyone wanted more time; **nos marchamos todos** all of us left
2: **con todo: con todo él me sigue gustando** even so I still like him
▷*adv* all; **vaya todo seguido** keep straight on *o* ahead
▷*nm*: **como un todo** as a whole; **del todo: no me agrada del todo** I don't entirely like it

todopoderoso, -a [toðopoðe'roso, a] *adj* all powerful; (*Rel*) almighty
todoterreno [toðote'rreno] *sm inv* four-wheel drive, SUV (ESP US)
toga ['toɤa] *nf* toga; (*Escol*) gown
Tokio ['tokjo] *n* Tokyo
toldo ['toldo] *nm* (*para el sol*) sunshade (BRIT), parasol; (*tienda*) marquee
tolerancia [tole'ranθja] *nf* tolerance; **tolerante** *adj* (*sociedad*) liberal; (*persona*) open-minded
tolerar [tole'rar] *vt* to tolerate; (*resistir*) to endure
toma ['toma] *nf* (*acto*) taking; (*Med*) dose; **toma de corriente** socket; **toma de tierra** earth (wire); **tomacorriente** (LAM) *nm* socket
tomar [to'mar] *vt* to take; (*aspecto*) to take on; (*beber*) to drink ▷*vi* to take; (LAM: *beber*) to drink; **tomarse** *vr* to take; **~se por** to consider o.s. to be; **~ a bien/mal** to take well/badly; **~ en serio** to take seriously; **~ el pelo a algn** to pull sb's leg; **~la con algn** to pick a quarrel with sb; **¡tome!** here you are!; **~ el sol** to sunbathe
tomate [to'mate] *nm* tomato
tomillo [to'miʎo] *nm* thyme
tomo ['tomo] *nm* (*libro*) volume
ton [ton] *abr* = **tonelada** ▷*nm*: **sin ~ ni son** without rhyme or reason
tonalidad [tonali'ðað] *nf* tone
tonel [to'nel] *nm* barrel
tonelada [tone'laða] *nf* ton; **tonelaje** *nm* tonnage
tónica ['tonika] *nf* (*Mús*) tonic; (*fig*) keynote
tónico, -a ['toniko, a] *adj* tonic ▷*nm* (*Med*) tonic
tono ['tono] *nm* tone; **fuera de ~** inappropriate
tontería [tonte'ria] *nf* (*estupidez*) foolishness; (*cosa*) stupid thing; (*acto*)

foolish act; **tonterías** *nfpl* (*disparates*) rubbish *sg*, nonsense *sg*

tonto, -a ['tonto, a] *adj* stupid, silly ▷ *nm/f* fool

topar [to'par] *vi*: **~ contra** *o* **en** to run into; **~ con** to run up against

tope ['tope] *adj* maximum ▷ *nm* (*fin*) end; (*límite*) limit; (*Ferro*) buffer; (*Auto*) bumper; **al ~** end to end

tópico, -a ['topiko, a] *adj* topical ▷ *nm* platitude

topo ['topo] *nm* (*Zool*) mole; (*fig*) blunderer

toque *etc* ['toke] *vb V* **tocar** ▷ *nm* touch; (*Mús*) beat; (*de campana*) peal; **dar un ~ a** to warn; **toque de queda** curfew

toqué *etc vb V* **tocar**

toquetear [tokete'ar] *vt* to finger

toquilla [to'kiʎa] *nf* (*pañuelo*) headscarf; (*chal*) shawl

tórax ['toraks] *nm* thorax

torbellino [torbe'ʎino] *nm* whirlwind; (*fig*) whirl

torcedura [torθe'ðura] *nf* twist; (*Med*) sprain

torcer [tor'θer] *vt* to twist; (*la esquina*) to turn; (*Med*) to sprain ▷ *vi* (*desviar*) to turn off; **torcerse** *vr* (*ladearse*) to bend; (*desviarse*) to go astray; (*fracasar*) to go wrong; **torcido, -a** *adj* twisted; (*fig*) crooked ▷ *nm* curl

tordo, -a ['torðo, a] *adj* dappled ▷ *nm* thrush

torear [tore'ar] *vt* (*fig: evadir*) to avoid; (*jugar con*) to tease ▷ *vi* to fight bulls; **toreo** *nm* bullfighting; **torero, -a** *nm/f* bullfighter

tormenta [tor'menta] *nf* storm; (*fig: confusión*) turmoil

tormento [tor'mento] *nm* torture; (*fig*) anguish

tornar [tor'nar] *vt* (*devolver*) to return, give back; (*transformar*) to transform ▷ *vi* to go back

tornasolado, -a [tornaso'laðo, a] *adj* (*brillante*) iridescent; (*reluciente*) shimmering

torneo [tor'neo] *nm* tournament

tornillo [tor'niʎo] *nm* screw

torniquete [torni'kete] *nm* (*Med*) tourniquet

torno ['torno] *nm* (*Tec*) winch; (*tambor*) drum; **en ~ (a)** round, about

toro ['toro] *nm* bull; (*fam*) he-man; **los ~s** bullfighting

toronja [to'ronxa] *nf* grapefruit

torpe ['torpe] *adj* (*poco hábil*) clumsy, awkward; (*necio*) dim; (*lento*) slow

torpedo [tor'peðo] *nm* torpedo

torpeza [tor'peθa] *nf* (*falta de agilidad*) clumsiness; (*lentitud*) slowness; (*error*) mistake

torre ['torre] *nf* tower; (*de petróleo*) derrick

torrefacto, -a [torre'facto, a] *adj* roasted

torrente [to'rrente] *nm* torrent

torrija [to'rrixa] *nf* French toast

torsión [tor'sjon] *nf* twisting

torso ['torso] *nm* torso

torta ['torta] *nf* cake; (*fam*) slap

tortícolis [tor'tikolis] *nm inv* stiff neck

tortilla [tor'tiʎa] *nf* omelette; (LAM: *de maíz*) maize pancake; **tortilla de papas** (LAM) potato omelette; **tortilla de patatas** (ESP) potato omelette; **tortilla francesa** (ESP) plain omelette

tórtola ['tortola] *nf* turtledove

tortuga [tor'tuɣa] *nf* tortoise

tortuoso, -a [tor'twoso, a] *adj* winding

tortura [tor'tura] *nf* torture; **torturar** *vt* to torture

tos [tos] *nf* cough; **tos ferina** whooping cough

toser [to'ser] *vi* to cough

tostada [tos'taða] *nf* piece of toast; **tostado, -a** *adj* toasted; (*por el sol*) dark brown; (*piel*) tanned

tostador [tosta'ðor] (ESP) *nm* toaster; **tostadora** (LAM) *nf* = **tostador**

tostar [tos'tar] *vt* to toast; (*café*) to roast; (*persona*) to tan; **tostarse** *vr* to get brown

total [to'tal] *adj* total ▷ *adv* in short; (*al fin y al cabo*) when all is said and done ▷ *nm* total; **en ~** in all; **~ que ...** to cut (BRIT) *o* make (US) a long story short ...

totalidad [totali'ðað] *nf* whole

totalitario, -a [totali'tarjo, a] *adj* totalitarian

tóxico, -a ['toksiko, a] *adj* toxic ▷ *nm* poison; **toxicómano, -a** *nm/f* drug addict

toxina [to'ksina] *nf* toxin

tozudo, -a [to'θuðo, a] *adj* obstinate

trabajador, a [traβaxa'ðor, a] *adj* hard-working ▷ *nm/f* worker; **trabajador autónomo** *o* **por cuenta propia** self-employed person

trabajar [traβa'xar] *vt* to work; (*Agr*) to till; (*empeñarse en*) to work at; (*convencer*) to persuade ▷ *vi* to work; (*esforzarse*) to strive; **trabajo** *nm* work; (*tarea*) task; (*Pol*) labour; (*fig*) effort; **tomarse el trabajo de** to take the trouble to; **trabajo a destajo** piecework; **trabajo en equipo** teamwork; **trabajo por turnos** shift work; **trabajos forzados** hard labour *sg*

trabalenguas [traβa'lengwas] *nm inv* tongue twister

tracción [trak'θjon] *nf* traction; **tracción delantera/trasera** front-wheel/rear-wheel drive

t

tractor [trak'tor] *nm* tractor
tradición [traði'θjon] *nf* tradition; **tradicional** *adj* traditional
traducción [traðuk'θjon] *nf* translation
traducir [traðu'θir] *vt* to translate; **traductor, a** *nm/f* translator
traer [tra'er] *vt* to bring; (*llevar*) to carry; (*llevar puesto*) to wear; (*incluir*) to carry; (*causar*) to cause; **traerse** *vr*: **~se algo** to be up to sth
traficar [trafi'kar] *vi* to trade
tráfico ['trafiko] *nm* (*Com*) trade; (*Auto*) traffic
tragaluz [traɣa'luθ] *nm* skylight
tragamonedas [traɣamo'neðas] (LAM) *nf inv* slot machine
tragaperras [traɣa'perras] (ESP) *nf inv* slot machine
tragar [tra'ɣar] *vt* to swallow; (*devorar*) to devour, bolt down; **tragarse** *vr* to swallow
tragedia [tra'xeðja] *nf* tragedy; **trágico, -a** *adj* tragic
trago ['traɣo] *nm* (*líquido*) drink; (*bocado*) gulp; (*fam: de bebida*) swig; (*desgracia*) blow; **echar un ~** to have a drink
traición [trai'θjon] *nf* treachery; (*Jur*) treason; (*una traición*) act of treachery; **traicionar** *vt* to betray
traidor, a [trai'ðor, a] *adj* treacherous ▷ *nm/f* traitor
traigo *etc vb V* **traer**
traje ['traxe] *vb V* **traer** ▷ *nm* (*de hombre*) suit; (*de mujer*) dress; (*vestido típico*) costume; **traje de baño/chaqueta** swimsuit/suit; **traje de etiqueta** dress suit; **traje de luces** bullfighter's costume
trajera *etc vb V* **traer**
trajín [tra'xin] *nm* (*fam: movimiento*) bustle; **trajinar** *vi* (*moverse*) to bustle about
trama ['trama] *nf* (*intriga*) plot; (*de tejido*) weft (BRIT), woof (US); **tramar** *vt* to plot; (*Tec*) to weave
tramitar [trami'tar] *vt* (*asunto*) to transact; (*negociar*) to negotiate
trámite ['tramite] *nm* (*paso*) step; (*Jur*) transaction; **trámites** *nmpl* (*burocracia*) procedure *sg*; (*Jur*) proceedings
tramo ['tramo] *nm* (*de tierra*) plot; (*de escalera*) flight; (*de vía*) section
trampa ['trampa] *nf* trap; (*en el suelo*) trapdoor; (*truco*) trick; (*engaño*) fiddle; **trampear** *vt, vi* to cheat
trampolín [trampo'lin] *nm* (*de piscina etc*) diving board
tramposo, -a [tram'poso, a] *adj* crooked, cheating ▷ *nm/f* crook, cheat
tranca ['tranka] *nf* (*palo*) stick; (*de puerta, ventana*) bar; **trancar** *vt* to bar
trance ['tranθe] *nm* (*momento difícil*) difficult moment *o* juncture; (*estado hipnotizado*) trance
tranquilidad [trankili'ðað] *nf* (*calma*) calmness, stillness; (*paz*) peacefulness
tranquilizar [trankili'θar] *vt* (*calmar*) to calm (down); (*asegurar*) to reassure; **tranquilizarse** *vr* to calm down; **tranquilo, -a** *adj* (*calmado*) calm; (*apacible*) peaceful; (*mar*) calm; (*mente*) untroubled
transacción [transak'θjon] *nf* transaction
transbordador [transβorða'ðor] *nm* ferry
transbordo [trans'βorðo] *nm* transfer; **hacer ~** to change (trains *etc*)
transcurrir [transku'rrir] *vi* (*tiempo*) to pass; (*hecho*) to take place
transcurso [trans'kurso] *nm*: **~ del tiempo** lapse (of time)
transeúnte [transe'unte] *nmf* passer-by
transferencia [transfe'renθja] *nf* transference; (*Com*) transfer
transferir [transfe'rir] *vt* to transfer
transformador [transforma'ðor] *nm* (*Elec*) transformer
transformar [transfor'mar] *vt* to transform; (*convertir*) to convert
transfusión [transfu'sjon] *nf* transfusion
transgénico, -a [trans'xeniko, a] *adj* genetically modified, GM
transición [transi'θjon] *nf* transition
transigir [transi'xir] *vi* to compromise, make concessions
transitar [transi'tar] *vi* to go (from place to place); **tránsito** *nm* transit; (*Auto*) traffic; **transitorio, -a** *adj* transitory
transmisión [transmi'sjon] *nf* (*Tec*) transmission; (*transferencia*) transfer; **transmisión exterior/en directo** outside/live broadcast
transmitir [transmi'tir] *vt* to transmit; (*Radio, TV*) to broadcast
transparencia [transpa'renθja] *nf* transparency; (*claridad*) clearness, clarity; (*foto*) slide
transparentar [transparen'tar] *vt* to reveal ▷ *vi* to be transparent; **transparente** *adj* transparent; (*claro*) clear
transpirar [transpi'rar] *vi* to perspire
transportar [transpor'tar] *vt* to transport; (*llevar*) to carry; **transporte** *nm* transport; (*Com*) haulage
transversal [transβer'sal] *adj* transverse, cross
tranvía [tram'bia] *nm* tram
trapeador [trapea'ðor] (LAM) *nm* mop; **trapear** (LAM) *vt* to mop

trapecio [tra'peθjo] *nm* trapeze; **trapecista** *nmf* trapeze artist
trapero, -a [tra'pero, a] *nm/f* ragman
trapicheo [trapi'tʃeo] (*fam*) *nm* scheme, fiddle
trapo ['trapo] *nm* (*tela*) rag; (*de cocina*) cloth
tráquea ['trakea] *nf* windpipe
traqueteo [trake'teo] *nm* rattling
tras [tras] *prep* (*detrás*) behind; (*después*) after
trasatlántico [trasat'lantiko] *nm* (*barco*) (cabin) cruiser
trascendencia [trasθen'denθja] *nf* (*importancia*) importance; (*Filosofía*) transcendence
trascendental [trasθenden'tal] *adj* important; (*Filosofía*) transcendental
trasero, -a [tra'sero, a] *adj* back, rear ▷ *nm* (*Anat*) bottom
trasfondo [tras'fondo] *nm* background
trasgredir [trasɣre'ðir] *vt* to contravene
trashumante [trasu'mante] *adj* (*animales*) migrating
trasladar [trasla'ðar] *vt* to move; (*persona*) to transfer; (*postergar*) to postpone; (*copiar*) to copy; **trasladarse** *vr* (*mudarse*) to move; **traslado** *nm* move; (*mudanza*) move, removal
traslucir [traslu'θir] *vt* to show
trasluz [tras'luθ] *nm* reflected light; **al ~** against *o* up to the light
trasnochador, a [trasnotʃa'ðor, a] *nm/f* night owl
trasnochar [trasno'tʃar] *vi* (*acostarse tarde*) to stay up late
traspapelar [traspape'lar] *vt* (*documento, carta*) to mislay, misplace
traspasar [traspa'sar] *vt* (*suj: bala etc*) to pierce, go through; (*propiedad*) to sell, transfer; (*calle*) to cross over; (*límites*) to go beyond; (*ley*) to break; **traspaso** *nm* (*venta*) transfer, sale
traspatio [tras'patjo] (LAM) *nm* backyard
traspié [tras'pje] *nm* (*tropezón*) trip; (*error*) blunder
trasplantar [trasplan'tar] *vt* to transplant
traste ['traste] *nm* (*Mús*) fret; **dar al ~ con algo** to ruin sth
trastero [tras'tero] *nm* storage room
trastienda [tras'tjenda] *nf* back of shop
trasto ['trasto] (*pey*) *nm* (*cosa*) piece of junk; (*persona*) dead loss
trastornado, -a [trastor'naðo, a] *adj* (*loco*) mad, crazy
trastornar [trastor'nar] *vt* (*fig: planes*) to disrupt; (*: nervios*) to shatter; (*: persona*) to drive crazy; **trastornarse** *vr* (*volverse loco*) to go mad *o* crazy; **trastorno** *nm* (*acto*) overturning; (*confusión*) confusion
tratable [tra'taβle] *adj* friendly
tratado [tra'taðo] *nm* (*Pol*) treaty; (*Com*) agreement
tratamiento [trata'mjento] *nm* treatment; **tratamiento de textos** (*Inform*) word processing *cpd*
tratar [tra'tar] *vt* (*ocuparse de*) to treat; (*manejar, Tec*) to handle; (*Med*) to treat; (*dirigirse a: persona*) to address ▷ *vi*: **~ de** (*hablar sobre*) to deal with, be about; (*intentar*) to try to; **tratarse** *vr* to treat each other; **~ con** (*Com*) to trade in; (*negociar*) to negotiate with; (*tener contactos*) to have dealings with; **¿de qué se trata?** what's it about?; **trato** *nm* dealings *pl*; (*relaciónes*) relationship; (*comportamiento*) manner; (*Com*) agreement
trauma ['trauma] *nm* trauma
través [tra'βes] *nm* (*fig*) reverse; **al ~** across, crossways; **a ~ de** across; (*sobre*) over; (*por*) through
travesaño [traβe'saɲo] *nm* (*Arq*) crossbeam; (*Deporte*) crossbar
travesía [traβe'sia] *nf* (*calle*) cross-street; (*Náut*) crossing
travesura [traβe'sura] *nf* (*broma*) prank; (*ingenio*) wit
travieso, -a [tra'βjeso, a] *adj* (*niño*) naughty
trayecto [tra'jekto] *nm* (*ruta*) road, way; (*viaje*) journey; (*tramo*) stretch; **trayectoria** *nf* trajectory; (*fig*) path
traza ['traθa] *nf* (*aspecto*) looks *pl*; (*señal*) sign; **trazado, -a** *adj*: **bien trazado** shapely, well-formed ▷ *nm* (*Arq*) plan, design; (*fig*) outline
trazar [tra'θar] *vt* (*Arq*) to plan; (*Arte*) to sketch; (*fig*) to trace; (*plan*) to draw up; **trazo** *nm* (*línea*) line; (*bosquejo*) sketch
trébol ['treβol] *nm* (*Bot*) clover
trece ['treθe] *num* thirteen
trecho ['tretʃo] *nm* (*distancia*) distance; (*tiempo*) while
tregua ['treɣwa] *nf* (*Mil*) truce; (*fig*) respite
treinta ['treinta] *num* thirty
tremendo, -a [tre'mendo, a] *adj* (*terrible*) terrible; (*imponente: cosa*) imposing; (*fam: fabuloso*) tremendous
tren [tren] *nm* train; **tren de aterrizaje** undercarriage; **tren de cercanías** suburban train
trenca ['trenka] *nf* duffel coat
trenza ['trenθa] *nf* (*de pelo*) plait (BRIT), braid (US)
trepadora [trepa'ðora] *nf* (*Bot*) climber
trepar [tre'par] *vt, vi* to climb

tres [tres] *num* three
tresillo [tre'siʎo] *nm* three-piece suite; (*Mús*) triplet
treta ['treta] *nf* trick
triángulo ['trjangulo] *nm* triangle
tribu ['triβu] *nf* tribe
tribuna [tri'βuna] *nf* (*plataforma*) platform; (*Deporte*) (grand)stand
tribunal [triβu'nal] *nm* (*Jur*) court; (*comisión, fig*) tribunal; **~ popular** jury
tributo [tri'βuto] *nm* (*Com*) tax
trigal [tri'ɣal] *nm* wheat field
trigo ['triɣo] *nm* wheat
trigueño, -a [tri'ɣeɲo, a] *adj* (*pelo*) corn-coloured
trillar [tri'ʎar] *vt* (*Agr*) to thresh
trimestral [trimes'tral] *adj* quarterly; (*Escol*) termly
trimestre [tri'mestre] *nm* (*Escol*) term
trinar [tri'nar] *vi* (*pájaros*) to sing; (*rabiar*) to fume, be angry
trinchar [trin'tʃar] *vt* to carve
trinchera [trin'tʃera] *nf* (*fosa*) trench
trineo [tri'neo] *nm* sledge
trinidad [trini'ðað] *nf* trio; (*Rel*): **la T~** the Trinity
tripa ['tripa] *nf* (*Anat*) intestine; (*fam*: *tb*: **~s**) insides *pl*
triple ['triple] *adj* triple
triplicado, -a [tripli'kaðo, a] *adj*: **por ~** in triplicate
tripulación [tripula'θjon] *nf* crew
tripulante [tripu'lante] *nmf* crewman/woman
tripular [tripu'lar] *vt* (*barco*) to man; (*Auto*) to drive
triquiñuela [triki'ɲwela] *nf* trick
tris [tris] *nm inv* crack
triste ['triste] *adj* sad; (*lamentable*) sorry, miserable; **tristeza** *nf* (*aflicción*) sadness; (*melancolía*) melancholy
triturar [tritu'rar] *vt* (*moler*) to grind; (*mascar*) to chew
triunfar [trjun'far] *vi* (*tener éxito*) to triumph; (*ganar*) to win; **triunfo** *nm* triumph
trivial [tri'βjal] *adj* trivial
triza ['triθa] *nf*: **hacer ~s** to smash to bits; (*papel*) to tear to shreds
trocear [troθe'ar] *vt* (*carne, manzana*) to cut up, cut into pieces
trocha ['trotʃa] *nf* short cut
trofeo [tro'feo] *nm* (*premio*) trophy; (*éxito*) success
tromba ['tromba] *nf* downpour
trombón [trom'bon] *nm* trombone
trombosis [trom'bosis] *nf inv* thrombosis
trompa ['trompa] *nf* horn; (*trompo*) humming top; (*hocico*) snout; (*fam*): **cogerse una ~** to get tight
trompazo [trom'paθo] *nm* bump, bang
trompeta [trom'peta] *nf* trumpet; (*clarín*) bugle
trompicón [trompi'kon]: **a trompicones** *adv* in fits and starts
trompo ['trompo] *nm* spinning top
trompón [trom'pon] *nm* bump
tronar [tro'nar] *vt* (*MÉX, CAM*: *fusilar*) to shoot; (*MÉX*: *examen*) to flunk ▷ *vi* to thunder; (*fig*) to rage
tronchar [tron'tʃar] *vt* (*árbol*) to chop down; (*fig*: *vida*) to cut short; (: *esperanza*) to shatter; (*persona*) to tire out; **troncharse** *vr* to fall down
tronco ['tronko] *nm* (*de árbol, Anat*) trunk
trono ['trono] *nm* throne
tropa ['tropa] *nf* (*Mil*) troop; (*soldados*) soldiers *pl*
tropezar [trope'θar] *vi* to trip, stumble; (*errar*) to slip up; **~ con** to run into; (*topar con*) to bump into; **tropezón** *nm* trip; (*fig*) blunder
tropical [tropi'kal] *adj* tropical
trópico ['tropiko] *nm* tropic
tropiezo [tro'pjeθo] *vb V* **tropezar** ▷ *nm* (*error*) slip, blunder; (*desgracia*) misfortune; (*obstáculo*) snag
trotamundos [trota'mundos] *nm inv* globetrotter
trotar [tro'tar] *vi* to trot; **trote** *nm* trot; (*fam*) travelling; **de mucho trote** hard-wearing
trozar [tro'θar] (*LAM*) *vt* to cut up, cut into pieces
trozo ['troθo] *nm* bit, piece
trucha ['trutʃa] *nf* trout
truco ['truko] *nm* (*habilidad*) knack; (*engaño*) trick
trueno ['trweno] *nm* thunder; (*estampido*) bang
trueque *etc* ['trweke] *vb V* **trocar** ▷ *nm* exchange; (*Com*) barter
trufa ['trufa] *nf* (*Bot*) truffle
truhán, -ana [tru'an, ana] *nm/f* rogue
truncar [trun'kar] *vt* (*cortar*) to truncate; (*fig*: *la vida etc*) to cut short; (: *el desarrollo*) to stunt
tu [tu] *adj* your
tú [tu] *pron* you
tubérculo [tu'βerkulo] *nm* (*Bot*) tuber
tuberculosis [tuβerku'losis] *nf inv* tuberculosis
tubería [tuβe'ria] *nf* pipes *pl*; (*conducto*) pipeline
tubo ['tuβo] *nm* tube, pipe; **tubo de ensayo** test tube; **tubo de escape** exhaust

(pipe)
tuerca ['twerka] *nf* nut
tuerto, -a ['twerto, a] *adj* blind in one eye ▷ *nm/f* one-eyed person
tuerza *etc vb V* **torcer**
tuétano ['twetano] *nm* marrow; (*Bot*) pith
tufo ['tufo] *nm* (*hedor*) stench
tul [tul] *nm* tulle
tulipán [tuli'pan] *nm* tulip
tullido, -a [tu'ʎiðo, a] *adj* crippled
tumba ['tumba] *nf* (*sepultura*) tomb
tumbar [tum'bar] *vt* to knock down; **tumbarse** *vr* (*echarse*) to lie down; (*extenderse*) to stretch out
tumbo ['tumbo] *nm*: **dar ~s** to stagger
tumbona [tum'bona] *nf* (*butaca*) easy chair; (*de playa*) deckchair (BRIT), beach chair (US)
tumor [tu'mor] *nm* tumour
tumulto [tu'multo] *nm* turmoil
tuna ['tuna] *nf* (*Mús*) *student music group*; *V tb* **tuno**

TUNA

A **tuna** is a musical group made up of university students or former students who dress up in costumes from the "Edad de Oro", the Spanish Golden Age. These groups go through the town playing their guitars, lutes and tambourines and serenade the young ladies in the halls of residence or make impromptu appearances at weddings or parties singing traditional Spanish songs for a few coins.

tunante [tu'nante] *nmf* rascal
tunear [tune'ar] *vt* (*Auto*) to style, mod (*inf*)
túnel ['tunel] *nm* tunnel
tuning ['tunin] *nm* (*Auto*) car styling, modding (*inf*)
tuno, -a ['tuno, a] *nm/f* (*fam*) rogue ▷ *nm member of student music group*
tupido, -a [tu'piðo, a] *adj* (*denso*) dense; (*tela*) close-woven
turbante [tur'βante] *nm* turban
turbar [tur'βar] *vt* (*molestar*) to disturb; (*incomodar*) to upset
turbina [tur'βina] *nf* turbine
turbio, -a ['turβjo, a] *adj* cloudy; (*tema etc*) confused
turbulencia [turβu'lenθja] *nf* turbulence; (*fig*) restlessness; **turbulento, -a** *adj* turbulent; (*fig: intranquilo*) restless; (*: ruidoso*) noisy
turco, -a ['turko, a] *adj* Turkish ▷ *nm/f* Turk
turismo [tu'rismo] *nm* tourism; (*coche*) car; **turista** *nmf* tourist; **turístico, -a** *adj* tourist *cpd*
turnar [tur'nar] *vi* to take (it in) turns; **turnarse** *vr* to take (it in) turns; **turno** *nm* (*de trabajo*) shift; (*en juegos etc*) turn
turquesa [tur'kesa] *nf* turquoise
Turquía [tur'kia] *nf* Turkey
turrón [tu'rron] *nm* (*dulce*) nougat
tutear [tute'ar] *vt* to address as familiar "tú"; **tutearse** *vr* to be on familiar terms
tutela [tu'tela] *nf* (*legal*) guardianship; **tutelar** *adj* tutelary ▷ *vt* to protect
tutor, a [tu'tor, a] *nm/f* (*legal*) guardian; (*Escol*) tutor
tuve *etc vb V* **tener**
tuviera *etc vb V* **tener**
tuyo, -a ['tujo, a] *adj* yours, of yours ▷ *pron* yours; **un amigo ~** a friend of yours; **los ~s** (*fam*) your relations *o* family
TV *nf abr* (= *televisión*) TV
TVE *nf abr* = **Televisión Española**

u [u] *conj* or
ubicar [uβi'kar] *vt* to place, situate; (*LAM*: *encontrar*) to find; **ubicarse** *vr* (*LAM*: *encontrarse*) to lie, be located
ubre ['uβre] *nf* udder
UCI *nf abr* (= *Unidad de Cuidados Intensivos*) ICU
Ud(s) *abr* = **usted(es)**
UE *nf abr* (= *Unión Europea*) EU
ufanarse [ufa'narse] *vr* to boast; **ufano, -a** *adj* (*arrogante*) arrogant; (*presumido*) conceited
UGT (*ESP*) *nf abr* = **Unión General de Trabajadores**
úlcera ['ulθera] *nf* ulcer
ulterior [ulte'rjor] *adj* (*más allá*) farther, further; (*subsecuente, siguiente*) subsequent
últimamente ['ultimamente] *adv* (*recientemente*) lately, recently
ultimar [ulti'mar] *vt* to finish; (*finalizar*) to finalize; (*LAM*: *matar*) to kill
ultimátum [ulti'matum] (*pl* **~s**) *nm* ultimatum
último, -a ['ultimo, a] *adj* last; (*más reciente*) latest, most recent; (*más bajo*) bottom; (*más alto*) top; **en las últimas** on one's last legs; **por ~** finally
ultra ['ultra] *adj* ultra ▷ *nmf* extreme right-winger
ultraje [ul'traxe] *nm* outrage; insult
ultramar [ultra'mar] *nm*: **de** *o* **en ~** abroad, overseas
ultramarinos [ultrama'rinos] *nmpl* groceries; **tienda de ~** grocer's (shop)
ultranza [ul'tranθa]: **a ~** *adv* (*a todo trance*) at all costs; (*completo*) outright
umbral [um'bral] *nm* (*gen*) threshold

PALABRA CLAVE

un, una [un, 'una] *art indef* a; (*antes de vocal*) an; **una mujer/naranja** a woman/ an orange
▷ *adj*: **unos (o unas): hay unos regalos para ti** there are some presents for you; **hay unas cervezas en la nevera** there are some beers in the fridge

unánime [u'nanime] *adj* unanimous; **unanimidad** *nf* unanimity
undécimo, -a [un'deθimo, a] *adj* eleventh
ungir [un'xir] *vt* to anoint
ungüento [un'gwento] *nm* ointment
único, -a ['uniko, a] *adj* only, sole; (*sin par*) unique
unidad [uni'ðað] *nf* unity; (*Com, Tec etc*) unit
unido, -a [u'niðo, a] *adj* joined, linked; (*fig*) united
unificar [unifi'kar] *vt* to unite, unify
uniformar [unifor'mar] *vt* to make uniform, level up; (*persona*) to put into uniform
uniforme [uni'forme] *adj* uniform, equal; (*superficie*) even ▷ *nm* uniform
unilateral [unilate'ral] *adj* unilateral
unión [u'njon] *nf* union; (*acto*) uniting, joining; (*unidad*) unity; (*Tec*) joint; **Unión Europea** European Union
unir [u'nir] *vt* (*juntar*) to join, unite; (*atar*) to tie, fasten; (*combinar*) to combine; **unirse** *vr* to join together, unite; (*empresas*) to merge
unísono [u'nisono] *nm*: **al ~** in unison
universal [uniβer'sal] *adj* universal; (*mundial*) world *cpd*
universidad [uniβersi'ðað] *nf* university
universitario, -a [uniβersi'tarjo, a] *adj* university *cpd* ▷ *nm/f* (*profesor*) lecturer; (*estudiante*) (university) student; (*graduado*) graduate
universo [uni'βerso] *nm* universe

PALABRA CLAVE

uno, -a ['uno, a] *adj* one; **unos pocos** a few; **unos cien** about a hundred ▷ *pron*
1 one; **quiero sólo uno** I only want one; **uno de ellos** one of them
2 (*alguien*) somebody, someone; **conozco a uno que se te parece** I know somebody *o* someone who looks like you; **uno mismo** oneself; **unos querían quedarse** some (people) wanted to stay
3 **(los) unos ... (los) otros ...** some ... others
▷ *nf* one; **es la una** it's one o'clock
▷ *nm* (number) one

untar [un'tar] *vt* (*mantequilla*) to spread; (*engrasar*) to grease, oil
uña ['uɲa] *nf* (*Anat*) nail; (*garra*) claw; (*casco*) hoof; (*arrancaclavos*) claw
uranio [u'ranjo] *nm* uranium
urbanización [urβaniθa'θjon] *nf* (*barrio, colonia*) housing estate
urbanizar [urβani'θar] *vt* (*zona*) to develop, urbanize
urbano, -a [ur'βano, a] *adj* (*de ciudad*) urban; (*cortés*) courteous, polite
urbe ['urβe] *nf* large city
urdir [ur'ðir] *vt* to warp; (*complot*) to plot, contrive
urgencia [ur'xenθja] *nf* urgency; (*prisa*) haste, rush; (*emergencia*) emergency; **servicios de ~** emergency services; **"U~s"** "Casualty"; **urgente** *adj* urgent
urgir [ur'xir] *vi* to be urgent; **me urge** I'm in a hurry for it
urinario, -a [uri'narjo, a] *adj* urinary ▷ *nm* urinal
urna ['urna] *nf* urn; (*Pol*) ballot box
urraca [u'rraka] *nf* magpie
URSS [urs] *nf* (*Hist*): **la URSS** the USSR
Uruguay [uru'ɣwai] *nm* (*tb*: **el ~**) Uruguay; **uruguayo, -a** *adj, nm/f* Uruguayan
usado, -a [u'saðo, a] *adj* used; (*de segunda mano*) secondhand
usar [u'sar] *vt* to use; (*ropa*) to wear; (*tener costumbre*) to be in the habit of; **usarse** *vr* to be used; **uso** *nm* use; wear; (*costumbre*) usage, custom; (*moda*) fashion; **al uso** in keeping with custom; **al uso de** in the style of; **de uso externo** (*Med*) for external use
usted [us'teð] *pron* (*sg*) you *sg*; (*pl*): **~es** you *pl*
usual [u'swal] *adj* usual
usuario, -a [usu'arjo, a] *nm/f* user
usurpar [usur'par] *vt* to usurp
utensilio [uten'siljo] *nm* tool; (*Culin*) utensil
útero ['utero] *nm* uterus, womb
útil ['util] *adj* useful ▷ *nm* tool; **utilidad** *nf* usefulness; (*Com*) profit; **utilizar** *vt* to use, utilize
uva ['uβa] *nf* grape

LAS UVAS

In Spain **Las uvas** play a big part on New Year's Eve (**Nochevieja**), when on the stroke of midnight people gather at home, in restaurants or in the **plaza mayor** and eat a grape for each stroke of the clock of the **Puerta del Sol** in Madrid. It is said to bring luck for the following year.

v *abr* (= *voltio*) v
va *vb V* **ir**
vaca ['baka] *nf* (*animal*) cow; **carne de ~** beef
vacaciones [baka'θjones] *nfpl* holidays
vacante [ba'kante] *adj* vacant, empty ▷ *nf* vacancy
vaciar [ba'θjar] *vt* to empty out; (*ahuecar*) to hollow out; (*moldear*) to cast; **vaciarse** *vr* to empty
vacilar [baθi'lar] *vi* to be unsteady; (*al hablar*) to falter; (*dudar*) to hesitate, waver; (*memoria*) to fail
vacío, -a [ba'θio, a] *adj* empty; (*puesto*) vacant; (*desocupado*) idle; (*vano*) vain ▷ *nm* emptiness; (*Física*) vacuum; (*un vacío*) (empty) space
vacuna [ba'kuna] *nf* vaccine; **vacunar** *vt* to vaccinate
vacuno, -a [ba'kuno, a] *adj* cow *cpd*; **ganado ~** cattle
vadear [baðe'ar] *vt* (*río*) to ford; **vado** *nm* ford
vagabundo, -a [baɣa'βundo, a] *adj* wandering ▷ *nm* tramp
vagancia [ba'ɣanθja] *nf* (*pereza*) idleness, laziness
vagar [ba'ɣar] *vi* to wander; (*no hacer nada*) to idle
vagina [ba'xina] *nf* vagina
vago, -a ['baɣo, a] *adj* vague; (*perezoso*) lazy ▷ *nm/f* (*vagabundo*) tramp; (*flojo*) lazybones *sg*, idler
vagón [ba'ɣon] *nm* (*Ferro*: *de pasajeros*) carriage; (: *de mercancías*) wagon
vaho ['bao] *nm* (*vapor*) vapour, steam; (*respiración*) breath
vaina ['baina] *nf* sheath
vainilla [bai'niʎa] *nf* vanilla
vais *vb V* **ir**
vaivén [bai'βen] *nm* to-and-fro

movement; (*de tránsito*) coming and going; **vaivenes** *nmpl* (*fig*) ups and downs

vajilla [ba'xiʎa] *nf* crockery, dishes *pl*; (*juego*) service, set

valdré *etc vb V* **valer**

vale ['bale] *nm* voucher; (*recibo*) receipt; (*pagaré*) IOU

valedero, -a [bale'ðero, a] *adj* valid

valenciano, -a [balen'θjano, a] *adj* Valencian

valentía [balen'tia] *nf* courage, bravery

valer [ba'ler] *vt* to be worth; (*Mat*) to equal; (*costar*) to cost ▷*vi* (*ser útil*) to be useful; (*ser válido*) to be valid; **valerse** *vr* to take care of oneself; **~se de** to make use of, take advantage of; **~ la pena** to be worthwhile; **¿vale?** (ESP) OK?; **más vale que nos vayamos** we'd better go; **¡eso a mí no me vale!** (MÉX: *fam: no importar*) I couldn't care less about that

valeroso, -a [bale'roso, a] *adj* brave, valiant

valgo *etc vb V* **valer**

valía [ba'lia] *nf* worth, value

validar [bali'ðar] *vt* to validate; **validez** *nf* validity; **válido, -a** *adj* valid

valiente [ba'ljente] *adj* brave, valiant ▷*nm* hero

valija [ba'lixa] (CS) *nf* (suit)case

valioso, -a [ba'ljoso, a] *adj* valuable

valla ['baʎa] *nf* fence; (*Deporte*) hurdle; **valla publicitaria** hoarding; **vallar** *vt* to fence in

valle ['baʎe] *nm* valley

valor [ba'lor] *nm* value, worth; (*precio*) price; (*valentía*) valour, courage; (*importancia*) importance; **valores** *nmpl* (*Com*) securities; **valorar** *vt* to value

vals [bals] *nm inv* waltz

válvula ['balβula] *nf* valve

vamos *vb V* **ir**

vampiro, -resa [bam'piro, 'resa] *nm/f* vampire

van *vb V* **ir**

vanguardia [ban'gwardja] *nf* vanguard; (*Arte etc*) avant-garde

vanidad [bani'ðað] *nf* vanity; **vanidoso, -a** *adj* vain, conceited

vano, -a ['bano, a] *adj* vain

vapor [ba'por] *nm* vapour; (*vaho*) steam; **al ~** (*Culin*) steamed; **vapor de agua** water vapour; **vaporizador** *nm* atomizer; **vaporizar** *vt* to vaporize; **vaporoso, -a** *adj* vaporous

vaquero, -a [ba'kero, a] *adj* cattle *cpd* ▷*nm* cowboy; **vaqueros** *nmpl* (*pantalones*) jeans

vaquilla [ba'kiʎa] *nf* (*Zool*) heifer

vara ['bara] *nf* stick; (*Tec*) rod

variable [ba'rjaβle] *adj, nf* variable

variación [baria'θjon] *nf* variation

variar [bar'jar] *vt* to vary; (*modificar*) to modify; (*cambiar de posición*) to switch around ▷*vi* to vary

varicela [bari'θela] *nf* chickenpox

varices [ba'riθes] *nfpl* varicose veins

variedad [barje'ðað] *nf* variety

varilla [ba'riʎa] *nf* stick; (*Bot*) twig; (*Tec*) rod; (*de rueda*) spoke

vario, -a ['barjo, a] *adj* varied; **~s** various, several

varita [ba'rita] *nf* (*tb*: **~ mágica**) magic wand

varón [ba'ron] *nm* male, man; **varonil** *adj* manly, virile

Varsovia [bar'soβja] *n* Warsaw

vas *vb V* **ir**

vasco, -a ['basko, a] *adj, nm/f* Basque; **vascongado, -a** [baskon'gaðo, a] *adj* Basque; **las Vascongadas** the Basque Country

vaselina [base'lina] *nf* Vaseline®

vasija [ba'sixa] *nf* container, vessel

vaso ['baso] *nm* glass, tumbler; (*Anat*) vessel

> No confundir **vaso** con la palabra inglesa *vase*.

vástago ['bastaɣo] *nm* (*Bot*) shoot; (*Tec*) rod; (*fig*) offspring

vasto, -a ['basto, a] *adj* vast, huge

Vaticano [bati'kano] *nm*: **el ~** the Vatican

vatio ['batjo] *nm* (*Elec*) watt

vaya *etc vb V* **ir**

Vd(s) *abr* = **usted(es)**

ve [be] *vb V* **ir; ver**

vecindad [beθin'dað] *nf* neighbourhood; (*habitantes*) residents *pl*

vecindario [beθin'darjo] *nm* neighbourhood; residents *pl*

vecino, -a [be'θino, a] *adj* neighbouring ▷*nm/f* neighbour; (*residente*) resident

veda ['beða] *nf* prohibition; **vedar** [be'ðar] *vt* (*prohibir*) to ban, prohibit; (*impedir*) to stop, prevent

vegetación [bexeta'θjon] *nf* vegetation

vegetal [bexe'tal] *adj, nm* vegetable

vegetariano, -a [bexeta'rjano, a] *adj, nm/f* vegetarian

vehículo [be'ikulo] *nm* vehicle; (*Med*) carrier

veía *etc vb V* **ver**

veinte ['beinte] *num* twenty

vejar [be'xar] *vt* (*irritar*) to annoy, vex; (*humillar*) to humiliate

vejez [be'xeθ] *nf* old age

vejiga [be'xiɣa] *nf* (*Anat*) bladder

vela ['bela] *nf* (*de cera*) candle; (*Náut*) sail; (*insomnio*) sleeplessness; (*vigilia*) vigil; (*Mil*) sentry duty; **estar a dos ~s** (*fam*: *sin dinero*) to be skint
velado, -a [be'laðo, a] *adj* veiled; (*sonido*) muffled; (*Foto*) blurred ▷ *nf* soirée
velar [be'lar] *vt* (*vigilar*) to keep watch over ▷ *vi* to stay awake; **~ por** to watch over, look after
velatorio [bela'torjo] *nm* (funeral) wake
velero [be'lero] *nm* (*Náut*) sailing ship; (*Aviac*) glider
veleta [be'leta] *nf* weather vane
veliz [be'lis] (*MÉX*) *nm* (suit)case
vello ['beʎo] *nm* down, fuzz
velo ['belo] *nm* veil
velocidad [beloθi'ðað] *nf* speed; (*Tec, Auto*) gear
velocímetro [belo'θimetro] *nm* speedometer
velorio [be'lorjo] (*LAM*) *nm* (funeral) wake
veloz [be'loθ] *adj* fast
ven *vb V* **venir**
vena ['bena] *nf* vein
venado [be'naðo] *nm* deer
vencedor, a [benθe'ðor, a] *adj* victorious ▷ *nm/f* victor, winner
vencer [ben'θer] *vt* (*dominar*) to defeat, beat; (*derrotar*) to vanquish; (*superar, controlar*) to overcome, master ▷ *vi* (*triunfar*) to win (through), triumph; (*plazo*) to expire; **vencido, -a** *adj* (*derrotado*) defeated, beaten; (*Com*) due ▷ *adv*: **pagar vencido** to pay in arrears
venda ['benda] *nf* bandage; **vendaje** *nm* bandage, dressing; **vendar** *vt* to bandage; **vendar los ojos** to blindfold
vendaval [benda'βal] *nm* (*viento*) gale
vendedor, a [bende'ðor, a] *nm/f* seller
vender [ben'der] *vt* to sell; **venderse** *vr* (*estar a la venta*) to be on sale; **~ al contado/al por mayor/al por menor** to sell for cash/wholesale/retail; **"se vende"** "for sale"
vendimia [ben'dimja] *nf* grape harvest
vendré *etc vb V* **venir**
veneno [be'neno] *nm* poison; (*de serpiente*) venom; **venenoso, -a** *adj* poisonous; venomous
venerable [bene'raβle] *adj* venerable; **venerar** *vt* (*respetar*) to revere; (*adorar*) to worship
venéreo, -a [be'nereo, a] *adj*: **enfermedad venérea** venereal disease
venezolano, -a [beneθo'lano, a] *adj* Venezuelan
Venezuela [bene'θwela] *nf* Venezuela
venganza [ben'ganθa] *nf* vengeance, revenge; **vengar** *vt* to avenge; **vengarse** *vr* to take revenge; **vengativo, -a** *adj* (*persona*) vindictive
vengo *etc vb V* **venir**
venia ['benja] *nf* (*perdón*) pardon; (*permiso*) consent
venial [be'njal] *adj* venial
venida [be'niða] *nf* (*llegada*) arrival; (*regreso*) return
venidero, -a [beni'ðero, a] *adj* coming, future
venir [be'nir] *vi* to come; (*llegar*) to arrive; (*ocurrir*) to happen; (*fig*): **~ de** to stem from; **~ bien/mal** to be suitable/unsuitable; **el año que viene** next year; **~se abajo** to collapse
venta ['benta] *nf* (*Com*) sale; **"en ~"** "for sale"; **estar a la** *o* **en ~** to be (up) for sale *o* on the market; **venta a domicilio** door-to-door selling; **venta a plazos** hire purchase; **venta al contado/al por mayor/al por menor** cash sale/wholesale/retail
ventaja [ben'taxa] *nf* advantage; **ventajoso, -a** *adj* advantageous
ventana [ben'tana] *nf* window; **ventanilla** *nf* (*de taquilla*) window (*of booking office etc*)
ventilación [bentila'θjon] *nf* ventilation; (*corriente*) draught
ventilador [bentila'ðor] *nm* fan
ventilar [benti'lar] *vt* to ventilate; (*para secar*) to put out to dry; (*asunto*) to air, discuss
ventisca [ben'tiska] *nf* blizzard
ventrílocuo, -a [ben'trilokwo, a] *nm/f* ventriloquist
ventura [ben'tura] *nf* (*felicidad*) happiness; (*buena suerte*) luck; (*destino*) fortune; **a la (buena) ~** at random; **venturoso, -a** *adj* happy; (*afortunado*) lucky, fortunate
veo *etc vb V* **ver**
ver [ber] *vt* to see; (*mirar*) to look at, watch; (*entender*) to understand; (*investigar*) to look into ▷ *vi* to see; to understand; **verse** *vr* (*encontrarse*) to meet; (*dejarse ver*) to be seen; (*hallarse*: *en un apuro*) to find o.s., be; **(vamos) a ~** let's see; **no tener nada que ~ con** to have nothing to do with; **a mi modo de ~** as I see it; **ya ~emos** we'll see
vera ['bera] *nf* edge, verge; (*de río*) bank
veranear [berane'ar] *vi* to spend the summer; **veraneo** *nm* summer holiday; **veraniego, -a** *adj* summer *cpd*
verano [be'rano] *nm* summer
veras ['beras] *nfpl* truth *sg*; **de ~** really, truly
verbal [ber'βal] *adj* verbal
verbena [ber'βena] *nf* (*baile*) open-air dance

V

verbo ['berβo] *nm* verb
verdad [ber'ðað] *nf* truth; (*fiabilidad*) reliability; **de ~** real, proper; **a decir ~** to tell the truth; **verdadero, -a** *adj* (*veraz*) true, truthful; (*fiable*) reliable; (*fig*) real
verde ['berðe] *adj* green; (*chiste*) blue, dirty ▷*nm* green; **viejo ~** dirty old man; **verdear** *vi* to turn green; **verdor** *nm* greenness
verdugo [ber'ðuɣo] *nm* executioner
verdulero, -a [berðu'lero, a] *nm/f* greengrocer
verduras [ber'ðuras] *nfpl* (*Culin*) greens
vereda [be'reða] *nf* path; (cs: *acera*) pavement (BRIT), sidewalk (US)
veredicto [bere'ðikto] *nm* verdict
vergonzoso, -a [berɣon'θoso, a] *adj* shameful; (*tímido*) timid, bashful
vergüenza [ber'ɣwenθa] *nf* shame, sense of shame; (*timidez*) bashfulness; (*pudor*) modesty; **me da ~** I'm ashamed
verídico, -a [be'riðiko, a] *adj* true, truthful
verificar [berifi'kar] *vt* to check; (*corroborar*) to verify; (*llevar a cabo*) to carry out; **verificarse** *vr* (*predicción*) to prove to be true
verja ['berxa] *nf* (*cancela*) iron gate; (*valla*) iron railings *pl*; (*de ventana*) grille
vermut [ber'mut] (*pl* **~s**) *nm* vermouth
verosímil [bero'simil] *adj* likely, probable; (*relato*) credible
verruga [be'rruɣa] *nf* wart
versátil [ber'satil] *adj* versatile
versión [ber'sjon] *nf* version
verso ['berso] *nm* verse; **un ~** a line of poetry
vértebra ['berteβra] *nf* vertebra
verter [ber'ter] *vt* (*líquido: adrede*) to empty, pour (out); (*: sin querer*) to spill; (*basura*) to dump ▷*vi* to flow
vertical [berti'kal] *adj* vertical
vértice ['bertiθe] *nm* vertex, apex
vertidos [ber'tiðos] *nmpl* waste *sg*
vertiente [ber'tjente] *nf* slope; (*fig*) aspect
vértigo ['bertiɣo] *nm* vertigo; (*mareo*) dizziness
vesícula [be'sikula] *nf* blister
vespino® [bes'pino] *nm o nf* moped
vestíbulo [bes'tiβulo] *nm* hall; (*de teatro*) foyer
vestido [bes'tiðo] *nm* (*ropa*) clothes *pl*, clothing; (*de mujer*) dress, frock ▷*pp de* **vestir**; **~ de azul/marinero** dressed in blue/as a sailor
vestidor [besti'ðor] (MÉX) *nm* (*Deporte*) changing (BRIT) *o* locker (US) room
vestimenta [besti'menta] *nf* clothing
vestir [bes'tir] *vt* (*poner: ropa*) to put on; (*llevar: ropa*) to wear; (*proveer de ropa a*) to clothe; (*sastre*) to make clothes for ▷*vi* to dress; (*verse bien*) to look good; **vestirse** *vr* to get dressed, dress o.s.
vestuario [bes'twarjo] *nm* clothes *pl*, wardrobe; (*Teatro: cuarto*) dressing room; (*Deporte*) changing (BRIT) *o* locker (US) room
vetar [be'tar] *vt* to veto
veterano, -a [bete'rano, a] *adj, nm* veteran
veterinaria [beteri'narja] *nf* veterinary science; *V tb* **veterinario**
veterinario, -a [beteri'narjo, a] *nm/f* vet(erinary surgeon)
veto ['beto] *nm* veto
vez [beθ] *nf* time; (*turno*) turn; **a la ~ que** at the same time as; **a su ~** in its turn; **otra ~** again; **una ~** once; **de una ~** in one go; **de una ~ para siempre** once and for all; **en ~ de** instead of; **a** *o* **algunas veces** sometimes; **una y otra ~** repeatedly; **de ~ en cuando** from time to time; **7 veces 9** 7 times 9; **hacer las veces de** to stand in for; **tal ~** perhaps
vía ['bia] *nf* track, route; (*Ferro*) line; (*fig*) way; (*Anat*) passage, tube ▷*prep* via, by way of; **por ~ judicial** by legal means; **en ~s de** in the process of; **vía aérea** airway; **Vía Láctea** Milky Way; **vía pública** public road *o* thoroughfare
viable ['bjaβle] *adj* (*solución, plan, alternativa*) feasible
viaducto [bja'ðukto] *nm* viaduct
viajante [bja'xante] *nm* commercial traveller
viajar [bja'xar] *vi* to travel; **viaje** *nm* journey; (*gira*) tour; (*Náut*) voyage; **estar de viaje** to be on a trip; **viaje de ida y vuelta** round trip; **viaje de novios** honeymoon; **viajero, -a** *adj* travelling; (*Zool*) migratory ▷*nm/f* (*quien viaja*) traveller; (*pasajero*) passenger
víbora ['biβora] *nf* (*Zool*) viper; (: (MÉX: *venenoso*) poisonous snake
vibración [biβra'θjon] *nf* vibration
vibrar [bi'βrar] *vt, vi* to vibrate
vicepresidente [biθepresi'ðente] *nmf* vice-president
viceversa [biθe'βersa] *adv* vice versa
vicio ['biθjo] *nm* vice; (*mala costumbre*) bad habit; **vicioso, -a** *adj* (*muy malo*) vicious; (*corrompido*) depraved ▷*nm/f* depraved person
víctima ['biktima] *nf* victim
victoria [bik'torja] *nf* victory; **victorioso, -a** *adj* victorious
vid [bið] *nf* vine
vida ['biða] *nf* (*gen*) life; (*duración*) lifetime;

de por ~ for life; **en la** *o* **mi ~** never; **estar con ~** to be still alive; **ganarse la ~** to earn one's living

vídeo ['biðeo] *nm* video ▷ *adj inv*: **película de ~** video film; **videocámara** *nf* camcorder; **videocasete** *nm* video cassette, videotape; **videoclub** *nm* video club; **videojuego** *nm* video game; **videollamada** *nf* video call; **videoteléfono** *nf* videophone

vidrio ['biðrjo] *nm* glass

vieira ['bjeira] *nf* scallop

viejo, -a ['bjexo, a] *adj* old ▷ *nm/f* old man/woman; **hacerse ~** to get old

Viena ['bjena] *n* Vienna

vienes *etc vb V* **venir**

vienés, -esa [bje'nes, esa] *adj* Viennese

viento ['bjento] *nm* wind; **hacer ~** to be windy

vientre ['bjentre] *nm* belly; (*matriz*) womb

viernes ['bjernes] *nm inv* Friday; **Viernes Santo** Good Friday

Vietnam [bjet'nam] *nm* Vietnam; **vietnamita** *adj* Vietnamese

viga ['biɣa] *nf* beam, rafter; (*de metal*) girder

vigencia [bi'xenθja] *nf* validity; **estar en ~** to be in force; **vigente** *adj* valid, in force; (*imperante*) prevailing

vigésimo, -a [bi'xesimo, a] *adj* twentieth

vigía [bi'xia] *nm* look-out

vigilancia [bixi'lanθja] *nf*: **tener a algn bajo ~** to keep watch on sb

vigilar [bixi'lar] *vt* to watch over ▷ *vi* (*gen*) to be vigilant; (*hacer guardia*) to keep watch; **~ por** to take care of

vigilia [vi'xilja] *nf* wakefulness, being awake; (*Rel*) fast

vigor [bi'ɣor] *nm* vigour, vitality; **en ~** in force; **entrar/poner en ~** to come/put into effect; **vigoroso, -a** *adj* vigorous

VIH *nm abr* (= *virus de la inmunodeficiencia humana*) HIV; **VIH negativo/positivo** HIV-negative/-positive

vil [bil] *adj* vile, low

villa ['biʎa] *nf* (*casa*) villa; (*pueblo*) small town; (*municipalidad*) municipality

villancico [biʎan'θiko] *nm* (Christmas) carol

vilo ['bilo]: **en ~** *adv* in the air, suspended; (*fig*) on tenterhooks, in suspense

vinagre [bi'naɣre] *nm* vinegar

vinagreta [bina'ɣreta] *nf* vinaigrette, French dressing

vinculación [binkula'θjon] *nf* (*lazo*) link, bond; (*acción*) linking

vincular [binku'lar] *vt* to link, bind; **vínculo** *nm* link, bond

vine *etc vb V* **venir**

vinicultura [binikul'tura] *nf* wine growing

viniera *etc vb V* **venir**

vino ['bino] *vb V* **venir** ▷ *nm* wine; **vino blanco/tinto** white/red wine

viña ['biɲa] *nf* vineyard; **viñedo** *nm* vineyard

viola ['bjola] *nf* viola

violación [bjola'θjon] *nf* violation; (*sexual*) rape

violar [bjo'lar] *vt* to violate; (*sexualmente*) to rape

violencia [bjo'lenθja] *nf* violence, force; (*incomodidad*) embarrassment; (*acto injusto*) unjust act; **violentar** *vt* to force; (*casa*) to break into; (*agredir*) to assault; (*violar*) to violate; **violento, -a** *adj* violent; (*furioso*) furious; (*situación*) embarrassing; (*acto*) forced, unnatural

violeta [bjo'leta] *nf* violet

violín [bjo'lin] *nm* violin

violón [bjo'lon] *nm* double bass

virar [bi'rar] *vi* to change direction

virgen ['birxen] *adj, nf* virgin

Virgo ['birɣo] *nm* Virgo

viril [bi'ril] *adj* virile; **virilidad** *nf* virility

virtud [bir'tuð] *nf* virtue; **en ~ de** by virtue of; **virtuoso, -a** *adj* virtuous ▷ *nm/f* virtuoso

viruela [bi'rwela] *nf* smallpox

virulento, -a [biru'lento, a] *adj* virulent

virus ['birus] *nm inv* virus

visa ['bisa] (LAM) *nf* = **visado**

visado [bi'saðo] (ESP) *nm* visa

víscera ['bisθera] *nf* (*Anat, Zool*) gut, bowel; **vísceras** *nfpl* entrails

visceral [bisθe'ral] *adj* (*odio*) intense; **reacción ~** gut reaction

visera [bi'sera] *nf* visor

visibilidad [bisiβili'ðað] *nf* visibility; **visible** *adj* visible; (*fig*) obvious

visillos [bi'siʎos] *nmpl* lace curtains

visión [bi'sjon] *nf* (*Anat*) vision, (eye)sight; (*fantasía*) vision, fantasy

visita [bi'sita] *nf* call, visit; (*persona*) visitor; **hacer una ~** to pay a visit; **visitar** [bisi'tar] *vt* to visit, call on

visón [bi'son] *nm* mink

visor [bi'sor] *nm* (*Foto*) viewfinder

víspera ['bispera] *nf*: **la ~ de ...** the day before ...

vista ['bista] *nf* sight, vision; (*capacidad de ver*) (eye)sight; (*mirada*) look(s) (*pl*); **a primera ~** at first glance; **hacer la ~ gorda** to turn a blind eye; **volver la ~** to look back; **está a la ~ que** it's obvious that; **en ~ de** in

view of; **en ~ de que** in view of the fact that; **¡hasta la ~!** so long!, see you!; **con ~s a** with a view to; **vistazo** *nm* glance; **dar** *o* **echar un vistazo a** to glance at
visto, -a ['bisto, a] *pp de* **ver** ▷ *vb V tb* **vestir** ▷ *adj* seen; (*considerado*) considered ▷ *nm*: **~ bueno** approval; **por lo ~** apparently; **está ~ que** it's clear that; **está bien/mal ~** it's acceptable/unacceptable; **~ que** since, considering that
vistoso, -a [bis'toso, a] *adj* colourful
visual [bi'swal] *adj* visual
vital [bi'tal] *adj* life *cpd*, living *cpd*; (*fig*) vital; (*persona*) lively, vivacious; **vitalicio, -a** *adj* for life; **vitalidad** *nf* (*de persona, negocio*) energy; (*de ciudad*) liveliness
vitamina [bita'mina] *nf* vitamin
vitorear [bitore'ar] *vt* to cheer, acclaim
vitrina [bi'trina] *nf* show case; (LAM: *escaparate*) shop window
viudo, -a ['bjuðo, a] *nm/f* widower/widow
viva ['biβa] *excl* hurrah!; **¡~ el rey!** long live the king!
vivaracho, -a [biβa'ratʃo, a] *adj* jaunty, lively; (*ojos*) bright, twinkling
vivaz [bi'βaθ] *adj* lively
víveres ['biβeres] *nmpl* provisions
vivero [bi'βero] *nm* (*para plantas*) nursery; (*para peces*) fish farm; (*fig*) hotbed
viveza [bi'βeθa] *nf* liveliness; (*agudeza*: *mental*) sharpness
vivienda [bi'βjenda] *nf* housing; (*una vivienda*) house; (*piso*) flat (BRIT), apartment (US)
viviente [bi'βjente] *adj* living
vivir [bi'βir] *vt, vi* to live ▷ *nm* life, living
vivo, -a ['biβo, a] *adj* living, alive; (*fig*: *descripción*) vivid; (*persona*: *astuto*) smart, clever; **en ~** (*transmisión etc*) live
vocablo [bo'kaβlo] *nm* (*palabra*) word; (*término*) term
vocabulario [bokaβu'larjo] *nm* vocabulary
vocación [boka'θjon] *nf* vocation; **vocacional** (LAM) *nf* ≈ technical college
vocal [bo'kal] *adj* vocal ▷ *nf* vowel; **vocalizar** *vt* to vocalize
vocero [bo'θero] (LAM) *nmf* spokesman/woman
voces ['boθes] *pl de* **voz**
vodka ['boðka] *nm o f* vodka
vol *abr* = **volumen**
volado [bo'laðo] (MÉX) *adv* in a rush, hastily
volador, a [bola'ðor, a] *adj* flying
volandas [bo'landas]: **en ~** *adv* in the air
volante [bo'lante] *adj* flying ▷ *nm* (*de coche*) steering wheel; (*de reloj*) balance
volar [bo'lar] *vt* (*edificio*) to blow up ▷ *vi* to fly
volátil [bo'latil] *adj* volatile
volcán [bol'kan] *nm* volcano; **volcánico, -a** *adj* volcanic
volcar [bol'kar] *vt* to upset, overturn; (*tumbar, derribar*) to knock over; (*vaciar*) to empty out ▷ *vi* to overturn; **volcarse** *vr* to tip over
voleibol [bolei'βol] *nm* volleyball
volqué *etc vb V* **volcar**
voltaje [bol'taxe] *nm* voltage
voltear [bolte'ar] *vt* to turn over; (*volcar*) to turn upside down
voltereta [bolte'reta] *nf* somersault
voltio ['boltjo] *nm* volt
voluble [bo'luβle] *adj* fickle
volumen [bo'lumen] (*pl* **volúmenes**) *nm* volume; **voluminoso, -a** *adj* voluminous; (*enorme*) massive
voluntad [bolun'tað] *nf* will; (*resolución*) willpower; (*deseo*) desire, wish
voluntario, -a [bolun'tarjo, a] *adj* voluntary ▷ *nm/f* volunteer
volver [bol'βer] *vt* (*gen*) to turn; (*dar vuelta a*) to turn (over); (*voltear*) to turn round, turn upside down; (*poner al revés*) to turn inside out; (*devolver*) to return ▷ *vi* to return, go back, come back; **volverse** *vr* to turn round; **~ la espalda** to turn one's back; **~ triste** *etc* **a algn** to make sb sad *etc*; **~ a hacer** to do again; **~ en sí** to come to; **~se insoportable/muy caro** to get *o* become unbearable/very expensive; **~se loco** to go mad
vomitar [bomi'tar] *vt, vi* to vomit; **vómito** *nm* vomit
voraz [bo'raθ] *adj* voracious
vos [bos] (LAM) *pron* you
vosotros, -as [bo'sotros, as] (ESP) *pron* you; (*reflexivo*): **entre/para ~** among/for yourselves
votación [bota'θjon] *nf* (*acto*) voting; (*voto*) vote
votar [bo'tar] *vi* to vote; **voto** *nm* vote; (*promesa*) vow; **votos** *nmpl* (good) wishes
voy *vb V* **ir**
voz [boθ] *nf* voice; (*grito*) shout; (*rumor*) rumour; (*Ling*) word; **dar voces** to shout, yell; **de viva ~** verbally; **en ~ alta** aloud; **en ~ baja** in a low voice, in a whisper; **voz de mando** command
vuelco ['bwelko] *vb V* **volcar** ▷ *nm* spill, overturning
vuelo ['bwelo] *vb V* **volar** ▷ *nm* flight; (*encaje*) lace, frill; **coger al ~** to catch in flight; **vuelo chárter/regular** charter/

scheduled flight; **vuelo libre** (*Deporte*) hang-gliding

vuelque *etc vb V* **volcar**

vuelta ['bwelta] *nf* (*gen*) turn; (*curva*) bend, curve; (*regreso*) return; (*revolución*) revolution; (*de circuito*) lap; (*de papel, tela*) reverse; (*cambio*) change; **a la ~** on one's return; **a la ~ (de la esquina)** round the corner; **a ~ de correo** by return of post; **dar ~s** (*cabeza*) to spin; **dar(se) la ~** (*volverse*) to turn round; **dar ~s a una idea** to turn over an idea (in one's head); **estar de ~** to be back; **dar una ~** to go for a walk; (*en coche*) to go for a drive; **vuelta ciclista** (*Deporte*) (cycle) tour

vuelto ['bwelto] *pp de* **volver**

vuelvo *etc vb V* **volver**

vuestro, -a ['bwestro, a] *adj pos* your; **un amigo ~** a friend of yours ▷ *pron*: **el ~/la vuestra, los ~s/las vuestras** yours

vulgar [bul'ɣar] *adj* (*ordinario*) vulgar; (*común*) common; **vulgaridad** *nf* commonness; (*acto*) vulgarity; (*expresión*) coarse expression

vulnerable [bulne'raβle] *adj* vulnerable

vulnerar [bulne'rar] *vt* (*ley, acuerdo*) to violate, breach; (*derechos, intimidad*) to violate; (*reputación*) to damage

walkie-talkie [walki-'talki] (*pl* **~s**) *nm* walkie-talkie

Walkman® ['walkman] *nm* Walkman®

wáter ['bater] *nm* (*taza*) toilet; (*LAM*: *lugar*) toilet (BRIT), rest room (US)

web [web] *nm o f* (*página*) website; (*red*) (World Wide) Web; **webcam** *nf* webcam; **webmaster** *nmf* webmaster; **website** *nm* website

western ['western] (*pl* **~s**) *nm* western

whisky ['wiski] *nm* whisky, whiskey

windsurf ['winsurf] *nm* windsurfing; **hacer ~** to go windsurfing

X

Y

xenofobia [kseno'foβja] *nf* xenophobia
xilófono [ksi'lofono] *nm* xylophone
xocoyote, -a [ksoko'yote, a] (MÉX) *nm/f* baby of the family, youngest child

y [i] *conj* and
ya [ja] *adv* (*gen*) already; (*ahora*) now; (*en seguida*) at once; (*pronto*) soon ▷ *excl* all right! ▷ *conj* (*ahora que*) now that; **~ lo sé** I know; **~ que ...** since; **¡~ está bien!** that's (quite) enough!; **¡~ voy!** coming!
yacaré [jaka're] (CS) *nm* cayman
yacer [ja'θer] *vi* to lie
yacimiento [jaθi'mjento] *nm* (*de mineral*) deposit; (*arqueológico*) site
yanqui ['janki] *adj, nmf* Yankee
yate ['jate] *nm* yacht
yazco *etc vb V* **yacer**
yedra ['jeðra] *nf* ivy
yegua ['jeɣwa] *nf* mare
yema ['jema] *nf* (*del huevo*) yolk; (*Bot*) leaf bud; (*fig*) best part; **yema del dedo** fingertip
yerno ['jerno] *nm* son-in-law
yeso ['jeso] *nm* plaster
yo [jo] *pron* I; **soy ~** it's me
yodo ['joðo] *nm* iodine
yoga ['joɣa] *nm* yoga
yogur(t) [jo'ɣur(t)] *nm* yoghurt
yuca ['juka] *nf* (*alimento*) cassava, manioc root
Yugoslavia [juɣos'laβja] *nf* (*Hist*) Yugoslavia
yugular [juɣu'lar] *adj* jugular
yunque ['junke] *nm* anvil
yuyo ['jujo] (RPL) *nm* (*mala hierba*) weed

Z

zafar [θa'far] *vt* (*soltar*) to untie; (*superficie*) to clear; **zafarse** *vr* (*escaparse*) to escape; (*Tec*) to slip off
zafiro [θa'firo] *nm* sapphire
zaga ['θaɣa] *nf*: **a la ~** behind
zaguán [θa'ɣwan] *nm* hallway
zalamero, -a [θala'mero, a] *adj* flattering; (*cobista*) suave
zamarra [θa'marra] *nf* (*chaqueta*) sheepskin jacket
zambullirse [θambu'ʎirse] *vr* to dive
zampar [θam'par] *vt* to gobble down
zanahoria [θana'orja] *nf* carrot
zancadilla [θanka'ðiʎa] *nf* trip
zanco ['θanko] *nm* stilt
zanja ['θanxa] *nf* ditch; **zanjar** *vt* (*resolver*) to resolve
zapata [θa'pata] *nf* (*Mecánica*) shoe
zapatería [θapate'ria] *nf* (*oficio*) shoemaking; (*tienda*) shoe shop; (*fábrica*) shoe factory; **zapatero, -a** *nm/f* shoemaker
zapatilla [θapa'tiʎa] *nf* slipper; **zapatilla de deporte** training shoe
zapato [θa'pato] *nm* shoe
zapping ['θapin] *nm* channel-hopping; **hacer ~** to channel-hop
zar [θar] *nm* tsar, czar
zarandear [θaranðe'ar] (*fam*) *vt* to shake vigorously
zarpa ['θarpa] *nf* (*garra*) claw
zarpar [θar'par] *vi* to weigh anchor
zarza ['θarθa] *nf* (*Bot*) bramble; **zarzamora** *nf* blackberry
zarzuela [θar'θwela] *nf Spanish light opera*
zigzag [θiɣ'θaɣ] *nm* zigzag
zinc [θink] *nm* zinc
zíper ['θiper] (*MÉX, CAM*) *nm* zip (fastener) (*BRIT*), zipper (*US*)
zócalo ['θokalo] *nm* (*Arq*) plinth, base; (*de pared*) skirting board (*BRIT*), baseboard (*US*); (*MÉX*: *plaza*) main *o* public square
zoclo ['θoklo] (*MÉX*) *nm* skirting board (*BRIT*), baseboard (*US*)
zodíaco [θo'ðiako] *nm* zodiac
zona ['θona] *nf* zone; **zona fronteriza** border area; **zona roja** (*LAM*) red-light district
zonzo, -a (*LAM*: *fam*) ['θonθo, a] *adj* silly ▷ *nm/f* fool
zoo ['θoo] *nm* zoo
zoología [θoolo'xia] *nf* zoology; **zoológico, -a** *adj* zoological ▷ *nm* (*tb*: **parque zoológico**) zoo; **zoólogo, -a** *nm/f* zoologist
zoom [θum] *nm* zoom lens
zopilote [θopi'lote] (*MÉX, CAM*) *nm* buzzard
zoquete [θo'kete] *nm* (*fam*) blockhead
zorro, -a ['θorro, a] *adj* crafty ▷ *nm/f* fox/vixen
zozobrar [θoθo'βrar] *vi* (*hundirse*) to capsize; (*fig*) to fail
zueco ['θweko] *nm* clog
zumbar [θum'bar] *vt* (*golpear*) to hit ▷ *vi* to buzz; **zumbido** *nm* buzzing
zumo ['θumo] *nm* juice
zurcir [θur'θir] *vt* (*coser*) to darn
zurdo, -a ['θurðo, a] *adj* left-handed
zurrar [θu'rrar] (*fam*) *vt* to wallop

a

A [eɪ] *n* (*Mus*) la *m*

KEYWORD

a [ə] (*before vowel or silent h: an*) *indef art*
1 un(a); **a book** un libro; **an apple** una manzana; **she's a doctor** (ella) es médica
2 (*instead of the number "one"*) un(a); **a year ago** hace un año; **a hundred/thousand** *etc* **pounds** cien/mil *etc* libras
3 (*in expressing ratios, prices etc*): **3 a day/ week** 3 al día/a la semana; **10 km an hour** 10 km por hora; **£5 a person** £5 por persona; **30p a kilo** 30p el kilo

A2 (BRIT: *Scol*) *n segunda parte de los "A levels"*
A.A. *n abbr* (BRIT: = *Automobile Association*) ≈ RACE *m* (SP); (= *Alcoholics Anonymous*) Alcohólicos Anónimos
A.A.A. (US) *n abbr* (= *American Automobile Association*) ≈ RACE *m* (SP)
aback [ə'bæk] *adv*: **to be taken ~** quedar desconcertado
abandon [ə'bændən] *vt* abandonar; (*give up*) renunciar a
abattoir ['æbətwɑː*] (BRIT) *n* matadero
abbey ['æbɪ] *n* abadía
abbreviation [əbriːvɪ'eɪʃən] *n* (*short form*) abreviatura
abdomen ['æbdəmən] *n* abdomen *m*
abduct [æb'dʌkt] *vt* raptar, secuestrar
abide [ə'baɪd] *vt*: **I can't ~ it/him** no lo/le puedo ver; **abide by** *vt fus* atenerse a
ability [ə'bɪlɪtɪ] *n* habilidad *f*, capacidad *f*; (*talent*) talento
able ['eɪbl] *adj* capaz; (*skilled*) hábil; **to be ~ to do sth** poder hacer algo
abnormal [æb'nɔːməl] *adj* anormal
aboard [ə'bɔːd] *adv* a bordo ▷ *prep* a bordo de
abolish [ə'bɔlɪʃ] *vt* suprimir, abolir
abolition [æbəu'lɪʃən] *n* supresión *f*, abolición *f*
abort [ə'bɔːt] *vt*, *vi* abortar; **abortion** [ə'bɔːʃən] *n* aborto; **to have an abortion** abortar, hacerse abortar

KEYWORD

about [ə'baut] *adv* **1** (*approximately*) más o menos, aproximadamente; **about a hundred/thousand** *etc* unos(unas) cien/ mil *etc*; **it takes about 10 hours** se tarda unas *or* más o menos 10 horas; **at about 2 o'clock** sobre las dos; **I've just about finished** casi he terminado
2 (*referring to place*) por todas partes; **to leave things lying about** dejar las cosas (tiradas) por ahí; **to run about** correr por todas partes; **to walk about** pasearse, ir y venir
3: **to be about to do sth** estar a punto de hacer algo
▷ *prep* **1** (*relating to*) de, sobre, acerca de; **a book about London** un libro sobre *or* acerca de Londres; **what is it about?** ¿de qué se trata?; **we talked about it** hablamos de eso *or* ello; **what** *or* **how about doing this?** ¿qué tal si hacemos esto?
2 (*referring to place*) por; **to walk about the town** caminar por la ciudad

above [ə'bʌv] *adv* encima, por encima, arriba ▷ *prep* encima de; (*greater than*: *in number*) más de; (: *in rank*) superior a; **mentioned ~** susodicho; **~ all** sobre todo
abroad [ə'brɔːd] *adv* (*to be*) en el extranjero; (*to go*) al extranjero
abrupt [ə'brʌpt] *adj* (*sudden*) brusco; (*curt*) áspero
abscess ['æbsɪs] *n* absceso
absence ['æbsəns] *n* ausencia
absent ['æbsənt] *adj* ausente; **absent-minded** *adj* distraído
absolute ['æbsəluːt] *adj* absoluto; **absolutely** [-'luːtlɪ] *adv* (*totally*) totalmente; (*certainly!*) ¡por supuesto (que sí)!
absorb [əb'zɔːb] *vt* absorber; **to be ~ed in a book** estar absorto en un libro; **absorbent cotton** (US) *n* algodón *m* hidrófilo; **absorbing** *adj* absorbente
abstain [əb'steɪn] *vi*: **to ~ (from)** abstenerse (de)
abstract ['æbstrækt] *adj* abstracto
absurd [əb'səːd] *adj* absurdo
abundance [ə'bʌndəns] *n* abundancia
abundant [ə'bʌndənt] *adj* abundante
abuse [*n* ə'bjuːs, *vb* ə'bjuːz] *n* (*insults*)

insultos *mpl*, injurias *fpl*; (*ill-treatment*) malos tratos *mpl*; (*misuse*) abuso ▷ *vt* insultar; maltratar; abusar de; **abusive** *adj* ofensivo

abysmal [ə'bɪzməl] *adj* pésimo; (*failure*) garrafal; (*ignorance*) supino

academic [ækə'dɛmɪk] *adj* académico, universitario; (*pej: issue*) puramente teórico ▷ *n* estudioso/a, profesor(a) *m/f* universitario/a; **academic year** *n* (*Univ*) año *m* académico; (*Scol*) año *m* escolar

academy [ə'kædəmɪ] *n* (*learned body*) academia; (*school*) instituto, colegio; **~ of music** conservatorio

accelerate [æk'sɛləreɪt] *vt*, *vi* acelerar; **acceleration** [æksɛlə'reɪʃən] *n* aceleración *f*; **accelerator** (BRIT) *n* acelerador *m*

accent ['æksɛnt] *n* acento; (*fig*) énfasis *m*

accept [ək'sɛpt] *vt* aceptar; (*responsibility, blame*) admitir; **acceptable** *adj* aceptable; **acceptance** *n* aceptación *f*

access ['æksɛs] *n* acceso; **to have ~ to** tener libre acceso a; **accessible** [-'sɛsəbl] *adj* (*place, person*) accesible; (*knowledge etc*) asequible

accessory [æk'sɛsərɪ] *n* accesorio; (*Law*): **~ to** cómplice de

accident ['æksɪdənt] *n* accidente *m*; (*chance event*) casualidad *f*; **by ~** (*unintentionally*) sin querer; (*by chance*) por casualidad; **accidental** [-'dɛntl] *adj* accidental, fortuito; **accidentally** [-'dɛntəlɪ] *adv* sin querer; por casualidad; **Accident and Emergency Department** *n* (BRIT) Urgencias *fpl*; **accident insurance** *n* seguro contra accidentes

acclaim [ə'kleɪm] *vt* aclamar, aplaudir ▷ *n* aclamación *f*, aplausos *mpl*

accommodate [ə'kɔmədeɪt] *vt* (*person*) alojar, hospedar; (*: car, hotel etc*) tener cabida para; (*oblige, help*) complacer

accommodation [əkɔmə'deɪʃən] (US **accommodations**) *n* alojamiento

accompaniment [ə'kʌmpənɪmənt] *n* acompañamiento

accompany [ə'kʌmpənɪ] *vt* acompañar

accomplice [ə'kʌmplɪs] *n* cómplice *mf*

accomplish [ə'kʌmplɪʃ] *vt* (*finish*) concluir; (*achieve*) lograr; **accomplishment** *n* (*skill: gen pl*) talento; (*completion*) realización *f*

accord [ə'kɔ:d] *n* acuerdo ▷ *vt* conceder; **of his own ~** espontáneamente; **accordance** *n*: **in accordance with** de acuerdo con; **according** ▷ **according to** *prep* según; (*in accordance with*) conforme a; **accordingly** *adv* (*appropriately*) de acuerdo con esto; (*as a result*) en consecuencia

account [ə'kaunt] *n* (*Comm*) cuenta; (*report*) informe *m*; **accounts** *npl* (*Comm*) cuentas *fpl*; **of no ~** de ninguna importancia; **on ~** a cuenta; **on no ~** bajo ningún concepto; **on ~ of** a causa de, por motivo de; **to take into ~, take ~ of** tener en cuenta; **account for** *vt fus* (*explain*) explicar; (*represent*) representar; **accountable** *adj*: **accountable (to)** responsable (ante); **accountant** *n* contable *mf*, contador(a) *m/f*; **account number** *n* (*at bank etc*) número de cuenta

accumulate [ə'kju:mjuleɪt] *vt* acumular ▷ *vi* acumularse

accuracy ['ækjurəsɪ] *n* (*of total*) exactitud *f*; (*of description etc*) precisión *f*

accurate ['ækjurɪt] *adj* (*total*) exacto; (*description*) preciso; (*person*) cuidadoso; (*device*) de precisión; **accurately** *adv* con precisión

accusation [ækju'zeɪʃən] *n* acusación *f*

accuse [ə'kju:z] *vt*: **to ~ sb (of sth)** acusar a algn (de algo); **accused** *n* (*Law*) acusado/a

accustomed [ə'kʌstəmd] *adj*: **~ to** acostumbrado a

ace [eɪs] *n* as *m*

ache [eɪk] *n* dolor *m* ▷ *vi* doler; **my head ~s** me duele la cabeza

achieve [ə'tʃi:v] *vt* (*aim, result*) alcanzar; (*success*) lograr, conseguir; **achievement** *n* (*completion*) realización *f*; (*success*) éxito

acid ['æsɪd] *adj* ácido; (*taste*) agrio ▷ *n* (*Chem, inf: LSD*) ácido

acknowledge [ək'nɔlɪdʒ] *vt* (*letter: also*: **~ receipt of**) acusar recibo de; (*fact, situation, person*) reconocer; **acknowledgement** *n* acuse *m* de recibo

acne ['æknɪ] *n* acné *m*

acorn ['eɪkɔ:n] *n* bellota

acoustic [ə'ku:stɪk] *adj* acústico

acquaintance [ə'kweɪntəns] *n* (*person*) conocido/a; (*with person, subject*) conocimiento

acquire [ə'kwaɪə*] *vt* adquirir; **acquisition** [ækwɪ'zɪʃən] *n* adquisición *f*

acquit [ə'kwɪt] *vt* absolver, exculpar; **to ~ o.s. well** salir con éxito

acre ['eɪkə*] *n* acre *m*

acronym ['ækrənɪm] *n* siglas *fpl*

across [ə'krɔs] *prep* (*on the other side of*) al otro lado de, del otro lado de; (*crosswise*) a través de ▷ *adv* de un lado a otro, de una parte a otra; a través, al través; (*measurement*): **the road is 10m ~** la carretera tiene 10m de ancho; **to run/swim ~** atravesar corriendo/nadando; **~ from** enfrente de

acrylic [ə'krɪlɪk] *adj* acrílico ▷ *n* acrílica

act [ækt] *n* acto, acción *f*; (*of play*) acto; (*in music hall etc*) número; (*Law*) decreto, ley *f* ▷ *vi* (*behave*) comportarse; (*have effect: drug, chemical*) hacer efecto; (*Theatre*) actuar; (*pretend*) fingir; (*take action*) obrar ▷ *vt* (*part*) hacer el papel de; **in the ~ of: to catch sb in the ~ of ...** pillar a algn en el momento en que ...; **to ~ as** actuar *or* hacer de; **act up** (*inf*) *vi* (*person*) portarse mal; **acting** *adj* suplente ▷ *n* (*activity*) actuación *f*; (*profession*) profesión *f* de actor

action ['ækʃən] *n* acción *f*, acto; (*Mil*) acción *f*, batalla; (*Law*) proceso, demanda; **out of ~** (*person*) fuera de combate; (*thing*) estropeado; **to take ~** tomar medidas; **action replay** *n* (*TV*) repetición *f*

activate ['æktɪveɪt] *vt* activar

active ['æktɪv] *adj* activo, enérgico; (*volcano*) en actividad; **actively** *adv* (*participate*) activamente; (*discourage, dislike*) enérgicamente

activist ['æktɪvɪst] *n* activista *m/f*

activity [-'tɪvɪtɪ] *n* actividad *f*; **activity holiday** *n vacaciones con actividades organizadas*

actor ['æktə*] *n* actor *m*, actriz *f*

actress ['aektrɪs] *n* actriz *f*

actual ['æktjuəl] *adj* verdadero, real; (*emphatic use*) propiamente dicho

> Be careful not to translate **actual** by the Spanish word *actual*.

actually ['æktjuəlɪ] *adv* realmente, en realidad; (*even*) incluso

> Be careful not to translate **actually** by the Spanish word *actualmente*.

acupuncture ['ækjupʌŋktʃə*] *n* acupuntura

acute [ə'kju:t] *adj* agudo

ad [æd] *n abbr* = **advertisement**

A.D. *adv abbr* (= *anno Domini*) DC

adamant ['ædəmənt] *adj* firme, inflexible

adapt [ə'dæpt] *vt* adaptar ▷ *vi*: **to ~ (to)** adaptarse (a), ajustarse (a); **adapter** (*US* **adaptor**) *n* (*Elec*) adaptador *m*; (*for several plugs*) ladrón *m*

add [æd] *vt* añadir, agregar; **add up** *vt* (*figures*) sumar ▷ *vi* (*fig*): **it doesn't add up** no tiene sentido; **add up to** *vt fus* (*Math*) sumar, ascender a; (*fig: mean*) querer decir, venir a ser

addict ['ædɪkt] *n* adicto/a; (*enthusiast*) entusiasta *mf*; **addicted** [ə'dɪktɪd] *adj*: **to be addicted to** ser adicto a, ser fanático de; **addiction** [ə'dɪkʃən] *n* (*to drugs etc*) adicción *f*; **addictive** [ə'dɪktɪv] *adj* que causa adicción

addition [ə'dɪʃən] *n* (*adding up*) adición *f*; (*thing added*) añadidura, añadido; **in ~** además, por añadidura; **in ~ to** además de; **additional** *adj* adicional

additive ['ædɪtɪv] *n* aditivo

address [ə'drɛs] *n* dirección *f*, señas *fpl*; (*speech*) discurso ▷ *vt* (*letter*) dirigir; (*speak to*) dirigirse a, dirigir la palabra a; (*problem*) tratar; **address book** *n* agenda (de direcciones)

adequate ['ædɪkwɪt] *adj* (*satisfactory*) adecuado; (*enough*) suficiente

adhere [əd'hɪə*] *vi*: **to ~ to** (*stick to*) pegarse a; (*fig: abide by*) observar; (*: belief etc*) ser partidario de

adhesive [əd'hi:zɪv] *n* adhesivo; **adhesive tape** *n* (BRIT) cinta adhesiva; (*US Med*) esparadrapo

adjacent [ə'dʒeɪsənt] *adj*: **~ to** contiguo a, inmediato a

adjective ['ædʒɛktɪv] *n* adjetivo

adjoining [ə'dʒɔɪnɪŋ] *adj* contiguo, vecino

adjourn [ə'dʒə:n] *vt* aplazar ▷ *vi* suspenderse

adjust [ə'dʒʌst] *vt* (*change*) modificar; (*clothing*) arreglar; (*machine*) ajustar ▷ *vi*: **to ~ (to)** adaptarse (a); **adjustable** *adj* ajustable; **adjustment** *n* adaptación *f*; (*to machine, prices*) ajuste *m*

administer [əd'mɪnɪstə*] *vt* administrar; **administration** [-'treɪʃən] *n* (*management*) administración *f*; (*government*) gobierno; **administrative** [-trətɪv] *adj* administrativo

administrator [əd'mɪnɪstreɪtə*] *n* administrador(a) *m/f*

admiral ['ædmərəl] *n* almirante *m*

admiration [ædmə'reɪʃən] *n* admiración *f*

admire [əd'maɪə*] *vt* admirar; **admirer** *n* (*fan*) admirador(a) *m/f*

admission [əd'mɪʃən] *n* (*to university, club*) ingreso; (*entry fee*) entrada; (*confession*) confesión *f*

admit [əd'mɪt] *vt* (*confess*) confesar; (*permit to enter*) dejar entrar, dar entrada a; (*to club, organization*) admitir; (*accept: defeat*) reconocer; **to be ~ted to hospital** ingresar en el hospital; **admit to** *vt fus* confesarse culpable de; **admittance** *n* entrada; **admittedly** *adv* es cierto *or* verdad que

adolescent [ædəu'lɛsnt] *adj, n* adolescente *mf*

adopt [ə'dɔpt] *vt* adoptar; **adopted** *adj* adoptivo; **adoption** [ə'dɔpʃən] *n* adopción *f*

adore [ə'dɔ:*] *vt* adorar

adorn [ə'dɔ:n] *vt* adornar

Adriatic [eɪdrɪ'ætɪk] *n*: **the ~ (Sea)** el (Mar) Adriático

adrift [ə'drɪft] *adv* a la deriva
adult ['ædʌlt] *n* adulto/a ▷ *adj* (*grown-up*) adulto; (*for adults*) para adultos; **adult education** *n* educación *f* para adultos
adultery [ə'dʌltərɪ] *n* adulterio
advance [əd'vɑːns] *n* (*progress*) adelanto, progreso; (*money*) anticipo, préstamo; (*Mil*) avance *m* ▷ *adj*: **~ booking** venta anticipada; **~ notice, ~ warning** previo aviso ▷ *vt* (*money*) anticipar; (*theory, idea*) proponer (para la discusión) ▷ *vi* avanzar, adelantarse; **to make ~s (to sb)** hacer proposiciones (a algn); **in ~** por adelantado; **advanced** *adj* avanzado; (*Scol*: *studies*) adelantado
advantage [əd'vɑːntɪdʒ] *n* (*also Tennis*) ventaja; **to take ~ of** (*person*) aprovecharse de; (*opportunity*) aprovechar
advent ['ædvənt] *n* advenimiento; **A~** Adviento
adventure [əd'vɛntʃə*] *n* aventura; **adventurous** [-tʃərəs] *adj* atrevido; aventurero
adverb ['ædvəːb] *n* adverbio
adversary ['ædvəsərɪ] *n* adversario, contrario
adverse ['ædvəːs] *adj* adverso, contrario
advert ['ædvəːt] (BRIT) *n abbr* = **advertisement**
advertise ['ædvətaɪz] *vi* (*in newspaper etc*) anunciar, hacer publicidad; **to ~ for** (*staff, accommodation etc*) buscar por medio de anuncios ▷ *vt* anunciar; **advertisement** [əd'vəːtɪsmənt] *n* (*Comm*) anuncio; **advertiser** *n* anunciante *mf*; **advertising** *n* publicidad *f*, anuncios *mpl*; (*industry*) industria publicitaria
advice [əd'vaɪs] *n* consejo, consejos *mpl*; (*notification*) aviso; **a piece of ~** un consejo; **to take legal ~** consultar con un abogado
advisable [əd'vaɪzəbl] *adj* aconsejable, conveniente
advise [əd'vaɪz] *vt* aconsejar; (*inform*): **to ~ sb of sth** informar a algn de algo; **to ~ sb against sth/doing sth** desaconsejar algo a algn/aconsejar a algn que no haga algo; **adviser, advisor** *n* consejero/a; (*consultant*) asesor(a) *m/f*; **advisory** *adj* consultivo
advocate [*vb* 'ædvəkeɪt, *n* -kɪt] *vt* abogar por ▷ *n* (*lawyer*) abogado/a; (*supporter*): **~ of** defensor(a) *m/f* de
Aegean [iː'dʒiːən] *n*: **the ~ (Sea)** el (Mar) Egeo
aerial ['ɛərɪəl] *n* antena ▷ *adj* aéreo
aerobics [ɛə'rəubɪks] *n* aerobic *m*
aeroplane ['ɛərəpleɪn] (BRIT) *n* avión *m*
aerosol ['ɛərəsɔl] *n* aerosol *m*
affair [ə'fɛə*] *n* asunto; (*also*: **love ~**) aventura (amorosa)
affect [ə'fɛkt] *vt* (*influence*) afectar, influir en; (*afflict, concern*) afectar; (*move*) conmover; **affected** *adj* afectado; **affection** *n* afecto, cariño; **affectionate** *adj* afectuoso, cariñoso
afflict [ə'flɪkt] *vt* afligir
affluent ['aefluənt] *adj* (*wealthy*) acomodado; **the ~ society** la sociedad opulenta
afford [ə'fɔːd] *vt* (*provide*) proporcionar; **can we ~ (to buy) it?** ¿tenemos bastante dinero para comprarlo?; **affordable** *adj* asequible
Afghanistan [æf'gænɪstæn] *n* Afganistán *m*
afraid [ə'freɪd] *adj*: **to be ~ of** (*person*) tener miedo a; (*thing*) tener miedo de; **to be ~ to** tener miedo de, temer; **I am ~ that** me temo que; **I am ~ not/so** lo siento, pero no/es así
Africa ['æfrɪkə] *n* África; **African** *adj, n* africano/a *m/f*; **African-American** *adj, n* afroamericano/a
after ['ɑːftə*] *prep* (*time*) después de; (*place, order*) detrás de, tras ▷ *adv* después ▷ *conj* después (de) que; **what/who are you ~?** ¿qué/a quién busca usted?; **~ having done/he left** después de haber hecho/después de que se marchó; **to name sb ~ sb** llamar a algn por algn; **it's twenty ~ eight** (US) son las ocho y veinte; **to ask ~ sb** preguntar por algn; **~ all** después de todo, al fin y al cabo; **~ you!** ¡pase usted!; **after-effects** *npl* consecuencias *fpl*, efectos *mpl*; **aftermath** *n* consecuencias *fpl*, resultados *mpl*; **afternoon** *n* tarde *f*; **after-shave (lotion)** *n* aftershave *m*; **aftersun (lotion/cream)** *n* loción *f*/crema para después del sol, aftersun *m*; **afterwards** (US **afterward**) *adv* después, más tarde
again [ə'gɛn] *adv* otra vez, de nuevo; **to do sth ~** volver a hacer algo; **~ and ~** una y otra vez
against [ə'gɛnst] *prep* (*in opposition to*) en contra de; (*leaning on, touching*) contra, junto a
age [eɪdʒ] *n* edad *f*; (*period*) época ▷ *vi* envejecer(se) ▷ *vt* envejecer; **she is 20 years of ~** tiene 20 años; **to come of ~** llegar a la mayoría de edad; **it's been ~s since I saw you** hace siglos que no te veo; **~d 10** de 10 años de edad; **age group** *n*: **to be in the same age group** tener la misma edad; **age limit** *n* edad *f* mínima (*or* máxima)
agency ['eɪdʒənsɪ] *n* agencia
agenda [ə'dʒɛndə] *n* orden *m* del día
Be careful not to translate **agenda** by the

Spanish word *agenda*.
agent ['eɪdʒənt] *n* agente *mf*; (*Comm: holding concession*) representante *mf*, delegado/a; (*Chem, fig*) agente *m*
aggravate ['ægrəveɪt] *vt* (*situation*) agravar; (*person*) irritar
aggression [ə'grɛʃən] *n* agresión *f*
aggressive [ə'grɛsɪv] *adj* (*belligerent*) agresivo; (*assertive*) enérgico
agile ['ædʒaɪl] *adj* ágil
agitated ['ædʒɪteɪtɪd] *adj* agitado
AGM *n abbr* (= *annual general meeting*) asamblea anual
ago [ə'gəu] *adv*: **2 days ~** hace 2 días; **not long ~** hace poco; **how long ~?** ¿hace cuánto tiempo?
agony ['ægənɪ] *n* (*pain*) dolor *m* agudo; (*distress*) angustia; **to be in ~** retorcerse de dolor
agree [ə'gri:] *vt* (*price, date*) acordar, quedar en ▷ *vi* (*have same opinion*): **to ~ (with/that)** estar de acuerdo (con/que); (*correspond*) coincidir, concordar; (*consent*) acceder; **to ~ with** (*person*) estar de acuerdo con, ponerse de acuerdo con; (: *food*) sentar bien a; (*Ling*) concordar con; **to ~ to sth/ to do sth** consentir en algo/aceptar hacer algo; **to ~ that** (*admit*) estar de acuerdo en que; **agreeable** *adj* (*sensation*) agradable; (*person*) simpático; (*willing*) de acuerdo, conforme; **agreed** *adj* (*time, place*) convenido; **agreement** *n* acuerdo; (*contract*) contrato; **in agreement** de acuerdo, conforme
agricultural [ægrɪ'kʌltʃərəl] *adj* agrícola
agriculture ['ægrɪkʌltʃə*] *n* agricultura
ahead [ə'hɛd] *adv* (*in front*) delante; (*into the future*): **she had no time to think ~** no tenía tiempo de hacer planes para el futuro; **~ of** delante de; (*in advance of*) antes de; **~ of time** antes de la hora; **go right** *or* **straight ~** (*direction*) siga adelante; (*permission*) hazlo (*or* hágalo)
aid [eɪd] *n* ayuda, auxilio; (*device*) aparato ▷ *vt* ayudar, auxiliar; **in ~ of** a beneficio de
aide [eɪd] *n* (*person, also Mil*) ayudante *mf*
AIDS [eɪdz] *n abbr* (= *acquired immune deficiency syndrome*) SIDA *m*
ailing ['eɪlɪŋ] *adj* (*person, economy*) enfermizo
ailment ['eɪlmənt] *n* enfermedad *f*, achaque *m*
aim [eɪm] *vt* (*gun, camera*) apuntar; (*missile, remark*) dirigir; (*blow*) asestar ▷ *vi* (*also*: **take ~**) apuntar ▷ *n* (*in shooting: skill*) puntería; (*objective*) propósito, meta; **to ~ at** (*with weapon*) apuntar a; (*objective*) aspirar a, pretender; **to ~ to do** tener la intención de hacer
ain't [eɪnt] (*inf*) = **am not; aren't; isn't**
air [ɛə*] *n* aire *m*; (*appearance*) aspecto ▷ *vt* (*room*) ventilar; (*clothes, ideas*) airear ▷ *cpd* aéreo; **to throw sth into the ~** (*ball etc*) lanzar algo al aire; **by ~** (*travel*) en avión; **to be on the ~** (*Radio, TV*) estar en antena; **airbag** *n* airbag *m inv*; **airbed** (BRIT) *n* colchón *m* neumático; **airborne** *adj* (*in the air*) en el aire; **as soon as the plane was airborne** tan pronto como el avión estuvo en el aire; **air-conditioned** *adj* climatizado; **air conditioning** *n* aire acondicionado; **aircraft** *n inv* avión *m*; **airfield** *n* campo de aviación; **Air Force** *n* fuerzas *fpl* aéreas, aviación *f*; **air hostess** (BRIT) *n* azafata; **airing cupboard** *n* (BRIT) armario *m* para oreo; **airlift** *n* puente *m* aéreo; **airline** *n* línea aérea; **airliner** *n* avión *m* de pasajeros; **airmail** *n*: **by airmail** por avión; **airplane** (US) *n* avión *m*; **airport** *n* aeropuerto; **air raid** *n* ataque *m* aéreo; **airsick** *adj*: **to be airsick** marearse (en avión); **airspace** *n* espacio aéreo; **airstrip** *n* pista de aterrizaje; **air terminal** *n* terminal *f*; **airtight** *adj* hermético; **air-traffic controller** *n* controlador(a) *m/f* aéreo/a; **airy** *adj* (*room*) bien ventilado; (*fig: manner*) desenfadado
aisle [aɪl] *n* (*of church*) nave *f*; (*of theatre, supermarket*) pasillo; **aisle seat** *n* (*on plane*) asiento de pasillo
ajar [ə'dʒɑ:*] *adj* entreabierto
à la carte [ælæ'kɑ:t] *adv* a la carta
alarm [ə'lɑ:m] *n* (*in shop, bank*) alarma; (*anxiety*) inquietud *f* ▷ *vt* asustar, inquietar; **alarm call** *n* (*in hotel etc*) alarma; **alarm clock** *n* despertador *m*; **alarmed** *adj* (*person*) alarmado, asustado; (*house, car etc*) con alarma; **alarming** *adj* alarmante
Albania [æl'beɪnɪə] *n* Albania
albeit [ɔ:l'bi:ɪt] *conj* aunque
album ['ælbəm] *n* álbum *m*; (*L.P.*) elepé *m*
alcohol ['ælkəhɔl] *n* alcohol *m*; **alcohol-free** *adj* sin alcohol; **alcoholic** [-'hɔlɪk] *adj*, *n* alcohólico/a *m/f*
alcove ['ælkəuv] *n* nicho, hueco
ale [eɪl] *n* cerveza
alert [ə'lə:t] *adj* (*attentive*) atento; (*to danger, opportunity*) alerta ▷ *n* alerta *m*, alarma ▷ *vt* poner sobre aviso; **to be on the ~** (*also Mil*) estar alerta *or* sobre aviso
algebra ['ældʒɪbrə] *n* álgebra
Algeria [æl'dʒɪərɪə] *n* Argelia
alias ['eɪlɪəs] *adv* alias, conocido por ▷ *n* (*of criminal*) apodo; (*of writer*) seudónimo
alibi ['ælɪbaɪ] *n* coartada
alien ['eɪlɪən] *n* (*foreigner*) extranjero/a;

(*extraterrestrial*) extraterrestre *mf* ▷ *adj*: **~ to** ajeno a; **alienate** *vt* enajenar, alejar
alight [ə'laɪt] *adj* ardiendo; (*eyes*) brillante ▷ *vi* (*person*) apearse, bajar; (*bird*) posarse
align [ə'laɪn] *vt* alinear
alike [ə'laɪk] *adj* semejantes, iguales ▷ *adv* igualmente, del mismo modo; **to look ~** parecerse
alive [ə'laɪv] *adj* vivo; (*lively*) alegre

KEYWORD

all [ɔ:l] *adj* (*sg*) todo/a; (*pl*) todos/as; **all day** todo el día; **all night** toda la noche; **all men** todos los hombres; **all five came** vinieron los cinco; **all the books** todos los libros; **all his life** toda su vida
▷ *pron* **1** todo; **I ate it all, I ate all of it** me lo comí todo; **all of us went** fuimos todos; **all the boys went** fueron todos los chicos; **is that all?** ¿eso es todo?, ¿algo más?; (*in shop*) ¿algo más?, ¿alguna cosa más?
2 (*in phrases*): **above all** sobre todo; por encima de todo; **after all** después de todo; **at all: not at all** (*in answer to question*) en absoluto; (*in answer to thanks*) ¡de nada!, ¡no hay de qué!; **I'm not at all tired** no estoy nada cansado/a; **anything at all will do** cualquier cosa viene bien; **all in all** a fin de cuentas
▷ *adv*: **all alone** completamente solo/a; **it's not as hard as all that** no es tan difícil como lo pintas; **all the more/the better** tanto más/mejor; **all but** casi; **the score is 2 all** están empatados a 2

Allah ['ælə] *n* Alá *m*
allegation [ælɪ'geɪʃən] *n* alegato
alleged [ə'lɛdʒd] *adj* supuesto, presunto; **allegedly** *adv* supuestamente, según se afirma
allegiance [ə'li:dʒəns] *n* lealtad *f*
allergic [ə'lə:dʒɪk] *adj*: **~ to** alérgico a
allergy ['ælədʒɪ] *n* alergia
alleviate [ə'li:vɪeɪt] *vt* aliviar
alley ['ælɪ] *n* callejuela
alliance [ə'laɪəns] *n* alianza
allied ['ælaɪd] *adj* aliado
alligator ['ælɪgeɪtə*] *n* (*Zool*) caimán *m*
all-in (BRIT) ['ɔ:lɪn] *adj, adv* (*charge*) todo incluido
allocate ['æləkeɪt] *vt* (*money etc*) asignar
allot [ə'lɔt] *vt* asignar
all-out ['ɔ:laut] *adj* (*effort etc*) supremo
allow [ə'lau] *vt* permitir, dejar; (*a claim*) admitir; (*sum, time etc*) dar, conceder; (*concede*): **to ~ that** reconocer que; **to ~ sb to do** permitir a algn hacer; **he is ~ed to ...** se le permite ...; **allow for** *vt fus* tener en cuenta; **allowance** *n* subvención *f*; (*welfare payment*) subsidio, pensión *f*; (*pocket money*) dinero de bolsillo; (*tax allowance*) desgravación *f*; **to make allowances for** (*person*) disculpar a; (*thing*) tener en cuenta
all right *adv* bien; (*as answer*) ¡conforme!, ¡está bien!
ally ['ælaɪ] *n* aliado/a ▷ *vt*: **to ~ o.s. with** aliarse con
almighty [ɔ:l'maɪtɪ] *adj* todopoderoso; (*row etc*) imponente
almond ['ɑ:mənd] *n* almendra
almost ['ɔ:lməust] *adv* casi
alone [ə'ləun] *adj, adv* solo; **to leave sb ~** dejar a algn en paz; **to leave sth ~** no tocar algo, dejar algo sin tocar; **let ~ ...** y mucho menos ...
along [ə'lɔŋ] *prep* a lo largo de, por ▷ *adv*: **is he coming ~ with us?** ¿viene con nosotros?; **he was limping ~** iba cojeando; **~ with** junto con; **all ~** (*all the time*) desde el principio; **alongside** *prep* al lado de ▷ *adv* al lado
aloof [ə'lu:f] *adj* reservado ▷ *adv*: **to stand ~** mantenerse apartado
aloud [ə'laud] *adv* en voz alta
alphabet ['ælfəbɛt] *n* alfabeto
Alps [ælps] *npl*: **the ~** los Alpes
already [ɔ:l'rɛdɪ] *adv* ya
alright ['ɔ:l'raɪt] (BRIT) *adv* = **all right**
also ['ɔ:lsəu] *adv* también, además
altar ['ɔltə*] *n* altar *m*
alter ['ɔltə*] *vt* cambiar, modificar ▷ *vi* cambiar; **alteration** [ɔltə'reɪʃən] *n* cambio; (*to clothes*) arreglo; (*to building*) arreglos *mpl*
alternate [*adj* ɔl'tə:nɪt, *vb* 'ɔltə:neɪt] *adj* (*actions etc*) alternativo; (*events*) alterno; (US) = **alternative** ▷ *vi*: **to ~ (with)** alternar (con); **on ~ days** un día sí y otro no
alternative [ɔl'tə:nətɪv] *adj* alternativo ▷ *n* alternativa; **~ medicine** medicina alternativa; **alternatively** *adv*: **alternatively one could ...** por otra parte se podría ...
although [ɔ:l'ðəu] *conj* aunque
altitude ['æltɪtju:d] *n* altura
altogether [ɔ:ltə'gɛðə*] *adv* completamente, del todo; (*on the whole*) en total, en conjunto
aluminium [ælju'mɪnɪəm] (BRIT), **aluminum** [ə'lu:mɪnəm] (US) *n* aluminio
always ['ɔ:lweɪz] *adv* siempre
Alzheimer's (disease) ['æltshaɪməz-] *n* enfermedad *f* de Alzheimer
am [æm] *vb see* **be**
amalgamate [ə'mælgəmeɪt] *vi*

amalgamarse ▷ *vt* amalgamar, unir
amass [ə'mæs] *vt* amontonar, acumular
amateur ['æmətə*] *n* aficionado/a, amateur *mf*
amaze [ə'meɪz] *vt* asombrar, pasmar; **to be ~d (at)** quedar pasmado (de); **amazed** *adj* asombrado; **amazement** *n* asombro, sorpresa; **amazing** *adj* extraordinario; (*fantastic*) increíble
Amazon ['æməzən] *n* (*Geo*) Amazonas *m*
ambassador [æm'bæsədə*] *n* embajador(a) *m/f*
amber ['æmbə*] *n* ámbar *m*; **at ~** (BRIT *Aut*) en el amarillo
ambiguous [æm'bɪgjuəs] *adj* ambiguo
ambition [æm'bɪʃən] *n* ambición *f*; **ambitious** [-ʃəs] *adj* ambicioso
ambulance ['æmbjuləns] *n* ambulancia
ambush ['æmbuʃ] *n* emboscada ▷ *vt* tender una emboscada a
amen [ɑː'mɛn] *excl* amén
amend [ə'mɛnd] *vt* enmendar; **to make ~s** dar cumplida satisfacción; **amendment** *n* enmienda
amenities [ə'miːnɪtɪz] *npl* comodidades *fpl*
America [ə'mɛrɪkə] *n* (*USA*) Estados *mpl* Unidos; **American** *adj, n* norteamericano/a; estadounidense *mf*; **American football** *n* (BRIT) fútbol *m* americano
amicable ['æmɪkəbl] *adj* amistoso, amigable
amid(st) [ə'mɪd(st)] *prep* entre, en medio de
ammunition [æmju'nɪʃən] *n* municiones *fpl*
amnesty ['æmnɪstɪ] *n* amnistía
among(st) [ə'mʌŋ(st)] *prep* entre, en medio de
amount [ə'maunt] *n* (*gen*) cantidad *f*; (*of bill etc*) suma, importe *m* ▷ *vi*: **to ~ to** sumar; (*be same as*) equivaler a, significar
amp(ère) ['æmp(ɛə*)] *n* amperio
ample ['æmpl] *adj* (*large*) grande; (*abundant*) abundante; (*enough*) bastante, suficiente
amplifier ['æmplɪfaɪə*] *n* amplificador *m*
amputate ['æmpjuteɪt] *vt* amputar
Amtrak ['æmtræk] (US) *n empresa nacional de ferrocarriles de los EEUU*
amuse [ə'mjuːz] *vt* divertir; (*distract*) distraer, entretener; **amusement** *n* diversión *f*; (*pastime*) pasatiempo; (*laughter*) risa; **amusement arcade** *n* salón *m* de juegos; **amusement park** *n* parque *m* de atracciones
amusing [ə'mjuːzɪŋ] *adj* divertido
an [æn] *indef art see* **a**
anaemia [ə'niːmɪə] (US **anemia**) *n* anemia
anaemic [ə'niːmɪk] (US **anemic**) *adj* anémico; (*fig*) soso, insípido
anaesthetic [ænɪs'θɛtɪk] (US **anesthetic**) *n* anestesia
analog(ue) ['ænəlɔg] *adj* (*computer, watch*) analógico
analogy [ə'nælədʒɪ] *n* analogía
analyse ['ænəlaɪz] (US **analyze**) *vt* analizar; **analysis** [ə'næləsɪs] (*pl* **analyses**) *n* análisis *m inv*; **analyst** [-lɪst] *n* (*political analyst, psychoanalyst*) analista *mf*
analyze ['ænəlaɪz] (US) *vt* = **analyse**
anarchy ['ænəkɪ] *n* anarquía, desorden *m*
anatomy [ə'nætəmɪ] *n* anatomía
ancestor ['ænsɪstə*] *n* antepasado
anchor ['æŋkə*] *n* ancla, áncora ▷ *vi* (*also*: **to drop ~**) anclar ▷ *vt* anclar; **to weigh ~** levar anclas
anchovy ['æntʃəvɪ] *n* anchoa
ancient ['eɪnʃənt] *adj* antiguo
and [ænd] *conj* y; (*before i-, hi- + consonant*) e; **men ~ women** hombres y mujeres; **father ~ son** padre e hijo; **trees ~ grass** árboles y hierba; **~ so on** etcétera, y así sucesivamente; **try ~ come** procura venir; **he talked ~ talked** habló sin parar; **better ~ better** cada vez mejor
Andes ['ændiːz] *npl*: **the ~** los Andes
Andorra [æn'dɔːrə] *n* Andorra
anemia *etc* [ə'niːmɪə] (US) = **anaemia** *etc*
anesthetic [ænɪs'θɛtɪk] (US) = **anaesthetic**
angel ['eɪndʒəl] *n* ángel *m*
anger ['æŋgə*] *n* cólera
angina [æn'dʒaɪnə] *n* angina (del pecho)
angle ['æŋgl] *n* ángulo; **from their ~** desde su punto de vista
angler ['æŋglə*] *n* pescador(a) *m/f* (de caña)
Anglican ['æŋglɪkən] *adj, n* anglicano/a *m/f*
angling ['æŋglɪŋ] *n* pesca con caña
angrily ['æŋgrɪlɪ] *adv* coléricamente, airadamente
angry ['æŋgrɪ] *adj* enfadado, airado; (*wound*) inflamado; **to be ~ with sb/at sth** estar enfadado con algn/por algo; **to get ~** enfadarse, enojarse
anguish ['æŋgwɪʃ] *n* (*physical*) tormentos *mpl*; (*mental*) angustia
animal ['ænɪməl] *n* animal *m*; (*pej: person*) bestia ▷ *adj* animal
animated [-meɪtɪd] *adj* animado
animation [ænɪ'meɪʃən] *n* animación *f*
aniseed ['ænɪsiːd] *n* anís *m*
ankle ['æŋkl] *n* tobillo

annex [*n* 'ænɛks, *vb* æ'nɛks] *n* (BRIT: *also*: **~e**: *building*) edificio anexo ▷ *vt* (*territory*) anexionar

anniversary [ænɪ'vəːsərɪ] *n* aniversario

announce [ə'nauns] *vt* anunciar; **announcement** *n* anuncio; (*official*) declaración *f*; **announcer** *n* (*Radio*) locutor(a) *m/f*; (*TV*) presentador(a) *m/f*

annoy [ə'nɔɪ] *vt* molestar, fastidiar; **don't get ~ed!** ¡no se enfade!; **annoying** *adj* molesto, fastidioso; (*person*) pesado

annual ['ænjuəl] *adj* anual ▷ *n* (*Bot*) anual *m*; (*book*) anuario; **annually** *adv* anualmente, cada año

annum ['ænəm] *n* *see* **per**

anonymous [ə'nɔnɪməs] *adj* anónimo

anorak ['ænəræk] *n* anorak *m*

anorexia [ænə'rɛksɪə] *n* (*Med*: *also*: **~ nervosa**) anorexia

anorexic [ænə'rɛksɪk] *adj*, *n* anoréxico/a *m/f*

another [ə'nʌðə*] *adj* (*one more, a different one*) otro ▷ *pron* otro; *see* **one**

answer ['ɑːnsə*] *n* contestación *f*, respuesta; (*to problem*) solución *f* ▷ *vi* contestar, responder ▷ *vt* (*reply to*) contestar a, responder a; (*problem*) resolver; (*prayer*) escuchar; **in ~ to your letter** contestando *or* en contestación a su carta; **to ~ the phone** contestar *or* coger el teléfono; **to ~ the bell** *or* **the door** acudir a la puerta; **answer back** *vi* replicar, ser respondón/ona; **answerphone** *n* (*esp* BRIT) contestador *m* (automático)

ant [ænt] *n* hormiga

Antarctic [ænt'ɑːktɪk] *n*: **the ~** el Antártico

antelope ['æntɪləup] *n* antílope *m*

antenatal ['æntɪ'neɪtl] *adj* antenatal, prenatal

antenna [æn'tɛnə, *pl* -niː] (*pl* **antennae**) *n* antena

anthem ['ænθəm] *n*: **national ~** himno nacional

anthology [æn'θɔlədʒɪ] *n* antología

anthrax ['ænθræks] *n* ántrax *m*

anthropology [ænθrə'pɔlədʒɪ] *n* antropología

anti [æntɪ] *prefix* anti; **antibiotic** [-baɪ'ɔtɪk] *n* antibiótico; **antibody** ['æntɪbɔdɪ] *n* anticuerpo

anticipate [æn'tɪsɪpeɪt] *vt* prever; (*expect*) esperar, contar con; (*look forward to*) esperar con ilusión; (*do first*) anticiparse a, adelantarse a; **anticipation** [-'peɪʃən] *n* (*expectation*) previsión *f*; (*eagerness*) ilusión *f*, expectación *f*

anticlimax [æntɪ'klaɪmæks] *n* decepción *f*

anticlockwise [æntɪ'klɔkwaɪz] (BRIT) *adv* en dirección contraria a la de las agujas del reloj

antics ['æntɪks] *npl* gracias *fpl*

anti: antidote ['æntɪdəut] *n* antídoto; **antifreeze** ['æntɪfriːz] *n* anticongelante *m*; **antihistamine** [-'hɪstəmiːn] *n* antihistamínico; **antiperspirant** ['æntɪpəːspɪrənt] *n* antitranspirante *m*

antique [æn'tiːk] *n* antigüedad *f* ▷ *adj* antiguo; **antique shop** *n* tienda de antigüedades

antiseptic [æntɪ'sɛptɪk] *adj*, *n* antiséptico

antisocial [æntɪ'səuʃəl] *adj* antisocial

antivirus [æntɪ'vaɪərəs] *adj* (*program, software*) antivirus *inv*

antlers ['æntləz] *npl* cuernas *fpl*, cornamenta *sg*

anxiety [æŋ'zaɪətɪ] *n* inquietud *f*; (*Med*) ansiedad *f*; **~ to do** deseo de hacer

anxious ['æŋkʃəs] *adj* inquieto, preocupado; (*worrying*) preocupante; (*keen*): **to be ~ to do** tener muchas ganas de hacer

KEYWORD

any ['ɛnɪ] *adj* **1** (*in questions etc*) algún/alguna; **have you any butter/children?** ¿tienes mantequilla/hijos?; **if there are any tickets left** si quedan billetes, si queda algún billete

2 (*with negative*): **I haven't any money/books** no tengo dinero/libros

3 (*no matter which*) cualquier; **any excuse will do** valdrá *or* servirá cualquier excusa; **choose any book you like** escoge el libro que quieras

4 (*in phrases*): **in any case** de todas formas, en cualquier caso; **any day now** cualquier día (de estos); **at any moment** en cualquier momento, de un momento a otro; **at any rate** en todo caso; **any time: come (at) any time** ven cuando quieras; **he might come (at) any time** podría llegar de un momento a otro

▷ *pron* **1** (*in questions etc*): **have you got any?** ¿tienes alguno(s)/a(s)?; **can any of you sing?** ¿sabe cantar alguno de vosotros/ustedes?

2 (*with negative*): **I haven't any (of them)** no tengo ninguno

3 (*no matter which one(s)*): **take any of those books (you like)** toma el libro que quieras de ésos

▷ *adv* **1** (*in questions etc*): **do you want any**

more soup/sandwiches? ¿quieres más sopa/bocadillos?; **are you feeling any better?** ¿te sientes algo mejor?
2 (*with negative*): **I can't hear him any more** ya no le oigo; **don't wait any longer** no esperes más

any: anybody *pron* cualquiera; (*in interrogative sentences*) alguien; (*in negative sentences*): **I don't see anybody** no veo a nadie; **if anybody should phone ...** si llama alguien ...; **anyhow** *adv* (*at any rate*) de todos modos, de todas formas; (*haphazard*): **do it anyhow you like** hazlo como quieras; **she leaves things just anyhow** deja las cosas como quiera *or* de cualquier modo; **I shall go anyhow** de todos modos iré; **anyone** *pron* = **anybody**; **anything** *pron* (*in questions etc*) algo, alguna cosa; (*with negative*) nada; **can you see anything?** ¿ves algo?; **if anything happens to me ...** si algo me ocurre ...; (*no matter what*): **you can say anything you like** puedes decir lo que quieras; **anything will do** vale todo *or* cualquier cosa; **he'll eat anything** come de todo *or* lo que sea; **anytime** *adv* (*at any moment*) en cualquier momento, de un momento a otro; (*whenever*) no importa cuándo, cuando quiera; **anyway** *adv* (*at any rate*) de todos modos, de todas formas; **I shall go anyway** iré de todos modos; (*besides*): **anyway, I couldn't come even if I wanted to** además, no podría venir aunque quisiera; **why are you phoning, anyway?** ¿entonces, por qué llamas?, ¿por qué llamas, pues?; **anywhere** *adv* (*in questions etc*): **can you see him anywhere?** ¿le ves por algún lado?; **are you going anywhere?** ¿vas a algún sitio?; (*with negative*): **I can't see him anywhere** no le veo por ninguna parte; **anywhere in the world** (*no matter where*) en cualquier parte (del mundo); **put the books down anywhere** deja los libros donde quieras
apart [ə'pɑːt] *adv* (*aside*) aparte; (*situation*): **~ (from)** separado (de); (*movement*): **to pull ~** separar; **10 miles ~** separados por 10 millas; **to take ~** desmontar; **~ from** *prep* aparte de
apartment [ə'pɑːtmənt] *n* (US) piso (SP), departamento (LAM), apartamento; (*room*) cuarto; **apartment building** (US) *n* edificio de apartamentos
apathy ['æpəθɪ] *n* apatía, indiferencia
ape [eɪp] *n* mono ▷*vt* imitar, remedar
aperitif [ə'pɛrɪtɪf] *n* aperitivo
aperture ['æpətʃjuə*] *n* rendija, resquicio; (*Phot*) abertura
APEX ['eɪpɛks] *n abbr* (= *Advanced Purchase Excursion Fare*) tarifa *f* APEX
apologize [ə'pɔlədʒaɪz] *vi*: **to ~ (for sth to sb)** disculparse (con algn de algo)
apology [ə'pɔlədʒɪ] *n* disculpa, excusa

> Be careful not to translate **apology** by the Spanish word *apología*.

apostrophe [ə'pɔstrəfɪ] *n* apóstrofo
appal [ə'pɔːl] (US **appall**) *vt* horrorizar, espantar; **appalling** *adj* espantoso; (*awful*) pésimo
apparatus [æpə'reɪtəs] *n* (*equipment*) equipo; (*organization*) aparato; (*in gymnasium*) aparatos *mpl*
apparent [ə'pærənt] *adj* aparente; (*obvious*) evidente; **apparently** *adv* por lo visto, al parecer
appeal [ə'piːl] *vi* (*Law*) apelar ▷*n* (*Law*) apelación *f*; (*request*) llamamiento; (*plea*) petición *f*; (*charm*) atractivo; **to ~ for** reclamar; **to ~ to** (*be attractive to*) atraer; **it doesn't ~ to me** no me atrae, no me llama la atención; **appealing** *adj* (*attractive*) atractivo
appear [ə'pɪə*] *vi* aparecer, presentarse; (*Law*) comparecer; (*publication*) salir (a luz), publicarse; (*seem*) parecer; **to ~ on TV/in "Hamlet"** salir por la tele/hacer un papel en "Hamlet"; **it would ~ that** parecería que; **appearance** *n* aparición *f*; (*look*) apariencia, aspecto
appendices [ə'pɛndɪsiːz] *npl of* **appendix**
appendicitis [əpɛndɪ'saɪtɪs] *n* apendicitis *f*
appendix [ə'pɛndɪks] (*pl* **appendices**) *n* apéndice *m*
appetite ['æpɪtaɪt] *n* apetito; (*fig*) deseo, anhelo
appetizer ['æpɪtaɪzə*] *n* (*drink*) aperitivo; (*food*) tapas *fpl* (SP)
applaud [ə'plɔːd] *vt, vi* aplaudir
applause [ə'plɔːz] *n* aplausos *mpl*
apple ['æpl] *n* manzana; **apple pie** *n* pastel *m* de manzana, pay *m* de manzana (LAM)
appliance [ə'plaɪəns] *n* aparato
applicable [ə'plɪkəbl] *adj* (*relevant*): **to be ~ (to)** referirse (a)
applicant ['æplɪkənt] *n* candidato/a; solicitante *mf*
application [æplɪ'keɪʃən] *n* aplicación *f*; (*for a job etc*) solicitud *f*, petición *f*; **application form** *n* solicitud *f*
apply [ə'plaɪ] *vt* (*paint etc*) poner; (*law etc: put into practice*) poner en vigor ▷*vi*: **to ~ to** (*ask*) dirigirse a; (*be applicable*) ser aplicable a; **to ~ for** (*permit, grant, job*)

solicitar; **to ~ o.s. to** aplicarse a, dedicarse a
appoint [ə'pɔɪnt] *vt* (*to post*) nombrar a
Be careful not to translate **appoint** by the Spanish word *apuntar*.
appointment *n* (*with client*) cita; (*act*) nombramiento; (*post*) puesto; (*at hairdresser etc*): **to have an appointment** tener hora; **to make an appointment (with sb)** citarse (con algn)
appraisal [ə'preɪzl] *n* valoración *f*
appreciate [ə'pri:ʃɪeɪt] *vt* apreciar, tener en mucho; (*be grateful for*) agradecer; (*be aware*) comprender ▷ *vi* (*Comm*) aumentar(se) en valor; **appreciation** [-'eɪʃən] *n* apreciación *f*; (*gratitude*) reconocimiento, agradecimiento; (*Comm*) aumento en valor
apprehension [æprɪ'hɛnʃən] *n* (*fear*) aprensión *f*
apprehensive [æprɪ'hɛnsɪv] *adj* aprensivo
apprentice [ə'prɛntɪs] *n* aprendiz(a) *m/f*
approach [ə'prəutʃ] *vi* acercarse ▷ *vt* acercarse a; (*ask, apply to*) dirigirse a; (*situation, problem*) abordar ▷ *n* acercamiento; (*access*) acceso; (*to problem, situation*): **~ (to)** actitud *f* (ante)
appropriate [*adj* ə'prəuprɪɪt, *vb* ə'prəuprɪeɪt] *adj* apropiado, conveniente ▷ *vt* (*take*) apropiarse de
approval [ə'pru:vəl] *n* aprobación *f*, visto bueno; (*permission*) consentimiento; **on ~** (*Comm*) a prueba
approve [ə'pru:v] *vt* aprobar; **approve of** *vt fus* (*thing*) aprobar; (*person*): **they don't approve of her** (ella) no les parece bien
approximate [ə'prɔksɪmɪt] *adj* aproximado; **approximately** *adv* aproximadamente, más o menos
Apr. *abbr* (= *April*) abr
apricot ['eɪprɪkɔt] *n* albaricoque *m*, chabacano (MEX), damasco (RPL)
April ['eɪprəl] *n* abril *m*; **April Fools' Day** *n* el primero de abril, ≈ día *m* de los Inocentes (*28 December*)
apron ['eɪprən] *n* delantal *m*
apt [æpt] *adj* acertado, apropiado; (*likely*): **~ to do** propenso a hacer
aquarium [ə'kwɛərɪəm] *n* acuario
Aquarius [ə'kwɛərɪəs] *n* Acuario
Arab ['ærəb] *adj, n* árabe *mf*
Arabia [ə'reɪbɪə] *n* Arabia; **Arabian** *adj* árabe; **Arabic** ['ærəbɪk] *adj* árabe; (*numerals*) arábigo ▷ *n* árabe *m*
arbitrary ['ɑ:bɪtrərɪ] *adj* arbitrario
arbitration [ɑ:bɪ'treɪʃən] *n* arbitraje *m*
arc [ɑ:k] *n* arco
arcade [ɑ:'keɪd] *n* (*round a square*) soportales *mpl*; (*shopping mall*) galería comercial
arch [ɑ:tʃ] *n* arco; (*of foot*) arco del pie ▷ *vt* arquear
archaeology [ɑ:kɪ'ɔlədʒɪ] (US **archeology**) *n* arqueología
archbishop [ɑ:tʃ'bɪʃəp] *n* arzobispo
archeology [ɑ:kɪ'ɔlədʒɪ] (US) = **archaeology**
architect ['ɑ:kɪtɛkt] *n* arquitecto/a; **architectural** [ɑ:kɪ'tɛktʃərəl] *adj* arquitectónico; **architecture** *n* arquitectura
archive ['ɑ:kaɪv] *n* (*often pl: also Comput*) archivo
Arctic ['ɑ:ktɪk] *adj* ártico ▷ *n*: **the ~** el Ártico
are [ɑ:*] *vb see* **be**
area ['ɛərɪə] *n* área, región *f*; (*part of place*) zona; (*Math etc*) área, superficie *f*; (*in room: e.g. dining area*) parte *f*; (*of knowledge, experience*) campo; **area code** (US) *n* (*Tel*) prefijo
arena [ə'ri:nə] *n* estadio; (*of circus*) pista
aren't [ɑ:nt] = **are not**
Argentina [ɑ:dʒən'ti:nə] *n* Argentina; **Argentinian** [-'tɪnɪən] *adj, n* argentino/a *m/f*
arguably ['ɑ:gjuəblɪ] *adv* posiblemente
argue ['ɑ:gju:] *vi* (*quarrel*) discutir, pelearse; (*reason*) razonar, argumentar; **to ~ that** sostener que
argument ['ɑ:gjumənt] *n* discusión *f*, pelea; (*reasons*) argumento
Aries ['ɛərɪz] *n* Aries *m*
arise [ə'raɪz] (*pt* **arose**, *pp* **arisen**) *vi* surgir, presentarse
arithmetic [ə'rɪθmətɪk] *n* aritmética
arm [ɑ:m] *n* brazo ▷ *vt* armar; **arms** *npl* armas *fpl*; **~ in ~** cogidos del brazo; **armchair** ['ɑ:mtʃɛə*] *n* sillón *m*, butaca
armed [ɑ:md] *adj* armado; **armed robbery** *n* robo a mano armada
armour ['ɑ:mə*] (US **armor**) *n* armadura; (*Mil: tanks*) blindaje *m*
armpit ['ɑ:mpɪt] *n* sobaco, axila
armrest ['ɑ:mrɛst] *n* apoyabrazos *m inv*
army ['ɑ:mɪ] *n* ejército; (*fig*) multitud *f*
A road *n* (BRIT) ≈ carretera *f* nacional
aroma [ə'rəumə] *n* aroma *m*, fragancia; **aromatherapy** *n* aromaterapia
arose [ə'rəuz] *pt of* **arise**
around [ə'raund] *adv* alrededor; (*in the area*): **there is no one else ~** no hay nadie más por aquí ▷ *prep* alrededor de
arouse [ə'rauz] *vt* despertar; (*anger*) provocar
arrange [ə'reɪndʒ] *vt* arreglar, ordenar;

(*organize*) organizar; **to ~ to do sth** quedar en hacer algo; **arrangement** *n* arreglo; (*agreement*) acuerdo; **arrangements** *npl* (*preparations*) preparativos *mpl*

array [ə'reɪ] *n*: **~ of** (*things*) serie *f* de; (*people*) conjunto de

arrears [ə'rɪəz] *npl* atrasos *mpl*; **to be in ~ with one's rent** estar retrasado en el pago del alquiler

arrest [ə'rɛst] *vt* detener; (*sb's attention*) llamar ▷ *n* detención *f*; **under ~** detenido

arrival [ə'raɪvəl] *n* llegada; **new ~** recién llegado/a; (*baby*) recién nacido

arrive [ə'raɪv] *vi* llegar; (*baby*) nacer; **arrive at** *vt fus* (*decision, solution*) llegar a

arrogance ['ærəgəns] *n* arrogancia, prepotencia (LAM)

arrogant ['ærəgənt] *adj* arrogante

arrow ['ærəu] *n* flecha

arse [ɑ:s] (BRIT: *inf!*) *n* culo, trasero

arson ['ɑ:sn] *n* incendio premeditado

art [ɑ:t] *n* arte *m*; (*skill*) destreza; **art college** *n* escuela *f* de Bellas Artes

artery ['ɑ:tərɪ] *n* arteria

art gallery *n* pinacoteca; (*saleroom*) galería de arte

arthritis [ɑ:'θraɪtɪs] *n* artritis *f*

artichoke ['ɑ:tɪtʃəuk] *n* alcachofa; **Jerusalem ~** aguaturma

article ['ɑ:tɪkl] *n* artículo

articulate [*adj* ɑ:'tɪkjulɪt, *vb* ɑ:'tɪkjuleɪt] *adj* claro, bien expresado ▷ *vt* expresar

artificial [ɑ:tɪ'fɪʃəl] *adj* artificial; (*affected*) afectado

artist ['ɑ:tɪst] *n* artista *mf*; (*Mus*) intérprete *mf*; **artistic** [ɑ:'tɪstɪk] *adj* artístico

art school *n* escuela de bellas artes

○ KEYWORD

as [æz] *conj* **1** (*referring to time*) cuando, mientras; a medida que; **as the years went by** con el paso de los años; **he came in as I was leaving** entró cuando me marchaba; **as from tomorrow** desde *or* a partir de mañana

2 (*in comparisons*): **as big as** tan grande como; **twice as big as** el doble de grande que; **as much money/many books as** tanto dinero/tantos libros como; **as soon as** en cuanto

3 (*since, because*) como, ya que; **he left early as he had to be home by 10** se fue temprano ya que tenía que estar en casa a las 10

4 (*referring to manner, way*): **do as you wish** haz lo que quieras; **as she said** como dijo; **he gave it to me as a present** me lo dio de regalo

5 (*in the capacity of*): **he works as a barman** trabaja de barman; **as chairman of the company, he ...** como presidente de la compañía ...

6 (*concerning*): **as for** *or* **to that** por *or* en lo que respecta a eso

7: **as if** *or* **though** como si; **he looked as if he was ill** parecía como si estuviera enfermo, tenía aspecto de enfermo; *see also* **long; such; well**

a.s.a.p. *abbr* (= *as soon as possible*) cuanto antes

asbestos [æz'bɛstəs] *n* asbesto, amianto

ascent [ə'sɛnt] *n* subida; (*slope*) cuesta, pendiente *f*

ash [æʃ] *n* ceniza; (*tree*) fresno

ashamed [ə'ʃeɪmd] *adj* avergonzado, apenado (LAM); **to be ~ of** avergonzarse de

ashore [ə'ʃɔ:*] *adv* en tierra; (*swim etc*) a tierra

ashtray ['æʃtreɪ] *n* cenicero

Ash Wednesday *n* miércoles *m* de Ceniza

Asia ['eɪʃə] *n* Asia; **Asian** *adj, n* asiático/a *m/f*

aside [ə'saɪd] *adv* a un lado ▷ *n* aparte *m*

ask [ɑ:sk] *vt* (*question*) preguntar; (*invite*) invitar; **to ~ sb sth/to do sth** preguntar algo a algn/pedir a algn que haga algo; **to ~ sb about sth** preguntar algo a algn; **to ~ (sb) a question** hacer una pregunta (a algn); **to ~ sb out to dinner** invitar a cenar a algn; **ask for** *vt fus* pedir; (*trouble*) buscar

asleep [ə'sli:p] *adj* dormido; **to fall ~** dormirse, quedarse dormido

asparagus [əs'pærəgəs] *n* (*plant*) espárrago; (*food*) espárragos *mpl*

aspect ['æspɛkt] *n* aspecto, apariencia; (*direction in which a building etc faces*) orientación *f*

aspirations [æspə'reɪʃənz] *npl* aspiraciones *fpl*; (*ambition*) ambición *f*

aspire [əs'paɪə*] *vi*: **to ~ to** aspirar a, ambicionar

aspirin ['æsprɪn] *n* aspirina

ass [æs] *n* asno, burro; (*inf*: *idiot*) imbécil *mf*; (US: *inf!*) culo, trasero

assassin [ə'sæsɪn] *n* asesino/a; **assassinate** *vt* asesinar

assault [ə'sɔ:lt] *n* asalto; (*Law*) agresión *f* ▷ *vt* asaltar, atacar; (*sexually*) violar

assemble [ə'sɛmbl] *vt* reunir, juntar; (*Tech*) montar ▷ *vi* reunirse, juntarse

assembly [ə'sɛmblɪ] *n* reunión *f*, asamblea; (*parliament*) parlamento; (*construction*) montaje *m*

assert [ə'sə:t] *vt* afirmar; (*authority*) hacer valer; **assertion** [-ʃən] *n* afirmación *f*
assess [ə'sɛs] *vt* valorar, calcular; (*tax, damages*) fijar; (*for tax*) gravar; **assessment** *n* valoración *f*; (*for tax*) gravamen *m*
asset ['æsɛt] *n* ventaja; **assets** *npl* (*Comm*) activo; (*property, funds*) fondos *mpl*
assign [ə'saɪn] *vt*: **to ~ (to)** (*date*) fijar (para); (*task*) asignar (a); (*resources*) destinar (a); **assignment** *n* tarea
assist [ə'sɪst] *vt* ayudar; **assistance** *n* ayuda, auxilio; **assistant** *n* ayudante *mf*; (BRIT: *also*: **shop assistant**) dependiente/a *m/f*
associate [*adj, n* ə'səuʃɪɪt, *vb* ə'səuʃɪeɪt] *adj* asociado ▷ *n* (*at work*) colega *mf* ▷ *vt* asociar; (*ideas*) relacionar ▷ *vi*: **to ~ with sb** tratar con algn
association [əsəusɪ'eɪʃən] *n* asociación *f*
assorted [ə'sɔ:tɪd] *adj* surtido, variado
assortment [ə'sɔ:tmənt] *n* (*of shapes, colours*) surtido; (*of books*) colección *f*; (*of people*) mezcla
assume [ə'sju:m] *vt* suponer; (*responsibilities*) asumir; (*attitude*) adoptar, tomar
assumption [ə'sʌmpʃən] *n* suposición *f*, presunción *f*; (*of power etc*) toma
assurance [ə'ʃuərəns] *n* garantía, promesa; (*confidence*) confianza, aplomo; (*insurance*) seguro
assure [ə'ʃuə*] *vt* asegurar
asterisk ['æstərɪsk] *n* asterisco
asthma ['æsmə] *n* asma
astonish [ə'stɔnɪʃ] *vt* asombrar, pasmar; **astonished** *adj* estupefacto, pasmado; **to be astonished (at)** asombrarse (de); **astonishing** *adj* asombroso, pasmoso; **I find it astonishing that ...** me asombra *or* pasma que ...; **astonishment** *n* asombro, sorpresa
astound [ə'staund] *vt* asombrar, pasmar
astray [ə'streɪ] *adv*: **to go ~** extraviarse; **to lead ~** (*morally*) llevar por mal camino
astrology [æs'trɔlədʒɪ] *n* astrología
astronaut ['æstrənɔ:t] *n* astronauta *mf*
astronomer [əs'trɔnəmə*] *n* astrónomo/a
astronomical [æstrə'nɔmɪkəl] *adj* astronómico
astronomy [æs'trɔnəmɪ] *n* astronomía
astute [əs'tju:t] *adj* astuto
asylum [ə'saɪləm] *n* (*refuge*) asilo; (*mental hospital*) manicomio

KEYWORD

at [æt] *prep* **1** (*referring to position*) en; (*direction*) a; **at the top** en lo alto; **at home/school** en casa/la escuela; **to look at sth/sb** mirar algo/a algn
2 (*referring to time*): **at 4 o'clock** a las 4; **at night** por la noche; **at Christmas** en Navidad; **at times** a veces
3 (*referring to rates, speed etc*): **at £1 a kilo** a una libra el kilo; **two at a time** de dos en dos; **at 50 km/h** a 50 km/h
4 (*referring to manner*): **at a stroke** de un golpe; **at peace** en paz
5 (*referring to activity*): **to be at work** estar trabajando; (*in the office etc*) estar en el trabajo; **to play at cowboys** jugar a los vaqueros; **to be good at sth** ser bueno en algo
6 (*referring to cause*): **shocked/surprised/annoyed at sth** asombrado/sorprendido/fastidiado por algo; **I went at his suggestion** fui a instancias suyas
7 (*symbol*) arroba

ate [eɪt] *pt of* **eat**
atheist ['eɪθɪɪst] *n* ateo/a
Athens ['æθɪnz] *n* Atenas
athlete ['æθli:t] *n* atleta *mf*
athletic [æθ'lɛtɪk] *adj* atlético; **athletics** *n* atletismo
Atlantic [ət'læntɪk] *adj* atlántico ▷ *n*: **the ~ (Ocean)** el (Océano) Atlántico
atlas ['ætləs] *n* atlas *m inv*
A.T.M. *n abbr* (= *automated telling machine*) cajero automático
atmosphere ['ætməsfɪə*] *n* atmósfera; (*of place*) ambiente *m*
atom ['ætəm] *n* átomo; **atomic** [ə'tɔmɪk] *adj* atómico; **atom(ic) bomb** *n* bomba atómica
A to Z® *n* (*map*) callejero
atrocity [ə'trɔsɪtɪ] *n* atrocidad *f*
attach [ə'tætʃ] *vt* (*fasten*) atar; (*join*) unir, sujetar; (*document, letter*) adjuntar; (*importance etc*) dar, conceder; **to be ~ed to sb/sth** (*to like*) tener cariño a algn/algo; **attachment** *n* (*tool*) accesorio; (*Comput*) archivo, documento adjunto; (*love*): **attachment (to)** apego (a)
attack [ə'tæk] *vt* (*Mil*) atacar; (*criminal*) agredir, asaltar; (*criticize*) criticar; (*task*) emprender ▷ *n* ataque *m*, asalto; (*on sb's life*) atentado; (*fig: criticism*) crítica; (*of illness*) ataque *m*; **heart ~** infarto (de miocardio); **attacker** *n* agresor(a) *m/f*, asaltante *mf*
attain [ə'teɪn] *vt* (*also*: **~ to**) alcanzar; (*achieve*) lograr, conseguir
attempt [ə'tɛmpt] *n* tentativa, intento; (*attack*) atentado ▷ *vt* intentar
attend [ə'tɛnd] *vt* asistir a; (*patient*)

atender; **attend to** *vt fus* ocuparse de; (*customer, patient*) atender a; **attendance** *n* asistencia, presencia; (*people present*) concurrencia; **attendant** *n* ayudante *mf*; (*in garage etc*) encargado/a ▷ *adj* (*dangers*) concomitante

attention [ə'tɛnʃən] *n* atención *f*; (*care*) atenciones *fpl* ▷ *excl* (*Mil*) ¡firme(s)!; **for the ~ of ...** (*Admin*) atención ...

attic ['ætɪk] *n* desván *m*

attitude ['ætɪtju:d] *n* actitud *f*; (*disposition*) disposición *f*

attorney [ə'tə:nɪ] *n* (*lawyer*) abogado/a; **Attorney General** *n* (BRIT) ≈ Presidente *m* del Consejo del Poder Judicial (SP); (US) ≈ ministro de Justicia

attract [ə'trækt] *vt* atraer; (*sb's attention*) llamar; **attraction** [ə'trækʃən] *n* encanto; (*gen pl*: *amusements*) diversiones *fpl*; (*Physics*) atracción *f*; (*fig*: *towards sb, sth*) atractivo; **attractive** *adj* guapo; (*interesting*) atrayente

attribute [*n* 'ætrɪbju:t, *vb* ə'trɪbju:t] *n* atributo ▷ *vt*: **to ~ sth to** atribuir algo a

aubergine ['əubəʒi:n] (BRIT) *n* berenjena; (*colour*) morado

auburn ['ɔ:bən] *adj* color castaño rojizo

auction ['ɔ:kʃən] *n* (*also*: **sale by ~**) subasta ▷ *vt* subastar

audible ['ɔ:dɪbl] *adj* audible, que se puede oír

audience ['ɔ:dɪəns] *n* público; (*Radio*) radioescuchas *mpl*; (*TV*) telespectadores *mpl*; (*interview*) audiencia

audit ['ɔ:dɪt] *vt* revisar, intervenir

audition [ɔ:'dɪʃən] *n* audición *f*

auditor ['ɔ:dɪtə*] *n* interventor(a) *m/f*, censor(a) *m/f* de cuentas

auditorium [ɔ:dɪ'tɔ:rɪəm] *n* auditorio

Aug. *abbr* (= *August*) ag

August ['ɔ:gəst] *n* agosto

aunt [ɑ:nt] *n* tía; **auntie** *n diminutive of* **aunt**; **aunty** *n diminutive of* **aunt**

au pair ['əu'pɛə*] *n* (*also*: **~ girl**) (chica) au pair *f*

aura ['ɔ:rə] *n* aura; (*atmosphere*) ambiente *m*

austerity [ɔ'stɛrɪtɪ] *n* austeridad *f*

Australia [ɔs'treɪlɪə] *n* Australia; **Australian** *adj, n* australiano/a *m/f*

Austria ['ɔstrɪə] *n* Austria; **Austrian** *adj, n* austríaco/a *m/f*

authentic [ɔ:'θɛntɪk] *adj* auténtico

author ['ɔ:θə*] *n* autor(a) *m/f*

authority [ɔ:'θɔrɪtɪ] *n* autoridad *f*; (*official permission*) autorización *f*; **the authorities** *npl* las autoridades

authorize ['ɔ:θəraɪz] *vt* autorizar

auto ['ɔ:təu] (US) *n* coche *m* (SP), carro (LAM), automóvil *m*

auto: autobiography [ɔ:təbaɪ'ɔgrəfɪ] *n* autobiografía; **autograph** ['ɔ:təgrɑ:f] *n* autógrafo ▷ *vt* (*photo etc*) dedicar; (*programme*) firmar; **automatic** [ɔ:tə'mætɪk] *adj* automático ▷ *n* (*gun*) pistola automática; (*car*) coche *m* automático; **automatically** *adv* automáticamente; **automobile** ['ɔ:təməbi:l] (US) *n* coche *m* (SP), carro (LAM), automóvil *m*; **autonomous** [ɔ:'tɔnəməs] *adj* autónomo; **autonomy** [ɔ:'tɔnəmɪ] *n* autonomía

autumn ['ɔ:təm] *n* otoño

auxiliary [ɔ:g'zɪlɪərɪ] *adj, n* auxiliar *mf*

avail [ə'veɪl] *vt*: **to ~ o.s. of** aprovechar(se) de ▷ *n*: **to no ~** en vano, sin resultado

availability [əveɪlə'bɪlɪtɪ] *n* disponibilidad *f*

available [ə'veɪləbl] *adj* disponible; (*unoccupied*) libre; (*person*: *unattached*) soltero y sin compromiso

avalanche ['ævəlɑ:nʃ] *n* alud *m*, avalancha

Ave. *abbr* = **avenue**

avenue ['ævənju:] *n* avenida; (*fig*) camino

average ['ævərɪdʒ] *n* promedio, término medio ▷ *adj* medio, de término medio; (*ordinary*) regular, corriente ▷ *vt* sacar un promedio de; **on ~** por regla general

avert [ə'və:t] *vt* prevenir; (*blow*) desviar; (*one's eyes*) apartar

avid ['ævɪd] *adj* ávido

avocado [ævə'kɑ:dəu] *n* (*also* BRIT: **~ pear**) aguacate *m*, palta (SC)

avoid [ə'vɔɪd] *vt* evitar, eludir

await [ə'weɪt] *vt* esperar, aguardar

awake [ə'weɪk] (*pt* **awoke**, *pp* **awoken** *or* **awaked**) *adj* despierto ▷ *vt* despertar ▷ *vi* despertarse; **to be ~** estar despierto

award [ə'wɔ:d] *n* premio; (*Law*: *damages*) indemnización *f* ▷ *vt* otorgar, conceder; (*Law*: *damages*) adjudicar

aware [ə'wɛə*] *adj*: **~ (of)** consciente (de); **to become ~ of/that** (*realize*) darse cuenta de/de que; (*learn*) enterarse de/de que; **awareness** *n* conciencia; (*knowledge*) conocimiento

away [ə'weɪ] *adv* fuera; (*movement*): **she went ~** se marchó; **far ~** lejos; **two kilometres ~** a dos kilómetros de distancia; **two hours ~ by car** a dos horas en coche; **the holiday was two weeks ~** faltaban dos semanas para las vacaciones; **he's ~ for a week** estará ausente una semana; **to take ~ (from)** quitar (a); (*subtract*) substraer (de); **to work/pedal ~** seguir trabajando/pedaleando; **to fade ~** (*colour*) desvanecerse; (*sound*) apagarse

awe [ɔ:] *n* admiración *f* respetuosa; **awesome** ['ɔ:səm] (US) *adj* (*excellent*) formidable

awful ['ɔ:fəl] *adj* horroroso; (*quantity*): **an ~ lot (of)** cantidad (de); **awfully** *adv* (*very*) terriblemente

awkward ['ɔ:kwəd] *adj* desmañado, torpe; (*shape*) incómodo; (*embarrassing*) delicado, difícil

awoke [ə'wəuk] *pt of* **awake**

awoken [ə'wəukən] *pp of* **awake**

axe [æks] (US **ax**) *n* hacha ▷ *vt* (*project*) cortar; (*jobs*) reducir

axle ['æksl] *n* eje *m*, árbol *m*

ay(e) [aɪ] *excl* sí

azalea [ə'zeɪlɪə] *n* azalea

B [bi:] *n* (*Mus*) si *m*

B.A. *abbr* = **Bachelor of Arts**

baby ['beɪbɪ] *n* bebé *mf*; (US: *inf*: *darling*) mi amor; **baby carriage** (US) *n* cochecito; **baby-sit** *vi* hacer de canguro; **baby-sitter** *n* canguro/a; **baby wipe** *n* toallita húmeda (*para bebés*)

bachelor ['bætʃələ*] *n* soltero; **B~ of Arts/Science** licenciado/a en Filosofía y Letras/Ciencias

back [bæk] *n* (*of person*) espalda; (*of animal*) lomo; (*of hand*) dorso; (*as opposed to front*) parte *f* de atrás; (*of chair*) respaldo; (*of page*) reverso; (*of book*) final *m*; (*Football*) defensa *m*; (*of crowd*): **the ones at the ~** los del fondo ▷ *vt* (*candidate*: *also*: **~ up**) respaldar, apoyar; (*horse*: *at races*) apostar a; (*car*) dar marcha atrás a *or* con ▷ *vi* (*car etc*) ir (*or* salir *or* entrar) marcha atrás ▷ *adj* (*payment, rent*) atrasado; (*seats, wheels*) de atrás ▷ *adv* (*not forward*) (hacia) atrás; (*returned*): **he's ~** está de vuelta, ha vuelto; **he ran ~** volvió corriendo; (*restitution*): **throw the ball ~** devuelve la pelota; **can I have it ~?** ¿me lo devuelve?; (*again*): **he called ~** llamó de nuevo; **back down** *vi* echarse atrás; **back out** *vi* (*of promise*) volverse atrás; **back up** *vt* (*person*) apoyar, respaldar; (*theory*) defender; (*Comput*) hacer una copia preventiva *or* de reserva; **backache** *n* dolor *m* de espalda; **backbencher** (BRIT) *n* *miembro del parlamento sin cargo relevante*; **backbone** *n* columna vertebral; **back door** *n* puerta *f* trasera; **backfire** *vi* (*Aut*) petardear; (*plans*) fallar, salir mal; **backgammon** *n* backgammon *m*; **background** *n* fondo; (*of events*) antecedentes *mpl*; (*basic knowledge*) bases *fpl*; (*experience*) conocimientos *mpl*, educación *f*; **family background** origen *m*, antecedentes *mpl*; **backing** *n* (*fig*) apoyo, respaldo; **backlog** *n*: **backlog of work** trabajo atrasado; **backpack** *n* mochila; **backpacker** *n* mochilero/a; **backslash** *n* pleca, barra inversa; **backstage** *adv* entre bastidores; **backstroke** *n* espalda; **backup** *adj* suplementario; (*Comput*) de reserva ▷ *n* (*support*) apoyo; (*also*: **backup file**) copia preventiva *or* de reserva; **backward** *adj* (*person, country*) atrasado; **backwards** *adv* hacia atrás; (*read a list*) al revés; (*fall*) de espaldas; **backyard** *n* traspatio

bacon [ˈbeɪkən] *n* tocino, beicon *m*

bacteria [bækˈtɪərɪə] *npl* bacterias *fpl*

bad [bæd] *adj* malo; (*mistake, accident*) grave; (*food*) podrido, pasado; **his ~ leg** su pierna lisiada; **to go ~** (*food*) pasarse

badge [bædʒ] *n* insignia; (*policeman's*) chapa, placa

badger [ˈbædʒə*] *n* tejón *m*

badly [ˈbædlɪ] *adv* mal; **to reflect ~ on sb** influir negativamente en la reputación de algn; **~ wounded** gravemente herido; **he needs it ~** le hace gran falta; **to be ~ off (for money)** andar mal de dinero

bad-mannered [ˈbædˈmænəd] *adj* mal educado

badminton [ˈbædmɪntən] *n* bádminton *m*

bad-tempered [ˈbædˈtɛmpəd] *adj* de mal genio *or* carácter; (*temporarily*) de mal humor

bag [bæg] *n* bolsa; (*handbag*) bolso; (*satchel*) mochila; (*case*) maleta; **~s of** (*inf*) un montón de; **baggage** *n* equipaje *m*; **baggage allowance** *n* límite *m* de equipaje; **baggage reclaim** *n* recogida de equipajes; **baggy** *adj* amplio; **bagpipes** *npl* gaita

bail [beɪl] *n* fianza ▷ *vt* (*prisoner: gen: grant bail to*) poner en libertad bajo fianza; (*boat: also:* **~ out**) achicar; **on ~** (*prisoner*) bajo fianza; **to ~ sb out** obtener la libertad de algn bajo fianza

bait [beɪt] *n* cebo ▷ *vt* poner cebo en; (*tease*) tomar el pelo a

bake [beɪk] *vt* cocer (al horno) ▷ *vi* cocerse; **baked beans** *npl* judías *fpl* en salsa de tomate; **baked potato** *n* patata al horno; **baker** *n* panadero; **bakery** *n* panadería; (*for cakes*) pastelería; **baking** *n* (*act*) amasar *m*; (*batch*) hornada; **baking powder** *n* levadura (en polvo)

balance [ˈbæləns] *n* equilibrio; (*Comm: sum*) balance *m*; (*remainder*) resto; (*scales*) balanza ▷ *vt* equilibrar; (*budget*) nivelar; (*account*) saldar; (*make equal*) equilibrar; **~ of trade/payments** balanza de comercio/pagos; **balanced** *adj* (*personality, diet*) equilibrado; (*report*) objetivo; **balance sheet** *n* balance *m*

balcony [ˈbælkənɪ] *n* (*open*) balcón *m*; (*closed*) galería; (*in theatre*) anfiteatro

bald [bɔːld] *adj* calvo; (*tyre*) liso

Balearics [bælɪˈærɪks] *npl*: **the ~** las Baleares

ball [bɔːl] *n* pelota; (*football*) balón *m*; (*of wool, string*) ovillo; (*dance*) baile *m*; **to play ~** (*fig*) cooperar

ballerina [bæləˈriːnə] *n* bailarina

ballet [ˈbæleɪ] *n* ballet *m*; **ballet dancer** *n* bailarín/ina *m/f*

balloon [bəˈluːn] *n* globo

ballot [ˈbælət] *n* votación *f*

ballpoint (pen) [ˈbɔːlpɔɪnt-] *n* bolígrafo

ballroom [ˈbɔːlrum] *n* salón *m* de baile

Baltic [ˈbɔːltɪk] *n*: **the ~ (Sea)** el (Mar) Báltico

bamboo [bæmˈbuː] *n* bambú *m*

ban [bæn] *n* prohibición *f*, proscripción *f* ▷ *vt* prohibir, proscribir

banana [bəˈnɑːnə] *n* plátano, banana (LAM), banano (CAM)

band [bænd] *n* grupo; (*strip*) faja, tira; (*stripe*) lista; (*Mus: jazz*) orquesta; (*: rock*) grupo; (*Mil*) banda

bandage [ˈbændɪdʒ] *n* venda, vendaje *m* ▷ *vt* vendar

Band-Aid® [ˈbændeɪd] (US) *n* tirita

bandit [ˈbændɪt] *n* bandido

bang [bæŋ] *n* (*of gun, exhaust*) estallido, detonación *f*; (*of door*) portazo; (*blow*) golpe *m* ▷ *vt* (*door*) cerrar de golpe; (*one's head*) golpear ▷ *vi* estallar; (*door*) cerrar de golpe

Bangladesh [bɑːŋgləˈdɛʃ] *n* Bangladesh *m*

bangle [ˈbæŋgl] *n* brazalete *m*, ajorca

bangs [bæŋz] (US) *npl* flequillo

banish [ˈbænɪʃ] *vt* desterrar

banister(s) [ˈbænɪstə(z)] *n(pl)* barandilla, pasamanos *m inv*

banjo [ˈbændʒəu] (*pl* **~es** *or* **~s**) *n* banjo

bank [bæŋk] *n* (*Comm*) banco; (*of river, lake*) ribera, orilla; (*of earth*) terraplén *m* ▷ *vi* (*Aviat*) ladearse; **bank on** *vt fus* contar con; **bank account** *n* cuenta de banco; **bank balance** *n* saldo; **bank card** *n* tarjeta bancaria; **bank charges** *npl* comisión *fsg*; **banker** *n* banquero; **bank holiday** *n* (BRIT) día *m* festivo *or* de fiesta; **banking** *n* banca; **bank manager** *n* director(a) *m/f* (de sucursal) de banco; **banknote** *n* billete *m* de banco

BANK HOLIDAY

El término **bank holiday** se aplica en el Reino Unido a todo día festivo oficial en el que cierran bancos y comercios.

Los más importantes son en Navidad, Semana Santa, finales de mayo y finales de agosto y, al contrario que en los países de tradición católica, no coinciden necesariamente con una celebración religiosa.

bankrupt ['bæŋkrʌpt] *adj* quebrado, insolvente; **to go ~** hacer bancarrota; **to be ~** estar en quiebra; **bankruptcy** *n* quiebra
bank statement *n* balance *m or* detalle *m* de cuenta
banner ['bænə*] *n* pancarta
bannister(s) ['bænɪstə(z)] *n(pl)* = **banister(s)**
banquet ['bæŋkwɪt] *n* banquete *m*
baptism ['bæptɪzəm] *n* bautismo; (*act*) bautizo
baptize [bæp'taɪz] *vt* bautizar
bar [bɑ:*] *n* (*pub*) bar *m*; (*counter*) mostrador *m*; (*rod*) barra; (*of window, cage*) reja; (*of soap*) pastilla; (*of chocolate*) tableta; (*fig: hindrance*) obstáculo; (*prohibition*) proscripción *f*; (*Mus*) barra ▷ *vt* (*road*) obstruir; (*person*) excluir; (*activity*) prohibir; **the B~** (*Law*) la abogacía; **behind ~s** entre rejas; **~ none** sin excepción
barbaric [bɑ:'bærɪk] *adj* bárbaro
barbecue ['bɑ:bɪkju:] *n* barbacoa
barbed wire ['bɑ:bd-] *n* alambre *m* de púas
barber ['bɑ:bə*] *n* peluquero, barbero; **barber's (shop)** (*US* **barber (shop)**) *n* peluquería
bar code *n* código de barras
bare [bɛə*] *adj* desnudo; (*trees*) sin hojas; (*necessities etc*) básico ▷ *vt* desnudar; (*teeth*) enseñar; **barefoot** *adj, adv* descalzo; **barely** *adv* apenas
bargain ['bɑ:gɪn] *n* pacto, negocio; (*good buy*) ganga ▷ *vi* negociar; (*haggle*) regatear; **into the ~** además, por añadidura; **bargain for** *vt fus*: **he got more than he bargained for** le resultó peor de lo que esperaba
barge [bɑ:dʒ] *n* barcaza; **barge in** *vi* irrumpir; (*interrupt: conversation*) interrumpir
bark [bɑ:k] *n* (*of tree*) corteza; (*of dog*) ladrido ▷ *vi* ladrar
barley ['bɑ:lɪ] *n* cebada
barmaid ['bɑ:meɪd] *n* camarera
barman ['bɑ:mən] (*irreg*) *n* camarero, barman *m*
barn [bɑ:n] *n* granero
barometer [bə'rɔmɪtə*] *n* barómetro
baron ['bærən] *n* barón *m*; (*press baron etc*) magnate *m*; **baroness** *n* baronesa
barracks ['bærəks] *npl* cuartel *m*
barrage ['bærɑ:ʒ] *n* (*Mil*) descarga, bombardeo; (*dam*) presa; (*of criticism*) lluvia, aluvión *m*
barrel ['bærəl] *n* barril *m*; (*of gun*) cañón *m*
barren ['bærən] *adj* estéril
barrette [bə'rɛt] (*US*) *n* pasador *m* (*LAM, SP*), broche *m* (*MEX*)
barricade [bærɪ'keɪd] *n* barricada
barrier ['bærɪə*] *n* barrera
barring ['bɑ:rɪŋ] *prep* excepto, salvo
barrister ['bærɪstə*] (*BRIT*) *n* abogado/a
barrow ['bærəu] *n* (*cart*) carretilla (de mano)
bartender ['bɑ:tɛndə*] (*US*) *n* camarero, barman *m*
base [beɪs] *n* base *f* ▷ *vt*: **to ~ sth on** basar *or* fundar algo en ▷ *adj* bajo, infame
baseball ['beɪsbɔ:l] *n* béisbol *m*; **baseball cap** *n* gorra *f* de béisbol
basement ['beɪsmənt] *n* sótano
bases[1] ['beɪsi:z] *npl of* **basis**
bases[2] ['beɪsɪz] *npl of* **base**
bash [bæʃ] (*inf*) *vt* golpear
basic ['beɪsɪk] *adj* básico; **basically** *adv* fundamentalmente, en el fondo; (*simply*) sencillamente; **basics** *npl*: **the basics** los fundamentos
basil ['bæzl] *n* albahaca
basin ['beɪsn] *n* cuenco, tazón *m*; (*Geo*) cuenca; (*also*: **wash~**) lavabo
basis ['beɪsɪs] (*pl* **bases**) *n* base *f*; **on a part-time/trial ~** a tiempo parcial/a prueba
basket ['bɑ:skɪt] *n* cesta, cesto; canasta; **basketball** *n* baloncesto
bass [beɪs] *n* (*Mus: instrument*) bajo; (*double bass*) contrabajo; (*singer*) bajo
bastard ['bɑ:stəd] *n* bastardo; (*inf!*) hijo de puta (!)
bat [bæt] *n* (*Zool*) murciélago; (*for ball games*) palo; (*BRIT: for table tennis*) pala ▷ *vt*: **he didn't ~ an eyelid** ni pestañeó
batch [bætʃ] *n* (*of bread*) hornada; (*of letters etc*) lote *m*
bath [bɑ:θ, *pl* bɑ:ðz] *n* (*action*) baño; (*bathtub*) bañera (*SP*), tina (*LAM*), bañadera (*RPL*) ▷ *vt* bañar; **to have a ~** bañarse, tomar un baño; *see also* **baths**
bathe [beɪð] *vi* bañarse ▷ *vt* (*wound*) lavar
bathing ['beɪðɪŋ] *n* el bañarse; **bathing costume** (*US* **bathing suit**) *n* traje *m* de baño
bath: bathrobe *n* (*man's*) batín *m*; (*woman's*) bata; **bathroom** *n* (cuarto de) baño; **baths** [bɑ:ðz] *npl* (*also*: **swimming baths**) piscina; **bath towel** *n* toalla de baño; **bathtub** *n* bañera
baton ['bætən] *n* (*Mus*) batuta; (*Athletics*) testigo; (*weapon*) porra

batter ['bætə*] *vt* maltratar; (*rain etc*) azotar ▷ *n* masa (para rebozar); **battered** *adj* (*hat, pan*) estropeado
battery ['bætərɪ] *n* (*Aut*) batería; (*of torch*) pila; **battery farming** *n* cría intensiva
battle ['bætl] *n* batalla; (*fig*) lucha ▷ *vi* luchar; **battlefield** *n* campo *m* de batalla
bay [beɪ] *n* (*Geo*) bahía; **B~ of Biscay** ≈ mar Cantábrico; **to hold sb at ~** mantener a algn a raya
bazaar [bə'zɑ:*] *n* bazar *m*; (*fete*) *venta con fines benéficos*
B. & B. *n abbr* = **bed and breakfast**; (*place*) pensión *f*; (*terms*) cama y desayuno
BBC *n abbr* (= *British Broadcasting Corporation*) *cadena de radio y televisión estatal británica*
B.C. *adv abbr* (= *before Christ*) a. de C.

KEYWORD

be [bi:] (*pt* **was, were**, *pp* **been**) *aux vb*
1 (*with present participle: forming continuous tenses*): **what are you doing?** ¿qué estás haciendo?, ¿qué haces?; **they're coming tomorrow** vienen mañana; **I've been waiting for you for hours** llevo horas esperándote
2 (*with pp: forming passives*) ser (*but often replaced by active or reflexive constructions*); **to be murdered** ser asesinado; **the box had been opened** habían abierto la caja; **the thief was nowhere to be seen** no se veía al ladrón por ninguna parte
3 (*in tag questions*): **it was fun, wasn't it?** fue divertido, ¿no? *or* ¿verdad?; **he's good-looking, isn't he?** es guapo, ¿no te parece?; **she's back again, is she?** entonces, ¿ha vuelto?
4 (*+to +infin*): **the house is to be sold** (*necessity*) hay que vender la casa; (*future*) van a vender la casa; **he's not to open it** no tiene que abrirlo ▷ *vb +complement*
1 (*with n or num complement, but see also 3, 4, 5 and impers vb below*) ser; **he's a doctor** es médico; **2 and 2 are 4** 2 y 2 son 4
2 (*with adj complement: expressing permanent or inherent quality*) ser; (*: expressing state seen as temporary or reversible*) estar; **I'm English** soy inglés/esa; **she's tall/pretty** es alta/bonita; **he's young** es joven; **be careful/good/quiet** ten cuidado/pórtate bien/cállate; **I'm tired** estoy cansado/a; **it's dirty** está sucio/a
3 (*of health*) estar; **how are you?** ¿cómo estás?; **he's very ill** está muy enfermo; **I'm better now** ya estoy mejor
4 (*of age*) tener; **how old are you?** ¿cuántos años tienes?; **I'm sixteen (years old)** tengo dieciséis años
5 (*cost*) costar; ser; **how much was the meal?** ¿cuánto fue *or* costó la comida?; **that'll be £5.75, please** son £5.75, por favor; **this shirt is £17** esta camisa cuesta £17
▷ *vi* **1** (*exist, occur etc*) existir, haber; **the best singer that ever was** el mejor cantante que existió jamás; **is there a God?** ¿hay un Dios?, ¿existe Dios?; **be that as it may** sea como sea; **so be it** así sea
2 (*referring to place*) estar; **I won't be here tomorrow** no estaré aquí mañana
3 (*referring to movement*): **where have you been?** ¿dónde has estado?
▷ *impers vb* **1** (*referring to time*): **it's 5 o'clock** son las 5; **it's the 28th of April** estamos a 28 de abril
2 (*referring to distance*): **it's 10 km to the village** el pueblo está a 10 km
3 (*referring to the weather*): **it's too hot/cold** hace demasiado calor/frío; **it's windy today** hace viento hoy
4 (*emphatic*): **it's me** soy yo; **it was Maria who paid the bill** fue María la que pagó la cuenta

beach [bi:tʃ] *n* playa ▷ *vt* varar
beacon ['bi:kən] *n* (*lighthouse*) faro; (*marker*) guía
bead [bi:d] *n* cuenta; (*of sweat etc*) gota; **beads** *npl* (*necklace*) collar *m*
beak [bi:k] *n* pico
beam [bi:m] *n* (*Arch*) viga, travesaño; (*of light*) rayo, haz *m* de luz ▷ *vi* brillar; (*smile*) sonreír
bean [bi:n] *n* judía; **runner/broad ~** habichuela/haba; **coffee ~** grano de café; **beansprouts** *npl* brotes *mpl* de soja
bear [bɛə*] (*pt* **bore**, *pp* **borne**) *n* oso ▷ *vt* (*weight etc*) llevar; (*cost*) pagar; (*responsibility*) tener; (*endure*) soportar, aguantar; (*children*) parir, tener; (*fruit*) dar ▷ *vi*: **to ~ right/left** torcer a la derecha/izquierda
beard [bɪəd] *n* barba
bearer ['bɛərə*] *n* portador(a) *m/f*
bearing ['bɛərɪŋ] *n* porte *m*, comportamiento; (*connection*) relación *f*
beast [bi:st] *n* bestia; (*inf*) bruto, salvaje *m*
beat [bi:t] (*pt* **~**, *pp* **beaten**) *n* (*of heart*) latido; (*Mus*) ritmo, compás *m*; (*of policeman*) ronda ▷ *vt* pegar, golpear; (*eggs*) batir; (*defeat: opponent*) vencer, derrotar; (*: record*) sobrepasar ▷ *vi* (*heart*) latir; (*drum*) redoblar; (*rain, wind*) azotar; **off the ~en track** aislado; **to ~ it** (*inf*) largarse; **beat up** *vt* (*attack*) dar una paliza a; **beating** *n* paliza
beautiful ['bju:tɪful] *adj* precioso,

hermoso, bello; **beautifully** *adv* maravillosamente

beauty ['bju:tɪ] *n* belleza; **beauty parlour** (*US* **beauty parlor**) *n* salón *m* de belleza; **beauty salon** *n* salón *m* de belleza; **beauty spot** *n* (*Tourism*) lugar *m* pintoresco

beaver ['bi:və*] *n* castor *m*

became [bɪ'keɪm] *pt of* **become**

because [bɪ'kɔz] *conj* porque; **~ of** debido a, a causa de

beckon ['bɛkən] *vt* (*also*: **~ to**) llamar con señas

become [bɪ'kʌm] (*pt* **became**, *pp* **~**) *vt* (*suit*) favorecer, sentar bien a ▷ *vi* (+ *n*) hacerse, llegar a ser; (+ *adj*) ponerse, volverse; **to ~ fat** engordar

bed [bɛd] *n* cama; (*of flowers*) macizo; (*of coal, clay*) capa; (*of river*) lecho; (*of sea*) fondo; **to go to ~** acostarse; **bed and breakfast** *n* (*place*) pensión *f*; (*terms*) cama y desayuno; **bedclothes** *npl* ropa de cama; **bedding** *n* ropa de cama; **bed linen** *n* (BRIT) ropa *f* de cama

BED AND BREAKFAST

Se llama **bed and breakfast** a una forma de alojamiento, en el campo o la ciudad, que ofrece cama y desayuno a precios inferiores a los de un hotel. El servicio se suele anunciar con carteles en los que a menudo se usa únicamente la abreviatura **B. & B.**

bed: bedroom *n* dormitorio; **bedside** *n*: **at the bedside of** a la cabecera de; **bedside lamp** *n* lámpara de noche; **bedside table** *n* mesilla de noche; **bedsit(ter)** (BRIT) *n* cuarto de alquiler; **bedspread** *n* cubrecama *m*, colcha; **bedtime** *n* hora de acostarse

bee [bi:] *n* abeja

beech [bi:tʃ] *n* haya

beef [bi:f] *n* carne *f* de vaca; **roast ~** rosbif *m*; **beefburger** *n* hamburguesa; **Beefeater** *n alabardero de la Torre de Londres*

been [bi:n] *pp of* **be**

beer [bɪə*] *n* cerveza; **beer garden** *n* (BRIT) terraza *f* de verano, jardín *m* (de un bar)

beet [bi:t] (*US*) *n* (*also*: **red ~**) remolacha

beetle ['bi:tl] *n* escarabajo

beetroot ['bi:tru:t] (BRIT) *n* remolacha

before [bɪ'fɔ:*] *prep* (*of time*) antes de; (*of space*) delante de ▷ *conj* antes (de) que ▷ *adv* antes, anteriormente; delante, adelante; **~ going** antes de marcharse; **~ she goes** antes de que se vaya; **the week ~** la semana anterior; **I've never seen it ~** no lo he visto nunca; **beforehand** *adv* de antemano, con anticipación

beg [bɛg] *vi* pedir limosna ▷ *vt* pedir, rogar; (*entreat*) suplicar; **to ~ sb to do sth** rogar a algn que haga algo; *see also* **pardon**

began [bɪ'gæn] *pt of* **begin**

beggar ['bɛgə*] *n* mendigo/a

begin [bɪ'gɪn] (*pt* **began**, *pp* **begun**) *vt, vi* empezar, comenzar; **to ~ doing** *or* **to do sth** empezar a hacer algo; **beginner** *n* principiante *mf*; **beginning** *n* principio, comienzo

begun [bɪ'gʌn] *pp of* **begin**

behalf [bɪ'hɑ:f] *n*: **on ~ of** en nombre de, por; (*for benefit of*) en beneficio de; **on my/his ~** por mí/él

behave [bɪ'heɪv] *vi* (*person*) portarse, comportarse; (*well*: *also*: **~ o.s.**) portarse bien; **behaviour** (*US* **behavior**) *n* comportamiento, conducta

behind [bɪ'haɪnd] *prep* detrás de; (*supporting*): **to be ~ sb** apoyar a algn ▷ *adv* detrás, por detrás, atrás ▷ *n* trasero; **to be ~ (schedule)** ir retrasado; **~ the scenes** (*fig*) entre bastidores

beige [beɪʒ] *adj* color beige

Beijing ['beɪ'dʒɪŋ] *n* Pekín *m*

being ['bi:ɪŋ] *n* ser *m*; (*existence*): **in ~** existente; **to come into ~** aparecer

belated [bɪ'leɪtɪd] *adj* atrasado, tardío

belch [bɛltʃ] *vi* eructar ▷ *vt* (*gen*: *belch out*: *smoke etc*) arrojar

Belgian ['bɛldʒən] *adj, n* belga *mf*

Belgium ['bɛldʒəm] *n* Bélgica

belief [bɪ'li:f] *n* opinión *f*; (*faith*) fe *f*

believe [bɪ'li:v] *vt, vi* creer; **to ~ in** creer en; **believer** *n* partidario/a; (*Rel*) creyente *mf*, fiel *mf*

bell [bɛl] *n* campana; (*small*) campanilla; (*on door*) timbre *m*

bellboy ['bɛlbɔɪ] (BRIT) *n* botones *m inv*

bellhop ['bɛlhɔp] (*US*) *n* = **bellboy**

bellow ['bɛləu] *vi* bramar; (*person*) rugir

bell pepper *n* (*esp US*) pimiento, pimentón *m* (LAM)

belly ['bɛlɪ] *n* barriga, panza; **belly button** (*inf*) *n* ombligo

belong [bɪ'lɔŋ] *vi*: **to ~ to** pertenecer a; (*club etc*) ser socio de; **this book ~s here** este libro va aquí; **belongings** *npl* pertenencias *fpl*

beloved [bɪ'lʌvɪd] *adj* querido/a

below [bɪ'ləu] *prep* bajo, debajo de; (*less than*) inferior a ▷ *adv* abajo, (por) debajo; **see ~** véase más abajo

belt [bɛlt] *n* cinturón *m*; (*Tech*) correa, cinta ▷ *vt* (*thrash*) pegar con correa; **beltway** (*US*)

n (*Aut*) carretera de circunvalación
bemused [bɪˈmjuːzd] *adj* perplejo
bench [bɛntʃ] *n* banco; (BRIT *Pol*): **the Government/Opposition ~es** (los asientos de) los miembros del Gobierno/de la Oposición; **the B~** (*Law: judges*) magistratura
bend [bɛnd] (*pt, pp* **bent**) *vt* doblar ▷ *vi* inclinarse ▷ *n* (BRIT: *in road, river*) curva; (*in pipe*) codo; **bend down** *vi* inclinarse, doblarse; **bend over** *vi* inclinarse
beneath [bɪˈniːθ] *prep* bajo, debajo de; (*unworthy*) indigno de ▷ *adv* abajo, (por) debajo
beneficial [bɛnɪˈfɪʃəl] *adj* beneficioso
benefit [ˈbɛnɪfɪt] *n* beneficio; (*allowance of money*) subsidio ▷ *vt* beneficiar ▷ *vi*: **he'll ~ from it** le sacará provecho
benign [bɪˈnaɪn] *adj* benigno; (*smile*) afable
bent [bɛnt] *pt, pp of* **bend** ▷ *n* inclinación *f* ▷ *adj*: **to be ~ on** estar empeñado en
bereaved [bɪˈriːvd] *npl*: **the ~** *los íntimos de una persona afligidos por su muerte*
beret [ˈbɛreɪ] *n* boina
Berlin [bəːˈlɪn] *n* Berlín
Bermuda [bəːˈmjuːdə] *n* las Bermudas
berry [ˈbɛrɪ] *n* baya
berth [bəːθ] *n* (*bed*) litera; (*cabin*) camarote *m*; (*for ship*) amarradero ▷ *vi* atracar, amarrar
beside [bɪˈsaɪd] *prep* junto a, al lado de; **to be ~ o.s. with anger** estar fuera de sí; **that's ~ the point** eso no tiene nada que ver; **besides** *adv* además ▷ *prep* además de
best [bɛst] *adj* (el/la) mejor ▷ *adv* (lo) mejor; **the ~ part of** (*quantity*) la mayor parte de; **at ~** en el mejor de los casos; **to make the ~ of sth** sacar el mejor partido de algo; **to do one's ~** hacer todo lo posible; **to the ~ of my knowledge** que yo sepa; **to the ~ of my ability** como mejor puedo; **best-before date** *n* fecha de consumo preferente; **best man** (*irreg*) *n* padrino de boda; **bestseller** *n* éxito de librería, bestseller *m*
bet [bɛt] (*pt, pp* **~** *or* **~ted**) *n* apuesta ▷ *vt*: **to ~ money on** apostar dinero por ▷ *vi* apostar; **to ~ sb sth** apostar algo a algn
betray [bɪˈtreɪ] *vt* traicionar; (*trust*) faltar a
better [ˈbɛtə*] *adj, adv* mejor ▷ *vt* superar ▷ *n*: **to get the ~ of sb** quedar por encima de algn; **you had ~ do it** más vale que lo hagas; **he thought ~ of it** cambió de parecer; **to get ~** (*Med*) mejorar(se)
betting [ˈbɛtɪŋ] *n* juego, el apostar; **betting shop** (BRIT) *n* agencia de apuestas
between [bɪˈtwiːn] *prep* entre ▷ *adv* (*time*) mientras tanto; (*place*) en medio
beverage [ˈbɛvərɪdʒ] *n* bebida
beware [bɪˈwɛə*] *vi*: **to ~ (of)** tener cuidado (con); **"~ of the dog"** "perro peligroso"
bewildered [bɪˈwɪldəd] *adj* aturdido, perplejo
beyond [bɪˈjɔnd] *prep* más allá de; (*past: understanding*) fuera de; (*after: date*) después de, más allá de; (*above*) superior a ▷ *adv* (*in space*) más allá; (*in time*) posteriormente; **~ doubt** fuera de toda duda; **~ repair** irreparable
bias [ˈbaɪəs] *n* (*prejudice*) prejuicio, pasión *f*; (*preference*) predisposición *f*; **bias(s)ed** *adj* parcial
bib [bɪb] *n* babero
Bible [ˈbaɪbl] *n* Biblia
bicarbonate of soda [baɪˈkɑːbənɪt-] *n* bicarbonato sódico
biceps [ˈbaɪsɛps] *n* bíceps *m*
bicycle [ˈbaɪsɪkl] *n* bicicleta; **bicycle pump** *n* bomba de bicicleta
bid [bɪd] (*pt* **bade** *or* **~**, *pp* **bidden** *or* **~**) *n* oferta, postura; (*in tender*) licitación *f*; (*attempt*) tentativa, conato ▷ *vi* hacer una oferta ▷ *vt* (*offer*) ofrecer; **to ~ sb good day** dar a algn los buenos días; **bidder** *n*: **the highest bidder** el mejor postor
bidet [ˈbiːdeɪ] *n* bidet *m*
big [bɪg] *adj* grande; (*brother, sister*) mayor; **bigheaded** *adj* engreído; **big toe** *n* dedo gordo (del pie)
bike [baɪk] *n* bici *f*; **bike lane** *n* carril-bici *m*
bikini [bɪˈkiːnɪ] *n* bikini *m*
bilateral [baɪˈlætərl] *adj* (*agreement*) bilateral
bilingual [baɪˈlɪŋgwəl] *adj* bilingüe
bill [bɪl] *n* cuenta; (*invoice*) factura; (*Pol*) proyecto de ley; (US: *banknote*) billete *m*; (*of bird*) pico; (*of show*) programa *m*; **"post no ~s"** "prohibido fijar carteles"; **to fit** *or* **fill the ~** (*fig*) cumplir con los requisitos; **billboard** (US) *n* cartelera; **billfold** [ˈbɪlfəuld] (US) *n* cartera
billiards [ˈbɪljədz] *n* billar *m*
billion [ˈbɪljən] *n* (BRIT) billón *m* (*millón de millones*); (US) mil millones *mpl*
bin [bɪn] *n* (*for rubbish*) cubo *or* bote *m* (MEX) *or* tacho (SC) de la basura; (*container*) recipiente *m*
bind [baɪnd] (*pt, pp* **bound**) *vt* atar; (*book*) encuadernar; (*oblige*) obligar ▷ *n* (*inf: nuisance*) lata
binge [bɪndʒ] (*inf*) *n*: **to go on a ~** ir de juerga
bingo [ˈbɪŋgəu] *n* bingo *m*

b

binoculars [bɪ'nɔkjuləz] *npl* prismáticos *mpl*

bio... [baɪə'] *prefix*: **biochemistry** *n* bioquímica; **biodegradable** [baɪəudɪ'greɪdəbl] *adj* biodegradable; **biography** [baɪ'ɔgrəfɪ] *n* biografía; **biological** *adj* biológico; **biology** [baɪ'ɔlədʒɪ] *n* biología; **biometric** [baɪə'mɛtrɪk] *adj* biométrico

birch [bə:tʃ] *n* (*tree*) abedul *m*

bird [bə:d] *n* ave *f*, pájaro; (BRIT: *inf*: *girl*) chica; **bird flu** *n* gripe *f* aviar; **bird of prey** *n* ave *f* de presa; **birdwatching** *n*: **he likes to go birdwatching on Sundays** los domingos le gusta ir a ver pájaros

Biro® ['baɪrəu] *n* boli

birth [bə:θ] *n* nacimiento; **to give ~ to** parir, dar a luz; **birth certificate** *n* partida de nacimiento; **birth control** *n* (*policy*) control *m* de natalidad; (*methods*) métodos *mpl* anticonceptivos; **birthday** *n* cumpleaños *m inv* ▷ *cpd* (*cake, card etc*) de cumpleaños; **birthmark** *n* antojo, marca de nacimiento; **birthplace** *n* lugar *m* de nacimiento

biscuit ['bɪskɪt] (BRIT) *n* galleta

bishop ['bɪʃəp] *n* obispo; (*Chess*) alfil *m*

bistro ['bi:strəu] *n* café-bar *m*

bit [bɪt] *pt of* **bite** ▷ *n* trozo, pedazo, pedacito; (*Comput*) bit *m*, bitio; (*for horse*) freno, bocado; **a ~ of** un poco de; **a ~ mad** un poco loco; **~ by ~** poco a poco

bitch [bɪtʃ] *n* perra; (*inf!*: *woman*) zorra (!)

bite [baɪt] (*pt* **bit**, *pp* **bitten**) *vt, vi* morder; (*insect etc*) picar ▷ *n* (*insect bite*) picadura; (*mouthful*) bocado; **to ~ one's nails** comerse las uñas; **let's have a ~ (to eat)** (*inf*) vamos a comer algo

bitten ['bɪtn] *pp of* **bite**

bitter ['bɪtə*] *adj* amargo; (*wind*) cortante, penetrante; (*battle*) encarnizado ▷ *n* (BRIT: *beer*) *cerveza típica británica a base de lúpulos*

bizarre [bɪ'zɑ:*] *adj* raro, extraño

black [blæk] *adj* negro; (*tea, coffee*) solo ▷ *n* color *m* negro; (*person*): **B~** negro/a ▷ *vt* (BRIT *Industry*) boicotear; **to give sb a ~ eye** ponerle a algn el ojo morado; **~ and blue** (*bruised*) amoratado; **to be in the ~** (*bank account*) estar en números negros; **black out** *vi* (*faint*) desmayarse; **blackberry** *n* zarzamora; **blackbird** *n* mirlo; **blackboard** *n* pizarra; **black coffee** *n* café *m* solo; **blackcurrant** *n* grosella negra; **black ice** *n* hielo invisible en la carretera; **blackmail** *n* chantaje *m* ▷ *vt* chantajear; **black market** *n* mercado negro; **blackout** *n* (*Mil*) oscurecimiento; (*power cut*) apagón *m*; (*TV, Radio*) interrupción *f* de programas; (*fainting*) desvanecimiento; **black pepper** *n* pimienta *f* negra; **black pudding** *n* morcilla; **Black Sea** *n*: **the Black Sea** el Mar Negro

bladder ['blædə*] *n* vejiga

blade [bleɪd] *n* hoja; (*of propeller*) paleta; **a ~ of grass** una brizna de hierba

blame [bleɪm] *n* culpa ▷ *vt*: **to ~ sb for sth** echar a algn la culpa de algo; **to be to ~ (for)** tener la culpa (de)

bland [blænd] *adj* (*music, taste*) soso

blank [blæŋk] *adj* en blanco; (*look*) sin expresión ▷ *n* (*of memory*): **my mind is a ~** no puedo recordar nada; (*on form*) blanco, espacio en blanco; (*cartridge*) cartucho sin bala *or* de fogueo

blanket ['blæŋkɪt] *n* manta (SP), cobija (LAM); (*of snow*) capa; (*of fog*) manto

blast [blɑ:st] *n* (*of wind*) ráfaga, soplo; (*of explosive*) explosión *f* ▷ *vt* (*blow up*) volar

blatant ['bleɪtənt] *adj* descarado

blaze [bleɪz] *n* (*fire*) fuego; (*fig*: *of colour*) despliegue *m*; (: *of glory*) esplendor *m* ▷ *vi* arder en llamas; (*fig*) brillar ▷ *vt*: **to ~ a trail** (*fig*) abrir (un) camino; **in a ~ of publicity** con gran publicidad

blazer ['bleɪzə*] *n chaqueta de uniforme de colegial o de socio de club*

bleach [bli:tʃ] *n* (*also*: **household ~**) lejía ▷ *vt* blanquear; **bleachers** (US) *npl* (*Sport*) gradas *fpl* al sol

bleak [bli:k] *adj* (*countryside*) desierto; (*prospect*) poco prometedor(a); (*weather*) crudo; (*smile*) triste

bled [blɛd] *pt, pp of* **bleed**

bleed [bli:d] (*pt, pp* **bled**) *vt, vi* sangrar; **my nose is ~ing** me está sangrando la nariz

blemish ['blɛmɪʃ] *n* marca, mancha; (*on reputation*) tacha

blend [blɛnd] *n* mezcla ▷ *vt* mezclar; (*colours etc*) combinar, mezclar ▷ *vi* (*colours etc*: *also*: **~ in**) combinarse, mezclarse; **blender** *n* (*Culin*) batidora

bless [blɛs] (*pt, pp* **~ed** *or* **blest**) *vt* bendecir; **~ you!** (*after sneeze*) ¡Jesús!; **blessing** *n* (*approval*) aprobación *f*; (*godsend*) don *m* del cielo, bendición *f*; (*advantage*) beneficio, ventaja

blew [blu:] *pt of* **blow**

blight [blaɪt] *vt* (*hopes etc*) frustrar, arruinar

blind [blaɪnd] *adj* ciego; (*fig*): **~ (to)** ciego (a) ▷ *n* (*for window*) persiana ▷ *vt* cegar; (*dazzle*) deslumbrar; (*deceive*): **to ~ sb to ...** cegar a algn a ... ; **the blind** *npl* los ciegos; **blind alley** *n* callejón *m* sin salida; **blindfold** *n* venda ▷ *adv* con los ojos

vendados ▷*vt* vendar los ojos a
blink [blɪŋk] *vi* parpadear, pestañear; (*light*) oscilar
bliss [blɪs] *n* felicidad *f*
blister ['blɪstə*] *n* ampolla ▷*vi* (*paint*) ampollarse
blizzard ['blɪzəd] *n* ventisca
bloated ['bləutɪd] *adj* hinchado; (*person: full*) ahíto
blob [blɔb] *n* (*drop*) gota; (*indistinct object*) bulto
block [blɔk] *n* bloque *m*; (*in pipes*) obstáculo; (*of buildings*) manzana (SP), cuadra (LAM) ▷*vt* obstruir, cerrar; (*progress*) estorbar; **~ of flats** (BRIT) bloque *m* de pisos; **mental ~** bloqueo mental; **block up** *vt* tapar, obstruir; (*pipe*) atascar; **blockade** [-'keɪd] *n* bloqueo ▷*vt* bloquear; **blockage** *n* estorbo, obstrucción *f*; **blockbuster** *n* (*book*) bestseller *m*; (*film*) éxito de público; **block capitals** *npl* mayúsculas *fpl*; **block letters** *npl* mayúsculas *fpl*
blog [blɔg] *n* blog *m*
bloke [bləuk] (BRIT: *inf*) *n* tipo, tío
blond(e) [blɔnd] *adj, n* rubio/a *m/f*
blood [blʌd] *n* sangre *f*; **blood donor** *n* donante *mf* de sangre; **blood group** *n* grupo sanguíneo; **blood poisoning** *n* envenenamiento de la sangre; **blood pressure** *n* presión *f* sanguínea; **bloodshed** *n* derramamiento de sangre; **bloodshot** *adj* inyectado en sangre; **bloodstream** *n* corriente *f* sanguínea; **blood test** *n* análisis *m inv* de sangre; **blood transfusion** *n* transfusión *f* de sangre; **blood type** *n* grupo sanguíneo; **blood vessel** *n* vaso sanguíneo; **bloody** *adj* sangriento; (*nose etc*) lleno de sangre; (BRIT: *inf!*): **this bloody ...** este condenado *o* puñetero ... (!) ▷*adv*: **bloody strong/good** (BRIT: *inf!*) terriblemente fuerte/bueno
bloom [blu:m] *n* flor *f* ▷*vi* florecer
blossom ['blɔsəm] *n* flor *f* ▷*vi* florecer
blot [blɔt] *n* borrón *m*; (*fig*) mancha ▷*vt* (*stain*) manchar
blouse [blauz] *n* blusa
blow [bləu] (*pt* **blew**, *pp* **blown**) *n* golpe *m*; (*with sword*) espadazo ▷*vi* soplar; (*dust, sand etc*) volar; (*fuse*) fundirse ▷*vt* (*wind*) llevarse; (*fuse*) quemar; (*instrument*) tocar; **to ~ one's nose** sonarse; **blow away** *vt* llevarse, arrancar; **blow out** *vi* apagarse; **blow up** *vi* estallar ▷*vt* volar; (*tyre*) inflar; (*Phot*) ampliar; **blow-dry** *n* moldeado (con secador)
blown [bləun] *pp of* **blow**
blue [blu:] *adj* azul; (*depressed*) deprimido; **~ film/joke** película/chiste *m* verde; **out of the ~** (*fig*) de repente; **bluebell** *n* campanilla, campánula azul; **blueberry** *n* arándano; **blue cheese** *n* queso azul; **blues** *npl*: **the blues** (*Mus*) el blues; **to have the blues** estar triste; **bluetit** *n* herrerillo *m* (común)
bluff [blʌf] *vi* tirarse un farol, farolear ▷*n* farol *m*; **to call sb's ~** coger a algn la palabra
blunder ['blʌndə*] *n* patinazo, metedura de pata ▷*vi* cometer un error, meter la pata
blunt [blʌnt] *adj* (*pencil*) despuntado; (*knife*) desafilado, romo; (*person*) franco, directo
blur [blə:*] *n* (*shape*): **to become a ~** hacerse borroso ▷*vt* (*vision*) enturbiar; (*distinction*) borrar; **blurred** *adj* borroso
blush [blʌʃ] *vi* ruborizarse, ponerse colorado ▷*n* rubor *m*; **blusher** *n* colorete *m*
board [bɔ:d] *n* (*cardboard*) cartón *m*; (*wooden*) tabla, tablero; (*on wall*) tablón *m*; (*for chess etc*) tablero; (*committee*) junta, consejo; (*in firm*) mesa *or* junta directiva; (*Naut, Aviat*): **on ~** a bordo ▷*vt* (*ship*) embarcarse en; (*train*) subir a; **full ~** (BRIT) pensión completa; **half ~** (BRIT) media pensión; **to go by the ~** (*fig*) ser abandonado *or* olvidado; **board game** *n* juego de tablero; **boarding card** (BRIT) *n* tarjeta de embarque; **boarding pass** (US) *n* = **boarding card**; **boarding school** *n* internado; **board room** *n* sala de juntas
boast [bəust] *vi*: **to ~ (about** *or* **of)** alardear (de)
boat [bəut] *n* barco, buque *m*; (*small*) barca, bote *m*
bob [bɔb] *vi* (*also*: **~ up and down**) menearse, balancearse
bobby pin ['bɔbɪ-] (US) *n* horquilla
body ['bɔdɪ] *n* cuerpo; (*corpse*) cadáver *m*; (*of car*) caja, carrocería; (*fig: group*) grupo; (*: organization*) organismo; **body-building** *n* culturismo; **bodyguard** *n* guardaespaldas *m inv*; **bodywork** *n* carrocería
bog [bɔg] *n* pantano, ciénaga ▷*vt*: **to get ~ged down** (*fig*) empantanarse, atascarse
bogus ['bəugəs] *adj* falso, fraudulento
boil [bɔɪl] *vt* (*water*) hervir; (*eggs*) pasar por agua, cocer ▷*vi* hervir; (*fig: with anger*) estar furioso; (*: with heat*) asfixiarse ▷*n* (*Med*) furúnculo, divieso; **to come to the ~**, **to come to a ~** (US) comenzar a hervir; **to ~ down to** (*fig*) reducirse a; **boil over** *vi* salirse, rebosar; (*anger etc*) llegar al colmo; **boiled egg** *n* (*soft*) huevo tibio (MEX) *or* pasado por agua *or* a la copa (SC); (*hard*) huevo duro; **boiled potatoes** *npl* patatas *fpl* (SP) *or* papas *fpl* (LAM) cocidas; **boiler** *n*

caldera; **boiling** ['bɔɪlɪŋ] *adj*: **I'm boiling (hot)** (*inf*) estoy asado; **boiling point** *n* punto de ebullición

bold [bəuld] *adj* valiente, audaz; (*pej*) descarado; (*colour*) llamativo

Bolivia [bə'lɪvɪə] *n* Bolivia; **Bolivian** *adj, n* boliviano/a *m/f*

bollard ['bɔləd] (BRIT) *n* (*Aut*) poste *m*

bolt [bəult] *n* (*lock*) cerrojo; (*with nut*) perno, tornillo ▷ *adv*: **~ upright** rígido, erguido ▷ *vt* (*door*) echar el cerrojo a; (*also*: **~ together**) sujetar con tornillos; (*food*) engullir ▷ *vi* fugarse; (*horse*) desbocarse

bomb [bɔm] *n* bomba ▷ *vt* bombardear; **bombard** [bɔm'bɑːd] *vt* bombardear; (*fig*) asediar; **bomber** *n* (*Aviat*) bombardero; **bomb scare** *n* amenaza de bomba

bond [bɔnd] *n* (*promise*) fianza; (*Finance*) bono; (*link*) vínculo, lazo; (*Comm*): **in ~** en depósito bajo fianza; **bonds** *npl* (*chains*) cadenas *fpl*

bone [bəun] *n* hueso; (*of fish*) espina ▷ *vt* deshuesar; quitar las espinas a

bonfire ['bɔnfaɪə*] *n* hoguera, fogata

bonnet ['bɔnɪt] *n* gorra; (BRIT: *of car*) capó *m*

bonus ['bəunəs] *n* (*payment*) paga extraordinaria, plus *m*; (*fig*) bendición *f*

boo [buː] *excl* ¡uh! ▷ *vt* abuchear, rechiflar

book [buk] *n* libro; (*of tickets*) taco; (*of stamps etc*) librito ▷ *vt* (*ticket*) sacar; (*seat, room*) reservar; **books** *npl* (*Comm*) cuentas *fpl*, contabilidad *f*; **book in** *vi* (*at hotel*) registrarse; **book up** *vt*: **to be booked up** (*hotel*) estar completo; **bookcase** *n* librería, estante *m* para libros; **booking** *n* reserva; **booking office** *n* (BRIT *Rail*) despacho de billetes (SP) *or* boletos (LAM); (*Theatre*) taquilla (SP), boletería (LAM); **book-keeping** *n* contabilidad *f*; **booklet** *n* folleto; **bookmaker** *n* corredor *m* de apuestas; **bookmark** *n* (*also Comput*) marcador; **bookseller** *n* librero; **bookshelf** *n* estante *m* (para libros); **bookshop, book store** *n* librería

boom [buːm] *n* (*noise*) trueno, estampido; (*in prices etc*) alza rápida; (*Econ, in population*) boom *m* ▷ *vi* (*cannon*) hacer gran estruendo, retumbar; (*Econ*) estar en alza

boost [buːst] *n* estímulo, empuje *m* ▷ *vt* estimular, empujar

boot [buːt] *n* bota; (BRIT: *of car*) maleta, maletero ▷ *vt* (*Comput*) arrancar; **to ~** (*in addition*) además, por añadidura

booth [buːð] *n* (*telephone booth, voting booth*) cabina

booze [buːz] (*inf*) *n* bebida

border ['bɔːdə*] *n* borde *m*, margen *m*; (*of a country*) frontera; (*for flowers*) arriate *m* ▷ *vt* (*road*) bordear; (*another country*: *also*: **~ on**) lindar con; **borderline** *n*: **on the borderline** en el límite

bore [bɔː*] *pt of* **bear** ▷ *vt* (*hole*) hacer un agujero en; (*well*) perforar; (*person*) aburrir ▷ *n* (*person*) pelmazo, pesado; (*of gun*) calibre *m*; **bored** *adj* aburrido; **he's bored to tears** *or* **to death** *or* **stiff** está aburrido como una ostra, está muerto de aburrimiento; **boredom** *n* aburrimiento

boring ['bɔːrɪŋ] *adj* aburrido

born [bɔːn] *adj*: **to be ~** nacer; **I was ~ in 1960** nací en 1960

borne [bɔːn] *pp of* **bear**

borough ['bʌrə] *n* municipio

borrow ['bɔrəu] *vt*: **to ~ sth (from sb)** tomar algo prestado (a algn)

Bosnia(-Herzegovina) ['bɔːsnɪə(hɛrzə'gəuviːnə)] *n* Bosnia(-Herzegovina); **Bosnian** ['bɔznɪən] *adj, n* bosnio/a

bosom ['buzəm] *n* pecho

boss [bɔs] *n* jefe *m* ▷ *vt* (*also*: **~ about or around**) mangonear; **bossy** *adj* mandón/ona

both [bəuθ] *adj, pron* ambos/as, los dos(las dos); **~ of us went, we ~ went** fuimos los dos, ambos fuimos ▷ *adv*: **~ A and B** tanto A como B

bother ['bɔðə*] *vt* (*worry*) preocupar; (*disturb*) molestar, fastidiar ▷ *vi* (*also*: **~ o.s.**) molestarse ▷ *n* (*trouble*) dificultad *f*; (*nuisance*) molestia, lata; **to ~ doing** tomarse la molestia de hacer

bottle ['bɔtl] *n* botella; (*small*) frasco; (*baby's*) biberón *m* ▷ *vt* embotellar; **bottle bank** *n* contenedor *m* de vidrio; **bottle-opener** *n* abrebotellas *m inv*

bottom ['bɔtəm] *n* (*of box, sea*) fondo; (*buttocks*) trasero, culo; (*of page*) pie *m*; (*of list*) final *m*; (*of class*) último/a ▷ *adj* (*lowest*) más bajo; (*last*) último

bought [bɔːt] *pt, pp of* **buy**

boulder ['bəuldə*] *n* canto rodado

bounce [bauns] *vi* (*ball*) (re)botar; (*cheque*) ser rechazado ▷ *vt* hacer (re)botar ▷ *n* (*rebound*) (re)bote *m*; **bouncer** (*inf*) *n* gorila *m* (*que echa a los alborotadores de un bar, club etc*)

bound [baund] *pt, pp of* **bind** ▷ *n* (*leap*) salto; (*gen pl*: *limit*) límite *m* ▷ *vi* (*leap*) saltar ▷ *vt* (*border*) rodear ▷ *adj*: **~ by** rodeado de; **to be ~ to do sth** (*obliged*) tener el deber de hacer algo; **he's ~ to come** es seguro que vendrá; **out of ~s** prohibido el paso; **~ for** con destino a

boundary ['baundrɪ] *n* límite *m*

bouquet ['bukeɪ] *n* (*of flowers*) ramo
bourbon ['buəbən] (US) *n* (*also*: **~ whiskey**) whisky *m* americano, bourbon *m*
bout [baut] *n* (*of malaria etc*) ataque *m*; (*of activity*) período; (*Boxing etc*) combate *m*, encuentro
boutique [bu:'ti:k] *n* boutique *f*, tienda de ropa
bow¹ [bəu] *n* (*knot*) lazo; (*weapon, Mus*) arco
bow² [bau] *n* (*of the head*) reverencia; (*Naut*: *also*: **~s**) proa ▷ *vi* inclinarse, hacer una reverencia
bowels [bauəlz] *npl* intestinos *mpl*, vientre *m*; (*fig*) entrañas *fpl*
bowl [bəul] *n* tazón *m*, cuenco; (*ball*) bola ▷ *vi* (*Cricket*) arrojar la pelota; *see also* **bowls**; **bowler** *n* (*Cricket*) lanzador *m* (de la pelota); (BRIT: *also*: **bowler hat**) hongo, bombín *m*; **bowling** *n* (*game*) bochas *fpl*, bolos *mpl*; **bowling alley** *n* bolera; **bowling green** *n* pista para bochas; **bowls** *n* juego de las bochas, bolos *mpl*
bow tie ['bəu-] *n* corbata de lazo, pajarita
box [bɔks] *n* (*also*: **cardboard ~**) caja, cajón *m*; (*Theatre*) palco ▷ *vt* encajonar ▷ *vi* (*Sport*) boxear; **boxer** ['bɔksə*] *n* (*person*) boxeador *m*; **boxer shorts** ['bɔksəʃɔ:ts] *pl n* bóxers; **a pair of boxer shorts** unos bóxers; **boxing** ['bɔksɪŋ] *n* (*Sport*) boxeo; **Boxing Day** (BRIT) *n día en que se dan los aguinaldos, 26 de diciembre*; **boxing gloves** *npl* guantes *mpl* de boxeo; **boxing ring** *n* ring *m*, cuadrilátero; **box office** *n* taquilla (SP), boletería (LAM)
boy [bɔɪ] *n* (*young*) niño; (*older*) muchacho, chico; (*son*) hijo; **boy band** *n* boy band *m* (*grupo musical de chicos*)
boycott ['bɔɪkɔt] *n* boicot *m* ▷ *vt* boicotear
boyfriend ['bɔɪfrɛnd] *n* novio
bra [brɑ:] *n* sostén *m*, sujetador *m*
brace [breɪs] *n* (BRIT: *also*: **~s**: *on teeth*) corrector *m*, aparato; (*tool*) berbiquí *m* ▷ *vt* (*knees, shoulders*) tensionar; **braces** *npl* (BRIT) tirantes *mpl*; **to ~ o.s.** (*fig*) prepararse
bracelet ['breɪslɪt] *n* pulsera, brazalete *m*
bracket ['brækɪt] *n* (*Tech*) soporte *m*, puntal *m*; (*group*) clase *f*, categoría; (*also*: **brace ~**) soporte *m*, abrazadera; (*also*: **round ~**) paréntesis *m inv*; (*also*: **square ~**) corchete *m* ▷ *vt* (*word etc*) poner entre paréntesis
brag [bræg] *vi* jactarse
braid [breɪd] *n* (*trimming*) galón *m*; (*of hair*) trenza
brain [breɪn] *n* cerebro; **brains** *npl* sesos *mpl*; **she's got ~s** es muy lista
braise [breɪz] *vt* cocer a fuego lento
brake [breɪk] *n* (*on vehicle*) freno ▷ *vi* frenar; **brake light** *n* luz *f* de frenado
bran [bræn] *n* salvado
branch [brɑ:ntʃ] *n* rama; (*Comm*) sucursal *f*; **branch off** *vi*: **a small road branches off to the right** hay una carretera pequeña que sale hacia la derecha; **branch out** *vi* (*fig*) extenderse
brand [brænd] *n* marca; (*fig*: *type*) tipo ▷ *vt* (*cattle*) marcar con hierro candente; **brand name** *n* marca; **brand-new** *adj* flamante, completamente nuevo
brandy ['brændɪ] *n* coñac *m*
brash [bræʃ] *adj* (*forward*) descarado
brass [brɑ:s] *n* latón *m*; **the ~** (*Mus*) los cobres; **brass band** *n* banda de metal
brat [bræt] (*pej*) *n* mocoso/a
brave [breɪv] *adj* valiente, valeroso ▷ *vt* (*face up to*) desafiar; **bravery** *n* valor *m*, valentía
brawl [brɔ:l] *n* pelea, reyerta
Brazil [brə'zɪl] *n* (el) Brasil; **Brazilian** *adj, n* brasileño/a *m/f*
breach [bri:tʃ] *vt* abrir brecha en ▷ *n* (*gap*) brecha; (*breaking*): **~ of contract** infracción *f* de contrato; **~ of the peace** perturbación *f* del órden público
bread [brɛd] *n* pan *m*; **breadbin** *n* panera; **breadbox** (US) *n* panera; **breadcrumbs** *npl* migajas *fpl*; (*Culin*) pan rallado
breadth [brɛtθ] *n* anchura; (*fig*) amplitud *f*
break [breɪk] (*pt* **broke**, *pp* **broken**) *vt* romper; (*promise*) faltar a; (*law*) violar, infringir; (*record*) batir ▷ *vi* romperse, quebrarse; (*storm*) estallar; (*weather*) cambiar; (*dawn*) despuntar; (*news etc*) darse a conocer ▷ *n* (*gap*) abertura; (*fracture*) fractura; (*time*) intervalo; (*: at school*) (período de) recreo; (*chance*) oportunidad *f*; **to ~ the news to sb** comunicar la noticia a algn; **break down** *vt* (*figures, data*) analizar, descomponer ▷ *vi* (*machine*) estropearse; (*Aut*) averiarse; (*person*) romper a llorar; (*talks*) fracasar; **break in** *vt* (*horse etc*) domar ▷ *vi* (*burglar*) forzar una entrada; (*interrupt*) interrumpir; **break into** *vt fus* (*house*) forzar; **break off** *vi* (*speaker*) pararse, detenerse; (*branch*) partir; **break out** *vi* estallar; (*prisoner*) escaparse; **to break out in spots** salirle a algn granos; **break up** *vi* (*ship*) hacerse pedazos; (*crowd, meeting*) disolverse; (*marriage*) deshacerse; (*Scol*) terminar (el curso); (*line*) cortarse ▷ *vt* (*rocks etc*) partir; (*journey*) partir; (*fight etc*) acabar con; **the line's** *or* **you're breaking up** se corta; **breakdown** *n* (*Aut*) avería; (*in communications*) interrupción *f*; (*Med*: *also*: **nervous breakdown**) colapso, crisis *f* nerviosa; (*of marriage, talks*) fracaso; (*of

statistics) análisis *m inv*; **breakdown truck, breakdown van** *n* (camión *m*) grúa
breakfast ['brɛkfəst] *n* desayuno
break: break-in *n* robo con allanamiento de morada; **breakthrough** *n* (*also fig*) avance *m*
breast [brɛst] *n* (*of woman*) pecho, seno; (*chest*) pecho; (*of bird*) pechuga; **breast-feed** (*pt, pp* **breast-fed**) *vt, vi* amamantar, criar a los pechos; **breast-stroke** *n* braza (de pecho)
breath [brɛθ] *n* aliento, respiración *f*; **to take a deep ~** respirar hondo; **out of ~** sin aliento, sofocado
Breathalyser® ['brɛθəlaɪzə*] (BRIT) *n* alcoholímetro
breathe [bri:ð] *vt, vi* respirar; **breathe in** *vt, vi* aspirar; **breathe out** *vt, vi* espirar; **breathing** *n* respiración *f*
breath: breathless *adj* sin aliento, jadeante; **breathtaking** *adj* imponente, pasmoso; **breath test** *n* prueba de la alcoholemia
bred [bred] *pt, pp of* **breed**
breed [bri:d] (*pt, pp* **bred**) *vt* criar ▷ *vi* reproducirse, procrear ▷ *n* (*Zool*) raza, casta; (*type*) tipo
breeze [bri:z] *n* brisa
breezy ['bri:zɪ] *adj* de mucho viento, ventoso; (*person*) despreocupado
brew [bru:] *vt* (*tea*) hacer; (*beer*) elaborar ▷ *vi* (*fig: trouble*) prepararse; (*storm*) amenazar; **brewery** *n* fábrica de cerveza, cervecería
bribe [braɪb] *n* soborno ▷ *vt* sobornar, cohechar; **bribery** *n* soborno, cohecho
bric-a-brac ['brɪkabræk] *n inv* baratijas *fpl*
brick [brɪk] *n* ladrillo; **bricklayer** *n* albañil *m*
bride [braɪd] *n* novia; **bridegroom** *n* novio; **bridesmaid** *n* dama de honor
bridge [brɪdʒ] *n* puente *m*; (*Naut*) puente *m* de mando; (*of nose*) caballete *m*; (*Cards*) bridge *m* ▷ *vt* (*fig*): **to ~ a gap** llenar un vacío
bridle ['braɪdl] *n* brida, freno
brief [bri:f] *adj* breve, corto ▷ *n* (*Law*) escrito; (*task*) cometido, encargo ▷ *vt* informar; **briefs** *npl* (*for men*) calzoncillos *mpl*; (*for women*) bragas *fpl*; **briefcase** *n* cartera (SP), portafolio (LAM); **briefing** *n* (*Press*) informe *m*; **briefly** *adv* (*glance*) fugazmente; (*say*) en pocas palabras
brigadier [brɪgə'dɪə*] *n* general *m* de brigada
bright [braɪt] *adj* brillante; (*room*) luminoso; (*day*) de sol; (*person: clever*) listo, inteligente; (*: lively*) alegre; (*colour*) vivo; (*future*) prometedor(a)
brilliant ['brɪljənt] *adj* brillante; (*inf*) fenomenal
brim [brɪm] *n* borde *m*; (*of hat*) ala
brine [braɪn] *n* (*Culin*) salmuera
bring [brɪŋ] (*pt, pp* **brought**) *vt* (*thing, person: with you*) traer; (*: to sb*) llevar, conducir; (*trouble, satisfaction*) causar; **bring about** *vt* ocasionar, producir; **bring back** *vt* volver a traer; (*return*) devolver; **bring down** *vt* (*government, plane*) derribar; (*price*) rebajar; **bring in** *vt* (*harvest*) recoger; (*person*) hacer entrar *or* pasar; (*object*) traer; (*Pol: bill, law*) presentar; (*produce: income*) producir, rendir; **bring on** *vt* (*illness, attack*) producir, causar; (*player, substitute*) sacar (de la reserva), hacer salir; **bring out** *vt* sacar; (*book etc*) publicar; (*meaning*) subrayar; **bring up** *vt* subir; (*person*) educar, criar; (*question*) sacar a colación; (*food: vomit*) devolver, vomitar
brink [brɪŋk] *n* borde *m*
brisk [brɪsk] *adj* (*abrupt: tone*) brusco; (*person*) enérgico, vigoroso; (*pace*) rápido; (*trade*) activo
bristle ['brɪsl] *n* cerda ▷ *vi*: **to ~ in anger** temblar de rabia
Brit [brɪt] *n abbr* (*inf: = British person*) británico/a
Britain ['brɪtən] *n* (*also*: **Great ~**) Gran Bretaña
British ['brɪtɪʃ] *adj* británico ▷ *npl*: **the ~** los británicos; **British Isles** *npl*: **the British Isles** las Islas Británicas
Briton ['brɪtən] *n* británico/a
brittle ['brɪtl] *adj* quebradizo, frágil
broad [brɔ:d] *adj* ancho; (*range*) amplio; (*smile*) abierto; (*general: outlines etc*) general; (*accent*) cerrado; **in ~ daylight** en pleno día; **broadband** *n* banda ancha; **broad bean** *n* haba; **broadcast** (*pt, pp* **~**) *n* emisión *f* ▷ *vt* (*Radio*) emitir; (*TV*) transmitir ▷ *vi* emitir; transmitir; **broaden** *vt* ampliar ▷ *vi* ensancharse; **to broaden one's mind** hacer más tolerante a algn; **broadly** *adv* en general; **broad-minded** *adj* tolerante, liberal
broccoli ['brɔkəlɪ] *n* brécol *m*
brochure ['brəuʃjuə*] *n* folleto
broil [brɔɪl] *vt* (*Culin*) asar a la parrilla
broiler ['brɔɪlə*] *n* (*grill*) parrilla
broke [brəuk] *pt of* **break** ▷ *adj* (*inf*) pelado, sin blanca
broken ['brəukən] *pp of* **break** ▷ *adj* roto; (*machine: also*: **~ down**) averiado; **~ leg** pierna rota; **in ~ English** en un inglés imperfecto

broker ['brəukə*] *n* agente *mf*, bolsista *mf*; (*insurance broker*) agente de seguros
bronchitis [brɔŋ'kaɪtɪs] *n* bronquitis *f*
bronze [brɔnz] *n* bronce *m*
brooch [brəutʃ] *n* prendedor *m*, broche *m*
brood [bru:d] *n* camada, cría ▷*vi* (*person*) dejarse obsesionar
broom [brum] *n* escoba; (*Bot*) retama
Bros. *abbr* (= *Brothers*) Hnos
broth [brɔθ] *n* caldo
brothel ['brɔθl] *n* burdel *m*
brother ['brʌðə*] *n* hermano; **brother-in-law** *n* cuñado
brought [brɔ:t] *pt, pp of* **bring**
brow [brau] *n* (*forehead*) frente *m*; (*eyebrow*) ceja; (*of hill*) cumbre *f*
brown [braun] *adj* (*colour*) marrón; (*hair*) castaño; (*tanned*) bronceado, moreno ▷*n* (*colour*) color *m* marrón *or* pardo ▷*vt* (*Culin*) dorar; **brown bread** *n* pan integral
Brownie ['braunɪ] *n* niña exploradora
brown rice *n* arroz *m* integral
brown sugar *n* azúcar *m* terciado
browse [brauz] *vi* (*through book*) hojear; (*in shop*) mirar; **browser** *n* (*Comput*) navegador *m*
bruise [bru:z] *n* cardenal *m* (SP), moretón *m* ▷*vt* magullar
brunette [bru:'nɛt] *n* morena
brush [brʌʃ] *n* cepillo; (*for painting, shaving etc*) brocha; (*artist's*) pincel *m*; (*with police etc*) roce *m* ▷*vt* (*sweep*) barrer; (*groom*) cepillar; (*also*: **~ against**) rozar al pasar
Brussels ['brʌslz] *n* Bruselas
Brussels sprout *n* col *f* de Bruselas
brutal ['bru:tl] *adj* brutal
B.Sc. *abbr* (= *Bachelor of Science*) *licenciado en Ciencias*
BSE *n abbr* (= *bovine spongiform encephalopathy*) encefalopatía espongiforme bovina
bubble ['bʌbl] *n* burbuja ▷*vi* burbujear, borbotar; **bubble bath** *n* espuma para el baño; **bubble gum** *n* chicle *m* de globo; **bubblejet printer** ['bʌbldʒɛt-] *n* impresora de injección por burbujas
buck [bʌk] *n* (*rabbit*) conejo macho; (*deer*) gamo; (US: *inf*) dólar *m* ▷*vi* corcovear; **to pass the ~ (to sb)** echar (a algn) el muerto
bucket ['bʌkɪt] *n* cubo, balde *m*
buckle ['bʌkl] *n* hebilla ▷*vt* abrochar con hebilla ▷*vi* combarse
bud [bʌd] *n* (*of plant*) brote *m*, yema; (*of flower*) capullo ▷*vi* brotar, echar brotes
Buddhism ['budɪzm] *n* Budismo
Buddhist ['budɪst] *adj, n* budista *m/f*
buddy ['bʌdɪ] (US) *n* compañero, compinche *m*
budge [bʌdʒ] *vt* mover; (*fig*) hacer ceder ▷*vi* moverse, ceder
budgerigar ['bʌdʒərɪgɑ:*] *n* periquito
budget ['bʌdʒɪt] *n* presupuesto ▷*vi*: **to ~ for sth** presupuestar algo
budgie ['bʌdʒɪ] *n* = **budgerigar**
buff [bʌf] *adj* (*colour*) color de ante ▷*n* (*inf*: *enthusiast*) entusiasta *mf*
buffalo ['bʌfələu] (*pl* **~** *or* **~es**) *n* (BRIT) búfalo; (US: *bison*) bisonte *m*
buffer ['bʌfə*] *n* (*Comput*) memoria intermedia; (*Rail*) tope *m*
buffet¹ ['bʌfɪt] *vt* golpear
buffet² ['bufeɪ] *n* (BRIT: *in station*) bar *m*, cafetería; (*food*) buffet *m*; **buffet car** (BRIT) *n* (*Rail*) coche-comedor *m*
bug [bʌg] *n* (*esp* US: *insect*) bicho, sabandija; (*Comput*) error *m*; (*germ*) microbio, bacilo; (*spy device*) micrófono oculto ▷*vt* (*inf*: *annoy*) fastidiar; (*room*) poner micrófono oculto en
buggy ['bʌgɪ] *n* cochecito de niño
build [bɪld] (*pt, pp* **built**) *n* (*of person*) tipo ▷*vt* construir, edificar; **build up** *vt* (*morale, forces, production*) acrecentar; (*stocks*) acumular; **builder** *n* (*contractor*) contratista *mf*; **building** *n* construcción *f*; (*structure*) edificio; **building site** *n* obra; **building society** (BRIT) *n* sociedad *f* inmobiliaria
built [bɪlt] *pt, pp of* **build**; **built-in** *adj* (*cupboard*) empotrado; (*device*) interior, incorporado; **built-up** *adj* (*area*) urbanizado
bulb [bʌlb] *n* (*Bot*) bulbo; (*Elec*) bombilla, foco (MEX), bujía (CAM), bombita (RPL)
Bulgaria [bʌl'gɛərɪə] *n* Bulgaria; **Bulgarian** *adj, n* búlgaro/a *m/f*
bulge [bʌldʒ] *n* bulto, protuberancia ▷*vi* bombearse, pandearse; (*pocket etc*): **to ~ (with)** rebosar (de)
bulimia [bə'lɪmɪə] *n* bulimia
bulimic [bju:'lɪmɪk] *adj, n* bulímico/a *m/f*
bulk [bʌlk] *n* masa, mole *f*; **in ~** (*Comm*) a granel; **the ~ of** la mayor parte de; **bulky** *adj* voluminoso, abultado
bull [bul] *n* toro; (*male elephant, whale*) macho
bulldozer ['buldəuzə*] *n* bulldozer *m*
bullet ['bulɪt] *n* bala
bulletin ['bulɪtɪn] *n* anuncio, parte *m*; (*journal*) boletín *m*; **bulletin board** *n* (US) tablón *m* de anuncios; (*Comput*) tablero de noticias
bullfight ['bulfaɪt] *n* corrida de toros; **bullfighter** *n* torero; **bullfighting** *n* los toros, el toreo
bully ['bulɪ] *n* valentón *m*, matón *m* ▷*vt*

intimidar, tiranizar
bum [bʌm] *n* (*inf: backside*) culo; (*esp* US: *tramp*) vagabundo
bumblebee ['bʌmblbi:] *n* abejorro
bump [bʌmp] *n* (*blow*) tope *m*, choque *m*; (*jolt*) sacudida; (*on road etc*) bache *m*; (*on head etc*) chichón *m* ▷ *vt* (*strike*) chocar contra; **bump into** *vt fus* chocar contra, tropezar con; (*person*) topar con; **bumper** *n* (*Aut*) parachoques *m inv* ▷ *adj*: **bumper crop** *or* **harvest** cosecha abundante; **bumpy** *adj* (*road*) lleno de baches
bun [bʌn] *n* (BRIT: *cake*) pastel *m*; (US: *bread*) bollo; (*of hair*) moño
bunch [bʌntʃ] *n* (*of flowers*) ramo; (*of keys*) manojo; (*of bananas*) piña; (*of people*) grupo; **bunches** *npl* (*in hair*) coletas *fpl*
bundle ['bʌndl] *n* bulto, fardo; (*of sticks*) haz *m*; (*of papers*) legajo ▷ *vt* (*also*: **~ up**) atar, envolver; **to ~ sth/sb into** meter algo/a algn precipitadamente en
bungalow ['bʌŋgələu] *n* bungalow *m*, chalé *m*
bungee jumping ['bʌndʒi:'dʒʌmpɪŋ] *n* puenting *m*, banyi *m*
bunion ['bʌnjən] *n* juanete *m*
bunk [bʌŋk] *n* litera; **bunk beds** *npl* literas *fpl*
bunker ['bʌŋkə*] *n* (*coal store*) carbonera; (*Mil*) refugio; (*Golf*) bunker *m*
bunny ['bʌnɪ] *n* (*inf*: *also*: **~ rabbit**) conejito
buoy [bɔɪ] *n* boya; **buoyant** *adj* (*ship*) capaz de flotar; (*economy*) boyante; (*person*) optimista
burden ['bə:dn] *n* carga ▷ *vt* cargar
bureau [bjuə'rəu] (*pl* **~x**) *n* (BRIT: *writing desk*) escritorio, buró *m*; (US: *chest of drawers*) cómoda; (*office*) oficina, agencia
bureaucracy [bjuə'rɔkrəsɪ] *n* burocracia
bureaucrat ['bjuərəkræt] *n* burócrata *m/f*
bureau de change [-də'ʃɑ̃ʒ] (*pl* **bureaux de change**) *n* caja *f* de cambio
bureaux ['bjuərəuz] *npl of* **bureau**
burger ['bə:gə*] *n* hamburguesa
burglar ['bə:glə*] *n* ladrón/ona *m/f*; **burglar alarm** *n* alarma *f* antirrobo; **burglary** *n* robo con allanamiento, robo de una casa
burial ['bɛrɪəl] *n* entierro
burn [bə:n] (*pt, pp* **~ed** *or* **~t**) *vt* quemar; (*house*) incendiar ▷ *vi* quemarse, arder; incendiarse; (*sting*) escocer ▷ *n* quemadura; **burn down** *vt* incendiar; **burn out** *vt* (*writer etc*): **to burn o.s. out** agotarse; **burning** *adj* (*building etc*) en llamas; (*hot*: *sand etc*) abrasador(a); (*ambition*) ardiente
Burns' Night [bə:nz-] *n ver abajo*

BURNS' NIGHT

Cada veinticinco de enero los escoceses celebran la llamada **Burns' Night** (noche de Burns), en honor al poeta escocés Robert Burns (1759–1796). Es tradición hacer una cena en la que, al son de la música de la gaita escocesa, se sirve "haggis", plato tradicional de asadura de cordero cocida en el estómago del animal, acompañado de nabos y puré de patatas. Durante la misma se recitan poemas del autor y varios discursos conmemorativos de carácter festivo.

burnt [bə:nt] *pt, pp of* **burn**
burp [bə:p] (*inf*) *n* eructo ▷ *vi* eructar
burrow ['bʌrəu] *n* madriguera ▷ *vi* hacer una madriguera; (*rummage*) hurgar
burst [bə:st] (*pt, pp* **~**) *vt* reventar; (*river: banks etc*) romper ▷ *vi* reventarse; (*tyre*) pincharse ▷ *n* (*of gunfire*) ráfaga; (*also*: **~ pipe**) reventón *m*; **a ~ of energy/speed/enthusiasm** una explosión de energía/un ímpetu de velocidad/un arranque de entusiasmo; **to ~ into flames** estallar en llamas; **to ~ into tears** deshacerse en lágrimas; **to ~ out laughing** soltar la carcajada; **to ~ open** abrirse de golpe; **to be ~ing with** (*container*) estar lleno a rebosar de; (*: person*) reventar por *or* de; **burst into** *vt fus* (*room etc*) irrumpir en
bury ['bɛrɪ] *vt* enterrar; (*body*) enterrar, sepultar
bus [bʌs] (*pl* **~es**) *n* autobús *m*
bush [buʃ] *n* arbusto; (*scrub land*) monte *m*; **to beat about the ~** andar(se) con rodeos
business ['bɪznɪs] *n* (*matter*) asunto; (*trading*) comercio, negocios *mpl*; (*firm*) empresa, casa; (*occupation*) oficio; **to be away on ~** estar en viaje de negocios; **it's my ~ to ...** me toca *or* corresponde ...; **it's none of my ~** yo no tengo nada que ver; **he means ~** habla en serio; **business class** *n* (*Aer*) clase *f* preferente; **businesslike** *adj* eficiente; **businessman** (*irreg*) *n* hombre *m* de negocios; **business trip** *n* viaje *m* de negocios; **businesswoman** (*irreg*) *n* mujer *f* de negocios
busker ['bʌskə*] (BRIT) *n* músico/a ambulante
bus: bus pass *n* bonobús; **bus shelter** *n* parada cubierta; **bus station** *n* estación *f* de autobuses; **bus stop** *n* parada de autobús
bust [bʌst] *n* (*Anat*) pecho; (*sculpture*) busto

▷*adj* (*inf: broken*) roto, estropeado; **to go ~** quebrar

bustling ['bʌslɪŋ] *adj* (*town*) animado, bullicioso

busy ['bɪzɪ] *adj* ocupado, atareado; (*shop, street*) concurrido, animado; (*Tel: line*) comunicando ▷*vt*: **to ~ o.s. with** ocuparse en; **busy signal** (*US*) *n* (*Tel*) señal *f* de comunicando

KEYWORD

but [bʌt] *conj* **1** pero; **he's not very bright, but he's hard-working** no es muy inteligente, pero es trabajador
2 (*in direct contradiction*) sino; **he's not English but French** no es inglés sino francés; **he didn't sing but he shouted** no cantó sino que gritó
3 (*showing disagreement, surprise etc*): **but that's far too expensive!** ¡pero eso es carísimo!; **but it does work!** ¡(pero) sí que funciona!
▷*prep* (*apart from, except*) menos, salvo; **we've had nothing but trouble** no hemos tenido más que problemas; **no-one but him can do it** nadie más que él puede hacerlo; **who but a lunatic would do such a thing?** ¡sólo un loco haría una cosa así!; **but for you/your help** si no fuera por ti/tu ayuda; **anything but that** cualquier cosa menos eso
▷*adv* (*just, only*): **she's but a child** no es más que una niña; **had I but known** si lo hubiera sabido; **I can but try** al menos lo puedo intentar; **it's all but finished** está casi acabado

butcher ['butʃə*] *n* carnicero ▷*vt* hacer una carnicería con; (*cattle etc*) matar; **butcher's (shop)** *n* carnicería

butler ['bʌtlə*] *n* mayordomo

butt [bʌt] *n* (*barrel*) tonel *m*; (*of gun*) culata; (*of cigarette*) colilla; (BRIT: *fig: target*) blanco ▷*vt* dar cabezadas contra, top(et)ar

butter ['bʌtə*] *n* mantequilla ▷*vt* untar con mantequilla; **buttercup** *n* botón *m* de oro

butterfly ['bʌtəflaɪ] *n* mariposa; (*Swimming: also*: **~ stroke**) braza de mariposa

buttocks ['bʌtəks] *npl* nalgas *fpl*

button ['bʌtn] *n* botón *m*; (*US*) placa, chapa ▷*vt* (*also*: **~ up**) abotonar, abrochar ▷*vi* abrocharse

buy [baɪ] (*pt, pp* **bought**) *vt* comprar ▷*n* compra; **to ~ sb sth/sth from sb** comprarle algo a algn; **to ~ sb a drink** invitar a algn a tomar algo; **buy out** *vt* (*partner*) comprar la parte de; **buy up** *vt* (*property*) acaparar; (*stock*) comprar todas las existencias de; **buyer** *n* comprador(a) *m/f*

buzz [bʌz] *n* zumbido; (*inf: phone call*) llamada (por teléfono) ▷*vi* zumbar; **buzzer** *n* timbre *m*

KEYWORD

by [baɪ] *prep* **1** (*referring to cause, agent*) por; de; **killed by lightning** muerto por un relámpago; **a painting by Picasso** un cuadro de Picasso
2 (*referring to method, manner, means*): **by bus/car/train** en autobús/coche/tren; **to pay by cheque** pagar con un cheque; **by moonlight/candlelight** a la luz de la luna/una vela; **by saving hard he ...** ahorrando ...
3 (*via, through*) por; **we came by Dover** vinimos por Dover
4 (*close to, past*): **the house by the river** la casa junto al río; **she rushed by me** pasó a mi lado como una exhalación; **I go by the post office every day** paso por delante de Correos todos los días
5 (*time: not later than*) para; (*: during*): **by daylight** de día; **by 4 o'clock** para las cuatro; **by this time tomorrow** mañana a estas horas; **by the time I got here it was too late** cuando llegué ya era demasiado tarde
6 (*amount*): **by the metre/kilo** por metro/kilo; **paid by the hour** pagado por hora
7 (*Math, measure*): **to divide/multiply by 3** dividir/multiplicar por 3; **a room 3 metres by 4** una habitación de 3 metros por 4; **it's broader by a metre** es un metro más ancho
8 (*according to*) según, de acuerdo con; **it's 3 o'clock by my watch** según mi reloj, son las tres; **it's all right by me** por mí, está bien
9: **(all) by oneself** *etc* todo solo; **he did it (all) by himself** lo hizo él solo; **he was standing (all) by himself in a corner** estaba de pie solo en un rincón
10: **by the way** a propósito, por cierto; **this wasn't my idea, by the way** pues, no fue idea mía
▷*adv* **1** *see* **go; pass** *etc*
2: **by and by** finalmente; **they'll come back by and by** acabarán volviendo; **by and large** en líneas generales, en general

bye(-bye) ['baɪ('baɪ)] *excl* adiós, hasta luego

by-election (BRIT) *n* elección *f* parcial

bypass ['baɪpɑːs] *n* carretera de circunvalación; (*Med*) (operación *f* de) by-pass *f* ▷*vt* evitar

byte [baɪt] *n* (*Comput*) byte *m*, octeto

C

C [siː] *n* (*Mus*) do *m*
cab [kæb] *n* taxi *m*; (*of truck*) cabina
cabaret ['kæbəreɪ] *n* cabaret *m*
cabbage ['kæbɪdʒ] *n* col *f*, berza
cabin ['kæbɪn] *n* cabaña; (*on ship*) camarote *m*; (*on plane*) cabina; **cabin crew** *n* tripulación *f* de cabina
cabinet ['kæbɪnɪt] *n* (*Pol*) consejo de ministros; (*furniture*) armario; (*also*: **display ~**) vitrina; **cabinet minister** *n* ministro/a (del gabinete)
cable ['keɪbl] *n* cable *m* ▷ *vt* cablegrafiar; **cable car** *n* teleférico; **cable television** *n* televisión *f* por cable
cactus ['kæktəs] (*pl* **cacti**) *n* cacto
café ['kæfeɪ] *n* café *m*
cafeteria [kæfɪ'tɪərɪə] *n* cafetería
caffein(e) ['kæfiːn] *n* cafeína
cage [keɪdʒ] *n* jaula
cagoule [kə'guːl] *n* chubasquero
cake [keɪk] *n* (*Culin*: *large*) tarta; (: *small*) pastel *m*; (*of soap*) pastilla
calcium ['kælsɪəm] *n* calcio
calculate ['kælkjuleɪt] *vt* calcular; **calculation** [-'leɪʃən] *n* cálculo, cómputo; **calculator** *n* calculadora
calendar ['kæləndə*] *n* calendario
calf [kɑːf] (*pl* **calves**) *n* (*of cow*) ternero, becerro; (*of other animals*) cría; (*also*: **~skin**) piel *f* de becerro; (*Anat*) pantorrilla
calibre ['kælɪbə*] (*US* **caliber**) *n* calibre *m*
call [kɔːl] *vt* llamar; (*meeting*) convocar ▷ *vi* (*shout*) llamar; (*Tel*) llamar (por teléfono); (*visit*: *also*: **~ in, ~ round**) hacer una visita ▷ *n* llamada; (*of bird*) canto; **to be ~ed** llamarse; **on ~** (*on duty*) de guardia; **call back** *vi* (*return*) volver; (*Tel*) volver a llamar; **call for** *vt fus* (*demand*) pedir, exigir; (*fetch*) pasar a recoger; **call in** *vt* (*doctor, expert, police*) llamar; **call off** *vt* (*cancel*: *meeting, race*) cancelar; (: *deal*) anular; (: *strike*) desconvocar; **call on** *vt fus* (*visit*) visitar; (*turn to*) acudir a; **call out** *vi* gritar; **call up** *vt* (*Mil*) llamar al servicio militar; (*Tel*) llamar; **callbox** (BRIT) *n* cabina telefónica; **call centre** (*US* **call center**) *n* centro de atención al cliente; **caller** *n* visita; (*Tel*) usuario/a
callous ['kæləs] *adj* insensible, cruel
calm [kɑːm] *adj* tranquilo; (*sea*) liso, en calma ▷ *n* calma, tranquilidad *f* ▷ *vt* calmar, tranquilizar; **calm down** *vi* calmarse, tranquilizarse ▷ *vt* calmar, tranquilizar; **calmly** ['kɑːmlɪ] *adv* tranquilamente, con calma
Calor gas® ['kælə*-] *n* butano
calorie ['kælərɪ] *n* caloría
calves [kɑːvz] *npl of* **calf**
camcorder ['kæmkɔːdə*] *n* videocámara
came [keɪm] *pt of* **come**
camel ['kæməl] *n* camello
camera ['kæmərə] *n* máquina fotográfica; (*Cinema, TV*) cámara; **in ~** (*Law*) a puerta cerrada; **cameraman** (*irreg*) *n* cámara *m*; **camera phone** *n* teléfono con cámara
camouflage ['kæməflɑːʒ] *n* camuflaje *m* ▷ *vt* camuflar
camp [kæmp] *n* campamento, camping *m*; (*Mil*) campamento; (*for prisoners*) campo; (*fig*: *faction*) bando ▷ *vi* acampar ▷ *adj* afectado, afeminado
campaign [kæm'peɪn] *n* (*Mil, Pol etc*) campaña ▷ *vi* hacer campaña; **campaigner** *n*: **campaigner for** defensor(a) *m/f* de
camp: campbed (BRIT) *n* cama de campaña; **camper** *n* campista *mf*; (*vehicle*) caravana; **campground** (*US*) *n* camping *m*, campamento; **camping** *n* camping *m*; **to go camping** hacer camping; **campsite** *n* camping *m*
campus ['kæmpəs] *n* ciudad *f* universitaria
can¹ [kæn] *n* (*of oil, water*) bidón *m*; (*tin*) lata, bote *m* ▷ *vt* enlatar

KEYWORD

can² [kæn] (*negative* **cannot, can't**, *conditional and pt* **could**) *aux vb* **1** (*be able to*) poder; **you can do it if you try** puedes hacerlo si lo intentas; **I can't see you** no te veo
2 (*know how to*) saber; **I can swim/play tennis/drive** sé nadar/jugar al tenis/conducir; **can you speak French?** ¿hablas *or* sabes hablar francés?
3 (*may*) poder; **can I use your phone?** ¿me dejas *or* puedo usar tu teléfono?
4 (*expressing disbelief, puzzlement etc*): **it can't**

be true! ¡no puede ser (verdad)!; **what CAN he want?** ¿qué querrá?
5 (*expressing possibility, suggestion etc*): **he could be in the library** podría estar en la biblioteca; **she could have been delayed** pudo haberse retrasado

Canada ['kænədə] *n* (el) Canadá; **Canadian** [kə'neɪdɪən] *adj, n* canadiense *mf*
canal [kə'næl] *n* canal *m*
canary [kə'nɛərɪ] *n* canario
Canary Islands [kə'nɛərɪ'aɪləndz] *npl*: **the ~** las (Islas) Canarias
cancel ['kænsəl] *vt* cancelar; (*train*) suprimir; (*cross out*) tachar, borrar; **cancellation** [-'leɪʃən] *n* cancelación *f*; supresión *f*
Cancer ['kænsə*] *n* (*Astrology*) Cáncer *m*
cancer ['kænsə*] *n* cáncer *m*
candidate ['kændɪdeɪt] *n* candidato/a
candle ['kændl] *n* vela; (*in church*) cirio; **candlestick** *n* (*single*) candelero; (*low*) palmatoria; (*bigger, ornate*) candelabro
candy ['kændɪ] *n* azúcar *m* cande; (*US*) caramelo; **candy bar** (*US*) *n* barrita (*dulce*); **candyfloss** (BRIT) *n* algodón *m* (azucarado)
cane [keɪn] *n* (*Bot*) caña; (*stick*) vara, palmeta; (*for furniture*) mimbre *f* ▷ *vt* (BRIT: *Scol*) castigar (con vara)
canister ['kænɪstə*] *n* bote *m*, lata; (*of gas*) bombona
cannabis ['kænəbɪs] *n* marijuana
canned [kænd] *adj* en lata, de lata
cannon ['kænən] (*pl* **~** *or* **~s**) *n* cañón *m*
cannot ['kænɔt] = **can not**
canoe [kə'nu:] *n* canoa; (*Sport*) piragua; **canoeing** *n* piragüismo
canon ['kænən] *n* (*clergyman*) canónigo; (*standard*) canon *m*
can-opener ['kænəupnə*] *n* abrelatas *m inv*
can't [kænt] = **can not**
canteen [kæn'ti:n] *n* (*eating place*) cantina; (BRIT: *of cutlery*) juego
canter ['kæntə*] *vi* ir a medio galope
canvas ['kænvəs] *n* (*material*) lona; (*painting*) lienzo; (*Naut*) velas *fpl*
canvass ['kænvəs] *vi* (*Pol*): **to ~ for** solicitar votos por ▷ *vt* (*Comm*) sondear
canyon ['kænjən] *n* cañón *m*
cap [kæp] *n* (*hat*) gorra; (*of pen*) capuchón *m*; (*of bottle*) tapa, tapón *m*; (*contraceptive*) diafragma *m*; (*for toy gun*) cápsula ▷ *vt* (*outdo*) superar; (*limit*) recortar
capability [keɪpə'bɪlɪtɪ] *n* capacidad *f*
capable ['keɪpəbl] *adj* capaz
capacity [kə'pæsɪtɪ] *n* capacidad *f*; (*position*) calidad *f*
cape [keɪp] *n* capa; (*Geo*) cabo
caper ['keɪpə*] *n* (*Culin: gen pl*) alcaparra; (*prank*) broma
capital ['kæpɪtl] *n* (*also*: **~ city**) capital *f*; (*money*) capital *m*; (*also*: **~ letter**) mayúscula; **capitalism** *n* capitalismo; **capitalist** *adj, n* capitalista *mf*; **capital punishment** *n* pena de muerte
Capitol ['kæpɪtl] *n* ver abajo

CAPITOL

El Capitolio **(Capitol)** es el edificio del Congreso **(Congress)** de los Estados Unidos, situado en la ciudad de Washington. Por extensión, también se suele llamar así al edificio en el que tienen lugar las sesiones parlamentarias de la cámara de representantes de muchos de los estados.

Capricorn ['kæprɪkɔ:n] *n* Capricornio
capsize [kæp'saɪz] *vt* volcar, hacer zozobrar ▷ *vi* volcarse, zozobrar
capsule ['kæpsju:l] *n* cápsula
captain ['kæptɪn] *n* capitán *m*
caption ['kæpʃən] *n* (*heading*) título; (*to picture*) leyenda
captivity [kæp'tɪvɪtɪ] *n* cautiverio
capture ['kæptʃə*] *vt* prender, apresar; (*animal, Comput*) capturar; (*place*) tomar; (*attention*) captar, llamar ▷ *n* apresamiento; captura; toma; (*data capture*) formulación *f* de datos
car [kɑ:*] *n* coche *m*, carro (LAM), automóvil *m*; (*US Rail*) vagón *m*
carafe [kə'ræf] *n* jarra
caramel ['kærəməl] *n* caramelo
carat ['kærət] *n* quilate *m*
caravan ['kærəvæn] *n* (BRIT) caravana, ruló *f*; (*in desert*) caravana; **caravan site** (BRIT) *n* camping *m* para caravanas
carbohydrate [kɑ:bəu'haɪdreɪt] *n* hidrato de carbono; (*food*) fécula
carbon ['kɑ:bən] *n* carbono; **carbon dioxide** *n* dióxido de carbono, anhídrido carbónico; **carbon monoxide** *n* monóxido de carbono
car boot sale *n mercadillo organizado en un aparcamiento, en el que se exponenlas mercancías en el maletero del coche*
carburettor [kɑ:bju'rɛtə*] (*US* **carburetor**) *n* carburador *m*
card [kɑ:d] *n* (*material*) cartulina; (*index card etc*) ficha; (*playing card*) carta, naipe *m*; (*visiting card, greetings card etc*) tarjeta; **cardboard** *n* cartón *m*; **card game** *n*

juego de naipes *or* cartas
cardigan ['kɑ:dɪgən] *n* rebeca
cardinal ['kɑ:dɪnl] *adj* cardinal; (*importance, principal*) esencial ▷*n* cardenal *m*
cardphone ['kɑ:dfəun] *n cabina que funciona con tarjetas telefónicas*
care [kɛə*] *n* cuidado; (*worry*) inquietud *f*; (*charge*) cargo, custodia ▷*vi*: **to ~ about** (*person, animal*) tener cariño a; (*thing, idea*) preocuparse por; **~ of** en casa de, al cuidado de; **in sb's ~** a cargo de algn; **to take ~ to** cuidarse de, tener cuidado de; **to take ~ of** cuidar; (*problem etc*) ocuparse de; **I don't ~** no me importa; **I couldn't ~ less** eso me trae sin cuidado; **care for** *vt fus* cuidar a; (*like*) querer
career [kə'rɪə*] *n* profesión *f*; (*in work, school*) carrera ▷*vi* (*also*: **~ along**) correr a toda velocidad
care: carefree *adj* despreocupado; **careful** *adj* cuidadoso; (*cautious*) cauteloso; **(be) careful!** ¡tenga cuidado!; **carefully** *adv* con cuidado, cuidadosamente; con cautela; **caregiver** (US) *n* (*professional*) enfermero/a *m/f*; (*unpaid*) *persona que cuida a un pariente o vecino*; **careless** *adj* descuidado; (*heedless*) poco atento; **carelessness** *n* descuido, falta de atención; **carer** ['kɛərə*] *n* (*professional*) enfermero/a *m/f*; (*unpaid*) *persona que cuida a un pariente o vecino*; **caretaker** *n* portero/a, conserje *mf*
car-ferry ['kɑ:fɛrɪ] *n* transbordador *m* para coches
cargo ['kɑ:gəu] (*pl* **~es**) *n* cargamento, carga
car hire *n* alquiler *m* de automóviles
Caribbean [kærɪ'bi:ən] *n*: **the ~ (Sea)** el (Mar) Caribe
caring ['kɛərɪŋ] *adj* humanitario; (*behaviour*) afectuoso
carnation [kɑ:'neɪʃən] *n* clavel *m*
carnival ['kɑ:nɪvəl] *n* carnaval *m*; (US: *funfair*) parque *m* de atracciones
carol ['kærəl] *n*: **(Christmas) ~** villancico
carousel [kærə'sɛl] (US) *n* tiovivo, caballitos *mpl*
car park (BRIT) *n* aparcamiento, parking *m*
carpenter ['kɑ:pɪntə*] *n* carpintero/a
carpet ['kɑ:pɪt] *n* alfombra; (*fitted*) moqueta ▷*vt* alfombrar
car rental (US) *n* alquiler *m* de coches
carriage ['kærɪdʒ] *n* (BRIT *Rail*) vagón *m*; (*horse-drawn*) coche *m*; (*of goods*) transporte *m*; (: *cost*) porte *m*, flete *m*; **carriageway** (BRIT) *n* (*part of road*) calzada
carrier ['kærɪə*] *n* (*transport company*) transportista, empresa de transportes; (*Med*) portador(a) *m/f*; **carrier bag** (BRIT) *n* bolsa de papel *or* plástico
carrot ['kærət] *n* zanahoria
carry ['kærɪ] *vt* (*person*) llevar; (*transport*) transportar; (*involve*: *responsibilities etc*) entrañar, implicar; (*Med*) ser portador de ▷*vi* (*sound*) oírse; **to get carried away** (*fig*) entusiasmarse; **carry on** *vi* (*continue*) seguir (adelante), continuar ▷*vt* proseguir, continuar; **carry out** *vt* (*orders*) cumplir; (*investigation*) llevar a cabo, realizar
cart [kɑ:t] *n* carro, carreta ▷*vt* (*inf*: *transport*) acarrear
carton ['kɑ:tən] *n* (*box*) caja (de cartón); (*of milk etc*) bote *m*; (*of yogurt*) tarrina
cartoon [kɑ:'tu:n] *n* (*Press*) caricatura; (*comic strip*) tira cómica; (*film*) dibujos *mpl* animados
cartridge ['kɑ:trɪdʒ] *n* cartucho; (*of pen*) recambio
carve [kɑ:v] *vt* (*meat*) trinchar; (*wood, stone*) cincelar, esculpir; (*initials etc*) grabar; **carving** *n* (*object*) escultura; (*design*) talla; (*art*) tallado
car wash *n* lavado de coches
case [keɪs] *n* (*container*) caja; (*Med*) caso; (*for jewels etc*) estuche *m*; (*Law*) causa, proceso; (BRIT: *also*: **suit~**) maleta; **in ~ of** en caso de; **in any ~** en todo caso; **just in ~** por si acaso
cash [kæʃ] *n* dinero en efectivo, dinero contante ▷*vt* cobrar, hacer efectivo; **to pay (in) ~** pagar al contado; **~ on delivery** cóbrese al entregar; **cashback** *n* (*discount*) devolución *f*; (*at supermarket etc*) *retirada de dinero en efectivo de un establecimiento donde se ha pagado con tarjeta; también dinero retirado*; **cash card** *n* tarjeta *f* dinero; **cash desk** (BRIT) *n* caja; **cash dispenser** *n* cajero automático
cashew [kæ'ʃu:] *n* (*also*: **~ nut**) anacardo
cashier [kæ'ʃɪə*] *n* cajero/a
cashmere ['kæʃmɪə*] *n* cachemira
cash point *n* cajero automático
cash register *n* caja
casino [kə'si:nəu] *n* casino
casket ['kɑ:skɪt] *n* cofre *m*, estuche *m*; (US: *coffin*) ataúd *m*
casserole ['kæsərəul] *n* (*food, pot*) cazuela
cassette [kæ'sɛt] *n* casete *f*; **cassette player, cassette recorder** *n* casete *m*
cast [kɑ:st] (*pt, pp* **~**) *vt* (*throw*) echar, arrojar, lanzar; (*glance, eyes*) dirigir; (*Theatre*): **to ~ sb as Othello** dar a algn el papel de Otelo ▷*vi* (*Fishing*) lanzar ▷*n* (*Theatre*) reparto; (*also*: **plaster ~**) vaciado; **to ~ one's vote** votar; **to ~ doubt on** suscitar dudas acerca de; **cast off** *vi* (*Naut*)

desamarrar; (*Knitting*) cerrar (los puntos)
castanets [kæstə'nɛts] *npl* castañuelas *fpl*
caster sugar ['kɑːstə*-] (BRIT) *n* azúcar *m* extrafino
Castile [kæs'tiːl] *n* Castilla; **Castilian** *adj, n* castellano/a *m/f*
cast-iron ['kɑːstaɪən] *adj* (*lit*) (hecho) de hierro fundido; (*fig: case*) irrebatible
castle ['kɑːsl] *n* castillo; (*Chess*) torre *f*
casual ['kæʒjul] *adj* fortuito; (*irregular: work etc*) eventual, temporero; (*unconcerned*) despreocupado; (*clothes*) informal

> Be careful not to translate **casual** by the Spanish word *casual*.

casualty ['kæʒjultɪ] *n* víctima, herido/a; (*dead*) muerto/a; (*Med: department*) urgencias *fpl*
cat [kæt] *n* gato; (*big cat*) felino
Catalan ['kætəlæn] *adj, n* catalán/ana *m/f*
catalogue ['kætəlɔg] (US **catalog**) *n* catálogo ▷ *vt* catalogar
Catalonia [kætə'ləunɪə] *n* Cataluña
catalytic converter [kætə'lɪtɪkkən'vəːtə*] *n* catalizador *m*
cataract ['kætərækt] *n* (*Med*) cataratas *fpl*
catarrh [kə'tɑː*] *n* catarro
catastrophe [kə'tæstrəfɪ] *n* catástrofe *f*
catch [kætʃ] (*pt, pp* **caught**) *vt* coger (SP), agarrar (LAM); (*arrest*) detener; (*grasp*) asir; (*breath*) contener; (*surprise: person*) sorprender; (*attract: attention*) captar; (*hear*) oír; (*Med*) contagiarse de, coger; (*also:* **~ up**) alcanzar ▷ *vi* (*fire*) encenderse; (*in branches etc*) enredarse ▷ *n* (*fish etc*) pesca; (*act of catching*) cogida; (*hidden problem*) dificultad *f*; (*game*) pilla-pilla; (*of lock*) pestillo, cerradura; **to ~ fire** encenderse; **to ~ sight of** divisar; **catch up** *vi* (*fig*) ponerse al día; **catching** ['kætʃɪŋ] *adj* (*Med*) contagioso
category ['kætɪgərɪ] *n* categoría, clase *f*
cater ['keɪtə*] *vi*: **to ~ for** (BRIT) abastecer a; (*needs*) atender a; (*Comm: parties etc*) proveer comida a
caterpillar ['kætəpɪlə*] *n* oruga, gusano
cathedral [kə'θiːdrəl] *n* catedral *f*
Catholic ['kæθəlɪk] *adj, n* (*Rel*) católico/a *m/f*
Catseye® ['kæts'aɪ] (BRIT) *n* (*Aut*) catafoto
cattle ['kætl] *npl* ganado
catwalk ['kætwɔːk] *n* pasarela
caught [kɔːt] *pt, pp of* **catch**
cauliflower ['kɔlɪflauə*] *n* coliflor *f*
cause [kɔːz] *n* causa, motivo, razón *f*; (*principle: also Pol*) causa ▷ *vt* causar
caution ['kɔːʃən] *n* cautela, prudencia; (*warning*) advertencia, amonestación *f* ▷ *vt* amonestar; **cautious** *adj* cauteloso, prudente, precavido
cave [keɪv] *n* cueva, caverna; **cave in** *vi* (*roof etc*) derrumbarse, hundirse
caviar(e) ['kævɪɑː*] *n* caviar *m*
cavity ['kævɪtɪ] *n* hueco, cavidad *f*
cc *abbr* (= *cubic centimetres*) c.c.; (= *carbon copy*) copia hecha con papel del carbón
CCTV *n abbr* (= *closed-circuit television*) circuito cerrado de televisión
CD *n abbr* (= *compact disc*) CD *m*; (*player*) (reproductor *m* de) CD; **CD player** *n* reproductor *m* de CD; **CD-ROM** [siːdiː'rɔm] *n abbr* CD-ROM *m*; **CD writer** *n* grabadora de CD
cease [siːs] *vt, vi* cesar; **ceasefire** *n* alto *m* el fuego
cedar ['siːdə*] *n* cedro
ceilidh ['keɪlɪ] *n* *baile con música y danzas tradicionales escocesas o irlandesas*
ceiling ['siːlɪŋ] *n* techo; (*fig*) límite *m*
celebrate ['sɛlɪbreɪt] *vt* celebrar ▷ *vi* divertirse; **celebration** [-'breɪʃən] *n* fiesta, celebración *f*
celebrity [sɪ'lɛbrɪtɪ] *n* celebridad *f*
celery ['sɛlərɪ] *n* apio
cell [sɛl] *n* celda; (*Biol*) célula; (*Elec*) elemento
cellar ['sɛlə*] *n* sótano; (*for wine*) bodega
cello ['tʃɛləu] *n* violoncelo
Cellophane® ['sɛləfeɪn] *n* celofán *m*
cellphone ['sɛlfəʊn] *n* teléfono celular
Celsius ['sɛlsɪəs] *adj* centígrado
Celtic ['kɛltɪk] *adj* celta
cement [sə'mɛnt] *n* cemento
cemetery ['sɛmɪtrɪ] *n* cementerio
censor ['sɛnsə*] *n* censor *m* ▷ *vt* (*cut*) censurar; **censorship** *n* censura
census ['sɛnsəs] *n* censo
cent [sɛnt] *n* (*unit of dollar*) centavo, céntimo; (*unit of euro*) céntimo; *see also* **per**
centenary [sɛn'tiːnərɪ] *n* centenario
centennial [sɛn'tɛniəl] (US) *n* centenario
center ['sɛntə*] (US) = **centre**
centi... [sɛntɪ] *prefix*: **centigrade** *adj* centígrado; **centimetre** (US **centimeter**) *n* centímetro; **centipede** ['sɛntɪpiːd] *n* ciempiés *m inv*
central ['sɛntrəl] *adj* central; (*of house etc*) céntrico; **Central America** *n* Centroamérica; **central heating** *n* calefacción *f* central; **central reservation** *n* (BRIT *Aut*) mediana
centre ['sɛntə*] (US **center**) *n* centro; (*fig*) núcleo ▷ *vt* centrar; **centre-forward** *n* (*Sport*) delantero centro; **centre-half** *n* (*Sport*) medio centro
century ['sɛntjurɪ] *n* siglo; **20th ~** siglo

veinte
CEO *n abbr* = **chief executive officer**
ceramic [sɪ'ræmɪk] *adj* cerámico
cereal ['si:rɪəl] *n* cereal *m*
ceremony ['sɛrɪmənɪ] *n* ceremonia; **to stand on ~** hacer ceremonias, estar de cumplido
certain ['sə:tən] *adj* seguro; (*person*): **a ~ Mr Smith** un tal Sr. Smith; (*particular, some*) cierto; **for ~** a ciencia cierta; **certainly** *adv* (*undoubtedly*) ciertamente; (*of course*) desde luego, por supuesto; **certainty** *n* certeza, certidumbre *f*, seguridad *f*; (*inevitability*) certeza
certificate [sə'tɪfɪkɪt] *n* certificado
certify ['sə:tɪfaɪ] *vt* certificar; (*award diploma to*) conceder un diploma a; (*declare insane*) declarar loco
cf. *abbr* (= *compare*) cfr
CFC *n abbr* (= *chlorofluorocarbon*) CFC *m*
chain [tʃeɪn] *n* cadena; (*of mountains*) cordillera; (*of events*) sucesión *f* ▷ *vt* (*also*: **~ up**) encadenar; **chain-smoke** *vi* fumar un cigarrillo tras otro
chair [tʃɛə*] *n* silla; (*armchair*) sillón *m*, butaca; (*of university*) cátedra; (*of meeting etc*) presidencia ▷ *vt* (*meeting*) presidir; **chairlift** *n* telesilla; **chairman** (*irreg*) *n* presidente *m*; **chairperson** *n* presidente/a *m/f*; **chairwoman** (*irreg*) *n* presidenta
chalet ['ʃæleɪ] *n* chalet *m* (de madera)
chalk [tʃɔ:k] *n* (*Geo*) creta; (*for writing*) tiza, gis *m* (MEX); **chalkboard** (US) *n* pizarrón (LAM), pizarra (SP)
challenge ['tʃælɪndʒ] *n* desafío, reto ▷ *vt* desafiar, retar; (*statement, right*) poner en duda; **to ~ sb to do sth** retar a algn a que haga algo; **challenging** *adj* exigente; (*tone*) de desafío
chamber ['tʃeɪmbə*] *n* cámara, sala; (*Pol*) cámara; (BRIT *Law*: *gen pl*) despacho; **~ of commerce** cámara de comercio; **chambermaid** *n* camarera
champagne [ʃæm'peɪn] *n* champaña *m*, champán *m*
champion ['tʃæmpɪən] *n* campeón/ona *m/f*; (*of cause*) defensor(a) *m/f*; **championship** *n* campeonato
chance [tʃɑ:ns] *n* (*opportunity*) ocasión *f*, oportunidad *f*; (*likelihood*) posibilidad *f*; (*risk*) riesgo ▷ *vt* arriesgar, probar ▷ *adj* fortuito, casual; **to ~ it** arriesgarse, intentarlo; **to take a ~** arriesgarse; **by ~** por casualidad
chancellor ['tʃɑ:nsələ*] *n* canciller *m*; **Chancellor of the Exchequer** (BRIT) *n* Ministro de Hacienda
chandelier [ʃændə'lɪə*] *n* araña (de luces)
change [tʃeɪndʒ] *vt* cambiar; (*replace*) cambiar, reemplazar; (*gear, clothes, job*) cambiar de; (*transform*) transformar ▷ *vi* cambiar(se); (*change trains*) hacer transbordo; (*traffic lights*) cambiar de color; (*be transformed*): **to ~ into** transformarse en ▷ *n* cambio; (*alteration*) modificación *f*; (*transformation*) transformación *f*; (*of clothes*) muda; (*coins*) suelto, sencillo; (*money returned*) vuelta; **to ~ gear** (*Aut*) cambiar de marcha; **to ~ one's mind** cambiar de opinión *or* idea; **for a ~** para variar; **change over** *vi* (*from sth to sth*) cambiar; (*players etc*) cambiar(se) ▷ *vt* cambiar; **changeable** *adj* (*weather*) cambiable; **change machine** *n* máquina de cambio; **changing room** (BRIT) *n* vestuario
channel ['tʃænl] *n* (*TV*) canal *m*; (*of river*) cauce *m*; (*groove*) conducto; (*fig*: *medium*) medio ▷ *vt* (*river etc*) encauzar; **the (English) C~** el Canal (de la Mancha); **the C~ Islands** las Islas Normandas; **Channel Tunnel** *n*: **the Channel Tunnel** el túnel del Canal de la Mancha, el Eurotúnel
chant [tʃɑ:nt] *n* (*of crowd*) gritos *mpl*; (*Rel*) canto ▷ *vt* (*slogan, word*) repetir a gritos
chaos ['keɪɔs] *n* caos *m*
chaotic [keɪ'ɔtɪk] *adj* caótico
chap [tʃæp] (BRIT: *inf*) *n* (*man*) tío, tipo
chapel ['tʃæpəl] *n* capilla
chapped [tʃæpt] *adj* agrietado
chapter ['tʃæptə*] *n* capítulo
character ['kærɪktə*] *n* carácter *m*, naturaleza, índole *f*; (*moral strength, personality*) carácter; (*in novel, film*) personaje *m*; **characteristic** [-'rɪstɪk] *adj* característico ▷ *n* característica; **characterize** ['kærɪktəraɪz] *vt* caracterizar
charcoal ['tʃɑ:kəul] *n* carbón *m* vegetal; (*Art*) carboncillo
charge [tʃɑ:dʒ] *n* (*Law*) cargo, acusación *f*; (*cost*) precio, coste *m*; (*responsibility*) cargo ▷ *vt* (*Law*): **to ~ (with)** acusar (de); (*battery*) cargar; (*price*) pedir; (*customer*) cobrar ▷ *vi* precipitarse; (*Mil*) cargar, atacar; **charge card** *n* tarjeta de cuenta; **charger** *n* (*also*: **battery charger**) cargador *m* (de baterías)
charismatic [kærɪz'mætɪk] *adj* carismático
charity ['tʃærɪtɪ] *n* caridad *f*; (*organization*) sociedad *f* benéfica; (*money, gifts*) limosnas *fpl*; **charity shop** *n* (BRIT) *tienda de artículos de segunda mano que dedica su recaudación a causas benéficas*
charm [tʃɑ:m] *n* encanto, atractivo; (*talisman*) hechizo; (*on bracelet*) dije *m* ▷ *vt* encantar; **charming** *adj* encantador(a)

chart [tʃɑːt] *n* (*diagram*) cuadro; (*graph*) gráfica; (*map*) carta de navegación ▷ *vt* (*course*) trazar; (*progress*) seguir; **charts** *npl* (*Top 40*): **the ~s** ≈ los 40 principales (SP)
charter ['tʃɑːtə*] *vt* (*plane*) alquilar; (*ship*) fletar ▷ *n* (*document*) carta; (*of university, company*) estatutos *mpl*; **chartered accountant** (BRIT) *n* contable *m/f* diplomado/a; **charter flight** *n* vuelo chárter
chase [tʃeɪs] *vt* (*pursue*) perseguir; (*also*: **~ away**) ahuyentar ▷ *n* persecución *f*
chat [tʃæt] *vi* (*also*: **have a ~**) charlar; (*on Internet*) chatear ▷ *n* charla; **chat up** *vt* (*inf*: *girl*) ligar con, enrollarse con; **chat room** *n* (*Internet*) chat *m*, canal *m* de charla; **chat show** (BRIT) *n* programa *m* de entrevistas
chatter ['tʃætə*] *vi* (*person*) charlar; (*teeth*) castañetear ▷ *n* (*of birds*) parloteo; (*of people*) charla, cháchara
chauffeur ['ʃəufə*] *n* chófer *m*
chauvinist ['ʃəuvɪnɪst] *n* (*male chauvinist*) machista *m*; (*nationalist*) chovinista *mf*
cheap [tʃiːp] *adj* barato; (*joke*) de mal gusto; (*poor quality*) de mala calidad ▷ *adv* barato; **cheap day return** *n* *billete de ida y vuelta el mismo día*; **cheaply** *adv* barato, a bajo precio
cheat [tʃiːt] *vi* hacer trampa ▷ *vt*: **to ~ sb (out of sth)** estafar (algo) a algn ▷ *n* (*person*) tramposo/a; **cheat on** *vt fus* engañar
Chechnya [tʃɪtʃ'njɑː] *n* Chechenia
check [tʃɛk] *vt* (*examine*) controlar; (*facts*) comprobar; (*halt*) parar, detener; (*restrain*) refrenar, restringir ▷ *n* (*inspection*) control *m*, inspección *f*; (*curb*) freno; (*US*: *bill*) nota, cuenta; (US) = **cheque**; (*pattern*: *gen pl*) cuadro; **check in** *vi* (*at hotel*) firmar el registro; (*at airport*) facturar el equipaje ▷ *vt* (*luggage*) facturar; **check off** *vt* (*esp US*: *check*) comprobar; (*cross off*) tachar; **check out** *vi* (*of hotel*) marcharse; **check up** *vi*: **to check up on sth** comprobar algo; **to check up on sb** investigar a algn; **checkbook** (US) = **chequebook**; **checked** *adj* a cuadros; **checkers** (US) *n* juego de damas; **check-in** *n* (*also*: **check-in desk**: *at airport*) mostrador *m* de facturación; **checking account** (US) *n* cuenta corriente; **checklist** *n* lista (de control); **checkmate** *n* jaque *m* mate; **checkout** *n* caja; **checkpoint** *n* (punto de) control *m*; **checkroom** (US) *n* consigna; **checkup** *n* (*Med*) reconocimiento general
cheddar ['tʃedə*] *n* (*also*: **~ cheese**) queso *m* cheddar
cheek [tʃiːk] *n* mejilla; (*impudence*) descaro; **what a ~!** ¡qué cara!; **cheekbone** *n* pómulo; **cheeky** *adj* fresco, descarado
cheer [tʃɪə*] *vt* vitorear, aplaudir; (*gladden*) alegrar, animar ▷ *vi* dar vivas ▷ *n* viva *m*; **cheer up** *vi* animarse ▷ *vt* alegrar, animar; **cheerful** *adj* alegre
cheerio [tʃɪərɪ'əu] (BRIT) *excl* ¡hasta luego!
cheerleader ['tʃɪəliːdə*] *n* animador(a) *m/f*
cheese [tʃiːz] *n* queso; **cheeseburger** *n* hamburguesa con queso; **cheesecake** *n* pastel *m* de queso
chef [ʃɛf] *n* jefe/a *m/f* de cocina
chemical ['kɛmɪkəl] *adj* químico ▷ *n* producto químico
chemist ['kɛmɪst] *n* (BRIT: *pharmacist*) farmacéutico/a; (*scientist*) químico/a; **chemistry** *n* química; **chemist's (shop)** (BRIT) *n* farmacia
cheque [tʃɛk] (US **check**) *n* cheque *m*; **chequebook** *n* talonario de cheques (SP), chequera (LAM); **cheque card** *n* tarjeta de cheque
cherry ['tʃɛrɪ] *n* cereza; (*also*: **~ tree**) cerezo
chess [tʃɛs] *n* ajedrez *m*
chest [tʃɛst] *n* (*Anat*) pecho; (*box*) cofre *m*, cajón *m*
chestnut ['tʃɛsnʌt] *n* castaña; (*also*: **~ tree**) castaño
chest of drawers *n* cómoda
chew [tʃuː] *vt* mascar, masticar; **chewing gum** *n* chicle *m*
chic [ʃiːk] *adj* elegante
chick [tʃɪk] *n* pollito, polluelo; (*inf*: *girl*) chica
chicken ['tʃɪkɪn] *n* gallina, pollo; (*food*) pollo; (*inf*: *coward*) gallina *mf*; **chicken out** (*inf*) *vi* rajarse; **chickenpox** *n* varicela
chickpea ['tʃɪkpiː] *n* garbanzo
chief [tʃiːf] *n* jefe/a *m/f* ▷ *adj* principal; **chief executive (officer)** *n* director(a) *m/f* general; **chiefly** *adv* principalmente
child [tʃaɪld] (*pl* **~ren**) *n* niño/a; (*offspring*) hijo/a; **child abuse** *n* (*with violence*) malos tratos *mpl* a niños; (*sexual*) abuso *m* sexual de niños; **child benefit** *n* (BRIT) *subsidio por cada hijo pequeño*; **childbirth** *n* parto; **childcare** *n* cuidado de los niños; **childhood** *n* niñez *f*, infancia; **childish** *adj* pueril, aniñado; **child minder** (BRIT) *n* madre *f* de día; **children** ['tʃɪldrən] *npl of* **child**
Chile ['tʃɪlɪ] *n* Chile *m*; **Chilean** *adj, n* chileno/a *m/f*
chill [tʃɪl] *n* frío; (*Med*) resfriado ▷ *vt* enfriar; (*Culin*) congelar; **chill out** *vi* (*esp US*: *inf*) tranquilizarse
chil(l)i ['tʃɪlɪ] (BRIT) *n* chile *m*, ají *m* (SC)
chilly ['tʃɪlɪ] *adj* frío

chimney ['tʃɪmnɪ] *n* chimenea
chimpanzee [tʃɪmpæn'zi:] *n* chimpancé *m*
chin [tʃɪn] *n* mentón *m*, barbilla
China ['tʃaɪnə] *n* China
china ['tʃaɪnə] *n* porcelana; (*crockery*) loza
Chinese [tʃaɪ'ni:z] *adj* chino ▷ *n inv* chino/a *m/f*; (*Ling*) chino
chip [tʃɪp] *n* (*gen pl*: *Culin*: BRIT) patata (SP) *or* papa (LAM) frita; (: US: *also*: **potato ~**) patata *or* papa frita; (*of wood*) astilla; (*of glass, stone*) lasca; (*at poker*) ficha; (*Comput*) chip *m* ▷ *vt* (*cup, plate*) desconchar; **chip shop** pescadería (*donde se vende principalmente pescado rebozado y patatas fritas*)
chiropodist [kɪ'rɔpədɪst] (BRIT) *n* pedicuro/a, callista *m/f*
chisel ['tʃɪzl] *n* (*for wood*) escoplo; (*for stone*) cincel *m*
chives [tʃaɪvz] *npl* cebollinos *mpl*
chlorine ['klɔ:ri:n] *n* cloro
choc-ice ['tʃɔkaɪs] *n* (BRIT) helado *m* cubierto de chocolate
chocolate ['tʃɔklɪt] *n* chocolate *m*; (*sweet*) bombón *m*
choice [tʃɔɪs] *n* elección *f*, selección *f*; (*option*) opción *f*; (*preference*) preferencia ▷ *adj* escogido
choir ['kwaɪə*] *n* coro
choke [tʃəuk] *vi* ahogarse; (*on food*) atragantarse ▷ *vt* estrangular, ahogar; (*block*): **to be ~d with** estar atascado de ▷ *n* (*Aut*) estárter *m*
cholesterol [kə'lɛstərul] *n* colesterol *m*
choose [tʃu:z] (*pt* **chose**, *pp* **chosen**) *vt* escoger, elegir; (*team*) seleccionar; **to ~ to do sth** optar por hacer algo
chop [tʃɔp] *vt* (*wood*) cortar, tajar; (*Culin*: *also*: **~ up**) picar ▷ *n* (*Culin*) chuleta; **chop down** *vt* (*tree*) talar; **chop off** *vt* cortar (de un tajo); **chopsticks** ['tʃɔpstɪks] *npl* palillos *mpl*
chord [kɔ:d] *n* (*Mus*) acorde *m*
chore [tʃɔ:*] *n* faena, tarea; (*routine task*) trabajo rutinario
chorus ['kɔ:rəs] *n* coro; (*repeated part of song*) estribillo
chose [tʃəuz] *pt of* **choose**
chosen ['tʃəuzn] *pp of* **choose**
Christ [kraɪst] *n* Cristo
christen ['krɪsn] *vt* bautizar; **christening** *n* bautizo
Christian ['krɪstɪən] *adj*, *n* cristiano/a *m/f*; **Christianity** [-'ænɪtɪ] *n* cristianismo; **Christian name** *n* nombre *m* de pila
Christmas ['krɪsməs] *n* Navidad *f*; **Merry ~!** ¡Felices Pascuas!; **Christmas card** *n* crismas *m inv*, tarjeta de Navidad; **Christmas carol** *n* villancico *m*; **Christmas Day** *n* día *m* de Navidad; **Christmas Eve** *n* Nochebuena; **Christmas pudding** *n* (*esp* BRIT) pudin *m* de Navidad; **Christmas tree** *n* árbol *m* de Navidad
chrome [krəum] *n* cromo
chronic ['krɔnɪk] *adj* crónico
chrysanthemum [krɪ'sænθəməm] *n* crisantemo
chubby ['tʃʌbɪ] *adj* regordete
chuck [tʃʌk] (*inf*) *vt* lanzar, arrojar; (BRIT: *also*: **~ up**) abandonar; **chuck out** *vt* (*person*) echar (fuera); (*rubbish etc*) tirar
chuckle ['tʃʌkl] *vi* reírse entre dientes
chum [tʃʌm] *n* compañero/a
chunk [tʃʌŋk] *n* pedazo, trozo
church [tʃə:tʃ] *n* iglesia; **churchyard** *n* cementerio
churn [tʃə:n] *n* (*for butter*) mantequera; (*for milk*) lechera
chute [ʃu:t] *n* (*also*: **rubbish ~**) vertedero; (*for coal etc*) rampa de caída
chutney ['tʃʌtnɪ] *n* *condimento a base de frutas de la India*
CIA (US) *n abbr* (= *Central Intelligence Agency*) CIA *f*
CID (BRIT) *n abbr* (= *Criminal Investigation Department*) ≈ B.I.C. *f* (SP)
cider ['saɪdə*] *n* sidra
cigar [sɪ'gɑ:*] *n* puro
cigarette [sɪgə'rɛt] *n* cigarrillo; **cigarette lighter** *n* mechero
cinema ['sɪnəmə] *n* cine *m*
cinnamon ['sɪnəmən] *n* canela
circle ['sə:kl] *n* círculo; (*in theatre*) anfiteatro ▷ *vi* dar vueltas ▷ *vt* (*surround*) rodear, cercar; (*move round*) dar la vuelta a
circuit ['sə:kɪt] *n* circuito; (*tour*) gira; (*track*) pista; (*lap*) vuelta
circular ['sə:kjulə*] *adj* circular ▷ *n* circular *f*
circulate ['sə:kjuleɪt] *vi* circular; (*person*: *at party etc*) hablar con los invitados ▷ *vt* poner en circulación; **circulation** [-'leɪʃən] *n* circulación *f*; (*of newspaper*) tirada
circumstances ['sə:kəmstənsɪz] *npl* circunstancias *fpl*; (*financial condition*) situación *f* económica
circus ['sə:kəs] *n* circo
cite [saɪt] *vt* citar
citizen ['sɪtɪzn] *n* (*Pol*) ciudadano/a; (*of city*) vecino/a, habitante *mf*; **citizenship** *n* ciudadanía; (BRIT: *Scol*) civismo
citrus fruits ['sɪtrəs-] *npl* agrios *mpl*
city ['sɪtɪ] *n* ciudad *f*; **the C~** *centro financiero de Londres*; **city centre** (BRIT)

n centro de la ciudad; **city technology college** *n* centro de formación profesional (*centro de enseñanza secundaria que da especial importancia a la ciencia y tecnología*.)
civic ['sɪvɪk] *adj* cívico; (*authorities*) municipal
civil ['sɪvɪl] *adj* civil; (*polite*) atento, cortés; **civilian** [sɪ'vɪlɪən] *adj* civil (*no militar*) ▷ *n* civil *mf*, paisano/a
civilization [sɪvɪlaɪ'zeɪʃən] *n* civilización *f*
civilized ['sɪvɪlaɪzd] *adj* civilizado
civil: civil law *n* derecho civil; **civil rights** *npl* derechos *mpl* civiles; **civil servant** *n* funcionario/a del Estado; **Civil Service** *n* administración *f* pública; **civil war** *n* guerra civil
CJD *n abbr* (= *Creutzfeldt-Jakob disease*) *enfermedad de Creutzfeldt-Jakob*
claim [kleɪm] *vt* exigir, reclamar; (*rights etc*) reivindicar; (*assert*) pretender ▷ *vi* (*for insurance*) reclamar ▷ *n* reclamación *f*; pretensión *f*; **claim form** *n* solicitud *f*
clam [klæm] *n* almeja
clamp [klæmp] *n* abrazadera, grapa ▷ *vt* (*two things together*) cerrar fuertemente; (*one thing on another*) afianzar (con abrazadera); (*Aut: wheel*) poner el cepo a
clan [klæn] *n* clan *m*
clap [klæp] *vi* aplaudir
claret ['klærət] *n* burdeos *m inv*
clarify ['klærɪfaɪ] *vt* aclarar
clarinet [klærɪ'nɛt] *n* clarinete *m*
clarity ['klærɪtɪ] *n* claridad *f*
clash [klæʃ] *n* enfrentamiento; choque *m*; desacuerdo; estruendo ▷ *vi* (*fight*) enfrentarse; (*beliefs*) chocar; (*disagree*) estar en desacuerdo; (*colours*) desentonar; (*two events*) coincidir
clasp [klɑːsp] *n* (*hold*) apretón *m*; (*of necklace, bag*) cierre *m* ▷ *vt* apretar; abrazar
class [klɑːs] *n* clase *f* ▷ *vt* clasificar
classic ['klæsɪk] *adj*, *n* clásico; **classical** *adj* clásico
classification [klæsɪfɪ'keɪʃən] *n* clasificación *f*
classify ['klæsɪfaɪ] *vt* clasificar
classmate ['klɑːsmeɪt] *n* compañero/a de clase
classroom ['klɑːsrum] *n* aula; **classroom assistant** *n* profesor(a) *m/f* de apoyo
classy ['klɑːsɪ] *adj* (*inf*) elegante, con estilo
clatter ['klætə*] *n* estrépito ▷ *vi* hacer ruido *or* estrépito
clause [klɔːz] *n* cláusula; (*Ling*) oración *f*
claustrophobic [klɔːstrə'fəubɪk] *adj* claustrofóbico; **I feel ~** me entra claustrofobia
claw [klɔː] *n* (*of cat*) uña; (*of bird of prey*) garra; (*of lobster*) pinza
clay [kleɪ] *n* arcilla
clean [kliːn] *adj* limpio; (*record, reputation*) bueno, intachable; (*joke*) decente ▷ *vt* limpiar; (*hands etc*) lavar; **clean up** *vt* limpiar, asear; **cleaner** *n* (*person*) asistenta; (*substance*) producto para la limpieza; **cleaner's** *n* tintorería; **cleaning** *n* limpieza
cleanser ['klɛnzə*] *n* (*for face*) crema limpiadora
clear [klɪə*] *adj* claro; (*road, way*) libre; (*conscience*) limpio, tranquilo; (*skin*) terso; (*sky*) despejado ▷ *vt* (*space*) despejar, limpiar; (*Law: suspect*) absolver; (*obstacle*) salvar, saltar por encima de; (*cheque*) aceptar ▷ *vi* (*fog etc*) despejarse ▷ *adv*: **~ of** a distancia de; **to ~ the table** recoger *or* levantar la mesa; **clear away** *vt* (*things, clothes etc*) quitar (de en medio); (*dishes*) retirar; **clear up** *vt* limpiar; (*mystery*) aclarar, resolver; **clearance** *n* (*removal*) despeje *m*; (*permission*) acreditación *f*; **clear-cut** *adj* bien definido, nítido; **clearing** *n* (*in wood*) claro; **clearly** *adv* claramente; (*evidently*) sin duda; **clearway** (BRIT) *n* *carretera donde no se puede parar*
clench [klɛntʃ] *vt* apretar, cerrar
clergy ['kləːdʒɪ] *n* clero
clerk [klɑːk, (US) kləːrk] *n* (BRIT) oficinista *mf*; (US) dependiente/a *m/f*
clever ['klɛvə*] *adj* (*intelligent*) inteligente, listo; (*skilful*) hábil; (*device, arrangement*) ingenioso
cliché ['kliːʃeɪ] *n* cliché *m*, frase *f* hecha
click [klɪk] *vt* (*tongue*) chasquear; (*heels*) taconear ▷ *vi* (*Comput*) hacer clic; **to ~ on an icon** hacer clic en un icono
client ['klaɪənt] *n* cliente *m/f*
cliff [klɪf] *n* acantilado
climate ['klaɪmɪt] *n* clima *m*; **climate change** *n* cambio climático
climax ['klaɪmæks] *n* (*of battle, career*) apogeo; (*of film, book*) punto culminante; (*sexual*) orgasmo
climb [klaɪm] *vi* subir; (*plant*) trepar; (*move with effort*): **to ~ over a wall/into a car** trepar a una tapia/subir a un coche ▷ *vt* (*stairs*) subir; (*tree*) trepar a; (*mountain*) escalar ▷ *n* subida; **climb down** *vi* (*fig*) volverse atrás; **climber** *n* alpinista *mf* (SP, MEX), andinista *mf* (LAM); **climbing** *n* alpinismo (SP, MEX), andinismo (LAM)
clinch [klɪntʃ] *vt* (*deal*) cerrar; (*argument*) remachar
cling [klɪŋ] (*pt, pp* **clung**) *vi*: **to ~ to** agarrarse a; (*clothes*) pegarse a
Clingfilm® ['klɪŋfɪlm] *n* plástico

adherente
clinic ['klınık] *n* clínica
clip [klıp] *n* (*for hair*) horquilla; (*also*: **paper ~**) sujetapapeles *m inv*, clip *m*; (*TV, Cinema*) fragmento ▷ *vt* (*cut*) cortar; (*also*: **~ together**) unir; **clipping** *n* (*newspaper*) recorte *m*
cloak [kləuk] *n* capa, manto ▷ *vt* (*fig*) encubrir, disimular; **cloakroom** *n* guardarropa; (BRIT: *WC*) lavabo (SP), aseos *mpl* (SP), baño (LAM)
clock [klɔk] *n* reloj *m*; **clock in** *or* **on** *vi* (*with card*) fichar, picar; (*start work*) entrar a trabajar; **clock off** *or* **out** *vi* (*with card*) fichar *or* picar la salida; (*leave work*) salir del trabajar; **clockwise** *adv* en el sentido de las agujas del reloj; **clockwork** *n* aparato de relojería ▷ *adj* (*toy*) de cuerda
clog [klɔg] *n* zueco, chanclo ▷ *vt* atascar ▷ *vi* (*also*: **~ up**) atascarse
clone [kləun] *n* clon *m* ▷ *vt* clonar
close¹ [kləus] *adj* (*near*): **~ (to)** cerca (de); (*friend*) íntimo; (*connection*) estrecho; (*examination*) detallado, minucioso; (*weather*) bochornoso ▷ *adv* cerca; **~ by, ~ at hand** muy cerca; **to have a ~ shave** (*fig*) escaparse por un pelo
close² [kləuz] *vt* (*shut*) cerrar; (*end*) concluir, terminar ▷ *vi* (*shop etc*) cerrarse; (*end*) concluirse, terminarse ▷ *n* (*end*) fin *m*, final *m*, conclusión *f*; **close down** *vi* cerrarse definitivamente; **closed** *adj* (*shop etc*) cerrado
closely ['kləuslı] *adv* (*study*) con detalle; (*watch*) de cerca; (*resemble*) estrechamente
closet ['klɔzıt] *n* armario
close-up ['kləusʌp] *n* primer plano
closing time *n* hora de cierre
closure ['kləuʒə*] *n* cierre *m*
clot [klɔt] *n* (*gen*) coágulo; (*inf*: *idiot*) imbécil *m/f* ▷ *vi* (*blood*) coagularse
cloth [klɔθ] *n* (*material*) tela, paño; (*rag*) trapo
clothes [kləuðz] *npl* ropa; **clothes line** *n* cuerda (para tender la ropa); **clothes peg** (US **clothes pin**) *n* pinza
clothing ['kləuðıŋ] *n* = **clothes**
cloud [klaud] *n* nube *f*; **cloud over** *vi* (*also fig*) nublarse; **cloudy** *adj* nublado, nubloso; (*liquid*) turbio
clove [kləuv] *n* clavo; **~ of garlic** diente *m* de ajo
clown [klaun] *n* payaso ▷ *vi* (*also*: **~ about, ~ around**) hacer el payaso
club [klʌb] *n* (*society*) club *m*; (*weapon*) porra, cachiporra; (*also*: **golf ~**) palo ▷ *vt* aporrear ▷ *vi*: **to ~ together** (*for gift*) comprar entre todos; **clubs** *npl* (*Cards*) tréboles *mpl*; **club class** *n* (*Aviat*) clase *f* preferente
clue [klu:] *n* pista; (*in crosswords*) indicación *f*; **I haven't a ~** no tengo ni idea
clump [klʌmp] *n* (*of trees*) grupo
clumsy ['klʌmzı] *adj* (*person*) torpe, desmañado; (*tool*) difícil de manejar; (*movement*) desgarbado
clung [klʌŋ] *pt, pp of* **cling**
cluster ['klʌstə*] *n* grupo ▷ *vi* agruparse, apiñarse
clutch [klʌtʃ] *n* (*Aut*) embrague *m*; (*grasp*): **~es** garras *fpl* ▷ *vt* asir; agarrar
cm *abbr* (= *centimetre*) cm
Co. *abbr* = **county; company**
c/o *abbr* (= *care of*) c/a, a/c
coach [kəutʃ] *n* autocar *m* (SP), coche *m* de línea; (*horse-drawn*) coche *m*; (*of train*) vagón *m*, coche *m*; (*Sport*) entrenador(a) *m/f*, instructor(a) *m/f*; (*tutor*) profesor(a) *m/f* particular ▷ *vt* (*Sport*) entrenar; (*student*) preparar, enseñar; **coach station** *n* (BRIT) estación *f* de autobuses *etc*; **coach trip** *n* excursión *f* en autocar
coal [kəul] *n* carbón *m*
coalition [kəuə'lıʃən] *n* coalición *f*
coarse [kɔ:s] *adj* basto, burdo; (*vulgar*) grosero, ordinario
coast [kəust] *n* costa, litoral *m* ▷ *vi* (*Aut*) ir en punto muerto; **coastal** *adj* costero, costanero; **coastguard** *n* guardacostas *m inv*; **coastline** *n* litoral *m*
coat [kəut] *n* abrigo; (*of animal*) pelaje *m*, lana; (*of paint*) mano *f*, capa ▷ *vt* cubrir, revestir; **coat hanger** *n* percha (SP), gancho (LAM); **coating** *n* capa, baño
coax [kəuks] *vt* engatusar
cob [kɔb] *n see* **corn**
cobbled ['kɔbld] *adj*: **~ street** calle *f* empedrada, calle *f* adoquinada
cobweb ['kɔbwɛb] *n* telaraña
cocaine [kə'keın] *n* cocaína
cock [kɔk] *n* (*rooster*) gallo; (*male bird*) macho ▷ *vt* (*gun*) amartillar; **cockerel** *n* gallito
cockney ['kɔknı] *n* *habitante de ciertos barrios de Londres*
cockpit ['kɔkpıt] *n* cabina
cockroach ['kɔkrəutʃ] *n* cucaracha
cocktail ['kɔkteıl] *n* coctel *m*, cóctel *m*
cocoa ['kəukəu] *n* cacao; (*drink*) chocolate *m*
coconut ['kəukənʌt] *n* coco
cod [kɔd] *n* bacalao
C.O.D. *abbr* (= *cash on delivery*) C.A.E.
code [kəud] *n* código; (*cipher*) clave *f*; (*dialling code*) prefijo; (*post code*) código postal

coeducational [kəuɛdju'keɪʃənl] *adj* mixto

coffee ['kɔfɪ] *n* café *m*; **coffee bar** (BRIT) *n* cafetería; **coffee bean** *n* grano de café; **coffee break** *n* descanso (para tomar café); **coffee maker** *n* máquina de hacer café, cafetera; **coffeepot** *n* cafetera; **coffee shop** *n* café *m*; **coffee table** *n* mesita (para servir el café)

coffin ['kɔfɪn] *n* ataúd *m*

cog [kɔg] *n* (*wheel*) rueda dentada; (*tooth*) diente *m*

cognac ['kɔnjæk] *n* coñac *m*

coherent [kəu'hɪərənt] *adj* coherente

coil [kɔɪl] *n* rollo; (*Elec*) bobina, carrete *m*; (*contraceptive*) espiral *f* ▷ *vt* enrollar

coin [kɔɪn] *n* moneda ▷ *vt* (*word*) inventar, idear

coincide [kəuɪn'saɪd] *vi* coincidir; (*agree*) estar de acuerdo; **coincidence** [kəu'ɪnsɪdəns] *n* casualidad *f*

Coke® [kəuk] *n* Coca-Cola®

coke [kəuk] *n* (*coal*) coque *m*

colander ['kɔləndə*] *n* colador *m*, escurridor *m*

cold [kəuld] *adj* frío ▷ *n* frío; (*Med*) resfriado; **it's ~** hace frío; **to be ~** (*person*) tener frío; **to catch (a) ~** resfriarse; **in ~ blood** a sangre fría; **cold sore** *n* herpes *mpl or fpl*

coleslaw ['kəulslɔː] *n especie de ensalada de col*

colic ['kɔlɪk] *n* cólico

collaborate [kə'læbəreɪt] *vi* colaborar

collapse [kə'læps] *vi* hundirse, derrumbarse; (*Med*) sufrir un colapso ▷ *n* hundimiento, derrumbamiento; (*Med*) colapso

collar ['kɔlə*] *n* (*of coat, shirt*) cuello; (*of dog etc*) collar; **collarbone** *n* clavícula

colleague ['kɔliːg] *n* colega *mf*; (*at work*) compañero/a

collect [kə'lɛkt] *vt* (*litter, mail etc*) recoger; (*as a hobby*) coleccionar; (BRIT: *call and pick up*) recoger; (*debts, subscriptions etc*) recaudar ▷ *vi* reunirse; (*dust*) acumularse; **to call ~** (US *Tel*) llamar a cobro revertido; **collection** [kə'lɛkʃən] *n* colección *f*; (*of mail, for charity*) recogida; **collective** [kə'lɛktɪv] *adj* colectivo; **collector** *n* coleccionista *mf*

college ['kɔlɪdʒ] *n* colegio mayor; (*of agriculture, technology*) escuela universitaria

collide [kə'laɪd] *vi* chocar

collision [kə'lɪʒən] *n* choque *m*

cologne [kə'ləun] *n* (*also*: **eau de ~**) (agua de) colonia

Colombia [kə'lɔmbɪə] *n* Colombia; **Colombian** *adj, n* colombiano/a

colon ['kəulən] *n* (*sign*) dos puntos; (*Med*) colon *m*

colonel ['kəːnl] *n* coronel *m*

colonial [kə'ləunɪəl] *adj* colonial

colony ['kɔlənɪ] *n* colonia

colour *etc* ['kʌlə*] (US **color** *etc*) *n* color *m* ▷ *vt* color(e)ar; (*dye*) teñir; (*fig*: *account*) adornar; (:*judgement*) distorsionar ▷ *vi* (*blush*) sonrojarse; **colour in** *vt* colorear; **colour-blind** *adj* daltónico; **coloured** *adj* de color; (*photo*) en color; **colour film** *n* película en color; **colourful** *adj* lleno de color; (*story*) fantástico; (*person*) excéntrico; **colouring** *n* (*complexion*) tez *f*; (*in food*) colorante *m*; **colour television** *n* televisión *f* en color

column ['kɔləm] *n* columna

coma ['kəumə] *n* coma *m*

comb [kəum] *n* peine *m*; (*ornamental*) peineta ▷ *vt* (*hair*) peinar; (*area*) registrar a fondo

combat ['kɔmbæt] *n* combate *m* ▷ *vt* combatir

combination [kɔmbɪ'neɪʃən] *n* combinación *f*

combine [*vb* kəm'baɪn, *n* 'kɔmbaɪn] *vt* combinar; (*qualities*) reunir ▷ *vi* combinarse ▷ *n* (*Econ*) cartel *m*

KEYWORD

come [kʌm] (*pt* **came**, *pp* **come**) *vi*

1 (*movement towards*) venir; **to come running** venir corriendo

2 (*arrive*) llegar; **he's come here to work** ha venido aquí para trabajar; **to come home** volver a casa

3 (*reach*): **to come to** llegar a; **the bill came to £40** la cuenta ascendía a cuarenta libras

4 (*occur*): **an idea came to me** se me ocurrió una idea

5 (*be, become*): **to come loose/undone** *etc* aflojarse/desabrocharse/desatarse *etc*; **I've come to like him** por fin ha llegado a gustarme

come across *vt fus* (*person*) topar con; (*thing*) dar con

come along *vi* (BRIT: *progress*) ir

come back *vi* (*return*) volver

come down *vi* (*price*) bajar; (*tree, building*) ser derribado

come from *vt fus* (*place, source*) ser de

come in *vi* (*visitor*) entrar; (*train, report*) llegar; (*fashion*) ponerse de moda; (*on deal etc*) entrar

come off *vi* (*button*) soltarse, desprenderse; (*attempt*) salir bien

come on *vi* (*pupil*) progresar; (*work, project*)

desarrollarse; (*lights*) encenderse; (*electricity*) volver; **come on!** ¡vamos!
come out *vi* (*fact*) salir a la luz; (*book, sun*) salir; (*stain*) quitarse
come round *vi* (*after faint, operation*) volver en sí
come to *vi* (*wake*) volver en sí
come up *vi* (*sun*) salir; (*problem*) surgir; (*event*) aproximarse; (*in conversation*) mencionarse
come up with *vt fus* (*idea*) sugerir; (*money*) conseguir

comeback ['kʌmbæk] *n*: **to make a ~** (*Theatre*) volver a las tablas
comedian [kə'mi:dɪən] *n* humorista *mf*
comedy ['kɔmɪdɪ] *n* comedia; (*humour*) comicidad *f*
comet ['kɔmɪt] *n* cometa *m*
comfort ['kʌmfət] *n* bienestar *m*; (*relief*) alivio ▷ *vt* consolar; **comfortable** *adj* cómodo; (*financially*) acomodado; (*easy*) fácil; **comfort station** (US) *n* servicios *mpl*
comic ['kɔmɪk] *adj* (*also*: **~al**) cómico ▷ *n* (*comedian*) cómico; (BRIT: *for children*) tebeo; (BRIT: *for adults*) comic *m*; **comic book** (US) *n* libro *m* de cómics; **comic strip** *n* tira cómica
comma ['kɔmə] *n* coma
command [kə'mɑ:nd] *n* orden *f*, mandato; (*Mil: authority*) mando; (*mastery*) dominio ▷ *vt* (*troops*) mandar; (*give orders to*): **to ~ sb to do** mandar *or* ordenar a algn hacer; **commander** *n* (*Mil*) comandante *mf*, jefe/a *m/f*
commemorate [kə'mɛməreɪt] *vt* conmemorar
commence [kə'mɛns] *vt, vi* comenzar, empezar; **commencement** (US) *n* (*Univ*) (ceremonia de) graduación *f*
commend [kə'mɛnd] *vt* elogiar, alabar; (*recommend*) recomendar
comment ['kɔmɛnt] *n* comentario ▷ *vi*: **to ~ on** hacer comentarios sobre; **"no ~"** (*written*) "sin comentarios"; (*spoken*) "no tengo nada que decir"; **commentary** ['kɔməntərɪ] *n* comentario; **commentator** ['kɔmənteɪtə*] *n* comentarista *mf*
commerce ['kɔmə:s] *n* comercio
commercial [kə'mə:ʃəl] *adj* comercial ▷ *n* (*TV, Radio*) anuncio; **commercial break** *n* intermedio para publicidad
commission [kə'mɪʃən] *n* (*committee, fee*) comisión *f* ▷ *vt* (*work of art*) encargar; **out of ~** fuera de servicio; **commissioner** *n* (*Police*) comisario de policía
commit [kə'mɪt] *vt* (*act*) cometer; (*resources*) dedicar; (*to sb's care*) entregar; **to ~ o.s. (to do)** comprometerse (a hacer); **to ~ suicide** suicidarse; **commitment** *n* compromiso; (*to ideology etc*) entrega
committee [kə'mɪtɪ] *n* comité *m*
commodity [kə'mɔdɪtɪ] *n* mercancía
common ['kɔmən] *adj* común; (*pej*) ordinario ▷ *n* campo común; **commonly** *adv* comúnmente; **commonplace** *adj* de lo más común; **Commons** (BRIT) *npl* (*Pol*): **the Commons** (la Cámara de) los Comunes; **common sense** *n* sentido común; **Commonwealth** *n*: **the Commonwealth** la Commonwealth
communal ['kɔmju:nl] *adj* (*property*) comunal; (*kitchen*) común
commune [*n* 'kɔmju:n, *vb* kə'mju:n] *n* (*group*) comuna ▷ *vi*: **to ~ with** comulgar *or* conversar con
communicate [kə'mju:nɪkeɪt] *vt* comunicar ▷ *vi*: **to ~ (with)** comunicarse (con); (*in writing*) estar en contacto (con)
communication [kəmju:nɪ'keɪʃən] *n* comunicación *f*
communion [kə'mju:nɪən] *n* (*also*: **Holy ~**) comunión *f*
communism ['kɔmjunɪzəm] *n* comunismo; **communist** *adj, n* comunista *mf*
community [kə'mju:nɪtɪ] *n* comunidad *f*; (*large group*) colectividad *f*; **community centre** (US **community center**) *n* centro social; **community service** *n* trabajo *m* comunitario (*prestado en lugar de cumplir una pena de prisión*)
commute [kə'mju:t] *vi* *viajar a diario de la casa al trabajo* ▷ *vt* conmutar; **commuter** *n* *persona que viaja a diario de la casa al trabajo*
compact [*adj* kəm'pækt, *n* 'kɔmpækt] *adj* compacto ▷ *n* (*also*: **powder ~**) polvera; **compact disc** *n* compact disc *m*; **compact disc player** *n* reproductor *m* de disco compacto, compact disc *m*
companion [kəm'pænɪən] *n* compañero/a
company ['kʌmpənɪ] *n* compañía; (*Comm*) sociedad *f*, compañía; **to keep sb ~** acompañar a algn; **company car** *n* coche *m* de la empresa; **company director** *n* director(a) *m/f* de empresa
comparable ['kɔmpərəbl] *adj* comparable
comparative [kəm'pærətɪv] *adj* relativo; (*study*) comparativo; **comparatively** *adv* (*relatively*) relativamente
compare [kəm'pɛə*] *vt*: **to ~ sth/sb with** *or* **to** comparar algo/a algn con ▷ *vi*: **to ~ (with)** compararse (con); **comparison** [-'pærɪsn] *n* comparación *f*

compartment [kəm'pɑːtmənt] *n* (*also: Rail*) compartim(i)ento
compass ['kʌmpəs] *n* brújula; **compasses** *npl* (*Math*) compás *m*
compassion [kəm'pæʃən] *n* compasión *f*
compatible [kəm'pætɪbl] *adj* compatible
compel [kəm'pɛl] *vt* obligar; **compelling** *adj* (*fig: argument*) convincente
compensate ['kɔmpənseɪt] *vt* compensar ▷*vi*: **to ~ for** compensar; **compensation** [-'seɪʃən] *n* (*for loss*) indemnización *f*
compete [kəm'piːt] *vi* (*take part*) tomar parte, concurrir; (*vie with*): **to ~ with** competir con, hacer competencia a
competent ['kɔmpɪtənt] *adj* competente, capaz
competition [kɔmpɪ'tɪʃən] *n* (*contest*) concurso; (*rivalry*) competencia
competitive [kəm'pɛtɪtɪv] *adj* (*Econ, Sport*) competitivo
competitor [kəm'pɛtɪtə*] *n* (*rival*) competidor(a) *m/f*; (*participant*) concursante *mf*
complacent [kəm'pleɪsənt] *adj* autocomplaciente
complain [kəm'pleɪn] *vi* quejarse; (*Comm*) reclamar; **complaint** *n* queja; reclamación *f*; (*Med*) enfermedad *f*
complement [*n* 'kɔmplɪmənt, *vb* 'kɔmplɪmɛnt] *n* complemento; (*esp of ship's crew*) dotación *f* ▷*vt* (*enhance*) complementar; **complementary** [kɔmplɪ'mɛntərɪ] *adj* complementario
complete [kəm'pliːt] *adj* (*full*) completo; (*finished*) acabado ▷*vt* (*fulfil*) completar; (*finish*) acabar; (*a form*) llenar; **completely** *adv* completamente; **completion** [-'pliːʃən] *n* terminación *f*; (*of contract*) realización *f*
complex ['kɔmplɛks] *adj, n* complejo
complexion [kəm'plɛkʃən] *n* (*of face*) tez *f*, cutis *m*
compliance [kəm'plaɪəns] *n* (*submission*) sumisión *f*; (*agreement*) conformidad *f*; **in ~ with** de acuerdo con
complicate ['kɔmplɪkeɪt] *vt* complicar; **complicated** *adj* complicado; **complication** [-'keɪʃən] *n* complicación *f*
compliment ['kɔmplɪmənt] *n* (*formal*) cumplido ▷*vt* felicitar; **complimentary** [-'mɛntərɪ] *adj* lisonjero; (*free*) de favor
comply [kəm'plaɪ] *vi*: **to ~ with** cumplir con
component [kəm'pəunənt] *adj* componente ▷*n* (*Tech*) pieza
compose [kəm'pəuz] *vt*: **to be ~d of** componerse de; (*music etc*) componer; **to ~ o.s.** tranquilizarse; **composer** *n* (*Mus*) compositor(a) *m/f*; **composition** [kɔmpə'zɪʃən] *n* composición *f*
composure [kəm'pəuʒə*] *n* serenidad *f*, calma
compound ['kɔmpaund] *n* (*Chem*) compuesto; (*Ling*) palabra compuesta; (*enclosure*) recinto ▷*adj* compuesto; (*fracture*) complicado
comprehension [-'hɛnʃən] *n* comprensión *f*
comprehensive [kɔmprɪ'hɛnsɪv] *adj* exhaustivo; (*Insurance*) contra todo riesgo; **comprehensive (school)** *n centro estatal de enseñanza secundaria* ≈ Instituto Nacional de Bachillerato (SP)
compress [*vb* kəm'prɛs, *n* 'kɔmprɛs] *vt* comprimir; (*information*) condensar ▷*n* (*Med*) compresa
comprise [kəm'praɪz] *vt* (*also:* **be ~d of**) comprender, constar de; (*constitute*) constituir
compromise ['kɔmprəmaɪz] *n* (*agreement*) arreglo ▷*vt* comprometer ▷*vi* transigir
compulsive [kəm'pʌlsɪv] *adj* compulsivo; (*viewing, reading*) obligado
compulsory [kəm'pʌlsərɪ] *adj* obligatorio
computer [kəm'pjuːtə*] *n* ordenador *m*, computador *m*, computadora; **computer game** *n* juego para ordenador; **computer-generated** *adj* realizado por ordenador, creado por ordenador; **computerize** *vt* (*data*) computerizar; (*system*) informatizar; **we're computerized now** ya nos hemos informatizado; **computer programmer** *n* programador(a) *m/f*; **computer programming** *n* programación *f*; **computer science** *n* informática; **computer studies** *npl* informática *fsg*, computación *fsg* (LAM); **computing** [kəm'pjuːtɪŋ] *n* (*activity, science*) informática
con [kɔn] *vt* (*deceive*) engañar; (*cheat*) estafar ▷*n* estafa
conceal [kən'siːl] *vt* ocultar
concede [kən'siːd] *vt* (*point, argument*) reconocer; (*territory*) ceder; **to ~ (defeat)** darse por vencido; **to ~ that** admitir que
conceited [kən'siːtɪd] *adj* presumido
conceive [kən'siːv] *vt, vi* concebir
concentrate ['kɔnsəntreɪt] *vi* concentrarse ▷*vt* concentrar
concentration [kɔnsən'treɪʃən] *n* concentración *f*
concept ['kɔnsɛpt] *n* concepto
concern [kən'səːn] *n* (*matter*) asunto; (*Comm*) empresa; (*anxiety*) preocupación

f ▷ *vt* (*worry*) preocupar; (*involve*) afectar; (*relate to*) tener que ver con; **to be ~ed (about)** interesarse (por), preocuparse (por); **concerning** *prep* sobre, acerca de

concert ['kɔnsət] *n* concierto; **concert hall** *n* sala de conciertos

concerto [kən'tʃəːtəu] *n* concierto

concession [kən'sɛʃən] *n* concesión *f*; **tax ~** privilegio fiscal

concise [kən'saɪs] *adj* conciso

conclude [kən'kluːd] *vt* concluir; (*treaty etc*) firmar; (*agreement*) llegar a; (*decide*) llegar a la conclusión de; **conclusion** [-'kluːʒən] *n* conclusión *f*; firma

concrete ['kɔnkriːt] *n* hormigón *m* ▷ *adj* de hormigón; (*fig*) concreto

concussion [kən'kʌʃən] *n* conmoción *f* cerebral

condemn [kən'dɛm] *vt* condenar; (*building*) declarar en ruina

condensation [kɔndɛn'seɪʃən] *n* condensación *f*

condense [kən'dɛns] *vi* condensarse ▷ *vt* condensar, abreviar

condition [kən'dɪʃən] *n* condición *f*, estado; (*requirement*) condición *f* ▷ *vt* condicionar; **on ~ that** a condición (de) que; **conditional** [kən'dɪʃənl] *adj* condicional; **conditioner** *n* suavizante

condo ['kɔndəu] (US) *n* (*inf*) = **condominium**

condom ['kɔndəm] *n* condón *m*

condominium [kɔndə'mɪnɪəm] (US) *n* (*building*) bloque *m* de pisos *or* apartamentos (*propiedad de quienes lo habitan*), condominio (LAM); (*apartment*) piso *or* apartamento (en propiedad), condominio (LAM)

condone [kən'dəun] *vt* condonar

conduct [*n* 'kɔndʌkt, *vb* kən'dʌkt] *n* conducta, comportamiento ▷ *vt* (*lead*) conducir; (*manage*) llevar a cabo, dirigir; (*Mus*) dirigir; **to ~ o.s.** comportarse; **conducted tour** (BRIT) *n* visita acompañada; **conductor** *n* (*of orchestra*) director *m*; (US: *on train*) revisor(a) *m/f*; (*on bus*) cobrador *m*; (*Elec*) conductor *m*

cone [kəun] *n* cono; (*pine cone*) piña; (*on road*) pivote *m*; (*for ice-cream*) cucurucho

confectionery [kən'fɛkʃənʀɪ] *n* dulces *mpl*

confer [kən'fəː*] *vt*: **to ~ sth on** otorgar algo a ▷ *vi* conferenciar

conference ['kɔnfərns] *n* (*meeting*) reunión *f*; (*convention*) congreso

confess [kən'fɛs] *vt* confesar ▷ *vi* admitir; **confession** [-'fɛʃən] *n* confesión *f*

confide [kən'faɪd] *vi*: **to ~ in** confiar en

confidence ['kɔnfɪdns] *n* (*also*: **self-~**) confianza; (*secret*) confidencia; **in ~** (*speak, write*) en confianza; **confident** *adj* seguro de sí mismo; (*certain*) seguro; **confidential** [kɔnfɪ'dɛnʃəl] *adj* confidencial

confine [kən'faɪn] *vt* (*limit*) limitar; (*shut up*) encerrar; **confined** *adj* (*space*) reducido

confirm [kən'fəːm] *vt* confirmar; **confirmation** [kɔnfə'meɪʃən] *n* confirmación *f*

confiscate ['kɔnfɪskeɪt] *vt* confiscar

conflict [*n* 'kɔnflɪkt, *vb* kən'flɪkt] *n* conflicto ▷ *vi* (*opinions*) chocar

conform [kən'fɔːm] *vi* conformarse; **to ~ to** ajustarse a

confront [kən'frʌnt] *vt* (*problems*) hacer frente a; (*enemy, danger*) enfrentarse con; **confrontation** [kɔnfrən'teɪʃən] *n* enfrentamiento

confuse [kən'fjuːz] *vt* (*perplex*) aturdir, desconcertar; (*mix up*) confundir; (*complicate*) complicar; **confused** *adj* confuso; (*person*) perplejo; **confusing** *adj* confuso; **confusion** [-'fjuːʒən] *n* confusión *f*

congestion [kən'dʒɛstʃən] *n* congestión *f*

congratulate [kən'grætjuleɪt] *vt*: **to ~ sb (on)** felicitar a algn (por); **congratulations** [-'leɪʃənz] *npl* felicitaciones *fpl*; **congratulations!** ¡enhorabuena!

congregation [-'geɪʃən] *n* (*of a church*) feligreses *mpl*

congress ['kɔŋgrɛs] *n* congreso; (US): **C~** Congreso; **congressman** (*irreg*: US) *n* miembro del Congreso; **congresswoman** (*irreg*: US) *n* diputada, miembro *f* del Congreso

conifer ['kɔnɪfə*] *n* conífera

conjugate ['kɔndʒugeɪt] *vt* conjugar

conjugation [kɔndʒə'geɪʃən] *n* conjugación *f*

conjunction [kən'dʒʌŋkʃən] *n* conjunción *f*; **in ~ with** junto con

conjure ['kʌndʒə*] *vi* hacer juegos de manos

connect [kə'nɛkt] *vt* juntar, unir; (*Elec*) conectar; (*Tel*: *subscriber*) poner; (*: caller*) poner al habla; (*fig*) relacionar, asociar ▷ *vi*: **to ~ with** (*train*) enlazar con; **to be ~ed with** (*associated*) estar relacionado con; **connecting flight** *n* vuelo *m* de enlace; **connection** [-ʃən] *n* juntura, unión *f*; (*Elec*) conexión *f*; (*Rail*) enlace *m*; (*Tel*) comunicación *f*; (*fig*) relación *f*

conquer ['kɔŋkə*] *vt* (*territory*) conquistar; (*enemy, feelings*) vencer

conquest ['kɔŋkwɛst] *n* conquista

cons [kɔnz] *npl* *see* **convenience; pro; mod**

conscience ['kɔnʃəns] *n* conciencia
conscientious [kɔnʃɪ'ɛnʃəs] *adj* concienzudo; (*objection*) de conciencia
conscious ['kɔnʃəs] *adj* (*deliberate*) deliberado; (*awake, aware*) consciente; **consciousness** *n* conciencia; (*Med*) conocimiento
consecutive [kən'sɛkjutɪv] *adj* consecutivo; **on 3 ~ occasions** en 3 ocasiones consecutivas
consensus [kən'sɛnsəs] *n* consenso
consent [kən'sɛnt] *n* consentimiento ▷ *vi*: **to ~ (to)** consentir (en)
consequence ['kɔnsɪkwəns] *n* consecuencia; (*significance*) importancia
consequently ['kɔnsɪkwəntlɪ] *adv* por consiguiente
conservation [kɔnsə'veɪʃən] *n* conservación *f*
conservative [kən'sə:vətɪv] *adj* conservador(a); (*estimate etc*) cauteloso; **Conservative** (BRIT) *adj, n* (*Pol*) conservador(a) *m/f*
conservatory [kən'sə:vətrɪ] *n* invernadero; (*Mus*) conservatorio
consider [kən'sɪdə*] *vt* considerar; (*take into account*) tener en cuenta; (*study*) estudiar, examinar; **to ~ doing sth** pensar en (la posibilidad de) hacer algo; **considerable** *adj* considerable; **considerably** *adv* notablemente; **considerate** *adj* considerado; **consideration** [-'reɪʃən] *n* consideración *f*; (*factor*) factor *m*; **to give sth further consideration** estudiar algo más a fondo; **considering** *prep* teniendo en cuenta
consignment [kən'saɪnmənt] *n* envío
consist [kən'sɪst] *vi*: **to ~ of** consistir en
consistency [kən'sɪstənsɪ] *n* (*of argument etc*) coherencia; consecuencia; (*thickness*) consistencia
consistent [kən'sɪstənt] *adj* (*person*) consecuente; (*argument etc*) coherente
consolation [kɔnsə'leɪʃən] *n* consuelo
console[1] [kən'səul] *vt* consolar
console[2] ['kɔnsəul] *n* consola
consonant ['kɔnsənənt] *n* consonante *f*
conspicuous [kən'spɪkjuəs] *adj* (*visible*) visible
conspiracy [kən'spɪrəsɪ] *n* conjura, complot *m*
constable ['kʌnstəbl] (BRIT) *n* policía *mf*; **chief ~** ≈ jefe *m* de policía
constant ['kɔnstənt] *adj* constante; **constantly** *adv* constantemente
constipated ['kɔnstɪpeɪtəd] *adj* estreñido

Be careful not to translate **constipated** by the Spanish word *constipado*.

constipation [kɔnstɪ'peɪʃən] *n* estreñimiento
constituency [kən'stɪtjuənsɪ] *n* (*Pol*: *area*) distrito electoral; (: *electors*) electorado
constitute ['kɔnstɪtju:t] *vt* constituir
constitution [kɔnstɪ'tju:ʃən] *n* constitución *f*
constraint [kən'streɪnt] *n* obligación *f*; (*limit*) restricción *f*
construct [kən'strʌkt] *vt* construir; **construction** [-ʃən] *n* construcción *f*; **constructive** *adj* constructivo
consul ['kɔnsl] *n* cónsul *mf*; **consulate** ['kɔnsjulɪt] *n* consulado
consult [kən'sʌlt] *vt* consultar; **consultant** *n* (BRIT *Med*) especialista *mf*; (*other specialist*) asesor(a) *m/f*; **consultation** [kɔnsəl'teɪʃən] *n* consulta; **consulting room** (BRIT) *n* consultorio
consume [kən'sju:m] *vt* (*eat*) comerse; (*drink*) beberse; (*fire etc, Comm*) consumir; **consumer** *n* consumidor(a) *m/f*
consumption [kən'sʌmpʃən] *n* consumo
cont. *abbr* (= *continued*) sigue
contact ['kɔntækt] *n* contacto; (*person*) contacto; (: *pej*) enchufe *m* ▷ *vt* ponerse en contacto con; **contact lenses** *npl* lentes *fpl* de contacto
contagious [kən'teɪdʒəs] *adj* contagioso
contain [kən'teɪn] *vt* contener; **to ~ o.s.** contenerse; **container** *n* recipiente *m*; (*for shipping etc*) contenedor *m*
contaminate [kən'tæmɪneɪt] *vt* contaminar
cont'd *abbr* (= *continued*) sigue
contemplate ['kɔntəmpleɪt] *vt* contemplar; (*reflect upon*) considerar
contemporary [kən'tɛmpərərɪ] *adj, n* contemporáneo/a *m/f*
contempt [kən'tɛmpt] *n* desprecio; **~ of court** (*Law*) desacato (a los tribunales)
contend [kən'tɛnd] *vt* (*argue*) afirmar ▷ *vi*: **to ~ with/for** luchar contra/por
content [*adj, vb* kən'tɛnt, *n* 'kɔntɛnt] *adj* (*happy*) contento; (*satisfied*) satisfecho ▷ *vt* contentar; satisfacer ▷ *n* contenido; **contents** *npl* contenido; **(table of) ~s** índice *m* de materias; **contented** *adj* contento; satisfecho
contest [*n* 'kɔntɛst, *vb* kən'tɛst] *n* lucha; (*competition*) concurso ▷ *vt* (*dispute*) impugnar; (*Pol*) presentarse como candidato/a en

Be careful not to translate **contest** by the Spanish word *contestar*.

contestant [kən'tɛstənt] *n* concursante

mf; (*in fight*) contendiente *mf*

context ['kɔntɛkst] *n* contexto

continent ['kɔntɪnənt] *n* continente *m*; **the C~** (BRIT) el continente europeo; **continental** [-'nɛntl] *adj* continental; **continental breakfast** *n* desayuno estilo europeo; **continental quilt** (BRIT) *n* edredón *m*

continual [kən'tɪnjuəl] *adj* continuo; **continually** *adv* constantemente

continue [kən'tɪnju:] *vi, vt* seguir, continuar

continuity [kɔntɪ'njuɪtɪ] *n* (*also Cine*) continuidad *f*

continuous [kən'tɪnjuəs] *adj* continuo; **continuous assessment** *n* (BRIT) evaluación *f* continua; **continuously** *adv* continuamente

contour ['kɔntuə*] *n* contorno; (*also*: **~ line**) curva de nivel

contraception [kɔntrə'sɛpʃən] *n* contracepción *f*

contraceptive [kɔntrə'sɛptɪv] *adj, n* anticonceptivo

contract [*n* 'kɔntrækt, *vb* kən'trækt] *n* contrato ▷*vi* (*Comm*): **to ~ to do sth** comprometerse por contrato a hacer algo; (*become smaller*) contraerse, encogerse ▷*vt* contraer; **contractor** *n* contratista *mf*

contradict [kɔntrə'dɪkt] *vt* contradecir; **contradiction** [-ʃən] *n* contradicción *f*

contrary[1] ['kɔntrərɪ] *adj* contrario ▷*n* lo contrario; **on the ~** al contrario; **unless you hear to the ~** a no ser que le digan lo contrario

contrary[2] [kən'trɛərɪ] *adj* (*perverse*) terco

contrast [*n* 'kɔntrɑ:st, *vt* kən'trɑ:st] *n* contraste *m* ▷*vt* comparar; **in ~ to** en contraste con

contribute [kən'trɪbju:t] *vi* contribuir ▷*vt*: **to ~ £10/an article to** contribuir con 10 libras/un artículo a; **to ~ to** (*charity*) donar a; (*newspaper*) escribir para; (*discussion*) intervenir en; **contribution** [kɔntrɪ'bju:ʃən] *n* (*donation*) donativo; (BRIT: *for social security*) cotización *f*; (*to debate*) intervención *f*; (*to journal*) colaboración *f*; **contributor** *n* contribuyente *mf*; (*to newspaper*) colaborador(a) *m/f*

control [kən'trəul] *vt* controlar; (*process etc*) dirigir; (*machinery*) manejar; (*temper*) dominar; (*disease*) contener ▷*n* control *m*; **controls** *npl* (*of vehicle*) instrumentos *mpl* de mando; (*of radio*) controles *mpl*; (*governmental*) medidas *fpl* de control; **under ~** bajo control; **to be in ~ of** tener el mando de; **the car went out of ~** se perdió el control del coche; **control tower** *n* (*Aviat*) torre *f* de control

controversial [kɔntrə'və:ʃl] *adj* polémico

controversy ['kɔntrəvə:sɪ] *n* polémica

convenience [kən'vi:nɪəns] *n* (*easiness*) comodidad *f*; (*suitability*) idoneidad *f*; (*advantage*) ventaja; **at your ~** cuando le sea conveniente; **all modern ~s, all mod cons** (BRIT) todo confort

convenient [kən'vi:nɪənt] *adj* (*useful*) útil; (*place, time*) conveniente

convent ['kɔnvənt] *n* convento

convention [kən'vɛnʃən] *n* convención *f*; (*meeting*) asamblea; (*agreement*) convenio; **conventional** *adj* convencional

conversation [kɔnvə'seɪʃən] *n* conversación *f*

conversely [-'və:slɪ] *adv* a la inversa

conversion [kən'və:ʃən] *n* conversión *f*

convert [*vb* kən'və:t, *n* 'kɔnvə:t] *vt* (*Rel, Comm*) convertir; (*alter*): **to ~ sth into/to** transformar algo en/convertir algo a ▷*n* converso/a; **convertible** *adj* convertible ▷*n* descapotable *m*

convey [kən'veɪ] *vt* llevar; (*thanks*) comunicar; (*idea*) expresar; **conveyor belt** *n* cinta transportadora

convict [*vb* kən'vɪkt, *n* 'kɔnvɪkt] *vt* (*find guilty*) declarar culpable a ▷*n* presidiario/a; **conviction** [-ʃən] *n* condena; (*belief, certainty*) convicción *f*

convince [kən'vɪns] *vt* convencer; **convinced** *adj*: **convinced of/that** convencido de/de que; **convincing** *adj* convincente

convoy ['kɔnvɔɪ] *n* convoy *m*

cook [kuk] *vt* (*stew etc*) guisar; (*meal*) preparar ▷*vi* cocer; (*person*) cocinar ▷*n* cocinero/a; **cook book** *n* libro de cocina; **cooker** *n* cocina; **cookery** *n* cocina; **cookery book** (BRIT) *n* = **cook book**; **cookie** (US) *n* galleta; **cooking** *n* cocina

cool [ku:l] *adj* fresco; (*not afraid*) tranquilo; (*unfriendly*) frío ▷*vt* enfriar ▷*vi* enfriarse; **cool down** *vi* enfriarse; (*fig: person, situation*) calmarse; **cool off** *vi* (*become calmer*) calmarse, apaciguarse; (*lose enthusiasm*) perder (el) interés, enfriarse

cop [kɔp] (*inf*) *n* poli *mf* (SP), tira *mf* (MEX)

cope [kəup] *vi*: **to ~ with** (*problem*) hacer frente a

copper ['kɔpə*] *n* (*metal*) cobre *m*; (BRIT: *inf*) poli *mf*, tira *mf* (MEX)

copy ['kɔpɪ] *n* copia; (*of book etc*) ejemplar *m* ▷*vt* copiar; **copyright** *n* derechos *mpl* de autor

coral ['kɔrəl] *n* coral *m*

cord [kɔ:d] *n* cuerda; (*Elec*) cable *m*; (*fabric*) pana; **cords** *npl* (*trousers*) pantalones *mpl* de

pana; **cordless** *adj* sin hilos
corduroy ['kɔːdərɔɪ] *n* pana
core [kɔː*] *n* centro, núcleo; (*of fruit*) corazón *m*; (*of problem*) meollo ▷*vt* quitar el corazón de
coriander [kɔrɪ'ændə*] *n* culantro
cork [kɔːk] *n* corcho; (*tree*) alcornoque *m*; **corkscrew** *n* sacacorchos *m inv*
corn [kɔːn] *n* (BRIT: *cereal crop*) trigo; (US: *maize*) maíz *m*; (*on foot*) callo; **~ on the cob** (*Culin*) mazorca, elote *m* (MEX), choclo (SC)
corned beef ['kɔːnd-] *n* carne *f* acecinada (en lata)
corner ['kɔːnə*] *n* (*outside*) esquina; (*inside*) rincón *m*; (*in road*) curva; (*Football*) córner *m*; (*Boxing*) esquina ▷*vt* (*trap*) arrinconar; (*Comm*) acaparar ▷*vi* (*in car*) tomar las curvas; **corner shop** (BRIT) tienda de la esquina
cornflakes ['kɔːnfleɪks] *npl* copos *mpl* de maíz, cornflakes *mpl*
cornflour ['kɔːnflauə*] (BRIT) *n* harina de maíz
cornstarch ['kɔːnstɑːtʃ] (US) *n* = **cornflour**
Cornwall ['kɔːnwəl] *n* Cornualles *m*
coronary ['kɔrənərɪ] *n* (*also*: **~ thrombosis**) infarto
coronation [kɔrə'neɪʃən] *n* coronación *f*
coroner ['kɔrənə*] *n* juez *mf* de instrucción
corporal ['kɔːpərl] *n* cabo ▷*adj*: **~ punishment** castigo corporal
corporate ['kɔːpərɪt] *adj* (*action, ownership*) colectivo; (*finance, image*) corporativo
corporation [kɔːpə'reɪʃən] *n* (*of town*) ayuntamiento; (*Comm*) corporación *f*
corps [kɔː*, *pl* kɔːz] *n inv* cuerpo; **diplomatic ~** cuerpo diplomático; **press ~** gabinete *m* de prensa
corpse [kɔːps] *n* cadáver *m*
correct [kə'rɛkt] *adj* justo, exacto; (*proper*) correcto ▷*vt* corregir; (*exam*) corregir, calificar; **correction** [-ʃən] *n* (*act*) corrección *f*; (*instance*) rectificación *f*
correspond [kɔrɪs'pɔnd] *vi* (*write*): **to ~ (with)** escribirse (con); (*be equivalent to*): **to ~ (to)** corresponder (a); (*be in accordance*): **to ~ (with)** corresponder (con); **correspondence** *n* correspondencia; **correspondent** *n* corresponsal *mf*; **corresponding** *adj* correspondiente
corridor ['kɔrɪdɔː*] *n* pasillo
corrode [kə'rəud] *vt* corroer ▷*vi* corroerse
corrupt [kə'rʌpt] *adj* (*person*) corrupto; (*Comput*) corrompido ▷*vt* corromper; (*Comput*) degradar; **corruption** *n* corrupción *f*; (*of data*) alteración *f*
Corsica ['kɔːsɪkə] *n* Córcega
cosmetic [kɔz'mɛtɪk] *adj, n* cosmético; **cosmetic surgery** *n* cirugía *f* estética
cosmopolitan [kɔzmə'pɔlɪtn] *adj* cosmopolita
cost [kɔst] (*pt, pp* **~**) *n* (*price*) precio ▷*vi* costar, valer ▷*vt* preparar el presupuesto de; **how much does it ~?** ¿cuánto cuesta?; **to ~ sb time/effort** costarle a algn tiempo/esfuerzo; **it ~ him his life** le costó la vida; **at all ~s** cueste lo que cueste; **costs** *npl* (*Comm*) costes *mpl*; (*Law*) costas *fpl*
co-star ['kəustɑː*] *n* coprotagonista *mf*
Costa Rica ['kɔstə'riːkə] *n* Costa Rica; **Costa Rican** *adj, n* costarriqueño/a
costly ['kɔstlɪ] *adj* costoso
cost of living *n* costo *or* coste *m* (*Sp*) de la vida
costume ['kɔstjuːm] *n* traje *m*; (BRIT: *also*: **swimming ~**) traje de baño
cosy ['kəuzɪ] (US **cozy**) *adj* (*person*) cómodo; (*room*) acogedor(a)
cot [kɔt] *n* (BRIT: *child's*) cuna; (US: *campbed*) cama de campaña
cottage ['kɔtɪdʒ] *n* casita de campo; (*rustic*) barraca; **cottage cheese** *n* requesón *m*
cotton ['kɔtn] *n* algodón *m*; (*thread*) hilo; **cotton on** *vi* (*inf*): **to cotton on (to sth)** caer en la cuenta (de algo); **cotton bud** *n* (BRIT) bastoncillo *m* de algodón; **cotton candy** (US) *n* algodón *m* (azucarado); **cotton wool** (BRIT) *n* algodón *m* (hidrófilo)
couch [kautʃ] *n* sofá *m*; (*doctor's etc*) diván *m*
cough [kɔf] *vi* toser ▷*n* tos *f*; **cough mixture** *n* jarabe *m* para la tos
could [kud] *pt of* **can²**; **couldn't** = **could not**
council ['kaunsl] *n* consejo; **city** *or* **town ~** consejo municipal; **council estate** (BRIT) *n urbanización de viviendas municipales de alquiler*; **council house** (BRIT) *n vivienda municipal de alquiler*; **councillor** (US **councilor**) *n* concejal(a) *m/f*; **council tax** *n* (BRIT) contribución *f* municipal (*dependiente del valor de la vivienda*)
counsel ['kaunsl] *n* (*advice*) consejo; (*lawyer*) abogado/a ▷*vt* aconsejar; **counselling** (US **counseling**) *n* (*Psych*) asistencia *f* psicológica; **counsellor** (US **counselor**) *n* consejero/a, abogado/a
count [kaunt] *vt* contar; (*include*) incluir ▷*vi* contar ▷*n* cuenta; (*of votes*) escrutinio; (*level*) nivel *m*; (*nobleman*) conde *m*; **count in** (*inf*) *vt*: **to count sb in on sth** contar con

algn para algo; **count on** *vt fus* contar con; **countdown** *n* cuenta atrás
counter ['kauntə*] *n* (*in shop*) mostrador *m*; (*in games*) ficha ▷*vt* contrarrestar ▷*adv*: **to run ~ to** ser contrario a, ir en contra de; **counter clockwise** (US) *adv* en sentido contrario al de las agujas del reloj
counterfeit ['kauntəfɪt] *n* falsificación *f*, simulación *f* ▷*vt* falsificar ▷*adj* falso, falsificado
counterpart ['kauntəpɑ:t] *n* homólogo/a
countess ['kauntɪs] *n* condesa
countless ['kauntlɪs] *adj* innumerable
country ['kʌntrɪ] *n* país *m*; (*native land*) patria; (*as opposed to town*) campo; (*region*) región *f*, tierra; **country and western (music)** *n* música country; **country house** *n* casa de campo; **countryside** *n* campo
county ['kauntɪ] *n* condado
coup [ku:] (*pl* **~s**) *n* (*also*: **~ d'état**) golpe *m* (de estado); (*achievement*) éxito
couple ['kʌpl] *n* (*of things*) par *m*; (*of people*) pareja; (*married couple*) matrimonio; **a ~ of** un par de
coupon ['ku:pɔn] *n* cupón *m*; (*voucher*) valé *m*
courage ['kʌrɪdʒ] *n* valor *m*, valentía; **courageous** [kə'reɪdʒəs] *adj* valiente
courgette [kuə'ʒɛt] (BRIT) *n* calabacín *m*, calabacita (MEX)
courier ['kurɪə*] *n* mensajero/a; (*for tourists*) guía *mf* (de turismo)
course [kɔ:s] *n* (*direction*) dirección *f*; (*of river, Scol*) curso; (*process*) transcurso; (*Med*): **~ of treatment** tratamiento; (*of ship*) rumbo; (*part of meal*) plato; (*Golf*) campo; **of ~** desde luego, naturalmente; **of ~!** ¡claro!
court [kɔ:t] *n* (*royal*) corte *f*; (*Law*) tribunal *m*, juzgado; (*Tennis etc*) pista, cancha ▷*vt* (*woman*) cortejar a; **to take to ~** demandar
courtesy ['kə:təsɪ] *n* cortesía; **(by) ~ of** por cortesía de; **courtesy bus, courtesy coach** *n* autobús *m* gratuito
court: court-house ['kɔ:thaus] (US) *n* palacio de justicia; **courtroom** ['kɔ:trum] *n* sala de justicia; **courtyard** ['kɔ:tjɑ:d] *n* patio
cousin ['kʌzn] *n* primo/a; **first ~** primo/a carnal, primo/a hermano/a
cover ['kʌvə*] *vt* cubrir; (*feelings, mistake*) ocultar; (*with lid*) tapar; (*book etc*) forrar; (*distance*) recorrer; (*include*) abarcar; (*protect: also: Insurance*) cubrir; (*Press*) investigar; (*discuss*) tratar ▷*n* cubierta; (*lid*) tapa; (*for chair etc*) funda; (*envelope*) sobre *m*; (*for book*) forro; (*of magazine*) portada; (*shelter*) abrigo; (*Insurance*) cobertura; (*of spy*) cobertura; **covers** *npl* (*on bed*) sábanas; mantas; **to take ~** (*shelter*) protegerse, resguardarse; **under ~** (*indoors*) bajo techo; **under ~ of darkness** al amparo de la oscuridad; **under separate ~** (*Comm*) por separado; **cover up** *vi*: **to cover up for sb** encubrir a algn; **coverage** *n* (*TV, Press*) cobertura; **cover charge** *n* precio del cubierto; **cover-up** *n* encubrimiento
cow [kau] *n* vaca; (*inf!: woman*) bruja ▷*vt* intimidar
coward ['kauəd] *n* cobarde *mf*; **cowardly** *adj* cobarde
cowboy ['kaubɔɪ] *n* vaquero
cozy ['kəuzɪ] (US) *adj* = **cosy**
crab [kræb] *n* cangrejo
crack [kræk] *n* grieta; (*noise*) crujido; (*drug*) crack *m* ▷*vt* agrietar, romper; (*nut*) cascar; (*solve: problem*) resolver; (*: code*) descifrar; (*whip etc*) chasquear; (*knuckles*) crujir; (*joke*) contar ▷*adj* (*expert*) de primera; **crack down on** *vt fus* adoptar fuertes medidas contra; **cracked** *adj* (*cup, window*) rajado; (*wall*) resquebrajado; **cracker** *n* (*biscuit*) cráčker *m*; (*Christmas cracker*) petardo sorpresa
crackle ['krækl] *vi* crepitar
cradle ['kreɪdl] *n* cuna
craft [krɑ:ft] *n* (*skill*) arte *m*; (*trade*) oficio; (*cunning*) astucia; (*boat: pl inv*) barco; (*plane: pl inv*) avión *m*; **craftsman** (*irreg*) *n* artesano; **craftsmanship** *n* (*quality*) destreza
cram [kræm] *vt* (*fill*): **to ~ sth with** llenar algo (a reventar) de; (*put*): **to ~ sth into** meter algo a la fuerza en ▷*vi* (*for exams*) empollar
cramp [kræmp] *n* (*Med*) calambre *m*; **cramped** *adj* apretado, estrecho
cranberry ['krænbərɪ] *n* arándano agrio
crane [kreɪn] *n* (*Tech*) grúa; (*bird*) grulla
crap [kræp] *n* (*inf!*) mierda (*!*)
crash [kræʃ] *n* (*noise*) estrépito; (*of cars etc*) choque *m*; (*of plane*) accidente *m* de aviación; (*Comm*) quiebra ▷*vt* (*car, plane*) estrellar ▷*vi* (*car, plane*) estrellarse; (*two cars*) chocar; (*Comm*) quebrar; **crash course** *n* curso acelerado; **crash helmet** *n* casco (protector)
crate [kreɪt] *n* cajón *m* de embalaje; (*for bottles*) caja
crave [kreɪv] *vt, vi*: **to ~ (for)** ansiar, anhelar
crawl [krɔ:l] *vi* (*drag o.s.*) arrastrarse; (*child*) andar a gatas, gatear; (*vehicle*) avanzar (lentamente) ▷*n* (*Swimming*) crol *m*
crayfish ['kreɪfɪʃ] *n inv* (*freshwater*) cangrejo de río; (*saltwater*) cigala

crayon ['kreɪən] *n* lápiz *m* de color
craze [kreɪz] *n* (*fashion*) moda
crazy ['kreɪzɪ] *adj* (*person*) loco; (*idea*) disparatado; (*inf*: *keen*): **~ about sb/sth** loco por algn/algo
creak [kri:k] *vi* (*floorboard*) crujir; (*hinge etc*) chirriar, rechinar
cream [kri:m] *n* (*of milk*) nata, crema; (*lotion*) crema; (*fig*) flor *f* y nata ▷ *adj* (*colour*) color crema; **cream cheese** *n* queso blanco; **creamy** *adj* cremoso; (*colour*) color crema
crease [kri:s] *n* (*fold*) pliegue *m*; (*in trousers*) raya; (*wrinkle*) arruga ▷ *vt* (*wrinkle*) arrugar ▷ *vi* (*wrinkle up*) arrugarse
create [kri:'eɪt] *vt* crear; **creation** [-ʃən] *n* creación *f*; **creative** *adj* creativo; **creator** *n* creador(a) *m/f*
creature ['kri:tʃə*] *n* (*animal*) animal *m*, bicho; (*person*) criatura
crèche [krɛʃ] *n* guardería (infantil)
credentials [krɪ'dɛnʃlz] *npl* (*references*) referencias *fpl*; (*identity papers*) documentos *mpl* de identidad
credibility [krɛdɪ'bɪlɪtɪ] *n* credibilidad *f*
credible ['krɛdɪbl] *adj* creíble; (*trustworthy*) digno de confianza
credit ['krɛdɪt] *n* crédito; (*merit*) honor *m*, mérito ▷ *vt* (*Comm*) abonar; (*believe*: *also*: **give ~ to**) creer, prestar fe a ▷ *adj* crediticio; **credits** *npl* (*Cinema*) fichas *fpl* técnicas; **to be in ~** (*person*) tener saldo a favor; **to ~ sb with** (*fig*) reconocer a algn el mérito de; **credit card** *n* tarjeta de crédito
creek [kri:k] *n* cala, ensenada; (*US*) riachuelo
creep [kri:p] (*pt, pp* **crept**) *vi* arrastrarse
cremate [krɪ'meɪt] *vt* incinerar
crematorium [krɛmə'tɔ:rɪəm] (*pl* **crematoria**) *n* crematorio
crept [krɛpt] *pt, pp of* **creep**
crescent ['krɛsnt] *n* media luna; (*street*) calle *f* (*en forma de semicírculo*)
cress [krɛs] *n* berro
crest [krɛst] *n* (*of bird*) cresta; (*of hill*) cima, cumbre *f*; (*of coat of arms*) blasón *m*
crew [kru:] *n* (*of ship etc*) tripulación *f*; (*TV, Cinema*) equipo; **crew-neck** *n* cuello a la caja
crib [krɪb] *n* cuna ▷ *vt* (*inf*) plagiar
cricket ['krɪkɪt] *n* (*insect*) grillo; (*game*) críquet *m*; **cricketer** *n* jugador(a) *m/f* de críquet
crime [kraɪm] *n* (*no pl*: *illegal activities*) crimen *m*; (*illegal action*) delito; **criminal** ['krɪmɪnl] *n* criminal *mf*, delincuente *mf* ▷ *adj* criminal; (*illegal*) delictivo; (*law*) penal
crimson ['krɪmzn] *adj* carmesí
cringe [krɪndʒ] *vi* agacharse, encogerse
cripple ['krɪpl] *n* lisiado/a, cojo/a ▷ *vt* lisiar, mutilar
crisis ['kraɪsɪs] (*pl* **crises**) *n* crisis *f inv*
crisp [krɪsp] *adj* fresco; (*vegetables etc*) crujiente; (*manner*) seco; **crispy** *adj* crujiente
criterion [kraɪ'tɪərɪən] (*pl* **criteria**) *n* criterio
critic ['krɪtɪk] *n* crítico/a; **critical** *adj* crítico; (*illness*) grave; **criticism** ['krɪtɪsɪzm] *n* crítica; **criticize** ['krɪtɪsaɪz] *vt* criticar
Croat ['krəuæt] *adj, n* = **Croatian**
Croatia [krəu'eɪʃə] *n* Croacia; **Croatian** *adj, n* croata *m/f* ▷ *n* (*Ling*) croata *m*
crockery ['krɔkərɪ] *n* loza, vajilla
crocodile ['krɔkədaɪl] *n* cocodrilo
crocus ['krəukəs] *n* croco, crocus *m*
croissant ['krwasŋ] *n* croissant *m*, medialuna (*esp* LAM)
crook [kruk] *n* ladrón/ona *m/f*; (*of shepherd*) cayado; **crooked** ['krukɪd] *adj* torcido; (*dishonest*) nada honrado
crop [krɔp] *n* (*produce*) cultivo; (*amount produced*) cosecha; (*riding crop*) látigo de montar ▷ *vt* cortar, recortar; **crop up** *vi* surgir, presentarse
cross [krɔs] *n* cruz *f*; (*hybrid*) cruce *m* ▷ *vt* (*street etc*) cruzar, atravesar ▷ *adj* de mal humor, enojado; **cross off** *vt* tachar; **cross out** *vt* tachar; **cross over** *vi* cruzar; **cross-Channel ferry** ['krɔs'tʃænl-] *n* transbordador *m* que cruza el Canal de la Mancha; **crosscountry (race)** *n* carrera a campo traviesa, cross *m*; **crossing** *n* (*sea passage*) travesía; (*also*: **pedestrian crossing**) paso para peatones; **crossing guard** (US) *n* *persona encargada de ayudar a los niños a cruzar la calle*; **crossroads** *n* cruce *m*, encrucijada; **crosswalk** (US) *n* paso de peatones; **crossword** *n* crucigrama *m*
crotch [krɔtʃ] *n* (*Anat, of garment*) entrepierna
crouch [krautʃ] *vi* agacharse, acurrucarse
crouton ['kru:tɔn] *n* cubito de pan frito
crow [krəu] *n* (*bird*) cuervo; (*of cock*) canto, cacareo ▷ *vi* (*cock*) cantar
crowd [kraud] *n* muchedumbre *f*, multitud *f* ▷ *vt* (*fill*) llenar ▷ *vi* (*gather*): **to ~ round** reunirse en torno a; (*cram*): **to ~ in** entrar en tropel; **crowded** *adj* (*full*) atestado; (*densely populated*) superpoblado
crown [kraun] *n* corona; (*of head*) coronilla; (*for tooth*) funda; (*of hill*) cumbre *f* ▷ *vt* coronar; (*fig*) completar, rematar; **crown jewels** *npl* joyas *fpl* reales
crucial ['kru:ʃl] *adj* decisivo
crucifix ['kru:sɪfɪks] *n* crucifijo

crude [kruːd] *adj* (*materials*) bruto; (*fig*: *basic*) tosco; (: *vulgar*) ordinario; **crude (oil)** *n* (petróleo) crudo
cruel ['kruəl] *adj* cruel; **cruelty** *n* crueldad *f*
cruise [kruːz] *n* crucero ▷*vi* (*ship*) hacer un crucero; (*car*) ir a velocidad de crucero
crumb [krʌm] *n* miga, migaja
crumble ['krʌmbl] *vt* desmenuzar ▷*vi* (*building, also fig*) desmoronarse
crumpet ['krʌmpɪt] *n* ≈ bollo para tostar
crumple ['krʌmpl] *vt* (*paper*) estrujar; (*material*) arrugar
crunch [krʌntʃ] *vt* (*with teeth*) mascar; (*underfoot*) hacer crujir ▷*n* (*fig*) hora *or* momento de la verdad; **crunchy** *adj* crujiente
crush [krʌʃ] *n* (*crowd*) aglomeración *f*; (*infatuation*): **to have a ~ on sb** estar loco por algn; (*drink*): **lemon ~** limonada ▷*vt* aplastar; (*paper*) estrujar; (*cloth*) arrugar; (*fruit*) exprimir; (*opposition*) aplastar; (*hopes*) destruir
crust [krʌst] *n* corteza; (*of snow, ice*) costra; **crusty** *adj* (*bread*) crujiente; (*person*) de mal carácter
crutch [krʌtʃ] *n* muleta
cry [kraɪ] *vi* llorar ▷*n* (*shriek*) chillido; (*shout*) grito; **cry out** *vi* (*call out, shout*) lanzar un grito, echar un grito ▷*vt* gritar
crystal ['krɪstl] *n* cristal *m*
cub [kʌb] *n* cachorro; (*also*: **~ scout**) niño explorador
Cuba ['kjuːbə] *n* Cuba; **Cuban** *adj, n* cubano/a *m/f*
cube [kjuːb] *n* cubo ▷*vt* (*Math*) cubicar
cubicle ['kjuːbɪkl] *n* (*at pool*) caseta; (*for bed*) cubículo
cuckoo ['kukuː] *n* cuco
cucumber ['kjuːkʌmbə*] *n* pepino
cuddle ['kʌdl] *vt* abrazar ▷*vi* abrazarse
cue [kjuː] *n* (*snooker cue*) taco; (*Theatre etc*) señal *f*
cuff [kʌf] *n* (*of sleeve*) puño; (*US*: *of trousers*) vuelta; (*blow*) bofetada ▷ **off the ~** *adv* de improviso; **cufflinks** *npl* gemelos *mpl*
cuisine [kwɪ'ziːn] *n* cocina
cul-de-sac ['kʌldəsæk] *n* callejón *m* sin salida
cull [kʌl] *vt* (*idea*) sacar ▷*n* (*of animals*) matanza selectiva
culminate ['kʌlmɪneɪt] *vi*: **to ~ in** terminar en
culprit ['kʌlprɪt] *n* culpable *mf*
cult [kʌlt] *n* culto
cultivate ['kʌltɪveɪt] *vt* cultivar
cultural ['kʌltʃərəl] *adj* cultural
culture ['kʌltʃə*] *n* (*also fig*) cultura; (*Biol*) cultivo
cumin ['kʌmɪn] *n* (*spice*) comino
cunning ['kʌnɪŋ] *n* astucia ▷*adj* astuto
cup [kʌp] *n* taza; (*as prize*) copa
cupboard ['kʌbəd] *n* armario; (*in kitchen*) alacena
cup final *n* (*Football*) final *f* de copa
curator [kjuə'reɪtə*] *n* director(a) *m/f*
curb [kəːb] *vt* refrenar; (*person*) reprimir ▷*n* freno; (*US*) bordillo
curdle ['kəːdl] *vi* cuajarse
cure [kjuə*] *vt* curar ▷*n* cura, curación *f*; (*fig*: *solution*) remedio
curfew ['kəːfjuː] *n* toque *m* de queda
curiosity [kjuərɪ'ɔsɪtɪ] *n* curiosidad *f*
curious ['kjuərɪəs] *adj* curioso; (*person*: *interested*): **to be ~** sentir curiosidad
curl [kəːl] *n* rizo ▷*vt* (*hair*) rizar ▷*vi* rizarse; **curl up** *vi* (*person*) hacerse un ovillo; **curler** *n* rulo; **curly** *adj* rizado
currant ['kʌrnt] *n* pasa (de Corinto); (*blackcurrant, redcurrant*) grosella
currency ['kʌrnsɪ] *n* moneda; **to gain ~** (*fig*) difundirse
current ['kʌrnt] *n* corriente *f* ▷*adj* (*accepted*) corriente; (*present*) actual; **current account** (BRIT) *n* cuenta corriente; **current affairs** *npl* noticias *fpl* de actualidad; **currently** *adv* actualmente
curriculum [kə'rɪkjuləm] (*pl* **~s** *or* **curricula**) *n* plan *m* de estudios; **curriculum vitae** *n* currículum *m*
curry ['kʌrɪ] *n* curry *m* ▷*vt*: **to ~ favour with** buscar favores con; **curry powder** *n* curry *m* en polvo
curse [kəːs] *vi* soltar tacos ▷*vt* maldecir ▷*n* maldición *f*; (*swearword*) palabrota, taco
cursor ['kəːsə*] *n* (*Comput*) cursor *m*
curt [kəːt] *adj* corto, seco
curtain ['kəːtn] *n* cortina; (*Theatre*) telón *m*
curve [kəːv] *n* curva ▷*vi* (*road*) hacer una curva; (*line etc*) curvarse; **curved** *adj* curvo
cushion ['kuʃən] *n* cojín *m*; (*of air*) colchón *m* ▷*vt* (*shock*) amortiguar
custard ['kʌstəd] *n* natillas *fpl*
custody ['kʌstədɪ] *n* custodia; **to take into ~** detener
custom ['kʌstəm] *n* costumbre *f*; (*Comm*) clientela
customer ['kʌstəmə*] *n* cliente *m/f*
customized ['kʌstəmaɪzd] *adj* (*car etc*) hecho a encargo
customs ['kʌstəmz] *npl* aduana; **customs officer** *n* aduanero/a
cut [kʌt] (*pt, pp* **~**) *vt* cortar; (*price*) rebajar; (*text, programme*) acortar; (*reduce*) reducir ▷*vi* cortar ▷*n* (*of garment*) corte *m*; (*in skin*) cortadura; (*in salary etc*) rebaja; (*in spending*)

reducción *f*, recorte *m*; (*slice of meat*) tajada; **to ~ a tooth** echar un diente; **to ~ and paste** (*Comput*) cortar y pegar; **cut back** *vt* (*plants*) podar; (*production, expenditure*) reducir; **cut down** *vt* (*tree*) derribar; (*reduce*) reducir; **cut off** *vt* cortar; (*person, place*) aislar; (*Tel*) desconectar; **cut out** *vt* (*shape*) recortar; (*stop: activity etc*) dejar; (*remove*) quitar; **cut up** *vt* cortar (en pedazos); **cutback** *n* reducción *f*
cute [kju:t] *adj* mono
cutlery ['kʌtlərɪ] *n* cubiertos *mpl*
cutlet ['kʌtlɪt] *n* chuleta; (*nut etc cutlet*) *plato vegetariano hecho con nueces y verdura en forma de chuleta*
cut-price ['kʌt'praɪs] (BRIT) *adj* a precio reducido
cut-rate ['kʌt'reɪt] (US) *adj* = **cut-price**
cutting ['kʌtɪŋ] *adj* (*remark*) mordaz ▷ *n* (BRIT: *from newspaper*) recorte *m*; (*from plant*) esqueje *m*
CV *n abbr* = **curriculum vitae**
cwt *abbr* = **hundredweight(s)**
cybercafé ['saɪbəkæfeɪ] *n* cibercafé *m*
cyberspace ['saɪbəspeɪs] *n* ciberespacio
cycle ['saɪkl] *n* ciclo; (*bicycle*) bicicleta ▷ *vi* ir en bicicleta; **cycle hire** *n* alquiler *m* de bicicletas; **cycle lane** *n* carril-bici *m*; **cycle path** *n* carril-bici *m*; **cycling** *n* ciclismo; **cyclist** *n* ciclista *mf*
cyclone ['saɪkləun] *n* ciclón *m*
cylinder ['sɪlɪndə*] *n* cilindro; (*of gas*) bombona
cymbal ['sɪmbl] *n* címbalo, platillo
cynical ['sɪnɪkl] *adj* cínico
Cypriot ['sɪprɪət] *adj, n* chipriota *m/f*
Cyprus ['saɪprəs] *n* Chipre *f*
cyst [sɪst] *n* quiste *m*; **cystitis** [-'taɪtɪs] *n* cistitis *f*
czar [zɑ:*] *n* zar *m*
Czech [tʃɛk] *adj, n* checo/a *m/f*; **Czech Republic** *n*: **the Czech Republic** la República Checa

d

D [di:] *n* (*Mus*) re *m*
dab [dæb] *vt* (*eyes, wound*) tocar (ligeramente); (*paint, cream*) poner un poco de
dad [dæd] *n* = **daddy**
daddy ['dædɪ] *n* papá *m*
daffodil ['dæfədɪl] *n* narciso
daft [dɑ:ft] *adj* tonto
dagger ['dægə*] *n* puñal *m*, daga
daily ['deɪlɪ] *adj* diario, cotidiano ▷ *adv* todos los días, cada día
dairy ['dɛərɪ] *n* (*shop*) lechería; (*on farm*) vaquería; **dairy produce** *n* productos *mpl* lácteos
daisy ['deɪzɪ] *n* margarita
dam [dæm] *n* presa ▷ *vt* construir una presa sobre, represar
damage ['dæmɪdʒ] *n* lesión *f*; daño; (*dents etc*) desperfectos *mpl*; (*fig*) perjuicio ▷ *vt* dañar, perjudicar; (*spoil, break*) estropear; **damages** *npl* (*Law*) daños *mpl* y perjuicios
damn [dæm] *vt* condenar; (*curse*) maldecir ▷ *n* (*inf*): **I don't give a ~** me importa un pito ▷ *adj* (*inf*: *also*: **~ed**) maldito; **~ (it)!** ¡maldito sea!
damp [dæmp] *adj* húmedo, mojado ▷ *n* humedad *f* ▷ *vt* (*also*: **~en**: *cloth, rag*) mojar; (: *enthusiasm*) enfriar
dance [dɑ:ns] *n* baile *m* ▷ *vi* bailar; **dance floor** *n* pista *f* de baile; **dancer** *n* bailador(a) *m/f*; (*professional*) bailarín/ina *m/f*; **dancing** *n* baile *m*
dandelion ['dændɪlaɪən] *n* diente *m* de león
dandruff ['dændrəf] *n* caspa
Dane [deɪn] *n* danés/esa *m/f*
danger ['deɪndʒə*] *n* peligro; (*risk*) riesgo; **~!** (*on sign*) ¡peligro de muerte!; **to be in ~ of** correr riesgo de; **dangerous** *adj* peligroso
dangle ['dæŋgl] *vt* colgar ▷ *vi* pender, colgar

Danish ['deɪnɪʃ] *adj* danés/esa ▷*n* (*Ling*) danés *m*

dare [dɛə*] *vt*: **to ~ sb to do** desafiar a algn a hacer ▷*vi*: **to ~ (to) do sth** atreverse a hacer algo; **I ~ say** (*I suppose*) puede ser (que); **daring** *adj* atrevido, osado ▷*n* atrevimiento, osadía

dark [dɑ:k] *adj* oscuro; (*hair, complexion*) moreno ▷*n*: **in the ~** a oscuras; **to be in the ~ about** (*fig*) no saber nada de; **after ~** después del anochecer; **darken** *vt* (*colour*) hacer más oscuro ▷*vi* oscurecerse; **darkness** *n* oscuridad *f*; **darkroom** *n* cuarto oscuro

darling ['dɑ:lɪŋ] *adj, n* querido/a *m/f*

dart [dɑ:t] *n* dardo; (*in sewing*) sisa ▷*vi* precipitarse; **dartboard** *n* diana; **darts** *n* (*game*) dardos *mpl*

dash [dæʃ] *n* (*small quantity*: *of liquid*) gota, chorrito; (*sign*) raya ▷*vt* (*throw*) tirar; (*hopes*) defraudar ▷*vi* precipitarse, ir de prisa

dashboard ['dæʃbɔ:d] *n* (*Aut*) salpicadero

data ['deɪtə] *npl* datos *mpl*; **database** *n* base *f* de datos; **data processing** *n* proceso de datos

date [deɪt] *n* (*day*) fecha; (*with friend*) cita; (*fruit*) dátil *m* ▷*vt* fechar; (*person*) salir con; **~ of birth** fecha de nacimiento; **to ~** *adv* hasta la fecha; **dated** *adj* anticuado

daughter ['dɔ:tə*] *n* hija; **daughter-in-law** *n* nuera, hija política

daunting ['dɔ:ntɪŋ] *adj* desalentador(a)

dawn [dɔ:n] *n* alba, amanecer *m*; (*fig*) nacimiento ▷*vi* (*day*) amanecer; (*fig*): **it ~ed on him that ...** cayó en la cuenta de que ...

day [deɪ] *n* día *m*; (*working day*) jornada; (*heyday*) tiempos *mpl*, días *mpl*; **the ~ before/after** el día anterior/siguiente; **the ~ after tomorrow** pasado mañana; **the ~ before yesterday** anteayer; **the following ~** el día siguiente; **by ~** de día; **day-care centre** ['deɪkɛə-] *n* centro de día; (*for children*) guardería infantil; **daydream** *vi* soñar despierto; **daylight** *n* luz *f* (del día); **day return** (BRIT) *n* billete *m* de ida y vuelta (en un día); **daytime** *n* día *m*; **day-to-day** *adj* cotidiano; **day trip** *n* excursión *f* (de un día)

dazed [deɪzd] *adj* aturdido

dazzle ['dæzl] *vt* deslumbrar; **dazzling** *adj* (*light, smile*) deslumbrante; (*colour*) fuerte

DC *abbr* (= *direct current*) corriente *f* continua

dead [dɛd] *adj* muerto; (*limb*) dormido; (*telephone*) cortado; (*battery*) agotado ▷*adv* (*completely*) totalmente; (*exactly*) exactamente; **to shoot sb ~** matar a algn a tiros; **~ tired** muerto (de cansancio); **to stop ~** parar en seco; **dead end** *n* callejón *m* sin salida; **deadline** *n* fecha (*or* hora) tope; **deadly** *adj* mortal, fatal; **Dead Sea** *n*: **the Dead Sea** el Mar Muerto

deaf [dɛf] *adj* sordo; **deafen** *vt* ensordecer; **deafening** *adj* ensordecedor/a

deal [di:l] (*pt, pp* **~t**) *n* (*agreement*) pacto, convenio; (*business deal*) trato ▷*vt* dar; (*card*) repartir; **a great ~ (of)** bastante, mucho; **deal with** *vt fus* (*people*) tratar con; (*problem*) ocuparse de; (*subject*) tratar de; **dealer** *n* comerciante *m/f*; (*Cards*) mano *f*; **dealings** *npl* (*Comm*) transacciones *fpl*; (*relations*) relaciones *fpl*

dealt [dɛlt] *pt, pp of* **deal**

dean [di:n] *n* (*Rel*) deán *m*; (*Scol*: BRIT) decano; (: US) decano; rector *m*

dear [dɪə*] *adj* querido; (*expensive*) caro ▷*n*: **my ~** mi querido/a ▷*excl*: **~ me!** ¡Dios mío!; **D~ Sir/Madam** (*in letter*) Muy Señor Mío, Estimado Señor/Estimada Señora; **D~ Mr/Mrs X** Estimado/a Señor(a) X; **dearly** *adv* (*love*) mucho; (*pay*) caro

death [dɛθ] *n* muerte *f*; **death penalty** *n* pena de muerte; **death sentence** *n* condena a muerte

debate [dɪ'beɪt] *n* debate *m* ▷*vt* discutir

debit ['dɛbɪt] *n* debe *m* ▷*vt*: **to ~ a sum to sb** *or* **to sb's account** cargar una suma en cuenta a algn; **debit card** *n* tarjeta *f* de débito

debris ['dɛbri:] *n* escombros *mpl*

debt [dɛt] *n* deuda; **to be in ~** tener deudas

debut [deɪ'bju:] *n* presentación *f*

Dec. *abbr* (= *December*) dic

decade ['dɛkeɪd] *n* decenio, década

decaffeinated [dɪ'kæfɪneɪtɪd] *adj* descafeinado

decay [dɪ'keɪ] *n* (*of building*) desmoronamiento; (*of tooth*) caries *f inv* ▷*vi* (*rot*) pudrirse

deceased [dɪ'si:st] *n*: **the ~** el(la) difunto/a

deceit [dɪ'si:t] *n* engaño; **deceive** [dɪ'si:v] *vt* engañar

December [dɪ'sɛmbə*] *n* diciembre *m*

decency ['di:sənsɪ] *n* decencia

decent ['di:sənt] *adj* (*proper*) decente; (*person*: *kind*) amable, bueno

deception [dɪ'sɛpʃən] *n* engaño

deceptive [dɪ'sɛptɪv] *adj* engañoso

Be careful not to translate **deception** by the Spanish word *decepción*.

decide [dɪ'saɪd] *vt* (*person*) decidir; (*question, argument*) resolver ▷*vi* decidir; **to ~ to do/that** decidir hacer/que; **to ~ on sth** decidirse por algo

decimal ['dɛsɪməl] *adj* decimal ▷*n* decimal *m*

decision [dɪ'sɪʒən] *n* decisión *f*
decisive [dɪ'saɪsɪv] *adj* decisivo; (*person*) decidido
deck [dɛk] *n* (*Naut*) cubierta; (*of bus*) piso; (*record deck*) platina; (*of cards*) baraja; **deckchair** *n* tumbona
declaration [dɛklə'reɪʃən] *n* declaración *f*
declare [dɪ'klɛə*] *vt* declarar
decline [dɪ'klaɪn] *n* disminución *f*, descenso ▷ *vt* rehusar ▷ *vi* (*person, business*) decaer; (*strength*) disminuir
decorate ['dɛkəreɪt] *vt* (*adorn*): **to ~ (with)** adornar (de), decorar (de); (*paint*) pintar; (*paper*) empapelar; **decoration** [-'reɪʃən] *n* adorno; (*act*) decoración *f*; (*medal*) condecoración *f*; **decorator** *n* (*workman*) pintor *m* (decorador)
decrease [*n* 'di:kri:s, *vb* dɪ'kri:s] *n*: **~ (in)** disminución *f* (de) ▷ *vt* disminuir, reducir ▷ *vi* reducirse
decree [dɪ'kri:] *n* decreto
dedicate ['dɛdɪkeɪt] *vt* dedicar; **dedicated** *adj* dedicado; (*Comput*) especializado; **dedicated word processor** procesador *m* de textos especializado *or* dedicado; **dedication** [-'keɪʃən] *n* (*devotion*) dedicación *f*; (*in book*) dedicatoria
deduce [dɪ'dju:s] *vt* deducir
deduct [dɪ'dʌkt] *vt* restar; descontar; **deduction** [dɪ'dʌkʃən] *n* (*amount deducted*) descuento; (*conclusion*) deducción *f*, conclusión *f*
deed [di:d] *n* hecho, acto; (*feat*) hazaña; (*Law*) escritura
deem [di:m] *vt* (*formal*) juzgar, considerar
deep [di:p] *adj* profundo; (*expressing measurements*) de profundidad; (*voice*) bajo; (*breath*) profundo; (*colour*) intenso ▷ *adv*: **the spectators stood 20 ~** los espectadores se formaron de 20 en fondo; **to be 4 metres ~** tener 4 metros de profundidad; **deep-fry** *vt* freír en aceite abundante; **deeply** *adv* (*breathe*) a pleno pulmón; (*interested, moved, grateful*) profundamente, hondamente
deer [dɪə*] *n inv* ciervo
default [dɪ'fɔ:lt] *n*: **by ~** (*win*) por incomparecencia ▷ *adj* (*Comput*) por defecto
defeat [dɪ'fi:t] *n* derrota ▷ *vt* derrotar, vencer
defect [*n* 'di:fɛkt, *vb* dɪ'fɛkt] *n* defecto ▷ *vi*: **to ~ to the enemy** pasarse al enemigo; **defective** [dɪ'fɛktɪv] *adj* defectuoso
defence [dɪ'fɛns] (*US* **defense**) *n* defensa
defend [dɪ'fɛnd] *vt* defender; **defendant** *n* acusado/a; (*in civil case*) demandado/a; **defender** *n* defensor(a) *m/f*; (*Sport*) defensa *mf*
defense [dɪ'fɛns] (*US*) = **defence**
defensive [dɪ'fɛnsɪv] *adj* defensivo ▷ *n*: **on the ~** a la defensiva
defer [dɪ'fə:*] *vt* aplazar
defiance [dɪ'faɪəns] *n* desafío; **in ~ of** en contra de; **defiant** [dɪ'faɪənt] *adj* (*challenging*) desafiante, retador(a)
deficiency [dɪ'fɪʃənsɪ] *n* (*lack*) falta; (*defect*) defecto; **deficient** [dɪ'fɪʃənt] *adj* deficiente
deficit ['dɛfɪsɪt] *n* déficit *m*
define [dɪ'faɪn] *vt* (*word etc*) definir; (*limits etc*) determinar
definite ['dɛfɪnɪt] *adj* (*fixed*) determinado; (*obvious*) claro; (*certain*) indudable; **he was ~ about it** no dejó lugar a dudas (sobre ello); **definitely** *adv* desde luego, por supuesto
definition [dɛfɪ'nɪʃən] *n* definición *f*; (*clearness*) nitidez *f*
deflate [di:'fleɪt] *vt* desinflar
deflect [dɪ'flɛkt] *vt* desviar
defraud [dɪ'frɔ:d] *vt*: **to ~ sb of sth** estafar algo a algn
defrost [di:'frɔst] *vt* descongelar
defuse [di:'fju:z] *vt* desactivar; (*situation*) calmar
defy [dɪ'faɪ] *vt* (*resist*) oponerse a; (*challenge*) desafiar; (*fig*): **it defies description** resulta imposible describirlo
degree [dɪ'gri:] *n* grado; (*Scol*) título; **to have a ~ in maths** tener una licenciatura en matemáticas; **by ~s** (*gradually*) poco a poco, por etapas; **to some ~** hasta cierto punto
dehydrated [di:haɪ'dreɪtɪd] *adj* deshidratado; (*milk*) en polvo
de-icer [di:'aɪsə*] *n* descongelador *m*
delay [dɪ'leɪ] *vt* demorar, aplazar; (*person*) entretener; (*train*) retrasar ▷ *vi* tardar ▷ *n* demora, retraso; **to be ~ed** retrasarse; **without ~** en seguida, sin tardar
delegate [*n* 'dɛlɪgɪt, *vb* 'dɛlɪgeɪt] *n* delegado/a ▷ *vt* (*person*) delegar en; (*task*) delegar
delete [dɪ'li:t] *vt* suprimir, tachar
deli ['dɛlɪ] *n* = **delicatessen**
deliberate [*adj* dɪ'lɪbərɪt, *vb* dɪ'lɪbəreɪt] *adj* (*intentional*) intencionado; (*slow*) pausado, lento ▷ *vi* deliberar; **deliberately** *adv* (*on purpose*) a propósito
delicacy ['dɛlɪkəsɪ] *n* delicadeza; (*choice food*) manjar *m*
delicate ['dɛlɪkɪt] *adj* delicado; (*fragile*) frágil
delicatessen [dɛlɪkə'tɛsn] *n* ultramarinos *mpl* finos
delicious [dɪ'lɪʃəs] *adj* delicioso
delight [dɪ'laɪt] *n* (*feeling*) placer *m*, deleite *m*; (*person, experience etc*) encanto,

d

delicia ▷*vt* encantar, deleitar; **to take ~ in** deleitarse en; **delighted** *adj*: **delighted (at** *or* **with/to do)** encantado (con/de hacer); **delightful** *adj* encantador(a), delicioso

delinquent [dɪ'lɪŋkwənt] *adj*, *n* delincuente *mf*

deliver [dɪ'lɪvə*] *vt* (*distribute*) repartir; (*hand over*) entregar; (*message*) comunicar; (*speech*) pronunciar; (*Med*) asistir al parto de; **delivery** *n* reparto; entrega; (*of speaker*) modo de expresarse; (*Med*) parto, alumbramiento; **to take delivery of** recibir

delusion [dɪ'lu:ʒən] *n* ilusión *f*, engaño

de luxe [də'lʌks] *adj* de lujo

delve [dɛlv] *vi*: **to ~ into** hurgar en

demand [dɪ'mɑ:nd] *vt* (*gen*) exigir; (*rights*) reclamar ▷*n* exigencia; (*claim*) reclamación *f*; (*Econ*) demanda; **to be in ~** ser muy solicitado; **on ~** a solicitud; **demanding** *adj* (*boss*) exigente; (*work*) absorbente

demise [dɪ'maɪz] *n* (*death*) fallecimiento

demo ['dɛməu] (*inf*) *n abbr* (= *demonstration*) manifestación *f*

democracy [dɪ'mɔkrəsɪ] *n* democracia; **democrat** ['dɛməkræt] *n* demócrata *mf*; **democratic** [dɛmə'krætɪk] *adj* democrático; (US) demócrata

demolish [dɪ'mɔlɪʃ] *vt* derribar, demoler; (*fig*: *argument*) destruir

demolition [dɛmə'lɪʃən] *n* derribo, demolición *f*

demon ['di:mən] *n* (*evil spirit*) demonio

demonstrate ['dɛmənstreɪt] *vt* demostrar; (*skill, appliance*) mostrar ▷*vi* manifestarse; **demonstration** [-'streɪʃən] *n* (*Pol*) manifestación *f*; (*proof, exhibition*) demostración *f*; **demonstrator** *n* (*Pol*) manifestante *mf*; (*Comm*) demostrador(a) *m/f*; vendedor(a) *m/f*

demote [dɪ'məut] *vt* degradar

den [dɛn] *n* (*of animal*) guarida; (*room*) habitación *f*

denial [dɪ'naɪəl] *n* (*refusal*) negativa; (*of report etc*) negación *f*

denim ['dɛnɪm] *n* tela vaquera; **denims** *npl* vaqueros *mpl*

Denmark ['dɛnmɑ:k] *n* Dinamarca

denomination [dɪnɔmɪ'neɪʃən] *n* valor *m*; (*Rel*) confesión *f*

denounce [dɪ'nauns] *vt* denunciar

dense [dɛns] *adj* (*crowd*) denso; (*thick*) espeso; (: *foliage etc*) tupido; (*inf*: *stupid*) torpe

density ['dɛnsɪtɪ] *n* densidad *f* ▷**single/double-~ disk** *n* (*Comput*) disco de densidad sencilla/de doble densidad

dent [dɛnt] *n* abolladura ▷*vt* (*also*: **make a ~ in**) abollar

dental ['dɛntl] *adj* dental; **dental floss** [-flɔs] *n* seda dental; **dental surgery** *n* clínica *f* dental, consultorio *m* dental

dentist ['dɛntɪst] *n* dentista *mf*

dentures ['dɛntʃəz] *npl* dentadura (postiza)

deny [dɪ'naɪ] *vt* negar; (*charge*) rechazar

deodorant [di:'əudərənt] *n* desodorante *m*

depart [dɪ'pɑ:t] *vi* irse, marcharse; (*train*) salir; **to ~ from** (*fig*: *differ from*) apartarse de

department [dɪ'pɑ:tmənt] *n* (*Comm*) sección *f*; (*Scol*) departamento; (*Pol*) ministerio; **department store** *n* gran almacén *m*

departure [dɪ'pɑ:tʃə*] *n* partida, ida; (*of train*) salida; (*of employee*) marcha; **a new ~** un nuevo rumbo; **departure lounge** *n* (*at airport*) sala de embarque

depend [dɪ'pɛnd] *vi*: **to ~ on** depender de; (*rely on*) contar con; **it ~s** depende, según; **~ing on the result** según el resultado; **dependant** *n* dependiente *mf*; **dependent** *adj*: **to be dependent on** depender de ▷*n* = **dependant**

depict [dɪ'pɪkt] *vt* (*in picture*) pintar; (*describe*) representar

deport [dɪ'pɔ:t] *vt* deportar

deposit [dɪ'pɔzɪt] *n* depósito; (*Chem*) sedimento; (*of ore, oil*) yacimiento ▷*vt* (*gen*) depositar; **deposit account** (BRIT) *n* cuenta de ahorros

depot ['dɛpəu] *n* (*storehouse*) depósito; (*for vehicles*) parque *m*; (US) estación *f*

depreciate [dɪ'pri:ʃɪeɪt] *vi* depreciarse, perder valor

depress [dɪ'prɛs] *vt* deprimir; (*wages etc*) hacer bajar; (*press down*) apretar; **depressed** *adj* deprimido; **depressing** *adj* deprimente; **depression** [dɪ'prɛʃən] *n* depresión *f*

deprive [dɪ'praɪv] *vt*: **to ~ sb of** privar a algn de; **deprived** *adj* necesitado

dept. *abbr* (= *department*) dto

depth [dɛpθ] *n* profundidad *f*; (*of cupboard*) fondo; **to be in the ~s of despair** sentir la mayor desesperación; **to be out of one's ~** (*in water*) no hacer pie; (*fig*) sentirse totalmente perdido

deputy ['dɛpjutɪ] *adj*: **~ head** subdirector(a) *m/f* ▷*n* sustituto/a, suplente *mf*; (US *Pol*) diputado/a; (US: *also*: **~ sheriff**) agente *m* del sheriff

derail [dɪ'reɪl] *vt*: **to be ~ed** descarrilarse

derelict ['dɛrɪlɪkt] *adj* abandonado

derive [dɪ'raɪv] *vt* (*benefit etc*) obtener ▷*vi*: **to ~ from** derivarse de

descend [dɪ'sɛnd] *vt*, *vi* descender, bajar;

to ~ from descender de; **to ~ to** rebajarse a; **descendant** *n* descendiente *mf*
descent [dɪ'sɛnt] *n* descenso; (*origin*) descendencia
describe [dɪs'kraɪb] *vt* describir; **description** [-'krɪpʃən] *n* descripción *f*; (*sort*) clase *f*, género
desert [*n* 'dɛzət, *vb* dɪ'zəːt] *n* desierto ▷*vt* abandonar ▷*vi* (*Mil*) desertar; **deserted** [dɪ'zəːtɪd] *adj* desierto
deserve [dɪ'zəːv] *vt* merecer, ser digno de
design [dɪ'zaɪn] *n* (*sketch*) bosquejo; (*layout, shape*) diseño; (*pattern*) dibujo; (*intention*) intención *f* ▷*vt* diseñar; **design and technology** (BRIT: *Scol*) *n* ≈ dibujo y tecnología
designate [*vb* 'dɛzɪgneɪt, *adj* 'dɛzɪgnɪt] *vt* (*appoint*) nombrar; (*destine*) designar ▷*adj* designado
designer [dɪ'zaɪnə*] *n* diseñador(a) *m/f*; (*fashion designer*) modisto/a, diseñador(a) *m/f* de moda
desirable [dɪ'zaɪərəbl] *adj* (*proper*) deseable; (*attractive*) atractivo
desire [dɪ'zaɪə*] *n* deseo ▷*vt* desear
desk [dɛsk] *n* (*in office*) escritorio; (*for pupil*) pupitre *m*; (*in hotel, at airport*) recepción *f*; (BRIT: *in shop, restaurant*) caja; **desk-top publishing** ['dɛsktɔp-] *n* autoedición *f*
despair [dɪs'pɛə*] *n* desesperación *f* ▷*vi*: **to ~ of** perder la esperanza de
despatch [dɪs'pætʃ] *n, vt* = **dispatch**
desperate ['dɛspərɪt] *adj* desesperado; (*fugitive*) peligroso; **to be ~ for sth/to do** necesitar urgentemente algo/hacer; **desperately** *adv* desesperadamente; (*very*) terriblemente, gravemente
desperation [dɛspə'reɪʃən] *n* desesperación *f*; **in (sheer) ~** (absolutamente) desesperado
despise [dɪs'paɪz] *vt* despreciar
despite [dɪs'paɪt] *prep* a pesar de, pese a
dessert [dɪ'zəːt] *n* postre *m*; **dessertspoon** *n* cuchara (de postre)
destination [dɛstɪ'neɪʃən] *n* destino
destined ['dɛstɪnd] *adj*: **~ for London** con destino a Londres
destiny ['dɛstɪnɪ] *n* destino
destroy [dɪs'trɔɪ] *vt* destruir; (*animal*) sacrificar
destruction [dɪs'trʌkʃən] *n* destrucción *f*
destructive [dɪs'trʌktɪv] *adj* destructivo, destructor(a)
detach [dɪ'tætʃ] *vt* separar; (*unstick*) despegar; **detached** *adj* (*attitude*) objetivo, imparcial; **detached house** *n* ≈ chalé *m*, ≈ chalet *m*
detail ['diːteɪl] *n* detalle *m*; (*no pl*; (: *in picture etc*) detalles *mpl*; (*trifle*) pequeñez *f* ▷*vt* detallar; (*Mil*) destacar; **in ~** detalladamente; **detailed** *adj* detallado
detain [dɪ'teɪn] *vt* retener; (*in captivity*) detener
detect [dɪ'tɛkt] *vt* descubrir; (*Med, Police*) identificar; (*Mil, Radar, Tech*) detectar; **detection** [dɪ'tɛkʃən] *n* descubrimiento; identificación *f*; **detective** *n* detective *mf*; **detective story** *n* novela policíaca
detention [dɪ'tɛnʃən] *n* detención *f*, arresto; (*Scol*) castigo
deter [dɪ'təː*] *vt* (*dissuade*) disuadir
detergent [dɪ'təːdʒənt] *n* detergente *m*
deteriorate [dɪ'tɪərɪəreɪt] *vi* deteriorarse
determination [dɪtəːmɪ'neɪʃən] *n* resolución *f*
determine [dɪ'təːmɪn] *vt* determinar; **determined** *adj* (*person*) resuelto, decidido; **determined to do** resuelto a hacer
deterrent [dɪ'tɛrənt] *n* (*Mil*) fuerza de disuasión
detest [dɪ'tɛst] *vt* aborrecer
detour ['diːtuə*] *n* (*gen*, *US Aut*) desviación *f*
detract [dɪ'trækt] *vt*: **to ~ from** quitar mérito a, desvirtuar
detrimental [dɛtrɪ'mɛntl] *adj*: **~ (to)** perjudicial (a)
devastating ['dɛvəsteɪtɪŋ] *adj* devastador(a); (*fig*) arrollador(a)
develop [dɪ'vɛləp] *vt* desarrollar; (*Phot*) revelar; (*disease*) coger; (*habit*) adquirir; (*fault*) empezar a tener ▷*vi* desarrollarse; (*advance*) progresar; (*facts, symptoms*) aparecer; **developing country** *n* país *m* en (vías de) desarrollo; **development** *n* desarrollo; (*advance*) progreso; (*of affair, case*) desenvolvimiento; (*of land*) urbanización *f*
device [dɪ'vaɪs] *n* (*apparatus*) aparato, mecanismo
devil ['dɛvl] *n* diablo, demonio
devious ['diːvɪəs] *adj* taimado
devise [dɪ'vaɪz] *vt* idear, inventar
devote [dɪ'vəut] *vt*: **to ~ sth to** dedicar algo a; **devoted** *adj* (*loyal*) leal, fiel; **to be devoted to sb** querer con devoción a algn; **the book is devoted to politics** el libro trata de la política; **devotion** *n* dedicación *f*; (*Rel*) devoción *f*
devour [dɪ'vauə*] *vt* devorar
devout [dɪ'vaut] *adj* devoto
dew [djuː] *n* rocío
diabetes [daɪə'biːtiːz] *n* diabetes *f*
diabetic [daɪə'bɛtɪk] *adj, n* diabético/a *m/f*
diagnose ['daɪəgnəuz] *vt* diagnosticar
diagnosis [daɪəg'nəusɪs] (*pl* **-ses**) *n*

diagnóstico
diagonal [daɪ'ægənl] *adj, n* diagonal *f*
diagram ['daɪəgræm] *n* diagrama *m*, esquema *m*
dial ['daɪəl] *n* esfera (SP), cara (LAM); (*on radio etc*) dial *m*; (*of phone*) disco ▷ *vt* (*number*) marcar
dialect ['daɪəlɛkt] *n* dialecto
dialling code ['daɪəlɪŋ-] *n* prefijo
dialling tone (US **dial tone**) *n* (BRIT) señal *f* or tono de marcar
dialogue ['daɪəlɔg] (US **dialog**) *n* diálogo
diameter [daɪ'æmɪtə*] *n* diámetro
diamond ['daɪəmənd] *n* diamante *m*; (*shape*) rombo; **diamonds** *npl* (*Cards*) diamantes *mpl*
diaper ['daɪəpə*] (US) *n* pañal *m*
diarrhoea [daɪə'ri:ə] (US **diarrhea**) *n* diarrea
diary ['daɪərɪ] *n* (*daily account*) diario; (*book*) agenda
dice [daɪs] *n inv* dados *mpl* ▷ *vt* (*Culin*) cortar en cuadritos
dictate [dɪk'teɪt] *vt* dictar; (*conditions*) imponer; **dictation** [-'teɪʃən] *n* dictado; (*giving of orders*) órdenes *fpl*
dictator [dɪk'teɪtə*] *n* dictador *m*
dictionary ['dɪkʃənrɪ] *n* diccionario
did [dɪd] *pt of* **do**
didn't ['dɪdənt] = **did not**
die [daɪ] *vi* morir; (*fig: fade*) desvanecerse, desaparecer; **to be dying for sth/to do sth** morirse por algo/de ganas de hacer algo; **die down** *vi* apagarse; (*wind*) amainar; **die out** *vi* desaparecer
diesel ['di:zəl] *n* vehículo con motor Diesel
diet ['daɪət] *n* dieta; (*restricted food*) régimen *m* ▷ *vi* (*also*: **be on a ~**) estar a dieta, hacer régimen
differ ['dɪfə*] *vi*: **to ~ (from)** (*be different*) ser distinto (a), diferenciarse (de); (*disagree*) discrepar (de); **difference** *n* diferencia; (*disagreement*) desacuerdo; **different** *adj* diferente, distinto; **differentiate** [-'rɛnʃɪeɪt] *vi*: **to differentiate (between)** distinguir (entre); **differently** *adv* de otro modo, en forma distinta
difficult ['dɪfɪkəlt] *adj* difícil; **difficulty** *n* dificultad *f*
dig [dɪg] (*pt, pp* **dug**) *vt* (*hole, ground*) cavar ▷ *n* (*prod*) empujón *m*; (*archaeological*) excavación *f*; (*remark*) indirecta; **to ~ one's nails into** clavar las uñas en; **dig up** *vt* (*information*) desenterrar; (*plant*) desarraigar
digest [*vb* daɪ'dʒɛst, *n* 'daɪdʒɛst] *vt* (*food*) digerir; (*facts*) asimilar ▷ *n* resumen *m*; **digestion** [dɪ'dʒɛstʃən] *n* digestión *f*
digit ['dɪdʒɪt] *n* (*number*) dígito; (*finger*) dedo; **digital** *adj* digital; **digital camera** *n* cámara digital; **digital TV** *n* televisión *f* digital
dignified ['dɪgnɪfaɪd] *adj* grave, solemne
dignity ['dɪgnɪtɪ] *n* dignidad *f*
digs [dɪgz] (BRIT: *inf*) *npl* pensión *f*, alojamiento
dilemma [daɪ'lɛmə] *n* dilema *m*
dill [dɪl] *n* eneldo
dilute [daɪ'lu:t] *vt* diluir
dim [dɪm] *adj* (*light*) débil; (*outline*) indistinto; (*room*) oscuro; (*inf: stupid*) lerdo ▷ *vt* (*light*) bajar
dime [daɪm] (US) *n* *moneda de diez centavos*
dimension [dɪ'mɛnʃən] *n* dimensión *f*
diminish [dɪ'mɪnɪʃ] *vt, vi* disminuir
din [dɪn] *n* estruendo, estrépito
dine [daɪn] *vi* cenar; **diner** *n* (*person*) comensal *mf*
dinghy ['dɪŋgɪ] *n* bote *m*; (*also*: **rubber ~**) lancha (neumática)
dingy ['dɪndʒɪ] *adj* (*room*) sombrío; (*colour*) sucio
dining car ['daɪnɪŋ-] (BRIT) *n* (*Rail*) coche-comedor *m*
dining room ['daɪnɪŋ-] *n* comedor *m*
dining table *n* mesa *f* de comedor
dinner ['dɪnə*] *n* (*evening meal*) cena; (*lunch*) comida; (*public*) cena, banquete *m*; **dinner jacket** *n* smoking *m*; **dinner party** *n* cena; **dinner time** *n* (*evening*) hora de cenar; (*midday*) hora de comer
dinosaur ['daɪnəsɔ:*] *n* dinosaurio
dip [dɪp] *n* (*slope*) pendiente *m*; (*in sea*) baño; (*Culin*) salsa ▷ *vt* (*in water*) mojar; (*ladle etc*) meter; (BRIT *Aut*): **to ~ one's lights** poner luces de cruce ▷ *vi* (*road etc*) descender, bajar
diploma [dɪ'pləumə] *n* diploma *m*
diplomacy [dɪ'pləuməsɪ] *n* diplomacia
diplomat ['dɪpləmæt] *n* diplomático/a; **diplomatic** [dɪplə'mætɪk] *adj* diplomático
dipstick ['dɪpstɪk] (BRIT) *n* (*Aut*) varilla de nivel (del aceite)
dire [daɪə*] *adj* calamitoso
direct [daɪ'rɛkt] *adj* directo; (*challenge*) claro; (*person*) franco ▷ *vt* dirigir; (*order*): **to ~ sb to do sth** mandar a algn hacer algo ▷ *adv* derecho; **can you ~ me to ...?** ¿puede indicarme dónde está ...?; **direct debit** (BRIT) *n* domiciliación *f* bancaria de recibos
direction [dɪ'rɛkʃən] *n* dirección *f*; **sense of ~** sentido de la dirección; **directions** *npl* (*instructions*) instrucciones *fpl*; **~s for use** modo de empleo
directly [dɪ'rɛktlɪ] *adv* (*in straight line*) directamente; (*at once*) en seguida
director [dɪ'rɛktə*] *n* director(a) *m/f*

directory [dɪ'rɛktərɪ] *n* (*Tel*) guía (telefónica); (*Comput*) directorio; **directory enquiries** (*US* **directory assistance**) *n* (servicio de) información *f*
dirt [dəːt] *n* suciedad *f*; (*earth*) tierra; **dirty** *adj* sucio; (*joke*) verde, colorado (*MEX*) ▷*vt* ensuciar; (*stain*) manchar
disability [dɪsə'bɪlɪtɪ] *n* incapacidad *f*
disabled [dɪs'eɪbld] *adj*: **to be physically ~** ser minusválido/a; **to be mentally ~** ser deficiente mental
disadvantage [dɪsəd'vɑːntɪdʒ] *n* desventaja, inconveniente *m*
disagree [dɪsə'griː] *vi* (*differ*) discrepar; **to ~ (with)** no estar de acuerdo (con); **disagreeable** *adj* desagradable; (*person*) antipático; **disagreement** *n* desacuerdo
disappear [dɪsə'pɪə*] *vi* desaparecer; **disappearance** *n* desaparición *f*
disappoint [dɪsə'pɔɪnt] *vt* decepcionar, defraudar; **disappointed** *adj* decepcionado; **disappointing** *adj* decepcionante; **disappointment** *n* decepción *f*
disapproval [dɪsə'pruːvəl] *n* desaprobación *f*
disapprove [dɪsə'pruːv] *vi*: **to ~ of** ver mal
disarm [dɪs'ɑːm] *vt* desarmar; **disarmament** [dɪs'ɑːməmənt] *n* desarme *m*
disaster [dɪ'zɑːstə*] *n* desastre *m*
disastrous [dɪ'zɑːstrəs] *adj* desastroso
disbelief [dɪsbə'liːf] *n* incredulidad *f*
disc [dɪsk] *n* disco; (*Comput*) = **disk**
discard [dɪs'kɑːd] *vt* (*old things*) tirar; (*fig*) descartar
discharge [*vb* dɪs'tʃɑːdʒ, *n* 'dɪstʃɑːdʒ] *vt* (*task, duty*) cumplir; (*waste*) verter; (*patient*) dar de alta; (*employee*) despedir; (*soldier*) licenciar; (*defendant*) poner en libertad ▷*n* (*Elec*) descarga; (*Med*) supuración *f*; (*dismissal*) despedida; (*of duty*) desempeño; (*of debt*) pago, descargo
discipline ['dɪsɪplɪn] *n* disciplina ▷*vt* disciplinar; (*punish*) castigar
disc jockey *n* pinchadiscos *mf inv*
disclose [dɪs'kləuz] *vt* revelar
disco ['dɪskəu] *n abbr* discoteca
discoloured [dɪs'kʌləd] (*US* **discolored**) *adj* descolorido
discomfort [dɪs'kʌmfət] *n* incomodidad *f*; (*unease*) inquietud *f*; (*physical*) malestar *m*
disconnect [dɪskə'nɛkt] *vt* separar; (*Elec etc*) desconectar
discontent [dɪskən'tɛnt] *n* descontento
discontinue [dɪskən'tɪnjuː] *vt* interrumpir; (*payments*) suspender; **"~d"** (*Comm*) "ya no se fabrica"
discount [*n* 'dɪskaunt, *vb* dɪs'kaunt] *n* descuento ▷*vt* descontar
discourage [dɪs'kʌrɪdʒ] *vt* desalentar; (*advise against*): **to ~ sb from doing** disuadir a algn de hacer
discover [dɪs'kʌvə*] *vt* descubrir; (*error*) darse cuenta de; **discovery** *n* descubrimiento
discredit [dɪs'krɛdɪt] *vt* desacreditar
discreet [dɪ'skriːt] *adj* (*tactful*) discreto; (*careful*) prudente
discrepancy [dɪ'skrɛpənsɪ] *n* diferencia
discretion [dɪ'skrɛʃən] *n* (*tact*) discreción *f*; **at the ~ of** a criterio de
discriminate [dɪ'skrɪmɪneɪt] *vi*: **to ~ between** distinguir entre; **to ~ against** discriminar contra; **discrimination** [-'neɪʃən] *n* (*discernment*) perspicacia; (*bias*) discriminación *f*
discuss [dɪ'skʌs] *vt* discutir; (*a theme*) tratar; **discussion** [dɪ'skʌʃən] *n* discusión *f*
disease [dɪ'ziːz] *n* enfermedad *f*
disembark [dɪsɪm'bɑːk] *vt, vi* desembarcar
disgrace [dɪs'greɪs] *n* ignominia; (*shame*) vergüenza, escándalo ▷*vt* deshonrar; **disgraceful** *adj* vergonzoso
disgruntled [dɪs'grʌntld] *adj* disgustado, descontento
disguise [dɪs'gaɪz] *n* disfraz *m* ▷*vt* disfrazar; **in ~** disfrazado
disgust [dɪs'gʌst] *n* repugnancia ▷*vt* repugnar, dar asco a

> Be careful not to translate **disgust** by the Spanish word *disgustar*.

disgusted [dɪs'gʌstɪd] *adj* indignado

> Be careful not to translate **disgusted** by the Spanish word *disgustado*.

disgusting [dɪs'gʌstɪŋ] *adj* repugnante, asqueroso; (*behaviour etc*) vergonzoso
dish [dɪʃ] *n* (*gen*) plato; **to do** *or* **wash the ~es** fregar los platos; **dishcloth** *n* estropajo
dishonest [dɪs'ɔnɪst] *adj* (*person*) poco honrado, tramposo; (*means*) fraudulento
dishtowel ['dɪʃtauəl] (*US*) *n* estropajo
dishwasher ['dɪʃwɔʃə*] *n* lavaplatos *m inv*
disillusion [dɪsɪ'luːʒən] *vt* desilusionar
disinfectant [dɪsɪn'fɛktənt] *n* desinfectante *m*
disintegrate [dɪs'ɪntɪgreɪt] *vi* disgregarse, desintegrarse
disk [dɪsk] *n* (*esp US*) = **disc**; (*Comput*) disco, disquete *m*; **single-/double-sided ~** disco de una cara/dos caras; **disk drive** *n* disc drive *m*; **diskette** *n* = **disk**
dislike [dɪs'laɪk] *n* antipatía, aversión *f* ▷*vt* tener antipatía a
dislocate ['dɪsləkeɪt] *vt* dislocar

d

disloyal [dɪs'lɔɪəl] *adj* desleal
dismal ['dɪzml] *adj* (*gloomy*) deprimente, triste; (*very bad*) malísimo, fatal
dismantle [dɪs'mæntl] *vt* desmontar, desarmar
dismay [dɪs'meɪ] *n* consternación *f* ▷ *vt* consternar
dismiss [dɪs'mɪs] *vt* (*worker*) despedir; (*pupils*) dejar marchar; (*soldiers*) dar permiso para irse; (*idea*, *Law*) rechazar; (*possibility*) descartar; **dismissal** *n* despido
disobedient [dɪsə'bi:dɪənt] *adj* desobediente
disobey [dɪsə'beɪ] *vt* desobedecer
disorder [dɪs'ɔ:də*] *n* desorden *m*; (*rioting*) disturbios *mpl*; (*Med*) trastorno
disorganized [dɪs'ɔ:gənaɪzd] *adj* desorganizado
disown [dɪs'əun] *vt* (*action*) renegar de; (*person*) negar cualquier tipo de relación con
dispatch [dɪs'pætʃ] *vt* enviar ▷ *n* (*sending*) envío; (*Press*) informe *m*; (*Mil*) parte *m*
dispel [dɪs'pɛl] *vt* disipar
dispense [dɪs'pɛns] *vt* (*medicines*) preparar; **dispense with** *vt fus* prescindir de; **dispenser** *n* (*container*) distribuidor *m* automático
disperse [dɪs'pə:s] *vt* dispersar ▷ *vi* dispersarse
display [dɪs'pleɪ] *n* (*in shop window*) escaparate *m*; (*exhibition*) exposición *f*; (*Comput*) visualización *f*; (*of feeling*) manifestación *f* ▷ *vt* exponer; manifestar; (*ostentatiously*) lucir
displease [dɪs'pli:z] *vt* (*offend*) ofender; (*annoy*) fastidiar
disposable [dɪs'pəuzəbl] *adj* desechable; (*income*) disponible
disposal [dɪs'pəuzl] *n* (*of rubbish*) destrucción *f*; **at one's ~** a su disposición
dispose [dɪs'pəuz] *vi*: **to ~ of** (*unwanted goods*) deshacerse de; (*problem etc*) resolver; **disposition** [dɪspə'zɪʃən] *n* (*nature*) temperamento; (*inclination*) propensión *f*
disproportionate [dɪsprə'pɔ:ʃənət] *adj* desproporcionado
dispute [dɪs'pju:t] *n* disputa; (*also*: **industrial ~**) conflicto (laboral) ▷ *vt* (*argue*) disputar, discutir; (*question*) cuestionar
disqualify [dɪs'kwɔlɪfaɪ] *vt* (*Sport*) desclasificar; **to ~ sb for sth/from doing sth** incapacitar a algn para algo/hacer algo
disregard [dɪsrɪ'gɑ:d] *vt* (*ignore*) no hacer caso de
disrupt [dɪs'rʌpt] *vt* (*plans*) desbaratar, trastornar; (*conversation*) interrumpir; **disruption** [dɪs'rʌpʃən] *n* trastorno, desbaratamiento; interrupción *f*
dissatisfaction [dɪssætɪs'fækʃən] *n* disgusto, descontento
dissatisfied [dɪs'sætɪsfaɪd] *adj* insatisfecho
dissect [dɪ'sɛkt] *vt* disecar
dissent [dɪ'sɛnt] *n* disensión *f*
dissertation [dɪsə'teɪʃən] *n* tesina
dissolve [dɪ'zɔlv] *vt* disolver ▷ *vi* disolverse; **to ~ in(to) tears** deshacerse en lágrimas
distance ['dɪstəns] *n* distancia; **in the ~** a lo lejos
distant ['dɪstənt] *adj* lejano; (*manner*) reservado, frío
distil [dɪs'tɪl] (*US* **distill**) *vt* destilar; **distillery** *n* destilería
distinct [dɪs'tɪŋkt] *adj* (*different*) distinto; (*clear*) claro; (*unmistakeable*) inequívoco; **as ~ from** a diferencia de; **distinction** [dɪs'tɪŋkʃən] *n* distinción *f*; (*honour*) honor *m*; (*in exam*) sobresaliente *m*; **distinctive** *adj* distintivo
distinguish [dɪs'tɪŋgwɪʃ] *vt* distinguir; **to ~ o.s.** destacarse; **distinguished** *adj* (*eminent*) distinguido
distort [dɪs'tɔ:t] *vt* distorsionar; (*shape*, *image*) deformar
distract [dɪs'trækt] *vt* distraer; **distracted** *adj* distraído; **distraction** [dɪs'trækʃən] *n* distracción *f*; (*confusion*) aturdimiento
distraught [dɪs'trɔ:t] *adj* loco de inquietud
distress [dɪs'trɛs] *n* (*anguish*) angustia, aflicción *f* ▷ *vt* afligir; **distressing** *adj* angustioso; doloroso
distribute [dɪs'trɪbju:t] *vt* distribuir; (*share out*) repartir; **distribution** [-'bju:ʃən] *n* distribución *f*, reparto; **distributor** *n* (*Aut*) distribuidor *m*; (*Comm*) distribuidora
district ['dɪstrɪkt] *n* (*of country*) zona, región *f*; (*of town*) barrio; (*Admin*) distrito; **district attorney** (*US*) *n* fiscal *mf*
distrust [dɪs'trʌst] *n* desconfianza ▷ *vt* desconfiar de
disturb [dɪs'tə:b] *vt* (*person*: *bother*, *interrupt*) molestar; (: *upset*) perturbar, inquietar; (*disorganize*) alterar; **disturbance** *n* (*upheaval*) perturbación *f*; (*political etc*: *gen pl*) disturbio; (*of mind*) trastorno; **disturbed** *adj* (*worried*, *upset*) preocupado, angustiado; **emotionally disturbed** trastornado; (*childhood*) inseguro; **disturbing** *adj* inquietante, perturbador(a)
ditch [dɪtʃ] *n* zanja; (*irrigation ditch*) acequia ▷ *vt* (*inf*: *partner*) deshacerse de; (: *plan*, *car etc*) abandonar
ditto ['dɪtəu] *adv* ídem, lo mismo

dive [daɪv] *n* (*from board*) salto; (*underwater*) buceo; (*of submarine*) sumersión *f* ▷ *vi* (*swimmer: into water*) saltar; (*: under water*) zambullirse, bucear; (*fish, submarine*) sumergirse; (*bird*) lanzarse en picado; **to ~ into** (*bag etc*) meter la mano en; (*place*) meterse de prisa en; **diver** *n* (*underwater*) buzo

diverse [daɪ'vəːs] *adj* diversos/as, varios/as

diversion [daɪ'vəːʃən] *n* (BRIT *Aut*) desviación *f*; (*distraction, Mil*) diversión *f*; (*of funds*) distracción *f*

diversity [daɪ'vəːsɪtɪ] *n* diversidad *f*

divert [daɪ'vəːt] *vt* (*turn aside*) desviar

divide [dɪ'vaɪd] *vt* dividir; (*separate*) separar ▷ *vi* dividirse; (*road*) bifurcarse; **divided highway** (US) *n* carretera de doble calzada

divine [dɪ'vaɪn] *adj* (*also fig*) divino

diving ['daɪvɪŋ] *n* (*Sport*) salto; (*underwater*) buceo; **diving board** *n* trampolín *m*

division [dɪ'vɪʒən] *n* división *f*; (*sharing out*) reparto; (*disagreement*) diferencias *fpl*; (*Comm*) sección *f*

divorce [dɪ'vɔːs] *n* divorcio ▷ *vt* divorciarse de; **divorced** *adj* divorciado; **divorcee** [-'siː] *n* divorciado/a

D.I.Y. (BRIT) *adj, n abbr* = **do-it-yourself**

dizzy ['dɪzɪ] *adj* (*spell*) de mareo; **to feel ~** marearse

DJ *n abbr* = **disc jockey**

DNA *n abbr* (= *deoxyribonucleic acid*) ADN *m*

KEYWORD

do [duː] (*pt* **did**, *pp* **done**) *n* (*inf: party etc*): **we're having a little do on Saturday** damos una fiestecita el sábado; **it was rather a grand do** fue un acontecimiento a lo grande

▷ *aux vb* **1** (*in negative constructions: not translated*): **I don't understand** no entiendo

2 (*to form questions: not translated*): **didn't you know?** ¿no lo sabías?; **what do you think?** ¿qué opinas?

3 (*for emphasis, in polite expressions*): **people do make mistakes sometimes** sí que se cometen errores a veces; **she does seem rather late** a mí también me parece que se ha retrasado; **do sit down/help yourself** siéntate/sírvete por favor; **do take care!** ¡ten cuidado(, te pido)!

4 (*used to avoid repeating vb*): **she sings better than I do** canta mejor que yo; **do you agree? – yes, I do/no, I don't** ¿estás de acuerdo? – sí (lo estoy)/no (lo estoy); **she lives in Glasgow – so do I** vive en Glasgow – yo también; **he didn't like it and neither did we** no le gustó y a nosotros tampoco; **who made this mess? – I did** ¿quién hizo esta chapuza? – yo; **he asked me to help him and I did** me pidió que le ayudara y lo hice

5 (*in question tags*): **you like him, don't you?** te gusta, ¿verdad? *or* ¿no?; **I don't know him, do I?** creo que no le conozco

▷ *vt* **1** (*gen, carry out, perform etc*): **what are you doing tonight?** ¿qué haces esta noche?; **what can I do for you?** ¿en qué puedo servirle?; **to do the washing-up/cooking** fregar los platos/cocinar; **to do one's teeth/hair/nails** lavarse los dientes/arreglarse el pelo/arreglarse las uñas

2 (*Aut etc*): **the car was doing 100** el coche iba a 100; **we've done 200 km already** ya hemos hecho 200 km; **he can do 100 in that car** puede ir a 100 en ese coche

▷ *vi* **1** (*act, behave*) hacer; **do as I do** haz como yo

2 (*get on, fare*): **he's doing well/badly at school** va bien/mal en la escuela; **the firm is doing well** la empresa anda *or* va bien; **how do you do?** mucho gusto; (*less formal*) ¿qué tal?

3 (*suit*): **will it do?** ¿sirve?, ¿está *or* va bien?

4 (*be sufficient*) bastar; **will £10 do?** ¿será bastante con £10?; **that'll do** así está bien; **that'll do!** (*in annoyance*) ¡ya está bien!, ¡basta ya!; **to make do (with)** arreglárselas (con)

do up *vt* (*laces*) atar; (*zip, dress, shirt*) abrochar; (*renovate: room, house*) renovar

do with *vt fus* (*need*): **I could do with a drink/some help** no me vendría mal un trago/un poco de ayuda; (*be connected*) tener que ver con; **what has it got to do with you?** ¿qué tiene que ver contigo?

do without *vi* pasar sin; **if you're late for tea then you'll do without** si llegas tarde tendrás que quedarte sin cenar

▷ *vt fus* pasar sin; **I can do without a car** puedo pasar sin coche

dock [dɔk] *n* (*Naut*) muelle *m*; (*Law*) banquillo (de los acusados) ▷ *vi* (*enter dock*) atracar (la) muelle; (*Space*) acoplarse; **docks** *npl* (*Naut*) muelles *mpl*, puerto *sg*

doctor ['dɔktə*] *n* médico/a; (*Ph.D. etc*) doctor(a) *m/f* ▷ *vt* (*drink etc*) adulterar; **Doctor of Philosophy** *n* Doctor en Filosofía y Letras

document ['dɔkjumənt] *n* documento; **documentary** [-'mɛntərɪ] *adj* documental ▷ *n* documental *m*; **documentation** [-mɛn'teɪʃən] *n* documentación *f*

dodge [dɔdʒ] *n* (*fig*) truco ▷ *vt* evadir; (*blow*) esquivar
dodgy ['dɔdʒɪ] *adj* (*inf: uncertain*) dudoso; (*suspicious*) sospechoso; (*risky*) arriesgado
does [dʌz] *vb see* **do**
doesn't ['dʌznt] = **does not**
dog [dɔg] *n* perro ▷ *vt* seguir los pasos de; (*bad luck*) perseguir; **doggy bag** ['dɔgɪ-] *n bolsa para llevarse las sobras de la comida*
do-it-yourself ['du:ɪtjɔ:'sɛlf] *n* bricolaje *m*
dole [dəul] (BRIT) *n* (*payment*) subsidio de paro; **on the ~** parado
doll [dɔl] *n* muñeca; (US: *inf: woman*) muñeca, gachí *f*
dollar ['dɔlə*] *n* dólar *m*
dolphin ['dɔlfɪn] *n* delfín *m*
dome [dəum] *n* (*Arch*) cúpula
domestic [də'mɛstɪk] *adj* (*animal, duty*) doméstico; (*flight, policy*) nacional; **domestic appliance** *n* aparato *m* doméstico, aparato *m* de uso doméstico
dominant ['dɔmɪnənt] *adj* dominante
dominate ['dɔmɪneɪt] *vt* dominar
domino ['dɔmɪnəu] (*pl* **~es**) *n* ficha de dominó; **dominoes** *n* (*game*) dominó
donate [də'neɪt] *vt* donar; **donation** [də'neɪʃən] *n* donativo
done [dʌn] *pp of* **do**
donkey ['dɔŋkɪ] *n* burro
donor ['dəunə*] *n* donante *mf*; **donor card** *n* carnet *m* de donante
don't [dəunt] = **do not**
donut ['dəunʌt] (US) *n* = **doughnut**
doodle ['du:dl] *vi* hacer dibujitos *or* garabatos
doom [du:m] *n* (*fate*) suerte *f* ▷ *vt*: **to be ~ed to failure** estar condenado al fracaso
door [dɔ:*] *n* puerta; **doorbell** *n* timbre *m*; **door handle** *n* tirador *m*; (*of car*) manija; **doorknob** *n* pomo *m* de la puerta, manilla *f* (LAM); **doorstep** *n* peldaño; **doorway** *n* entrada, puerta
dope [dəup] *n* (*inf: illegal drug*) droga; (*: person*) imbécil *mf* ▷ *vt* (*horse etc*) drogar
dormitory ['dɔ:mɪtrɪ] *n* (BRIT) dormitorio; (US) colegio mayor
DOS *n abbr* (= *disk operating system*) DOS *m*
dosage ['dəusɪdʒ] *n* dosis *f inv*
dose [dəus] *n* dosis *f inv*
dot [dɔt] *n* punto ▷ *vi*: **~ted with** salpicado de; **on the ~** en punto; **dotcom** [dɔt'kɔm] *n* puntocom *f inv*; **dotted line** ['dɔtɪd-] *n*: **to sign on the dotted line** firmar
double ['dʌbl] *adj* doble ▷ *adv* (*twice*): **to cost ~** costar el doble ▷ *n* doble *m* ▷ *vt* doblar ▷ *vi* doblarse; **on the ~, at the ~** (BRIT) corriendo; **double back** *vi* (*person*) volver sobre sus pasos; **double bass** *n* contrabajo; **double bed** *n* cama de matrimonio; **double-check** *vt* volver a revisar ▷ *vi*: **I'll double-check** voy a revisarlo otra vez; **double-click** *vi* (*Comput*) hacer doble clic; **double-cross** *vt* (*trick*) engañar; (*betray*) traicionar; **doubledecker** *n* autobús *m* de dos pisos; **double glazing** (BRIT) *n* doble acristalamiento; **double room** *n* habitación *f* doble; **doubles** *n* (*Tennis*) juego de dobles; **double yellow lines** *npl* (BRIT: *Aut*) *línea doble amarilla de prohibido aparcar*, ≈ línea *fsg* amarilla continua
doubt [daut] *n* duda ▷ *vt* dudar; (*suspect*) dudar de; **to ~ that** dudar que; **doubtful** *adj* dudoso; (*person*): **to be doubtful about sth** tener dudas sobre algo; **doubtless** *adv* sin duda
dough [dəu] *n* masa, pasta; **doughnut** (US **donut**) *n* ≈ rosquilla
dove [dʌv] *n* paloma
down [daun] *n* (*feathers*) plumón *m*, flojel *m* ▷ *adv* (*downwards*) abajo, hacia abajo; (*on the ground*) por *or* en tierra ▷ *prep* abajo ▷ *vt* (*inf: drink*) beberse; **~ with X!** ¡abajo X!; **down-and-out** *n* vagabundo/a; **downfall** *n* caída, ruina; **downhill** *adv*: **to go downhill** (*also fig*) ir cuesta abajo
Downing Street ['daunɪŋ-] *n* (BRIT) Downing Street *f*
down: download *vt* (*Comput*) bajar; **downright** *adj* (*nonsense, lie*) manifiesto; (*refusal*) terminante
Down's syndrome ['daunz-] *n* síndrome *m* de Down
down: downstairs *adv* (*below*) (en el piso de) abajo; (*downwards*) escaleras abajo; **down-to-earth** *adj* práctico; **downtown** *adv* en el centro de la ciudad; **down under** *adv* en Australia (*or* Nueva Zelanda); **downward** [-wəd] *adj, adv* hacia abajo; **downwards** [-wədz] *adv* hacia abajo
doz. *abbr* = **dozen**
doze [dəuz] *vi* dormitar
dozen ['dʌzn] *n* docena; **a ~ books** una docena de libros; **~s of** cantidad de
Dr. *abbr* = **doctor; drive**
drab [dræb] *adj* gris, monótono
draft [drɑ:ft] *n* (*first copy*) borrador *m*; (*Pol: of bill*) anteproyecto; (US: *call-up*) quinta ▷ *vt* (*plan*) preparar; (*write roughly*) hacer un borrador de; *see also* **draught**
drag [dræg] *vt* arrastrar; (*river*) dragar, rastrear ▷ *vi* (*time*) pasar despacio; (*play, film etc*) hacerse pesado ▷ *n* (*inf*) lata; (*women's clothing*): **in ~** vestido de travesti; **to ~ and drop** (*Comput*) arrastrar y soltar

dragon ['drægən] *n* dragón *m*
dragonfly ['drægənflaɪ] *n* libélula
drain [dreɪn] *n* desaguadero; (*in street*) sumidero; (*source of loss*): **to be a ~ on** consumir, agotar ▷ *vt* (*land, marshes*) desaguar; (*reservoir*) desecar; (*vegetables*) escurrir ▷ *vi* escurrirse; **drainage** *n* (*act*) desagüe *m*; (*Med, Agr*) drenaje *m*; (*sewage*) alcantarillado; **drainpipe** *n* tubo de desagüe
drama ['drɑːmə] *n* (*art*) teatro; (*play*) drama *m*; (*excitement*) emoción *f*; **dramatic** [drə'mætɪk] *adj* dramático; (*sudden, marked*) espectacular
drank [dræŋk] *pt of* **drink**
drape [dreɪp] *vt* (*cloth*) colocar; (*flag*) colgar; **drapes** *npl* (US) cortinas *fpl*
drastic ['dræstɪk] *adj* (*measure*) severo; (*change*) radical, drástico
draught [drɑːft] (US **draft**) *n* (*of air*) corriente *f* de aire; (*Naut*) calado; **on ~** (*beer*) de barril; **draught beer** *n* cerveza de barril; **draughts** (BRIT) *n* (*game*) juego de damas
draw [drɔː] (*pt* **drew**, *pp* **drawn**) *vt* (*picture*) dibujar; (*cart*) tirar de; (*curtain*) correr; (*take out*) sacar; (*attract*) atraer; (*money*) retirar; (*wages*) cobrar ▷ *vi* (*Sport*) empatar ▷ *n* (*Sport*) empate *m*; (*lottery*) sorteo; **draw out** *vi* (*lengthen*) alargarse ▷ *vt* sacar; **draw up** *vi* (*stop*) pararse ▷ *vt* (*chair*) acercar; (*document*) redactar; **drawback** *n* inconveniente *m*, desventaja
drawer [drɔː*] *n* cajón *m*
drawing ['drɔːɪŋ] *n* dibujo; **drawing pin** (BRIT) *n* chincheta; **drawing room** *n* salón *m*
drawn [drɔːn] *pp of* **draw**
dread [drɛd] *n* pavor *m*, terror *m* ▷ *vt* temer, tener miedo *or* pavor a; **dreadful** *adj* horroroso
dream [driːm] (*pt, pp* **~ed** *or* **~t**) *n* sueño ▷ *vt, vi* soñar; **dreamer** *n* soñador(a) *m/f*
dreamt [drɛmt] *pt, pp of* **dream**
dreary ['drɪərɪ] *adj* monótono
drench [drɛntʃ] *vt* empapar
dress [drɛs] *n* vestido; (*clothing*) ropa ▷ *vt* vestir; (*wound*) vendar ▷ *vi* vestirse; **to get ~ed** vestirse; **dress up** *vi* vestirse de etiqueta; (*in fancy dress*) disfrazarse; **dress circle** (BRIT) *n* principal *m*; **dresser** *n* (*furniture*) aparador *m*; (: US) cómoda (con espejo); **dressing** *n* (*Med*) vendaje *m*; (*Culin*) aliño; **dressing gown** (BRIT) *n* bata; **dressing room** *n* (*Theatre*) camarín *m*; (*Sport*) vestuario; **dressing table** *n* tocador *m*; **dressmaker** *n* modista, costurera
drew [druː] *pt of* **draw**
dribble ['drɪbl] *vi* (*baby*) babear ▷ *vt* (*ball*) regatear
dried [draɪd] *adj* (*fruit*) seco; (*milk*) en polvo
drier ['draɪə*] *n* = **dryer**
drift [drɪft] *n* (*of current etc*) flujo; (*of snow*) ventisquero; (*meaning*) significado ▷ *vi* (*boat*) ir a la deriva; (*sand, snow*) amontonarse
drill [drɪl] *n* (*drill bit*) broca; (*tool for DIY etc*) taladro; (*of dentist*) fresa; (*for mining etc*) perforadora, barrena; (*Mil*) instrucción *f* ▷ *vt* perforar, taladrar; (*troops*) enseñar la instrucción a ▷ *vi* (*for oil*) perforar
drink [drɪŋk] (*pt* **drank**, *pp* **drunk**) *n* bebida; (*sip*) trago ▷ *vt, vi* beber; **to have a ~** tomar algo; tomar una copa *or* un trago; **a ~ of water** un trago de agua; **drink-driving** *n*: **to be charged with drink-driving** ser acusado de conducir borracho *or* en estado de embriaguez; **drinker** *n* bebedor(a) *m/f*; **drinking water** *n* agua potable
drip [drɪp] *n* (*act*) goteo; (*one drip*) gota; (*Med*) gota a gota *m* ▷ *vi* gotear
drive [draɪv] (*pt* **drove**, *pp* **driven**) *n* (*journey*) viaje *m* (en coche); (*also*: **~way**) entrada; (*energy*) energía, vigor *m*; (*Comput*: *also*: **disk ~**) drive *m* ▷ *vt* (*car*) conducir (SP), manejar (LAM); (*nail*) clavar; (*push*) empujar; (*Tech*: *motor*) impulsar ▷ *vi* (*Aut*: *at controls*) conducir; (: *travel*) pasearse en coche; **left-/right-hand ~** conducción *f* a la izquierda/derecha; **to ~ sb mad** volverle loco a algn; **drive out** *vt* (*force out*) expulsar, echar; **drive-in** *adj* (*esp* US): **drive-in cinema** autocine *m*
driven ['drɪvn] *pp of* **drive**
driver ['draɪvə*] *n* conductor(a) *m/f* (SP), chofer *mf* (LAM); (*of taxi, bus*) chófer *mf* (SP), chofer *mf* (LAM); **driver's license** (US) *n* carnet *m* de conducir
driveway ['draɪvweɪ] *n* entrada
driving ['draɪvɪŋ] *n* el conducir (SP), el manejar (LAM); **driving instructor** *n* profesor(a) *m/f* de autoescuela (SP), instructor(a) *m/f* de manejo (LAM); **driving lesson** *n* clase *f* de conducir (SP) *or* manejar (LAM); **driving licence** (BRIT) *n* licencia de manejo (LAM), carnet *m* de conducir (SP); **driving test** *n* examen *m* de conducir (SP) *or* manejar (LAM)
drizzle ['drɪzl] *n* llovizna
droop [druːp] *vi* (*flower*) marchitarse; (*shoulders*) encorvarse; (*head*) inclinarse
drop [drɔp] *n* (*of water*) gota; (*lessening*) baja; (*fall*) caída ▷ *vt* dejar caer; (*voice, eyes, price*) bajar; (*passenger*) dejar; (*omit*) omitir ▷ *vi* (*object*) caer; (*wind*) amainar; **drop in** *vi* (*inf*: *visit*): **to drop in (on)** pasar por casa (de); **drop off** *vi* (*sleep*) dormirse ▷ *vt*

(*passenger*) dejar; **drop out** *vi* (*withdraw*) retirarse

drought [draut] *n* sequía

drove [drəuv] *pt of* **drive**

drown [draun] *vt* ahogar ▷*vi* ahogarse

drowsy ['drauzɪ] *adj* soñoliento; **to be ~** tener sueño

drug [drʌg] *n* medicamento; (*narcotic*) droga ▷*vt* drogar; **to be on ~s** drogarse; **drug addict** *n* drogadicto/a; **drug dealer** *n* traficante *mf* de drogas; **druggist** (*US*) *n* farmacéutico; **drugstore** (*US*) *n* farmacia

drum [drʌm] *n* tambor *m*; (*for oil, petrol*) bidón *m*; **drums** *npl* batería; **drummer** *n* tambor *m*

drunk [drʌŋk] *pp of* **drink** ▷*adj* borracho ▷*n* (*also*: **~ard**) borracho/a; **drunken** *adj* borracho; (*laughter, party*) de borrachos

dry [draɪ] *adj* seco; (*day*) sin lluvia; (*climate*) árido, seco ▷*vt* secar; (*tears*) enjugarse ▷*vi* secarse; **dry off** *vi* secarse ▷*vt* secar; **dry up** *vi* (*river*) secarse; **dry-cleaner's** *n* tintorería; **dry-cleaning** *n* lavado en seco; **dryer** *n* (*for hair*) secador *m*; (*US*: *for clothes*) secadora

DSS *n abbr* = **Department of Social Security**

D&T (BRIT: *Scol*) *n abbr* (= *design and technology*) ≈ dibujo y tecnología

DTP *n abbr* (= *desk-top publishing*) autoedición *f*

dual ['djuəl] *adj* doble; **dual carriageway** (BRIT) *n* carretera de doble calzada

dubious ['dju:bɪəs] *adj* indeciso; (*reputation, company*) sospechoso

duck [dʌk] *n* pato ▷*vi* agacharse

due [dju:] *adj* (*owed*): **he is ~ £10** se le deben 10 libras; (*expected*: *event*): **the meeting is ~ on Wednesday** la reunión tendrá lugar el miércoles; (: *arrival*): **the train is ~ at 8am** el tren tiene su llegada para las 8; (*proper*) debido ▷*n*: **to give sb his (*or* her) ~** ser justo con algn ▷*adv*: **~ north** derecho al norte

duel ['djuəl] *n* duelo

duet [dju:'ɛt] *n* dúo

dug [dʌg] *pt, pp of* **dig**

duke [dju:k] *n* duque *m*

dull [dʌl] *adj* (*light*) débil; (*stupid*) torpe; (*boring*) pesado; (*sound, pain*) sordo; (*weather, day*) gris ▷*vt* (*pain, grief*) aliviar; (*mind, senses*) entorpecer

dumb [dʌm] *adj* mudo; (*pej*: *stupid*) estúpido

dummy ['dʌmɪ] *n* (*tailor's dummy*) maniquí *m*; (*mock-up*) maqueta; (BRIT: *for baby*) chupete *m* ▷*adj* falso, postizo

dump [dʌmp] *n* (*also*: **rubbish ~**) basurero, vertedero; (*inf*: *place*) cuchitril *m* ▷*vt* (*put down*) dejar; (*get rid of*) deshacerse de; (*Comput*: *data*) transferir

dumpling ['dʌmplɪŋ] *n bola de masa hervida*

dune [dju:n] *n* duna

dungarees [dʌŋgə'ri:z] *npl* mono

dungeon ['dʌndʒən] *n* calabozo

duplex ['dju:plɛks] *n* dúplex *m*

duplicate [*n* 'dju:plɪkət, *vb* 'dju:plɪkeɪt] *n* duplicado ▷*vt* duplicar; (*photocopy*) fotocopiar; (*repeat*) repetir; **in ~** por duplicado

durable ['djuərəbl] *adj* duradero

duration [djuə'reɪʃən] *n* duración *f*

during ['djuərɪŋ] *prep* durante

dusk [dʌsk] *n* crepúsculo, anochecer *m*

dust [dʌst] *n* polvo ▷*vt* quitar el polvo a, desempolvar; (*cake etc*): **to ~ with** espolvorear de; **dustbin** (BRIT) *n* cubo *or* bote *m* (MEX) *or* tacho (SC) de la basura; **duster** *n* paño, trapo; **dustman** (BRIT: *irreg*) *n* basurero; **dustpan** *n* cogedor *m*; **dusty** *adj* polvoriento

Dutch [dʌtʃ] *adj* holandés/esa ▷*n* (*Ling*) holandés *m*; **the Dutch** *npl* los holandeses; **to go ~** (*inf*) pagar cada uno lo suyo; **Dutchman** (*irreg*) *n* holandés *m*; **Dutchwoman** (*irreg*) *n* holandésa

duty ['dju:tɪ] *n* deber *m*; (*tax*) derechos *mpl* de aduana; **on ~** de servicio; (*at night etc*) de guardia; **off ~** libre (de servicio); **duty-free** *adj* libre de impuestos

duvet ['du:veɪ] (BRIT) *n* edredón *m*

DVD *n abbr* (= *digital versatile or video disc*) DVD *m*; **DVD player** *n* lector *m* de DVD; **DVD writer** *n* grabadora de DVD

dwarf [dwɔ:f] (*pl* **dwarves**) *n* enano/a ▷*vt* empequeñecer

dwell [dwɛl] (*pt, pp* **dwelt**) *vi* morar; **dwell on** *vt fus* explayarse en

dwelt [dwɛlt] *pt, pp of* **dwell**

dwindle ['dwɪndl] *vi* disminuir

dye [daɪ] *n* tinte *m* ▷*vt* teñir

dying ['daɪɪŋ] *adj* moribundo

dynamic [daɪ'næmɪk] *adj* dinámico

dynamite ['daɪnəmaɪt] *n* dinamita

dyslexia [dɪs'lɛksɪə] *n* dislexia

dyslexic [dɪs'lɛksɪk] *adj, n* disléxico/a *m/f*

e

E [iː] *n* (*Mus*) mi *m*
E111 *n abbr* (= *form E111*) impreso E111
each [iːtʃ] *adj* cada *inv* ▷ *pron* cada uno; **~ other** el uno al otro; **they hate ~ other** se odian (entre ellos *or* mutuamente); **they have 2 books ~** tienen 2 libros por persona
eager [ˈiːgə*] *adj* (*keen*) entusiasmado; **to be ~ to do sth** tener muchas ganas de hacer algo, impacientarse por hacer algo; **to be ~ for** tener muchas ganas de
eagle [ˈiːgl] *n* águila
ear [ɪə*] *n* oreja; oído; (*of corn*) espiga; **earache** *n* dolor *m* de oídos; **eardrum** *n* tímpano
earl [əːl] *n* conde *m*
earlier [ˈəːlɪə*] *adj* anterior ▷ *adv* antes
early [ˈəːlɪ] *adv* temprano; (*before time*) con tiempo, con anticipación ▷ *adj* temprano; (*settlers etc*) primitivo; (*death, departure*) prematuro; (*reply*) pronto; **to have an ~ night** acostarse temprano; **in the ~** *or* **~ in the spring/19th century** a principios de primavera/del siglo diecinueve; **early retirement** *n* jubilación *f* anticipada
earmark [ˈɪəmɑːk] *vt*: **to ~ (for)** reservar (para), destinar (a)
earn [əːn] *vt* (*salary*) percibir; (*interest*) devengar; (*praise*) merecerse
earnest [ˈəːnɪst] *adj* (*wish*) fervoroso; (*person*) serio, formal; **in ~** en serio
earnings [ˈəːnɪŋz] *npl* (*personal*) sueldo, ingresos *mpl*; (*company*) ganancias *fpl*
ear: earphones *npl* auriculares *mpl*; **earplugs** *npl* tapones *mpl* para los oídos; **earring** *n* pendiente *m*, arete *m*
earth [əːθ] *n* tierra; (BRIT *Elec*) cable *m* de toma de tierra ▷ *vt* (BRIT *Elec*) conectar a tierra; **earthquake** *n* terremoto
ease [iːz] *n* facilidad *f*; (*comfort*) comodidad *f* ▷ *vt* (*lessen: problem*) mitigar; (: *pain*) aliviar; (: *tension*) reducir; **to ~ sth in/out** meter/sacar algo con cuidado; **at ~!** (*Mil*) ¡descansen!
easily [ˈiːzɪlɪ] *adv* fácilmente
east [iːst] *n* este *m* ▷ *adj* del este, oriental; (*wind*) este ▷ *adv* al este, hacia el este; **the E~** el Oriente; (*Pol*) los países del Este; **eastbound** *adj* en dirección este
Easter [ˈiːstə*] *n* Pascua (de Resurrección); **Easter egg** *n* huevo de Pascua
eastern [ˈiːstən] *adj* del este, oriental; (*oriental*) oriental
Easter Sunday *n* Domingo de Resurrección
easy [ˈiːzɪ] *adj* fácil; (*simple*) sencillo; (*comfortable*) holgado, cómodo; (*relaxed*) tranquilo ▷ *adv*: **to take it** *or* **things ~** (*not worry*) tomarlo con calma; (*rest*) descansar; **easy-going** *adj* acomodadizo
eat [iːt] (*pt* **ate**, *pp* **eaten**) *vt* comer; **eat out** *vi* comer fuera
eavesdrop [ˈiːvzdrɔp] *vi*: **to ~ (on)** escuchar a escondidas
e-book [ˈiːbuk] *n* libro electrónico
e-business [ˈiːbɪznɪs] *n* (*company*) negocio electrónico; (*commerce*) comercio electrónico
EC *n abbr* (= *European Community*) CE *f*
eccentric [ɪkˈsɛntrɪk] *adj, n* excéntrico/a *m/f*
echo [ˈɛkəu] (*pl* **~es**) *n* eco ▷ *vt* (*sound*) repetir ▷ *vi* resonar, hacer eco
eclipse [ɪˈklɪps] *n* eclipse *m*
eco-friendly [ˈiːkəufrɛndlɪ] *adj* ecológico
ecological [iːkəˈlɔdʒɪkl] *adj* ecológico
ecology [ɪˈkɔlədʒɪ] *n* ecología
e-commerce *n abbr* comercio electrónico
economic [iːkəˈnɔmɪk] *adj* económico; (*business etc*) rentable; **economical** *adj* económico; **economics** *n* (*Scol*) economía ▷ *npl* (*of project etc*) rentabilidad *f*
economist [ɪˈkɔnəmɪst] *n* economista *m/f*
economize [ɪˈkɔnəmaɪz] *vi* economizar, ahorrar
economy [ɪˈkɔnəmɪ] *n* economía; **economy class** *n* (*Aviat*) clase *f* económica; **economy class syndrome** *n* síndrome *m* de la clase turista
ecstasy [ˈɛkstəsɪ] *n* éxtasis *m inv*; (*drug*) éxtasis *m inv*; **ecstatic** [ɛksˈtætɪk] *adj* extático
eczema [ˈɛksɪmə] *n* eczema *m*
edge [ɛdʒ] *n* (*of knife*) filo; (*of object*) borde *m*; (*of lake*) orilla ▷ *vt* (*Sewing*) ribetear; **on ~** (*fig*) = **edgy**; **to ~ away from** alejarse poco a poco de
edgy [ˈɛdʒɪ] *adj* nervioso, inquieto
edible [ˈɛdɪbl] *adj* comestible

Edinburgh ['ɛdɪnbərə] *n* Edimburgo
edit ['ɛdɪt] *vt* (*be editor of*) dirigir; (*text, report*) corregir, preparar; **edition** [ɪ'dɪʃən] *n* edición *f*; **editor** *n* (*of newspaper*) director(a) *m/f*; (*of column*): **foreign/political editor** encargado de la sección de extranjero/ política; (*of book*) redactor(a) *m/f*; **editorial** [-'tɔ:rɪəl] *adj* editorial ▷*n* editorial *m*
educate ['ɛdjukeɪt] *vt* (*gen*) educar; (*instruct*) instruir; **educated** ['ɛdjukeɪtɪd] *adj* culto
education [ɛdju'keɪʃən] *n* educación *f*; (*schooling*) enseñanza; (*Scol*) pedagogía; **educational** *adj* (*policy etc*) educacional; (*experience*) docente; (*toy*) educativo
eel [i:l] *n* anguila
eerie ['ɪərɪ] *adj* misterioso
effect [ɪ'fɛkt] *n* efecto ▷*vt* efectuar, llevar a cabo; **to take ~** (*law*) entrar en vigor *or* vigencia; (*drug*) surtir efecto; **in ~** en realidad; **effects** *npl* (*property*) efectos *mpl*; **effective** *adj* eficaz; (*actual*) verdadero; **effectively** *adv* eficazmente; (*in reality*) efectivamente
efficiency [ɪ'fɪʃənsɪ] *n* eficiencia; rendimiento
efficient [ɪ'fɪʃənt] *adj* eficiente; (*machine*) de buen rendimiento; **efficiently** *adv* eficientemente, de manera eficiente
effort ['ɛfət] *n* esfuerzo; **effortless** *adj* sin ningún esfuerzo; (*style*) natural
e.g. *adv abbr* (= *exempli gratia*) p. ej.
egg [ɛg] *n* huevo; **hard-boiled/soft-boiled ~** huevo duro/pasado por agua; **eggcup** *n* huevera; **eggplant** (*esp* US) *n* berenjena; **eggshell** *n* cáscara de huevo; **egg white** *n* clara de huevo; **egg yolk** *n* yema de huevo
ego ['i:gəu] *n* ego
Egypt ['i:dʒɪpt] *n* Egipto; **Egyptian** [ɪ'dʒɪpʃən] *adj, n* egipcio/a *m/f*
eight [eɪt] *num* ocho; **eighteen** *num* diez y ocho, dieciocho; **eighteenth** *adj* decimoctavo; **the eighteenth floor** la planta dieciocho; **the eighteenth of August** el dieciocho de agosto; **eighth** *num* octavo; **eightieth** ['eɪtɪɪθ] *adj* octogésimo
eighty ['eɪtɪ] *num* ochenta
Eire ['ɛərə] *n* Eire *m*
either ['aɪðə*] *adj* cualquiera de los dos; (*both, each*) cada ▷*pron*: **~ (of them)** cualquiera (de los dos) ▷*adv* tampoco ▷*conj*: **~ yes or no** o sí o no; **on ~ side** en ambos lados; **I don't like ~** no me gusta ninguno/a de los(las) dos; **no, I don't ~** no, yo tampoco
eject [ɪ'dʒɛkt] *vt* echar, expulsar; (*tenant*) desahuciar
elaborate [*adj* ɪ'læbərɪt, *vb* ɪ'læbəreɪt] *adj* (*complex*) complejo ▷*vt* (*expand*) ampliar; (*refine*) refinar ▷*vi* explicar con más detalles
elastic [ɪ'læstɪk] *n* elástico ▷*adj* elástico; (*fig*) flexible; **elastic band** (BRIT) *n* gomita
elbow ['ɛlbəu] *n* codo
elder ['ɛldə*] *adj* mayor ▷*n* (*tree*) saúco; (*person*) mayor; **elderly** *adj* de edad, mayor ▷*npl*: **the elderly** los mayores
eldest ['ɛldɪst] *adj, n* el/la mayor
elect [ɪ'lɛkt] *vt* elegir ▷*adj*: **the president ~** el presidente electo; **to ~ to do** optar por hacer; **election** *n* elección *f*; **electoral** *adj* electoral; **electorate** *n* electorado
electric [ɪ'lɛktrɪk] *adj* eléctrico; **electrical** *adj* eléctrico; **electric blanket** *n* manta eléctrica; **electric fire** *n* estufa eléctrica; **electrician** [ɪlɛk'trɪʃən] *n* electricista *mf*; **electricity** [ɪlɛk'trɪsɪtɪ] *n* electricidad *f*; **electric shock** *n* electrochoque *m*; **electrify** [ɪ'lɛktrɪfaɪ] *vt* (*Rail*) electrificar; (*fig: audience*) electrizar
electronic [ɪlɛk'trɔnɪk] *adj* electrónico; **electronic mail** *n* correo electrónico; **electronics** *n* electrónica
elegance ['ɛlɪgəns] *n* elegancia
elegant ['ɛlɪgənt] *adj* elegante
element ['ɛlɪmənt] *n* elemento; (*of kettle etc*) resistencia
elementary [ɛlɪ'mɛntərɪ] *adj* elemental; (*primitive*) rudimentario; **elementary school** (US) *n* escuela de enseñanza primaria
elephant ['ɛlɪfənt] *n* elefante *m*
elevate ['ɛlɪveɪt] *vt* (*gen*) elevar; (*in rank*) ascender
elevator ['ɛlɪveɪtə*] (US) *n* ascensor *m*; (*in warehouse etc*) montacargas *m inv*
eleven [ɪ'lɛvn] *num* once; **eleventh** *num* undécimo
eligible ['ɛlɪdʒəbl] *adj*: **an ~ young man/ woman** un buen partido; **to be ~ for sth** llenar los requisitos para algo
eliminate [ɪ'lɪmɪneɪt] *vt* (*suspect, possibility*) descartar
elm [ɛlm] *n* olmo
eloquent ['ɛləkwənt] *adj* elocuente
else [ɛls] *adv*: **something ~** otra cosa; **somewhere ~** en otra parte; **everywhere ~** en todas partes menos aquí; **where ~?** ¿dónde más?, ¿en qué otra parte?; **there was little ~ to do** apenas quedaba otra cosa que hacer; **nobody ~ spoke** no habló nadie más; **elsewhere** *adv* (*be*) en otra parte; (*go*) a otra parte
elusive [ɪ'lu:sɪv] *adj* esquivo; (*quality*) difícil de encontrar
e-mail ['i:meɪl] *n abbr* (= *electronic mail*) correo electrónico, e-mail *m*; **e-mail**

address *n* dirección *f* electrónica, email *m*
embankment [ɪm'bæŋkmənt] *n* terraplén *m*
embargo [ɪm'bɑːgəu] (*pl* **~es**) *n* (*Comm, Naut*) embargo; (*prohibition*) prohibición *f*; **to put an ~ on sth** poner un embargo en algo
embark [ɪm'bɑːk] *vi* embarcarse ▷ *vt* embarcar; **to ~ on** (*journey*) emprender; (*course of action*) lanzarse a
embarrass [ɪm'bærəs] *vt* avergonzar; (*government etc*) dejar en mal lugar; **embarrassed** *adj* (*laugh, silence*) embarazoso

Be careful not to translate **embarrassed** by the Spanish word *embarazada*.

embarrassing *adj* (*situation*) violento; (*question*) embarazoso; **embarrassment** *n* (*shame*) vergüenza; (*problem*): **to be an embarrassment for sb** poner en un aprieto a algn
embassy ['ɛmbəsɪ] *n* embajada
embrace [ɪm'breɪs] *vt* abrazar, dar un abrazo a; (*include*) abarcar ▷ *vi* abrazarse ▷ *n* abrazo
embroider [ɪm'brɔɪdə*] *vt* bordar; **embroidery** *n* bordado
embryo ['ɛmbrɪəu] *n* embrión *m*
emerald ['ɛmərəld] *n* esmeralda
emerge [ɪ'məːdʒ] *vi* salir; (*arise*) surgir
emergency [ɪ'məːdʒənsɪ] *n* crisis *f inv*; **in an ~** en caso de urgencia; **state of ~** estado de emergencia; **emergency brake** (*US*) *n* freno de mano; **emergency exit** *n* salida de emergencia; **emergency landing** *n* aterrizaje *m* forzoso; **emergency room** (*US*: *Med*) *n* sala *f* de urgencias; **emergency services** *npl* (*fire, police, ambulance*) servicios *mpl* de urgencia *or* emergencia
emigrate ['ɛmɪgreɪt] *vi* emigrar; **emigration** [ɛmɪ'greɪʃən] *n* emigración *f*
eminent ['ɛmɪnənt] *adj* eminente
emissions [ɪ'mɪʃənz] *npl* emisión *f*
emit [ɪ'mɪt] *vt* emitir; (*smoke*) arrojar; (*smell*) despedir; (*sound*) producir
emotion [ɪ'məuʃən] *n* emoción *f*; **emotional** *adj* (*needs*) emocional; (*person*) sentimental; (*scene*) conmovedor(a), emocionante; (*speech*) emocionado
emperor ['ɛmpərə*] *n* emperador *m*
emphasis ['ɛmfəsɪs] (*pl* **-ses**) *n* énfasis *m inv*
emphasize ['ɛmfəsaɪz] *vt* (*word, point*) subrayar, recalcar; (*feature*) hacer resaltar
empire ['ɛmpaɪə*] *n* imperio
employ [ɪm'plɔɪ] *vt* emplear; **employee** [-'iː] *n* empleado/a; **employer** *n* patrón/ona *m/f*; empresario; **employment** *n* (*work*) trabajo; **employment agency** *n* agencia de colocaciones
empower [ɪm'pauə*] *vt*: **to ~ sb to do sth** autorizar a algn para hacer algo
empress ['ɛmprɪs] *n* emperatriz *f*
emptiness ['ɛmptɪnɪs] *n* vacío; (*of life etc*) vaciedad *f*
empty ['ɛmptɪ] *adj* vacío; (*place*) desierto; (*house*) desocupado; (*threat*) vano ▷ *vt* vaciar; (*place*) dejar vacío ▷ *vi* vaciarse; (*house etc*) quedar desocupado; **empty-handed** *adj* con las manos vacías
EMU *n abbr* (= *European Monetary Union*) UME *f*
emulsion [ɪ'mʌlʃən] *n* emulsión *f*; (*also*: **~ paint**) pintura emulsión
enable [ɪ'neɪbl] *vt*: **to ~ sb to do sth** permitir a algn hacer algo
enamel [ɪ'næməl] *n* esmalte *m*; (*also*: **~ paint**) pintura esmaltada
enchanting [ɪn'tʃɑːntɪŋ] *adj* encantador(a)
encl. *abbr* (= *enclosed*) adj
enclose [ɪn'kləuz] *vt* (*land*) cercar; (*letter etc*) adjuntar; **please find ~d** le mandamos adjunto
enclosure [ɪn'kləuʒə*] *n* cercado, recinto
encore [ɔŋ'kɔː*] *excl* ¡otra!, ¡bis! ▷ *n* bis *m*
encounter [ɪn'kauntə*] *n* encuentro ▷ *vt* encontrar, encontrarse con; (*difficulty*) tropezar con
encourage [ɪn'kʌrɪdʒ] *vt* alentar, animar; (*activity*) fomentar; (*growth*) estimular; **encouragement** *n* estímulo; (*of industry*) fomento
encouraging [ɪn'kʌrɪdʒɪŋ] *adj* alentador(a)
encyclop(a)edia [ɛnsaɪkləu'piːdɪə] *n* enciclopedia
end [ɛnd] *n* fin *m*; (*of table*) extremo; (*of street*) final *m*; (*Sport*) lado ▷ *vt* terminar, acabar; (*also*: **bring to an ~, put an ~ to**) acabar con ▷ *vi* terminar, acabar; **in the ~** al fin; **on ~** (*object*) de punta, de cabeza; **to stand on ~** (*hair*) erizarse; **for hours on ~** hora tras hora; **end up** *vi*: **to end up in** terminar en; (*place*) ir a parar en
endanger [ɪn'deɪndʒə*] *vt* poner en peligro; **an ~ed species** una especie en peligro de extinción
endearing [ɪn'dɪərɪŋ] *adj* simpático, atractivo
endeavour [ɪn'dɛvə*] (*US* **endeavor**) *n* esfuerzo; (*attempt*) tentativa ▷ *vi*: **to ~ to do** esforzarse por hacer; (*try*) procurar hacer
ending ['ɛndɪŋ] *n* (*of book*) desenlace *m*; (*Ling*) terminación *f*
endless ['ɛndlɪs] *adj* interminable, inacabable

e

endorse [ɪn'dɔːs] *vt* (*cheque*) endosar; (*approve*) aprobar; **endorsement** *n* (*on driving licence*) nota de inhabilitación
endurance [ɪn'djuərəns] *n* resistencia
endure [ɪn'djuə*] *vt* (*bear*) aguantar, soportar ▷ *vi* (*last*) durar
enemy ['ɛnəmɪ] *adj*, *n* enemigo/a *m/f*
energetic [ɛnə'dʒɛtɪk] *adj* enérgico
energy ['ɛnədʒɪ] *n* energía
enforce [ɪn'fɔːs] *vt* (*Law*) hacer cumplir
engaged [ɪn'geɪdʒd] *adj* (BRIT: *busy, in use*) ocupado; (*betrothed*) prometido; **to get ~** prometerse; **engaged tone** (BRIT) *n* (*Tel*) señal *f* de comunicando
engagement [ɪn'geɪdʒmənt] *n* (*appointment*) compromiso, cita; (*booking*) contratación *f*; (*to marry*) compromiso; (*period*) noviazgo; **engagement ring** *n* anillo de prometida
engaging [ɪn'geɪdʒɪŋ] *adj* atractivo
engine ['ɛndʒɪn] *n* (*Aut*) motor *m*; (*Rail*) locomotora
engineer [ɛndʒɪ'nɪə*] *n* ingeniero; (BRIT: *for repairs*) mecánico; (*on ship*, US *Rail*) maquinista *m*; **engineering** *n* ingeniería
England ['ɪŋglənd] *n* Inglaterra
English ['ɪŋglɪʃ] *adj* inglés/esa ▷ *n* (*Ling*) inglés *m*; **the English** *npl* los ingleses *mpl*; **English Channel** *n*: **the English Channel** (el Canal de) la Mancha; **Englishman** (*irreg*) *n* inglés *m*; **Englishwoman** (*irreg*) *n* inglésa
engrave [ɪn'greɪv] *vt* grabar
engraving [ɪn'greɪvɪŋ] *n* grabado
enhance [ɪn'hɑːns] *vt* (*gen*) aumentar; (*beauty*) realzar
enjoy [ɪn'dʒɔɪ] *vt* (*health, fortune*) disfrutar de, gozar de; (*like*) gustarle a algn; **to ~ o.s.** divertirse; **enjoyable** *adj* agradable; (*amusing*) divertido; **enjoyment** *n* (*joy*) placer *m*; (*activity*) diversión *f*
enlarge [ɪn'lɑːdʒ] *vt* aumentar; (*broaden*) extender; (*Phot*) ampliar ▷ *vi*: **to ~ on** (*subject*) tratar con más detalles; **enlargement** *n* (*Phot*) ampliación *f*
enlist [ɪn'lɪst] *vt* alistar; (*support*) conseguir ▷ *vi* alistarse
enormous [ɪ'nɔːməs] *adj* enorme
enough [ɪ'nʌf] *adj*: **~ time/books** bastante tiempo/bastantes libros ▷ *pron* bastante(s) ▷ *adv*: **big ~** bastante grande; **he has not worked ~** no ha trabajado bastante; **have you got ~?** ¿tiene usted bastante(s)?; **~ to eat** (lo) suficiente *or* (lo) bastante para comer; **~!** ¡basta ya!; **that's ~, thanks** con eso basta, gracias; **I've had ~ of him** estoy harto de él; **... which, funnily** *or* **oddly ~ ...** ... lo que, por extraño que parezca ...
enquire [ɪn'kwaɪə*] *vt*, *vi* = **inquire**
enquiry [ɪn'kwaɪərɪ] *n* (*official investigation*) investigación
enrage [ɪn'reɪdʒ] *vt* enfurecer
enrich [ɪn'rɪtʃ] *vt* enriquecer
enrol [ɪn'rəul] (US **enroll**) *vt* (*members*) inscribir; (*Scol*) matricular ▷ *vi* inscribirse; matricularse; **enrolment** (US **enrollment**) *n* inscripción *f*; matriculación *f*
en route [ɔn'ruːt] *adv* durante el viaje
en suite [ɔn'swiːt] *adj*: **with ~ bathroom** con baño
ensure [ɪn'ʃuə*] *vt* asegurar
entail [ɪn'teɪl] *vt* suponer
enter ['ɛntə*] *vt* (*room*) entrar en; (*club*) hacerse socio de; (*army*) alistarse en; (*sb for a competition*) inscribir; (*write down*) anotar, apuntar; (*Comput*) meter ▷ *vi* entrar
enterprise ['ɛntəpraɪz] *n* empresa; (*spirit*) iniciativa; **free ~** la libre empresa; **private ~** la iniciativa privada; **enterprising** *adj* emprendedor(a)
entertain [ɛntə'teɪn] *vt* (*amuse*) divertir; (*invite*: *guest*) invitar (a casa); (*idea*) abrigar; **entertainer** *n* artista *mf*; **entertaining** *adj* divertido, entretenido; **entertainment** *n* (*amusement*) diversión *f*; (*show*) espectáculo
enthusiasm [ɪn'θuːzɪæzəm] *n* entusiasmo
enthusiast [ɪn'θuːzɪæst] *n* entusiasta *mf*; **enthusiastic** [-'æstɪk] *adj* entusiasta; **to be enthusiastic about** entusiasmarse por
entire [ɪn'taɪə*] *adj* entero; **entirely** *adv* totalmente
entitle [ɪn'taɪtl] *vt*: **to ~ sb to sth** dar a algn derecho a algo; **entitled** *adj* (*book*) titulado; **to be entitled to do** tener derecho a hacer
entrance [*n* 'ɛntrəns, *vb* ɪn'trɑːns] *n* entrada ▷ *vt* encantar, hechizar; **to gain ~ to** (*university etc*) ingresar en; **entrance examination** *n* examen *m* de ingreso; **entrance fee** *n* cuota; **entrance ramp** (US) *n* (*Aut*) rampa de acceso
entrant ['ɛntrənt] *n* (*in race, competition*) participante *mf*; (*in examination*) candidato/a
entrepreneur [ɔntrəprə'nəː] *n* empresario
entrust [ɪn'trʌst] *vt*: **to ~ sth to sb** confiar algo a algn
entry ['ɛntrɪ] *n* entrada; (*in competition*) participación *f*; (*in register*) apunte *m*; (*in account*) partida; (*in reference book*) artículo; **"no ~"** "prohibido el paso"; (*Aut*) "dirección prohibida"; **entry phone** *n* portero automático
envelope ['ɛnvələup] *n* sobre *m*
envious ['ɛnvɪəs] *adj* envidioso; (*look*) de

envidia
environment [ɪn'vaɪərnmənt] *n* (*surroundings*) entorno; (*natural world*): **the ~** el medio ambiente; **environmental** [-'mɛntl] *adj* ambiental; medioambiental; **environmentally** [-'mɛntəlɪ] *adv*: **environmentally sound/friendly** ecológico
envisage [ɪn'vɪzɪdʒ] *vt* prever
envoy ['ɛnvɔɪ] *n* enviado
envy ['ɛnvɪ] *n* envidia ▷*vt* tener envidia a; **to ~ sb sth** envidiar algo a algn
epic ['ɛpɪk] *n* épica ▷*adj* épico
epidemic [ɛpɪ'dɛmɪk] *n* epidemia
epilepsy ['ɛpɪlɛpsɪ] *n* epilepsia
epileptic [ɛpɪ'lɛptɪk] *adj*, *n* epiléptico/a *m/f*; **epileptic fit** [ɛpɪ'lɛptɪk-] *n* ataque *m* de epilepsia, acceso *m* epiléptico
episode ['ɛpɪsəud] *n* episodio
equal ['i:kwl] *adj* igual; (*treatment*) equitativo ▷*n* igual *mf* ▷*vt* ser igual a; (*fig*) igualar; **to be ~ to** (*task*) estar a la altura de; **equality** [i:'kwɔlɪtɪ] *n* igualdad *f*; **equalize** *vi* (*Sport*) empatar; **equally** *adv* igualmente; (*share etc*) a partes iguales
equation [ɪ'kweɪʒən] *n* (*Math*) ecuación *f*
equator [ɪ'kweɪtə*] *n* ecuador *m*
equip [ɪ'kwɪp] *vt* equipar; (*person*) proveer; **to be well ~ped** estar bien equipado; **equipment** *n* equipo; (*tools*) avíos *mpl*
equivalent [ɪ'kwɪvələnt] *adj*: **~ (to)** equivalente (a) ▷*n* equivalente *m*
ER *abbr* (BRIT: = *Elizabeth Regina*) *la reina Isabel*; (US: *Med*) = **emergency room**
era ['ɪərə] *n* era, época
erase [ɪ'reɪz] *vt* borrar; **eraser** *n* goma de borrar
erect [ɪ'rɛkt] *adj* erguido ▷*vt* erigir, levantar; (*assemble*) montar; **erection** [-ʃən] *n* construcción *f*; (*assembly*) montaje *m*; (*Physiol*) erección *f*
ERM *n abbr* (= *Exchange Rate Mechanism*) *tipo de cambio europeo*
erode [ɪ'rəud] *vt* (*Geo*) erosionar; (*metal*) corroer, desgastar; (*fig*) desgastar
erosion [ɪ'rəuʒən] *n* erosión *f*; desgaste *m*
erotic [ɪ'rɔtɪk] *adj* erótico
errand ['ɛrnd] *n* recado (SP), mandado (LAM)
erratic [ɪ'rætɪk] *adj* desigual, poco uniforme
error ['ɛrə*] *n* error *m*, equivocación *f*
erupt [ɪ'rʌpt] *vi* entrar en erupción; (*fig*) estallar; **eruption** [ɪ'rʌpʃən] *n* erupción *f*; (*of war*) estallido
escalate ['ɛskəleɪt] *vi* extenderse, intensificarse
escalator ['ɛskəleɪtə*] *n* escalera móvil
escape [ɪ'skeɪp] *n* fuga ▷*vi* escaparse; (*flee*) huir, evadirse; (*leak*) fugarse ▷*vt* (*responsibility etc*) evitar, eludir; (*consequences*) escapar a; (*elude*): **his name ~s me** no me sale su nombre; **to ~ from** (*place*) escaparse de; (*person*) escaparse a
escort [*n* 'ɛskɔ:t, *vb* ɪ'skɔ:t] *n* acompañante *mf*; (*Mil*) escolta *mf* ▷*vt* acompañar
especially [ɪ'spɛʃlɪ] *adv* (*above all*) sobre todo; (*particularly*) en particular, especialmente
espionage ['ɛspɪənɑ:ʒ] *n* espionaje *m*
essay ['ɛseɪ] *n* (*Literature*) ensayo; (*Scol*: *short*) redacción *f*; (: *long*) trabajo
essence ['ɛsns] *n* esencia
essential [ɪ'sɛnʃl] *adj* (*necessary*) imprescindible; (*basic*) esencial; **essentially** *adv* esencialmente; **essentials** *npl* lo imprescindible, lo esencial
establish [ɪ'stæblɪʃ] *vt* establecer; (*prove*) demostrar; (*relations*) entablar; (*reputation*) ganarse; **establishment** *n* establecimiento; **the Establishment** la clase dirigente
estate [ɪ'steɪt] *n* (*land*) finca, hacienda; (*inheritance*) herencia; (BRIT: *also*: **housing ~**) urbanización *f*; **estate agent** (BRIT) *n* agente *mf* inmobiliario/a; **estate car** (BRIT) *n* furgoneta
estimate [*n* 'ɛstɪmət, *vb* 'ɛstɪmeɪt] *n* estimación *f*, apreciación *f*; (*assessment*) tasa, cálculo; (*Comm*) presupuesto ▷*vt* estimar, tasar; calcular
etc *abbr* (= *et cetera*) etc
eternal [ɪ'tə:nl] *adj* eterno
eternity [ɪ'tə:nɪtɪ] *n* eternidad *f*
ethical ['ɛθɪkl] *adj* ético; **ethics** ['ɛθɪks] *n* ética ▷*npl* moralidad *f*
Ethiopia [i:θɪ'əupɪə] *n* Etiopia
ethnic ['ɛθnɪk] *adj* étnico; **ethnic minority** *n* minoría étnica
e-ticket ['i:tɪkɪt] *n* billete *m* electrónico (SP), boleto electrónico (LAM)
etiquette ['ɛtɪkɛt] *n* etiqueta
EU *n abbr* (= *European Union*) UE *f*
euro *n* euro
Europe ['juərəp] *n* Europa; **European** [-'pi:ən] *adj*, *n* europeo/a *m/f*; **European Community** *n* Comunidad *f* Europea; **European Union** *n* Unión *f* Europea
Eurostar® ['juərəustɑ:*] *n* Eurostar® *m*
evacuate [ɪ'vækjueɪt] *vt* (*people*) evacuar; (*place*) desocupar
evade [ɪ'veɪd] *vt* evadir, eludir
evaluate [ɪ'væljueɪt] *vt* evaluar; (*value*) tasar; (*evidence*) interpretar
evaporate [ɪ'væpəreɪt] *vi* evaporarse; (*fig*)

desvanecerse
eve [i:v] *n*: **on the ~ of** en vísperas de
even ['i:vn] *adj* (*level*) llano; (*smooth*) liso; (*speed, temperature*) uniforme; (*number*) par ▷ *adv* hasta, incluso; (*introducing a comparison*) aún, todavía; **~ if, ~ though** aunque *+subjun*; **~ more** aun más; **~ so** aun así; **not ~** ni siquiera; **~ he was there** hasta él estuvo allí; **~ on Sundays** incluso los domingos; **to get ~ with sb** ajustar cuentas con algn
evening ['i:vnɪŋ] *n* tarde *f*; (*late*) noche *f*; **in the ~** por la tarde; **evening class** *n* clase *f* nocturna; **evening dress** *n* (*no pl*: *formal clothes*) traje *m* de etiqueta; (*woman's*) traje *m* de noche
event [ɪ'vɛnt] *n* suceso, acontecimiento; (*Sport*) prueba; **in the ~ of** en caso de; **eventful** *adj* (*life*) activo; (*day*) ajetreado
eventual [ɪ'vɛntʃuəl] *adj* final

> Be careful not to translate **eventual** by the Spanish word *eventual*.

eventually *adv* (*finally*) finalmente; (*in time*) con el tiempo
ever ['ɛvə*] *adv* (*at any time*) nunca, jamás; (*at all times*) siempre; (*in question*): **why ~ not?** ¿y por qué no?; **the best ~** lo nunca visto; **have you ~ seen it?** ¿lo ha visto usted alguna vez?; **better than ~** mejor que nunca; **~ since** *adv* desde entonces ▷ *conj* después de que; **evergreen** *n* árbol *m* de hoja perenne

KEYWORD

every ['ɛvrɪ] *adj* **1** (*each*) cada; **every one of them** (*persons*) todos ellos/as; (*objects*) cada uno de ellos/as; **every shop in the town was closed** todas las tiendas de la ciudad estaban cerradas
2 (*all possible*) todo/a; **I gave you every assistance** te di toda la ayuda posible; **I have every confidence in him** tiene toda mi confianza; **we wish you every success** te deseamos toda suerte de éxitos
3 (*showing recurrence*) todo/a; **every day/week** todos los días/todas las semanas; **every other car had been broken into** habían forzado uno de cada dos coches; **she visits me every other/third day** me visita cada dos/tres días; **every now and then** de vez en cuando

every: everybody *pron* = **everyone**; **everyday** *adj* (*daily*) cotidiano, de todos los días; (*usual*) acostumbrado; **everyone** *pron* todos/as, todo el mundo; **everything** *pron* todo; **this shop sells everything** esta tienda vende de todo; **everywhere** *adv*: **I've been looking for you everywhere** te he estado buscando por todas partes; **everywhere you go you meet ...** en todas partes encuentras ...
evict [ɪ'vɪkt] *vt* desahuciar
evidence ['ɛvɪdəns] *n* (*proof*) prueba; (*of witness*) testimonio; (*sign*) indicios *mpl*; **to give ~** prestar declaración, dar testimonio
evident ['ɛvɪdənt] *adj* evidente, manifiesto; **evidently** *adv* por lo visto
evil ['i:vl] *adj* malo; (*influence*) funesto ▷ *n* mal *m*
evoke [ɪ'vəuk] *vt* evocar
evolution [i:və'lu:ʃən] *n* evolución *f*
evolve [ɪ'vɔlv] *vt* desarrollar ▷ *vi* evolucionar, desarrollarse
ewe [ju:] *n* oveja
ex [eks] (*inf*) *n*: **my ~** mi ex
ex- [ɛks] *prefix* ex
exact [ɪg'zækt] *adj* exacto; (*person*) meticuloso ▷ *vt*: **to ~ sth (from)** exigir algo (de); **exactly** *adv* exactamente; (*indicating agreement*) exacto
exaggerate [ɪg'zædʒəreɪt] *vt, vi* exagerar; **exaggeration** [-'reɪʃən] *n* exageración *f*
exam [ɪg'zæm] *n abbr* (*Scol*) = **examination**
examination [ɪgzæmɪ'neɪʃən] *n* examen *m*; (*Med*) reconocimiento
examine [ɪg'zæmɪn] *vt* examinar; (*inspect*) inspeccionar, escudriñar; (*Med*) reconocer; **examiner** *n* examinador(a) *m/f*
example [ɪg'zɑ:mpl] *n* ejemplo; **for ~** por ejemplo
exasperated [ɪg'zɑ:spəreɪtɪd] *adj* exasperado
excavate ['ɛkskəveɪt] *vt* excavar
exceed [ɪk'si:d] *vt* (*amount*) exceder; (*number*) pasar de; (*speed limit*) sobrepasar; (*powers*) excederse en; (*hopes*) superar; **exceedingly** *adv* sumamente, sobremanera
excel [ɪk'sɛl] *vi* sobresalir; **to ~ o.s** lucirse
excellence ['ɛksələns] *n* excelencia
excellent ['ɛksələnt] *adj* excelente
except [ɪk'sɛpt] *prep* (*also*: **~ for, ~ing**) excepto, salvo ▷ *vt* exceptuar, excluir; **~ if/when** excepto si/cuando; **~ that** salvo que; **exception** [ɪk'sɛpʃən] *n* excepción *f*; **to take exception to** ofenderse por; **exceptional** [ɪk'sɛpʃənl] *adj* excepcional; **exceptionally** [ɪk'sepʃənəlɪ] *adv* excepcionalmente, extraordinariamente
excerpt ['ɛksə:pt] *n* extracto
excess [ɪk'sɛs] *n* exceso; **excess baggage** *n* exceso de equipaje; **excessive** *adj* excesivo
exchange [ɪks'tʃeɪndʒ] *n* intercambio; (*conversation*) diálogo; (*also*: **telephone ~**)

central *f* (telefónica) ▷ *vt*: **to ~ (for)** cambiar (por); **exchange rate** *n* tipo de cambio
excite [ɪk'saɪt] *vt* (*stimulate*) estimular; (*arouse*) excitar; **excited** *adj*: **to get excited** emocionarse; **excitement** *n* (*agitation*) excitación *f*; (*exhilaration*) emoción *f*; **exciting** *adj* emocionante
exclaim [ɪk'skleɪm] *vi* exclamar; **exclamation** [ɛksklə'meɪʃən] *n* exclamación *f*; **exclamation mark** *n* punto de admiración; **exclamation point** (US) = **exclamation mark**
exclude [ɪk'sklu:d] *vt* excluir; exceptuar
excluding [ɪks'klu:dɪŋ] *prep*: **~ VAT** IVA no incluido
exclusion [ɪk'sklu:ʒən] *n* exclusión *f*; **to the ~ of** con exclusión de
exclusive [ɪk'sklu:sɪv] *adj* exclusivo; (*club, district*) selecto; **~ of tax** excluyendo impuestos; **exclusively** *adv* únicamente
excruciating [ɪk'skru:ʃɪeɪtɪŋ] *adj* (*pain*) agudísimo, atroz; (*noise, embarrassment*) horrible
excursion [ɪk'skə:ʃən] *n* (*tourist excursion*) excursión *f*
excuse [*n* ɪk'skju:s, *vb* ɪk'skju:z] *n* disculpa, excusa; (*pretext*) pretexto ▷ *vt* (*justify*) justificar; (*forgive*) disculpar, perdonar; **to ~ sb from doing sth** dispensar a algn de hacer algo; **~ me!** (*attracting attention*) ¡por favor!; (*apologizing*) ¡perdón!; **if you will ~ me** con su permiso
ex-directory ['ɛksdɪ'rɛktərɪ] (BRIT) *adj* que no consta en la guía
execute ['ɛksɪkju:t] *vt* (*plan*) realizar; (*order*) cumplir; (*person*) ajusticiar, ejecutar; **execution** [-'kju:ʃən] *n* realización *f*; cumplimiento; ejecución *f*
executive [ɪg'zɛkjutɪv] *n* (*person, committee*) ejecutivo; (*Pol: committee*) poder *m* ejecutivo ▷ *adj* ejecutivo
exempt [ɪg'zɛmpt] *adj*: **~ from** exento de ▷ *vt*: **to ~ sb from** eximir a algn de
exercise ['ɛksəsaɪz] *n* ejercicio ▷ *vt* (*patience*) usar de; (*right*) valerse de; (*dog*) llevar de paseo; (*mind*) preocupar ▷ *vi* (*also*: **to take ~**) hacer ejercicio(s); **exercise book** *n* cuaderno
exert [ɪg'zə:t] *vt* ejercer; **to ~ o.s.** esforzarse; **exertion** [-ʃən] *n* esfuerzo
exhale [eks'heɪl] *vt* despedir ▷ *vi* exhalar
exhaust [ɪg'zɔ:st] *n* (*Aut*: *also*: **~ pipe**) escape *m*; (*: fumes*) gases *mpl* de escape ▷ *vt* agotar; **exhausted** *adj* agotado; **exhaustion** [ɪg'zɔ:stʃən] *n* agotamiento; **nervous exhaustion** postración *f* nerviosa
exhibit [ɪg'zɪbɪt] *n* (*Art*) obra expuesta; (*Law*) objeto expuesto ▷ *vt* (*show: emotions*) manifestar; (*: courage, skill*) demostrar; (*paintings*) exponer; **exhibition** [ɛksɪ'bɪʃən] *n* exposición *f*; (*of talent etc*) demostración *f*
exhilarating [ɪg'zɪləreɪtɪŋ] *adj* estimulante, tónico
exile ['ɛksaɪl] *n* exilio; (*person*) exiliado/a ▷ *vt* desterrar, exiliar
exist [ɪg'zɪst] *vi* existir; (*live*) vivir; **existence** *n* existencia; **existing** *adj* existente, actual
exit ['ɛksɪt] *n* salida ▷ *vi* (*Theatre*) hacer mutis; (*Comput*) salir (del sistema)

Be careful not to translate **exit** by the Spanish word *éxito*.

exit ramp (US) *n* (*Aut*) vía de acceso
exotic [ɪg'zɔtɪk] *adj* exótico
expand [ɪk'spænd] *vt* ampliar; (*number*) aumentar ▷ *vi* (*population*) aumentar; (*trade etc*) expandirse; (*gas, metal*) dilatarse
expansion [ɪk'spænʃən] *n* (*of population*) aumento; (*of trade*) expansión *f*
expect [ɪk'spɛkt] *vt* esperar; (*require*) contar con; (*suppose*) suponer ▷ *vi*: **to be ~ing** (*pregnant woman*) estar embarazada; **expectation** [ɛkspɛk'teɪʃən] *n* (*hope*) esperanza; (*belief*) expectativa
expedition [ɛkspə'dɪʃən] *n* expedición *f*
expel [ɪk'spɛl] *vt* arrojar; (*from place*) expulsar
expenditure [ɪks'pɛndɪtʃə*] *n* gastos *mpl*, desembolso; consumo
expense [ɪk'spɛns] *n* gasto, gastos *mpl*; (*high cost*) costa; **expenses** *npl* (*Comm*) gastos *mpl*; **at the ~ of** a costa de; **expense account** *n* cuenta de gastos
expensive [ɪk'spɛnsɪv] *adj* caro, costoso
experience [ɪk'spɪərɪəns] *n* experiencia ▷ *vt* experimentar; (*suffer*) sufrir; **experienced** *adj* experimentado
experiment [ɪk'spɛrɪmənt] *n* experimento ▷ *vi* hacer experimentos; **experimental** [-'mɛntl] *adj* experimental; **the process is still at the experimental stage** el proceso está todavía en prueba
expert ['ɛkspə:t] *adj* experto, perito ▷ *n* experto/a, perito/a; (*specialist*) especialista *mf*; **expertise** [-'ti:z] *n* pericia
expire [ɪk'spaɪə*] *vi* caducar, vencer; **expiry** *n* vencimiento; **expiry date** *n* (*of medicine, food item*) fecha de caducidad
explain [ɪk'spleɪn] *vt* explicar; **explanation** [ɛksplə'neɪʃən] *n* explicación *f*
explicit [ɪk'splɪsɪt] *adj* explícito
explode [ɪk'spləud] *vi* estallar, explotar; (*population*) crecer rápidamente; (*with anger*) reventar
exploit [*n* 'ɛksplɔɪt, *vb* ɪk'splɔɪt] *n* hazaña

▷ *vt* explotar; **exploitation** [-'teɪʃən] *n* explotación *f*

explore [ɪk'splɔ:*] *vt* explorar; (*fig*) examinar; investigar; **explorer** *n* explorador(a) *m/f*

explosion [ɪk'spləuʒən] *n* explosión *f*; **explosive** [ɪks'pləusɪv] *adj, n* explosivo

export [*vb* ɛk'spɔ:t, *n, cpd* 'ɛkspɔ:t] *vt* exportar ▷ *n* (*process*) exportación *f*; (*product*) producto de exportación ▷ *cpd* de exportación; **exporter** *n* exportador *m*

expose [ɪk'spəuz] *vt* exponer; (*unmask*) desenmascarar; **exposed** *adj* expuesto

exposure [ɪk'spəuʒə*] *n* exposición *f*; (*publicity*) publicidad *f*; (*Phot: speed*) velocidad *f* de obturación; (*: shot*) fotografía; **to die from ~** (*Med*) morir de frío

express [ɪk'sprɛs] *adj* (*definite*) expreso, explícito; (BRIT: *letter etc*) urgente ▷ *n* (*train*) rápido ▷ *vt* expresar; **expression** [ɪk'sprɛʃən] *n* expresión *f*; (*of actor etc*) sentimiento; **expressway** (US) *n* (*urban motorway*) autopista

exquisite [ɛk'skwɪzɪt] *adj* exquisito

extend [ɪk'stɛnd] *vt* (*visit, street*) prolongar; (*building*) ampliar; (*invitation*) ofrecer ▷ *vi* (*land*) extenderse; (*period of time*) prolongarse

extension [ɪk'stɛnʃən] *n* extensión *f*; (*building*) ampliación *f*; (*of time*) prolongación *f*; (*Tel: in private house*) línea derivada; (*: in office*) extensión *f*; **extension lead** *n* alargador *m*, alargadera

extensive [ɪk'stɛnsɪv] *adj* extenso; (*damage*) importante; (*knowledge*) amplio

extent [ɪk'stɛnt] *n* (*breadth*) extensión *f*; (*scope*) alcance *m*; **to some ~** hasta cierto punto; **to the ~ of ...** hasta el punto de ...; **to such an ~ that ...** hasta tal punto que ...; **to what ~?** ¿hasta qué punto?

exterior [ɛk'stɪərɪə*] *adj* exterior, externo ▷ *n* exterior *m*

external [ɛk'stə:nl] *adj* externo

extinct [ɪk'stɪŋkt] *adj* (*volcano*) extinguido; (*race*) extinto; **extinction** *n* extinción *f*

extinguish [ɪk'stɪŋgwɪʃ] *vt* extinguir, apagar

extra ['ɛkstrə] *adj* adicional ▷ *adv* (*in addition*) de más ▷ *n* (*luxury, addition*) extra *m*; (*Cinema, Theatre*) extra *mf*, comparsa *mf*

extract [*vb* ɪk'strækt, *n* 'ɛkstrækt] *vt* sacar; (*tooth*) extraer; (*money, promise*) obtener ▷ *n* extracto

extradite ['ɛkstrədaɪt] *vt* extraditar

extraordinary [ɪk'strɔ:dnrɪ] *adj* extraordinario; (*odd*) raro

extravagance [ɪk'strævəgəns] *n* derroche *m*, despilfarro; (*thing bought*) extravagancia

extravagant [ɪk'strævəgənt] *adj* (*lavish: person*) pródigo; (*: gift*) (demasiado) caro; (*wasteful*) despilfarrador(a)

extreme [ɪk'stri:m] *adj* extremo, extremado ▷ *n* extremo; **extremely** *adv* sumamente, extremadamente

extremist [ɪk'stri:mɪst] *adj, n* extremista *m/f*

extrovert ['ɛkstrəvə:t] *n* extrovertido/a

eye [aɪ] *n* ojo ▷ *vt* mirar de soslayo, ojear; **to keep an ~ on** vigilar; **eyeball** *n* globo ocular; **eyebrow** *n* ceja; **eyedrops** *npl* gotas *fpl* para los ojos, colino; **eyelash** *n* pestaña; **eyelid** *n* párpado; **eyeliner** *n* delineador *m* (de ojos); **eyeshadow** *n* sombreador *m* de ojos; **eyesight** *n* vista; **eye witness** *n* testigo *mf* presencial

F [ɛf] *n* (*Mus*) fa *m*
fabric ['fæbrɪk] *n* tejido, tela

Be careful not to translate **fabric** by the Spanish word *fábrica*.

fabulous ['fæbjuləs] *adj* fabuloso
face [feɪs] *n* (*Anat*) cara, rostro; (*of clock*) esfera (SP), cara (LAM); (*of mountain*) cara, ladera; (*of building*) fachada ▷ *vt* (*direction*) estar de cara a; (*situation*) hacer frente a; (*facts*) aceptar; **~ down** (*person, card*) boca abajo; **to lose ~** desprestigiarse; **to make** *or* **pull a ~** hacer muecas; **in the ~ of** (*difficulties etc*) ante; **on the ~ of it** a primera vista; **~ to ~** cara a cara; **face up to** *vt fus* hacer frente a, arrostrar; **face cloth** (BRIT) *n* manopla; **face pack** *n* (BRIT) mascarilla
facial ['feɪʃəl] *adj* de la cara ▷ *n* (*also*: **beauty ~**) tratamiento facial, limpieza
facilitate [fə'sɪlɪteɪt] *vt* facilitar
facilities [fə'sɪlɪtɪz] *npl* (*buildings*) instalaciones *fpl*; (*equipment*) servicios *mpl*; **credit ~** facilidades *fpl* de crédito
fact [fækt] *n* hecho; **in ~** en realidad
faction ['fækʃən] *n* facción *f*
factor ['fæktə*] *n* factor *m*
factory ['fæktərɪ] *n* fábrica
factual ['fæktjuəl] *adj* basado en los hechos
faculty ['fækəltɪ] *n* facultad *f*; (US: *teaching staff*) personal *m* docente
fad [fæd] *n* novedad *f*, moda
fade [feɪd] *vi* desteñirse; (*sound, smile*) desvanecerse; (*light*) apagarse; (*flower*) marchitarse; (*hope, memory*) perderse; **fade away** *vi* (*sound*) apagarse
fag [fæg] (BRIT: *inf*) *n* (*cigarette*) pitillo (SP), cigarro
Fahrenheit ['fɑːrənhaɪt] *n* Fahrenheit *m*
fail [feɪl] *vt* (*candidate, test*) suspender (SP), reprobar (LAM); (*memory etc*) fallar a ▷ *vi* suspender (SP), reprobar (LAM); (*be unsuccessful*) fracasar; (*strength, brakes*) fallar; (*light*) acabarse; **to ~ to do sth** (*neglect*) dejar de hacer algo; (*be unable*) no poder hacer algo; **without ~** sin falta; **failing** *n* falta, defecto ▷ *prep* a falta de; **failure** ['feɪljə*] *n* fracaso; (*person*) fracasado/a; (*mechanical etc*) fallo
faint [feɪnt] *adj* débil; (*recollection*) vago; (*mark*) apenas visible ▷ *n* desmayo ▷ *vi* desmayarse; **to feel ~** estar mareado, marearse; **faintest** *adj*: **I haven't the faintest idea** no tengo la más remota idea; **faintly** *adv* débilmente; (*vaguely*) vagamente
fair [fɛə*] *adj* justo; (*hair, person*) rubio; (*weather*) bueno; (*good enough*) regular; (*considerable*) considerable ▷ *adv* (*play*) limpio ▷ *n* feria; (BRIT: *funfair*) parque *m* de atracciones; **fairground** *n* recinto ferial; **fair-haired** *adj* (*person*) rubio; **fairly** *adv* (*justly*) con justicia; (*quite*) bastante; **fair trade** *n* comercio justo; **fairway** *n* (*Golf*) calle *f*
fairy ['fɛərɪ] *n* hada; **fairy tale** *n* cuento de hadas
faith [feɪθ] *n* fe *f*; (*trust*) confianza; (*sect*) religión *f*; **faithful** *adj* (*loyal*: *troops etc*) leal; (*spouse*) fiel; (*account*) exacto; **faithfully** *adv* fielmente; **yours faithfully** (BRIT: *in letters*) le saluda atentamente
fake [feɪk] *n* (*painting etc*) falsificación *f*; (*person*) impostor(a) *m/f* ▷ *adj* falso ▷ *vt* fingir; (*painting etc*) falsificar
falcon ['fɔːlkən] *n* halcón *m*
fall [fɔːl] (*pt* **fell**, *pp* **fallen**) *n* caída; (*in price etc*) descenso; (US) otoño ▷ *vi* caer(se); (*price*) bajar, descender; **falls** *npl* (*waterfall*) cascada, salto de agua; **to ~ flat** (*on one's face*) caerse (boca abajo); (*plan*) fracasar; (*joke, story*) no hacer gracia; **fall apart** *vi* deshacerse; **fall down** *vi* (*person*) caerse; (*building, hopes*) derrumbarse; **fall for** *vt fus* (*trick*) dejarse engañar por; (*person*) enamorarse de; **fall off** *vi* caerse; (*diminish*) disminuir; **fall out** *vi* (*friends etc*) reñir; (*hair, teeth*) caerse; **fall over** *vi* caer(se); **fall through** *vi* (*plan, project*) fracasar
fallen ['fɔːlən] *pp of* **fall**
fallout ['fɔːlaut] *n* lluvia radioactiva
false [fɔːls] *adj* falso; **under ~ pretences** con engaños; **false alarm** *n* falsa alarma; **false teeth** (BRIT) *npl* dentadura postiza
fame [feɪm] *n* fama
familiar [fə'mɪlɪə*] *adj* conocido, familiar; (*tone*) de confianza; **to be ~ with** (*subject*) conocer (bien); **familiarize** [fə'mɪlɪəraɪz] *vt*: **to familiarize o.s. with** familiarizarse con

family ['fæmılı] *n* familia; **family doctor** *n* médico/a de cabecera; **family planning** *n* planificación *f* familiar
famine ['fæmın] *n* hambre *f*, hambruna
famous ['feıməs] *adj* famoso, célebre
fan [fæn] *n* abanico; (*Elec*) ventilador *m*; (*of pop star*) fan *mf*; (*Sport*) hincha *mf* ▷ *vt* abanicar; (*fire, quarrel*) atizar
fanatic [fə'nætık] *n* fanático/a
fan belt *n* correa del ventilador
fan club *n* club *m* de fans
fancy ['fænsı] *n* (*whim*) capricho, antojo; (*imagination*) imaginación *f* ▷ *adj* (*luxury*) lujoso, de lujo ▷ *vt* (*feel like, want*) tener ganas de; (*imagine*) imaginarse; (*think*) creer; **to take a ~ to sb** tomar cariño a algn; **he fancies her** (*inf*) le gusta (ella) mucho; **fancy dress** *n* disfraz *m*
fan heater *n* calefactor *m* de aire
fantasize ['fæntəsaız] *vi* fantasear, hacerse ilusiones
fantastic [fæn'tæstık] *adj* (*enormous*) enorme; (*strange, wonderful*) fantástico
fantasy ['fæntəzı] *n* (*dream*) sueño; (*unreality*) fantasía
fanzine ['fænzi:n] *n* fanzine *m*
FAQs *abbr* (= *frequently asked questions*) preguntas frecuentes
far [fɑ:*] *adj* (*distant*) lejano ▷ *adv* lejos; (*much, greatly*) mucho; **~ away, ~ off** (a lo) lejos; **~ better** mucho mejor; **~ from** lejos de; **by ~** con mucho; **go as ~ as the farm** vaya hasta la granja; **as ~ as I know** que yo sepa; **how ~?** ¿hasta dónde?; (*fig*) ¿hasta qué punto?
farce [fɑ:s] *n* farsa
fare [fɛə*] *n* (*on trains, buses*) precio (del billete); (*in taxi: cost*) tarifa; (*food*) comida; **half ~** medio pasaje *m*; **full ~** pasaje completo
Far East *n*: **the ~** el Extremo Oriente
farewell [fɛə'wɛl] *excl, n* adiós *m*
farm [fɑ:m] *n* cortijo (SP), hacienda (LAM), rancho (MEX), estancia (RPL) ▷ *vt* cultivar; **farmer** *n* granjero, hacendado (LAM), ranchero (MEX), estanciero (RPL); **farmhouse** *n* granja, casa del hacendado (LAM), rancho (MEX), casco de la estancia (RPL); **farming** *n* agricultura; (*of crops*) cultivo; (*of animals*) cría; **farmyard** *n* corral *m*
far-reaching [fɑ:'ri:tʃıŋ] *adj* (*reform, effect*) de gran alcance
fart [fɑ:t] (*inf!*) *vi* tirarse un pedo (*!*)
farther ['fɑ:ðə*] *adv* más lejos, más allá ▷ *adj* más lejano
farthest ['fɑ:ðıst] *superlative of* **far**
fascinate ['fæsıneıt] *vt* fascinar; **fascinated** *adj* fascinado
fascinating ['fæsıneıtıŋ] *adj* fascinante
fascination [-'neıʃən] *n* fascinación *f*
fascist ['fæʃıst] *adj, n* fascista *m/f*
fashion ['fæʃən] *n* moda; (*fashion industry*) industria de la moda; (*manner*) manera ▷ *vt* formar; **in ~** a la moda; **out of ~** pasado de moda; **fashionable** *adj* de moda; **fashion show** *n* desfile *m* de modelos
fast [fɑ:st] *adj* rápido; (*dye, colour*) resistente; (*clock*): **to be ~** estar adelantado ▷ *adv* rápidamente, de prisa; (*stuck, held*) firmemente ▷ *n* ayuno ▷ *vi* ayunar; **~ asleep** profundamente dormido
fasten ['fɑ:sn] *vt* atar, sujetar; (*coat, belt*) abrochar ▷ *vi* atarse; abrocharse
fast food *n* comida rápida, platos *mpl* preparados
fat [fæt] *adj* gordo; (*book*) grueso; (*profit*) grande, pingüe ▷ *n* grasa; (*on person*) carnes *fpl*; (*lard*) manteca
fatal ['feıtl] *adj* (*mistake*) fatal; (*injury*) mortal; **fatality** [fə'tælıtı] *n* (*road death etc*) víctima; **fatally** *adv* fatalmente; mortalmente
fate [feıt] *n* destino; (*of person*) suerte *f*
father ['fɑ:ðə*] *n* padre *m*; **Father Christmas** *n* Papá *m* Noel; **father-in-law** *n* suegro
fatigue [fə'ti:g] *n* fatiga, cansancio
fattening ['fætnıŋ] *adj* (*food*) que hace engordar
fatty ['fætı] *adj* (*food*) graso ▷ *n* (*inf*) gordito/a, gordinflón/ona *m/f*
faucet ['fɔ:sıt] (US) *n* grifo (SP), llave *f*, canilla (RPL)
fault [fɔ:lt] *n* (*blame*) culpa; (*defect: in person, machine*) defecto; (*Geo*) falla ▷ *vt* criticar; **it's my ~** es culpa mía; **to find ~ with** criticar, poner peros a; **at ~** culpable; **faulty** *adj* defectuoso
fauna ['fɔ:nə] *n* fauna
favour *etc* ['feıvə*] (US **favor** *etc*) *n* favor *m*; (*approval*) aprobación *f* ▷ *vt* (*proposition*) estar a favor de, aprobar; (*assist*) ser propicio a; **to do sb a ~** hacer un favor a algn; **to find ~ with sb** caer en gracia a algn; **in ~ of** a favor de; **favourable** *adj* favorable; **favourite** ['feıvrıt] *adj, n* favorito, preferido
fawn [fɔ:n] *n* cervato ▷ *adj* (*also*: **~-coloured**) color de cervato, leonado ▷ *vi*: **to ~ (up)on** adular
fax [fæks] *n* (*document*) fax *m*; (*machine*) telefax *m* ▷ *vt* mandar por telefax
FBI (US) *n abbr* (= *Federal Bureau of Investigation*) ≈ BIC *f* (SP)
fear [fıə*] *n* miedo, temor *m* ▷ *vt* tener

miedo de, temer; **for ~ of** por si; **fearful** *adj* temeroso, miedoso; (*awful*) terrible; **fearless** *adj* audaz
feasible ['fi:zəbl] *adj* factible
feast [fi:st] *n* banquete *m*; (*Rel*: *also*: **~ day**) fiesta ▷ *vi* festejar
feat [fi:t] *n* hazaña
feather ['fɛðə*] *n* pluma
feature ['fi:tʃə*] *n* característica; (*article*) artículo de fondo ▷ *vt* (*film*) presentar ▷ *vi*: **to ~ in** tener un papel destacado en; **features** *npl* (*of face*) facciones *fpl*; **feature film** *n* largometraje *m*
Feb. *abbr* (= *February*) feb
February ['fɛbruərɪ] *n* febrero
fed [fɛd] *pt, pp of* **feed**
federal ['fɛdərəl] *adj* federal
federation [fɛdə'reɪʃən] *n* federación *f*
fed up [fɛd'ʌp] *adj*: **to be ~ (with)** estar harto (de)
fee [fi:] *n* pago; (*professional*) derechos *mpl*, honorarios *mpl*; (*of club*) cuota; **school ~s** matrícula
feeble ['fi:bl] *adj* débil; (*joke*) flojo
feed [fi:d] (*pt, pp* **fed**) *n* comida; (*of animal*) pienso; (*on printer*) dispositivo de alimentación ▷ *vt* alimentar; (BRIT: *baby*: *breastfeed*) dar el pecho a; (*animal*) dar de comer a; (*data, information*): **to ~ into** meter en; **feedback** *n* reacción *f*, feedback *m*
feel [fi:l] (*pt, pp* **felt**) *n* (*sensation*) sensación *f*; (*sense of touch*) tacto; (*impression*): **to have the ~ of** parecerse a ▷ *vt* tocar; (*pain etc*) sentir; (*think, believe*) creer; **to ~ hungry/cold** tener hambre/frío; **to ~ lonely/better** sentirse solo/mejor; **I don't ~ well** no me siento bien; **it ~s soft** es suave al tacto; **to ~ like** (*want*) tener ganas de; **feeling** *n* (*physical*) sensación *f*; (*foreboding*) presentimiento; (*emotion*) sentimiento
feet [fi:t] *npl of* **foot**
fell [fɛl] *pt of* **fall** ▷ *vt* (*tree*) talar
fellow ['fɛləu] *n* tipo, tío (SP); (*comrade*) compañero; (*of learned society*) socio/a; **fellow citizen** *n* conciudadano/a; **fellow countryman** (*irreg*) *n* compatriota *m*; **fellow men** *npl* semejantes *mpl*; **fellowship** *n* compañerismo; (*grant*) beca
felony ['fɛlənɪ] *n* crimen *m*
felt [fɛlt] *pt, pp of* **feel** ▷ *n* fieltro; **felt-tip** *n* (*also*: **felt-tip pen**) rotulador *m*
female ['fi:meɪl] *n* (*pej*: *woman*) mujer *f*, tía; (*Zool*) hembra ▷ *adj* femenino; hembra
feminine ['fɛmɪnɪn] *adj* femenino
feminist ['fɛmɪnɪst] *n* feminista
fence [fɛns] *n* valla, cerca ▷ *vt* (*also*: **~ in**) cercar ▷ *vi* (*Sport*) hacer esgrima; **fencing** *n* esgrima
fend [fɛnd] *vi*: **to ~ for o.s.** valerse por sí mismo; **fend off** *vt* (*attack*) rechazar; (*questions*) evadir
fender ['fɛndə*] (US) *n* guardafuego; (*Aut*) parachoques *m inv*
fennel ['fɛnl] *n* hinojo
ferment [*vb* fə'mɛnt, *n* 'fə:mɛnt] *vi* fermentar ▷ *n* (*fig*) agitación *f*
fern [fə:n] *n* helecho
ferocious [fə'rəuʃəs] *adj* feroz
ferret ['fɛrɪt] *n* hurón *m*
ferry ['fɛrɪ] *n* (*small*) barca (de pasaje), balsa; (*large*: *also*: **~boat**) transbordador *m*, ferry *m* ▷ *vt* transportar
fertile ['fə:taɪl] *adj* fértil; (*Biol*) fecundo; **fertilize** ['fə:tɪlaɪz] *vt* (*Biol*) fecundar; (*Agr*) abonar; **fertilizer** *n* abono
festival ['fɛstɪvəl] *n* (*Rel*) fiesta; (*Art, Mus*) festival *m*
festive ['fɛstɪv] *adj* festivo; **the ~ season** (BRIT: *Christmas*) las Navidades
fetch [fɛtʃ] *vt* ir a buscar; (*sell for*) venderse por
fête [feɪt] *n* fiesta
fetus ['fi:təs] (US) *n* = **foetus**
feud [fju:d] *n* (*hostility*) enemistad *f*; (*quarrel*) disputa
fever ['fi:və*] *n* fiebre *f*; **feverish** *adj* febril
few [fju:] *adj* (*not many*) pocos ▷ *pron* pocos; algunos; **a ~** *adj* unos pocos, algunos; **fewer** *adj* menos; **fewest** *adj* los(las) menos
fiancé [fɪ'ɑ̃:ŋseɪ] *n* novio, prometido; **fiancée** *n* novia, prometida
fiasco [fɪ'æskəu] *n* fiasco
fib [fɪb] *n* mentirilla
fibre ['faɪbə*] (US **fiber**) *n* fibra; **fibreglass** (US **Fiberglass**®) *n* fibra de vidrio
fickle ['fɪkl] *adj* inconstante
fiction ['fɪkʃən] *n* ficción *f*; **fictional** *adj* novelesco
fiddle ['fɪdl] *n* (*Mus*) violín *m*; (*cheating*) trampa ▷ *vt* (BRIT: *accounts*) falsificar; **fiddle with** *vt fus* juguetear con
fidelity [fɪ'dɛlɪtɪ] *n* fidelidad *f*
field [fi:ld] *n* campo; (*fig*) campo, esfera; (*Sport*) campo (SP), cancha (LAM); **field marshal** *n* mariscal *m*
fierce [fɪəs] *adj* feroz; (*wind, heat*) fuerte; (*fighting, enemy*) encarnizado
fifteen [fɪf'ti:n] *num* quince; **fifteenth** *adj* decimoquinto; **the fifteenth floor** la planta quince; **the fifteenth of August** el quince de agosto
fifth [fɪfθ] *num* quinto
fiftieth ['fɪftɪɪθ] *adj* quincuagésimo
fifty ['fɪftɪ] *num* cincuenta; **fifty-fifty** *adj*

f

(*deal, split*) a medias ▷ *adv* a medias, mitad por mitad
fig [fɪg] *n* higo
fight [faɪt] (*pt, pp* **fought**) *n* (*gen*) pelea; (*Mil*) combate *m*; (*struggle*) lucha ▷ *vt* luchar contra; (*cancer, alcoholism*) combatir; (*election*) intentar ganar; (*emotion*) resistir ▷ *vi* pelear, luchar; **fight back** *vi* defenderse; (*after illness*) recuperarse ▷ *vt* (*tears*) contener; **fight off** *vt* (*attack, attacker*) rechazar; (*disease, sleep, urge*) luchar contra; **fighting** *n* combate *m*, pelea
figure ['fɪgə*] *n* (*Drawing, Geom*) figura, dibujo; (*number, cipher*) cifra; (*body, outline*) tipo; (*personality*) figura ▷ *vt* (*esp* US) imaginar ▷ *vi* (*appear*) figurar; **figure out** *vt* (*work out*) resolver
file [faɪl] *n* (*tool*) lima; (*dossier*) expediente *m*; (*folder*) carpeta; (*Comput*) fichero; (*row*) fila ▷ *vt* limar; (*Law: claim*) presentar; (*store*) archivar; **filing cabinet** *n* fichero, archivador *m*
Filipino [fɪlɪ'pi:nəu] *adj* filipino ▷ *n* (*person*) filipino/a *m/f*; (*Ling*) tagalo
fill [fɪl] *vt* (*space*): **to ~ (with)** llenar (de); (*vacancy, need*) cubrir ▷ *n*: **to eat one's ~** llenarse; **fill in** *vt* rellenar; **fill out** *vt* (*form, receipt*) rellenar; **fill up** *vt* llenar (hasta el borde) ▷ *vi* (*Aut*) poner gasolina
fillet ['fɪlɪt] *n* filete *m*; **fillet steak** *n* filete *m* de ternera
filling ['fɪlɪŋ] *n* (*Culin*) relleno; (*for tooth*) empaste *m*; **filling station** *n* estación *f* de servicio
film [fɪlm] *n* película ▷ *vt* (*scene*) filmar ▷ *vi* rodar (una película); **film star** *n* astro, estrella de cine
filter ['fɪltə*] *n* filtro ▷ *vt* filtrar; **filter lane** (BRIT) *n* carril *m* de selección
filth [fɪlθ] *n* suciedad *f*; **filthy** *adj* sucio; (*language*) obsceno
fin [fɪn] *n* (*gen*) aleta
final ['faɪnl] *adj* (*last*) final, último; (*definitive*) definitivo, terminante ▷ *n* (BRIT *Sport*) final *f*; **finals** *npl* (*Scol*) examen *m* final; (US *Sport*) final *f*
finale [fɪ'nɑ:lɪ] *n* final *m*
final: finalist *n* (*Sport*) finalista *mf*; **finalize** *vt* concluir, completar; **finally** *adv* (*lastly*) por último, finalmente; (*eventually*) por fin
finance [faɪ'næns] *n* (*money*) fondos *mpl* ▷ *vt* financiar; **finances** *npl* finanzas *fpl*; (*personal finances*) situación *f* económica; **financial** [-'nænʃəl] *adj* financiero; **financial year** *n* ejercicio (financiero)
find [faɪnd] (*pt, pp* **found**) *vt* encontrar, hallar; (*come upon*) descubrir ▷ *n* hallazgo; descubrimiento; **to ~ sb guilty** (*Law*) declarar culpable a algn; **find out** *vt* averiguar; (*truth, secret*) descubrir; **to find out about** (*subject*) informarse sobre; (*by chance*) enterarse de; **findings** *npl* (*Law*) veredicto, fallo; (*of report*) recomendaciones *fpl*
fine [faɪn] *adj* excelente; (*thin*) fino ▷ *adv* (*well*) bien ▷ *n* (*Law*) multa ▷ *vt* (*Law*) multar; **to be ~** (*person*) estar bien; (*weather*) hacer buen tiempo; **fine arts** *npl* bellas artes *fpl*
finger ['fɪŋgə*] *n* dedo ▷ *vt* (*touch*) manosear; **little/index ~** (dedo) meñique *m*/índice *m*; **fingernail** *n* uña; **fingerprint** *n* huella dactilar; **fingertip** *n* yema del dedo
finish ['fɪnɪʃ] *n* (*end*) fin *m*; (*Sport*) meta; (*polish etc*) acabado ▷ *vt, vi* terminar; **to ~ doing sth** acabar de hacer algo; **to ~ third** llegar el tercero; **finish off** *vt* acabar, terminar; (*kill*) acabar con; **finish up** *vt* acabar, terminar ▷ *vi* ir a parar, terminar
Finland ['fɪnlənd] *n* Finlandia
Finn [fɪn] *n* finlandés/esa *m/f*; **Finnish** *adj* finlandés/esa ▷ *n* (*Ling*) finlandés *m*
fir [fə:*] *n* abeto
fire ['faɪə*] *n* fuego; (*in hearth*) lumbre *f*; (*accidental*) incendio; (*heater*) estufa ▷ *vt* (*gun*) disparar; (*interest*) despertar; (*inf: dismiss*) despedir ▷ *vi* (*shoot*) disparar; **on ~** ardiendo, en llamas; **fire alarm** *n* alarma de incendios; **firearm** *n* arma de fuego; **fire brigade** (US **fire department**) *n* (cuerpo de) bomberos *mpl*; **fire engine** (BRIT) *n* coche *m* de bomberos; **fire escape** *n* escalera de incendios; **fire exit** *n* salida de incendios; **fire extinguisher** *n* extintor *m* (de incendios); **fireman** (*irreg*) *n* bombero; **fireplace** *n* chimenea; **fire station** *n* parque *m* de bomberos; **firetruck** (US) *n* = **fire engine**; **firewall** *n* (*Internet*) firewall *m*; **firewood** *n* leña; **fireworks** *npl* fuegos *mpl* artificiales
firm [fə:m] *adj* firme; (*look, voice*) resuelto ▷ *n* firma, empresa; **firmly** *adv* firmemente; resueltamente
first [fə:st] *adj* primero ▷ *adv* (*before others*) primero; (*when listing reasons etc*) en primer lugar, primeramente ▷ *n* (*person: in race*) primero/a; (*Aut*) primera; (BRIT *Scol*) *título de licenciado con calificación de sobresaliente*; **at ~** al principio; **~ of all** ante todo; **first aid** *n* primera ayuda, primeros auxilios *mpl*; **first-aid kit** *n* botiquín *m*; **first-class** *adj* (*excellent*) de primera (categoría); (*ticket etc*) de primera clase; **first-hand** *adj* de primera mano; **first lady** *n* (*esp* US) primera dama; **firstly** *adv* en primer lugar; **first**

name *n* nombre *m* (de pila); **first-rate** *adj* estupendo
fiscal ['fɪskəl] *adj* fiscal; **fiscal year** *n* año fiscal, ejercicio
fish [fɪʃ] *n inv* pez *m*; (*food*) pescado ▷ *vt, vi* pescar; **to go ~ing** ir de pesca; **~ and chips** pescado frito con patatas fritas; **fisherman** (*irreg*) *n* pescador *m*; **fish fingers** (BRIT) *npl* croquetas *fpl* de pescado; **fishing** *n* pesca; **fishing boat** *n* barca de pesca; **fishing line** *n* sedal *m*; **fishmonger** *n* (BRIT) pescadero/a; **fishmonger's (shop)** (BRIT) *n* pescadería; **fish sticks** (US) *npl* = **fish fingers**; **fishy** (*inf*) *adj* sospechoso
fist [fɪst] *n* puño
fit [fɪt] *adj* (*healthy*) en (buena) forma; (*proper*) adecuado, apropiado ▷ *vt* (*clothes*) estar *or* sentar bien a; (*instal*) poner; (*equip*) proveer, dotar; (*facts*) cuadrar *or* corresponder con ▷ *vi* (*clothes*) sentar bien; (*in space, gap*) caber; (*facts*) coincidir ▷ *n* (*Med*) ataque *m*; **~ to** (*ready*) a punto de; **~ for** apropiado para; **a ~ of anger/pride** un arranque de cólera/orgullo; **this dress is a good ~** este vestido me sienta bien; **by ~s and starts** a rachas; **fit in** *vi* (*fig: person*) llevarse bien (con todos); **fitness** *n* (*Med*) salud *f*; **fitted** *adj* (*jacket, shirt*) entallado; (*sheet*) de cuatro picos; **fitted carpet** *n* moqueta; **fitted kitchen** *n* cocina amueblada; **fitting** *adj* apropiado ▷ *n* (*of dress*) prueba; (*of piece of equipment*) instalación *f*; **fitting room** *n* probador *m*; **fittings** *npl* instalaciones *fpl*
five [faɪv] *num* cinco; **fiver** (*inf*) *n* (BRIT) billete *m* de cinco libras; (US) billete *m* de cinco dólares
fix [fɪks] *vt* (*secure*) fijar, asegurar; (*mend*) arreglar; (*prepare*) preparar ▷ *n*: **to be in a ~** estar en un aprieto; **fix up** *vt* (*meeting*) arreglar; **to fix sb up with sth** proveer a algn de algo; **fixed** *adj* (*prices etc*) fijo; **fixture** *n* (*Sport*) encuentro
fizzy ['fɪzɪ] *adj* (*drink*) gaseoso
flag [flæg] *n* bandera; (*stone*) losa ▷ *vi* decaer ▷ *vt*: **to ~ sb down** hacer señas a algn para que se pare; **flagpole** *n* asta de bandera
flair [flɛə*] *n* aptitud *f* especial
flak [flæk] *n* (*Mil*) fuego antiaéreo; (*inf: criticism*) lluvia de críticas
flake [fleɪk] *n* (*of rust, paint*) escama; (*of snow, soap powder*) copo ▷ *vi* (*also*: **~ off**) desconcharse
flamboyant [flæm'bɔɪənt] *adj* (*dress*) vistoso; (*person*) extravagante
flame [fleɪm] *n* llama
flamingo [flə'mɪŋgəu] *n* flamenco
flammable ['flæməbl] *adj* inflamable
flan [flæn] (BRIT) *n* tarta

> Be careful not to translate **flan** by the Spanish word *flan*.

flank [flæŋk] *n* (*of animal*) ijar *m*; (*of army*) flanco ▷ *vt* flanquear
flannel ['flænl] *n* (BRIT: *also*: **face ~**) manopla; (*fabric*) franela
flap [flæp] *n* (*of pocket, envelope*) solapa ▷ *vt* (*wings, arms*) agitar ▷ *vi* (*sail, flag*) ondear
flare [flɛə*] *n* llamarada; (*Mil*) bengala; (*in skirt etc*) vuelo; **flares** *npl* (*trousers*) pantalones *mpl* de campana; **flare up** *vi* encenderse; (*fig: person*) encolerizarse; (*: revolt*) estallar
flash [flæʃ] *n* relámpago; (*also*: **news ~**) noticias *fpl* de última hora; (*Phot*) flash *m* ▷ *vt* (*light, headlights*) lanzar un destello con; (*news, message*) transmitir; (*smile*) lanzar ▷ *vi* brillar; (*hazard light etc*) lanzar destellos; **in a ~** en un instante; **he ~ed by** *or* **past** pasó como un rayo; **flashback** *n* (*Cinema*) flashback *m*; **flashbulb** *n* bombilla fusible; **flashlight** *n* linterna
flask [flɑːsk] *n* frasco; (*also*: **vacuum ~**) termo
flat [flæt] *adj* llano; (*smooth*) liso; (*tyre*) desinflado; (*battery*) descargado; (*beer*) muerto; (*refusal etc*) rotundo; (*Mus*) desafinado; (*rate*) fijo ▷ *n* (BRIT: *apartment*) piso (SP), departamento (LAM), apartamento; (*Aut*) pinchazo; (*Mus*) bemol *m*; **to work ~ out** trabajar a toda mecha; **flatten** *vt* (*also*: **flatten out**) allanar; (*smooth out*) alisar; (*building, plants*) arrasar
flatter ['flætə*] *vt* adular, halagar; **flattering** *adj* halagüeño; (*dress*) que favorece
flaunt [flɔːnt] *vt* ostentar, lucir
flavour *etc* ['fleɪvə*] (US **flavor** *etc*) *n* sabor *m*, gusto ▷ *vt* sazonar, condimentar; **strawberry-flavoured** con sabor a fresa; **flavouring** *n* (*in product*) aromatizante *m*
flaw [flɔː] *n* defecto; **flawless** *adj* impecable
flea [fliː] *n* pulga; **flea market** *n* rastro, mercadillo
flee [fliː] (*pt, pp* **fled**) *vt* huir de ▷ *vi* huir, fugarse
fleece [fliːs] *n* vellón *m*; (*wool*) lana; (*top*) forro polar ▷ *vt* (*inf*) desplumar
fleet [fliːt] *n* flota; (*of lorries etc*) escuadra
fleeting ['fliːtɪŋ] *adj* fugaz
Flemish ['flɛmɪʃ] *adj* flamenco
flesh [flɛʃ] *n* carne *f*; (*skin*) piel *f*; (*of fruit*) pulpa
flew [fluː] *pt of* **fly**
flex [flɛks] *n* cordón *m* ▷ *vt* (*muscles*)

tensar; **flexibility** *n* flexibilidad *f*; **flexible** *adj* flexible; **flexitime** (*US* **flextime**) *n* horario flexible

flick [flɪk] *n* capirotazo; chasquido ▷ *vt* (*with hand*) dar un capirotazo a; (*whip etc*) chasquear; (*switch*) accionar; **flick through** *vt fus* hojear

flicker ['flɪkə*] *vi* (*light*) parpadear; (*flame*) vacilar

flies [flaɪz] *npl of* **fly**

flight [flaɪt] *n* vuelo; (*escape*) huida, fuga; (*also*: **~ of steps**) tramo (de escaleras); **flight attendant** *n* auxiliar *mf* de vuelo

flimsy ['flɪmzɪ] *adj* (*thin*) muy ligero; (*building*) endeble; (*excuse*) flojo

flinch [flɪntʃ] *vi* encogerse; **to ~ from** retroceder ante

fling [flɪŋ] (*pt, pp* **flung**) *vt* arrojar

flint [flɪnt] *n* pedernal *m*; (*in lighter*) piedra

flip [flɪp] *vt* dar la vuelta a; (*switch: turn on*) encender; (*turn*) apagar; (*coin*) echar a cara o cruz

flip-flops ['flɪpflɔps] *npl* (*esp* BRIT) chancletas *fpl*

flipper ['flɪpə*] *n* aleta

flirt [flə:t] *vi* coquetear, flirtear ▷ *n* coqueta

float [fləut] *n* flotador *m*; (*in procession*) carroza; (*money*) reserva ▷ *vi* flotar; (*swimmer*) hacer la plancha

flock [flɔk] *n* (*of sheep*) rebaño; (*of birds*) bandada ▷ *vi*: **to ~ to** acudir en tropel a

flood [flʌd] *n* inundación *f*; (*of letters, imports etc*) avalancha ▷ *vt* inundar ▷ *vi* (*place*) inundarse; (*people*): **to ~ into** inundar; **flooding** *n* inundaciones *fpl*; **floodlight** *n* foco

floor [flɔ:*] *n* suelo; (*storey*) piso; (*of sea*) fondo ▷ *vt* (*question*) dejar sin respuesta; (: *blow*) derribar; **ground ~, first ~** (*US*) planta baja; **first ~, second ~** (*US*) primer piso; **floorboard** *n* tabla; **flooring** *n* suelo; (*material*) solería; **floor show** *n* cabaret *m*

flop [flɔp] *n* fracaso ▷ *vi* (*fail*) fracasar; (*fall*) derrumbarse; **floppy** *adj* flojo ▷ *n* (*Comput*: *also*: **floppy disk**) floppy *m*

flora ['flɔ:rə] *n* flora

floral ['flɔ:rl] *adj* (*pattern*) floreado

florist ['flɔrɪst] *n* florista *mf*; **florist's (shop)** *n* floristería

flotation [fləu'teɪʃən] *n* (*of shares*) emisión *f*; (*of company*) lanzamiento

flour ['flauə*] *n* harina

flourish ['flʌrɪʃ] *vi* florecer ▷ *n* ademán *m*, movimiento (ostentoso)

flow [fləu] *n* (*movement*) flujo; (*of traffic*) circulación *f*; (*tide*) corriente *f* ▷ *vi* (*river, blood*) fluir; (*traffic*) circular

flower ['flauə*] *n* flor *f* ▷ *vi* florecer; **flower bed** *n* macizo; **flowerpot** *n* tiesto

flown [fləun] *pp of* **fly**

fl. oz. *abbr* (= *fluid ounce*)

flu [flu:] *n*: **to have ~** tener la gripe

fluctuate ['flʌktjueɪt] *vi* fluctuar

fluent ['flu:ənt] *adj* (*linguist*) que habla perfectamente; (*speech*) elocuente; **he speaks ~ French, he's ~ in French** domina el francés

fluff [flʌf] *n* pelusa; **fluffy** *adj* de pelo suave

fluid ['flu:ɪd] *adj* (*movement*) fluido, líquido; (*situation*) inestable ▷ *n* fluido, líquido; **fluid ounce** *n* onza *f* líquida

fluke [flu:k] (*inf*) *n* chiripa

flung [flʌŋ] *pt, pp of* **fling**

fluorescent [fluə'rɛsnt] *adj* fluorescente

fluoride ['fluəraɪd] *n* fluoruro

flurry ['flʌrɪ] *n* (*of snow*) temporal *m*; **~ of activity** frenesí *m* de actividad

flush [flʌʃ] *n* rubor *m*; (*fig*: *of youth etc*) resplandor *m* ▷ *vt* limpiar con agua ▷ *vi* ruborizarse ▷ *adj*: **~ with** a ras de; **to ~ the toilet** hacer funcionar la cisterna

flute [flu:t] *n* flauta

flutter ['flʌtə*] *n* (*of wings*) revoloteo, aleteo; (*fig*): **a ~ of panic/excitement** una oleada de pánico/excitación ▷ *vi* revolotear

fly [flaɪ] (*pt* **flew**, *pp* **flown**) *n* mosca; (*on trousers*: *also*: **flies**) bragueta ▷ *vt* (*plane*) pilot(e)ar; (*cargo*) transportar (en avión); (*distances*) recorrer (en avión) ▷ *vi* volar; (*passengers*) ir en avión; (*escape*) evadirse; (*flag*) ondear; **fly away, fly off** *vi* emprender el vuelo; **fly-drive** *n*: **fly-drive holiday** *vacaciones que incluyen vuelo y alquiler de coche*; **flying** *n* (*activity*) (el) volar; (*action*) vuelo ▷ *adj*: **flying visit** visita relámpago; **with flying colours** con lucimiento; **flying saucer** *n* platillo volante; **flyover** (BRIT) *n* paso a desnivel *or* superior

FM *abbr* (*Radio*) (= *frequency modulation*) FM

foal [fəul] *n* potro

foam [fəum] *n* espuma ▷ *vi* hacer espuma

focus ['fəukəs] (*pl* **~es**) *n* foco; (*centre*) centro ▷ *vt* (*field glasses etc*) enfocar ▷ *vi*: **to ~ (on)** enfocar (a); (*issue etc*) centrarse en; **in/out of ~** enfocado/desenfocado

foetus ['fi:təs] (*US* **fetus**) *n* feto

fog [fɔg] *n* niebla; **foggy** *adj*: **it's foggy** hay niebla, está brumoso; **fog lamp** (*US* **fog light**) *n* (*Aut*) faro de niebla

foil [fɔɪl] *vt* frustrar ▷ *n* hoja; (*kitchen foil*) papel *m* (de) aluminio; (*complement*) complemento; (*Fencing*) florete *m*

fold [fəuld] *n* (*bend, crease*) pliegue *m*; (*Agr*)

redil *m* ▷ *vt* doblar; (*arms*) cruzar; **fold up** *vi* plegarse, doblarse; (*business*) quebrar ▷ *vt* (*map etc*) plegar; **folder** *n* (*for papers*) carpeta; (*Comput*) directorio; **folding** *adj* (*chair, bed*) plegable

foliage ['fəulɪɪdʒ] *n* follaje *m*

folk [fəuk] *npl* gente *f* ▷ *adj* popular, folklórico; **folks** *npl* (*family*) familia *sg*, parientes *mpl*; **folklore** ['fəuklɔ:*] *n* folklore *m*; **folk music** *n* música folk; **folk song** *n* canción *f* popular

follow ['fɔləu] *vt* seguir ▷ *vi* seguir; (*result*) resultar; **to ~ suit** hacer lo mismo; **follow up** *vt* (*letter, offer*) responder a; (*case*) investigar; **follower** *n* (*of person, belief*) partidario/a; **following** *adj* siguiente ▷ *n* afición *f*, partidarios *mpl*; **follow-up** *n* continuación *f*

fond [fɔnd] *adj* (*memory, smile etc*) cariñoso; (*hopes*) ilusorio; **to be ~ of** tener cariño a; (*pastime, food*) ser aficionado a

food [fu:d] *n* comida; **food mixer** *n* batidora; **food poisoning** *n* intoxicación *f* alimenticia; **food processor** *n* robot *m* de cocina; **food stamp** (US) *n* vale *m* para comida

fool [fu:l] *n* tonto/a; (*Culin*) puré *m* de frutas con nata ▷ *vt* engañar ▷ *vi* (*gen*) bromear; **fool about, fool around** *vi* hacer el tonto; **foolish** *adj* tonto; (*careless*) imprudente; **foolproof** *adj* (*plan etc*) infalible

foot [fut] (*pl* **feet**) *n* pie *m*; (*measure*) pie *m* (= 304 *mm*); (*of animal*) pata ▷ *vt* (*bill*) pagar; **on ~** a pie; **footage** *n* (*Cinema*) imágenes *fpl*; **foot-and-mouth (disease)** [futənd'mauθ-] *n* fiebre *f* aftosa; **football** *n* balón *m*; (*game*: BRIT) fútbol *m*; (: US) fútbol *m* americano; **footballer** *n* (BRIT) = **football player**; **football match** *n* partido de fútbol; **football player** *n* (BRIT) futbolista *mf*; (US) jugador *m* de fútbol americano; **footbridge** *n* puente *m* para peatones; **foothills** *npl* estribaciones *fpl*; **foothold** *n* pie *m* firme; **footing** *n* (*fig*) posición *f*; **to lose one's footing** perder el pie; **footnote** *n* nota (al pie de la página); **footpath** *n* sendero; **footprint** *n* huella, pisada; **footstep** *n* paso; **footwear** *n* calzado

KEYWORD

for [fɔ:] *prep* **1** (*indicating destination, intention*) para; **the train for London** el tren con destino a *or* de Londres; **he left for Rome** marchó para Roma; **he went for the paper** fue por el periódico; **is this for me?** ¿es esto para mí?; **it's time for lunch** es la hora de comer

2 (*indicating purpose*) para; **what('s it) for?** ¿para qué (es)?; **to pray for peace** rezar por la paz

3 (*on behalf of, representing*): **the MP for Hove** el diputado por Hove; **he works for the government/a local firm** trabaja para el gobierno/en una empresa local; **I'll ask him for you** se lo pediré por ti; **G for George** G de Gerona

4 (*because of*) por esta razón; **for fear of being criticized** por temor a ser criticado

5 (*with regard to*) para; **it's cold for July** hace frío para julio; **he has a gift for languages** tiene don de lenguas

6 (*in exchange for*) por; **I sold it for £5** lo vendí por £5; **to pay 50 pence for a ticket** pagar 50 peniques por un billete

7 (*in favour of*): **are you for or against us?** ¿estás con nosotros o contra nosotros?; **I'm all for it** estoy totalmente a favor; **vote for X** vote (a) X

8 (*referring to distance*): **there are roadworks for 5 km** hay obras en 5 km; **we walked for miles** caminamos kilómetros y kilómetros

9 (*referring to time*): **he was away for two years** estuvo fuera (durante) dos años; **it hasn't rained for 3 weeks** no ha llovido durante *or* en 3 semanas; **I have known her for years** la conozco desde hace años; **can you do it for tomorrow?** ¿lo podrás hacer para mañana?

10 (*with infinitive clauses*): **it is not for me to decide** la decisión no es cosa mía; **it would be best for you to leave** sería mejor que te fueras; **there is still time for you to do it** todavía te queda tiempo para hacerlo; **for this to be possible ...** para que esto sea posible ...

11 (*in spite of*) a pesar de; **for all his complaints** a pesar de sus quejas ▷ *conj* (*since, as*: *rather formal*) puesto que

forbid [fə'bɪd] (*pt* **forbad(e)**, *pp* **forbidden**) *vt* prohibir; **to ~ sb to do sth** prohibir a algn hacer algo; **forbidden** *pt of* **forbid** ▷ *adj* (*food, area*) prohibido; (*word, subject*) tabú

force [fɔ:s] *n* fuerza ▷ *vt* forzar; (*push*) meter a la fuerza; **to ~ o.s. to do** hacer un esfuerzo por hacer; **forced** *adj* forzado; **forceful** *adj* enérgico

ford [fɔ:d] *n* vado

fore [fɔ:*] *n*: **to come to the ~** empezar a destacar; **forearm** *n* antebrazo; **forecast** (*pt, pp* **forecast**) *n* pronóstico ▷ *vt* pronosticar; **forecourt** *n* patio; **forefinger** *n* (dedo) índice *m*; **forefront** *n*: **in the forefront of** en la vanguardia de;

foreground *n* primer plano; **forehead** ['fɔrɪd] *n* frente *f*

foreign ['fɔrɪn] *adj* extranjero; (*trade*) exterior; (*object*) extraño; **foreign currency** *n* divisas *fpl*; **foreigner** *n* extranjero/a; **foreign exchange** *n* divisas *fpl*; **Foreign Office** (BRIT) *n* Ministerio de Asuntos Exteriores; **Foreign Secretary** (BRIT) *n* Ministro de Asuntos Exteriores

fore: foreman (*irreg*) *n* capataz *m*; (*in construction*) maestro de obras; **foremost** *adj* principal ▷ *adv*: **first and foremost** ante todo; **forename** *n* nombre *m* (de pila)

forensic [fə'rɛnsɪk] *adj* forense

foresee [fɔː'siː] (*pt* **foresaw**, *pp* **foreseen**) *vt* prever; **foreseeable** *adj* previsible

forest ['fɔrɪst] *n* bosque *m*; **forestry** *n* silvicultura

forever [fə'rɛvə*] *adv* para siempre; (*endlessly*) constantemente

foreword ['fɔːwəːd] *n* prefacio

forfeit ['fɔːfɪt] *vt* perder

forgave [fə'geɪv] *pt of* **forgive**

forge [fɔːdʒ] *n* herrería ▷ *vt* (*signature, money*) falsificar; (*metal*) forjar; **forger** *n* falsificador(a) *m/f*; **forgery** *n* falsificación *f*

forget [fə'gɛt] (*pt* **forgot**, *pp* **forgotten**) *vt* olvidar ▷ *vi* olvidarse; **forgetful** *adj* despistado

forgive [fə'gɪv] (*pt* **forgave**, *pp* **forgiven**) *vt* perdonar; **to ~ sb for sth** perdonar algo a algn

forgot [fə'gɔt] *pt of* **forget**

forgotten [fə'gɔtn] *pp of* **forget**

fork [fɔːk] *n* (*for eating*) tenedor *m*; (*for gardening*) horca; (*of roads*) bifurcación *f* ▷ *vi* (*road*) bifurcarse

forlorn [fə'lɔːn] *adj* (*person*) triste, melancólico; (*place*) abandonado; (*attempt, hope*) desesperado

form [fɔːm] *n* forma; (BRIT *Scol*) clase *f*; (*document*) formulario ▷ *vt* formar; (*idea*) concebir; (*habit*) adquirir; **in top ~** en plena forma; **to ~ a queue** hacer cola

formal ['fɔːməl] *adj* (*offer, receipt*) por escrito; (*person etc*) correcto; (*occasion, dinner*) de etiqueta; (*dress*) correcto; (*garden*) (de estilo) clásico; **formality** [-'mælɪtɪ] *n* (*procedure*) trámite *m*; corrección *f*; etiqueta

format ['fɔːmæt] *n* formato ▷ *vt* (*Comput*) formatear

formation [fɔː'meɪʃən] *n* formación *f*

former ['fɔːmə*] *adj* anterior; (*earlier*) antiguo; (*ex*) ex; **the ~ ... the latter ...** aquél ... éste ...; **formerly** *adv* antes

formidable ['fɔːmɪdəbl] *adj* formidable

formula ['fɔːmjulə] *n* fórmula

fort [fɔːt] *n* fuerte *m*

forthcoming [fɔːθ'kʌmɪŋ] *adj* próximo, venidero; (*help, information*) disponible; (*character*) comunicativo

fortieth ['fɔːtɪɪθ] *adj* cuadragésimo

fortify ['fɔːtɪfaɪ] *vt* (*city*) fortificar; (*person*) fortalecer

fortnight ['fɔːtnaɪt] (BRIT) *n* quince días *mpl*; quincena; **fortnightly** *adj* de cada quince días, quincenal ▷ *adv* cada quince días, quincenalmente

fortress ['fɔːtrɪs] *n* fortaleza

fortunate ['fɔːtʃənɪt] *adj* afortunado; **it is ~ that ...** (es una) suerte que ...; **fortunately** *adv* afortunadamente

fortune ['fɔːtʃən] *n* suerte *f*; (*wealth*) fortuna; **fortune-teller** *n* adivino/a

forty ['fɔːtɪ] *num* cuarenta

forum ['fɔːrəm] *n* foro

forward ['fɔːwəd] *adj* (*movement, position*) avanzado; (*front*) delantero; (*in time*) adelantado; (*not shy*) atrevido ▷ *n* (*Sport*) delantero ▷ *vt* (*letter*) remitir; (*career*) promocionar; **to move ~** avanzar; **forwarding address** *n* destinatario; **forward(s)** *adv* (hacia) adelante; **forward slash** *n* barra diagonal

fossil ['fɔsl] *n* fósil *m*

foster ['fɔstə*] *vt* (*child*) acoger en una familia; fomentar; **foster child** *n* hijo/a adoptivo/a; **foster mother** *n* madre *f* adoptiva

fought [fɔːt] *pt, pp of* **fight**

foul [faul] *adj* sucio, puerco; (*weather, smell etc*) asqueroso; (*language*) grosero; (*temper*) malísimo ▷ *n* (*Sport*) falta ▷ *vt* (*dirty*) ensuciar; **foul play** *n* (*Law*) muerte *f* violenta

found [faund] *pt, pp of* **find** ▷ *vt* fundar; **foundation** [-'deɪʃən] *n* (*act*) fundación *f*; (*basis*) base *f*; (*also*: **foundation cream**) crema base; **foundations** *npl* (*of building*) cimientos *mpl*

founder ['faundə*] *n* fundador(a) *m/f* ▷ *vi* hundirse

fountain ['fauntɪn] *n* fuente *f*; **fountain pen** *n* (pluma) estilográfica (SP), pluma-fuente *f* (LAM)

four [fɔː*] *num* cuatro; **on all ~s** a gatas; **four-letter word** *n* taco; **four-poster** *n* (*also*: **four-poster bed**) cama de columnas; **fourteen** *num* catorce; **fourteenth** *adj* decimocuarto; **fourth** *num* cuarto; **four-wheel drive** *n* tracción *f* a las cuatro ruedas

fowl [faul] *n* ave *f* (de corral)

fox [fɔks] *n* zorro ▷ *vt* confundir

foyer ['fɔɪeɪ] *n* vestíbulo

fraction ['frækʃən] *n* fracción *f*

fracture ['fræktʃə*] *n* fractura

fragile ['frædʒaɪl] *adj* frágil
fragment ['frægmənt] *n* fragmento
fragrance ['freɪgrəns] *n* fragancia
frail [freɪl] *adj* frágil; (*person*) débil
frame [freɪm] *n* (*Tech*) armazón *m*; (*of person*) cuerpo; (*of picture, door etc*) marco; (*of spectacles*: *also*: **~s**) montura ▷ *vt* enmarcar; **framework** *n* marco
France [frɑːns] *n* Francia
franchise ['fræntʃaɪz] *n* (*Pol*) derecho de votar, sufragio; (*Comm*) licencia, concesión *f*
frank [fræŋk] *adj* franco ▷ *vt* (*letter*) franquear; **frankly** *adv* francamente
frantic ['fræntɪk] *adj* (*distraught*) desesperado; (*hectic*) frenético
fraud [frɔːd] *n* fraude *m*; (*person*) impostor(a) *m/f*
fraught [frɔːt] *adj*: **~ with** lleno de
fray [freɪ] *vi* deshilacharse
freak [friːk] *n* (*person*) fenómeno; (*event*) suceso anormal
freckle ['frɛkl] *n* peca
free [friː] *adj* libre; (*gratis*) gratuito ▷ *vt* (*prisoner etc*) poner en libertad; (*jammed object*) soltar; **~ (of charge), for ~** gratis; **freedom** *n* libertad *f*; **Freefone®** *n* número gratuito; **free gift** *n* prima; **free kick** *n* tiro libre; **freelance** *adj* independiente ▷ *adv* por cuenta propia; **freely** *adv* libremente; (*liberally*) generosamente; **Freepost®** *n* porte *m* pagado; **free-range** *adj* (*hen, eggs*) de granja; **freeway** (*US*) *n* autopista; **free will** *n* libre albedrío; **of one's own free will** por su propia voluntad
freeze [friːz] (*pt* **froze**, *pp* **frozen**) *vi* (*weather*) helar; (*liquid, pipe, person*) helarse, congelarse ▷ *vt* helar; (*food, prices, salaries*) congelar ▷ *n* helada; (*on arms, wages*) congelación *f*; **freezer** *n* congelador *m*, freezer *m* (*SC*)
freezing ['friːzɪŋ] *adj* helado; **three degrees below ~** tres grados bajo cero; **freezing point** *n* punto de congelación
freight [freɪt] *n* (*goods*) carga; (*money charged*) flete *m*; **freight train** (*US*) *n* tren *m* de mercancías
French [frɛntʃ] *adj* francés/esa ▷ *n* (*Ling*) francés *m*; **the French** *npl* los franceses; **French bean** *n* judía verde; **French bread** *n* pan *m* francés; **French dressing** *n* (*Culin*) vinagreta; **French fried potatoes, French fries** (*US*) *npl* patatas *fpl* (*SP*) *or* papas *fpl* (*LAM*) fritas; **Frenchman** (*irreg*) *n* francés *m*; **Frenchwoman** (*irreg*) *n* francésa; **French stick** *n* barra de pan; **French window** *n* puerta de cristal
frenzy ['frɛnzɪ] *n* frenesí *m*
frequency ['friːkwənsɪ] *n* frecuencia
frequent [*adj* 'friːkwənt, *vb* frɪ'kwɛnt] *adj* frecuente ▷ *vt* frecuentar; **frequently** [-əntlɪ] *adv* frecuentemente, a menudo
fresh [frɛʃ] *adj* fresco; (*bread*) tierno; (*new*) nuevo; **freshen** *vi* (*wind, air*) soplar más recio; **freshen up** *vi* (*person*) arreglarse, lavarse; **fresher** (*BRIT*: *inf*) *n* (*Univ*) estudiante *mf* de primer año; **freshly** *adv* (*made, painted etc*) recién; **freshman** (*US*: *irreg*) *n* = **fresher**; **freshwater** *adj* (*fish*) de agua dulce
fret [frɛt] *vi* inquietarse
Fri *abbr* (= *Friday*) vier
friction ['frɪkʃən] *n* fricción *f*
Friday ['fraɪdɪ] *n* viernes *m inv*
fridge [frɪdʒ] (*BRIT*) *n* frigorífico (*SP*), nevera (*SP*), refrigerador *m* (*LAM*), heladera (*RPL*)
fried [fraɪd] *adj* frito
friend [frɛnd] *n* amigo/a; **friendly** *adj* simpático; (*government*) amigo; (*place*) acogedor(a); (*match*) amistoso; **friendship** *n* amistad *f*
fries [fraɪz] (*esp US*) *npl* = **French fried potatoes**
frigate ['frɪgɪt] *n* fragata
fright [fraɪt] *n* (*terror*) terror *m*; (*scare*) susto; **to take ~** asustarse; **frighten** *vt* asustar; **frightened** *adj* asustado; **frightening** *adj* espantoso; **frightful** *adj* espantoso, horrible
frill [frɪl] *n* volante *m*
fringe [frɪndʒ] *n* (*BRIT*: *of hair*) flequillo; (*on lampshade etc*) flecos *mpl*; (*of forest etc*) borde *m*, margen *m*
Frisbee® ['frɪzbɪ] *n* frisbee® *m*
fritter ['frɪtə*] *n* buñuelo
frivolous ['frɪvələs] *adj* frívolo
fro [frəu] *see* **to**
frock [frɔk] *n* vestido
frog [frɔg] *n* rana; **frogman** (*irreg*) *n* hombre-rana *m*

KEYWORD

from [frɔm] *prep* **1** (*indicating starting place*) de, desde; **where do you come from?** ¿de dónde eres?; **from London to Glasgow** de Londres a Glasgow; **to escape from sth/sb** escaparse de algo/algn
2 (*indicating origin etc*) de; **a letter/telephone call from my sister** una carta/llamada de mi hermana; **tell him from me that ...** dígale de mi parte que ...
3 (*indicating time*): **from one o'clock to** *or* **until** *or* **till two** de(sde) la una a *or* hasta las dos; **from January (on)** a partir de enero

4 (*indicating distance*) de; **the hotel is 1 km from the beach** el hotel está a 1 km de la playa
5 (*indicating price, number etc*) de; **prices range from £10 to £50** los precios van desde £10 a *or* hasta £50; **the interest rate was increased from 9% to 10%** el tipo de interés fue incrementado de un 9% a un 10%
6 (*indicating difference*) de; **he can't tell red from green** no sabe distinguir el rojo del verde; **to be different from sb/sth** ser diferente a algn/algo
7 (*because of, on the basis of*): **from what he says** por lo que dice; **weak from hunger** debilitado por el hambre

front [frʌnt] *n* (*foremost part*) parte *f* delantera; (*of house*) fachada; (*of dress*) delantero; (*promenade*: *also*: **sea ~**) paseo marítimo; (*Mil, Pol, Meteorology*) frente *m*; (*fig*: *appearances*) apariencias *fpl* ▷ *adj* (*wheel, leg*) delantero; (*row, line*) primero; **in ~ (of)** delante (de); **front door** *n* puerta principal; **frontier** ['frʌntɪə*] *n* frontera; **front page** *n* primera plana; **front-wheel drive** *n* tracción *f* delantera
frost [frɔst] *n* helada; (*also*: **hoar~**) escarcha; **frostbite** *n* congelación *f*; **frosting** *n* (*esp* US: *icing*) glaseado; **frosty** *adj* (*weather*) de helada; (*welcome etc*) glacial
froth [frɔθ] *n* espuma
frown [fraun] *vi* fruncir el ceño
froze [frəuz] *pt of* **freeze**
frozen ['frəuzn] *pp of* **freeze**
fruit [fru:t] *n inv* fruta; fruto; (*fig*) fruto; resultados *mpl*; **fruit juice** *n* zumo (SP) *or* jugo (LAM) de fruta; **fruit machine** (BRIT) *n* máquina *f* tragaperras; **fruit salad** *n* macedonia (SP) *or* ensalada (LAM) de frutas
frustrate [frʌs'treɪt] *vt* frustrar; **frustrated** *adj* frustrado
fry [fraɪ] (*pt, pp* **fried**) *vt* freír; **small ~** gente *f* menuda; **frying pan** *n* sartén *f*
ft. *abbr* = **foot; feet**
fudge [fʌdʒ] *n* (*Culin*) *caramelo blando*
fuel [fjuəl] *n* (*for heating*) combustible *m*; (*coal*) carbón *m*; (*wood*) leña; (*for engine*) carburante *m*; **fuel tank** *n* depósito (de combustible)
fulfil [ful'fɪl] *vt* (*function*) cumplir con; (*condition*) satisfacer; (*wish, desire*) realizar
full [ful] *adj* lleno; (*fig*) pleno; (*complete*) completo; (*maximum*) máximo; (*information*) detallado; (*price*) íntegro; (*skirt*) amplio ▷ *adv*: **to know ~ well that** saber perfectamente que; **I'm ~ (up)** no puedo más; **~ employment** pleno empleo; **a ~ two hours** dos horas completas; **at ~ speed** a máxima velocidad; **in ~** (*reproduce, quote*) íntegramente; **full-length** *adj* (*novel etc*) entero; (*coat*) largo; (*portrait*) de cuerpo entero; **full moon** *n* luna llena; **full-scale** *adj* (*attack, war*) en gran escala; (*model*) de tamaño natural; **full stop** *n* punto; **full-time** *adj* (*work*) de tiempo completo ▷ *adv*: **to work full-time** trabajar a tiempo completo; **fully** *adv* completamente; (*at least*) por lo menos
fumble ['fʌmbl] *vi*: **to ~ with** manejar torpemente
fume [fju:m] *vi* (*rage*) estar furioso; **fumes** *npl* humo, gases *mpl*
fun [fʌn] *n* (*amusement*) diversión *f*; **to have ~** divertirse; **for ~** en broma; **to make ~ of** burlarse de
function ['fʌŋkʃən] *n* función *f* ▷ *vi* funcionar
fund [fʌnd] *n* fondo; (*reserve*) reserva; **funds** *npl* (*money*) fondos *mpl*
fundamental [fʌndə'mɛntl] *adj* fundamental
funeral ['fju:nərəl] *n* (*burial*) entierro; (*ceremony*) funerales *mpl*; **funeral director** *n* director(a) *m/f* de pompas fúnebres; **funeral parlour** (BRIT) *n* funeraria
funfair ['fʌnfɛə*] (BRIT) *n* parque *m* de atracciones
fungus ['fʌŋgəs] (*pl* **fungi**) *n* hongo; (*mould*) moho
funnel ['fʌnl] *n* embudo; (*of ship*) chimenea
funny ['fʌnɪ] *adj* gracioso, divertido; (*strange*) curioso, raro
fur [fə:*] *n* piel *f*; (BRIT: *in kettle etc*) sarro; **fur coat** *n* abrigo de pieles
furious ['fjuərɪəs] *adj* furioso; (*effort*) violento
furnish ['fə:nɪʃ] *vt* amueblar; (*supply*) suministrar; (*information*) facilitar; **furnishings** *npl* muebles *mpl*
furniture ['fə:nɪtʃə*] *n* muebles *mpl*; **piece of ~** mueble *m*
furry ['fə:rɪ] *adj* peludo
further ['fə:ðə*] *adj* (*new*) nuevo, adicional ▷ *adv* más lejos; (*more*) más; (*moreover*) además ▷ *vt* promover, adelantar; **further education** *n* educación *f* superior; **furthermore** *adv* además
furthest ['fə:ðɪst] *superlative of* **far**
fury ['fjuərɪ] *n* furia
fuse [fju:z] (US **fuze**) *n* fusible *m*; (*for bomb etc*) mecha ▷ *vt* (*metal*) fundir; (*fig*) fusionar ▷ *vi* fundirse; fusionarse; (BRIT *Elec*): **to ~ the lights** fundir los plomos; **fuse box** *n* caja de fusibles
fusion ['fju:ʒən] *n* fusión *f*

fuss [fʌs] *n* (*excitement*) conmoción *f*; (*trouble*) alboroto; **to make a ~** armar un lío *or* jaleo; **to make a ~ of sb** mimar a algn; **fussy** *adj* (*person*) exigente; (*too ornate*) recargado

future ['fju:tʃə*] *adj* futuro; (*coming*) venidero ▷ *n* futuro; (*prospects*) porvenir *m*; **in ~** de ahora en adelante; **futures** *npl* (*Comm*) operaciones *fpl* a término, futuros *mpl*

fuze [fju:z] (US) = **fuse**

fuzzy ['fʌzɪ] *adj* (*Phot*) borroso; (*hair*) muy rizado

g

G [dʒi:] *n* (*Mus*) sol *m*

g. *abbr* (= *gram(s)*) gr.

gadget ['gædʒɪt] *n* aparato

Gaelic ['geɪlɪk] *adj, n* (*Ling*) gaélico

gag [gæg] *n* (*on mouth*) mordaza; (*joke*) chiste *m* ▷ *vt* amordazar

gain [geɪn] *n*: **~ (in)** aumento (de); (*profit*) ganancia ▷ *vt* ganar ▷ *vi* (*watch*) adelantarse; **to ~ from/by sth** sacar provecho de algo; **to ~ on sb** ganar terreno a algn; **to ~ 3 lbs (in weight)** engordar 3 libras

gal. *abbr* = **gallon**

gala ['gɑ:lə] *n* fiesta

galaxy ['gæləksɪ] *n* galaxia

gale [geɪl] *n* (*wind*) vendaval *m*

gall bladder ['gɔ:l-] *n* vesícula biliar

gallery ['gælərɪ] *n* (*also*: **art ~**: *public*) pinacoteca; (: *private*) galería de arte; (*for spectators*) tribuna

gallon ['gæln] *n* galón *m* (*BRIT* = 4,546 *litros*, *US* = 3,785 *litros*)

gallop ['gæləp] *n* galope *m* ▷ *vi* galopar

gallstone ['gɔ:lstəun] *n* cálculo biliario

gamble ['gæmbl] *n* (*risk*) riesgo ▷ *vt* jugar, apostar ▷ *vi* (*take a risk*) jugárselas; (*bet*) apostar; **to ~ on** apostar a; (*success etc*) contar con; **gambler** *n* jugador(a) *m/f*; **gambling** *n* juego

game [geɪm] *n* juego; (*match*) partido; (*of cards*) partida; (*Hunting*) caza ▷ *adj* (*willing*): **to be ~ for anything** atreverse a todo; **big ~** caza mayor (*contest*) juegos; (BRIT: *Scol*) deportes *mpl*; **games console** [geɪmz-] *n* consola de juegos; **game show** *n* programa *m* concurso *m*, concurso

gammon ['gæmən] *n* (*bacon*) tocino ahumado; (*ham*) jamón *m* ahumado

gang [gæŋ] *n* (*of criminals*) pandilla; (*of friends etc*) grupo; (*of workmen*) brigada

gangster ['gæŋstə*] *n* gángster *m*

gap [gæp] *n* vacío (SP), hueco (LAM);

(*in trees, traffic*) claro; (*in time*) intervalo; (*difference*): **~ (between)** diferencia (entre)

gape [geɪp] *vi* mirar boquiabierto; (*shirt etc*) abrirse (completamente)

gap year *n* año sabático (antes de empezar a estudiar en la universidad)

garage ['gærɑ:ʒ] *n* garaje *m*; (*for repairs*) taller *m*; **garage sale** *n* venta de objetos usados (*en el jardín de una casa particular*)

garbage ['gɑ:bɪdʒ] (US) *n* basura; (*inf: nonsense*) tonterías *fpl*; **garbage can** *n* cubo *or* bote *m* (MEX) *or* tacho (SC) de la basura; **garbage collector** (US) *n* basurero/a

garden ['gɑ:dn] *n* jardín *m*; **gardens** *npl* (*park*) parque *m*; **garden centre** (BRIT) *n* centro de jardinería; **gardener** *n* jardinero/a; **gardening** *n* jardinería

garlic ['gɑ:lɪk] *n* ajo

garment ['gɑ:mənt] *n* prenda (de vestir)

garnish ['gɑ:nɪʃ] *vt* (*Culin*) aderezar

garrison ['gærɪsn] *n* guarnición *f*

gas [gæs] *n* gas *m*; (*fuel*) combustible *m*; (*US: gasoline*) gasolina ▷*vt* asfixiar con gas; **gas cooker** (BRIT) *n* cocina de gas; **gas cylinder** *n* bombona de gas; **gas fire** *n* estufa de gas

gasket ['gæskɪt] *n* (*Aut*) junta de culata

gasoline ['gæsəli:n] (US) *n* gasolina

gasp [gɑ:sp] *n* boqueada; (*of shock etc*) grito sofocado ▷*vi* (*pant*) jadear

gas: gas pedal *n* (*esp US*) acelerador *m*; **gas station** (US) *n* gasolinera; **gas tank** (US) *n* (*Aut*) depósito (de gasolina)

gate [geɪt] *n* puerta; (*iron gate*) verja

gateau ['gætəu] (*pl* **~x**) *n* tarta

gatecrash ['geɪtkræʃ] (BRIT) *vt* colarse en

gateway ['geɪtweɪ] *n* puerta

gather ['gæðə*] *vt* (*flowers, fruit*) coger (SP), recoger; (*assemble*) reunir; (*pick up*) recoger; (*Sewing*) fruncir; (*understand*) entender ▷*vi* (*assemble*) reunirse; **to ~ speed** ganar velocidad; **gathering** *n* reunión *f*, asamblea

gauge [geɪdʒ] *n* (*instrument*) indicador *m* ▷*vt* medir; (*fig*) juzgar

gave [geɪv] *pt of* **give**

gay [geɪ] *adj* (*homosexual*) gay; (*joyful*) alegre; (*colour*) vivo

gaze [geɪz] *n* mirada fija ▷*vi*: **to ~ at sth** mirar algo fijamente

GB *abbr* = **Great Britain**

GCSE (BRIT) *n abbr* (= *General Certificate of Secondary Education*) *examen de reválida que se hace a los 16 años*

gear [gɪə*] *n* equipo, herramientas *fpl*; (*Tech*) engranaje *m*; (*Aut*) velocidad *f*, marcha ▷*vt* (*fig: adapt*): **to ~ sth to** adaptar *or* ajustar algo a; **top** *or* **high** (US)**/low ~** cuarta/primera velocidad; **in ~** en marcha; **gear up** *vi* prepararse; **gear box** *n* caja de cambios; **gear lever** *n* palanca de cambio; **gear shift** (US) *n* = **gear lever**; **gear stick** *n* (BRIT) palanca de cambios

geese [gi:s] *npl of* **goose**

gel [dʒɛl] *n* gel *m*

gem [dʒɛm] *n* piedra preciosa

Gemini ['dʒɛmɪnaɪ] *n* Géminis *m*, Gemelos *mpl*

gender ['dʒɛndə*] *n* género

gene [dʒi:n] *n* gen(e) *m*

general ['dʒɛnərl] *n* general *m* ▷*adj* general; **in ~** en general; **general anaesthetic** (US **general anesthetic**) *n* anestesia general; **general election** *n* elecciones *fpl* generales; **generalize** *vi* generalizar; **generally** *adv* generalmente, en general; **general practitioner** *n* médico general; **general store** *n* tienda (*que vende de todo*) (LAM, SP), almacén *m* (SC, SP)

generate ['dʒɛnəreɪt] *vt* (*Elec*) generar; (*jobs, profits*) producir

generation [dʒɛnə'reɪʃən] *n* generación *f*

generator ['dʒɛnəreɪtə*] *n* generador *m*

generosity [dʒɛnə'rɔsɪtɪ] *n* generosidad *f*

generous ['dʒɛnərəs] *adj* generoso

genetic [dʒɪ'nɛtɪk] *adj*: **~ engineering** ingeniería genética; **~ fingerprinting** identificación *f* genética; **genetically modified** *adj* transgénico; **genetics** *n* genética

genitals ['dʒɛnɪtlz] *npl* (órganos *mpl*) genitales *mpl*

genius ['dʒi:nɪəs] *n* genio

genome ['gi:nəum] *n* genoma *m*

gent [dʒɛnt] *n abbr* (BRIT *inf*) = **gentleman**

gentle ['dʒɛntl] *adj* apacible, dulce; (*animal*) manso; (*breeze, curve etc*) suave

> Be careful not to translate **gentle** by the Spanish word *gentil*.

gentleman ['dʒɛntlmən] (*irreg*) *n* señor *m*; (*well-bred man*) caballero

gently ['dʒɛntlɪ] *adv* dulcemente; suavemente

gents [dʒɛnts] *n* aseos *mpl* (de caballeros)

genuine ['dʒɛnjuɪn] *adj* auténtico; (*person*) sincero; **genuinely** *adv* sinceramente

geographic(al) [dʒɪə'græfɪk(l)] *adj* geográfico

geography [dʒɪ'ɔgrəfɪ] *n* geografía

geology [dʒɪ'ɔlədʒɪ] *n* geología

geometry [dʒɪ'ɔmətrɪ] *n* geometría

geranium [dʒɪ'reɪnjəm] *n* geranio

geriatric [dʒɛrɪ'ætrɪk] *adj, n* geriátrico/a *m/f*

germ [dʒəːm] *n* (*microbe*) microbio, bacteria; (*seed, fig*) germen *m*
German ['dʒəːmən] *adj* alemán/ana ▷ *n* alemán/ana *m/f*; (*Ling*) alemán *m*; **German measles** *n* rubéola
Germany ['dʒəːmənɪ] *n* Alemania
gesture ['dʒɛstjə*] *n* gesto; (*symbol*) muestra

KEYWORD

get [gɛt] (*pt, pp* **got**, *pp* **gotten** (*US*)) *vi*
1 (*become, be*) ponerse, volverse; **to get old/tired** envejecer/cansarse; **to get drunk** emborracharse; **to get dirty** ensuciarse; **to get married** casarse; **when do I get paid?** ¿cuándo me pagan *or* se me paga?; **it's getting late** se está haciendo tarde
2 (*go*): **to get to/from** llegar a/de; **to get home** llegar a casa
3 (*begin*) empezar a; **to get to know sb** (llegar a) conocer a algn; **I'm getting to like him** me está empezando a gustar; **let's get going** *or* **started** ¡vamos (a empezar)!
4 (*modal aux vb*): **you've got to do it** tienes que hacerlo
▷ *vt* 1: **to get sth done** (*finish*) terminar algo; (*have done*) mandar hacer algo; **to get one's hair cut** cortarse el pelo; **to get the car going** *or* **to go** arrancar el coche; **to get sb to do sth** conseguir *or* hacer que algn haga algo; **to get sth/sb ready** preparar algo/a algn
2 (*obtain: money, permission, results*) conseguir; (*find: job, flat*) encontrar; (*fetch: person, doctor*) buscar; (*object*) ir a buscar, traer; **to get sth for sb** conseguir algo para algn; **get me Mr Jones, please** (*Tel*) póngame (*SP*) *or* comuníqueme (*LAM*) con el Sr. Jones, por favor; **can I get you a drink?** ¿quieres algo de beber?
3 (*receive: present, letter*) recibir; (*acquire: reputation*) alcanzar; (*: prize*) ganar; **what did you get for your birthday?** ¿qué te regalaron por tu cumpleaños?; **how much did you get for the painting?** ¿cuánto sacaste por el cuadro?
4 (*catch*) coger (*SP*), agarrar (*LAM*); (*hit: target etc*) dar en; **to get sb by the arm/throat** coger *or* agarrar a algn por el brazo/cuello; **get him!** ¡cógelo! (*SP*), ¡atrápalo! (*LAM*); **the bullet got him in the leg** la bala le dio en la pierna
5 (*take, move*) llevar; **to get sth to sb** hacer llegar algo a algn; **do you think we'll get it through the door?** ¿crees que lo podremos meter por la puerta?
6 (*catch, take: plane, bus etc*) coger (*SP*), tomar (*LAM*); **where do I get the train for Birmingham?** ¿dónde se coge *or* se toma el tren para Birmingham?
7 (*understand*) entender; (*hear*) oír; **I've got it!** ¡ya lo tengo!, ¡eureka!; **I don't get your meaning** no te entiendo; **I'm sorry, I didn't get your name** lo siento, no cogí tu nombre
8 (*have, possess*): **to have got** tener
get away *vi* marcharse; (*escape*) escaparse
get away with *vt fus* hacer impunemente
get back *vi* (*return*) volver ▷ *vt* recobrar
get in *vi* entrar; (*train*) llegar; (*arrive home*) volver a casa, regresar
get into *vt fus* entrar en; (*vehicle*) subir a; **to get into a rage** enfadarse
get off *vi* (*from train etc*) bajar; (*depart: person, car*) marcharse ▷ *vt* (*remove*) quitar ▷ *vt fus* (*train, bus*) bajar de
get on *vi* (*at exam etc*): **how are you getting on?** ¿cómo te va?; (*agree*): **to get on (with)** llevarse bien (con) ▷ *vt fus* subir a
get out *vi* salir; (*of vehicle*) bajar ▷ *vt* sacar
get out of *vt fus* salir de; (*duty etc*) escaparse de
get over *vt fus* (*illness*) recobrarse de
get through *vi* (*Tel*) (lograr) comunicarse
get up *vi* (*rise*) levantarse ▷ *vt fus* subir

getaway ['gɛtəweɪ] *n* fuga
Ghana ['gɑːnə] *n* Ghana
ghastly ['gɑːstlɪ] *adj* horrible
ghetto ['gɛtəu] *n* gueto
ghost [gəust] *n* fantasma *m*
giant ['dʒaɪənt] *n* gigante *mf* ▷ *adj* gigantesco, gigante
gift [gɪft] *n* regalo; (*ability*) talento; **gifted** *adj* dotado; **gift shop** (*US* **gift store**) *n* tienda de regalos; **gift token, gift voucher** *n* vale *m* canjeable por un regalo
gig [gɪg] *n* (*inf: concert*) actuación *f*
gigabyte ['dʒɪgəbaɪt] *n* gigabyte *m*
gigantic [dʒaɪ'gæntɪk] *adj* gigantesco
giggle ['gɪgl] *vi* reírse tontamente
gills [gɪlz] *npl* (*of fish*) branquias *fpl*, agallas *fpl*
gilt [gɪlt] *adj, n* dorado
gimmick ['gɪmɪk] *n* truco
gin [dʒɪn] *n* ginebra
ginger ['dʒɪndʒə*] *n* jengibre *m*
gipsy ['dʒɪpsɪ] *n* = **gypsy**
giraffe [dʒɪ'rɑːf] *n* jirafa
girl [gəːl] *n* (*small*) niña; (*young woman*) chica, joven *f*, muchacha; (*daughter*) hija; **an English ~** una (chica) inglesa; **girl band** *n* girl band *m* (*grupo musical de chicas*); **girlfriend** *n* (*of girl*) amiga; (*of boy*) novia; **Girl Scout** (*US*) *n* = **Girl Guide**
gist [dʒɪst] *n* lo esencial

g

give [gɪv] (*pt* **gave**, *pp* **given**) *vt* dar; (*deliver*) entregar; (*as gift*) regalar ▷ *vi* (*break*) romperse; (*stretch*: *fabric*) dar de sí; **to ~ sb sth, ~ sth to sb** dar algo a algn; **give away** *vt* (*give free*) regalar; (*betray*) traicionar; (*disclose*) revelar; **give back** *vt* devolver; **give in** *vi* ceder ▷ *vt* entregar; **give out** *vt* distribuir; **give up** *vi* rendirse, darse por vencido ▷ *vt* renunciar a; **to give up smoking** dejar de fumar; **to give o.s. up** entregarse

given ['gɪvn] *pp of* **give** ▷ *adj* (*fixed*: *time, amount*) determinado ▷ *conj*: **~ (that) ...** dado (que) ...; **~ the circumstances ...** dadas las circunstancias ...

glacier ['glæsɪə*] *n* glaciar *m*

glad [glæd] *adj* contento; **gladly** ['-lɪ] *adv* con mucho gusto

glamour ['glæmər] (*US* **glamor**) *n* encanto, atractivo; **glamorous** *adj* encantador(a), atractivo

glance [glɑːns] *n* ojeada, mirada ▷ *vi*: **to ~ at** echar una ojeada a

gland [glænd] *n* glándula

glare [glɛə*] *n* (*of anger*) mirada feroz; (*of light*) deslumbramiento, brillo; **to be in the ~ of publicity** ser el foco de la atención pública ▷ *vi* deslumbrar; **to ~ at** mirar con odio a; **glaring** *adj* (*mistake*) manifiesto

glass [glɑːs] *n* vidrio, cristal *m*; (*for drinking*) vaso; (*: with stem*) copa; **glasses** *npl* (*spectacles*) gafas *fpl*

glaze [gleɪz] *vt* (*window*) poner cristales a; (*pottery*) vidriar ▷ *n* vidriado

gleam [gliːm] *vi* brillar

glen [glɛn] *n* cañada

glide [glaɪd] *vi* deslizarse; (*Aviat*: *birds*) planear; **glider** *n* (*Aviat*) planeador *m*

glimmer ['glɪmə*] *n* luz *f* tenue; (*of interest*) muestra; (*of hope*) rayo

glimpse [glɪmps] *n* vislumbre *m* ▷ *vt* vislumbrar, entrever

glint [glɪnt] *vi* centellear

glisten ['glɪsn] *vi* relucir, brillar

glitter ['glɪtə*] *vi* relucir, brillar

global ['gləubl] *adj* mundial; **globalization** *n* globalización *f*; **global warming** *n* (re)calentamiento global *or* de la tierra

globe [gləub] *n* globo; (*model*) globo terráqueo

gloom [gluːm] *n* oscuridad *f*; (*sadness*) tristeza; **gloomy** *adj* (*dark*) oscuro; (*sad*) triste; (*pessimistic*) pesimista

glorious ['glɔːrɪəs] *adj* glorioso; (*weather etc*) magnífico

glory ['glɔːrɪ] *n* gloria

gloss [glɔs] *n* (*shine*) brillo; (*paint*) pintura de aceite

glossary ['glɔsərɪ] *n* glosario

glossy ['glɔsɪ] *adj* lustroso; (*magazine*) de lujo

glove [glʌv] *n* guante *m*; **glove compartment** *n* (*Aut*) guantera

glow [gləu] *vi* brillar

glucose ['gluːkəus] *n* glucosa

glue [gluː] *n* goma (de pegar), cemento ▷ *vt* pegar

GM *adj abbr* (= *genetically modified*) transgénico

gm *abbr* (= *gram*) g

GMO *n abbr* (= *genetically modified organism*) organismo transgénico

GMT *abbr* (= *Greenwich Mean Time*) GMT

gnaw [nɔː] *vt* roer

go [gəu] (*pt* **went**, *pp* **gone**, *pl* **~es**) *vi* ir; (*travel*) viajar; (*depart*) irse, marcharse; (*work*) funcionar, marchar; (*be sold*) venderse; (*time*) pasar; (*fit, suit*): **to ~ with** hacer juego con; (*become*) ponerse; (*break etc*) estropearse, romperse ▷ *n*: **to have a ~ (at)** probar suerte (con); **to be on the ~** no parar; **whose ~ is it?** ¿a quién le toca?; **he's ~ing to do it** va a hacerlo; **to ~ for a walk** ir de paseo; **to ~ dancing** ir a bailar; **how did it ~?** ¿qué tal salió *or* resultó?, ¿cómo ha ido?; **to ~ round the back** pasar por detrás; **go ahead** *vi* seguir adelante; **go away** *vi* irse, marcharse; **go back** *vi* volver; **go by** *vi* (*time*) pasar ▷ *vt fus* guiarse por; **go down** *vi* bajar; (*ship*) hundirse; (*sun*) ponerse ▷ *vt fus* bajar; **go for** *vt fus* (*fetch*) ir por; (*like*) gustar; (*attack*) atacar; **go in** *vi* entrar; **go into** *vt fus* entrar en; (*investigate*) investigar; (*embark on*) dedicarse a; **go off** *vi* irse, marcharse; (*food*) pasarse; (*explode*) estallar; (*event*) realizarse ▷ *vt fus* dejar de gustar; **I'm going off him/the idea** ya no me gusta tanto él/la idea; **go on** *vi* (*continue*) seguir, continuar; (*happen*) pasar, ocurrir; **to go on doing sth** seguir haciendo algo; **go out** *vi* salir; (*fire, light*) apagarse; **go over** *vi* (*ship*) zozobrar ▷ *vt fus* (*check*) revisar; **go past** *vi, vt fus* pasar; **go round** *vi* (*circulate*: *news, rumour*) correr; (*suffice*) alcanzar, bastar; (*revolve*) girar, dar vueltas; (*visit*): **to go round (to sb's)** pasar a ver (a algn); **to go round (by)** (*make a detour*) dar la vuelta (por); **go through** *vt fus* (*town etc*) atravesar; **go up** *vi, vt fus* subir; **go with** *vt fus* (*accompany*) ir con, acompañar a; **go without** *vt fus* pasarse sin

go-ahead ['gəuəhɛd] *adj* (*person*) dinámico; (*firm*) innovador(a) ▷ *n* luz *f* verde

goal [gəul] *n* meta; (*score*) gol *m*;

goalkeeper *n* portero; **goal-post** *n* poste *m* (de la portería)
goat [gəut] *n* cabra
gobble ['gɔbl] *vt* (*also*: **~ down, ~ up**) tragarse, engullir
God [gɔd] *n* Dios *m*; **godchild** *n* ahijado/a; **goddaughter** *n* ahijada; **goddess** *n* diosa; **godfather** *n* padrino; **godmother** *n* madrina; **godson** *n* ahijado
goggles ['gɔglz] *npl* gafas *fpl*
going ['gəuɪŋ] *n* (*conditions*) estado del terreno ▷ *adj*: **the ~ rate** la tarifa corriente *or* en vigor
gold [gəuld] *n* oro ▷ *adj* de oro; **golden** *adj* (*made of gold*) de oro; (*gold in colour*) dorado; **goldfish** *n* pez *m* de colores; **goldmine** *n* (*also fig*) mina de oro; **gold-plated** *adj* chapado en oro
golf [gɔlf] *n* golf *m*; **golf ball** *n* (*for game*) pelota de golf; (*on typewriter*) esfera; **golf club** *n* club *m* de golf; (*stick*) palo (de golf); **golf course** *n* campo de golf; **golfer** *n* golfista *mf*
gone [gɔn] *pp of* **go**
gong [gɔŋ] *n* gong *m*
good [gud] *adj* bueno; (*pleasant*) agradable; (*kind*) bueno, amable; (*well-behaved*) educado ▷ *n* bien *m*, provecho; **goods** *npl* (*Comm*) mercancías *fpl*; **~!** ¡qué bien!; **to be ~ at** tener aptitud para; **to be ~ for** servir para; **it's ~ for you** te hace bien; **would you be ~ enough to ...?** ¿podría hacerme el favor de ...?, ¿sería tan amable de ...?; **a ~ deal (of)** mucho; **a ~ many** muchos; **to make ~** reparar; **it's no ~ complaining** no vale la pena (de) quejarse; **for ~** para siempre, definitivamente; **~ morning/afternoon!** ¡buenos días/buenas tardes!; **~ evening!** ¡buenas noches!; **~ night!** ¡buenas noches!
goodbye [gud'baɪ] *excl* ¡adiós!; **to say ~ (to)** (*person*) despedirse (de)
good: Good Friday *n* Viernes *m* Santo; **good-looking** *adj* guapo; **good-natured** *adj* amable, simpático; **goodness** *n* (*of person*) bondad *f*; **for goodness sake!** ¡por Dios!; **goodness gracious!** ¡Dios mío!; **goods train** (BRIT) *n* tren *m* de mercancías; **goodwill** *n* buena voluntad *f*
Google® ['gu:gəl] *n* Google® *m* ▷ *vi* hacer búsquedas en Internet ▷ *vt* buscar información en Internet sobre
goose [gu:s] (*pl* **geese**) *n* ganso, oca
gooseberry ['guzbərɪ] *n* grosella espinosa; **to play ~** hacer de carabina
goose bumps, goose pimples *npl* carne *f* de gallina
gorge [gɔ:dʒ] *n* barranco ▷ *vr*: **to ~ o.s. (on)** atracarse (de)
gorgeous ['gɔ:dʒəs] *adj* (*thing*) precioso; (*weather*) espléndido; (*person*) guapísimo
gorilla [gə'rɪlə] *n* gorila *m*
gosh [gɔʃ] (*inf*) *excl* ¡cielos!
gospel ['gɔspl] *n* evangelio
gossip ['gɔsɪp] *n* (*scandal*) cotilleo, chismes *mpl*; (*chat*) charla; (*scandalmonger*) cotilla *m/f*, chismoso/a ▷ *vi* cotillear; **gossip column** *n* ecos *mpl* de sociedad
got [gɔt] *pt, pp of* **get**
gotten (US) ['gɔtn] *pp of* **get**
gourmet ['guəmeɪ] *n* gastrónomo/a *m/f*
govern ['gʌvən] *vt* gobernar; (*influence*) dominar; **government** *n* gobierno; **governor** *n* gobernador(a) *m/f*; (*of school etc*) miembro del consejo; (*of jail*) director(a) *m/f*
gown [gaun] *n* traje *m*; (*of teacher*, BRIT: *of judge*) toga
G.P. *n abbr* = **general practitioner**
grab [græb] *vt* coger (SP), agarrar (LAM), arrebatar ▷ *vi*: **to ~ at** intentar agarrar
grace [greɪs] *n* gracia ▷ *vt* honrar; (*adorn*) adornar; **5 days' ~** un plazo de 5 días; **graceful** *adj* grácil, ágil; (*style, shape*) elegante, gracioso; **gracious** ['greɪʃəs] *adj* amable
grade [greɪd] *n* (*quality*) clase *f*, calidad *f*; (*in hierarchy*) grado; (*Scol: mark*) nota; (US: *school class*) curso ▷ *vt* clasificar; **grade crossing** (US) *n* paso a nivel; **grade school** (US) *n* escuela primaria
gradient ['greɪdɪənt] *n* pendiente *f*
gradual ['grædjuəl] *adj* paulatino; **gradually** *adv* paulatinamente
graduate [*n* 'grædjuɪt, *vb* 'grædjueɪt] *n* (US: *of high school*) graduado/a; (*of university*) licenciado/a ▷ *vi* graduarse; licenciarse; **graduation** [-'eɪʃən] *n* (*ceremony*) entrega del título
graffiti [grə'fi:tɪ] *n* pintadas *fpl*
graft [grɑ:ft] *n* (*Agr, Med*) injerto; (BRIT: *inf*) trabajo duro; (*bribery*) corrupción *f* ▷ *vt* injertar
grain [greɪn] *n* (*single particle*) grano; (*corn*) granos *mpl*, cereales *mpl*; (*of wood*) fibra
gram [græm] *n* gramo
grammar ['græmə*] *n* gramática; **grammar school** (BRIT) *n* ≈ instituto de segunda enseñanza, liceo (SP)
gramme [græm] *n* = **gram**
gran [græn] (*inf*) *n* (BRIT) abuelita
grand [grænd] *adj* magnífico, imponente; (*wonderful*) estupendo; (*gesture etc*) grandioso; **grandad** (*inf*) *n* = **granddad**; **grandchild** (*pl* **grandchildren**) *n* nieto/a *m/f*; **granddad** (*inf*) *n* yayo, abuelito;

granddaughter *n* nieta; **grandfather** *n* abuelo; **grandma** (*inf*) *n* yaya, abuelita; **grandmother** *n* abuela; **grandpa** (*inf*) *n* = **granddad**; **grandparents** *npl* abuelos *mpl*; **grand piano** *n* piano de cola; **Grand Prix** ['grɑ̃:'pri:] *n* (*Aut*) gran premio, Grand Prix *m*; **grandson** *n* nieto

granite ['grænɪt] *n* granito

granny ['grænɪ] (*inf*) *n* abuelita, yaya

grant [grɑ:nt] *vt* (*concede*) conceder; (*admit*) reconocer ▷ *n* (*Scol*) beca; (*Admin*) subvención *f*; **to take sth/sb for ~ed** dar algo por sentado/no hacer ningún caso a algn

grape [greɪp] *n* uva

grapefruit ['greɪpfru:t] *n* pomelo (SP, SC), toronja (LAM)

graph [grɑ:f] *n* gráfica; **graphic** ['græfɪk] *adj* gráfico; **graphics** *n* artes *fpl* gráficas ▷ *npl* (*drawings*) dibujos *mpl*

grasp [grɑ:sp] *vt* agarrar, asir; (*understand*) comprender ▷ *n* (*grip*) asimiento; (*understanding*) comprensión *f*

grass [grɑ:s] *n* hierba; (*lawn*) césped *m*; **grasshopper** *n* saltamontes *m inv*

grate [greɪt] *n* parrilla de chimenea ▷ *vi*: **to ~ (on)** chirriar (sobre) ▷ *vt* (*Culin*) rallar

grateful ['greɪtful] *adj* agradecido

grater ['greɪtə*] *n* rallador *m*

gratitude ['grætɪtju:d] *n* agradecimiento

grave [greɪv] *n* tumba ▷ *adj* serio, grave

gravel ['grævl] *n* grava

gravestone ['greɪvstəun] *n* lápida

graveyard ['greɪvjɑ:d] *n* cementerio

gravity ['grævɪtɪ] *n* gravedad *f*

gravy ['greɪvɪ] *n* salsa de carne

gray [greɪ] *adj* = **grey**

graze [greɪz] *vi* pacer ▷ *vt* (*touch lightly*) rozar; (*scrape*) raspar ▷ *n* (*Med*) abrasión *f*

grease [gri:s] *n* (*fat*) grasa; (*lubricant*) lubricante *m* ▷ *vt* engrasar; lubrificar; **greasy** *adj* grasiento

great [greɪt] *adj* grande; (*inf*) magnífico, estupendo; **Great Britain** *n* Gran Bretaña; **great-grandfather** *n* bisabuelo; **great-grandmother** *n* bisabuela; **greatly** *adv* muy; (*with verb*) mucho

Greece [gri:s] *n* Grecia

greed [gri:d] *n* (*also*: **~iness**) codicia, avaricia; (*for food*) gula; (*for power etc*) avidez *f*; **greedy** *adj* avaro; (*for food*) glotón/ona

Greek [gri:k] *adj* griego ▷ *n* griego/a; (*Ling*) griego

green [gri:n] *adj* (*also Pol*) verde; (*inexperienced*) novato ▷ *n* verde *m*; (*stretch of grass*) césped *m*; (*Golf*) green; *m* **greens** *npl* (*vegetables*) verduras *fpl*; **green card** *n* (*Aut*) carta verde; (*US*: *work permit*) *permiso de trabajo para los extranjeros en EE. UU.*; **greengage** *n* (ciruela) claudia; **greengrocer** (BRIT) *n* verdulero/a; **greenhouse** *n* invernadero; **greenhouse effect** *n* efecto invernadero

Greenland ['gri:nlənd] *n* Groenlandia

green salad *n* ensalada *f* (*de lechuga, pepino, pimiento verde, etc*)

greet [gri:t] *vt* (*welcome*) dar la bienvenida a; (*receive*: *news*) recibir; **greeting** *n* (*welcome*) bienvenida; **greeting(s) card** *n* tarjeta de felicitación

grew [gru:] *pt of* **grow**

grey [greɪ] (*US* **gray**) *adj* gris; (*weather*) sombrío; **grey-haired** *adj* canoso; **greyhound** *n* galgo

grid [grɪd] *n* reja; (*Elec*) red *f*; **gridlock** *n* (*traffic jam*) retención *f*

grief [gri:f] *n* dolor *m*, pena

grievance ['gri:vəns] *n* motivo de queja, agravio

grieve [gri:v] *vi* afligirse, acongojarse ▷ *vt* dar pena a; **to ~ for** llorar por

grill [grɪl] *n* (*on cooker*) parrilla; (*also*: **mixed ~**) parillada ▷ *vt* (BRIT) asar a la parrilla; (*inf*: *question*) interrogar

grille [grɪl] *n* reja; (*Aut*) rejilla

grim [grɪm] *adj* (*place*) sombrío; (*situation*) triste; (*person*) ceñudo

grime [graɪm] *n* mugre *f*, suciedad *f*

grin [grɪn] *n* sonrisa abierta ▷ *vi* sonreír abiertamente

grind [graɪnd] (*pt, pp* **ground**) *vt* (*coffee, pepper etc*) moler; (*US*: *meat*) picar; (*make sharp*) afilar ▷ *n* (*work*) rutina

grip [grɪp] *n* (*hold*) asimiento; (*control*) control *m*, dominio; (*of tyre etc*): **to have a good/bad ~** agarrarse bien/mal; (*handle*) asidero; (*holdall*) maletín *m* ▷ *vt* agarrar; (*viewer, reader*) fascinar; **to get to ~s with** enfrentarse con; **gripping** *adj* absorbente

grit [grɪt] *n* gravilla; (*courage*) valor *m* ▷ *vt* (*road*) poner gravilla en; **to ~ one's teeth** apretar los dientes

grits [grɪts] (*US*) *npl* maíz *msg* a medio moler

groan [grəun] *n* gemido; quejido ▷ *vi* gemir; quejarse

grocer ['grəusə*] *n* tendero (de ultramarinos (SP)); **groceries** *npl* comestibles *mpl*; **grocer's (shop)** *n* tienda de comestibles *or* (MEX, CAM) abarrotes, almacén (SC); **grocery** *n* (*shop*) tienda de ultramarinos

groin [grɔɪn] *n* ingle *f*

groom [gru:m] *n* mozo/a de cuadra; (*also*: **bride~**) novio ▷ *vt* (*horse*) almohazar;

(*fig*): **to ~ sb for** preparar a algn para; **well-~ed** de buena presencia
groove [gru:v] *n* ranura, surco
grope [grəup] *vi*: **to ~ for** buscar a tientas
gross [grəus] *adj* (*neglect, injustice*) grave; (*vulgar: behaviour*) grosero; (: *appearance*) de mal gusto; (*Comm*) bruto; **grossly** *adv* (*greatly*) enormemente
grotesque [grə'tɛsk] *adj* grotesco
ground [graund] *pt, pp of* **grind** ▷ *n* suelo, tierra; (*Sport*) campo, terreno; (*reason: gen pl*) causa, razón *f*; (*US: also*: **~ wire**) tierra ▷ *vt* (*plane*) mantener en tierra; (*US Elec*) conectar con tierra; **grounds** *npl* (*of coffee etc*) poso; (*gardens etc*) jardines *mpl*, parque *m*; **on the ~** en el suelo; **to the ~** al suelo; **to gain/lose ~** ganar/perder terreno; **ground floor** *n* (BRIT) planta baja; **groundsheet** (BRIT) *n* tela impermeable; suelo; **groundwork** *n* preparación *f*
group [gru:p] *n* grupo; (*musical*) conjunto ▷ *vt* (*also*: **~ together**) agrupar ▷ *vi* (*also*: **~ together**) agruparse
grouse [graus] *n inv* (*bird*) urogallo ▷ *vi* (*complain*) quejarse
grovel ['grɔvl] *vi* (*fig*): **to ~ before** humillarse ante
grow [grəu] (*pt* **grew**, *pp* **grown**) *vi* crecer; (*increase*) aumentar; (*expand*) desarrollarse; (*become*) volverse; **to ~ rich/weak** enriquecerse/debilitarse ▷ *vt* cultivar; (*hair, beard*) dejar crecer; **grow on** *vt fus*: **that painting is growing on me** ese cuadro me gusta cada vez más; **grow up** *vi* crecer, hacerse hombre/mujer
growl [graul] *vi* gruñir
grown [grəun] *pp of* **grow**; **grown-up** *n* adulto/a, mayor *mf*
growth [grəuθ] *n* crecimiento, desarrollo; (*what has grown*) brote *m*; (*Med*) tumor *m*
grub [grʌb] *n* larva, gusano; (*inf: food*) comida
grubby ['grʌbɪ] *adj* sucio, mugriento
grudge [grʌdʒ] *n* (motivo de) rencor *m* ▷ *vt*: **to ~ sb sth** dar algo a algn de mala gana; **to bear sb a ~** guardar rencor a algn
gruelling ['gruəlɪŋ] (*US* **grueling**) *adj* penoso, duro
gruesome ['gru:səm] *adj* horrible
grumble ['grʌmbl] *vi* refunfuñar, quejarse
grumpy ['grʌmpɪ] *adj* gruñón/ona
grunt [grʌnt] *vi* gruñir
guarantee [gærən'ti:] *n* garantía ▷ *vt* garantizar
guard [gɑ:d] *n* (*squad*) guardia; (*one man*) guardia *mf*; (BRIT *Rail*) jefe *m* de tren; (*on machine*) dispositivo de seguridad; (*also*: **fire~**) rejilla de protección ▷ *vt* guardar; (*prisoner*) vigilar; **to be on one's ~** estar alerta; **guardian** *n* guardián/ana *m/f*; (*of minor*) tutor(a) *m/f*
guerrilla [gə'rɪlə] *n* guerrillero/a
guess [gɛs] *vi* adivinar; (*US*) suponer ▷ *vt* adivinar; suponer ▷ *n* suposición *f*, conjetura; **to take** *or* **have a ~** tratar de adivinar
guest [gɛst] *n* invitado/a; (*in hotel*) huésped *mf*; **guest house** *n* casa de huéspedes, pensión *f*; **guest room** *n* cuarto de huéspedes
guidance ['gaɪdəns] *n* (*advice*) consejos *mpl*
guide [gaɪd] *n* (*person*) guía *mf*; (*book, fig*) guía; (*also*: **Girl ~**) guía ▷ *vt* (*round museum etc*) guiar; (*lead*) conducir; (*direct*) orientar; **guidebook** *n* guía; **guide dog** *n* perro *m* guía; **guided tour** *n* visita *f* con guía; **guidelines** *npl* (*advice*) directrices *fpl*
guild [gɪld] *n* gremio
guilt [gɪlt] *n* culpabilidad *f*; **guilty** *adj* culpable
guinea pig ['gɪnɪ-] *n* cobaya; (*fig*) conejillo de Indias
guitar [gɪ'tɑ:*] *n* guitarra; **guitarist** *n* guitarrista *m/f*
gulf [gʌlf] *n* golfo; (*abyss*) abismo
gull [gʌl] *n* gaviota
gulp [gʌlp] *vi* tragar saliva ▷ *vt* (*also*: **~ down**) tragarse
gum [gʌm] *n* (*Anat*) encía; (*glue*) goma, cemento; (*sweet*) caramelo de goma; (*also*: **chewing-~**) chicle *m* ▷ *vt* pegar con goma
gun [gʌn] *n* (*small*) pistola, revólver *m*; (*shotgun*) escopeta; (*rifle*) fusil *m*; (*cannon*) cañón *m*; **gunfire** *n* disparos *mpl*; **gunman** (*irreg*) *n* pistolero; **gunpoint** *n*: **at gunpoint** a mano armada; **gunpowder** *n* pólvora; **gunshot** *n* escopetazo
gush [gʌʃ] *vi* salir a raudales; (*person*) deshacerse en efusiones
gust [gʌst] *n* (*of wind*) ráfaga
gut [gʌt] *n* intestino; **guts** *npl* (*Anat*) tripas *fpl*; (*courage*) valor *m*
gutter ['gʌtə*] *n* (*of roof*) canalón *m*; (*in street*) cuneta
guy [gaɪ] *n* (*also*: **~rope**) cuerda; (*inf: man*) tío (SP), tipo; (*figure*) monigote *m*
Guy Fawkes' Night [gaɪ'fɔ:ks-] *n* ver abajo

GUY FAWKES' NIGHT

La noche del cinco de noviembre, **Guy Fawkes' Night**, se celebra en el Reino Unido el fracaso de la conspiración de la pólvora ("Gunpowder Plot"), un intento fallido de volar el parlamento de Jaime I en 1605. Esa noche se lanzan fuegos artificiales y se hacen hogueras en las que se queman unos muñecos de trapo que representan a **Guy Fawkes**, uno de los cabecillas de la revuelta. Días antes, los niños tienen por costumbre pedir a los transeúntes "a penny for the guy", dinero que emplean en comprar cohetes y petardos.

gym [dʒɪm] *n* gimnasio; **gymnasium** *n* gimnasio *mf*; **gymnast** *n* gimnasta *mf*; **gymnastics** *n* gimnasia; **gym shoes** *npl* zapatillas *fpl* (de deporte)

gynaecologist [gaɪnɪ'kɔlədʒɪst] (US **gynecologist**) *n* ginecólogo/a

gypsy ['dʒɪpsɪ] *n* gitano/a

haberdashery [hæbə'dæʃərɪ] (BRIT) *n* mercería

habit ['hæbɪt] *n* hábito, costumbre *f*; (*drug habit*) adicción *f*; (*costume*) hábito

habitat ['hæbɪtæt] *n* hábitat *m*

hack [hæk] *vt* (*cut*) cortar; (*slice*) tajar ▷ *n* (*pej*: *writer*) escritor(a) *m/f* a sueldo; **hacker** *n* (*Comput*) pirata *mf* informático/a

had [hæd] *pt, pp of* **have**

haddock ['hædək] (*pl* ~ *or* **~s**) *n* *especie de merluza*

hadn't ['hædnt] = **had not**

haemorrhage ['hɛmərɪdʒ] (US **hemorrhage**) *n* hemorragia

haemorrhoids ['hɛmərɔɪdz] (US **hemorrhoids**) *npl* hemorroides *fpl*

haggle ['hægl] *vi* regatear

Hague [heɪg] *n*: **The ~** La Haya

hail [heɪl] *n* granizo; (*fig*) lluvia ▷ *vt* saludar; (*taxi*) llamar a; (*acclaim*) aclamar ▷ *vi* granizar; **hailstone** *n* (piedra de) granizo

hair [hɛə*] *n* pelo, cabellos *mpl*; (*one hair*) pelo, cabello; (*on legs etc*) vello; **to do one's ~** arreglarse el pelo; **to have grey ~** tener canas *fpl*; **hairband** *n* cinta; **hairbrush** *n* cepillo (para el pelo); **haircut** *n* corte *m* (de pelo); **hairdo** *n* peinado; **hairdresser** *n* peluquero/a; **hairdresser's** *n* peluquería; **hair dryer** *n* secador *m* de pelo; **hair gel** *n* fijador; **hair spray** *n* laca; **hairstyle** *n* peinado; **hairy** *adj* peludo; velludo; (*inf*: *frightening*) espeluznante

hake [heɪk] (*pl* ~ *or* **~s**) *n* merluza

half [hɑːf] (*pl* **halves**) *n* mitad *f*; (*of beer*) ≈ caña (SP), media pinta; (*Rail, Bus*) billete *m* de niño ▷ *adj* medio ▷ *adv* medio, a medias; **two and a ~** dos y media; **~ a dozen** media docena; **~ a pound** media libra; **to cut sth in ~** cortar algo por la mitad; **half board** *n* (BRIT: *in hotel*) media pensión; **half-**

brother *n* hermanastro; **half day** *n* medio día *m*, media jornada; **half fare** *n* medio pasaje *m*; **half-hearted** *adj* indiferente, poco entusiasta; **half-hour** *n* media hora; **half-price** *adj, adv* a mitad de precio; **half term** (BRIT) *n* (*Scol*) *vacaciones de mediados del trimestre*; **half-time** *n* descanso; **halfway** *adv* a medio camino; **halfway through** a mitad de

hall [hɔːl] *n* (*for concerts*) sala; (*entrance way*) hall *m*; vestíbulo

hallmark ['hɔːlmɑːk] *n* sello

hallo [hə'ləu] *excl* = **hello**

hall of residence (BRIT) *n* residencia

Hallowe'en [hæləu'iːn] *n* víspera de Todos los Santos

HALLOWE'EN

La tradición anglosajona dice que en la noche del 31 de octubre, **Hallowe'en**, víspera de Todos los Santos, es posible ver a brujas y fantasmas. En este día los niños se disfrazan y van de puerta en puerta llevando un farol hecho con una calabaza en forma de cabeza humana. Cuando se les abre la puerta gritan "trick or treat", amenazando con gastar una broma a quien no les dé golosinas o algo de calderilla.

hallucination [həluːsɪ'neɪʃən] *n* alucinación *f*

hallway ['hɔːlweɪ] *n* vestíbulo

halo ['heɪləu] *n* (*of saint*) halo, aureola

halt [hɔːlt] *n* (*stop*) alto, parada ▷ *vt* parar; interrumpir ▷ *vi* pararse

halve [hɑːv] *vt* partir por la mitad

halves [hɑːvz] *npl of* **half**

ham [hæm] *n* jamón *m* (cocido)

hamburger ['hæmbəːgə*] *n* hamburguesa

hamlet ['hæmlɪt] *n* aldea

hammer ['hæmə*] *n* martillo ▷ *vt* (*nail*) clavar; (*force*): **to ~ an idea into sb/a message home** meter una idea en la cabeza a algn/machacar una idea ▷ *vi* dar golpes

hammock ['hæmək] *n* hamaca

hamper ['hæmpə*] *vt* estorbar ▷ *n* cesto

hamster ['hæmstə*] *n* hámster *m*

hamstring ['hæmstrɪŋ] *n* (*Anat*) tendón *m* de la corva

hand [hænd] *n* mano *f*; (*of clock*) aguja; (*writing*) letra; (*worker*) obrero ▷ *vt* dar, pasar; **to give** *or* **lend sb a ~** echar una mano a algn, ayudar a algn; **at ~** a mano; **in ~** (*time*) libre; (*job etc*) entre manos; **on ~** (*person, services*) a mano, al alcance; **to ~** (*information etc*) a mano; **on the one ~ ..., on the other ~ ...** por una parte ... por otra (parte) ...; **hand down** *vt* pasar, bajar; (*tradition*) transmitir; (*heirloom*) dejar en herencia; (*US: sentence, verdict*) imponer; **hand in** *vt* entregar; **hand out** *vt* distribuir; **hand over** *vt* (*deliver*) entregar; **handbag** *n* bolso (SP), cartera (LAM), bolsa (MEX); **hand baggage** *n* = **hand luggage**; **handbook** *n* manual *m*; **handbrake** *n* freno de mano; **handcuffs** *npl* esposas *fpl*; **handful** *n* puñado

handicap ['hændɪkæp] *n* minusvalía; (*disadvantage*) desventaja; (*Sport*) handicap *m* ▷ *vt* estorbar; **to be mentally ~ped** ser mentalmente *m/f* discapacitado; **to be physically ~ped** ser minusválido/a

handkerchief ['hæŋkətʃɪf] *n* pañuelo

handle ['hændl] *n* (*of door etc*) tirador *m*; (*of cup etc*) asa; (*of knife etc*) mango; (*for winding*) manivela ▷ *vt* (*touch*) tocar; (*deal with*) encargarse de; (*treat: people*) manejar; **"~ with care"** "(manéjese) con cuidado"; **to fly off the ~** perder los estribos; **handlebar(s)** *n(pl)* manillar *m*

hand: hand luggage *n* equipaje *m* de mano; **handmade** *adj* hecho a mano; **handout** *n* (*money etc*) limosna; (*leaflet*) folleto; **hands-free** *adj* (*phone*) manos libres *inv*; **hands-free kit** *n* manos libres *m inv*

handsome ['hænsəm] *adj* guapo; (*building*) bello; (*fig: profit*) considerable

handwriting ['hændraɪtɪŋ] *n* letra

handy ['hændɪ] *adj* (*close at hand*) a la mano; (*tool etc*) práctico; (*skilful*) hábil, diestro

hang [hæŋ] (*pt, pp* **hung**) *vt* colgar; (*criminal: pt, pp hanged*) ahorcar ▷ *vi* (*painting, coat etc*) colgar; (*hair, drapery*) caer; **to get the ~ of sth** (*inf*) lograr dominar algo; **hang about** *or* **around** *vi* haraganear; **hang down** *vi* colgar, pender; **hang on** *vi* (*wait*) esperar; **hang out** *vt* (*washing*) tender, colgar ▷ *vi* (*inf: live*) vivir; (*spend time*) pasar el rato; **to hang out of sth** colgar fuera de algo; **hang round** *vi* = **hang around**; **hang up** *vi* (*Tel*) colgar ▷ *vt* colgar

hanger ['hæŋə*] *n* percha

hang-gliding ['-glaɪdɪŋ] *n* vuelo libre

hangover ['hæŋəuvə*] *n* (*after drinking*) resaca

hankie, hanky ['hæŋkɪ] *n abbr* = **handkerchief**

happen ['hæpən] *vi* suceder, ocurrir; (*chance*): **he ~ed to hear/see** dió la casualidad de que oyó/vió; **as it ~s** da la casualidad de que

happily ['hæpɪlɪ] *adv* (*luckily*)

afortunadamente; (*cheerfully*) alegremente
happiness ['hæpɪnɪs] *n* felicidad *f*; (*cheerfulness*) alegría
happy ['hæpɪ] *adj* feliz; (*cheerful*) alegre; **to be ~ (with)** estar contento (con); **to be ~ to do** estar encantado de hacer; **~ birthday!** ¡feliz cumpleaños!
harass ['hærəs] *vt* acosar, hostigar; **harassment** *n* persecución *f*
harbour ['hɑːbə*] (*US* **harbor**) *n* puerto ▷ *vt* (*fugitive*) dar abrigo a; (*hope etc*) abrigar
hard [hɑːd] *adj* duro; (*difficult*) difícil; (*work*) arduo; (*person*) severo; (*fact*) innegable ▷ *adv* (*work*) mucho, duro; (*think*) profundamente; **to look ~ at** clavar los ojos en; **to try ~** esforzarse; **no ~ feelings!** ¡sin rencor(es)!; **to be ~ of hearing** ser duro de oído; **to be ~ done by** ser tratado injustamente; **hardback** *n* libro en cartoné; **hardboard** *n* aglomerado *m* (*de madera*); **hard disk** *n* (*Comput*) disco duro *or* rígido; **harden** *vt* endurecer; (*fig*) curtir ▷ *vi* endurecerse; curtirse
hardly ['hɑːdlɪ] *adv* apenas; **~ ever** casi nunca
hard: hardship *n* privación *f*; **hard shoulder** (*BRIT*) *n* (*Aut*) arcén *m*; **hard-up** (*inf*) *adj* sin un duro (*SP*), pelado, sin un centavo (*MEX*), pato (*SC*); **hardware** *n* ferretería; (*Comput*) hardware *m*; (*Mil*) armamento; **hardware shop** (*US* **hardware store**) ferretería; **hard-working** *adj* trabajador(a)
hardy ['hɑːdɪ] *adj* fuerte; (*plant*) resistente
hare [hɛə*] *n* liebre *f*
harm [hɑːm] *n* daño, mal *m* ▷ *vt* (*person*) hacer daño a; (*health, interests*) perjudicar; (*thing*) dañar; **out of ~'s way** a salvo; **harmful** *adj* dañino; **harmless** *adj* (*person*) inofensivo; (*joke etc*) inocente
harmony ['hɑːmənɪ] *n* armonía
harness ['hɑːnɪs] *n* arreos *mpl*; (*for child*) arnés *m*; (*safety harness*) arneses *mpl* ▷ *vt* (*horse*) enjaezar; (*resources*) aprovechar
harp [hɑːp] *n* arpa ▷ *vi*: **to ~ on (about)** machacar (con)
harsh [hɑːʃ] *adj* (*cruel*) duro, cruel; (*severe*) severo; (*sound*) áspero; (*light*) deslumbrador(a)
harvest ['hɑːvɪst] *n* (*harvest time*) siega; (*of cereals etc*) cosecha; (*of grapes*) vendimia ▷ *vt* cosechar
has [hæz] *vb see* **have**
hasn't ['hæznt] = **has not**
hassle ['hæsl] (*inf*) *n* lata
haste [heɪst] *n* prisa; **hasten** ['heɪsn] *vt* acelerar ▷ *vi* darse prisa; **hastily** *adv* de prisa; precipitadamente; **hasty** *adj* apresurado; (*rash*) precipitado
hat [hæt] *n* sombrero
hatch [hætʃ] *n* (*Naut*: *also*: **~way**) escotilla; (*also*: **service ~**) ventanilla ▷ *vi* (*bird*) salir del cascarón ▷ *vt* incubar; (*plot*) tramar; **5 eggs have ~ed** han salido 5 pollos
hatchback ['hætʃbæk] *n* (*Aut*) tres *or* cinco puertas *m*
hate [heɪt] *vt* odiar, aborrecer ▷ *n* odio; **hatred** ['heɪtrɪd] *n* odio
haul [hɔːl] *vt* tirar ▷ *n* (*of fish*) redada; (*of stolen goods etc*) botín *m*
haunt [hɔːnt] *vt* (*ghost*) aparecerse en; (*obsess*) obsesionar ▷ *n* guarida; **haunted** *adj* (*castle etc*) embrujado; (*look*) de angustia

KEYWORD

have [haev] (*pt, pp* **had**) *aux vb* **1** (*gen*) haber; **to have arrived/eaten** haber llegado/comido; **having finished** *or* **when he had finished, he left** cuando hubo acabado, se fue
2 (*in tag questions*): **you've done it, haven't you?** lo has hecho, ¿verdad? *or* ¿no?
3 (*in short answers and questions*): **I haven't** no; **so I have** pues, es verdad; **we haven't paid – yes we have!** no hemos pagado – ¡sí que hemos pagado!; **I've been there before, have you?** he estado allí antes, ¿y tú?
▷ *modal aux vb* (*be obliged*): **to have (got) to do sth** tener que hacer algo; **you haven't to tell her** no hay que *or* no debes decírselo
▷ *vt* **1** (*possess*): **he has (got) blue eyes/dark hair** tiene los ojos azules/el pelo negro
2 (*referring to meals etc*): **to have breakfast/lunch/dinner** desayunar/comer/cenar; **to have a drink/a cigarette** tomar algo/fumar un cigarrillo
3 (*receive*) recibir; (*obtain*) obtener; **may I have your address?** ¿puedes darme tu dirección?; **you can have it for £5** te lo puedes quedar por £5; **I must have it by tomorrow** lo necesito para mañana; **to have a baby** tener un niño *or* bebé
4 (*maintain, allow*): **I won't have it/this nonsense!** ¡no lo permitiré!/¡no permitiré estas tonterías!; **we can't have that** no podemos permitir eso
5 to have sth done hacer *or* mandar hacer algo; **to have one's hair cut** cortarse el pelo; **to have sb do sth** hacer que algn haga algo
6 (*experience, suffer*): **to have a cold/flu** tener un resfriado/la gripe; **she had her bag stolen/her arm broken** le robaron el bolso/se rompió un brazo; **to have an**

operation operarse
7 (+ *noun*): **to have a swim/walk/bath/ rest** nadar/dar un paseo/darse un baño/ descansar; **let's have a look** vamos a ver; **to have a meeting/party** celebrar una reunión/una fiesta; **let me have a try** déjame intentarlo

haven ['heɪvn] *n* puerto; (*fig*) refugio
haven't ['hævnt] = **have not**
havoc ['hævək] *n* estragos *mpl*
Hawaii [hə'waii:] *n* (Islas *fpl*) Hawai *fpl*
hawk [hɔ:k] *n* halcón *m*
hawthorn ['hɔ:θɔ:n] *n* espino
hay [heɪ] *n* heno; **hay fever** *n* fiebre *f* del heno; **haystack** *n* almiar *m*
hazard ['hæzəd] *n* peligro ▷ *vt* aventurar; **hazardous** *adj* peligroso; **hazard warning lights** *npl* (*Aut*) señales *fpl* de emergencia
haze [heɪz] *n* neblina
hazel ['heɪzl] *n* (*tree*) avellano ▷ *adj* (*eyes*) color *m* de avellano; **hazelnut** *n* avellana
hazy ['heɪzɪ] *adj* brumoso; (*idea*) vago
he [hi:] *pron* él; **~ who ...** él que ..., quien ...
head [hɛd] *n* cabeza; (*leader*) jefe/a *m/f*; (*of school*) director(a) *m/f* ▷ *vt* (*list*) encabezar; (*group*) capitanear; (*company*) dirigir; **~s (or tails)** cara (o cruz); **~ first** de cabeza; **~ over heels** (*in love*) perdidamente; **to ~ the ball** cabecear (la pelota); **head for** *vt fus* dirigirse a; (*disaster*) ir camino de; **head off** *vt* (*threat, danger*) evitar; **headache** *n* dolor *m* de cabeza; **heading** *n* título; **headlamp** (BRIT) *n* = **headlight**; **headlight** *n* faro; **headline** *n* titular *m*; **head office** *n* oficina central, central *f*; **headphones** *npl* auriculares *mpl*; **headquarters** *npl* sede *f* central; (*Mil*) cuartel *m* general; **headroom** *n* (*in car*) altura interior; (*under bridge*) (límite *m* de) altura; **headscarf** *n* pañuelo; **headset** *n* cascos *mpl*; **headteacher** *n* director(directora); **head waiter** *n* maître *m*
heal [hi:l] *vt* curar ▷ *vi* cicatrizarse
health [hɛlθ] *n* salud *f*; **health care** *n* asistencia sanitaria; **health centre** (BRIT) *n* ambulatorio, centro médico; **health food** *n* alimentos *mpl* orgánicos; **Health Service** (BRIT) *n* el servicio de salud pública, ≈ el Insalud (SP); **healthy** *adj* sano, saludable
heap [hi:p] *n* montón *m* ▷ *vt*: **to ~ (up)** amontonar; **to ~ sth with** llenar algo hasta arriba de; **~s of** un montón de
hear [hɪə*] (*pt, pp* **~d**) *vt* (*also Law*) oír; (*news*) saber ▷ *vi* oír; **to ~ about** oír hablar de; **to ~ from sb** tener noticias de algn
heard [hə:d] *pt, pp of* **hear**
hearing [hɪərɪŋ] *n* (*sense*) oído; (*Law*) vista; **hearing aid** *n* audífono
hearse [hə:s] *n* coche *m* fúnebre
heart [hɑ:t] *n* corazón *m*; (*fig*) valor *m*; (*of lettuce*) cogollo; **hearts** *npl* (*Cards*) corazones *mpl*; **to lose/take ~** descorazonarse/cobrar ánimo; **at ~** en el fondo; **by ~** (*learn, know*) de memoria; **heart attack** *n* infarto (de miocardio); **heartbeat** *n* latido (del corazón); **heartbroken** *adj*: **she was heartbroken about it** esto le partió el corazón; **heartburn** *n* acedía; **heart disease** *n* enfermedad *f* cardíaca
hearth [hɑ:θ] *n* (*fireplace*) chimenea
heartless ['hɑ:tlɪs] *adj* despiadado
hearty ['hɑ:tɪ] *adj* (*person*) campechano; (*laugh*) sano; (*dislike, support*) absoluto
heat [hi:t] *n* calor *m*; (*Sport*: *also*: **qualifying ~**) prueba eliminatoria ▷ *vt* calentar; **heat up** *vi* calentarse ▷ *vt* calentar; **heated** *adj* caliente; (*fig*) acalorado; **heater** *n* estufa; (*in car*) calefacción *f*
heather ['hɛðə*] *n* brezo
heating ['hi:tɪŋ] *n* calefacción *f*
heatwave ['hi:tweɪv] *n* ola de calor
heaven ['hɛvn] *n* cielo; (*fig*) una maravilla; **heavenly** *adj* celestial; (*fig*) maravilloso
heavily ['hɛvɪlɪ] *adv* pesadamente; (*drink, smoke*) con exceso; (*sleep, sigh*) profundamente; (*depend*) mucho
heavy ['hɛvɪ] *adj* pesado; (*work, blow*) duro; (*sea, rain, meal*) fuerte; (*drinker, smoker*) grande; (*responsibility*) grave; (*schedule*) ocupado; (*weather*) bochornoso
Hebrew ['hi:bru:] *adj, n* (*Ling*) hebreo
hectare ['hɛktɑ:*] *n* (BRIT) hectárea
hectic ['hɛktɪk] *adj* agitado
he'd [hi:d] = **he would; he had**
hedge [hɛdʒ] *n* seto ▷ *vi* contestar con evasivas; **to ~ one's bets** (*fig*) cubrirse
hedgehog ['hɛdʒhɔg] *n* erizo
heed [hi:d] *vt* (*also*: **take ~**: *pay attention to*) hacer caso de
heel [hi:l] *n* talón *m*; (*of shoe*) tacón *m* ▷ *vt* (*shoe*) poner tacón a
hefty ['hɛftɪ] *adj* (*person*) fornido; (*parcel, profit*) gordo
height [haɪt] *n* (*of person*) estatura; (*of building*) altura; (*high ground*) cerro; (*altitude*) altitud *f*; (*fig*: *of season*): **at the ~ of summer** en los días más calurosos del verano; (: *of power etc*) cúspide *f*; (: *of stupidity etc*) colmo; **heighten** *vt* elevar; (*fig*) aumentar
heir [ɛə*] *n* heredero; **heiress** *n* heredera
held [hɛld] *pt, pp of* **hold**
helicopter ['hɛlɪkɔptə*] *n* helicóptero
hell [hɛl] *n* infierno; **~!** (*inf*) ¡demonios!

h

he'll [hi:l] = **he will; he shall**
hello [hə'ləu] *excl* ¡hola!; (*to attract attention*) ¡oiga!; (*surprise*) ¡caramba!
helmet ['hɛlmɪt] *n* casco
help [hɛlp] *n* ayuda; (*cleaner etc*) criada, asistenta ▷ *vt* ayudar; **~!** ¡socorro!; **~ yourself** sírvete; **he can't ~ it** no es culpa suya; **help out** *vi* ayudar, echar una mano ▷ *vt*: **to help sb out** ayudar a algn, echar una mano a algn; **helper** *n* ayudante *mf*; **helpful** *adj* útil; (*person*) servicial; (*advice*) útil; **helping** *n* ración *f*; **helpless** *adj* (*incapable*) incapaz; (*defenceless*) indefenso; **helpline** *n* teléfono de asistencia al público
hem [hɛm] *n* dobladillo ▷ *vt* poner *or* coser el dobladillo de
hemisphere ['hɛmɪsfɪə*] *n* hemisferio
hemorrhage ['hɛmərɪdʒ] (US) *n* = **haemorrhage**
hemorrhoids ['hɛmərɔɪdz] (US) *npl* = **haemorrhoids**
hen [hɛn] *n* gallina; (*female bird*) hembra
hence [hɛns] *adv* (*therefore*) por lo tanto; **2 years ~** de aquí a 2 años
hen night, hen party *n* (*inf*) despedida de soltera
hepatitis [hɛpə'taɪtɪs] *n* hepatitis *f*
her [hə:*] *pron* (*direct*) la; (*indirect*) le; (*stressed, after prep*) ella ▷ *adj* su; *see also* **me; my**
herb [hə:b] *n* hierba; **herbal** *adj* de hierbas; **herbal tea** *n* infusión *f* de hierbas
herd [hə:d] *n* rebaño
here [hɪə*] *adv* aquí; (*at this point*) en este punto; **~!** (*present*) ¡presente!; **~ is/are** aquí está/están; **~ she is** aquí está
hereditary [hɪ'rɛdɪtrɪ] *adj* hereditario
heritage ['hɛrɪtɪdʒ] *n* patrimonio
hernia ['hə:nɪə] *n* hernia
hero ['hɪərəu] (*pl* **~es**) *n* héroe *m*; (*in book, film*) protagonista *m*; **heroic** [hɪ'rəuɪk] *adj* heroico
heroin ['hɛrəuɪn] *n* heroína
heroine ['hɛrəuɪn] *n* heroína; (*in book, film*) protagonista
heron ['hɛrən] *n* garza
herring ['hɛrɪŋ] *n* arenque *m*
hers [hə:z] *pron* (el) suyo((la) suya) *etc*; *see also* **mine'**
herself [hə:'sɛlf] *pron* (*reflexive*) se; (*emphatic*) ella misma; (*after prep*) sí (misma); *see also* **oneself**
he's [hi:z] = **he is; he has**
hesitant ['hɛzɪtənt] *adj* vacilante
hesitate ['hɛzɪteɪt] *vi* vacilar; (*in speech*) titubear; (*be unwilling*) resistirse a; **hesitation** ['-teɪʃən] *n* indecisión *f*; titubeo; dudas *fpl*
heterosexual [hɛtərəu'sɛksjuəl] *adj* heterosexual
hexagon ['hɛksəgən] *n* hexágono
hey [heɪ] *excl* ¡oye!, ¡oiga!
heyday ['heɪdeɪ] *n*: **the ~ of** el apogeo de
HGV *n abbr* (= *heavy goods vehicle*) vehículo pesado
hi [haɪ] *excl* ¡hola!; (*to attract attention*) ¡oiga!
hibernate ['haɪbəneɪt] *vi* invernar
hiccough ['hɪkʌp] = **hiccup**
hiccup ['hɪkʌp] *vi* hipar
hid [hɪd] *pt of* **hide**
hidden ['hɪdn] *pp of* **hide** ▷ *adj*: **~ agenda** plan *m* encubierto
hide [haɪd] (*pt* **hid**, *pp* **hidden**) *n* (*skin*) piel *f* ▷ *vt* esconder, ocultar ▷ *vi*: **to ~ (from sb)** esconderse *or* ocultarse (de algn)
hideous ['hɪdɪəs] *adj* horrible
hiding ['haɪdɪŋ] *n* (*beating*) paliza; **to be in ~** (*concealed*) estar escondido
hi-fi ['haɪfaɪ] *n* estéreo, hifi *m* ▷ *adj* de alta fidelidad
high [haɪ] *adj* alto; (*speed, number*) grande; (*price*) elevado; (*wind*) fuerte; (*voice*) agudo ▷ *adv* alto, a gran altura; **it is 20 m ~** tiene 20 m de altura; **~ in the air** en las alturas; **highchair** *n* silla alta; **high-class** *adj* (*hotel*) de lujo; (*person*) distinguido, de categoría; (*food*) de alta categoría; **higher education** *n* educación *f* or enseñanza superior; **high heels** *npl* (*heels*) tacones *mpl* altos; (*shoes*) zapatos *mpl* de tacón; **high jump** *n* (*Sport*) salto de altura; **highlands** ['haɪləndz] *npl* tierras *fpl* altas; **the Highlands** (*in Scotland*) las Tierras Altas de Escocia; **highlight** *n* (*fig: of event*) punto culminante ▷ *vt* subrayar; **highlights** *npl* (*in hair*) reflejos *mpl*; **highlighter** *n* rotulador; **highly** *adv* (*paid*) muy bien; (*critical, confidential*) sumamente; (*a lot*): **to speak/think highly of** hablar muy bien de/tener en mucho a; **highness** *n* altura; **Her/His Highness** Su Alteza; **high-rise** *n* (*also*: **high-rise block, high-rise building**) torre *f* de pisos; **high school** *n* ≈ Instituto Nacional de Bachillerato (SP); **high season** (BRIT) *n* temporada alta; **high street** (BRIT) *n* calle *f* mayor; **high-tech** (*inf*) *adj* al-tec (*inf*), de alta tecnología; **highway** *n* carretera; (US) carretera nacional; autopista; **Highway Code** (BRIT) *n* código de la circulación
hijack ['haɪdʒæk] *vt* secuestrar; **hijacker** *n* secuestrador(a) *m/f*
hike [haɪk] *vi* (*go walking*) ir de excursión (a pie) ▷ *n* caminata; **hiker** *n* excursionista *mf*; **hiking** *n* senderismo

hilarious [hɪˈlɛərɪəs] *adj* divertidísimo
hill [hɪl] *n* colina; (*high*) montaña; (*slope*) cuesta; **hillside** *n* ladera; **hill walking** *n* senderismo (de montaña); **hilly** *adj* montañoso
him [hɪm] *pron* (*direct*) le, lo; (*indirect*) le; (*stressed, after prep*) él; *see also* **me**; **himself** *pron* (*reflexive*) se; (*emphatic*) él mismo; (*after prep*) sí (mismo); *see also* **oneself**
hind [haɪnd] *adj* posterior
hinder [ˈhɪndə*] *vt* estorbar, impedir
hindsight [ˈhaɪndsaɪt] *n*: **with ~** en retrospectiva
Hindu [ˈhɪndu:] *n* hindú *mf*; **Hinduism** *n* (*Rel*) hinduismo
hinge [hɪndʒ] *n* bisagra, gozne *m* ▷ *vi* (*fig*): **to ~ on** depender de
hint [hɪnt] *n* indirecta; (*advice*) consejo; (*sign*) dejo ▷ *vt*: **to ~ that** insinuar que ▷ *vi*: **to ~ at** hacer alusión a
hip [hɪp] *n* cadera
hippie [ˈhɪpɪ] *n* hippie *m/f*, jipi *m/f*
hippo [ˈhɪpəu] (*pl* **~s**) *n* hipopótamo
hippopotamus [hɪpəˈpɔtəməs] (*pl* **~es** *or* **hippopotami**) *n* hipopótamo
hippy [ˈhɪpɪ] *n* = **hippie**
hire [ˈhaɪə*] *vt* (BRIT: *car, equipment*) alquilar; (*worker*) contratar ▷ *n* alquiler *m*; **for ~** se alquila; (*taxi*) libre; **hire(d) car** (BRIT) *n* coche *m* de alquiler; **hire purchase** (BRIT) *n* compra a plazos
his [hɪz] *pron* (el) suyo((la) suya) *etc* ▷ *adj* su; *see also* **mine[1]; my**
Hispanic [hɪsˈpænɪk] *adj* hispánico
hiss [hɪs] *vi* silbar
historian [hɪˈstɔ:rɪən] *n* historiador(a) *m/f*
historic(al) [hɪˈstɔrɪk(l)] *adj* histórico
history [ˈhɪstərɪ] *n* historia
hit [hɪt] (*pt, pp* **~**) *vt* (*strike*) golpear, pegar; (*reach*: *target*) alcanzar; (*collide with*: *car*) chocar contra; (*fig*: *affect*) afectar ▷ *n* golpe *m*; (*success*) éxito; (*on website*) visita; (*in web search*) correspondencia; **to ~ it off with sb** llevarse bien con algn; **hit back** *vi* defenderse; (*fig*) devolver golpe por golpe
hitch [hɪtʃ] *vt* (*fasten*) atar, amarrar; (*also*: **~ up**) remangar ▷ *n* (*difficulty*) dificultad *f*; **to ~ a lift** hacer autostop
hitch-hike [ˈhɪtʃhaɪk] *vi* hacer autostop; **hitch-hiker** *n* autostopista *m/f*; **hitch-hiking** *n* autostop *m*
hi-tech [haɪˈtɛk] *adj* de alta tecnología
hitman [ˈhɪtmæn] (*irreg*) *n* asesino a sueldo
HIV *n abbr* (= *human immunodeficiency virus*) VIH *m*; **~-negative/positive** VIH negativo/positivo
hive [haɪv] *n* colmena
hoard [hɔ:d] *n* (*treasure*) tesoro; (*stockpile*) provisión *f* ▷ *vt* acumular; (*goods in short supply*) acaparar
hoarse [hɔ:s] *adj* ronco
hoax [həuks] *n* trampa
hob [hɔb] *n* quemador *m*
hobble [ˈhɔbl] *vi* cojear
hobby [ˈhɔbɪ] *n* pasatiempo, afición *f*
hobo [ˈhəubəu] (US) *n* vagabundo
hockey [ˈhɔkɪ] *n* hockey *m*; **hockey stick** *n* palo *m* de hockey
hog [hɔg] *n* cerdo, puerco ▷ *vt* (*fig*) acaparar; **to go the whole ~** poner toda la carne en el asador
Hogmanay [hɔgməˈneɪ] *n* *ver abajo*

HOGMANAY

La Nochevieja o "New Year's Eve" se conoce como "Hogmanay" en Escocia, donde se festeje de forma especial. La familia y los amigos se suelen juntar para oír las campanadas del reloj y luego se hace el "first-footing", costumbre que consiste en visitar a los amigos y vecinos llevando algo de beber (generalmente whisky) y un trozo de carbón que se supone que traerá buena suerte para el año entrante.

hoist [hɔɪst] *n* (*crane*) grúa ▷ *vt* levantar, alzar; (*flag, sail*) izar
hold [həuld] (*pt, pp* **held**) *vt* sostener; (*contain*) contener; (*have*: *power, qualification*) tener; (*keep back*) retener; (*believe*) sostener; (*consider*) considerar; (*keep in position*): **to ~ one's head up** mantener la cabeza alta; (*meeting*) celebrar ▷ *vi* (*withstand pressure*) resistir; (*be valid*) valer ▷ *n* (*grasp*) asimiento; (*fig*) dominio; **~ the line!** (*Tel*) ¡no cuelgue!; **to ~ one's own** (*fig*) defenderse; **to catch** *or* **get (a) ~ of** agarrarse *or* asirse de; **hold back** *vt* retener; (*secret*) ocultar; **hold on** *vi* agarrarse bien; (*wait*) esperar; **hold on!** (*Tel*) ¡(espere) un momento!; **hold out** *vt* ofrecer ▷ *vi* (*resist*) resistir; **hold up** *vt* (*raise*) levantar; (*support*) apoyar; (*delay*) retrasar; (*rob*) asaltar; **holdall** (BRIT) *n* bolsa; **holder** *n* (*container*) receptáculo; (*of ticket, record*) poseedor(a) *m/f*; (*of office, title etc*) titular *mf*
hole [həul] *n* agujero
holiday [ˈhɔlədɪ] *n* vacaciones *fpl*; (*public holiday*) (día *m* de) fiesta, día *m* feriado; **on ~** de vacaciones; **holiday camp** *n* (BRIT: *also*: **holiday centre**) centro de vacaciones; **holiday job** *n* (BRIT) trabajillo extra para las

h

vacaciones; **holiday-maker** (BRIT) *n* turista *mf*; **holiday resort** *n* centro turístico
Holland ['hɔlənd] *n* Holanda
hollow ['hɔləu] *adj* hueco; (*claim*) vacío; (*eyes*) hundido; (*sound*) sordo ▷ *n* hueco; (*in ground*) hoyo ▷ *vt*: **to ~ out** excavar
holly ['hɔlɪ] *n* acebo
Hollywood ['hɔlɪwud] *n* Hollywood *m*
holocaust ['hɔləkɔ:st] *n* holocausto
holy ['həulɪ] *adj* santo, sagrado; (*water*) bendito
home [həum] *n* casa; (*country*) patria; (*institution*) asilo ▷ *cpd* (*domestic*) casero, de casa; (*Econ, Pol*) nacional ▷ *adv* (*direction*) a casa; (*right in: nail etc*) a fondo; **at ~** en casa; (*in country*) en el país; (*fig*) como pez en el agua; **to go/come ~** ir/volver a casa; **make yourself at ~** ¡estás en tu casa!; **home address** *n* domicilio; **homeland** *n* tierra natal; **homeless** *adj* sin hogar, sin casa; **homely** *adj* (*simple*) sencillo; **home-made** *adj* casero; **home match** *n* partido en casa; **Home Office** (BRIT) *n* Ministerio del Interior; **home owner** *n* propietario/a *m/f* de una casa; **home page** *n* página de inicio; **Home Secretary** (BRIT) *n* Ministro del Interior; **homesick** *adj*: **to be homesick** tener morriña, sentir nostalgia; **home town** *n* ciudad *f* natal; **homework** *n* deberes *mpl*
homicide ['hɔmɪsaɪd] (US) *n* homicidio
homoeopathic [həumɪɔ'pəθɪk] (US **homeopathic**) *adj* homeopático
homoeopathy [həumɪ'ɔpəθɪ] (US **homeopathy**) *n* homeopatía
homosexual [hɔməu'sɛksjuəl] *adj, n* homosexual *mf*
honest ['ɔnɪst] *adj* honrado; (*sincere*) franco, sincero; **honestly** *adv* honradamente; francamente; **honesty** *n* honradez *f*
honey ['hʌnɪ] *n* miel *f*; **honeymoon** *n* luna de miel; **honeysuckle** *n* madreselva
Hong Kong ['hɔŋ'kɔŋ] *n* Hong-Kong *m*
honorary ['ɔnərərɪ] *adj* (*member, president*) de honor; (*title*) honorífico; **~ degree** doctorado honoris causa
honour ['ɔnə*] (US **honor**) *vt* honrar; (*commitment, promise*) cumplir con ▷ *n* honor *m*, honra; **to graduate with ~s** ≈ licenciarse con matrícula (de honor); **honourable** (US **honorable**) *adj* honorable; **honours degree** *n* (*Scol*) *título de licenciado con calificación alta*
hood [hud] *n* capucha; (BRIT *Aut*) capota; (US *Aut*) capó *m*; (*of cooker*) campana de humos; **hoodie** *n* (*top*) jersey *m* con capucha
hoof [hu:f] (*pl* **hooves**) *n* pezuña
hook [huk] *n* gancho; (*on dress*) corchete *m*, broche *m*; (*for fishing*) anzuelo ▷ *vt* enganchar; (*fish*) pescar
hooligan ['hu:lɪgən] *n* gamberro
hoop [hu:p] *n* aro
hooray [hu:'reɪ] *excl* = **hurray**
hoot [hu:t] (BRIT) *vi* (*Aut*) tocar el pito, pitar; (*siren*) (hacer) sonar; (*owl*) ulular
Hoover® ['hu:və*] (BRIT) *n* aspiradora ▷ *vt*: **to hoover** pasar la aspiradora por
hooves [hu:vz] *npl of* **hoof**
hop [hɔp] *vi* saltar, brincar; (*on one foot*) saltar con un pie
hope [həup] *vt, vi* esperar ▷ *n* esperanza; **I ~ so/not** espero que sí/no; **hopeful** *adj* (*person*) optimista; (*situation*) prometedor(a); **hopefully** *adv* con esperanza; (*one hopes*): **hopefully he will recover** esperamos que se recupere; **hopeless** *adj* desesperado; (*person*): **to be hopeless** ser un desastre
hops [hɔps] *npl* lúpulo
horizon [hə'raɪzn] *n* horizonte *m*; **horizontal** [hɔrɪ'zɔntl] *adj* horizontal
hormone ['hɔ:məun] *n* hormona
horn [hɔ:n] *n* cuerno; (*Mus: also*: **French ~**) trompa; (*Aut*) pito, claxon *m*
horoscope ['hɔrəskəup] *n* horóscopo
horrendous [hɔ'rɛndəs] *adj* horrendo
horrible ['hɔrɪbl] *adj* horrible
horrid ['hɔrɪd] *adj* horrible, horroroso
horrific [hɔ'rɪfɪk] *adj* (*accident*) horroroso; (*film*) horripilante
horrifying ['hɔrɪfaɪɪŋ] *adj* horroroso
horror ['hɔrə*] *n* horror *m*; **horror film** *n* película de horror
hors d'œuvre [ɔ:'də:vrə] *n* entremeses *mpl*
horse [hɔ:s] *n* caballo; **horseback** *n*: **on horseback** a caballo; **horse chestnut** *n* (*tree*) castaño de Indias; (*nut*) castaña de Indias; **horsepower** *n* caballo (de fuerza); **horse-racing** *n* carreras *fpl* de caballos; **horseradish** *n* rábano picante; **horse riding** *n* (BRIT) equitación *f*
hose [həuz] *n* manguera; **hosepipe** *n* manguera
hospital ['hɔspɪtl] *n* hospital *m*
hospitality [hɔspɪ'tælɪtɪ] *n* hospitalidad *f*
host [həust] *n* anfitrión *m*; (*TV, Radio*) presentador *m*; (*Rel*) hostia; (*large number*): **a ~ of** multitud de
hostage ['hɔstɪdʒ] *n* rehén *m*
hostel ['hɔstl] *n* hostal *m*; **(youth) ~** albergue *m* juvenil
hostess ['həustɪs] *n* anfitriona; (BRIT: *air hostess*) azafata; (*TV, Radio*) presentadora

hostile ['hɔstaɪl] *adj* hostil
hostility [hɔ'stɪlɪtɪ] *n* hostilidad *f*
hot [hɔt] *adj* caliente; (*weather*) caluroso, de calor; (*as opposed to warm*) muy caliente; (*spicy*) picante; **to be ~** (*person*) tener calor; (*object*) estar caliente; (*weather*) hacer calor; **hot dog** *n* perro caliente
hotel [həu'tɛl] *n* hotel *m*
hot-water bottle [hɔt'wɔːtə*-] *n* bolsa de agua caliente
hound [haund] *vt* acosar ▷*n* perro (de caza)
hour ['auə*] *n* hora; **hourly** *adj* (de) cada hora
house [*n* haus, *pl* 'hauzɪz, *vb* hauz] *n* (*gen, firm*) casa; (*Pol*) cámara; (*Theatre*) sala ▷*vt* (*person*) alojar; (*collection*) albergar; **on the ~** (*fig*) la casa invita; **household** *n* familia; (*home*) casa; **householder** *n* propietario/a; (*head of house*) cabeza de familia; **housekeeper** *n* ama de llaves; **housekeeping** *n* (*work*) trabajos *mpl* domésticos; **housewife** (*irreg*) *n* ama de casa; **house wine** *n* vino *m* de la casa; **housework** *n* faenas *fpl* (de la casa)
housing ['hauzɪŋ] *n* (*act*) alojamiento; (*houses*) viviendas *fpl*; **housing development, housing estate** (BRIT) *n* urbanización *f*
hover ['hɔvə*] *vi* flotar (en el aire); **hovercraft** *n* aerodeslizador *m*
how [hau] *adv* (*in what way*) cómo; **~ are you?** ¿cómo estás?; **~ much milk/many people?** ¿cuánta leche/gente?; **~ much does it cost?** ¿cuánto cuesta?; **~ long have you been here?** ¿cuánto hace que estás aquí?; **~ old are you?** ¿cuántos años tienes?; **~ tall is he?** ¿cómo es de alto?; **~ is school?** ¿cómo (te) va (en) la escuela?; **~ was the film?** ¿qué tal la película?; **~ lovely/awful!** ¡qué bonito/horror!
however [hau'ɛvə*] *adv*: **~ I do it** lo haga como lo haga; **~ cold it is** por mucho frío que haga; **~ fast he runs** por muy rápido que corra; **~ did you do it?** ¿cómo lo hiciste? ▷*conj* sin embargo, no obstante
howl [haul] *n* aullido ▷*vi* aullar; (*person*) dar alaridos; (*wind*) ulular
H.P. *n abbr* = **hire purchase**
h.p. *abbr* = **horsepower**
HQ *n abbr* = **headquarters**
hr(s) *abbr* (= *hour(s)*) h
HTML *n abbr* (= *hypertext markup language*) lenguaje *m* de hipertexto
hubcap ['hʌbkæp] *n* tapacubos *m inv*
huddle ['hʌdl] *vi*: **to ~ together** acurrucarse
huff [hʌf] *n*: **in a ~** enojado
hug [hʌg] *vt* abrazar; (*thing*) apretar con los brazos
huge [hjuːdʒ] *adj* enorme
hull [hʌl] *n* (*of ship*) casco
hum [hʌm] *vt* tararear, canturrear ▷*vi* tararear, canturrear; (*insect*) zumbar
human ['hjuːmən] *adj, n* humano
humane [hjuː'meɪn] *adj* humano, humanitario
humanitarian [hjuːmænɪ'tɛərɪən] *adj* humanitario
humanity [hjuː'mænɪtɪ] *n* humanidad *f*
human rights *npl* derechos *mpl* humanos
humble ['hʌmbl] *adj* humilde
humid ['hjuːmɪd] *adj* húmedo; **humidity** [-'mɪdɪtɪ] *n* humedad *f*
humiliate [hjuː'mɪlɪeɪt] *vt* humillar
humiliating [hjuː'mɪlɪeɪtɪŋ] *adj* humillante, vergonzoso
humiliation [hjuːmɪlɪ'eɪʃən] *n* humillación *f*
hummus ['huməs] *n* *paté de garbanzos*
humorous ['hjuːmərəs] *adj* gracioso, divertido
humour ['hjuːmə*] (US **humor**) *n* humorismo, sentido del humor; (*mood*) humor *m* ▷*vt* (*person*) complacer
hump [hʌmp] *n* (*in ground*) montículo; (*camel's*) giba
hunch [hʌntʃ] *n* (*premonition*) presentimiento
hundred ['hʌndrəd] *num* ciento; (*before n*) cien; **~s of** centenares de; **hundredth** [-ɪdθ] *adj* centésimo
hung [hʌŋ] *pt, pp of* **hang**
Hungarian [hʌŋ'gɛərɪən] *adj, n* húngaro/a *m/f*
Hungary ['hʌŋgərɪ] *n* Hungría
hunger ['hʌŋgə*] *n* hambre *f* ▷*vi*: **to ~ for** (*fig*) tener hambre de, anhelar
hungry ['hʌŋgrɪ] *adj*: **~ (for)** hambriento (de); **to be ~** tener hambre
hunt [hʌnt] *vt* (*seek*) buscar; (*Sport*) cazar ▷*vi* (*search*): **to ~ (for)** buscar; (*Sport*) cazar ▷*n* búsqueda; caza, cacería; **hunter** *n* cazador(a) *m/f*; **hunting** *n* caza
hurdle ['həːdl] *n* (*Sport*) valla; (*fig*) obstáculo
hurl [həːl] *vt* lanzar, arrojar
hurrah [huː'rɑː] *excl* = **hurray**
hurray [hu'reɪ] *excl* ¡viva!
hurricane ['hʌrɪkən] *n* huracán *m*
hurry ['hʌrɪ] *n* prisa ▷*vt* (*also*: **~ up**: *person*) dar prisa a; (: *work*) apresurar, hacer de prisa; **to be in a ~** tener prisa; **hurry up** *vi* darse prisa, apurarse (LAM)
hurt [həːt] (*pt, pp* **~**) *vt* hacer daño a ▷*vi* doler ▷*adj* lastimado

husband ['hʌzbənd] *n* marido
hush [hʌʃ] *n* silencio ▷*vt* hacer callar; **~!** ¡chitón!, ¡cállate!
husky ['hʌskɪ] *adj* ronco ▷*n* perro esquimal
hut [hʌt] *n* cabaña; (*shed*) cobertizo
hyacinth ['haɪəsɪnθ] *n* jacinto
hydrangea [haɪ'dreɪnʒə] *n* hortensia
hydrofoil ['haɪdrəfɔɪl] *n* aerodeslizador *m*
hydrogen ['haɪdrədʒən] *n* hidrógeno
hygiene ['haɪdʒiːn] *n* higiene *f*; **hygienic** [-'dʒiːnɪk] *adj* higiénico
hymn [hɪm] *n* himno
hype [haɪp] (*inf*) *n* bombardeo publicitario
hyphen ['haɪfn] *n* guión *m*
hypnotize ['hɪpnətaɪz] *vt* hipnotizar
hypocrite ['hɪpəkrɪt] *n* hipócrita *mf*
hypocritical [hɪpə'krɪtɪkl] *adj* hipócrita
hypothesis [haɪ'pɔθɪsɪs] (*pl* **hypotheses**) *n* hipótesis *f inv*
hysterical [hɪ'stɛrɪkl] *adj* histérico; (*funny*) para morirse de risa
hysterics [hɪ'stɛrɪks] *npl* histeria; **to be in ~** (*fig*) morirse de risa

I

I [aɪ] *pron* yo
ice [aɪs] *n* hielo; (*ice cream*) helado ▷*vt* (*cake*) alcorzar ▷*vi* (*also*: **~ over, ~ up**) helarse; **iceberg** *n* iceberg *m*; **ice cream** *n* helado; **ice cube** *n* cubito de hielo; **ice hockey** *n* hockey *m* sobre hielo
Iceland ['aɪslənd] *n* Islandia; **Icelander** *n* islandés/esa *m/f*; **Icelandic** [aɪs'lændɪk] *adj* islandés/esa ▷*n* (*Ling*) islandés *m*
ice: ice lolly (BRIT) *n* polo; **ice rink** *n* pista de hielo; **ice skating** *n* patinaje *m* sobre hielo
icing ['aɪsɪŋ] *n* (*Culin*) alcorza; **icing sugar** (BRIT) *n* azúcar *m* glas(eado)
icon ['aɪkɔn] *n* icono
ICT (BRIT: *Scol*) *n abbr* (= *information and communications technology*) informática
icy ['aɪsɪ] *adj* helado
I'd [aɪd] = **I would; I had**
ID card *n* (*identity card*) DNI *m*
idea [aɪ'dɪə] *n* idea
ideal [aɪ'dɪəl] *n* ideal *m* ▷*adj* ideal; **ideally** [-dɪəlɪ] *adv* idealmente; **they're ideally suited** hacen una pareja ideal
identical [aɪ'dɛntɪkl] *adj* idéntico
identification [aɪdɛntɪfɪ'keɪʃən] *n* identificación *f*; **(means of) ~** documentos *mpl* personales
identify [aɪ'dɛntɪfaɪ] *vt* identificar
identity [aɪ'dɛntɪtɪ] *n* identidad *f*; **identity card** *n* carnet *m* de identidad; **identity theft** *n* robo de identidad
ideology [aɪdɪ'ɔlədʒɪ] *n* ideología
idiom ['ɪdɪəm] *n* modismo; (*style of speaking*) lenguaje *m*

> Be careful not to translate **idiom** by the Spanish word *idioma*.

idiot ['ɪdɪət] *n* idiota *mf*
idle ['aɪdl] *adj* (*inactive*) ocioso; (*lazy*) holgazán/ana; (*unemployed*) parado, desocupado; (*machinery etc*) parado; (*talk etc*)

frívolo ▷ *vi* (*machine*) marchar en vacío
idol ['aɪdl] *n* ídolo
idyllic [ɪ'dɪlɪk] *adj* idílico
i.e. *abbr* (= *that is*) esto es
if [ɪf] *conj* si; **~ necessary** si fuera necesario, si hiciese falta; **~ I were you** yo en tu lugar; **~ so/not** de ser así/si no; **~ only I could!** ¡ojalá pudiera!; *see also* **as; even**
ignite [ɪg'naɪt] *vt* (*set fire to*) encender ▷ *vi* encenderse
ignition [ɪg'nɪʃən] *n* (*Aut: process*) ignición *f*; (: *mechanism*) encendido; **to switch on/off the ~** arrancar/apagar el motor
ignorance ['ɪgnərəns] *n* ignorancia
ignorant ['ɪgnərənt] *adj* ignorante; **to be ~ of** ignorar
ignore [ɪg'nɔː*] *vt* (*person, advice*) no hacer caso de; (*fact*) pasar por alto
I'll [aɪl] = **I will; I shall**
ill [ɪl] *adj* enfermo, malo ▷ *n* mal *m* ▷ *adv* mal; **to be taken ~** ponerse enfermo
illegal [ɪ'liːgl] *adj* ilegal
illegible [ɪ'lɛdʒɪbl] *adj* ilegible
illegitimate [ɪlɪ'dʒɪtɪmət] *adj* ilegítimo
ill health *n* mala salud *f*; **to be in ~** estar mal de salud
illiterate [ɪ'lɪtərət] *adj* analfabeto
illness ['ɪlnɪs] *n* enfermedad *f*
illuminate [ɪ'luːmɪneɪt] *vt* (*room, street*) iluminar, alumbrar
illusion [ɪ'luːʒən] *n* ilusión *f*; (*trick*) truco
illustrate ['ɪləstreɪt] *vt* ilustrar
illustration [ɪlə'streɪʃən] *n* (*act of illustrating*) ilustración *f*; (*example*) ejemplo, ilustración *f*; (*in book*) lámina
I'm [aɪm] = **I am**
image ['ɪmɪdʒ] *n* imagen *f*
imaginary [ɪ'mædʒɪnərɪ] *adj* imaginario
imagination [ɪmædʒɪ'neɪʃən] *n* imaginación *f*; (*inventiveness*) inventiva
imaginative [ɪ'mædʒɪnətɪv] *adj* imaginativo
imagine [ɪ'mædʒɪn] *vt* imaginarse
imbalance [ɪm'bæləns] *n* desequilibrio
imitate ['ɪmɪteɪt] *vt* imitar; **imitation** [ɪmɪ'teɪʃən] *n* imitación *f*; (*copy*) copia
immaculate [ɪ'mækjulət] *adj* inmaculado
immature [ɪmə'tjuə*] *adj* (*person*) inmaduro
immediate [ɪ'miːdɪət] *adj* inmediato; (*pressing*) urgente, apremiante; (*nearest: family*) próximo; (: *neighbourhood*) inmediato; **immediately** *adv* (*at once*) en seguida; (*directly*) inmediatamente; **immediately next to** muy junto a
immense [ɪ'mɛns] *adj* inmenso, enorme; (*importance*) enorme; **immensely** *adv* enormemente
immerse [ɪ'məːs] *vt* (*submerge*) sumergir; **to be ~d in** (*fig*) estar absorto en
immigrant ['ɪmɪgrənt] *n* inmigrante *mf*; **immigration** [ɪmɪ'greɪʃən] *n* inmigración *f*
imminent ['ɪmɪnənt] *adj* inminente
immoral [ɪ'mɔrl] *adj* inmoral
immortal [ɪ'mɔːtl] *adj* inmortal
immune [ɪ'mjuːn] *adj*: **~ (to)** inmune (a); **immune system** *n* sistema *m* inmunitario
immunize ['ɪmjunaɪz] *vt* inmunizar
impact ['ɪmpækt] *n* impacto
impair [ɪm'pɛə*] *vt* perjudicar
impartial [ɪm'pɑːʃl] *adj* imparcial
impatience [ɪm'peɪʃəns] *n* impaciencia
impatient [ɪm'peɪʃənt] *adj* impaciente; **to get** *or* **grow ~** impacientarse
impeccable [ɪm'pɛkəbl] *adj* impecable
impending [ɪm'pɛndɪŋ] *adj* inminente
imperative [ɪm'pɛrətɪv] *adj* (*tone*) imperioso; (*need*) imprescindible
imperfect [ɪm'pəːfɪkt] *adj* (*goods etc*) defectuoso ▷ *n* (*Ling: also:* **~ tense**) imperfecto
imperial [ɪm'pɪərɪəl] *adj* imperial
impersonal [ɪm'pəːsənl] *adj* impersonal
impersonate [ɪm'pəːsəneɪt] *vt* hacerse pasar por; (*Theatre*) imitar
impetus ['ɪmpətəs] *n* ímpetu *m*; (*fig*) impulso
implant [ɪm'plɑːnt] *vt* (*Med*) injertar, implantar; (*fig: idea, principle*) inculcar
implement [*n* 'ɪmplɪmənt, *vb* 'ɪmplɪmɛnt] *n* herramienta; (*for cooking*) utensilio ▷ *vt* (*regulation*) hacer efectivo; (*plan*) realizar
implicate ['ɪmplɪkeɪt] *vt* (*compromise*) comprometer; **to ~ sb in sth** comprometer a algn en algo
implication [ɪmplɪ'keɪʃən] *n* consecuencia; **by ~** indirectamente
implicit [ɪm'plɪsɪt] *adj* implícito; (*belief, trust*) absoluto
imply [ɪm'plaɪ] *vt* (*involve*) suponer; (*hint*) dar a entender que
impolite [ɪmpə'laɪt] *adj* mal educado
import [*vb* ɪm'pɔːt, *n* 'ɪmpɔːt] *vt* importar ▷ *n* (*Comm*) importación *f*; (: *article*) producto importado; (*meaning*) significado, sentido
importance [ɪm'pɔːtəns] *n* importancia
important [ɪm'pɔːtənt] *adj* importante; **it's not ~** no importa, no tiene importancia
importer [ɪm'pɔːtə*] *n* importador(a) *m/f*
impose [ɪm'pəuz] *vt* imponer ▷ *vi*: **to ~ on sb** abusar de algn; **imposing** *adj* imponente, impresionante
impossible [ɪm'pɔsɪbl] *adj* imposible;

(*person*) insoportable
impotent [ˈɪmpətənt] *adj* impotente
impoverished [ɪmˈpɔvərɪʃt] *adj* necesitado
impractical [ɪmˈpræktɪkl] *adj* (*person, plan*) poco práctico
impress [ɪmˈprɛs] *vt* impresionar; (*mark*) estampar; **to ~ sth on sb** hacer entender algo a algn
impression [ɪmˈprɛʃən] *n* impresión *f*; (*imitation*) imitación *f*; **to be under the ~ that** tener la impresión de que
impressive [ɪmˈprɛsɪv] *adj* impresionante
imprison [ɪmˈprɪzn] *vt* encarcelar; **imprisonment** *n* encarcelamiento; (*term of imprisonment*) cárcel *f*
improbable [ɪmˈprɔbəbl] *adj* improbable, inverosímil
improper [ɪmˈprɔpə*] *adj* (*unsuitable: conduct etc*) incorrecto; (*: activities*) deshonesto
improve [ɪmˈpru:v] *vt* mejorar; (*foreign language*) perfeccionar ▷*vi* mejorarse; **improvement** *n* mejoramiento; perfección *f*; progreso
improvise [ˈɪmprəvaɪz] *vt, vi* improvisar
impulse [ˈɪmpʌls] *n* impulso; **to act on ~** obrar sin reflexión; **impulsive** [ɪmˈpʌlsɪv] *adj* irreflexivo

KEYWORD

in [ɪn] *prep* **1** (*indicating place, position, with place names*) en; **in the house/garden** en (la) casa/el jardín; **in here/there** aquí/ahí *or* allí dentro; **in London/England** en Londres/Inglaterra
2 (*indicating time*) en; **in spring** en (la) primavera; **in the afternoon** por la tarde; **at 4 o'clock in the afternoon** a las 4 de la tarde; **I did it in 3 hours/days** lo hice en 3 horas/días; **I'll see you in 2 weeks** *or* **in 2 weeks' time** te veré dentro de 2 semanas
3 (*indicating manner etc*) en; **in a loud/soft voice** en voz alta/baja; **in pencil/ink** a lápiz/bolígrafo; **the boy in the blue shirt** el chico de la camisa azul
4 (*indicating circumstances*): **in the sun/shade/rain** al sol/a la sombra/bajo la lluvia; **a change in policy** un cambio de política
5 (*indicating mood, state*): **in tears** en lágrimas, llorando; **in anger/despair** enfadado/desesperado; **to live in luxury** vivir lujosamente
6 (*with ratios, numbers*): **1 in 10 households, 1 household in 10** una de cada 10 familias; **20 pence in the pound** 20 peniques por libra; **they lined up in twos** se alinearon de dos en dos
7 (*referring to people, works*) en; entre; **the disease is common in children** la enfermedad es común entre los niños; **in (the works of) Dickens** en (las obras de) Dickens
8 (*indicating profession etc*): **to be in teaching** estar en la enseñanza
9 (*after superlative*) de; **the best pupil in the class** el(la) mejor alumno/a de la clase
10 (*with present participle*): **in saying this** al decir esto
▷ *adv*: **to be in** (*person: at home*) estar en casa; (*at work*) estar; (*train, ship, plane*) haber llegado; (*in fashion*) estar de moda; **she'll be in later today** llegará más tarde hoy; **to ask sb in** hacer pasar a algn; **to run/limp** *etc* **in** entrar corriendo/cojeando *etc*
▷ *n*: **the ins and outs** (*of proposal, situation etc*) los detalles

inability [ɪnəˈbɪlɪtɪ] *n*: **~ (to do)** incapacidad *f* (de hacer)
inaccurate [ɪnˈækjurət] *adj* inexacto, incorrecto
inadequate [ɪnˈædɪkwət] *adj* (*income, reply etc*) insuficiente; (*person*) incapaz
inadvertently [ɪnədˈvə:tntlɪ] *adv* por descuido
inappropriate [ɪnəˈprəuprɪət] *adj* inadecuado; (*improper*) poco oportuno
inaugurate [ɪˈnɔ:gjureɪt] *vt* inaugurar; (*president, official*) investir
Inc. (US) *abbr* (= *incorporated*) S.A.
incapable [ɪnˈkeɪpəbl] *adj* incapaz
incense [*n* ˈɪnsɛns, *vb* ɪnˈsɛns] *n* incienso ▷*vt* (*anger*) indignar, encolerizar
incentive [ɪnˈsɛntɪv] *n* incentivo, estímulo
inch [ɪntʃ] *n* pulgada; **to be within an ~ of** estar a dos dedos de; **he didn't give an ~** no dio concesión alguna
incidence [ˈɪnsɪdns] *n* (*of crime, disease*) incidencia
incident [ˈɪnsɪdnt] *n* incidente *m*
incidentally [ɪnsɪˈdɛntəlɪ] *adv* (*by the way*) a propósito
inclination [ɪnklɪˈneɪʃən] *n* (*tendency*) tendencia, inclinación *f*; (*desire*) deseo; (*disposition*) propensión *f*
incline [*n* ˈɪnklaɪn, *vb* ɪnˈklaɪn] *n* pendiente *m*, cuesta ▷*vt* (*head*) poner de lado ▷*vi* inclinarse; **to be ~d to** (*tend*) tener tendencia a hacer algo
include [ɪnˈklu:d] *vt* (*incorporate*) incluir; (*in letter*) adjuntar; **including** *prep* incluso,

inclusive

inclusion [ɪn'klu:ʒən] *n* inclusión *f*

inclusive [ɪn'klusɪv] *adj* inclusivo; **~ of tax** incluidos los impuestos

income ['ɪŋkʌm] *n* (*earned*) ingresos *mpl*; (*from property etc*) renta; (*from investment etc*) rédito; **income support** *n* (BRIT) ≈ ayuda familiar; **income tax** *n* impuesto sobre la renta

incoming ['ɪnkʌmɪŋ] *adj* (*flight, government etc*) entrante

incompatible [ɪnkəm'pætɪbl] *adj* incompatible

incompetence [ɪn'kɔmpɪtəns] *n* incompetencia

incompetent [ɪn'kɔmpɪtənt] *adj* incompetente

incomplete [ɪnkəm'pli:t] *adj* (*partial: achievement etc*) incompleto; (*unfinished: painting etc*) inacabado

inconsistent [ɪnkən'sɪstənt] *adj* inconsecuente; (*contradictory*) incongruente; **~ with** (que) no concuerda con

inconvenience [ɪnkən'vi:njəns] *n* inconvenientes *mpl*; (*trouble*) molestia, incomodidad *f* ▷ *vt* incomodar

inconvenient [ɪnkən'vi:njənt] *adj* incómodo, poco práctico; (*time, place, visitor*) inoportuno

incorporate [ɪn'kɔ:pəreɪt] *vt* incorporar; (*contain*) comprender; (*add*) agregar

incorrect [ɪnkə'rɛkt] *adj* incorrecto

increase [*n* 'ɪnkri:s, *vb* ɪn'kri:s] *n* aumento ▷ *vi* aumentar; (*grow*) crecer; (*price*) subir ▷ *vt* aumentar; (*price*) subir; **increasingly** *adv* cada vez más, más y más

incredible [ɪn'krɛdɪbl] *adj* increíble; **incredibly** *adv* increíblemente

incur [ɪn'kə:*] *vt* (*expenditure*) incurrir; (*loss*) sufrir; (*anger, disapproval*) provocar

indecent [ɪn'di:snt] *adj* indecente

indeed [ɪn'di:d] *adv* efectivamente, en realidad; (*in fact*) en efecto; (*furthermore*) es más; **yes ~!** ¡claro que sí!

indefinitely [ɪn'dɛfɪnɪtlɪ] *adv* (*wait*) indefinidamente

independence [ɪndɪ'pɛndns] *n* independencia; **Independence Day** (US) *n* Día *m* de la Independencia

INDEPENDENCE DAY

El cuatro de julio es **Independence Day**, la fiesta nacional de Estados Unidos, que se celebra en conmemoración de la Declaración de Independencia, escrita por Thomas Jefferson y aprobada en 1776. En ella se proclamaba la independencia total de Gran Bretaña de las trece colonias americanas que serían el origen de los Estados Unidos de América.

independent [ɪndɪ'pɛndənt] *adj* independiente; **independent school** *n* (BRIT) escuela *f* privada, colegio *m* privado

index ['ɪndɛks] (*pl* **~es**) *n* (*in book*) índice *m*; (: *in library etc*) catálogo; (*pl* **indices**: *ratio, sign*) exponente *m*

India ['ɪndɪə] *n* la India; **Indian** *adj, n* indio/a; **Red Indian** piel roja *mf*

indicate ['ɪndɪkeɪt] *vt* indicar; **indication** [-'keɪʃən] *n* indicio, señal *f*; **indicative** [ɪn'dɪkətɪv] *adj*: **to be indicative of** indicar; **indicator** *n* indicador *m*; (*Aut*) intermitente *m*

indices ['ɪndɪsi:z] *npl of* **index**

indict [ɪn'daɪt] *vt* acusar; **indictment** *n* acusación *f*

indifference [ɪn'dɪfrəns] *n* indiferencia

indifferent [ɪn'dɪfrənt] *adj* indiferente; (*mediocre*) regular

indigenous [ɪn'dɪdʒɪnəs] *adj* indígena

indigestion [ɪndɪ'dʒɛstʃən] *n* indigestión *f*

indignant [ɪn'dɪgnənt] *adj*: **to be ~ at sth/with sb** indignarse por algo/con algn

indirect [ɪndɪ'rɛkt] *adj* indirecto

indispensable [ɪndɪ'spɛnsəbl] *adj* indispensable, imprescindible

individual [ɪndɪ'vɪdjuəl] *n* individuo ▷ *adj* individual; (*personal*) personal; (*particular*) particular; **individually** *adv* (*singly*) individualmente

Indonesia [ɪndə'ni:zɪə] *n* Indonesia

indoor ['ɪndɔ:*] *adj* (*swimming pool*) cubierto; (*plant*) de interior; (*sport*) bajo cubierta; **indoors** [ɪn'dɔ:z] *adv* dentro

induce [ɪn'dju:s] *vt* inducir, persuadir; (*bring about*) producir; (*labour*) provocar

indulge [ɪn'dʌldʒ] *vt* (*whim*) satisfacer; (*person*) complacer; (*child*) mimar ▷ *vi*: **to ~ in** darse el gusto de; **indulgent** *adj* indulgente

industrial [ɪn'dʌstrɪəl] *adj* industrial; **industrial estate** (BRIT) *n* polígono (SP) *or* zona (LAM) industrial; **industrialist** *n* industrial *mf*; **industrial park** (US) *n* = **industrial estate**

industry ['ɪndəstrɪ] *n* industria; (*diligence*) aplicación *f*

inefficient [ɪnɪ'fɪʃənt] *adj* ineficaz, ineficiente

inequality [ɪnɪ'kwɔlɪtɪ] *n* desigualdad *f*

inevitable [ɪn'ɛvɪtəbl] *adj* inevitable; **inevitably** *adv* inevitablemente

i

inexpensive [ɪnɪk'spɛnsɪv] *adj* económico
inexperienced [ɪnɪk'spɪərɪənst] *adj* inexperto
inexplicable [ɪnɪk'splɪkəbl] *adj* inexplicable
infamous ['ɪnfəməs] *adj* infame
infant ['ɪnfənt] *n* niño/a; (*baby*) niño/a pequeño/a, bebé *mf*; (*pej*) aniñado
infantry ['ɪnfəntrɪ] *n* infantería
infant school (BRIT) *n* parvulario
infect [ɪn'fɛkt] *vt* (*wound*) infectar; (*food*) contaminar; (*person, animal*) contagiar; **infection** [ɪn'fɛkʃən] *n* infección *f*; (*fig*) contagio; **infectious** [ɪn'fɛkʃəs] *adj* (*also fig*) contagioso
infer [ɪn'fəː*] *vt* deducir, inferir
inferior [ɪn'fɪərɪə*] *adj, n* inferior *mf*
infertile [ɪn'fəːtaɪl] *adj* estéril; (*person*) infecundo
infertility [ɪnfəː'tɪlɪtɪ] *n* esterilidad *f*; infecundidad *f*
infested [ɪn'fɛstɪd] *adj*: **~ with** plagado de
infinite ['ɪnfɪnɪt] *adj* infinito; **infinitely** *adv* infinitamente
infirmary [ɪn'fəːmərɪ] *n* hospital *m*
inflamed [ɪn'fleɪmd] *adj*: **to become ~** inflamarse
inflammation [ɪnflə'meɪʃən] *n* inflamación *f*
inflatable [ɪn'fleɪtəbl] *adj* (*ball, boat*) inflable
inflate [ɪn'fleɪt] *vt* (*tyre, price etc*) inflar; (*fig*) hinchar; **inflation** [ɪn'fleɪʃən] *n* (*Econ*) inflación *f*
inflexible [ɪn'flɛksəbl] *adj* (*rule*) rígido; (*person*) inflexible
inflict [ɪn'flɪkt] *vt*: **to ~ sth on sb** infligir algo en algn
influence ['ɪnfluəns] *n* influencia ▷*vt* influir en, influenciar; **under the ~ of alcohol** en estado de embriaguez; **influential** [-'ɛnʃl] *adj* influyente
influx ['ɪnflʌks] *n* afluencia
info (*inf*) ['ɪnfəu] *n* = **information**
inform [ɪn'fɔːm] *vt*: **to ~ sb of sth** informar a algn sobre *or* de algo ▷*vi*: **to ~ on sb** delatar a algn
informal [ɪn'fɔːməl] *adj* (*manner, tone*) familiar; (*dress, interview, occasion*) informal; (*visit, meeting*) extraoficial
information [ɪnfə'meɪʃən] *n* información *f*; (*knowledge*) conocimientos *mpl*; **a piece of ~** un dato; **information office** *n* información *f*; **information technology** *n* informática
informative [ɪn'fɔːmətɪv] *adj* informativo
infra-red [ɪnfrə'rɛd] *adj* infrarrojo
infrastructure ['ɪnfrəstrʌktʃə*] *n* (*of system etc*) infraestructura
infrequent [ɪn'friːkwənt] *adj* infrecuente
infuriate [ɪn'fjuərɪeɪt] *vt*: **to become ~d** ponerse furioso
infuriating [ɪn'fjuərɪeɪtɪŋ] *adj* (*habit, noise*) enloquecedor(a)
ingenious [ɪn'dʒiːnjəs] *adj* ingenioso
ingredient [ɪn'griːdɪənt] *n* ingrediente *m*
inhabit [ɪn'hæbɪt] *vt* vivir en; **inhabitant** *n* habitante *mf*
inhale [ɪn'heɪl] *vt* inhalar ▷*vi* (*breathe in*) aspirar; (*in smoking*) tragar; **inhaler** *n* inhalador *m*
inherent [ɪn'hɪərənt] *adj*: **~ in** *or* **to** inherente a
inherit [ɪn'hɛrɪt] *vt* heredar; **inheritance** *n* herencia; (*fig*) patrimonio
inhibit [ɪn'hɪbɪt] *vt* inhibir, impedir; **inhibition** [-'bɪʃən] *n* cohibición *f*
initial [ɪ'nɪʃl] *adj* primero ▷*n* inicial *f* ▷*vt* firmar con las iniciales; **initials** *npl* (*as signature*) iniciales *fpl*; (*abbreviation*) siglas *fpl*; **initially** *adv* al principio
initiate [ɪ'nɪʃɪeɪt] *vt* iniciar; **to ~ proceedings against sb** (*Law*) entablar proceso contra algn
initiative [ɪ'nɪʃətɪv] *n* iniciativa
inject [ɪn'dʒɛkt] *vt* inyectar; **to ~ sb with sth** inyectar algo a algn; **injection** [ɪn'dʒɛkʃən] *n* inyección *f*
injure ['ɪndʒə*] *vt* (*hurt*) herir, lastimar; (*fig: reputation etc*) perjudicar; **injured** *adj* (*person, arm*) herido, lastimado; **injury** *n* herida, lesión *f*; (*wrong*) perjuicio, daño

Be careful not to translate **injury** by the Spanish word *injuria*.

injustice [ɪn'dʒʌstɪs] *n* injusticia
ink [ɪŋk] *n* tinta; **ink-jet printer** ['ɪŋkdʒɛt-] *n* impresora de chorro de tinta
inland [*adj* 'ɪnlənd, *adv* ɪn'lænd] *adj* (*waterway, port etc*) interior ▷*adv* tierra adentro; **Inland Revenue** (BRIT) *n* departamento de impuestos ≈ Hacienda (SP)
in-laws ['ɪnlɔːz] *npl* suegros *mpl*
inmate ['ɪnmeɪt] *n* (*in prison*) preso/a, presidiario/a; (*in asylum*) internado/a
inn [ɪn] *n* posada, mesón *m*
inner ['ɪnə*] *adj* (*courtyard, calm*) interior; (*feelings*) íntimo; **inner-city** *adj* (*schools, problems*) de las zonas céntricas pobres, de los barrios céntricos pobres
inning ['ɪnɪŋ] *n* (US: *Baseball*) inning *m*, entrada; **~s** (*Cricket*) entrada, turno
innocence ['ɪnəsns] *n* inocencia
innocent ['ɪnəsnt] *adj* inocente

innovation [ɪnəu'veɪʃən] *n* novedad *f*
innovative ['ɪnəu'veɪtɪv] *adj* innovador
in-patient ['ɪnpeɪʃənt] *n* paciente *m/f* interno/a
input ['ɪnput] *n* entrada; (*of resources*) inversión *f*; (*Comput*) entrada de datos
inquest ['ɪnkwɛst] *n* (*coroner's*) encuesta judicial
inquire [ɪn'kwaɪə*] *vi* preguntar ▷ *vt*: **to ~ whether** preguntar si; **to ~ about** (*person*) preguntar por; (*fact*) informarse de; **inquiry** *n* pregunta; (*investigation*) investigación *f*, pesquisa; **"Inquiries"** "Información"
ins. *abbr* = **inches**
insane [ɪn'seɪn] *adj* loco; (*Med*) demente
insanity [ɪn'sænɪtɪ] *n* demencia, locura
insect ['ɪnsɛkt] *n* insecto; **insect repellent** *n* loción *f* contra insectos
insecure [ɪnsɪ'kjuə*] *adj* inseguro
insecurity [ɪnsɪ'kjuərɪtɪ] *n* inseguridad *f*
insensitive [ɪn'sɛnsɪtɪv] *adj* insensible
insert [*vb* ɪn'səːt, *n* 'ɪnsəːt] *vt* (*into sth*) introducir ▷ *n* encarte *m*
inside ['ɪn'saɪd] *n* interior *m* ▷ *adj* interior, interno ▷ *adv* (*be*) (por) dentro; (*go*) hacia dentro ▷ *prep* dentro de; (*of time*): **~ 10 minutes** en menos de 10 minutos; **inside lane** *n* (*Aut*: *in Britain*) carril *m* izquierdo; (: *in US, Europe etc*) carril *m* derecho; **inside out** *adv* (*turn*) al revés; (*know*) a fondo
insight ['ɪnsaɪt] *n* perspicacia
insignificant [ɪnsɪg'nɪfɪknt] *adj* insignificante
insincere [ɪnsɪn'sɪə*] *adj* poco sincero
insist [ɪn'sɪst] *vi* insistir; **to ~ on** insistir en; **to ~ that** insistir en que; (*claim*) exigir que; **insistent** *adj* insistente; (*noise, action*) persistente
insomnia [ɪn'sɔmnɪə] *n* insomnio
inspect [ɪn'spɛkt] *vt* inspeccionar, examinar; (*troops*) pasar revista a; **inspection** [ɪn'spɛkʃən] *n* inspección *f*, examen *m*; (*of troops*) revista; **inspector** *n* inspector(a) *m/f*; (BRIT: *on buses, trains*) revisor(a) *m/f*
inspiration [ɪnspə'reɪʃən] *n* inspiración *f*; **inspire** [ɪn'spaɪə*] *vt* inspirar; **inspiring** *adj* inspirador(a)
instability [ɪnstə'bɪlɪtɪ] *n* inestabilidad *f*
install [ɪn'stɔːl] (US **instal**) *vt* instalar; (*official*) nombrar; **installation** [ɪnstə'leɪʃən] *n* instalación *f*
instalment [ɪn'stɔːlmənt] (US **installment**) *n* plazo; (*of story*) entrega; (*of TV serial etc*) capítulo; **in ~s** (*pay, receive*) a plazos
instance ['ɪnstəns] *n* ejemplo, caso; **for ~** por ejemplo; **in the first ~** en primer lugar
instant ['ɪnstənt] *n* instante *m*, momento ▷ *adj* inmediato; (*coffee etc*) instantáneo; **instantly** *adv* en seguida; **instant messaging** *n* mensajería instantánea
instead [ɪn'stɛd] *adv* en cambio; **~ of** en lugar de, en vez de
instinct ['ɪnstɪŋkt] *n* instinto; **instinctive** *adj* instintivo
institute ['ɪnstɪtjuːt] *n* instituto; (*professional body*) colegio ▷ *vt* (*begin*) iniciar, empezar; (*proceedings*) entablar; (*system, rule*) establecer
institution [ɪnstɪ'tjuːʃən] *n* institución *f*; (*Med*: *home*) asilo; (: *asylum*) manicomio; (*of system etc*) establecimiento; (*of custom*) iniciación *f*
instruct [ɪn'strʌkt] *vt*: **to ~ sb in sth** instruir a algn en *or* sobre algo; **to ~ sb to do sth** dar instrucciones a algn de hacer algo; **instruction** [ɪn'strʌkʃən] *n* (*teaching*) instrucción *f*; **instructions** *npl* (*orders*) órdenes *fpl*; **instructions (for use)** modo de empleo; **instructor** *n* instructor(a) *m/f*
instrument ['ɪnstrəmənt] *n* instrumento; **instrumental** [-'mɛntl] *adj* (*Mus*) instrumental; **to be instrumental in** ser (el) artífice de
insufficient [ɪnsə'fɪʃənt] *adj* insuficiente
insulate ['ɪnsjuleɪt] *vt* aislar; **insulation** [-'leɪʃən] *n* aislamiento
insulin ['ɪnsjulɪn] *n* insulina
insult [*n* 'ɪnsʌlt, *vb* ɪn'sʌlt] *n* insulto ▷ *vt* insultar; **insulting** *adj* insultante
insurance [ɪn'ʃuərəns] *n* seguro; **fire/life ~** seguro contra incendios/sobre la vida; **insurance company** *n* compañía *f* de seguros; **insurance policy** *n* póliza (de seguros)
insure [ɪn'ʃuə*] *vt* asegurar
intact [ɪn'tækt] *adj* íntegro; (*unharmed*) intacto
intake ['ɪnteɪk] *n* (*of food*) ingestión *f*; (*of air*) consumo; (BRIT *Scol*): **an ~ of 200 a year** 200 matriculados al año
integral ['ɪntɪgrəl] *adj* (*whole*) íntegro; (*part*) integrante
integrate ['ɪntɪgreɪt] *vt* integrar ▷ *vi* integrarse
integrity [ɪn'tɛgrɪtɪ] *n* honradez *f*, rectitud *f*
intellect ['ɪntəlɛkt] *n* intelecto; **intellectual** [-'lɛktjuəl] *adj*, *n* intelectual *mf*
intelligence [ɪn'tɛlɪdʒəns] *n* inteligencia
intelligent [ɪn'tɛlɪdʒənt] *adj* inteligente
intend [ɪn'tɛnd] *vt* (*gift etc*): **to ~ sth for** destinar algo a; **to ~ to do sth** tener intención de *or* pensar hacer algo

intense [ɪn'tɛns] *adj* intenso
intensify [ɪn'tɛnsɪfaɪ] *vt* intensificar; (*increase*) aumentar
intensity [ɪn'tɛnsɪtɪ] *n* (*gen*) intensidad *f*
intensive [ɪn'tɛnsɪv] *adj* intensivo; **intensive care** *n*: **to be in intensive care** estar bajo cuidados intensivos; **intensive care unit** *n* unidad *f* de vigilancia intensiva
intent [ɪn'tɛnt] *n* propósito; (*Law*) premeditación *f* ▷ *adj* (*absorbed*) absorto; (*attentive*) atento; **to all ~s and purposes** prácticamente; **to be ~ on doing sth** estar resuelto a hacer algo
intention [ɪn'tɛnʃən] *n* intención *f*, propósito; **intentional** *adj* deliberado
interact [ɪntər'ækt] *vi* influirse mutuamente; **interaction** [ɪntər'ækʃən] *n* interacción *f*, acción *f* recíproca; **interactive** *adj* (*Comput*) interactivo
intercept [ɪntə'sɛpt] *vt* interceptar; (*stop*) detener
interchange ['ɪntətʃeɪndʒ] *n* intercambio; (*on motorway*) intersección *f*
intercourse ['ɪntəkɔːs] *n* (*sexual*) relaciones *fpl* sexuales
interest ['ɪntrɪst] *n* (*also Comm*) interés *m* ▷ *vt* interesar; **interested** *adj* interesado; **to be interested in** interesarse por; **interesting** *adj* interesante; **interest rate** *n* tipo *or* tasa de interés
interface ['ɪntəfeɪs] *n* (*Comput*) junción *f*
interfere [ɪntə'fɪə*] *vi*: **to ~ in** entrometerse en; **to ~ with** (*hinder*) estorbar; (*damage*) estropear
interference [ɪntə'fɪərəns] *n* intromisión *f*; (*Radio, TV*) interferencia
interim ['ɪntərɪm] *n*: **in the ~** en el ínterin ▷ *adj* provisional
interior [ɪn'tɪərɪə*] *n* interior *m* ▷ *adj* interior; **interior design** *n* interiorismo, decoración *f* de interiores
intermediate [ɪntə'miːdɪət] *adj* intermedio
intermission [ɪntə'mɪʃən] *n* intermisión *f*; (*Theatre*) descanso
intern [*vb* ɪn'təːn, *n* 'ɪntəːn] (US) *vt* internar ▷ *n* interno/a
internal [ɪn'təːnl] *adj* (*layout, pipes, security*) interior; (*injury, structure, memo*) internal; **Internal Revenue Service** (US) *n* departamento de impuestos, ≈ Hacienda (SP)
international [ɪntə'næʃənl] *adj* internacional ▷ *n* (BRIT: *match*) partido internacional
Internet ['ɪntənɛt] *n*: **the ~** Internet *m or f*; **Internet café** *n* cibercafé *m*; **Internet Service Provider** *n* proveedor *m* de (acceso a) Internet; **Internet user** *n* internauta *mf*
interpret [ɪn'təːprɪt] *vt* interpretar; (*translate*) traducir; (*understand*) entender ▷ *vi* hacer de intérprete; **interpretation** [ɪntəːprɪ'teɪʃən] *n* interpretación *f*; traducción *f*; **interpreter** *n* intérprete *mf*
interrogate [ɪn'tɛrəugeɪt] *vt* interrogar; **interrogation** [-'geɪʃən] *n* interrogatorio
interrogative [ɪntə'rɔgətɪv] *adj* interrogativo
interrupt [ɪntə'rʌpt] *vt, vi* interrumpir; **interruption** [-'rʌpʃən] *n* interrupción *f*
intersection [ɪntə'sɛkʃən] *n* (*of roads*) cruce *m*
interstate ['ɪntərsteɪt] (US) *n* carretera interestatal
interval ['ɪntəvl] *n* intervalo; (BRIT *Theatre, Sport*) descanso; (*Scol*) recreo; **at ~s** a ratos, de vez en cuando
intervene [ɪntə'viːn] *vi* intervenir; (*event*) interponerse; (*time*) transcurrir
interview ['ɪntəvjuː] *n* entrevista ▷ *vt* entrevistarse con; **interviewer** *n* entrevistador(a) *m/f*
intimate [*adj* 'ɪntɪmət, *vb* 'ɪntɪmeɪt] *adj* íntimo; (*friendship*) estrecho; (*knowledge*) profundo ▷ *vt* dar a entender
intimidate [ɪn'tɪmɪdeɪt] *vt* intimidar, amedrentar
intimidating [ɪn'tɪmɪdeɪtɪŋ] *adj* amedrentador, intimidante
into ['ɪntuː] *prep* en; (*towards*) a; (*inside*) hacia el interior de; **~ 3 pieces/French** en 3 pedazos/al francés
intolerant [ɪn'tɔlərənt] *adj*: **~ (of)** intolerante (con *or* para)
intranet ['ɪntrənet] *n* intranet *f*
intransitive [ɪn'trænsɪtɪv] *adj* intransitivo
intricate ['ɪntrɪkət] *adj* (*design, pattern*) intrincado
intrigue [ɪn'triːg] *n* intriga ▷ *vt* fascinar; **intriguing** *adj* fascinante
introduce [ɪntrə'djuːs] *vt* introducir, meter; (*speaker, TV show etc*) presentar; **to ~ sb (to sb)** presentar a algn (a algn); **to ~ sb to** (*pastime, technique*) introducir a algn a; **introduction** [-'dʌkʃən] *n* introducción *f*; (*of person*) presentación *f*; **introductory** [-'dʌktərɪ] *adj* introductorio; (*lesson, offer*) de introducción
intrude [ɪn'truːd] *vi* (*person*) entrometerse; **to ~ on** estorbar; **intruder** *n* intruso/a
intuition [ɪntjuː'ɪʃən] *n* intuición *f*
inundate ['ɪnʌndeɪt] *vt*: **to ~ with** inundar de
invade [ɪn'veɪd] *vt* invadir

invalid [*n* 'ɪnvəlɪd, *adj* ɪn'vælɪd] *n* (*Med*) minusválido/a ▷ *adj* (*not valid*) inválido, nulo
invaluable [ɪn'væljuəbl] *adj* inestimable
invariably [ɪn'vɛərɪəblɪ] *adv* sin excepción, siempre; **she is ~ late** siempre llega tarde
invasion [ɪn'veɪʒən] *n* invasión *f*
invent [ɪn'vɛnt] *vt* inventar; **invention** [ɪn'vɛnʃən] *n* invento; (*lie*) ficción *f*, mentira; **inventor** *n* inventor(a) *m/f*
inventory ['ɪnvəntrɪ] *n* inventario
inverted commas [ɪn'vəːtɪd-] (BRIT) *npl* comillas *fpl*
invest [ɪn'vɛst] *vt* invertir ▷ *vi*: **to ~ in** (*company etc*) invertir dinero en; (*fig*: *sth useful*) comprar
investigate [ɪn'vɛstɪgeɪt] *vt* investigar; **investigation** [-'geɪʃən] *n* investigación *f*, pesquisa
investigator [ɪn'vɛstɪgeɪtə*] *n* investigador(a) *m/f*; **private ~** investigador(a) *m/f* privado/a
investment [ɪn'vɛstmənt] *n* inversión *f*
investor [ɪn'vɛstə*] *n* inversionista *mf*
invisible [ɪn'vɪzɪbl] *adj* invisible
invitation [ɪnvɪ'teɪʃən] *n* invitación *f*
invite [ɪn'vaɪt] *vt* invitar; (*opinions etc*) solicitar, pedir; **inviting** *adj* atractivo; (*food*) apetitoso
invoice ['ɪnvɔɪs] *n* factura ▷ *vt* facturar
involve [ɪn'vɔlv] *vt* suponer, implicar; tener que ver con; (*concern, affect*) corresponder; **to ~ sb (in sth)** comprometer a algn (con algo); **involved** *adj* complicado; **to be involved in** (*take part*) tomar parte en; (*be engrossed*) estar muy metido en; **involvement** *n* participación *f*; dedicación *f*
inward ['ɪnwəd] *adj* (*movement*) interior, interno; (*thought, feeling*) íntimo; **inward(s)** *adv* hacia dentro
iPod® ['aɪpɔd] *n* iPod® *m*
IQ *n abbr* (= *intelligence quotient*) cociente *m* intelectual
IRA *n abbr* (= *Irish Republican Army*) IRA *m*
Iran [ɪ'rɑːn] *n* Irán *m*; **Iranian** [ɪ'reɪnɪən] *adj, n* iraní *mf*
Iraq [ɪ'rɑːk] *n* Iraq; **Iraqi** *adj, n* iraquí *mf*
Ireland ['aɪələnd] *n* Irlanda
iris ['aɪrɪs] (*pl* **~es**) *n* (*Anat*) iris *m*; (*Bot*) lirio
Irish ['aɪrɪʃ] *adj* irlandés/esa ▷ *npl*: **the ~** los irlandeses; **Irishman** (*irreg*) *n* irlandés *m*; **Irishwoman** (*irreg*) *n* irlandésa
iron ['aɪən] *n* hierro; (*for clothes*) plancha ▷ *cpd* de hierro ▷ *vt* (*clothes*) planchar
ironic(al) [aɪ'rɔnɪk(l)] *adj* irónico; **ironically** *adv* irónicamente
ironing ['aɪənɪŋ] *n* (*activity*) planchado; (*clothes*: *ironed*) ropa planchada; (: *to be ironed*) ropa por planchar; **ironing board** *n* tabla de planchar
irony ['aɪrənɪ] *n* ironía
irrational [ɪ'ræʃənl] *adj* irracional
irregular [ɪ'rɛgjulə*] *adj* irregular; (*surface*) desigual; (*action, event*) anómalo; (*behaviour*) poco ortodoxo
irrelevant [ɪ'rɛləvənt] *adj* fuera de lugar, inoportuno
irresistible [ɪrɪ'zɪstɪbl] *adj* irresistible
irresponsible [ɪrɪ'spɔnsɪbl] *adj* (*act*) irresponsable; (*person*) poco serio
irrigation [ɪrɪ'geɪʃən] *n* riego
irritable ['ɪrɪtəbl] *adj* (*person*) de mal humor
irritate ['ɪrɪteɪt] *vt* fastidiar; (*Med*) picar; **irritating** *adj* fastidioso; **irritation** [-'teɪʃən] *n* fastidio; enfado; picazón *f*
IRS (US) *n abbr* = **Internal Revenue Service**
is [ɪz] *vb see* **be**
ISDN *n abbr* (= *Integrated Services Digital Network*) RDSI *f*
Islam ['ɪzlɑːm] *n* Islam *m*; **Islamic** [ɪz'læmɪk] *adj* islámico
island ['aɪlənd] *n* isla; **islander** *n* isleño/a
isle [aɪl] *n* isla
isn't ['ɪznt] = **is not**
isolated ['aɪsəleɪtɪd] *adj* aislado
isolation [aɪsə'leɪʃən] *n* aislamiento
ISP *n abbr* = **Internet Service Provider**
Israel ['ɪzreɪl] *n* Israel *m*; **Israeli** [ɪz'reɪlɪ] *adj, n* israelí *mf*
issue ['ɪsjuː] *n* (*problem, subject*) cuestión *f*; (*outcome*) resultado; (*of banknotes etc*) emisión *f*; (*of newspaper etc*) edición *f* ▷ *vt* (*rations, equipment*) distribuir, repartir; (*orders*) dar; (*certificate, passport*) expedir; (*decree*) promulgar; (*magazine*) publicar; (*cheques*) extender; (*banknotes, stamps*) emitir; **at ~** en cuestión; **to take ~ with sb (over)** estar en desacuerdo con algn (sobre); **to make an ~ of sth** hacer una cuestión de algo
IT *n abbr* = **information technology**

KEYWORD

it [ɪt] *pron* **1** (*specific subject*: *not generally translated*) él (ella); (: *direct object*) lo, la; (: *indirect object*) le; (*after prep*) él (ella); (*abstract concept*) ello; **it's on the table** está en la mesa; **I can't find it** no lo (*or* la) encuentro; **give it to me** dámelo (*or* dámela); **I spoke to him about it** le hablé del asunto; **what did you learn from it?** ¿qué aprendiste de él (*or* ella)?; **did you go**

to it? (*party, concert etc*) ¿fuiste?
2 (*impersonal*): **it's raining** llueve, está lloviendo; **it's 6 o'clock/the 10th of August** son las 6/es el 10 de agosto; **how far is it? – it's 10 miles/2 hours on the train** ¿a qué distancia está? – a 10 millas/2 horas en tren; **who is it? – it's me** ¿quién es? – soy yo

Italian [ɪ'tæljən] *adj* italiano ▷ *n* italiano/a; (*Ling*) italiano
italics [ɪ'tælɪks] *npl* cursiva
Italy ['ɪtəlɪ] *n* Italia
itch [ɪtʃ] *n* picazón *f* ▷ *vi* (*part of body*) picar; **to ~ to do sth** rabiar por hacer algo; **itchy** *adj*: **my hand is itchy** me pica la mano
it'd ['ɪtd] = **it would; it had**
item ['aɪtəm] *n* artículo; (*on agenda*) asunto (a tratar); (*also*: **news ~**) noticia
itinerary [aɪ'tɪnərərɪ] *n* itinerario
it'll ['ɪtl] = **it will; it shall**
its [ɪts] *adj* su; sus *pl*
it's [ɪts] = **it is; it has**
itself [ɪt'sɛlf] *pron* (*reflexive*) sí mismo/a; (*emphatic*) él mismo(ella misma)
ITV *n abbr* (BRIT: = *Independent Television*) *cadena de televisión comercial independiente del Estado*
I've [aɪv] = **I have**
ivory ['aɪvərɪ] *n* marfil *m*
ivy ['aɪvɪ] *n* (*Bot*) hiedra

jab [dʒæb] *vt*: **to ~ sth into sth** clavar algo en algo ▷ *n* (*inf*: *Med*) pinchazo
jack [dʒæk] *n* (*Aut*) gato; (*Cards*) sota
jacket ['dʒækɪt] *n* chaqueta, americana (SP), saco (LAM); (*of book*) sobrecubierta; **jacket potato** *n* patata asada (con piel)
jackpot ['dʒækpɔt] *n* premio gordo
Jacuzzi® [dʒə'ku:zɪ] *n* jacuzzi® *m*
jagged ['dʒægɪd] *adj* dentado
jail [dʒeɪl] *n* cárcel *f* ▷ *vt* encarcelar; **jail sentence** *n* pena *f* de cárcel
jam [dʒæm] *n* mermelada; (*also*: **traffic ~**) embotellamiento; (*inf*: *difficulty*) apuro ▷ *vt* (*passage etc*) obstruir; (*mechanism, drawer etc*) atascar; (*Radio*) interferir ▷ *vi* atascarse, trabarse; **to ~ sth into sth** meter algo a la fuerza en algo
Jamaica [dʒə'meɪkə] *n* Jamaica
jammed [dʒæmd] *adj* atascado
Jan *abbr* (= *January*) ene
janitor ['dʒænɪtə*] *n* (*caretaker*) portero, conserje *m*
January ['dʒænjuərɪ] *n* enero
Japan [dʒə'pæn] *n* (el) Japón; **Japanese** [dʒæpə'ni:z] *adj* japonés/esa ▷ *n inv* japonés/esa *m/f*; (*Ling*) japonés *m*
jar [dʒɑ:*] *n* tarro, bote *m* ▷ *vi* (*sound*) chirriar; (*colours*) desentonar
jargon ['dʒɑ:gən] *n* jerga
javelin ['dʒævlɪn] *n* jabalina
jaw [dʒɔ:] *n* mandíbula
jazz [dʒæz] *n* jazz *m*
jealous ['dʒɛləs] *adj* celoso; (*envious*) envidioso; **jealousy** *n* celos *mpl*; envidia
jeans [dʒi:nz] *npl* vaqueros *mpl*, tejanos *mpl*
Jello® ['dʒɛləu] (US) *n* gelatina
jelly ['dʒɛlɪ] *n* (*jam*) jalea; (*dessert etc*) gelatina; **jellyfish** *n inv* medusa, aguaviva (RPL)
jeopardize ['dʒɛpədaɪz] *vt* arriesgar, poner en peligro

jerk [dʒəːk] *n* (*jolt*) sacudida; (*wrench*) tirón *m*; (*inf*) imbécil *mf* ▷ *vt* tirar bruscamente de ▷ *vi* (*vehicle*) traquetear
Jersey ['dʒəːzɪ] *n* Jersey *m*
jersey ['dʒəːzɪ] *n* jersey *m*; (*fabric*) (tejido de) punto
Jesus ['dʒiːzəs] *n* Jesús *m*
jet [dʒɛt] *n* (*of gas, liquid*) chorro; (*Aviat*) avión *m* a reacción; **jet lag** *n* desorientación *f* después de un largo vuelo; **jet-ski** *vi* practicar el motociclismo acuático
jetty ['dʒɛtɪ] *n* muelle *m*, embarcadero
Jew [dʒuː] *n* judío/a
jewel ['dʒuːəl] *n* joya; (*in watch*) rubí *m*; **jeweller** (US **jeweler**) *n* joyero/a; **jeweller's (shop)** (US **jewelry store**) *n* joyería; **jewellery** (US **jewelry**) *n* joyas *fpl*, alhajas *fpl*
Jewish ['dʒuːɪʃ] *adj* judío
jigsaw ['dʒɪgsɔː] *n* (*also*: **~ puzzle**) rompecabezas *m inv*, puzle *m*
job [dʒɔb] *n* (*task*) tarea; (*post*) empleo; **it's not my ~** no me incumbe a mí; **it's a good ~ that ...** menos mal que ...; **just the ~!** ¡estupendo!; **job centre** (BRIT) *n oficina estatal de colocaciones*; **jobless** *adj* sin trabajo
jockey ['dʒɔkɪ] *n* jockey *mf* ▷ *vi*: **to ~ for position** maniobrar para conseguir una posición
jog [dʒɔg] *vt* empujar (ligeramente) ▷ *vi* (*run*) hacer footing; **to ~ sb's memory** refrescar la memoria a algn; **jogging** *n* footing *m*
join [dʒɔɪn] *vt* (*things*) juntar, unir; (*club*) hacerse socio de; (*Pol: party*) afiliarse a; (*queue*) ponerse en; (*meet: people*) reunirse con ▷ *vi* (*roads*) juntarse; (*rivers*) confluir ▷ *n* juntura; **join in** *vi* tomar parte, participar ▷ *vt fus* tomar parte *or* participar en; **join up** *vi* reunirse; (*Mil*) alistarse
joiner ['dʒɔɪnə*] (BRIT) *n* carpintero/a
joint [dʒɔɪnt] *n* (*Tech*) junta, unión *f*; (*Anat*) articulación *f*; (BRIT *Culin*) pieza de carne (para asar); (*inf: place*) tugurio; (*: of cannabis*) porro ▷ *adj* (*common*) común; (*combined*) combinado; **joint account** *n* (*with bank etc*) cuenta común; **jointly** *adv* (*gen*) en común; (*together*) conjuntamente
joke [dʒəuk] *n* chiste *m*; (*also*: **practical ~**) broma ▷ *vi* bromear; **to play a ~ on** gastar una broma a; **joker** *n* (*Cards*) comodín *m*
jolly ['dʒɔlɪ] *adj* (*merry*) alegre; (*enjoyable*) divertido ▷ *adv* (BRIT: *inf*) muy, terriblemente
jolt [dʒəult] *n* (*jerk*) sacudida; (*shock*) susto ▷ *vt* (*physically*) sacudir; (*emotionally*) asustar
Jordan ['dʒɔːdən] *n* (*country*) Jordania; (*river*) Jordán *m*
journal ['dʒəːnl] *n* (*magazine*) revista; (*diary*) periódico, diario; **journalism** *n* periodismo; **journalist** *n* periodista *mf*, reportero/a
journey ['dʒəːnɪ] *n* viaje *m*; (*distance covered*) trayecto
joy [dʒɔɪ] *n* alegría; **joyrider** *n gamberro que roba un coche para dar una vuelta y luego abandonarlo*; **joy stick** *n* (*Aviat*) palanca de mando; (*Comput*) palanca de control
Jr *abbr* = **junior**
judge [dʒʌdʒ] *n* juez *mf*; (*fig: expert*) perito ▷ *vt* juzgar; (*consider*) considerar
judo ['dʒuːdəu] *n* judo
jug [dʒʌg] *n* jarra
juggle ['dʒʌgl] *vi* hacer juegos malabares; **juggler** *n* malabarista *mf*
juice [dʒuːs] *n* zumo (SP), jugo (LAM); **juicy** *adj* jugoso
Jul *abbr* (= *July*) jul
July [dʒuː'laɪ] *n* julio
jumble ['dʒʌmbl] *n* revoltijo ▷ *vt* (*also*: **~ up**) revolver; **jumble sale** (BRIT) *n venta de objetos usados con fines benéficos*

JUMBLE SALE

Los **jumble sales** son unos mercadillos que se organizan con fines benéficos en los locales de un colegio, iglesia u otro centro público. En ellos puede comprarse todo tipo de artículos baratos de segunda mano, sobre todo ropa, juguetes, libros, vajillas o muebles.

jumbo ['dʒʌmbəu] *n* (*also*: **~ jet**) jumbo
jump [dʒʌmp] *vi* saltar, dar saltos; (*with fear etc*) pegar un bote; (*increase*) aumentar ▷ *vt* saltar ▷ *n* salto; aumento; **to ~ the queue** (BRIT) colarse
jumper ['dʒʌmpə*] *n* (BRIT: *pullover*) suéter *m*, jersey *m*; (US: *dress*) mandil *m*
jumper cables (US) *npl* = **jump leads**
jump leads (BRIT) *npl* cables *mpl* puente de batería
Jun. *abbr* = **junior**
junction ['dʒʌŋkʃən] *n* (BRIT: *of roads*) cruce *m*; (*Rail*) empalme *m*
June [dʒuːn] *n* junio
jungle ['dʒʌŋgl] *n* selva, jungla
junior ['dʒuːnɪə*] *adj* (*in age*) menor, más joven; (*brother/sister etc*): **seven years her ~** siete años menor que ella; (*position*) subalterno ▷ *n* menor *mf*, joven *mf*; **junior high school** (US) *n centro de educación*

secundaria; *see also* **high school**; **junior school** (BRIT) *n* escuela primaria
junk [dʒʌŋk] *n* (*cheap goods*) baratijas *fpl*; (*rubbish*) basura; **junk food** *n* *alimentos preparados y envasados de escaso valor nutritivo*
junkie ['dʒʌŋkɪ] (*inf*) *n* drogadicto/a, yonqui *mf*
junk mail *n* propaganda de buzón
Jupiter ['dʒu:pɪtə*] *n* (*Mythology*, *Astrology*) Júpiter *m*
jurisdiction [dʒuərɪs'dɪkʃən] *n* jurisdicción *f*; **it falls** *or* **comes within/outside our ~** es/no es de nuestra competencia
jury ['dʒuərɪ] *n* jurado
just [dʒʌst] *adj* justo ▷ *adv* (*exactly*) exactamente; (*only*) sólo, solamente; **he's ~ done it/left** acaba de hacerlo/irse; **~ right** perfecto; **~ two o'clock** las dos en punto; **she's ~ as clever as you** (ella) es tan lista como tú; **~ as well that ...** menos mal que ...; **~ as he was leaving** en el momento en que se marchaba; **~ before/enough** justo antes/lo suficiente; **~ here** aquí mismo; **he ~ missed** ha fallado por poco; **~ listen to this** escucha esto un momento
justice ['dʒʌstɪs] *n* justicia; (*US*: *judge*) juez *mf*; **to do ~ to** (*fig*) hacer justicia a
justification [dʒʌstɪfɪ'keɪʃən] *n* justificación *f*
justify ['dʒʌstɪfaɪ] *vt* justificar; (*text*) alinear
jut [dʒʌt] *vi* (*also*: **~ out**) sobresalir
juvenile ['dʒu:vənaɪl] *adj* (*court*) de menores; (*humour*, *mentality*) infantil ▷ *n* menor *m* de edad

K *abbr* (= *one thousand*) mil; (= *kilobyte*) kilobyte *m*, kiloocteto
kangaroo [kæŋgə'ru:] *n* canguro
karaoke [kɑ:rə'əukɪ] *n* karaoke
karate [kə'rɑ:tɪ] *n* karate *m*
kebab [kə'bæb] *n* pincho moruno
keel [ki:l] *n* quilla; **on an even ~** (*fig*) en equilibrio
keen [ki:n] *adj* (*interest*, *desire*) grande, vivo; (*eye*, *intelligence*) agudo; (*competition*) reñido; (*edge*) afilado; (*eager*) entusiasta; **to be ~ to do** *or* **on doing sth** tener muchas ganas de hacer algo; **to be ~ on sth/sb** interesarse por algo/algn
keep [ki:p] (*pt*, *pp* **kept**) *vt* (*preserve*, *store*) guardar; (*hold back*) quedarse con; (*maintain*) mantener; (*detain*) detener; (*shop*) ser propietario de; (*feed*: *family etc*) mantener; (*promise*) cumplir; (*chickens*, *bees etc*) criar; (*accounts*) llevar; (*diary*) escribir; (*prevent*): **to ~ sb from doing sth** impedir a algn hacer algo ▷ *vi* (*food*) conservarse; (*remain*) seguir, continuar ▷ *n* (*of castle*) torreón *m*; (*food etc*) comida, subsistencia; (*inf*): **for ~s** para siempre; **to ~ doing sth** seguir haciendo algo; **to ~ sb happy** tener a algn contento; **to ~ a place tidy** mantener un lugar limpio; **to ~ sth to o.s.** guardar algo para sí mismo; **to ~ sth (back) from sb** ocultar algo a algn; **to ~ time** (*clock*) mantener la hora exacta; **keep away** *vt*: **to keep sth/sb away from sb** mantener algo/a algn apartado de algn ▷ *vi*: **to keep away (from)** mantenerse apartado (de); **keep back** *vt* (*crowd*, *tears*) contener; (*money*) quedarse con; (*conceal*: *information*): **to keep sth back from sb** ocultar algo a algn ▷ *vi* hacerse a un lado; **keep off** *vt* (*dog*, *person*) mantener a distancia ▷ *vi*: **if the rain keeps off** so no lleuve; **keep your hands off!** ¡no toques!; **"keep off the grass"** "prohibido

pisar el césped"; **keep on** *vi*: **to keep on doing** seguir *or* continuar haciendo; **to keep on (about sth)** no parar de hablar (de algo); **keep out** *vi* (*stay out*) permanecer fuera; **"keep out"** "prohibida la entrada"; **keep up** *vt* mantener, conservar ▷*vi* no retrasarse; **to keep up with** (*pace*) ir al paso de; (*level*) mantenerse a la altura de; **keeper** *n* guardián/ana *m/f*; **keeping** *n* (*care*) cuidado; **in keeping with** de acuerdo con

kennel ['kɛnl] *n* perrera; **kennels** *npl* residencia canina

Kenya ['kɛnjə] *n* Kenia

kept [kɛpt] *pt, pp of* **keep**

kerb [kə:b] (BRIT) *n* bordillo

kerosene ['kɛrəsi:n] *n* keroseno

ketchup ['kɛtʃəp] *n* salsa de tomate, catsup *m*

kettle ['kɛtl] *n* hervidor *m* de agua

key [ki:] *n* llave *f*; (*Mus*) tono; (*of piano, typewriter*) tecla ▷*adj* (*issue etc*) clave *inv* ▷*vt* (*also*: **~ in**) teclear; **keyboard** *n* teclado; **keyhole** *n* ojo (de la cerradura); **keyring** *n* llavero

kg *abbr* (= *kilogram*) kg

khaki ['kɑ:kɪ] *n* caqui

kick [kɪk] *vt* dar una patada *or* un puntapié a; (*inf: habit*) quitarse de ▷*vi* (*horse*) dar coces ▷*n* patada; puntapié *m*; (*of animal*) coz *f*; (*thrill*): **he does it for ~s** lo hace por pura diversión; **kick off** *vi* (*Sport*) hacer el saque inicial; **kick-off** *n* saque inicial; **the kick-off is at 10 o'clock** el partido empieza a las diez

kid [kɪd] *n* (*inf: child*) chiquillo/a; (*animal*) cabrito; (*leather*) cabritilla ▷*vi* (*inf*) bromear

kidnap ['kɪdnæp] *vt* secuestrar; **kidnapping** *n* secuestro

kidney ['kɪdnɪ] *n* riñón *m*; **kidney bean** *n* judía, alubia

kill [kɪl] *vt* matar; (*murder*) asesinar ▷*n* matanza; **to ~ time** matar el tiempo; **killer** *n* asesino/a; **killing** *n* (*one*) asesinato; (*several*) matanza; **to make a killing** (*fig*) hacer su agosto

kiln [kɪln] *n* horno

kilo ['ki:ləu] *n* kilo; **kilobyte** *n* (*Comput*) kilobyte *m*, kiloocteto; **kilogram(me)** *n* kilo, kilogramo; **kilometre** ['kɪləmi:tə*] (US **kilometer**) *n* kilómetro; **kilowatt** *n* kilovatio

kilt [kɪlt] *n* falda escocesa

kin [kɪn] *n see* **next-of-kin**

kind [kaɪnd] *adj* amable, atento ▷*n* clase *f*, especie *f*; (*species*) género; **in ~** (*Comm*) en especie; **a ~ of** una especie de; **to be two of a ~** ser tal para cual

kindergarten ['kɪndəgɑ:tn] *n* jardín *m* de la infancia

kindly ['kaɪndlɪ] *adj* bondadoso; cariñoso ▷*adv* bondadosamente, amablemente; **will you ~ ...** sea usted tan amable de ...

kindness ['kaɪndnɪs] *n* (*quality*) bondad *f*, amabilidad *f*; (*act*) favor *m*

king [kɪŋ] *n* rey *m*; **kingdom** *n* reino; **kingfisher** *n* martín *m* pescador; **king-size(d) bed** *n* cama de matrimonio extragrande

kiosk ['ki:ɔsk] *n* quiosco; (BRIT *Tel*) cabina

kipper ['kɪpə*] *n* arenque *m* ahumado

kiss [kɪs] *n* beso ▷*vt* besar; **to ~ (each other)** besarse; **kiss of life** *n* respiración *f* boca a boca

kit [kɪt] *n* (*equipment*) equipo; (*tools etc*) (caja de) herramientas *fpl*; (*assembly kit*) juego de armar

kitchen ['kɪtʃɪn] *n* cocina

kite [kaɪt] *n* (*toy*) cometa

kitten ['kɪtn] *n* gatito/a

kiwi ['ki:wi:-] *n* (*also*: **~ fruit**) kiwi *m*

km *abbr* (= *kilometre*) km

km/h *abbr* (= *kilometres per hour*) km/h

knack [næk] *n*: **to have the ~ of doing sth** tener el don de hacer algo

knee [ni:] *n* rodilla; **kneecap** *n* rótula

kneel [ni:l] (*pt, pp* **knelt**) *vi* (*also*: **~ down**) arrodillarse

knelt [nɛlt] *pt, pp of* **kneel**

knew [nju:] *pt of* **know**

knickers ['nɪkəz] (BRIT) *npl* bragas *fpl*

knife [naɪf] (*pl* **knives**) *n* cuchillo ▷*vt* acuchillar

knight [naɪt] *n* caballero; (*Chess*) caballo

knit [nɪt] *vt* tejer, tricotar ▷*vi* hacer punto, tricotar; (*bones*) soldarse; **to ~ one's brows** fruncir el ceño; **knitting** *n* labor *f* de punto; **knitting needle** *n* aguja de hacer punto; **knitwear** *n* prendas *fpl* de punto

knives [naɪvz] *npl of* **knife**

knob [nɔb] *n* (*of door*) tirador *m*; (*of stick*) puño; (*on radio, TV*) botón *m*

knock [nɔk] *vt* (*strike*) golpear; (*bump into*) chocar contra; (*inf*) criticar ▷*vi* (*at door etc*): **to ~ at/on** llamar a ▷*n* golpe *m*; (*on door*) llamada; **knock down** *vt* atropellar; **knock off** (*inf*) *vi* (*finish*) salir del trabajo ▷*vt* (*from price*) descontar; (*inf: steal*) birlar; **knock out** *vt* dejar sin sentido; (*Boxing*) poner fuera de combate, dejar K.O.; (*in competition*) eliminar; **knock over** *vt* (*object*) tirar; (*person*) atropellar; **knockout** *n* (*Boxing*) K.O. *m*, knockout *m* ▷*cpd* (*competition etc*) eliminatorio

knot [nɔt] *n* nudo ▷*vt* anudar

know [nəu] (*pt* **knew**, *pp* **known**) *vt* (*facts*) saber; (*be acquainted with*) conocer;

(*recognize*) reconocer, conocer; **to ~ how to swim** saber nadar; **to ~ about** *or* **of sb/sth** saber de algn/algo; **know-all** *n* sabelotodo *mf*; **know-how** *n* conocimientos *mpl*; **knowing** *adj* (*look*) de complicidad; **knowingly** *adv* (*purposely*) adrede; (*smile, look*) con complicidad; **know-it-all** (US) *n* = **know-all**

knowledge ['nɔlɪdʒ] *n* conocimiento; (*learning*) saber *m*, conocimientos *mpl*; **knowledgeable** *adj* entendido

known [nəun] *pp of* **know** ▷ *adj* (*thief, facts*) conocido; (*expert*) reconocido

knuckle ['nʌkl] *n* nudillo

koala [kəu'ɑːlə] *n* (*also*: **~ bear**) koala *m*

Koran [kɔ'rɑːn] *n* Corán *m*

Korea [kə'rɪə] *n* Corea; **Korean** *adj, n* coreano/a *m/f*

kosher ['kəuʃə*] *adj* autorizado por la ley judía

Kosovar ['kɔsəvɑ*], **Kosovan** ['kɔːsəvən] *adj* kosovar

Kosovo ['kɔsəvəu] *n* Kosovo

Kremlin ['kremlɪn] *n*: **the ~** el Kremlin

Kuwait [ku'weɪt] *n* Kuwait *m*

l

L (BRIT) *abbr* = **learner driver**

l. *abbr* (= *litre*) l

lab [læb] *n abbr* = **laboratory**

label ['leɪbl] *n* etiqueta ▷ *vt* poner etiqueta a

labor *etc* ['leɪbə*] (US) = **labour** *etc*

laboratory [lə'bɔrətərɪ] *n* laboratorio

Labor Day (US) *n* día *m* de los trabajadores (*primer lunes de septiembre*)

labor union (US) *n* sindicato

labour ['leɪbə*] (US **labor**) *n* (*hard work*) trabajo; (*labour force*) mano *f* de obra; (*Med*): **to be in ~** estar de parto ▷ *vi*: **to ~ (at sth)** trabajar (en algo) ▷ *vt*: **to ~ a point** insistir en un punto; **L~, the L~ party** (BRIT) el partido laborista, los laboristas *mpl*; **labourer** *n* peón *m*; **farm labourer** peón *m*; (*day labourer*) jornalero

lace [leɪs] *n* encaje *m*; (*of shoe etc*) cordón *m* ▷ *vt* (*shoes*: *also*: **~ up**) atarse (los zapatos)

lack [læk] *n* (*absence*) falta ▷ *vt* faltarle a algn, carecer de; **through** *or* **for ~ of** por falta de; **to be ~ing** faltar, no haber; **to be ~ing in sth** faltarle a algn algo

lacquer ['lækə*] *n* laca

lacy ['leɪsɪ] *adj* (*of lace*) de encaje; (*like lace*) como de encaje

lad [læd] *n* muchacho, chico

ladder ['lædə*] *n* escalera (de mano); (BRIT: *in tights*) carrera

ladle ['leɪdl] *n* cucharón *m*

lady ['leɪdɪ] *n* señora; (*dignified, graceful*) dama; **"ladies and gentlemen ..."** "señoras y caballeros ..."; **young ~** señorita; **the ladies' (room)** los servicios de señoras; **ladybird** (US **ladybug**) *n* mariquita

lag [læg] *n* retraso ▷ *vi* (*also*: **~ behind**) retrasarse, quedarse atrás ▷ *vt* (*pipes*) revestir

lager ['lɑːgə*] *n* cerveza (rubia)

lagoon [lə'guːn] *n* laguna

laid [leɪd] *pt, pp of* **lay**; **laid back** *(inf) adj* relajado
lain [leɪn] *pp of* **lie**
lake [leɪk] *n* lago
lamb [læm] *n* cordero; *(meat)* (carne *f* de) cordero
lame [leɪm] *adj* cojo; *(excuse)* poco convincente
lament [lə'mɛnt] *n* quejo ▷*vt* lamentarse de
lamp [læmp] *n* lámpara; **lamppost** (BRIT) *n* (poste *m* de) farol *m*; **lampshade** *n* pantalla
land [lænd] *n* tierra; *(country)* país *m*; *(piece of land)* terreno; *(estate)* tierras *fpl*, finca ▷*vi* *(from ship)* desembarcar; *(Aviat)* aterrizar; *(fig: fall)* caer, terminar ▷*vt* *(passengers, goods)* desembarcar; **to ~ sb with sth** *(inf)* hacer cargar a algn con algo; **landing** *n* aterrizaje *m*; *(of staircase)* rellano; **landing card** *n* tarjeta de desembarque; **landlady** *n* *(of rented house, pub etc)* dueña; **landlord** *n* propietario; *(of pub etc)* patrón *m*; **landmark** *n* lugar *m* conocido; **to be a landmark** *(fig)* marcar un hito histórico; **landowner** *n* terrateniente *mf*; **landscape** *n* paisaje *m*; **landslide** *n* *(Geo)* corrimiento de tierras; *(fig: Pol)* victoria arrolladora
lane [leɪn] *n* *(in country)* camino; *(Aut)* carril *m*; *(in race)* calle *f*
language ['læŋgwɪdʒ] *n* lenguaje *m*; *(national tongue)* idioma *m*, lengua; **bad ~** palabrotas *fpl*; **language laboratory** *n* laboratorio de idiomas; **language school** *n* academia de idiomas
lantern ['læntn] *n* linterna, farol *m*
lap [læp] *n* *(of track)* vuelta; *(of body)* regazo ▷*vt* *(also:* **~ up**) beber a lengüetadas ▷*vi* *(waves)* chapotear; **to sit on sb's ~** sentarse en las rodillas de algn
lapel [lə'pɛl] *n* solapa
lapse [læps] *n* fallo; *(moral)* desliz *m*; *(of time)* intervalo ▷*vi* *(expire)* caducar; *(time)* pasar, transcurrir; **to ~ into bad habits** caer en malos hábitos
laptop (computer) ['læptɔp-] *n* (ordenador *m*) portátil *m*
lard [lɑ:d] *n* manteca (de cerdo)
larder ['lɑ:də*] *n* despensa
large [lɑ:dʒ] *adj* grande; **at ~** *(free)* en libertad; *(generally)* en general

> Be careful not to translate **large** by the Spanish word *largo*.

largely *adv* *(mostly)* en su mayor parte; *(introducing reason)* en gran parte; **large-scale** *adj* *(map)* en gran escala; *(fig)* importante
lark [lɑ:k] *n* *(bird)* alondra; *(joke)* broma
laryngitis [lærɪn'dʒaɪtɪs] *n* laringitis *f*
lasagne [lə'zænjə] *n* lasaña
laser ['leɪzə*] *n* láser *m*; **laser printer** *n* impresora (por) láser
lash [læʃ] *n* latigazo; *(also:* **eye~**) pestaña ▷*vt* azotar; *(tie)*: **to ~ to/together** atar a/atar; **lash out** *vi*: **to lash out (at sb)** *(hit)* arremeter (contra algn); **to lash out against sb** lanzar invectivas contra algn
lass [læs] (BRIT) *n* chica
last [lɑ:st] *adj* último; *(end: of series etc)* final ▷*adv* *(most recently)* la última vez; *(finally)* por último ▷*vi* durar; *(continue)* continuar, seguir; **~ night** anoche; **~ week** la semana pasada; **at ~** por fin; **~ but one** penúltimo; **lastly** *adv* por último, finalmente; **last-minute** *adj* de última hora
latch [lætʃ] *n* pestillo; **latch onto** *vt fus* *(person, group)* pegarse a; *(idea)* agarrarse a
late [leɪt] *adj* *(far on: in time, process etc)* al final de; *(not on time)* tarde, atrasado; *(dead)* fallecido ▷*adv* tarde; *(behind time, schedule)* con retraso; **of ~** últimamente; **~ at night** a última hora de la noche; **in ~ May** hacia fines de mayo; **the ~ Mr X** el difunto Sr X; **latecomer** *n* recién llegado/a; **lately** *adv* últimamente; **later** *adj* *(date etc)* posterior; *(version etc)* más reciente ▷*adv* más tarde, después; **latest** ['leɪtɪst] *adj* último; **at the latest** a más tardar
lather ['lɑ:ðə*] *n* espuma (de jabón) ▷*vt* enjabonar
Latin ['lætɪn] *n* latín *m* ▷*adj* latino; **Latin America** *n* América latina; **Latin American** *adj, n* latinoamericano/a *m/f*
latitude ['lætɪtju:d] *n* latitud *f*; *(fig)* libertad *f*
latter ['lætə*] *adj* último; *(of two)* segundo ▷*n*: **the ~** el último, éste
laugh [lɑ:f] *n* risa ▷*vi* reír(se); **(to do sth) for a ~** (hacer algo) en broma; **laugh at** *vt fus* reírse de; **laughter** *n* risa
launch [lɔ:ntʃ] *n* lanzamiento; *(boat)* lancha ▷*vt* *(ship)* botar; *(rocket etc)* lanzar; *(fig)* comenzar; **launch into** *vt fus* lanzarse a
launder ['lɔ:ndə*] *vt* lavar
Launderette® [lɔ:n'drɛt] (BRIT) *n* lavandería (automática)
Laundromat® ['lɔ:ndrəmæt] (US) *n* = **Launderette**
laundry ['lɔ:ndrɪ] *n* *(dirty)* ropa sucia; *(clean)* colada; *(room)* lavadero
lava ['lɑ:və] *n* lava
lavatory ['lævətərɪ] *n* wáter *m*
lavender ['lævəndə*] *n* lavanda
lavish ['lævɪʃ] *adj* *(amount)* abundante;

(*person*): **~ with** pródigo en ▷ *vt*: **to ~ sth on sb** colmar a algn de algo

law [lɔː] *n* ley *f*; (*Scol*) derecho; (*a rule*) regla; (*professions connected with law*) jurisprudencia; **lawful** *adj* legítimo, lícito; **lawless** *adj* (*action*) criminal

lawn [lɔːn] *n* césped *m*; **lawnmower** *n* cortacésped *m*

lawsuit ['lɔːsuːt] *n* pleito

lawyer ['lɔːjə*] *n* abogado/a; (*for sales, wills etc*) notario/a

lax [læks] *adj* laxo

laxative ['læksətɪv] *n* laxante *m*

lay [leɪ] (*pt, pp* **laid**) *pt of* **lie** ▷ *adj* laico; (*not expert*) lego ▷ *vt* (*place*) colocar; (*eggs, table*) poner; (*cable*) tender; (*carpet*) extender; **lay down** *vt* (*pen etc*) dejar; (*rules etc*) establecer; **to lay down the law** (*pej*) imponer las normas; **lay off** *vt* (*workers*) despedir; **lay on** *vt* (*meal, facilities*) proveer; **lay out** *vt* (*spread out*) disponer, exponer; **lay-by** *n* (BRIT *Aut*) área de aparcamiento

layer ['leɪə*] *n* capa

layman ['leɪmən] (*irreg*) *n* lego

layout ['leɪaut] *n* (*design*) plan *m*, trazado; (*Press*) composición *f*

lazy ['leɪzɪ] *adj* perezoso, vago; (*movement*) lento

lb. *abbr* = **pound** (*weight*)

lead¹ [liːd] (*pt, pp* **led**) *n* (*front position*) delantera; (*clue*) pista; (*Elec*) cable *m*; (*for dog*) correa; (*Theatre*) papel *m* principal ▷ *vt* (*walk etc in front*) ir a la cabeza de; (*guide*): **to ~ sb somewhere** conducir a algn a algún sitio; (*be leader*) dirigir; (*start, guide: activity*) protagonizar ▷ *vi* (*road, pipe etc*) conducir a; (*Sport*) ir primero; **to be in the ~** (*Sport*) llevar la delantera; (*fig*) ir a la cabeza; **to ~ the way** llevar la delantera; **lead up to** *vt fus* (*events*) conducir a; (*in conversation*) preparar el terreno para

lead² [lɛd] *n* (*metal*) plomo; (*in pencil*) mina

leader ['liːdə*] *n* jefe/a *m/f*, líder *mf*; (*Sport*) líder *mf*; **leadership** *n* dirección *f*; (*position*) mando; (*quality*) iniciativa

lead-free ['lɛdfriː] *adj* sin plomo

leading ['liːdɪŋ] *adj* (*main*) principal; (*first*) primero; (*front*) delantero

lead singer [liːd-] *n* cantante *mf*

leaf [liːf] (*pl* **leaves**) *n* hoja ▷ *vi*: **to ~ through** hojear; **to turn over a new ~** reformarse

leaflet ['liːflɪt] *n* folleto

league [liːg] *n* sociedad *f*; (*Football*) liga; **to be in ~ with** haberse confabulado con

leak [liːk] *n* (*of liquid, gas*) escape *m*, fuga; (*in pipe*) agujero; (*in roof*) gotera; (*in security*) filtración *f* ▷ *vi* (*shoes, ship*) hacer agua; (*pipe*) tener (un) escape; (*roof*) gotear; (*liquid, gas*) escaparse, fugarse; (*fig*) divulgarse ▷ *vt* (*fig*) filtrar

lean [liːn] (*pt, pp* **~ed** *or* **~t**) *adj* (*thin*) flaco; (*meat*) magro ▷ *vt*: **to ~ sth on sth** apoyar algo en algo ▷ *vi* (*slope*) inclinarse; **to ~ against** apoyarse contra; **to ~ on** apoyarse en; **lean forward** *vi* inclinarse hacia adelante; **lean over** *vi* inclinarse; **leaning** *n*: **leaning (towards)** inclinación *f* (hacia)

leant [lɛnt] *pt, pp of* **lean**

leap [liːp] (*pt, pp* **~ed** *or* **~t**) *n* salto ▷ *vi* saltar

leapt [lɛpt] *pt, pp of* **leap**

leap year *n* año bisiesto

learn [ləːn] (*pt, pp* **~ed** *or* **~t**) *vt* aprender ▷ *vi* aprender; **to ~ about sth** enterarse de algo; **to ~ to do sth** aprender a hacer algo; **learner** *n* (BRIT: *also*: **learner driver**) principiante *mf*; **learning** *n* el saber *m*, conocimientos *mpl*

learnt [ləːnt] *pp of* **learn**

lease [liːs] *n* arriendo ▷ *vt* arrendar

leash [liːʃ] *n* correa

least [liːst] *adj*: **the ~** (*slightest*) el menor, el más pequeño; (*smallest amount of*) mínimo ▷ *adv* (+ *vb*) menos; (+ *adj*): **the ~ expensive** el (la) menos costoso/a; **the ~ possible effort** el menor esfuerzo posible; **at ~** por lo menos, al menos; **you could at ~ have written** por lo menos podías haber escrito; **not in the ~** en absoluto

leather ['lɛðə*] *n* cuero

leave [liːv] (*pt, pp* **left**) *vt* dejar; (*go away from*) abandonar; (*place etc: permanently*) salir de ▷ *vi* irse; (*train etc*) salir ▷ *n* permiso; **to ~ sth to sb** (*money etc*) legar algo a algn; (*responsibility etc*) encargar a algn de algo; **to be left** quedar, sobrar; **there's some milk left over** sobra *or* queda algo de leche; **on ~** de permiso; **leave behind** *vt* (*on purpose*) dejar; (*accidentally*) dejarse; **leave out** *vt* omitir

leaves [liːvz] *npl of* **leaf**

Lebanon ['lɛbənən] *n*: **the ~** el Líbano

lecture ['lɛktʃə*] *n* conferencia; (*Scol*) clase *f* ▷ *vi* dar una clase ▷ *vt* (*scold*): **to ~ sb on** *or* **about sth** echar una reprimenda a algn por algo; **to give a ~ on** dar una conferencia sobre; **lecture hall** *n* sala de conferencias; (*Univ*) aula; **lecturer** *n* conferenciante *mf*; (BRIT: *at university*) profesor(a) *m/f*; **lecture theatre** *n* = **lecture hall**

led [lɛd] *pt, pp of* **lead¹**

ledge [lɛdʒ] *n* repisa; (*of window*) alféizar *m*; (*of mountain*) saliente *m*

leek [liːk] *n* puerro

left [lɛft] *pt, pp of* **leave** ▷ *adj* izquierdo;

(*remaining*): **there are two ~** quedan dos ▷*n* izquierda ▷*adv* a la izquierda; **on** *or* **to the ~** a la izquierda; **the L~** (*Pol*) la izquierda; **left-hand** *adj*: **the left-hand side** la izquierda; **left-hand drive** *adj*: **a left-hand drive car** un coche con el volante a la izquierda; **left-handed** *adj* zurdo; **left-luggage locker** *n* (BRIT) consigna *f* automática; **left-luggage (office)** (BRIT) *n* consigna; **left-overs** *npl* sobras *fpl*; **left-wing** *adj* (*Pol*) de izquierdas, izquierdista

leg [lɛg] *n* pierna; (*of animal, chair*) pata; (*trouser leg*) pernera; (*Culin*: *of lamb*) pierna; (: *of chicken*) pata; (*of journey*) etapa

legacy ['lɛgəsɪ] *n* herencia

legal ['li:gl] *adj* (*permitted by law*) lícito; (*of law*) legal; **legal holiday** (US) *n* fiesta oficial; **legalize** *vt* legalizar; **legally** *adv* legalmente

legend ['lɛdʒənd] *n* (*also fig*: *person*) leyenda; **legendary** [-ərɪ] *adj* legendario

leggings ['legɪŋz] *npl* mallas *fpl*, leggins *mpl*

legible ['lɛdʒəbl] *adj* legible

legislation [lɛdʒɪs'leɪʃən] *n* legislación *f*

legislative ['lɛdʒɪslətɪv] *adj* legislativo

legitimate [lɪ'dʒɪtɪmət] *adj* legítimo

leisure ['lɛʒə*] *n* ocio, tiempo libre; **at ~** con tranquilidad; **leisure centre** (BRIT) *n* centro de recreo; **leisurely** *adj* sin prisa; lento

lemon ['lɛmən] *n* limón *m*; **lemonade** *n* (*fizzy*) gaseosa; **lemon tea** *n* té *m* con limón

lend [lɛnd] (*pt, pp* **lent**) *vt*: **to ~ sth to sb** prestar algo a algn

length [lɛŋθ] *n* (*size*) largo, longitud *f*; (*distance*): **the ~ of** todo lo largo de; (*of swimming pool, cloth*) largo; (*of wood, string*) trozo; (*amount of time*) duración *f*; **at ~** (*at last*) por fin, finalmente; (*lengthily*) largamente; **lengthen** *vt* alargar ▷*vi* alargarse; **lengthways** *adv* a lo largo; **lengthy** *adj* largo, extenso

lens [lɛnz] *n* (*of spectacles*) lente *f*; (*of camera*) objetivo

Lent [lɛnt] *n* Cuaresma

lent [lɛnt] *pt, pp of* **lend**

lentil ['lɛntl] *n* lenteja

Leo ['li:əu] *n* Leo

leopard ['lɛpəd] *n* leopardo

leotard ['li:ətɑ:d] *n* mallas *fpl*

leprosy ['lɛprəsɪ] *n* lepra

lesbian ['lɛzbɪən] *n* lesbiana

less [lɛs] *adj* (*in size, degree etc*) menor; (*in quality*) menos ▷*pron, adv* menos ▷*prep*: **~ tax/10% discount** menos impuestos/el 10 por ciento de descuento; **~ than half** menos de la mitad; **~ than ever** menos que nunca; **~ and ~** cada vez menos; **the ~ he works ...** cuanto menos trabaja ...; **lessen** *vi* disminuir, reducirse ▷*vt* disminuir, reducir; **lesser** ['lɛsə*] *adj* menor; **to a lesser extent** en menor grado

lesson ['lɛsn] *n* clase *f*; (*warning*) lección *f*

let [lɛt] (*pt, pp* **~**) *vt* (*allow*) dejar, permitir; (BRIT: *lease*) alquilar; **to ~ sb do sth** dejar que algn haga algo; **to ~ sb know sth** comunicar algo a algn; **~'s go** ¡vamos!; **~ him come** que venga; **"to ~"** "se alquila"; **let down** *vt* (*tyre*) desinflar; (*disappoint*) defraudar; **let in** *vt* dejar entrar; (*visitor etc*) hacer pasar; **let off** *vt* (*culprit*) dejar escapar; (*gun*) disparar; (*bomb*) accionar; (*firework*) hacer estallar; **let out** *vt* dejar salir; (*sound*) soltar

lethal ['li:θl] *adj* (*weapon*) mortífero; (*poison, wound*) mortal

letter ['lɛtə*] *n* (*of alphabet*) letra; (*correspondence*) carta; **letterbox** (BRIT) *n* buzón *m*

lettuce ['lɛtɪs] *n* lechuga

leukaemia [lu:'ki:mɪə] (US **leukemia**) *n* leucemia

level ['lɛvl] *adj* (*flat*) llano ▷*adv*: **to draw ~ with** llegar a la altura de ▷*n* nivel *m*; (*height*) altura ▷*vt* nivelar; allanar; (*destroy*: *building*) derribar; (: *forest*) arrasar; **to be ~ with** estar a nivel de; **A ~s** (BRIT) ≈ exámenes *mpl* de bachillerato superior, B.U.P.; **AS ~** (BRIT) *asignatura aprobada entre los "GCSEs" y los "A levels"*; **on the ~** (*fig*: *honest*) serio; **level crossing** (BRIT) *n* paso a nivel

lever ['li:və*] *n* (*also fig*) palanca ▷*vt*: **to ~ up** levantar con palanca; **leverage** *n* (*using bar etc*) apalancamiento; (*fig*: *influence*) influencia

levy ['lɛvɪ] *n* impuesto ▷*vt* exigir, recaudar

liability [laɪə'bɪlətɪ] *n* (*pej*: *person, thing*) estorbo, lastre *m*; (*Jur*: *responsibility*) responsabilidad *f*

liable ['laɪəbl] *adj* (*subject*): **~ to** sujeto a; (*responsible*): **~ for** responsable de; (*likely*): **~ to do** propenso a hacer

liaise [lɪ'eɪz] *vi*: **to ~ with** enlazar con

liar ['laɪə*] *n* mentiroso/a

liberal ['lɪbərəl] *adj* liberal; (*offer, amount etc*) generoso; **Liberal Democrat** *n* (BRIT) demócrata *m/f* liberal

liberate ['lɪbəreɪt] *vt* (*people*: *from poverty etc*) librar; (*prisoner*) libertar; (*country*) liberar

liberation [lɪbə'reɪʃən] *n* liberación *f*

liberty ['lɪbətɪ] *n* libertad *f*; **to be at ~** (*criminal*) estar en libertad; **to be at ~ to do** estar libre para hacer; **to take the ~ of doing sth** tomarse la libertad de hacer algo

Libra ['li:brə] *n* Libra

librarian [laɪ'brɛərɪən] *n* bibliotecario/a
library ['laɪbrərɪ] *n* biblioteca

Be careful not to translate **library** by the Spanish word *librería*.

Libya ['lɪbɪə] *n* Libia
lice [laɪs] *npl of* **louse**
licence ['laɪsəns] (*US* **license**) *n* licencia; (*permit*) permiso; (*also*: **driving ~**) carnet *m* de conducir (*SP*), licencia de manejo (*LAM*)
license ['laɪsəns] *n* (*US*) = **licence** ▷ *vt* autorizar, dar permiso a; **licensed** *adj* (*for alcohol*) autorizado para vender bebidas alcohólicas; (*car*) matriculado; **license plate** (*US*) *n* placa (de matrícula); **licensing hours** (*BRIT*) *npl horas durante las cuales se permite la venta y consumo de alcohol (en un bar etc)*
lick [lɪk] *vt* lamer; (*inf*: *defeat*) dar una paliza a; **to ~ one's lips** relamerse
lid [lɪd] *n* (*of box, case*) tapa; (*of pan*) tapadera
lie [laɪ] (*pt* **lay**, *pp* **lain**) *vi* (*rest*) estar echado, estar acostado; (*of object*: *be situated*) estar, encontrarse; (*tell lies*: *pt, pp* **lied**) mentir ▷ *n* mentira; **to ~ low** (*fig*) mantenerse a escondidas; **lie about** *or* **around** *vi* (*things*) estar tirado; (*BRIT*: *people*) estar tumbado; **lie down** *vi* echarse, tumbarse
Liechtenstein ['lɪktənstaɪn] *n* Liechtenstein *m*
lie-in ['laɪɪn] (*BRIT*) *n*: **to have a ~** quedarse en la cama
lieutenant [lɛf'tɛnənt, *US* lu:'tɛnənt] *n* (*Mil*) teniente *mf*
life [laɪf] (*pl* **lives**) *n* vida; **to come to ~** animarse; **life assurance** (*BRIT*) *n* seguro de vida; **lifeboat** *n* lancha de socorro; **lifeguard** *n* vigilante *mf*, socorrista *mf*; **life insurance** *n* = **life assurance**; **life jacket** *n* chaleco salvavidas; **lifelike** *adj* (*model etc*) que parece vivo; (*realistic*) realista; **life preserver** (*US*) *n* cinturón *m*/chaleco salvavidas; **life sentence** *n* cadena perpetua; **lifestyle** *n* estilo de vida; **lifetime** *n* (*of person*) vida; (*of thing*) período de vida
lift [lɪft] *vt* levantar; (*end*: *ban, rule*) levantar, suprimir ▷ *vi* (*fog*) disiparse ▷ *n* (*BRIT*: *machine*) ascensor *m*; **to give sb a ~** (*BRIT*) llevar a algn en el coche; **lift up** *vt* levantar; **lift-off** *n* despegue *m*
light [laɪt] (*pt, pp* **~ed** *or* **lit**) *n* luz *f*; (*lamp*) luz *f*, lámpara; (*Aut*) faro; (*for cigarette etc*): **have you got a ~?** ¿tienes fuego? ▷ *vt* (*candle, cigarette, fire*) encender (*SP*), prender (*LAM*); (*room*) alumbrar ▷ *adj* (*colour*) claro; (*not heavy, also fig*) ligero; (*room*) con mucha luz; (*gentle, graceful*) ágil; **lights** *npl* (*traffic lights*) semáforos *mpl*; **to come to ~** salir a luz; **in the ~ of** (*new evidence etc*) a la luz de; **light up** *vi* (*smoke*) encender un cigarrillo; (*face*) iluminarse ▷ *vt* (*illuminate*) iluminar, alumbrar; (*set fire to*) encender; **light bulb** *n* bombilla (*SP*), foco (*MEX*), bujía (*CAM*), bombita (*RPL*); **lighten** *vt* (*make less heavy*) aligerar; **lighter** *n* (*also*: **cigarette lighter**) encendedor *m*, mechero; **light-hearted** *adj* (*person*) alegre; (*remark etc*) divertido; **lighthouse** *n* faro; **lighting** *n* (*system*) alumbrado; **lightly** *adv* ligeramente; (*not seriously*) con poca seriedad; **to get off lightly** ser castigado con poca severidad
lightning ['laɪtnɪŋ] *n* relámpago, rayo
lightweight ['laɪtweɪt] *adj* (*suit*) ligero ▷ *n* (*Boxing*) peso ligero
like [laɪk] *vt* gustarle a algn ▷ *prep* como ▷ *adj* parecido, semejante ▷ *n*: **and the ~** y otros por el estilo; **his ~s and dislikes** sus gustos y aversiones; **I would ~, I'd ~** me gustaría; (*for purchase*) quisiera; **would you ~ a coffee?** ¿te apetece un café?; **I ~ swimming** me gusta nadar; **she ~s apples** le gustan las manzanas; **to be** *or* **look ~ sb/sth** parecerse a algn/algo; **what does it look/taste/sound ~?** ¿cómo es/a qué sabe/cómo suena?; **that's just ~ him** es muy de él, es característico de él; **do it ~ this** hazlo así; **it is nothing ~ ...** no tiene parecido alguno con ...; **likeable** *adj* simpático, agradable
likelihood ['laɪklɪhud] *n* probabilidad *f*
likely ['laɪklɪ] *adj* probable; **he's ~ to leave** es probable que se vaya; **not ~!** ¡ni hablar!
likewise ['laɪkwaɪz] *adv* igualmente; **to do ~** hacer lo mismo
liking ['laɪkɪŋ] *n*: **~ (for)** (*person*) cariño (a); (*thing*) afición (a); **to be to sb's ~** ser del gusto de algn
lilac ['laɪlək] *n* (*tree*) lilo; (*flower*) lila
Lilo® ['laɪləu] *n* colchoneta inflable
lily ['lɪlɪ] *n* lirio, azucena; **~ of the valley** lirio de los valles
limb [lɪm] *n* miembro
limbo ['lɪmbəu] *n*: **to be in ~** (*fig*) quedar a la expectativa
lime [laɪm] *n* (*tree*) limero; (*fruit*) lima; (*Geo*) cal *f*
limelight ['laɪmlaɪt] *n*: **to be in the ~** (*fig*) ser el centro de atención
limestone ['laɪmstəun] *n* piedra caliza
limit ['lɪmɪt] *n* límite *m* ▷ *vt* limitar; **limited** *adj* limitado; **to be limited to** limitarse a
limousine ['lɪməzi:n] *n* limusina
limp [lɪmp] *n*: **to have a ~** tener cojera ▷ *vi*

cojear ▷ *adj* flojo; (*material*) fláccido
line [laɪn] *n* línea; (*rope*) cuerda; (*for fishing*) sedal *m*; (*wire*) hilo; (*row, series*) fila, hilera; (*of writing*) renglón *m*, línea; (*of song*) verso; (*on face*) arruga; (*Rail*) vía ▷ *vt* (*road etc*) llenar; (*Sewing*) forrar; **to ~ the streets** llenar las aceras; **in ~ with** alineado con; (*according to*) de acuerdo con; **line up** *vi* hacer cola ▷ *vt* alinear; (*prepare*) preparar; organizar
linear ['lɪnɪə*] *adj* lineal
linen ['lɪnɪn] *n* ropa blanca; (*cloth*) lino
liner ['laɪnə*] *n* vapor *m* de línea, transatlántico; (*for bin*) bolsa (de basura)
line-up ['laɪnʌp] *n* (US: *queue*) cola; (*Sport*) alineación *f*
linger ['lɪŋgə*] *vi* retrasarse, tardar en marcharse; (*smell, tradition*) persistir
lingerie ['lænʒəri:] *n* lencería
linguist ['lɪŋgwɪst] *n* lingüista *mf*; **linguistic** *adj* lingüístico
lining ['laɪnɪŋ] *n* forro; (*Anat*) (membrana) mucosa
link [lɪŋk] *n* (*of a chain*) eslabón *m*; (*relationship*) relación *f*, vínculo; (*Internet*) link *m*, enlace *m* ▷ *vt* vincular, unir; (*associate*): **to ~ with** *or* **to** relacionar con; **links** *npl* (*Golf*) campo de golf; **link up** *vt* acoplar ▷ *vi* unirse
lion ['laɪən] *n* león *m*; **lioness** *n* leona
lip [lɪp] *n* labio; **lipread** *vi* leer los labios; **lip salve** *n* crema protectora para labios; **lipstick** *n* lápiz *m* de labios, carmín *m*
liqueur [lɪ'kjuə*] *n* licor *m*
liquid ['lɪkwɪd] *adj, n* líquido; **liquidizer** [-aɪzə*] *n* licuadora
liquor ['lɪkə*] *n* licor *m*, bebidas *fpl* alcohólicas; **liquor store** (US) *n* bodega, *tienda de vinos y bebidas alcohólicas*
Lisbon ['lɪzbən] *n* Lisboa
lisp [lɪsp] *n* ceceo ▷ *vi* cecear
list [lɪst] *n* lista ▷ *vt* (*mention*) enumerar; (*put on a list*) poner en una lista
listen ['lɪsn] *vi* escuchar, oír; **to ~ to sb/sth** escuchar a algn/algo; **listener** *n* oyente *mf*; (*Radio*) radioyente *mf*
lit [lɪt] *pt, pp of* **light**
liter ['li:tə*] (US) *n* = **litre**
literacy ['lɪtərəsɪ] *n* capacidad *f* de leer y escribir
literal ['lɪtərl] *adj* literal; **literally** *adv* literalmente
literary ['lɪtərərɪ] *adj* literario
literate ['lɪtərət] *adj* que sabe leer y escribir; (*educated*) culto
literature ['lɪtərɪtʃə*] *n* literatura; (*brochures etc*) folletos *mpl*
litre ['li:tə*] (US **liter**) *n* litro
litter ['lɪtə*] *n* (*rubbish*) basura; (*young animals*) camada, cría; **litter bin** (BRIT) *n* papelera; **littered** *adj*: **littered with** (*scattered*) lleno de
little ['lɪtl] *adj* (*small*) pequeño; (*not much*) poco ▷ *adv* poco; **a ~** un poco (de); **~ house/bird** casita/pajarito; **a ~ bit** un poquito; **~ by ~** poco a poco; **little finger** *n* dedo meñique
live¹ [laɪv] *adj* (*animal*) vivo; (*wire*) conectado; (*broadcast*) en directo; (*shell*) cargado
live² [lɪv] *vi* vivir; **live together** *vi* vivir juntos; **live up to** *vt fus* (*fulfil*) cumplir con
livelihood ['laɪvlɪhud] *n* sustento
lively ['laɪvlɪ] *adj* vivo; (*interesting: place, book etc*) animado
liven up ['laɪvn-] *vt* animar ▷ *vi* animarse
liver ['lɪvə*] *n* hígado
lives [laɪvz] *npl of* **life**
livestock ['laɪvstɔk] *n* ganado
living ['lɪvɪŋ] *adj* (*alive*) vivo ▷ *n*: **to earn** *or* **make a ~** ganarse la vida; **living room** *n* sala (de estar)
lizard ['lɪzəd] *n* lagarto; (*small*) lagartija
load [ləud] *n* carga; (*weight*) peso ▷ *vt* (*Comput*) cargar; (*also*: **~ up**): **to ~ (with)** cargar (con *or* de); **a ~ of rubbish** (*inf*) tonterías *fpl*; **a ~ of, ~s of** (*fig*) (gran) cantidad de, montones de; **loaded** *adj* (*vehicle*): **to be loaded with** estar cargado de
loaf [ləuf] (*pl* **loaves**) *n* (barra de) pan *m*
loan [ləun] *n* préstamo ▷ *vt* prestar; **on ~** prestado
loathe [ləuð] *vt* aborrecer; (*person*) odiar
loaves [ləuvz] *npl of* **loaf**
lobby ['lɔbɪ] *n* vestíbulo, sala de espera; (*Pol: pressure group*) grupo de presión ▷ *vt* presionar
lobster ['lɔbstə*] *n* langosta
local ['ləukl] *adj* local ▷ *n* (*pub*) bar *m*; **the locals** *npl* los vecinos, los del lugar; **local anaesthetic** *n* (*Med*) anestesia local; **local authority** *n* municipio, ayuntamiento (SP); **local government** *n* gobierno municipal; **locally** [-kəlɪ] *adv* en la vecindad; por aquí
locate [ləu'keɪt] *vt* (*find*) localizar; (*situate*): **to be ~d in** estar situado en
location [ləu'keɪʃən] *n* situación *f*; **on ~** (*Cinema*) en exteriores
loch [lɔx] *n* lago
lock [lɔk] *n* (*of door, box*) cerradura; (*of canal*) esclusa; (*of hair*) mechón *m* ▷ *vt* (*with key*) cerrar (con llave) ▷ *vi* (*door etc*) cerrarse (con llave); (*wheels*) trabarse; **lock in** *vt* encerrar; **lock out** *vt* (*person*) cerrar la puerta a; **lock up** *vt* (*criminal*) meter en la cárcel; (*mental patient*) encerrar; (*house*)

cerrar (con llave) ▷ *vi* echar la llave
locker ['lɔkə*] *n* casillero; **locker-room** (*US*) *n* (*Sport*) vestuario
locksmith ['lɔksmɪθ] *n* cerrajero/a
locomotive [ləukə'məutɪv] *n* locomotora
lodge [lɔdʒ] *n* casita (del guarda) ▷ *vi* (*person*): **to ~ (with)** alojarse (en casa de); (*bullet, bone*) incrustarse ▷ *vt* presentar; **lodger** *n* huésped *mf*
lodging ['lɔdʒɪŋ] *n* alojamiento, hospedaje *m*
loft [lɔft] *n* desván *m*
log [lɔg] *n* (*of wood*) leño, tronco; (*written account*) diario ▷ *vt* anotar; **log in, log on** *vi* (*Comput*) entrar en el sistema; **log off, log out** *vi* (*Comput*) salir del sistema
logic ['lɔdʒɪk] *n* lógica; **logical** *adj* lógico
logo ['ləugəu] *n* logotipo
lollipop ['lɔlɪpɔp] *n* pirulí *m*; **lollipop man/lady** (BRIT: *irreg*) *n persona encargada de ayudar a los niños a cruzar la calle*
lolly ['lɔlɪ] *n* (*inf: ice cream*) polo; (*: lollipop*) piruleta; (*: money*) guita
London ['lʌndən] *n* Londres; **Londoner** *n* londinense *mf*
lone [ləun] *adj* solitario
loneliness ['ləunlɪnɪs] *n* soledad *f*; aislamiento
lonely ['ləunlɪ] *adj* (*situation*) solitario; (*person*) solo; (*place*) aislado
long [lɔŋ] *adj* largo ▷ *adv* mucho tiempo, largamente ▷ *vi*: **to ~ for sth** anhelar algo; **so** *or* **as ~ as** mientras, con tal que; **don't be ~!** ¡no tardes!, ¡vuelve pronto!; **how ~ is the street?** ¿cuánto tiene la calle de largo?; **how ~ is the lesson?** ¿cuánto dura la clase?; **6 metres ~** que mide 6 metros, de 6 metros de largo; **6 months ~** que dura 6 meses, de 6 meses de duración; **all night ~** toda la noche; **he no ~er comes** ya no viene; **I can't stand it any ~er** ya no lo aguanto más; **~ before** mucho antes; **before ~** (*+ future*) dentro de poco; (*+ past*) poco tiempo después; **at ~ last** al fin, por fin; **long-distance** *adj* (*race*) de larga distancia; (*call*) interurbano; **long-haul** *adj* (*flight*) de larga distancia; **longing** *n* anhelo, ansia; (*nostalgia*) nostalgia ▷ *adj* anhelante
longitude ['lɔŋgɪtju:d] *n* longitud *f*
long: long jump *n* salto de longitud; **long-life** *adj* (*batteries*) de larga duración; (*milk*) uperizado; **long-sighted** (BRIT) *adj* présbita; **long-standing** *adj* de mucho tiempo; **long-term** *adj* a largo plazo
loo [lu:] (BRIT: *inf*) *n* wáter *m*
look [luk] *vi* mirar; (*seem*) parecer; (*building etc*): **to ~ south/on to the sea** dar al sur/al mar ▷ *n* (*gen*): **to have a ~** mirar; (*glance*) mirada; (*appearance*) aire *m*, aspecto; **looks** *npl* (*good looks*) belleza; **~ (here)!** (*expressing annoyance etc*) ¡oye!; **~!** (*expressing surprise*) ¡mira!; **look after** *vt fus* (*care for*) cuidar a; (*deal with*) encargarse de; **look around** *vi* echar una mirada alrededor; **look at** *vt fus* mirar; (*read quickly*) echar un vistazo a; **look back** *vi* mirar hacia atrás; **look down on** *vt fus* (*fig*) despreciar, mirar con desprecio; **look for** *vt fus* buscar; **look forward to** *vt fus* esperar con ilusión; (*in letters*): **we look forward to hearing from you** quedamos a la espera de sus gratas noticias; **look into** *vt* investigar; **look out** *vi* (*beware*): **to look out (for)** tener cuidado (de); **look out for** *vt fus* (*seek*) buscar; (*await*) esperar; **look round** *vi* volver la cabeza; **look through** *vt fus* (*examine*) examinar; **look up** *vi* mirar hacia arriba; (*improve*) mejorar ▷ *vt* (*word*) buscar; **look up to** *vt fus* admirar; **lookout** *n* (*tower etc*) puesto de observación; (*person*) vigía *mf*; **to be on the lookout for sth** estar al acecho de algo
loom [lu:m] *vi*: **~ (up)** (*threaten*) surgir, amenazar; (*event: approach*) aproximarse
loony ['lu:nɪ] (*inf*) *n, adj* loco/a *m/f*
loop [lu:p] *n* lazo ▷ *vt*: **to ~ sth round sth** pasar algo alrededor de algo; **loophole** *n* escapatoria
loose [lu:s] *adj* suelto; (*clothes*) ancho; (*morals, discipline*) relajado; **to be on the ~** estar en libertad; **to be at a ~ end** *or* **at ~ ends** (*US*) no saber qué hacer; **loosely** *adv* libremente, aproximadamente; **loosen** *vt* aflojar
loot [lu:t] *n* botín *m* ▷ *vt* saquear
lop-sided ['lɔp'saɪdɪd] *adj* torcido
lord [lɔ:d] *n* señor *m*; **L~ Smith** Lord Smith; **the L~** el Señor; **my ~** (*to bishop*) Ilustrísima; (*to noble etc*) Señor; **good L~!** ¡Dios mío!; **Lords** *npl* (BRIT: *Pol*): **the (House of) Lords** la Cámara de los Lores
lorry ['lɔrɪ] (BRIT) *n* camión *m*; **lorry driver** (BRIT) *n* camionero/a
lose [lu:z] (*pt, pp* **lost**) *vt* perder ▷ *vi* perder, ser vencido; **to ~ (time)** (*clock*) atrasarse; **lose out** *vi* salir perdiendo; **loser** *n* perdedor(a) *m/f*
loss [lɔs] *n* pérdida; **heavy ~es** (*Mil*) grandes pérdidas; **to be at a ~** no saber qué hacer; **to make a ~** sufrir pérdidas
lost [lɔst] *pt, pp of* **lose** ▷ *adj* perdido; **lost property** (*US* **lost and found**) *n* objetos *mpl* perdidos
lot [lɔt] *n* (*group: of things*) grupo; (*at auctions*) lote *m*; **the ~** el todo, todos; **a ~** (*large number: of books etc*) muchos; (*a great deal*) mucho, bastante; **a ~ of, ~s**

of mucho(s) *(pl)*; **I read a ~** leo bastante; **to draw ~s (for sth)** echar suertes (para decidir algo)
lotion ['ləuʃən] *n* loción *f*
lottery ['lɔtərɪ] *n* lotería
loud [laud] *adj* *(voice, sound)* fuerte; *(laugh, shout)* estrepitoso; *(condemnation etc)* enérgico; *(gaudy)* chillón/ona ▷ *adv* *(speak etc)* fuerte; **out ~** en voz alta; **loudly** *adv* *(noisily)* fuerte; *(aloud)* en voz alta; **loudspeaker** *n* altavoz *m*
lounge [laundʒ] *n* salón *m*, sala (de estar); *(at airport etc)* sala; (BRIT: *also*: **~-bar**) salón-bar *m* ▷ *vi* (*also*: **~ about** *or* **around**) reposar, holgazanear
louse [laus] (*pl* **lice**) *n* piojo
lousy ['lauzɪ] *(inf)* *adj* *(bad quality)* malísimo, asqueroso; *(ill)* fatal
love [lʌv] *n* *(romantic, sexual)* amor *m*; *(kind, caring)* cariño ▷ *vt* amar, querer; *(thing, activity)* encantarle a algn; **"~ from Anne"** *(on letter)* "un abrazo (de) Anne"; **to ~ to do** encantarle a algn hacer; **to be/fall in ~ with** estar enamorado/enamorarse de; **to make ~** hacer el amor; **for the ~ of** por amor de; **"15 ~"** *(Tennis)* "15 a cero"; **I ~ you** te quiero; **I ~ paella** me encanta la paella; **love affair** *n* aventura sentimental; **love life** *n* vida sentimental
lovely ['lʌvlɪ] *adj* *(delightful)* encantador(a); *(beautiful)* precioso
lover ['lʌvə*] *n* amante *mf*; *(person in love)* enamorado; *(amateur)*: **a ~ of** un(a) aficionado/a *or* un(a) amante de
loving ['lʌvɪŋ] *adj* amoroso, cariñoso; *(action)* tierno
low [ləu] *adj, adv* bajo ▷ *n* *(Meteorology)* área de baja presión; **to be ~ on** *(supplies etc)* andar mal de; **to feel ~** sentirse deprimido; **to turn (down) ~** bajar; **low-alcohol** *adj* de bajo contenido en alcohol; **low-calorie** *adj* bajo en calorías
lower ['ləuə*] *adj* más bajo; *(less important)* menos importante ▷ *vt* bajar; *(reduce)* reducir ▷ *vr*: **to ~ o.s. to** *(fig)* rebajarse a
low-fat *adj* *(milk, yoghurt)* desnatado; *(diet)* bajo en calorías
loyal ['lɔɪəl] *adj* leal; **loyalty** *n* lealtad *f*; **loyalty card** *n* tarjeta cliente
L.P. *n abbr* (= *long-playing record*) elepé *m*
L-plates ['ɛl-] (BRIT) *npl* placas *fpl* de aprendiz de conductor

L-PLATES

En el Reino Unido las personas que están aprendiendo a conducir deben llevar en la parte delantera y trasera de su vehículo unas placas blancas con una L en rojo conocidas como **L-Plates** (de **learner**). No es necesario que asistan a clases teóricas sino que, desde el principio, se le sentrega un carnet de conducir provisional ("provisional driving licence") para que realicen sus prácticas, aunque no pueden circular por las autopistas y deben ir siempre acompañadas por un conductor con carnet definitivo ("full driving licence").

Lt *abbr* (= *lieutenant*) Tte.
Ltd *abbr* (= *limited company*) S.A.
luck [lʌk] *n* suerte *f*; **bad ~** mala suerte; **good ~!** ¡que tengas suerte!, ¡suerte!; **bad** *or* **hard** *or* **tough ~!** ¡qué pena!; **luckily** *adv* afortunadamente; **lucky** *adj* afortunado; *(at cards etc)* con suerte; *(object)* que trae suerte
lucrative ['lu:krətɪv] *adj* lucrativo
ludicrous ['lu:dɪkrəs] *adj* absurdo
luggage ['lʌgɪdʒ] *n* equipaje *m*; **luggage rack** *n* *(on car)* baca, portaequipajes *m inv*
lukewarm ['lu:kwɔ:m] *adj* tibio
lull [lʌl] *n* tregua ▷ *vt*: **to ~ sb to sleep** arrullar a algn; **to ~ sb into a false sense of security** dar a algn una falsa sensación de seguridad
lullaby ['lʌləbaɪ] *n* nana
lumber ['lʌmbə*] *n* *(junk)* trastos *mpl* viejos; *(wood)* maderos *mpl*
luminous ['lu:mɪnəs] *adj* luminoso
lump [lʌmp] *n* terrón *m*; *(fragment)* trozo; *(swelling)* bulto ▷ *vt* (*also*: **~ together**) juntar; **lump sum** *n* suma global; **lumpy** *adj* *(sauce)* lleno de grumos; *(mattress)* lleno de bultos
lunatic ['lu:nətɪk] *adj* loco
lunch [lʌntʃ] *n* almuerzo, comida ▷ *vi* almorzar; **lunch break, lunch hour** *n* hora del almuerzo; **lunch time** *n* hora de comer
lung [lʌŋ] *n* pulmón *m*
lure [luə*] *n* *(attraction)* atracción *f* ▷ *vt* tentar
lurk [lə:k] *vi* *(person, animal)* estar al acecho; *(fig)* acechar
lush [lʌʃ] *adj* exuberante
lust [lʌst] *n* lujuria; *(greed)* codicia
Luxembourg ['lʌksəmbə:g] *n* Luxemburgo
luxurious [lʌg'zjuərɪəs] *adj* lujoso
luxury ['lʌkʃərɪ] *n* lujo ▷ *cpd* de lujo
Lycra® ['laɪkrə] *n* licra®
lying ['laɪɪŋ] *n* mentiras *fpl* ▷ *adj* mentiroso
lyrics ['lɪrɪks] *npl* *(of song)* letra

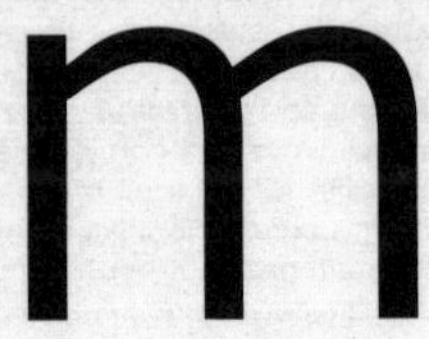

m. *abbr* = **metre; mile; million**
M.A. *abbr* = **Master of Arts**
ma (*inf*) [mɑː] *n* mamá
mac [mæk] (BRIT) *n* impermeable *m*
macaroni [mækəˈrəunɪ] *n* macarrones *mpl*
Macedonia [mæsɪˈdəunɪə] *n* Macedonia; **Macedonian** [-ˈdəunɪən] *adj* macedonio ▷*n* macedonio/a; (*Ling*) macedonio
machine [məˈʃiːn] *n* máquina ▷*vt* (*dress etc*) coser a máquina; (*Tech*) hacer a máquina; **machine gun** *n* ametralladora; **machinery** *n* maquinaria; (*fig*) mecanismo; **machine washable** *adj* lavable a máquina
macho [ˈmætʃəu] *adj* machista
mackerel [ˈmækrl] *n inv* caballa
mackintosh [ˈmækɪntɔʃ] (BRIT) *n* impermeable *m*
mad [mæd] *adj* loco; (*idea*) disparatado; (*angry*) furioso; (*keen*): **to be ~ about sth** volverle loco a algn algo
Madagascar [mædəˈgæskə*] *n* Madagascar *m*
madam [ˈmædəm] *n* señora
mad cow disease *n* encefalopatía espongiforme bovina
made [meɪd] *pt, pp of* **make**; **made-to-measure** (BRIT) *adj* hecho a la medida; **made-up** [ˈmeɪdʌp] *adj* (*story*) ficticio
madly [ˈmædlɪ] *adv* locamente
madman [ˈmædmən] (*irreg*) *n* loco
madness [ˈmædnɪs] *n* locura
Madrid [məˈdrɪd] *n* Madrid
Mafia [ˈmæfɪə] *n* Mafia
mag [mæg] *n abbr* (BRIT *inf*) = **magazine**
magazine [mægəˈziːn] *n* revista; (*Radio, TV*) programa *m* magazina
maggot [ˈmægət] *n* gusano
magic [ˈmædʒɪk] *n* magia ▷*adj* mágico; **magical** *adj* mágico; **magician** [məˈdʒɪʃən] *n* mago/a; (*conjurer*) prestidigitador(a) *m/f*
magistrate [ˈmædʒɪstreɪt] *n* juez *mf* (municipal)
magnet [ˈmægnɪt] *n* imán *m*; **magnetic** [-ˈnɛtɪk] *adj* magnético; (*personality*) atrayente
magnificent [mægˈnɪfɪsənt] *adj* magnífico
magnify [ˈmægnɪfaɪ] *vt* (*object*) ampliar; (*sound*) aumentar; **magnifying glass** *n* lupa
magpie [ˈmægpaɪ] *n* urraca
mahogany [məˈhɔgənɪ] *n* caoba
maid [meɪd] *n* criada; **old ~** (*pej*) solterona
maiden name *n* nombre *m* de soltera
mail [meɪl] *n* correo; (*letters*) cartas *fpl* ▷*vt* echar al correo; **mailbox** (US) *n* buzón *m*; **mailing list** *n* lista de direcciones; **mailman** (US: *irreg*) *n* cartero; **mail-order** *n* pedido postal
main [meɪn] *adj* principal, mayor ▷*n* (*pipe*) cañería maestra; (US) red *f* eléctrica ▷**the ~s** *npl* (BRIT *Elec*) la red eléctrica; **in the ~** en general; **main course** *n* (*Culin*) plato principal; **mainland** *n* tierra firme; **mainly** *adv* principalmente; **main road** *n* carretera; **mainstream** *n* corriente *f* principal; **main street** *n* calle *f* mayor
maintain [meɪnˈteɪn] *vt* mantener; **maintenance** [ˈmeɪntənəns] *n* mantenimiento; (*Law*) manutención *f*
maisonette [meɪzəˈnɛt] *n* dúplex *m*
maize [meɪz] (BRIT) *n* maíz *m*, choclo (SC)
majesty [ˈmædʒɪstɪ] *n* majestad *f*; (*title*): **Your M~** Su Majestad
major [ˈmeɪdʒə*] *n* (*Mil*) comandante *mf* ▷*adj* principal; (*Mus*) mayor
Majorca [məˈjɔːkə] *n* Mallorca
majority [məˈdʒɔrɪtɪ] *n* mayoría
make [meɪk] (*pt, pp* **made**) *vt* hacer; (*manufacture*) fabricar; (*mistake*) cometer; (*speech*) pronunciar; (*cause to be*): **to ~ sb sad** poner triste a algn; (*force*): **to ~ sb do sth** obligar a algn a hacer algo; (*earn*) ganar; (*equal*): **2 and 2 ~ 4** 2 y 2 son 4 ▷*n* marca; **to ~ the bed** hacer la cama; **to ~ a fool of sb** poner a algn en ridículo; **to ~ a profit/loss** obtener ganancias/sufrir pérdidas; **to ~ it** (*arrive*) llegar; (*achieve sth*) tener éxito; **what time do you ~ it?** ¿qué hora tienes?; **to ~ do with** contentarse con; **make off** *vi* largarse; **make out** *vt* (*decipher*) descifrar; (*understand*) entender; (*see*) distinguir; (*cheque*) extender; **make up** *vt* (*invent*) inventar; (*prepare*) hacer; (*constitute*) constituir ▷*vi* reconciliarse; (*with cosmetics*) maquillarse; **make up for** *vt*

fus compensar; **makeover** ['meɪkəuvə*] *n* (*by beautician*) sesión *f* de maquillaje y peluquería; (*change of image*) lavado de cara; **maker** *n* fabricante *mf*; (*of film, programme*) autor(a) *m/f*; **makeshift** *adj* improvisado; **make-up** *n* maquillaje *m*

making ['meɪkɪŋ] *n* (*fig*): **in the ~** en vías de formación; **to have the ~s of** (*person*) tener madera de

malaria [mə'lɛərɪə] *n* malaria

Malaysia [mə'leɪzɪə] *n* Malasia, Malaysia

male [meɪl] *n* (*Biol*) macho ▷ *adj* (*sex, attitude*) masculino; (*child etc*) varón

malicious [mə'lɪʃəs] *adj* malicioso; rencoroso

malignant [mə'lɪgnənt] *adj* (*Med*) maligno

mall [mɔːl] (*US*) *n* (*also*: **shopping ~**) centro comercial

mallet ['mælɪt] *n* mazo

malnutrition [mælnjuː'trɪʃən] *n* desnutrición *f*

malpractice [mæl'præktɪs] *n* negligencia profesional

malt [mɔːlt] *n* malta; (*whisky*) whisky *m* de malta

Malta ['mɔːltə] *n* Malta; **Maltese** [-'tiːz] *adj, n inv* maltés/esa *m/f*

mammal ['mæml] *n* mamífero

mammoth ['mæməθ] *n* mamut *m* ▷ *adj* gigantesco

man [mæn] (*pl* **men**) *n* hombre *m*; (*mankind*) el hombre ▷ *vt* (*Naut*) tripular; (*Mil*) guarnecer; (*operate: machine*) manejar; **an old ~** un viejo; **~ and wife** marido y mujer

manage ['mænɪdʒ] *vi* arreglárselas, ir tirando ▷ *vt* (*be in charge of*) dirigir; (*control: person*) manejar; (*: ship*) gobernar; **manageable** *adj* manejable; **management** *n* dirección *f*; **manager** *n* director(a) *m/f*; (*of pop star*) mánager *mf*; (*Sport*) entrenador(a) *m/f*; **manageress** *n* directora; entrenadora; **managerial** [-ə'dʒɪerɪəl] *adj* directivo; **managing director** *n* director(a) *m/f* general

mandarin ['mændərɪn] *n* (*also*: **~ orange**) mandarina; (*person*) mandarín *m*

mandate ['mændeɪt] *n* mandato

mandatory ['mændətərɪ] *adj* obligatorio

mane [meɪn] *n* (*of horse*) crin *f*; (*of lion*) melena

maneuver [mə'nuːvə*] (*US*) = **manoeuvre**

mangetout [mɔnʒ'tuː] *n* tirabeque *m*

mango ['mæŋgəu] (*pl* **~es**) *n* mango

man: manhole *n* agujero de acceso; **manhood** *n* edad *f* viril; (*state*) virilidad *f*

mania ['meɪnɪə] *n* manía; **maniac** ['meɪnɪæk] *n* maníaco/a; (*fig*) maniático

manic ['mænɪk] *adj* frenético

manicure ['mænɪkjuə*] *n* manicura

manifest ['mænɪfɛst] *vt* manifestar, mostrar ▷ *adj* manifiesto

manifesto [mænɪ'fɛstəu] *n* manifiesto

manipulate [mə'nɪpjuleɪt] *vt* manipular

man: mankind [mæn'kaɪnd] *n* humanidad *f*, género humano; **manly** *adj* varonil; **man-made** *adj* artificial

manner ['mænə*] *n* manera, modo; (*behaviour*) conducta, manera de ser; (*type*): **all ~ of things** toda clase de cosas; **manners** *npl* (*behaviour*) modales *mpl*; **bad ~s** mala educación

manoeuvre [mə'nuːvə*] (*US* **maneuver**) *vt, vi* maniobrar ▷ *n* maniobra

manpower ['mænpauə*] *n* mano *f* de obra

mansion ['mænʃən] *n* palacio, casa grande

manslaughter ['mænslɔːtə*] *n* homicidio no premeditado

mantelpiece ['mæntlpiːs] *n* repisa, chimenea

manual ['mænjuəl] *adj* manual ▷ *n* manual *m*

manufacture [mænju'fæktʃə*] *vt* fabricar ▷ *n* fabricación *f*; **manufacturer** *n* fabricante *mf*

manure [mə'njuə*] *n* estiércol *m*

manuscript ['mænjuskrɪpt] *n* manuscrito

many ['mɛnɪ] *adj, pron* muchos/as; **a great ~** muchísimos, un buen número de; **~ a time** muchas veces

map [mæp] *n* mapa *m* ▷ **to ~ out** *vt* proyectar

maple ['meɪpl] *n* arce *m*, maple *m* (*LAM*)

Mar *abbr* (= *March*) mar

mar [mɑː*] *vt* estropear

marathon ['mærəθən] *n* maratón *m*

marble ['mɑːbl] *n* mármol *m*; (*toy*) canica

March [mɑːtʃ] *n* marzo

march [mɑːtʃ] *vi* (*Mil*) marchar; (*demonstrators*) manifestarse ▷ *n* marcha; (*demonstration*) manifestación *f*

mare [mɛə*] *n* yegua

margarine [mɑːdʒə'riːn] *n* margarina

margin ['mɑːdʒɪn] *n* margen *m*; (*Comm: profit margin*) margen *m* de beneficios; **marginal** *adj* marginal; **marginally** *adv* ligeramente

marigold ['mærɪgəuld] *n* caléndula

marijuana [mærɪ'wɑːnə] *n* marijuana

marina [mə'riːnə] *n* puerto deportivo

marinade [mærɪ'neɪd] *n* adobo

marinate ['mærɪneɪt] *vt* marinar

marine [mə'ri:n] *adj* marino ▷*n* soldado de marina

marital ['mærɪtl] *adj* matrimonial; **marital status** *n* estado *m* civil

maritime ['mærɪtaɪm] *adj* marítimo

marjoram ['mɑ:dʒərəm] *n* mejorana

mark [mɑ:k] *n* marca, señal *f*; (*in snow, mud etc*) huella; (*stain*) mancha; (BRIT *Scol*) nota ▷*vt* marcar; manchar; (*damage: furniture*) rayar; (*indicate: place etc*) señalar; (BRIT *Scol*) calificar, corregir; **to ~ time** marcar el paso; (*fig*) marcar(se) un ritmo; **marked** *adj* (*obvious*) marcado, acusado; **marker** *n* (*sign*) marcador *m*; (*bookmark*) señal *f* (de libro)

market ['mɑ:kɪt] *n* mercado ▷*vt* (*Comm*) comercializar; **marketing** *n* márketing *m*; **marketplace** *n* mercado; **market research** *n* análisis *m inv* de mercados

marmalade ['mɑ:məleɪd] *n* mermelada de naranja

maroon [mə'ru:n] *vt*: **to be ~ed** quedar aislado; (*fig*) quedar abandonado ▷*n* (*colour*) granate *m*

marquee [mɑ:'ki:] *n* entoldado

marriage ['mærɪdʒ] *n* (*relationship, institution*) matrimonio; (*wedding*) boda; (*act*) casamiento; **marriage certificate** *n* partida de casamiento

married ['mærɪd] *adj* casado; (*life, love*) conyugal

marrow ['mærəu] *n* médula; (*vegetable*) calabacín *m*

marry ['mærɪ] *vt* casarse con; (*father, priest etc*) casar ▷*vi* (*also*: **get married**) casarse

Mars [mɑ:z] *n* Marte *m*

marsh [mɑ:ʃ] *n* pantano; (*salt marsh*) marisma

marshal ['mɑ:ʃl] *n* (*Mil*) mariscal *m*; (*at sports meeting etc*) oficial *m*; (US: *of police, fire department*) jefe/a *m/f* ▷*vt* (*thoughts etc*) ordenar; (*soldiers*) formar

martyr ['mɑ:tə*] *n* mártir *mf*

marvel ['mɑ:vl] *n* maravilla, prodigio ▷*vi*: **to ~ (at)** maravillarse (de); **marvellous** (US **marvelous**) *adj* maravilloso

Marxism ['mɑ:ksɪzəm] *n* marxismo

Marxist ['mɑ:ksɪst] *adj, n* marxista *mf*

marzipan ['mɑ:zɪpæn] *n* mazapán *m*

mascara [mæs'kɑ:rə] *n* rímel *m*

mascot ['mæskət] *n* mascota

masculine ['mæskjulɪn] *adj* masculino

mash [mæʃ] *vt* machacar; **mashed potato(es)** *n(pl)* puré *m* de patatas (SP) *or* papas (LAM)

mask [mɑ:sk] *n* máscara ▷*vt* (*cover*): **to ~ one's face** ocultarse la cara; (*hide: feelings*) esconder

mason ['meɪsn] *n* (*also*: **stone~**) albañil *m*; (*also*: **free~**) masón *m*; **masonry** *n* (*in building*) mampostería

mass [mæs] *n* (*people*) muchedumbre *f*; (*of air, liquid etc*) masa; (*of detail, hair etc*) gran cantidad *f*; (*Rel*) misa ▷*cpd* masivo ▷*vi* reunirse; concentrarse; **the masses** *npl* las masas; **~es of** (*inf*) montones de

massacre ['mæsəkə*] *n* masacre *f*

massage ['mæsɑ:ʒ] *n* masaje *m* ▷*vt* dar masaje en

massive ['mæsɪv] *adj* enorme; (*support, changes*) masivo

mass media *npl* medios *mpl* de comunicación

mass-produce ['mæsprə'dju:s] *vt* fabricar en serie

mast [mɑ:st] *n* (*Naut*) mástil *m*; (*Radio etc*) torre *f*

master ['mɑ:stə*] *n* (*of servant*) amo; (*of situation*) dueño, maestro; (*in primary school*) maestro; (*in secondary school*) profesor *m*; (*title for boys*): **M~ X** Señorito X ▷*vt* dominar; **mastermind** *n* inteligencia superior ▷*vt* dirigir, planear; **Master of Arts/Science** *n* licenciatura superior en Letras/Ciencias; **masterpiece** *n* obra maestra

masturbate ['mæstəbeɪt] *vi* masturbarse

mat [mæt] *n* estera; (*also*: **door~**) felpudo; (*also*: **table ~**) salvamanteles *m inv*, posavasos *m inv* ▷*adj* = **matt**

match [mætʃ] *n* cerilla, fósforo; (*game*) partido; (*equal*) igual *m/f* ▷*vt* (*go well with*) hacer juego con; (*equal*) igualar; (*correspond to*) corresponderse con; (*pair: also*: **~ up**) casar con ▷*vi* hacer juego; **to be a good ~** hacer juego; **matchbox** *n* caja de cerillas; **matching** *adj* que hace juego

mate [meɪt] *n* (*workmate*) colega *mf*; (*inf: friend*) amigo/a; (*animal*) macho/hembra; (*in merchant navy*) segundo de a bordo ▷*vi* acoplarse, aparearse ▷*vt* aparear

material [mə'tɪərɪəl] *n* (*substance*) materia; (*information*) material *m*; (*cloth*) tela, tejido ▷*adj* material; (*important*) esencial; **materials** *npl* materiales *mpl*

materialize [mə'tɪərɪəlaɪz] *vi* materializarse

maternal [mə'tə:nl] *adj* maternal

maternity [mə'tə:nɪtɪ] *n* maternidad *f*; **maternity hospital** *n* hospital *m* de maternidad; **maternity leave** *n* baja por maternidad

math [mæθ] (US) *n* = **mathematics**

mathematical [mæθə'mætɪkl] *adj* matemático

mathematician [mæθəmə'tɪʃən] *n* matemático/a
mathematics [mæθə'mætɪks] *n* matemáticas *fpl*
maths [mæθs] (*BRIT*) *n* = **mathematics**
matinée ['mætɪneɪ] *n* sesión *f* de tarde
matron ['meɪtrən] *n* enfermera *f* jefe; (*in school*) ama de llaves
matt [mæt] *adj* mate
matter ['mætə*] *n* cuestión *f*, asunto; (*Physics*) sustancia, materia; (*reading matter*) material *m*; (*Med: pus*) pus *m* ▷ *vi* importar; **matters** *npl* (*affairs*) asuntos *mpl*, temas *mpl*; **it doesn't ~** no importa; **what's the ~?** ¿qué pasa?; **no ~ what** pase lo que pase; **as a ~ of course** por rutina; **as a ~ of fact** de hecho
mattress ['mætrɪs] *n* colchón *m*
mature [mə'tjuə*] *adj* maduro ▷ *vi* madurar; **mature student** *n estudiante de más de 21 años*; **maturity** *n* madurez *f*
maul [mɔ:l] *vt* magullar
mauve [məuv] *adj* de color malva (*SP*) *or* guinda (*LAM*)
max *abbr* = **maximum**
maximize ['mæksɪmaɪz] *vt* (*profits etc*) llevar al máximo; (*chances*) maximizar
maximum ['mæksɪməm] (*pl* **maxima**) *adj* máximo ▷ *n* máximo
May [meɪ] *n* mayo
may [meɪ] (*conditional* **might**) *vi* (*indicating possibility*): **he ~ come** puede que venga; (*be allowed to*): **~ I smoke?** ¿puedo fumar?; (*wishes*): **~ God bless you!** ¡que Dios le bendiga!; **you ~ as well go** bien puedes irte
maybe ['meɪbi:] *adv* quizá(s)
May Day *n* el primero de Mayo
mayhem ['meɪhɛm] *n* caos *m* total
mayonnaise [meɪə'neɪz] *n* mayonesa
mayor [mɛə*] *n* alcalde *m*; **mayoress** *n* alcaldesa
maze [meɪz] *n* laberinto
MD *n abbr* = **managing director**
me [mi:] *pron* (*direct*) me; (*stressed, after pron*) mí; **can you hear ~?** ¿me oyes?; **he heard ME** ¡me oyó a mí!; **it's ~** soy yo; **give them to ~** dámelos/las; **with/without ~** conmigo/sin mí
meadow ['mɛdəu] *n* prado, pradera
meagre ['mi:gə*] (*US* **meager**) *adj* escaso, pobre
meal [mi:l] *n* comida; (*flour*) harina; **mealtime** *n* hora de comer
mean [mi:n] (*pt, pp* **~t**) *adj* (*with money*) tacaño; (*unkind*) mezquino, malo; (*shabby*) humilde; (*average*) medio ▷ *vt* (*signify*) querer decir, significar; (*refer to*) referirse a; (*intend*): **to ~ to do sth** pensar *or* pretender hacer algo ▷ *n* medio, término medio; **means** *npl* (*way*) medio, manera; (*money*) recursos *mpl*, medios *mpl*; **by ~s of** mediante, por medio de; **by all ~s!** ¡naturalmente!, ¡claro que sí!; **do you ~ it?** ¿lo dices en serio?; **what do you ~?** ¿qué quiere decir?; **to be ~t for sb/sth** ser para algn/algo
meaning ['mi:nɪŋ] *n* significado, sentido; (*purpose*) sentido, propósito; **meaningful** *adj* significativo; **meaningless** *adj* sin sentido
meant [mɛnt] *pt, pp of* **mean**
meantime ['mi:ntaɪm] *adv* (*also*: **in the ~**) mientras tanto
meanwhile ['mi:nwaɪl] *adv* = **meantime**
measles ['mi:zlz] *n* sarampión *m*
measure ['mɛʒə*] *vt, vi* medir ▷ *n* medida; (*ruler*) regla; **measurement** ['mɛʒəmənt] *n* (*measure*) medida; (*act*) medición *f*; **to take sb's measurements** tomar las medidas a algn
meat [mi:t] *n* carne *f*; **cold ~** fiambre *m*; **meatball** *n* albóndiga
Mecca ['mɛkə] *n* La Meca
mechanic [mɪ'kænɪk] *n* mecánico/a; **mechanical** *adj* mecánico
mechanism ['mɛkənɪzəm] *n* mecanismo
medal ['mɛdl] *n* medalla; **medallist** (*US* **medalist**) *n* (*Sport*) medallista *mf*
meddle ['mɛdl] *vi*: **to ~ in** entrometerse en; **to ~ with sth** manosear algo
media ['mi:dɪə] *npl* medios *mpl* de comunicación ▷ *npl of* **medium**
mediaeval [mɛdɪ'i:vl] *adj* = **medieval**
mediate ['mi:dɪeɪt] *vi* mediar
medical ['mɛdɪkl] *adj* médico ▷ *n* reconocimiento médico; **medical certificate** *n* certificado *m* médico
medicated ['mɛdɪkeɪtɪd] *adj* medicinal
medication [mɛdɪ'keɪʃən] *n* medicación *f*
medicine ['mɛdsɪn] *n* medicina; (*drug*) medicamento
medieval [mɛdɪ'i:vl] *adj* medieval
mediocre [mi:dɪ'əukə*] *adj* mediocre
meditate ['mɛdɪteɪt] *vi* meditar
meditation [mɛdɪ'teɪʃən] *n* meditación *f*
Mediterranean [mɛdɪtə'reɪnɪən] *adj* mediterráneo; **the ~ (Sea)** el (Mar) Mediterráneo
medium ['mi:dɪəm] (*pl* **media**) *adj* mediano, regular ▷ *n* (*means*) medio; (*pl mediums: person*) médium *mf*; **medium-sized** *adj* de tamaño mediano; (*clothes*) de (la) talla mediana; **medium wave** *n* onda media
meek [mi:k] *adj* manso, sumiso
meet [mi:t] (*pt, pp* **met**) *vt* encontrar;

(*accidentally*) encontrarse con, tropezar con; (*by arrangement*) reunirse con; (*for the first time*) conocer; (*go and fetch*) ir a buscar; (*opponent*) enfrentarse con; (*obligations*) cumplir; (*encounter: problem*) hacer frente a; (*need*) satisfacer ▷ *vi* encontrarse; (*in session*) reunirse; (*join: objects*) unirse; (*for the first time*) conocerse; **meet up** *vi*: **to meet up with sb** reunirse con algn; **meet with** *vt fus* (*difficulty*) tropezar con; **to meet with success** tener éxito; **meeting** *n* encuentro; (*arranged*) cita, compromiso; (*business meeting*) reunión *f*; (*Pol*) mítin *m*; **meeting place** *n* lugar *m* de reunión *or* encuentro

megabyte ['mɛgəbaɪt] *n* (*Comput*) megabyte *m*, megaocteto

megaphone ['mɛgəfəun] *n* megáfono

megapixel ['mɛgəpɪksl] *n* megapíxel *m*

melancholy ['mɛlənkəlɪ] *n* melancolía ▷ *adj* melancólico

melody ['mɛlədɪ] *n* melodía

melon ['mɛlən] *n* melón *m*

melt [mɛlt] *vi* (*metal*) fundirse; (*snow*) derretirse ▷ *vt* fundir

member ['mɛmbə*] *n* (*gen, Anat*) miembro; (*of club*) socio/a; **Member of Congress** (US) *n* miembro *mf* del Congreso; **Member of Parliament** *n* (BRIT) diputado/a *m/f*, parlamentario/a *m/f*; **Member of the European Parliament** *n* diputado/a *m/f* del Parlamento Europeo, eurodiputado/a *m/f*; **Member of the Scottish Parliament** (BRIT) diputado/a del Parlamento escocés; **membership** *n* (*members*) número de miembros; (*state*) filiación *f*; **membership card** *n* carnet *m* de socio

memento [mə'mɛntəu] *n* recuerdo

memo ['mɛməu] *n* apunte *m*, nota

memorable ['mɛmərəbl] *adj* memorable

memorandum [mɛmə'rændəm] (*pl* **memoranda**) *n* apunte *m*, nota; (*official note*) acta

memorial [mɪ'mɔːrɪəl] *n* monumento conmemorativo ▷ *adj* conmemorativo

memorize ['mɛməraɪz] *vt* aprender de memoria

memory ['mɛmərɪ] *n* (*also: Comput*) memoria; (*instance*) recuerdo; (*of dead person*): **in ~ of** a la memoria de; **memory card** *n* (*for digital camera*) tarjeta de memoria

men [mɛn] *npl of* **man**

menace ['mɛnəs] *n* amenaza ▷ *vt* amenazar

mend [mɛnd] *vt* reparar, arreglar; (*darn*) zurcir ▷ *vi* reponerse ▷ *n* arreglo, reparación *f* zurcido ▷ *n*: **to be on the ~** ir mejorando; **to ~ one's ways** enmendarse

meningitis [mɛnɪn'dʒaɪtɪs] *n* meningitis *f*

menopause ['mɛnəupɔːz] *n* menopausia

men's room (US) *n*: **the ~** el servicio de caballeros

menstruation [mɛnstru'eɪʃən] *n* menstruación *f*

menswear ['mɛnzwɛə*] *n* confección *f* de caballero

mental ['mɛntl] *adj* mental; **mental hospital** *n* (hospital *m*) psiquiátrico; **mentality** [mɛn'tælɪtɪ] *n* mentalidad *f*; **mentally** *adv*: **to be mentally ill** tener una enfermedad mental

menthol ['mɛnθɔl] *n* mentol *m*

mention ['mɛnʃən] *n* mención *f* ▷ *vt* mencionar; (*speak*) hablar de; **don't ~ it!** ¡de nada!

menu ['mɛnjuː] *n* (*set menu*) menú *m*; (*printed*) carta; (*Comput*) menú *m*

MEP *n abbr* = **Member of the European Parliament**

mercenary ['məːsɪnərɪ] *adj, n* mercenario/a

merchandise ['məːtʃəndaɪz] *n* mercancías *fpl*

merchant ['məːtʃənt] *n* comerciante *mf*; **merchant navy** (US), **merchant marine** *n* marina mercante

merciless ['məːsɪlɪs] *adj* despiadado

mercury ['məːkjurɪ] *n* mercurio

mercy ['məːsɪ] *n* compasión *f*; (*Rel*) misericordia; **at the ~ of** a la merced de

mere [mɪə*] *adj* simple, mero; **merely** *adv* simplemente, sólo

merge [məːdʒ] *vt* (*join*) unir ▷ *vi* unirse; (*Comm*) fusionarse; (*colours etc*) fundirse; **merger** *n* (*Comm*) fusión *f*

meringue [mə'ræŋ] *n* merengue *m*

merit ['mɛrɪt] *n* mérito ▷ *vt* merecer

mermaid ['məːmeɪd] *n* sirena

merry ['mɛrɪ] *adj* alegre; **M~ Christmas!** ¡Felices Pascuas!; **merry-go-round** *n* tiovivo

mesh [mɛʃ] *n* malla

mess [mɛs] *n* (*muddle: of situation*) confusión *f*; (*: of room*) revoltijo; (*dirt*) porquería; (*Mil*) comedor *m*; **mess about** *or* **around** (*inf*) *vi* perder el tiempo; (*pass the time*) entretenerse; **mess up** *vt* (*spoil*) estropear; (*dirty*) ensuciar; **mess with** (*inf*) *vt fus* (*challenge, confront*) meterse con (*inf*); (*interfere with*) interferir con

message ['mɛsɪdʒ] *n* recado, mensaje *m*

messenger ['mɛsɪndʒə*] *n* mensajero/a

Messrs *abbr* (*on letters*) (= *Messieurs*) Sres

messy ['mɛsɪ] *adj* (*dirty*) sucio; (*untidy*) desordenado

met [mɛt] *pt, pp of* **meet**
metabolism [mɛ'tæbəlɪzəm] *n* metabolismo
metal ['mɛtl] *n* metal *m*; **metallic** [-'tælɪk] *adj* metálico
metaphor ['mɛtəfə*] *n* metáfora
meteor ['mi:tɪə*] *n* meteoro; **meteorite** [-aɪt] *n* meteorito
meteorology [mi:tɪɔ'rɔlədʒɪ] *n* meteorología
meter ['mi:tə*] *n* (*instrument*) contador *m*; (*US: unit*) = **metre** ▷ *vt* (*US Post*) franquear
method ['mɛθəd] *n* método; **methodical** [mɪ'θɔdɪkl] *adj* metódico
meths [mɛθs] *n* (BRIT) alcohol *m* metilado *or* desnaturalizado
meticulous [mɛ'tɪkjuləs] *adj* meticuloso
metre ['mi:tə*] (*US* **meter**) *n* metro
metric ['mɛtrɪk] *adj* métrico
metro ['metrəu] *n* metro
metropolitan [mɛtrə'pɔlɪtən] *adj* metropolitano; **the M~ Police** (BRIT) la policía londinense
Mexican ['mɛksɪkən] *adj, n* mexicano/a , mejicano/a
Mexico ['mɛksɪkəu] *n* México, Méjico (SP)
mg *abbr* (= *milligram*) mg
mice [maɪs] *npl of* **mouse**
micro... [maɪkrəu] *prefix* micro...; **microchip** *n* microplaqueta; **microphone** *n* micrófono; **microscope** *n* microscopio; **microwave** *n* (*also*: **microwave oven**) horno microondas
mid [mɪd] *adj*: **in ~ May** a mediados de mayo; **in ~ afternoon** a media tarde; **in ~ air** en el aire; **midday** *n* mediodía *m*
middle ['mɪdl] *n* centro; (*half-way point*) medio; (*waist*) cintura ▷ *adj* de en medio; (*course, way*) intermedio; **in the ~ of the night** en plena noche; **middle-aged** *adj* de mediana edad; **Middle Ages** *npl*: **the Middle Ages** la Edad Media; **middle-class** *adj* de clase media; **the middle class(es)** la clase media; **Middle East** *n* Oriente *m* Medio; **middle name** *n* segundo nombre; **middle school** *n* (*US*) *colegio para niños de doce a catorce años*; (BRIT) *colegio para niños de ocho o nueve a doce o trece años*
midge [mɪdʒ] *n* mosquito
midget ['mɪdʒɪt] *n* enano/a
midnight ['mɪdnaɪt] *n* medianoche *f*
midst [mɪdst] *n*: **in the ~ of** (*crowd*) en medio de; (*situation, action*) en mitad de
midsummer [mɪd'sʌmə*] *n*: **in ~** en pleno verano
midway [mɪd'weɪ] *adj, adv*: **~ (between)** a medio camino (entre); **~ through** a la mitad (de)
midweek [mɪd'wi:k] *adv* entre semana
midwife ['mɪdwaɪf] (*irreg*) *n* comadrona, partera
midwinter [mɪd'wɪntə*] *n*: **in ~** en pleno invierno
might [maɪt] *vb see* **may** ▷ *n* fuerza, poder *m*; **mighty** *adj* fuerte, poderoso
migraine ['mi:greɪn] *n* jaqueca
migrant ['maɪgrənt] *n, adj* (*bird*) migratorio; (*worker*) emigrante
migrate [maɪ'greɪt] *vi* emigrar
migration [maɪ'greɪʃən] *n* emigración *f*
mike [maɪk] *n abbr* (= *microphone*) micro
mild [maɪld] *adj* (*person*) apacible; (*climate*) templado; (*slight*) ligero; (*taste*) suave; (*illness*) leve; **mildly** ['-lɪ] *adv* ligeramente; suavemente; **to put it mildly** para no decir más
mile [maɪl] *n* milla; **mileage** *n* número de millas ≈ kilometraje *m*; **mileometer** [maɪ'lɔmɪtə] *n* ≈ cuentakilómetros *m inv*; **milestone** *n* mojón *m*
military ['mɪlɪtərɪ] *adj* militar
militia [mɪ'lɪʃə] *n* milicia
milk [mɪlk] *n* leche *f* ▷ *vt* (*cow*) ordeñar; (*fig*) chupar; **milk chocolate** *n* chocolate *m* con leche; **milkman** (*irreg*) *n* lechero; **milky** *adj* lechoso
mill [mɪl] *n* (*windmill etc*) molino; (*coffee mill*) molinillo; (*factory*) fábrica ▷ *vt* moler ▷ *vi* (*also*: **~ about**) arremolinarse
millennium [mɪ'lɛnɪəm] (*pl* **~s** *or* **millennia**) *n* milenio, milenario
milli... ['mɪlɪ] *prefix*: **milligram(me)** *n* miligramo; **millilitre** (*US* **milliliter**) ['mɪlɪli:tə*] *n* mililitro; **millimetre** (*US* **millimeter**) *n* milímetro
million ['mɪljən] *n* millón *m*; **a ~ times** un millón de veces; **millionaire** [-jə'nɛə*] *n* millonario/a; **millionth** [-θ] *adj* millonésimo
milometer [maɪ'lɔmɪtə*] (BRIT) *n* = **mileometer**
mime [maɪm] *n* mímica; (*actor*) mimo/a ▷ *vt* remedar ▷ *vi* actuar de mimo
mimic ['mɪmɪk] *n* imitador(a) *m/f* ▷ *adj* mímico ▷ *vt* remedar, imitar
min. *abbr* = **minimum; minute(s)**
mince [mɪns] *vt* picar ▷ *n* (BRIT *Culin*) carne *f* picada; **mincemeat** *n conserva de fruta picada*; (*US*: *meat*) carne *f* picada; **mince pie** *n empanadilla rellena de fruta picada*
mind [maɪnd] *n* mente *f*; (*intellect*) intelecto; (*contrasted with matter*) espíritu *m* ▷ *vt* (*attend to, look after*) ocuparse de, cuidar; (*be careful*) tener cuidado con; (*object to*): **I don't ~ the noise** no me molesta el ruido; **it is on my ~** me preocupa; **to bear**

sth in ~ tomar *or* tener algo en cuenta; **to make up one's ~** decidirse; **I don't ~** me es igual; **~ you ...** te advierto que ...; **never ~!** ¡es igual!, ¡no importa!; (*don't worry*) ¡no te preocupes!; **"~ the step"** "cuidado con el escalón"; **mindless** *adj* (*crime*) sin motivo; (*work*) de autómata

mine[1] [maɪn] *pron* el mío/la mía etc; **a friend of ~** un(a) amigo/a mío/mía ▷ *adj*: **this book is ~** este libro es mío

mine[2] [maɪn] *n* mina ▷ *vt* (*coal*) extraer; (*bomb: beach etc*) minar; **minefield** *n* campo de minas; **miner** *n* minero/a

mineral ['mɪnərəl] *adj* mineral ▷ *n* mineral *m*; **mineral water** *n* agua mineral

mingle ['mɪŋgl] *vi*: **to ~ with** mezclarse con

miniature ['mɪnətʃə*] *adj* (en) miniatura ▷ *n* miniatura

minibar ['mɪnɪbɑː*] *n* minibar *m*

minibus ['mɪnɪbʌs] *n* microbús *m*

minicab ['mɪnɪkæb] *n* taxi *m* (*que sólo puede pedirse por teléfono*)

minimal ['mɪnɪml] *adj* mínimo

minimize ['mɪnɪmaɪz] *vt* minimizar; (*play down*) empequeñecer

minimum ['mɪnɪməm] (*pl* **minima**) *n, adj* mínimo

mining ['maɪnɪŋ] *n* explotación *f* minera

miniskirt ['mɪnɪskəːt] *n* minifalda

minister ['mɪnɪstə*] *n* (BRIT *Pol*) ministro/a (SP), secretario/a (LAM); (*Rel*) pastor *m* ▷ *vi*: **to ~ to** atender a

ministry ['mɪnɪstrɪ] *n* (BRIT *Pol*) ministerio, secretaría (MEX); (*Rel*) sacerdocio

minor ['maɪnə*] *adj* (*repairs, injuries*) leve; (*poet, planet*) menor; (*Mus*) menor ▷ *n* (*Law*) menor *m* de edad

Minorca [mɪ'nɔːkə] *n* Menorca

minority [maɪ'nɔrɪtɪ] *n* minoría

mint [mɪnt] *n* (*plant*) menta, hierbabuena; (*sweet*) caramelo de menta ▷ *vt* (*coins*) acuñar; **the (Royal) M~, the (US) M~** la Casa de la Moneda; **in ~ condition** en perfecto estado

minus ['maɪnəs] *n* (*also*: **~ sign**) signo de menos ▷ *prep* menos; **12 ~ 6 equals 6** 12 menos 6 son 6; **~ 24°C** menos 24 grados

minute[1] ['mɪnɪt] *n* minuto; (*fig*) momento; **minutes** *npl* (*of meeting*) actas *fpl*; **at the last ~** a última hora

minute[2] [maɪ'njuːt] *adj* diminuto; (*search*) minucioso

miracle ['mɪrəkl] *n* milagro

miraculous [mɪ'rækjuləs] *adj* milagroso

mirage ['mɪrɑːʒ] *n* espejismo

mirror ['mɪrə*] *n* espejo; (*in car*) retrovisor *m*

misbehave [mɪsbɪ'heɪv] *vi* portarse mal

misc. *abbr* = **miscellaneous**

miscarriage ['mɪskærɪdʒ] *n* (*Med*) aborto; **~ of justice** error *m* judicial

miscellaneous [mɪsɪ'leɪnɪəs] *adj* varios/as, diversos/as

mischief ['mɪstʃɪf] *n* travesuras *fpl*, diabluras *fpl*; (*maliciousness*) malicia; **mischievous** [-ʃɪvəs] *adj* travieso

misconception [mɪskən'sɛpʃən] *n* idea equivocada; equivocación *f*

misconduct [mɪs'kɔndʌkt] *n* mala conducta; **professional ~** falta profesional

miser ['maɪzə*] *n* avaro/a

miserable ['mɪzərəbl] *adj* (*unhappy*) triste, desgraciado; (*unpleasant, contemptible*) miserable

misery ['mɪzərɪ] *n* tristeza; (*wretchedness*) miseria, desdicha

misfortune [mɪs'fɔːtʃən] *n* desgracia

misgiving [mɪs'gɪvɪŋ] *n* (*apprehension*) presentimiento; **to have ~s about sth** tener dudas acerca de algo

misguided [mɪs'gaɪdɪd] *adj* equivocado

mishap ['mɪshæp] *n* desgracia, contratiempo

misinterpret [mɪsɪn'təːprɪt] *vt* interpretar mal

misjudge [mɪs'dʒʌdʒ] *vt* juzgar mal

mislay [mɪs'leɪ] *vt* extraviar, perder

mislead [mɪs'liːd] *vt* llevar a conclusiones erróneas; **misleading** *adj* engañoso

misplace [mɪs'pleɪs] *vt* extraviar

misprint ['mɪsprɪnt] *n* errata, error *m* de imprenta

misrepresent [mɪsrɛprɪ'zɛnt] *vt* falsificar

Miss [mɪs] *n* Señorita

miss [mɪs] *vt* (*train etc*) perder; (*fail to hit: target*) errar; (*regret the absence of*): **I ~ him** (yo) le echo de menos *or* a faltar; (*fail to see*): **you can't ~ it** no tiene pérdida ▷ *vi* fallar ▷ *n* (*shot*) tiro fallido *or* perdido; **miss out** (BRIT) *vt* omitir; **miss out on** *vt fus* (*fun, party, opportunity*) perderse

missile ['mɪsaɪl] *n* (*Aviat*) mísil *m*; (*object thrown*) proyectil *m*

missing ['mɪsɪŋ] *adj* (*pupil*) ausente; (*thing*) perdido; (*Mil*): **~ in action** desaparecido en combate

mission ['mɪʃən] *n* misión *f*; (*official representation*) delegación *f*; **missionary** *n* misionero/a

misspell [mɪs'spɛl] (*pt, pp* **misspelt** (BRIT) *or* **~ed**) *vt* escribir mal

mist [mɪst] *n* (*light*) neblina; (*heavy*) niebla; (*at sea*) bruma ▷ *vi* (*eyes: also*: **~ over, ~ up**) llenarse de lágrimas; (BRIT: *windows: also*: **~**

over, ~ up) empañarse
mistake [mɪs'teɪk] (*vt: irreg*) *n* error *m* ▷ *vt* entender mal; **by ~** por equivocación; **to make a ~** equivocarse; **to ~ A for B** confundir A con B; **mistaken** *pp of* **mistake** ▷ *adj* equivocado; **to be mistaken** equivocarse, engañarse
mister ['mɪstə*] (*inf*) *n* señor *m*; *see* **Mr**
mistletoe ['mɪsltəu] *n* muérdago
mistook [mɪs'tuk] *pt of* **mistake**
mistress ['mɪstrɪs] *n* (*lover*) amante *f*; (*of house*) señora (de la casa); (BRIT: *in primary school*) maestra; (*in secondary school*) profesora; (*of situation*) dueña
mistrust [mɪs'trʌst] *vt* desconfiar de
misty ['mɪstɪ] *adj* (*day*) de niebla; (*glasses etc*) empañado
misunderstand [mɪsʌndə'stænd] (*irreg*) *vt, vi* entender mal; **misunderstanding** *n* malentendido
misunderstood [mɪsʌndə'stud] *pt, pp of* **misunderstand** ▷ *adj* (*person*) incomprendido
misuse [*n* mɪs'ju:s, *vb* mɪs'ju:z] *n* mal uso; (*of power*) abuso; (*of funds*) malversación *f* ▷ *vt* abusar de; malversar
mitt(en) ['mɪt(n)] *n* manopla
mix [mɪks] *vt* mezclar; (*combine*) unir ▷ *vi* mezclarse; (*people*) llevarse bien ▷ *n* mezcla; **mix up** *vt* mezclar; (*confuse*) confundir; **mixed** *adj* mixto; (*feelings etc*) encontrado; **mixed grill** *n* (BRIT) parrillada mixta; **mixed salad** *n* ensalada mixta; **mixed-up** *adj* (*confused*) confuso, revuelto; **mixer** *n* (*for food*) licuadora; (*for drinks*) coctelera; (*person*): **he's a good mixer** tiene don de gentes; **mixture** *n* mezcla; (*also*: **cough mixture**) jarabe *m*; **mix-up** *n* confusión *f*
ml *abbr* (= *millilitre(s)*) ml
mm *abbr* (= *millimetre*) mm
moan [məun] *n* gemido ▷ *vi* gemir; (*inf: complain*): **to ~ (about)** quejarse (de)
moat [məut] *n* foso
mob [mɔb] *n* multitud *f* ▷ *vt* acosar
mobile ['məubaɪl] *adj* móvil ▷ *n* móvil *m*; **mobile home** *n* caravana; **mobile phone** *n* teléfono móvil
mobility [məu'bɪlɪtɪ] *n* movilidad *f*
mobilize ['məubɪlaɪz] *vt* movilizar
mock [mɔk] *vt* (*ridicule*) ridiculizar; (*laugh at*) burlarse de ▷ *adj* fingido; **~ exam** *examen preparatorio antes de los exámenes oficiales** (BRIT: *Scol: inf*) exámenes *mpl* de prueba; **mockery** *n* burla
mod cons ['mɔd'kɔnz] *npl abbr* (= *modern conveniences*) *see* **convenience**
mode [məud] *n* modo
model ['mɔdl] *n* modelo; (*fashion model, artist's model*) modelo *mf* ▷ *adj* modelo ▷ *vt* (*with clay etc*) modelar; (*copy*): **to ~ o.s. on** tomar como modelo a ▷ *vi* ser modelo; **to ~ clothes** pasar modelos, ser modelo
modem ['məudəm] *n* modem *m*
moderate [*adj* 'mɔdərət, *vb* 'mɔdəreɪt] *adj* moderado/a ▷ *vi* moderarse, calmarse ▷ *vt* moderar
moderation [mɔdə'reɪʃən] *n* moderación *f*; **in ~** con moderación
modern ['mɔdən] *adj* moderno; **modernize** *vt* modernizar; **modern languages** *npl* lenguas *fpl* modernas
modest ['mɔdɪst] *adj* modesto; (*small*) módico; **modesty** *n* modestia
modification [mɔdɪfɪ'keɪʃən] *n* modificación *f*
modify ['mɔdɪfaɪ] *vt* modificar
module ['mɔdju:l] *n* (*unit, component, Space*) módulo
mohair ['məuhɛə*] *n* mohair *m*
Mohammed [mə'hæmɛd] *n* Mahoma *m*
moist [mɔɪst] *adj* húmedo; **moisture** ['mɔɪstʃə*] *n* humedad *f*; **moisturizer** ['mɔɪstʃəraɪzə*] *n* crema hidratante
mold *etc* [məuld] (US) = **mould** *etc*
mole [məul] *n* (*animal, spy*) topo; (*spot*) lunar *m*
molecule ['mɔlɪkju:l] *n* molécula
molest [məu'lɛst] *vt* importunar; (*assault sexually*) abusar sexualmente de

> Be careful not to translate **molest** by the Spanish word *molestar*.

molten ['məultən] *adj* fundido; (*lava*) líquido
mom [mɔm] (US) *n* = **mum**
moment ['məumənt] *n* momento; **at the ~** de momento, por ahora; **momentarily** *adv* momentáneamente; (US: *very soon*) de un momento a otro; **momentary** *adj* momentáneo; **momentous** [-'mɛntəs] *adj* trascendental, importante
momentum [məu'mɛntəm] *n* momento; (*fig*) ímpetu *m*; **to gather ~** cobrar velocidad; (*fig*) ganar fuerza
mommy ['mɔmɪ] (US) *n* = **mummy**
Mon *abbr* (= *Monday*) lun
Monaco ['mɔnəkəu] *n* Mónaco
monarch ['mɔnək] *n* monarca *mf*; **monarchy** *n* monarquía
monastery ['mɔnəstərɪ] *n* monasterio
Monday ['mʌndɪ] *n* lunes *m inv*
monetary ['mʌnɪtərɪ] *adj* monetario
money ['mʌnɪ] *n* dinero; (*currency*) moneda; **to make ~** ganar dinero; **money belt** *n* riñonera; **money order** *n* giro
mongrel ['mʌŋgrəl] *n* (*dog*) perro mestizo
monitor ['mɔnɪtə*] *n* (*Scol*) monitor *m*;

(*also*: **television ~**) receptor *m* de control; (*of computer*) monitor *m* ▷ *vt* controlar
monk [mʌŋk] *n* monje *m*
monkey ['mʌŋkɪ] *n* mono
monologue ['mɔnəlɔg] *n* monólogo
monopoly [mə'nɔpəlɪ] *n* monopolio
monosodium glutamate [mɔnə'səu-dɪəm'glu:təmeɪt] *n* glutamato monosódico
monotonous [mə'nɔtənəs] *adj* monótono
monsoon [mɔn'su:n] *n* monzón *m*
monster ['mɔnstə*] *n* monstruo
month [mʌnθ] *n* mes *m*; **monthly** *adj* mensual ▷ *adv* mensualmente
monument ['mɔnjumənt] *n* monumento
mood [mu:d] *n* humor *m*; (*of crowd, group*) clima *m*; **to be in a good/bad ~** estar de buen/mal humor; **moody** *adj* (*changeable*) de humor variable; (*sullen*) malhumorado
moon [mu:n] *n* luna; **moonlight** *n* luz *f* de la luna
moor [muə*] *n* páramo ▷ *vt* (*ship*) amarrar ▷ *vi* echar las amarras
moose [mu:s] *n inv* alce *m*
mop [mɔp] *n* fregona; (*of hair*) greña, melena ▷ *vt* fregar; **mop up** *vt* limpiar
mope [məup] *vi* estar *or* andar deprimido
moped ['məupɛd] *n* ciclomotor *m*
moral ['mɔrl] *adj* moral ▷ *n* moraleja; **morals** *npl* moralidad *f*, moral *f*
morale [mɔ'rɑ:l] *n* moral *f*
morality [mə'rælɪtɪ] *n* moralidad *f*
morbid ['mɔ:bɪd] *adj* (*interest*) morboso; (*Med*) mórbido

KEYWORD

more [mɔ:*] *adj* **1** (*greater in number etc*) más; **more people/work than before** más gente/trabajo que antes
2 (*additional*) más; **do you want (some) more tea?** ¿quieres más té?; **is there any more wine?** ¿queda vino?; **it'll take a few more weeks** tardará unas semanas más; **it's 2 kms more to the house** faltan 2 kms para la casa; **more time/letters than we expected** más tiempo del que/más cartas de las que esperábamos
▷ *pron* (*greater amount, additional amount*) más; **more than 10** más de 10; **it cost more than the other one/than we expected** costó más que el otro/más de lo que esperábamos; **is there any more?** ¿hay más?; **many/much more** muchos(as)/ mucho(a) más
▷ *adv* más; **more dangerous/easily (than)** más peligroso/fácilmente (que); **more and more expensive** cada vez más caro; **more or less** más o menos; **more than ever** más que nunca

moreover [mɔ:'rəuvə*] *adv* además, por otra parte
morgue [mɔ:g] *n* depósito de cadáveres
morning ['mɔ:nɪŋ] *n* mañana; (*early morning*) madrugada ▷ *cpd* matutino, de la mañana; **in the ~** por la mañana; **7 o'clock in the ~** las 7 de la mañana; **morning sickness** *n* náuseas *fpl* matutinas
Moroccan [mə'rɔkən] *adj, n* marroquí *m/f*
Morocco [mə'rɔkəu] *n* Marruecos *m*
moron ['mɔ:rɔn] (*inf*) *n* imbécil *mf*
morphine ['mɔ:fi:n] *n* morfina
Morse [mɔ:s] *n* (*also*: **~ code**) (código) Morse
mortal ['mɔ:tl] *adj, n* mortal *m*
mortar ['mɔ:tə*] *n* argamasa
mortgage ['mɔ:gɪdʒ] *n* hipoteca ▷ *vt* hipotecar
mortician [mɔ:'tɪʃən] (US) *n* director/a *m/f* de pompas fúnebres
mortified ['mɔ:tɪfaɪd] *adj*: **I was ~** me dio muchísima vergüenza
mortuary ['mɔ:tjuərɪ] *n* depósito de cadáveres
mosaic [məu'zeɪɪk] *n* mosaico
Moslem ['mɔzləm] *adj, n* = **Muslim**
mosque [mɔsk] *n* mezquita
mosquito [mɔs'ki:təu] (*pl* **~es**) *n* mosquito (SP), zancudo (LAM)
moss [mɔs] *n* musgo
most [məust] *adj* la mayor parte de, la mayoría de ▷ *pron* la mayor parte, la mayoría ▷ *adv* el más; (*very*) muy; **the ~** (*also*: + *adj*) el más; **~ of them** la mayor parte de ellos; **I saw the ~** yo vi el que más; **at the (very) ~** a lo sumo, todo lo más; **to make the ~ of** aprovechar (al máximo); **a ~ interesting book** un libro interesantísimo; **mostly** *adv* en su mayor parte, principalmente
MOT (BRIT) *n abbr* = **Ministry of Transport**; **the ~ (test)** *inspección (anual) obligatoria de coches y camiones*
motel [məu'tɛl] *n* motel *m*
moth [mɔθ] *n* mariposa nocturna; (*clothes moth*) polilla
mother ['mʌðə*] *n* madre *f* ▷ *adj* materno ▷ *vt* (*care for*) cuidar (como una madre); **motherhood** *n* maternidad *f*; **mother-in-law** *n* suegra; **mother-of-pearl** *n* nácar *m*; **Mother's Day** *n* Día *m* de la Madre; **mother-to-be** *n* futura madre *f*; **mother tongue** *n* lengua materna

motif [məu'ti:f] *n* motivo
motion ['məuʃən] *n* movimiento; (*gesture*) ademán *m*, señal *f*; (*at meeting*) moción *f* ▷ *vt, vi*: **to ~ (to) sb to do sth** hacer señas a algn para que haga algo; **motionless** *adj* inmóvil; **motion picture** *n* película
motivate ['məutɪveɪt] *vt* motivar
motivation [məutɪ'veɪʃən] *n* motivación *f*
motive ['məutɪv] *n* motivo
motor ['məutə*] *n* motor *m*; (BRIT: *inf*: *vehicle*) coche *m* (SP), carro (LAM), automóvil *m* ▷ *adj* motor (*f*: *motora or motriz*); **motorbike** *n* moto *f*; **motorboat** *n* lancha motora; **motorcar** (BRIT) *n* coche *m*, carro, automóvil *m*; **motorcycle** *n* motocicleta; **motorcyclist** *n* motociclista *mf*; **motoring** (BRIT) *n* automovilismo; **motorist** *n* conductor(a) *m/f*, automovilista *mf*; **motor racing** (BRIT) *n* carreras *fpl* de coches, automovilismo; **motorway** (BRIT) *n* autopista
motto ['mɔtəu] (*pl* **~es**) *n* lema *m*; (*watchword*) consigna
mould [məuld] (US **mold**) *n* molde *m*; (*mildew*) moho ▷ *vt* moldear; (*fig*) formar; **mouldy** *adj* enmohecido
mound [maund] *n* montón *m*, montículo
mount [maunt] *n* monte *m* ▷ *vt* montar, subir a; (*jewel*) engarzar; (*picture*) enmarcar; (*exhibition etc*) organizar ▷ *vi* (*increase*) aumentar; **mount up** *vi* aumentar
mountain ['mauntɪn] *n* montaña ▷ *cpd* de montaña; **mountain bike** *n* bicicleta de montaña; **mountaineer** *n* alpinista *mf* (SP, MEX), andinista *mf* (LAM); **mountaineering** *n* alpinismo (SP, MEX), andinismo (LAM); **mountainous** *adj* montañoso; **mountain range** *n* sierra
mourn [mɔ:n] *vt* llorar, lamentar ▷ *vi*: **to ~ for** llorar la muerte de; **mourner** *n* doliente *mf*; dolorido/a; **mourning** *n* luto; **in mourning** de luto
mouse [maus] (*pl* **mice**) *n* (*Zool, Comput*) ratón *m*; **mouse mat** *n* (*Comput*) alfombrilla
moussaka [mu'sɑ:kə] *n* musaca
mousse [mu:s] *n* (*Culin*) crema batida; (*for hair*) espuma (moldeadora)
moustache [məs'tɑ:ʃ] (US **mustache**) *n* bigote *m*
mouth [mauð, *pl* mauðz] *n* boca; (*of river*) desembocadura; **mouthful** *n* bocado; **mouth organ** *n* armónica; **mouthpiece** *n* (*of musical instrument*) boquilla; (*spokesman*) portavoz *mf*; **mouthwash** *n* enjuague *m*
move [mu:v] *n* (*movement*) movimiento; (*in game*) jugada; (: *turn to play*) turno; (*change*: *of house*) mudanza; (: *of job*) cambio de trabajo ▷ *vt* mover; (*emotionally*) conmover; (*Pol*: *resolution etc*) proponer ▷ *vi* moverse; (*traffic*) circular; (*also*: **~ house**) trasladarse, mudarse; **to ~ sb to do sth** mover a algn a hacer algo; **to get a ~ on** darse prisa; **move back** *vi* retroceder; **move in** *vi* (*to a house*) instalarse; (*police, soldiers*) intervenir; **move off** *vi* ponerse en camino; **move on** *vi* ponerse en camino; **move out** *vi* (*of house*) mudarse; **move over** *vi* apartarse, hacer sitio; **move up** *vi* (*employee*) ser ascendido; **movement** *n* movimiento
movie ['mu:vɪ] *n* película; **to go to the ~s** ir al cine; **movie theater** (US) *n* cine *m*
moving ['mu:vɪŋ] *adj* (*emotional*) conmovedor(a); (*that moves*) móvil
mow [məu] (*pt* **~ed**, *pp* **mowed** *or* **mown**) *vt* (*grass, corn*) cortar, segar; **mower** *n* (*also*: **lawnmower**) cortacéspedes *m inv*
Mozambique [məuzæm'bi:k] *n* Mozambique *m*
MP *n abbr* = **Member of Parliament**
MP3 *n* MP3; **MP3 player** *n* reproductor *m* (de) MP3
mpg *n abbr* = **miles per gallon**
m.p.h. *abbr* = **miles per hour** (60 *m.p.h.* = 96 *k.p.h.*)
Mr ['mɪstə*] (US **Mr.**) *n*: **~ Smith** (el) Sr. Smith
Mrs ['mɪsɪz] (US **Mrs.**) *n*: **~ Smith** (la) Sra. Smith
Ms [mɪz] (US **Ms.**) *n* = **Miss** *or* **Mrs**; **~ Smith** (la) Sr(t)a. Smith
MSP *n abbr* = **Member of the Scottish Parliament**
Mt *abbr* (*Geo*) (= *mount*) m
much [mʌtʃ] *adj* mucho ▷ *adv* mucho; (*before pp*) muy ▷ *n or pron* mucho; **how ~ is it?** ¿cuánto es?, ¿cuánto cuesta?; **too ~** demasiado; **it's not ~** no es mucho; **as ~ as** tanto como; **however ~ he tries** por mucho que se esfuerce
muck [mʌk] *n* suciedad *f*; **muck up** (*inf*) *vt* arruinar, estropear; **mucky** *adj* (*dirty*) sucio
mucus ['mju:kəs] *n* mucosidad *f*, moco
mud [mʌd] *n* barro, lodo
muddle ['mʌdl] *n* desorden *m*, confusión *f*; (*mix-up*) embrollo, lío ▷ *vt* (*also*: **~ up**) embrollar, confundir
muddy ['mʌdɪ] *adj* fangoso, cubierto de lodo
mudguard ['mʌdgɑ:d] *n* guardabarros *m inv*
muesli ['mju:zlɪ] *n* muesli *m*
muffin ['mʌfɪn] *n* panecillo dulce
muffled ['mʌfld] *adj* (*noise etc*) amortiguado, apagado

muffler (US) ['mʌflə*] *n* (*Aut*) silenciador *m*
mug [mʌg] *n* taza grande (*sin platillo*); (*for beer*) jarra; (*inf: face*) jeta ▷*vt* (*assault*) asaltar; **mugger** ['mʌgə*] *n* atracador(a) *m/f*; **mugging** *n* asalto
muggy ['mʌgɪ] *adj* bochornoso
mule [mju:l] *n* mula
multicoloured ['mʌltɪkʌləd] (US), **multicolored** *adj* multicolor
multimedia ['mʌltɪ'mi:dɪə] *adj* multimedia
multinational [mʌltɪ'næʃənl] *n* multinacional *f* ▷*adj* multinacional
multiple ['mʌltɪpl] *adj* múltiple ▷*n* múltiplo; **multiple choice (test)** *n* examen *m* de tipo test; **multiple sclerosis** *n* esclerosis *f* múltiple
multiplex cinema ['mʌltɪplɛks-] *n* multicines *mpl*
multiplication [mʌltɪplɪ'keɪʃən] *n* multiplicación *f*
multiply ['mʌltɪplaɪ] *vt* multiplicar ▷*vi* multiplicarse
multistorey [mʌltɪ'stɔ:rɪ] (BRIT) *adj* de muchos pisos
mum [mʌm] (BRIT: *inf*) *n* mamá ▷*adj*: **to keep ~** mantener la boca cerrada
mumble ['mʌmbl] *vt, vi* hablar entre dientes, refunfuñar
mummy ['mʌmɪ] *n* (BRIT: *mother*) mamá; (*embalmed*) momia
mumps [mʌmps] *n* paperas *fpl*
munch [mʌntʃ] *vt, vi* mascar
municipal [mju:'nɪsɪpl] *adj* municipal
mural ['mjuərl] *n* (pintura) mural *m*
murder ['mə:də*] *n* asesinato; (*in law*) homicidio ▷*vt* asesinar, matar; **murderer** *n* asesino
murky ['mə:kɪ] *adj* (*water*) turbio; (*street, night*) lóbrego
murmur ['mə:mə*] *n* murmullo ▷*vt, vi* murmurar
muscle ['mʌsl] *n* músculo; (*fig: strength*) garra, fuerza; **muscular** ['mʌskjulə*] *adj* muscular; (*person*) musculoso
museum [mju:'zɪəm] *n* museo
mushroom ['mʌʃrum] *n* seta, hongo; (*Culin*) champiñón *m* ▷*vi* crecer de la noche a la mañana
music ['mju:zɪk] *n* música; **musical** *adj* musical; (*sound*) melodioso; (*person*) con talento musical ▷*n* (*show*) comedia musical; **musical instrument** *n* instrumento musical; **musician** [-'zɪʃən] *n* músico/a
Muslim ['mʌzlɪm] *adj, n* musulmán/ana *m/f*
muslin ['mʌzlɪn] *n* muselina
mussel ['mʌsl] *n* mejillón *m*
must [mʌst] *aux vb* (*obligation*): **I ~ do it** debo hacerlo, tengo que hacerlo; (*probability*): **he ~ be there by now** ya debe (de) estar allí ▷*n*: **it's a ~** es imprescindible
mustache ['mʌstæʃ] (US) *n* = **moustache**
mustard ['mʌstəd] *n* mostaza
mustn't ['mʌsnt] = **must not**
mute [mju:t] *adj, n* mudo/a *m/f*
mutilate ['mju:tɪleɪt] *vt* mutilar
mutiny ['mju:tɪnɪ] *n* motín *m* ▷*vi* amotinarse
mutter ['mʌtə*] *vt, vi* murmurar
mutton ['mʌtn] *n* carne *f* de cordero
mutual ['mju:tʃuəl] *adj* mutuo; (*interest*) común
muzzle ['mʌzl] *n* hocico; (*for dog*) bozal *m*; (*of gun*) boca ▷*vt* (*dog*) poner un bozal a
my [maɪ] *adj* mi(s); **~ house/brother/sisters** mi casa/mi hermano/mis hermanas; **I've washed ~ hair/cut ~ finger** me he lavado el pelo/cortado un dedo; **is this ~ pen or yours?** ¿es este bolígrafo mío o tuyo?
myself [maɪ'sɛlf] *pron* (*reflexive*) me; (*emphatic*) yo mismo; (*after prep*) mí (mismo); *see also* **oneself**
mysterious [mɪs'tɪərɪəs] *adj* misterioso
mystery ['mɪstərɪ] *n* misterio
mystical ['mɪstɪkl] *adj* místico
mystify ['mɪstɪfaɪ] *vt* (*perplex*) dejar perplejo
myth [mɪθ] *n* mito; **mythology** [mɪ'θɔlədʒɪ] *n* mitología

n/a *abbr* (= *not applicable*) no interesa
nag [næg] *vt* (*scold*) regañar
nail [neɪl] *n* (*human*) uña; (*metal*) clavo ▷ *vt* clavar; **to ~ sth to sth** clavar algo en algo; **to ~ sb down to doing sth** comprometer a algn a que haga algo; **nailbrush** *n* cepillo para las uñas; **nailfile** *n* lima para las uñas; **nail polish** *n* esmalte *m or* laca para las uñas; **nail polish remover** *n* quitaesmalte *m*; **nail scissors** *npl* tijeras *fpl* para las uñas; **nail varnish** (BRIT) *n* = **nail polish**
naïve [naɪ'iːv] *adj* ingenuo
naked ['neɪkɪd] *adj* (*nude*) desnudo; (*flame*) expuesto al aire
name [neɪm] *n* nombre *m*; (*surname*) apellido; (*reputation*) fama, renombre *m* ▷ *vt* (*child*) poner nombre a; (*criminal*) identificar; (*price, date etc*) fijar; **what's your ~?** ¿cómo se llama?; **by ~** de nombre; **in the ~ of** en nombre de; **to give one's ~ and address** dar sus señas; **namely** *adv* a saber
nanny ['nænɪ] *n* niñera
nap [næp] *n* (*sleep*) sueñecito, siesta
napkin ['næpkɪn] *n* (*also*: **table ~**) servilleta
nappy ['næpɪ] (BRIT) *n* pañal *m*
narcotics *npl* (*illegal drugs*) estupefacientes *mpl*, narcóticos *mpl*
narrative ['nærətɪv] *n* narrativa ▷ *adj* narrativo
narrator [nə'reɪtə*] *n* narrador(a) *m/f*
narrow ['nærəu] *adj* estrecho, angosto; (*fig: majority etc*) corto; (*: ideas etc*) estrecho ▷ *vi* (*road*) estrecharse; (*diminish*) reducirse; **to have a ~ escape** escaparse por los pelos; **narrow down** *vt* (*search, investigation, possibilities*) restringir, limitar; (*list*) reducir; **narrowly** *adv* (*miss*) por poco; **narrow-minded** *adj* de miras estrechas
nasal ['neɪzl] *adj* nasal
nasty ['nɑːstɪ] *adj* (*remark*) feo; (*person*) antipático; (*revolting: taste, smell*) asqueroso; (*wound, disease etc*) peligroso, grave
nation ['neɪʃən] *n* nación *f*
national ['næʃənl] *adj, n* nacional *m/f*; **national anthem** *n* himno nacional; **national dress** *n* vestido nacional; **National Health Service** (BRIT) *n* servicio nacional de salud pública ≈ Insalud *m* (SP); **National Insurance** (BRIT) *n* seguro social nacional; **nationalist** *adj, n* nacionalista *mf*; **nationality** [-'nælɪtɪ] *n* nacionalidad *f*; **nationalize** *vt* nacionalizar; **national park** (BRIT) *n* parque *m* nacional; **National Trust** *n* (BRIT) *organización encargada de preservar el patrimonio histórico británico*
nationwide ['neɪʃənwaɪd] *adj* en escala *or* a nivel nacional
native ['neɪtɪv] *n* (*local inhabitant*) natural *mf*, nacional *mf* ▷ *adj* (*indigenous*) indígena; (*country*) natal; (*innate*) natural, innato; **a ~ of Russia** un(a) natural *mf* de Rusia; **Native American** *adj, n* americano/a indígena, amerindio/a; **native speaker** *n* hablante *mf* nativo/a
NATO ['neɪtəu] *n abbr* (= *North Atlantic Treaty Organization*) OTAN *f*
natural ['nætʃrəl] *adj* natural; **natural gas** *n* gas *m* natural; **natural history** *n* historia natural; **naturally** *adv* (*speak etc*) naturalmente; (*of course*) desde luego, por supuesto; **natural resources** *npl* recursos *mpl* naturales
nature ['neɪtʃə*] *n* (*also*: **N~**) naturaleza; (*group, sort*) género, clase *f*; (*character*) carácter *m*, genio; **by ~** por *or* de naturaleza; **nature reserve** *n* reserva natural
naughty ['nɔːtɪ] *adj* (*child*) travieso
nausea ['nɔːsɪə] *n* náuseas *fpl*
naval ['neɪvl] *adj* naval, de marina
navel ['neɪvl] *n* ombligo
navigate ['nævɪgeɪt] *vt* gobernar ▷ *vi* navegar; (*Aut*) ir de copiloto; **navigation** [-'geɪʃən] *n* (*action*) navegación *f*; (*science*) náutica
navy ['neɪvɪ] *n* marina de guerra; (*ships*) armada, flota
Nazi ['nɑːtsɪ] *n* nazi *mf*
NB *abbr* (= *nota bene*) nótese
near [nɪə*] *adj* (*place, relation*) cercano; (*time*) próximo ▷ *adv* cerca ▷ *prep* (*also*: **~ to**: *space*) cerca de, junto a; (*: time*) cerca de ▷ *vt* acercarse a, aproximarse a; **nearby** [nɪə'baɪ] *adj* cercano, próximo ▷ *adv* cerca; **nearly** *adv* casi, por poco; **I nearly fell** por poco me caigo; **near-sighted** *adj* miope, corto de vista
neat [niːt] *adj* (*place*) ordenado, bien cuidado; (*person*) pulcro; (*plan*) ingenioso;

(*spirits*) solo; **neatly** *adv* (*tidily*) con esmero; (*skilfully*) ingeniosamente

necessarily ['nɛsɪsrɪlɪ] *adv* necesariamente

necessary ['nɛsɪsrɪ] *adj* necesario, preciso

necessity [nɪ'sɛsɪtɪ] *n* necesidad *f*

neck [nɛk] *n* (*of person, garment, bottle*) cuello; (*of animal*) pescuezo ▷ *vi* (*inf*) besuquearse; **~ and ~** parejos; **necklace** ['nɛklɪs] *n* collar *m*; **necktie** ['nɛktaɪ] *n* corbata

nectarine ['nɛktərɪn] *n* nectarina

need [ni:d] *n* (*lack*) escasez *f*, falta; (*necessity*) necesidad *f* ▷ *vt* (*require*) necesitar; **I ~ to do it** tengo que *or* debo hacerlo; **you don't ~ to go** no hace falta que (te) vayas

needle ['ni:dl] *n* aguja ▷ *vt* (*fig: inf*) picar, fastidiar

needless ['ni:dlɪs] *adj* innecesario; **~ to say** huelga decir que

needlework ['ni:dlwə:k] *n* (*activity*) costura, labor *f* de aguja

needn't ['ni:dnt] = **need not**

needy ['ni:dɪ] *adj* necesitado

negative ['nɛgətɪv] *n* (*Phot*) negativo; (*Ling*) negación *f* ▷ *adj* negativo

neglect [nɪ'glɛkt] *vt* (*one's duty*) faltar a, no cumplir con; (*child*) descuidar, desatender ▷ *n* (*of house, garden etc*) abandono; (*of child*) desatención *f*; (*of duty*) incumplimiento

negotiate [nɪ'gəuʃɪeɪt] *vt* (*treaty, loan*) negociar; (*obstacle*) franquear; (*bend in road*) tomar ▷ *vi*: **to ~ (with)** negociar (con)

negotiations [nɪgəuʃɪ'eɪʃənz] *pl n* negociaciones

negotiator [nɪ'gəuʃɪeɪtə*] *n* negociador(a) *m/f*

neighbour ['neɪbə*] (*US* **neighbor** *etc*) *n* vecino/a; **neighbourhood** *n* (*place*) vecindad *f*, barrio; (*people*) vecindario; **neighbouring** *adj* vecino

neither ['naɪðə*] *adj* ni ▷ *conj*: **I didn't move and ~ did John** no me he movido, ni Juan tampoco ▷ *pron* ninguno ▷ *adv*: **~ good nor bad** ni bueno ni malo; **~ is true** ninguno/a de los(las) dos es cierto/a

neon ['ni:ɔn] *n* neón *m*

Nepal [nɪ'pɔ:l] *n* Nepal *m*

nephew ['nɛvju:] *n* sobrino

nerve [nə:v] *n* (*Anat*) nervio; (*courage*) valor *m*; (*impudence*) descaro, frescura (*nervousness*) nerviosismo *msg*, nervios *mpl*; **a fit of ~s** un ataque de nervios

nervous ['nə:vəs] *adj* (*anxious, Anat*) nervioso; (*timid*) tímido, miedoso; **nervous breakdown** *n* crisis *f* nerviosa

nest [nɛst] *n* (*of bird*) nido; (*wasps' nest*) avispero ▷ *vi* anidar

net [nɛt] *n* (*gen*) red *f*; (*fabric*) tul *m* ▷ *adj* (*Comm*) neto, líquido ▷ *vt* coger (SP) *or* agarrar (LAM) con red; (*Sport*) marcar; **netball** *n* básquet *m*

Netherlands ['nɛðələndz] *npl*: **the ~** los Países Bajos

nett [nɛt] *adj* = **net**

nettle ['nɛtl] *n* ortiga

network ['nɛtwə:k] *n* red *f*

neurotic [njuə'rɔtɪk] *adj* neurótico/a

neuter ['nju:tə*] *adj* (*Ling*) neutro ▷ *vt* castrar, capar

neutral ['nju:trəl] *adj* (*person*) neutral; (*colour etc, Elec*) neutro ▷ *n* (*Aut*) punto muerto

never ['nɛvə*] *adv* nunca, jamás; **I ~ went** no fui nunca; **~ in my life** jamás en la vida; *see also* **mind**; **never-ending** *adj* interminable, sin fin; **nevertheless** [nɛvəðə'lɛs] *adv* sin embargo, no obstante

new [nju:] *adj* nuevo; (*brand new*) a estrenar; (*recent*) reciente; **New Age** *n* Nueva Era; **newborn** *adj* recién nacido; **newcomer** ['nju:kʌmə*] *n* recién venido/a *or* llegado/a; **newly** *adv* nuevamente, recién

news [nju:z] *n* noticias *fpl*; **a piece of ~** una noticia; **the ~** (*Radio, TV*) las noticias *fpl*; **news agency** *n* agencia de noticias; **newsagent** (BRIT) *n* vendedor(a) *m/f* de periódicos; **newscaster** *n* presentador(a) *m/f*, locutor(a) *m/f*; **news dealer** (*US*) *n* = **newsagent**; **newsletter** *n* hoja informativa, boletín *m*; **newspaper** *n* periódico, diario; **newsreader** *n* = **newscaster**

newt [nju:t] *n* tritón *m*

New Year *n* Año Nuevo; **New Year's Day** *n* Día *m* de Año Nuevo; **New Year's Eve** *n* Nochevieja

New Zealand [nju:'zi:lənd] *n* Nueva Zelanda; **New Zealander** *n* neozelandés/esa *m/f*

next [nɛkst] *adj* (*house, room*) vecino; (*bus stop, meeting*) próximo; (*following: page etc*) siguiente ▷ *adv* después; **the ~ day** el día siguiente; **~ time** la próxima vez; **~ year** el año próximo *or* que viene; **~ to** junto a, al lado de; **~ to nothing** casi nada; **~ please!** ¡el siguiente!; **next door** *adv* en la casa de al lado ▷ *adj* vecino, de al lado; **next-of-kin** *n* pariente *m* más cercano

NHS *n abbr* = **National Health Service**

nibble ['nɪbl] *vt* mordisquear, mordiscar

nice [naɪs] *adj* (*likeable*) simpático; (*kind*) amable; (*pleasant*) agradable;

(*attractive*) bonito, lindo (LAM); **nicely** *adv* amablemente; bien
niche [ni:ʃ] *n* (*Arch*) nicho, hornacina
nick [nɪk] *n* (*wound*) rasguño; (*cut, indentation*) mella, muesca ▷ *vt* (*inf*) birlar, robar; **in the ~ of time** justo a tiempo
nickel ['nɪkl] *n* níquel *m*; (US) *moneda de 5 centavos*
nickname ['nɪkneɪm] *n* apodo, mote *m* ▷ *vt* apodar
nicotine ['nɪkəti:n] *n* nicotina
niece [ni:s] *n* sobrina
night [naɪt] *n* noche *f*; (*evening*) tarde *f*; **the ~ before last** anteanoche; **at ~, by ~** de noche, por la noche; **night club** *n* cabaret *m*; **nightdress** (BRIT) *n* camisón *m*; **nightie** ['naɪtɪ] *n* = **nightdress**; **nightlife** *n* vida nocturna; **nightly** *adj* de todas las noches ▷ *adv* todas las noches, cada noche; **nightmare** *n* pesadilla; **night school** *n* clase(s) *f(pl)* nocturna(s); **night shift** *n* turno nocturno *or* de noche; **night-time** *n* noche *f*
nil [nɪl] (BRIT) *n* (*Sport*) cero, nada
nine [naɪn] *num* nueve; **nineteen** *num* diecinueve, diez y nueve; **nineteenth** [naɪn'ti:nθ] *adj* decimonoveno, decimonono; **ninetieth** ['naɪntɪɪθ] *adj* nonagésimo; **ninety** *num* noventa
ninth [naɪnθ] *adj* noveno
nip [nɪp] *vt* (*pinch*) pellizcar; (*bite*) morder
nipple ['nɪpl] *n* (*Anat*) pezón *m*
nitrogen ['naɪtrədʒən] *n* nitrógeno

KEYWORD

no [nəu] (*pl* **noes**) *adv* (*opposite of "yes"*) no; **are you coming? – no (I'm not)** ¿vienes? – no; **would you like some more? – no thank you** ¿quieres más? – no gracias ▷ *adj* (*not any*): **I have no money/time/books** no tengo dinero/tiempo/libros; **no other man would have done it** ningún otro lo hubiera hecho; **"no entry"** "prohibido el paso"; **"no smoking"** "prohibido fumar"
▷ *n* no *m*

nobility [nəu'bɪlɪtɪ] *n* nobleza
noble ['nəubl] *adj* noble
nobody ['nəubədɪ] *pron* nadie
nod [nɔd] *vi* saludar con la cabeza; (*in agreement*) decir que sí con la cabeza; (*doze*) dar cabezadas ▷ *vt*: **to ~ one's head** inclinar la cabeza ▷ *n* inclinación *f* de cabeza; **nod off** *vi* dar cabezadas
noise [nɔɪz] *n* ruido; (*din*) escándalo, estrépito; **noisy** *adj* ruidoso; (*child*) escandaloso
nominal ['nɔmɪnl] *adj* nominal
nominate ['nɔmɪneɪt] *vt* (*propose*) proponer; (*appoint*) nombrar; **nomination** [nɔmɪ'neɪʃən] *n* propuesta; nombramiento; **nominee** [-'ni:] *n* candidato/a
none [nʌn] *pron* ninguno/a ▷ *adv* de ninguna manera; **~ of you** ninguno de vosotros; **I've ~ left** no me queda ninguno/a; **he's ~ the worse for it** no le ha hecho ningún mal
nonetheless [nʌnðə'lɛs] *adv* sin embargo, no obstante
non-fiction [nɔn'fɪkʃən] *n* literatura no novelesca
nonsense ['nɔnsəns] *n* tonterías *fpl*, disparates *fpl*; **~!** ¡qué tonterías!
non: non-smoker *n* no fumador(a) *m/f*; **non-smoking** *adj* (de) no fumador; **non-stick** *adj* (*pan, surface*) antiadherente
noodles ['nu:dlz] *npl* tallarines *mpl*
noon [nu:n] *n* mediodía *m*
no-one ['nəuwʌn] *pron* = **nobody**
nor [nɔ:*] *conj* = **neither** ▷ *adv see* **neither**
norm [nɔ:m] *n* norma
normal ['nɔ:ml] *adj* normal; **normally** *adv* normalmente
north [nɔ:θ] *n* norte *m* ▷ *adj* del norte, norteño ▷ *adv* al *or* hacia el norte; **North America** *n* América del Norte; **North American** *adj, n* norteamericano/a *m/f*; **northbound** ['nɔ:θbaund] *adj* (*traffic*) que se dirige al norte; (*carriageway*) de dirección norte; **north-east** *n* nor(d)este *m*; **northeastern** *adj* nor(d)este, del nor(d)este; **northern** ['nɔ:ðən] *adj* norteño, del norte; **Northern Ireland** *n* Irlanda del Norte; **North Korea** *n* Corea del Norte; **North Pole** *n* Polo Norte; **North Sea** *n* Mar *m* del Norte; **north-west** *n* nor(d)oeste *m*; **northwestern** ['nɔ:θ'westən] *adj* noroeste, del noroeste
Norway ['nɔ:weɪ] *n* Noruega; **Norwegian** [-'wi:dʒən] *adj* noruego/a ▷ *n* noruego/a; (*Ling*) noruego
nose [nəuz] *n* (*Anat*) nariz *f*; (*Zool*) hocico; (*sense of smell*) olfato ▷ *vi*: **to ~ about** curiosear; **nosebleed** *n* hemorragia nasal; **nosey** (*inf*) *adj* curioso, fisgón/ona
nostalgia [nɔs'tældʒɪə] *n* nostalgia
nostalgic [nɔs'tældʒɪk] *adj* nostálgico
nostril ['nɔstrɪl] *n* ventana de la nariz
nosy ['nəuzɪ] (*inf*) *adj* = **nosey**
not [nɔt] *adv* no; **~ that ...** no es que ...; **it's too late, isn't it?** es demasiado tarde, ¿verdad *or* no?; **~ yet/now** todavía/ahora no; **why ~?** ¿por qué no?; *see also* **all; only**

notable ['nəutəbl] *adj* notable; **notably** *adv* especialmente
notch [nɔtʃ] *n* muesca, corte *m*
note [nəut] *n* (*Mus, record, letter*) nota; (*banknote*) billete *m*; (*tone*) tono ▷ *vt* (*observe*) notar, observar; (*write down*) apuntar, anotar; **notebook** *n* libreta, cuaderno; **noted** ['nəutɪd] *adj* célebre, conocido; **notepad** *n* bloc *m*; **notepaper** *n* papel *m* para cartas
nothing ['nʌθɪŋ] *n* nada; (*zero*) cero; **he does ~** no hace nada; **~ new** nada nuevo; **~ much** no mucho; **for ~** (*free*) gratis, sin pago; (*in vain*) en balde
notice ['nəutɪs] *n* (*announcement*) anuncio; (*warning*) aviso; (*dismissal*) despido; (*resignation*) dimisión *f*; (*period of time*) plazo ▷ *vt* (*observe*) notar, observar; **to bring sth to sb's ~** (*attention*) llamar la atención de algn sobre algo; **to take ~ of** tomar nota de, prestar atención a; **at short ~** con poca anticipación; **until further ~** hasta nuevo aviso; **to hand in one's ~** dimitir

Be careful not to translate **notice** by the Spanish word *noticia*.

noticeable *adj* evidente, obvio
notify ['nəutɪfaɪ] *vt*: **to ~ sb (of sth)** comunicar (algo) a algn
notion ['nəuʃən] *n* idea; (*opinion*) opinión *f*; **notions** *npl* (US) mercería
notorious [nəu'tɔ:rɪəs] *adj* notorio
notwithstanding [nɔtwɪθ'stændɪŋ] *adv* no obstante, sin embargo; **~ this** a pesar de esto
nought [nɔ:t] *n* cero
noun [naun] *n* nombre *m*, sustantivo
nourish ['nʌrɪʃ] *vt* nutrir; (*fig*) alimentar; **nourishment** *n* alimento, sustento
Nov. *abbr* (= *November*) nov
novel ['nɔvl] *n* novela ▷ *adj* (*new*) nuevo, original; (*unexpected*) insólito; **novelist** *n* novelista *mf*; **novelty** *n* novedad *f*
November [nəu'vɛmbə*] *n* noviembre *m*
novice ['nɔvɪs] *n* (*Rel*) novicio/a
now [nau] *adv* (*at the present time*) ahora; (*these days*) actualmente, hoy día ▷ *conj*: **~ (that)** ya que, ahora que; **right ~** ahora mismo; **by ~** ya; **just ~** ahora mismo; **~ and then, ~ and again** de vez en cuando; **from ~ on** de ahora en adelante; **nowadays** ['nauədeɪz] *adv* hoy (en) día, actualmente
nowhere ['nəuwɛə*] *adv* (*direction*) a ninguna parte; (*location*) en ninguna parte
nozzle ['nɔzl] *n* boquilla
nr *abbr* (BRIT) = **near**
nuclear ['nju:klɪə*] *adj* nuclear
nucleus ['nju:klɪəs] (*pl* **nuclei**) *n* núcleo
nude [nju:d] *adj*, *n* desnudo/a *m/f*; **in the ~** desnudo
nudge [nʌdʒ] *vt* dar un codazo a
nudist ['nju:dɪst] *n* nudista *mf*
nudity ['nju:dɪtɪ] *n* desnudez *f*
nuisance ['nju:sns] *n* molestia, fastidio; (*person*) pesado, latoso; **what a ~!** ¡qué lata!
numb [nʌm] *adj*: **~ with cold/fear** entumecido por el frío/paralizado de miedo
number ['nʌmbə*] *n* número; (*quantity*) cantidad *f* ▷ *vt* (*pages etc*) numerar, poner número a; (*amount to*) sumar, ascender a; **to be ~ed among** figurar entre; **a ~ of** varios, algunos; **they were ten in ~** eran diez; **number plate** (BRIT) *n* matrícula, placa; **Number Ten** *n* (BRIT: 10 *Downing Street*) *residencia del primer ministro*
numerical [nju:'mɛrɪkl] *adj* numérico
numerous ['nju:mərəs] *adj* numeroso
nun [nʌn] *n* monja, religiosa
nurse [nə:s] *n* enfermero/a; (*also*: **~maid**) niñera ▷ *vt* (*patient*) cuidar, atender
nursery ['nə:sərɪ] *n* (*institution*) guardería infantil; (*room*) cuarto de los niños; (*for plants*) criadero, semillero; **nursery rhyme** *n* canción *f* infantil; **nursery school** *n* parvulario, escuela de párvulos; **nursery slope** (BRIT) *n* (*Ski*) cuesta para principiantes
nursing ['nə:sɪŋ] *n* (*profession*) profesión *f* de enfermera; (*care*) asistencia, cuidado; **nursing home** *n* clínica de reposo
nurture ['nə:tʃə*] *vt* (*child, plant*) alimentar, nutrir
nut [nʌt] *n* (*Tech*) tuerca; (*Bot*) nuez *f*
nutmeg ['nʌtmɛg] *n* nuez *f* moscada
nutrient ['nju:trɪənt] *adj* nutritivo ▷ *n* elemento nutritivo
nutrition [nju:'trɪʃən] *n* nutrición *f*, alimentación *f*
nutritious [nju:'trɪʃəs] *adj* nutritivo, alimenticio
nuts [nʌts] (*inf*) *adj* loco
NVQ *n abbr* (BRIT) = **National Vocational Qualification**
nylon ['naɪlɔn] *n* nilón *m* ▷ *adj* de nilón

oath [əuθ] *n* juramento; (*swear word*) palabrota; **on** (BRIT) *or* **under ~** bajo juramento
oak [əuk] *n* roble *m* ▷ *adj* de roble
O.A.P. (BRIT) *n, abbr* = **old-age pensioner**
oar [ɔ:*] *n* remo
oasis [əu'eɪsɪs] (*pl* **oases**) *n* oasis *m inv*
oath [əuθ] *n* juramento; (*swear word*) palabrota; **on** (BRIT) *or* **under ~** bajo juramento
oatmeal ['əutmi:l] *n* harina de avena
oats [əuts] *npl* avena
obedience [ə'bi:dɪəns] *n* obediencia
obedient [ə'bi:dɪənt] *adj* obediente
obese [əu'bi:s] *adj* obeso
obesity [əu'bi:sɪtɪ] *n* obesidad *f*
obey [ə'beɪ] *vt* obedecer; (*instructions, regulations*) cumplir
obituary [ə'bɪtjuərɪ] *n* necrología
object [*n* 'ɔbdʒɪkt, *vb* əb'dʒɛkt] *n* objeto; (*purpose*) objeto, propósito; (*Ling*) complemento ▷ *vi*: **to ~ to** estar en contra de; (*proposal*) oponerse a; **to ~ that** objetar que; **expense is no ~** no importa cuánto cuesta; **I ~!** ¡yo protesto!; **objection** [əb'dʒɛkʃən] *n* protesta; **I have no objection to ...** no tengo inconveniente en que ...; **objective** *adj, n* objetivo
obligation [ɔblɪ'geɪʃən] *n* obligación *f*; (*debt*) deber *m*; **without ~** sin compromiso
obligatory [ə'blɪgətərɪ] *adj* obligatorio
oblige [ə'blaɪdʒ] *vt* (*do a favour for*) complacer, hacer un favor a; **to ~ sb to do sth** forzar *or* obligar a algn a hacer algo; **to be ~d to sb for sth** estarle agradecido a algn por algo
oblique [ə'bli:k] *adj* oblicuo; (*allusion*) indirecto
obliterate [ə'blɪtəreɪt] *vt* borrar
oblivious [ə'blɪvɪəs] *adj*: **~ of** inconsciente de
oblong ['ɔblɔŋ] *adj* rectangular ▷ *n* rectángulo
obnoxious [əb'nɔkʃəs] *adj* odioso, detestable; (*smell*) nauseabundo
oboe ['əubəu] *n* oboe *m*
obscene [əb'si:n] *adj* obsceno
obscure [əb'skjuə*] *adj* oscuro ▷ *vt* oscurecer; (*hide*: *sun*) esconder
observant [əb'zə:vnt] *adj* observador(a)
observation [ɔbzə'veɪʃən] *n* observación *f*; (*Med*) examen *m*
observatory [əb'zə:vətrɪ] *n* observatorio
observe [əb'zə:v] *vt* observar; (*rule*) cumplir; **observer** *n* observador(a) *m/f*
obsess [əb'sɛs] *vt* obsesionar; **obsession** [əb'sɛʃən] *n* obsesión *f*; **obsessive** *adj* obsesivo; obsesionante
obsolete ['ɔbsəli:t] *adj*: **to be ~** estar en desuso
obstacle ['ɔbstəkl] *n* obstáculo; (*nuisance*) estorbo
obstinate ['ɔbstɪnɪt] *adj* terco, porfiado; (*determined*) obstinado
obstruct [əb'strʌkt] *vt* obstruir; (*hinder*) estorbar, obstaculizar; **obstruction** [əb'strʌkʃən] *n* (*action*) obstrucción *f*; (*object*) estorbo, obstáculo
obtain [əb'teɪn] *vt* obtener; (*achieve*) conseguir
obvious ['ɔbvɪəs] *adj* obvio, evidente; **obviously** *adv* evidentemente, naturalmente; **obviously not** por supuesto que no
occasion [ə'keɪʒən] *n* oportunidad *f*, ocasión *f*; (*event*) acontecimiento; **occasional** *adj* poco frecuente, ocasional; **occasionally** *adv* de vez en cuando
occult [ɔ'kʌlt] *adj* (*gen*) oculto
occupant ['ɔkjupənt] *n* (*of house*) inquilino/a; (*of car*) ocupante *mf*
occupation [ɔkju'peɪʃən] *n* ocupación *f*; (*job*) trabajo; (*pastime*) ocupaciones *fpl*
occupy ['ɔkjupaɪ] *vt* (*seat, post, time*) ocupar; (*house*) habitar; **to ~ o.s. in doing** pasar el tiempo haciendo
occur [ə'kə:*] *vi* pasar, suceder; **to ~ to sb** ocurrírsele a algn; **occurrence** [ə'kʌrəns] *n* acontecimiento; (*existence*) existencia
ocean ['əuʃən] *n* océano
o'clock [ə'klɔk] *adv*: **it is 5 ~** son las 5
Oct. *abbr* (= *October*) oct
October [ɔk'təubə*] *n* octubre *m*
octopus ['ɔktəpəs] *n* pulpo
odd [ɔd] *adj* extraño, raro; (*number*) impar; (*sock, shoe etc*) suelto; **60-~** 60 y pico; **at ~ times** de vez en cuando; **to be the ~ one out** estar de más; **oddly** *adv* curiosamente, extrañamente; *see also* **enough**; **odds** *npl*

(*in betting*) puntos *mpl* de ventaja; **it makes no odds** da lo mismo; **at odds** reñidos/as; **odds and ends** minucias *fpl*

odometer [ɔ'dɔmɪtə*] (US) *n* cuentakilómetros *m inv*

odour ['əudə*] (US **odor**) *n* olor *m*; (*unpleasant*) hedor *m*

KEYWORD

of [ɔv, əv] *prep* **1** (*gen*) de; **a friend of ours** un amigo nuestro; **a boy of 10** un chico de 10 años; **that was kind of you** eso fue muy amable por *or* de tu parte
2 (*expressing quantity, amount, dates etc*) de; **a kilo of flour** un kilo de harina; **there were three of them** había tres; **three of us went** tres de nosotros fuimos; **the 5th of July** el 5 de julio
3 (*from, out of*) de; **made of wood** (hecho) de madera

off [ɔf] *adj, adv* (*engine*) desconectado; (*light*) apagado; (*tap*) cerrado; (BRIT: *food*: *bad*) pasado, malo; (: *milk*) cortado; (*cancelled*) cancelado ▷ *prep* de; **to be ~** (*to leave*) irse, marcharse; **to be ~ sick** estar enfermo *or* de baja; **a day ~** un día libre *or* sin trabajar; **to have an ~ day** tener un día malo; **he had his coat ~** se había quitado el abrigo; **10% ~** (*Comm*) (con el) 10% de descuento; **5 km ~ (the road)** a 5 km (de la carretera); **~ the coast** frente a la costa; **I'm ~ meat** (*no longer eat/like it*) paso de la carne; **on the ~ chance** por si acaso; **~ and on** de vez en cuando

offence [ə'fɛns] (US **offense**) *n* (*crime*) delito; **to take ~ at** ofenderse por

offend [ə'fɛnd] *vt* (*person*) ofender; **offender** *n* delincuente *mf*

offense [ə'fɛns] (US) *n* = **offence**

offensive [ə'fɛnsɪv] *adj* ofensivo; (*smell etc*) repugnante ▷ *n* (*Mil*) ofensiva

offer ['ɔfə*] *n* oferta, ofrecimiento; (*proposal*) propuesta ▷ *vt* ofrecer; (*opportunity*) facilitar; **"on ~"** (*Comm*) "en oferta"

offhand [ɔf'hænd] *adj* informal ▷ *adv* de improviso

office ['ɔfɪs] *n* (*place*) oficina; (*room*) despacho; (*position*) carga, oficio; **doctor's ~** (US) consultorio; **to take ~** entrar en funciones; **office block** (US), **office building** *n* bloque *m* de oficinas; **office hours** *npl* horas *fpl* de oficina; (US *Med*) horas *fpl* de consulta

officer ['ɔfɪsə*] *n* (*Mil etc*) oficial *mf*; (*also*: **police ~**) agente *mf* de policía; (*of organization*) director(a) *m/f*

office worker *n* oficinista *mf*

official [ə'fɪʃl] *adj* oficial, autorizado ▷ *n* funcionario/a, oficial *mf*

off: off-licence (BRIT) *n* (*shop*) bodega *tienda de vinos y bebidas alcohólicas*; **off-line** *adj, adv* (*Comput*) fuera de línea; **off-peak** *adj* (*electricity*) de banda económica; (*ticket*) *billete de precio reducido por viajar fuera de las horas punta*; **off-putting** (BRIT) *adj* (*person*) asqueroso; (*remark*) desalentador(a); **off-season** *adj, adv* fuera de temporada

OFF-LICENCE

En el Reino Unido la venta de bebidas alcohólicas está estrictamente regulada y se necesita una licencia especial, con la que cuentan los bares, restaurantes y los establecimientos de **off-licence**, los únicos lugares en donde se pueden adquirir bebidas alcohólicas para su consumo fuera del local, de donde viene su nombre. También venden bebidas no alcohólicas, tabaco, chocolatinas, patatas fritas, etc. y a menudo forman parte de una cadena nacional.

offset ['ɔfsɛt] *vt* contrarrestar, compensar

offshore [ɔf'ʃɔ:*] *adj* (*breeze, island*) costera; (*fishing*) de bajura

offside ['ɔf'saɪd] *adj* (*Sport*) fuera de juego; (*Aut*: *in UK*) del lado derecho; (: *in US, Europe etc*) del lado izquierdo

offspring ['ɔfsprɪŋ] *n inv* descendencia

often ['ɔfn] *adv* a menudo, con frecuencia; **how ~ do you go?** ¿cada cuánto vas?

oh [əu] *excl* ¡ah!

oil [ɔɪl] *n* aceite *m*; (*petroleum*) petróleo; (*for heating*) aceite *m* combustible ▷ *vt* engrasar; **oil filter** *n* (*Aut*) filtro de aceite; **oil painting** *n* pintura al óleo; **oil refinery** *n* refinería de petróleo; **oil rig** *n* torre *f* de perforación; **oil slick** *n* marea negra; **oil tanker** *n* petrolero; (*truck*) camión *m* cisterna; **oil well** *n* pozo (de petróleo); **oily** *adj* aceitoso; (*food*) grasiento

ointment ['ɔɪntmənt] *n* ungüento

O.K., okay ['əu'keɪ] *excl* ¡O.K.!, ¡está bien!, ¡vale! (SP) ▷ *adj* bien ▷ *vt* dar el visto bueno a

old [əuld] *adj* viejo; (*former*) antiguo; **how ~ are you?** ¿cuántos años tienes?, ¿qué edad tienes?; **he's 10 years ~** tiene 10 años; **~er brother** hermano mayor; **old age** *n* vejez *f*; **old-age pension** *n* (BRIT) jubilación *f*, pensión *f*; **old-age pensioner** (BRIT) *n* jubilado/a; **old-fashioned** *adj* anticuado,

pasado de moda; **old people's home** *n* (*esp* BRIT) residencia *f* de ancianos
olive ['ɔlɪv] *n* (*fruit*) aceituna; (*tree*) olivo ▷ *adj* (*also*: **~-green**) verde oliva; **olive oil** *n* aceite *m* de oliva
Olympic [əu'lɪmpɪk] *adj* olímpico; **the ~ Games, the ~s** las Olimpiadas
omelet(te) ['ɔmlɪt] *n* tortilla francesa (SP), omelette *f* (LAM)
omen ['əumən] *n* presagio
ominous ['ɔmɪnəs] *adj* de mal agüero, amenazador(a)
omit [əu'mɪt] *vt* omitir

KEYWORD

on [ɔn] *prep* **1** (*indicating position*) en; sobre; **on the wall** en la pared; **it's on the table** está sobre *or* en la mesa; **on the left** a la izquierda
2 (*indicating means, method, condition etc*): **on foot** a pie; **on the train/plane** (*go*) en tren/avión; (*be*) en el tren/el avión; **on the radio/television/telephone** por *or* en la radio/televisión/al teléfono; **to be on drugs** drogarse; (*Med*) estar a tratamiento; **to be on holiday/business** estar de vacaciones/en viaje de negocios
3 (*referring to time*): **on Friday** el viernes; **on Fridays** los viernes; **on June 20th** el 20 de junio; **a week on Friday** del viernes en una semana; **on arrival** al llegar; **on seeing this** al ver esto
4 (*about, concerning*) sobre, acerca de; **a book on physics** un libro de *or* sobre física
▷ *adv* **1** (*referring to dress*): **to have one's coat on** tener *or* llevar el abrigo puesto; **she put her gloves on** se puso los guantes
2 (*referring to covering*): **"screw the lid on tightly"** "cerrar bien la tapa"
3 (*further, continuously*): **to walk** *etc* **on** seguir caminando *etc*
▷ *adj* **1** (*functioning, in operation*: *machine, radio, TV, light*) encendido/a (SP), prendido/a (LAM); (: *tap*) abierto/a; (: *brakes*) echado/a, puesto/a; **is the meeting still on?** (*in progress*) ¿todavía continúa la reunión?; (*not cancelled*) ¿va a haber reunión al fin?; **there's a good film on at the cinema** ponen una buena película en el cine
2 **that's not on!** (*inf*: *not possible*) ¡eso ni hablar!; (: *not acceptable*) ¡eso no se hace!

once [wʌns] *adv* una vez; (*formerly*) antiguamente ▷ *conj* una vez que; **~ he had left/it was done** una vez que se había marchado/se hizo; **at ~** en seguida, inmediatamente; (*simultaneously*) a la vez; **~ a week** una vez por semana; **~ more** otra vez; **~ and for all** de una vez por todas; **~ upon a time** érase una vez
oncoming ['ɔnkʌmɪŋ] *adj* (*traffic*) que viene de frente

KEYWORD

one [wʌn] *num* un(o)/una; **one hundred and fifty** ciento cincuenta; **one by one** uno a uno
▷ *adj* **1** (*sole*) único; **the one book which** el único libro que; **the one man who** el único que
2 (*same*) mismo/a; **they came in the one car** vinieron en un solo coche
▷ *pron* **1** **this one** éste(ésta); **that one** ése(ésa); (*more remote*) aquél(aquella); **I've already got (a red) one** ya tengo uno/a rojo/a; **one by one** uno/a por uno/a
2 **one another** os (SP), se (+ *el uno al otro, unos a otros etc*); **do you two ever see one another?** ¿vosotros dos os veis alguna vez? (SP), ¿se ven ustedes dos alguna vez?; **the boys didn't dare look at one another** los chicos no se atrevieron a mirarse (el uno al otro); **they all kissed one another** se besaron unos a otros
3 (*impers*): **one never knows** nunca se sabe; **to cut one's finger** cortarse el dedo; **one needs to eat** hay que comer
one-off (BRIT: *inf*) *n* (*event*) acontecimiento único

oneself [wʌn'sɛlf] *pron* (*reflexive*) se; (*after prep*) sí; (*emphatic*) uno/a mismo/a; **to hurt ~** hacerse daño; **to keep sth for ~** guardarse algo; **to talk to ~** hablar solo
one: one-shot [wʌn'ʃɔt] (US) *n* = **one-off**; **one-sided** *adj* (*argument*) parcial; **one-to-one** *adj* (*relationship*) de dos; **one-way** *adj* (*street*) de sentido único
ongoing ['ɔngəuɪŋ] *adj* continuo
onion ['ʌnjən] *n* cebolla
on-line ['ɔnlaɪn] *adj, adv* (*Comput*) en línea
onlooker ['ɔnlukə*] *n* espectador(a) *m/f*
only ['əunlɪ] *adv* solamente, sólo ▷ *adj* único, solo ▷ *conj* solamente que, pero; **an ~ child** un hijo único; **not ~ ... but also ...** no sólo ... sino también ...
on-screen [ɔn'skri:n] *adj* (*Comput etc*) en pantalla; (*romance, kiss*) cinematográfico
onset ['ɔnsɛt] *n* comienzo
onto ['ɔntu] *prep* = **on to**
onward(s) ['ɔnwəd(z)] *adv* (*move*) (hacia) adelante; **from that time ~** desde entonces en adelante
oops [ups] *excl* (*also*: **~-a-daisy!**) ¡huy!

ooze [uːz] *vi* rezumar
opaque [əu'peɪk] *adj* opaco
open ['əupn] *adj* abierto; (*car*) descubierto; (*road, view*) despejado; (*meeting*) público; (*admiration*) manifiesto ▷ *vt* abrir ▷ *vi* abrirse; (*book etc: commence*) comenzar; **in the ~ (air)** al aire libre; **open up** *vt* abrir; (*blocked road*) despejar ▷ *vi* abrirse, empezar; **open-air** *adj* al aire libre; **opening** *n* abertura; (*start*) comienzo; (*opportunity*) oportunidad *f*; **opening hours** *npl* horario de apertura; **open learning** *n enseñanza flexible a tiempo parcial*; **openly** *adv* abiertamente; **open-minded** *adj* imparcial; **open-necked** *adj* (*shirt*) desabrochado; sin corbata; **open-plan** *adj*: **open-plan office** *gran oficina sin particiones*; **Open University** *n* (BRIT) ≈ Universidad *f* Nacional de Enseñanza a Distancia, UNED *f*

OPEN UNIVERSITY

La **Open University**, fundada en 1969, está especializada en impartir cursos a distancia que no exigen una dedicación exclusiva. Cuenta con sus propios materiales de apoyo, entre ellos programas de radio y televisión emitidos por la **BBC** y para conseguir los créditos de la licenciatura es necesaria la presentación de unos trabajos y la asistencia a los cursos de verano.

opera ['ɔpərə] *n* ópera; **opera house** *n* teatro de la ópera; **opera singer** *n* cantante *m/f* de ópera
operate ['ɔpəreɪt] *vt* (*machine*) hacer funcionar; (*company*) dirigir ▷ *vi* funcionar; **to ~ on sb** (*Med*) operar a algn
operating room ['ɔpəreɪtɪŋ-] (US) *n* quirófano, sala de operaciones
operating theatre (BRIT) *n* sala de operaciones
operation [ɔpə'reɪʃən] *n* operación *f*; (*of machine*) funcionamiento; **to be in ~** estar funcionando *or* en funcionamiento; **to have an ~** (*Med*) ser operado; **operational** *adj* operacional, en buen estado
operative ['ɔpərətɪv] *adj* en vigor
operator ['ɔpəreɪtə*] *n* (*of machine*) maquinista *mf*, operario/a; (*Tel*) operador(a) *m/f*, telefonista *mf*
opinion [ə'pɪnɪən] *n* opinión *f*; **in my ~** en mi opinión, a mi juicio; **opinion poll** *n* encuesta, sondeo
opponent [ə'pəunənt] *n* adversario/a, contrincante *mf*
opportunity [ɔpə'tjuːnɪtɪ] *n* oportunidad *f*; **to take the ~ of doing** aprovechar la ocasión para hacer
oppose [ə'pəuz] *vt* oponerse a; **to be ~d to sth** oponerse a algo; **as ~d to** a diferencia de
opposite ['ɔpəzɪt] *adj* opuesto, contrario a; (*house etc*) de enfrente ▷ *adv* en frente ▷ *prep* en frente de, frente a ▷ *n* lo contrario
opposition [ɔpə'zɪʃən] *n* oposición *f*
oppress [ə'prɛs] *vt* oprimir
opt [ɔpt] *vi*: **to ~ for** optar por; **to ~ to do** optar por hacer; **opt out** *vi*: **to opt out of** optar por no hacer
optician [ɔp'tɪʃən] *n* óptico *m/f*
optimism ['ɔptɪmɪzəm] *n* optimismo
optimist ['ɔptɪmɪst] *n* optimista *mf*; **optimistic** [-'mɪstɪk] *adj* optimista
optimum ['ɔptɪməm] *adj* óptimo
option ['ɔpʃən] *n* opción *f*; **optional** *adj* facultativo, discrecional
or [ɔː*] *conj* o; (*before o, ho*) u; (*with negative*): **he hasn't seen ~ heard anything** no ha visto ni oído nada; **~ else** si no
oral ['ɔːrəl] *adj* oral ▷ *n* examen *m* oral
orange ['ɔrɪndʒ] *n* (*fruit*) naranja ▷ *adj* color naranja; **orange juice** *n* jugo *m* de naranja, zumo *m* de naranja (SP); **orange squash** *n* naranjada
orbit ['ɔːbɪt] *n* órbita ▷ *vt, vi* orbitar
orchard ['ɔːtʃəd] *n* huerto
orchestra ['ɔːkɪstrə] *n* orquesta; (US: *seating*) platea
orchid ['ɔːkɪd] *n* orquídea
ordeal [ɔː'diːl] *n* experiencia horrorosa
order ['ɔːdə*] *n* orden *m*; (*command*) orden *f*; (*good order*) buen estado; (*Comm*) pedido ▷ *vt* (*also*: **put in ~**) arreglar, poner en orden; (*Comm*) pedir; (*command*) mandar, ordenar; **in ~** en orden; (*of document*) en regla; **in (working) ~** en funcionamiento; **in ~ to do/that** para hacer/que; **on ~** (*Comm*) pedido; **to be out of ~** estar desordenado; (*not working*) no funcionar; **to ~ sb to do sth** mandar a algn hacer algo; **order form** *n* hoja de pedido; **orderly** *n* (*Mil*) ordenanza *m*; (*Med*) enfermero/a (auxiliar) ▷ *adj* ordenado
ordinary ['ɔːdnrɪ] *adj* corriente, normal; (*pej*) común y corriente; **out of the ~** fuera de lo común
ore [ɔː*] *n* mineral *m*
oregano [ɔrɪ'gɑːnəu] *n* orégano
organ ['ɔːgən] *n* órgano; **organic** [ɔː'gænɪk] *adj* orgánico; **organism** *n* organismo
organization [ɔːgənaɪ'zeɪʃən] *n* organización *f*
organize ['ɔːgənaɪz] *vt* organizar;

organized ['ɔːgənaizd] *adj* organizado; **organizer** *n* organizador(a) *m/f*
orgasm ['ɔːgæzəm] *n* orgasmo
orgy ['ɔːdʒɪ] *n* orgía
oriental [ɔːrɪ'ɛntl] *adj* oriental
orientation [ɔːrɪen'teɪʃən] *n* orientación *f*
origin ['ɔrɪdʒɪn] *n* origen *m*
original [ə'rɪdʒɪnl] *adj* original; (*first*) primero; (*earlier*) primitivo ▷ *n* original *m*; **originally** *adv* al principio
originate [ə'rɪdʒɪneɪt] *vi*: **to ~ from, to ~ in** surgir de, tener su origen en
Orkneys ['ɔːknɪz] *npl*: **the ~** (*also*: **the Orkney Islands**) las Orcadas
ornament ['ɔːnəmənt] *n* adorno; (*trinket*) chuchería; **ornamental** [-'mɛntl] *adj* decorativo, de adorno
ornate [ɔː'neɪt] *adj* muy ornado, vistoso
orphan ['ɔːfn] *n* huérfano/a
orthodox ['ɔːθədɔks] *adj* ortodoxo
orthopaedic [ɔːθə'piːdɪk] (*US* **orthopedic**) *adj* ortopédico
osteopath ['ɔstɪəpæθ] *n* osteópata *mf*
ostrich ['ɔstrɪtʃ] *n* avestruz *m*
other ['ʌðə*] *adj* otro ▷ *pron*: **the ~ (one)** el(la) otro/a ▷ *adv*: **~ than** aparte de; **otherwise** *adv* de otra manera ▷ *conj* (*if not*) si no
otter ['ɔtə*] *n* nutria
ouch [autʃ] *excl* ¡ay!
ought [ɔːt] (*pt* **~**) *aux vb*: **I ~ to do it** debería hacerlo; **this ~ to have been corrected** esto debiera haberse corregido; **he ~ to win** (*probability*) debe *or* debiera ganar
ounce [auns] *n* onza (*28.35g*)
our ['auə*] *adj* nuestro; *see also* **my**; **ours** *pron* (el) nuestro/(la) nuestra *etc*; *see also* **mine**[1]; **ourselves** *pron pl* (*reflexive, after prep*) nosotros; (*emphatic*) nosotros mismos; *see also* **oneself**
oust [aust] *vt* desalojar
out [aut] *adv* fuera, afuera; (*not at home*) fuera (de casa); (*light, fire*) apagado; **~ there** allí (fuera); **he's ~** (*absent*) no está, ha salido; **to be ~ in one's calculations** equivocarse (en sus cálculos); **to run ~** salir corriendo; **~ loud** en alta voz; **~ of** (*outside*) fuera de; (*because of*: *anger etc*) por; **~ of petrol** sin gasolina; **"~ of order"** "no funciona"; **outback** *n* interior *m*; **outbound** *adj* (*flight*) de salida; (*flight*: *not return*) de ida; **outbreak** *n* (*of war*) comienzo; (*of disease*) epidemia; (*of violence etc*) ola; **outburst** *n* explosión *f*, arranque *m*; **outcast** *n* paria *mf*; **outcome** *n* resultado; **outcry** *n* protestas *fpl*; **outdated** *adj* anticuado, fuera de moda; **outdoor** *adj* exterior, de aire libre; (*clothes*) de calle; **outdoors** *adv* al aire libre
outer ['autə*] *adj* exterior, externo; **outer space** *n* espacio exterior
outfit ['autfɪt] *n* (*clothes*) conjunto
out: outgoing *adj* (*character*) extrovertido; (*retiring*: *president etc*) saliente; **outgoings** (*BRIT*) *npl* gastos *mpl*; **outhouse** *n* dependencia
outing ['autɪŋ] *n* excursión *f*, paseo
out: outlaw *n* proscrito ▷ *vt* proscribir; **outlay** *n* inversión *f*; **outlet** *n* salida; (*of pipe*) desagüe *m*; (*US Elec*) toma de corriente; (*also*: **retail outlet**) punto de venta; **outline** *n* (*shape*) contorno, perfil *m*; (*sketch, plan*) esbozo ▷ *vt* (*plan etc*) esbozar; **in outline** (*fig*) a grandes rasgos; **outlook** *n* (*fig*: *prospects*) perspectivas *fpl*; (: *for weather*) pronóstico; **outnumber** *vt* superar en número; **out-of-date** *adj* (*passport*) caducado; (*clothes*) pasado de moda; **out-of-doors** *adv* al aire libre; **out-of-the-way** *adj* apartado; **out-of-town** *adj* (*shopping centre etc*) en las afueras; **outpatient** *n* paciente *mf* externo/a; **outpost** *n* puesto avanzado; **output** *n* (volumen *m* de) producción *m*, rendimiento; (*Comput*) salida
outrage ['autreɪdʒ] *n* escándalo; (*atrocity*) atrocidad *f* ▷ *vt* ultrajar; **outrageous** [-'reɪdʒəs] *adj* monstruoso
outright [*adv* aut'raɪt, *adj* 'autraɪt] *adv* (*ask, deny*) francamente; (*refuse*) rotundamente; (*win*) de manera absoluta; (*be killed*) en el acto ▷ *adj* franco; rotundo
outset ['autsɛt] *n* principio
outside [aut'saɪd] *n* exterior *m* ▷ *adj* exterior, externo ▷ *adv* fuera ▷ *prep* fuera de; (*beyond*) más allá de; **at the ~** (*fig*) a lo sumo; **outside lane** *n* (*Aut*: *in Britain*) carril *m* de la derecha; (: *in US, Europe etc*) carril *m* de la izquierda; **outside line** *n* (*Tel*) línea (exterior); **outsider** *n* (*stranger*) extraño, forastero
out: outsize *adj* (*clothes*) de talla grande; **outskirts** *npl* alrededores *mpl*, afueras *fpl*; **outspoken** *adj* muy franco; **outstanding** *adj* excepcional, destacado; (*remaining*) pendiente
outward ['autwəd] *adj* externo; (*journey*) de ida; **outwards** *adv* (*esp BRIT*) = **outward**
outweigh [aut'weɪ] *vt* pesar más que
oval ['əuvl] *adj* ovalado ▷ *n* óvalo
ovary ['əuvərɪ] *n* ovario
oven ['ʌvn] *n* horno; **oven glove** *n* guante *m* para el horno, manopla para el horno; **ovenproof** *adj* resistente al horno; **oven-ready** *adj* listo para el horno
over ['əuvə*] *adv* encima, por encima ▷ *adj or adv* (*finished*) terminado; (*surplus*)

de sobra ▷ *prep* (por) encima de; (*above*) sobre; (*on the other side of*) al otro lado de; (*more than*) más de; (*during*) durante; **~ here** (por) aquí; **~ there** (por) allí *or* allá; **all ~** (*everywhere*) por todas partes; **~ and ~ (again)** una y otra vez; **~ and above** además de; **to ask sb ~** invitar a algn a casa; **to bend ~** inclinarse

overall [*adj, n* 'əuvərɔ:l, *adv* əuvər'ɔ:l] *adj* (*length etc*) total; (*study*) de conjunto ▷ *adv* en conjunto ▷ *n* (BRIT) guardapolvo; **overalls** *npl* (*boiler suit*) mono (SP) *or* overol *m* (LAM) (de trabajo)

overboard *adv* (*Naut*) por la borda

overcame [əuvə'keɪm] *pt of* **overcome**

overcast ['əuvəka:st] *adj* encapotado

overcharge [əuvə'tʃa:dʒ] *vt*: **to ~ sb** cobrar un precio excesivo a algn

overcoat ['əuvəkəut] *n* abrigo, sobretodo

overcome [əuvə'kʌm] *vt* vencer; (*difficulty*) superar

over: overcrowded *adj* atestado de gente; (*city, country*) superpoblado; **overdo** (*irreg*) *vt* exagerar; (*overcook*) cocer demasiado; **to overdo it** (*work etc*) pasarse; **overdone** [əuvə'dʌn] *adj* (*vegetables*) recocido; (*steak*) demasiado hecho; **overdose** *n* sobredosis *f inv*; **overdraft** *n* saldo deudor; **overdrawn** *adj* (*account*) en descubierto; **overdue** *adj* retrasado; **overestimate** *vt* sobreestimar

overflow [*vb* əuvə'fləu, *n* 'əuvəfləu] *vi* desbordarse ▷ *n* (*also*: **~ pipe**) (cañería de) desagüe *m*

overgrown [əuvə'grəun] *adj* (*garden*) invadido por la vegetación

overhaul [*vb* əuvə'hɔ:l, *n* 'əuvəhɔ:l] *vt* revisar, repasar ▷ *n* revisión *f*

overhead [*adv* əuvə'hɛd, *adj, n* 'əuvəhɛd] *adv* por arriba *or* encima ▷ *adj* (*cable*) aéreo ▷ *n* (US) = **overheads**; **overhead projector** *n* retroproyector; **overheads** *npl* (*expenses*) gastos *mpl* generales

over: overhear (*irreg*) *vt* oír por casualidad; **overheat** *vi* (*engine*) recalentarse; **overland** *adj, adv* por tierra; **overlap** [əuvə'læp] *vi* traslaparse; **overleaf** *adv* al dorso; **overload** *vt* sobrecargar; **overlook** *vt* (*have view of*) dar a, tener vistas a; (*miss: by mistake*) pasar por alto; (*excuse*) perdonar

overnight [əuvə'naɪt] *adv* durante la noche; (*fig*) de la noche a la mañana ▷ *adj* de noche; **to stay ~** pasar la noche; **overnight bag** *n* fin *m* de semana, neceser *m* de viaje

overpass (US) ['əuvəpa:s] *n* paso superior

overpower [əuvə'pauə*] *vt* dominar; (*fig*) embargar; **overpowering** *adj* (*heat*) agobiante; (*smell*) penetrante

over: overreact [əuvəri'ækt] *vi* reaccionar de manera exagerada; **overrule** *vt* (*decision*) anular; (*claim*) denegar; **overrun** (*irreg*) *vt* (*country*) invadir; (*time limit*) rebasar, exceder

overseas [əuvə'si:z] *adv* (*abroad: live*) en el extranjero; (*travel*) al extranjero ▷ *adj* (*trade*) exterior; (*visitor*) extranjero

oversee [əuvə'si:] (*irreg*) *vt* supervisar

overshadow [əuvə'ʃædəu] *vt*: **to be ~ed by** estar a la sombra de

oversight ['əuvəsaɪt] *n* descuido

oversleep [əuvə'sli:p] (*irreg*) *vi* quedarse dormido

overspend [əuvə'spɛnd] (*irreg*) *vi* gastar más de la cuenta; **we have overspent by 5 pounds** hemos excedido el presupuesto en 5 libras

overt [əu'və:t] *adj* abierto

overtake [əuvə'teɪk] (*irreg*) *vt* sobrepasar; (BRIT *Aut*) adelantar

over: overthrow (*irreg*) *vt* (*government*) derrocar; **overtime** *n* horas *fpl* extraordinarias

overtook [əuvə'tuk] *pt of* **overtake**

over: overturn *vt* volcar; (*fig: plan*) desbaratar; (*: government*) derrocar ▷ *vi* volcar; **overweight** *adj* demasiado gordo *or* pesado; **overwhelm** *vt* aplastar; (*emotion*) sobrecoger; **overwhelming** *adj* (*victory, defeat*) arrollador(a); (*feeling*) irresistible

ow [au] *excl* ¡ay!

owe [əu] *vt*: **to ~ sb sth, to ~ sth to sb** deber algo a algn; **owing to** *prep* debido a, por causa de

owl [aul] *n* búho, lechuza

own [əun] *vt* tener, poseer ▷ *adj* propio; **a room of my ~** una habitación propia; **to get one's ~ back** tomar revancha; **on one's ~** solo, a solas; **own up** *vi* confesar; **owner** *n* dueño/a; **ownership** *n* posesión *f*

ox [ɔks] (*pl* **~en**) *n* buey *m*

Oxbridge ['ɔksbrɪdʒ] *n universidades de Oxford y Cambridge*

oxen ['ɔksən] *npl of* **ox**

oxygen ['ɔksɪdʒən] *n* oxígeno

oyster ['ɔɪstə*] *n* ostra

oz. *abbr* = **ounce(s)**

ozone ['əuzəun] *n* ozono; **ozone friendly** *adj* que no daña la capa de ozono; **ozone layer** *n* capa *f* de ozono

p

p [pi:] *abbr* = **penny; pence**

P.A. *n abbr* = **personal assistant; public address system**

p.a. *abbr* = **per annum**

pace [peɪs] *n* paso ▷ *vi*: **to ~ up and down** pasearse de un lado a otro; **to keep ~ with** llevar el mismo paso que; **pacemaker** *n* (*Med*) regulador *m* cardíaco, marcapasos *m inv*; (*Sport*: *also*: **pacesetter**) liebre *f*

Pacific [pəˈsɪfɪk] *n*: **the ~ (Ocean)** el (Océano) Pacífico

pacifier [ˈpæsɪfaɪə*] (US) *n* (*dummy*) chupete *m*

pack [pæk] *n* (*packet*) paquete *m*; (*of hounds*) jauría; (*of people*) manada, bando; (*of cards*) baraja; (*bundle*) fardo; (US: *of cigarettes*) paquete *m*; (*back pack*) mochila ▷ *vt* (*fill*) llenar; (*in suitcase etc*) meter, poner; (*cram*) llenar, atestar; **to ~ (one's bags)** hacerse la maleta; **to ~ sb off** despachar a algn; **pack in** *vi* (*watch, car*) estropearse ▷ *vt* (*inf*) dejar; **pack it in!** ¡para!, ¡basta ya!; **pack up** *vi* (*inf*: *machine*) estropearse; (*person*) irse ▷ *vt* (*belongings, clothes*) recoger; (*goods, presents*) empaquetar, envolver

package [ˈpækɪdʒ] *n* paquete *m*; (*bulky*) bulto; (*also*: **~ deal**) acuerdo global; **package holiday** *n* vacaciones *fpl* organizadas; **package tour** *n* viaje *m* organizado

packaging [ˈpækɪdʒɪŋ] *n* envase *m*

packed [pækt] *adj* abarrotado; **packed lunch** *n* almuerzo frío

packet [ˈpækɪt] *n* paquete *m*

packing [ˈpækɪŋ] *n* embalaje *m*

pact [pækt] *n* pacto

pad [pæd] *n* (*of paper*) bloc *m*; (*cushion*) cojinete *m*; (*inf*: *home*) casa ▷ *vt* rellenar; **padded** *adj* (*jacket*) acolchado; (*bra*) reforzado

paddle [ˈpædl] *n* (*oar*) canalete *m*; (US: *for table tennis*) paleta ▷ *vt* impulsar con canalete ▷ *vi* (*with feet*) chapotear; **paddling pool** (BRIT) *n* estanque *m* de juegos

paddock [ˈpædək] *n* corral *m*

padlock [ˈpædlɔk] *n* candado

paedophile [ˈpi:dəufaɪl] (US **pedophile**) *adj* de pedófilos ▷ *n* pedófilo/a

page [peɪdʒ] *n* (*of book*) página; (*of newspaper*) plana; (*also*: **~ boy**) paje *m* ▷ *vt* (*in hotel etc*) llamar por altavoz a

pager [ˈpeɪdʒə*] *n* (*Tel*) busca *m*

paid [peɪd] *pt, pp of* **pay** ▷ *adj* (*work*) remunerado; (*holiday*) pagado; (*official etc*) a sueldo; **to put ~ to** (BRIT) acabar con

pain [peɪn] *n* dolor *m*; **to be in ~** sufrir; **to take ~s to do sth** tomarse grandes molestias en hacer algo; **painful** *adj* doloroso; (*difficult*) penoso; (*disagreeable*) desagradable; **painkiller** *n* analgésico; **painstaking** [ˈpeɪnzteɪkɪŋ] *adj* (*person*) concienzudo, esmerado

paint [peɪnt] *n* pintura ▷ *vt* pintar; **to ~ the door blue** pintar la puerta de azul; **paintbrush** *n* (*of artist*) pincel *m*; (*of decorator*) brocha; **painter** *n* pintor(a) *m/f*; **painting** *n* pintura

pair [pɛə*] *n* (*of shoes, gloves etc*) par *m*; (*of people*) pareja; **a ~ of scissors** unas tijeras; **a ~ of trousers** unos pantalones, un pantalón

pajamas [pəˈdʒɑ:məz] (US) *npl* pijama *m*

Pakistan [pɑ:kɪˈstɑ:n] *n* Paquistán *m*; **Pakistani** *adj, n* paquistaní *mf*

pal [pæl] (*inf*) *n* compinche *mf*, compañero/a

palace [ˈpæləs] *n* palacio

pale [peɪl] *adj* (*gen*) pálido; (*colour*) claro ▷ *n*: **to be beyond the ~** pasarse de la raya

Palestine [ˈpælɪstaɪn] *n* Palestina; **Palestinian** [-ˈtɪnɪən] *adj, n* palestino/a *m/f*

palm [pɑ:m] *n* (*Anat*) palma; (*also*: **~ tree**) palmera, palma ▷ *vt*: **to ~ sth off on sb** (*inf*) encajar algo a algn

pamper [ˈpæmpə*] *vt* mimar

pamphlet [ˈpæmflət] *n* folleto

pan [pæn] *n* (*also*: **sauce~**) cacerola, cazuela, olla; (*also*: **frying ~**) sartén *f*

pancake [ˈpænkeɪk] *n* crepe *f*

panda [ˈpændə] *n* panda *m*

pane [peɪn] *n* cristal *m*

panel [ˈpænl] *n* (*of wood etc*) panel *m*; (*Radio, TV*) panel *m* de invitados

panhandler [ˈpænhændlə*] (US) *n* (*inf*) mendigo/a

panic [ˈpænɪk] *n* terror *m* pánico ▷ *vi* dejarse llevar por el pánico

panorama [pænəˈrɑ:mə] *n* panorama *m*

pansy [ˈpænzɪ] *n* (*Bot*) pensamiento; (*inf*,

pej) maricón *m*
pant [pænt] *vi* jadear
panther ['pænθə*] *n* pantera
panties ['pæntɪz] *npl* bragas *fpl*, pantis *mpl*
pantomime ['pæntəmaɪm] (BRIT) *n* *revista musical representada en Navidad, basada en cuentos dehadas*

PANTOMIME

En época navideña se ponen en escena en los teatros británicos las llamadas **pantomimes**, que son versiones libres de cuentos tradicionales como Aladino o El gato con botas. En ella nunca faltan personajes como la dama ("dame"), papel que siempre interpreta un actor, el protagonista joven ("principal boy"), normalmente interpretado por una actriz, y el malvado ("villain"). Es un espectáculo familiar en el que se anima al público a participar y aunque va dirigido principalmente a los niños, cuenta con grandes dosis de humor para adultos.

pants [pænts] *n* (BRIT: *underwear: woman's*) bragas *fpl*; (: *man's*) calzoncillos *mpl*; (US: *trousers*) pantalones *mpl*
paper ['peɪpə*] *n* papel *m*; (*also*: **news~**) periódico, diario; (*academic essay*) ensayo; (*exam*) examen *m* ▷ *adj* de papel ▷ *vt* empapelar, tapizar (MEX); **papers** *npl* (*also*: **identity ~s**) papeles *mpl*, documentos *mpl*; **paperback** *n* libro en rústica; **paper bag** *n* bolsa de papel; **paper clip** *n* clip *m*; **paper shop** (BRIT) *n* tienda de periódicos; **paperwork** *n* trabajo administrativo
paprika ['pæprɪkə] *n* pimentón *m*
par [pɑ:*] *n* par *f*; (*Golf*) par *m*; **to be on a ~ with** estar a la par con
paracetamol [pærə'si:təmɔl] (BRIT) *n* paracetamol *m*
parachute ['pærəʃu:t] *n* paracaídas *m inv*
parade [pə'reɪd] *n* desfile *m* ▷ *vt* (*show*) hacer alarde de ▷ *vi* desfilar; (*Mil*) pasar revista
paradise ['pærədaɪs] *n* paraíso
paradox ['pærədɔks] *n* paradoja
paraffin ['pærəfɪn] (BRIT) *n* (*also*: **~ oil**) parafina
paragraph ['pærəgrɑ:f] *n* párrafo
parallel ['pærəlɛl] *adj* en paralelo; (*fig*) semejante ▷ *n* (*line*) paralela; (*fig, Geo*) paralelo
paralysed ['pærəlaɪzd] *adj* paralizado
paralysis [pə'rælɪsɪs] *n* parálisis *f inv*
paramedic [pærə'mɛdɪk] *n* auxiliar *m/f* sanitario/a
paranoid ['pærənɔɪd] *adj* (*person, feeling*) paranoico
parasite ['pærəsaɪt] *n* parásito/a
parcel ['pɑ:sl] *n* paquete *m* ▷ *vt* (*also*: **~ up**) empaquetar, embalar
pardon ['pɑ:dn] *n* (*Law*) indulto ▷ *vt* perdonar; **~ me!, I beg your ~!** (*I'm sorry!*) ¡perdone usted!; **(I beg your) ~?, ~ me?** (US: *what did you say?*) ¿cómo?
parent ['pɛərənt] *n* (*mother*) madre *f*; (*father*) padre *m*; **parents** *npl* padres *mpl*

Be careful not to translate **parent** by the Spanish word *pariente*.

parental [pə'rɛntl] *adj* paternal/maternal
Paris ['pærɪs] *n* París
parish ['pærɪʃ] *n* parroquia
Parisian [pə'rɪzɪən] *adj, n* parisiense *mf*
park [pɑ:k] *n* parque *m* ▷ *vt* aparcar, estacionar ▷ *vi* aparcar, estacionarse
parking ['pɑ:kɪŋ] *n* aparcamiento, estacionamiento; **"no ~"** "prohibido estacionarse"; **parking lot** (US) *n* parking *m*; **parking meter** *n* parquímetro; **parking ticket** *n* multa de aparcamiento
parkway ['pɑ:kweɪ] (US) *n* alameda
parliament ['pɑ:ləmənt] *n* parlamento; (*Spanish*) Cortes *fpl*; **parliamentary** [-'mɛntərɪ] *adj* parlamentario

PARLIAMENT

El Parlamento británico (**Parliament**) tiene como sede el palacio de Westminster, también llamado "Houses of Parliament" y consta de dos cámaras. La Cámara de los Comunes ("House of Commons"), compuesta por 650 diputados (**Members of Parliament**) elegidos por sufragio universal en su respectiva circunscripción electoral (constituency), se reúne 175 días al año y sus sesiones son moderadas por el Presidente de la Cámara (**Speaker**). La cámara alta es la Cámara de los Lores ("House of Lords") y está formada por miembros que han sido nombrados por el monarca o que han heredado su escaño. Su poder es limitado, aunque actúa como tribunal supremo de apelación, excepto en Escocia.

Parmesan [pɑ:mɪ'zæn] *n* (*also*: **~ cheese**) queso parmesano
parole [pə'rəul] *n*: **on ~** libre bajo palabra
parrot ['pærət] *n* loro, papagayo
parsley ['pɑ:slɪ] *n* perejil *m*
parsnip ['pɑ:snɪp] *n* chirivía

parson ['pɑːsn] *n* cura *m*

part [pɑːt] *n* (*gen, Mus*) parte *f*; (*bit*) trozo; (*of machine*) pieza; (*Theatre etc*) papel *m*; (*of serial*) entrega; (US: *in hair*) raya ▷ *adv* = **partly** ▷ *vt* separar ▷ *vi* (*people*) separarse; (*crowd*) apartarse; **to take ~ in** tomar parte *or* participar en; **to take sth in good ~** tomar algo en buena parte; **to take sb's ~** defender a algn; **for my ~** por mi parte; **for the most ~** en su mayor parte; **to ~ one's hair** hacerse la raya; **part with** *vt fus* ceder, entregar; (*money*) pagar; **part of speech** *n* parte *f* de la oración, categoría *f* gramatical

partial ['pɑːʃl] *adj* parcial; **to be ~ to** ser aficionado a

participant [pɑː'tɪsɪpənt] *n* (*in competition*) concursante *mf*; (*in campaign etc*) participante *mf*

participate [pɑː'tɪsɪpeɪt] *vi*: **to ~ in** participar en

particle ['pɑːtɪkl] *n* partícula; (*of dust*) grano

particular [pə'tɪkjulə*] *adj* (*special*) particular; (*concrete*) concreto; (*given*) determinado; (*fussy*) quisquilloso; (*demanding*) exigente; **in ~** en particular; **particularly** *adv* (*in particular*) sobre todo; (*difficult, good etc*) especialmente; **particulars** *npl* (*information*) datos *mpl*; (*details*) pormenores *mpl*

parting ['pɑːtɪŋ] *n* (*act*) separación *f*; (*farewell*) despedida; (BRIT: *in hair*) raya ▷ *adj* de despedida

partition [pɑː'tɪʃən] *n* (*Pol*) división *f*; (*wall*) tabique *m*

partly ['pɑːtlɪ] *adv* en parte

partner ['pɑːtnə*] *n* (*Comm*) socio/a; (*Sport, at dance*) pareja; (*spouse*) cónyuge *mf*; (*lover*) compañero/a; **partnership** *n* asociación *f*; (*Comm*) sociedad *f*

partridge ['pɑːtrɪdʒ] *n* perdiz *f*

part-time ['pɑːt'taɪm] *adj, adv* a tiempo parcial

party ['pɑːtɪ] *n* (*Pol*) partido; (*celebration*) fiesta; (*group*) grupo; (*Law*) parte *f* interesada ▷ *cpd* (*Pol*) de partido

pass [pɑːs] *vt* (*time, object*) pasar; (*place*) pasar por; (*overtake*) rebasar; (*exam*) aprobar; (*approve*) aprobar ▷ *vi* pasar; (*Scol*) aprobar, ser aprobado ▷ *n* (*permit*) permiso; (*membership card*) carnet *m*; (*in mountains*) puerto, desfiladero; (*Sport*) pase *m*; (*Scol*: *also*: **~ mark**): **to get a ~ in** aprobar en; **to ~ sth through sth** pasar algo por algo; **to make a ~ at sb** (*inf*) hacer proposiciones a algn; **pass away** *vi* fallecer; **pass by** *vi* pasar ▷ *vt* (*ignore*) pasar por alto; **pass on** *vt* transmitir; **pass out** *vi* desmayarse; **pass over** *vi, vt* omitir, pasar por alto; **pass up** *vt* (*opportunity*) renunciar a; **passable** *adj* (*road*) transitable; (*tolerable*) pasable

passage ['pæsɪdʒ] *n* (*also*: **~way**) pasillo; (*act of passing*) tránsito; (*fare, in book*) pasaje *m*; (*by boat*) travesía; (*Anat*) tubo

passenger ['pæsɪndʒə*] *n* pasajero/a, viajero/a

passer-by [pɑːsə'baɪ] *n* transeúnte *mf*

passing place *n* (*Aut*) apartadero

passion ['pæʃən] *n* pasión *f*; **passionate** *adj* apasionado; **passion fruit** *n* fruta de la pasión, granadilla

passive ['pæsɪv] *adj* (*gen, also Ling*) pasivo

passport ['pɑːspɔːt] *n* pasaporte *m*; **passport control** *n* control *m* de pasaporte; **passport office** *n* oficina de pasaportes

password ['pɑːswəːd] *n* contraseña

past [pɑːst] *prep* (*in front of*) por delante de; (*further than*) más allá de; (*later than*) después de ▷ *adj* pasado; (*president etc*) antiguo ▷ *n* (*time*) pasado; (*of person*) antecedentes *mpl*; **he's ~ forty** tiene más de cuarenta años; **ten/quarter ~ eight** las ocho y diez/cuarto; **for the ~ few/3 days** durante los últimos días/últimos 3 días; **to run ~ sb** pasar a algn corriendo

pasta ['pæstə] *n* pasta

paste [peɪst] *n* pasta; (*glue*) engrudo ▷ *vt* pegar

pastel ['pæstl] *adj* pastel; (*painting*) al pastel

pasteurized ['pæstəraɪzd] *adj* pasteurizado

pastime ['pɑːstaɪm] *n* pasatiempo

pastor ['pɑːstə*] *n* pastor *m*

past participle [-'pɑːtɪsɪpl] *n* (*Ling*) participio *m* (de) pasado *or* (de) pretérito *or* pasivo

pastry ['peɪstrɪ] *n* (*dough*) pasta; (*cake*) pastel *m*

pasture ['pɑːstʃə*] *n* pasto

pasty[1] ['pæstɪ] *n* empanada

pasty[2] ['peɪstɪ] *adj* (*complexion*) pálido

pat [pæt] *vt* dar una palmadita a; (*dog etc*) acariciar

patch [pætʃ] *n* (*of material,: eye patch*) parche *m*; (*mended part*) remiendo; (*of land*) terreno ▷ *vt* remendar; **(to go through) a bad ~** (pasar por) una mala racha; **patchy** *adj* desigual

pâté ['pæteɪ] *n* paté *m*

patent ['peɪtnt] *n* patente *f* ▷ *vt* patentar ▷ *adj* patente, evidente

paternal [pə'təːnl] *adj* paternal; (*relation*) paterno

paternity leave [pə'təːnɪtɪ-] *n* permiso *m*

por paternidad, licencia por paternidad
path [pɑːθ] *n* camino, sendero; (*trail, track*) pista; (*of missile*) trayectoria
pathetic [pəˈθɛtɪk] *adj* patético, lastimoso; (*very bad*) malísimo
pathway [ˈpɑːθweɪ] *n* sendero, vereda
patience [ˈpeɪʃns] *n* paciencia; (BRIT *Cards*) solitario
patient [ˈpeɪʃnt] *n* paciente *mf* ▷ *adj* paciente, sufrido
patio [ˈpætɪəu] *n* patio
patriotic [pætrɪˈɔtɪk] *adj* patriótico
patrol [pəˈtrəul] *n* patrulla ▷ *vt* patrullar por; **patrol car** *n* coche *m* patrulla
patron [ˈpeɪtrən] *n* (*in shop*) cliente *mf*; (*of charity*) patrocinador(a) *m/f*; **~ of the arts** mecenas *m*
patronizing [ˈpætrənaɪzɪŋ] *adj* condescendiente
pattern [ˈpætən] *n* (*Sewing*) patrón *m*; (*design*) dibujo; **patterned** *adj* (*material*) estampado
pause [pɔːz] *n* pausa ▷ *vi* hacer una pausa
pave [peɪv] *vt* pavimentar; **to ~ the way for** preparar el terreno para
pavement [ˈpeɪvmənt] (BRIT) *n* acera, banqueta (MEX), andén *m* (CAM), vereda (SC)
pavilion [pəˈvɪlɪən] *n* (*Sport*) caseta
paving [ˈpeɪvɪŋ] *n* pavimento, enlosado
paw [pɔː] *n* pata
pawn [pɔːn] *n* (*Chess*) peón *m*; (*fig*) instrumento ▷ *vt* empeñar; **pawn broker** *n* prestamista *mf*
pay [peɪ] (*pt, pp* **paid**) *n* (*wage etc*) sueldo, salario ▷ *vt* pagar ▷ *vi* (*be profitable*) rendir; **to ~ attention (to)** prestar atención (a); **to ~ sb a visit** hacer una visita a algn; **to ~ one's respects to sb** presentar sus respetos a algn; **pay back** *vt* (*money*) reembolsar; (*person*) pagar; **pay for** *vt fus* pagar; **pay in** *vt* ingresar; **pay off** *vt* saldar ▷ *vi* (*scheme, decision*) dar resultado; **pay out** *vt* (*money*) gastar, desembolsar; **pay up** *vt* pagar (de mala gana); **payable** *adj*: **payable to** pagadero a; **pay day** *n* día *m* de paga; **pay envelope** (US) *n* = **pay packet**; **payment** *n* pago; **monthly payment** mensualidad *f*; **payout** *n* pago; (*in competition*) premio en metálico; **pay packet** (BRIT) *n* sobre *m* (de paga); **pay phone** *n* teléfono público; **payroll** *n* nómina; **pay slip** *n* recibo de sueldo; **pay television** *n* televisión *f* de pago
PC *n abbr* = **personal computer**; (BRIT) (= *police constable*) policía *mf* ▷ *adv abbr* = **politically correct**
p.c. *abbr* = **per cent**
PDA *n abbr* (= *personal digital assistant*) agenda electrónica
PE *n abbr* (= *physical education*) ed. física
pea [piː] *n* guisante *m* (SP), arveja (LAM), chícharo (MEX, CAM)
peace [piːs] *n* paz *f*; (*calm*) paz *f*, tranquilidad *f*; **peaceful** *adj* (*gentle*) pacífico; (*calm*) tranquilo, sosegado
peach [piːtʃ] *n* melocotón *m* (SP), durazno (LAM)
peacock [ˈpiːkɔk] *n* pavo real
peak [piːk] *n* (*of mountain*) cumbre *f*, cima; (*of cap*) visera; (*fig*) cumbre *f*; **peak hours** *npl* horas *fpl* punta
peanut [ˈpiːnʌt] *n* cacahuete *m* (SP), maní *m* (LAM), cacahuate *m* (MEX); **peanut butter** *n* manteca de cacahuete *or* maní
pear [pɛə*] *n* pera
pearl [pəːl] *n* perla
peasant [ˈpɛznt] *n* campesino/a
peat [piːt] *n* turba
pebble [ˈpɛbl] *n* guijarro
peck [pɛk] *vt* (*also*: **~ at**) picotear ▷ *n* picotazo; (*kiss*) besito; **peckish** (BRIT: *inf*) *adj*: **I feel peckish** tengo ganas de picar algo
peculiar [pɪˈkjuːlɪə*] *adj* (*odd*) extraño, raro; (*typical*) propio, característico; **~ to** propio de
pedal [ˈpɛdl] *n* pedal *m* ▷ *vi* pedalear
pedalo [ˈpedələu] *n* patín *m* a pedal
pedestal [ˈpɛdəstl] *n* pedestal *m*
pedestrian [pɪˈdɛstrɪən] *n* peatón/ona *m/f* ▷ *adj* pedestre; **pedestrian crossing** (BRIT) *n* paso de peatones; **pedestrianized** *adj*: **a pedestrianized street** una calle peatonal; **pedestrian precinct** (US **pedestrian zone**) *n* zona peatonal
pedigree [ˈpɛdɪgriː] *n* genealogía; (*of animal*) raza, pedigrí *m* ▷ *cpd* (*animal*) de raza, de casta
pedophile [ˈpiːdəufaɪl] (US) *n* = **paedophile**
pee [piː] (*inf*) *vi* mear
peek [piːk] *vi* mirar a hurtadillas
peel [piːl] *n* piel *f*; (*of orange, lemon*) cáscara; (*: removed*) peladuras *fpl* ▷ *vt* pelar ▷ *vi* (*paint etc*) desconcharse; (*wallpaper*) despegarse, desprenderse; (*skin*) pelar
peep [piːp] *n* (BRIT: *look*) mirada furtiva; (*sound*) pío ▷ *vi* (BRIT: *look*) mirar furtivamente
peer [pɪə*] *vi*: **to ~ at** esudriñar ▷ *n* (*noble*) par *m*; (*equal*) igual *m*; (*contemporary*) contemporáneo/a
peg [pɛg] *n* (*for coat etc*) gancho, colgadero; (BRIT: *also*: **clothes ~**) pinza
pelican [ˈpɛlɪkən] *n* pelícano; **pelican crossing** (BRIT) *n* (*Aut*) paso de peatones señalizado

pelt [pɛlt] *vt*: **to ~ sb with sth** arrojarle algo a algn ▷*vi* (*rain*) llover a cántaros; (*inf*: *run*) correr ▷*n* pellejo
pelvis ['pɛlvɪs] *n* pelvis *f*
pen [pɛn] *n* (*fountain pen*) pluma; (*ballpoint pen*) bolígrafo; (*for sheep*) redil *m*
penalty ['pɛnltɪ] *n* (*gen*) pena; (*fine*) multa
pence [pɛns] *npl of* **penny**
pencil ['pɛnsl] *n* lápiz *m*; **pencil in** *vt* (*appointment*) apuntar con carácter provisional; **pencil case** *n* estuche *m*; **pencil sharpener** *n* sacapuntas *m inv*
pendant ['pɛndnt] *n* pendiente *m*
pending ['pɛndɪŋ] *prep* antes de ▷*adj* pendiente
penetrate ['pɛnɪtreɪt] *vt* penetrar
penfriend ['pɛnfrɛnd] (BRIT) *n* amigo/a por carta
penguin ['pɛŋgwɪn] *n* pingüino
penicillin [pɛnɪ'sɪlɪn] *n* penicilina
peninsula [pə'nɪnsjulə] *n* península
penis ['pi:nɪs] *n* pene *m*
penitentiary [pɛnɪ'tɛnʃərɪ] (US) *n* cárcel *f*, presidio
penknife ['pɛnnaɪf] *n* navaja
penniless ['pɛnɪlɪs] *adj* sin dinero
penny ['pɛnɪ] (*pl* **pennies** *or* **pence**) (BRIT) *n* penique *m*; (US) centavo
penpal ['pɛnpæl] *n* amigo/a por carta
pension ['pɛnʃən] *n* (*state benefit*) jubilación *f*; **pensioner** (BRIT) *n* jubilado/a
pentagon ['pɛntəgən] (US) *n*: **the P~** (*Pol*) el Pentágono

PENTAGON

Se conoce como **Pentagon** al edificio de planta pentagonal que acoge las dependencias del Ministerio de Defensa estadounidense ("Department of Defense") en Arlington, Virginia. En lenguaje periodístico se aplica también a la dirección militar del país.

penthouse ['pɛnthaus] *n* ático de lujo
penultimate [pɛ'nʌltɪmət] *adj* penúltimo
people ['pi:pl] *npl* gente *f*; (*citizens*) pueblo, ciudadanos *mpl*; (*Pol*): **the ~** el pueblo ▷*n* (*nation, race*) pueblo, nación *f*; **several ~ came** vinieron varias personas; **~ say that ...** dice la gente que ...
pepper ['pɛpə*] *n* (*spice*) pimienta; (*vegetable*) pimiento ▷*vt*: **to ~ with** (*fig*) salpicar de; **peppermint** *n* (*sweet*) pastilla de menta
per [pə:*] *prep* por; **~ day/~son** por día/persona; **~ annum** al año
perceive [pə'si:v] *vt* percibir; (*realize*) darse cuenta de
per cent *n* por ciento
percentage [pə'sɛntɪdʒ] *n* porcentaje *m*
perception [pə'sɛpʃən] *n* percepción *f*; (*insight*) perspicacia; (*opinion etc*) opinión *f*
perch [pə:tʃ] *n* (*fish*) perca; (*for bird*) percha ▷*vi*: **to ~ (on)** (*bird*) posarse (en); (*person*) encaramarse (en)
percussion [pə'kʌʃən] *n* percusión *f*
perfect [*adj, n* 'pə:fɪkt, *vb* pə'fɛkt] *adj* perfecto ▷*n* (*also*: **~ tense**) perfecto ▷*vt* perfeccionar; **perfection** [pə'fɛkʃən] *n* perfección *f*; **perfectly** ['pə:fɪktlɪ] *adv* perfectamente
perform [pə'fɔ:m] *vt* (*carry out*) realizar, llevar a cabo; (*Theatre*) representar; (*piece of music*) interpretar ▷*vi* (*well, badly*) funcionar; **performance** *n* (*of a play*) representación *f*; (*of actor, athlete etc*) actuación *f*; (*of car, engine, company*) rendimiento; (*of economy*) resultados *mpl*; **performer** *n* (*actor*) actor *m*, actriz *f*
perfume ['pə:fju:m] *n* perfume *m*
perhaps [pə'hæps] *adv* quizá(s), tal vez
perimeter [pə'rɪmɪtə*] *n* perímetro
period ['pɪərɪəd] *n* período; (*Scol*) clase *f*; (*full stop*) punto; (*Med*) regla ▷*adj* (*costume, furniture*) de época; **periodical** [pɪərɪ'ɔdɪkl] *n* periódico; **periodically** *adv* de vez en cuando, cada cierto tiempo
perish ['pɛrɪʃ] *vi* perecer; (*decay*) echarse a perder
perjury ['pə:dʒərɪ] *n* (*Law*) perjurio
perk [pə:k] *n* extra *m*
perm [pə:m] *n* permanente *f*
permanent ['pə:mənənt] *adj* permanente; **permanently** *adv* (*lastingly*) para siempre, de modo definitivo; (*all the time*) permanentemente
permission [pə'mɪʃən] *n* permiso
permit [*n* 'pə:mɪt, *vt* pə'mɪt] *n* permiso, licencia ▷*vt* permitir
perplex [pə'plɛks] *vt* dejar perplejo
persecute ['pə:sɪkju:t] *vt* perseguir
persecution [pə:sɪ'kju:ʃən] *n* persecución *f*
persevere [pə:sɪ'vɪə*] *vi* persistir
Persian ['pə:ʃən] *adj, n* persa *mf*; **the ~ Gulf** el Golfo Pérsico
persist [pə'sɪst] *vi*: **to ~ (in doing sth)** persistir (en hacer algo); **persistent** *adj* persistente; (*determined*) porfiado
person ['pə:sn] *n* persona; **in ~** en persona; **personal** *adj* personal; individual; (*visit*) en persona; **personal assistant** *n* ayudante *mf* personal; **personal computer** *n* ordenador *m* personal; **personality**

[-'nælɪtɪ] *n* personalidad *f*; **personally** *adv* personalmente; (*in person*) en persona; **to take sth personally** tomarse algo a mal; **personal organizer** *n* agenda; **personal stereo** *n* Walkman® *m*

personnel [pə:sə'nɛl] *n* personal *m*

perspective [pə'spɛktɪv] *n* perspectiva

perspiration [pə:spɪ'reɪʃən] *n* transpiración *f*

persuade [pə'sweɪd] *vt*: **to ~ sb to do sth** persuadir a algn para que haga algo

persuasion [pə'sweɪʒən] *n* persuasión *f*; (*persuasiveness*) persuasiva

persuasive [pə'sweɪsɪv] *adj* persuasivo

perverse [pə'və:s] *adj* perverso; (*wayward*) travieso

pervert [*n* 'pə:və:t, *vb* pə'və:t] *n* pervertido/a ▷*vt* pervertir; (*truth, sb's words*) tergiversar

pessimism ['pɛsɪmɪzəm] *n* pesimismo

pessimist ['pɛsɪmɪst] *n* pesimista *mf*; **pessimistic** [-'mɪstɪk] *adj* pesimista

pest [pɛst] *n* (*insect*) insecto nocivo; (*fig*) lata, molestia

pester ['pɛstə*] *vt* molestar, acosar

pesticide ['pɛstɪsaɪd] *n* pesticida *m*

pet [pɛt] *n* animal *m* doméstico ▷*cpd* favorito ▷*vt* acariciar; **teacher's ~** favorito/a (del profesor); **~ hate** manía

petal ['pɛtl] *n* pétalo

petite [pə'ti:t] *adj* chiquita

petition [pə'tɪʃən] *n* petición *f*

petrified ['pɛtrɪfaɪd] *adj* horrorizado

petrol ['pɛtrəl] (BRIT) *n* gasolina

petroleum [pə'trəulɪəm] *n* petróleo

petrol: petrol pump (BRIT) *n* (*in garage*) surtidor *m* de gasolina; **petrol station** (BRIT) *n* gasolinera; **petrol tank** (BRIT) *n* depósito (de gasolina)

petticoat ['pɛtɪkəut] *n* enaguas *fpl*

petty ['pɛtɪ] *adj* (*mean*) mezquino; (*unimportant*) insignificante

pew [pju:] *n* banco

pewter ['pju:tə*] *n* peltre *m*

phantom ['fæntəm] *n* fantasma *m*

pharmacist ['fɑ:məsɪst] *n* farmacéutico/a

pharmacy ['fɑ:məsɪ] *n* farmacia

phase [feɪz] *n* fase *f*; **phase in** *vt* introducir progresivamente; **phase out** *vt* (*machinery, product*) retirar progresivamente; (*job, subsidy*) eliminar por etapas

Ph.D. *abbr* = **Doctor of Philosophy**

pheasant ['fɛznt] *n* faisán *m*

phenomena [fə'nɔmɪnə] *npl of* **phenomenon**

phenomenal [fɪ'nɔmɪnl] *adj* fenomenal, extraordinario

phenomenon [fə'nɔmɪnən] (*pl* **phenomena**) *n* fenómeno

Philippines ['fɪlɪpi:nz] *npl*: **the ~** las Filipinas

philosopher [fɪ'lɔsəfə*] *n* filósofo/a

philosophical [fɪlə'sɔfɪkl] *adj* filosófico

philosophy [fɪ'lɔsəfɪ] *n* filosofía

phlegm [flɛm] *n* flema

phobia ['fəubjə] *n* fobia

phone [fəun] *n* teléfono ▷*vt* telefonear, llamar por teléfono; **to be on the ~** tener teléfono; (*be calling*) estar hablando por teléfono; **phone back** *vt, vi* volver a llamar; **phone up** *vt, vi* llamar por teléfono; **phone book** *n* guía telefónica; **phone booth** *n* cabina telefónica; **phone box** (BRIT) *n* = **phone booth**; **phone call** *n* llamada (telefónica); **phonecard** *n* teletarjeta; **phone number** *n* número de teléfono

phonetics [fə'nɛtɪks] *n* fonética

phoney ['fəunɪ] *adj* falso

photo ['fəutəu] *n* foto *f*; **photo album** *n* álbum *m* de fotos; **photocopier** *n* fotocopiadora; **photocopy** *n* fotocopia ▷*vt* fotocopiar

photograph ['fəutəgrɑ:f] *n* fotografía ▷*vt* fotografiar; **photographer** [fə'tɔgrəfə*] *n* fotógrafo; **photography** [fə'tɔgrəfɪ] *n* fotografía

phrase [freɪz] *n* frase *f* ▷*vt* expresar; **phrase book** *n* libro de frases

physical ['fɪzɪkl] *adj* físico; **physical education** *n* educación *f* física; **physically** *adv* físicamente

physician [fɪ'zɪʃən] *n* médico/a

physicist ['fɪzɪsɪst] *n* físico/a

physics ['fɪzɪks] *n* física

physiotherapist [fɪzɪəu'θɛrəpɪst] *n* fisioterapeuta

physiotherapy [fɪzɪəu'θɛrəpɪ] *n* fisioterapia

physique [fɪ'zi:k] *n* físico

pianist ['pi:ənɪst] *n* pianista *mf*

piano [pɪ'ænəu] *n* piano

pick [pɪk] *n* (*tool*: *also*: **~-axe**) pico, piqueta ▷*vt* (*select*) elegir, escoger; (*gather*) coger (SP), recoger; (*remove, take out*) sacar, quitar; (*lock*) abrir con ganzúa; **take your ~** escoja lo que quiera; **the ~ of** lo mejor de; **to ~ one's nose/teeth** hurgarse las narices/limpiarse los dientes; **to ~ a quarrel with sb** meterse con algn; **pick on** *vt fus* (*person*) meterse con; **pick out** *vt* escoger; (*distinguish*) identificar; **pick up** *vi* (*improve*: *sales*) ir mejor; (*: patient*) reponerse; (*Finance*) recobrarse ▷*vt* recoger; (*learn*) aprender; (*Police*: *arrest*) detener; (*person*: *for sex*) ligar; (*Radio*) captar; **to pick up speed**

acelerarse; **to pick o.s. up** levantarse

pickle ['pɪkl] *n* (*also*: **~s**: *as condiment*) escabeche *m*; (*fig*: *mess*) apuro ▷ *vt* encurtir

pickpocket ['pɪkpɔkɪt] *n* carterista *mf*

pick-up ['pɪkʌp] *n* (*also*: **~ truck**) furgoneta, camioneta

picnic ['pɪknɪk] *n* merienda ▷ *vi* ir de merienda; **picnic area** *n* zona de picnic; (*Aut*) área de descanso

picture ['pɪktʃə*] *n* cuadro; (*painting*) pintura; (*photograph*) fotografía; (*TV*) imagen *f*; (*film*) película; (*fig*: *description*) descripción *f*; (: *situation*) situación *f* ▷ *vt* (*imagine*) imaginar; **pictures** *npl*: **the ~s** (BRIT) el cine; **picture frame** *n* marco; **picture messaging** *n* (envío de) mensajes con imágenes

picturesque [pɪktʃə'rɛsk] *adj* pintoresco

pie [paɪ] *n* pastel *m*; (*open*) tarta; (*small*: *of meat*) empanada

piece [pi:s] *n* pedazo, trozo; (*of cake*) trozo; (*item*): **a ~ of clothing/furniture/advice** una prenda (de vestir)/un mueble/un consejo ▷ *vt*: **to ~ together** juntar; (*Tech*) armar; **to take to ~s** desmontar

pie chart *n* gráfico de sectores *or* tarta

pier [pɪə*] *n* muelle *m*, embarcadero

pierce [pɪəs] *vt* perforar; **pierced** *adj*: **I've got pierced ears** tengo los agujeros hechos en las orejas

pig [pɪg] *n* cerdo, chancho (LAM); (*pej*: *unkind person*) asqueroso; (: *greedy person*) glotón/ ona *m/f*

pigeon ['pɪdʒən] *n* paloma; (*as food*) pichón *m*

piggy bank ['pɪgɪ-] *n* hucha (*en forma de cerdito*)

pigsty ['pɪgstaɪ] *n* pocilga

pigtail *n* (*girl's*) trenza

pike [paɪk] *n* (*fish*) lucio

pilchard ['pɪltʃəd] *n* sardina

pile [paɪl] *n* montón *m*; (*of carpet, cloth*) pelo; **pile up** *vi +adv* (*accumulate*: *work*) amontonarse, acumularse ▷ *vt +adv* (*put in a heap*: *books, clothes*) apilar, amontonar; (*accumulate*) acumular; **piles** *npl* (*Med*) almorranas *fpl*, hemorroides *mpl*; **pile-up** *n* (*Aut*) accidente *m* múltiple

pilgrimage ['pɪlgrɪmɪdʒ] *n* peregrinación *f*, romería

pill [pɪl] *n* píldora; **the ~** la píldora

pillar ['pɪlə*] *n* pilar *m*

pillow ['pɪləu] *n* almohada; **pillowcase** *n* funda

pilot ['paɪlət] *n* piloto ▷ *cpd* (*scheme etc*) piloto ▷ *vt* pilotar; **pilot light** *n* piloto

pimple ['pɪmpl] *n* grano

PIN *n abbr* (= *personal identification number*) número personal

pin [pɪn] *n* alfiler *m* ▷ *vt* prender (con alfiler); **~s and needles** hormigueo; **to ~ sb down** (*fig*) hacer que algn concrete; **to ~ sth on sb** (*fig*) colgarle a algn el sambenito de algo

pinafore ['pɪnəfɔ:*] *n* delantal *m*

pinch [pɪntʃ] *n* (*of salt etc*) pizca ▷ *vt* pellizcar; (*inf*: *steal*) birlar; **at a ~** en caso de apuro

pine [paɪn] *n* (*also*: **~ tree**) pino ▷ *vi*: **to ~ for** suspirar por

pineapple ['paɪnæpl] *n* piña, ananás *m*

ping [pɪŋ] *n* (*noise*) sonido agudo; **ping-pong®** *n* pingpong® *m*

pink [pɪŋk] *adj* rosado, (color de) rosa ▷ *n* (*colour*) rosa; (*Bot*) clavel *m*, clavellina

pinpoint ['pɪnpɔɪnt] *vt* precisar

pint [paɪnt] *n* pinta (BRIT = *568cc*, US = *473cc*); (BRIT: *inf*: *of beer*) pinta de cerveza ≈ jarra (SP)

pioneer [paɪə'nɪə*] *n* pionero/a

pious ['paɪəs] *adj* piadoso, devoto

pip [pɪp] *n* (*seed*) pepita; **the ~s** (BRIT) la señal

pipe [paɪp] *n* tubo, caño; (*for smoking*) pipa ▷ *vt* conducir en cañerías; **pipeline** *n* (*for oil*) oleoducto; (*for gas*) gasoducto; **piper** *n* gaitero/a

pirate ['paɪərət] *n* pirata *mf* ▷ *vt* (*cassette, book*) piratear

Pisces ['paɪsi:z] *n* Piscis *m*

piss [pɪs] (*inf!*) *vi* mear; **pissed** (*inf!*) *adj* (*drunk*) borracho

pistol ['pɪstl] *n* pistola

piston ['pɪstən] *n* pistón *m*, émbolo

pit [pɪt] *n* hoyo; (*also*: **coal ~**) mina; (*in garage*) foso de inspección; (*also*: **orchestra ~**) platea ▷ *vt*: **to ~ one's wits against sb** medir fuerzas con algn

pitch [pɪtʃ] *n* (*Mus*) tono; (BRIT *Sport*) campo, terreno; (*fig*) punto; (*tar*) brea ▷ *vt* (*throw*) arrojar, lanzar ▷ *vi* (*fall*) caer(se); **to ~ a tent** montar una tienda (de campaña); **pitch-black** *adj* negro como boca de lobo

pitfall ['pɪtfɔ:l] *n* riesgo

pith [pɪθ] *n* (*of orange*) médula

pitiful ['pɪtɪful] *adj* (*touching*) lastimoso, conmovedor(a)

pity ['pɪtɪ] *n* compasión *f*, piedad *f* ▷ *vt* compadecer(se de); **what a ~!** ¡qué pena!

pizza ['pi:tsə] *n* pizza

placard ['plækɑ:d] *n* letrero; (*in march etc*) pancarta

place [pleɪs] *n* lugar *m*, sitio; (*seat*) plaza, asiento; (*post*) puesto; (*home*): **at/to his ~** en/a su casa; (*role*: *in society etc*) papel *m* ▷ *vt* (*object*) poner, colocar; (*identify*) reconocer;

P

to take ~ tener lugar; **to be ~d** (*in race, exam*) colocarse; **out of ~** (*not suitable*) fuera de lugar; **in the first ~** en primer lugar; **to change ~s with sb** cambiarse de sitio con algn; **~ of birth** lugar *m* de nacimiento; **place mat** *n* (*wooden etc*) salvamanteles *m inv*; (*linen etc*) mantel *m* individual; **placement** *n* (*positioning*) colocación *f*; (*at work*) emplazamiento

placid ['plæsɪd] *adj* apacible

plague [pleɪg] *n* plaga; (*Med*) peste *f* ▷ *vt* (*fig*) acosar, atormentar

plaice [pleɪs] *n inv* platija

plain [pleɪn] *adj* (*unpatterned*) liso; (*clear*) claro, evidente; (*simple*) sencillo; (*not handsome*) poco atractivo ▷ *adv* claramente ▷ *n* llano, llanura; **plain chocolate** *n* chocolate *m* amargo; **plainly** *adv* claramente

plaintiff ['pleɪntɪf] *n* demandante *mf*

plait [plæt] *n* trenza

plan [plæn] *n* (*drawing*) plano; (*scheme*) plan *m*, proyecto ▷ *vt* proyectar, planificar ▷ *vi* hacer proyectos; **to ~ to do** pensar hacer

plane [pleɪn] *n* (*Aviat*) avión *m*; (*Math, fig*) plano; (*also*: **~ tree**) plátano; (*tool*) cepillo

planet ['plænɪt] *n* planeta *m*

plank [plæŋk] *n* tabla

planning ['plænɪŋ] *n* planificación *f*; **family ~** planificación familiar

plant [plɑːnt] *n* planta; (*machinery*) maquinaria; (*factory*) fábrica ▷ *vt* plantar; (*field*) sembrar; (*bomb*) colocar

plantation [plæn'teɪʃən] *n* plantación *f*; (*estate*) hacienda

plaque [plæk] *n* placa

plaster ['plɑːstə*] *n* (*for walls*) yeso; (*also*: **~ of Paris**) yeso mate, escayola (SP); (BRIT: *also*: **sticking ~**) tirita (SP), curita (LAM) ▷ *vt* enyesar; (*cover*): **to ~ with** llenar *or* cubrir de; **plaster cast** *n* (*Med*) escayola; (*model, statue*) vaciado de yeso

plastic ['plæstɪk] *n* plástico ▷ *adj* de plástico; **plastic bag** *n* bolsa de plástico; **plastic surgery** *n* cirujía plástica

plate [pleɪt] *n* (*dish*) plato; (*metal, in book*) lámina; (*dental plate*) placa de dentadura postiza

plateau ['plætəu] (*pl* **~s** *or* **~x**) *n* meseta, altiplanicie *f*

platform ['plætfɔːm] *n* (*Rail*) andén *m*; (*stage*, BRIT: *on bus*) plataforma; (*at meeting*) tribuna; (*Pol*) programa *m* (electoral)

platinum ['plætɪnəm] *adj*, *n* platino

platoon [plə'tuːn] *n* pelotón *m*

platter ['plætə*] *n* fuente *f*

plausible ['plɔːzɪbl] *adj* verosímil; (*person*) convincente

play [pleɪ] *n* (*Theatre*) obra, comedia ▷ *vt* (*game*) jugar; (*compete against*) jugar contra; (*instrument*) tocar; (*part*: *in play etc*) hacer el papel de; (*tape, record*) poner ▷ *vi* jugar; (*band*) tocar; (*tape, record*) sonar; **to ~ safe** ir a lo seguro; **play back** *vt* (*tape*) poner; **play up** *vi* (*cause trouble to*) dar guerra; **player** *n* jugador(a) *m/f*; (*Theatre*) actor(actriz) *m/f*; (*Mus*) músico/a; **playful** *adj* juguetón/ona; **playground** *n* (*in school*) patio de recreo; (*in park*) parque *m* infantil; **playgroup** *n* jardín *m* de niños; **playing card** *n* naipe *m*, carta; **playing field** *n* campo de deportes; **playschool** *n* = **playgroup**; **playtime** *n* (*Scol*) recreo; **playwright** *n* dramaturgo/a

plc *abbr* (= *public limited company*) ≈ S.A.

plea [pliː] *n* súplica, petición *f*; (*Law*) alegato, defensa

plead [pliːd] *vt* (*Law*): **to ~ sb's case** defender a algn; (*give as excuse*) poner como pretexto ▷ *vi* (*Law*) declararse; (*beg*): **to ~ with sb** suplicar *or* rogar a algn

pleasant ['plɛznt] *adj* agradable

please [pliːz] *excl* ¡por favor! ▷ *vt* (*give pleasure to*) dar gusto a, agradar ▷ *vi* (*think fit*): **do as you ~** haz lo que quieras; **~ yourself!** (*inf*) ¡haz lo que quieras!, ¡como quieras!; **pleased** *adj* (*happy*) alegre, contento; **pleased (with)** satisfecho (de); **pleased to meet you** ¡encantado!, ¡tanto gusto!

pleasure ['plɛʒə*] *n* placer *m*, gusto; **"it's a ~"** "el gusto es mío"

pleat [pliːt] *n* pliegue *m*

pledge [plɛdʒ] *n* (*promise*) promesa, voto ▷ *vt* prometer

plentiful ['plɛntɪful] *adj* copioso, abundante

plenty ['plɛntɪ] *n*: **~ of** mucho(s)/a(s)

pliers ['plaɪəz] *npl* alicates *mpl*, tenazas *fpl*

plight [plaɪt] *n* situación *f* difícil

plod [plɔd] *vi* caminar con paso pesado; (*fig*) trabajar laboriosamente

plonk [plɔŋk] (*inf*) *n* (BRIT: *wine*) vino peleón ▷ *vt*: **to ~ sth down** dejar caer algo

plot [plɔt] *n* (*scheme*) complot *m*, conjura; (*of story, play*) argumento; (*of land*) terreno ▷ *vt* (*mark out*) trazar; (*conspire*) tramar, urdir ▷ *vi* conspirar

plough [plau] (US **plow**) *n* arado ▷ *vt* (*earth*) arar; **to ~ money into** invertir dinero en; **ploughman's lunch** (BRIT) *n* *almuerzo de pub a base de pan, queso y encurtidos*

plow [plau] (US) = **plough**

ploy [plɔɪ] *n* truco, estratagema

pluck [plʌk] *vt* (*fruit*) coger (SP), recoger (LAM); (*musical instrument*) puntear; (*bird*) desplumar; (*eyebrows*) depilar; **to ~ up courage** hacer de tripas corazón

plug [plʌg] *n* tapón *m*; (*Elec*) enchufe *m*, clavija; (*Aut*: *also*: **spark(ing) ~**) bujía ▷ *vt* (*hole*) tapar; (*inf*: *advertise*) dar publicidad a; **plug in** *vt* (*Elec*) enchufar; **plughole** *n* desagüe *m*

plum [plʌm] *n* (*fruit*) ciruela

plumber ['plʌmə*] *n* fontanero/a (SP, CAM), plomero/a (LAM)

plumbing ['plʌmɪŋ] *n* (*trade*) fontanería, plomería; (*piping*) cañería

plummet ['plʌmɪt] *vi*: **to ~ (down)** caer a plomo

plump [plʌmp] *adj* rechoncho, rollizo ▷ *vi*: **to ~ for** (*inf*: *choose*) optar por

plunge [plʌndʒ] *n* zambullida ▷ *vt* sumergir, hundir ▷ *vi* (*fall*) caer; (*dive*) saltar; (*person*) arrojarse; **to take the ~** lanzarse

plural ['pluərl] *adj* plural ▷ *n* plural *m*

plus [plʌs] *n* (*also*: **~ sign**) signo más ▷ *prep* más, y, además de; **ten/twenty ~** más de diez/veinte

ply [plaɪ] *vt* (*a trade*) ejercer ▷ *vi* (*ship*) ir y venir ▷ *n* (*of wool, rope*) cabo; **to ~ sb with drink** insistir en ofrecer a algn muchas copas; **plywood** *n* madera contrachapada

P.M. *n abbr* = **Prime Minister**

p.m. *adv abbr* (= *post meridiem*) de la tarde *or* noche

PMS *n abbr* (= *premenstrual syndrome*) SPM *m*

PMT *n abbr* (= *premenstrual tension*) SPM *m*

pneumatic drill [nju:'mætɪk-] *n* martillo neumático

pneumonia [nju:'məunɪə] *n* pulmonía

poach [pəutʃ] *vt* (*cook*) escalfar; (*steal*) cazar (*or* pescar) en vedado ▷ *vi* cazar (*or* pescar) en vedado; **poached** *adj* escalfado

P.O. Box *n abbr* (= *Post Office Box*) apdo., aptdo.

pocket ['pɔkɪt] *n* bolsillo; (*fig*: *small area*) bolsa ▷ *vt* meter en el bolsillo; (*steal*) embolsar; **to be out of ~** (BRIT) salir perdiendo; **pocketbook** (US) *n* cartera; **pocket money** *n* asignación *f*

pod [pɔd] *n* vaina

podiatrist [pɔ'di:ətrɪst] (US) *n* pedicuro/a

podium ['pəudɪəm] *n* podio

poem ['pəuɪm] *n* poema *m*

poet ['pəuɪt] *n* poeta *m/f*; **poetic** [-'ɛtɪk] *adj* poético; **poetry** *n* poesía

poignant ['pɔɪnjənt] *adj* conmovedor(a)

point [pɔɪnt] *n* punto; (*tip*) punta; (*purpose*) fin *m*, propósito; (*use*) utilidad *f*; (*significant part*) lo significativo; (*moment*) momento; (*Elec*) toma (de corriente); (*also*: **decimal ~**): **2 ~ 3 (2.3)** dos coma tres (2,3) ▷ *vt* señalar; (*gun etc*): **to ~ sth at sb** apuntar algo a algn ▷ *vi*: **to ~ at** señalar; **points** *npl* (*Aut*) contactos *mpl*; (*Rail*) agujas *fpl*; **to be on the ~ of doing sth** estar a punto de hacer algo; **to make a ~ of** poner empeño en; **to get/miss the ~** comprender/no comprender; **to come to the ~** ir al meollo; **there's no ~ (in doing)** no tiene sentido (hacer); **point out** *vt* señalar; **point-blank** *adv* (*say, refuse*) sin más hablar; (*also*: **at point-blank range**) a quemarropa; **pointed** *adj* (*shape*) puntiagudo, afilado; (*remark*) intencionado; **pointer** *n* (*needle*) aguja, indicador *m*; **pointless** *adj* sin sentido; **point of view** *n* punto de vista

poison ['pɔɪzn] *n* veneno ▷ *vt* envenenar; **poisonous** *adj* venenoso; (*fumes etc*) tóxico

poke [pəuk] *vt* (*jab with finger, stick etc*) empujar; (*put*): **to ~ sth in(to)** introducir algo en; **poke about** *or* **around** *vi* fisgonear; **poke out** *vi* (*stick out*) salir

poker ['pəukə*] *n* atizador *m*; (*Cards*) póker *m*

Poland ['pəulənd] *n* Polonia

polar ['pəulə*] *adj* polar; **polar bear** *n* oso polar

Pole [pəul] *n* polaco/a

pole [pəul] *n* palo; (*fixed*) poste *m*; (*Geo*) polo; **pole bean** (US) *n* ≈ judía verde; **pole vault** *n* salto con pértiga

police [pə'li:s] *n* policía ▷ *vt* vigilar; **police car** *n* coche-patrulla *m*; **police constable** (BRIT) *n* guardia *m*, policía *m*; **police force** *n* cuerpo de policía; **policeman** (*irreg*) *n* policía *m*, guardia *m*; **police officer** *n* guardia *m*, policía *m*; **police station** *n* comisaría; **policewoman** (*irreg*) *n* mujer *f* policía

policy ['pɔlɪsɪ] *n* política; (*also*: **insurance ~**) póliza

polio ['pəulɪəu] *n* polio *f*

Polish ['pəulɪʃ] *adj* polaco ▷ *n* (*Ling*) polaco

polish ['pɔlɪʃ] *n* (*for shoes*) betún *m*; (*for floor*) cera (de lustrar); (*shine*) brillo, lustre *m*; (*fig*: *refinement*) educación *f* ▷ *vt* (*shoes*) limpiar; (*make shiny*) pulir, sacar brillo a; **polish off** *vt* (*food*) despachar; **polished** *adj* (*fig*: *person*) elegante

polite [pə'laɪt] *adj* cortés, atento; **politeness** *n* cortesía

political [pə'lɪtɪkl] *adj* político; **politically** *adv* políticamente; **politically correct** políticamente correcto

politician [pɔlɪ'tɪʃən] *n* político/a

politics ['pɔlɪtɪks] *n* política

poll [pəul] *n* (*election*) votación *f*; (*also*: **opinion ~**) sondeo, encuesta ▷ *vt* encuestar; (*votes*) obtener

P

pollen ['pɔlən] *n* polen *m*
polling station ['pəulɪŋ-] *n* centro electoral
pollute [pə'lu:t] *vt* contaminar
pollution [pə'lu:ʃən] *n* polución *f*, contaminación *f* del medio ambiente
polo ['pəuləu] *n* (*sport*) polo; **polo-neck** *adj* de cuello vuelto ▷ *n* (*sweater*) suéter *m* de cuello vuelto; **polo shirt** *n* polo, niqui *m*
polyester [pɔlɪ'ɛstə*] *n* poliéster *m*
polystyrene [pɔlɪ'staɪri:n] *n* poliestireno
polythene ['pɔlɪθi:n] (BRIT) *n* politeno; **polythene bag** *n* bolsa de plástico
pomegranate ['pɔmɪgrænɪt] *n* granada
pompous ['pɔmpəs] *adj* pomposo
pond [pɔnd] *n* (*natural*) charca; (*artificial*) estanque *m*
ponder ['pɔndə*] *vt* meditar
pony ['pəunɪ] *n* poni *m*; **ponytail** *n* coleta; **pony trekking** (BRIT) *n* excursión *f* a caballo
poodle ['pu:dl] *n* caniche *m*
pool [pu:l] *n* (*natural*) charca; (*also*: **swimming ~**) piscina, alberca (MEX), pileta (RPL); (*fig*: *of light etc*) charco; (*Sport*) chapolín *m* ▷ *vt* juntar; **pools** *npl* quinielas *fpl*
poor [puə*] *adj* pobre; (*bad*) de mala calidad ▷ *npl*: **the ~** los pobres; **poorly** *adj* mal, enfermo ▷ *adv* mal
pop [pɔp] *n* (*sound*) ruido seco; (*Mus*) (música) pop *m*; (*inf*: *father*) papá *m*; (*drink*) gaseosa ▷ *vt* (*put quickly*) meter (de prisa) ▷ *vi* reventar; (*cork*) saltar; **pop in** *vi* entrar un momento; **pop out** *vi* salir un momento; **popcorn** *n* palomitas *fpl*
poplar ['pɔplə*] *n* álamo
popper ['pɔpə*] (BRIT) *n* automático
poppy ['pɔpɪ] *n* amapola
Popsicle® ['pɔpsɪkl] (US) *n* polo
pop star *n* estrella del pop
popular ['pɔpjulə*] *adj* popular; **popularity** [pɔpju'lærɪtɪ] *n* popularidad *f*
population [pɔpju'leɪʃən] *n* población *f*
pop-up ['pɔpʌp] (*Comput*) *adj* (*menu, window*) emergente ▷ *n* ventana emergente, (ventana *f*) pop-up *f*
porcelain ['pɔ:slɪn] *n* porcelana
porch [pɔ:tʃ] *n* pórtico, entrada; (US) veranda
pore [pɔ:*] *n* poro ▷ *vi*: **to ~ over** engolfarse en
pork [pɔ:k] *n* carne *f* de cerdo *or* (LAM) chancho; **pork chop** *n* chuleta de cerdo; **pork pie** *n* (BRIT: *Culin*) empanada de carne de cerdo
porn [pɔ:n] *adj* (*inf*) porno *inv* ▷ *n* porno; **pornographic** [pɔ:nə'græfɪk] *adj* pornográfico; **pornography** [pɔ:'nɔgrəfɪ] *n* pornografía
porridge ['pɔrɪdʒ] *n* gachas *fpl* de avena
port [pɔ:t] *n* puerto; (*Naut*: *left side*) babor *m*; (*wine*) vino de Oporto; **~ of call** puerto de escala
portable ['pɔ:təbl] *adj* portátil
porter ['pɔ:tə*] *n* (*for luggage*) maletero; (*doorkeeper*) portero/a, conserje *m/f*
portfolio [pɔ:t'fəulɪəu] *n* cartera
portion ['pɔ:ʃən] *n* porción *f*; (*of food*) ración *f*
portrait ['pɔ:treɪt] *n* retrato
portray [pɔ:'treɪ] *vt* retratar; (*actor*) representar
Portugal ['pɔ:tjugl] *n* Portugal *m*
Portuguese [pɔ:tju'gi:z] *adj* portugués/esa ▷ *n inv* portugués/esa *m/f*; (*Ling*) portugués *m*
pose [pəuz] *n* postura, actitud *f* ▷ *vi* (*pretend*): **to ~ as** hacerse pasar por ▷ *vt* (*question*) plantear; **to ~ for** posar para
posh [pɔʃ] (*inf*) *adj* elegante, de lujo
position [pə'zɪʃən] *n* posición *f*; (*job*) puesto; (*situation*) situación *f* ▷ *vt* colocar
positive ['pɔzɪtɪv] *adj* positivo; (*certain*) seguro; (*definite*) definitivo; **positively** *adv* (*affirmatively, enthusiastically*) de forma positiva; (*inf*: *really*) absolutamente
possess [pə'zɛs] *vt* poseer; **possession** [pə'zɛʃən] *n* posesión *f*; **possessions** *npl* (*belongings*) pertenencias *fpl*; **possessive** *adj* posesivo
possibility [pɔsɪ'bɪlɪtɪ] *n* posibilidad *f*
possible ['pɔsɪbl] *adj* posible; **as big as ~** lo más grande posible; **possibly** *adv* posiblemente; **I cannot possibly come** me es imposible venir
post [pəust] *n* (BRIT: *system*) correos *mpl*; (BRIT: *letters, delivery*) correo; (*job, situation*) puesto; (*pole*) poste *m* ▷ *vt* (BRIT: *send by post*) echar al correo; (BRIT: *appoint*): **to ~ to** enviar a; **postage** *n* porte *m*, franqueo; **postal** *adj* postal, de correos; **postal order** *n* giro postal; **postbox** (BRIT) *n* buzón *m*; **postcard** *n* tarjeta postal; **postcode** (BRIT) *n* código postal
poster ['pəustə*] *n* cartel *m*
postgraduate ['pəust'grædjuət] *n* posgraduado/a
postman ['pəustmən] (BRIT: *irreg*) *n* cartero
postmark ['pəustmɑ:k] *n* matasellos *m inv*
post-mortem [-'mɔ:təm] *n* autopsia
post office *n* (*building*) (oficina de) correos *m*; (*organization*): **the Post Office** Correos *m inv* (SP), Dirección *f* General de Correos (LAM)
postpone [pəs'pəun] *vt* aplazar

posture ['pɔstʃə*] *n* postura, actitud *f*
postwoman ['pəustwumən] (BRIT: *irreg*) *n* cartera
pot [pɔt] *n* (*for cooking*) olla; (*teapot*) tetera; (*coffeepot*) cafetera; (*for flowers*) maceta; (*for jam*) tarro, pote *m*; (*inf*: *marijuana*) chocolate *m* ▷ *vt* (*plant*) poner en tiesto; **to go to ~** (*inf*) irse al traste
potato [pə'teɪtəu] (*pl* **~es**) *n* patata (SP), papa (LAM); **potato peeler** *n* pelapatatas *m inv*
potent ['pəutnt] *adj* potente, poderoso; (*drink*) fuerte
potential [pə'tɛnʃl] *adj* potencial, posible ▷ *n* potencial *m*
pothole ['pɔthəul] *n* (*in road*) bache *m*; (BRIT: *underground*) gruta
pot plant ['pɔtplɑːnt] *n* planta de interior
potter ['pɔtə*] *n* alfarero/a ▷ *vi*: **to ~ around** *or* **about** (BRIT) hacer trabajitos; **pottery** *n* cerámica; (*factory*) alfarería
potty ['pɔtɪ] *n* orinal *m* de niño
pouch [pautʃ] *n* (*Zool*) bolsa; (*for tobacco*) petaca
poultry ['pəultrɪ] *n* aves *fpl* de corral; (*meat*) pollo
pounce [pauns] *vi*: **to ~ on** precipitarse sobre
pound [paund] *n* libra (*weight = 453g or 16oz; money = 100 pence*) ▷ *vt* (*beat*) golpear; (*crush*) machacar ▷ *vi* (*heart*) latir; **pound sterling** *n* libra esterlina
pour [pɔː*] *vt* echar; (*tea etc*) servir ▷ *vi* correr, fluir; **to ~ sb a drink** servirle a algn una copa; **pour in** *vi* (*people*) entrar en tropel; **pour out** *vi* salir en tropel ▷ *vt* (*drink*) echar, servir; (*fig*): **to pour out one's feelings** desahogarse; **pouring** *adj*: **pouring rain** lluvia torrencial
pout [paut] *vi* hacer pucheros
poverty ['pɔvətɪ] *n* pobreza, miseria
powder ['paudə*] *n* polvo; (*also*: **face ~**) polvos *mpl* ▷ *vt* polvorear; **to ~ one's face** empolvarse la cara; **powdered milk** *n* leche *f* en polvo
power ['pauə*] *n* poder *m*; (*strength*) fuerza; (*nation, Tech*) potencia; (*drive*) empuje *m*; (*Elec*) fuerza, energía ▷ *vt* impulsar; **to be in ~** (*Pol*) estar en el poder; **power cut** (BRIT) *n* apagón *m*; **power failure** *n* = **power cut**; **powerful** *adj* poderoso; (*engine*) potente; (*speech etc*) convincente; **powerless** *adj*: **powerless (to do)** incapaz (de hacer); **power point** (BRIT) *n* enchufe *m*; **power station** *n* central *f* eléctrica
p.p. *abbr* (= *per procurationem*); **p.p. J. Smith** p.p. (por poder de) J. Smith; (= *pages*) págs
PR *n abbr* = **public relations**

practical ['præktɪkl] *adj* práctico; **practical joke** *n* broma pesada; **practically** *adv* (*almost*) casi
practice ['præktɪs] *n* (*habit*) costumbre *f*; (*exercise*) práctica, ejercicio; (*training*) adiestramiento; (*Med*: *of profession*) práctica, ejercicio; (*Med, Law*: *business*) consulta ▷ *vt, vi* (US) = **practise**; **in ~** (*in reality*) en la práctica; **out of ~** desentrenado
practise ['præktɪs] (US **practice**) *vt* (*carry out*) practicar; (*profession*) ejercer; (*train at*) practicar ▷ *vi* ejercer; (*train*) practicar; **practising** *adj* (*Christian etc*) practicante; (*lawyer*) en ejercicio
practitioner [præk'tɪʃənə*] *n* (*Med*) médico/a
pragmatic [præg'mætɪk] *adj* pragmático
prairie ['prɛərɪ] *n* pampa
praise [preɪz] *n* alabanza(s) *f(pl)*, elogio(s) *m(pl)* ▷ *vt* alabar, elogiar
pram [præm] (BRIT) *n* cochecito de niño
prank [præŋk] *n* travesura
prawn [prɔːn] *n* gamba; **prawn cocktail** *n* cóctel *m* de gambas
pray [preɪ] *vi* rezar; **prayer** [prɛə*] *n* oración *f*, rezo; (*entreaty*) ruego, súplica
preach [priːtʃ] *vi* predicar; **preacher** *n* predicador(a) *m/f*
precarious [prɪ'kɛərɪəs] *adj* precario
precaution [prɪ'kɔːʃən] *n* precaución *f*
precede [prɪ'siːd] *vt, vi* preceder; **precedent** ['prɛsɪdənt] *n* precedente *m*; **preceding** [prɪ'siːdɪŋ] *adj* anterior
precinct ['priːsɪŋkt] *n* recinto
precious ['prɛʃəs] *adj* precioso
precise [prɪ'saɪs] *adj* preciso, exacto; **precisely** *adv* precisamente, exactamente
precision [prɪ'sɪʒən] *n* precisión *f*
predator ['prɛdətə*] *n* depredador *m*
predecessor ['priːdɪsɛsə*] *n* antecesor(a) *m/f*
predicament [prɪ'dɪkəmənt] *n* apuro
predict [prɪ'dɪkt] *vt* pronosticar; **predictable** *adj* previsible; **prediction** [-'dɪkʃən] *n* predicción *f*
predominantly [prɪ'dɔmɪnəntlɪ] *adv* en su mayoría
preface ['prɛfəs] *n* prefacio
prefect ['priːfɛkt] (BRIT) *n* (*in school*) monitor(a) *m/f*
prefer [prɪ'fəː*] *vt* preferir; **to ~ doing** *or* **to do** preferir hacer; **preferable** ['prɛfrəbl] *adj* preferible; **preferably** ['prɛfrəblɪ] *adv* de preferencia; **preference** ['prɛfrəns] *n* preferencia; (*priority*) prioridad *f*
prefix ['priːfɪks] *n* prefijo
pregnancy ['prɛgnənsɪ] *n* (*of woman*) embarazo; (*of animal*) preñez *f*

pregnant ['prɛgnənt] *adj* (*woman*) embarazada; (*animal*) preñada
prehistoric ['pri:hɪs'tɔrɪk] *adj* prehistórico
prejudice ['prɛdʒudɪs] *n* prejuicio; **prejudiced** *adj* (*person*) predispuesto
preliminary [prɪ'lɪmɪnərɪ] *adj* preliminar
prelude ['prɛlju:d] *n* preludio
premature ['prɛmətʃuə*] *adj* prematuro
premier ['prɛmɪə*] *adj* primero, principal ▷ *n* (*Pol*) primer(a) ministro/a
première ['prɛmɪɛə*] *n* estreno
Premier League [prɛmɪə'li:g] *n* primera división
premises ['prɛmɪsɪz] *npl* (*of business etc*) local *m*; **on the ~** en el lugar mismo
premium ['pri:mɪəm] *n* premio; (*insurance*) prima; **to be at a ~** ser muy solicitado
premonition [prɛmə'nɪʃən] *n* presentimiento
preoccupied [pri:'ɔkjupaɪd] *adj* ensimismado
prepaid [pri:'peɪd] *adj* porte pagado
preparation [prɛpə'reɪʃən] *n* preparación *f*; **preparations** *npl* preparativos *mpl*
preparatory school [prɪ'pærətərɪ-] *n* escuela preparatoria
prepare [prɪ'pɛə*] *vt* preparar, disponer; (*Culin*) preparar ▷ *vi*: **to ~ for** (*action*) prepararse *or* disponerse para; (*event*) hacer preparativos para; **~d to** dispuesto a; **~d for** listo para
preposition [prɛpə'zɪʃən] *n* preposición *f*
prep school [prɛp-] *n* = **preparatory school**
prerequisite [pri:'rɛkwɪzɪt] *n* requisito
preschool ['pri:'sku:l] *adj* preescolar
prescribe [prɪ'skraɪb] *vt* (*Med*) recetar
prescription [prɪ'skrɪpʃən] *n* (*Med*) receta
presence ['prɛzns] *n* presencia; **in sb's ~** en presencia de algn; **~ of mind** aplomo
present [*adj, n* 'prɛznt, *vb* prɪ'zɛnt] *adj* (*in attendance*) presente; (*current*) actual ▷ *n* (*gift*) regalo; (*actuality*): **the ~** la actualidad, el presente ▷ *vt* (*introduce, describe*) presentar; (*expound*) exponer; (*give*) presentar, dar, ofrecer; (*Theatre*) representar; **to give sb a ~** regalar algo a algn; **at ~** actualmente; **presentable** [prɪ'zɛntəbl] *adj*: **to make o.s. presentable** arreglarse; **presentation** [-'teɪʃən] *n* presentación *f*; (*of report etc*) exposición *f*; (*formal ceremony*) entrega de un regalo; **present-day** *adj* actual; **presenter** [prɪ'zɛntə*] *n* (*Radio, TV*) locutor(a) *m/f*; **presently** *adv* (*soon*) dentro de poco; (*now*) ahora; **present participle** *n* participio (de) presente
preservation [prɛzə'veɪʃən] *n* conservación *f*
preservative [prɪ'zə:vətɪv] *n* conservante *m*
preserve [prɪ'zə:v] *vt* (*keep safe*) preservar, proteger; (*maintain*) mantener; (*food*) conservar ▷ *n* (*for game*) coto, vedado; (*often pl: jam*) conserva, confitura
preside [prɪ'zaɪd] *vi* presidir
president ['prɛzɪdənt] *n* presidente *m/f*; **presidential** [-'dɛnʃl] *adj* presidencial
press [prɛs] *n* (*newspapers*): **the P~** la prensa; (*printer's*) imprenta; (*of button*) pulsación *f* ▷ *vt* empujar; (*button etc*) apretar; (*clothes: iron*) planchar; (*put pressure on: person*) presionar; (*insist*): **to ~ sth on sb** insistir en que algn acepte algo ▷ *vi* (*squeeze*) apretar; (*pressurize*): **to ~ for** presionar por; **we are ~ed for time/money** estamos apurados de tiempo/dinero; **press conference** *n* rueda de prensa; **pressing** *adj* apremiante; **press stud** (BRIT) *n* botón *m* de presión; **press-up** (BRIT) *n* plancha
pressure ['prɛʃə*] *n* presión *f*; **to put ~ on sb** presionar a algn; **pressure cooker** *n* olla a presión; **pressure group** *n* grupo de presión
prestige [prɛs'ti:ʒ] *n* prestigio
prestigious [prɛs'tɪdʒəs] *adj* prestigioso
presumably [prɪ'zju:məblɪ] *adv* es de suponer que, cabe presumir que
presume [prɪ'zju:m] *vt*: **to ~ (that)** presumir (que), suponer (que)
pretence [prɪ'tɛns] (US **pretense**) *n* fingimiento; **under false ~s** con engaños
pretend [prɪ'tɛnd] *vt, vi* (*feign*) fingir

> Be careful not to translate **pretend** by the Spanish word *pretender*.

pretense [prɪ'tɛns] (US) *n* = **pretence**
pretentious [prɪ'tɛnʃəs] *adj* presumido; (*ostentatious*) ostentoso, aparatoso
pretext ['pri:tɛkst] *n* pretexto
pretty ['prɪtɪ] *adj* bonito, lindo (LAM) ▷ *adv* bastante
prevail [prɪ'veɪl] *vi* (*gain mastery*) prevalecer; (*be current*) predominar; **prevailing** *adj* (*dominant*) predominante
prevalent ['prɛvələnt] *adj* (*widespread*) extendido
prevent [prɪ'vɛnt] *vt*: **to ~ sb from doing sth** impedir a algn hacer algo; **to ~ sth from happening** evitar que ocurra algo; **prevention** [prɪ'vɛnʃən] *n* prevención *f*; **preventive** *adj* preventivo
preview ['pri:vju:] *n* (*of film*) preestreno
previous ['pri:vɪəs] *adj* previo, anterior; **previously** *adv* antes
prey [preɪ] *n* presa ▷ *vi*: **to ~ on** (*feed on*)

alimentarse de; **it was ~ing on his mind** le preocupaba, le obsesionaba
price [praɪs] *n* precio ▷*vt* (*goods*) fijar el precio de; **priceless** *adj* que no tiene precio; **price list** *n* tarifa
prick [prɪk] *n* (*sting*) picadura ▷*vt* pinchar; (*hurt*) picar; **to ~ up one's ears** aguzar el oído
prickly ['prɪklɪ] *adj* espinoso; (*fig: person*) enojadizo
pride [praɪd] *n* orgullo; (*pej*) soberbia ▷*vt*: **to ~ o.s. on** enorgullecerse de
priest [pri:st] *n* sacerdote *m*
primarily ['praɪmərɪlɪ] *adv* ante todo
primary ['praɪmərɪ] *adj* (*first in importance*) principal ▷*n* (*US Pol*) elección *f* primaria; **primary school** (BRIT) *n* escuela primaria
prime [praɪm] *adj* primero, principal; (*excellent*) selecto, de primera clase ▷*n*: **in the ~ of life** en la flor de la vida ▷*vt* (*wood: fig*) preparar; **~ example** ejemplo típico; **Prime Minister** *n* primer(a) ministro/a
primitive ['prɪmɪtɪv] *adj* primitivo; (*crude*) rudimentario
primrose ['prɪmrəuz] *n* primavera, prímula
prince [prɪns] *n* príncipe *m*
princess [prɪn'sɛs] *n* princesa
principal ['prɪnsɪpl] *adj* principal, mayor ▷*n* director(a) *m/f*; **principally** *adv* principalmente
principle ['prɪnsɪpl] *n* principio; **in ~** en principio; **on ~** por principio
print [prɪnt] *n* (*footprint*) huella; (*fingerprint*) huella dactilar; (*letters*) letra de molde; (*fabric*) estampado; (*Art*) grabado; (*Phot*) impresión *f* ▷*vt* imprimir; (*cloth*) estampar; (*write in capitals*) escribir en letras de molde; **out of ~** agotado; **print out** *vt* (*Comput*) imprimir; **printer** *n* (*person*) impresor(a) *m/f*; (*machine*) impresora; **printout** *n* (*Comput*) impresión *f*
prior ['praɪə*] *adj* anterior, previo; (*more important*) más importante; **~ to** antes de
priority [praɪ'ɔrɪtɪ] *n* prioridad *f*; **to have ~ (over)** tener prioridad (sobre)
prison ['prɪzn] *n* cárcel *f*, prisión *f* ▷*cpd* carcelario; **prisoner** *n* (*in prison*) preso/a; (*captured person*) prisionero; **prisoner-of-war** *n* prisionero de guerra
pristine ['prɪsti:n] *adj* pristino
privacy ['prɪvəsɪ] *n* intimidad *f*
private ['praɪvɪt] *adj* (*personal*) particular; (*property, industry, discussion etc*) privado; (*person*) reservado; (*place*) tranquilo ▷*n* soldado raso; **"~"** (*on envelope*) "confidencial"; (*on door*) "prohibido el paso"; **in ~** en privado; **privately** *adv* en privado; (*in o.s.*) en secreto; **private property** *n* propiedad *f* privada; **private school** *n* colegio particular
privatize ['praɪvɪtaɪz] *vt* privatizar
privilege ['prɪvɪlɪdʒ] *n* privilegio; (*prerogative*) prerrogativa
prize [praɪz] *n* premio ▷*adj* de primera clase ▷*vt* apreciar, estimar; **prize-giving** *n* distribución *f* de premios; **prizewinner** *n* premiado/a
pro [prəu] *n* (*Sport*) profesional *mf* ▷*prep* a favor de; **the ~s and cons** los pros y los contras
probability [prɔbə'bɪlɪtɪ] *n* probabilidad *f*; **in all ~** con toda probabilidad
probable ['prɔbəbl] *adj* probable
probably ['prɔbəblɪ] *adv* probablemente
probation [prə'beɪʃən] *n*: **on ~** (*employee*) a prueba; (*Law*) en libertad condicional
probe [prəub] *n* (*Med, Space*) sonda; (*enquiry*) encuesta, investigación *f* ▷*vt* sondar; (*investigate*) investigar
problem ['prɔbləm] *n* problema *m*
procedure [prə'si:dʒə*] *n* procedimiento; (*bureaucratic*) trámites *mpl*
proceed [prə'si:d] *vi* (*do afterwards*): **to ~ to do sth** proceder a hacer algo; (*continue*): **to ~ (with)** continuar *or* seguir (con); **proceedings** *npl* acto(s) (*pl*); (*Law*) proceso; **proceeds** ['prəusi:dz] *npl* (*money*) ganancias *fpl*, ingresos *mpl*
process ['prəusɛs] *n* proceso ▷*vt* tratar, elaborar
procession [prə'sɛʃən] *n* desfile *m*; **funeral ~** cortejo fúnebre
proclaim [prə'kleɪm] *vt* (*announce*) anunciar
prod [prɔd] *vt* empujar ▷*n* empujón *m*
produce [*n* 'prɔdju:s, *vt* prə'dju:s] *n* (*Agr*) productos *mpl* agrícolas ▷*vt* producir; (*play, film, programme*) presentar; **producer** *n* productor(a) *m/f*; (*of film, programme*) director(a) *m/f*; (*of record*) productor(a) *m/f*
product ['prɔdʌkt] *n* producto; **production** [prə'dʌkʃən] *n* producción *f*; (*Theatre*) presentación *f*; **productive** [prə'dʌktɪv] *adj* productivo; **productivity** [prɔdʌk'tɪvɪtɪ] *n* productividad *f*
Prof. [prɔf] *abbr* (= *professor*) Prof
profession [prə'fɛʃən] *n* profesión *f*; **professional** *adj* profesional ▷*n* profesional *mf*; (*skilled person*) perito
professor [prə'fɛsə*] *n* (BRIT) catedrático/a; (US, CANADA) profesor(a) *m/f*
profile ['prəufaɪl] *n* perfil *m*
profit ['prɔfɪt] *n* (*Comm*) ganancia ▷*vi*: **to ~ by** *or* **from** aprovechar *or* sacar provecho

P

de; **profitable** *adj* (*Econ*) rentable
profound [prə'faund] *adj* profundo
programme ['prəugræm] (*US* **program**) *n* programa *m* ▷*vt* programar; **programmer** (*US* **programer**) *n* programador(a) *m/f*; **programming** (*US* **programing**) *n* programación *f*
progress [*n* 'prəugrɛs, *vi* prə'grɛs] *n* progreso; (*development*) desarrollo ▷*vi* progresar, avanzar; **in ~** en curso; **progressive** [-'grɛsɪv] *adj* progresivo; (*person*) progresista
prohibit [prə'hɪbɪt] *vt* prohibir; **to ~ sb from doing sth** prohibir a algn hacer algo
project [*n* 'prɔdʒɛkt, *vb* prə'dʒɛkt] *n* proyecto ▷*vt* proyectar ▷*vi* (*stick out*) salir, sobresalir; **projection** [prə'dʒɛkʃən] *n* proyección *f*; (*overhang*) saliente *m*; **projector** [prə'dʒɛktə*] *n* proyector *m*
prolific [prə'lɪfɪk] *adj* prolífico
prolong [prə'lɔŋ] *vt* prolongar, extender
prom [prɔm] *n abbr* = **promenade** (*US*: *ball*) baile *m* de gala; **the P~s** *ver abajo*

PROM

El ciclo de conciertos de música clásica más conocido de Londres es el llamado **the Proms** (promenade concerts), que se celebra anualmente en el Royal Albert Hall. Su nombre se debe a que originalmente el público paseaba durante las actuaciones, costumbre que en la actualidad se mantiene de forma simbólica, permitiendo que parte de los asistentes permanezcan de pie. En Estados Unidos se llama **prom** a un baile de gala en un centro de educación secundaria o universitaria.

promenade [prɔmə'nɑ:d] *n* (*by sea*) paseo marítimo
prominent ['prɔmɪnənt] *adj* (*standing out*) saliente; (*important*) eminente, importante
promiscuous [prə'mɪskjuəs] *adj* (*sexually*) promiscuo
promise ['prɔmɪs] *n* promesa ▷*vt, vi* prometer; **promising** *adj* prometedor(a)
promote [prə'məut] *vt* (*employee*) ascender; (*product, pop star*) hacer propaganda por; (*ideas*) fomentar; **promotion** [-'məuʃən] *n* (*advertising campaign*) campaña *f* de promoción; (*in rank*) ascenso
prompt [prɔmpt] *adj* rápido ▷*adv*: **at 6 o'clock ~** a las seis en punto ▷*n* (*Comput*) aviso ▷*vt* (*urge*) mover, incitar; (*when talking*) instar; (*Theatre*) apuntar; **to ~ sb to do sth** instar a algn a hacer algo; **promptly** *adv* rápidamente; (*exactly*) puntualmente
prone [prəun] *adj* (*lying*) postrado; **~ to** propenso a
prong [prɔŋ] *n* diente *m*, punta
pronoun ['prəunaun] *n* pronombre *m*
pronounce [prə'nauns] *vt* pronunciar
pronunciation [prənʌnsɪ'eɪʃən] *n* pronunciación *f*
proof [pru:f] *n* prueba ▷*adj*: **~ against** a prueba de
prop [prɔp] *n* apoyo; (*fig*) sostén *m* accesorios *mpl*, at(t)rezzo *msg*; **prop up** *vt* (*roof, structure*) apuntalar; (*economy*) respaldar
propaganda [prɔpə'gændə] *n* propaganda
propeller [prə'pɛlə*] *n* hélice *f*
proper ['prɔpə*] *adj* (*suited, right*) propio; (*exact*) justo; (*seemly*) correcto, decente; (*authentic*) verdadero; (*referring to place*): **the village ~** el pueblo mismo; **properly** *adv* (*adequately*) correctamente; (*decently*) decentemente; **proper noun** *n* nombre *m* propio
property ['prɔpətɪ] *n* propiedad *f*; (*personal*) bienes *mpl* muebles
prophecy ['prɔfɪsɪ] *n* profecía
prophet ['prɔfɪt] *n* profeta *m*
proportion [prə'pɔ:ʃən] *n* proporción *f*; (*share*) parte *f*; **proportions** *npl* (*size*) dimensiones *fpl*; **proportional** *adj*: **proportional (to)** en proporción (con)
proposal [prə'pəuzl] *n* (*offer of marriage*) oferta de matrimonio; (*plan*) proyecto
propose [prə'pəuz] *vt* proponer ▷*vi* declararse; **to ~ to do** tener intención de hacer
proposition [prɔpə'zɪʃən] *n* propuesta
proprietor [prə'praɪətə*] *n* propietario/a, dueño/a
prose [prəuz] *n* prosa
prosecute ['prɔsɪkju:t] *vt* (*Law*) procesar; **prosecution** [-'kju:ʃən] *n* proceso, causa; (*accusing side*) acusación *f*; **prosecutor** *n* acusador(a) *m/f*; (*also*: **public prosecutor**) fiscal *mf*
prospect [*n* 'prɔspɛkt, *vb* prə'spɛkt] *n* (*possibility*) posibilidad *f*; (*outlook*) perspectiva ▷*vi*: **to ~ for** buscar; **prospects** *npl* (*for work etc*) perspectivas *fpl*; **prospective** [prə'spɛktɪv] *adj* futuro
prospectus [prə'spɛktəs] *n* prospecto
prosper ['prɔspə*] *vi* prosperar; **prosperity** [-'spɛrɪtɪ] *n* prosperidad *f*; **prosperous** *adj* próspero
prostitute ['prɔstɪtju:t] *n* prostituta; (*male*) *hombre que se dedica a la prostitución*

protect [prə'tɛkt] *vt* proteger; **protection** [-'tɛkʃən] *n* protección *f*; **protective** *adj* protector(a)
protein ['prəuti:n] *n* proteína
protest [*n* 'prəutɛst, *vb* prə'tɛst] *n* protesta ▷ *vi*: **to ~ about** *or* **at/against** protestar de/contra ▷ *vt* (*insist*): **to ~ (that)** insistir en (que)
Protestant ['prɔtɪstənt] *adj, n* protestante *mf*
protester [prə'tɛstə*] *n* manifestante *mf*
protractor [prə'træktə*] *n* (*Geom*) transportador *m*
proud [praud] *adj* orgulloso; (*pej*) soberbio, altanero
prove [pru:v] *vt* probar; (*show*) demostrar ▷ *vi*: **to ~ (to be) correct** resultar correcto; **to ~ o.s.** probar su valía
proverb ['prɔvə:b] *n* refrán *m*
provide [prə'vaɪd] *vt* proporcionar, dar; **to ~ sb with sth** proveer a algn de algo; **provide for** *vt fus* (*person*) mantener a; (*problem etc*) tener en cuenta; **provided** *conj*: **provided (that)** con tal de que, a condición de que; **providing** [prə'vaɪdɪŋ] *conj*: **providing (that)** a condición de que, con tal de que
province ['prɔvɪns] *n* provincia; (*fig*) esfera; **provincial** [prə'vɪnʃəl] *adj* provincial; (*pej*) provinciano
provision [prə'vɪʒən] *n* (*supplying*) suministro, abastecimiento; (*of contract etc*) disposición *f*; **provisions** *npl* (*food*) comestibles *mpl*; **provisional** *adj* provisional
provocative [prə'vɔkətɪv] *adj* provocativo
provoke [prə'vəuk] *vt* (*cause*) provocar, incitar; (*anger*) enojar
prowl [praul] *vi* (*also*: **~ about, ~ around**) merodear ▷ *n*: **on the ~** de merodeo
proximity [prɔk'sɪmɪtɪ] *n* proximidad *f*
proxy ['prɔksɪ] *n*: **by ~** por poderes
prudent ['pru:dənt] *adj* prudente
prune [pru:n] *n* ciruela pasa ▷ *vt* podar
pry [praɪ] *vi*: **to ~ (into)** entrometerse (en)
PS *n abbr* (= *postscript*) P.D.
pseudonym ['sju:dəunɪm] *n* seudónimo
PSHE (BRIT: *Scol*) *n abbr* (= *personal, social and health education*) *formación social y sanitaria*
psychiatric [saɪkɪ'ætrɪk] *adj* psiquiátrico
psychiatrist [saɪ'kaɪətrɪst] *n* psiquiatra *mf*
psychic ['saɪkɪk] *adj* (*also*: **~al**) psíquico
psychoanalysis [saɪkəuə'nælɪsɪs] *n* psicoanálisis *m inv*
psychological [saɪkə'lɔdʒɪkl] *adj* psicológico
psychologist [saɪ'kɔlədʒɪst] *n* psicólogo/a
psychology [saɪ'kɔlədʒɪ] *n* psicología
psychotherapy [saɪkəu'θɛrəpɪ] *n* psicoterapia
pt *abbr* = **pint(s); point(s)**
PTO *abbr* (= *please turn over*) sigue
pub [pʌb] *n abbr* (= *public house*) pub *m*, bar *m*
puberty ['pju:bətɪ] *n* pubertad *f*
public ['pʌblɪk] *adj* público ▷ *n*: **the ~** el público; **in ~** en público; **to make ~** hacer público
publication [pʌblɪ'keɪʃən] *n* publicación *f*
public: public company *n* sociedad *f* anónima; **public convenience** (BRIT) *n* aseos *mpl* públicos (SP), sanitarios *mpl* (LAM); **public holiday** *n* (día *m* de) fiesta (SP), (día *m*) feriado (LAM); **public house** (BRIT) *n* bar *m*, pub *m*
publicity [pʌb'lɪsɪtɪ] *n* publicidad *f*
publicize ['pʌblɪsaɪz] *vt* publicitar
public: public limited company *n* sociedad *f* anónima (S.A.); **publicly** *adv* públicamente, en público; **public opinion** *n* opinión *f* pública; **public relations** *n* relaciones *fpl* públicas; **public school** *n* (BRIT) escuela privada; (US) instituto; **public transport** *n* transporte *m* público
publish ['pʌblɪʃ] *vt* publicar; **publisher** *n* (*person*) editor(a) *m/f*; (*firm*) editorial *f*; **publishing** *n* (*industry*) industria del libro
pub lunch *n almuerzo que se sirve en un pub*; **to go for a ~** almorzar *o* comer en un pub
pudding ['pudɪŋ] *n* pudín *m*; (BRIT: *dessert*) postre *m*; **black ~** morcilla
puddle ['pʌdl] *n* charco
Puerto Rico [pwɛ:təu'ri:kəu] *n* Puerto Rico
puff [pʌf] *n* soplo; (*of smoke, air*) bocanada; (*of breathing*) resoplido ▷ *vt*: **to ~ one's pipe** chupar la pipa ▷ *vi* (*pant*) jadear; **puff pastry** *n* hojaldre *m*
pull [pul] *n* (*tug*): **to give sth a ~** dar un tirón a algo ▷ *vt* tirar de; (*press: trigger*) apretar; (*haul*) tirar, arrastrar; (*close: curtain*) echar ▷ *vi* tirar; **to ~ to pieces** hacer pedazos; **not to ~ one's punches** no andarse con bromas; **to ~ one's weight** hacer su parte; **to ~ o.s. together** sobreponerse; **to ~ sb's leg** tomar el pelo a algn; **pull apart** *vt* (*break*) romper; **pull away** *vi* (*vehicle: move off*) salir, arrancar; (*draw back*) apartarse bruscamente; **pull back** *vt* (*lever etc*) tirar hacia sí; (*curtains*) descorrer ▷ *vi* (*refrain*) contenerse; (*Mil: withdraw*) retirarse; **pull down** *vt*

(*building*) derribar; **pull in** *vi* (*car etc*) parar (junto a la acera); (*train*) llegar a la estación; **pull off** *vt* (*deal etc*) cerrar; **pull out** *vi* (*car, train etc*) salir ▷ *vt* sacar, arrancar; **pull over** *vi* (*Aut*) hacerse a un lado; **pull up** *vi* (*stop*) parar ▷ *vt* (*raise*) levantar; (*uproot*) arrancar, desarraigar

pulley ['pulı] *n* polea

pullover ['puləuvə*] *n* jersey *m*, suéter *m*

pulp [pʌlp] *n* (*of fruit*) pulpa

pulpit ['pulpıt] *n* púlpito

pulse [pʌls] *n* (*Anat*) pulso; (*rhythm*) pulsación *f*; (*Bot*) legumbre *f*; **pulses** *pl n* legumbres

puma ['pju:mə] *n* puma *m*

pump [pʌmp] *n* bomba; (*shoe*) zapatilla ▷ *vt* sacar con una bomba; **pump up** *vt* inflar

pumpkin ['pʌmpkın] *n* calabaza

pun [pʌn] *n* juego de palabras

punch [pʌntʃ] *n* (*blow*) golpe *m*, puñetazo; (*tool*) punzón *m*; (*drink*) ponche *m* ▷ *vt* (*hit*): **to ~ sb/sth** dar un puñetazo *or* golpear a algn/algo; **punch-up** (BRIT: *inf*) *n* riña

punctual ['pʌŋktjuəl] *adj* puntual

punctuation [pʌŋktju'eıʃən] *n* puntuación *f*

puncture ['pʌŋktʃə*] (BRIT) *n* pinchazo ▷ *vt* pinchar

punish ['pʌnıʃ] *vt* castigar; **punishment** *n* castigo

punk [pʌŋk] *n* (*also*: **~ rocker**) punki *mf*; (*also*: **~ rock**) música punk; (US: *inf*: *hoodlum*) rufián *m*

pup [pʌp] *n* cachorro

pupil ['pju:pl] *n* alumno/a; (*of eye*) pupila

puppet ['pʌpıt] *n* títere *m*

puppy ['pʌpı] *n* cachorro, perrito

purchase ['pə:tʃıs] *n* compra ▷ *vt* comprar

pure [pjuə*] *adj* puro; **purely** *adv* puramente

purify ['pjuərıfaı] *vt* purificar, depurar

purity ['pjuərıtı] *n* pureza

purple ['pə:pl] *adj* purpúreo; morado

purpose ['pə:pəs] *n* propósito; **on ~** a propósito, adrede

purr [pə:*] *vi* ronronear

purse [pə:s] *n* monedero; (US: *handbag*) bolso (SP), cartera (LAM), bolsa (MEX) ▷ *vt* fruncir

pursue [pə'sju:] *vt* seguir

pursuit [pə'sju:t] *n* (*chase*) caza; (*occupation*) actividad *f*

pus [pʌs] *n* pus *m*

push [puʃ] *n* empuje *m*, empujón *m*; (*of button*) presión *f*; (*drive*) empuje *m* ▷ *vt* empujar; (*button*) apretar; (*promote*) promover ▷ *vi* empujar; (*demand*): **to ~ for** luchar por; **push in** *vi* colarse; **push off** (*inf*) *vi* largarse; **push on** *vi* seguir adelante; **push over** *vt* (*cause to fall*) hacer caer, derribar; (*knock over*) volcar; **push through** *vi* (*crowd*) abrirse paso a empujones ▷ *vt* (*measure*) despachar; **pushchair** (BRIT) *n* sillita de ruedas; **pusher** *n* (*drug pusher*) traficante *mf* de drogas; **push-up** (US) *n* plancha

pussy(-cat) ['pusı-] (*inf*) *n* minino (*inf*)

put [put] (*pt, pp* **~**) *vt* (*place*) poner, colocar; (*put into*) meter; (*say*) expresar; (*a question*) hacer; (*estimate*) estimar; **put aside** *vt* (*lay down*: *book etc*) dejar *or* poner a un lado; (*save*) ahorrar; (*in shop*) guardar; **put away** *vt* (*store*) guardar; **put back** *vt* (*replace*) devolver a su lugar; (*postpone*) aplazar; **put by** *vt* (*money*) guardar; **put down** *vt* (*on ground*) poner en el suelo; (*animal*) sacrificar; (*in writing*) apuntar; (*revolt etc*) sofocar; (*attribute*): **to put sth down to** atribuir algo a; **put forward** *vt* (*ideas*) presentar, proponer; **put in** *vt* (*complaint*) presentar; (*time*) dedicar; **put off** *vt* (*postpone*) aplazar; (*discourage*) desanimar; **put on** *vt* ponerse; (*light etc*) encender; (*play etc*) presentar; (*gain*): **to put on weight** engordar; (*brake*) echar; (*record, kettle etc*) poner; (*assume*) adoptar; **put out** *vt* (*fire, light*) apagar; (*rubbish etc*) sacar; (*cat etc*) echar; (*one's hand*) alargar; (*inf*: *person*): **to be put out** alterarse; **put through** *vt* (*Tel*) poner; (*plan etc*) hacer aprobar; **put together** *vt* unir, reunir; (*assemble*: *furniture*) armar, montar; (*meal*) preparar; **put up** *vt* (*raise*) levantar, alzar; (*hang*) colgar; (*build*) construir; (*increase*) aumentar; (*accommodate*) alojar; **put up with** *vt fus* aguantar

putt [pʌt] *n* putt *m*, golpe *m* corto; **putting green** *n* green *m*; minigolf *m*

puzzle ['pʌzl] *n* rompecabezas *m inv*; (*also*: **crossword ~**) crucigrama *m*; (*mystery*) misterio ▷ *vt* dejar perplejo, confundir ▷ *vi*: **to ~ over sth** devanarse los sesos con algo; **puzzled** *adj* perplejo; **puzzling** *adj* misterioso, extraño

pyjamas [pı'dʒɑ:məz] (BRIT) *npl* pijama *m*

pylon ['paılən] *n* torre *f* de conducción eléctrica

pyramid ['pırəmıd] *n* pirámide *f*

q

quack [kwæk] *n* graznido; (*pej*: *doctor*) curandero/a
quadruple [kwɔ'drupl] *vt*, *vi* cuadruplicar
quail [kweɪl] *n* codorniz *f* ▷ *vi*: **to ~ at** *or* **before** amedrentarse ante
quaint [kweɪnt] *adj* extraño; (*picturesque*) pintoresco
quake [kweɪk] *vi* temblar ▷ *n abbr* = **earthquake**
qualification [kwɔlɪfɪ'keɪʃən] *n* (*ability*) capacidad *f*; (*often pl*: *diploma etc*) título; (*reservation*) salvedad *f*
qualified ['kwɔlɪfaɪd] *adj* capacitado; (*professionally*) titulado; (*limited*) limitado
qualify ['kwɔlɪfaɪ] *vt* (*make competent*) capacitar; (*modify*) modificar ▷ *vi* (*in competition*): **to ~ (for)** calificarse (para); (*pass examination(s)*: **to ~ (as)** calificarse (de), graduarse (en); (*be eligible*): **to ~ (for)** reunir los requisitos (para)
quality ['kwɔlɪtɪ] *n* calidad *f*; (*of person*) cualidad *f*
qualm [kwɑ:m] *n* escrúpulo
quantify ['kwɔntɪfaɪ] *vt* cuantificar
quantity ['kwɔntɪtɪ] *n* cantidad *f*; **in ~** en grandes cantidades
quarantine ['kwɔrnti:n] *n* cuarentena
quarrel ['kwɔrl] *n* riña, pelea ▷ *vi* reñir, pelearse
quarry ['kwɔrɪ] *n* cantera
quart [kwɔ:t] *n* ≈ litro
quarter ['kwɔ:tə*] *n* cuarto, cuarta parte *f*; (US: *coin*) *moneda de 25 centavos*; (*of year*) trimestre *m*; (*district*) barrio ▷ *vt* dividir en cuartos; (*Mil*: *lodge*) alojar; **quarters** *npl* (*barracks*) cuartel *m*; (*living quarters*) alojamiento; **a ~ of an hour** un cuarto de hora; **quarter final** *n* cuarto de final; **quarterly** *adj* trimestral ▷ *adv* cada 3 meses, trimestralmente
quartet(te) [kwɔ:'tɛt] *n* cuarteto
quartz [kwɔ:ts] *n* cuarzo
quay [ki:] *n* (*also*: **~side**) muelle *m*
queasy ['kwi:zɪ] *adj*: **to feel ~** tener náuseas
queen [kwi:n] *n* reina; (*Cards etc*) dama
queer [kwɪə*] *adj* raro, extraño ▷ *n* (*inf*: *highly offensive*) maricón *m*
quench [kwɛntʃ] *vt*: **to ~ one's thirst** apagar la sed
query ['kwɪərɪ] *n* (*question*) pregunta ▷ *vt* dudar de
quest [kwɛst] *n* busca, búsqueda
question ['kwɛstʃən] *n* pregunta; (*doubt*) duda; (*matter*) asunto, cuestión *f* ▷ *vt* (*doubt*) dudar de; (*interrogate*) interrogar, hacer preguntas a; **beyond ~** fuera de toda duda; **out of the ~** imposible; ni hablar; **questionable** *adj* dudoso; **question mark** *n* punto de interrogación; **questionnaire** [-'nɛə*] *n* cuestionario
queue [kju:] (BRIT) *n* cola ▷ *vi* (*also*: **~ up**) hacer cola
quiche [ki:ʃ] *n* quiche *m*
quick [kwɪk] *adj* rápido; (*agile*) ágil; (*mind*) listo ▷ *n*: **cut to the ~** (*fig*) herido en lo vivo; **be ~!** ¡date prisa!; **quickly** *adv* rápidamente, de prisa
quid [kwɪd] (BRIT: *inf*) *n inv* libra
quiet ['kwaɪət] *adj* (*voice, music etc*) bajo; (*person, place*) tranquilo; (*ceremony*) íntimo ▷ *n* silencio; (*calm*) tranquilidad *f* ▷ *vt*, *vi* (US) = **quieten**

Be careful not to translate **quiet** by the Spanish word *quieto*.

quietly *adv* tranquilamente; (*silently*) silenciosamente
quilt [kwɪlt] *n* edredón *m*
quirky ['kw´:kɪ] *adj* raro, estrafalario
quit [kwɪt] (*pt*, *pp* **~** *or* **~ted**) *vt* dejar, abandonar; (*premises*) desocupar ▷ *vi* (*give up*) renunciar; (*resign*) dimitir
quite [kwaɪt] *adv* (*rather*) bastante; (*entirely*) completamente; **that's not ~ big enough** no acaba de ser lo bastante grande; **~ a few of them** un buen número de ellos; **~ (so)!** ¡así es!, ¡exactamente!
quits [kwɪts] *adj*: **~ (with)** en paz (con); **let's call it ~** dejémoslo en tablas
quiver ['kwɪvə*] *vi* estremecerse
quiz [kwɪz] *n* concurso ▷ *vt* interrogar
quota ['kwəutə] *n* cuota
quotation [kwəu'teɪʃən] *n* cita; (*estimate*) presupuesto; **quotation marks** *npl* comillas *fpl*
quote [kwəut] *n* cita; (*estimate*) presupuesto ▷ *vt* citar; (*price*) cotizar ▷ *vi*: **to ~ from** citar de; **quotes** *npl* (*inverted commas*) comillas *fpl*

rabbi ['ræbaɪ] *n* rabino
rabbit ['ræbɪt] *n* conejo
rabies ['reɪbi:z] *n* rabia
RAC (BRIT) *n abbr* (= *Royal Automobile Club*) ≈ RACE *m*
rac(c)oon [rə'ku:n] *n* mapache *m*
race [reɪs] *n* carrera; (*species*) raza ▷ *vt* (*horse*) hacer correr; (*engine*) acelerar ▷ *vi* (*compete*) competir; (*run*) correr; (*pulse*) latir a ritmo acelerado; **race car** (US) *n* = **racing car**; **racecourse** *n* hipódromo; **racehorse** *n* caballo de carreras; **racetrack** *n* pista; (*for cars*) autódromo
racial ['reɪʃl] *adj* racial
racing ['reɪsɪŋ] *n* carreras *fpl*; **racing car** (BRIT) *n* coche *m* de carreras; **racing driver** (BRIT) *n* piloto *mf* de carreras
racism ['reɪsɪzəm] *n* racismo; **racist** [-sɪst] *adj*, *n* racista *mf*
rack [ræk] *n* (*also*: **luggage ~**) rejilla; (*shelf*) estante *m*; (*also*: **roof ~**) baca, portaequipajes *m inv*; (*dish rack*) escurreplatos *m inv*; (*clothes rack*) percha ▷ *vt* atormentar; **to ~ one's brains** devanarse los sesos
racket ['rækɪt] *n* (*for tennis*) raqueta; (*noise*) ruido, estrépito; (*swindle*) estafa, timo
racquet ['rækɪt] *n* raqueta
radar ['reɪdɑ:*] *n* radar *m*
radiation [reɪdɪ'eɪʃən] *n* radiación *f*
radiator ['reɪdɪeɪtə*] *n* radiador *m*
radical ['rædɪkl] *adj* radical
radio ['reɪdɪəu] *n* radio *f*; **on the ~** por radio; **radioactive** *adj* radioactivo; **radio station** *n* emisora
radish ['rædɪʃ] *n* rábano
RAF *n abbr* (= *Royal Air Force*) las Fuerzas Aéreas Británicas
raffle ['ræfl] *n* rifa, sorteo
raft [rɑ:ft] *n* balsa; (*also*: **life ~**) balsa salvavidas
rag [ræg] *n* (*piece of cloth*) trapo; (*torn cloth*) harapo; (*pej*: *newspaper*) periodicucho; (*for charity*) *actividades estudiantiles benéficas*; **rags** *npl* (*torn clothes*) harapos *mpl*
rage [reɪdʒ] *n* rabia, furor *m* ▷ *vi* (*person*) rabiar, estar furioso; (*storm*) bramar; **it's all the ~** (*very fashionable*) está muy de moda
ragged ['rægɪd] *adj* (*edge*) desigual, mellado; (*appearance*) andrajoso, harapiento
raid [reɪd] *n* (*Mil*) incursión *f*; (*criminal*) asalto; (*by police*) redada ▷ *vt* invadir, atacar; asaltar
rail [reɪl] *n* (*on stair*) barandilla, pasamanos *m inv*; (*on bridge, balcony*) pretil *m*; (*of ship*) barandilla; (*also*: **towel ~**) toallero; **railcard** *n* (BRIT) *tarjeta para obtener descuentos en el tren*; **railing(s)** *n(pl)* vallado; **railroad** (US) *n* = **railway**; **railway** (BRIT) *n* ferrocarril *m*, vía férrea; **railway line** (BRIT) *n* línea (de ferrocarril); **railway station** (BRIT) *n* estación *f* de ferrocarril
rain [reɪn] *n* lluvia ▷ *vi* llover; **in the ~** bajo la lluvia; **it's ~ing** llueve, está lloviendo; **rainbow** *n* arco iris; **raincoat** *n* impermeable *m*; **raindrop** *n* gota de lluvia; **rainfall** *n* lluvia; **rainforest** *n* selvas *fpl* tropicales; **rainy** *adj* lluvioso
raise [reɪz] *n* aumento ▷ *vt* levantar; (*increase*) aumentar; (*improve*: *morale*) subir; (: *standards*) mejorar; (*doubts*) suscitar; (*a question*) plantear; (*cattle, family*) criar; (*crop*) cultivar; (*army*) reclutar; (*loan*) obtener; **to ~ one's voice** alzar la voz
raisin ['reɪzn] *n* pasa de Corinto
rake [reɪk] *n* (*tool*) rastrillo; (*person*) libertino ▷ *vt* (*garden*) rastrillar
rally ['rælɪ] *n* (*Pol etc*) reunión *f*, mitin *m*; (*Aut*) rallye *m*; (*Tennis*) peloteo ▷ *vt* reunir ▷ *vi* recuperarse
RAM [ræm] *n abbr* (= *random access memory*) RAM *f*
ram [ræm] *n* carnero; (*also*: **battering ~**) ariete *m* ▷ *vt* (*crash into*) dar contra, chocar con; (*push*: *fist etc*) empujar con fuerza
Ramadan [ræmə'dæn] *n* ramadán *m*
ramble ['ræmbl] *n* caminata, excursión *f* en el campo ▷ *vi* (*pej*: *also*: **~ on**) divagar; **rambler** *n* excursionista *mf*; (*Bot*) trepadora; **rambling** *adj* (*speech*) inconexo; (*house*) laberíntico; (*Bot*) trepador(a)
ramp [ræmp] *n* rampa; **on/off ~** (US *Aut*) vía de acceso/salida
rampage [ræm'peɪdʒ] *n*: **to be on the ~** desmandarse ▷ *vi*: **they went rampaging through the town** recorrieron la ciudad armando alboroto
ran [ræn] *pt of* **run**
ranch [rɑ:ntʃ] *n* hacienda, estancia

random ['rændəm] *adj* fortuito, sin orden; (*Comput, Math*) aleatorio ▷ *n*: **at ~** al azar
rang [ræŋ] *pt of* **ring**
range [reɪndʒ] *n* (*of mountains*) cadena de montañas, cordillera; (*of missile*) alcance *m*; (*of voice*) registro; (*series*) serie *f*; (*of products*) surtido; (*Mil*: *also*: **shooting ~**) campo de tiro; (*also*: **kitchen ~**) fogón *m* ▷ *vt* (*place*) colocar; (*arrange*) arreglar ▷ *vi*: **to ~ over** (*extend*) extenderse por; **to ~ from ... to ...** oscilar entre ... y ...
ranger [reɪndʒə*] *n* guardabosques *mf inv*
rank [ræŋk] *n* (*row*) fila; (*Mil*) rango; (*status*) categoría; (BRIT: *also*: **taxi ~**) parada de taxis ▷ *vi*: **to ~ among** figurar entre ▷ *adj* fétido, rancio; **the ~ and file** (*fig*) la base
ransom ['rænsəm] *n* rescate *m*; **to hold to ~** (*fig*) hacer chantaje a
rant [rænt] *vi* divagar, desvariar
rap [ræp] *vt* golpear, dar un golpecito en ▷ *n* (*music*) rap *m*
rape [reɪp] *n* violación *f*; (*Bot*) colza ▷ *vt* violar
rapid ['ræpɪd] *adj* rápido; **rapidly** *adv* rápidamente; **rapids** *npl* (*Geo*) rápidos *mpl*
rapist ['reɪpɪst] *n* violador *m*
rapport [ræ'pɔː*] *n* simpatía
rare [rɛə*] *adj* raro, poco común; (*Culin*: *steak*) poco hecho; **rarely** *adv* pocas veces
rash [ræʃ] *adj* imprudente, precipitado ▷ *n* (*Med*) sarpullido, erupción *f* (cutánea); (*of events*) serie *f*
rasher ['ræʃə*] *n* lonja
raspberry ['rɑːzbərɪ] *n* frambuesa
rat [ræt] *n* rata
rate [reɪt] *n* (*ratio*) razón *f*; (*price*) precio; (: *of hotel etc*) tarifa; (*of interest*) tipo; (*speed*) velocidad *f* ▷ *vt* (*value*) tasar; (*estimate*) estimar; **rates** *npl* (BRIT: *property tax*) impuesto municipal; (*fees*) tarifa; **to ~ sth/sb as** considerar algo/a algn como
rather ['rɑːðə*] *adv*: **it's ~ expensive** es algo caro; (*too much*) es demasiado caro; (*to some extent*) más bien; **there's ~ a lot** hay bastante; **I would** *or* **I'd ~ go** preferiría ir; **or ~** mejor dicho
rating ['reɪtɪŋ] *n* tasación *f*; (*score*) índice *m*; (*of ship*) clase *f*; **ratings** *npl* (*Radio, TV*) niveles *mpl* de audiencia
ratio ['reɪʃɪəu] *n* razón *f*; **in the ~ of 100 to 1** a razón de 100 a 1
ration ['ræʃən] *n* ración *f* ▷ *vt* racionar; **rations** *npl* víveres *mpl*
rational ['ræʃənl] *adj* (*solution, reasoning*) lógico, razonable; (*person*) cuerdo, sensato
rattle ['rætl] *n* golpeteo; (*of train etc*) traqueteo; (*for baby*) sonaja, sonajero ▷ *vi* castañetear; (*car, bus*): **to ~ along** traquetear ▷ *vt* hacer sonar agitando
rave [reɪv] *vi* (*in anger*) encolerizarse; (*with enthusiasm*) entusiasmarse; (*Med*) delirar, desvariar ▷ *n* (*inf*: *party*) rave *m*
raven ['reɪvən] *n* cuervo
ravine [rə'viːn] *n* barranco
raw [rɔː] *adj* crudo; (*not processed*) bruto; (*sore*) vivo; (*inexperienced*) novato, inexperto; **~ materials** materias primas
ray [reɪ] *n* rayo; **~ of hope** (rayo de) esperanza
razor ['reɪzə*] *n* (*open*) navaja; (*safety razor*) máquina de afeitar; (*electric razor*) máquina (eléctrica) de afeitar; **razor blade** *n* hoja de afeitar
Rd *abbr* = **road**
RE *n abbr* (BRIT) = **religious education**
re [riː] *prep* con referencia a
reach [riːtʃ] *n* alcance *m*; (*of river etc*) extensión *f* entre dos recodos ▷ *vt* alcanzar, llegar a; (*achieve*) lograr ▷ *vi* extenderse; **within ~** al alcance (de la mano); **out of ~** fuera del alcance; **reach out** *vt* (*hand*) tender ▷ *vi*: **to reach out for sth** alargar *or* tender la mano para tomar algo
react [riː'ækt] *vi* reaccionar; **reaction** [-'ækʃən] *n* reacción *f*; **reactor** [riː'æktə*] *n* (*also*: **nuclear reactor**) reactor *m* (nuclear)
read [riːd, *pt, pp* rɛd] (*pt, pp* **~**) *vi* leer ▷ *vt* leer; (*understand*) entender; (*study*) estudiar; **read out** *vt* leer en alta voz; **reader** *n* lector(a) *m/f*; (BRIT: *at university*) profesor(a) *m/f* adjunto/a
readily ['rɛdɪlɪ] *adv* (*willingly*) de buena gana; (*easily*) fácilmente; (*quickly*) en seguida
reading ['riːdɪŋ] *n* lectura; (*on instrument*) indicación *f*
ready ['rɛdɪ] *adj* listo, preparado; (*willing*) dispuesto; (*available*) disponible ▷ *adv*: **~-cooked** listo para comer ▷ *n*: **at the ~** (*Mil*) listo para tirar ▷ **to get ~** *vi* prepararse ▷ **to get ~** *vt* preparar; **ready-made** *adj* confeccionado
real [rɪəl] *adj* verdadero, auténtico; **in ~ terms** en términos reales; **real ale** *n* cerveza elaborada tradicionalmente; **real estate** *n* bienes *mpl* raíces; **realistic** [-'lɪstɪk] *adj* realista; **reality** [riː'ælɪtɪ] *n* realidad *f*; **reality TV** *n* telerrealidad *f*
realization [rɪəlaɪ'zeɪʃən] *n* comprensión *f*; (*fulfilment, Comm*) realización *f*
realize ['rɪəlaɪz] *vt* (*understand*) darse cuenta de
really ['rɪəlɪ] *adv* realmente; (*for emphasis*) verdaderamente; (*actually*): **what ~ happened** lo que pasó en realidad; **~?** ¿de

r

veras?; **~!** (*annoyance*) ¡vamos!, ¡por favor!
realm [rɛlm] *n* reino; (*fig*) esfera
realtor ['rɪəltɔ:*] (US) *n* agente *mf* inmobiliario/a
reappear [ri:ə'pɪə*] *vi* reaparecer
rear [rɪə*] *adj* trasero ▷ *n* parte *f* trasera ▷ *vt* (*cattle, family*) criar ▷ *vi* (*also*: **~ up**: *animal*) encabritarse
rearrange [ri:ə'reɪndʒ] *vt* ordenar *or* arreglar de nuevo
rear: rear-view mirror *n* (*Aut*) (espejo) retrovisor *m*; **rear-wheel drive** *n* tracción *f* trasera
reason ['ri:zn] *n* razón *f* ▷ *vi*: **to ~ with sb** tratar de que algn entre en razón; **it stands to ~ that ...** es lógico que ...; **reasonable** *adj* razonable; (*sensible*) sensato; **reasonably** *adv* razonablemente; **reasoning** *n* razonamiento, argumentos *mpl*
reassurance [ri:ə'ʃuərəns] *n* consuelo
reassure [ri:ə'ʃuə*] *vt* tranquilizar, alentar; **to ~ sb that ...** tranquilizar a algn asegurando que ...
rebate ['ri:beɪt] *n* (*on tax etc*) desgravación *f*
rebel [*n* 'rɛbl, *vi* rɪ'bɛl] *n* rebelde *mf* ▷ *vi* rebelarse, sublevarse; **rebellion** [rɪ'bɛljən] *n* rebelión *f*, sublevación *f*; **rebellious** [rɪ'bɛljəs] *adj* rebelde; (*child*) revoltoso
rebuild [ri:'bɪld] *vt* reconstruir
recall [*vb* rɪ'kɔ:l, *n* 'ri:kɔl] *vt* (*remember*) recordar; (*ambassador etc*) retirar ▷ *n* recuerdo; retirada
rec'd *abbr* (= *received*) rbdo
receipt [rɪ'si:t] *n* (*document*) recibo; (*for parcel etc*) acuse *m* de recibo; (*act of receiving*) recepción *f*; **receipts** *npl* (*Comm*) ingresos *mpl*

> Be careful not to translate **receipt** by the Spanish word *receta*.

receive [rɪ'si:v] *vt* recibir; (*guest*) acoger; (*wound*) sufrir; **receiver** *n* (*Tel*) auricular *m*; (*Radio*) receptor *m*; (*of stolen goods*) perista *mf*; (*Comm*) administrador *m* jurídico
recent ['ri:snt] *adj* reciente; **recently** *adv* recientemente; **recently arrived** recién llegado
reception [rɪ'sɛpʃən] *n* recepción *f*; (*welcome*) acogida; **reception desk** *n* recepción *f*; **receptionist** *n* recepcionista *mf*
recession [rɪ'sɛʃən] *n* recesión *f*
recharge [ri:'tʃɑ:dʒ] *vt* (*battery*) recargar
recipe ['rɛsɪpɪ] *n* receta; (*for disaster, success*) fórmula
recipient [rɪ'sɪpɪənt] *n* recibidor(a) *m/f*; (*of letter*) destinatario/a
recital [rɪ'saɪtl] *n* recital *m*
recite [rɪ'saɪt] *vt* (*poem*) recitar
reckless ['rɛkləs] *adj* temerario, imprudente; (*driving, driver*) peligroso
reckon ['rɛkən] *vt* calcular; (*consider*) considerar; (*think*): **I ~ that ...** me parece que ...
reclaim [rɪ'kleɪm] *vt* (*land, waste*) recuperar; (*land: from sea*) rescatar; (*demand back*) reclamar
recline [rɪ'klaɪn] *vi* reclinarse
recognition [rɛkəg'nɪʃən] *n* reconocimiento; **transformed beyond ~** irreconocible
recognize ['rɛkəgnaɪz] *vt*: **to ~ (by/as)** reconocer (por/como)
recollection [rɛkə'lɛkʃən] *n* recuerdo
recommend [rɛkə'mɛnd] *vt* recomendar; **recommendation** [rɛkəmɛn'deɪʃən] *n* recomendación *f*
reconcile ['rɛkənsaɪl] *vt* (*two people*) reconciliar; (*two facts*) compaginar; **to ~ o.s. to sth** conformarse a algo
reconsider [ri:kən'sɪdə*] *vt* repensar
reconstruct [ri:kən'strʌkt] *vt* reconstruir
record [*n, adj* 'rɛkɔ:d, *vt* rɪ'kɔ:d] *n* (*Mus*) disco; (*of meeting etc*) acta; (*register*) registro, partida; (*file*) archivo; (*also*: **criminal ~**) antecedentes *mpl*; (*written*) expediente *m*; (*Sport, Comput*) récord *m* ▷ *adj* récord, sin precedentes ▷ *vt* registrar; (*Mus: song etc*) grabar; **in ~ time** en un tiempo récord; **off the ~** *adj* no oficial ▷ *adv* confidencialmente; **recorded delivery** (BRIT) *n* (*Post*) entrega con acuse de recibo; **recorder** *n* (*Mus*) flauta de pico; **recording** *n* (*Mus*) grabación *f*; **record player** *n* tocadiscos *m inv*
recount [rɪ'kaunt] *vt* contar
recover [rɪ'kʌvə*] *vt* recuperar ▷ *vi* (*from illness, shock*) recuperarse; **recovery** *n* recuperación *f*
recreate [ri:krɪ'eɪt] *vt* recrear
recreation [rɛkrɪ'eɪʃən] *n* recreo; **recreational vehicle** (US) *n* caravan *or* rulota pequeña; **recreational drug** droga recreativa
recruit [rɪ'kru:t] *n* recluta *mf* ▷ *vt* reclutar; (*staff*) contratar; **recruitment** *n* reclutamiento
rectangle ['rɛktæŋgl] *n* rectángulo; **rectangular** [-'tæŋgjulə*] *adj* rectangular
rectify ['rɛktɪfaɪ] *vt* rectificar
rector ['rɛktə*] *n* (*Rel*) párroco
recur [rɪ'kə:*] *vi* repetirse; (*pain, illness*) producirse de nuevo; **recurring** *adj* (*problem*) repetido, constante
recyclable [ri:'saɪkləbl] *adj* reciclable
recycle [ri:'saɪkl] *vt* reciclar

recycling [riːˈsaɪklɪŋ] *n* reciclaje

red [rɛd] *n* rojo ▷*adj* rojo; (*hair*) pelirrojo; (*wine*) tinto; **to be in the ~** (*account*) estar en números rojos; (*business*) tener un saldo negativo; **to give sb the ~ carpet treatment** recibir a algn con todos los honores; **Red Cross** *n* Cruz *f* Roja; **redcurrant** *n* grosella roja

redeem [rɪˈdiːm] *vt* redimir; (*promises*) cumplir; (*sth in pawn*) desempeñar; (*fig, also Rel*) rescatar

red: red-haired *adj* pelirrojo; **redhead** *n* pelirrojo/a; **red-hot** *adj* candente; **red light** *n*: **to go through a red light** (*Aut*) pasar la luz roja; **red-light district** *n* barrio chino

red meat *n* carne *f* roja

reduce [rɪˈdjuːs] *vt* reducir; **to ~ sb to tears** hacer llorar a algn; **"~ speed now"** (*Aut*) "reduzca la velocidad"; **reduced** *adj* (*decreased*) reducido, rebajado; **at a reduced price** con rebaja *or* descuento; **"greatly reduced prices"** "grandes rebajas"; **reduction** [rɪˈdʌkʃən] *n* reducción *f*; (*of price*) rebaja; (*discount*) descuento; (*smaller-scale copy*) copia reducida

redundancy [rɪˈdʌndənsɪ] *n* (*dismissal*) despido; (*unemployment*) desempleo

redundant [rɪˈdʌndnt] *adj* (BRIT: *worker*) parado, sin trabajo; (*detail, object*) superfluo; **to be made ~** quedar(se) sin trabajo

reed [riːd] *n* (*Bot*) junco, caña; (*Mus*) lengüeta

reef [riːf] *n* (*at sea*) arrecife *m*

reel [riːl] *n* carrete *m*, bobina; (*of film*) rollo; (*dance*) *baile escocés* ▷*vt* (*also*: **~ up**) devanar; (*also*: **~ in**) sacar ▷*vi* (*sway*) tambalear(se)

ref [rɛf] (*inf*) *n abbr* = **referee**

refectory [rɪˈfɛktərɪ] *n* comedor *m*

refer [rɪˈfəː*] *vt* (*send*: *patient*) referir; (: *matter*) remitir ▷*vi*: **to ~ to** (*allude to*) referirse a, aludir a; (*apply to*) relacionarse con; (*consult*) consultar

referee [rɛfəˈriː] *n* árbitro; (BRIT: *for job application*): **to be a ~ for sb** proporcionar referencias a algn ▷*vt* (*match*) arbitrar en

reference [ˈrɛfrəns] *n* referencia; (*for job application*: *letter*) carta de recomendación; **with ~ to** (*Comm*: *in letter*) me remito a; **reference number** *n* número de referencia

refill [*vt* riːˈfɪl, *n* ˈriːfɪl] *vt* rellenar ▷*n* repuesto, recambio

refine [rɪˈfaɪn] *vt* refinar; **refined** *adj* (*person*) fino; **refinery** *n* refinería

reflect [rɪˈflɛkt] *vt* reflejar ▷*vi* (*think*) reflexionar, pensar; **it ~s badly/well on him** le perjudica/le hace honor; **reflection** [-ˈflɛkʃən] *n* (*act*) reflexión *f*; (*image*) reflejo; (*criticism*) crítica; **on reflection** pensándolo bien

reflex [ˈriːflɛks] *adj, n* reflejo

reform [rɪˈfɔːm] *n* reforma ▷*vt* reformar

refrain [rɪˈfreɪn] *vi*: **to ~ from doing** abstenerse de hacer ▷*n* estribillo

refresh [rɪˈfrɛʃ] *vt* refrescar; **refreshing** *adj* refrescante; **refreshments** *npl* refrescos *mpl*

refrigerator [rɪˈfrɪdʒəreɪtə*] *n* frigorífico (SP), nevera (SP), refrigerador *m* (LAM), heladera (RPL)

refuel [riːˈfjuəl] *vi* repostar (combustible)

refuge [ˈrɛfjuːdʒ] *n* refugio, asilo; **to take ~ in** refugiarse en; **refugee** [rɛfjuˈdʒiː] *n* refugiado/a

refund [*n* ˈriːfʌnd, *vb* rɪˈfʌnd] *n* reembolso ▷*vt* devolver, reembolsar

refurbish [riːˈfəːbɪʃ] *vt* restaurar, renovar

refusal [rɪˈfjuːzəl] *n* negativa; **to have first ~ on** tener la primera opción a

refuse¹ [ˈrɛfjuːs] *n* basura

refuse² [rɪˈfjuːz] *vt* rechazar; (*invitation*) declinar; (*permission*) denegar ▷*vi*: **to ~ to do sth** negarse a hacer algo; (*horse*) rehusar

regain [rɪˈgeɪn] *vt* recobrar, recuperar

regard [rɪˈgɑːd] *n* mirada; (*esteem*) respeto; (*attention*) consideración *f* ▷*vt* (*consider*) considerar; **to give one's ~s to** saludar de su parte a; **"with kindest ~s"** "con muchos recuerdos"; **as ~s, with ~ to** con respecto a, en cuanto a; **regarding** *prep* con respecto a, en cuanto a; **regardless** *adv* a pesar de todo; **regardless of** sin reparar en

regenerate [rɪˈdʒɛnəreɪt] *vt* regenerar

reggae [ˈrɛgeɪ] *n* reggae *m*

regiment [ˈrɛdʒɪmənt] *n* regimiento

region [ˈriːdʒən] *n* región *f*; **in the ~ of** (*fig*) alrededor de; **regional** *adj* regional

register [ˈrɛdʒɪstə*] *n* registro ▷*vt* registrar; (*birth*) declarar; (*car*) matricular; (*letter*) certificar; (*instrument*) marcar, indicar ▷*vi* (*at hotel*) registrarse; (*as student*) matricularse; (*make impression*) producir impresión; **registered** *adj* (*letter, parcel*) certificado

registrar [ˈrɛdʒɪstrɑː*] *n* secretario/a (del registro civil)

registration [rɛdʒɪsˈtreɪʃən] *n* (*act*) declaración *f*; (*Aut*: *also*: **~ number**) matrícula

registry office [ˈrɛdʒɪstrɪ-] (BRIT) *n* registro civil; **to get married in a ~** casarse por lo civil

regret [rɪˈgrɛt] *n* sentimiento, pesar *m* ▷*vt* sentir, lamentar; **regrettable** *adj* lamentable

regular [ˈrɛgjulə*] *adj* regular; (*soldier*)

r

profesional; (*usual*) habitual; (: *doctor*) de cabecera ▷ *n* (*client etc*) cliente/a *m/f* habitual; **regularly** *adv* con regularidad; (*often*) repetidas veces

regulate ['rɛgjuleɪt] *vt* controlar; **regulation** [-'leɪʃən] *n* (*rule*) regla, reglamento

rehabilitation ['riːəbɪlɪ'teɪʃən] *n* rehabilitación *f*

rehearsal [rɪ'həːsəl] *n* ensayo

rehearse [rɪ'həːs] *vt* ensayar

reign [reɪn] *n* reinado; (*fig*) predominio ▷ *vi* reinar; (*fig*) imperar

reimburse [riːɪm'bəːs] *vt* reembolsar

rein [reɪn] *n* (*for horse*) rienda

reincarnation [riːɪnkɑː'neɪʃən] *n* reencarnación *f*

reindeer ['reɪndɪə*] *n inv* reno

reinforce [riːɪn'fɔːs] *vt* reforzar; **reinforcements** *npl* (*Mil*) refuerzos *mpl*

reinstate [riːɪn'steɪt] *vt* reintegrar; (*tax, law*) reinstaurar

reject [*n* 'riːdʒɛkt, *vb* rɪ'dʒɛkt] *n* (*thing*) desecho ▷ *vt* rechazar; (*suggestion*) descartar; (*coin*) expulsar; **rejection** [rɪ'dʒɛkʃən] *n* rechazo

rejoice [rɪ'dʒɔɪs] *vi*: **to ~ at** *or* **over** regocijarse *or* alegrarse de

relate [rɪ'leɪt] *vt* (*tell*) contar, relatar; (*connect*) relacionar ▷ *vi* relacionarse; **related** *adj* afín; (*person*) emparentado; **related to** (*subject*) relacionado con; **relating to** *prep* referente a

relation [rɪ'leɪʃən] *n* (*person*) familiar *mf*, pariente *mf*; (*link*) relación *f*; **relations** *npl* (*relatives*) familiares *mpl*; **relationship** *n* relación *f*; (*personal*) relaciones *fpl*; (*also*: **family relationship**) parentesco

relative ['rɛlətɪv] *n* pariente *mf*, familiar *mf* ▷ *adj* relativo; **relatively** *adv* (*comparatively*) relativamente

relax [rɪ'læks] *vi* descansar; (*unwind*) relajarse ▷ *vt* (*one's grip*) soltar, aflojar; (*control*) relajar; (*mind, person*) descansar; **relaxation** [riːlæk'seɪʃən] *n* descanso; (*of rule, control*) relajamiento; (*entertainment*) diversión *f*; **relaxed** *adj* relajado; (*tranquil*) tranquilo; **relaxing** *adj* relajante

relay ['riːleɪ] *n* (*race*) carrera de relevos ▷ *vt* (*Radio, TV*) retransmitir

release [rɪ'liːs] *n* (*liberation*) liberación *f*; (*from prison*) puesta en libertad; (*of gas etc*) escape *m*; (*of film etc*) estreno; (*of record*) lanzamiento ▷ *vt* (*prisoner*) poner en libertad; (*gas*) despedir, arrojar; (*from wreckage*) soltar; (*catch, spring etc*) desenganchar; (*film*) estrenar; (*book*) publicar; (*news*) difundir

relegate ['rɛləgeɪt] *vt* relegar; (BRIT *Sport*): **to be ~d to** bajar a

relent [rɪ'lɛnt] *vi* ablandarse; **relentless** *adj* implacable

relevant ['rɛləvənt] *adj* (*fact*) pertinente; **~ to** relacionado con

reliable [rɪ'laɪəbl] *adj* (*person, firm*) de confianza, de fiar; (*method, machine*) seguro; (*source*) fidedigno

relic ['rɛlɪk] *n* (*Rel*) reliquia; (*of the past*) vestigio

relief [rɪ'liːf] *n* (*from pain, anxiety*) alivio; (*help, supplies*) socorro, ayuda; (*Art, Geo*) relieve *m*

relieve [rɪ'liːv] *vt* (*pain*) aliviar; (*bring help to*) ayudar, socorrer; (*take over from*) sustituir; (: *guard*) relevar; **to ~ sb of sth** quitar algo a algn; **to ~ o.s.** hacer sus necesidades; **relieved** *adj*: **to be relieved** sentir un gran alivio

religion [rɪ'lɪdʒən] *n* religión *f*

religious [rɪ'lɪdʒəs] *adj* religioso; **religious education** *n* educación *f* religiosa

relish ['rɛlɪʃ] *n* (*Culin*) salsa; (*enjoyment*) entusiasmo ▷ *vt* (*food etc*) saborear; (*enjoy*): **to ~ sth** hacerle mucha ilusión a algn algo

relocate [riːləu'keɪt] *vt* cambiar de lugar, mudar ▷ *vi* mudarse

reluctance [rɪ'lʌktəns] *n* renuencia

reluctant [rɪ'lʌktənt] *adj* renuente; **reluctantly** *adv* de mala gana

rely on [rɪ'laɪ-] *vt fus* depender de; (*trust*) contar con

remain [rɪ'meɪn] *vi* (*survive*) quedar; (*be left*) sobrar; (*continue*) quedar(se), permanecer; **remainder** *n* resto; **remaining** *adj* que queda(n); (*surviving*) restante(s); **remains** *npl* restos *mpl*

remand [rɪ'mɑːnd] *n*: **on ~** detenido (bajo custodia) ▷ *vt*: **to be ~ed in custody** quedar detenido bajo custodia

remark [rɪ'mɑːk] *n* comentario ▷ *vt* comentar; **remarkable** *adj* (*outstanding*) extraordinario

remarry [riː'mærɪ] *vi* volver a casarse

remedy ['rɛmədɪ] *n* remedio ▷ *vt* remediar, curar

remember [rɪ'mɛmbə*] *vt* recordar, acordarse de; (*bear in mind*) tener presente; (*send greetings to*): **~ me to him** dale recuerdos de mi parte; **Remembrance Day** *n* ≈ día en el que se recuerda a los caídos en las dos guerrasmundiales

REMEMBRANCE DAY

En el Reino Unido el domingo más

próximo al 11 de noviembre se conoce como **Remembrance Sunday** o **Remembrance Day**, aniversario de la firma del armisticio de 1918 que puso fin a la Primera Guerra Mundial. Ese día, a las once de la mañana (hora en que se firmó el armisticio), se recuerda a los que murieron en las dos guerras mundiales con dos minutos de silencio ante los monumentos a los caídos. Allí se colocan coronas de amapolas, flor que también se suele llevar prendida en el pecho tras pagar un donativo destinado a los inválidos de guerra.

remind [rɪ'maɪnd] *vt*: **to ~ sb to do sth** recordar a algn que haga algo; **to ~ sb of sth** (*of fact*) recordar algo a algn; **she ~s me of her mother** me recuerda a su madre; **reminder** *n* notificación *f*; (*memento*) recuerdo
reminiscent [rɛmɪ'nɪsnt] *adj*: **to be ~ of sth** recordar algo
remnant ['rɛmnənt] *n* resto; (*of cloth*) retal *m*
remorse [rɪ'mɔːs] *n* remordimientos *mpl*
remote [rɪ'məut] *adj* (*distant*) lejano; (*person*) distante; **remote control** *n* telecontrol *m*; **remotely** *adv* remotamente; (*slightly*) levemente
removal [rɪ'muːvəl] *n* (*taking away*) el quitar; (BRIT: *from house*) mudanza; (*from office*: *dismissal*) destitución *f*; (*Med*) extirpación *f*; **removal man** (*irreg*) *n* (BRIT) mozo de mudanzas; **removal van** (BRIT) *n* camión *m* de mudanzas
remove [rɪ'muːv] *vt* quitar; (*employee*) destituir; (*name*: *from list*) tachar, borrar; (*doubt*) disipar; (*abuse*) suprimir, acabar con; (*Med*) extirpar
Renaissance [rɪ'neɪsɑ̃ns] *n*: **the ~** el Renacimiento
rename [riː'neɪm] *vt* poner nuevo nombre a
render ['rɛndə*] *vt* (*thanks*) dar; (*aid*) proporcionar, prestar; (*make*): **to ~ sth useless** hacer algo inútil
rendezvous ['rɔndɪvuː] *n* cita
renew [rɪ'njuː] *vt* renovar; (*resume*) reanudar; (*loan etc*) prorrogar
renovate ['rɛnəveɪt] *vt* renovar
renowned [rɪ'naund] *adj* renombrado
rent [rɛnt] *n* (*for house*) arriendo, renta ▷*vt* alquilar; **rental** *n* (*for television, car*) alquiler *m*
reorganize [riː'ɔːgənaɪz] *vt* reorganizar
rep [rɛp] *n abbr* = **representative**
repair [rɪ'pɛə*] *n* reparación *f*, compostura ▷*vt* reparar, componer; (*shoes*) remendar; **in good/bad ~** en buen/mal estado; **repair kit** *n* caja de herramientas
repay [riː'peɪ] *vt* (*money*) devolver, reembolsar; (*person*) pagar; (*debt*) liquidar; (*sb's efforts*) devolver, corresponder a; **repayment** *n* reembolso, devolución *f*; (*sum of money*) recompensa
repeat [rɪ'piːt] *n* (*Radio, TV*) reposición *f* ▷*vt* repetir ▷*vi* repetirse; **repeatedly** *adv* repetidas veces; **repeat prescription** *n* (BRIT) receta renovada
repellent [rɪ'pɛlənt] *adj* repugnante ▷*n*: **insect ~** crema *or* loción *f* anti-insectos
repercussions [riːpə'kʌʃənz] *npl* consecuencias *fpl*
repetition [rɛpɪ'tɪʃən] *n* repetición *f*
repetitive [rɪ'pɛtɪtɪv] *adj* repetitivo
replace [rɪ'pleɪs] *vt* (*put back*) devolver a su sitio; (*take the place*) reemplazar, sustituir; **replacement** *n* (*act*) reposición *f*; (*thing*) recambio; (*person*) suplente *mf*
replay ['riːpleɪ] *n* (*Sport*) desempate *m*; (*of tape, film*) repetición *f*
replica ['rɛplɪkə] *n* copia, reproducción *f* (exacta)
reply [rɪ'plaɪ] *n* respuesta, contestación *f* ▷*vi* contestar, responder
report [rɪ'pɔːt] *n* informe *m*; (*Press etc*) reportaje *m*; (BRIT: *also*: **school ~**) boletín *m* escolar; (*of gun*) estallido ▷*vt* informar de; (*Press etc*) hacer un reportaje sobre; (*notify*: *accident, culprit*) denunciar ▷*vi* (*make a report*) presentar un informe; (*present o.s.*): **to ~ (to sb)** presentarse (ante algn); **report card** *n* (US, SCOTTISH) cartilla escolar; **reportedly** *adv* según se dice; **reporter** *n* periodista *mf*
represent [rɛprɪ'zɛnt] *vt* representar; (*Comm*) ser agente de; (*describe*): **to ~ sth as** describir algo como; **representation** [-'teɪʃən] *n* representación *f*; **representative** *n* representante *mf*; (US *Pol*) diputado/a *m/f* ▷*adj* representativo
repress [rɪ'prɛs] *vt* reprimir; **repression** [-'prɛʃən] *n* represión *f*
reprimand ['rɛprɪmɑːnd] *n* reprimenda ▷*vt* reprender
reproduce [riːprə'djuːs] *vt* reproducir ▷*vi* reproducirse; **reproduction** [-'dʌkʃən] *n* reproducción *f*
reptile ['rɛptaɪl] *n* reptil *m*
republic [rɪ'pʌblɪk] *n* república; **republican** *adj, n* republicano/a *m/f*
reputable ['rɛpjutəbl] *adj* (*make etc*) de renombre
reputation [rɛpju'teɪʃən] *n* reputación *f*
request [rɪ'kwɛst] *n* petición *f*; (*formal*)

r

solicitud *f* ▷ *vt*: **to ~ sth of** *or* **from sb** solicitar algo a algn; **request stop** (BRIT) *n* parada discrecional

require [rɪ'kwaɪə*] *vt* (*need*: *person*) necesitar, tener necesidad de; (: *thing*, *situation*) exigir; (*want*) pedir; **to ~ sb to do sth** pedir a algn que haga algo; **requirement** *n* requisito; (*need*) necesidad *f*

resat [ri:'sæt] *pt, pp of* **resit**

rescue ['rɛskju:] *n* rescate *m* ▷ *vt* rescatar

research [rɪ'sə:tʃ] *n* investigaciones *fpl* ▷ *vt* investigar

resemblance [rɪ'zɛmbləns] *n* parecido

resemble [rɪ'zɛmbl] *vt* parecerse a

resent [rɪ'zɛnt] *vt* tomar a mal; **resentful** *adj* resentido; **resentment** *n* resentimiento

reservation [rɛzə'veɪʃən] *n* reserva; **reservation desk** (US) *n* (*in hotel*) recepción *f*

reserve [rɪ'zə:v] *n* reserva; (*Sport*) suplente *mf* ▷ *vt* (*seats etc*) reservar; **reserved** *adj* reservado

reservoir ['rɛzəvwɑ:*] *n* (*artificial lake*) embalse *m*, tank; (*small*) depósito

residence ['rɛzɪdəns] *n* (*formal*: *home*) domicilio; (*length of stay*) permanencia; **residence permit** (BRIT) *n* permiso de permanencia

resident ['rɛzɪdənt] *n* (*of area*) vecino/a; (*in hotel*) huésped *mf* ▷ *adj* (*population*) permanente; (*doctor*) residente; **residential** [-'dɛnʃəl] *adj* residencial

residue ['rɛzɪdju:] *n* resto

resign [rɪ'zaɪn] *vt* renunciar a ▷ *vi* dimitir; **to ~ o.s. to** (*situation*) resignarse a; **resignation** [rɛzɪg'neɪʃən] *n* dimisión *f*; (*state of mind*) resignación *f*

resin ['rɛzɪn] *n* resina

resist [rɪ'zɪst] *vt* resistir, oponerse a; **resistance** *n* resistencia

resit ['ri:sɪt] (BRIT) (*pt, pp* **resat**) *vt* (*exam*) volver a presentarse a; (*subject*) recuperar, volver a examinarse de (SP)

resolution [rɛzə'lu:ʃən] *n* resolución *f*

resolve [rɪ'zɔlv] *n* resolución *f* ▷ *vt* resolver ▷ *vi*: **to ~ to do** resolver hacer

resort [rɪ'zɔ:t] *n* (*town*) centro turístico; (*recourse*) recurso ▷ *vi*: **to ~ to** recurrir a; **in the last ~** como último recurso

resource [rɪ'sɔ:s] *n* recurso; **resourceful** *adj* despabilado, ingenioso

respect [rɪs'pɛkt] *n* respeto ▷ *vt* respetar; **respectable** *adj* respetable; (*large*: *amount*) apreciable; (*passable*) tolerable; **respectful** *adj* respetuoso; **respective** *adj* respectivo; **respectively** *adv* respectivamente

respite ['rɛspaɪt] *n* respiro

respond [rɪs'pɔnd] *vi* responder; (*react*) reaccionar; **response** [-'pɔns] *n* respuesta; reacción *f*

responsibility [rɪspɔnsɪ'bɪlɪtɪ] *n* responsabilidad *f*

responsible [rɪs'pɔnsɪbl] *adj* (*character*) serio, formal; (*job*) de confianza; (*liable*): **~ (for)** responsable (de); **responsibly** *adv* con seriedad

responsive [rɪs'pɔnsɪv] *adj* sensible

rest [rɛst] *n* descanso, reposo; (*Mus, pause*) pausa, silencio; (*support*) apoyo; (*remainder*) resto ▷ *vi* descansar; (*be supported*): **to ~ on** descansar sobre ▷ *vt*: **to ~ sth on/against** apoyar algo en *or* sobre/contra; **the ~ of them** (*people, objects*) los demás; **it ~s with him to ...** depende de él el que ...

restaurant ['rɛstərɔŋ] *n* restaurante *m*; **restaurant car** (BRIT) *n* (*Rail*) coche-comedor *m*

restless ['rɛstlɪs] *adj* inquieto

restoration [rɛstə'reɪʃən] *n* restauración *f*; devolución *f*

restore [rɪ'stɔ:*] *vt* (*building*) restaurar; (*sth stolen*) devolver; (*health*) restablecer; (*to power*) volver a poner a

restrain [rɪs'treɪn] *vt* (*feeling*) contener, refrenar; (*person*): **to ~ (from doing)** disuadir (de hacer); **restraint** *n* (*restriction*) restricción *f*; (*moderation*) moderación *f*; (*of manner*) reserva

restrict [rɪs'trɪkt] *vt* restringir, limitar; **restriction** [-kʃən] *n* restricción *f*, limitación *f*

rest room (US) *n* aseos *mpl*

restructure [ri:'strʌktʃə*] *vt* reestructurar

result [rɪ'zʌlt] *n* resultado ▷ *vi*: **to ~ in** terminar en, tener por resultado; **as a ~ of** a consecuencia de

resume [rɪ'zju:m] *vt* reanudar ▷ *vi* comenzar de nuevo

Be careful not to translate **resume** by the Spanish word *resumir*.

résumé ['reɪzju:meɪ] *n* resumen *m*; (US) currículum *m*

resuscitate [rɪ'sʌsɪteɪt] *vt* (*Med*) resucitar

retail ['ri:teɪl] *adj, adv* al por menor; **retailer** *n* detallista *mf*

retain [rɪ'teɪn] *vt* (*keep*) retener, conservar

retaliation [rɪtælɪ'eɪʃən] *n* represalias *fpl*

retarded [rɪ'tɑ:dɪd] *adj* retrasado

retire [rɪ'taɪə*] *vi* (*give up work*) jubilarse; (*withdraw*) retirarse; (*go to bed*) acostarse; **retired** *adj* (*person*) jubilado; **retirement** *n* (*giving up work*: *state*) retiro; (: *act*) jubilación *f*

retort [rɪ'tɔ:t] *vi* contestar
retreat [rɪ'tri:t] *n* (*place*) retiro; (*Mil*) retirada ▷ *vi* retirarse
retrieve [rɪ'tri:v] *vt* recobrar; (*situation, honour*) salvar; (*Comput*) recuperar; (*error*) reparar
retrospect ['rɛtrəspɛkt] *n*: **in ~** retrospectivamente; **retrospective** [-'spɛktɪv] *adj* retrospectivo; (*law*) retroactivo
return [rɪ'tə:n] *n* (*going or coming back*) vuelta, regreso; (*of sth stolen etc*) devolución *f*; (*Finance: from land, shares*) ganancia, ingresos *mpl* ▷ *cpd* (*journey*) de regreso; (BRIT: *ticket*) de ida y vuelta; (*match*) de vuelta ▷ *vi* (*person etc: come or go back*) volver, regresar; (*symptoms etc*) reaparecer; (*regain*): **to ~ to** recuperar ▷ *vt* devolver; (*favour, love etc*) corresponder a; (*verdict*) pronunciar; (*Pol: candidate*) elegir; **returns** *npl* (*Comm*) ingresos *mpl*; **in ~ (for)** a cambio (de); **by ~ of post** a vuelta de correo; **many happy ~s (of the day)!** ¡feliz cumpleaños!; **return ticket** *n* (*esp* BRIT) billete *m* (SP) *or* boleto *m* (LAM) de ida y vuelta, billete *m* redondo (MEX)
reunion [ri:'ju:nɪən] *n* (*of family*) reunión *f*; (*of two people, school*) reencuentro
reunite [ri:ju:'naɪt] *vt* reunir; (*reconcile*) reconciliar
revamp [ri:'væmp] *vt* renovar
reveal [rɪ'vi:l] *vt* revelar; **revealing** *adj* revelador(a)
revel ['rɛvl] *vi*: **to ~ in sth/in doing sth** gozar de algo/con hacer algo
revelation [rɛvə'leɪʃən] *n* revelación *f*
revenge [rɪ'vɛndʒ] *n* venganza; **to take ~ on** vengarse de
revenue ['rɛvənju:] *n* ingresos *mpl*, rentas *fpl*
Reverend ['rɛvərənd] *adj* (*in titles*): **the ~ John Smith** (*Anglican*) el Reverendo John Smith; (*Catholic*) el Padre John Smith; (*Protestant*) el Pastor John Smith
reversal [rɪ'və:sl] *n* (*of order*) inversión *f*; (*of direction, policy*) cambio; (*of decision*) revocación *f*
reverse [rɪ'və:s] *n* (*opposite*) contrario; (*back: of cloth*) revés *m*; (*: of coin*) reverso; (*: of paper*) dorso; (*Aut*: *also*: **~ gear**) marcha atrás, revés *m* ▷ *adj* (*order*) inverso; (*direction*) contrario; (*process*) opuesto ▷ *vt* (*decision, Aut*) dar marcha atrás a; (*position, function*) invertir ▷ *vi* (BRIT *Aut*) dar marcha atrás; **reverse-charge call** (BRIT) *n* llamada a cobro revertido; **reversing lights** (BRIT) *npl* (*Aut*) luces *fpl* de retroceso
revert [rɪ'və:t] *vi*: **to ~ to** volver a
review [rɪ'vju:] *n* (*magazine, Mil*) revista; (*of book, film*) reseña; (US: *examination*) repaso, examen *m* ▷ *vt* repasar, examinar; (*Mil*) pasar revista a; (*book, film*) reseñar
revise [rɪ'vaɪz] *vt* (*manuscript*) corregir; (*opinion*) modificar; (*price, procedure*) revisar ▷ *vi* (*study*) repasar; **revision** [rɪ'vɪʒən] *n* corrección *f*; modificación *f*; (*for exam*) repaso
revival [rɪ'vaɪvəl] *n* (*recovery*) reanimación *f*; (*of interest*) renacimiento; (*Theatre*) reestreno; (*of faith*) despertar *m*
revive [rɪ'vaɪv] *vt* resucitar; (*custom*) restablecer; (*hope*) despertar; (*play*) reestrenar ▷ *vi* (*person*) volver en sí; (*business*) reactivarse
revolt [rɪ'vəult] *n* rebelión *f* ▷ *vi* rebelarse, sublevarse ▷ *vt* dar asco a, repugnar; **revolting** *adj* asqueroso, repugnante
revolution [rɛvə'lu:ʃən] *n* revolución *f*; **revolutionary** *adj, n* revolucionario/a *m/f*
revolve [rɪ'vɔlv] *vi* dar vueltas, girar; (*life, discussion*): **to ~ (a)round** girar en torno a
revolver [rɪ'vɔlvə*] *n* revólver *m*
reward [rɪ'wɔ:d] *n* premio, recompensa ▷ *vt*: **to ~ (for)** recompensar *or* premiar (por); **rewarding** *adj* (*fig*) valioso
rewind [ri:'waɪnd] *vt* rebobinar
rewritable [ri:'raɪtəbl] *adj* (*CD, DVD*) reescribible
rewrite [ri:'raɪt] (*pt* **rewrote**, *pp* **rewritten**) *vt* reescribir
rheumatism ['ru:mətɪzəm] *n* reumatismo, reúma *m*
rhinoceros [raɪ'nɔsərəs] *n* rinoceronte *m*
rhubarb ['ru:bɑ:b] *n* ruibarbo
rhyme [raɪm] *n* rima; (*verse*) poesía
rhythm ['rɪðm] *n* ritmo
rib [rɪb] *n* (*Anat*) costilla ▷ *vt* (*mock*) tomar el pelo a
ribbon ['rɪbən] *n* cinta; **in ~s** (*torn*) hecho trizas
rice [raɪs] *n* arroz *m*; **rice pudding** *n* arroz *m* con leche
rich [rɪtʃ] *adj* rico; (*soil*) fértil; (*food*) pesado; (*: sweet*) empalagoso; (*abundant*): **~ in** (*minerals etc*) rico en
rid [rɪd] (*pt, pp* **~**) *vt*: **to ~ sb of sth** librar a algn de algo; **to get ~ of** deshacerse *or* desembarazarse de
riddle ['rɪdl] *n* (*puzzle*) acertijo; (*mystery*) enigma *m*, misterio ▷ *vt*: **to be ~d with** ser lleno *or* plagado de
ride [raɪd] (*pt* **rode**, *pp* **ridden**) *n* paseo; (*distance covered*) viaje *m*, recorrido ▷ *vi* (*as sport*) montar; (*go somewhere: on horse, bicycle*) dar un paseo, pasearse; (*travel: on bicycle, motorcycle, bus*) viajar ▷ *vt* (*a horse*)

r

montar a; (*a bicycle, motorcycle*) andar en; (*distance*) recorrer; **to take sb for a ~** (*fig*) engañar a algn; **rider** *n* (*on horse*) jinete *mf*; (*on bicycle*) ciclista *mf*; (*on motorcycle*) motociclista *mf*

ridge [rɪdʒ] *n* (*of hill*) cresta; (*of roof*) caballete *m*; (*wrinkle*) arruga

ridicule ['rɪdɪkjuːl] *n* irrisión *f*, burla ▷ *vt* poner en ridículo, burlarse de; **ridiculous** [-'dɪkjuləs] *adj* ridículo

riding ['raɪdɪŋ] *n* equitación *f*; **I like ~** me gusta montar a caballo; **riding school** *n* escuela de equitación

rife [raɪf] *adj*: **to be ~** ser muy común; **to be ~ with** abundar en

rifle ['raɪfl] *n* rifle *m*, fusil *m* ▷ *vt* saquear

rift [rɪft] *n* (*in clouds*) claro; (*fig*: *disagreement*) desavenencia

rig [rɪg] *n* (*also*: **oil ~**: *at sea*) plataforma petrolera ▷ *vt* (*election etc*) amañar

right [raɪt] *adj* (*correct*) correcto, exacto; (*suitable*) indicado, debido; (*proper*) apropiado; (*just*) justo; (*morally good*) bueno; (*not left*) derecho ▷ *n* bueno; (*title, claim*) derecho; (*not left*) derecha ▷ *adv* bien, correctamente; (*not left*) a la derecha; (*exactly*): **~ now** ahora mismo ▷ *vt* enderezar; (*correct*) corregir ▷ *excl* ¡bueno!, ¡está bien!; **to be ~** (*person*) tener razón; (*answer*) ser correcto; **is that the ~ time?** (*of clock*) ¿es esa la hora buena?; **by ~s** en justicia; **on the ~** a la derecha; **to be in the ~** tener razón; **~ away** en seguida; **~ in the middle** exactamente en el centro; **right angle** *n* ángulo recto; **rightful** *adj* legítimo; **right-hand** *adj*: **right-hand drive** conducción *f* por la derecha; **the right-hand side** derecha; **right-handed** *adj* diestro; **rightly** *adv* correctamente, debidamente; (*with reason*) con razón; **right of way** *n* (*on path etc*) derecho de paso; (*Aut*) prioridad *f*; **right-wing** *adj* (*Pol*) derechista

rigid ['rɪdʒɪd] *adj* rígido; (*person, ideas*) inflexible

rigorous ['rɪgərəs] *adj* riguroso

rim [rɪm] *n* borde *m*; (*of spectacles*) aro; (*of wheel*) llanta

rind [raɪnd] *n* (*of bacon*) corteza; (*of lemon etc*) cáscara; (*of cheese*) costra

ring [rɪŋ] (*pt* **rang**, *pp* **rung**) *n* (*of metal*) aro; (*on finger*) anillo; (*of people*) corro; (*of objects*) círculo; (*gang*) banda; (*for boxing*) cuadrilátero; (*of circus*) pista; (*bull ring*) ruedo, plaza; (*sound of bell*) toque *m* ▷ *vi* (*on telephone*) llamar por teléfono; (*bell*) repicar; (*doorbell, phone*) sonar; (*also*: **~ out**) sonar; (*ears*) zumbar ▷ *vt* (BRIT *Tel*) llamar, telefonear; (*bell etc*) hacer sonar; (*doorbell*) tocar; **to give sb a ~** (BRIT *Tel*) llamar *or* telefonear a algn; **ring back** (BRIT) *vt, vi* (*Tel*) devolver la llamada; **ring off** (BRIT) *vi* (*Tel*) colgar, cortar la comunicación; **ring up** (BRIT) *vt* (*Tel*) llamar, telefonear; **ringing tone** *n* (*Tel*) tono de llamada; **ringleader** *n* (*of gang*) cabecilla *m*; **ring road** (BRIT) *n* carretera periférica *or* de circunvalación; **ringtone** *n* (*on mobile*) tono de llamada

rink [rɪŋk] *n* (*also*: **ice ~**) pista de hielo

rinse [rɪns] *n* aclarado; (*dye*) tinte *m* ▷ *vt* aclarar; (*mouth*) enjuagar

riot ['raɪət] *n* motín *m*, disturbio ▷ *vi* amotinarse; **to run ~** desmandarse

rip [rɪp] *n* rasgón *m*, rasgadura ▷ *vt* rasgar, desgarrar ▷ *vi* rasgarse, desgarrarse; **rip off** *vt* (*inf*: *cheat*) estafar; **rip up** *vt* hacer pedazos

ripe [raɪp] *adj* maduro

rip-off ['rɪpɔf] *n* (*inf*): **it's a ~!** ¡es una estafa!, ¡es un timo!

ripple ['rɪpl] *n* onda, rizo; (*sound*) murmullo ▷ *vi* rizarse

rise [raɪz] (*pt* **rose**, *pp* **risen**) *n* (*slope*) cuesta, pendiente *f*; (*hill*) altura; (BRIT: *in wages*) aumento; (*in prices, temperature*) subida; (*fig*: *to power etc*) ascenso ▷ *vi* subir; (*waters*) crecer; (*sun, moon*) salir; (*person*: *from bed etc*) levantarse; (*also*: **~ up**: *rebel*) sublevarse; (*in rank*) ascender; **to give ~ to** dar lugar *or* origen a; **to ~ to the occasion** ponerse a la altura de las circunstancias; **risen** ['rɪzn] *pp of* **rise**; **rising** *adj* (*increasing*: *number*) creciente; (*: prices*) en aumento *or* alza; (*tide*) creciente; (*sun, moon*) naciente

risk [rɪsk] *n* riesgo, peligro ▷ *vt* arriesgar; (*run the risk of*) exponerse a; **to take** *or* **run the ~ of doing** correr el riesgo de hacer; **at ~** en peligro; **at one's own ~** bajo su propia responsabilidad; **risky** *adj* arriesgado, peligroso

rite [raɪt] *n* rito; **last ~s** exequias *fpl*

ritual ['rɪtjuəl] *adj* ritual ▷ *n* ritual *m*, rito

rival ['raɪvl] *n* rival *mf*; (*in business*) competidor(a) *m/f* ▷ *adj* rival, opuesto ▷ *vt* competir con; **rivalry** *n* competencia

river ['rɪvə*] *n* río ▷ *cpd* (*port*) de río; (*traffic*) fluvial; **up/down ~** río arriba/abajo; **riverbank** *n* orilla (del río)

rivet ['rɪvɪt] *n* roblón *m*, remache *m* ▷ *vt* (*fig*) captar

road [rəud] *n* camino; (*motorway etc*) carretera; (*in town*) calle *f* ▷ *cpd* (*accident*) de tráfico; **major/minor ~** carretera principal/secundaria; **roadblock** *n* barricada; **road map** *n* mapa *m* de carreteras; **road rage** *n* *agresividad en la carretera*; **road safety** *n*

seguridad *f* vial; **roadside** *n* borde *m* (del camino); **roadsign** *n* señal *f* de tráfico; **road tax** *n* (BRIT) impuesto de rodaje; **roadworks** *npl* obras *fpl*
roam [rəum] *vi* vagar
roar [rɔː*] *n* rugido; (*of vehicle, storm*) estruendo; (*of laughter*) carcajada ▷*vi* rugir; hacer estruendo; **to ~ with laughter** reírse a carcajadas; **to do a ~ing trade** hacer buen negocio
roast [rəust] *n* carne *f* asada, asado ▷*vt* asar; (*coffee*) tostar; **roast beef** *n* rosbif *m*
rob [rɔb] *vt* robar; **to ~ sb of sth** robar algo a algn; (*fig: deprive*) quitar algo a algn; **robber** *n* ladrón/ona *m/f*; **robbery** *n* robo
robe [rəub] *n* (*for ceremony etc*) toga; (*also*: **bath~**) albornoz *m*
robin ['rɔbɪn] *n* petirrojo
robot ['rəubɔt] *n* robot *m*
robust [rəu'bʌst] *adj* robusto, fuerte
rock [rɔk] *n* roca; (*boulder*) peña, peñasco; (US: *small stone*) piedrecita; (BRIT: *sweet*) ≈ pirulí ▷*vt* (*swing gently: cradle*) balancear, mecer; (*: child*) arrullar; (*shake*) sacudir ▷*vi* mecerse, balancearse; sacudirse; **on the ~s** (*drink*) con hielo; (*marriage etc*) en ruinas; **rock and roll** *n* rocanrol *m*; **rock climbing** *n* (*Sport*) escalada
rocket ['rɔkɪt] *n* cohete *m*; **rocking chair** ['rɔkɪŋ-] *n* mecedora
rocky ['rɔkɪ] *adj* rocoso
rod [rɔd] *n* vara, varilla; (*also*: **fishing ~**) caña
rode [rəud] *pt of* **ride**
rodent ['rəudnt] *n* roedor *m*
rogue [rəug] *n* pícaro, pillo
role [rəul] *n* papel *m*; **role-model** *n* modelo a imitar
roll [rəul] *n* rollo; (*of bank notes*) fajo; (*also*: **bread ~**) panecillo; (*register, list*) lista, nómina; (*sound of drums etc*) redoble *m* ▷*vt* hacer rodar; (*also*: **~ up**: *string*) enrollar; (*cigarette*) liar; (*also*: **~ out**: *pastry*) aplanar; (*flatten: road, lawn*) apisonar ▷*vi* rodar; (*drum*) redoblar; (*ship*) balancearse; **roll over** *vi* dar una vuelta; **roll up** *vi* (*inf: arrive*) aparecer ▷*vt* (*carpet*) arrollar; (*: sleeves*) arremangar; **roller** *n* rodillo; (*wheel*) rueda; (*for road*) apisonadora; (*for hair*) rulo; **Rollerblades®** *npl* patines *mpl* en línea; **roller coaster** *n* montaña rusa; **roller skates** *npl* patines *mpl* de rueda; **roller-skating** *n* patinaje sobre ruedas; **to go roller-skating** ir a patinar (*sobre ruedas*); **rolling pin** *n* rodillo (de cocina)
ROM [rɔm] *n abbr* (*Comput*: = *read only memory*) ROM *f*
Roman ['rəumən] (*irreg*) *adj* romano/a; **Roman Catholic** (*irreg*) *adj, n* católico/a *m/f* (romano/a)
romance [rə'mæns] *n* (*love affair*) amor *m*; (*charm*) lo romántico; (*novel*) novela de amor
Romania *etc* [ruː'meɪnɪə] *n* = **Rumania** *etc*
Roman numeral *n* número romano
romantic [rə'mæntɪk] *adj* romántico
Rome [rəum] *n* Roma
roof [ruːf] (*pl* **~s**) *n* techo; (*of house*) techo, tejado ▷*vt* techar, poner techo a; **the ~ of the mouth** el paladar; **roof rack** *n* (*Aut*) baca, portaequipajes *m inv*
rook [ruk] *n* (*bird*) graja; (*Chess*) torre *f*
room [ruːm] *n* cuarto, habitación *f*; (*also*: **bed~**) dormitorio, recámara (MEX), pieza (SC); (*in school etc*) sala; (*space, scope*) sitio, cabida; **roommate** *n* compañero/a de cuarto; **room service** *n* servicio de habitaciones; **roomy** *adj* espacioso; (*garment*) amplio
rooster ['ruːstə*] *n* gallo
root [ruːt] *n* raíz *f* ▷*vi* arraigarse
rope [rəup] *n* cuerda; (*Naut*) cable *m* ▷*vt* (*tie*) atar *or* amarrar con (una) cuerda; (*climbers: also*: **~ together**) encordarse; (*an area: also*: **~ off**) acordonar; **to know the ~s** (*fig*) conocer los trucos (del oficio)
rose [rəuz] *pt of* **rise** ▷*n* rosa; (*shrub*) rosal *m*; (*on watering can*) roseta
rosé ['rəuzeɪ] *n* vino rosado
rosemary ['rəuzmərɪ] *n* romero
rosy ['rəuzɪ] *adj* rosado, sonrosado; **a ~ future** un futuro prometedor
rot [rɔt] *n* podredumbre *f*; (*fig: pej*) tonterías *fpl* ▷*vt* pudrir ▷*vi* pudrirse
rota ['rəutə] *n* (sistema *m* de) turnos *m*
rotate [rəu'teɪt] *vt* (*revolve*) hacer girar, dar vueltas a; (*jobs*) alternar ▷*vi* girar, dar vueltas
rotten ['rɔtn] *adj* podrido; (*dishonest*) corrompido; (*inf: bad*) pocho; **to feel ~** (*ill*) sentirse fatal
rough [rʌf] *adj* (*skin, surface*) áspero; (*terrain*) quebrado; (*road*) desigual; (*voice*) bronco; (*person, manner*) tosco, grosero; (*weather*) borrascoso; (*treatment*) brutal; (*sea*) picado; (*town, area*) peligroso; (*cloth*) basto; (*plan*) preliminar; (*guess*) aproximado ▷*n* (*Golf*): **in the ~** en las hierbas altas; **to ~ it** vivir sin comodidades; **to sleep ~** (BRIT) pasar la noche al raso; **roughly** *adv* (*handle*) torpemente; (*make*) toscamente; (*speak*) groseramente; (*approximately*) aproximadamente
roulette [ruː'lɛt] *n* ruleta
round [raund] *adj* redondo ▷*n* círculo; (BRIT: *of toast*) rebanada; (*of policeman*) ronda; (*of milkman*) recorrido; (*of doctor*)

visitas *fpl*; (*game*: *of cards, in competition*) partida; (*of ammunition*) cartucho; (*Boxing*) asalto; (*of talks*) ronda ▷ *vt* (*corner*) doblar ▷ *prep* alrededor de; (*surrounding*): **~ his neck/the table** en su cuello/alrededor de la mesa; (*in a circular movement*): **to move ~ the room/sail ~ the world** dar una vuelta a la habitación/circumnavigar el mundo; (*in various directions*): **to move ~ a room/house** moverse por toda la habitación/casa; (*approximately*) alrededor de ▷ *adv*: **all ~** por todos lados; **the long way ~** por el camino menos directo; **all (the) year ~** durante todo el año; **it's just ~ the corner** (*fig*) está a la vuelta de la esquina; **~ the clock** *adv* las 24 horas; **to go ~ to sb's (house)** ir a casa de algn; **to go ~ the back** pasar por atrás; **enough to go ~** bastante (para todos); **a ~ of applause** una salva de aplausos; **a ~ of drinks/sandwiches** una ronda de bebidas/bocadillos; **round off** *vt* (*speech etc*) acabar, poner término a; **round up** *vt* (*cattle*) acorralar; (*people*) reunir; (*price*) redondear; **roundabout** (BRIT) *n* (*Aut*) isleta; (*at fair*) tiovivo ▷ *adj* (*route, means*) indirecto; **round trip** *n* viaje *m* de ida y vuelta; **roundup** *n* rodeo; (*of criminals*) redada; (*of news*) resumen *m*

rouse [rauz] *vt* (*wake up*) despertar; (*stir up*) suscitar

route [ruːt] *n* ruta, camino; (*of bus*) recorrido; (*of shipping*) derrota

routine [ruːˈtiːn] *adj* rutinario ▷ *n* rutina; (*Theatre*) número

row¹ [rəu] *n* (*line*) fila, hilera; (*Knitting*) pasada ▷ *vi* (*in boat*) remar ▷ *vt* conducir remando; **4 days in a ~** 4 días seguidos

row² [rau] *n* (*racket*) escándalo; (*dispute*) bronca, pelea; (*scolding*) regaño ▷ *vi* pelear(se)

rowboat [ˈrəubəut] (US) = **rowing boat**

rowing [ˈrəuɪŋ] *n* remo; **rowing boat** (BRIT) *n* bote *m* de remos

royal [ˈrɔɪəl] *adj* real; **royalty** *n* (*royal persons*) familia real; (*payment to author*) derechos *mpl* de autor

rpm *abbr* (= *revs per minute*) r.p.m.

R.S.V.P. *abbr* (= *répondez s'il vous plaôt*) SRC

Rt. Hon. *abbr* (BRIT) (= *Right Honourable*) *título honorífico de diputado*

rub [rʌb] *vt* frotar; (*scrub*) restregar ▷ *n*: **to give sth a ~** frotar algo; **to ~ sb up** *or* **~ sb** (US) **the wrong way** entrarle algn por mal ojo; **rub in** *vt* (*ointment*) aplicar frotando; **rub off** *vi* borrarse; **rub out** *vt* borrar

rubber [ˈrʌbə*] *n* caucho, goma; (BRIT: *eraser*) goma de borrar; **rubber band** *n* goma, gomita; **rubber gloves** *npl* guantes *mpl* de goma

rubbish [ˈrʌbɪʃ] (BRIT) *n* basura; (*waste*) desperdicios *mpl*; (*fig*: *pej*) tonterías *fpl*; (*junk*) pacotilla; **rubbish bin** (BRIT) *n* cubo *or* bote *m* (MEX) *or* tacho (SC) de la basura; **rubbish dump** (BRIT) *n* vertedero, basurero

rubble [ˈrʌbl] *n* escombros *mpl*

ruby [ˈruːbɪ] *n* rubí *m*

rucksack [ˈrʌksæk] *n* mochila

rudder [ˈrʌdə*] *n* timón *m*

rude [ruːd] *adj* (*impolite*: *person*) mal educado; (: *word, manners*) grosero; (*crude*) crudo; (*indecent*) indecente

ruffle [ˈrʌfl] *vt* (*hair*) despeinar; (*clothes*) arrugar; **to get ~d** (*fig*: *person*) alterarse

rug [rʌg] *n* alfombra; (BRIT: *blanket*) manta

rugby [ˈrʌgbɪ] *n* rugby *m*

rugged [ˈrʌgɪd] *adj* (*landscape*) accidentado; (*features*) robusto

ruin [ˈruːɪn] *n* ruina ▷ *vt* arruinar; (*spoil*) estropear; **ruins** *npl* ruinas *fpl*, restos *mpl*

rule [ruːl] *n* (*norm*) norma, costumbre *f*; (*regulation, ruler*) regla; (*government*) dominio ▷ *vt* (*country, person*) gobernar ▷ *vi* gobernar; (*Law*) fallar; **as a ~** por regla general; **rule out** *vt* excluir; **ruler** *n* (*sovereign*) soberano; (*for measuring*) regla; **ruling** *adj* (*party*) gobernante; (*class*) dirigente ▷ *n* (*Law*) fallo, decisión *f*

rum [rʌm] *n* ron *m*

Rumania [ruːˈmeɪnɪə] *n* Rumanía; **Rumanian** *adj* rumano/a ▷ *n* rumano/a *m/f*; (*Ling*) rumano

rumble [ˈrʌmbl] *n* (*noise*) ruido sordo ▷ *vi* retumbar, hacer un ruido sordo; (*stomach, pipe*) sonar

rumour [ˈruːmə*] (US **rumor**) *n* rumor *m* ▷ *vt*: **it is ~ed that ...** se rumorea que ...

rump steak *n* filete *m* de lomo

run [rʌn] (*pt* **ran**, *pp* **run**) *n* (*fast pace*): **at a ~** corriendo; (*Sport, in tights*) carrera; (*outing*) paseo, excursión *f*; (*distance travelled*) trayecto; (*series*) serie *f*; (*Theatre*) temporada; (*Ski*) pista ▷ *vt* correr; (*operate*: *business*) dirigir; (: *competition, course*) organizar; (: *hotel, house*) administrar, llevar; (*Comput*) ejecutar; (*pass*: *hand*) pasar; (*Press*: *feature*) publicar ▷ *vi* correr; (*work*: *machine*) funcionar, marchar; (*bus, train*: *operate*) circular, ir; (: *travel*) ir; (*continue*: *play*) seguir; (*contract*) ser válido; (*flow*: *river*) fluir; (*colours, washing*) desteñirse; (*in election*) ser candidato; **there was a ~ on** (*meat, tickets*) hubo mucha demanda de; **in the long ~** a la larga; **on the ~** en fuga; **I'll ~ you to the station** te llevaré a la estación (en coche); **to ~ a risk** correr un riesgo; **to ~ a bath** llenar la bañera; **run after** *vt fus* (*to* *catch up*) correr tras; (*chase*) perseguir; **run away** *vi* huir; **run down** *vt* (*production*) ir reduciendo; (*factory*) ir restringiendo la producción en; (*car*) atropellar; (*criticize*) criticar; **to be run down** (*person*: *tired*) estar debilitado; **run into** *vt fus* (*meet*: *person, trouble*) tropezar con; (*collide with*) chocar con; **run off** *vt* (*water*) dejar correr; (*copies*) sacar ▷ *vi* huir corriendo; **run out** *vi* (*person*) salir corriendo; (*liquid*) irse; (*lease*) caducar, vencer; (*money etc*) acabarse; **run out of** *vt fus* quedar sin; **run over** *vt* (*Aut*) atropellar ▷ *vt fus* (*revise*) repasar; **run through** *vt fus* (*instructions*) repasar; **run up** *vt* (*debt*) contraer; **to run up against** (*difficulties*) tropezar con; **runaway** *adj* (*horse*) desbocado; (*truck*) sin frenos; (*child*) escapado de casa

rung [rʌŋ] *pp of* **ring** ▷ *n* (*of ladder*) escalón *m*, peldaño

runner ['rʌnə*] *n* (*in race*: *person*) corredor(a) *m/f*; (: *horse*) caballo; (*on sledge*) patín *m*; **runner bean** (BRIT) *n* ≈ judía verde; **runner-up** *n* subcampeón/ona *m/f*

running ['rʌnɪŋ] *n* (*sport*) atletismo; (*of business*) administración *f* ▷ *adj* (*water, costs*) corriente; (*commentary*) continuo; **to be in/out of the ~ for sth** tener/no tener posibilidades de ganar algo; **6 days ~** 6 días seguidos

runny ['rʌnɪ] *adj* fluido; (*nose, eyes*) gastante

run-up ['rʌnʌp] *n*: **~ to** (*election etc*) período previo a

runway ['rʌnweɪ] *n* (*Aviat*) pista de aterrizaje

rupture ['rʌptʃə*] *n* (*Med*) hernia ▷ *vt*: **to ~ o.s** causarse una hernia

rural ['ruərl] *adj* rural

rush [rʌʃ] *n* ímpetu *m*; (*hurry*) prisa; (*Comm*) demanda repentina; (*current*) corriente *f* fuerte; (*of feeling*) torrente *m*; (*Bot*) junco ▷ *vt* apresurar; (*work*) hacer de prisa ▷ *vi* correr, precipitarse; **rush hour** *n* horas *fpl* punta

Russia ['rʌʃə] *n* Rusia; **Russian** *adj* ruso/a ▷ *n* ruso/a *m/f*; (*Ling*) ruso

rust [rʌst] *n* herrumbre *f*, moho ▷ *vi* oxidarse

rusty ['rʌstɪ] *adj* oxidado

ruthless ['ru:θlɪs] *adj* despiadado

RV (US) *n abbr* = **recreational vehicle**

rye [raɪ] *n* centeno

S

Sabbath ['sæbəθ] *n* domingo; (*Jewish*) sábado

sabotage ['sæbətɑ:ʒ] *n* sabotaje *m* ▷ *vt* sabotear

saccharin(e) ['sækərɪn] *n* sacarina

sachet ['sæʃeɪ] *n* sobrecito

sack [sæk] *n* (*bag*) saco, costal *m* ▷ *vt* (*dismiss*) despedir; (*plunder*) saquear; **to get the ~** ser despedido

sacred ['seɪkrɪd] *adj* sagrado, santo

sacrifice ['sækrɪfaɪs] *n* sacrificio ▷ *vt* sacrificar

sad [sæd] *adj* (*unhappy*) triste; (*deplorable*) lamentable

saddle ['sædl] *n* silla (de montar); (*of cycle*) sillín *m* ▷ *vt* (*horse*) ensillar; **to be ~d with sth** (*inf*) quedar cargado con algo

sadistic [sə'dɪstɪk] *adj* sádico

sadly ['sædlɪ] *adv* lamentablemente; **to be ~ lacking in** estar por desgracia carente de

sadness ['sædnɪs] *n* tristeza

s.a.e. *abbr* (= *stamped addressed envelope*) *sobre con las propias señas de uno y con sello*

safari [sə'fɑ:rɪ] *n* safari *m*

safe [seɪf] *adj* (*out of danger*) fuera de peligro; (*not dangerous, sure*) seguro; (*unharmed*) ileso ▷ *n* caja de caudales, caja fuerte; **~ and sound** sano y salvo; **(just) to be on the ~ side** para mayor seguridad; **safely** *adv* seguramente, con seguridad; **to arrive safely** llegar bien; **safe sex** *n* sexo seguro *or* sin riesgo

safety ['seɪftɪ] *n* seguridad *f*; **safety belt** *n* cinturón *m* (de seguridad); **safety pin** *n* imperdible *m*, seguro (MEX), alfiler *m* de gancho (SC)

saffron ['sæfrən] *n* azafrán *m*

sag [sæg] *vi* aflojarse

sage [seɪdʒ] *n* (*herb*) salvia; (*man*) sabio

Sagittarius [sædʒɪ'tɛərɪəs] *n* Sagitario

Sahara [sə'hɑ:rə] *n*: **the ~ (Desert)** el

(desierto del) Sáhara

said [sɛd] *pt, pp of* **say**

sail [seɪl] *n* (*on boat*) vela; (*trip*): **to go for a ~** dar un paseo en barco ▷ *vt* (*boat*) gobernar ▷ *vi* (*travel: ship*) navegar; (*Sport*) hacer vela; (*begin voyage*) salir; **they ~ed into Copenhagen** arribaron a Copenhague; **sailboat** (US) *n* = **sailing boat**; **sailing** *n* (*Sport*) vela; **to go sailing** hacer vela; **sailing boat** *n* barco de vela; **sailor** *n* marinero, marino

saint [seɪnt] *n* santo

sake [seɪk] *n*: **for the ~ of** por

salad ['sæləd] *n* ensalada; **salad cream** (BRIT) *n* (especie *f* de) mayonesa; **salad dressing** *n* aliño

salami [sə'lɑ:mɪ] *n* salami *m*, salchichón *m*

salary ['sælərɪ] *n* sueldo

sale [seɪl] *n* venta; (*at reduced prices*) liquidación *f*, saldo; (*auction*) subasta; **sales** *npl* (*total amount sold*) ventas *fpl*, facturación *f*; **"for ~"** "se vende"; **on ~** en venta; **on ~ or return** (*goods*) venta por reposición; **sales assistant** (US), **sales clerk** *n* dependiente/a *m/f*; **salesman/woman** (*irreg*) *n* (*in shop*) dependiente/a *m/f*; **salesperson** (*irreg*) *n* vendedor(a) *m/f*, dependiente/a *m/f*; **sales rep** *n* representante *mf*, agente *mf* comercial

saline ['seɪlaɪn] *adj* salino

saliva [sə'laɪvə] *n* saliva

salmon ['sæmən] *n inv* salmón *m*

salon ['sælɔn] *n* (*hairdressing salon*) peluquería; (*beauty salon*) salón *m* de belleza

saloon [sə'lu:n] *n* (US) bar *m*, taberna; (BRIT *Aut*) coche *m* (de) turismo; (*ship's lounge*) cámara, salón *m*

salt [sɔlt] *n* sal *f* ▷ *vt* salar; (*put salt on*) poner sal en; **saltwater** *adj* de agua salada; **salty** *adj* salado

salute [sə'lu:t] *n* saludo; (*of guns*) salva ▷ *vt* saludar

salvage ['sælvɪdʒ] *n* (*saving*) salvamento, recuperación *f*; (*things saved*) objetos *mpl* salvados ▷ *vt* salvar

Salvation Army [sæl'veɪʃən-] *n* Ejército de Salvación

same [seɪm] *adj* mismo ▷ *pron*: **the ~** el(la) mismo/a, los(las) mismos/as; **the ~ book as** el mismo libro que; **at the ~ time** (*at the same moment*) al mismo tiempo; (*yet*) sin embargo; **all** *or* **just the ~** sin embargo, aun así; **to do the ~ (as sb)** hacer lo mismo (que algn); **the ~ to you!** ¡igualmente!

sample ['sɑ:mpl] *n* muestra ▷ *vt* (*food*) probar; (*wine*) catar

sanction ['sæŋkʃən] *n* aprobación *f* ▷ *vt* sancionar; aprobar; **sanctions** *npl* (*Pol*) sanciones *fpl*

sanctuary ['sæŋktjuərɪ] *n* santuario; (*refuge*) asilo, refugio; (*for wildlife*) reserva

sand [sænd] *n* arena; (*beach*) playa ▷ *vt* (*also*: **~ down**) lijar

sandal ['sændl] *n* sandalia

sand: sandbox (US) *n* = **sandpit**; **sandcastle** *n* castillo de arena; **sand dune** *n* duna; **sandpaper** *n* papel *m* de lija; **sandpit** *n* (*for children*) cajón *m* de arena; **sands** *npl* playa *sg* de arena; **sandstone** ['sændstəun] *n* piedra arenisca

sandwich ['sændwɪtʃ] *n* sandwich *m* ▷ *vt* intercalar; **~ed between** apretujado entre; **cheese/ham ~** sandwich de queso/jamón

sandy ['sændɪ] *adj* arenoso; (*colour*) rojizo

sane [seɪn] *adj* cuerdo; (*sensible*) sensato

Be careful not to translate **sane** by the Spanish word *sano*.

sang [sæŋ] *pt of* **sing**

sanitary towel (US **sanitary napkin**) *n* paño higiénico, compresa

sanity ['sænɪtɪ] *n* cordura; (*of judgment*) sensatez *f*

sank [sæŋk] *pt of* **sink**

Santa Claus [sæntə'klɔ:z] *n* San Nicolás, Papá Noel

sap [sæp] *n* (*of plants*) savia ▷ *vt* (*strength*) minar, agotar

sapphire ['sæfaɪə*] *n* zafiro

sarcasm ['sɑ:kæzm] *n* sarcasmo

sarcastic [sɑ:'kæstɪk] *adj* sarcástico

sardine [sɑ:'di:n] *n* sardina

SASE (US) *n abbr* (*= self-addressed stamped envelope*) *sobre con las propias señas de uno y con sello*

Sat. *abbr* (*= Saturday*) sáb

sat [sæt] *pt, pp of* **sit**

satchel ['sætʃl] *n* (*child's*) mochila, cartera (SP)

satellite ['sætəlaɪt] *n* satélite *m*; **satellite dish** *n* antena de televisión por satélite; **satellite television** *n* televisión *f* vía satélite

satin ['sætɪn] *n* raso ▷ *adj* de raso

satire ['sætaɪə*] *n* sátira

satisfaction [sætɪs'fækʃən] *n* satisfacción *f*

satisfactory [sætɪs'fæktərɪ] *adj* satisfactorio

satisfied ['sætɪsfaɪd] *adj* satisfecho; **to be ~ (with sth)** estar satisfecho (de algo)

satisfy ['sætɪsfaɪ] *vt* satisfacer; (*convince*) convencer

Saturday ['sætədɪ] *n* sábado

sauce [sɔ:s] *n* salsa; (*sweet*) crema; jarabe *m*; **saucepan** *n* cacerola, olla

saucer ['sɔ:sə*] *n* platillo; **Saudi Arabia** *n*

Arabia Saudí *or* Saudita
sauna ['sɔːnə] *n* sauna
sausage ['sɔsɪdʒ] *n* salchicha; **sausage roll** *n* empanadita de salchicha
sautéed ['səuteɪd] *adj* salteado
savage ['sævɪdʒ] *adj* (*cruel, fierce*) feroz, furioso; (*primitive*) salvaje ▷ *n* salvaje *mf* ▷ *vt* (*attack*) embestir
save [seɪv] *vt* (*rescue*) salvar, rescatar; (*money, time*) ahorrar; (*put by, keep: seat*) guardar; (*Comput*) salvar (y guardar); (*avoid: trouble*) evitar; (*Sport*) parar ▷ *vi* (*also:* **~ up**) ahorrar ▷ *n* (*Sport*) parada ▷ *prep* salvo, excepto
savings ['seɪvɪŋz] *npl* ahorros *mpl*; **savings account** *n* cuenta de ahorros; **savings and loan association** (US) *n* sociedad *f* de ahorro y préstamo
savoury ['seɪvərɪ] (US **savory**) *adj* sabroso; (*dish: not sweet*) salado
saw [sɔː] (*pt* **~ed**, *pp* **~ed** *or* **~n**) *pt of* **see** ▷ *n* (*tool*) sierra ▷ *vt* serrar; **sawdust** *n* (a) serrín *m*
sawn [sɔːn] *pp of* **saw**
saxophone ['sæksəfəun] *n* saxófono
say [seɪ] (*pt, pp* **said**) *n*: **to have one's ~** expresar su opinión ▷ *vt* decir; **to have a** *or* **some ~ in sth** tener voz *or* tener que ver en algo; **to ~ yes/no** decir que sí/no; **could you ~ that again?** ¿podría repetir eso?; **that is to ~** es decir; **that goes without ~ing** ni que decir tiene; **saying** *n* dicho, refrán *m*
scab [skæb] *n* costra; (*pej*) esquirol *m*
scaffolding ['skæfəldɪŋ] *n* andamio, andamiaje *m*
scald [skɔːld] *n* escaldadura ▷ *vt* escaldar
scale [skeɪl] *n* (*gen, Mus*) escala; (*of fish*) escama; (*of salaries, fees etc*) escalafón *m* ▷ *vt* (*mountain*) escalar; (*tree*) trepar; **scales** *npl* (*for weighing: small*) balanza; (*: large*) báscula; **on a large ~** en gran escala; **~ of charges** tarifa, lista de precios
scallion ['skæljən] (US) *n* cebolleta
scallop ['skɔləp] *n* (*Zool*) venera; (*Sewing*) festón *m*
scalp [skælp] *n* cabellera ▷ *vt* escalpar
scalpel ['skælpl] *n* bisturí *m*
scam [skæm] *n* (*inf*) estafa, timo
scampi ['skæmpɪ] *npl* gambas *fpl*
scan [skæn] *vt* (*examine*) escudriñar; (*glance at quickly*) dar un vistazo a; (*TV, Radar*) explorar, registrar ▷ *n* (*Med*): **to have a ~** pasar por el escáner
scandal ['skændl] *n* escándalo; (*gossip*) chismes *mpl*
Scandinavia [skændɪ'neɪvɪə] *n* Escandinavia; **Scandinavian** *adj, n* escandinavo/a *m/f*
scanner ['skænə*] *n* (*Radar, Med*) escáner *m*
scapegoat ['skeɪpgəut] *n* cabeza de turco, chivo expiatorio
scar [skɑː] *n* cicatriz *f*; (*fig*) señal *f* ▷ *vt* dejar señales en
scarce [skɛəs] *adj* escaso; **to make o.s. ~** (*inf*) esfumarse; **scarcely** *adv* apenas
scare [skɛə*] *n* susto, sobresalto; (*panic*) pánico ▷ *vt* asustar, espantar; **to ~ sb stiff** dar a algn un susto de muerte; **bomb ~** amenaza de bomba; **scarecrow** *n* espantapájaros *m inv*; **scared** *adj*: **to be scared** estar asustado
scarf [skɑːf] (*pl* **~s** *or* **scarves**) *n* (*long*) bufanda; (*square*) pañuelo
scarlet ['skɑːlɪt] *adj* escarlata
scarves [skɑːvz] *npl of* **scarf**
scary ['skɛərɪ] (*inf*) *adj* espeluznante
scatter ['skætə*] *vt* (*spread*) esparcir, desparramar; (*put to flight*) dispersar ▷ *vi* desparramarse; dispersarse
scenario [sɪ'nɑːrɪəu] *n* (*Theatre*) argumento; (*Cinema*) guión *m*; (*fig*) escenario
scene [siːn] *n* (*Theatre, fig etc*) escena; (*of crime etc*) escenario; (*view*) panorama *m*; (*fuss*) escándalo; **scenery** *n* (*Theatre*) decorado; (*landscape*) paisaje *m*

> Be careful not to translate **scenery** by the Spanish word *escenario*.

scenic *adj* pintoresco
scent [sɛnt] *n* perfume *m*, olor *m*; (*fig: track*) rastro, pista
sceptical ['skɛptɪkl] *adj* escéptico
schedule ['ʃɛdjuːl] (US) ['skɛdjuːl] *n* (*timetable*) horario; (*of events*) programa *m*; (*list*) lista ▷ *vt* (*visit*) fijar la hora de; **to arrive on ~** llegar a la hora debida; **to be ahead of/behind ~** estar adelantado/en retraso; **scheduled flight** *n* vuelo regular
scheme [skiːm] *n* (*plan*) plan *m*, proyecto; (*plot*) intriga; (*arrangement*) disposición *f*; (*pension scheme etc*) sistema *m* ▷ *vi* (*intrigue*) intrigar
schizophrenic [skɪtzə'frɛnɪk] *adj* esquizofrénico
scholar ['skɔlə*] *n* (*pupil*) alumno/a; (*learned person*) sabio/a, erudito/a; **scholarship** *n* erudición *f*; (*grant*) beca
school [skuːl] *n* escuela, colegio; (*in university*) facultad *f* ▷ *cpd* escolar; **schoolbook** *n* libro de texto; **schoolboy** *n* alumno; **school children** *npl* alumnos *mpl*; **schoolgirl** *n* alumna; **schooling** *n* enseñanza; **schoolteacher** *n* (*primary*) maestro/a; (*secondary*) profesor(a) *m/f*
science ['saɪəns] *n* ciencia; **science**

fiction *n* ciencia-ficción *f*; **scientific** [-'tɪfɪk] *adj* científico; **scientist** *n* científico/a

sci-fi ['saɪfaɪ] *n abbr* (*inf*) = **science fiction**

scissors ['sɪzəz] *npl* tijeras *fpl*; **a pair of ~** unas tijeras

scold [skəuld] *vt* regañar

scone [skɔn] *n pastel de pan*

scoop [sku:p] *n* (*for flour etc*) pala; (*Press*) exclusiva

scooter ['sku:tə*] *n* moto *f*; (*toy*) patinete *m*

scope [skəup] *n* (*of plan*) ámbito; (*of person*) competencia; (*opportunity*) libertad *f* (de acción)

scorching ['skɔ:tʃɪŋ] *adj* (*heat, sun*) abrasador(a)

score [skɔ:*] *n* (*points etc*) puntuación *f*; (*Mus*) partitura; (*twenty*) veintena ▷ *vt* (*goal, point*) ganar; (*mark*) rayar; (*achieve: success*) conseguir ▷ *vi* marcar un tanto; (*Football*) marcar (un) gol; (*keep score*) llevar el tanteo; **~s of** (*lots of*) decenas de; **on that ~** en lo que se refiere a eso; **to ~ 6 out of 10** obtener una puntuación de 6 sobre 10; **score out** *vt* tachar; **scoreboard** *n* marcador *m*; **scorer** *n* marcador *m*; (*keeping score*) encargado/a del marcador

scorn [skɔ:n] *n* desprecio

Scorpio ['skɔ:pɪəu] *n* Escorpión *m*

scorpion ['skɔ:pɪən] *n* alacrán *m*

Scot [skɔt] *n* escocés/esa *m/f*

Scotch tape® (US) *n* cinta adhesiva, celo, scotch® *m*

Scotland ['skɔtlənd] *n* Escocia

Scots [skɔts] *adj* escocés/esa; **Scotsman** (*irreg*) *n* escocés; **Scotswoman** (*irreg*) *n* escocésa; **Scottish** ['skɔtɪʃ] *adj* escocés/esa; **Scottish Parliament** *n* Parlamento escocés

scout [skaut] *n* (*Mil: also:* **boy ~**) explorador *m*; **girl ~** (US) niña exploradora

scowl [skaul] *vi* fruncir el ceño; **to ~ at sb** mirar con ceño a algn

scramble ['skræmbl] *n* (*climb*) subida (difícil); (*struggle*) pelea ▷ *vi*: **to ~ through/out** abrirse paso/salir con dificultad; **to ~ for** pelear por; **scrambled eggs** *npl* huevos *mpl* revueltos

scrap [skræp] *n* (*bit*) pedacito; (*fig*) pizca; (*fight*) riña, bronca; (*also:* **~ iron**) chatarra, hierro viejo ▷ *vt* (*discard*) desechar, descartar ▷ *vi* reñir, armar una bronca; **scraps** *npl* (*waste*) sobras *fpl*, desperdicios *mpl*; **scrapbook** *n* álbum *m* de recortes

scrape [skreɪp] *n*: **to get into a ~** meterse en un lío ▷ *vt* raspar; (*skin etc*) rasguñar; (*scrape against*) rozar ▷ *vi*: **to ~ through** (*exam*) aprobar por los pelos; **scrap paper** *n* pedazos *mpl* de papel

scratch [skrætʃ] *n* rasguño; (*from claw*) arañazo ▷ *vt* (*paint, car*) rayar; (*with claw, nail*) rasguñar, arañar; (*rub: nose etc*) rascarse ▷ *vi* rascarse; **to start from ~** partir de cero; **to be up to ~** cumplir con los requisitos; **scratch card** *n* (BRIT) tarjeta *f* de "rasque y gane"

scream [skri:m] *n* chillido ▷ *vi* chillar

screen [skri:n] *n* (*Cinema, TV*) pantalla; (*movable barrier*) biombo ▷ *vt* (*conceal*) tapar; (*from the wind etc*) proteger; (*film*) proyectar; (*candidates etc*) investigar a; **screening** *n* (*Med*) investigación *f* médica; **screenplay** *n* guión *m*; **screen saver** *n* (*Comput*) protector *m* de pantalla

screw [skru:] *n* tornillo ▷ *vt* (*also:* **~ in**) atornillar; **screw up** *vt* (*paper etc*) arrugar; **to screw up one's eyes** arrugar el entrecejo; **screwdriver** *n* destornillador *m*

scribble ['skrɪbl] *n* garabatos *mpl* ▷ *vt, vi* garabatear

script [skrɪpt] *n* (*Cinema etc*) guión *m*; (*writing*) escritura, letra

scroll [skrəul] *n* rollo

scrub [skrʌb] *n* (*land*) maleza ▷ *vt* fregar, restregar; (*inf: reject*) cancelar, anular

scruffy ['skrʌfɪ] *adj* desaliñado, piojoso

scrum(mage) ['skrʌm(mɪdʒ)] *n* (*Rugby*) melée *f*

scrutiny ['skru:tɪnɪ] *n* escrutinio, examen *m*

scuba diving ['sku:bə'daɪvɪŋ] *n* submarinismo

sculptor ['skʌlptə*] *n* escultor(a) *m/f*

sculpture ['skʌlptʃə*] *n* escultura

scum [skʌm] *n* (*on liquid*) espuma; (*pej: people*) escoria

scurry ['skʌrɪ] *vi* correr; **to ~ off** escabullirse

sea [si:] *n* mar *m* ▷ *cpd* de mar, marítimo; **by ~** (*travel*) en barco; **on the ~** (*boat*) en el mar; (*town*) junto al mar; **to be all at ~** (*fig*) estar despistado; **out to ~**, **at ~** en alta mar; **seafood** *n* mariscos *mpl*; **sea front** *n* paseo marítimo; **seagull** *n* gaviota

seal [si:l] *n* (*animal*) foca; (*stamp*) sello ▷ *vt* (*close*) cerrar; **seal off** *vt* (*area*) acordonar

sea level *n* nivel *m* del mar

seam [si:m] *n* costura; (*of metal*) juntura; (*of coal*) veta, filón *m*

search [sə:tʃ] *n* (*for person, thing*) busca, búsqueda; (*Comput*) búsqueda; (*inspection: of sb's home*) registro ▷ *vt* (*look in*) buscar en; (*examine*) examinar; (*person, place*) registrar ▷ *vi*: **to ~ for** buscar; **in ~ of** en busca de; **search engine** *n* (*Comput*) buscador *m*;

search party *n* pelotón *m* de salvamento
sea: seashore *n* playa, orilla del mar; **seasick** *adj* mareado; **seaside** *n* playa, orilla del mar; **seaside resort** *n* centro turístico costero
season ['si:zn] *n* (*of year*) estación *f*; (*sporting etc*) temporada; (*of films etc*) ciclo ▷ *vt* (*food*) sazonar; **in/out of ~** en sazón/fuera de temporada; **seasonal** *adj* estacional; **seasoning** *n* condimento, aderezo; **season ticket** *n* abono
seat [si:t] *n* (*in bus, train*) asiento; (*chair*) silla; (*Parliament*) escaño; (*buttocks*) culo, trasero; (*of trousers*) culera ▷ *vt* sentar; (*have room for*) tener cabida para; **to be ~ed** sentarse; **seat belt** *n* cinturón *m* de seguridad; **seating** *n* asientos *mpl*
sea: sea water *n* agua del mar; **seaweed** *n* alga marina
sec. *abbr* = **second(s)**
secluded [si'klu:dɪd] *adj* retirado
second ['sɛkənd] *adj* segundo ▷ *adv* en segundo lugar ▷ *n* segundo; (*Aut: also:* **~ gear**) segunda; (*Comm*) artículo con algún desperfecto; (BRIT *Scol: degree*) *título de licenciado con calificación de notable* ▷ *vt* (*motion*) apoyar; **secondary** *adj* secundario; **secondary school** *n* escuela secundaria; **second-class** *adj* de segunda clase ▷ *adv* (*Rail*) en segunda; **secondhand** *adj* de segunda mano, usado; **secondly** *adv* en segundo lugar; **second-rate** *adj* de segunda categoría; **second thoughts**: **to have second thoughts** cambiar de opinión; **on second thoughts** *or* **thought** (US) pensándolo bien
secrecy ['si:krəsɪ] *n* secreto
secret ['si:krɪt] *adj, n* secreto; **in ~** en secreto
secretary ['sɛkrətərɪ] *n* secretario/a; **S~ of State (for)** (BRIT *Pol*) Ministro (de)
secretive ['si:krətɪv] *adj* reservado, sigiloso
secret service *n* servicio secreto
sect [sɛkt] *n* secta
section ['sɛkʃən] *n* sección *f*; (*part*) parte *f*; (*of document*) artículo; (*of opinion*) sector *m*; (*cross-section*) corte *m* transversal
sector ['sɛktə*] *n* sector *m*
secular ['sɛkjulə*] *adj* secular, seglar
secure [sɪ'kjuə*] *adj* seguro; (*firmly fixed*) firme, fijo ▷ *vt* (*fix*) asegurar, afianzar; (*get*) conseguir
security [sɪ'kjuərɪtɪ] *n* seguridad *f*; (*for loan*) fianza; (*: object*) prenda; **securities** *npl* (*Comm*) valores *mpl*, títulos *mpl*; **security guard** *n* guardia *m/f* de seguridad
sedan [sɪ'dæn] (US) *n* (*Aut*) sedán *m*
sedate [sɪ'deɪt] *adj* tranquilo ▷ *vt* tratar con sedantes
sedative ['sɛdɪtɪv] *n* sedante *m*, sedativo
seduce [sɪ'dju:s] *vt* seducir; **seductive** [-'dʌktɪv] *adj* seductor(a)
see [si:] (*pt* **saw**, *pp* **seen**) *vt* ver; (*accompany*): **to ~ sb to the door** acompañar a algn a la puerta; (*understand*) ver, comprender ▷ *vi* ver ▷ *n* (arz)obispado; **to ~ that** (*ensure*) asegurar que; **~ you soon!** ¡hasta pronto!; **see off** *vt* despedir; **see out** *vt* (*take to the door*) acompañar hasta la puerta; **see through** *vt fus* (*fig*) calar ▷ *vt* (*plan*) llevar a cabo; **see to** *vt fus* atender a, encargarse de
seed [si:d] *n* semilla; (*in fruit*) pepita; (*fig: gen pl*) germen *m*; (*Tennis etc*) preseleccionado/a; **to go to ~** (*plant*) granar; (*fig*) descuidarse
seeing ['si:ɪŋ] *conj*: **~ (that)** visto que, en vista de que
seek [si:k] (*pt, pp* **sought**) *vt* buscar; (*post*) solicitar
seem [si:m] *vi* parecer; **there ~s to be ...** parece que hay ...; **seemingly** *adv* aparentemente, según parece
seen [si:n] *pp of* **see**
seesaw ['si:sɔ:] *n* subibaja
segment ['sɛgmənt] *n* (*part*) sección *f*; (*of orange*) gajo
segregate ['sɛgrɪgeɪt] *vt* segregar
seize [si:z] *vt* (*grasp*) agarrar, asir; (*take possession of*) secuestrar; (*: territory*) apoderarse de; (*opportunity*) aprovecharse de
seizure ['si:ʒə*] *n* (*Med*) ataque *m*; (*Law, of power*) incautación *f*
seldom ['sɛldəm] *adv* rara vez
select [sɪ'lɛkt] *adj* selecto, escogido ▷ *vt* escoger, elegir; (*Sport*) seleccionar; **selection** *n* selección *f*, elección *f*; (*Comm*) surtido; **selective** *adj* selectivo
self [sɛlf] (*pl* **selves**) *n* uno mismo; **the ~** el yo ▷ *prefix* auto...; **self-assured** *adj* seguro de sí mismo; **self-catering** (BRIT) *adj* (*flat etc*) con cocina; **self-centred** (US **self-centered**) *adj* egocéntrico; **self-confidence** *n* confianza en sí mismo; **self-confident** *adj* seguro de sí (mismo), lleno de confianza en sí mismo; **self-conscious** *adj* cohibido; **self-contained** (BRIT) *adj* (*flat*) con entrada particular; **self-control** *n* autodominio; **self-defence** (US **self-defense**) *n* defensa propia; **self-drive** *adj* (BRIT) sin chofer *or* (SP) chófer; **self-employed** *adj* que trabaja por cuenta propia; **self-esteem** *n* amor *m* propio; **self-indulgent** *adj* autocomplaciente; **self-interest** *n* egoísmo; **selfish** *adj*

S

egoísta; **self-pity** *n* lástima de sí mismo; **self-raising** [sɛlfˈreɪzɪŋ] (*US* **self-rising**) *adj*: **self-raising flour** harina con levadura; **self-respect** *n* amor *m* propio; **self-service** *adj* de autoservicio

sell [sɛl] (*pt, pp* **sold**) *vt* vender ▷ *vi* venderse; **to ~ at** *or* **for £10** venderse a 10 libras; **sell off** *vt* liquidar; **sell out** *vi*: **to sell out of tickets/milk** vender todas las entradas/toda la leche; **sell-by date** *n* fecha de caducidad; **seller** *n* vendedor(a) *m/f*

Sellotape® [ˈsɛləuteɪp] (*BRIT*) *n* celo (*SP*), cinta Scotch® (*LAM*) *or* Dúrex® (*MEX, ARG*)

selves [sɛlvz] *npl of* **self**

semester [sɪˈmɛstə*] (*US*) *n* semestre *m*

semi... [sɛmɪ] *prefix* semi..., medio...; **semicircle** *n* semicírculo; **semidetached (house)** *n* (casa) semiseparada; **semi-final** *n* semi-final *m*

seminar [ˈsɛmɪnɑː*] *n* seminario

semi-skimmed [sɛmɪˈskɪmd] *adj* semidesnatado; **semi-skimmed (milk)** *n* leche semidesnatada

senate [ˈsɛnɪt] *n* senado; **the S~** (*US*) el Senado; **senator** *n* senador(a) *m/f*

send [sɛnd] (*pt, pp* **sent**) *vt* mandar, enviar; (*signal*) transmitir; **send back** *vt* devolver; **send for** *vt fus* mandar traer; **send in** *vt* (*report, application, resignation*) mandar; **send off** *vt* (*goods*) despachar; (*BRIT Sport: player*) expulsar; **send on** *vt* (*letter, luggage*) remitir; (*person*) mandar; **send out** *vt* (*invitation*) mandar; (*signal*) emitir; **send up** *vt* (*person, price*) hacer subir; (*BRIT: parody*) parodiar; **sender** *n* remitente *mf*; **send-off** *n*: **a good send-off** una buena despedida

senile [ˈsiːnaɪl] *adj* senil

senior [ˈsiːnɪə*] *adj* (*older*) mayor, más viejo; (*: on staff*) de más antigüedad; (*of higher rank*) superior; **senior citizen** *n* persona de la tercera edad; **senior high school** (*US*) *n* ≈ instituto de enseñanza media; *see also* **high school**

sensation [sɛnˈseɪʃən] *n* sensación *f*; **sensational** *adj* sensacional

sense [sɛns] *n* (*faculty, meaning*) sentido; (*feeling*) sensación *f*; (*good sense*) sentido común, juicio ▷ *vt* sentir, percibir; **it makes ~** tiene sentido; **senseless** *adj* estúpido, insensato; (*unconscious*) sin conocimiento; **sense of humour** (*BRIT*) *n* sentido del humor

sensible [ˈsɛnsɪbl] *adj* sensato; (*reasonable*) razonable, lógico

Be careful not to translate **sensible** by the Spanish word *sensible*.

sensitive [ˈsɛnsɪtɪv] *adj* sensible; (*touchy*) susceptible

sensual [ˈsɛnsjuəl] *adj* sensual

sensuous [ˈsɛnsjuəs] *adj* sensual

sent [sɛnt] *pt, pp of* **send**

sentence [ˈsɛntns] *n* (*Ling*) oración *f*; (*Law*) sentencia, fallo ▷ *vt*: **to ~ sb to death/ to 5 years (in prison)** condenar a algn a muerte/a 5 años de cárcel

sentiment [ˈsɛntɪmənt] *n* sentimiento; (*opinion*) opinión *f*; **sentimental** [-ˈmɛntl] *adj* sentimental

Sep. *abbr* (= *September*) sep., set.

separate [*adj* ˈsɛprɪt, *vb* ˈsɛpəreɪt] *adj* separado; (*distinct*) distinto ▷ *vt* separar; (*part*) dividir ▷ *vi* separarse; **separately** *adv* por separado; **separates** *npl* (*clothes*) coordinados *mpl*; **separation** [-ˈreɪʃən] *n* separación *f*

September [sɛpˈtɛmbə*] *n* se(p)tiembre *m*

septic [ˈsɛptɪk] *adj* séptico; **septic tank** *n* fosa séptica

sequel [ˈsiːkwl] *n* consecuencia, resultado; (*of story*) continuación *f*

sequence [ˈsiːkwəns] *n* sucesión *f*, serie *f*; (*Cinema*) secuencia

sequin [ˈsiːkwɪn] *n* lentejuela

Serb [səːb] *adj, n* = **Serbian**

Serbian [ˈsəːbɪən] *adj* serbio ▷ *n* serbio/a; (*Ling*) serbio

sergeant [ˈsɑːdʒənt] *n* sargento

serial [ˈsɪərɪəl] *n* (*TV*) telenovela, serie *f* televisiva; (*Book*) serie *f*; **serial killer** *n* asesino/a múltiple; **serial number** *n* número de serie

series [ˈsɪəriːs] *n inv* serie *f*

serious [ˈsɪərɪəs] *adj* serio; (*grave*) grave; **seriously** *adv* en serio; (*ill, wounded etc*) gravemente

sermon [ˈsəːmən] *n* sermón *m*

servant [ˈsəːvənt] *n* servidor(a) *m/f*; (*house servant*) criado/a

serve [səːv] *vt* servir; (*customer*) atender; (*train*) pasar por; (*apprenticeship*) hacer; (*prison term*) cumplir ▷ *vi* (*at table*) servir; (*Tennis*) sacar; **to ~ as/for/to do** servir de/ para/para hacer ▷ *n* (*Tennis*) saque *m*; **it ~s him right** se lo tiene merecido; **server** *n* (*Comput*) servidor *m*

service [ˈsəːvɪs] *n* servicio; (*Rel*) misa; (*Aut*) mantenimiento; (*dishes etc*) juego ▷ *vt* (*car etc*) revisar; (*: repair*) reparar; **to be of ~ to sb** ser útil a algn; **~ included/not included** servicio incluido/no incluido (*Econ: tertiary sector*) sector *m* terciario *or* (de) servicios; (*BRIT: on motorway*) área de servicio; (*Mil*): **the S~s** las fuerzas armadas; **service area** *n* (*on motorway*) área de servicio; **service charge** (BRIT) *n* servicio; **serviceman** (*irreg*) *n* militar *m*; **service station** *n* estación *f* de servicio

serviette [sə:vɪ'ɛt] (BRIT) *n* servilleta

session ['sɛʃən] *n* sesión *f*; **to be in ~** estar en sesión

set [sɛt] (*pt, pp* **~**) *n* juego; (*Radio*) aparato; (*TV*) televisor *m*; (*of utensils*) batería; (*of cutlery*) cubierto; (*of books*) colección *f*; (*Tennis*) set *m*; (*group of people*) grupo; (*Cinema*) plató *m*; (*Theatre*) decorado; (*Hairdressing*) marcado ▷ *adj* (*fixed*) fijo; (*ready*) listo ▷ *vt* (*place*) poner, colocar; (*fix*) fijar; (*adjust*) ajustar, arreglar; (*decide*: *rules etc*) establecer, decidir ▷ *vi* (*sun*) ponerse; (*jam, jelly*) cuajarse; (*concrete*) fraguar; (*bone*) componerse; **to be ~ on doing sth** estar empeñado en hacer algo; **to ~ to music** poner música a; **to ~ on fire** incendiar, poner fuego a; **to ~ free** poner en libertad; **to ~ sth going** poner algo en marcha; **to ~ sail** zarpar, hacerse a la vela; **set aside** *vt* poner aparte, dejar de lado; (*money, time*) reservar; **set down** *vt* (*bus, train*) dejar; **set in** *vi* (*infection*) declararse; (*complications*) comenzar; **the rain has set in for the day** parece que va a llover todo el día; **set off** *vi* partir ▷ *vt* (*bomb*) hacer estallar; (*events*) poner en marcha; (*show up well*) hacer resaltar; **set out** *vi* partir ▷ *vt* (*arrange*) disponer; (*state*) exponer; **to set out to do sth** proponerse hacer algo; **set up** *vt* establecer; **setback** *n* revés *m*, contratiempo; **set menu** *n* menú *m*

settee [sɛ'ti:] *n* sofá *m*

setting ['sɛtɪŋ] *n* (*scenery*) marco; (*position*) disposición *f*; (*of sun*) puesta; (*of jewel*) engaste *m*, montadura

settle ['sɛtl] *vt* (*argument*) resolver; (*accounts*) ajustar, liquidar; (*Med*: *calm*) calmar, sosegar ▷ *vi* (*dust etc*) depositarse; (*weather*) serenarse; **to ~ for sth** convenir en aceptar algo; **to ~ on sth** decidirse por algo; **settle down** *vi* (*get comfortable*) ponerse cómodo, acomodarse; (*calm down*) calmarse, tranquilizarse; (*live quietly*) echar raíces; **settle in** *vi* instalarse; **settle up** *vi*: **to settle up with sb** ajustar cuentas con algn; **settlement** *n* (*payment*) liquidación *f*; (*agreement*) acuerdo, convenio; (*village etc*) pueblo

setup ['sɛtʌp] *n* sistema *m*; (*situation*) situación *f*

seven ['sɛvn] *num* siete; **seventeen** *num* diez y siete, diecisiete; **seventeenth** [sevn'ti:nθ] *adj* decimoséptimo; **seventh** *num* séptimo; **seventieth** ['sevntɪɪθ] *adj* septuagésimo; **seventy** *num* setenta

sever ['sɛvə*] *vt* cortar; (*relations*) romper

several ['sɛvərl] *adj, pron* varios/as *m/fpl*, algunos/as *m/fpl*; **~ of us** varios de nosotros

severe [sɪ'vɪə*] *adj* severo; (*serious*) grave; (*hard*) duro; (*pain*) intenso

sew [səu] (*pt* **~ed**, *pp* **~n**) *vt, vi* coser

sewage ['su:ɪdʒ] *n* aguas *fpl* residuales

sewer ['su:ə*] *n* alcantarilla, cloaca

sewing ['səuɪŋ] *n* costura; **sewing machine** *n* máquina de coser

sewn [səun] *pp of* **sew**

sex [sɛks] *n* sexo; (*lovemaking*): **to have ~** hacer el amor; **sexism** ['sɛksɪzəm] *n* sexismo; **sexist** *adj, n* sexista *mf*; **sexual** ['sɛksjuəl] *adj* sexual; **sexual intercourse** *n* relaciones *fpl* sexuales; **sexuality** [seksju'ælɪtɪ] *n* sexualidad *f*; **sexy** *adj* sexy

shabby ['ʃæbɪ] *adj* (*person*) desharrapado; (*clothes*) raído, gastado; (*behaviour*) ruin *inv*

shack [ʃæk] *n* choza, chabola

shade [ʃeɪd] *n* sombra; (*for lamp*) pantalla; (*for eyes*) visera; (*of colour*) matiz *m*, tonalidad *f*; (*small quantity*): **a ~ (too big/more)** un poquitín (grande/más) ▷ *vt* dar sombra a; (*eyes*) proteger del sol; **in the ~** en la sombra; **shades** *npl* (*sunglasses*) gafas *fpl* de sol

shadow ['ʃædəu] *n* sombra ▷ *vt* (*follow*) seguir y vigilar; **shadow cabinet** (BRIT) *n* (*Pol*) *gabinete paralelo formado por el partido de oposición*

shady ['ʃeɪdɪ] *adj* sombreado; (*fig*: *dishonest*) sospechoso; (: *deal*) turbio

shaft [ʃɑ:ft] *n* (*of arrow, spear*) astil *m*; (*Aut, Tech*) eje *m*, árbol *m*; (*of mine*) pozo; (*of lift*) hueco, caja; (*of light*) rayo

shake [ʃeɪk] (*pt* **shook**, *pp* **shaken**) *vt* sacudir; (*building*) hacer temblar; (*bottle, cocktail*) agitar ▷ *vi* (*tremble*) temblar; **to ~ one's head** (*in refusal*) negar con la cabeza; (*in dismay*) mover *or* menear la cabeza, incrédulo; **to ~ hands with sb** estrechar la mano a algn; **shake off** *vt* sacudirse; (*fig*) deshacerse de; **shake up** *vt* agitar; (*fig*) reorganizar; **shaky** *adj* (*hand, voice*) trémulo; (*building*) inestable

shall [ʃæl] *aux vb*: **~ I help you?** ¿quieres que te ayude?; **I'll buy three, ~ I?** compro tres, ¿no te parece?

shallow ['ʃæləu] *adj* poco profundo; (*fig*) superficial

sham [ʃæm] *n* fraude *m*, engaño

shambles ['ʃæmblz] *n* confusión *f*

shame [ʃeɪm] *n* vergüenza ▷ *vt* avergonzar; **it is a ~ that/to do** es una lástima que/hacer; **what a ~!** ¡qué lástima!; **shameful** *adj* vergonzoso; **shameless** *adj* desvergonzado

shampoo [ʃæm'pu:] *n* champú *m* ▷ *vt*

lavar con champú
shandy ['ʃændɪ] *n mezcla de cerveza con gaseosa*
shan't [ʃɑ:nt] = **shall not**
shape [ʃeɪp] *n* forma ▷*vt* formar, dar forma a; (*sb's ideas*) formar; (*sb's life*) determinar; **to take ~** tomar forma
share [ʃɛə*] *n* (*part*) parte *f*, porción *f*; (*contribution*) cuota; (*Comm*) acción *f* ▷*vt* dividir; (*have in common*) compartir; **to ~ out (among** *or* **between)** repartir (entre); **shareholder** (BRIT) *n* accionista *mf*
shark [ʃɑ:k] *n* tiburón *m*
sharp [ʃɑ:p] *adj* (*blade, nose*) afilado; (*point*) puntiagudo; (*outline*) definido; (*pain*) intenso; (*Mus*) desafinado; (*contrast*) marcado; (*voice*) agudo; (*person*: *quick-witted*) astuto; (: *dishonest*) poco escrupuloso ▷*n* (*Mus*) sostenido ▷*adv*: **at 2 o'clock ~** a las 2 en punto; **sharpen** *vt* afilar; (*pencil*) sacar punta a; (*fig*) agudizar; **sharpener** *n* (*also*: **pencil sharpener**) sacapuntas *m inv*; **sharply** *adv* (*turn, stop*) bruscamente; (*stand out, contrast*) claramente; (*criticize, retort*) severamente
shatter ['ʃætə*] *vt* hacer añicos *or* pedazos; (*fig*: *ruin*) destruir, acabar con ▷*vi* hacerse añicos; **shattered** *adj* (*grief-stricken*) destrozado, deshecho; (*exhausted*) agotado, hecho polvo
shave [ʃeɪv] *vt* afeitar, rasurar ▷*vi* afeitarse, rasurarse ▷*n*: **to have a ~** afeitarse; **shaver** *n* (*also*: **electric shaver**) máquina de afeitar (eléctrica)
shavings ['ʃeɪvɪŋz] *npl* (*of wood etc*) virutas *fpl*
shaving cream ['ʃeɪvɪŋ-] *n* crema de afeitar
shaving foam *n* espuma de afeitar
shawl [ʃɔ:l] *n* chal *m*
she [ʃi:] *pron* ella
sheath [ʃi:θ] *n* vaina; (*contraceptive*) preservativo
shed [ʃɛd] (*pt, pp* **~**) *n* cobertizo ▷*vt* (*skin*) mudar; (*tears, blood*) derramar; (*load*) derramar; (*workers*) despedir
she'd [ʃi:d] = **she had; she would**
sheep [ʃi:p] *n inv* oveja; **sheepdog** *n* perro pastor; **sheepskin** *n* piel *f* de carnero
sheer [ʃɪə*] *adj* (*utter*) puro, completo; (*steep*) escarpado; (*material*) diáfano ▷*adv* verticalmente
sheet [ʃi:t] *n* (*on bed*) sábana; (*of paper*) hoja; (*of glass, metal*) lámina; (*of ice*) capa
sheik(h) [ʃeɪk] *n* jeque *m*
shelf [ʃɛlf] (*pl* **shelves**) *n* estante *m*
shell [ʃɛl] *n* (*on beach*) concha; (*of egg, nut etc*) cáscara; (*explosive*) proyectil *m*, obús *m*; (*of building*) armazón *f* ▷*vt* (*peas*) desenvainar; (*Mil*) bombardear
she'll [ʃi:l] = **she will; she shall**
shellfish ['ʃɛlfɪʃ] *n inv* crustáceo; (*as food*) mariscos *mpl*
shelter ['ʃɛltə*] *n* abrigo, refugio ▷*vt* (*aid*) amparar, proteger; (*give lodging to*) abrigar ▷*vi* abrigarse, refugiarse; **sheltered** *adj* (*life*) protegido; (*spot*) abrigado
shelves [ʃɛlvz] *npl of* **shelf**
shelving ['ʃɛlvɪŋ] *n* estantería
shepherd ['ʃɛpəd] *n* pastor *m* ▷*vt* (*guide*) guiar, conducir; **shepherd's pie** (BRIT) *n pastel de carne y patatas*
sheriff ['ʃɛrɪf] (US) *n* sheriff *m*
sherry ['ʃɛrɪ] *n* jerez *m*
she's [ʃi:z] = **she is; she has**
Shetland ['ʃɛtlənd] *n* (*also*: **the ~s, the ~ Isles**) las Islas de Zetlandia
shield [ʃi:ld] *n* escudo; (*protection*) blindaje *m* ▷*vt*: **to ~ (from)** proteger (de)
shift [ʃɪft] *n* (*change*) cambio; (*at work*) turno ▷*vt* trasladar; (*remove*) quitar ▷*vi* moverse
shin [ʃɪn] *n* espinilla
shine [ʃaɪn] (*pt, pp* **shone**) *n* brillo, lustre *m* ▷*vi* brillar, relucir ▷*vt* (*shoes*) lustrar, sacar brillo a; **to ~ a torch on sth** dirigir una linterna hacia algo
shingles ['ʃɪŋglz] *n* (*Med*) herpes *mpl or fpl*
shiny ['ʃaɪnɪ] *adj* brillante, lustroso
ship [ʃɪp] *n* buque *m*, barco ▷*vt* (*goods*) embarcar; (*send*) transportar *or* enviar por vía marítima; **shipment** *n* (*goods*) envío; **shipping** *n* (*act*) embarque *m*; (*traffic*) buques *mpl*; **shipwreck** *n* naufragio ▷*vt*: **to be shipwrecked** naufragar; **shipyard** *n* astillero
shirt [ʃə:t] *n* camisa; **in (one's) ~ sleeves** en mangas de camisa
shit [ʃɪt] (*inf!*) *excl* ¡mierda! (*!*)
shiver ['ʃɪvə*] *n* escalofrío ▷*vi* temblar, estremecerse; (*with cold*) tiritar
shock [ʃɔk] *n* (*impact*) choque *m*; (*Elec*) descarga (eléctrica); (*emotional*) conmoción *f*; (*start*) sobresalto, susto; (*Med*) postración *f* nerviosa ▷*vt* dar un susto a; (*offend*) escandalizar; **shocking** *adj* (*awful*) espantoso; (*outrageous*) escandaloso
shoe [ʃu:] (*pt, pp* **shod**) *n* zapato; (*for horse*) herradura ▷*vt* (*horse*) herrar; **shoelace** *n* cordón *m*; **shoe polish** *n* betún *m*; **shoeshop** *n* zapatería
shone [ʃɔn] *pt, pp of* **shine**
shook [ʃuk] *pt of* **shake**
shoot [ʃu:t] (*pt, pp* **shot**) *n* (*on branch, seedling*) retoño, vástago ▷*vt* disparar; (*kill*) matar a tiros; (*wound*) pegar un tiro; (*execute*)

fusilar; (*film*) rodar, filmar ▷ *vi* (*Football*) chutar; **shoot down** *vt* (*plane*) derribar; **shoot up** *vi* (*prices*) dispararse; **shooting** *n* (*shots*) tiros *mpl*; (*Hunting*) caza con escopeta

shop [ʃɔp] *n* tienda; (*workshop*) taller *m* ▷ *vi* (*also*: **go ~ping**) ir de compras; **shop assistant** (BRIT) *n* dependiente/a *m/f*; **shopkeeper** *n* tendero/a; **shoplifting** *n* mechería; **shopping** *n* (*goods*) compras *fpl*; **shopping bag** *n* bolsa (de compras); **shopping centre** (US **shopping center**) *n* centro comercial; **shopping mall** *n* centro comercial; **shopping trolley** *n* (BRIT) carrito de la compra; **shop window** *n* escaparate *m* (SP), vidriera (LAM)

shore [ʃɔː*] *n* orilla ▷ *vt*: **to ~ (up)** reforzar; **on ~** en tierra

short [ʃɔːt] *adj* corto; (*in time*) breve, de corta duración; (*person*) bajo; (*curt*) brusco, seco; (*insufficient*) insuficiente; **(a pair of) ~s** (unos) pantalones *mpl* cortos; **to be ~ of sth** estar falto de algo; **in ~** en pocas palabras; **~ of doing ...** fuera de hacer ...; **it is ~ for** es la forma abreviada de; **to cut ~** (*speech, visit*) interrumpir, terminar inesperadamente; **everything ~ of ...** todo menos ...; **to fall ~ of** no alcanzar; **to run ~ of** quedarle a algn poco; **to stop ~** parar en seco; **to stop ~ of** detenerse antes de; **shortage** *n*: **a shortage of** una falta de; **shortbread** *n especie de mantecada*; **shortcoming** *n* defecto, deficiencia; **short(crust) pastry** (BRIT) *n* pasta quebradiza; **shortcut** *n* atajo; **shorten** *vt* acortar; (*visit*) interrumpir; **shortfall** *n* déficit *m*; **shorthand** (BRIT) *n* taquigrafía; **short-lived** *adj* efímero; **shortly** *adv* en breve, dentro de poco; **shorts** *npl* pantalones *mpl* cortos; (US) calzoncillos *mpl*; **short-sighted** (BRIT) *adj* miope; (*fig*) imprudente; **short-sleeved** *adj* de manga corta; **short story** *n* cuento; **short-tempered** *adj* enojadizo; **short-term** *adj* (*effect*) a corto plazo

shot [ʃɔt] *pt, pp of* **shoot** ▷ *n* (*sound*) tiro, disparo; (*try*) tentativa; (*injection*) inyección *f*; (*Phot*) toma, fotografía; **to be a good/poor ~** (*person*) tener buena/mala puntería; **like a ~** (*without any delay*) como un rayo; **shotgun** *n* escopeta

should [ʃud] *aux vb*: **I ~ go now** debo irme ahora; **he ~ be there now** debe de haber llegado (ya); **I ~ go if I were you** yo en tu lugar me iría; **I ~ like to** me gustaría

shoulder [ˈʃəuldə*] *n* hombro ▷ *vt* (*fig*) cargar con; **shoulder blade** *n* omóplato

shouldn't [ˈʃudnt] = **should not**

shout [ʃaut] *n* grito ▷ *vt* gritar ▷ *vi* gritar, dar voces

shove [ʃʌv] *n* empujón *m* ▷ *vt* empujar; (*inf*: *put*): **to ~ sth in** meter algo a empellones

shovel [ˈʃʌvl] *n* pala; (*mechanical*) excavadora ▷ *vt* mover con pala

show [ʃəu] (*pt* **~ed**, *pp* **~n**) *n* (*of emotion*) demostración *f*; (*semblance*) apariencia; (*exhibition*) exposición *f*; (*Theatre*) función *f*, espectáculo; (*TV*) show *m* ▷ *vt* mostrar, enseñar; (*courage etc*) mostrar, manifestar; (*exhibit*) exponer; (*film*) proyectar ▷ *vi* mostrarse; (*appear*) aparecer; **for ~** para impresionar; **on ~** (*exhibits etc*) expuesto; **show in** *vt* (*person*) hacer pasar; **show off** (*pej*) *vi* presumir ▷ *vt* (*display*) lucir; **show out** *vt*: **to show sb out** acompañar a algn a la puerta; **show up** *vi* (*stand out*) destacar; (*inf*: *turn up*) aparecer ▷ *vt* (*unmask*) desenmascarar; **show business** *n* mundo del espectáculo

shower [ˈʃauə*] *n* (*rain*) chaparrón *m*, chubasco; (*of stones etc*) lluvia; (*for bathing*) ducha, regadera (MEX) ▷ *vi* llover ▷ *vt* (*fig*): **to ~ sb with sth** colmar a algn de algo; **to have a ~** ducharse; **shower cap** *n* gorro de baño; **shower gel** *n* gel *m* de ducha

showing [ˈʃəuɪŋ] *n* (*of film*) proyección *f*

show jumping *n* hípica

shown [ʃəun] *pp of* **show**

show: show-off (*inf*) *n* (*person*) presumido/a; **showroom** *n* sala de muestras

shrank [ʃræŋk] *pt of* **shrink**

shred [ʃrɛd] *n* (*gen pl*) triza, jirón *m* ▷ *vt* hacer trizas; (*Culin*) desmenuzar

shrewd [ʃruːd] *adj* astuto

shriek [ʃriːk] *n* chillido ▷ *vi* chillar

shrimp [ʃrɪmp] *n* camarón *m*

shrine [ʃraɪn] *n* santuario, sepulcro

shrink [ʃrɪŋk] (*pt* **shrank**, *pp* **shrunk**) *vi* encogerse; (*be reduced*) reducirse; (*also*: **~ away**) retroceder ▷ *vt* encoger ▷ *n* (*inf, pej*) loquero/a; **to ~ from (doing) sth** no atreverse a hacer algo

shrivel [ˈʃrɪvl] (*also*: **~ up**) *vt* (*dry*) secar ▷ *vi* secarse

shroud [ʃraud] *n* sudario ▷ *vt*: **~ed in mystery** envuelto en el misterio

Shrove Tuesday [ˈʃrəuv-] *n* martes *m* de carnaval

shrub [ʃrʌb] *n* arbusto

shrug [ʃrʌg] *n* encogimiento de hombros ▷ *vt, vi*: **to ~ (one's shoulders)** encogerse de hombros; **shrug off** *vt* negar importancia a

shrunk [ʃrʌŋk] *pp of* **shrink**

shudder [ˈʃʌdə*] *n* estremecimiento, escalofrío ▷ *vi* estremecerse

shuffle [ˈʃʌfl] *vt* (*cards*) barajar ▷ *vi*: **to ~**

S

(one's feet) arrastrar los pies
shun [ʃʌn] *vt* rehuir, esquivar
shut [ʃʌt] (*pt, pp* ~) *vt* cerrar ▷*vi* cerrarse; **shut down** *vt, vi* cerrar; **shut up** *vi* (*inf*: *keep quiet*) callarse ▷*vt* (*close*) cerrar; (*silence*) hacer callar; **shutter** *n* contraventana; (*Phot*) obturador *m*
shuttle ['ʃʌtl] *n* lanzadera; (*also*: **~ service**) servicio rápido y continuo entre dos puntos; (*Aviat*) puente *m* aéreo; **shuttlecock** *n* volante *m*
shy [ʃaɪ] *adj* tímido
sibling ['sɪblɪŋ] *n* (*formal*) hermano/a
Sicily ['sɪsɪlɪ] *n* Sicilia
sick [sɪk] *adj* (*ill*) enfermo; (*nauseated*) mareado; (*humour*) negro; (*vomiting*): **to be ~** (BRIT) vomitar; **to feel ~** tener náuseas; **to be ~ of** (*fig*) estar harto de; **sickening** *adj* (*fig*) asqueroso; **sick leave** *n* baja por enfermedad; **sickly** *adj* enfermizo; (*smell*) nauseabundo; **sickness** *n* enfermedad *f*, mal *m*; (*vomiting*) náuseas *fpl*
side [saɪd] *n* (*gen*) lado; (*of body*) costado; (*of lake*) orilla; (*of hill*) ladera; (*team*) equipo ▷*adj* (*door, entrance*) lateral ▷*vi*: **to ~ with sb** tomar el partido de algn; **by the ~ of** al lado de; **~ by ~** juntos/as; **from ~ to ~** de un lado para otro; **from all ~s** de todos lados; **to take ~s (with)** tomar partido (con); **sideboard** *n* aparador *m*; **sideboards** (BRIT) *npl* = **sideburns**; **sideburns** *npl* patillas *fpl*; **sidelight** *n* (*Aut*) luz *f* lateral; **sideline** *n* (*Sport*) línea de banda; (*fig*) empleo suplementario; **side order** *n* *plato de acompañamiento*; **side road** *n* (BRIT) calle *f* lateral; **side street** *n* calle *f* lateral; **sidetrack** *vt* (*fig*) desviar (de su propósito); **sidewalk** (US) *n* acera; **sideways** *adv* de lado
siege [si:dʒ] *n* cerco, sitio
sieve [sɪv] *n* colador *m* ▷*vt* cribar
sift [sɪft] *vt* cribar; (*fig*: *information*) escudriñar
sigh [saɪ] *n* suspiro ▷*vi* suspirar
sight [saɪt] *n* (*faculty*) vista; (*spectacle*) espectáculo; (*on gun*) mira, alza ▷*vt* divisar; **in ~** a la vista; **out of ~** fuera de (la) vista; **on ~** (*shoot*) sin previo aviso; **sightseeing** *n* excursionismo, turismo; **to go sightseeing** hacer turismo
sign [saɪn] *n* (*with hand*) señal *f*, seña; (*trace*) huella, rastro; (*notice*) letrero; (*written*) signo ▷*vt* firmar; (*Sport*) fichar; **to ~ sth over to sb** firmar el traspaso de algo a algn; **sign for** *vt fus* (*item*) firmar el recibo de; **sign in** *vi* firmar el registro (al entrar); **sign on** *vi* (BRIT: *as unemployed*) registrarse como desempleado; (*for course*) inscribirse ▷*vt* (*Mil*) alistar; (*employee*) contratar; **sign up** *vi* (*Mil*) alistarse; (*for course*) inscribirse ▷*vt* (*player*) fichar
signal ['sɪgnl] *n* señal *f* ▷*vi* señalizar ▷*vt* (*person*) hacer señas a; (*message*) comunicar por señales
signature ['sɪgnətʃə*] *n* firma
significance [sɪg'nɪfɪkəns] *n* (*importance*) trascendencia
significant [sɪg'nɪfɪkənt] *adj* significativo; (*important*) trascendente
signify ['sɪgnɪfaɪ] *vt* significar
sign language *n* lenguaje *m* para sordomudos
signpost ['saɪnpəust] *n* indicador *m*
Sikh [si:k] *adj, n* sij *mf*
silence ['saɪlns] *n* silencio ▷*vt* acallar; (*guns*) reducir al silencio
silent ['saɪlnt] *adj* silencioso; (*not speaking*) callado; (*film*) mudo; **to remain ~** guardar silencio
silhouette [sɪlu:'ɛt] *n* silueta
silicon chip ['sɪlɪkən-] *n* plaqueta de silicio
silk [sɪlk] *n* seda ▷*adj* de seda
silly ['sɪlɪ] *adj* (*person*) tonto; (*idea*) absurdo
silver ['sɪlvə*] *n* plata; (*money*) moneda suelta ▷*adj* de plata; (*colour*) plateado; **silver-plated** *adj* plateado
similar ['sɪmɪlə*] *adj*: **~ (to)** parecido *or* semejante (a); **similarity** [-'lærɪtɪ] *n* semejanza; **similarly** *adv* del mismo modo
simmer ['sɪmə*] *vi* hervir a fuego lento
simple ['sɪmpl] *adj* (*easy*) sencillo; (*foolish, Comm*: *interest*) simple; **simplicity** [-'plɪsɪtɪ] *n* sencillez *f*; **simplify** ['sɪmplɪfaɪ] *vt* simplificar; **simply** *adv* (*live, talk*) sencillamente; (*just, merely*) sólo
simulate ['sɪmju:leɪt] *vt* fingir, simular
simultaneous [sɪməl'teɪnɪəs] *adj* simultáneo; **simultaneously** *adv* simultáneamente
sin [sɪn] *n* pecado ▷*vi* pecar
since [sɪns] *adv* desde entonces, después ▷*prep* desde ▷*conj* (*time*) desde que; (*because*) ya que, puesto que; **~ then, ever ~** desde entonces
sincere [sɪn'sɪə*] *adj* sincero; **sincerely** *adv*: **yours sincerely** (*in letters*) le saluda atentamente
sing [sɪŋ] (*pt* **sang**, *pp* **sung**) *vt, vi* cantar
Singapore [sɪŋə'pɔ:*] *n* Singapur *m*
singer ['sɪŋə*] *n* cantante *mf*
singing ['sɪŋɪŋ] *n* canto
single ['sɪŋgl] *adj* único, solo; (*unmarried*) soltero; (*not double*) simple, sencillo ▷*n* (BRIT: *also*: **~ ticket**) billete *m* sencillo; (*record*) sencillo, single *m*; **singles** *npl*

(*Tennis*) individual *m*; **single out** *vt* (*choose*) escoger; **single bed** *n* cama individual; **single file** *n*: **in single file** en fila de uno; **single-handed** *adv* sin ayuda; **single-minded** *adj* resuelto, firme; **single parent** *n* padre *m* soltero, madre *f* soltera (*o divorciado etc*); **single parent family** familia monoparental; **single room** *n* cuarto individual

singular ['sɪŋgjulə*] *adj* (*odd*) raro, extraño; (*outstanding*) excepcional ▷ *n* (*Ling*) singular *m*

sinister ['sɪnɪstə*] *adj* siniestro

sink [sɪŋk] (*pt* **sank**, *pp* **sunk**) *n* fregadero ▷ *vt* (*ship*) hundir, echar a pique; (*foundations*) excavar ▷ *vi* hundirse; **to ~ sth into** hundir algo en; **sink in** *vi* (*fig*) penetrar, calar

sinus ['saɪnəs] *n* (*Anat*) seno

sip [sɪp] *n* sorbo ▷ *vt* sorber, beber a sorbitos

sir [sə*] *n* señor *m*; **S~ John Smith** Sir John Smith; **yes ~** sí, señor

siren ['saɪərn] *n* sirena

sirloin ['sə:lɔɪn] *n* (*also*: **~ steak**) solomillo

sister ['sɪstə*] *n* hermana; (BRIT: *nurse*) enfermera jefe; **sister-in-law** *n* cuñada

sit [sɪt] (*pt*, *pp* **sat**) *vi* sentarse; (*be sitting*) estar sentado; (*assembly*) reunirse; (*for painter*) posar ▷ *vt* (*exam*) presentarse a; **sit back** *vi* (*in seat*) recostarse; **sit down** *vi* sentarse; **sit on** *vt fus* (*jury, committee*) ser miembro de, formar parte de; **sit up** *vi* incorporarse; (*not go to bed*) velar

sitcom ['sɪtkɔm] *n abbr* (= *situation comedy*) comedia de situación

site [saɪt] *n* sitio; (*also*: **building ~**) solar *m* ▷ *vt* situar

sitting ['sɪtɪŋ] *n* (*of assembly etc*) sesión *f*; (*in canteen*) turno; **sitting room** *n* sala de estar

situated ['sɪtjueɪtɪd] *adj* situado

situation [sɪtju'eɪʃən] *n* situación *f*; **"~s vacant"** (BRIT) "ofrecen trabajo"

six [sɪks] *num* seis; **sixteen** *num* diez y seis, dieciséis; **sixteenth** [sɪks'ti:nθ] *adj* decimosexto; **sixth** [sɪksθ] *num* sexto; **sixth form** *n* (BRIT) clase *f* de alumnos del sexto año (*de 16 a 18 años de edad*); **sixth-form college** *n* instituto *m* para alumnos de 16 a 18 años; **sixtieth** ['sɪkstɪɪθ] *adj* sexagésimo; **sixty** *num* sesenta

size [saɪz] *n* tamaño; (*extent*) extensión *f*; (*of clothing*) talla; (*of shoes*) número; **sizeable** *adj* importante, considerable

sizzle ['sɪzl] *vi* crepitar

skate [skeɪt] *n* patín *m*; (*fish*: *pl inv*) raya ▷ *vi* patinar; **skateboard** *n* monopatín *m*; **skateboarding** *n* monopatín *m*; **skater** *n* patinador(a) *m/f*; **skating** *n* patinaje *m*; **skating rink** *n* pista de patinaje

skeleton ['skɛlɪtn] *n* esqueleto; (*Tech*) armazón *f*; (*outline*) esquema *m*

skeptical ['skɛptɪkl] (US) = **sceptical**

sketch [skɛtʃ] *n* (*drawing*) dibujo; (*outline*) esbozo, bosquejo; (*Theatre*) sketch *m* ▷ *vt* dibujar; (*plan etc*: *also*: **~ out**) esbozar

skewer ['skju:ə*] *n* broqueta

ski: [ski:] *n* esquí *m* ▷ *vi* esquiar; **ski boot** *n* bota de esquí

skid [skɪd] *n* patinazo ▷ *vi* patinar

ski: skier *n* esquiador(a) *m/f*; **skiing** *n* esquí *m*

skilful ['skɪlful] (US **skillful**) *adj* diestro, experto

ski lift *n* telesilla *m*, telesquí *m*

skill [skɪl] *n* destreza, pericia; técnica; **skilled** *adj* hábil, diestro; (*worker*) cualificado

skim [skɪm] *vt* (*milk*) desnatar; (*glide over*) rozar, rasar ▷ *vi*: **to ~ through** (*book*) hojear; **skimmed milk** (US **skim milk**) *n* leche *f* desnatada

skin [skɪn] *n* piel *f*; (*complexion*) cutis *m* ▷ *vt* (*fruit etc*) pelar; (*animal*) despellejar; **skinhead** *n* cabeza *m/f* rapada, skin(head) *m/f*; **skinny** *adj* flaco

skip [skɪp] *n* brinco, salto; (BRIT: *container*) contenedor *m* ▷ *vi* brincar; (*with rope*) saltar a la comba ▷ *vt* saltarse

ski: ski pass *n* forfait *m* (de esquí); **ski pole** *n* bastón *m* de esquiar

skipper ['skɪpə*] *n* (*Naut, Sport*) capitán *m*

skipping rope ['skɪpɪŋ-] (US **skip rope**) *n* comba

skirt [skə:t] *n* falda, pollera (SC) ▷ *vt* (*go round*) ladear

skirting board ['skə:tɪŋ-] (BRIT) *n* rodapié *m*

ski slope *n* pista de esquí

ski suit *n* traje *m* de esquiar

skull [skʌl] *n* calavera; (*Anat*) cráneo

skunk [skʌŋk] *n* mofeta

sky [skaɪ] *n* cielo; **skyscraper** *n* rascacielos *m inv*

slab [slæb] *n* (*stone*) bloque *m*; (*flat*) losa; (*of cake*) trozo

slack [slæk] *adj* (*loose*) flojo; (*slow*) de poca actividad; (*careless*) descuidado; **slacks** *npl* pantalones *mpl*

slain [sleɪn] *pp of* **slay**

slam [slæm] *vt* (*throw*) arrojar (violentamente); (*criticize*) criticar duramente ▷ *vi* (*door*) cerrarse de golpe; **to ~ the door** dar un portazo

slander ['slɑ:ndə*] *n* calumnia,

difamación *f*

slang [slæŋ] *n* argot *m*; (*jargon*) jerga

slant [slɑːnt] *n* sesgo, inclinación *f*; (*fig*) interpretación *f*

slap [slæp] *n* palmada; (*in face*) bofetada ▷ *vt* dar una palmada *or* bofetada a; (*paint etc*): **to ~ sth on sth** embadurnar algo con algo ▷ *adv* (*directly*) exactamente, directamente

slash [slæʃ] *vt* acuchillar; (*fig: prices*) fulminar

slate [sleɪt] *n* pizarra ▷ *vt* (*fig: criticize*) criticar duramente

slaughter ['slɔːtə*] *n* (*of animals*) matanza; (*of people*) carnicería ▷ *vt* matar; **slaughterhouse** *n* matadero

Slav [slɑːv] *adj* eslavo

slave [sleɪv] *n* esclavo/a ▷ *vi* (*also*: **~ away**) sudar tinta; **slavery** *n* esclavitud *f*

slay [sleɪ] (*pt* **slew**, *pp* **slain**) *vt* matar

sleazy ['sliːzɪ] *adj* de mala fama

sled [slɛd] (US) = **sledge**

sledge [slɛdʒ] *n* trineo

sleek [sliːk] *adj* (*shiny*) lustroso; (*car etc*) elegante

sleep [sliːp] (*pt, pp* **slept**) *n* sueño ▷ *vi* dormir; **to go to ~** quedarse dormido; **sleep in** *vi* (*oversleep*) quedarse dormido; **sleep together** *vi* (*have sex*) acostarse juntos; **sleeper** *n* (*person*) durmiente *mf*; (BRIT *Rail: on track*) traviesa; (*: train*) coche-cama *m*; **sleeping bag** *n* saco de dormir; **sleeping car** *n* coche-cama *m*; **sleeping pill** *n* somnífero; **sleepover** *n*: **we're having a sleepover at Jo's** nos vamos a quedar a dormir en casa de Jo; **sleepwalk** *vi* caminar dormido; (*habitually*) ser sonámbulo; **sleepy** *adj* soñoliento; (*place*) soporífero

sleet [sliːt] *n* aguanieve *f*

sleeve [sliːv] *n* manga; (*Tech*) manguito; (*of record*) portada; **sleeveless** *adj* sin mangas

sleigh [sleɪ] *n* trineo

slender ['slɛndə*] *adj* delgado; (*means*) escaso

slept [slɛpt] *pt, pp of* **sleep**

slew [sluː] *pt of* **slay** ▷ *vi* (BRIT: *veer*) torcerse

slice [slaɪs] *n* (*of meat*) tajada; (*of bread*) rebanada; (*of lemon*) rodaja; (*utensil*) pala ▷ *vt* cortar (en tajos), rebanar

slick [slɪk] *adj* (*skilful*) hábil, diestro; (*clever*) astuto ▷ *n* (*also*: **oil ~**) marea negra

slide [slaɪd] (*pt, pp* **slid**) *n* (*movement*) descenso, desprendimiento; (*in playground*) tobogán *m*; (*Phot*) diapositiva; (BRIT: *also*: **hair ~**) pasador *m* ▷ *vt* correr, deslizar ▷ *vi* (*slip*) resbalarse; (*glide*) deslizarse; **sliding** *adj* (*door*) corredizo

slight [slaɪt] *adj* (*slim*) delgado; (*frail*) delicado; (*pain etc*) leve; (*trivial*) insignificante; (*small*) pequeño ▷ *n* desaire *m* ▷ *vt* (*insult*) ofender, desairar; **not in the ~est** en absoluto; **slightly** *adv* ligeramente, un poco

slim [slɪm] *adj* delgado, esbelto; (*fig: chance*) remoto ▷ *vi* adelgazar; **slimming** *n* adelgazamiento

slimy ['slaɪmɪ] *adj* cenagoso

sling [slɪŋ] (*pt, pp* **slung**) *n* (*Med*) cabestrillo; (*weapon*) honda ▷ *vt* tirar, arrojar

slip [slɪp] *n* (*slide*) resbalón *m*; (*mistake*) descuido; (*underskirt*) combinación *f*; (*of paper*) papelito ▷ *vt* (*slide*) deslizar ▷ *vi* deslizarse; (*stumble*) resbalar(se); (*decline*) decaer; (*move smoothly*): **to ~ into/out of** (*room etc*) introducirse en/salirse de; **to give sb the ~** eludir a algn; **a ~ of the tongue** un lapsus; **to ~ sth on/off** ponerse/quitarse algo; **slip up** *vi* (*make mistake*) equivocarse; meter la pata

slipper ['slɪpə*] *n* zapatilla, pantufla

slippery ['slɪpərɪ] *adj* resbaladizo; **slip road** (BRIT) *n* carretera de acceso

slit [slɪt] (*pt, pp* **~**) *n* raja; (*cut*) corte *m* ▷ *vt* rajar; cortar

slog [slɔg] (BRIT) *vi* sudar tinta; **it was a ~** costó trabajo (hacerlo)

slogan ['sləugən] *n* eslogan *m*, lema *m*

slope [sləup] *n* (*up*) cuesta, pendiente *f*; (*down*) declive *m*; (*side of mountain*) falda, vertiente *m* ▷ *vi*: **to ~ down** estar en declive; **to ~ up** inclinarse; **sloping** *adj* en pendiente; en declive; (*writing*) inclinado

sloppy ['slɔpɪ] *adj* (*work*) descuidado; (*appearance*) desaliñado

slot [slɔt] *n* ranura ▷ *vt*: **to ~ into** encajar en; **slot machine** *n* (BRIT: *vending machine*) distribuidor *m* automático; (*for gambling*) tragaperras *m inv*

Slovakia [sləu'vækɪə] *n* Eslovaquia

Slovene [sləu'viːn] *adj* esloveno ▷ *n* esloveno/a; (*Ling*) esloveno; **Slovenia** [sləu'viːnɪə] *n* Eslovenia; **Slovenian** *adj*, *n* = **Slovene**

slow [sləu] *adj* lento; (*not clever*) lerdo; (*watch*): **to be ~** atrasar ▷ *adv* lentamente, despacio ▷ *vt, vi* retardar; **"~"** (*road sign*) "disminuir velocidad"; **slow down** *vi* reducir la marcha; **slowly** *adv* lentamente, despacio; **slow motion** *n*: **in slow motion** a cámara lenta

slug [slʌg] *n* babosa; (*bullet*) posta; **sluggish** *adj* lento; (*person*) perezoso

slum [slʌm] *n* casucha
slump [slʌmp] *n* (*economic*) depresión *f* ▷ *vi* hundirse; (*prices*) caer en picado
slung [slʌŋ] *pt, pp of* **sling**
slur [slə:*] *n*: **to cast a ~ on** insultar ▷ *vt* (*speech*) pronunciar mal
sly [slaɪ] *adj* astuto; (*smile*) taimado
smack [smæk] *n* bofetada ▷ *vt* dar con la mano a; (*child, on face*) abofetear ▷ *vi*: **to ~ of** saber a, oler a
small [smɔ:l] *adj* pequeño; **small ads** (BRIT) *npl* anuncios *mpl* por palabras; **small change** *n* suelto, cambio
smart [smɑ:t] *adj* elegante; (*clever*) listo, inteligente; (*quick*) rápido, vivo ▷ *vi* escocer, picar; **smartcard** *n* tarjeta inteligente
smash [smæʃ] *n* (*also*: **~-up**) choque *m*; (*Mus*) exitazo ▷ *vt* (*break*) hacer pedazos; (*car etc*) estrellar; (*Sport*: *record*) batir ▷ *vi* hacerse pedazos; (*against wall etc*) estrellarse; **smashing** (*inf*) *adj* estupendo
smear [smɪə*] *n* mancha; (*Med*) frotis *m inv* ▷ *vt* untar; **smear test** *n* (*Med*) citología, frotis *m inv* (cervical)
smell [smɛl] (*pt, pp* **smelt** *or* **~ed**) *n* olor *m*; (*sense*) olfato ▷ *vt, vi* oler; **smelly** *adj* maloliente
smelt [smɛlt] *pt, pp of* **smell**
smile [smaɪl] *n* sonrisa ▷ *vi* sonreír
smirk [smə:k] *n* sonrisa falsa *or* afectada
smog [smɔg] *n* esmog *m*
smoke [sməuk] *n* humo ▷ *vi* fumar; (*chimney*) echar humo ▷ *vt* (*cigarettes*) fumar; **smoke alarm** *n* detector *m* de humo, alarma contra incendios; **smoked** *adj* (*bacon, glass*) ahumado; **smoker** *n* fumador(a) *m/f*; (*Rail*) coche *m* fumador; **smoking** *n*: **"no smoking"** "prohibido fumar"

> Be careful not to translate **smoking** by the Spanish word *smoking*.

smoky *adj* (*room*) lleno de humo; (*taste*) ahumado
smooth [smu:ð] *adj* liso; (*sea*) tranquilo; (*flavour, movement*) suave; (*sauce*) fino; (*person*: *pej*) meloso ▷ *vt* (*also*: **~ out**) alisar; (*creases, difficulties*) allanar
smother ['smʌðə*] *vt* sofocar; (*repress*) contener
SMS *n abbr* (= *short message service*) (servicio) SMS; **SMS message** *n* (mensaje *m*) SMS
smudge [smʌdʒ] *n* mancha ▷ *vt* manchar
smug [smʌg] *adj* presumido; orondo
smuggle ['smʌgl] *vt* pasar de contrabando; **smuggling** *n* contrabando
snack [snæk] *n* bocado; **snack bar** *n* cafetería
snag [snæg] *n* problema *m*
snail [sneɪl] *n* caracol *m*
snake [sneɪk] *n* serpiente *f*
snap [snæp] *n* (*sound*) chasquido; (*photograph*) foto *f* ▷ *adj* (*decision*) instantáneo ▷ *vt* (*break*) quebrar; (*fingers*) castañetear ▷ *vi* quebrarse; (*fig*: *speak sharply*) contestar bruscamente; **to ~ shut** cerrarse de golpe; **snap at** *vt fus* (*dog*) intentar morder; **snap up** *vt* agarrar; **snapshot** *n* foto *f* (instantánea)
snarl [snɑ:l] *vi* gruñir
snatch [snætʃ] *n* (*small piece*) fragmento ▷ *vt* (*snatch away*) arrebatar; (*fig*) agarrar; **to ~ some sleep** encontrar tiempo para dormir
sneak [sni:k] (*pt* (US) **snuck**) *vi*: **to ~ in/out** entrar/salir a hurtadillas ▷ *n* (*inf*) soplón/ona *m/f*; **to ~ up on sb** aparecérsele de improviso a algn; **sneakers** *npl* zapatos *mpl* de lona
sneer [snɪə*] *vi* reír con sarcasmo; (*mock*): **to ~ at** burlarse de
sneeze [sni:z] *vi* estornudar
sniff [snɪf] *vi* sollozar ▷ *vt* husmear, oler; (*drugs*) esnifar
snigger ['snɪgə*] *vi* reírse con disimulo
snip [snɪp] *n* tijeretazo; (BRIT: *inf*: *bargain*) ganga ▷ *vt* tijeretear
sniper ['snaɪpə*] *n* francotirador(a) *m/f*
snob [snɔb] *n* (e)snob *mf*
snooker ['snu:kə*] *n especie de billar*
snoop [snu:p] *vi*: **to ~ about** fisgonear
snooze [snu:z] *n* siesta ▷ *vi* echar una siesta
snore [snɔ:*] *n* ronquido ▷ *vi* roncar
snorkel ['snɔ:kl] *n* (tubo) respirador *m*
snort [snɔ:t] *n* bufido ▷ *vi* bufar
snow [snəu] *n* nieve *f* ▷ *vi* nevar; **snowball** *n* bola de nieve ▷ *vi* (*fig*) agrandirse, ampliarse; **snowstorm** *n* nevada, nevasca
snub [snʌb] *vt* (*person*) desairar ▷ *n* desaire *m*, repulsa
snug [snʌg] *adj* (*cosy*) cómodo; (*fitted*) ajustado

KEYWORD

so [səu] *adv* **1** (*thus, likewise*) así, de este modo; **if so** de ser así; **I like swimming – so do I** a mí me gusta nadar – a mí también; **I've got work to do – so has Paul** tengo trabajo que hacer – Paul también; **it's 5 o'clock – so it is!** son las cinco – ¡pues es verdad!; **I hope/think so** espero/creo que sí; **so far** hasta ahora; (*in past*) hasta este momento
2 (*in comparisons etc*: *to such a degree*) tan; **so quickly (that)** tan rápido (que); **so big**

(that) tan grande (que); **she's not so clever as her brother** no es tan lista como su hermano; **we were so worried** estábamos preocupadísimos
3: **so much** *adj, adv* tanto; **so many** tantos/as
4 (*phrases*): **10 or so** unos 10, 10 o así; **so long!** (*inf: goodbye*) ¡hasta luego!
▷ *conj* **1** (*expressing purpose*): **so as to do** para hacer; **so (that)** para que *+subjun*
2 (*expressing result*) así que; **so you see, I could have gone** así que ya ves, (yo) podría haber ido

soak [səuk] *vt* (*drench*) empapar; (*steep in water*) remojar ▷*vi* remojarse, estar a remojo; **soak up** *vt* absorber; **soaking** *adj* (*also*: **soaking wet**) calado *or* empapado (hasta los huesos *or* el tuétano)
so-and-so ['səuənsəu] *n* (*somebody*) fulano/a de tal
soap [səup] *n* jabón *m*; **soap opera** *n* telenovela; **soap powder** *n* jabón *m* en polvo
soar [sɔː*] *vi* (*on wings*) remontarse; (*rocket: prices*) dispararse; (*building etc*) elevarse
sob [sɔb] *n* sollozo ▷*vi* sollozar
sober ['səubə*] *adj* (*serious*) serio; (*not drunk*) sobrio; (*colour, style*) discreto; **sober up** *vt* quitar la borrachera
so-called ['səu'kɔːld] *adj* así llamado
soccer ['sɔkə*] *n* fútbol *m*
sociable ['səuʃəbl] *adj* sociable
social ['səuʃl] *adj* social ▷*n* velada, fiesta; **socialism** *n* socialismo; **socialist** *adj, n* socialista *mf*; **socialize** *vi*: **to socialize (with)** alternar (con); **social life** *n* vida social; **socially** *adv* socialmente; **social security** *n* seguridad *f* social; **social services** *npl* servicios *mpl* sociales; **social work** *n* asistencia social; **social worker** *n* asistente/a *m/f* social
society [sə'saɪətɪ] *n* sociedad *f*; (*club*) asociación *f*; (*also*: **high ~**) alta sociedad
sociology [səusɪ'ɔlədʒi] *n* sociología
sock [sɔk] *n* calcetín *m*
socket ['sɔkɪt] *n* cavidad *f*; (BRIT *Elec*) enchufe *m*
soda ['səudə] *n* (*Chem*) sosa; (*also*: **~ water**) soda; (*US*: *also*: **~ pop**) gaseosa
sodium ['səudɪəm] *n* sodio
sofa ['səufə] *n* sofá *m*; **sofa bed** *n* sofá-cama *m*
soft [sɔft] *adj* (*lenient, not hard*) blando; (*gentle, not bright*) suave; **soft drink** *n* bebida no alcohólica; **soft drugs** *npl* drogas *fpl* blandas; **soften** ['sɔfn] *vt* ablandar; suavizar; (*effect*) amortiguar ▷*vi* ablandarse; suavizarse; **softly** *adv* suavemente; (*gently*) delicadamente, con delicadeza; **software** *n* (*Comput*) software *m*
soggy ['sɔgɪ] *adj* empapado
soil [sɔɪl] *n* (*earth*) tierra, suelo ▷*vt* ensuciar
solar ['səulə*] *adj* solar; **solar power** *n* energía solar; **solar system** *n* sistema *m* solar
sold [səuld] *pt, pp of* **sell**
soldier ['səuldʒə*] *n* soldado; (*army man*) militar *m*
sold out *adj* (*Comm*) agotado
sole [səul] *n* (*of foot*) planta; (*of shoe*) suela; (*fish: pl inv*) lenguado ▷*adj* único; **solely** *adv* únicamente, sólo, solamente; **I will hold you solely responsible** le consideraré el único responsable
solemn ['sɔləm] *adj* solemne
solicitor [sə'lɪsɪtə*] (BRIT) *n* (*for wills etc*) ≈ notario/a; (*in court*) ≈ abogado/a
solid ['sɔlɪd] *adj* sólido; (*gold etc*) macizo ▷*n* sólido
solitary ['sɔlɪtərɪ] *adj* solitario, solo
solitude ['sɔlɪtjuːd] *n* soledad *f*
solo ['səuləu] *n* solo ▷*adv* (*fly*) en solitario; **soloist** *n* solista *m/f*
soluble ['sɔljuːbl] *adj* soluble
solution [sə'luːʃən] *n* solución *f*
solve [sɔlv] *vt* resolver, solucionar
solvent ['sɔlvənt] *adj* (*Comm*) solvente ▷*n* (*Chem*) solvente *m*
sombre ['sɔmbə*] (US **somber**) *adj* sombrío

KEYWORD

some [sʌm] *adj* **1** (*a certain amount or number*): **some tea/water/biscuits** té/agua/(unas) galletas; **there's some milk in the fridge** hay leche en el frigo; **there were some people outside** había algunas personas fuera; **I've got some money, but not much** tengo algo de dinero, pero no mucho
2 (*certain: in contrasts*) algunos/as; **some people say that ...** hay quien dice que ...; **some films were excellent, but most were mediocre** hubo películas excelentes, pero la mayoría fueron mediocres
3 (*unspecified*): **some woman was asking for you** una mujer estuvo preguntando por ti; **he was asking for some book (or other)** pedía un libro; **some day** algún día; **some day next week** un día de la semana que viene

▷*pron* **1** (*a certain number*): **I've got some** (*books etc*) tengo algunos/as
2 (*a certain amount*) algo; **I've got some** (*money, milk*) tengo algo; **could I have some of that cheese?** ¿me puede dar un poco de ese queso?; **I've read some of the book** he leído parte del libro
▷*adv*: **some 10 people** unas 10 personas, una decena de personas

some: somebody ['sʌmbədɪ] *pron* = **someone**; **somehow** *adv* de alguna manera; (*for some reason*) por una u otra razón; **someone** *pron* alguien; **someplace** (US) *adv* = **somewhere**; **something** *pron* algo; **would you like something to eat/drink?** ¿te gustaría cenar/tomar algo?; **sometime** *adv* (*in future*) algún día, en algún momento; (*in past*): **sometime last month** durante el mes pasado; **sometimes** *adv* a veces; **somewhat** *adv* algo; **somewhere** *adv* (*be*) en alguna parte; (*go*) a alguna parte; **somewhere else** (*be*) en otra parte; (*go*) a otra parte
son [sʌn] *n* hijo
song [sɔŋ] *n* canción *f*
son-in-law ['sʌnɪnlɔː] *n* yerno
soon [suːn] *adv* pronto, dentro de poco; **~ afterwards** poco después; *see also* **as**; **sooner** *adv* (*time*) antes, más temprano; (*preference: rather*): **I would sooner do that** preferiría hacer eso; **sooner or later** tarde o temprano
soothe [suːð] *vt* tranquilizar; (*pain*) aliviar
sophisticated [sə'fɪstɪkeɪtɪd] *adj* sofisticado
sophomore ['sɔfəmɔː*] (US) *n* estudiante *mf* de segundo año
soprano [sə'prɑːnəu] *n* soprano *f*
sorbet ['sɔːbeɪ] *n* sorbete *m*
sordid ['sɔːdɪd] *adj* (*place etc*) sórdido; (*motive etc*) mezquino
sore [sɔː*] *adj* (*painful*) doloroso, que duele ▷*n* llaga
sorrow ['sɔrəu] *n* pena, dolor *m*
sorry ['sɔrɪ] *adj* (*regretful*) arrepentido; (*condition, excuse*) lastimoso; **~!** ¡perdón!, ¡perdone!; **~?** ¿cómo?; **to feel ~ for sb** tener lástima a algn; **I feel ~ for him** me da lástima
sort [sɔːt] *n* clase *f*, género, tipo; **sort out** *vt* (*papers*) clasificar; (*organize*) ordenar, organizar; (*resolve: problem, situation etc*) arreglar, solucionar
SOS *n* SOS *m*
so-so ['səusəu] *adv* regular, así así
sought [sɔːt] *pt, pp of* **seek**
soul [səul] *n* alma
sound [saund] *n* (*noise*) sonido, ruido; (*volume: on TV etc*) volumen *m*; (*Geo*) estrecho ▷*adj* (*healthy*) sano; (*safe, not damaged*) en buen estado; (*reliable: person*) digno de confianza; (*sensible*) sensato, razonable; (*secure: investment*) seguro ▷*adv*: **~ asleep** profundamente dormido ▷*vt* (*alarm*) sonar ▷*vi* sonar, resonar; (*fig: seem*) parecer; **to ~ like** sonar a; **soundtrack** *n* (*of film*) banda sonora
soup [suːp] *n* (*thick*) sopa; (*thin*) caldo
sour ['sauə*] *adj* agrio; (*milk*) cortado; **it's ~ grapes** (*fig*) están verdes
source [sɔːs] *n* fuente *f*
south [sauθ] *n* sur *m* ▷*adj* del sur, sureño ▷*adv* al sur, hacia el sur; **South Africa** *n* África del Sur; **South African** *adj, n* sudafricano/a *m/f*; **South America** *n* América del Sur, Sudamérica; **South American** *adj, n* sudamericano/a *m/f*; **southbound** *adj* (con) rumbo al sur; **southeastern** [sauθ'iːstən] *adj* sureste, del sureste; **southern** ['sʌðən] *adj* del sur, meridional; **South Korea** *n* Corea del Sur; **South Pole** *n* Polo Sur; **southward(s)** *adv* hacia el sur; **south-west** *n* suroeste *m*; **southwestern** [sauθ'westən] *adj* suroeste
souvenir [suːvə'nɪə*] *n* recuerdo
sovereign ['sɔvrɪn] *adj, n* soberano/a *m/f*
sow¹ [səu] (*pt* **~ed**, *pp* **sown**) *vt* sembrar
sow² [sau] *n* cerda, puerca
soya ['sɔɪə] (BRIT) *n* soja
spa [spɑː] *n* balneario
space [speɪs] *n* espacio; (*room*) sitio ▷*cpd* espacial ▷*vt* (*also*: **~ out**) espaciar; **spacecraft** *n* nave *f* espacial; **spaceship** *n* = **spacecraft**
spacious ['speɪʃəs] *adj* amplio
spade [speɪd] *n* (*tool*) pala, laya; **spades** *npl* (*Cards: British*) picas *fpl*; (*: Spanish*) espadas *fpl*
spaghetti [spə'gɛtɪ] *n* espaguetis *mpl*, fideos *mpl*
Spain [speɪn] *n* España
spam [spæm] *n* (*junk e-mail*) spam *m*
span [spæn] *n* (*of bird, plane*) envergadura; (*of arch*) luz *f*; (*in time*) lapso ▷*vt* extenderse sobre, cruzar; (*fig*) abarcar
Spaniard ['spænjəd] *n* español(a) *m/f*
Spanish ['spænɪʃ] *adj* español(a) ▷*n* (*Ling*) español *m*, castellano; **the Spanish** *npl* los españoles
spank [spæŋk] *vt* zurrar
spanner ['spænə*] (BRIT) *n* llave *f* (inglesa)
spare [spɛə*] *adj* de reserva; (*surplus*) sobrante, de más ▷*n* = **spare part** ▷*vt* (*do without*) pasarse sin; (*refrain from hurting*) perdonar; **to ~** (*surplus*) sobrante, de sobra; **spare part** *n* pieza de repuesto; **spare**

S

room *n* cuarto de los invitados; **spare time** *n* tiempo libre; **spare tyre** (*US* **spare tire**) *n* (*Aut*) neumático *or* llanta (*LAM*) de recambio; **spare wheel** *n* (*Aut*) rueda de recambio

spark [spɑːk] *n* chispa; (*fig*) chispazo; **spark(ing) plug** *n* bujía

sparkle ['spɑːkl] *n* centelleo, destello ▷ *vi* (*shine*) relucir, brillar

sparrow ['spærəu] *n* gorrión *m*

sparse [spɑːs] *adj* esparcido, escaso

spasm ['spæzəm] *n* (*Med*) espasmo

spat [spæt] *pt, pp of* **spit**

spate [speɪt] *n* (*fig*): **a ~ of** un torrente de

spatula ['spætjulə] *n* espátula

speak [spiːk] (*pt* **spoke**, *pp* **spoken**) *vt* (*language*) hablar; (*truth*) decir ▷ *vi* hablar; (*make a speech*) intervenir; **to ~ to sb/of** *or* **about sth** hablar con algn/de *or* sobre algo; **~ up!** ¡habla fuerte!; **speaker** *n* (*in public*) orador(a) *m/f*; (*also*: **loudspeaker**) altavoz *m*; (*for stereo etc*) bafle *m*; (*Pol*): **the Speaker** (*BRIT*) *el Presidente de la Cámara de los Comunes*; (*US*) *el Presidente del Congreso*

spear [spɪə*] *n* lanza ▷ *vt* alancear

special ['spɛʃl] *adj* especial; (*edition etc*) extraordinario; (*delivery*) urgente; **special delivery** *n* (*Post*): **by special delivery** por entrega urgente; **special effects** *npl* (*Cine*) efectos *mpl* especiales; **specialist** *n* especialista *mf*; **speciality** [spɛʃɪ'ælɪtɪ] (*BRIT*) *n* especialidad *f*; **specialize** *vi*: **to specialize (in)** especializarse (en); **specially** *adv* sobre todo, en particular; **special needs** *npl* (*BRIT*): **children with special needs** niños que requieren una atención diferenciada; **special offer** *n* (*Comm*) oferta especial; **special school** *n* (*BRIT*) colegio *m* de educación especial; **specialty** (*US*) *n* = **speciality**

species ['spiːʃiːz] *n inv* especie *f*

specific [spə'sɪfɪk] *adj* específico; **specifically** *adv* específicamente

specify ['spɛsɪfaɪ] *vt, vi* especificar, precisar

specimen ['spɛsɪmən] *n* ejemplar *m*; (*Med*: *of urine*) espécimen *m*; (: *of blood*) muestra

speck [spɛk] *n* grano, mota

spectacle ['spɛktəkl] *n* espectáculo; **spectacles** *npl* (*BRIT*: *glasses*) gafas *fpl* (*SP*), anteojos *mpl*; **spectacular** [-'tækjulə*] *adj* espectacular; (*success*) impresionante

spectator [spɛk'teɪtə*] *n* espectador(a) *m/f*

spectrum ['spɛktrəm] (*pl* **spectra**) *n* espectro

speculate ['spɛkjuleɪt] *vi*: **to ~ (on)** especular (en)

sped [spɛd] *pt, pp of* **speed**

speech [spiːtʃ] *n* (*faculty*) habla; (*formal talk*) discurso; (*spoken language*) lenguaje *m*; **speechless** *adj* mudo, estupefacto

speed [spiːd] *n* velocidad *f*; (*haste*) prisa; (*promptness*) rapidez *f*; **at full** *or* **top ~** a máxima velocidad; **speed up** *vi* acelerarse ▷ *vt* acelerar; **speedboat** *n* lancha motora; **speeding** *n* (*Aut*) exceso de velocidad; **speed limit** *n* límite *m* de velocidad, velocidad *f* máxima; **speedometer** [spɪ'dɔmɪtə*] *n* velocímetro; **speedy** *adj* (*fast*) veloz, rápido; (*prompt*) pronto

spell [spɛl] (*pt, pp* **spelt** (*BRIT*) *or* **~ed**) *n* (*also*: **magic ~**) encanto, hechizo; (*period of time*) rato, período ▷ *vt* deletrear; (*fig*) anunciar, presagiar; **to cast a ~ on sb** hechizar a algn; **he can't ~** pone faltas de ortografía; **spell out** *vt* (*explain*): **to spell sth out for sb** explicar algo a algn en detalle; **spellchecker** ['spɛltʃɛkə*] *n* corrector *m* ortográfico; **spelling** *n* ortografía

spelt [spɛlt] *pt, pp of* **spell**

spend [spɛnd] (*pt, pp* **spent**) *vt* (*money*) gastar; (*time*) pasar; (*life*) dedicar; **spending** *n*: **government spending** gastos *mpl* del gobierno

spent [spɛnt] *pt, pp of* **spend** ▷ *adj* (*cartridge, bullets, match*) usado

sperm [spəːm] *n* esperma

sphere [sfɪə*] *n* esfera

spice [spaɪs] *n* especia ▷ *vt* condimentar

spicy ['spaɪsɪ] *adj* picante

spider ['spaɪdə*] *n* araña

spike [spaɪk] *n* (*point*) punta; (*Bot*) espiga

spill [spɪl] (*pt, pp* **spilt** *or* **~ed**) *vt* derramar, verter ▷ *vi* derramarse; **to ~ over** desbordarse

spin [spɪn] (*pt, pp* **spun**) *n* (*Aviat*) barrena; (*trip in car*) paseo (en coche); (*on ball*) efecto ▷ *vt* (*wool etc*) hilar; (*ball etc*) hacer girar ▷ *vi* girar, dar vueltas

spinach ['spɪnɪtʃ] *n* espinaca; (*as food*) espinacas *fpl*

spinal ['spaɪnl] *adj* espinal

spin doctor *n* *informador(a) parcial al servicio de un partido político etc*

spin-dryer (*BRIT*) *n* secador *m* centrífugo

spine [spaɪn] *n* espinazo, columna vertebral; (*thorn*) espina

spiral ['spaɪərl] *n* espiral *f* ▷ *vi* (*fig*: *prices*) subir desorbitadamente

spire ['spaɪə*] *n* aguja, chapitel *m*

spirit ['spɪrɪt] *n* (*soul*) alma; (*ghost*) fantasma *m*; (*attitude, sense*) espíritu *m*; (*courage*) valor *m*, ánimo; **spirits** *npl* (*drink*) licor(es) *m(pl)*; **in good ~s** alegre, de buen

ánimo
spiritual ['spɪrɪtjuəl] *adj* espiritual ▷ *n* espiritual *m*
spit [spɪt] (*pt, pp* **spat**) *n* (*for roasting*) asador *m*, espetón *m*; (*saliva*) saliva ▷ *vi* escupir; (*sound*) chisporrotear; (*rain*) lloviznar
spite [spaɪt] *n* rencor *m*, ojeriza ▷ *vt* causar pena a, mortificar; **in ~ of** a pesar de, pese a; **spiteful** *adj* rencoroso, malévolo
splash [splæʃ] *n* (*sound*) chapoteo; (*of colour*) mancha ▷ *vt* salpicar ▷ *vi* (*also:* **~ about**) chapotear; **splash out** (*inf*) *vi* (BRIT) derrochar dinero
splendid ['splɛndɪd] *adj* espléndido
splinter ['splɪntə*] *n* (*of wood etc*) astilla; (*in finger*) espigón *m* ▷ *vi* astillarse, hacer astillas
split [splɪt] (*pt, pp* **~**) *n* hendedura, raja; (*fig*) división *f*; (*Pol*) escisión *f* ▷ *vt* partir, rajar; (*party*) dividir; (*share*) repartir ▷ *vi* dividirse, escindirse; **split up** *vi* (*couple*) separarse; (*meeting*) acabarse
spoil [spɔɪl] (*pt, pp* **~t** *or* **~ed**) *vt* (*damage*) dañar; (*mar*) estropear; (*child*) mimar, consentir
spoilt [spɔɪlt] *pt, pp of* **spoil** ▷ *adj* (*child*) mimado, consentido; (*ballot paper*) invalidado
spoke [spəuk] *pt of* **speak** ▷ *n* rayo, radio
spoken ['spəukn] *pp of* **speak**
spokesman ['spəuksmən] (*irreg*) *n* portavoz *m*
spokesperson ['spəukspə:sn] (*irreg*) *n* portavoz *m/f*, vocero/a (LAM)
spokeswoman ['spəukswumən] (*irreg*) *n* portavoz *f*
sponge [spʌndʒ] *n* esponja; (*also:* **~ cake**) bizcocho ▷ *vt* (*wash*) lavar con esponja ▷ *vi*: **to ~ off** *or* **on sb** vivir a costa de algn; **sponge bag** (BRIT) *n* esponjera
sponsor ['spɔnsə*] *n* patrocinador(a) *m/f* ▷ *vt* (*applicant, proposal etc*) proponer; **sponsorship** *n* patrocinio
spontaneous [spɔn'teɪnɪəs] *adj* espontáneo
spooky ['spu:kɪ] (*inf*) *adj* espeluznante, horripilante
spoon [spu:n] *n* cuchara; **spoonful** *n* cucharada
sport [spɔ:t] *n* deporte *m*; (*person*): **to be a good ~** ser muy majo ▷ *vt* (*wear*) lucir, ostentar; **sport jacket** (US) *n* = **sports jacket**; **sports car** *n* coche *m* deportivo; **sports centre** (BRIT) *n* polideportivo; **sports jacket** (BRIT) *n* chaqueta deportiva; **sportsman** (*irreg*) *n* deportista *m*; **sports utility vehicle** *n* todoterreno *m inv*; **sportswear** *n* trajes *mpl* de deporte *or* sport; **sportswoman** (*irreg*) *n* deportista; **sporty** *adj* deportista
spot [spɔt] *n* sitio, lugar *m*; (*dot: on pattern*) punto, mancha; (*pimple*) grano; (*Radio*) cuña publicitaria; (*TV*) espacio publicitario; (*small amount*): **a ~ of** un poquito de ▷ *vt* (*notice*) notar, observar; **on the ~** allí mismo; **spotless** *adj* perfectamente limpio; **spotlight** *n* foco, reflector *m*; (*Aut*) faro auxiliar
spouse [spauz] *n* cónyuge *mf*
sprain [spreɪn] *n* torcedura ▷ *vt*: **to ~ one's ankle/wrist** torcerse el tobillo/la muñeca
sprang [spræŋ] *pt of* **spring**
sprawl [sprɔ:l] *vi* tumbarse
spray [spreɪ] *n* rociada; (*of sea*) espuma; (*container*) atomizador *m*; (*for paint etc*) pistola rociadora; (*of flowers*) ramita ▷ *vt* rociar; (*crops*) regar
spread [sprɛd] (*pt, pp* **~**) *n* extensión *f*; (*for bread etc*) pasta para untar; (*inf: food*) comilona ▷ *vt* extender; (*butter*) untar; (*wings, sails*) desplegar; (*work, wealth*) repartir; (*scatter*) esparcir ▷ *vi* (*also:* **~ out**: *stain*) extenderse; (*news*) diseminarse; **spread out** *vi* (*move apart*) separarse; **spreadsheet** *n* hoja electrónica *or* de cálculo
spree [spri:] *n*: **to go on a ~** ir de juerga
spring [sprɪŋ] (*pt* **sprang**, *pp* **sprung**) *n* (*season*) primavera; (*leap*) salto, brinco; (*coiled metal*) resorte *m*; (*of water*) fuente *f*, manantial *m* ▷ *vi* saltar, brincar; **spring up** *vi* (*thing: appear*) aparecer; (*problem*) surgir; **spring onion** *n* cebolleta
sprinkle ['sprɪŋkl] *vt* (*pour: liquid*) rociar; (*: salt, sugar*) espolvorear; **to ~ water** *etc* **on, ~ with water** *etc* rociar *or* salpicar de agua *etc*
sprint [sprɪnt] *n* esprint *m* ▷ *vi* esprintar
sprung [sprʌŋ] *pp of* **spring**
spun [spʌn] *pt, pp of* **spin**
spur [spə:*] *n* espuela; (*fig*) estímulo, aguijón *m* ▷ *vt* (*also:* **~ on**) estimular, incitar; **on the ~ of the moment** de improviso
spurt [spə:t] *n* chorro; (*of energy*) arrebato ▷ *vi* chorrear
spy [spaɪ] *n* espía *mf* ▷ *vi*: **to ~ on** espiar a ▷ *vt* (*see*) divisar, lograr ver
sq. *abbr* = **square**
squabble ['skwɔbl] *vi* reñir, pelear
squad [skwɔd] *n* (*Mil*) pelotón *m*; (*Police*) brigada; (*Sport*) equipo
squadron ['skwɔdrn] *n* (*Mil*) escuadrón *m*; (*Aviat, Naut*) escuadra

squander ['skwɔndə*] *vt* (*money*) derrochar, despilfarrar; (*chances*) desperdiciar
square [skwɛə*] *n* cuadro; (*in town*) plaza; (*inf: person*) carca *m/f* ▷ *adj* cuadrado; (*inf: ideas, tastes*) trasnochado ▷ *vt* (*arrange*) arreglar; (*Math*) cuadrar; (*reconcile*) compaginar; **all ~** igual(es); **to have a ~ meal** comer caliente; **2 metres ~** 2 metros en cuadro; **2 ~ metres** 2 metros cuadrados; **square root** *n* raíz *f* cuadrada
squash [skwɔʃ] *n* (BRIT: *drink*): **lemon/orange ~** zumo (SP) *or* jugo (LAM) de limón/naranja; (*US Bot*) calabacín *m*; (*Sport*) squash *m* ▷ *vt* aplastar
squat [skwɔt] *adj* achaparrado ▷ *vi* (*also*: **~ down**) agacharse, sentarse en cuclillas; **squatter** *n* okupa *mf* (SP)
squeak [skwi:k] *vi* (*hinge*) chirriar, rechinar; (*mouse*) chillar
squeal [skwi:l] *vi* chillar, dar gritos agudos
squeeze [skwi:z] *n* presión *f*; (*of hand*) apretón *m*; (*Comm*) restricción *f* ▷ *vt* (*hand, arm*) apretar
squid [skwɪd] *n inv* calamar *m*; (*Culin*) calamares *mpl*
squint [skwɪnt] *vi* bizquear, ser bizco ▷ *n* (*Med*) estrabismo
squirm [skwə:m] *vi* retorcerse, revolverse
squirrel ['skwɪrəl] *n* ardilla
squirt [skwə:t] *vi* salir a chorros ▷ *vt* chiscar
Sr *abbr* = **senior**
Sri Lanka [srɪ'læŋkə] *n* Sri Lanka *m*
St *abbr* = **saint; street**
stab [stæb] *n* (*with knife*) puñalada; (*of pain*) pinchazo; (*inf: try*): **to have a ~ at (doing) sth** intentar (hacer) algo ▷ *vt* apuñalar
stability [stə'bɪlɪtɪ] *n* estabilidad *f*
stable ['steɪbl] *adj* estable ▷ *n* cuadra, caballeriza
stack [stæk] *n* montón *m*, pila ▷ *vt* amontonar, apilar
stadium ['steɪdɪəm] *n* estadio
staff [stɑ:f] *n* (*work force*) personal *m*, plantilla; (BRIT *Scol*) cuerpo docente ▷ *vt* proveer de personal
stag [stæg] *n* ciervo, venado
stage [steɪdʒ] *n* escena; (*point*) etapa; (*platform*) plataforma; (*profession*): **the ~** el teatro ▷ *vt* (*play*) poner en escena, representar; (*organize*) montar, organizar; **in ~s** por etapas
stagger ['stægə*] *vi* tambalearse ▷ *vt* (*amaze*) asombrar; (*hours, holidays*) escalonar; **staggering** *adj* asombroso
stagnant ['stægnənt] *adj* estancado
stag night, stag party *n* despedida de soltero
stain [steɪn] *n* mancha; (*colouring*) tintura ▷ *vt* manchar; (*wood*) teñir; **stained glass** *n* vidrio *m* de color; **stainless steel** *n* acero inoxidable
staircase ['stɛəkeɪs] *n* = **stairway**
stairs [stɛəz] *npl* escaleras *fpl*
stairway ['stɛəweɪ] *n* escalera
stake [steɪk] *n* estaca, poste *m*; (*Comm*) interés *m*; (*Betting*) apuesta ▷ *vt* (*money*) apostar; (*life*) arriesgar; (*reputation*) poner en juego; (*claim*) presentar una reclamación; **to be at ~** estar en juego
stale [steɪl] *adj* (*bread*) duro; (*food*) pasado; (*smell*) rancio; (*beer*) agrio
stalk [stɔ:k] *n* tallo, caña ▷ *vt* acechar, cazar al acecho
stall [stɔ:l] *n* (*in market*) puesto; (*in stable*) casilla (de establo) ▷ *vt* (*Aut*) calar; (*fig*) dar largas a ▷ *vi* (*Aut*) calarse; (*fig*) andarse con rodeos
stamina ['stæmɪnə] *n* resistencia
stammer ['stæmə*] *n* tartamudeo ▷ *vi* tartamudear
stamp [stæmp] *n* sello (SP), estampilla (LAM), timbre *m* (MEX); (*mark*) marca, huella; (*on document*) timbre *m* ▷ *vi* (*also*: **~ one's foot**) patear ▷ *vt* (*mark*) marcar; (*letter*) franquear; (*with rubber stamp*) sellar; **stamp out** *vt* (*fire*) apagar con el pie; (*crime, opposition*) acabar con; **stamped addressed envelope** *n* (BRIT) sobre *m* sellado con las señas propias
stampede [stæm'pi:d] *n* estampida
stance [stæns] *n* postura
stand [stænd] (*pt, pp* **stood**) *n* (*position*) posición *f*, postura; (*for taxis*) parada; (*hall stand*) perchero; (*music stand*) atril *m*; (*Sport*) tribuna; (*at exhibition*) stand *m* ▷ *vi* (*be*) estar, encontrarse; (*be on foot*) estar de pie; (*rise*) levantarse; (*remain*) quedar en pie; (*in election*) presentar candidatura ▷ *vt* (*place*) poner, colocar; (*withstand*) aguantar, soportar; (*invite to*) invitar; **to make a ~** (*fig*) mantener una postura firme; **to ~ for parliament** (BRIT) presentarse (como candidato) a las elecciones; **stand back** *vi* retirarse; **stand by** *vi* (*be ready*) estar listo ▷ *vt fus* (*opinion*) aferrarse a; (*person*) apoyar; **stand down** *vi* (*withdraw*) ceder el puesto; **stand for** *vt fus* (*signify*) significar; (*tolerate*) aguantar, permitir; **stand in for** *vt fus* suplir a; **stand out** *vi* destacarse; **stand up** *vi* levantarse, ponerse de pie; **stand up for** *vt fus* defender; **stand up to** *vt fus* hacer frente a
standard ['stændəd] *n* patrón *m*, norma; (*level*) nivel *m*; (*flag*) estandarte *m* ▷ *adj*

(*size etc*) normal, corriente; (*text*) básico; **standards** *npl* (*morals*) valores *mpl* morales; **standard of living** *n* nivel *m* de vida

standing ['stændɪŋ] *adj* (*on foot*) de pie, en pie; (*permanent*) permanente ▷ *n* reputación *f*; **of many years' ~** que lleva muchos años; **standing order** (BRIT) *n* (*at bank*) orden *f* de pago permanente

stand: standpoint *n* punto de vista; **standstill** *n*: **at a standstill** (*industry, traffic*) paralizado; (*car*) parado; **to come to a standstill** quedar paralizado; pararse

stank [stæŋk] *pt of* **stink**

staple ['steɪpl] *n* (*for papers*) grapa ▷ *adj* (*food etc*) básico ▷ *vt* grapar

star [stɑː*] *n* estrella; (*celebrity*) estrella, astro ▷ *vt* (*Theatre, Cinema*) ser el/la protagonista de; **the stars** *npl* (*Astrology*) el horóscopo

starboard ['stɑːbəd] *n* estribor *m*

starch [stɑːtʃ] *n* almidón *m*

stardom ['stɑːdəm] *n* estrellato

stare [stɛə*] *n* mirada fija ▷ *vi*: **to ~ at** mirar fijo

stark [stɑːk] *adj* (*bleak*) severo, escueto ▷ *adv*: **~ naked** en cueros

start [stɑːt] *n* principio, comienzo; (*departure*) salida; (*sudden movement*) salto, sobresalto; (*advantage*) ventaja ▷ *vt* empezar, comenzar; (*cause*) causar; (*found*) fundar; (*engine*) poner en marcha ▷ *vi* comenzar, empezar; (*with fright*) asustarse, sobresaltarse; (*train etc*) salir; **to ~ doing** *or* **to do sth** empezar a hacer algo; **start off** *vi* empezar, comenzar; (*leave*) salir, ponerse en camino; **start out** *vi* (*begin*) empezar; (*set out*) partir, salir; **start up** *vi* comenzar; (*car*) ponerse en marcha ▷ *vt* comenzar; poner en marcha; **starter** *n* (*Aut*) botón *m* de arranque; (*Sport: official*) juez *mf* de salida; (BRIT *Culin*) entrante *m*; **starting point** *n* punto de partida

startle ['stɑːtl] *vt* asustar, sobrecoger; **startling** *adj* alarmante

starvation [stɑː'veɪʃən] *n* hambre *f*

starve [stɑːv] *vi* tener mucha hambre; (*to death*) morir de hambre ▷ *vt* hacer pasar hambre

state [steɪt] *n* estado ▷ *vt* (*say, declare*) afirmar; **the S~s** los Estados Unidos; **to be in a ~** estar agitado; **statement** *n* afirmación *f*; **state school** *n* escuela *or* colegio estatal; **statesman** (*irreg*) *n* estadista *m*

static ['stætɪk] *n* (*Radio*) parásitos *mpl* ▷ *adj* estático

station ['steɪʃən] *n* estación *f*; (*Radio*) emisora; (*rank*) posición *f* social ▷ *vt* colocar, situar; (*Mil*) apostar

stationary ['steɪʃnərɪ] *adj* estacionario, fijo

stationer's (shop) (BRIT) *n* papelería

stationery [-nərɪ] *n* papel *m* de escribir, articulos *mpl* de escritorio

station wagon (US) *n* ranchera

statistic [stə'tɪstɪk] *n* estadística; **statistics** *n* (*science*) estadística

statue ['stætjuː] *n* estatua

stature ['stætʃə*] *n* estatura; (*fig*) talla

status ['steɪtəs] *n* estado; (*reputation*) estatus *m*; **status quo** *n* (e)statu quo *m*

statutory ['stætjutrɪ] *adj* estatutario

staunch [stɔːntʃ] *adj* leal, incondicional

stay [steɪ] *n* estancia ▷ *vi* quedar(se); (*as guest*) hospedarse; **to ~ put** seguir en el mismo sitio; **to ~ the night/5 days** pasar la noche/estar 5 días; **stay away** *vi* (*from person, building*) no acercarse; (*from event*) no acudir; **stay behind** *vi* quedar atrás; **stay in** *vi* quedarse en casa; **stay on** *vi* quedarse; **stay out** *vi* (*of house*) no volver a casa; (*on strike*) permanecer en huelga; **stay up** *vi* (*at night*) velar, no acostarse

steadily ['stɛdɪlɪ] *adv* constantemente; (*firmly*) firmemente; (*work, walk*) sin parar; (*gaze*) fijamente

steady ['stɛdɪ] *adj* (*firm*) firme; (*regular*) regular; (*person, character*) sensato, juicioso; (*boyfriend*) formal; (*look, voice*) tranquilo ▷ *vt* (*stabilize*) estabilizar; (*nerves*) calmar

steak [steɪk] *n* filete *m*; (*beef*) bistec *m*

steal [stiːl] (*pt* **stole**, *pp* **stolen**) *vt* robar ▷ *vi* robar; (*move secretly*) andar a hurtadillas

steam [stiːm] *n* vapor *m*; (*mist*) vaho, humo ▷ *vt* (*Culin*) cocer al vapor ▷ *vi* echar vapor; **steam up** *vi* (*window*) empañarse; **to get steamed up about sth** (*fig*) ponerse negro por algo; **steamy** *adj* (*room*) lleno de vapor; (*window*) empañado; (*heat, atmosphere*) bochornoso

steel [stiːl] *n* acero ▷ *adj* de acero

steep [stiːp] *adj* escarpado, abrupto; (*stair*) empinado; (*price*) exorbitante, excesivo ▷ *vt* empapar, remojar

steeple ['stiːpl] *n* aguja

steer [stɪə*] *vt* (*car*) conducir (SP), manejar (LAM); (*person*) dirigir ▷ *vi* conducir, manejar; **steering** *n* (*Aut*) dirección *f*; **steering wheel** *n* volante *m*

stem [stɛm] *n* (*of plant*) tallo; (*of glass*) pie *m* ▷ *vt* detener; (*blood*) restañar

step [stɛp] *n* paso; (*on stair*) peldaño, escalón *m* ▷ *vi*: **to ~ forward/back** dar un paso adelante/hacia atrás; **steps** *npl* (BRIT) = **stepladder**; **in/out of ~ (with)** acorde/en disonancia (con); **step down**

vi (*fig*) retirarse; **step in** *vi* entrar; (*fig*) intervenir; **step up** *vt* (*increase*) aumentar; **stepbrother** *n* hermanastro; **stepchild** (*pl* **stepchildren**) *n* hijastro/a *m/f*; **stepdaughter** *n* hijastra; **stepfather** *n* padrastro; **stepladder** *n* escalera doble *or* de tijera; **stepmother** *n* madrastra; **stepsister** *n* hermanastra; **stepson** *n* hijastro

stereo ['stɛrɪəu] *n* estéreo ▷ *adj* (*also*: **~phonic**) estéreo, estereofónico

stereotype ['stɪərɪətaɪp] *n* estereotipo ▷ *vt* estereotipar

sterile ['stɛraɪl] *adj* estéril; **sterilize** ['stɛrɪlaɪz] *vt* esterilizar

sterling ['stə:lɪŋ] *adj* (*silver*) de ley ▷ *n* (*Econ*) libras *fpl* esterlinas *fpl*; **one pound ~** una libra esterlina

stern [stə:n] *adj* severo, austero ▷ *n* (*Naut*) popa

steroid ['stɪərɔɪd] *n* esteroide *m*

stew [stju:] *n* estofado, guiso ▷ *vt* estofar, guisar; (*fruit*) cocer

steward ['stju:əd] *n* camarero; **stewardess** *n* (*esp on plane*) azafata

stick [stɪk] (*pt, pp* **stuck**) *n* palo; (*of dynamite*) barreno; (*as weapon*) porra; (*also*: **walking ~**) bastón *m* ▷ *vt* (*glue*) pegar; (*inf*: *put*) meter; (: *tolerate*) aguantar, soportar; (*thrust*): **to ~ sth into** clavar *or* hincar algo en ▷ *vi* pegarse; (*be unmoveable*) quedarse parado; (*in mind*) quedarse grabado; **stick out** *vi* sobresalir; **stick up** *vi* sobresalir; **stick up for** *vt fus* defender; **sticker** *n* (*label*) etiqueta engomada; (*with slogan*) pegatina; **sticking plaster** *n* esparadrapo; **stick shift** (US) *n* (*Aut*) palanca de cambios

sticky ['stɪkɪ] *adj* pegajoso; (*label*) engomado; (*fig*) difícil

stiff [stɪf] *adj* rígido, tieso; (*hard*) duro; (*manner*) estirado; (*difficult*) difícil; (*person*) inflexible; (*price*) exorbitante ▷ *adv*: **scared/bored ~** muerto de miedo/aburrimiento

stifling ['staɪflɪŋ] *adj* (*heat*) sofocante, bochornoso

stigma ['stɪgmə] *n* (*fig*) estigma *m*

stiletto [stɪ'lɛtəu] (BRIT) *n* (*also*: **~ heel**) tacón *m* de aguja

still [stɪl] *adj* inmóvil, quieto ▷ *adv* todavía; (*even*) aun; (*nonetheless*) sin embargo, aun así

stimulate ['stɪmjuleɪt] *vt* estimular

stimulus ['stɪmjuləs] (*pl* **stimuli**) *n* estímulo, incentivo

sting [stɪŋ] (*pt, pp* **stung**) *n* picadura; (*pain*) escozor *m*, picazón *f*; (*organ*) aguijón *m* ▷ *vt, vi* picar

stink [stɪŋk] (*pt* **stank**, *pp* **stunk**) *n* hedor *m*, tufo ▷ *vi* heder, apestar

stir [stə:*] *n* (*fig*: *agitation*) conmoción *f* ▷ *vt* (*tea etc*) remover; (*fig*: *emotions*) provocar ▷ *vi* moverse; **stir up** *vt* (*trouble*) fomentar; **stir-fry** *vt* sofreír removiendo ▷ *n* *plato preparado sofriendo y removiendo los ingredientes*

stitch [stɪtʃ] *n* (*Sewing*) puntada; (*Knitting*) punto; (*Med*) punto (de sutura); (*pain*) punzada ▷ *vt* coser; (*Med*) suturar

stock [stɔk] *n* (*Comm*: *reserves*) existencias *fpl*, stock *m*; (: *selection*) surtido; (*Agr*) ganado, ganadería; (*Culin*) caldo; (*descent*) raza, estirpe *f*; (*Finance*) capital *m* ▷ *adj* (*fig*: *reply etc*) clásico ▷ *vt* (*have in stock*) tener existencias de; **~s and shares** acciones y valores; **in ~** en existencia *or* almacén; **out of ~** agotado; **to take ~ of** (*fig*) asesorar, examinar; **stockbroker** ['stɔkbrəukə*] *n* agente *mf or* corredor *mf* de bolsa(a); **stock cube** (BRIT) *n* pastilla de caldo; **stock exchange** *n* bolsa; **stockholder** ['stɔk-həuldə*] (US) *n* accionista *m/f*

stocking ['stɔkɪŋ] *n* media

stock market *n* bolsa (de valores)

stole [stəul] *pt of* **steal** ▷ *n* estola

stolen ['stəuln] *pp of* **steal**

stomach ['stʌmək] *n* (*Anat*) estómago; (*belly*) vientre *m* ▷ *vt* tragar, aguantar; **stomachache** *n* dolor *m* de estómago

stone [stəun] *n* piedra; (*in fruit*) hueso (= *6.348 kg*; *14 libras*) ▷ *adj* de piedra ▷ *vt* apedrear; (*fruit*) deshuesar

stood [stud] *pt, pp of* **stand**

stool [stu:l] *n* taburete *m*

stoop [stu:p] *vi* (*also*: **~ down**) doblarse, agacharse; (*also*: **have a ~**) ser cargado de espaldas

stop [stɔp] *n* parada; (*in punctuation*) punto ▷ *vt* parar, detener; (*break*) suspender; (*block*: *pay*) suspender; (: *cheque*) invalidar; (*also*: **put a ~ to**) poner término a ▷ *vi* pararse, detenerse; (*end*) acabarse; **to ~ doing sth** dejar de hacer algo; **stop by** *vi* pasar por; **stop off** *vi* interrumpir el viaje; **stopover** *n* parada; (*Aviat*) escala; **stoppage** *n* (*strike*) paro; (*blockage*) obstrucción *f*

storage ['stɔ:rɪdʒ] *n* almacenaje *m*

store [stɔ:*] *n* (*stock*) provisión *f*; (*depot* (BRIT: *large shop*) almacén *m*; (US) tienda; (*reserve*) reserva, repuesto ▷ *vt* almacenar; **stores** *npl* víveres *mpl*; **to be in ~ for sb** (*fig*) esperarle a algn; **storekeeper** (US) *n* tendero/a

storey ['stɔ:rɪ] (US **story**) *n* piso

storm [stɔ:m] *n* tormenta; (*fig*: *of*

applause) salva; (: *of criticism*) nube *f* ▷ *vi* (*fig*) rabiar ▷ *vt* tomar por asalto; **stormy** *adj* tempestuoso

story ['stɔːrɪ] *n* historia; (*lie*) mentira; (*US*) = **storey**

stout [staut] *adj* (*strong*) sólido; (*fat*) gordo, corpulento; (*resolute*) resuelto ▷ *n* cerveza negra

stove [stəuv] *n* (*for cooking*) cocina; (*for heating*) estufa

straight [streɪt] *adj* recto, derecho; (*frank*) franco, directo; (*simple*) sencillo ▷ *adv* derecho, directamente; (*drink*) sin mezcla; **to put** *or* **get sth ~** dejar algo en claro; **~ away, ~ off** en seguida; **straighten** *vt* (*also*: **straighten out**) enderezar, poner derecho ▷ *vi* (*also*: **straighten up**) enderezarse, ponerse derecho; **straightforward** *adj* (*simple*) sencillo; (*honest*) honrado, franco

strain [streɪn] *n* tensión *f*; (*Tech*) presión *f*; (*Med*) torcedura; (*breed*) tipo, variedad *f* ▷ *vt* (*back etc*) torcerse; (*resources*) agotar; (*stretch*) estirar; (*food, tea*) colar; **strained** *adj* (*muscle*) torcido; (*laugh*) forzado; (*relations*) tenso; **strainer** *n* colador *m*

strait [streɪt] *n* (*Geo*) estrecho (*fig*): **to be in dire ~s** estar en un gran apuro

strand [strænd] *n* (*of thread*) hebra; (*of hair*) trenza; (*of rope*) ramal *m*; **stranded** *adj* (*person*: *without money*) desamparado; (: *without transport*) colgado

strange [streɪndʒ] *adj* (*not known*) desconocido; (*odd*) extraño, raro; **strangely** *adv* de un modo raro; **stranger** *n* desconocido/a; (*from another area*) forastero/a

Be careful not to translate **stranger** by the Spanish word *extranjero*.

strangle ['stræŋgl] *vt* estrangular

strap [stræp] *n* correa; (*of slip, dress*) tirante *m*

strategic [strə'tiːdʒɪk] *adj* estratégico

strategy ['strætɪdʒɪ] *n* estrategia

straw [strɔː] *n* paja; (*drinking straw*) caña, pajita; **that's the last ~!** ¡eso es el colmo!

strawberry ['strɔːbərɪ] *n* fresa, frutilla (*SC*)

stray [streɪ] *adj* (*animal*) extraviado; (*bullet*) perdido; (*scattered*) disperso ▷ *vi* extraviarse, perderse

streak [striːk] *n* raya; (*in hair*) raya ▷ *vt* rayar ▷ *vi*: **to ~ past** pasar como un rayo

stream [striːm] *n* riachuelo, arroyo; (*of people, vehicles*) riada, caravana; (*of smoke, insults etc*) chorro ▷ *vt* (*Scol*) dividir en grupos por habilidad ▷ *vi* correr, fluir; **to ~ in/out** (*people*) entrar/salir en tropel

street [striːt] *n* calle *f*; **streetcar** (*US*) *n* tranvía *m*; **street light** *n* farol *m* (*LAM*), farola (*SP*); **street map** *n* plano (de la ciudad); **street plan** *n* plano

strength [strɛŋθ] *n* fuerza; (*of girder, knot etc*) resistencia; (*fig*: *power*) poder *m*; **strengthen** *vt* fortalecer, reforzar

strenuous ['strɛnjuəs] *adj* (*energetic, determined*) enérgico

stress [strɛs] *n* presión *f*; (*mental strain*) estrés *m*; (*accent*) acento ▷ *vt* subrayar, recalcar; (*syllable*) acentuar; **stressed** *adj* (*tense* estresado, agobiado; (*syllable*) acentuado; **stressful** *adj* (*job*) estresante

stretch [strɛtʃ] *n* (*of sand etc*) trecho ▷ *vi* estirarse; (*extend*): **to ~ to** *or* **as far as** extenderse hasta ▷ *vt* extender, estirar; (*make demands*) exigir el máximo esfuerzo a; **stretch out** *vi* tenderse ▷ *vt* (*arm etc*) extender; (*spread*) estirar

stretcher ['strɛtʃə*] *n* camilla

strict [strɪkt] *adj* severo; (*exact*) estricto; **strictly** *adv* severamente; estrictamente

stride [straɪd] (*pt* **strode**, *pp* **stridden**) *n* zancada, tranco ▷ *vi* dar zancadas, andar a trancos

strike [straɪk] (*pt, pp* **struck**) *n* huelga; (*of oil etc*) descubrimiento; (*attack*) ataque *m* ▷ *vt* golpear, pegar; (*oil etc*) descubrir; (*bargain, deal*) cerrar ▷ *vi* declarar la huelga; (*attack*) atacar; (*clock*) dar la hora; **on ~** (*workers*) en huelga; **to ~ a match** encender un fósforo; **striker** *n* huelguista *mf*; (*Sport*) delantero; **striking** *adj* llamativo

string [strɪŋ] (*pt, pp* **strung**) *n* cuerda; (*row*) hilera ▷ *vt*: **to ~ together** ensartar; **to ~ out** extenderse; **the strings** *npl* (*Mus*) los instrumentos de cuerda; **to pull ~s** (*fig*) mover palancas

strip [strɪp] *n* tira; (*of land*) franja; (*of metal*) cinta, lámina ▷ *vt* desnudar; (*paint*) quitar; (*also*: **~ down**: *machine*) desmontar ▷ *vi* desnudarse; **strip off** *vt* (*paint etc*) quitar ▷ *vi* (*person*) desnudarse

stripe [straɪp] *n* raya; (*Mil*) galón *m*; **striped** *adj* a rayas, rayado

stripper ['strɪpə*] *n* artista *mf* de striptease

strip-search ['strɪpsəːtʃ] *vt*: **to ~ sb** desnudar y registrar a algn

strive [straɪv] (*pt* **strove**, *pp* **striven**) *vi*: **to ~ for sth/to do sth** luchar por conseguir/hacer algo

strode [strəud] *pt of* **stride**

stroke [strəuk] *n* (*blow*) golpe *m*; (*Swimming*) brazada; (*Med*) apoplejía; (*of paintbrush*) toque *m* ▷ *vt* acariciar; **at a ~** de un solo golpe

stroll [strəul] *n* paseo, vuelta ▷*vi* dar un paseo *or* una vuelta; **stroller** (US) *n* (*for child*) sillita de ruedas
strong [strɔŋ] *adj* fuerte; **they are 50 ~** son 50; **stronghold** *n* fortaleza; (*fig*) baluarte *m*; **strongly** *adv* fuertemente, con fuerza; (*believe*) firmemente
strove [strəuv] *pt of* **strive**
struck [strʌk] *pt, pp of* **strike**
structure ['strʌktʃə*] *n* estructura; (*building*) construcción *f*
struggle ['strʌgl] *n* lucha ▷*vi* luchar
strung [strʌŋ] *pt, pp of* **string**
stub [stʌb] *n* (*of ticket etc*) talón *m*; (*of cigarette*) colilla; **to ~ one's toe on sth** dar con el dedo (del pie) contra algo; **stub out** *vt* apagar
stubble ['stʌbl] *n* rastrojo; (*on chin*) barba (incipiente)
stubborn ['stʌbən] *adj* terco, testarudo
stuck [stʌk] *pt, pp of* **stick** ▷*adj* (*jammed*) atascado
stud [stʌd] *n* (*shirt stud*) corchete *m*; (*of boot*) taco; (*earring*) pendiente *m* (de bolita); (*also*: **~ farm**) caballeriza; (*also*: **~ horse**) caballo semental ▷*vt* (*fig*): **~ded with** salpicado de
student ['stju:dənt] *n* estudiante *mf* ▷*adj* estudiantil; **student driver** (US) *n* conductor(a) *mf* en prácticas; **students' union** *n* (*building*) centro de estudiantes; (BRIT: *association*) federación *f* de estudiantes
studio ['stju:dɪəu] *n* estudio; (*artist's*) taller *m*; **studio flat** *n* estudio
study ['stʌdɪ] *n* estudio ▷*vt* estudiar; (*examine*) examinar, investigar ▷*vi* estudiar
stuff [stʌf] *n* materia; (*substance*) material *m*, sustancia; (*things*) cosas *fpl* ▷*vt* llenar; (*Culin*) rellenar; (*animals*) disecar; (*inf: push*) meter; **stuffing** *n* relleno; **stuffy** *adj* (*room*) mal ventilado; (*person*) de miras estrechas
stumble ['stʌmbl] *vi* tropezar, dar un traspié; **to ~ across, ~ on** (*fig*) tropezar con
stump [stʌmp] *n* (*of tree*) tocón *m*; (*of limb*) muñón *m* ▷*vt*: **to be ~ed for an answer** no saber qué contestar
stun [stʌn] *vt* dejar sin sentido
stung [stʌŋ] *pt, pp of* **sting**
stunk [stʌŋk] *pp of* **stink**
stunned [stʌnd] *adj* (*dazed*) aturdido, atontado; (*amazed*) pasmado; (*shocked*) anonadado
stunning ['stʌnɪŋ] *adj* (*fig: news*) pasmoso; (*: outfit etc*) sensacional
stunt [stʌnt] *n* (*in film*) escena peligrosa; (*publicity stunt*) truco publicitario
stupid ['stju:pɪd] *adj* estúpido, tonto; **stupidity** [-'pɪdɪtɪ] *n* estupidez *f*
sturdy ['stə:dɪ] *adj* robusto, fuerte
stutter ['stʌtə*] *n* tartamudeo ▷*vi* tartamudear
style [staɪl] *n* estilo; **stylish** *adj* elegante, a la moda; **stylist** *n* (*hair stylist*) peluquero/a
sub... [sʌb] *prefix* sub...; **subconscious** *adj* subconsciente
subdued [səb'dju:d] *adj* (*light*) tenue; (*person*) sumiso, manso
subject [*n* 'sʌbdʒɪkt, *vb* səb'dʒɛkt] *n* súbdito; (*Scol*) asignatura; (*matter*) tema *m*; (*Grammar*) sujeto ▷*vt*: **to ~ sb to sth** someter a algn a algo; **to be ~ to** (*law*) estar sujeto a; (*person*) ser propenso a; **subjective** [-'dʒɛktɪv] *adj* subjetivo; **subject matter** *n* (*content*) contenido
subjunctive [səb'dʒʌŋktɪv] *adj, n* subjuntivo
submarine [sʌbmə'ri:n] *n* submarino
submission [səb'mɪʃən] *n* sumisión *f*
submit [səb'mɪt] *vt* someter ▷*vi*: **to ~ to sth** someterse a algo
subordinate [sə'bɔ:dɪnət] *adj, n* subordinado/a *m/f*
subscribe [səb'skraɪb] *vi* suscribir; **to ~ to** (*opinion, fund*) suscribir, aprobar; (*newspaper*) suscribirse a
subscription [səb'skrɪpʃən] *n* abono; (*to magazine*) subscripción *f*
subsequent ['sʌbsɪkwənt] *adj* subsiguiente, posterior; **subsequently** *adv* posteriormente, más tarde
subside [səb'saɪd] *vi* hundirse; (*flood*) bajar; (*wind*) amainar
subsidiary [səb'sɪdɪərɪ] *adj* secundario ▷*n* sucursal *f*, filial *f*
subsidize ['sʌbsɪdaɪz] *vt* subvencionar
subsidy ['sʌbsɪdɪ] *n* subvención *f*
substance ['sʌbstəns] *n* sustancia
substantial [səb'stænʃl] *adj* sustancial, sustancioso; (*fig*) importante
substitute ['sʌbstɪtju:t] *n* (*person*) suplente *mf*; (*thing*) sustituto ▷*vt*: **to ~ A for B** sustituir A por B, reemplazar B por A; **substitution** *n* sustitución *f*
subtle ['sʌtl] *adj* sutil
subtract [səb'trækt] *vt* restar, sustraer
suburb ['sʌbə:b] *n* barrio residencial; **the ~s** las afueras (de la ciudad); **suburban** [sə'bə:bən] *adj* suburbano; (*train etc*) de cercanías
subway ['sʌbweɪ] *n* (BRIT) paso subterráneo *or* inferior; (US) metro
succeed [sək'si:d] *vi* (*person*) tener éxito; (*plan*) salir bien ▷*vt* suceder a; **to ~ in**

doing lograr hacer
success [sək'sɛs] *n* éxito

Be careful not to translate **success** by the Spanish word *suceso*.

successful *adj* exitoso; (*business*) próspero; **to be successful (in doing)** lograr (hacer); **successfully** *adv* con éxito
succession [sək'sɛʃən] *n* sucesión *f*, serie *f*
successive [sək'sɛsɪv] *adj* sucesivo, consecutivo
successor [sək'sɛsə*] *n* sucesor(a) *m/f*
succumb [sə'kʌm] *vi* sucumbir
such [sʌtʃ] *adj* tal, semejante; (*of that kind*): **~ a book** tal libro; (*so much*): **~ courage** tanto valor ▷*adv* tan; **~ a long trip** un viaje tan largo; **~ a lot of** tanto(s)/a(s); **~ as** (*like*) tal como; **as ~** como tal; **such-and-such** *adj* tal o cual
suck [sʌk] *vt* chupar; (*bottle*) sorber; (*breast*) mamar
Sudan [su'dæn] *n* Sudán *m*
sudden ['sʌdn] *adj* (*rapid*) repentino, súbito; (*unexpected*) imprevisto; **all of a ~** de repente; **suddenly** *adv* de repente
sue [su:] *vt* demandar
suede [sweɪd] *n* ante *m*, gamuza
suffer ['sʌfə*] *vt* sufrir, padecer; (*tolerate*) aguantar, soportar ▷*vi* sufrir; **to ~ from** (*illness etc*) padecer; **suffering** *n* sufrimiento
suffice [sə'faɪs] *vi* bastar, ser suficiente
sufficient [sə'fɪʃənt] *adj* suficiente, bastante
suffocate ['sʌfəkeɪt] *vi* ahogarse, asfixiarse
sugar ['ʃugə*] *n* azúcar *m* ▷*vt* echar azúcar a, azucarar
suggest [sə'dʒɛst] *vt* sugerir; **suggestion** [-'dʒɛstʃən] *n* sugerencia
suicide ['suɪsaɪd] *n* suicidio; (*person*) suicida *mf*; *see also* **commit**; **suicide attack** *n* atentado suicida; **suicide bomber** *n* terrorista *mf* suicida; **suicide bombing** *n* atentado suicida
suit [su:t] *n* (*man's*) traje *m*; (*woman's*) conjunto; (*Law*) pleito; (*Cards*) palo ▷*vt* convenir; (*clothes*) sentar a, ir bien a; (*adapt*): **to ~ sth to** adaptar *or* ajustar algo a; **well ~ed** (*well matched*: *couple*) hecho el uno para el otro; **suitable** *adj* conveniente; (*apt*) indicado; **suitcase** *n* maleta, valija (RPL)
suite [swi:t] *n* (*of rooms, Mus*) suite *f*; (*furniture*): **bedroom/dining room ~** (juego de) dormitorio/comedor; *see also* **three-piece suite**
sulfur ['sʌlfə*] (US) *n* = **sulphur**
sulk [sʌlk] *vi* estar de mal humor
sulphur ['sʌlfə*] (US **sulfur**) *n* azufre *m*
sultana [sʌl'tɑ:nə] *n* (*fruit*) pasa de Esmirna
sum [sʌm] *n* suma; (*total*) total *m*; **sum up** *vt* resumir ▷*vi* hacer un resumen
summarize ['sʌməraɪz] *vt* resumir
summary ['sʌmərɪ] *n* resumen *m* ▷*adj* (*justice*) sumario
summer ['sʌmə*] *n* verano ▷*cpd* de verano; **in ~** en verano; **summer holidays** *npl* vacaciones *fpl* de verano; **summertime** *n* (*season*) verano
summit ['sʌmɪt] *n* cima, cumbre *f*; (*also*: **~ conference, ~ meeting**) (conferencia) cumbre *f*
summon ['sʌmən] *vt* (*person*) llamar; (*meeting*) convocar; (*Law*) citar
Sun. *abbr* (= *Sunday*) dom
sun [sʌn] *n* sol *m*; **sunbathe** *vi* tomar el sol; **sunbed** *n* cama solar; **sunblock** *n* filtro solar; **sunburn** *n* (*painful*) quemadura; (*tan*) bronceado; **sunburned, sunburnt** *adj* (*painfully*) quemado por el sol; (*tanned*) bronceado
Sunday ['sʌndɪ] *n* domingo
sunflower ['sʌnflauə*] *n* girasol *m*
sung [sʌŋ] *pp of* **sing**
sunglasses ['sʌnglɑ:sɪz] *npl* gafas *fpl* (SP) *or* anteojos *fpl* (LAM) de sol
sunk [sʌŋk] *pp of* **sink**
sun: sunlight *n* luz *f* del sol; **sun lounger** *n* tumbona, perezosa (LAM); **sunny** *adj* soleado; (*day*) de sol; (*fig*) alegre; **sunrise** *n* salida del sol; **sun roof** *n* (*Aut*) techo corredizo; **sunscreen** *n* protector *m* solar; **sunset** *n* puesta del sol; **sunshade** *n* (*over table*) sombrilla; **sunshine** *n* sol *m*; **sunstroke** *n* insolación *f*; **suntan** *n* bronceado; **suntan lotion** *n* bronceador *m*; **suntan oil** *n* aceite *m* bronceador
super ['su:pə*] (*inf*) *adj* genial
superb [su:'pə:b] *adj* magnífico, espléndido
superficial [su:pə'fɪʃəl] *adj* superficial
superintendent [su:pərɪn'tɛndənt] *n* director(a) *m/f*; (*Police*) subjefe/a *m/f*
superior [su'pɪərɪə*] *adj* superior; (*smug*) desdeñoso ▷*n* superior *m*
superlative [su'pə:lətɪv] *n* superlativo
supermarket ['su:pəmɑ:kɪt] *n* supermercado
supernatural [su:pə'nætʃərəl] *adj* sobrenatural ▷*n*: **the ~** lo sobrenatural
superpower ['su:pəpauə*] *n* (*Pol*) superpotencia
superstition [su:pə'stɪʃən] *n* superstición *f*
superstitious [su:pə'stɪʃəs] *adj* supersticioso

S

superstore ['su:pəstɔ:*] *n* (BRIT) hipermercado
supervise ['su:pəvaɪz] *vt* supervisar; **supervision** [-'vɪʒən] *n* supervisión *f*; **supervisor** *n* supervisor(a) *m/f*
supper ['sʌpə*] *n* cena
supple ['sʌpl] *adj* flexible
supplement [*n* 'sʌplɪmənt, *vb* sʌplɪ'mɛnt] *n* suplemento ▷ *vt* suplir
supplier [sə'plaɪə*] *n* (*Comm*) distribuidor(a) *m/f*
supply [sə'plaɪ] *vt* (*provide*) suministrar; (*equip*): **to ~ (with)** proveer (de) ▷ *n* provisión *f*; (*of gas, water etc*) suministro; **supplies** *npl* (*food*) víveres *mpl*; (*Mil*) pertrechos *mpl*
support [sə'pɔ:t] *n* apoyo; (*Tech*) soporte *m* ▷ *vt* apoyar; (*financially*) mantener; (*uphold, Tech*) sostener

> Be careful not to translate **support** by the Spanish word *soportar*.

supporter *n* (*Pol etc*) partidario/a; (*Sport*) aficionado/a
suppose [sə'pəuz] *vt* suponer; (*imagine*) imaginarse; (*duty*): **to be ~d to do sth** deber hacer algo; **supposedly** [sə'pəuzɪdlɪ] *adv* según cabe suponer; **supposing** *conj* en caso de que
suppress [sə'prɛs] *vt* suprimir; (*yawn*) ahogar
supreme [su'pri:m] *adj* supremo
surcharge ['sə:tʃɑ:dʒ] *n* sobretasa, recargo
sure [ʃuə*] *adj* seguro; (*definite, convinced*) cierto; **to make ~ of sth/that** asegurarse de algo/asegurar que; **~!** (*of course*) ¡claro!, ¡por supuesto!; **~ enough** efectivamente; **surely** *adv* (*certainly*) seguramente
surf [sə:f] *n* olas *fpl* ▷ *vt*: **to ~ the Net** navegar por Internet
surface ['sə:fɪs] *n* superficie *f* ▷ *vt* (*road*) revestir ▷ *vi* salir a la superficie; **by ~ mail** por vía terrestre
surfboard ['sə:fbɔ:d] *n* tabla (de surf)
surfer ['sə:fə*] *n* (*in sea*) surfista *mf*; **web** *or* **net ~** internauta *mf*
surfing ['sə:fɪŋ] *n* surf *m*
surge [sə:dʒ] *n* oleada, oleaje *m* ▷ *vi* (*wave*) romper; (*people*) avanzar en tropel
surgeon ['sə:dʒən] *n* cirujano/a
surgery ['sə:dʒərɪ] *n* cirugía; (BRIT: *room*) consultorio
surname ['sə:neɪm] *n* apellido
surpass [sə:'pɑ:s] *vt* superar, exceder
surplus ['sə:pləs] *n* excedente *m*; (*Comm*) superávit *m* ▷ *adj* excedente, sobrante
surprise [sə'praɪz] *n* sorpresa ▷ *vt* sorprender; **surprised** *adj* (*look, smile*) de sorpresa; **to be surprised** sorprenderse; **surprising** *adj* sorprendente; **surprisingly** *adv*: **it was surprisingly easy** me *etc* sorprendió lo fácil que fue
surrender [sə'rɛndə*] *n* rendición *f*, entrega ▷ *vi* rendirse, entregarse
surround [sə'raund] *vt* rodear, circundar; (*Mil etc*) cercar; **surrounding** *adj* circundante; **surroundings** *npl* alrededores *mpl*, cercanías *fpl*
surveillance [sə:'veɪləns] *n* vigilancia
survey [*n* 'sə:veɪ, *vb* sə:'veɪ] *n* inspección *f*, reconocimiento; (*inquiry*) encuesta ▷ *vt* examinar, inspeccionar; (*look at*) mirar, contemplar; **surveyor** *n* agrimensor(a) *m/f*
survival [sə'vaɪvl] *n* supervivencia
survive [sə'vaɪv] *vi* sobrevivir; (*custom etc*) perdurar ▷ *vt* sobrevivir a; **survivor** *n* superviviente *mf*
suspect [*adj, n* 'sʌspɛkt, *vb* səs'pɛkt] *adj, n* sospechoso/a *m/f* ▷ *vt* (*person*) sospechar de; (*think*) sospechar
suspend [səs'pɛnd] *vt* suspender; **suspended sentence** *n* (*Law*) libertad *f* condicional; **suspenders** *npl* (BRIT) ligas *fpl*; (US) tirantes *mpl*
suspense [səs'pɛns] *n* incertidumbre *f*, duda; (*in film etc*) suspense *m*; **to keep sb in ~** mantener a algn en suspense
suspension [səs'pɛnʃən] *n* (*gen, Aut*) suspensión *f*; (*of driving licence*) privación *f*; **suspension bridge** *n* puente *m* colgante
suspicion [səs'pɪʃən] *n* sospecha; (*distrust*) recelo; **suspicious** *adj* receloso; (*causing suspicion*) sospechoso
sustain [səs'teɪn] *vt* sostener, apoyar; (*suffer*) sufrir, padecer
SUV (*esp* US) *n abbr* (= *sports utility vehicle*) todoterreno *m inv*, 4x4 *m*
swallow ['swɔləu] *n* (*bird*) golondrina ▷ *vt* tragar; (*fig.: pride*) tragarse
swam [swæm] *pt of* **swim**
swamp [swɔmp] *n* pantano, ciénaga ▷ *vt* (*with water etc*) inundar; (*fig*) abrumar, agobiar
swan [swɔn] *n* cisne *m*
swap [swɔp] *n* canje *m*, intercambio ▷ *vt*: **to ~ (for)** cambiar (por)
swarm [swɔ:m] *n* (*of bees*) enjambre *m*; (*fig*) multitud *f* ▷ *vi* (*bees*) formar un enjambre; (*people*) pulular; **to be ~ing with** ser un hervidero de
sway [sweɪ] *vi* mecerse, balancearse ▷ *vt* (*influence*) mover, influir en
swear [swɛə*] (*pt* **swore**, *pp* **sworn**) *vi* (*curse*) maldecir; (*promise*) jurar ▷ *vt* jurar; **swear in** *vt*: **to be sworn in** prestar juramento; **swearword** *n* taco, palabrota

sweat [swɛt] *n* sudor *m* ▷ *vi* sudar
sweater ['swɛtə*] *n* suéter *m*
sweatshirt ['swɛtʃə:t] *n* suéter *m*
sweaty ['swɛtɪ] *adj* sudoroso
Swede [swi:d] *n* sueco/a
swede [swi:d] (BRIT) *n* nabo
Sweden ['swi:dn] *n* Suecia; **Swedish** ['swi:dɪʃ] *adj* sueco ▷ *n* (*Ling*) sueco
sweep [swi:p] (*pt, pp* **swept**) *n* (*act*) barrido; (*also*: **chimney ~**) deshollinador(a) *m/f* ▷ *vt* barrer; (*with arm*) empujar; (*current*) arrastrar ▷ *vi* barrer; (*arm etc*) moverse rápidamente; (*wind*) soplar con violencia
sweet [swi:t] *n* (*candy*) dulce *m*, caramelo; (BRIT: *pudding*) postre *m* ▷ *adj* dulce; (*fig*: *kind*) dulce, amable; (: *attractive*) mono; **sweetcorn** *n* maíz *m*; **sweetener** ['swi:tnə*] *n* (*Culin*) edulcorante *m*; **sweetheart** *n* novio/a; **sweetshop** *n* (BRIT) confitería, bombonería
swell [swɛl] (*pt* **~ed**, *pp* **swollen** *or* **~ed**) *n* (*of sea*) marejada, oleaje *m* ▷ *adj* (US: *inf*: *excellent*) estupendo, fenomenal ▷ *vt* hinchar, inflar ▷ *vi* (*also*: **~ up**) hincharse; (*numbers*) aumentar; (*sound, feeling*) ir aumentando; **swelling** *n* (*Med*) hinchazón *f*
swept [swɛpt] *pt, pp of* **sweep**
swerve [swə:v] *vi* desviarse bruscamente
swift [swɪft] *n* (*bird*) vencejo ▷ *adj* rápido, veloz
swim [swɪm] (*pt* **swam**, *pp* **swum**) *n*: **to go for a ~** ir a nadar *or* a bañarse ▷ *vi* nadar; (*head, room*) dar vueltas ▷ *vt* nadar; (*the Channel etc*) cruzar a nado; **swimmer** *n* nadador(a) *m/f*; **swimming** *n* natación *f*; **swimming costume** (BRIT) *n* bañador *m*, traje *m* de baño; **swimming pool** *n* piscina, alberca (MEX), pileta (RPL); **swimming trunks** *npl* bañador *m* (de hombre); **swimsuit** *n* = **swimming costume**
swing [swɪŋ] (*pt, pp* **swung**) *n* (*in playground*) columpio; (*movement*) balanceo, vaivén *m*; (*change of direction*) viraje *m*; (*rhythm*) ritmo ▷ *vt* balancear; (*also*: **~ round**) voltear, girar ▷ *vi* balancearse, columpiarse; (*also*: **~ round**) dar media vuelta; **to be in full ~** estar en plena marcha
swipe card [swaɪp-] *n* tarjeta magnética deslizante, tarjeta swipe
swirl [swə:l] *vi* arremolinarse
Swiss [swɪs] *adj, n inv* suizo/a *m/f*
switch [swɪtʃ] *n* (*for light etc*) interruptor *m*; (*change*) cambio ▷ *vt* (*change*) cambiar de; **switch off** *vt* apagar; (*engine*) parar; **switch on** *vt* encender (SP), prender (LAM); (*engine, machine*) arrancar; **switchboard** *n* (*Tel*) centralita (SP), conmutador *m* (LAM)
Switzerland ['swɪtsələnd] *n* Suiza
swivel ['swɪvl] *vi* (*also*: **~ round**) girar
swollen ['swəulən] *pp of* **swell**
swoop [swu:p] *n* (*by police etc*) redada ▷ *vi* (*also*: **~ down**) calarse
swop [swɔp] = **swap**
sword [sɔ:d] *n* espada; **swordfish** *n* pez *m* espada
swore [swɔ:*] *pt of* **swear**
sworn [swɔ:n] *pp of* **swear** ▷ *adj* (*statement*) bajo juramento; (*enemy*) implacable
swum [swʌm] *pp of* **swim**
swung [swʌŋ] *pt, pp of* **swing**
syllable ['sɪləbl] *n* sílaba
syllabus ['sɪləbəs] *n* programa *m* de estudios
symbol ['sɪmbl] *n* símbolo; **symbolic(al)** [sɪm'bɔlɪk(l)] *adj* simbólico; **to be symbolic(al) of sth** simbolizar algo
symmetrical [sɪ'mɛtrɪkl] *adj* simétrico
symmetry ['sɪmɪtrɪ] *n* simetría
sympathetic [sɪmpə'θɛtɪk] *adj* (*understanding*) comprensivo; (*showing support*): **~ to(wards)** bien dispuesto hacia

Be careful not to translate **sympathetic** by the Spanish word *simpático*.

sympathize ['sɪmpəθaɪz] *vi*: **to ~ with** (*person*) compadecerse de; (*feelings*) comprender; (*cause*) apoyar
sympathy ['sɪmpəθɪ] *n* (*pity*) compasión *f*
symphony ['sɪmfənɪ] *n* sinfonía
symptom ['sɪmptəm] *n* síntoma *m*, indicio
synagogue ['sɪnəgɔg] *n* sinagoga
syndicate ['sɪndɪkɪt] *n* sindicato; (*of newspapers*) agencia (de noticias)
syndrome ['sɪndrəum] *n* síndrome *m*
synonym ['sɪnənɪm] *n* sinónimo
synthetic [sɪn'θɛtɪk] *adj* sintético
Syria ['sɪrɪə] *n* Siria
syringe [sɪ'rɪndʒ] *n* jeringa
syrup ['sɪrəp] *n* jarabe *m*; (*also*: **golden ~**) almíbar *m*
system ['sɪstəm] *n* sistema *m*; (*Anat*) organismo; **systematic** [-'mætɪk] *adj* sistemático, metódico; **systems analyst** *n* analista *mf* de sistemas

ta [tɑː] (BRIT: *inf*) *excl* ¡gracias!
tab [tæb] *n* lengüeta; (*label*) etiqueta; **to keep ~s on** (*fig*) vigilar
table ['teɪbl] *n* mesa; (*of statistics etc*) cuadro, tabla ▷*vt* (BRIT: *motion etc*) presentar; **to lay** *or* **set the ~** poner la mesa; **tablecloth** *n* mantel *m*; **table d'hôte** [tɑːbl'dəut] *adj* del menú; **table lamp** *n* lámpara de mesa; **tablemat** *n* (*for plate*) posaplatos *m inv*; (*for hot dish*) salvamantel *m*; **tablespoon** *n* cuchara de servir; (*also*: **tablespoonful**: *as measurement*) cucharada
tablet ['tæblɪt] *n* (*Med*) pastilla, comprimido; (*of stone*) lápida
table tennis *n* ping-pong *m*, tenis *m* de mesa
tabloid ['tæblɔɪd] *n* periódico popular sensacionalista

TABLOID PRESS

El término **tabloid press** o **tabloids** se usa para referirse a la prensa popular británica, por el tamaño más pequeño de los periódicos. A diferencia de los de la llamada **quality press**, estas publicaciones se caracterizan por un lenguaje sencillo, una presentación llamativa y un contenido sensacionalista, centrado a veces en los escándalos financieros y sexuales de los famosos, por lo que también reciben el nombre peyorativo de "gutter press".

taboo [tə'buː] *adj, n* tabú *m*
tack [tæk] *n* (*nail*) tachuela; (*fig*) rumbo ▷*vt* (*nail*) clavar con tachuelas; (*stitch*) hilvanar ▷*vi* virar
tackle ['tækl] *n* (*fishing tackle*) aparejo (de pescar); (*for lifting*) aparejo ▷*vt* (*difficulty*) enfrentarse con; (*challenge*: *person*) hacer frente a; (*grapple with*) agarrar; (*Football*) cargar; (*Rugby*) placar
tacky ['tækɪ] *adj* pegajoso; (*pej*) cutre
tact [tækt] *n* tacto, discreción *f*; **tactful** *adj* discreto, diplomático
tactics ['tæktɪks] *npl* táctica
tactless ['tæktlɪs] *adj* indiscreto
tadpole ['tædpəul] *n* renacuajo
taffy ['tæfɪ] (US) *n* melcocha
tag [tæg] *n* (*label*) etiqueta
tail [teɪl] *n* cola; (*of shirt, coat*) faldón *m* ▷*vt* (*follow*) vigilar a; **tails** *npl* (*formal suit*) levita
tailor ['teɪlə*] *n* sastre *m*
Taiwan [taɪ'wɑːn] *n* Taiwán *m*; **Taiwanese** [taɪwə'niːz] *adj, n* taiwanés/esa *m/f*
take [teɪk] (*pt* **took**, *pp* **taken**) *vt* tomar; (*grab*) coger (SP), agarrar (LAM); (*gain*: *prize*) ganar; (*require*: *effort, courage*) exigir; (*tolerate*: *pain etc*) aguantar; (*hold*: *passengers etc*) tener cabida para; (*accompany, bring, carry*) llevar; (*exam*) presentarse a; **to ~ sth from** (*drawer etc*) sacar algo de; (*person*) quitar algo a; **I ~ it that ...** supongo que ...; **take after** *vt fus* parecerse a; **take apart** *vt* desmontar; **take away** *vt* (*remove*) quitar; (*carry*) llevar; (*Math*) restar; **take back** *vt* (*return*) devolver; (*one's words*) retractarse de; **take down** *vt* (*building*) derribar; (*letter etc*) apuntar; **take in** *vt* (*deceive*) engañar; (*understand*) entender; (*include*) abarcar; (*lodger*) acoger, recibir; **take off** *vi* (*Aviat*) despegar ▷*vt* (*remove*) quitar; **take on** *vt* (*work*) aceptar; (*employee*) contratar; (*opponent*) desafiar; **take out** *vt* sacar; **take over** *vt* (*business*) tomar posesión de; (*country*) tomar el poder ▷*vi*: **to take over from sb** reemplazar a algn; **take up** *vt* (*a dress*) acortar; (*occupy*: *time, space*) ocupar; (*engage in*: *hobby etc*) dedicarse a; (*accept*): **to take sb up on** aceptar algo de algn; **takeaway** (BRIT) *adj* (*food*) para llevar ▷*n* tienda *or* restaurante *m* de comida para llevar; **taken** *pp of* **take**; **takeoff** *n* (*Aviat*) despegue *m*; **takeout** (US) *n* = **takeaway**; **takeover** *n* (*Comm*) absorción *f*; **takings** *npl* (*Comm*) ingresos *mpl*
talc [tælk] *n* (*also*: **~um powder**) (polvos de) talco
tale [teɪl] *n* (*story*) cuento; (*account*) relación *f*; **to tell ~s** (*fig*) chivarse
talent ['tælnt] *n* talento; **talented** *adj* de talento
talk [tɔːk] *n* charla; (*conversation*) conversación *f*; (*gossip*) habladurías *fpl*, chismes *mpl* ▷*vi* hablar; **talks** *npl* (*Pol etc*) conversaciones *fpl*; **to ~ about** hablar de; **to ~ sb into doing sth** convencer a algn para que haga algo; **to ~ sb out of doing sth**

disuadir a algn de que haga algo; **to ~ shop** hablar del trabajo; **talk over** *vt* discutir; **talk show** *n* programa *m* de entrevistas

tall [tɔːl] *adj* alto; (*object*) grande; **to be 6 feet ~** (*person*) ≈ medir 1 metro 80

tambourine [tæmbəˈriːn] *n* pandereta

tame [teɪm] *adj* domesticado; (*fig*) mediocre

tamper [ˈtæmpə*] *vi*: **to ~ with** tocar, andar con

tampon [ˈtæmpən] *n* tampón *m*

tan [tæn] *n* (*also*: **sun~**) bronceado ▷ *vi* ponerse moreno ▷ *adj* (*colour*) marrón

tandem [ˈtændəm] *n* tándem *m*

tangerine [tændʒəˈriːn] *n* mandarina

tangle [ˈtæŋgl] *n* enredo; **to get in(to) a ~** enredarse

tank [tæŋk] *n* (*water tank*) depósito, tanque *m*; (*for fish*) acuario; (*Mil*) tanque *m*

tanker [ˈtæŋkə*] *n* (*ship*) buque *m*, cisterna; (*truck*) camión *m* cisterna

tanned [tænd] *adj* (*skin*) moreno

tantrum [ˈtæntrəm] *n* rabieta

Tanzania [tænzəˈnɪə] *n* Tanzania

tap [tæp] *n* (BRIT: *on sink etc*) grifo (SP), llave *f*, canilla (RPL); (*gas tap*) llave *f*; (*gentle blow*) golpecito ▷ *vt* (*hit gently*) dar golpecitos en; (*resources*) utilizar, explotar; (*telephone*) intervenir; **on ~** (*fig*: *resources*) a mano; **tap dancing** *n* claqué *m*

tape [teɪp] *n* (*also*: **magnetic ~**) cinta magnética; (*cassette*) cassette *f*, cinta; (*sticky tape*) cinta adhesiva; (*for tying*) cinta ▷ *vt* (*record*) grabar (en cinta); (*stick with tape*) pegar con cinta adhesiva; **tape measure** *n* cinta métrica, metro; **tape recorder** *n* grabadora

tapestry [ˈtæpɪstrɪ] *n* (*object*) tapiz *m*; (*art*) tapicería

tar [tɑː] *n* alquitrán *m*, brea

target [ˈtɑːgɪt] *n* blanco

tariff [ˈtærɪf] *n* (*on goods*) arancel *m*; (BRIT: *in hotels etc*) tarifa

tarmac [ˈtɑːmæk] *n* (BRIT: *on road*) asfaltado; (*Aviat*) pista (de aterrizaje)

tarpaulin [tɑːˈpɔːlɪn] *n* lona impermeabilizada

tarragon [ˈtærəgən] *n* estragón *m*

tart [tɑːt] *n* (*Culin*) tarta; (BRIT: *inf*: *prostitute*) puta ▷ *adj* agrio, ácido

tartan [ˈtɑːtn] *n* tejido escocés *m*

tartar(e) sauce [ˈtɑːtə-] *n* salsa tártara

task [tɑːsk] *n* tarea; **to take to ~** reprender

taste [teɪst] *n* (*sense*) gusto; (*flavour*) sabor *m*; (*sample*): **have a ~!** ¡prueba un poquito!; (*fig*) muestra, idea ▷ *vt* probar ▷ *vi*: **to ~ of** *or* **like** (*fish, garlic etc*) saber a; **you can ~ the garlic (in it)** se nota el sabor a ajo; **in good/bad ~** de buen/mal gusto; **tasteful** *adj* de buen gusto; **tasteless** *adj* (*food*) soso; (*remark etc*) de mal gusto; **tasty** *adj* sabroso, rico

tatters [ˈtætəz] *npl*: **in ~** hecho jirones

tattoo [təˈtuː] *n* tatuaje *m*; (*spectacle*) espectáculo militar ▷ *vt* tatuar

taught [tɔːt] *pt, pp of* **teach**

taunt [tɔːnt] *n* burla ▷ *vt* burlarse de

Taurus [ˈtɔːrəs] *n* Tauro

taut [tɔːt] *adj* tirante, tenso

tax [tæks] *n* impuesto ▷ *vt* gravar (con un impuesto); (*fig*: *memory*) poner a prueba; (: *patience*) agotar; **tax-free** *adj* libre de impuestos

taxi [ˈtæksɪ] *n* taxi *m* ▷ *vi* (*Aviat*) rodar por la pista; **taxi driver** *n* taxista *mf*; **taxi rank** (BRIT) *n* = **taxi stand**; **taxi stand** *n* parada de taxis

tax payer *n* contribuyente *mf*

TB *n abbr* = **tuberculosis**

tea [tiː] *n* té *m*; (BRIT: *meal*) ≈ merienda (SP); cena; **high ~** (BRIT) merienda-cena (SP); **tea bag** *n* bolsita de té; **tea break** (BRIT) *n* descanso para el té

teach [tiːtʃ] (*pt, pp* **taught**) *vt*: **to ~ sb sth, ~ sth to sb** enseñar algo a algn ▷ *vi* (*be a teacher*) ser profesor(a), enseñar; **teacher** *n* (*in secondary school*) profesor(a) *m/f*; (*in primary school*) maestro/a, profesor(a) de EGB; **teaching** *n* enseñanza

tea: tea cloth *n* (BRIT) paño de cocina, trapo de cocina (LAM); **teacup** *n* taza para el té

tea leaves *npl* hojas de té

team [tiːm] *n* equipo; (*of horses*) tiro; **team up** *vi* asociarse

teapot [ˈtiːpɔt] *n* tetera

tear[1] [tɪə*] *n* lágrima; **in ~s** llorando

tear[2] [tɛə*] (*pt* **tore**, *pp* **torn**) *n* rasgón *m*, desgarrón *m* ▷ *vt* romper, rasgar ▷ *vi* rasgarse; **tear apart** *vt* (*also fig*) hacer pedazos; **tear down** *vt +adv* (*building, statue*) derribar; (*poster, flag*) arrancar; **tear off** *vt* (*sheet of paper etc*) arrancar; (*one's clothes*) quitarse a tirones; **tear up** *vt* (*sheet of paper etc*) romper

tearful [ˈtɪəfəl] *adj* lloroso

tear gas [ˈtɪə-] *n* gas *m* lacrimógeno

tearoom [ˈtiːruːm] *n* salón *m* de té

tease [tiːz] *vt* tomar el pelo a

tea: teaspoon *n* cucharita; (*also*: **teaspoonful**: *as measurement*) cucharadita; **teatime** *n* hora del té; **tea towel** (BRIT) *n* paño de cocina

technical [ˈtɛknɪkl] *adj* técnico

technician [tɛkˈnɪʃn] *n* técnico/a

technique [tɛkˈniːk] *n* técnica

technology [tɛkˈnɔlədʒɪ] *n* tecnología

teddy (bear) ['tɛdɪ-] *n* osito de felpa
tedious ['tiːdɪəs] *adj* pesado, aburrido
tee [tiː] *n* (*Golf*) tee *m*
teen [tiːn] *adj* = **teenage** ▷ *n* (US) = **teenager**
teenage ['tiːneɪdʒ] *adj* (*fashions etc*) juvenil; (*children*) quinceañero; **teenager** *n* adolescente *mf*
teens [tiːnz] *npl*: **to be in one's ~** ser adolescente
teeth [tiːθ] *npl of* **tooth**
teetotal ['tiː'təutl] *adj* abstemio
telecommunications [tɛlɪkəmjuːnɪ'keɪʃənz] *n* telecomunicaciones *fpl*
telegram ['tɛlɪgræm] *n* telegrama *m*
telegraph pole ['tɛlɪgrɑːf-] *n* poste *m* telegráfico
telephone ['tɛlɪfəun] *n* teléfono ▷ *vt* llamar por teléfono, telefonear; (*message*) dar por teléfono; **to be on the ~** (*talking*) hablar por teléfono; (*possessing telephone*) tener teléfono; **telephone book** *n* guía *f* telefónica; **telephone booth, telephone box** (BRIT) *n* cabina telefónica; **telephone call** *n* llamada (telefónica); **telephone directory** *n* guía (telefónica); **telephone number** *n* número de teléfono
telesales ['tɛlɪseɪlz] *npl* televenta(s) (*f(pl)*
telescope ['tɛlɪskəup] *n* telescopio
televise ['tɛlɪvaɪz] *vt* televisar
television ['tɛlɪvɪʒən] *n* televisión *f*; **on ~** en la televisión; **television programme** *n* programa *m* de televisión
tell [tɛl] (*pt, pp* **told**) *vt* decir; (*relate: story*) contar; (*distinguish*): **to ~ sth from** distinguir algo de ▷ *vi* (*talk*): **to ~ (of)** contar; (*have effect*) tener efecto; **to ~ sb to do sth** mandar a algn hacer algo; **tell off** *vt*: **to tell sb off** regañar a algn; **teller** *n* (*in bank*) cajero/a
telly ['tɛlɪ] (BRIT: *inf*) *n abbr* (= *television*) tele *f*
temp [tɛmp] *n abbr* (BRIT) (= *temporary*) temporero/a
temper ['tɛmpə*] *n* (*nature*) carácter *m*; (*mood*) humor *m*; (*bad temper*) (mal) genio; (*fit of anger*) acceso de ira ▷ *vt* (*moderate*) moderar; **to be in a ~** estar furioso; **to lose one's ~** enfadarse, enojarse
temperament ['tɛmprəmənt] *n* (*nature*) temperamento; **temperamental** [tɛmprə'mɛntl] *adj* temperamental
temperature ['tɛmprətʃə*] *n* temperatura; **to have** *or* **run a ~** tener fiebre
temple ['tɛmpl] *n* (*building*) templo; (*Anat*) sien *f*
temporary ['tɛmpərərɪ] *adj* provisional; (*passing*) transitorio; (*worker*) temporero; (*job*) temporal
tempt [tɛmpt] *vt* tentar; **to ~ sb into doing sth** tentar *or* inducir a algn a hacer algo; **temptation** *n* tentación *f*; **tempting** *adj* tentador(a); (*food*) apetitoso/a
ten [tɛn] *num* diez
tenant ['tɛnənt] *n* inquilino/a
tend [tɛnd] *vt* cuidar ▷ *vi*: **to ~ to do sth** tener tendencia a hacer algo; **tendency** ['tɛndənsɪ] *n* tendencia
tender ['tɛndə*] *adj* (*person, care*) tierno, cariñoso; (*meat*) tierno; (*sore*) sensible ▷ *n* (*Comm: offer*) oferta; (*money*): **legal ~** moneda de curso legal ▷ *vt* ofrecer
tendon ['tɛndən] *n* tendón *m*
tenner ['tɛnə*] *n* (*inf*) (billete *m* de) diez libras *m*
tennis ['tɛnɪs] *n* tenis *m*; **tennis ball** *n* pelota de tenis; **tennis court** *n* cancha de tenis; **tennis match** *n* partido de tenis; **tennis player** *n* tenista *mf*; **tennis racket** *n* raqueta de tenis
tenor ['tɛnə*] *n* (*Mus*) tenor *m*
tenpin bowling ['tɛnpɪn-] *n* (juego de los) bolos
tense [tɛns] *adj* (*person*) nervioso; (*moment, atmosphere*) tenso; (*muscle*) tenso, en tensión ▷ *n* (*Ling*) tiempo
tension ['tɛnʃən] *n* tensión *f*
tent [tɛnt] *n* tienda (de campaña) (SP), carpa (LAM)
tentative ['tɛntətɪv] *adj* (*person, smile*) indeciso; (*conclusion, plans*) provisional
tenth [tɛnθ] *num* décimo
tent: tent peg *n* clavija, estaca; **tent pole** *n* mástil *m*
tepid ['tɛpɪd] *adj* tibio
term [təːm] *n* (*word*) término; (*period*) período; (*Scol*) trimestre *m* ▷ *vt* llamar; **terms** *npl* (*conditions, Comm*) condiciones *fpl*; **in the short/long ~** a corto/largo plazo; **to be on good ~s with sb** llevarse bien con algn; **to come to ~s with** (*problem*) aceptar
terminal ['təːmɪnl] *adj* (*disease*) mortal; (*patient*) terminal ▷ *n* (*Elec*) borne *m*; (*Comput*) terminal *m*; (*also*: **air ~**) terminal *f*; (BRIT: *also*: **coach ~**) estación *f* terminal *f*
terminate ['təːmɪneɪt] *vt* terminar
termini ['təːmɪnaɪ] *npl of* **terminus**
terminology [təːmɪ'nɔlədʒɪ] *n* terminología
terminus ['təːmɪnəs] (*pl* **termini**) *n* término, (estación *f*) terminal *f*
terrace ['tɛrəs] *n* terraza; (BRIT: *row of houses*) hilera de casas adosadas; **the ~s** (BRIT *Sport*) las gradas *fpl*; **terraced** *adj* (*garden*) en terrazas; (*house*) adosado

terrain [tɛ'reɪn] *n* terreno
terrestrial [tɪ'restrɪəl] *adj* (*life*) terrestre; (BRIT: *channel*) de transmisión (por) vía terrestre
terrible ['tɛrɪbl] *adj* terrible, horrible; (*inf*) atroz; **terribly** *adv* terriblemente; (*very badly*) malísimamente
terrier ['tɛrɪə*] *n* terrier *m*
terrific [tə'rɪfɪk] *adj* (*very great*) tremendo; (*wonderful*) fantástico, fenomenal
terrified ['tɛrɪfaɪd] *adj* aterrorizado
terrify ['tɛrɪfaɪ] *vt* aterrorizar; **terrifying** *adj* aterrador(a)
territorial [tɛrɪ'tɔ:rɪəl] *adj* territorial
territory ['tɛrɪtərɪ] *n* territorio
terror ['tɛrə*] *n* terror *m*; **terrorism** *n* terrorismo; **terrorist** *n* terrorista *mf*; **terrorist attack** *n* atentado (terrorista)
test [tɛst] *n* (*gen, Chem*) prueba; (*Med*) examen *m*; (*Scol*) examen *m*, test *m*; (*also*: **driving ~**) examen *m* de conducir ▷ *vt* probar, poner a prueba; (*Med, Scol*) examinar
testicle ['tɛstɪkl] *n* testículo
testify ['tɛstɪfaɪ] *vi* (*Law*) prestar declaración; **to ~ to sth** atestiguar algo
testimony ['tɛstɪmənɪ] *n* (*Law*) testimonio
test: test match *n* (*Cricket, Rugby*) partido internacional; **test tube** *n* probeta
tetanus ['tɛtənəs] *n* tétano
text [tɛkst] *n* texto; (*on mobile phone*) mensaje *m* de texto ▷ *vt*: **to ~ sb** (*inf*) enviar un mensaje (de texto) *or* un SMS a algn; **textbook** *n* libro de texto
textile ['tekstaɪl] *n* textil *m*, tejido
text message *n* mensaje *m* de texto
text messaging [-'mɛsɪdʒɪŋ] *n* (envío de) mensajes *mpl* de texto
texture ['tɛkstʃə*] *n* textura
Thai [taɪ] *adj, n* tailandés/esa *m/f*
Thailand ['taɪlænd] *n* Tailandia
than [ðaen] *conj* (*in comparisons*): **more ~ 10/once** más de 10/una vez; **I have more/less ~ you/Paul** tengo más/menos que tú/Paul; **she is older ~ you think** es mayor de lo que piensas
thank [θæŋk] *vt* dar las gracias a, agradecer; **~ you (very much)** muchas gracias; **~ God!** ¡gracias a Dios! ▷ *excl* (*also*: **many ~s, ~s a lot**) ¡gracias! ▷ **~s to** *prep* gracias a; **thanks** *npl* gracias *fpl*; **thankfully** *adv* (*fortunately*) afortunadamente; **Thanksgiving (Day)** *n* día *m* de Acción de Gracias

THANKSGIVING (DAY)

En Estados Unidos el cuarto jueves de noviembre es **Thanksgiving Day**, fiesta oficial en la que se recuerda la celebración que hicieron los primeros colonos norteamericanos ("Pilgrims" o "Pilgrim Fathers") tras la estupenda cosecha de 1621, por la que se dan gracias a Dios. En Canadá se celebra una fiesta semejante el segundo lunes de octubre, aunque no está relacionada con dicha fecha histórica.

KEYWORD

that [ðæt] (*pl* **those**) *adj* (*demonstrative*) ese/a; (*pl*) esos/as; (*more remote*) aquel(aquella); (*pl*) aquellos/as; **leave those books on the table** deja esos libros sobre la mesa; **that one** ése(ésa); (*more remote*) aquél(aquélla); **that one over there** ése(ésa) de ahí; aquél(aquélla) de allí
▷ *pron* **1** (*demonstrative*) ése/a; (*pl*) ésos/as; (*neuter*) eso; (*more remote*) aquél(aquélla); (*pl*) aquéllos/as; (*neuter*) aquello; **what's that?** ¿qué es eso (*or* aquello)?; **who's that?** ¿quién es ése/a (*or* aquél (aquella))?; **is that you?** ¿eres tú?; **will you eat all that?** ¿vas a comer todo eso?; **that's my house** ésa es mi casa; **that's what he said** eso es lo que dijo; **that is (to say)** es decir
2 (*relative*: *subject, object*) que; (*with preposition*) (el (la)) que *etc*, el(la) cual *etc*; **the book (that) I read** el libro que leí; **the books that are in the library** los libros que están en la biblioteca; **all (that) I have** todo lo que tengo; **the box (that) I put it in** la caja en la que *or* donde lo puse; **the people (that) I spoke to** la gente con la que hablé
3 (*relative*: *of time*) que; **the day (that) he came** el día (en) que vino
▷ *conj* que; **he thought that I was ill** creyó que yo estaba enfermo
▷ *adv* (*demonstrative*): **I can't work that much** no puedo trabajar tanto; **I didn't realise it was that bad** no creí que fuera tan malo; **that high** así de alto

thatched [θætʃt] *adj* (*roof*) de paja; (*cottage*) con tejado de paja
thaw [θɔ:] *n* deshielo ▷ *vi* (*ice*) derretirse; (*food*) descongelarse ▷ *vt* (*food*) descongelar

KEYWORD

the [ði:, ðə] *def art* **1** (*gen*) el *f*, la *pl*, los *fpl*, las (*NB 'el' immediately before f n beginning with stressed (h)a; a+ el =al; de + el = del*); **the boy/girl** el chico/la chica; **the books/flowers**

t

los libros/las flores; **to the postman/from the drawer** al cartero/del cajón; **I haven't the time/money** no tengo tiempo/dinero
2 (*+adj to form n*) los; lo; **the rich and the poor** los ricos y los pobres; **to attempt the impossible** intentar lo imposible
3 (*in titles*): **Elizabeth the First** Isabel primera; **Peter the Great** Pedro el Grande
4 (*in comparisons*): **the more he works the more he earns** cuanto más trabaja más gana

theatre ['θɪətə*] (*US* **theater**) *n* teatro; (*also*: **lecture ~**) aula; (*Med*: *also*: **operating ~**) quirófano
theft [θɛft] *n* robo
their [ðɛə*] *adj* su; **theirs** *pron* (el) suyo((la) suya etc); *see also* **my; mine**[1]
them [ðɛm, ðəm] *pron* (*direct*) los/las; (*indirect*) les; (*stressed, after prep*) ellos(ellas); *see also* **me**
theme [θi:m] *n* tema *m*; **theme park** *n* parque de atracciones (*en torno a un tema central*)
themselves [ðəm'sɛlvz] *pl pron* (*subject*) ellos mismos(ellas mismas); (*complement*) se; (*after prep*) sí (mismos(as)); *see also* **oneself**
then [ðɛn] *adv* (*at that time*) entonces; (*next*) después; (*later*) luego, después; (*and also*) además ▷ *conj* (*therefore*) en ese caso, entonces ▷ *adj*: **the ~ president** el entonces presidente; **by ~** para entonces; **from ~ on** desde entonces
theology [θɪ'ɔlədʒɪ] *n* teología
theory ['θɪərɪ] *n* teoría
therapist ['θɛrəpɪst] *n* terapeuta *mf*
therapy ['θɛrəpɪ] *n* terapia

KEYWORD

there ['ðɛə*] *adv* **1** **there is, there are** hay; **there is no-one here/no bread left** no hay nadie aquí/no queda pan; **there has been an accident** ha habido un accidente
2 (*referring to place*) ahí; (*distant*) allí; **it's there** está ahí; **put it in/on/up/down there** ponlo ahí dentro/encima/arriba/abajo; **I want that book there** quiero ese libro de ahí; **there he is!** ¡ahí está!
3 **there, there** (*esp to child*) ea, ea

there: thereabouts *adv* por ahí; **thereafter** *adv* después; **thereby** *adv* así, de ese modo; **therefore** *adv* por lo tanto; **there's** = **there is; there has**
thermal ['θə:ml] *adj* termal; (*paper*) térmico
thermometer [θə'mɔmɪtə*] *n* termómetro
thermostat ['θə:məustæt] *n* termostato
these [ði:z] *pl adj* estos/as ▷ *pl pron* éstos/as
thesis ['θi:sɪs] (*pl* **theses**) *n* tesis *f inv*
they [ðeɪ] *pl pron* ellos(ellas); (*stressed*) ellos (mismos)(ellas (mismas)); **~ say that ...** (*it is said that*) se dice que ...; **they'd** = **they had; they would**; **they'll** = **they shall; they will**; **they're** = **they are**; **they've** = **they have**
thick [θɪk] *adj* (*in consistency*) espeso; (*in size*) grueso; (*stupid*) torpe ▷ *n*: **in the ~ of the battle** en lo más reñido de la batalla; **it's 20 cm ~** tiene 20 cm de espesor; **thicken** *vi* espesarse ▷ *vt* (*sauce etc*) espesar; **thickness** *n* espesor *m*; grueso
thief [θi:f] (*pl* **thieves**) *n* ladrón/ona *m/f*
thigh [θaɪ] *n* muslo
thin [θɪn] *adj* (*person, animal*) flaco; (*in size*) delgado; (*in consistency*) poco espeso; (*hair, crowd*) escaso ▷ *vt*: **to ~ (down)** diluir
thing [θɪŋ] *n* cosa; (*object*) objeto, artículo; (*matter*) asunto; (*mania*): **to have a ~ about sb/sth** estar obsesionado con algn/algo; **things** *npl* (*belongings*) efectos *mpl* (personales); **the best ~ would be to ...** lo mejor sería ...; **how are ~s?** ¿qué tal?
think [θɪŋk] (*pt, pp* **thought**) *vi* pensar ▷ *vt* pensar, creer; **what did you ~ of them?** ¿qué te parecieron?; **to ~ about sth/sb** pensar en algo/algn; **I'll ~ about it** lo pensaré; **to ~ of doing sth** pensar en hacer algo; **I ~ so/not** creo que sí/no; **to ~ well of sb** tener buen concepto de algn; **think over** *vt* reflexionar sobre, meditar; **think up** *vt* (*plan etc*) idear
third [θə:d] *adj* (*before n*) tercer(a); (*following n*) tercero/a ▷ *n* tercero/a; (*fraction*) tercio; (*BRIT Scol: degree*) *título de licenciado con calificación de aprobado*; **thirdly** *adv* en tercer lugar; **third party insurance** (*BRIT*) *n* seguro contra terceros; **Third World** *n* Tercer Mundo
thirst [θə:st] *n* sed *f*; **thirsty** *adj* (*person, animal*) sediento; (*work*) que da sed; **to be thirsty** tener sed
thirteen ['θə:'ti:n] *num* trece; **thirteenth** [-'ti:nθ] *adj* decimotercero
thirtieth ['θə:tɪəθ] *adj* trigésimo
thirty ['θə:tɪ] *num* treinta

KEYWORD

this [ðɪs] (*pl* **these**) *adj* (*demonstrative*) este/a *pl*; estos/as; (*neuter*) esto; **this man/woman** este hombre(esta mujer); **these children/flowers** estos chicos/estas flores;

this one (here) éste/a, esto (de aquí) ▷ *pron* (*demonstrative*) éste/a *pl*, éstos/as; (*neuter*) esto; **who is this?** ¿quién es éste/ésta?; **what is this?** ¿qué es esto?; **this is where I live** aquí vivo; **this is what he said** esto es lo que dijo; **this is Mr Brown** (*in introductions*) le presento al Sr. Brown; (*photo*) éste es el Sr. Brown; (*on telephone*) habla el Sr. Brown
▷ *adv* (*demonstrative*): **this high/long** *etc* así de alto/largo *etc*; **this far** hasta aquí

thistle ['θɪsl] *n* cardo
thorn [θɔːn] *n* espina
thorough ['θʌrə] *adj* (*search*) minucioso; (*wash*) a fondo; (*knowledge, research*) profundo; (*person*) meticuloso; **thoroughly** *adv* (*search*) minuciosamente; (*study*) profundamente; (*wash*) a fondo; (*utterly: bad, wet etc*) completamente, totalmente
those [ðəuz] *pl adj* esos(esas); (*more remote*) aquellos/as
though [ðəu] *conj* aunque ▷ *adv* sin embargo
thought [θɔːt] *pt, pp of* **think** ▷ *n* pensamiento; (*opinion*) opinión *f*; **thoughtful** *adj* pensativo; (*serious*) serio; (*considerate*) atento; **thoughtless** *adj* desconsiderado
thousand ['θauzənd] *num* mil; **two ~** dos mil; **~s of** miles de; **thousandth** *num* milésimo
thrash [θræʃ] *vt* azotar; (*defeat*) derrotar
thread [θrɛd] *n* hilo; (*of screw*) rosca ▷ *vt* (*needle*) enhebrar
threat [θrɛt] *n* amenaza; **threaten** *vi* amenazar ▷ *vt*: **to threaten sb with/to do** amenazar a algn con/con hacer; **threatening** *adj* amenazador(a), amenazante
three [θriː] *num* tres; **three-dimensional** *adj* tridimensional; **three-piece suite** *n* tresillo; **three-quarters** *npl* tres cuartas partes; **three-quarters full** tres cuartas partes lleno
threshold ['θrɛʃhəuld] *n* umbral *m*
threw [θruː] *pt of* **throw**
thrill [θrɪl] *n* (*excitement*) emoción *f*; (*shudder*) estremecimiento ▷ *vt* emocionar; **to be ~ed** (*with gift etc*) estar encantado; **thrilled** *adj*: **I was thrilled** Estaba emocionada; **thriller** *n* novela (*or* obra *or* película) de suspense; **thrilling** *adj* emocionante
thriving ['θraɪvɪŋ] *adj* próspero
throat [θrəut] *n* garganta; **to have a sore ~** tener dolor de garganta
throb [θrɔb] *vi* latir; dar punzadas; vibrar
throne [θrəun] *n* trono
through [θruː] *prep* por, a través de; (*time*) durante; (*by means of*) por medio de, mediante; (*owing to*) gracias a ▷ *adj* (*ticket, train*) directo ▷ *adv* completamente, de parte a parte; de principio a fin; **to put sb ~ to sb** (*Tel*) poner *or* pasar a algn con algn; **to be ~** (*Tel*) tener comunicación; (*have finished*) haber terminado; **"no ~ road"** (BRIT) "calle sin salida"; **throughout** *prep* (*place*) por todas partes de, por todo; (*time*) durante todo ▷ *adv* por *or* en todas partes
throw [θrəu] (*pt* **threw**, *pp* **thrown**) *n* tiro; (*Sport*) lanzamiento ▷ *vt* tirar, echar; (*Sport*) lanzar; (*rider*) derribar; (*fig*) desconcertar; **to ~ a party** dar una fiesta; **throw away** *vt* tirar; (*money*) derrochar; **throw in** *vt* (*Sport: ball*) sacar; (*include*) incluir; **throw off** *vt* deshacerse de; **throw out** *vt* tirar; (*person*) echar; expulsar; **throw up** *vi* vomitar
thru [θruː] (US) = **through**
thrush [θrʌʃ] *n* zorzal *m*, tordo
thrust [θrʌst] (*pt, pp* **~**) *vt* empujar con fuerza
thud [θʌd] *n* golpe *m* sordo
thug [θʌg] *n* gamberro/a
thumb [θʌm] *n* (*Anat*) pulgar *m*; **to ~ a lift** hacer autostop; **thumbtack** (US) *n* chincheta (SP)
thump [θʌmp] *n* golpe *m*; (*sound*) ruido seco *or* sordo ▷ *vt* golpear ▷ *vi* (*heart etc*) palpitar
thunder ['θʌndə*] *n* trueno ▷ *vi* tronar; (*train etc*): **to ~ past** pasar como un trueno; **thunderstorm** *n* tormenta
Thur(s). *abbr* (= *Thursday*) juev
Thursday ['θəːzdɪ] *n* jueves *m inv*
thus [ðʌs] *adv* así, de este modo
thwart [θwɔːt] *vt* frustrar
thyme [taɪm] *n* tomillo
Tibet [tɪ'bɛt] *n* el Tibet
tick [tɪk] *n* (*sound: of clock*) tictac *m*; (*mark*) palomita; (*Zool*) garrapata; (BRIT: *inf*): **in a ~** en un instante ▷ *vi* hacer tictac ▷ *vt* marcar; **tick off** *vt* marcar; (*person*) reñir
ticket ['tɪkɪt] *n* billete *m* (SP), boleto (LAM); (*for cinema etc*) entrada; (*in shop: on goods*) etiqueta; (*for raffle*) papeleta; (*for library*) tarjeta; (*parking ticket*) multa de aparcamiento (SP) *or* por estacionamiento (indebido) (LAM); **ticket barrier** *n* (BRIT: *Rail*) *barrera más allá de la cual se necesita billete/boleto*; **ticket collector** *n* revisor(a) *m/f*; **ticket inspector** *n* revisor(a) *m/f*, inspector(a) *m/f* de boletos (LAM); **ticket machine** *n* máquina de billetes (SP) *or* boletos (LAM); **ticket office** *n*

(*Theatre*) taquilla (SP), boletería (LAM); (*Rail*) mostrador *m* de billetes (SP) *or* boletos (LAM)

tickle ['tɪkl] *vt* hacer cosquillas a ▷*vi* hacer cosquillas; **ticklish** *adj* (*person*) cosquilloso; (*problem*) delicado

tide [taɪd] *n* marea; (*fig*: *of events etc*) curso, marcha

tidy ['taɪdɪ] *adj* (*room etc*) ordenado; (*dress, work*) limpio; (*person*) (bien) arreglado ▷*vt* (*also*: **~ up**) poner en orden

tie [taɪ] *n* (*string etc*) atadura; (BRIT: *also*: **neck~**) corbata; (*fig*: *link*) vínculo, lazo; (*Sport etc*: *draw*) empate *m* ▷*vt* atar ▷*vi* (*Sport etc*) empatar; **to ~ in a bow** atar con un lazo; **to ~ a knot in sth** hacer un nudo en algo; **tie down** *vt* (*fig*: *person*: *restrict*) atar; (: *to price, date etc*) obligar a; **tie up** *vt* (*dog, person*) atar; (*arrangements*) concluir; **to be tied up** (*busy*) estar ocupado

tier [tɪə*] *n* grada; (*of cake*) piso

tiger ['taɪgə*] *n* tigre *m*

tight [taɪt] *adj* (*rope*) tirante; (*money*) escaso; (*clothes*) ajustado; (*bend*) cerrado; (*shoes, schedule*) apretado; (*budget*) ajustado; (*security*) estricto; (*inf*: *drunk*) borracho ▷*adv* (*squeeze*) muy fuerte; (*shut*) bien; **tighten** *vt* (*rope*) estirar; (*screw, grip*) apretar; (*security*) reforzar ▷*vi* estirarse; apretarse; **tightly** *adv* (*grasp*) muy fuerte; **tights** (BRIT) *npl* panti *mpl*

tile [taɪl] *n* (*on roof*) teja; (*on floor*) baldosa; (*on wall*) azulejo

till [tɪl] *n* caja (registradora) ▷*vt* (*land*) cultivar ▷*prep, conj* = **until**

tilt [tɪlt] *vt* inclinar ▷*vi* inclinarse

timber [tɪmbə*] *n* (*material*) madera

time [taɪm] *n* tiempo; (*epoch*: *often pl*) época; (*by clock*) hora; (*moment*) momento; (*occasion*) vez *f*; (*Mus*) compás *m* ▷*vt* calcular *or* medir el tiempo de; (*race*) cronometrar; (*remark, visit etc*) elegir el momento para; **a long ~** mucho tiempo; **4 at a ~** de 4 en 4; 4 a la vez; **for the ~ being** de momento, por ahora; **from ~ to ~** de vez en cuando; **at ~s** a veces; **in ~** (*soon enough*) a tiempo; (*after some time*) con el tiempo; (*Mus*) al compás; **in a week's ~** dentro de una semana; **in no ~** en un abrir y cerrar de ojos; **any ~** cuando sea; **on ~** a la hora; **5 ~s 5** 5 por 5; **what ~ is it?** ¿qué hora es?; **to have a good ~** pasarlo bien, divertirse; **time limit** *n* plazo; **timely** *adj* oportuno; **timer** *n* (*in kitchen etc*) programador *m* horario; **time-share** *n* apartamento (*or* casa) a tiempo compartido; **timetable** *n* horario; **time zone** *n* huso horario

timid ['tɪmɪd] *adj* tímido

timing ['taɪmɪŋ] *n* (*Sport*) cronometraje *m*; **the ~ of his resignation** el momento que eligió para dimitir

tin [tɪn] *n* estaño; (*also*: **~ plate**) hojalata; (BRIT: *can*) lata; **tinfoil** *n* papel *m* de estaño

tingle ['tɪŋgl] *vi* (*person*): **to ~ (with)** estremecerse (de); (*hands etc*) hormiguear

tinker ['tɪŋkə*]: **~ with** *vt fus* jugar con, tocar

tinned [tɪnd] (BRIT) *adj* (*food*) en lata, en conserva

tin opener [-əupnə*] (BRIT) *n* abrelatas *m inv*

tint [tɪnt] *n* matiz *m*; (*for hair*) tinte *m*; **tinted** *adj* (*hair*) teñido; (*glass, spectacles*) ahumado

tiny ['taɪnɪ] *adj* minúsculo, pequeñito

tip [tɪp] *n* (*end*) punta; (*gratuity*) propina; (BRIT: *for rubbish*) vertedero; (*advice*) consejo ▷*vt* (*waiter*) dar una propina a; (*tilt*) inclinar; (*empty*: *also*: **~ out**) vaciar, echar; (*overturn*: *also*: **~ over**) volcar; **tip off** *vt* avisar, poner sobreaviso a

tiptoe ['tɪptəu] *n*: **on ~** de puntillas

tire ['taɪə*] *n* (US) = **tyre** ▷*vt* cansar ▷*vi* cansarse; (*become bored*) aburrirse; **tired** *adj* cansado; **to be tired of sth** estar harto de algo; **tire pressure** (US) = **tyre pressure**; **tiring** *adj* cansado

tissue ['tɪʃu:] *n* tejido; (*paper handkerchief*) pañuelo de papel, kleenex® *m*; **tissue paper** *n* papel *m* de seda

tit [tɪt] *n* (*bird*) herrerillo común; **to give ~ for tat** dar ojo por ojo

title ['taɪtl] *n* título

T-junction ['ti:dʒʌŋkʃən] *n* cruce *m* en T

TM *abbr* = **trademark**

KEYWORD

to [tu:, tə] *prep* **1** (*direction*) a; **to go to France/London/school/the station** ir a Francia/Londres/al colegio/a la estación; **to go to Claude's/the doctor's** ir a casa de Claude/al médico; **the road to Edinburgh** la carretera de Edimburgo

2 (*as far as*) hasta, a; **from here to London** de aquí a *or* hasta Londres; **to count to 10** contar hasta 10; **from 40 to 50 people** entre 40 y 50 personas

3 (*with expressions of time*): **a quarter/twenty to 5** las 5 menos cuarto/veinte

4 (*for, of*): **the key to the front door** la llave de la puerta principal; **she is secretary to the director** es la secretaría del director; **a letter to his wife** una carta a *or* para su mujer

5 (*expressing indirect object*) a; **to give sth to sb** darle algo a algn; **to talk to sb** hablar con

algn; **to be a danger to sb** ser un peligro para algn; **to carry out repairs to sth** hacer reparaciones en algo
6 (*in relation to*): **3 goals to 2** 3 goles a 2; **30 miles to the gallon** ≈ 94 litros a los cien (kms)
7 (*purpose, result*): **to come to sb's aid** venir en auxilio *or* ayuda de algn; **to sentence sb to death** condenar a algn a muerte; **to my great surprise** con gran sorpresa mía
▷ *with vb* 1 (*simple infin*): **to go/eat** ir/comer
2 (*following another vb*): **to want/try/start to do** querer/intentar/empezar a hacer
3 (*with vb omitted*): **I don't want to** no quiero
4 (*purpose, result*) para; **I did it to help you** lo hice para ayudarte; **he came to see you** vino a verte
5 (*equivalent to relative clause*): **I have things to do** tengo cosas que hacer; **the main thing is to try** lo principal es intentarlo
6 (*after adj etc*): **ready to go** listo para irse; **too old to …** demasiado viejo (como) para …
▷ *adv*: **pull/push the door to** tirar de/empujar la puerta

toad [təud] *n* sapo; **toadstool** *n* hongo venenoso
toast [təust] *n* (*Culin*) tostada; (*drink, speech*) brindis *m* ▷ *vt* (*Culin*) tostar; (*drink to*) brindar por; **toaster** *n* tostador *m*
tobacco [tə'bækəu] *n* tabaco
toboggan [tə'bɔgən] *n* tobogán *m*
today [tə'deɪ] *adv, n* (*also fig*) hoy *m*
toddler ['tɔdlə*] *n* niño/a (que empieza a andar)
toe [təu] *n* dedo (del pie); (*of shoe*) punta; **to ~ the line** (*fig*) conformarse; **toenail** *n* uña del pie
toffee ['tɔfɪ] *n* toffee *m*
together [tə'gɛðə*] *adv* juntos; (*at same time*) al mismo tiempo, a la vez; **~ with** junto con
toilet ['tɔɪlət] *n* inodoro; (BRIT: *room*) (cuarto de) baño, servicio ▷ *cpd* (*soap etc*) de aseo; **toilet bag** *n* neceser *m*, bolsa de aseo; **toilet paper** *n* papel *m* higiénico; **toiletries** *npl* artículos *mpl* de tocador; **toilet roll** *n* rollo de papel higiénico
token ['təukən] *n* (*sign*) señal *f*, muestra; (*souvenir*) recuerdo; (*disc*) ficha ▷ *adj* (*strike, payment etc*) simbólico; **book/record ~** (BRIT) vale *m* para comprar libros/discos; **gift ~** (BRIT) vale-regalo
Tokyo ['təukjəu] *n* Tokio, Tokío
told [təuld] *pt, pp of* **tell**
tolerant ['tɔlərnt] *adj*: **~ of** tolerante con
tolerate ['tɔləreɪt] *vt* tolerar

toll [təul] *n* (*of casualties*) número de víctimas; (*tax, charge*) peaje *m* ▷ *vi* (*bell*) doblar; **toll call** *n* (*US Tel*) conferencia, llamada interurbana; **toll-free** (*US*) *adj, adv* gratis
tomato [tə'mɑːtəu] (*pl* **~es**) *n* tomate *m*; **tomato sauce** *n* salsa de tomate
tomb [tuːm] *n* tumba; **tombstone** *n* lápida
tomorrow [tə'mɔrəu] *adv, n* (*also: fig*) mañana; **the day after ~** pasado mañana; **~ morning** mañana por la mañana
ton [tʌn] *n* tonelada (BRIT = 1016 *kg*; US = 907 *kg*); (*metric ton*) tonelada métrica; **~s of** (*inf*) montones de
tone [təun] *n* tono ▷ *vi* (*also:* **~ in**) armonizar; **tone down** *vt* (*criticism*) suavizar; (*colour*) atenuar
tongs [tɔŋz] *npl* (*for coal*) tenazas *fpl*; (*curling tongs*) tenacillas *fpl*
tongue [tʌŋ] *n* lengua; **~ in cheek** irónicamente
tonic ['tɔnɪk] *n* (*Med*) tónico; (*also:* **~ water**) (agua) tónica
tonight [tə'naɪt] *adv, n* esta noche; esta tarde
tonne [tʌn] *n* tonelada (métrica) (1.000*kg*)
tonsil ['tɔnsl] *n* amígdala; **tonsillitis** [-'laɪtɪs] *n* amigdalitis *f*
too [tuː] *adv* (*excessively*) demasiado; (*also*) también; **~ much** demasiado; **~ many** demasiados/as
took [tuk] *pt of* **take**
tool [tuːl] *n* herramienta; **tool box** *n* caja de herramientas; **tool kit** *n* juego de herramientas
tooth [tuːθ] (*pl* **teeth**) *n* (*Anat, Tech*) diente *m*; (*molar*) muela; **toothache** *n* dolor *m* de muelas; **toothbrush** *n* cepillo de dientes; **toothpaste** *n* pasta de dientes; **toothpick** *n* palillo
top [tɔp] *n* (*of mountain*) cumbre *f*, cima; (*of tree*) copa; (*of head*) coronilla; (*of ladder, page*) lo alto; (*of table*) superficie *f*; (*of cupboard*) parte *f* de arriba; (*lid: of box*) tapa; (*: of bottle, jar*) tapón *m*; (*of list etc*) cabeza; (*toy*) peonza; (*garment*) blusa; camiseta ▷ *adj* de arriba; (*in rank*) principal, primero; (*best*) mejor ▷ *vt* (*exceed*) exceder; (*be first in*) encabezar; **on ~ of** (*above*) sobre, encima de; (*in addition to*) además de; **from ~ to bottom** de pies a cabeza; **top up** *vt* llenar; (*mobile phone*) recargar (el saldo de); **top floor** *n* último piso; **top hat** *n* sombrero de copa
topic ['tɔpɪk] *n* tema *m*; **topical** *adj* actual
topless ['tɔplɪs] *adj* (*bather, bikini*) topless *inv*
topping ['tɔpɪŋ] *n* (*Culin*): **with a ~ of**

cream con nata por encima
topple ['tɔpl] *vt* derribar ▷ *vi* caerse
top-up card *n* (*for mobile phone*) tarjeta prepago
torch [tɔːtʃ] *n* antorcha; (BRIT: *electric*) linterna
tore [tɔː*] *pt of* **tear²**
torment [*n* 'tɔːmɛnt, *vt* tɔː'mɛnt] *n* tormento ▷ *vt* atormentar; (*fig: annoy*) fastidiar
torn [tɔːn] *pp of* **tear²**
tornado [tɔː'neɪdəu] (*pl* **~es**) *n* tornado
torpedo [tɔː'piːdəu] (*pl* **~es**) *n* torpedo
torrent ['tɔrnt] *n* torrente *m*; **torrential** [tɔ'rɛnʃl] *adj* torrencial
tortoise ['tɔːtəs] *n* tortuga
torture ['tɔːtʃə*] *n* tortura ▷ *vt* torturar; (*fig*) atormentar
Tory ['tɔːrɪ] (BRIT) *adj*, *n* (*Pol*) conservador(a) *m/f*
toss [tɔs] *vt* tirar, echar; (*one's head*) sacudir; **to ~ a coin** echar a cara o cruz; **to ~ up for sth** jugar a cara o cruz algo; **to ~ and turn** (*in bed*) dar vueltas
total ['təutl] *adj* total, entero; (*emphatic: failure etc*) completo, total ▷ *n* total *m*, suma ▷ *vt* (*add up*) sumar; (*amount to*) ascender a
totalitarian [təutælɪ'tɛərɪən] *adj* totalitario
totally ['təutəlɪ] *adv* totalmente
touch [tʌtʃ] *n* tacto; (*contact*) contacto ▷ *vt* tocar; (*emotionally*) conmover; **a ~ of** (*fig*) un poquito de; **to get in ~ with sb** ponerse en contacto con algn; **to lose ~** (*friends*) perder contacto; **touch down** *vi* (*on land*) aterrizar; **touchdown** *n* aterrizaje *m*; (*on sea*) amerizaje *m*; (US *Football*) ensayo; **touched** *adj* (*moved*) conmovido; **touching** *adj* (*moving*) conmovedor(a); **touchline** *n* (*Sport*) línea de banda; **touch-sensitive** *adj* sensible al tacto
tough [tʌf] *adj* (*material*) resistente; (*meat*) duro; (*problem etc*) difícil; (*policy, stance*) inflexible; (*person*) fuerte
tour ['tuə*] *n* viaje *m*, vuelta; (*also*: **package ~**) viaje *m* todo comprendido; (*of town, museum*) visita; (*by band etc*) gira ▷ *vt* recorrer, visitar; **tour guide** *n* guía *mf* turístico/a
tourism ['tuərɪzm] *n* turismo
tourist ['tuərɪst] *n* turista *mf* ▷ *cpd* turístico; **tourist office** *n* oficina de turismo
tournament ['tuənəmənt] *n* torneo
tour operator *n* touroperador(a) *m/f*, operador(a) *m/f* turístico/a
tow [təu] *vt* remolcar; **"on** *or* **in** (US) **~"** (*Aut*) "a remolque"; **tow away** *vt* llevarse a remolque
toward(s) [tə'wɔːd(z)] *prep* hacia; (*attitude*) respecto a, con; (*purpose*) para
towel ['tauəl] *n* toalla; **towelling** *n* (*fabric*) felpa
tower ['tauə*] *n* torre *f*; **tower block** (BRIT) *n* torre *f* (de pisos)
town [taun] *n* ciudad *f*; **to go to ~** ir a la ciudad; (*fig*) echar la casa por la ventana; **town centre** (BRIT) *n* centro de la ciudad; **town hall** *n* ayuntamiento
tow truck (US) *n* camión *m* grúa
toxic ['tɔksɪk] *adj* tóxico
toy [tɔɪ] *n* juguete *m*; **toy with** *vt fus* jugar con; (*idea*) acariciar; **toyshop** *n* juguetería
trace [treɪs] *n* rastro ▷ *vt* (*draw*) trazar, delinear; (*locate*) encontrar; (*follow*) seguir la pista de
track [træk] *n* (*mark*) huella, pista; (*path: gen*) camino, senda; (: *of bullet etc*) trayectoria; (: *of suspect, animal*) pista, rastro; (*Rail*) vía; (*Sport*) pista; (*on tape, record*) canción *f* ▷ *vt* seguir la pista de; **to keep ~ of** mantenerse al tanto de, seguir; **track down** *vt* (*prey*) seguir el rastro de; (*sth lost*) encontrar; **tracksuit** *n* chandal *m*
tractor ['træktə*] *n* tractor *m*
trade [treɪd] *n* comercio; (*skill, job*) oficio ▷ *vi* negociar, comerciar ▷ *vt* (*exchange*): **to ~ sth (for sth)** cambiar algo (por algo); **trade in** *vt* (*old car etc*) ofrecer como parte del pago; **trademark** *n* marca de fábrica; **trader** *n* comerciante *mf*; **tradesman** (*irreg*) *n* (*shopkeeper*) tendero; **trade union** *n* sindicato
trading ['treɪdɪŋ] *n* comercio
tradition [trə'dɪʃən] *n* tradición *f*; **traditional** *adj* tradicional
traffic ['træfɪk] *n* (*gen, Aut*) tráfico, circulación *f* ▷ *vi*: **to ~ in** (*pej: liquor, drugs*) traficar en; **traffic circle** (US) *n* isleta; **traffic island** *n* refugio, isleta; **traffic jam** *n* embotellamiento; **traffic lights** *npl* semáforo; **traffic warden** *n* guardia *mf* de tráfico
tragedy ['trædʒədɪ] *n* tragedia
tragic ['trædʒɪk] *adj* trágico
trail [treɪl] *n* (*tracks*) rastro, pista; (*path*) camino, sendero; (*dust, smoke*) estela ▷ *vt* (*drag*) arrastrar; (*follow*) seguir la pista de ▷ *vi* arrastrar; (*in contest etc*) ir perdiendo; **trailer** *n* (*Aut*) remolque *m*; (*caravan*) caravana; (*Cinema*) trailer *m*, avance *m*
train [treɪn] *n* tren *m*; (*of dress*) cola; (*series*) serie *f* ▷ *vt* (*educate, teach skills to*) formar; (*sportsman*) entrenar; (*dog*) adiestrar; (*point: gun etc*): **to ~ on** apuntar

a ▷*vi* (*Sport*) entrenarse; (*learn a skill*): **to ~ as a teacher** *etc* estudiar para profesor *etc*; **one's ~ of thought** el razonamiento de algn; **trainee** [treɪ'ni:] *n* aprendiz(a) *m/f*; **trainer** *n* (*Sport*: *coach*) entrenador(a) *m/f*; (*of animals*) domador(a) *m/f*; **trainers** *npl* (*shoes*) zapatillas *fpl* (de deporte); **training** *n* formación *f*; entrenamiento; **to be in training** (*Sport*) estar entrenando; **training course** *n* curso de formación; **training shoes** *npl* zapatillas *fpl* (de deporte)

trait [treɪt] *n* rasgo

traitor ['treɪtə*] *n* traidor(a) *m/f*

tram [træm] (BRIT) *n* (*also*: **~car**) tranvía *m*

tramp [træmp] *n* (*person*) vagabundo/a; (*inf*: *pej*: *woman*) puta

trample ['træmpl] *vt*: **to ~ (underfoot)** pisotear

trampoline ['træmpəli:n] *n* trampolín *m*

tranquil ['træŋkwɪl] *adj* tranquilo; **tranquillizer** (*US* **tranquilizer**) *n* (*Med*) tranquilizante *m*

transaction [træn'zækʃən] *n* transacción *f*, operación *f*

transatlantic ['trænzət'læntɪk] *adj* transatlántico

transcript ['trænskrɪpt] *n* copia

transfer [*n* 'trænsfə:*, *vb* træns'fə:*] *n* (*of employees*) traslado; (*of money, power*) transferencia; (*Sport*) traspaso; (*picture, design*) calcomanía ▷*vt* trasladar; transferir; **to ~ the charges** (BRIT *Tel*) llamar a cobro revertido

transform [træns'fɔ:m] *vt* transformar; **transformation** *n* transformación *f*

transfusion [træns'fju:ʒən] *n* transfusión *f*

transit ['trænzɪt] *n*: **in ~** en tránsito

transition [træn'zɪʃən] *n* transición *f*

transitive ['trænzɪtɪv] *adj* (*Ling*) transitivo

translate [trænz'leɪt] *vt* traducir; **translation** [-'leɪʃən] *n* traducción *f*; **translator** *n* traductor(a) *m/f*

transmission [trænz'mɪʃən] *n* transmisión *f*

transmit [trænz'mɪt] *vt* transmitir; **transmitter** *n* transmisor *m*

transparent [træns'pærnt] *adj* transparente

transplant ['trænspla:nt] *n* (*Med*) transplante *m*

transport [*n* 'trænspɔ:t, *vt* træns'pɔ:t] *n* transporte *m*; (*car*) coche *m* (SP), carro (LAM), automóvil *m* ▷*vt* transportar; **transportation** [-'teɪʃən] *n* transporte *m*

transvestite [trænz'vɛstaɪt] *n* travestí *mf*

trap [træp] *n* (*snare, trick*) trampa; (*carriage*) cabriolé *m* ▷*vt* coger (SP) *or* agarrar (LAM) (en una trampa); (*trick*) engañar; (*confine*) atrapar

trash [træʃ] *n* (*rubbish*) basura; (*nonsense*) tonterías *fpl*; (*pej*): **the book/film is ~** el libro/la película no vale nada; **trash can** (*US*) *n* cubo *or* bote *m* (MEX) *or* tacho (SC) de la basura

trauma ['trɔ:mə] *n* trauma *m*; **traumatic** [trɔ:'mætɪk] *adj* traumático

travel ['trævl] *n* el viajar ▷*vi* viajar ▷*vt* (*distance*) recorrer; **travel agency** *n* agencia de viajes; **travel agent** *n* agente *mf* de viajes; **travel insurance** *n* seguro de viaje; **traveller** (*US* **traveler**) *n* viajero/a; **traveller's cheque** (*US* **traveler's check**) *n* cheque *m* de viajero; **travelling** (*US* **traveling**) *n* los viajes, el viajar; **travel-sick** *adj*: **to get travel-sick** marearse al viajar; **travel sickness** *n* mareo

tray [treɪ] *n* bandeja; (*on desk*) cajón *m*

treacherous ['trɛtʃərəs] *adj* traidor, traicionero; (*dangerous*) peligroso

treacle ['tri:kl] (BRIT) *n* melaza

tread [trɛd] (*pt* **trod**, *pp* **trodden**) *n* (*step*) paso, pisada; (*sound*) ruido de pasos; (*of stair*) escalón *m*; (*of tyre*) banda de rodadura ▷*vi* pisar; **tread on** *vt fus* pisar

treasure ['trɛʒə*] *n* tesoro ▷*vt* (*value*: *object, friendship*) apreciar; (: *memory*) guardar; **treasurer** *n* tesorero/a

treasury ['trɛʒərɪ] *n*: **the T~** el Ministerio de Hacienda

treat [tri:t] *n* (*present*) regalo ▷*vt* tratar; **to ~ sb to sth** invitar a algn a algo; **treatment** *n* tratamiento

treaty ['tri:tɪ] *n* tratado

treble ['trɛbl] *adj* triple ▷*vt* triplicar ▷*vi* triplicarse

tree [tri:] *n* árbol *m*; **~ trunk** tronco (de árbol)

trek [trɛk] *n* (*long journey*) viaje *m* largo y difícil; (*tiring walk*) caminata

tremble ['trɛmbl] *vi* temblar

tremendous [trɪ'mɛndəs] *adj* tremendo, enorme; (*excellent*) estupendo

trench [trɛntʃ] *n* zanja

trend [trɛnd] *n* (*tendency*) tendencia; (*of events*) curso; (*fashion*) moda; **trendy** *adj* de moda

trespass ['trɛspəs] *vi*: **to ~ on** entrar sin permiso en; **"no ~ing"** "prohibido el paso"

trial ['traɪəl] *n* (*Law*) juicio, proceso; (*test*: *of machine etc*) prueba; **trial period** *n* periodo de prueba

triangle ['traɪæŋgl] *n* (*Math, Mus*) triángulo

triangular [traɪ'æŋgjulə*] *adj* triangular
tribe [traɪb] *n* tribu *f*
tribunal [traɪ'bju:nl] *n* tribunal *m*
tribute ['trɪbju:t] *n* homenaje *m*, tributo; **to pay ~ to** rendir homenaje a
trick [trɪk] *n* (*skill, knack*) tino, truco; (*conjuring trick*) truco; (*joke*) broma; (*Cards*) baza ▷*vt* engañar; **to play a ~ on sb** gastar una broma a algn; **that should do the ~** a ver si funciona así
trickle ['trɪkl] *n* (*of water etc*) goteo ▷*vi* gotear
tricky ['trɪkɪ] *adj* difícil; delicado
tricycle ['traɪsɪkl] *n* triciclo
trifle ['traɪfl] *n* bagatela; (*Culin*) *dulce de bizcocho borracho, gelatina, fruta y natillas* ▷*adv*: **a ~ long** un poquito largo
trigger ['trɪgə*] *n* (*of gun*) gatillo
trim [trɪm] *adj* (*house, garden*) en buen estado; (*person, figure*) esbelto ▷*n* (*haircut etc*) recorte *m*; (*on car*) guarnición *f* ▷*vt* (*neaten*) arreglar; (*cut*) recortar; (*decorate*) adornar; (*Naut*: *a sail*) orientar
trio ['tri:əu] *n* trío
trip [trɪp] *n* viaje *m*; (*excursion*) excursión *f*; (*stumble*) traspié *m* ▷*vi* (*stumble*) tropezar; (*go lightly*) andar a paso ligero; **on a ~** de viaje; **trip up** *vi* tropezar, caerse ▷*vt* hacer tropezar *or* caer
triple ['trɪpl] *adj* triple
triplets ['trɪplɪts] *npl* trillizos/as *mpl/fpl*
tripod ['traɪpɔd] *n* trípode *m*
triumph ['traɪʌmf] *n* triunfo ▷*vi*: **to ~ (over)** vencer; **triumphant** [traɪ'ʌmfənt] *adj* (*team etc*) vencedor(a); (*wave, return*) triunfal
trivial ['trɪvɪəl] *adj* insignificante; (*commonplace*) banal
trod [trɔd] *pt of* **tread**
trodden ['trɔdn] *pp of* **tread**
trolley ['trɔlɪ] *n* carrito; (*also*: **~ bus**) trolebús *m*
trombone [trɔm'bəun] *n* trombón *m*
troop [tru:p] *n* grupo, banda; **troops** *npl* (*Mil*) tropas *fpl*
trophy ['trəufɪ] *n* trofeo
tropical ['trɔpɪkl] *adj* tropical
trot [trɔt] *n* trote *m* ▷*vi* trotar; **on the ~** (BRIT: *fig*) seguidos/as
trouble ['trʌbl] *n* problema *m*, dificultad *f*; (*worry*) preocupación *f*; (*bother, effort*) molestia, esfuerzo; (*unrest*) inquietud *f*; (*Med*): **stomach** *etc* **~** problemas *mpl* gástricos *etc* ▷*vt* (*disturb*) molestar; (*worry*) preocupar, inquietar ▷*vi*: **to ~ to do sth** molestarse en hacer algo; **troubles** *npl* (*Pol etc*) conflictos *mpl*; (*personal*) problemas *mpl*; **to be in ~** estar en un apuro; **it's no ~!** ¡no es molestia (ninguna)!; **what's the ~?** (*with broken TV etc*) ¿cuál es el problema?; (*doctor to patient*) ¿qué pasa?; **troubled** *adj* (*person*) preocupado; (*country, epoch, life*) agitado; **troublemaker** *n* agitador(a) *m/f*; (*child*) alborotador *m*; **troublesome** *adj* molesto
trough [trɔf] *n* (*also*: **drinking ~**) abrevadero; (*also*: **feeding ~**) comedero; (*depression*) depresión *f*
trousers ['trauzəz] *npl* pantalones *mpl*; **short ~** pantalones *mpl* cortos
trout [traut] *n inv* trucha
trowel ['trauəl] *n* (*of gardener*) palita; (*of builder*) paleta
truant ['truənt] *n*: **to play ~** (BRIT) hacer novillos
truce [tru:s] *n* tregua
truck [trʌk] *n* (*lorry*) camión *m*; (*Rail*) vagón *m*; **truck driver** *n* camionero
true [tru:] *adj* verdadero; (*accurate*) exacto; (*genuine*) auténtico; (*faithful*) fiel; **to come ~** realizarse
truly ['tru:lɪ] *adv* (*really*) realmente; (*truthfully*) verdaderamente; (*faithfully*): **yours ~** (*in letter*) le saluda atentamente
trumpet ['trʌmpɪt] *n* trompeta
trunk [trʌŋk] *n* (*of tree, person*) tronco; (*of elephant*) trompa; (*case*) baúl *m*; (US *Aut*) maletero; **trunks** *npl* (*also*: **swimming ~s**) bañador *m* (de hombre)
trust [trʌst] *n* confianza; (*responsibility*) responsabilidad *f*; (*Law*) fideicomiso ▷*vt* (*rely on*) tener confianza en; (*hope*) esperar; (*entrust*): **to ~ sth to sb** confiar algo a algn; **to take sth on ~** fiarse de algo; **trusted** *adj* de confianza; **trustworthy** *adj* digno de confianza
truth [tru:θ, *pl* tru:ðz] *n* verdad *f*; **truthful** *adj* veraz
try [traɪ] *n* tentativa, intento; (*Rugby*) ensayo ▷*vt* (*attempt*) intentar; (*test*: *also*: **~ out**) probar, someter a prueba; (*Law*) juzgar, procesar; (*strain*: *patience*) hacer perder ▷*vi* probar; **to have a ~** probar suerte; **to ~ to do sth** intentar hacer algo; **~ again!** ¡vuelve a probar!; **~ harder!** ¡esfuérzate más!; **well, I tried** al menos lo intenté; **try on** *vt* (*clothes*) probarse; **trying** *adj* (*experience*) cansado; (*person*) pesado
T-shirt ['ti:ʃə:t] *n* camiseta
tub [tʌb] *n* cubo (SP), cubeta (SP, MEX), balde *m* (LAM); (*bath*) bañera (SP), tina (LAM), bañadera (RPL)
tube [tju:b] *n* tubo; (BRIT: *underground*) metro; (*for tyre*) cámara de aire
tuberculosis [tjubə:kju'ləusɪs] *n* tuberculosis *f inv*

tube station (BRIT) *n* estación *f* de metro
tuck [tʌk] *vt* (*put*) poner; **tuck away** *vt* (*money*) guardar; (*building*): **to be tucked away** esconderse, ocultarse; **tuck in** *vt* meter dentro; (*child*) arropar ▷ *vi* (*eat*) comer con apetito; **tuck shop** *n* (*Scol*) tienda ≈ bar *m* (del colegio) (SP)
Tue(s). *abbr* (= *Tuesday*) mart
Tuesday ['tju:zdɪ] *n* martes *m inv*
tug [tʌg] *n* (*ship*) remolcador *m* ▷ *vt* tirar de
tuition [tju:'ɪʃən] *n* (BRIT) enseñanza; (: *private tuition*) clases *fpl* particulares; (US: *school fees*) matrícula
tulip ['tju:lɪp] *n* tulipán *m*
tumble ['tʌmbl] *n* (*fall*) caída ▷ *vi* caer; **to ~ to sth** (*inf*) caer en la cuenta de algo; **tumble dryer** (BRIT) *n* secadora
tumbler ['tʌmblə*] *n* (*glass*) vaso
tummy ['tʌmɪ] (*inf*) *n* barriga, tripa
tumour ['tju:mə*] (US **tumor**) *n* tumor *m*
tuna ['tju:nə] *n inv* (*also*: **~ fish**) atún *m*
tune [tju:n] *n* melodía ▷ *vt* (*Mus*) afinar; (*Radio, TV, Aut*) sintonizar; **to be in/out of ~** (*instrument*) estar afinado/desafinado; (*singer*) cantar afinadamente/desafinar; **to be in/out of ~ with** (*fig*) estar de acuerdo/en desacuerdo con; **tune in** *vi*: **to tune in (to)** (*Radio, TV*) sintonizar (con); **tune up** *vi* (*musician*) afinar (su instrumento)
tunic ['tju:nɪk] *n* túnica
Tunisia [tju:'nɪzɪə] *n* Túnez *m*
tunnel ['tʌnl] *n* túnel *m*; (*in mine*) galería ▷ *vi* construir un túnel/una galería
turbulence ['tə:bjuləns] *n* (*Aviat*) turbulencia
turf [tə:f] *n* césped *m*; (*clod*) tepe *m* ▷ *vt* cubrir con césped
Turk [tə:k] *n* turco/a
Turkey ['tə:kɪ] *n* Turquía
turkey ['tə:kɪ] *n* pavo
Turkish ['tə:kɪʃ] *adj, n* turco; (*Ling*) turco
turmoil ['tə:mɔɪl] *n*: **in ~** revuelto
turn [tə:n] *n* turno; (*in road*) curva; (*of mind, events*) rumbo; (*Theatre*) número; (*Med*) ataque *m* ▷ *vt* girar, volver; (*collar, steak*) dar la vuelta a; (*page*) pasar; (*change*): **to ~ sth into** convertir algo en ▷ *vi* volver; (*person*: *look back*) volverse; (*reverse direction*) dar la vuelta; (*milk*) cortarse; (*become*): **to ~ nasty/forty** ponerse feo/cumplir los cuarenta; **a good ~** un favor; **it gave me quite a ~** me dio un susto; **"no left ~"** (*Aut*) "prohibido girar a la izquierda"; **it's your ~** te toca a ti; **in ~** por turnos; **to take ~s (at)** turnarse (en); **turn around** *vi* (*person*) volverse, darse la vuelta ▷ *vt* (*object*) dar la vuelta a, voltear (LAM); **turn away** *vi* apartar la vista ▷ *vi* rechazar; **turn back** *vi* volverse atrás ▷ *vt* hacer retroceder; (*clock*) retrasar; **turn down** *vt* (*refuse*) rechazar; (*reduce*) bajar; (*fold*) doblar; **turn in** *vi* (*inf*: *go to bed*) acostarse ▷ *vt* (*fold*) doblar hacia dentro; **turn off** *vi* (*from road*) desviarse ▷ *vt* (*light, radio etc*) apagar; (*tap*) cerrar; (*engine*) parar; **turn on** *vt* (*light, radio etc*) encender (SP), prender (LAM); (*tap*) abrir; (*engine*) poner en marcha; **turn out** *vt* (*light, gas*) apagar; (*produce*) producir ▷ *vi* (*voters*) concurrir; **to turn out to be ...** resultar ser ...; **turn over** *vi* (*person*) volverse ▷ *vt* (*object*) dar la vuelta a; (*page*) volver; **turn round** *vi* volverse; (*rotate*) girar; **turn to** *vt fus*: **to turn to sb** acudir a algn; **turn up** *vi* (*person*) llegar, presentarse; (*lost object*) aparecer ▷ *vt* (*gen*) subir; **turning** *n* (*in road*) vuelta; **turning point** *n* (*fig*) momento decisivo
turnip ['tə:nɪp] *n* nabo
turn: turnout *n* concurrencia; **turnover** *n* (*Comm*: *amount of money*) volumen *m* de ventas; (: *of goods*) movimiento; **turnstile** *n* torniquete *m*; **turn-up** (BRIT) *n* (*on trousers*) vuelta
turquoise ['tə:kwɔɪz] *n* (*stone*) turquesa ▷ *adj* color turquesa
turtle ['tə:tl] *n* galápago; **turtleneck (sweater)** *n* jersey *m* de cuello vuelto
tusk [tʌsk] *n* colmillo
tutor ['tju:tə*] *n* profesor(a) *m/f*; **tutorial** [-'tɔ:rɪəl] *n* (*Scol*) seminario
tuxedo [tʌk'si:dəu] (US) *n* smóking *m*, esmoquin *m*
TV [ti:'vi:] *n abbr* (= *television*) tele *f*
tweed [twi:d] *n* tweed *m*
tweezers ['twi:zəz] *npl* pinzas *fpl* (de depilar)
twelfth [twɛlfθ] *num* duodécimo
twelve [twɛlv] *num* doce; **at ~ o'clock** (*midday*) a mediodía; (*midnight*) a medianoche
twentieth ['twɛntɪɪθ] *adj* vigésimo
twenty ['twɛntɪ] *num* veinte
twice [twaɪs] *adv* dos veces; **~ as much** dos veces más
twig [twɪg] *n* ramita
twilight ['twaɪlaɪt] *n* crepúsculo
twin [twɪn] *adj, n* gemelo/a *m/f* ▷ *vt* hermanar; **twin(-bedded) room** *n* habitación *f* doble; **twin beds** *npl* camas *fpl* gemelas
twinkle ['twɪŋkl] *vi* centellear; (*eyes*) brillar
twist [twɪst] *n* (*action*) torsión *f*; (*in road, coil*) vuelta; (*in wire, flex*) doblez *f*; (*in story*) giro ▷ *vt* torcer; (*weave*) trenzar; (*roll around*) enrollar; (*fig*) deformar ▷ *vi* serpentear

t

twit [twɪt] (*inf*) *n* tonto
twitch [twɪtʃ] *n* (*pull*) tirón *m*; (*nervous*) tic *m* ▷*vi* crisparse
two [tu:] *num* dos; **to put ~ and ~ together** (*fig*) atar cabos
type [taɪp] *n* (*category*) tipo, género; (*model*) tipo; (*Typ*) tipo, letra ▷*vt* (*letter etc*) escribir a máquina; **typewriter** *n* máquina de escribir
typhoid ['taɪfɔɪd] *n* tifoidea
typhoon [taɪ'fu:n] *n* tifón *m*
typical ['tɪpɪkl] *adj* típico; **typically** *adv* típicamente
typing ['taɪpɪŋ] *n* mecanografía
typist ['taɪpɪst] *n* mecanógrafo/a
tyre ['taɪə*] (*US* **tire**) *n* neumático, llanta (*LAM*); **tyre pressure** (*BRIT*) *n* presión *f* de los neumáticos

UFO ['ju:fəu] *n abbr* (= *unidentified flying object*) OVNI *m*
Uganda [ju:'gændə] *n* Uganda
ugly ['ʌglɪ] *adj* feo; (*dangerous*) peligroso
UHT *abbr* (= *UHT milk*) leche *f* UHT, leche *f* uperizada
UK *n abbr* = **United Kingdom**
ulcer ['ʌlsə*] *n* úlcera; (*mouth ulcer*) llaga
ultimate ['ʌltɪmət] *adj* último, final; (*greatest*) máximo; **ultimately** *adv* (*in the end*) por último, al final; (*fundamentally*) a *or* en fin de cuentas
ultimatum [ʌltɪ'meɪtəm] (*pl* **~s** *or* **ultimata**) *n* ultimátum *m*
ultrasound ['ʌltrəsaund] *n* (*Med*) ultrasonido
ultraviolet ['ʌltrə'vaɪəlɪt] *adj* ultravioleta
umbrella [ʌm'brɛlə] *n* paraguas *m inv*; (*for sun*) sombrilla
umpire ['ʌmpaɪə*] *n* árbitro
UN *n abbr* (= *United Nations*) NN. UU.
unable [ʌn'eɪbl] *adj*: **to be ~ to do sth** no poder hacer algo
unacceptable [ʌnək'sɛptəbl] *adj* (*proposal, behaviour, price*) inaceptable; **it's ~ that** no se puede aceptar que
unanimous [ju:'nænɪməs] *adj* unánime
unarmed [ʌn'ɑ:md] *adj* (*defenceless*) inerme; (*without weapon*) desarmado
unattended [ʌnə'tɛndɪd] *adj* desatendido
unattractive [ʌnə'træktɪv] *adj* poco atractivo
unavailable [ʌnə'veɪləbl] *adj* (*article, room, book*) no disponible; (*person*) ocupado
unavoidable [ʌnə'vɔɪdəbl] *adj* inevitable
unaware [ʌnə'wɛə*] *adj*: **to be ~ of** ignorar; **unawares** *adv*: **to catch sb unawares** pillar a algn desprevenido
unbearable [ʌn'bɛərəbl] *adj* insoportable
unbeatable [ʌn'bi:təbl] *adj* (*team*)

invencible; (*price*) inmejorable; (*quality*) insuperable
unbelievable [ʌnbɪ'li:vəbl] *adj* increíble
unborn [ʌn'bɔ:n] *adj* que va a nacer
unbutton [ʌn'bʌtn] *vt* desabrochar
uncalled-for [ʌn'kɔ:ldfɔ:*] *adj* gratuito, inmerecido
uncanny [ʌn'kænɪ] *adj* extraño
uncertain [ʌn'sə:tn] *adj* incierto; (*indecisive*) indeciso; **uncertainty** *n* incertidumbre *f*
unchanged [ʌn'tʃeɪndʒd] *adj* igual, sin cambios
uncle ['ʌŋkl] *n* tío
unclear [ʌn'klɪə*] *adj* poco claro; **I'm still ~ about what I'm supposed to do** todavía no tengo muy claro lo que tengo que hacer
uncomfortable [ʌn'kʌmfətəbl] *adj* incómodo; (*uneasy*) inquieto
uncommon [ʌn'kɔmən] *adj* poco común, raro
unconditional [ʌnkən'dɪʃənl] *adj* incondicional
unconscious [ʌn'kɔnʃəs] *adj* sin sentido; (*unaware*): **to be ~ of** no darse cuenta de ▷ *n*: **the ~** el inconsciente
uncontrollable [ʌnkən'trəuləbl] *adj* (*child etc*) incontrolable; (*temper*) indomable; (*laughter*) incontenible
unconventional [ʌnkən'vɛnʃənl] *adj* poco convencional
uncover [ʌn'kʌvə*] *vt* descubrir; (*take lid off*) destapar
undecided [ʌndɪ'saɪdɪd] *adj* (*character*) indeciso; (*question*) no resuelto
undeniable [ʌndɪ'naɪəbl] *adj* innegable
under ['ʌndə*] *prep* debajo de; (*less than*) menos de; (*according to*) según, de acuerdo con; (*sb's leadership*) bajo ▷ *adv* debajo, abajo; **~ there** allí abajo; **~ repair** en reparación; **undercover** *adj* clandestino; **underdone** *adj* (*Culin*) poco hecho; **underestimate** *vt* subestimar; **undergo** (*irreg*) *vt* sufrir; (*treatment*) recibir; **undergraduate** *n* estudiante *mf*; **underground** *n* (BRIT: *railway*) metro; (*Pol*) movimiento clandestino ▷ *adj* (*car park*) subterráneo ▷ *adv* (*work*) en la clandestinidad; **undergrowth** *n* maleza; **underline** *vt* subrayar; **undermine** *vt* socavar, minar; **underneath** [ʌndə'ni:θ] *adv* debajo ▷ *prep* debajo de, bajo; **underpants** *npl* calzoncillos *mpl*; **underpass** (BRIT) *n* paso subterráneo; **underprivileged** *adj* desposeído; **underscore** *vt* subrayar; **undershirt** (US) *n* camiseta; **underskirt** (BRIT) *n* enaguas *fpl*
understand [ʌndə'stænd] *vt, vi* entender, comprender; (*assume*) tener entendido; **understandable** *adj* comprensible; **understanding** *adj* comprensivo ▷ *n* comprensión *f*, entendimiento; (*agreement*) acuerdo
understatement ['ʌndəsteɪtmənt] *n* modestia (excesiva); **that's an ~!** ¡eso es decir poco!
understood [ʌndə'stud] *pt, pp of* **understand** ▷ *adj* (*agreed*) acordado; (*implied*): **it is ~ that** se sobreentiende que
undertake [ʌndə'teɪk] (*irreg*) *vt* emprender; **to ~ to do sth** comprometerse a hacer algo
undertaker ['ʌndəteɪkə*] *n* director(a) *m/f* de pompas fúnebres
undertaking ['ʌndəteɪkɪŋ] *n* empresa; (*promise*) promesa
under: underwater *adv* bajo el agua ▷ *adj* submarino; **underway** *adj*: **to be underway** (*meeting*) estar en marcha; (*investigation*) estar llevándose a cabo; **underwear** *n* ropa interior; **underwent** *vb see* **undergo**; **underworld** *n* (*of crime*) hampa, inframundo
undesirable [ʌndɪ'zaɪrəbl] *adj* (*person*) indeseable; (*thing*) poco aconsejable
undisputed [ʌndɪ'spju:tɪd] *adj* incontestable
undo [ʌn'du:] (*irreg*) *vt* (*laces*) desatar; (*button etc*) desabrochar; (*spoil*) deshacer
undone [ʌn'dʌn] *pp of* **undo** ▷ *adj*: **to come ~** (*clothes*) desabrocharse; (*parcel*) desatarse
undoubtedly [ʌn'dautɪdlɪ] *adv* indudablemente, sin duda
undress [ʌn'drɛs] *vi* desnudarse
unearth [ʌn'ə:θ] *vt* desenterrar
uneasy [ʌn'i:zɪ] *adj* intranquilo, preocupado; (*feeling*) desagradable; (*peace*) inseguro
unemployed [ʌnɪm'plɔɪd] *adj* parado, sin trabajo ▷ *npl*: **the ~** los parados
unemployment [ʌnɪm'plɔɪmənt] *n* paro, desempleo; **unemployment benefit** *n* (BRIT) subsidio de desempleo *or* paro
unequal [ʌn'i:kwəl] *adj* (*unfair*) desigual; (*size, length*) distinto
uneven [ʌn'i:vn] *adj* desigual; (*road etc*) lleno de baches
unexpected [ʌnɪk'spɛktɪd] *adj* inesperado; **unexpectedly** *adv* inesperadamente
unfair [ʌn'fɛə*] *adj*: **~ (to sb)** injusto (con algn)
unfaithful [ʌn'feɪθful] *adj* infiel
unfamiliar [ʌnfə'mɪlɪə*] *adj* extraño, desconocido; **to be ~ with** desconocer

unfashionable [ʌn'fæʃnəbl] *adj* pasado *or* fuera de moda
unfasten [ʌn'fɑːsn] *vt* (*knot*) desatar; (*dress*) desabrochar; (*open*) abrir
unfavourable [ʌn'feɪvərəbl] (*US* **unfavorable**) *adj* desfavorable
unfinished [ʌn'fɪnɪʃt] *adj* inacabado, sin terminar
unfit [ʌn'fɪt] *adj* bajo de forma; (*incompetent*): **~ (for)** incapaz (de); **~ for work** no apto para trabajar
unfold [ʌn'fəuld] *vt* desdoblar ▷ *vi* abrirse
unforgettable [ʌnfə'gɛtəbl] *adj* inolvidable
unfortunate [ʌn'fɔːtʃnət] *adj* desgraciado; (*event, remark*) inoportuno; **unfortunately** *adv* desgraciadamente
unfriendly [ʌn'frɛndlɪ] *adj* antipático; (*behaviour, remark*) hostil, poco amigable
unfurnished [ʌn'fəːnɪʃt] *adj* sin amueblar
unhappiness [ʌn'hæpɪnɪs] *n* tristeza, desdicha
unhappy [ʌn'haepɪ] *adj* (*sad*) triste; (*unfortunate*) desgraciado; (*childhood*) infeliz; **~ about/with** (*arrangements etc*) poco contento con, descontento de
unhealthy [ʌn'hɛlθɪ] *adj* (*place*) malsano; (*person*) enfermizo; (*fig: interest*) morboso
unheard-of [ʌn'həːdɔv] *adj* inaudito, sin precedente
unhelpful [ʌn'hɛlpful] *adj* (*person*) poco servicial; (*advice*) inútil
unhurt [ʌn'həːt] *adj* ileso
unidentified [ʌnaɪ'dɛntɪfaɪd] *adj* no identificado, sin identificar; *see also* **UFO**
uniform ['juːnɪfɔːm] *n* uniforme *m* ▷ *adj* uniforme
unify ['juːnɪfaɪ] *vt* unificar, unir
unimportant [ʌnɪm'pɔːtənt] *adj* sin importancia
uninhabited [ʌnɪn'hæbɪtɪd] *adj* desierto
unintentional [ʌnɪn'tɛnʃənəl] *adj* involuntario
union ['juːnjən] *n* unión *f*; (*also*: **trade ~**) sindicato ▷ *cpd* sindical; **Union Jack** *n* bandera del Reino Unido
unique [juː'niːk] *adj* único
unisex ['juːnɪsɛks] *adj* unisex
unit ['juːnɪt] *n* unidad *f*; (*section: of furniture etc*) elemento; (*team*) grupo; **kitchen ~** módulo de cocina
unite [juː'naɪt] *vt* unir ▷ *vi* unirse; **united** *adj* unido; (*effort*) conjunto; **United Kingdom** *n* Reino Unido; **United Nations (Organization)** *n* Naciones *fpl* Unidas; **United States (of America)** *n* Estados *mpl* Unidos
unity ['juːnɪtɪ] *n* unidad *f*
universal [juːnɪ'vəːsl] *adj* universal
universe ['juːnɪvəːs] *n* universo
university [juːnɪ'vəːsɪtɪ] *n* universidad *f*
unjust [ʌn'dʒʌst] *adj* injusto
unkind [ʌn'kaɪnd] *adj* poco amable; (*behaviour, comment*) cruel
unknown [ʌn'nəun] *adj* desconocido
unlawful [ʌn'lɔːful] *adj* ilegal, ilícito
unleaded [ʌn'lɛdɪd] *adj* (*petrol, fuel*) sin plombo
unleash [ʌn'liːʃ] *vt* desatar
unless [ʌn'lɛs] *conj* a menos que; **~ he comes** a menos que venga; **~ otherwise stated** salvo indicación contraria
unlike [ʌn'laɪk] *adj* (*not alike*) distinto de *or* a; (*not like*) poco propio de ▷ *prep* a diferencia de
unlikely [ʌn'laɪklɪ] *adj* improbable; (*unexpected*) inverosímil
unlimited [ʌn'lɪmɪtɪd] *adj* ilimitado
unlisted [ʌn'lɪstɪd] (*US*) *adj* (*Tel*) que no consta en la guía
unload [ʌn'ləud] *vt* descargar
unlock [ʌn'lɔk] *vt* abrir (con llave)
unlucky [ʌn'lʌkɪ] *adj* desgraciado; (*object, number*) que da mala suerte; **to be ~** tener mala suerte
unmarried [ʌn'mærɪd] *adj* soltero
unmistak(e)able [ʌnmɪs'teɪkəbl] *adj* inconfundible
unnatural [ʌn'nætʃrəl] *adj* (*gen*) antinatural; (*manner*) afectado; (*habit*) perverso
unnecessary [ʌn'nɛsəsərɪ] *adj* innecesario, inútil
UNO ['juːnəu] *n abbr* (= *United Nations Organization*) ONU *f*
unofficial [ʌnə'fɪʃl] *adj* no oficial; (*news*) sin confirmar
unpack [ʌn'pæk] *vi* deshacer las maletas ▷ *vt* deshacer
unpaid [ʌn'peɪd] *adj* (*bill, debt*) sin pagar, impagado; (*Comm*) pendiente; (*holiday*) sin sueldo; (*work*) sin pago, voluntario
unpleasant [ʌn'plɛznt] *adj* (*disagreeable*) desagradable; (*person, manner*) antipático
unplug [ʌn'plʌg] *vt* desenchufar, desconectar
unpopular [ʌn'pɔpjulə*] *adj* impopular, poco popular
unprecedented [ʌn'prɛsɪdəntɪd] *adj* sin precedentes
unpredictable [ʌnprɪ'dɪktəbl] *adj* imprevisible
unprotected ['ʌnprə'tɛktɪd] *adj* (*sex*) sin protección
unqualified [ʌn'kwɔlɪfaɪd] *adj* sin título, no cualificado; (*success*) total

unravel [ʌn'rævl] *vt* desenmarañar
unreal [ʌn'rɪəl] *adj* irreal; (*extraordinary*) increíble
unrealistic [ʌnrɪə'lɪstɪk] *adj* poco realista
unreasonable [ʌn'ri:znəbl] *adj* irrazonable; (*demand*) excesivo
unrelated [ʌnrɪ'leɪtɪd] *adj* sin relación; (*family*) no emparentado
unreliable [ʌnrɪ'laɪəbl] *adj* (*person*) informal; (*machine*) poco fiable
unrest [ʌn'rɛst] *n* inquietud *f*, malestar *m*; (*Pol*) disturbios *mpl*
unroll [ʌn'rəul] *vt* desenrollar
unruly [ʌn'ru:lɪ] *adj* indisciplinado
unsafe [ʌn'seɪf] *adj* peligroso
unsatisfactory ['ʌnsætɪs'fæktərɪ] *adj* poco satisfactorio
unscrew [ʌn'skru:] *vt* destornillar
unsettled [ʌn'sɛtld] *adj* inquieto, intranquilo; (*weather*) variable
unsettling [ʌn'sɛtlɪŋ] *adj* perturbador(a), inquietante
unsightly [ʌn'saɪtlɪ] *adj* feo
unskilled [ʌn'skɪld] *adj* (*work*) no especializado; (*worker*) no cualificado
unspoiled ['ʌn'spɔɪld], **unspoilt** ['ʌn'spɔɪlt] *adj* (*place*) que no ha perdido su belleza natural
unstable [ʌn'steɪbl] *adj* inestable
unsteady [ʌn'stɛdɪ] *adj* inestable
unsuccessful [ʌnsək'sɛsful] *adj* (*attempt*) infructuoso; (*writer, proposal*) sin éxito; **to be ~** (*in attempting sth*) no tener éxito, fracasar
unsuitable [ʌn'su:təbl] *adj* inapropiado; (*time*) inoportuno
unsure [ʌn'ʃuə*] *adj* inseguro, poco seguro
untidy [ʌn'taɪdɪ] *adj* (*room*) desordenado; (*appearance*) desaliñado
untie [ʌn'taɪ] *vt* desatar
until [ən'tɪl] *prep* hasta ▷ *conj* hasta que; **~ he comes** hasta que venga; **~ now** hasta ahora; **~ then** hasta entonces
untrue [ʌn'tru:] *adj* (*statement*) falso
unused [ʌn'ju:zd] *adj* sin usar
unusual [ʌn'ju:ʒuəl] *adj* insólito, poco común; (*exceptional*) inusitado; **unusually** *adv* (*exceptionally*) excepcionalmente; **he arrived unusually early** llegó más temprano que de costumbre
unveil [ʌn'veɪl] *vt* (*statue*) descubrir
unwanted [ʌn'wɔntɪd] *adj* (*clothing*) viejo; (*pregnancy*) no deseado
unwell [ʌn'wɛl] *adj*: **to be/feel ~** estar indispuesto/sentirse mal
unwilling [ʌn'wɪlɪŋ] *adj*: **to be ~ to do sth** estar poco dispuesto a hacer algo
unwind [ʌn'waɪnd] (*irreg*) *vt* desenvolver ▷ *vi* (*relax*) relajarse
unwise [ʌn'waɪz] *adj* imprudente
unwittingly [ʌn'wɪtɪŋlɪ] *adv* inconscientemente, sin darse cuenta
unwrap [ʌn'ræp] *vt* desenvolver
unzip [ʌn'zɪp] *vt* abrir la cremallera de; (*Comput*) descomprimir

KEYWORD

up [ʌp] *prep*: **to go/be up sth** subir/estar subido en algo; **he went up the stairs/the hill** subió las escaleras/la colina; **we walked/climbed up the hill** subimos la colina; **they live further up the street** viven más arriba en la calle; **go up that road and turn left** sigue por esa calle y gira a la izquierda
▷ *adv* **1** (*upwards, higher*) más arriba; **up in the mountains** en lo alto (de la montaña); **put it a bit higher up** ponlo un poco más arriba *or* alto; **up there** ahí *or* allí arriba; **up above** en lo alto, por encima, arriba
2: **to be up** (*out of bed*) estar levantado; (*prices, level*) haber subido
3: **up to** (*as far as*) hasta; **up to now** hasta ahora *or* la fecha
4: **to be up to: it's up to you** (*depending on*) depende de ti; **he's not up to it** (*job, task etc*) no es capaz de hacerlo; **his work is not up to the required standard** su trabajo no da la talla; (*inf*: *be doing*): **what is he up to?** ¿que estará tramando?
▷ *n*: **ups and downs** altibajos *mpl*

up-and-coming [ʌpənd'kʌmɪŋ] *adj* prometedor(a)
upbringing ['ʌpbrɪŋɪŋ] *n* educación *f*
update [ʌp'deɪt] *vt* poner al día
upfront [ʌp'frʌnt] *adj* claro, directo ▷ *adv* a las claras; (*pay*) por adelantado; **to be ~ about sth** admitir algo claramente
upgrade [ʌp'greɪd] *vt* (*house*) modernizar; (*employee*) ascender
upheaval [ʌp'hi:vl] *n* trastornos *mpl*; (*Pol*) agitación *f*
uphill [ʌp'hɪl] *adj* cuesta arriba; (*fig*: *task*) penoso, difícil ▷ *adv*: **to go ~** ir cuesta arriba
upholstery [ʌp'həulstərɪ] *n* tapicería
upmarket [ʌp'mɑ:kɪt] *adj* (*product*) de categoría
upon [ə'pɔn] *prep* sobre
upper ['ʌpə*] *adj* superior, de arriba ▷ *n* (*of shoe*: *also*: **~s**) empeine *m*; **upper-class** *adj* de clase alta
upright ['ʌpraɪt] *adj* derecho; (*vertical*) vertical; (*fig*) honrado
uprising ['ʌpraɪzɪŋ] *n* sublevación *f*
uproar ['ʌprɔ:*] *n* escándalo

upset [*n* 'ʌpsɛt, *vb, adj* ʌp'sɛt] *n* (*to plan etc*) revés *m*, contratiempo; (*Med*) trastorno ▷ *vt irreg* (*glass etc*) volcar; (*plan*) alterar; (*person*) molestar, disgustar ▷ *adj* molesto, disgustado; (*stomach*) revuelto
upside-down [ʌpsaɪd'daun] *adv* al revés; **to turn a place ~** (*fig*) revolverlo todo
upstairs [ʌp'stɛəz] *adv* arriba ▷ *adj* (*room*) de arriba ▷ *n* el piso superior
up-to-date ['ʌptə'deɪt] *adj* al día
uptown ['ʌptaun] (US) *adv* hacia las afueras ▷ *adj* exterior, de las afueras
upward ['ʌpwəd] *adj* ascendente; **upward(s)** *adv* hacia arriba; (*more than*): **upward(s) of** más de
uranium [juə'reɪnɪəm] *n* uranio
Uranus [juə'reɪnəs] *n* Urano
urban ['ə:bən] *adj* urbano
urge [ə:dʒ] *n* (*desire*) deseo ▷ *vt*: **to ~ sb to do sth** animar a algn a hacer algo
urgency ['ə:dʒənsɪ] *n* urgencia
urgent ['ə:dʒənt] *adj* urgente; (*voice*) perentorio
urinal ['juərɪnl] *n* (*building*) urinario; (*vessel*) orinal *m*
urinate ['juərɪneɪt] *vi* orinar
urine ['juərɪn] *n* orina, orines *mpl*
US *n abbr* (= *United States*) EE. UU.
us [ʌs] *pron* nos; (*after prep*) nosotros/as; *see also* **me**
USA *n abbr* (= *United States (of America)*) EE.UU.
use [*n* ju:s, *vb* ju:z] *n* uso, empleo; (*usefulness*) utilidad *f* ▷ *vt* usar, emplear; **she ~d to do it** (ella) solía *or* acostumbraba hacerlo; **in ~** en uso; **out of ~** en desuso; **to be of ~** servir; **it's no ~** (*pointless*) es inútil; (*not useful*) no sirve; **to be ~d to** estar acostumbrado a, acostumbrar; **use up** *vt* (*food*) consumir; (*money*) gastar; **used** [ju:zd] *adj* (*car*) usado; **useful** *adj* útil; **useless** *adj* (*unusable*) inservible; (*pointless*) inútil; (*person*) inepto; **user** *n* usuario/a; **user-friendly** *adj* (*computer*) amistoso
usual ['ju:ʒuəl] *adj* normal, corriente; **as ~** como de costumbre; **usually** *adv* normalmente
utensil [ju:'tɛnsl] *n* utensilio; **kitchen ~s** batería de cocina
utility [ju:'tɪlɪtɪ] *n* utilidad *f*; (*public utility*) (empresa de) servicio público
utilize ['ju:tɪlaɪz] *vt* utilizar
utmost ['ʌtməust] *adj* mayor ▷ *n*: **to do one's ~** hacer todo lo posible
utter ['ʌtə*] *adj* total, completo ▷ *vt* pronunciar, proferir; **utterly** *adv* completamente, totalmente
U-turn ['ju:'tə:n] *n* viraje *m* en redondo

V

v. *abbr* = **verse; versus**; (= *volt*) v; (= *vide*) véase
vacancy ['veɪkənsɪ] *n* (BRIT: *job*) vacante *f*; (*room*) habitación *f* libre; **"no vacancies"** "completo"
vacant ['veɪkənt] *adj* desocupado, libre; (*expression*) distraído
vacate [və'keɪt] *vt* (*house, room*) desocupar; (*job*) dejar (vacante)
vacation [və'keɪʃən] *n* vacaciones *fpl*; **vacationer** (US **vacationist**) *n* turista *m/f*
vaccination [væksɪ'neɪʃən] *n* vacunación *f*
vaccine ['væksi:n] *n* vacuna
vacuum ['vækjum] *n* vacío; **vacuum cleaner** *n* aspiradora
vagina [və'dʒaɪnə] *n* vagina
vague [veɪg] *adj* vago; (*memory*) borroso; (*ambiguous*) impreciso; (*person: absent-minded*) distraído; (: *evasive*): **to be ~** no decir las cosas claramente
vain [veɪn] *adj* (*conceited*) presumido; (*useless*) vano, inútil; **in ~** en vano
Valentine's Day ['væləntaɪnzdeɪ] *n* día de los enamorados
valid ['vælɪd] *adj* válido; (*ticket*) valedero; (*law*) vigente
valley ['vælɪ] *n* valle *m*
valuable ['væljuəbl] *adj* (*jewel*) de valor; (*time*) valioso; **valuables** *npl* objetos *mpl* de valor
value ['vælju:] *n* valor *m*; (*importance*) importancia ▷ *vt* (*fix price of*) tasar, valorar; (*esteem*) apreciar; **values** *npl* (*principles*) principios *mpl*
valve [vælv] *n* válvula
vampire ['væmpaɪə*] *n* vampiro
van [væn] *n* (*Aut*) furgoneta, camioneta
vandal ['vændl] *n* vándalo/a; **vandalism** *n* vandalismo; **vandalize** *vt* dañar, destruir
vanilla [və'nɪlə] *n* vainilla

vanish ['vænɪʃ] *vi* desaparecer
vanity ['vænɪtɪ] *n* vanidad *f*
vapour ['veɪpə*] (*US* **vapor**) *n* vapor *m*; (*on breath, window*) vaho
variable ['vɛərɪəbl] *adj* variable
variant ['vɛərɪənt] *n* variante *f*
variation [vɛərɪ'eɪʃən] *n* variación *f*
varied ['vɛərɪd] *adj* variado
variety [və'raɪətɪ] *n* (*diversity*) diversidad *f*; (*type*) variedad *f*
various ['vɛərɪəs] *adj* (*several: people*) varios/as; (*reasons*) diversos/as
varnish ['vɑːnɪʃ] *n* barniz *m*; (*nail varnish*) esmalte *m* ▷ *vt* barnizar; (*nails*) pintar (con esmalte)
vary ['vɛərɪ] *vt* variar; (*change*) cambiar ▷ *vi* variar
vase [vɑːz] *n* jarrón *m*

Be careful not to translate **vase** by the Spanish word *vaso*.

Vaseline® ['væsɪliːn] *n* vaselina®
vast [vɑːst] *adj* enorme
VAT [væt] (BRIT) *n abbr* (= *value added tax*) IVA *m*
vault [vɔːlt] *n* (*of roof*) bóveda; (*tomb*) panteón *m*; (*in bank*) cámara acorazada ▷ *vt* (*also*: **~ over**) saltar (por encima de)
VCR *n abbr* = **video cassette recorder**
VDU *n abbr* (= *visual display unit*) UPV *f*
veal [viːl] *n* ternera
veer [vɪə*] *vi* (*vehicle*) virar; (*wind*) girar
vegan ['viːgən] *n* vegetariano/a estricto/a, vegetaliano/a
vegetable ['vɛdʒtəbl] *n* (*Bot*) vegetal *m*; (*edible plant*) legumbre *f*, hortaliza ▷ *adj* vegetal
vegetarian [vɛdʒɪ'tɛərɪən] *adj, n* vegetariano/a *m/f*
vegetation [vɛdʒɪ'teɪʃən] *n* vegetación *f*
vehicle ['viːɪkl] *n* vehículo; (*fig*) medio
veil [veɪl] *n* velo ▷ *vt* velar
vein [veɪn] *n* vena; (*of ore etc*) veta
Velcro® ['vɛlkrəu] *n* velcro® *m*
velvet ['vɛlvɪt] *n* terciopelo
vending machine ['vɛndɪŋ-] *n* distribuidor *m* automático
vendor ['vɛndə*] *n* vendedor(a) *m/f*; **street ~** vendedor(a) *m/f* callejero/a
vengeance ['vɛndʒəns] *n* venganza; **with a ~** (*fig*) con creces
venison ['vɛnɪsn] *n* carne *f* de venado
venom ['vɛnəm] *n* veneno; (*bitterness*) odio
vent [vɛnt] *n* (*in jacket*) respiradero; (*in wall*) rejilla (de ventilación) ▷ *vt* (*fig: feelings*) desahogar
ventilation [vɛntɪ'leɪʃən] *n* ventilación *f*
venture ['vɛntʃə*] *n* empresa ▷ *vt* (*opinion*) ofrecer ▷ *vi* arriesgarse, lanzarse; **business ~** empresa comercial
venue ['vɛnjuː] *n* lugar *m*
Venus ['viːnəs] *n* Venus *m*
verb [vəːb] *n* verbo; **verbal** *adj* verbal
verdict ['vəːdɪkt] *n* veredicto, fallo; (*fig*) opinión *f*, juicio
verge [vəːdʒ] (BRIT) *n* borde *m*; **"soft ~s"** (*Aut*) "arcén *m* no asfaltado"; **to be on the ~ of doing sth** estar a punto de hacer algo
verify ['vɛrɪfaɪ] *vt* comprobar, verificar
versatile ['vəːsətaɪl] *adj* (*person*) polifacético; (*machine, tool etc*) versátil
verse [vəːs] *n* poesía; (*stanza*) estrofa; (*in bible*) versículo
version ['vəːʃən] *n* versión *f*
versus ['vəːsəs] *prep* contra
vertical ['vəːtɪkl] *adj* vertical
very ['vɛrɪ] *adv* muy ▷ *adj*: **the ~ book which** el mismo libro que; **the ~ last** el último de todos; **at the ~ least** al menos; **~ much** muchísimo
vessel ['vɛsl] *n* (*ship*) barco; (*container*) vasija; *see* **blood**
vest [vɛst] *n* (BRIT) camiseta; (*US: waistcoat*) chaleco
vet [vɛt] *vt* (*candidate*) investigar ▷ *n abbr* (BRIT) = **veterinary surgeon**
veteran ['vɛtərn] *n* excombatiente *mf*, veterano/a
veterinary surgeon ['vɛtrɪnərɪ-] (*US* **veterinarian**) *n* veterinario/a *m/f*
veto ['viːtəu] (*pl* **~es**) *n* veto ▷ *vt* prohibir, poner el veto a
via ['vaɪə] *prep* por, por medio de
viable ['vaɪəbl] *adj* viable
vibrate [vaɪ'breɪt] *vi* vibrar
vibration [vaɪ'breɪʃən] *n* vibración *f*
vicar ['vɪkə*] *n* párroco (de la Iglesia Anglicana)
vice [vaɪs] *n* (*evil*) vicio; (*Tech*) torno de banco; **vice-chairman** (*irreg*) *n* vicepresidente *m*
vice versa ['vaɪsɪ'vəːsə] *adv* viceversa
vicinity [vɪ'sɪnɪtɪ] *n*: **in the ~ (of)** cercano (a)
vicious ['vɪʃəs] *adj* (*attack*) violento; (*words*) cruel; (*horse, dog*) resabido
victim ['vɪktɪm] *n* víctima
victor ['vɪktə*] *n* vencedor(a) *m/f*
Victorian [vɪk'tɔːrɪən] *adj* victoriano
victorious [vɪk'tɔːrɪəs] *adj* vencedor(a)
victory ['vɪktərɪ] *n* victoria
video ['vɪdɪəu] *n* vídeo (SP), video (LAM); **video call** *n* videollamada; **video camera** *n* videocámara, cámara de vídeo; **video (cassette) recorder** *n* vídeo (SP), video (LAM); **video game** *n* videojuego;

videophone *n* videoteléfono; **video shop** *n* videoclub *m*; **video tape** *n* cinta de vídeo
vie [vaɪ] *vi*: **to ~ (with sb for sth)** competir (con algn por algo)
Vienna [vɪ'ɛnə] *n* Viena
Vietnam [vjɛt'næm] *n* Vietnam *m*; **Vietnamese** [-nə'mi:z] *n inv, adj* vietnamita *mf*
view [vju:] *n* vista; (*outlook*) perspectiva; (*opinion*) opinión *f*, criterio ▷ *vt* (*look at*) mirar; (*fig*) considerar; **on ~** (*in museum etc*) expuesto; **in full ~ (of)** en plena vista (de); **in ~ of the weather/the fact that** en vista del tiempo/del hecho de que; **in my ~** en mi opinión; **viewer** *n* espectador(a) *m/f*; (*TV*) telespectador(a) *m/f*; **viewpoint** *n* (*attitude*) punto de vista; (*place*) mirador *m*
vigilant ['vɪdʒɪlənt] *adj* vigilante
vigorous ['vɪgərəs] *adj* enérgico, vigoroso
vile [vaɪl] *adj* vil, infame; (*smell*) asqueroso; (*temper*) endemoniado
villa ['vɪlə] *n* (*country house*) casa de campo; (*suburban house*) chalet *m*
village ['vɪlɪdʒ] *n* aldea; **villager** *n* aldeano/a
villain ['vɪlən] *n* (*scoundrel*) malvado/a; (*in novel*) malo; (BRIT: *criminal*) maleante *mf*
vinaigrette [vɪneɪ'grɛt] *n* vinagreta
vine [vaɪn] *n* vid *f*
vinegar ['vɪnɪgə*] *n* vinagre *m*
vineyard ['vɪnjɑ:d] *n* viña, viñedo
vintage ['vɪntɪdʒ] *n* (*year*) vendimia, cosecha ▷ *cpd* de época
vinyl ['vaɪnl] *n* vinilo
viola [vɪ'əulə] *n* (*Mus*) viola
violate ['vaɪəleɪt] *vt* violar
violation [vaɪə'leɪʃən] *n* violación *f*; **in ~ of sth** en violación de algo
violence ['vaɪələns] *n* violencia
violent ['vaɪələnt] *adj* violento; (*intense*) intenso
violet ['vaɪələt] *adj* violado, violeta ▷ *n* (*plant*) violeta
violin [vaɪə'lɪn] *n* violín *m*
VIP *n abbr* (= *very important person*) VIP *m*
virgin ['və:dʒɪn] *n* virgen *f*
Virgo ['və:gəu] *n* Virgo
virtual ['və:tjuəl] *adj* virtual; **virtually** *adv* prácticamente; **virtual reality** *n* (*Comput*) mundo *or* realidad *f* virtual
virtue ['və:tju:] *n* virtud *f*; (*advantage*) ventaja; **by ~ of** en virtud de
virus ['vaɪərəs] *n* (*also Comput*) virus *m inv*
visa ['vɪ:zə] *n* visado (SP), visa (LAM)
vise [vaɪs] (US) *n* (*Tech*) = **vice**
visibility [vɪzɪ'bɪlɪtɪ] *n* visibilidad *f*
visible ['vɪzəbl] *adj* visible
vision ['vɪʒən] *n* (*sight*) vista; (*foresight, in dream*) visión *f*
visit ['vɪzɪt] *n* visita ▷ *vt* (*person* (US: *also*: **~ with**) visitar, hacer una visita a; (*place*) ir a, (ir a) conocer; **visiting hours** *npl* (*in hospital etc*) horas *fpl* de visita; **visitor** *n* (*in museum*) visitante *mf*; (*invited to house*) visita; (*tourist*) turista *mf*; **visitor centre** (US **visitor center**) *n* centro *m* de información
visual ['vɪzjuəl] *adj* visual; **visualize** *vt* imaginarse
vital ['vaɪtl] *adj* (*essential*) esencial; (*dynamic*) dinámico; (*organ*) vital
vitality [vaɪ'tælɪtɪ] *n* energía, vitalidad *f*
vitamin ['vɪtəmɪn] *n* vitamina
vivid ['vɪvɪd] *adj* (*account*) gráfico; (*light*) intenso; (*imagination, memory*) vivo
V-neck ['vi:nɛk] *n* cuello de pico
vocabulary [vəu'kæbjulərɪ] *n* vocabulario
vocal ['vəukl] *adj* vocal; (*articulate*) elocuente
vocational [vəu'keɪʃənl] *adj* profesional
vodka ['vɔdkə] *n* vodka *m*
vogue [vəug] *n*: **in ~** en boga
voice [vɔɪs] *n* voz *f* ▷ *vt* expresar; **voice mail** *n* fonobuzón *m*
void [vɔɪd] *n* vacío; (*hole*) hueco ▷ *adj* (*invalid*) nulo, inválido; (*empty*): **~ of** carente *or* desprovisto de
volatile ['vɔlətaɪl] *adj* (*situation*) inestable; (*person*) voluble; (*liquid*) volátil
volcano [vɔl'keɪnəu] (*pl* **~es**) *n* volcán *m*
volleyball ['vɔlɪbɔ:l] *n* vol(e)ibol *m*
volt [vəult] *n* voltio; **voltage** *n* voltaje *m*
volume ['vɔlju:m] *n* (*gen*) volumen *m*; (*book*) tomo
voluntarily ['vɔləntrɪlɪ] *adv* libremente, voluntariamente
voluntary ['vɔləntərɪ] *adj* voluntario
volunteer [vɔlən'tɪə*] *n* voluntario/a ▷ *vt* (*information*) ofrecer ▷ *vi* ofrecerse (de voluntario); **to ~ to do** ofrecerse a hacer
vomit ['vɔmɪt] *n* vómito ▷ *vt, vi* vomitar
vote [vəut] *n* voto; (*votes cast*) votación *f*; (*right to vote*) derecho de votar; (*franchise*) sufragio ▷ *vt* (*chairman*) elegir; (*propose*): **to ~ that** proponer que ▷ *vi* votar, ir a votar; **~ of thanks** voto de gracias; **voter** *n* votante *mf*; **voting** *n* votación *f*
voucher ['vautʃə*] *n* (*for meal etc*) vale *m*
vow [vau] *n* voto ▷ *vt*: **to ~ to do/that** jurar hacer/que
vowel ['vauəl] *n* vocal *f*
voyage ['vɔɪɪdʒ] *n* viaje *m*
vulgar ['vʌlgə*] *adj* (*rude*) ordinario, grosero; (*in bad taste*) de mal gusto
vulnerable ['vʌlnərəbl] *adj* vulnerable
vulture ['vʌltʃə*] *n* buitre *m*

waddle ['wɔdl] *vi* anadear
wade [weɪd] *vi*: **to ~ through** (*water*) vadear; (*fig*: *book*) leer con dificultad
wafer ['weɪfə*] *n* galleta, barquillo
waffle ['wɔfl] *n* (*Culin*) gofre *m* ▷ *vi* dar el rollo
wag [wæg] *vt* menear, agitar ▷ *vi* moverse, menearse
wage [weɪdʒ] *n* (*also*: **~s**) sueldo, salario ▷ *vt*: **to ~ war** hacer la guerra
wag(g)on ['wægən] *n* (*horse-drawn*) carro; (BRIT *Rail*) vagón *m*
wail [weɪl] *n* gemido ▷ *vi* gemir
waist [weɪst] *n* cintura, talle *m*; **waistcoat** (BRIT) *n* chaleco
wait [weɪt] *n* (*interval*) pausa ▷ *vi* esperar; **to lie in ~ for** acechar a; **I can't ~ to** (*fig*) estoy deseando; **to ~ for** esperar (a); **wait on** *vt fus* servir a; **waiter** *n* camarero; **waiting list** *n* lista de espera; **waiting room** *n* sala de espera; **waitress** ['weɪtrɪs] *n* camarera
waive [weɪv] *vt* suspender
wake [weɪk] (*pt* **woke** *or* **~d**, *pp* **woken** *or* **~d**) *vt* (*also*: **~ up**) despertar ▷ *vi* (*also*: **~ up**) despertarse ▷ *n* (*for dead person*) vela, velatorio; (*Naut*) estela
Wales [weɪlz] *n* País *m* de Gales; **the Prince of ~** el príncipe de Gales
walk [wɔ:k] *n* (*stroll*) paseo; (*hike*) excursión *f* a pie, caminata; (*gait*) paso, andar *m*; (*in park etc*) paseo, alameda ▷ *vi* andar, caminar; (*for pleasure, exercise*) pasear ▷ *vt* (*distance*) recorrer a pie, andar; (*dog*) pasear; **10 minutes' ~ from here** a 10 minutos de aquí andando; **people from all ~s of life** gente de todas las esferas; **walk out** *vi* (*audience*) salir; (*workers*) declararse en huelga; **walker** *n* (*person*) paseante *mf*, caminante *mf*; **walkie-talkie** ['wɔ:kɪ'tɔ:kɪ] *n* walkie-talkie *m*; **walking** *n* el andar; **walking shoes** *npl* zapatos *mpl* para andar; **walking stick** *n* bastón *m*; **Walkman®** *n* Walkman® *m*; **walkway** *n* paseo
wall [wɔ:l] *n* pared *f*; (*exterior*) muro; (*city wall etc*) muralla
wallet ['wɔlɪt] *n* cartera, billetera
wallpaper ['wɔ:lpeɪpə*] *n* papel *m* pintado ▷ *vt* empapelar
walnut ['wɔ:lnʌt] *n* nuez *f*; (*tree*) nogal *m*
walrus ['wɔ:lrəs] (*pl* **~** *or* **~es**) *n* morsa
waltz [wɔ:lts] *n* vals *m* ▷ *vi* bailar el vals
wand [wɔnd] *n* (*also*: **magic ~**) varita (mágica)
wander ['wɔndə*] *vi* (*person*) vagar; deambular; (*thoughts*) divagar ▷ *vt* recorrer, vagar por
want [wɔnt] *vt* querer, desear; (*need*) necesitar ▷ *n*: **for ~ of** por falta de; **wanted** *adj* (*criminal*) buscado; **"wanted"** (*in advertisements*) "se busca"
war [wɔ:*] *n* guerra; **to make ~ (on)** declarar la guerra (a)
ward [wɔ:d] *n* (*in hospital*) sala; (*Pol*) distrito electoral; (*Law*: *child*: *also*: **~ of court**) pupilo/a
warden ['wɔ:dn] *n* (BRIT: *of institution*) director(a) *m/f*; (*of park, game reserve*) guardián/ana *m/f*; (BRIT: *also*: **traffic ~**) guardia *mf*
wardrobe ['wɔ:drəub] *n* armario, ropero; (*clothes*) vestuario
warehouse ['wɛəhaus] *n* almacén *m*, depósito
warfare ['wɔ:fɛə*] *n* guerra
warhead ['wɔ:hɛd] *n* cabeza armada
warm [wɔ:m] *adj* caliente; (*thanks*) efusivo; (*clothes etc*) abrigado; (*welcome, day*) caluroso; **it's ~** hace calor; **I'm ~** tengo calor; **warm up** *vi* (*room*) calentarse; (*person*) entrar en calor; (*athlete*) hacer ejercicios de calentamiento ▷ *vt* calentar; **warmly** *adv* afectuosamente; **warmth** *n* calor *m*
warn [wɔ:n] *vt* avisar, advertir; **warning** *n* aviso, advertencia; **warning light** *n* luz *f* de advertencia
warrant ['wɔrnt] *n* autorización *f*; (*Law*: *to arrest*) orden *f* de detención; (: *to search*) mandamiento de registro
warranty ['wɔrəntɪ] *n* garantía
warrior ['wɔrɪə*] *n* guerrero/a
Warsaw ['wɔ:sɔ:] *n* Varsovia
warship ['wɔ:ʃɪp] *n* buque *m* *or* barco de guerra
wart [wɔ:t] *n* verruga
wartime ['wɔ:taɪm] *n*: **in ~** en tiempos de guerra, en la guerra
wary ['wɛərɪ] *adj* cauteloso

was [wɔz] *pt of* **be**

wash [wɔʃ] *vt* lavar ▷ *vi* lavarse; (*sea etc*): **to ~ against/over sth** llegar hasta/ cubrir algo ▷ *n* (*clothes etc*) lavado; (*of ship*) estela; **to have a ~** lavarse; **wash up** *vi* (BRIT) fregar los platos; (*US*) lavarse; **washbasin** (*US*) *n* lavabo; **wash cloth** (*US*) *n* manopla; **washer** *n* (*Tech*) arandela; **washing** *n* (*dirty*) ropa sucia; (*clean*) colada; **washing line** *n* cuerda de (colgar) la ropa; **washing machine** *n* lavadora; **washing powder** (BRIT) *n* detergente *m* (en polvo)

Washington ['wɔʃɪŋtən] *n* Washington *m*

wash: washing-up (BRIT) *n* fregado, platos *mpl* (para fregar); **washing-up liquid** (BRIT) *n* líquido lavavajillas; **washroom** (*US*) *n* servicios *mpl*

wasn't ['wɔznt] = **was not**

wasp [wɔsp] *n* avispa

waste [weɪst] *n* derroche *m*, despilfarro; (*of time*) pérdida; (*food*) sobras *fpl*; (*rubbish*) basura, desperdicios *mpl* ▷ *adj* (*material*) de desecho; (*left over*) sobrante; (*land*) baldío, descampado ▷ *vt* malgastar, derrochar; (*time*) perder; (*opportunity*) desperdiciar; **waste ground** (BRIT) *n* terreno baldío; **wastepaper basket** *n* papelera

watch [wɔtʃ] *n* (*also*: **wrist ~**) reloj *m*; (*Mil: group of guards*) centinela *m*; (*act*) vigilancia; (*Naut: spell of duty*) guardia ▷ *vt* (*look at*) mirar, observar; (*: match, programme*) ver; (*spy on, guard*) vigilar; (*be careful of*) cuidarse de, tener cuidado de ▷ *vi* ver, mirar; (*keep guard*) montar guardia; **watch out** *vi* cuidarse, tener cuidado; **watchdog** *n* perro guardián; (*fig*) *persona u organismo encargado de asegurarse de que las empresasactúan dentro de la legalidad*; **watch strap** *n* pulsera (de reloj)

water ['wɔːtə*] *n* agua ▷ *vt* (*plant*) regar ▷ *vi* (*eyes*) llorar; (*mouth*) hacerse la boca agua; **water down** *vt* (*milk etc*) aguar; (*fig: story*) dulcificar, diluir; **watercolour** (*US* **watercolor**) *n* acuarela; **watercress** *n* berro; **waterfall** *n* cascada, salto de agua; **watering can** *n* regadera; **watermelon** *n* sandía; **waterproof** *adj* impermeable; **water-skiing** *n* esquí *m* acuático

watt [wɔt] *n* vatio

wave [weɪv] *n* (*of hand*) señal *f* con la mano; (*on water*) ola; (*Radio, in hair*) onda; (*fig*) oleada ▷ *vi* agitar la mano; (*flag etc*) ondear ▷ *vt* (*handkerchief, gun*) agitar; **wavelength** *n* longitud *f* de onda

waver ['weɪvə*] *vi* (*voice, love etc*) flaquear; (*person*) vacilar

wavy ['weɪvɪ] *adj* ondulado

wax [wæks] *n* cera ▷ *vt* encerar ▷ *vi* (*moon*) crecer

way [weɪ] *n* camino; (*distance*) trayecto, recorrido; (*direction*) dirección *f*, sentido; (*manner*) modo, manera; (*habit*) costumbre *f*; **which ~? – this ~** ¿por dónde? *or* ¿en qué dirección? – por aquí; **on the ~** (*en route*) en (el) camino; **to be on one's ~** estar en camino; **to be in the ~** bloquear el camino; (*fig*) estorbar; **to go out of one's ~ to do sth** desvivirse por hacer algo; **under ~** en marcha; **to lose one's ~** extraviarse; **in a ~** en cierto modo *or* sentido; **no ~!** (*inf*) ¡de eso nada!; **by the ~ ...** a propósito ...; **"~ in"** (BRIT) "entrada"; **"~ out"** (BRIT) "salida"; **the ~ back** el camino de vuelta; **"give ~"** (BRIT *Aut*) "ceda el paso"

W.C. *n* (BRIT) wáter *m*

we [wiː] *pl pron* nosotros/as

weak [wiːk] *adj* débil, flojo; (*tea etc*) claro; **weaken** *vi* debilitarse; (*give way*) ceder ▷ *vt* debilitar; **weakness** *n* debilidad *f*; (*fault*) punto débil; **to have a weakness for** tener debilidad por

wealth [wɛlθ] *n* riqueza; (*of details*) abundancia; **wealthy** *adj* rico

weapon ['wɛpən] *n* arma; **~s of mass destruction** armas de destrucción masiva

wear [wɛə*] (*pt* **wore**, *pp* **worn**) *n* (*use*) uso; (*deterioration through use*) desgaste *m* ▷ *vt* (*clothes*) llevar; (*shoes*) calzar; (*damage: through use*) gastar, usar ▷ *vi* (*last*) durar; (*rub through etc*) desgastarse; **evening ~** ropa de etiqueta; **sports~/ baby~** ropa de deportes/de niños; **wear off** *vi* (*pain etc*) pasar, desaparecer; **wear out** *vt* desgastar; (*person, strength*) agotar

weary ['wɪərɪ] *adj* cansado; (*dispirited*) abatido ▷ *vi*: **to ~ of** cansarse de

weasel ['wiːzl] *n* (*Zool*) comadreja

weather ['wɛðə*] *n* tiempo ▷ *vt* (*storm, crisis*) hacer frente a; **under the ~** (*fig: ill*) indispuesto, pachucho; **weather forecast** *n* boletín *m* meteorológico

weave [wiːv] (*pt* **wove**, *pp* **woven**) *vt* (*cloth*) tejer; (*fig*) entretejer

web [wɛb] *n* (*of spider*) telaraña; (*on duck's foot*) membrana; (*network*) red *f*; **the (World Wide) W~** la Red; **web address** *n* dirección *f* de Internet; **webcam** *n* webcam *f*; **web page** *n* (página) web *m or f*; **website** *n* sitio web

Wed. *abbr* (= *Wednesday*) miérc

wed [wɛd] (*pt, pp* **~ded**) *vt* casar ▷ *vi* casarse

we'd [wiːd] = **we had; we would**

wedding ['wɛdɪŋ] *n* boda, casamiento; **silver/golden ~ (anniversary)** bodas *fpl* de plata/de oro; **wedding anniversary** *n*

aniversario de boda; **wedding day** *n* día *m* de la boda; **wedding dress** *n* traje *m* de novia; **wedding ring** *n* alianza
wedge [wɛdʒ] *n* (*of wood etc*) cuña; (*of cake*) trozo ▷ *vt* acuñar; (*push*) apretar
Wednesday ['wɛdnzdɪ] *n* miércoles *m inv*
wee [wi:] (SCOTTISH) *adj* pequeñito
weed [wi:d] *n* mala hierba, maleza ▷ *vt* escardar, desherbar; **weedkiller** *n* herbicida *m*
week [wi:k] *n* semana; **a ~ today/on Friday** de hoy/del viernes en ocho días; **weekday** *n* día *m* laborable; **weekend** *n* fin *m* de semana; **weekly** *adv* semanalmente, cada semana ▷ *adj* semanal ▷ *n* semanario
weep [wi:p] (*pt, pp* **wept**) *vi, vt* llorar
weigh [weɪ] *vt, vi* pesar; **to ~ anchor** levar anclas; **weigh up** *vt* sopesar
weight [weɪt] *n* peso; (*metal weight*) pesa; **to lose/put on ~** adelgazar/engordar; **weightlifting** *n* levantamiento de pesas
weir [wɪə*] *n* presa
weird [wɪəd] *adj* raro, extraño
welcome ['wɛlkəm] *adj* bienvenido ▷ *n* bienvenida ▷ *vt* dar la bienvenida a; (*be glad of*) alegrarse de; **thank you – you're ~** gracias – de nada
weld [wɛld] *n* soldadura ▷ *vt* soldar
welfare ['wɛlfɛə*] *n* bienestar *m*; (*social aid*) asistencia social; **welfare state** *n* estado del bienestar
well [wɛl] *n* fuente *f*, pozo ▷ *adv* bien ▷ *adj*: **to be ~** estar bien (de salud) ▷ *excl* ¡vaya!, ¡bueno!; **as ~** también; **as ~ as** además de; **~ done!** ¡bien hecho!; **get ~ soon!** ¡que te mejores pronto!; **to do ~** (*business*) ir bien; (*person*) tener éxito
we'll [wi:l] = **we will; we shall**
well: well-behaved *adj* bueno; **well-built** *adj* (*person*) fornido; **well-dressed** *adj* bien vestido
wellies ['welɪz] (*inf*) *npl* (BRIT) botas de goma
well: well-known *adj* (*person*) conocido; **well-off** *adj* acomodado; **well-paid** [wel'peɪd] *adj* bien pagado, bien retribuido
Welsh [wɛlʃ] *adj* galés/esa ▷ *n* (*Ling*) galés *m*; **Welshman** (*irreg*) *n* galés *m*; **Welshwoman** (*irreg*) *n* galesa
went [wɛnt] *pt of* **go**
wept [wɛpt] *pt, pp of* **weep**
were [wə:*] *pt of* **be**
we're [wɪə*] = **we are**
weren't [wə:nt] = **were not**
west [wɛst] *n* oeste *m* ▷ *adj* occidental, del oeste ▷ *adv* al *or* hacia el oeste; **the W~** el Oeste, el Occidente; **westbound** ['wɛstbaund] *adj* (*traffic, carriageway*) con rumbo al oeste; **western** *adj* occidental ▷ *n* (*Cinema*) película del oeste; **West Indian** *adj, n* antillano/a *m/f*
wet [wɛt] *adj* (*damp*) húmedo; (*soaked*): **~ through** mojado; (*rainy*) lluvioso ▷ *n* (BRIT: *Pol*) conservador(a) *m/f* moderado/a; **to get ~** mojarse; **"~ paint"** "recién pintado"; **wetsuit** *n* traje *m* térmico
we've [wi:v] = **we have**
whack [wæk] *vt* dar un buen golpe a
whale [weɪl] *n* (*Zool*) ballena
wharf [wɔ:f] (*pl* **wharves**) *n* muelle *m*

KEYWORD

what [wɔt] *adj* **1** (*in direct/indirect questions*) qué; **what size is he?** ¿qué talla usa?; **what colour/shape is it?** ¿de qué color/forma es?
2 (*in exclamations*): **what a mess!** ¡qué desastre!; **what a fool I am!** ¡qué tonto soy!
▷ *pron* **1** (*interrogative*) qué; **what are you doing?** ¿qué haces *or* estás haciendo?; **what is happening?** ¿qué pasa *or* está pasando?; **what is it called?** ¿cómo se llama?; **what about me?** ¿y yo qué?; **what about doing ...?** ¿qué tal si hacemos ...?
2 (*relative*) lo que; **I saw what you did/was on the table** vi lo que hiciste/había en la mesa
▷ *excl* (*disbelieving*) ¡cómo!; **what, no coffee!** ¡que no hay café!

whatever [wɔt'ɛvə*] *adj*: **~ book you choose** cualquier libro que elijas ▷ *pron*: **do ~ is necessary** haga lo que sea necesario; **~ happens** pase lo que pase; **no reason ~** *or* **whatsoever** ninguna razón sea la que sea; **nothing ~** nada en absoluto
whatsoever [wɔtsəu'ɛvə*] *adj see* **whatever**
wheat [wi:t] *n* trigo
wheel [wi:l] *n* rueda; (*Aut*: *also*: **steering ~**) volante *m*; (*Naut*) timón *m* ▷ *vt* (*pram etc*) empujar ▷ *vi* (*also*: **~ round**) dar la vuelta, girar; **wheelbarrow** *n* carretilla; **wheelchair** *n* silla de ruedas; **wheel clamp** *n* (*Aut*) cepo
wheeze [wi:z] *vi* resollar

KEYWORD

when [wɛn] *adv* cuando; **when did it happen?** ¿cuándo ocurrió?; **I know when it happened** sé cuándo ocurrió
▷ *conj* **1** (*at, during, after the time that*) cuando; **be careful when you cross the road** ten cuidado al cruzar la calle; **that**

was when I needed you fue entonces que te necesité
2 (*on, at which*): **on the day when I met him** el día en qué le conocí
3 (*whereas*) cuando

whenever [wɛn'ɛvə*] *conj* cuando; (*every time that*) cada vez que ▷*adv* cuando sea
where [wɛə*] *adv* dónde ▷*conj* donde; **this is ~** aquí es donde; **whereabouts** *adv* dónde ▷*n*: **nobody knows his whereabouts** nadie conoce su paradero; **whereas** *conj* visto que, mientras; **whereby** *pron* por lo cual; **wherever** *conj* dondequiera que; (*interrogative*) dónde
whether ['wɛðə*] *conj* si; **I don't know ~ to accept or not** no sé si aceptar o no; **~ you go or not** vayas o no vayas

KEYWORD

which [wɪtʃ] *adj* **1** (*interrogative: direct, indirect*) qué; **which picture(s) do you want?** ¿qué cuadro(s) quieres?; **which one?** ¿cuál?
2 in which case en cuyo caso; **we got there at 8 pm, by which time the cinema was full** llegamos allí a las 8, cuando el cine estaba lleno
▷*pron* **1** (*interrogative*) cual; **I don't mind which** el/la que sea
2 (*relative: replacing noun*) que; (*: replacing clause*) lo que; (*: after preposition*) (el(la)) que etc el/la cual etc; **the apple which you ate/which is on the table** la manzana que comiste/que está en la mesa; **the chair on which you are sitting** la silla en la que estás sentado; **he said he knew, which is true/I feared** dijo que lo sabía, lo cual *or* lo que es cierto/me temía

whichever [wɪtʃ'ɛvə*] *adj*: **take ~ book you prefer** coja (SP) el libro que prefiera; **~ book you take** cualquier libro que coja
while [waɪl] *n* rato, momento ▷*conj* mientras; (*although*) aunque; **for a ~** durante algún tiempo
whilst [waɪlst] *conj* = **while**
whim [wɪm] *n* capricho
whine [waɪn] *n* (*of pain*) gemido; (*of engine*) zumbido; (*of siren*) aullido ▷*vi* gemir; zumbar; (*fig: complain*) gimotear
whip [wɪp] *n* látigo; (*Pol: person*) *encargado de la disciplina partidaria en el parlamento* ▷*vt* azotar; (*Culin*) batir; (*move quickly*): **to ~ sth out/off** sacar/quitar algo de un tirón; **whipped cream** *n* nata *or* crema montada
whirl [wə:l] *vt* hacer girar, dar vueltas a ▷*vi* girar, dar vueltas; (*leaves etc*) arremolinarse
whisk [wɪsk] *n* (*Culin*) batidor *m* ▷*vt* (*Culin*) batir; **to ~ sb away** *or* **off** llevar volando a algn
whiskers ['wɪskəz] *npl* (*of animal*) bigotes *mpl*; (*of man*) patillas *fpl*
whiskey ['wɪskɪ] (US, IRELAND) *n* = **whisky**
whisky ['wɪskɪ] *n* whisky *m*
whisper ['wɪspə*] *n* susurro ▷*vi, vt* susurrar
whistle ['wɪsl] *n* (*sound*) silbido; (*object*) silbato ▷*vi* silbar
white [waɪt] *adj* blanco; (*pale*) pálido ▷*n* blanco; (*of egg*) clara; **whiteboard** *n* pizarra blanca; **interactive whiteboard** pizarra interactiva; **White House** (US) *n* Casa Blanca; **whitewash** *n* (*paint*) jalbegue *m*, cal *f* ▷*vt* blanquear
whiting ['waɪtɪŋ] *n inv* (*fish*) pescadilla
Whitsun ['wɪtsn] *n* pentecostés *m*
whittle ['wɪtl] *vt*: **to ~ away, ~ down** ir reduciendo
whizz [wɪz] *vi*: **to ~ past** *or* **by** pasar a toda velocidad

KEYWORD

who [hu:] *pron* **1** (*interrogative*) quién; **who is it?, who's there?** ¿quién es?; **who are you looking for?** ¿a quién buscas?; **I told her who I was** le dije quién era yo
2 (*relative*) que; **the man/woman who spoke to me** el hombre/la mujer que habló conmigo; **those who can swim** los que saben *or* sepan nadar

whoever [hu:'ɛvə*] *pron*: **~ finds it** cualquiera *or* quienquiera que lo encuentre; **ask ~ you like** pregunta a quien quieras; **~ he marries** no importa con quién se case
whole [həul] *adj* (*entire*) todo, entero; (*not broken*) intacto ▷*n* todo; (*all*): **the ~ of the town** toda la ciudad, la ciudad entera ▷*n* (*total*) total *m*; (*sum*) conjunto; **on the ~, as a ~** en general; **wholefood(s)** *n(pl)* alimento(s) *m(pl)* integral(es); **wholeheartedly** [həul'hɑ:tɪdlɪ] *adv* con entusiasmo; **wholemeal** *adj* integral; **wholesale** *n* venta al por mayor ▷*adj* al por mayor; (*fig: destruction*) sistemático; **wholewheat** *adj* = **wholemeal**; **wholly** *adv* totalmente, enteramente

KEYWORD

whom [hu:m] *pron* **1** (*interrogative*): **whom did you see?** ¿a quién viste?; **to**

whom did you give it? ¿a quién se lo diste?; **tell me from whom you received it** dígame de quién lo recibió
2 (*relative*) que; **to whom** a quien(es); **of whom** de quien(es), del/de la que *etc*; **the man whom I saw/to whom I wrote** el hombre que vi/a quien escribí; **the lady about/with whom I was talking** la señora de (la) que/con quien *or* (la) que hablaba

whore [hɔ:*] (*inf, pej*) *n* puta

KEYWORD

whose [hu:z] *adj*
1 (*possessive: interrogative*): **whose book is this?, whose is this book?** ¿de quién es este libro?; **whose pencil have you taken?** ¿de quién es el lápiz que has cogido?; **whose daughter are you?** ¿de quién eres hija?
2 (*possessive: relative*) cuyo/a, *pl* cuyos/as; **the man whose son you rescued** el hombre cuyo hijo rescataste; **those whose passports I have** aquellas personas cuyos pasaportes tengo; **the woman whose car was stolen** la mujer a quien le robaron el coche ▷ *pron* de quién; **whose is this?** ¿de quién es esto?; **I know whose it is** sé de quién es

KEYWORD

why [waɪ] *adv* por qué; **why not?** ¿por qué no?; **why not do it now?** ¿por qué no lo haces (*or* hacemos *etc*) ahora? ▷ *conj*: **I wonder why he said that** me pregunto por qué dijo eso; **that's not why I'm here** no es por eso (por lo) que estoy aquí; **the reason why** la razón por la que
▷ *excl* (*expressing surprise, shock, annoyance*) ¡hombre!, ¡vaya!; (*explaining*): **why, it's you!** ¡hombre, eres tú!; **why, that's impossible** ¡pero sí eso es imposible!

wicked ['wɪkɪd] *adj* malvado, cruel
wicket ['wɪkɪt] *n* (*Cricket: stumps*) palos *mpl*; (*: grass area*) terreno de juego
wide [waɪd] *adj* ancho; (*area, knowledge*) vasto, grande; (*choice*) amplio ▷ *adv*: **to open ~** abrir de par en par; **to shoot ~** errar el tiro; **widely** *adv* (*travelled*) mucho; (*spaced*) muy; **it is widely believed/known that ...** mucha gente piensa/sabe que ...; **widen** *vt* ensanchar; (*experience*) ampliar ▷ *vi* ensancharse; **wide open** *adj* abierto de par en par; **widespread** *adj* extendido, general

widow ['wɪdəu] *n* viuda; **widower** *n* viudo
width [wɪdθ] *n* anchura; (*of cloth*) ancho
wield [wi:ld] *vt* (*sword*) blandir; (*power*) ejercer
wife [waɪf] (*pl* **wives**) *n* mujer *f*, esposa
wig [wɪg] *n* peluca
wild [waɪld] *adj* (*animal*) salvaje; (*plant*) silvestre; (*person*) furioso, violento; (*idea*) descabellado; (*rough: sea*) bravo; (*: land*) agreste; (*: weather*) muy revuelto; **wilderness** ['wɪldənɪs] *n* desierto; **wildlife** *n* fauna; **wildly** *adv* (*behave*) locamente; (*lash out*) a diestro y siniestro; (*guess*) a lo loco; (*happy*) a más no poder

KEYWORD

will [wɪl] *aux vb* **1** (*forming future tense*): **I will finish it tomorrow** lo terminaré *or* voy a terminar mañana; **I will have finished it by tomorrow** lo habré terminado para mañana; **will you do it? – yes I will/no I won't** ¿lo harás? – sí/no
2 (*in conjectures, predictions*): **he will** *or* **he'll be there by now** ya habrá *or* debe (de) haber llegado; **that will be the postman** será *or* debe ser el cartero
3 (*in commands, requests, offers*): **will you be quiet!** ¿quieres callarte?; **will you help me?** ¿quieres ayudarme?; **will you have a cup of tea?** ¿te apetece un té?; **I won't put up with it!** ¡no lo soporto! ▷ *vt* (*pt, pp* **willed**): **to will sb to do sth** desear que algn haga algo; **he willed himself to go on** con gran fuerza de voluntad, continuó
▷ *n* voluntad *f*; (*testament*) testamento

willing ['wɪlɪŋ] *adj* (*with goodwill*) de buena voluntad; (*enthusiastic*) entusiasta; **he's ~ to do it** está dispuesto a hacerlo; **willingly** *adv* con mucho gusto
willow ['wɪləu] *n* sauce *m*
willpower ['wɪlpauə*] *n* fuerza de voluntad
wilt [wɪlt] *vi* marchitarse
win [wɪn] (*pt, pp* **won**) *n* victoria, triunfo ▷ *vt* ganar; (*obtain*) conseguir, lograr ▷ *vi* ganar; **win over** *vt* convencer a
wince [wɪns] *vi* encogerse
wind[1] [wɪnd] *n* viento; (*Med*) gases *mpl* ▷ *vt* (*take breath away from*) dejar sin aliento a
wind[2] [waɪnd] (*pt, pp* **wound**) *vt* enrollar; (*wrap*) envolver; (*clock, toy*) dar cuerda a ▷ *vi* (*road, river*) serpentear; **wind down** *vt* (*car window*) bajar; (*fig: production, business*) disminuir; **wind up** *vt* (*clock*) dar cuerda a; (*debate, meeting*) concluir, terminar

windfall ['wɪndfɔːl] *n* golpe *m* de suerte
winding ['waɪndɪŋ] *adj* (*road*) tortuoso; (*staircase*) de caracol
windmill ['wɪndmɪl] *n* molino de viento
window ['wɪndəu] *n* ventana; (*in car, train*) ventanilla; (*in shop etc*) escaparate *m* (SP), vidriera (LAM); **window box** *n* jardinera de ventana; **window cleaner** *n* (*person*) limpiacristales *mf inv*; **window pane** *n* cristal *m*; **window seat** *n* asiento junto a la ventana; **windowsill** *n* alféizar *m*, repisa
windscreen ['wɪndskriːn] (US **windshield**) *n* parabrisas *m inv*; **windscreen wiper** (US **windshield wiper**) *n* limpiaparabrisas *m inv*
windsurfing ['wɪndsəːfɪŋ] *n* windsurf *m*
windy ['wɪndɪ] *adj* de mucho viento; **it's ~** hace viento
wine [waɪn] *n* vino; **wine bar** *n* enoteca; **wine glass** *n* copa (para vino); **wine list** *n* lista de vinos; **wine tasting** *n* degustación *f* de vinos
wing [wɪŋ] *n* ala; (*Aut*) aleta; **wing mirror** *n* (espejo) retrovisor *m*
wink [wɪŋk] *n* guiño, pestañeo ▷ *vi* guiñar, pestañear
winner ['wɪnə*] *n* ganador(a) *m/f*
winning ['wɪnɪŋ] *adj* (*team*) ganador(a); (*goal*) decisivo; (*smile*) encantador(a)
winter ['wɪntə*] *n* invierno ▷ *vi* invernar; **winter sports** *npl* deportes *mpl* de invierno; **wintertime** *n* invierno
wipe [waɪp] *n*: **to give sth a ~** pasar un trapo sobre algo ▷ *vt* limpiar; (*tape*) borrar; **wipe out** *vt* (*debt*) liquidar; (*memory*) borrar; (*destroy*) destruir; **wipe up** *vt* limpiar
wire ['waɪə*] *n* alambre *m*; (*Elec*) cable *m* (eléctrico); (*Tel*) telegrama *m* ▷ *vt* (*house*) poner la instalación eléctrica en; (*also*: **~ up**) conectar; (*person*: *telegram*) telegrafiar
wiring ['waɪərɪŋ] *n* instalación *f* eléctrica
wisdom ['wɪzdəm] *n* sabiduría, saber *m*; (*good sense*) cordura; **wisdom tooth** *n* muela del juicio
wise [waɪz] *adj* sabio; (*sensible*) juicioso
wish [wɪʃ] *n* deseo ▷ *vt* querer; **best ~es** (*on birthday etc*) felicidades *fpl*; **with best ~es** (*in letter*) saludos *mpl*, recuerdos *mpl*; **to ~ sb goodbye** despedirse de algn; **he ~ed me well** me deseó mucha suerte; **to ~ to do/sb to do sth** querer hacer/que algn haga algo; **to ~ for** desear
wistful ['wɪstful] *adj* pensativo
wit [wɪt] *n* ingenio, gracia; (*also*: **~s**) inteligencia; (*person*) chistoso/a
witch [wɪtʃ] *n* bruja

KEYWORD

with [wɪð, wɪθ] *prep* **1** (*accompanying, in the company of*) con (*con +mí, ti, sí = conmigo, contigo, consigo*); **I was with him** estaba con él; **we stayed with friends** nos quedamos en casa de unos amigos; **I'm (not) with you** (*don't understand*) (no) te entiendo; **to be with it** (*inf*: *person*: *up-to-date*) estar al tanto; (: *alert*) ser despabilado
2 (*descriptive, indicating manner etc*) con; de; **a room with a view** una habitación con vistas; **the man with blue eyes** el hombre de los ojos azules; **red with anger** rojo de ira; **to shake with fear** temblar de miedo; **to fill sth with water** llenar algo de agua

withdraw [wɪθ'drɔː] *vt* retirar, sacar ▷ *vi* retirarse; **to ~ money (from the bank)** retirar fondos (del banco); **withdrawal** *n* retirada; (*of money*) reintegro; **withdrawn** *pp of* **withdraw** ▷ *adj* (*person*) reservado, introvertido
withdrew [wɪθ'druː] *pt of* **withdraw**
wither ['wɪðə*] *vi* marchitarse
withhold [wɪθ'həuld] *vt* (*money*) retener; (*decision*) aplazar; (*permission*) negar; (*information*) ocultar
within [wɪð'ɪn] *prep* dentro de ▷ *adv* dentro; **~ reach (of)** al alcance (de); **~ sight (of)** a la vista (de); **~ the week** antes de acabar la semana; **~ a mile (of)** a menos de una milla (de)
without [wɪð'aut] *prep* sin; **to go ~ sth** pasar sin algo
withstand [wɪθ'stænd] *vt* resistir a
witness ['wɪtnɪs] *n* testigo *mf* ▷ *vt* (*event*) presenciar; (*document*) atestiguar la veracidad de; **to bear ~ to** (*fig*) ser testimonio de
witty ['wɪtɪ] *adj* ingenioso
wives [waɪvz] *npl of* **wife**
wizard ['wɪzəd] *n* hechicero
wk *abbr* = **week**
wobble ['wɔbl] *vi* temblar; (*chair*) cojear
woe [wəu] *n* desgracia
woke [wəuk] *pt of* **wake**
woken ['wəukən] *pp of* **wake**
wolf [wulf] *n* lobo
woman ['wumən] (*pl* **women**) *n* mujer *f*
womb [wuːm] *n* matriz *f*, útero
won [wʌn] *pt, pp of* **win**
wonder ['wʌndə*] *n* maravilla, prodigio; (*feeling*) asombro ▷ *vi*: **to ~ whether/why** preguntarse si/por qué; **to ~ at** asombrarse de; **to ~ about** pensar sobre *or* en; **it's no**

~ (that) no es de extrañarse (que *+subjun*); **wonderful** *adj* maravilloso

won't [wəunt] = **will not**

wood [wud] *n* (*timber*) madera; (*forest*) bosque *m*; **wooden** *adj* de madera; **woodwind** *n* (*Mus*) instrumentos *mpl* de viento de madera; **woodwork** *n* carpintería

wool [wul] *n* lana; **to pull the ~ over sb's eyes** (*fig*) engatusar a algn; **woollen** (*US* **woolen**) *adj* de lana; **woolly** (*US* **wooly**) *adj* lanudo, de lana; (*fig*: *ideas*) confuso

word [wə:d] *n* palabra; (*news*) noticia; (*promise*) palabra (de honor) ▷ *vt* redactar; **in other ~s** en otras palabras; **to break/keep one's ~** faltar a la palabra/cumplir la promesa; **to have ~s with sb** reñir con algn; **word processing** *n* proceso de textos; **word processor** *n* procesador *m* de textos

wore [wɔ:*] *pt of* **wear**

work [wə:k] *n* trabajo; (*job*) empleo, trabajo; (*Art, Literature*) obra ▷ *vi* trabajar; (*mechanism*) funcionar, marchar; (*medicine*) ser eficaz, surtir efecto ▷ *vt* (*shape*) trabajar; (*stone etc*) tallar; (*mine etc*) explotar; (*machine*) manejar, hacer funcionar ▷ *npl* (*of clock, machine*) mecanismo; **to be out of ~** estar parado, no tener trabajo; **to ~ loose** (*part*) desprenderse; (*knot*) aflojarse; **works** *n* (BRIT: *factory*) fábrica; **work out** *vi* (*plans etc*) salir bien, funcionar; **works** *vt* (*problem*) resolver; (*plan*) elaborar; **it works out at £100** suma 100 libras; **worker** *n* trabajador(a) *m/f*, obrero/a; **work experience** *n*: **I'm going to do my work experience in a factory** voy a hacer las prácticas en una fábrica; **workforce** *n* mano de obra; **working class** *n* clase *f* obrera ▷ *adj*: **working-class** obrero; **working week** *n* semana laboral; **workman** (*irreg*) *n* obrero; **work of art** *n* obra de arte; **workout** *n* (*Sport*) sesión *f* de ejercicios; **work permit** *n* permiso de trabajo; **workplace** *n* lugar *m* de trabajo; **worksheet** *n* (*Scol*) hoja de ejercicios; **workshop** *n* taller *m*; **work station** *n* puesto *or* estación *f* de trabajo; **work surface** *n* encimera; **worktop** *n* encimera

world [wə:ld] *n* mundo ▷ *cpd* (*champion*) del mundo; (*power, war*) mundial; **to think the ~ of sb** (*fig*) tener un concepto muy alto de algn; **World Cup** *n* (*Football*): **the World Cup** el Mundial, los Mundiales; **world-wide** *adj* mundial, universal; **World-Wide Web** *n*: **the World-Wide Web** el World Wide Web

worm [wə:m] *n* (*also*: **earth ~**) lombriz *f*

worn [wɔ:n] *pp of* **wear** ▷ *adj* usado; **worn-out** *adj* (*object*) gastado; (*person*) rendido, agotado

worried ['wʌrɪd] *adj* preocupado

worry ['wʌrɪ] *n* preocupación *f* ▷ *vt* preocupar, inquietar ▷ *vi* preocuparse; **worrying** *adj* inquietante

worse [wə:s] *adj, adv* peor ▷ *n* lo peor; **a change for the ~** un empeoramiento; **worsen** *vt, vi* empeorar; **worse off** *adj* (*financially*): **to be worse off** tener menos dinero; (*fig*): **you'll be worse off this way** de esta forma estarás peor que nunca

worship ['wə:ʃɪp] *n* adoración *f* ▷ *vt* adorar; **Your W~** (BRIT: *to mayor*) señor alcalde; (: *to judge*) señor juez

worst [wə:st] *adj, adv* peor ▷ *n* lo peor; **at ~** en lo peor de los casos

worth [wə:θ] *n* valor *m* ▷ *adj*: **to be ~** valer; **it's ~ it** vale *or* merece la pena; **to be ~ one's while (to do)** merecer la pena (hacer); **worthless** *adj* sin valor; (*useless*) inútil; **worthwhile** *adj* (*activity*) que merece la pena; (*cause*) loable

worthy ['wə:ðɪ] *adj* respetable; (*motive*) honesto; **~ of** digno de

KEYWORD

would [wud] *aux vb* **1** (*conditional tense*): **if you asked him he would do it** si se lo pidieras, lo haría; **if you had asked him he would have done it** si se lo hubieras pedido, lo habría *or* hubiera hecho

2 (*in offers, invitations, requests*): **would you like a biscuit?** ¿quieres una galleta?; (*formal*) ¿querría una galleta?; **would you ask him to come in?** ¿quiere hacerle pasar?; **would you open the window please?** ¿quiere *or* podría abrir la ventana, por favor?

3 (*in indirect speech*): **I said I would do it** dije que lo haría

4 (*emphatic*): **it WOULD have to snow today!** ¡tenía que nevar precisamente hoy!

5 (*insistence*): **she wouldn't behave** no quiso comportarse bien

6 (*conjecture*): **it would have been midnight** sería medianoche; **it would seem so** parece ser que sí

7 (*indicating habit*): **he would go there on Mondays** iba allí los lunes

wouldn't ['wudnt] = **would not**

wound[1] [wu:nd] *n* herida ▷ *vt* herir

wound[2] [waund] *pt, pp of* **wind**[2]

wove [wəuv] *pt of* **weave**

woven ['wəuvən] *pp of* **weave**

wrap [ræp] *vt* (*also*: **~ up**) envolver; (*gift*) envolver, abrigar ▷ *vi* (*dress warmly*) abrigarse; **wrapper** *n* (*on chocolate*) papel *m*; (BRIT: *of book*) sobrecubierta; **wrapping** *n* envoltura, envase *m*; **wrapping paper** *n* papel *m* de envolver; (*fancy*) papel *m* de regalo

wreath [ri:ð, *pl* ri:ðz] *n* (*funeral wreath*) corona

wreck [rɛk] *n* (*ship: destruction*) naufragio; (*: remains*) restos *mpl* del barco; (*pej: person*) ruina ▷ *vt* (*car etc*) destrozar; (*chances*) arruinar; **wreckage** *n* restos *mpl*; (*of building*) escombros *mpl*

wren [rɛn] *n* (*Zool*) reyezuelo

wrench [rɛntʃ] *n* (*Tech*) llave *f* inglesa; (*tug*) tirón *m*; (*fig*) dolor *m* ▷ *vt* arrancar; **to ~ sth from sb** arrebatar algo violentamente a algn

wrestle ['rɛsl] *vi*: **to ~ (with sb)** luchar (con *or* contra algn); **wrestler** *n* luchador(a) *m/f* (de lucha libre); **wrestling** *n* lucha libre

wretched ['rɛtʃɪd] *adj* miserable

wriggle ['rɪgl] *vi* (*also*: **~ about**) menearse, retorcerse

wring [rɪŋ] (*pt, pp* **wrung**) *vt* retorcer; (*wet clothes*) escurrir; (*fig*): **to ~ sth out of sb** sacar algo por la fuerza a algn

wrinkle ['rɪŋkl] *n* arruga ▷ *vt* arrugar ▷ *vi* arrugarse

wrist [rɪst] *n* muñeca

writable ['raɪtəbl] *adj* (*CD, DVD*) escribible

write [raɪt] (*pt* **wrote**, *pp* **written**) *vt* escribir; (*cheque*) extender ▷ *vi* escribir; **write down** *vt* escribir; (*note*) apuntar; **write off** *vt* (*debt*) borrar (como incobrable); (*fig*) desechar por inútil; **write out** *vt* escribir; **write-off** *n* siniestro total; **writer** *n* escritor(a) *m/f*

writing ['raɪtɪŋ] *n* escritura; (*hand-writing*) letra; (*of author*) obras *fpl*; **in ~** por escrito; **writing paper** *n* papel *m* de escribir

written ['rɪtn] *pp of* **write**

wrong [rɔŋ] *adj* (*wicked*) malo; (*unfair*) injusto; (*incorrect*) equivocado, incorrecto; (*not suitable*) inoportuno, inconveniente; (*reverse*) del revés ▷ *adv* equivocadamente ▷ *n* injusticia ▷ *vt* ser injusto con; **you are ~ to do it** haces mal en hacerlo; **you are ~ about that, you've got it ~** en eso estás equivocado; **to be in the ~** no tener razón, tener la culpa; **what's ~?** ¿qué pasa?; **to go ~** (*person*) equivocarse; (*plan*) salir mal; (*machine*) estropearse; **wrongly** *adv* mal, incorrectamente; (*by mistake*) por error; **wrong number** *n* (*Tel*): **you've got the wrong number** se ha equivocado de número

wrote [rəut] *pt of* **write**

wrung [rʌŋ] *pt, pp of* **wring**

WWW *n abbr* (*=World Wide Web*) WWW *m*

XL *abbr* = **extra large**

Xmas ['ɛksməs] *n abbr* = **Christmas**

X-ray ['ɛksreɪ] *n* radiografía ▷ *vt* radiografiar, sacar radiografías de

xylophone ['zaɪləfəun] *n* xilófono

Y

yacht [jɔt] *n* yate *m*; **yachting** *n* (*sport*) balandrismo
yard [jɑːd] *n* patio; (*measure*) yarda; **yard sale** (US) *n* venta de objetos usados (*en el jardín de una casa particular*)
yarn [jɑːn] *n* hilo; (*tale*) cuento, historia
yawn [jɔːn] *n* bostezo ▷ *vi* bostezar
yd. *abbr* (= *yard*) yda
yeah [jɛə] (*inf*) *adv* sí
year [jɪə*] *n* año; **to be 8 ~s old** tener 8 años; **an eight-~-old child** un niño de ocho años (de edad); **yearly** *adj* anual ▷ *adv* anualmente, cada año
yearn [jəːn] *vi*: **to ~ for sth** añorar algo, suspirar por algo
yeast [jiːst] *n* levadura
yell [jɛl] *n* grito, alarido ▷ *vi* gritar
yellow ['jɛləu] *adj* amarillo; **Yellow Pages®** *npl* páginas *fpl* amarillas
yes [jɛs] *adv* sí ▷ *n* sí *m*; **to say/answer ~** decir/contestar que sí
yesterday ['jɛstədɪ] *adv* ayer ▷ *n* ayer *m*; **~ morning/evening** ayer por la mañana/tarde; **all day ~** todo el día de ayer
yet [jɛt] *adv* ya; (*negative*) todavía ▷ *conj* sin embargo, a pesar de todo; **it is not finished ~** todavía no está acabado; **the best ~** el/la mejor hasta ahora; **as ~** hasta ahora, todavía
yew [juː] *n* tejo
Yiddish ['jɪdɪʃ] *n* yiddish *m*
yield [jiːld] *n* (*Agr*) cosecha; (*Comm*) rendimiento ▷ *vt* ceder; (*results*) producir, dar; (*profit*) rendir ▷ *vi* rendirse, ceder; (*US Aut*) ceder el paso
yob(bo) ['jɔb(bəu)] *n* (BRIT *inf*) gamberro
yoga ['jəugə] *n* yoga *m*
yog(h)ourt ['jəugət] *n* yogur *m*
yog(h)urt ['jəugət] *n* = **yog(h)ourt**
yolk [jəuk] *n* yema (de huevo)

KEYWORD

you [juː] *pron* **1** (*subject: familiar*) tú; (*pl*) vosotros/as (SP), ustedes (LAM); (*polite*) usted; (*pl*) ustedes; **you are very kind** eres/es *etc* muy amable; **you Spanish enjoy your food** a vosotros (*or* ustedes) los españoles os (*or* les) gusta la comida; **you and I will go** iremos tú y yo
2 (*object: direct: familiar*) te; (*pl*) os (SP), les (LAM); (*polite*) le; (*pl*) les; (*f*) la; (*pl*) las; **I know you** te/le etc conozco
3 (*object: indirect: familiar*) te; (*pl*) os (SP), les (LAM); (*polite*) le; (*pl*) les; **I gave the letter to you yesterday** te/os *etc* di la carta ayer
4 (*stressed*): **I told you to do it** te dije a ti que lo hicieras, es a ti a quien dije que lo hicieras; *see also* **3; 5**
5 (*after prep: NB: con +ti = contigo: familiar*) ti; (*pl*) vosotros/as (SP), ustedes (LAM); (*: polite*) usted; (*pl*) ustedes; **it's for you** es para ti/vosotros *etc*
6 (*comparisons: familiar*) tú; (*pl*) vosotros/as (SP), ustedes (LAM); (*: polite*) usted; (*pl*) ustedes; **she's younger than you** es más joven que tú/vosotros etc
7 (*impersonal one*): **fresh air does you good** el aire puro (te) hace bien; **you never know** nunca se sabe; **you can't do that!** ¡eso no se hace!

you'd [juːd] = **you had; you would**
you'll [juːl] = **you will; you shall**
young [jʌŋ] *adj* joven ▷ *npl* (*of animal*) cría; (*people*): **the ~** los jóvenes, la juventud; **youngster** *n* joven *mf*
your [jɔː*] *adj* tu; (*pl*) vuestro; (*formal*) su; *see also* **my**
you're [juə*] = **you are**
yours [jɔːz] *pron* tuyo (*pl*), vuestro; (*formal*) suyo; *see also* **faithfully; mine¹** *see also* **sincerely**
yourself [jɔː'sɛlf] *pron* tú mismo; (*complement*) te; (*after prep*) tí (mismo); (*formal*) usted mismo; (*: complement*) se; (*: after prep*) sí (mismo); **yourselves** *pl pron* vosotros mismos; (*after prep*) vosotros (mismos); (*formal*) ustedes (mismos); (*: complement*) se; (*: after prep*) sí mismos; *see also* **oneself**
youth [*pl* juːðz *n* juventud *f*; (*young man*) joven *m*; **youth club** *n* club *m* juvenil; **youthful** *adj* juvenil; **youth hostel** *n* albergue *m* de juventud
you've [juːv] = **you have**

Z

zeal [zi:l] *n* celo, entusiasmo
zebra ['zi:brə] *n* cebra; **zebra crossing** (BRIT) *n* paso de peatones
zero ['zɪərəu] *n* cero
zest [zɛst] *n* ánimo, vivacidad *f*; (*of orange*) piel *f*
zigzag ['zɪgzæg] *n* zigzag *m* ▷ *vi* zigzaguear, hacer eses
Zimbabwe [zɪm'bɑ:bwɪ] *n* Zimbabwe *m*
zinc [zɪŋk] *n* cinc *m*, zinc *m*
zip [zip] *n* (*also*: **~ fastener,** (US) **~per**) cremallera (SP), cierre (AM) *m*, zíper *m* (MEX, CAM) ▷ *vt* (*also*: **~ up**) cerrar la cremallera de; (*file*) comprimir; **zip code** (US) *n* código postal; **zip file** *n* (*Comput*) archivo comprimido; **zipper** (US) *n* cremallera
zit [zɪt] *n* grano
zodiac ['zəudɪæk] *n* zodíaco
zone [zəun] *n* zona
zoo [zu:] *n* (jardín *m*) zoo *m*
zoology [zu'ɔlədʒɪ] *n* zoología
zoom [zu:m] *vi*: **to ~ past** pasar zumbando; **zoom lens** *n* zoom *m*
zucchini [zu:'ki:nɪ] (US) *n(pl)* calabacín(ines) *m(pl)*